Type Definitions

```
TYPE
   String20 = PACKED ARRAY [1..20] OF char;
   NameList = ARRAY [1..ClassSize] OF String20;
   AmountList = ARRAY [1..MaxSize] OF real;
   CurrentYears = 1950..2000;
   WeatherType = (Cloudy, Sunny, Rain, Snow, Balmy);
```

Record Definition

```
TYPE
   String20 = PACKED ARRAY [1..20] OF char;
   PatientInfo = RECORD
                     Name : String20;
                     Age : 0..100;
                     Weight : 0..300
                 END;  {  of RECORD PatientInfo  }
   PatientList = ARRAY [1..100] OF PatientInfo;
VAR
   Patient : PatientList;
```

Using Records

```
FOR J := 1 TO NumPatients DO
   BEGIN
     WITH Patient[J] DO
       BEGIN
         writeln (Name:30);
         writeln (Age:10, Weight:10)
       END;
     writeln; writeln
   END;  {  of FOR...TO loop  }
```

File Definition

```
TYPE
   String20 = PACKED ARRAY [1..20] OF char;
   PatientInfo = RECORD
                     Name : String20;
                     Age : 0..100;
                     Weight : 0..300
                 END;  {  of RECORD PatientInfo  }
   PatientFile = FILE OF PatientInfo;
VAR
   Patient : PatientFile;
   TempRec : PatientInfo;
```

Using Files

```
rewrite (Patient);
WHILE NOT eof(input) DO
   BEGIN
     GetData (Patient^);
     Process (Patient^);
     put (Patient)
   END;
```

Introduction to Computer Science: Programming,
Problem Solving, and Data Structures.
Second Alternate Edition
Thomas L. Naps and Douglas W. Nance
© 1992 West Publishing Company

Introduction to Computer Science:
Programming, Problem Solving, and Data Structures

SECOND ALTERNATE EDITION

Thomas L. Naps
LAWRENCE UNIVERSITY

Douglas W. Nance
CENTRAL MICHIGAN UNIVERSITY

WEST PUBLISHING COMPANY
ST. PAUL   NEW YORK   LOS ANGELES   SAN FRANCISCO

To Ruth and Marguerite

Copyeditor: Janet Hunter
Interior design: Paula Schlosser, Lucy Lesiak, and John Rokusek
Illustrations: Miyake Illustration and Design
Cover design: Miyake Illustration and Design
Indexer: Virginia Hobbs
Composition: Carlisle Communications
Production, PrePress, Printing and Binding:
  West Publishing Company

WEST'S COMMITMENT TO THE ENVIRONMENT
In 1906, West Publishing Company began recycling materials left over from the production of books. This began a tradition of efficient and responsible use of resources. Today, up to 95 percent of our legal books and 70% of our college texts are printed on recycled, acid-free stock. West also recycles nearly 22 million pounds of scrap paper annually—the equivalent of 181,717 trees. Since the 1960s, West has devised ways to capture and recycle waste inks, solvents, oils, and vapors created in the printing process. We also recycle plastics of all kinds, wood, glass, corrugated cardboard, and batteries, and have eliminated the use of styrofoam book packaging. We at West are proud of the longevity and the scope of our commitment to our environment.

Printed in the United States of America
99 98 97 96 95 94 93 92   8 7 6 5 4 3 2 1

Library of Congress Cataloging-in-Publication Data

Naps, Thomas L.
    Introduction to computer science: programming, problemsolving, and data structures.— 2nd alternate ed. / Thomas L. Naps. Douglas W. Nance.
        p. cm.
    Includes index.
    ISBN 0–314–93307–7
    1. Electronic digital computers—Programming.   2. Data structures (Computer science)   I. Nance, Douglas W.   II. Title.
QA76.6.N356   1992
005 —dc20   92–6949

CIP

▦ Contents

CHAPTER

2 ■ Arithmetic, Variables, Input, Constants, and Standard Functions   47

CHAPTER **3** ■ Subprograms: Procedures and
Functions for Problem Solving   85

CHAPTER   **6** ■ Text Files and Enumerated Data Types   263

CHAPTER   **7** ■ One-Dimensional Arrays   301

CHAPTER   **14 ■** Software Engineering and the System
Life Cycle   653

CHAPTER   **15 ■** Linked Lists and Pointers   711

CHAPTER   **16** ■ Stacks and Queues   777

CHAPTER   **19** ■ More Powerful Sorting Methods   967

CHAPTER   **20** ■ More Powerful Search Methods   1005

■ Appendixes

■ Glossary   G.1

■ Answers to Selected Exercises   AN.1

■ Index   I.1

⊞ Preface

Background and Objectives

In the recently released report, *Computing Curricula 1991,* the Association for Computing Machinery–(ACM–IEEE–CS) Joint Curriculum Task Force concludes that a computer science curriculum is "more than a set of isolated courses. There are unifying themes and goals that span the whole curriculum." Clearly, the place to make the student aware of these unifying themes and goals is at the introductory level. The disciplines of mathematics and the natural sciences have long recognized that one way to achieve this unification is to use one consistent text throughout the introductory sequence of courses. Although a student's introductory experience in computer science has matured into a two-semester sequence (typically labeled CS1 and CS2 following guidelines of the ACM's Curriculum Committee), we still find a dearth of texts designed to span such a sequence. Too often we find that CS1 is taught using a text that does not go much beyond Pascal programming. Then, in the CS2 course, students are asked to switch gears and adapt to a much more rigorous style of presentation.

Our goal in developing the first edition of *Introduction to Computer Science: Programming, Problem-Solving, and Data Structures,* Alternate Edition was to provide a text that viewed CS1 and CS2 as a unified whole. In particular, the first edition was designed with six objectives in mind.

1. To provide students with a comprehensive understanding of how to program in Pascal. Such knowledge of Pascal is viewed as one of the foundational blocks that allows students to explore the ideas and techniques of computer science.
2. To present Pascal in a context that emphasizes a structured, top-down approach to problem solving. Students should realize that computer science is primarily problem solving, not programming.
3. To demonstrate the application of software engineering principles in the design, coding, and testing of large programs.
4. To introduce students to essential data structures such as linked lists, queues, stacks, trees, and (to a lesser extent) graphs. This introduction emphasizes the definition of each structure as an abstract data type before discussing implementations and applications of that structure.

5. To provide a systematic approach to studying algorithms, an approach that focuses first on understanding the action of an algorithm and then on analyzing the algorithm from a time/space perspective. In particular, searching, sorting, and recursive algorithms are covered in detail.

6. To give students an overview of what lies ahead in their study of computer science.

In the second edition, we continue to follow these objectives and attempt to present them in more of a spiral, recurring style than we did in the first edition. Software engineering, abstraction, and the use of preconditions and postconditions for specifying algorithms are presented earlier in the second edition. This allows us to gradually build an increasing amount of formalism into the second half of the text. This formalism is best reflected in a completely revised style of specifying abstract data types (ADTs).

Organization

Chapters 1–11 constitute the core of a CS1 course. The material in Chapters 1 and 2 includes the basics of most programming languages: input, output, data types, arithmetic, and standard functions. Even if students are well versed in these mechanics from another programming language, they should not skip these two chapters. The fundamental issues of Computer Science as a science (1.1) and program development by top-down design (1.3) are contained in this material. We feel it is very important for students to have a broad perspective of the discipline of Computer Science and to use a problem-solving approach when designing solutions to solve problems. Chapters 1 and 2 set the stage for this kind of development.

Throughout the text, we have attempted to explain and develop concepts carefully. These are illustrated by frequent examples and diagrams. New concepts are then used in complete programs to show how they aid in solving problems. An early and consistent emphasis has been placed on good writing habits and on producing neat, attractive output. We firmly believe program documentation and readability are important. Thus, we frequently discuss them in the text and offer style tips where appropriate.

Subprograms are presented fairly early in this text. Procedures and user-defined functions are presented in their entirety in Chapter 3 before either selection statements (Chapter 4) or repetition statements (Chapter 5). This facilitates good problem solving habits in that a completely modular approach can be emphasized early in the course. Students are introduced to recursion at the end of Chapter 5 (this is Section 11.1 from the Nance, one semester Alternate Edition) so they are familiar with this important topic when it is explored more deeply in Chapter 17.

The first part of Chapter 6 introduces text files. From that point on examples and programming problems use a combination of interactive and non-interactive environments. If you prefer, it would be possible to present the material on text files (Section 6.1) earlier in the course.

Chapters 7 and 8 develop arrays. Due to the significance of this concept these chapters contain numerous examples, illustrations, and applications. Both the Selection Sort and Bubble Sort are presented in Chapter 7. Sequential and binary search algorithms are also covered in this chapter. Additional sorting algorithms are studied in Chapters 12 and 19. Records and files are discussed in Chapters 9 and 10, respectively. Their placement there is traditional. These chapters, combined with Chapters 7 and 8, present a detailed treatment of static data structures.

Chapter 11, Sets, could be presented any time after Chapter 6. Although a full chapter has been devoted to this topic, a working knowledge could be given to students in one or two days.

Chapters 12–20 contain material for what might typically be called a CS2 course. Collectively, Chapters 12–14 present more detailed treatment of the software engineering principles that were introduced in the earlier chapters. Chapter 12 introduces big-O analysis as the essential tool used by the computer scientist in evaluating alternative strategies from a time/space perspective. Simple sorting and searching algorithms are used as examples for the application of big-O analysis. By reviewing some of the algorithms already presented in Chapter 7, we allow the student to concentrate on the intricacies of big-O analysis without having to worry about unraveling new and complex algorithms.

Chapter 13 is a critical chapter since it presents the formalism by which ADTs are studied throughout the remainder of the text. This formalism consists of specifying an ADT's operations as a set of language-independent preconditions and postconditions before moving to a Pascal Interface for an ADT. Rules for using and implementing ADTs are developed. Strings, two-dimensional tables, and keyed lists are presented as examples of ADTs. Since students have studied big-O analysis in the previous chapter, they are well equipped to compare and contrast the efficiencies of various implementation techniques for these ADTs. These three examples recur frequently throughout the remainder of the text as we explore more advanced techniques for implementing ADTs.

Chapter 14 pulls together and expands upon the software engineering issues that have been introduced in earlier chapters. The first three sections of this chapter are critical in that they present a detailed treatment of the analysis, design, implementation, testing, maintenance, and obsolescence stages of the software system life cycle. The final three sections of the chapter discuss random access file processing, formal verification, and object-oriented programming respectively; these sections are independent of the rest of the text and can be covered at an instructor's discretion.

Chapters 15–18 cover essential data structures and recursion as advanced programming techniques. Each data structure is first defined as an abstract type; various implementations are then discussed and compared using the big-O terminology of Chapter 12. This provides a convincing demonstration of the utility of big-O analysis. Chapter 15, devoted to linked lists and pointers, discusses how linked lists might be used as an alternative implementation strategy for the ADTs that were introduced in Chapter 13. Chapter 16 covers stacks and queues, discussing simulation and parsing respectively as applications of these ADTs. As a follow-up to our discussion of recursion in Chapter 5, Chapter 17 explores recursion in depth. A graduated series of examples is presented, culminating with the use of trial-and-error backtracking as a problem-solving technique. Chapter 18 provides examples of the utility of recursion by using it as the primary technique for processing data in binary trees, general trees, and graphs. The importance of binary search trees as an alternative way of representing keyed lists is also discussed, with comparisons being drawn to the array and linked list implementations previously covered in Chapters 13 and 15. The material on general trees, graphs, and networks in the final two sections of Chapter 18 can be omitted without affecting a student's understanding of the chapters that follow.

The background in software engineering and data structures found in Chapters 13–18 prepares the student for the more complex sort and search algorithms of Chapters 19 and 20. In Chapter 19, sorting methods that break the $O(n^2)$ barrier are investigated. These methods include the shell sort, quick sort, heap sort, and merge sort. Chapter 20 scrutinizes search techniques such as hashing, indexing, indexed sequential search, B-trees, and tries.

 Throughout this text, algorithms are implemented in standard Pascal. Due to the increasing use of Turbo Pascal with personal computers, Turbo Pascal references are included in the margins to indicate where Turbo differs from standard Pascal.

 Both interactive and batch mode examples are used in this text. Interactive examples in the first half of the text are indicated by a logo in the left margin, as shown here.

 Features

This text has a number of noteworthy pedagogical features.

■ Objectives—a concise list of topics and learning objectives in each section.

■ Style tips—suggestions for programming style, intended to enhance readability.

■ Exercises—short answer questions at the end of each section.

■ Programming problems and projects—starting with Chapter 2, lengthy lists of suggestions for complete programs and projects given at ends of chapters. Many of the projects involve communication skills, as well as programming skills.

■ Module specifications for program modules.

■ Structure charts to reflect modular development. These include use of data flow arrows to emphasize transmission of data to and/or from each module. This sets the stage for understanding use of value and variable parameters when procedures are introduced.

■ Notes of Interest—vignettes intended to create awareness of and interest in various aspects of computer science. These provide a vehicle for giving students an overview of what lies ahead in their study of computer science.

■ Suggestions for test programs—ideas included in exercises that encourage the student to use the computer to determine answers to questions and to see how to implement concepts in short programs.

■ Focus on Program Design—beginning with Chapter 5, at the end of each chapter, a complete program is designed (and in some cases fully implemented) to illustrate the use of concepts developed within the chapter.

■ Running and debugging tips—beginning with Chapter 5, these hints precede each end-of-chapter summary section.

■ New terms are italicized when first introduced.

■ Extensive figures and graphic documentation—these allow students to visualize the effect of algorithms on data. Algorithms are pictorially traced in a way that will bring them to life in the students' minds.

■ Tables in chapter-end summaries—these are used frequently to compare and evaluate various Pascal features, data structures, and algorithms. Such compact, side-by-side comparisons emphasize the importance of knowing the relative advantages and disadvantages of the various techniques studied.

■ Appendixes and back matter—appendixes on reserved words, standard identifiers, syntax diagrams, character sets, compiler error messages, Turbo Pascal, the GOTO statement, packing and unpacking, and random numbers follow the chapters. In addition, the text presents a complete glossary, as well as answers to selected exercises.

Changes in the Second Edition

In writing the second edition of this text, we worked to better integrate the topics from the CS1 and CS2 portions of the text. Toward this end, we emphasized software engineering concepts earlier in the text and presented principles of abstraction more formally throughout. In doing so, we recognized that these changes must not destroy the pedagogical features that proved attractive in the first edition.

The second edition offers the following:

■ Continuing emphasis on the design of solutions to problems.

■ Three new sections on using assertions.

■ New material emphasizing communication in computer science. This includes text references and exercises in every chapter designed to encourage students to interview people, write reports, give oral reports, and write program specifications without writing code.

■ Replacement of case studies in the CS2 portion of the book with Focus on Program Design sections. In addition to sometimes presenting a complete program, these sections illustrate design issues and techniques for laboratory experimentation with complex algorithms.

■ Significantly more material on procedural and data abstraction in the CS1 portion of the text to prepare students for the more formal approach to ADTs in Chapter 13.

■ New material on software engineering in the CS1 portion of the text to complement the detailed presentation of this topic in Chapter 14.

■ Optional material on formal verification and object-oriented programming has been incorporated.

■ Material on stacks and queues has been combined in one chapter.

■ Recursion is now introduced in the CS1 portion of the text to prepare students for a new, in-depth presentation in Chapter 17.

■ In addition to use of graphic documentation to help students visualize algorithms, run-time trace diagrams are introduced as a means of analyzing recursive algorithms.

■ Additional material on heaps and priority queues has been added to the chapter on trees.

Ancillaries

It is our belief that a broad-based teaching support package is essential for an introductory course in Pascal. Thus, the following ancillary materials are available from West Publishing Company:

1. Laboratory Manuals—In keeping with our intent to provide a modern approach and to meet the growing need for laboratory experience as put forth by the new ACM Curriculum Guidelines, there are two laboratory manuals (one for users of standard Pascal and one for

users of Turbo Pascal) that are tied closely to the text's pedagogy. Authored by Carol Wilson and Tom Naps and class-tested with students at two universities, both provide excellent sets of lab exercises to promote students' understanding.

2. A Student's Solutions Manual—This contains solutions to all odd-numbered exercises at the end of each section. These solutions represent more thorough answers than those provided in the Answers to Selected Exercises section in the text. Explanation and development are given for appropriate problems. Complete solutions for two programming problems are included for each chapter.

3. An Instructor's Manual—This manual contains the following for each chapter:
   a. outline
   b. teaching test questions
   c. chapter test questions
   d. answers to test questions
   e. solutions to all even-numbered end-section exercises

4. A Set of Transparency Masters—More than 150 transparency masters are available to adopters of the text. These include figures, tables, and selected other material from the text.

5. Software with machine-readable Programming Problems—This software contains at least four complete programming problem solutions for each of the early chapters and at least two complete programming problem solutions for each chapter from Chapter 12 on. It also includes the complete Focus on Program Design problem. This software is available for IBM-PCs and compatibles, Apple MacIntoshes, and DEC Vaxes in both standard and Turbo Pascal.

6. A Computerized Test Bank—Adopters of this edition will receive a computerized test-generation system. This provides a test-bank system that allows you to edit, add, or delete as you wish.

7. West Publishing Company's videotape library—Adopters can choose from a list of relevant computer science videotapes. Contact your West representative for more information.

For students who may be uncertain about wanting to take CS2 and thus are using CS1 to explore their interest in taking more computer science courses, the material presented in this text may also be covered using two separate texts: *Pascal: Understanding Programming and Problem-Solving, Second Alternate Edition,* by Doug Nance and *Introduction to Program Design and Data Structures* by Tom Naps. These two texts are integrated with *Introduction to Computer Science* in a fashion that would allow students in the same class the choice of using the single combined text or the two separate texts. Contact your West representative for details and examination copies.

Acknowledgments

The patient support of our editors at West, Jerry Westby and Denis Ralling, and copyeditor Janet Hunter has been a key ingredient in producing this text. We have now worked with Jerry, Denis, and Janet on a variety of authoring endeavors. In addition to being experts at what they do, they each have become valued long-distance friends. The production staff at West, especially production assistant Lynette D'Amico, have battled a variety of obstacles to keep simultaneous projects on schedule.

As we revised and revised, the wisdom of many reviewers has woven itself into the text. They are:

Stephen J. Allan
Utah State University

Robert B. Anderson
University of Houston

Anthony Q. Baxter
University of Kentucky

Sid Bradley
McNeese State University

John Carroll
San Diego State University

Thomas J. Cheatham
Western Kentucky University

Robert Christiansen
University of Iowa

Timothy R. Colburn
University of Minnesota at Duluth

David Cordes
University of Alabama

Lee D. Cornell
Mankato State University

Aija Downing
University of Western Ontario

Linda J. Elliott
La Salle University

George Friedman
University of Illinois at Urbana-Champaign

Hugh Garraway
University of Southern Mississippi

C. Neil Harris
DeAnza College

Gary F. Hasman
Alfred University

Earl Hasz
Metropolitan State College of Denver

Linda Hayden
Elizabeth City State University

Michael Jenkin
York University

William C. Jones, Jr.
Central Connecticut State University

Donald Johnson
North Central College

Debbie C. Kaneko
Hampton University

Angela R. Keith
Elizabethtown Community College

S. B. Khleif
Tennessee Technological University

Danny Kopec
University of Maine

Howard Kurs
Normandale Community College

Kurk Lew
New River Community College

Doris K. Lidtke
Towson State University

Ronald A. Mann
University of Louisville

Timothy S. Margush
University of Akron

William A. Moy
University of Wisconsin-Parkside

Mostafa Nassar
Acadia University

Michael J. Murphy
University of Houston-Downtown

William R. Nico
California State-Hayward

Lynne O'Hanlon
Los Angeles Pierce College

Joshua D. Panar
Ryerson Polytechnical Institute

Sue Pilgreen
McNeese State University

Ingrid F. Russell
University of Hartford

James A. Schaefer
Rhode Island College

Paul S. Schnare
Eastern Kentucky University

Kay G. Schulze
United States Naval Academy

Patricia A. McQuaid
Auburn University

David J. Thuente
Indiana-Purdue University at Ft. Wayne

Winnie Y. Yu
Southern Connecticut State University

Debra Trantina
Arizona State University

Jim Cowles, Ohio University in Lancaster, has done yeoman's work in preparing many of the ancillaries. Carol Wilson, Western Kentucky University, contributed two Notes of Interest and prepared a Laboratory Manual that can be used with this text. Marilyn Jussell, Kearney State College, revised the Turbo Pascal Notes (Appendix 6) to make this text more practical for classroom use when Turbo is being used by students in the class. Lawrence students Chris Hundhausen, Beth Martinson, and Phoutha Keopanya all contributed solutions to selected exercises for the final section of back matter. We would also like to extend thanks to Bhagat Singh, who contributed to the first edition of this text.

Of course, our greatest debt is to our families. Our method of writing books has made it a true family project for each of us. Our families' contributions obviously go much beyond word processing, proofreading, and making backups. They offer continual reminders to put—and keep—computer science in its proper perspective.

*A computer will do what you
tell it to do, but that may be
much different from what you
had in mind.*

Joseph Weizenbaum

Computer Science: Architecture, Languages, Problem Solving, and Programs

This chapter provides a quick introduction to computer science, computer languages and computer programs. Section 1.1 provides a preview of the study of computer science. Section 1.2 begins to explore the relationship between computers, computer languages, and computer programs. Section 1.3 lays the foundation for what many consider is the most important aspect of entry-level courses in computer science: program development. The problem solving theme started in this section is continued throughout the text. The remainder of Chapter 1 is intended to enable you to write complete programs as early as possible. You will thus be able to use the computer as an active participant from the initial stages of your study of computer science.

As you read this chapter, do not be overly concerned about the introduction and early use of terminology. All terms will be subsequently developed. A good approach to an introductory chapter like this is to reread it periodically. This will help you maintain a good perspective as to how new concepts and techniques fit in the broader picture of using computers. Finally, remember that learning a language that will make a computer work can be exciting; being able to control such a machine can lead to quite a sense of power.

■ **1.1**
Computer Science: A Preview

Computer science is a very young discipline. Electronic computers were initially developed in the 1940s. Those who worked with computers in the 1940s and 1950s often did so by teaching themselves about computers; most schools did not then offer any instruction in computer science. However, as these early pioneers in computers learned more about the machines they were using, a collection of principles began to evolve into the discipline we now call computer science. Because it emerged from the efforts of people using computers in a variety of disciplines, the influence of these disciplines can often be seen in computer science. With that in mind, in the next sections I will briefly define what computer science is (and what it is not).

Computer Science Is Not Computer Literacy

In the 1990s, computer literate people will know how to use a variety of computer software to make their professional lives and home lives more productive and easier. This software includes, for instance, word processors for writing and data management systems for storing every conceivable form of information (from address lists to recipes).

However, knowing how to use specific pieces of computer software is not the same as acquiring an understanding of computer science, just as being able to drive a car does not qualify you as an expert mechanic. The user of computer software must merely be able to follow instructions about how to use the software. On the other hand, the modern computer scientist must, more than anything else, be a skillful problem-solver. The collection of problems that computer science encompasses and the techniques used to solve those problems are the real substance of this rapidly expanding discipline.

Computer Science Is Mathematics and Logic

The problem-solving emphasis of computer science borrows heavily from the areas of mathematics and logic. Faced with a problem, computer scientists must first formulate a solution. This method of solution, or *algorithm* as it is often called in computer science, must be thoroughly understood before the computer scientists make any attempt to implement the solution on the computer. Thus, at the early stages of problem solution, computer scientists work solely with their minds and do not rely upon the machine in any way.

Once the solution is understood, computer scientists must then state the solution to this problem in a formal language called a *programming language.* This parallels the fashion in which mathematicians or logicians must develop a proof or argument in the formal language of mathematics. This formal solution as stated in a programming language must then be evaluated in terms of its correctness, style, and efficiency. Part of this evaluation process involves entering the formally stated algorithm as a programmed series of steps for the computer to follow.

Another part of the evaluation process is distinctly separate from a consideration of whether or not the computer produces the "right answer" when the program is executed. Indeed, one of the main areas of emphasis throughout this book is in developing well-designed solutions to problems and in recognizing the difference between such solutions and ones that work, but inelegantly. True computer scientists seek not just solutions to problems, but the best possible solutions.

Computer Science Is Science

Perhaps nothing is as intrinsic to the scientific method as the formulation of hypotheses to explain phenomena and the careful testing of these hypotheses to prove them right or wrong. This same process plays an integral role in the way computer scientists work.

Upon observing a problem, such as a long list of names that we would like arranged in alphabetical order, computer scientists formulate a hypothesis in the form of an algorithm that they believe will effectively solve the problem. Using mathematical techniques, they can make predictions about how such a proposed algorithm will solve the problem. But because the problems facing computer scientists arise from the world of real applications, predictive techniques relying solely upon mathematical theory are not sufficient to prove an algorithm correct. Ultimately, computer scientists must implement their solutions on computers and test them in the complex situations that originally gave rise to the problems. Only after such thorough testing can the hypothetical solutions be declared right or wrong.

Moreover, just as many scientific principles are not 100 percent right or wrong, the hypothetical solutions posed by computer scientists are often subject to limitations. An understanding of those limitations—of when the method is appropriate and when it is not—is a crucial part of the knowledge that computer scientists must have. This is analogous to the way in which any scientist must be aware of the particular limitations of a scientific theory in explaining a given set of phenomena.

Do not forget the experimental nature of computer science as you study this book. You must participate in computer science to truly learn it. Although a good book can help, *you* must solve the problems, implement those solutions on the computer, and then test the results. View each of the problems you are assigned as an experiment for which you are to propose a solution and then verify the correctness of your solution by testing it on the computer. If the solution does not work exactly as you hypothesized, do not become discouraged. Instead, ask yourself why it did not work; by doing so you will acquire a deeper understanding of the problem and your solution. In this sense, the computer represents the experimental tool of the computer scientist. Do not be afraid to use it for exploration.

Computer Science Is Engineering

Whatever the area of specialization, an engineer must neatly combine a firm grasp of scientific principles with implementation techniques. Without knowledge of the principles, the engineer's ability to creatively design models for a problem's solution is severely limited. Such model-building is crucial to the engineering design process. The ultimate design of a bridge, for instance, is the result of the engineer's considering many possible models of the bridge and then selecting the best one. The transformation of abstract ideas into models of a problem's solution is thus central to the engineering design process. The ability to generate a variety of models that can be explored is the hallmark of creative engineering.

Similarly, the computer scientist is a model-builder. Faced with a problem, the computer scientist must construct models for its solution. Such models take the form of an information structure to hold the data pertinent to the problem and the algorithmic method to manipulate that information structure to actually solve the problem. Just as an engineer must have an in-depth understanding of scientific principles to build a model, so must a computer scientist. With these principles, the computer scientist may conceive of models that are elegant, efficient, and appropriate to the problem at hand.

An understanding of principles alone is not sufficient for either the engineer or the computer scientist. Experience in the actual implementation of hypothetical models is also necessary. Without such experience, you can have only very limited intuition about what is feasible and how a large-scale project should be organized to reach a successful conclusion. Ultimately, computers are used to solve problems in the real world. There, you will need to design programs that come in on time, that are within (if not under) the budget, and that solve all aspects of the original problem. The experience you acquire in designing problem solutions and then implementing them is vital to your being a complete computer scientist. Hence, remember that you cannot actually study computer science without actively doing it. To merely read about computer science techniques will leave you with an unrealistic perspective of what is possible.

Computer Science Is Communication

As the discipline of computer science continues to evolve, communication is assuming a more significant role in the undergraduate curriculum. The Association for Computing Machinery, Inc. Curriculum Guidelines for 1991 state, " . . . undergraduate programs should prepare students to . . . define a problem clearly; . . . document that solution; . . . and to communicate that solution to colleagues, professionals in other fields, and the general public." [page 7]

It is no longer sufficient to be content with a program that runs correctly. Extra attention should be devoted to the communication aspects associated with such a program. For instance, you might be asked to submit a written proposal prior to designing a solution; or to carefully and completely document a program as it is being designed; or to write a follow-up report after a program has been completed.

These are some ways in which communication can be emphasized as an integral part of computer science. Several opportunities will be provided in the Exercises and problem lists of this text for you to focus on the communication aspects associated with computer science.

Computer Science Is Interdisciplinary

The problems solved by computer scientists come from a variety of disciplines—mathematics, physics, chemistry, biology, geology, economics, business, engineering, linguistics, and psychology, to name a few. As a computer scientist working on a problem in one of these areas, you must be a quasi-expert in that discipline as well as in computer science. For instance, you cannot write a program to manage the checking account system of a bank unless you thoroughly understand how banks work and how that bank runs its checking accounts. At minimum, you must be literate enough in other disciplines to converse with the people for whom you are writing programs and to learn precisely what it is they want the computer to do for them. Since such people are often very naive about the computer and its capabilities, you

A NOTE OF INTEREST

Ethics and Computer Science

Ethical issues in computer science are rapidly gaining public attention. As evidence, consider the following article from the *Washington Post*.

Should law-enforcement agencies be allowed to use computers to help them determine whether a person ought to be jailed or allowed out on bond? Should the military let computers decide when and on whom nuclear weapons should be used?

While theft and computer viruses have not gone away as industry problems, a group of 30 computer engineers and ethicists who gathered in Washington recently agreed that questions about the proper use of computers is taking center stage. At issue is to what degree computers should be allowed to make significant decisions that human beings normally make.

Already, judges are consulting computers, which have been programmed to predict how certain personality types will behave. Judges are basing their decisions more on what the computer tells them than on their own analysis of the arrested person's history. Computers are helping doctors decide treatments for patients. They played a major role in the July 1988 shooting of the Iranian jetliner by the USS Vincennes, and they are the backbone of this country's Strategic Defense Initiative ("Star Wars").

Representatives from universities, IBM Corp., the Brookings Institution, and several Washington theological seminaries [recently discussed] what they could do to build a conscience in the computer field.

The computer industry has been marked by "creativity and drive for improvement and advancement," not by ethical concerns, said Robert Melford, chairman of the computing-ethics subcommittee of the Institute of Electrical and Electronics Engineers.

Computer professionals, Melford said, often spend much of their time in solitude, separated from the people affected by their programs who could provide valuable feedback.

Unlike hospitals, computer companies and most organized computer users have no staff ethicists or ethics committees to ponder the consequences of what they do. Few businesses have written policies about the proper way to govern computers. But there is evidence that technical schools, at least, are beginning to work an ethical component into their curricula. [For example, in recent years,] all computer engineering majors at Polytechnic University in Brooklyn [have been required to take a course in ethics.] The Massachusetts Institute of Technology is considering mandating five years of study instead of the current four to include work in ethics.

Affirmation that such questions should be addressed by computer scientists is contained in the 1991 curriculum guidelines of the Association for Computing Machinery, Inc. These guidelines state that "Undergraduates should also develop an understanding of the historical, social, and ethical context of the discipline and the profession."

You will see further Notes of Interest on this area of critical concern later in this book.

will have to possess considerable communication skills as well as a knowledge of that other discipline.

Are you beginning to think that a computer scientist must be knowledgeable about much more than just the computer? If so, you are correct. Too often, computer scientists are viewed as technicians, tucked away in their own little worlds and not thinking or caring about anything other than computers. Nothing could be further from the truth. The successful computer scientist must be able to communicate, to learn new ideas quickly, and to adapt to ever-changing conditions. Computer science is emerging from its early dark ages into a mature process, one that I hope you will find rewarding and exciting. In studying computer science, you will be developing many talents; this text can get you started on the road to that development process.

■ **1.2**
Computer Architecture and Language

This section is intended to provide you with a brief overview of what computers are and how they are used. Although there are various sizes, makes, and models of computers, you will see that they all operate in basically the same straightforward manner. Whether you work on a personal computer that costs a few hundred dollars or on a mainframe that costs in the millions, the principles of making the machine work are essentially the same.

In this section we will look at components of a computer and the idea of language for a computer. Also, we will continue to emphasize the notion of problem solving, which is independent of any particular language.

Modern Computers

The search for aids to perform calculations is almost as old as number systems. Early devices include the abacus, Napier's bones, the slide rule, and mechanical adding machines. More recently, calculators have changed the nature of personal computing as a result of their availability, low cost, and high speed. The development of computers over time is highlighted in Figure 1.1. For more complete information, see *People and Computers, Partners in Problem Solving*, by John F. Vinsonhaler, Christian C. Wagner, and Castelle G. Gentry, West Publishing Company, 1989.

The last few decades have seen the most significant change in computing machines in the world's history as a result of improvements that have led to modern computers. As recently as the 1960s, a computer required several rooms because of its size. However, the advent of silicon chips has reduced the size and increased the availability of computers so that parents are able to purchase personal computers as presents for their children. These computers are more powerful than the early behemoths.

What is a computer? According to *Webster's New World Dictionary of the American Language* (2nd College Edition), a computer is "an electronic machine which, by means of stored instructions and information, performs

FIGURE 1.1
Development of computers

Era	Early Computing Devices		Mechanical Computers	Electro-mechanical Computers
Year	1000 B.C. A.D. 1614	1650	1900	1945
Development	Abacus Napier's bones		Adding machine Slide rule Difference engine Analytic engine	Cogged wheels Instruction register Operation code Address Plug board Harvard Mark I Tabulating machine

rapid, often complex calculations or compiles, correlates, and selects data." Basically, a computer can be thought of as a machine that manipulates information in the form of numbers and characters. This information is referred to as *data*. What makes computers remarkable is the extreme speed and precision with which they can store, retrieve, and manipulate data.

Several types of computers currently are available. An oversimplification is to categorize computers as mainframe, minicomputer, or microcomputer. In this grouping, *mainframe* computers are the large machines used by major companies, government agencies, and universities. They have the capability of being used by as many as 100 or more people at the same time and can cost millions of dollars. *Minicomputers,* in a sense, are smaller versions of large computers. They can be used by several people at once but have less storage capacity and cost far less. *Microcomputers* are frequently referred to as personal computers. They have limited storage capacity (in a relative sense), are generally used by one person at a time, and can be purchased for as little as a few hundred dollars.

As you begin your work with computers, you will hear people talking about *hardware* and *software*. Hardware refers to the actual machine and its support devices. Software refers to programs that make the machine do something. Many software packages exist for today's computers. They include word processing, data-base programs, spreadsheets, games, operating systems, and compilers. You can (and will!) learn to create your own software. In fact, that is what this book is all about.

A *program* can be thought of as a set of instructions that tells the machine what to do. When you have written a program, the computer will behave exactly as you have instructed it. It will do no more or no less than what is contained in your specific instructions. For example,

Noncommercial Electronic Computers	Batch Processing	Time-Sharing Systems	Personal Computers
1945 1950	1965	1975	Present
First-generation computers	Second-generation computers	Third-generation computers	Fourth-generation computers
Vacuum tubes	Transistors	Integrated circuit technology	Fifth-generation computers (supercomputers)
Machine language programming	Magnetic core memory	Operating system software	Microprocessors
	Assemblers		
	Compilers	Teleprocessing	Workstations
ENIAC	UNIVAC I		
	IBM 704		

```
PROGRAM ComputeAverage (input, output);

VAR
  Score1, Score2, Score3 : integer;
  Average : real;

BEGIN
  writeln ('Enter three scores and press <RETURN>.');
  readln (Score1, Score2, Score3);
  Average := (Score1 + Score2 + Score3) / 3;
  writeln (Average:20:3)
END.
```

is a Pascal program that allows three scores to be entered from a keyboard, computes their average, and then prints the result. Do not be concerned about specific parts of this program. It is intended only to illustrate the idea of a set of instructions. Very soon, you will be able to write significantly more sophisticated programs.

Learning to write programs requires two skills.

1. You need to be able to use specific terminology and punctuation that can be understood by the machine: you need to learn a programming language.
2. You need to be able to develop a plan for solving a particular problem. This plan—or algorithm—is a sequence of steps that, when followed, will lead to a solution of the problem.

Initially, you may think that learning a language is the more difficult task because your problems will have relatively easy solutions. Nothing could be further from the truth! **The single most important thing you can do as a student of computer science is to develop the skill to solve problems.** Once you have this skill, you can learn to write programs in several different languages.

Computer Hardware

Let's take another look at the question: What is a computer? Our previous answer indicated it is a machine. Although there are several forms, names, and brands of computers, each consists of a *main unit* that is subsequently connected to peripheral devices. The main unit of a computer consists of a *central processing unit (CPU)* and *main (primary) memory*. The CPU is the "brain" of the computer. It contains an *arithmetic/logic unit (ALU),* which is capable of performing arithmetic operations and evaluating expressions to see if they are true or false, and the *control unit,* which controls the action of remaining components so your program can be followed step-by-step, or *executed*.

Main memory can be thought of as mailboxes in a post office. It is a sequence of locations where information representing instructions, numbers, characters, and so on can be stored. Main memory is usable while the computer is turned on. It is where the program being executed is stored along with data it is manipulating.

As you develop a greater appreciation of how the computer works, you might wonder: How are data stored in memory? Each memory location has an address and is capable of holding a sequence of *binary* (0 or 1) *digits,* which are commonly referred to as *bits*. Instructions, symbols, letters, numbers, and so on are translated into an appropriate pattern of binary digits and then stored in various memory locations. These are retrieved, used, and changed according to instructions in your program. In fact, the program itself is similarly translated and stored in part of main memory. Main memory can be envisioned as in Figure 1.2, and the main unit can be envisioned as in Figure 1.3.

FIGURE 1.2
Main memory

FIGURE 1.3
Main unit

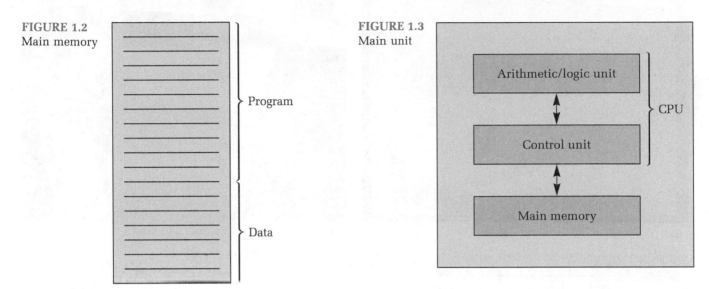

Peripherals can be divided into three categories: *input devices*, *output devices*, and *secondary (auxiliary) memory devices*. Input devices are necessary to give information to a computer. Programs are entered through an input device and then program statements are translated and stored as previously indicated. One input device (a typical keyboard) is shown in Figure 1.4.

FIGURE 1.4
Keyboard

Output devices are necessary to show the results of a program. These are normally in the form of a screen, line printer, impact printer, or laser printer (Figure 1.5). Input and output devices are frequently referred to as *I/O devices*.

Secondary (auxiliary) memory devices are used if additional memory is needed. On small computers, these secondary memory devices could be

FIGURE 1.5
(a) Screen, (b) line printer (mainframe), (c) impact printer (microcomputer), and (d) laser printer

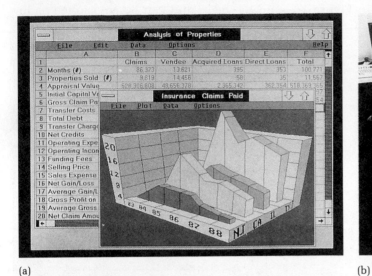

(a)

(b)

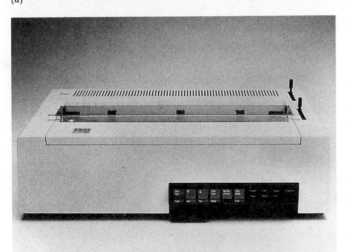

(c)

(d)

floppy disks or hard disks (Figure 1.6), magnetic tapes, or magnetic bubbles. Programs and data waiting to be executed are kept "waiting in the wings" in secondary memory.

Communication between components of a computer is frequently organized around a group of wires called a *bus*. The relationship between a bus and various computer components can be envisioned as in Figure 1.7

A photograph of a bus is shown in Figure 1.8. What appear to be lines between the slots are actually wires imprinted upon the underlying board. Boards with wires connected to peripheral devices may be inserted into the slots.

FIGURE 1.6
(a) Disk drive and (b) microcomputer with hard disk

(a)

(b)

FIGURE 1.7
Illustration of a bus

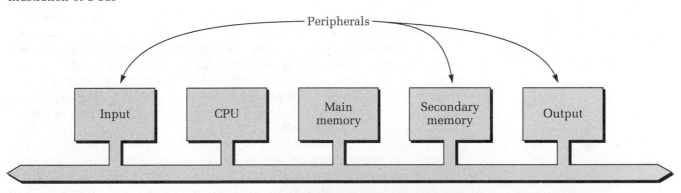

FIGURE 1.8
Bus

Data Loss on Floppy Disks

Why is it important to keep the dust covers on your diskettes? Look at the figure shown here. It illustrates how some very small particles look huge in comparison to the distance between the surface of a diskette and the read/write head. If these particles become lodged between the head and the surface of the diskette, the surface may be scratched, resulting in data loss. So consider yourself warned: handle your disks carefully.

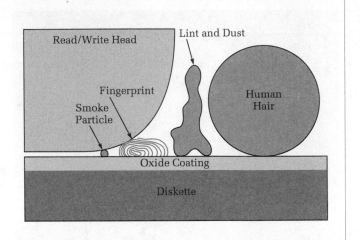

Computer Software

As previously stated, software refers to programs that make the machine do something. Software consists of two kinds of programs: *system software* and *applications software.*

System software includes what is often called the *operating system.* (You may have heard reference to DOS, which is an acronym for Disk Operating System.) The operating system for a computer is a large program and is usually supplied with a computer. This program allows the user to communicate with the hardware. More specifically, an operating system might control computer access (via passwords), allocate peripheral resources (perhaps with a printer queue), schedule shared resources (for CPU use), or control execution of other programs.

Applications software consists of programs designed for a specific use. Examples of applications software include programs for word processing, text editing, simulating spreadsheets, playing games, designing machinery, and figuring payrolls. Most computer users work with applications software and have little need for learning a computer language; the programs they require have already been written to accomplish their tasks.

Computer Languages

What is a computer language? All data transmission, manipulation, storage, and retrieval is actually done by the machine using electrical pulses generated by sequences of binary digits. If eight-digit binary codes are used, there are 256 numbered instructions from 00000000 to 11111111. Instructions for adding two numbers would consist of a sequence of these eight-digit codes.

Instructions written in this form are referred to as *machine language.* It is possible to write an entire program in machine language. However, this is very time consuming and difficult to read and understand.

Therefore, the next level of computer language allows words and symbols to be used in an unsophisticated manner to accomplish simple tasks. For example, the machine code for adding two integers might be

0100001100111010001111010100000100101011101000010

This is replaced by

        LOAD A
        ADD B
        STORE C

This causes the number in A to be added to the number in B and the result to be stored for later use in C. This computer language is an *assembly language,* which is generally referred to as a *low-level language.* What actually happens is that words and symbols are translated into appropriate binary digits and the machine uses the translated form.

Although assembly language is an improvement on machine language for readability and program development, it is still a bit cumbersome. Consequently, many *high-level languages* have been developed; these include Pascal, PL/I, FORTRAN, BASIC, COBOL, C, Ada, Modula-2, Logo, and others. These languages simplify even further the terminology and symbolism necessary for directing the machine to perform various manipulations of data. For example, in these languages, the task of adding two integers would be written as

        C := A + B;   (Pascal)
        C = A + B;   (PL/I)
        C = A + B   (FORTRAN)
        C = A + B   (BASIC)
        ADD A,B GIVING C   (COBOL)
        C = A + B;   (C)
        C := A + B;   (Ada)
        C := A + B;   (Modula-2)
        MAKE "C :A + :B   (Logo)

A high-level language makes it easier to read, write, and understand a program. This book develops the concepts, symbolism, and terminology necessary for using Pascal as a programming language for solving problems. After you have become proficient in using Pascal, you should find it relatively easy to learn the nuances of other high-level languages.

For a moment, let's consider how an instruction such as

        C := A + B;

gets translated into machine code. The actual bit pattern for this code varies according to the machine and software version, but it could be as previously indicated. In order for the translation to happen, a special program called a *compiler* "reads" the high-level instructions and translates them into machine code. This compiled version is then run using some appropriate data. The results are then presented through some form of output device. The special programs that activate the compiler, run the machine-code version, and cause output to be printed are examples of system programs (software). The written program is a *source program,* and the machine-code version generated by the compiler is an *object program* (also referred to as *object code*).

As you will soon see, the compiler does more than just translate instructions into machine code. It also detects certain errors in your source program and prints appropriate messages. For example, if you write the instruction

        C := (A + B;

where a parenthesis is missing, when the compiler attempts to translate this line into machine code, it will detect that ")" is needed to close the parenthetical expression. It will then give you an error message such as

```
ERROR IN VARIABLE
```

You will then need to correct the error (and any others) and recompile your source program before running it with the data.

Before leaving this introductory section let's consider the question: Why study Pascal? Various languages have differing strengths and weaknesses. Pascal's strong features include the following:

1. It incorporates program structure in a reasonable approximation of English. For example, if a certain process is to be repeated until some condition is met, this could be written in the program as

```
REPEAT
      } (process here)
UNTIL  (condition here)
```

2. It allows the use of descriptive words for variables and data types. Thus, programs for computing payrolls could use words like Hours-Worked, StateTax, FICA, TotalDeductions, and GrossPay.
3. It facilitates good problem-solving habits; in fact, many people consider this to be Pascal's main strength. As previously noted, developing the skill to solve a problem using a computer program is the most important trait to develop as a beginning programmer. Pascal is structured in such a manner that it encourages—indeed, almost requires—good problem-solving skills.

A NOTE OF INTEREST

Why Learn Pascal?

From the point of view of many potential users, Pascal's major drawback is that it is a compiled rather than an interpreted language. This means that developing and testing a small Pascal program can take a lot longer and involve many more steps than it would with an interpreted language like BASIC. The effect of this drawback has been lessened recently with the development of interpreter programs for Pascal. [For example, some current versions of Pascal, such as Turbo Pascal, have quick compilation, and are as easy to use as most interpreted languages.] Even so, most programs written by users of personal computers are small ones designed for quick solutions to particular problems, and the use of Pascal for such programs may be a form of overkill.

Ironically, the characteristics of Pascal that make it relatively unsuited for small programs are a direct consequence of its strengths as a programming language. The discipline imposed by the language makes it easier to understand large programs, but it may be more than a small program demands. For serious development of large programs or for the creation of tools that will be used over and over again (and require modifications from time to time), Pascal is clearly superior.

Experts generally consider Pascal an important language for people who are planning to study computer science or to learn programming. Indeed, the College Entrance Examination Board has designated Pascal as the required language for advanced-placement courses in computer science for high school students. While it is true that an experienced programmer can write clearly structured programs in any language, learning the principles of structured programming is much easier in Pascal.

Is Pascal difficult to learn? We don't think so, but the question is relative and may depend on which language you learn first. Programmers become accustomed to the first language they learn, making it the standard by which all others are judged. Even the poor features of the familiar language come to be seen as necessities, and a new language seems inferior. Don't let such subjective evaluations bar your way to learning Pascal, a powerful and elegant programming language.

You are now ready to begin a detailed study of Pascal. You will undoubtedly spend much time and encounter some frustration during the course of your work. I hope your efforts result in an exciting and rewarding learning experience. Good luck.

■ 1.3
Program Development— Top-Down Design

We are now ready to examine problems that computers can solve. First we need to know how to solve a problem and then we need to learn how to use a programming language to implement our solution on the computer.

Before looking at problem solving and writing programs for the computer, we should consider some psychological aspects of working in computer science. Studying computer science can cause a significant amount of frustration because

1. Planning is a critical issue. First, you must plan to develop instructions to solve your problem and then you should plan to translate those instructions into code before you sit down at the keyboard. You should not attempt to type in code "off the top of your head."
2. Time is a major problem. Writing programs is not like completing other assignments. You cannot expect to complete a programming assignment by staying up late the night before it is due. You must begin early and expect to make several revisions before your final version will be ready.
3. Successful problem solving and programming require extreme precision. Generally, concepts in computer science are not difficult; however, implementation of these concepts allows no room for error. For example, one misplaced semicolon in a 1,000-line program could prevent the program from working.

In other words, you must be prepared to plan well, start early, be patient, handle frustration, and work hard to succeed in computer science. If you cannot do this, you will probably neither enjoy computer science nor be successful at it.

The key to writing a successful program is planning. Good programs do not just happen; they are the result of careful design and patience. Just as an artist commissioned to paint a portrait would not start out by shading in the lips and eyes, a good computer programmer would not attack a problem by immediately trying to write code for a program to solve the problem. Writing a program is like writing an essay: an overall theme is envisioned, an outline of major ideas is developed, each major idea is subdivided into several parts, and each part is developed using individual sentences.

Six Steps to Good Programming Habits

In developing a program to solve a problem, six steps should be followed: analyze the problem, develop an algorithm, write code for the program, run the program, test the results and document the program. These steps will help develop good problem-solving habits and, in turn, solve programming problems correctly. A brief discussion of each of these steps follows:

Step 1. Analyze the Problem. This is not a trivial task. Before you can do anything, you must know exactly what it is you are to do. You must be able to formulate a clear and precise statement of what is to be done. You should understand completely what data are available and what may be assumed. You should also know exactly what output is desired and the form it should take.

Step 2. Develop an Algorithm. An algorithm is a finite sequence of effective statements that, when applied to the problem, will solve it. An *effective statement* is a clear, unambiguous instruction that can be carried out. Each algorithm you develop should have a specific beginning; at the completion of one step, have the next step uniquely determined; and have an ending that is reached in a reasonable amount of time.

Step 3. Write Code for the Program. When the algorithm correctly solves the problem, you can think about translating your algorithm into a high-level language. An effective algorithm will significantly reduce the time you need to complete this step.

Step 4. Run the Program. After writing the code, you are ready to run the program. This means that, using an editor, you type the program code into the computer, compile the program, and run the program. At this point, you may discover errors that can be as simple as typing errors or that may require a reevaluation of all or parts of your algorithm. The probability of having to make some corrections or changes is quite high.

Step 5. Test the Results. After your program has run, you need to be sure that the results are correct, that they are in a form you like, and that your program produces the correct solution in all cases. To be sure the results are correct, you must look at them and compare them with what you expect. In the case of using a program with arithmetic operations, this means checking some results with pencil and paper. With complex programs, you will need to thoroughly test the program by running it many times using data that you have carefully selected. Often you will need to make revisions and return to Step 4.

Step 6. Document the Program. It is very important to completely document a working program. The writer knows how the program works; if others are to modify it, they must know the logic used. As you develop the ability to write programs to solve more complex problems, you will find it helpful to include documentation in Step 3 as you write the code.

Developing Algorithms

Algorithms for solving a problem can be developed by stating the problem and then subdividing the problem into major subtasks. Each subtask can then be subdivided into smaller tasks. This process is repeated until each remaining task is one that is easily solved. This process is known as *top-down design,* and each successive subdivision is referred to as a *stepwise refinement.* Tasks identified at each stage of this process are called *modules.* The relationship between modules can be shown graphically in a *structure chart* (see Figure 1.9).

To illustrate developing an algorithm, we will use the problem of updating a checkbook after a transaction has been made. A first-level refinement is shown in Figure 1.10. An arrow pointing into a module means information is needed before the task can be performed. An arrow pointing out of a module means the module task has been completed and information required for subsequent work is available. Each of these modules could be further refined as shown in Figure 1.11. Finally, one of the last modules could be refined as shown in Figure 1.12. The complete top-down design

FIGURE 1.9
Structure chart illustrating top-down design

FIGURE 1.10
First-level refinement

FIGURE 1.11
Second-level refinement

FIGURE 1.12
Third-level refinement

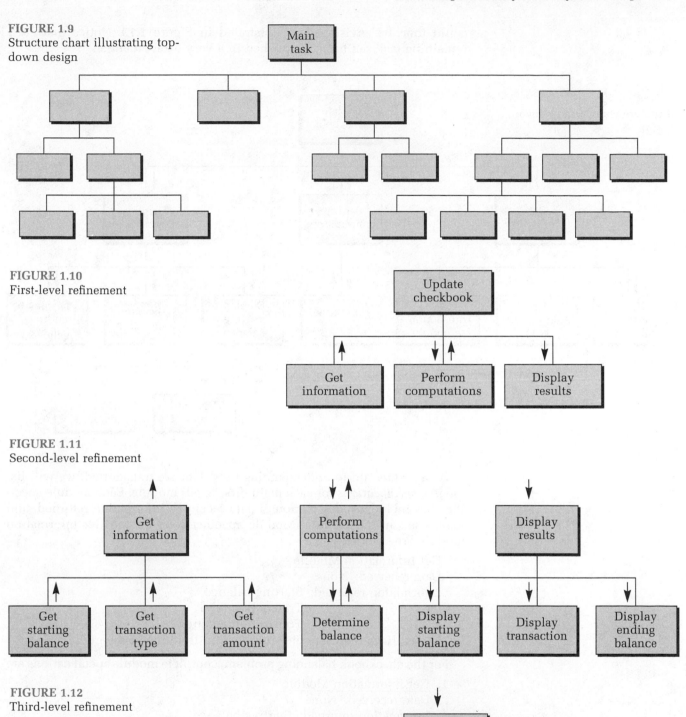

could then be envisioned as illustrated in Figure 1.13. Notice that each remaining task can be accomplished in a very direct manner.

FIGURE 1.13
Structure chart for top-down design

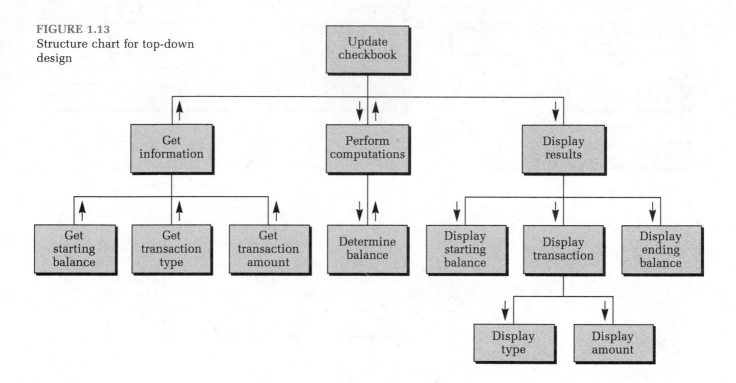

As a further aid to understanding how data are transmitted, we will list *module specifications* for each main (first-level) module. Each module specification includes a description of data received, information returned, and logic used in the module. Module specifications for the Get Information module are

Get Information Module
Data received: None
Information returned: Starting balance
                       Transaction type
                       Transaction amount
Logic: Have the user enter information from the keyboard.

For the checkbook-balancing problem, complete module specifications are

1. Get Information Module
    Data received: None
    Information returned: Starting balance
                          Transaction type
                          Transaction amount
    Logic: Have the user enter information from the keyboard.

2. Perform Computations Module
    Data received: Starting balance
                    Transaction type
                    Transaction amount

Information returned: Ending balance
Logic: If transaction is a deposit, add it to the starting balance; otherwise, subtract it.

3. Display Results Module
Data received: Starting balance
Transaction type
Transaction amount
Ending balance
Information returned: None
Logic: Display results in a readable form.

At least two comments should be made about top-down design. First, different people can (and probably will) have different designs for the solution of a problem. However, each good design will have well-defined modules with functional subtasks. Second, the graphic method just used helps to formulate general logic for solving a problem but is somewhat awkward for translating to code. Thus, we will use a stylized, half-English, half-code method called *pseudocode* to illustrate stepwise refinement in such a design. This will be written in English, but the sentence structure and indentations will suggest Pascal code. Major tasks will be numbered with whole numbers and subtasks with decimal numbers. First-level pseudocode for the checkbook-balancing problem is

1. Get information
2. Perform computations
3. Display results

A second-level pseudocode development produces

1. Get information
   1.1   get starting balance
   1.2   get transaction type
   1.3   get transaction amount
2. Perform computations
   2.1   **IF** deposit **THEN**
      add to balance
     ELSE
      subtract from balance
3. Display results
   3.1   display starting balance
   3.2   display transaction
   3.3   display ending balance

Finally, step 3.2 of the pseudocode is subdivided as previously indicated into

   3.2   display transaction
      3.2.1   display transaction type
      3.2.2   display transaction amount

Two final comments are in order. First, each module developed should be tested with data for that module. Once you are sure each module does what you want, the whole program should work when the modules are used together. Second, the process of dividing a task into subtasks is especially suitable for writing programs in Pascal. As you will see, the language supports development of subprograms for specific subtasks.

A NOTE OF INTEREST

Software Verification

Sitting 70 kilometers east of Toronto on the shore of Lake Ontario, the Darlington Nuclear Generating Station looks much like any other large nuclear power plant of the Canadian variety. But behind its ordinary exteriors lies an unusual design feature.

Darlington is the first Canadian nuclear station to use computers to operate the two emergency shutdown systems that safeguard each of its four reactors. In both shutdown systems, a computer program replaces an array of electrically operated mechanical devices— switches and relays—designed to respond to sensors monitoring conditions critical to a reactor's safe operation, such as water levels in boilers.

When completed in 1992, Darlington's four reactors will supply enough electricity to serve a city of 2 million people. Its Toronto-based builder, Ontario Hydro, opted for sophisticated software rather than old-fashioned hardware in the belief that a computer-operated shutdown system would be more economical, flexible, reliable and safe than one under mechanical control.

But that approach carried unanticipated costs. To satisfy regulators that the shutdown software would function as advertised, Ontario Hydro engineers had to go through a frustrating but essential checking process that required nearly three years of extra effort.

"There are lots of examples where software has gone wrong with serious consequences," says engineer GlennH. Archinoff of Ontario Hydro. "If you want a shutdown system to work when you need it, you have to have a high level of assurance."

The Darlington experience demonstrates the tremendous effort involved in establishing the correctness of even relatively short and straightforward computer programs. The 10,000 "lines" of instructions, or code, required for each shutdown system pale in comparison with the 100,000 lines that constitute a typical word-processing program or the millions of lines needed to operate a long-distance telephone network or a space shuttle.

A Pascal program for this problem follows:

```
PROGRAM Checkbook (input, output);

VAR
  StartingBalance,
  EndingBalance,
  TransAmount : real;
  TransType : char;

BEGIN  { Main program }

  { Module for getting the data  }

  writeln;
  writeln ('Enter the starting balance and press <RETURN>.');
  readln (StartingBalance);
  writeln ('Enter the transaction type (D) deposit or (W) withdrawal');
  writeln ('and press <RETURN>.');
  readln (Transtype);
  writeln ('Enter the transaction amount and press <RETURN>.');
  readln (TransAmount);
```

} 1*

*These numbers refer to the modules previously developed with module specifications.

```
     {  Module for performing computations  }

     IF TransType = 'D' THEN
        EndingBalance := StartingBalance + TransAmount
     ELSE
        EndingBalance := StartingBalance - TransAmount;

     {  Module for displaying results  }

     writeln;
     writeln ('Starting Balance           $', StartingBalance:8:2);
     writeln ('Transaction                $', TransAmount:8:2, TransType:2);
     writeln ('---------':33);
     writeln ('Ending Balance             $', EndingBalance:8:2)
END.  {  of main program  }
```

Notice how sections of the program correspond to module specifications. Sample runs of the program produce the output

```
Enter the starting balance and press <RETURN>.
235.16
Enter the transaction type (D) deposit or (W) withdrawal
and press <RETURN>.
D
Enter the transaction amount and press <RETURN>.
75.00

Starting Balance        $  235.16
Transaction             $   75.00 D
                        ---------
Ending Balance          $  310.16

Enter the starting balance and press <RETURN>.
310.16
Enter the transaction type (D) deposit or (W) withdrawal
and press <RETURN>.
W
Enter the transaction amount and press <RETURN>.
65.75

Starting Balance        $  310.16
Transaction             $   65.75 W
                        ---------
Ending Balance          $  244.41
```

You probably would not use the power of a computer for something as simple as this program. You could just press a few calculator keys instead. However, as you will see, the language supports development of subprograms for specific subtasks. You will, for example, soon be able to enhance this program to check for overdrafts, save the new balance for later use, and repeat the process for several transactions. Learning to think in terms of modular development now will aid you not just in creating algorithms to solve problems, but it will aid you in writing programs to solve problems.

Software Engineering

The phrase *software engineering* is used to refer to the process of developing and maintaining very large software systems. Before becoming engrossed in the specifics of solving problems and writing relatively small programs, it is instructive to consider the broader picture faced by those who develop software for "real world" use.

It is not unusual for software systems to be programs that, if written in this size type, would require between 100 and 150 pages of text. These systems must be reliable, economical, and subject to use by a diverse audience. Because of these requirements, software developers must be aware of and practice certain techniques.

As you might imagine, such large programs are not the work of a single individual but are developed by teams of programmers. Issues such as communication, writing style, and technique become as important as developing algorithms to solve particular parts of the problem. Management, coordination, and design are major considerations that need resolution very early in the process. Although you will not face these larger organizational issues in this course, you will see how some of what you learn has implications for larger design issues.

Software engineering has been so titled because techniques and principles from the more established engineering disciplines are used to guide the large-scale development required in major software. To illustrate, consider the problems faced by an engineer who is to design and supervise construction of a bridge. This analysis was presented by Alfred Spector and David Gifford in an article entitled "A Computer Science Perspective on Bridge Design" published in *Communications of the ACM* (April 1986).

Engineers designing a bridge view it first as a hierarchy of substructures. This decomposition process continues on the substructures themselves until a level of very fundamental objects (such as beams and plates) ultimately is reached. This decomposition technique is similar to the stepwise refinement technique used by software designers, who break a complex problem down into a hierarchy of subproblems each of which ultimately can be solved by a relatively simple algorithm.

Engineers build conceptual models before actually constructing a bridge. This model-building allows them to evaluate various design alternatives in a way which eventually leads to the best possible design for the application being considered. This process is analogous to the way in which a skilled software designer builds models of a software system using structure charts and first-level pseudocode descriptions of modules. The designer then studies these conceptual models and eventually chooses the most elegant and efficient model for the application.

By the fashion in which engineers initially break down the bridge design, they insure that different aspects of the design can be addressed by different subordinate groups of design engineers working in a relatively independent fashion. This is similar to the goal of a software designer who oversees a program development team. The design of the software system must insure that individual components may be developed simultaneously by separate groups whose work will not have harmful side effects when the components are finally pulled together.

This overview is presented to give you a better perspective on how developments in this text are part of a greater whole. As you progress through your study of Pascal, you will see specific illustrations of how concepts and techniques can be viewed as part of the software engineering process.

Software System Life Cycle

Software engineering is the process by which large software systems are produced. As you might imagine, these systems need to be maintained and modified; ultimately, they are replaced with other systems. This entire process parallels that of an organism. That is, there is a development, maintenance, and subsequent demise. Thus, this process is referred to as the *soft-*

ware system life cycle. Specifically, a system life cycle can be viewed in the following phases:

1. Analysis
2. Design
3. Coding
4. Testing/verification
5. Maintenance
6. Obsolescence

It probably comes as a surprise that computer scientists view this process as having a phase that precedes the design phase. However, it is extremely critical that a problem be completely understood before any attempt is made to design a solution. The analysis phase is complicated by the fact that potential users may not supply enough information when describing their intended use of a system. Analysis requires careful attention to items such as exact form of input, exact form of output, how data entry errors (there will be some) should be handled, how large the data bases will become, how much training in using the system will be provided, and what possible modifications might be required as the intended audience increases/decreases. Clearly, the analysis phase requires an experienced communicator.

The design phase is what much of this book is about. This is where the solution is developed using a modular approach. Attention must be paid to techniques which include communication, algorithm development, writing style, team work, and so on.

Coding closely follows design. Unfortunately, many beginning students want to write code too quickly. This can be a painful lesson if you have to scrap several days of work because your original design was not sufficient. You are encouraged to make sure your designs are complete before writing any code. In the real world, teams of designers work long hours before programmers ever get a chance to start writing code.

The testing phase of a large system is a significant undertaking. Early testing is done on individual modules to get them running properly. Larger data sets must then be run on the entire program to make sure the modules interact properly with the main program. When the system appears ready to the designers, it is usually field tested by selected users. Each of these testing levels is likely to require changes in the design and coding of the system.

Finally, the system is released to the public and the maintenance phase begins. This phase lasts throughout the remainder of the program's useful life. During this phase, we are concerned with repairing problems that arise with the system after is has been put into use. These problems are not necessarily bugs introduced during the coding phases. More often they are the result of user needs that change over time. For instance, annual changes in the tax laws necessitate changes in even the best payroll programs. Or problems may be due to misinterpretation of user needs during the early analysis phase. Whatever the reason, we must expect that a program will have to undergo numerous changes during its lifetime. During the maintenance phase, the time spent documenting the original program will be repaid many times over. One of the worst tasks imaginable in software development is to be asked to maintain an undocumented program. Undocumented code can quickly become virtually unintelligible, even to the program's original author. Indeed, one of the measures of a good program is how well it stands up to the maintenance phase.

Of course, no matter how good a program may be, it will eventually become obsolete. At that time, the system life cycle starts all over again with the development of a new system to replace the obsolete one. Hence, the system life cycle is never-ending, being itself part of a larger repetitive pattern that continues to evolve with changing user needs and more powerful technology.

Exercises 1.3

1. Which of the following can be considered effective statements; that is, clear, unambiguous instructions that can be carried out? For each statement, explain why it is effective or why it is not.

   a. Pay the cashier $9.15.

   b. Water the plants a day before they die.

   c. Determine all positive prime numbers less than 1,000,000.

   d. Choose X to be the smallest positive fraction.

   e. Invest your money in a stock that will increase in value.

2. What additional information must be obtained in order to understand each of the following problems?

   a. Find the largest number of a set of numbers.

   b. Alphabetize a list of names.

   c. Compute charges for a telephone bill.

3. Outline the main tasks for solving each of the following problems.

   a. Write a good term paper.

   b. Take a vacation.

   c. Choose a college.

   d. Get a summer job.

   e. Compute the semester average for a student in a computer science course and print all pertinent data.

4. Refine the main tasks in each part of Exercise 3 into a sufficient number of levels so that the problem can be solved in a well-defined manner.

5. Use pseudocode to write a solution for each of the following problems. Indicate each stage of your development.

   a. Compute the wages for two employees of a company. The input information will consist of the hourly wage and the number of hours worked in one week. The output should contain a list of all deductions, gross pay, and net pay. For this problem, assume deductions are made for federal withholding taxes, state withholding taxes, social security, and union dues.

   b. Compute the average test score for five students in a class. Input for this problem will consist of five scores. Output should include each score and the average of these scores.

6. Develop an algorithm to find the total, average, and largest number in a given list of 25 numbers.

7. Develop an algorithm for finding the greatest common divisor (GCD) of two positive integers.

8. Develop an algorithm for solving the system of equations

   $ax + by = c$
   $dx + ey = f$

9. Draw a structure chart and write module specifications for each of the following exercises.

   a. Exercise 5a.

   b. Exercise 5b.

   c. Exercise 6.

10. Discuss how the top-down design principles of software engineering are similar to the design problems faced by a construction engineer for a building. Be sure to include anticipated work with all subcontractors.

11. Using the construction analogy of Exercise 10, give an example of some specific communication required between electricians and the masons who finish the interior walls. Discuss why this information flow should be coordinated by a construction engineer.

12. State the phases of the software system life cycle.

13. Contact some company or major user of a software system to see what kinds of modifications might be required in a system after it has been released to the public. (Your own computer center might be sufficient.)

■ ■ ■ ■

■ 1.4
Writing Programs

Words in Pascal

Consider the following complete Pascal program.

```
PROGRAM Example (input, output);

CONST
  Skip = ' ';
  LoopLimit = 10;

VAR
  J, Number, Sum : integer;
  Average : real;

BEGIN
  Sum := 0;
  FOR J := 1 TO LoopLimit DO
    BEGIN
      writeln ('Enter a number and press <RETURN>.');
      readln (Number);
      Sum := Sum + Number
    END;
  Average := Sum / LoopLimit;
  writeln;
  writeln (Skip:10, 'The average is', Average:8:2);
  writeln;
  writeln (Skip:10, 'The number of scores is', LoopLimit:3)
END.
```

This program—and most programming languages—requires the use of words when writing code. In Pascal, words that have a predefined meaning that cannot be changed are called *reserved words*. Some other predefined words (*standard identifiers*) can have their meanings changed if the programmer has strong reasons for doing so. Other words (programmer-supplied *identifiers*) must be created according to a well-defined set of rules, but can have any meaning, subject to those rules.

In the body of this text, reserved words are capitalized and in bold type; standard identifiers are lowercase and in bold type. Reserved words used in the text's example programs are capitalized and standard identifiers are lowercase. This convention is not required by the language.

Reserved Words

In Pascal, reserved words are predefined and cannot be used in a program for anything other than the purpose for which they are reserved. Some examples are **AND, OR, NOT, BEGIN, END, IF,** and **FOR.** As you continue in Pascal, you will learn where and how these words are used. At this time, however, you need only become familiar with the reserved words in Table 1.1; they are also listed in Appendix 1.

TABLE 1.1
Reserved words

AND	ELSE	IF	OR	THEN
ARRAY	END	IN	PACKED	TO
BEGIN	FILE	LABEL	PROCEDURE	TYPE
CASE	FOR	MOD	PROGRAM	UNTIL
CONST	FORWARD	NIL	RECORD	VAR
DIV	FUNCTION	NOT	REPEAT	WHILE
DO	GOTO	OF	SET	WITH
DOWNTO				

Standard Identifiers

A second set of predefined words, standard identifiers, can have their meanings changed by the programmer. For example, if you could develop a better algorithm for the trigonometric function **sin,** you could then substitute it in the program. However, these words should not be used for anything other than their intended use. This list will vary somewhat from computer to computer, so you should obtain a list of standard identifiers used in your local implementation of Pascal. Some standard identifiers are listed in Table 1.2 and in Appendix 2. The term *keywords* is used to refer to both reserved words and standard identifiers in subsequent discussions.

TABLE 1.2
Standard identifiers

Data Types	Constants	Functions	Procedures	Files
boolean	false	abs	dispose	input
char	maxint	arctan	get	output
integer	true	chr	new	
real		cos	pack	
text		eof	page	
		eoln	put	
		exp	read	
		ln	readln	
		odd	reset	
		ord	rewrite	
		pred	unpack	
		round	write	
		sin	writeln	
		sqr		
		sqrt		
		succ		
		trunc		

Syntax and Syntax Diagrams

Syntax refers to the rules governing construction of valid statements. This includes the order in which statements occur, together with appropriate punctuation. *Syntax diagramming* is a method to describe formally the legal syntax of language structures. Syntax diagrams show the permissible alternatives for each part of each kind of sentence and where the parts may appear. The symbolism we use is shown in Figure 1.14. A combined listing of syntax diagrams is contained in Appendix 3.

FIGURE 1.14
Symbols used in syntax diagrams

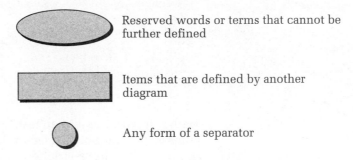

Reserved words or terms that cannot be further defined

Items that are defined by another diagram

Any form of a separator

Arrows are used to indicate possible alternatives. To illustrate, a syntax diagram for forming simple words in the English language is

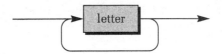

If the word must start with a vowel, the diagram is

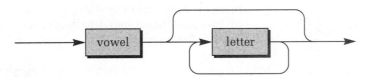

where vowel and letter are defined in a manner consistent with the English alphabet. Syntax diagrams are used throughout the text to illustrate formal constructs. You are encouraged to become familiar with them.

Identifiers

Reserved words and standard identifiers are restricted in their use. Most Pascal programs require other programmer-supplied identifiers; the more complicated the program, the more identifiers are needed. **A valid identifier must start with a letter of the alphabet and must consist of only letters and digits**. A syntax diagram for forming identifiers is

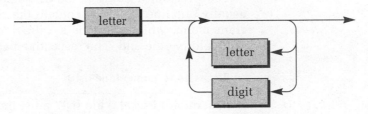

Table 1.3 gives some valid and invalid identifiers along with the reasons for those that are invalid. A valid identifier can be of any length. However, some versions of Pascal recognize only the first part of a long identifier, for example, the first eight or the first ten characters. Therefore, identifiers such as

TABLE 1.3
Valid and Invalid identifiers

Identifier	Valid	If Invalid, Reason
Sum	Yes	
X + Y	No	"+" is not allowed
Average	Yes	
Text1	Yes	
1stNum	No	Must start with a letter
X	Yes	
K mart	No	Spaces are not allowed
ThisIsaLongOne	Yes	

MathTestScore1 and MathTestScore2 might be the same identifier to a computer and could not be used as different identifiers in a program. Thus, you should learn what restrictions are imposed by your compiler.

The most common use of identifiers is to name the variables to be used in a program. Other uses for identifiers include the program name, symbolic constants, new data types, and subprogram names, all of which are discussed later. Always use descriptive names for identifiers, even though single-letter identifiers are permitted; as you'll see, descriptive names are easier to follow in a program.

Basic Program Components

A program in Pascal consists of three components: a *program heading,* an optional *declaration section,* and an *executable section.* These three components are illustrated in the program shown in Figure 1.15. The syntax diagram for a program is

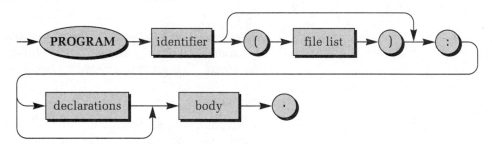

Figure 1.16 illustrates the program components of the sample program (**PROGRAM** Example) that started this section; appropriate program parts are indicated.

The program heading is the first statement of any Pascal program. It is usually one line and must contain the reserved word **PROGRAM;** the program name, which must be a valid identifier; a list of files used; and a semicolon at the end. The respective parts of a program heading are

> **PROGRAM** ⟨name⟩ (⟨file list⟩);

In standard Pascal, "file list" must include the files **input** and/or **output.** Some other versions, for example Turbo Pascal, do not have this requirement. *Note:* The symbol (T) appears in the margin to alert you to cases in which Turbo differs from standard Pascal. These differences are explained in Appendix 6.

⊤

FIGURE 1.15
Components of a program

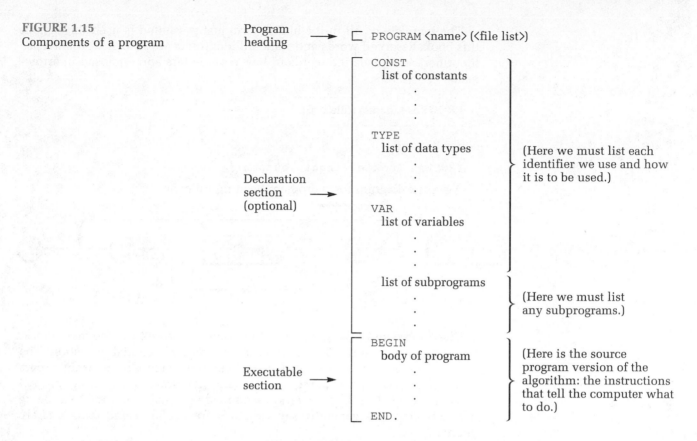

Program heading → ☐ PROGRAM ⟨name⟩ (⟨file list⟩)

CONST
  list of constants
    .
    .
    .
TYPE
  list of data types
    .
    .
    .
VAR
  list of variables
    .
    .
    .

(Here we must list each identifier we use and how it is to be used.)

Declaration section (optional) →

list of subprograms
    .
    .
    .

(Here we must list any subprograms.)

BEGIN
  body of program
    .
    .
    .
END.

Executable section →

(Here is the source program version of the algorithm: the instructions that tell the computer what to do.)

FIGURE 1.16
Components of **PROGRAM** Example

Program heading → ☐ PROGRAM Example (input, output);

Declaration section →
```
CONST
  Skip = ' ';
VAR
  J, X, Sum : integer;
  Average : real;
```

Executable section →
```
BEGIN
  Sum := 0;
  FOR J := 1 TO 30 DO
    BEGIN
      read (X)
      Sum := Sum + X
    END;
  Average := Sum / 30;
  writeln;
  writeln (Skip:10, 'The average is', Average:8:2);
  writeln;
  writeln (Skip:10, 'The number of scores is', 30:3)
END.
```

The template or fill-in-the-blanks form just presented is used throughout this book. Reserved words and standard identifiers are shown. You must use identifiers to replace the words in lowercase letters and enclosed in arrowheads "⟨ ⟩". Thus,

> **PROGRAM** ⟨name⟩ (⟨file list⟩);

could become

```
PROGRAM Rookie (input, output);
```

A syntax diagram for a program heading follows:

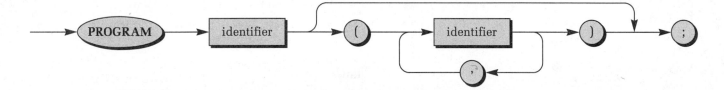

The remainder of the program is sometimes referred to as the main block; major divisions are the declaration section and the executable section. The declaration section is used to declare (name) all symbolic constants, data types, variables, and subprograms that are necessary to the program. All constants named in the declaration section are normally referred to as being defined. Thus, we generally say variables are declared and constants are defined.

When constants are defined, they appear in the *constant definition* portion of the declaration section after the reserved word **CONST.** The form for defining a constant is

> **CONST**
>   **⟨identifier1⟩** = ⟨value 1⟩;
>   **⟨identifier2⟩** = ⟨value 2⟩;
>   .
>   .
>   .
>   **⟨identifier*n*⟩** = ⟨value *n*⟩;

The syntax diagram for this part is

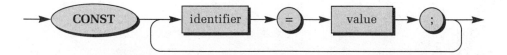

Values of constant identifiers cannot be changed during program execution.

If a value is one character or a string of characters, it must be enclosed in single quotation marks (apostrophes). For example,

```
CONST
  Date = 'July 4, 1776';
```

Any number of constants may be defined in this section. A typical constant definition portion of the declaration section could be

```
CONST
  Skip = ' ';
  Date = 'July 4, 1776';
  ClassSize = 35;
  SpeedLimit = 65;
  CmToInches = 0.3937;
  Found = true;
```

The **TYPE** portion of the declaration section will be explained in Section 6.2. For now, we assume all data used in a Pascal program must be one of the four *standard simple types*: **integer, real, char,** or **boolean.** Discussion of types **integer, real,** and **char** is in Section 2.3; discussion of **boolean** is in Section 5.1.

The *variable declaration* portion of the declaration section must be listed after the **TYPE** portion, if present, and must begin with the reserved word **VAR.** This section must contain all identifiers for variables to be used in the program; if a variable is used that has not been declared, an error will occur when the program is compiled.

The form required for declaring variables is somewhat different from that used for defining constants: it requires a colon instead of an equal sign and specific data types. The simplest correct form is

```
VAR
  ⟨identifier1⟩ : ⟨data type 1⟩;
      .
      .
      .
  ⟨identifiern⟩ : ⟨data type n⟩;
```

The syntax diagram is

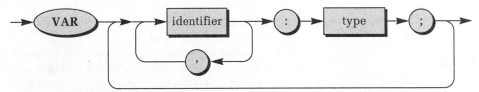

The reserved word **VAR** may appear only once in a program (exceptions will be noted when subprograms are developed). If no variables are to be used, a variable declaration section is not needed; however, this seldom happens. A typical variable declaration section could look like this:

```
VAR
  Sum : integer;
  Average : real;
  I, J, K : integer;
  Ch : char;
```

The third basic program component is the executable section. This section contains the statements that cause the computer to do something. It must start with the reserved word **BEGIN** and conclude with the reserved word **END.** Also, a period must follow the last **END** in the executable section. The syntax diagram is

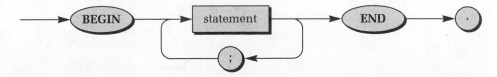

Writing Code in Pascal

We are now ready to examine the use of the executable section of a program. In Pascal, the basic unit of grammar is an *executable statement,* which consists of valid identifiers, standard identifiers, reserved words, numbers, and/ or characters together with appropriate punctuation.

One of the main rules for writing code in Pascal is that a semicolon is used to separate executable statements. For example, if the statement

```
writeln ('The results are':20, Sum:8, ' and', Aver:6:2)
```

were to be used in a program, it would (almost always) require a semicolon between it and the next executable statement. Thus, it should be

```
writeln ('The results are':20, Sum:8, ' and', Aver:6:2);
```

One instance exists where an executable statement does not need a following semicolon. When a statement is followed by the reserved word **END,** a semicolon is not required. This is because **END** is not a statement by itself, but part of a **BEGIN . . . END** pair. However, if a semicolon is included, it will not affect the program. You can visualize the executable section as shown in Figure 1.17.

FIGURE 1.17
Executable section

```
          ┌─ BEGIN
          │     ⟨statement 1⟩;
          │     ⟨statement 2⟩;
Executable│              .
section   →            .
          │              .
          │     ⟨statement n − 1⟩;
          │     ⟨statement n⟩
          └─ END.
```

Pascal does not require that each statement be on a separate line. Actually, you could write a program as one long line (which may wrap around to fit the screen) if you wish; however, it would be difficult to read. Compare, for example, the readability of the following two programs.

```
PROGRAM ReadCheck (output); CONST Name = 'George';
Age = 26; VAR J, Sum : integer; BEGIN Sum := 0;
FOR J := 1 TO 10 DO Sum := Sum + J; writeln
('My name is ':28, Name); writeln ('My age is ':27, Age);
writeln; writeln ('The sum is ':28, Sum) END.


PROGRAM ReadCheck (output);

CONST
  Name = 'George';
  Age = 26;
VAR
  J, Sum : integer;
BEGIN
  Sum := 0;
  FOR J := 1 TO 10 DO
    Sum := Sum + J;
  writeln ('My name is ':28, Name);
  writeln ('My age is ':27, Age);
  writeln;
  writeln ('The sum is ':28, Sum)
END.
```

A NOTE OF INTEREST

Blaise Pascal

Blaise Pascal (1623–1662) began a spectacular, if short, mathematical career at a very early age. He was a brilliant child. As a youngster of 14, he attended meetings of senior French mathematicians. At age 16, he had so impressed the famous mathematician Descartes with his writings that Descartes refused to believe the author could be so young.

Two years later, Pascal invented a calculating machine, the Pascaline, (shown at right) that stands as the very remote predecessor of the modern computer. The Pascaline could add and subtract; it functioned by a series of eight rotating gears, similar to an automobile's odometer. Pascal's machine was opposed by tax clerks of the era who viewed it as a threat to their jobs. Pascal presented his machine to Queen Christina of Sweden in 1650; it is not known what she did with it.

In spite of his obvious talent for mathematics, Pascal devoted most of his adult life to questions of theology;

his work in this area is still regularly studied. A man who often perceived omens in events around him, Pascal concluded that God's plan for him did not include mathematics and dropped the subject entirely. However, while experiencing a particularly nagging toothache when he was 35, Pascal let his thoughts wander to mathematics, and the pain disappeared.

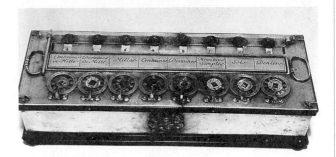

He took this as a heavenly sign and made a quick but intensive return to mathematical research. In barely a week, he managed to discover the fundamental properties of the cycloid curve. With that, Pascal again abandoned mathematics, and in 1662, at the age of 39, he died.

You are not expected to know what the statements mean at this point, but it should be obvious that the second program is much more readable than the first. In addition, it is easier to change if corrections are necessary.

These programs are executed similarly because Pascal ignores extra spaces and line boundaries.

Program Comments

Programming languages typically include some provision for putting *comments* in a program. These comments are nonexecutable and are used to document and explain various parts of the program. In Pascal, the form for including comments in a program is either

```
{ . . . comment . . . }
or
(* . . . comment . . . *)
```

Exercises 1.4

1. List the rules for forming valid identifiers.

2. Which of the following are valid identifiers? Give an explanation for those that are invalid.

   a. 7Up
   b. Payroll
   c. Room222
   d. Name List
   e. A
   f. A1

   g. 1A
   h. Time&Place
   i. CONST
   j. X*Y
   k. ListOfEmployees
   l. Lima,Ohio

3. Which of the following are valid program headings? Give an explanation for those that are invalid.

   a. `PROGRAM Rookie (output)`
   b. `PROGRAM Pro (input, output);`
   c. `TestProgram (input, output);`
   d. `PROGRAM (output);`
   e. `PROGRAM GettingBetter (output);`
   f. `PROGRAM Have Fun (input, output);`
   g. `PROGRAM 2ndOne (output);`

4. Name the three main sections of a Pascal program.

5. Write constant definition statements for the following:

   a. your name
   b. your age
   c. your birth date
   d. your birthplace

6. Find all errors in the following definitions and declarations:

   a.
   ```
   CONST
      Company : 'General Motors';
   VAR
      Salary : real;
   ```
   b.
   ```
   VAR
      Age = 25;
   ```
   c.
   ```
   VAR
      Days : integer;
      Ch : char;
   CONST
      Name = 'John Smith';
   ```
   d.
   ```
   CONST
      Car : 'Cadillac';
   ```
   e.
   ```
   CONST
      Score : integer;
   ```
   f.
   ```
   VAR
      X, Y, Z : real;
      Score,
      Num : integer;
   ```

7. Discuss the significance of a semicolon in writing Pascal statements. Include an explanation of when semicolons are not required in a program.

■ ■ ■ ■

■ **1.5**
Data Types and Output

Type integer

Pascal requires that all data used in a program be given a *data type*. Since numbers in some form will be used in computer programs, we will first look at numbers of type **integer,** which are integers that are positive, negative, or zero.

Some rules that must be observed when using integers are

1. Plus "+" signs do not have to be written before a positive integer.
2. Minus "−" signs must be written when using a negative number.
3. Leading zeros are ignored.
4. Decimal points cannot be used when writing integers. Although 14 and 14.0 have the same value, 14.0 is not of type **integer.**
5. Commas cannot be used when writing integers. 271,362 is not allowed; it must be written as 271362.

The syntax diagram for an integer is

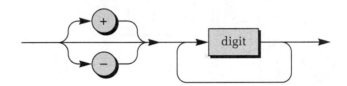

There is a limit on the largest and the smallest integer constant. The largest such constant is **maxint** and the smallest is usually −**maxint** or (−**maxint**−1). **maxint** and −**maxint** are recognized by every version of Pascal; however, different machines have different values for them. This section ends with a program that enables you to discover the value of **maxint** on your computer. Operations with integers will be examined in the next section and integer variables will be discussed in Section 2.2.

Type real

When using decimal notation, numbers of type **real** must be written with a decimal point with at least one digit on each side of the decimal. Thus, .2 is not a valid **real** but 0.2 is.

Plus "+" and minus "−" signs for data of type **real** are treated exactly as with integers. When working with reals, however, both leading and trailing zeros are ignored. Thus, +23.45, 23.45, 023.45, 23.450, and 0023.45000 have the same value.

All reals seen thus far have been in *fixed-point* form. The computer will also accept reals in *floating-point* or exponential form. Floating-point form is an equivalent method for writing numbers in scientific notation to accommodate numbers that may have very large or very small values. The difference is, instead of writing the base decimal times some power of 10, the base decimal is followed by E and the appropriate power of 10. For example, 231.6 in scientific notation would be 2.316×10^2 and in floating-point form would be 2.316E2. Table 1.4 sets forth several fixed-point decimal numbers with the equivalent scientific notation and floating-point form. Floating-point form for real numbers does not require exactly one digit on the left of the decimal point. In fact, it can be used with no decimal points written. To

TABLE 1.4
Forms for equivalent numbers

Fixed-point	Scientific Notation	Floating-point
46.345	4.6345×10	4.6345E1
59214.3	5.92143×10^4	5.92143E4
0.00042	4.2×10^{-4}	4.2E$-$4
36000000000.0	3.6×10^{10}	3.6E10
0.000000005	5.0×10^{-9}	5.0E$-$9
-341000.0	-3.41×10^5	-3.41E5

illustrate, 4.16E1, 41.6, 416.0E-1, and 416E-1 have the same value and all are permissible. However, it is not a good habit to use floating-point form for decimal numbers unless exactly one digit appears on the left of the decimal. In most other cases, fixed-point form is preferable.

The syntax diagram for a floating-point number is

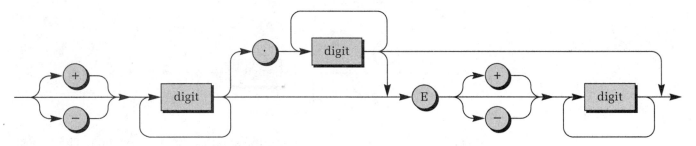

When using reals in a program, you may use either fixed-point or floating-point form. But the computer prints out reals in floating-point form unless you specify otherwise. Formatting of output is discussed later in this section.

Type char

Another data type available in Pascal is **char,** which is used to represent character data. In standard Pascal, data of type **char** can be only a single character (which could be a blank space). These characters come from an available character set that differs somewhat from computer to computer, but always includes the letters of the alphabet (uppercase and lowercase); the digits 0, 1, 2, 3, 4, 5, 6, 7, 8, and 9; and special symbols such as #, &, !, +, $-$, *, /, and so on. Two common character sets are given in Appendix 4.

Character constants of type **char** must be enclosed in single quotation marks when used in a program. Otherwise, they are treated as variables and subsequent use causes a compilation error. Thus, to use the letter A as a constant, you would type 'A'. The use of digits and standard operation symbols as characters is also permitted; for example, '7' would be considered a character, but 7 is an integer.

If a word of one or more characters is used as a constant in a program, it is referred to as a *string constant.* String constants, generally called *strings,* may be defined in the **CONST** portion of the declaration section. The entire string must be enclosed in single quotation marks.

Students with experience in BASIC usually expect the equivalent of a string variable for storing names, and other information. A string is not a standard Pascal data type; standard Pascal does not have such a feature. However, an analogous feature, packed arrays of characters, is presented in Section 7.5.

When a single quotation mark is needed within a string, it is represented by two single quotation marks. For example, if the name desired was O'Malley, it would be represented by

```
'O''Malley'
```

When a single quotation mark is needed as a single character, it can be represented by placing two single quotation marks within single quotation marks. When typed, this appears as ''''. Note that these are all single quotation marks; use of the double quotation mark character here will not produce the desired result.

Type string (Optional: Nonstandard)

As previously mentioned, standard Pascal does not provide for a **string** data type. However, since many versions of Pascal (particularly Turbo) do contain a **string** data type, we have decided to include mention of this data type in this edition of this book.

Having the data type **string** available allows a programmer to design programs that are capable of using strings of characters as well as numeric data. This is particularly useful when using names of people and companies, for example. Later we will see how such strings can be incorporated into a program; for now it is sufficient that you be aware that several versions of nonstandard Pascal provide a **string** data type. (Also see the discussion on reading strings, at the end of Section 2.3.)

Output

The goal of most programs is to print something. What gets printed (either on paper or on a screen) is referred to as output. The two program statements that produce output are **write** and **writeln** (pronounced "write line"). They are usually followed by character strings, numbers, numerical expressions, or variable names enclosed in parentheses. The general form is

> **write** (⟨expression 1⟩, ⟨expression 2⟩, . . . , ⟨expression *n*⟩)
>
> or
>
> **writeln** (⟨expression 1⟩, ⟨expression 2⟩, . . . , ⟨expression *n*⟩)

A simplified syntax diagram for **write** (applicable also for **writeln**) is

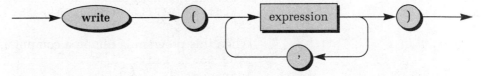

For more information on syntax diagrams for **write** and **writeln**, see Appendix 3.

A **writeln** can also be used as a complete statement:

```
writeln;
```

causes a blank line to be printed. This technique is frequently used to produce more readable output.

The **write** statement causes subsequent output to be on the same line; **writeln** causes the next output to be on the next line. This is because **writeln** is actually a **write** statement followed by a line feed. When output is to a monitor, **writeln** causes the cursor to move to the next line for the next I/O operation. To illustrate,

```
write ('This is a test.');
writeln ('How many lines are printed?');
```

causes the output

```
This is a test.How many lines are printed?
```

whereas,

```
writeln ('This is a test.');
writeln ('How many lines are printed?');
```

causes the output

```
This is a test.
How many lines are printed?
```

Some implementations require a **writeln** for the last output statement. Otherwise, output gathered in a buffer does not get printed.

Character strings can be printed by enclosing the string in single quotation marks within the parentheses. Numerical data can be printed by including the desired number or numbers within the parentheses. Thus,

```
writeln (100)
```

produces

```
      100
```

<hr>

EXAMPLE 1.1

Let's write a complete Pascal program to print the address

```
1403 South Drive
Apartment 3B
Pittsburgh, PA     15238
```

A complete program to print this is

```
PROGRAM Address (output);

BEGIN
  writeln ('1403 South Drive');
  writeln ('Apartment 3B');
  writeln ('Pittsburgh, PA', 15238)
END.
```

When this program is run on a computer, you may get

```
1403 South Drive
Apartment 3B
Pittsburgh, PA       15238
```

Formatting Integers

Output of integers can be controlled by *formatting*. Within a **write** or **writeln** statement, an integer, identifier, or integer expression can be followed by a colon and another integer to specify the field width. The value will then be printed on the right side of the specified field. Thus,

```
writeln (100, 50:10, 25:10);
```

produces

```
100--------50--------25
```

where each " − " indicates a blank.

The general form for formating integers is

```
write (⟨integer⟩ : ⟨n⟩);
or
writeln (⟨integer⟩ : ⟨n⟩);
```

Some illustrations for formatting integer output are

Program Statement	Output
`writeln (123:6);`	`---123`
`writeln (15, 10:5);`	`---------15---10` WRONG
`writeln (-263:7, 21:3);`	`---263_21`
`writeln (+5062:6);`	`--5062`
`writeln (65221:3);`	`65221`

Note that, in line five, an attempt is made to specify a field width smaller than the number of digits contained in the integer. Most versions of Pascal will automatically print the entire integer; however, some versions will print only in the specified width.

STYLE TIP

Using **writelns** at the beginning and end of the executable section will separate desired output from other messages or directions. Thus, the previous program for printing an address could have been

```
PROGRAM Address (output);
BEGIN
  writeln;
  writeln ('1403 South Drive');
  writeln ('Apartment 3B');
  writeln ('Pittsburgh, PA', 15238);
  writeln;
END.
```

Formatting Reals

Output of reals can also be controlled by formatting. The general form is

```
write (⟨real⟩ : ⟨n1⟩ : ⟨n2⟩);
or
writeln (⟨real⟩ : ⟨n1⟩ : ⟨n2⟩);
```

where $n1$ specifies the total field width and $n2$ specifies the number of positions to the right of the decimal. Thus,

```
writeln (736.23:8:2);
```

produces

```
--736.23
```

Formatting reals causes the following to happen:

1. The decimal uses one position in the specified field width.
2. Leading zeros are not printed.
3. Trailing zeros are printed to the specified number of positions to the right of the decimal.
4. Leading plus " + " signs are omitted.
5. Leading minus " − " signs are printed and use one position of the specified field.
6. Digits appearing to the right of the decimal have been rounded rather than truncated.

As with integers, if a field width is specified that is too small, most versions of Pascal will default to the minimum width required to present all digits to the left of the decimal as well as the specified digits to the right of the decimal. Reals in floating-point form can also be used in a formatted **writeln** statement. The following table illustrates how output using data of type **real** can be formatted.

Program Statement	Output
writeln (765.432:10:3)	---765.432
writeln (023.14:10:2)	-----23.14
writeln (65.50:10:2)	-----65.50
writeln (+341.2:10:2)	----341.20
writeln (-341.2:10:2)	----341.20
writeln (16.458:10:2)	-----16.46
writeln (0.00456:10:4)	----0.0046
writeln (136.51:4:2)	----136.51

Formatting Strings

Strings and string constants can be formatted using a colon followed by a positive integer "n" to specify field width. The general form for formatting strings is

```
write ('⟨string⟩' : ⟨n⟩);
or
writeln ('⟨string⟩' : ⟨n⟩);
```

The string will be right justified in the field. Unlike reals, strings are truncated when necessary. Thus,

```
writeln, ('field', 'width':10, 'check':15);
```
would produce
```
field-----width----------check
```
                :10   :15

Test Programs

Programmers should develop the habit of using *test programs* to improve their knowledge and programming skills. Test programs should be relatively short and written to provide an answer to a specific question. For example, **maxint** was discussed earlier in this section. It was mentioned that the value of **maxint** depended upon the machine being used. You could use a test

STYLE TIP

■ ■ ■ ■ ■ ■ ■ ■ ■ ■ ■

A constant consisting of a blank can be used as a formatting aid. For example, a constant section could include

```
CONST
  Skip = ' ';
  Indent = ' ';
```

Output statements can then use these constants as

```
writeln (Indent:6, message1, Skip:10, message2);
```

program to discover what your computer uses for **maxint.** A complete program that accomplishes this is

```
PROGRAM TestMax (output);

BEGIN
  writeln ('Maxint is ', maxint)
END.
```

Notice that a brief message, 'Maxint is ', is included to explain the output. Such a message or "output label" is almost always desirable.

Test programs allow you to play with the computer. You can answer "What if   " questions by adopting a "try it and see" attitude. This is an excellent way to become comfortable with your computer and the programming language you are using. For example, you might change the previous test program to

```
PROGRAM TestMax (output);

BEGIN
  writeln ('Maxint is ', maxint);
  writeln ('TooMuch is ', maxint + 1)
END.
```

Exercises 1.5

1. Which of the following are valid integers? Explain why the others are invalid.

   a. 521
   b. −32.0
   c. 5,621
   d. +00784
   e. +65
   f. 6521492183
   g. −0

2. Which of the following are valid reals? Explain why the others are invalid.

   a. 26.3
   b. +181.0
   c. −.14
   d. 492.
   e. +017.400
   f. 43E2
   g. −0.2E−3
   h. 43,162.3E5
   i. −176.52E+1
   j. 1.43000E+2

3. Change the following fixed-point decimals to floating-point decimals with exactly one nonzero digit to the left of the decimal.

   a. 173.0
   b. 743927000000.0
   c. −0.000000023
   d. +014.768
   e. −5.2

4. Change the following floating-point decimals to fixed-point decimals.

   a. −1.0046E+3
   b. 4.2E−8
   c. 9.020E10
   d. −4.615230E3
   e. −8.02E−3

5. Indicate the data type for each of the following:

   a. −720

   b. −720.0

   c. 150E3

   d. 150

   e. '150'

   f. '23.4E2'

   g. 23.4E−2

6. Write and run test programs for each of the following:

   a. Examine the output for a decimal number without field width specified; for example,

   ```
   writeln (2.31)
   ```

   b. Try to print a message without using quotation marks for a character string; for example,

   ```
   writeln (Hello);
   ```

7. For each of the following, write a program that would produce the indicated output.

   ```
   a. Score                              b.  Price
      -----                                  -------
         86                                    $ 19.94
         82                                    $100.00
         79                                    $ 58.95
   ```

   where "S" is in column 10.   where "P" is in column 50.

8. Assume the hourly wages of five students are

   ```
   3.65
   4.10
   2.89
   5.00
   4.50
   ```

   Write a program that produces this output, where the "E" of Employee is in column 20.

   ```
   ------------------------
   Employee    Hourly Wage
   ------------------------

      1          $ 3.65
      2          $ 4.10
      3          $ 2.89
      4          $ 5.00
      5          $ 4.50
   ------------------------
   ```

9. What is the output from the following segment of code on your printer or terminal?

   ```
   writeln ('My test average is', 87.5);
   writeln ('My test average is':20, 87.5:10);
   writeln ('My test average is':25, 87.5:10:2);
   writeln ('My test average is':25, 87.5:6:2);
   ```

10. Write a program that produces the following output. Start Student in column 20 and Test in Column 40.

    ```
    Student Name              Test Score

    Adams, Mike                  73
    Conley, Theresa              86
    Samson, Ron                  92
    O'Malley, Colleen            81
    ```

11. The Great Lakes Shipping Company is going to use a computer program to generate billing statements for their customers. The heading of each bill is to be

```
          GREAT LAKES SHIPPING COMPANY
           SAULT STE. MARIE, MICHIGAN
     ----------------------------------------------
     Thank you for doing business with our company.
     The information listed below was used to
     determine your total cargo fee. We hope you
     were satisfied with our service.
     ----------------------------------------------
     CARGO       TONNAGE       RATE/TON       TOTAL DUE
```

Write a complete Pascal program that produces this heading.

12. What output is produced by each of the following statements or sequence of statements when executed by the computer?

a. `writeln (1234, 1234:8, 1234:6);`

b. `writeln (12:4, -21:4, 120:4);`

c. `writeln ('FIGURE  AREA   PERIMETER');`
   `writeln ('----------------------');`
   `writeln;`
   `writeln ('SQUARE', 16:5, 16:12);`
   `writeln;`
   `writeln ('RECT ', 24:5, 20:12);`

13. Write a complete program that produces the following table:

```
WIDTH          LENGTH          AREA
  4              2               8
 21              5             105
```

14. What output is produced when each of the following is executed?

a. `writeln (2.134:15:2);`

b. `writeln (423.73:5:2);`

c. `writeln (-42.1:8:3);`

d. `writeln (-4.21E3:6:2);`

e. `writeln (10.25);`

f. `writeln (1.25, 1.25:6:2, 1.25:6:1);`

15. Write a complete program that produces the following output:

```
Hourly Wage          Hours Worked          Total
     5.0                 20.0              100.00
     7.50                15.25             114.375
```

16. What type of data would be used to print each of the following?

a. your age

b. your grade point average

c. your name

d. a test score

e. the average test score

f. your grade

■ ■ ■ ■

■ **Summary**

Key Terms

algorithm
applications software
arithmetic/logic unit
   (ALU)
assembly language
binary digits
bits
bus
central processing unit
   (CPU)
comments
compiler
constant definition
control unit
data
data type
declaration section
effective statement
executable section
executable statement
executed
fixed point

floating point
formatting
hardware
high-level language
identifier
input device
I/O devices
keyword
low-level language
machine language
main unit
main (primary) memory
mainframe
microcomputer
minicomputer
module
module specifications
object code
object program
operating system
output device
program
program heading

programming language
pseudocode
reserved word
secondary (auxiliary)
   memory devices
software
software engineering
software system life
   cycle
source program
standard identifier
standard simple type
stepwise refinement
string
string constant
structure chart
syntax
syntax diagram
system software
test program
top-down design
variable declaration

Keywords

BEGIN	**integer**	**real**
char	**maxint**	**VAR**
CONST	**output**	**write**
END	**PROGRAM**	**writeln**
input		

Keyword (Optional)

string

Key Concepts

■ Six steps in problem solving include: analyze the problem, develop an algorithm, write code for the program, run the program, test the results against answers manually computed with paper and pencil, and document the program.
■ Top-down design is a process of dividing tasks into subtasks until each subtask can be readily accomplished.
■ Stepwise refinement refers to refinements of tasks into subtasks.
■ A structure chart is a graphic representation of the relationship between modules.
■ Software engineering is the process of developing and maintaining large software systems.
■ The software system life cycle consists of the following phases: analysis, design, coding, testing/verification, maintenance, and obsolescence.
■ Valid identifiers must begin with a letter and they can contain only letters and digits.
■ The three components of a Pascal program are program heading, declaration section, and executable section.
■ Semicolons are used to separate executable statements.
■ Extra spaces and blank lines are ignored in Pascal.
■ Output is generated by using **write** or **writeln.**

- Strings are formatted using a single colon followed by a positive integer that specifies the total field width, for example

```
writeln ('This is a string,':30);
```

- The following table summarizes the use of the data types **integer, real,** and **char.**

Data Type	Permissible Data	Formatting
integer	numeric	one colon; for example `writeln (25:6);`
real	numeric	two colons; for example `writeln (1234.5:8:2);`
char	character	one colon; for example `writeln ('A':6);`

■ Programming Problems and Projects

Write and run a short program for each of the following:

1. A program to print your initials in block letters. Your output could look like

```
JJJJJ              A              CC
    J            A A           C   C
    J            A   A         C
    J            AAAAA         C
J   J            A   A         C   C
 JJ              A   A          CC
```

2. Design a simple picture and print it out using **writeln** statements. If you plan the picture using a sheet of graph paper, keeping track of spacing will be easier.

3. A program to print out your mailing address.

4. Our lady of Mercy Hospital prints billing statements for patients when they are ready to leave the hospital. Write a program that prints a heading for each statement as follows:

```
////////////////////////////////////////
/                                      /
/        Our Lady of Mercy Hospital    /
/        ---------------------------   /
/                                      /
/              1306 Central City       /
/              Phone (416) 333-5555    /
/                                      /
////////////////////////////////////////
```

5. Your computer science instructor wants course and program information included as part of every assignment. Write a program that can be used to print this information. Sample output is

```
*****************************************
*                                       *
*     Author:         Mary Smith        *
*     Course:         CPS-150           *
*     Assignment:     Program #3        *
*     Due Date:       September 18      *
*     Instructor:     Mr. Samson        *
*                                       *
*****************************************
```

6. As part of a programming project that will compute and print grades for each student in your class, you have been asked to write a program that produces a heading for each student report. The columns in which the various headings should be are as follows:

- the border for the class name starts in column 30
- Student Name starts in column 20
- Test Average starts in column 40
- Grade starts in column 55

Write a program to print the heading as follows:

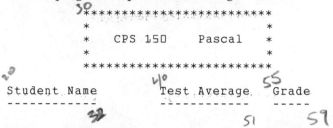

```
     ************************
     *                      *
     *   CPS 150    Pascal   *
     *                      *
     ************************

Student Name          Test Average   Grade
-----------           ------------   -----
```

CHAPTER

2

You will, I am sure, agree with me that if page 534 finds us only in the second chapter, the length of the first must have been really intolerable.

Sir Arthur Conan Doyle

Arithmetic, Variables, Input, Constants, and Standard Functions

In this chapter we will discuss arithmetic operations, using data in a program, obtaining input, and using constants and variables. We will also discuss the use of functions to perform standard operations such as finding the square root or absolute value of a number.

■ 2.1
Arithmetic in Pascal

Basic Operations for Integers

Integer arithmetic in Pascal allows the operations of addition, subtraction, and multiplication to be performed. The notation for these operations is

Symbol	Operation	Example	Value
+	Addition	3 + 5	8
−	Subtraction	43 − 25	18
*	Multiplication	4 * 7	28

Noticeably absent from this list is a division operation. This is because *integer arithmetic operations* are expected to produce integer answers. Since division problems might not produce integers, Pascal provides two operations, **MOD** and **DIV**, to produce integer answers.

In a standard division problem, there is a quotient and remainder. In Pascal, **DIV** produces the quotient and **MOD** produces the remainder when the first operand is positive. For example, in the problem 17 divided by 3, 17 **DIV** 3 produces 5, and 17 **MOD** 3 produces 2. Avoid using **DIV** 0 (zero) and **MOD** 0 (zero). A precise description of how **MOD** works is given on page 39 of the *Second Draft ANSI Standard for Pascal* as: "A term of the form *i* mod *j* shall be an error if *j* is zero or negative, otherwise the value of *i* mod *j* shall be that value of $(i - (k*j))$ for integral *k* such that $0 <= i$ mod $j < j$." Several integer expressions and their values are shown in Table 2.1. Notice that when 3 is multiplied by -2, the expression is written as $3 * (-2)$ rather than $3 * -2$. This is because consecutive operators cannot appear in an arithmetic expression. However, this expression could be written as $-2 * 3$.

TABLE 2.1
Values of integer expressions

Expression	Value
-3 + 2	-1
2 - 3	-1
-3 * 2	-6
3 * (-2)	-6
-3 * (-2)	6
17 DIV 3	5
17 MOD 3	2
17 DIV (-3)	-5
-17 DIV 3	-5
-17 MOD 3	1
-17 DIV (-3)	5

Order of Operations for Integers

Expressions involving more than one operation are frequently used when writing programs. When this happens, it is important to know the order in which these operations are performed. The priorities for these are:

1. All expressions within a set of parentheses are evaluated first. If there are parentheses within parentheses (the parentheses are nested), the innermost expressions are evaluated first.
2. The operations *, **MOD**, and **DIV** are evaluated next in order from left to right.
3. The operations + and − are evaluated last from left to right.

These operations are the operations of algebra and are summarized in Table 2.2.

TABLE 2.2
Integer arithmetic priority

Expression or Operation	Priority
( )	1. Evaluate from inside out
*, MOD, DIV	2. Evaluate from left to right
+, −	3. Evaluate from left to right

To illustrate how expressions are evaluated, consider the values of the expressions listed in Table 2.3. As expressions get more elaborate, it can be helpful to list partial evaluations in a manner similar to the order in which the computer performs the evaluations. For example, suppose the expression

```
(3 - 4) + 18 DIV 5 + 2
```

TABLE 2.3
Priority of operations

Expression	Value
3 - 4 * 5	−17
3 - (4 * 5)	−17
(3 - 4) * 5	−5
3 * 4 - 5	7
3 * (4 - 5)	−3
17 - 10 - 3	4
17 - (10 - 3)	10
(17 - 10) - 3	4
-42 + 50 MOD 17	−26

is to be evaluated. If we consider the order in which subexpressions are evaluated, we get

```
(3 - 4)  + 18 DIV 5 + 2
   ↓
  -1     + 18 DIV 5 + 2
              ↓
  -1     +     3     + 2
   ↓
           2         + 2
                ↓
                4
```

Using MOD and DIV

MOD and **DIV** can be used when it is necessary to perform conversions within arithmetic operations. For example, consider the problem of adding two weights given in units of pounds and ounces. This problem can be solved by converting both weights to ounces, adding the ounces, and then converting the total ounces to pounds and ounces. The conversion from ounces to pounds can be accomplished by using **MOD** and **DIV**. If the total number of ounces is 243, then

   243 **DIV** 16

yields the number of pounds (15), and

   243 **MOD** 16

yields the number of ounces (3).

Basic Operations for Reals

The operations of addition, subtraction, and multiplication are the same for data of type **real** as for integers. Additionally, division is now permitted. Since **MOD** and **DIV** are restricted to data of type **integer,** the symbol for division of data of type **real** is "/". The *real arithmetic operations* are as follows:

Symbol	Operation	Example	Value
+	Addition	4.2 + 19.36	23.56
−	Subtraction	19.36 - 4.2	15.16
*	Multiplication	3.1 * 2.0	6.2
/	Division	54.6 / 2.0	27.3

Division is given the same priority as multiplication when arithmetic expressions are evaluated by the computer. The rules for order of operation are the same as those for evaluating integer arithmetic expressions. A summary of these operations is shown in Table 2.4.

TABLE 2.4
Real arithmetic priority

Expression or Operation	Priority
( )	1. Evaluate from inside out
*, /	2. Evaluate from left to right
+, -	3. Evaluate from left to right

Some example calculations using data of type **real** are

Expression	Value
-1.0 + 3.5 + 2.0	4.5
-1.0 + 3.5 * 2.0	6.0
2.0 * (1.2 - 4.3)	-6.2
2.0 * 1.2 - 4.3	-1.9
-12.6 / 3.0 + 3.0	-1.2
-12.6 / (3.0 + 3.0)	-2.1

As with integers, consecutive operation signs are not allowed. Thus, if you want to multiply 4.3 by -2.0, you can use $-2.0 * 4.3$ or $4.3 * (-2.0)$, but you cannot use $4.3 * -2.0$. As expressions get a bit more complicated, it is again helpful to write out the expression and evaluate it step by step. For example,

```
18.2 + (-4.3) * (10.1 + (72.3 / 3.0 - 4.5))
                             ↓
18.2 + (-4.3) * (10.1 +    (24.1    - 4.5))
                              ↓
18.2 + (-4.3) * (10.1 +           19.6)
                     ↓
18.2 + (-4.3) *          29.7
            ↓
18.2 +          (-127.71)
        ↓
      -109.51
```

Note that exponentiation has not been listed as an available operation for either integers or reals. Pascal does not have an exponentiation operator. A method of overcoming this problem is presented in Section 3.4.

Overflow and Underflow

Arithmetic operations with computers have some limitations. One of these is the problem of *overflow*. Integer overflow occurs when an integer expression exceeds the absolute value of **maxint**. Thus, an attempt to use (**maxint** + 1) or (−**maxint** − 1) causes an overflow problem. Ideally, an error message would be printed when such a situation arises. Some systems do print a message such as ARITHMETIC OVERFLOW when this occurs; however, other systems merely assign a meaningless value and continue with the program. In Section 4.3 we discuss how to protect a program against this problem.

Real overflow occurs when the absolute value of a **real** is too large to fit into a memory location. Similar to the case for integer overflow, some systems do not print an error message when this occurs, but the manual for your system should include information on the limitations regarding storage of **real** numbers.

A second problem occurs when working with reals. If a real number is too small to be represented, it is replaced by zero. This is called *underflow*. Thus, your computations may produce a real of the magnitude $1.0 * 10^{-100}$, but your system could replace this with a zero.

In general, underflow is less of a problem than overflow; however, it cannot be completely ignored. Some mathematical approximations require use of numbers as they approach zero. Some financial calculations (such as computing interest) also require the use of very small numbers. If your computations do not require use of small numbers, you can ignore underflow. However, if you do use such numbers, you must know the system limitations before writing programs that need them. Consult your system manual to find the limitations of your system. Figure 2.1 illustrates the overflow and underflow possibilities.

FIGURE 2.1

Overflow and underflow

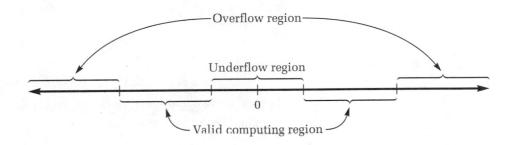

Mixed Expressions

Arithmetic expressions using data of two or more types are called *mixed-mode expressions*. In a mixed-mode expression involving both **integer** and **real** data types, the value will be of type **real**. A **real** also results if division (/) is used with integers. When formatting output, always format for reals. *Note:* Avoid using **MOD** and **DIV** with mixed-mode expressions.

Exercises 2.1

1. Find the value of each of the following expressions:
   a. 17 - 3 * 2
   b. -15 * 3 + 4
   c. 123 MOD 5
   d. 123 DIV 5
   e. 5 * 123 DIV 5 + 123 MOD 5
   f. -21 * 3 * (-1)
   g. 14 * (3 + 18 DIV 4) - 50
   h. 100 - (4 * (3 + 2)) * (-2)
   i. -56 MOD 3
   j. 14 * 8 MOD 5 - 23 DIV (-4)

2. Find the value of each of the following expressions:

   a. `3.21 + 5.02 - 6.1`

   b. `6.0 / 2.0 * 3.0`

   c. `6.0 / (2.0 + 3.0)`

   d. `-20.5 * (2.1 + 2.0)`

   e. `-2.0 * ((56.8 / 4.0 + 0.8) + 5.0)`

   f. `1.04E2 * 0.02E3`

   g. `800.0E-2 / 4.0 + 15.3`

3. Which of the following are valid expressions? For those that are, indicate whether they are of type **integer** or **real**.

   a. `18 - (5 * 2)`

   b. `(18 - 5) * 2`

   c. `18 - 5 * 2.0`

   d. `25 * (14 MOD 7.0)`

   e. `1.4E3 * 5`

   f. `28 / 7`

   g. `28.0 / 4`

   h. `10.5 + 14 DIV 3`

   i. `24 DIV 6 / 3`

   j. `24 DIV (6 / 3)`

4. Evaluate each of the valid expressions in Exercise 3.

5. What is the output produced by the following program?

```
PROGRAM MixedMode (output);
BEGIN
   writeln;
   writeln ('   Expression      Value');
   writeln ('   ----------      -----');
   writeln;
   writeln ('   10 / 5' , 10/5:12:3);
   writeln ('   2.0+7*(-1)', 2.0 + 7 * (-1));
   writeln
END.
```

6. Find all errors in the following Pascal statements:

   a. `writeln (-20 DIV 4.0:8:3);`

   b. `writeln (-20 DIV 4:8:3);`

   c. `writeln (-20 DIV 4:8);`

   d. `writeln (8 - 3.0 * 5:6);`

   e. `writeln (7 * 6 DIV 3 / 2:6:2);`

   f. `writeln (-17.1 + 5 * 20.0:8:3);`

■ ■ ■ ■

■ **2.2**
Using Variables

Memory Locations

It is frequently necessary to store values for later use. This is done by putting the value into a *memory location* by using a symbolic name to refer to this location. If the contents of the location are to be changed during a program,

A NOTE OF INTEREST

Herman Hollerith

Herman Hollerith (1860–1929) was hired by the United States Census Bureau in 1879 at the age of 19. Since the 1880 census was predicted to take a long time to complete (it actually took until 1887), Hollerith was assigned the task of developing a mechanical method of tabulating census data. He introduced his census machine in 1887. It consisted of four parts:

1. a punched paper card that represented data using a special code (Hollerith code),
2. a card punch apparatus,
3. a tabulator that read the punched cards, and
4. a sorting machine with 24 compartments.

The punched cards used by Hollerith were the same size as cards still in use today.

Using Hollerith's techniques and equipment, the 1890 census tabulation was completed in one-third the time required for the previous census tabulation. This included working with data for twelve million additional people.

Hollerith proceeded to form the Tabulating Machine Company (1896), which supplied equipment to census bureaus in the United States, Canada, and western Europe. After a disagreement with the census director, Hollerith began marketing his equipment in other commercial areas. Hollerith sold his company in 1911. It was later combined with twelve others to form the Computing-Tabulating-Recording Company, a direct ancestor of International Business Machines Corp.

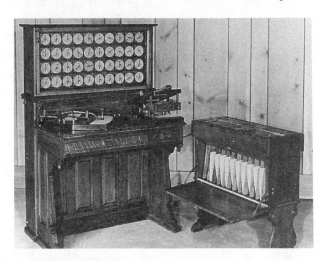

In the meantime, Hollerith's successor at the census bureau, James Powers, redesigned the census machine. He then formed his own company, which subsequently became Remington Rand and Sperry Univac.

the symbolic name is referred to as a *variable;* if the contents are not to be changed, it is referred to as a *constant.*

A graphic way to think about memory locations is to envision them as boxes; each box is named and a value is stored inside. For example, suppose a program is written to add a sequence of numbers. If we name the memory location to be used Sum, initially we have

```
┌──────┐
│      │
└──────┘
  Sum
```

which depicts a memory location that has been reserved and can be accessed by a reference to Sum. If we then add the integers 10, 20, and 30 and store them in Sum, we have

```
┌──────┐
│  60  │
└──────┘
  Sum
```

It is important to distinguish between the name of a memory location (Sum) and the value or contents of a memory location (60). The name does not change during a program, but the contents can be changed as often as necessary. (Contents of memory locations which are referred to by constants cannot be changed.) If 30 were added to the contents in the previous example, the new value stored in Sum could be depicted as

90

Sum

Those symbolic names representing memory locations whose values will be changing must be declared in the **VAR** section of the program (as indicated in Section 1.4); for example,

```
VAR
   Sum : integer;
```

Those that represent memory locations whose values will not be changing must be declared in the **CONST** section.

Assignment Statements

Let's now examine how the contents of variables are manipulated. A value may be put into a memory location with an *assignment statement* in the form of

⟨Variable name⟩ := ⟨value⟩;
or
⟨Variable name⟩ := ⟨expression⟩;

where "Variable name" is the name of the memory location. For example, if Sum had no value, then

```
Sum := 30;
```

changes

?	to	30

Sum   Sum

The syntax diagram for this is

Some important rules concerning assignment statements are:

1. The assignment is always made from right to left (←).
2. The syntax for assigning requires a colon followed immediately by an equal sign (:=).
3. Only one variable can be on the left of the assignment symbol.
4. Constants cannot be on the left side of the assignment symbol.
5. The expression may be a constant, a constant expression, a variable that has previously been assigned a value, or a combination of variables and constants.
6. Values on the right side of the assignment symbol are not changed by the assignment.
7. The variable and expression must match in data type.

Two common errors that beginners make are trying to assign from left to right and forgetting the colon when using an assignment statement.

Repeated assignments can be made. For example, if Sum is an integer variable, the statements

```
Sum := 50;
Sum := 70;
Sum := 100;
```

produce first 50, then 70, and finally 100 as shown.

```
50  70  100
```
Sum

In this sense, memory is destructive in that it retains only the last value assigned.

Pascal variables are symbolic addresses that can hold values. When a variable is declared, the type of values it will store must be specified (declared). Storing a value of the wrong type in a variable leads to a program error. This means that data types must match when using assignment statements: reals must be assigned to **real** variables, integers to **integer** variables, and characters to **char** variables. The only exception is that an integer can be assigned to a **real** variable; however, the integer is then converted to a real. If, for example, Average is a **real** variable and the assignment statement

```
Average := 21;
```

is made, the value is stored as the real 21.0.

Assignments to a character variable require that the constant be enclosed in single quotation marks. For example, if Letter is of type **char** and you want to store the letter C in Letter, use the assignment statement

```
Letter := 'C';
```

This could be pictured as

```
C
```
Letter

Furthermore, only one character can be assigned or stored in a character variable at a time.

To illustrate working with assignment statements, assume that the variable declaration portion of the program is

```
VAR
    Sum : integer;
    Average : real;
    Letter : char;
```

Examples of valid and invalid assignment statements using the variables just declared are shown in Table 2.5.

Expressions

Actual use of variables in a program is usually more elaborate than what we have just seen. Variables may be used in any manner that does not violate their type declarations. This includes both arithmetic operations and assignment statements. For example, if Score1, Score2, Score3, and Average are **real** variables,

TABLE 2.5
Assignment
statements

Statement	Valid	If Invalid, Reason
`Sum := 50;`	Yes	
`Sum := 10.5;`	No	Data types do not match
`Average := 15.6;`	Yes	
`Average := 33;`	Yes	
`Letter := 'A';`	Yes	
`Letter := 'HI';`	No	Not a single character
`Letter := 20;`	No	Data types do not match
`Letter := 'Z';`	Yes	
`Letter := A;`	?	Valid if A is a variable or constant of type **char**
`Sum := 7;`	Yes	
`Letter := '7';`	Yes	
`Letter := 7;`	No	Data types do not match
`Sum := '7';`	No	Data types do not match

```
Score1 := 72.3;
Score2 := 89.4;
Score3 := 95.6;
Average := (Score1 + Score2 + Score3) / 3.0;
```

is a valid fragment of code.

Let's now consider the problem of accumulating a total. Assuming New-Score and Total are integer variables, the following code is valid.

```
Total := 0;
NewScore := 5;
Total := Total + NewScore;
NewScore := 7;
Total := Total + NewScore;
```

As this code is executed, the values of memory locations for Total and NewScore could be depicted as

```
Total := 0;
```
0		
Total		NewScore

```
NewScore := 5;
```
0		5
Total		NewScore

```
Total := Total + NewScore;
```
5		5
Total		NewScore

```
NewScore := 7;
```
5		7
Total		NewScore

```
Total := Total + NewScore;
```
12		7
Total		NewScore

Output

Variables and variable expressions can be used when creating output. When used in a **writeln** statement, they perform the same function as a constant. For example, if the assignment statement

```
Age := 5;
```

has been made, these two statements

```
writeln (5);
writeln (Age);
```

produce the same output. If Age1, Age2, Age3, and Sum are integer variables and the assignments

```
Age1 := 21;
Age2 := 30;
Age3 := 12;
Sum := Age1 + Age2 + Age3;
```

are made,

```
writeln ('The sum is ', 21 + 30 + 12);
writeln ('The sum is ', Age1 + Age2 + Age3);
writeln ('The sum is ', Sum);
```

all produce the same output.

Formatting variables and variable expressions in **writeln** statements follows the same rules that were presented in Chapter 1 for formatting constants. The statements needed to write the sum of the problem we just saw in a field width of four are

```
writeln ('The sum is ', (21 + 30 + 12):4);
writeln ('The sum is ', (Age1 + Age2 + Age3):4);
writeln ('The sum is ', Sum:4);
```

■ **EXAMPLE 2.1**

Suppose you want a program to print data about the cost of three textbooks and the average price of the books. The variable declaration section could include:

```
VAR
   MathText, BioText,
   CompSciText,
   Total, Average : real;
```

A portion of the program could be

```
MathText := 23.95;
BioText := 27.50;
CompSciText := 19.95;
Total := MathText + BioText + CompSciText;
Average := Total / 3;
```

The output could be created by

```
writeln;
writeln ('Text            Price');
writeln ('----            -----');
writeln;
writeln ('Math', MathText:18:2);
writeln ('Biology', BioText:15:2);
writeln ('CompSci', CompSciText:15:2);
writeln;
writeln ('Total', Total:17:2);
writeln;
writeln ('The average price is', Average:7:2);
```

The output would be

```
Text            Price
----            -----

Math            23.95
Biology         27.50
CompSci         19.95

Total           71.40

The average price is   23.80
```

■   ■

Software Engineering

The communication aspect of software engineering can be simplified by judicious choices of meaningful identifiers. Systems programmers must be aware that over time many others will need to read and analyze the code. Some extra time spent thinking about and using descriptive identifiers provides great timesavings during the testing and maintenance phases. Code that is written using descriptive identifiers is referred to as *self-documenting code*.

Exercises 2.2

1. Assume the variable declaration section of a program is

```
VAR
   Age, IQ : integer;
   Income : real;
```

Indicate which of the following are valid assignment statements. Give the reason for each that is invalid.

a. `Age := 21;`

b. `IQ := Age + 100;`

c. `IQ := 120.5;`

d. `Age + IQ := 150;`

e. `Income := 22000;`

f. `Income := 100 * (Age + IQ);`

g. `Age := IQ / 3;`

h. `IQ := 3 * Age;`

2. Write and run a test program to illustrate what happens when values of one data type are assigned to variables of another type.

3. Suppose A, B, and Temp have been declared as integer variables. Indicate the contents of A and B at the end of each sequence of statements.

a.
```
A := 5;
B := -2;
A := A + B;
B := B - A;
```

b.
```
A := 31;
B := 26;
Temp := A;
A := B;
B := Temp;
```

c.
```
A := 0;
B := 7;
A := A + B MOD 2 * (-3);
B := B + 4 * A;
```

d.
```
A := -8;
B := 3;
Temp := A + B;
A := 3 * B;
B := A;
Temp := Temp + A + B;
```

4. Suppose X and Y are real variables and the assignments

```
X := 121.3;
Y := 98.6;
```

have been made. What **writeln** statements would cause the following output?

a. `The value of X is  121.3`

b. `The sum of X and Y is  219.9`

c.
```
X =     121.3
Y =      98.6
    -----
Total = 219.9
```

5. Assume the variable declaration section of a program is

```
VAR
   Age, Height : integer;
   Weight : real;
   Gender : char;
```

What output would be created by the following program fragment?

```
Age := 23;
Height := 73;
Weight := 186.5;
Gender := 'M';
writeln ('Gender', Gender:10);
writeln ('Age', Age:14);
writeln ('Height', Height:11, ' inches');
writeln ('Weight', Weight:14:1, ' lbs');
```

6. Write a complete program that allows you to add five integers and then print

a. The integers.

b. Their sum.

c. Their average.

7. Assume Ch and Age have been appropriately declared. What output is produced by the following?

```
Ch := 'M';
Age := 21;
writeln ('******************************':40);
writeln ('*':11, '*':29);
write ('*':11, 'Name':7, 'Age':9);
writeln ('Gender':6, '*':4);
writeln ('*':11, '____':7, '___':9, '___':9, '*':4);
writeln;
write ('*':11, 'Jones':8, Age:8, Ch:9, '*':4);
writeln;
writeln ('*':11, '*':29);
writeln ('******************************':40);
```

8. Assume the variable declaration section of a program is

```
VAR
   Weight1, Weight2 : integer;
   AverageWeight : real;
```

and the following assignment statements have been made:

```
Weight1 := 165;
Weight2 := 174;
AverageWeight := (Weight1 + Weight2) / 2;
```

a. What output would be produced by the following section of code?

```
writeln ('Weight');
writeln ('------');
writeln;
writeln (Weight1);
writeln (Weight2);
writeln;
writeln ('The average weight is', (Weight1 + Weight2) / 2);
```

b. Write a segment of code to produce the following output (use AverageWeight).

```
      Weight
      ------

        165
        174
        ---
Total   339
```

```
The average weight is 169.5 pounds.
```

9. Assume the variable declaration section of a program is

```
VAR
   Letter : char;
```

and the following assignment has been made:

```
Letter := 'A';
```

What output is produced from the following segment of code?

```
writeln ('This reviews string formatting,':40);
writeln ('When a letter', Letter, 'is used,');
writeln ('Oops!':14, 'I forgot to format.':20);
writeln ('When a letter':22, Letter:2, 'is used,':9);
writeln ('it is a string of length one.':38);
```

■ ■ ■ ■

■ 2.3
Input

Earlier, "running a program" was subdivided into the three general categories of getting the data, manipulating it appropriately, and printing the results. Our work thus far has centered on creating output and manipulating data. We are now going to focus on how to get data for a program.

Input Statements

Data for a program are usually obtained from an input device, which can be a keyboard, terminal, card reader, disk, or tape. When such data are obtained, ⊤ the standard file **input** must be included in the file list of the program heading. (Some interactive systems use a different method. Check with your instructor.) Your program heading will (probably) have the form

PROGRAM ⟨program name⟩ (**input, output**);

The Pascal statements used to get data are **read** and **readln**; they are analogous to **write** and **writeln** for output. General forms for these *input* statements are

> **read** (⟨variable name⟩);
> **read** (⟨variable 1⟩, ⟨variable 2⟩, . . . , ⟨variable *n*⟩);
> **readln** (⟨variable name⟩);
> **readln** (⟨variable 1⟩, ⟨variable 2⟩, . . . , ⟨variable *n*⟩);
> **readln;**

A simplified syntax diagram for **read** and **readln** statements is

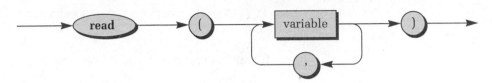

See Appendix 3 for a more detailed program.

When **read** or **readln** is used to get data, the value of the data item is stored in the indicated memory location. Data read into a program must match the type of variable in the variable list. To illustrate, if a variable declaration section includes

```
VAR
   Age : integer;
   Wage : real;
```

and the data items are

```
21          5.25
```

then

```
read (Age, Wage);
```

results in

21	5.25
Age	Wage

Interactive Input

Interactive input refers to entering values from the keyboard while the program is running. In this case, **read** or **readln** causes the program to halt and wait for data items to be typed. A *prompt* may appear on the screen. In this text, a prompt will be shown as ▢. For example, if you want to enter three scores at some point in a program, you can use

```
readln (Score1, Score2, Score3);
```

as a program statement. At this point, you must enter at least three integers and press "return" (or some sequence of integers and "return" until at least three numbers are read as data items). The remaining part of the program is then executed. To illustrate, the following program reads in three integers and prints the integers and their average as output.

```
PROGRAM Average (input, output);

CONST
   Skip = ' ';
```

```
VAR
   Score1, Score2, Score3 : integer;
   Average : real;

BEGIN
   readln (Score1, Score2, Score3);
   Average := (Score1 + Score2 + Score3) / 3;
   writeln;
   writeln (Skip:10, 'The numbers are', Score1:4, Score2:4, Score3:4);
   writeln;
   writeln (Skip:10, 'Their average is', Average:8:2);
   writeln
END.
```

When the program runs, if you type in

```
89 90 91
```

and press "return", output is

```
The numbers are  89  90  91
Their average is    90.00
```

Interactive programs should have a prompting message to the user so the user knows what to do when a prompt appears. For example, the problem in the previous example can be modified by the line

```
writeln ('Please enter 3 scores separated by spaces');
writeln ('and then press <RETURN>.');
```

before the line

```
readln (Score1, Score2, Score3);
```

The screen will display the message

```
Please enter 3 scores separated by spaces
and then press <RETURN>.
?
```

when the program is run.

Clearly stated screen messages to the person running a program are what make a program *user-friendly.* For long messages or several lines of output, you might wish to use **readln** as a complete statement to halt execution. When you press "return", the program will continue. When **readln** is used for input, "return" must be pressed before program execution will continue.

The difference between **read** and **readln** is that **readln** causes a line feed. This has two effects. First, all remaining (unread) data items on a line are skipped. Second, output from **write** or **writeln** statements will start on the next line rather than the same line. For example, consider the statements

```
read (A);
write (A);
```

and

```
readln (A);
write (A);
```

When you are working interactively, if you execute these statements, enter the number 45, and press "return", the first statement may cause

```
4545
```

to appear on the screen; the second causes

```
45
45
```

■ **EXAMPLE 2.2**

Pythagorean triples are sets of three integers that satisfy the Pythagorean theorem. That is, integers a, b, and c such that $a^2 + b^2 = c^2$. 3, 4, 5 is such a triple because $3^2 + 4^2 = 5^2$. Formulas for generating Pythagorean triples are $a = m^2 - n^2$, $b = 2mn$, and $c = m^2 + n^2$ where m and n are positive integers such that $m > n$. The following interactive program allows the user to enter values for m and n and then have the Pythagorean triple printed.

```
PROGRAM PythagoreanTriple (input, output);

VAR
   M, N, A, B, C : integer;

BEGIN
   writeln ('Enter a positive integer and press <RETURN>.');
   readln (N);
   write ('Enter a positive integer greater than ', N);
   writeln (' and press <RETURN>.');
   readln (M);
   A := (M * M) - (N * N);
   B := 2 * M * N;
   C := (M * M) + (N * N);
   writeln;
   writeln ('For M = ', M, ' and N = ', N);
   writeln ('the Pythagorean triple is ', A:5, B:5, C:5)
END.
```

Sample runs of this program (using data 1,2 and 2,5) produce the following:

```
Enter a positive integer and press <RETURN>.
?1
Enter a positive integer greater than 1 and press <RETURN>.
?2

For M = 2 and N = 1
the Pythagorean triple is     3    4    5

Enter a positive integer and press <RETURN>.
?2
Enter a positive integer greater than 2 and press <RETURN>.
?5
For M = 5 and N = 2
the Pythagorean triple is    21   20   29
```

■   ■

Reading Numeric Data

Reading numeric data into a program is reasonably straightforward. At least one blank must be used to separate numbers. The ⟨RETURN⟩ character is read as a blank, so any sequence of numbers and spaces or ⟨RETURN⟩ can be used to enter the required data.

Since the type of data items entered must match the data types for variables in an input statement, exercise some caution when using both reals and integers as input. To illustrate, suppose a variable declaration section is

```
VAR
   A : integer;
   X : real;
```

and you wish to enter the data items 97.5 and 86 respectively, **readln** (X,A) achieves the desired result. However, **readln** (A,X) results in an error. Since A is of type **integer,** only the 97 is read into A. The next character is a period and when an attempt is made to read this period into the memory location for X, a type mismatch error occurs. One exception is that an integer can be read into a variable of type **real.** However, it is stored as a **real** and must be used accordingly.

Data items can be entered using various combinations of **read** and **readln.** For example,

```
readln (Score1, Score2, Score3);
```

can be replaced by any of the following:

1. ```
   read (Score1);
   readln (Score2, Score3);
   ```
2. ```
   read (Score1, Score2);
   readln (Score3);
   ```
3. ```
   read (Score1);
   read (Score2);
   readln (Score3);
   ```

Note that in each case, three integers are to be entered in such a manner that the first one is stored in Score1, the second in Score2, and the third in Score3.

Character Sets

Before we look at reading character data, we need to examine the way in which character data are stored. In the **char** data type, each character is associated with an integer. Thus, the sequence of characters is associated with a sequence of integers. The particular sequence used by a machine for this purpose is referred to as the *collating sequence* for that *character set.* Two such sequences currently in use are

1. American Standard Code for Information Interchange (ASCII) and
2. Extended Binary Coded Decimal Interchange Code (EBCDIC).

Each collating sequence contains an ordering of the characters in a character set and is listed in Appendix 4. For programs in this text, we use the ASCII code. As shown in Table 2.6, fifty-two of these characters are letters, ten are digits, and the rest are special characters.

TABLE 2.6
ASCII code

ƀ ! " # $ % & ' ( ) * + , - . / 0 1 2 3 4 5 6 7 8 9 : ; < = > ? @
A B C D E F G H I J K L M N O P Q R S T U V W X Y Z [\ ] ^ — `
a b c d e f g h i j k l m n o p q r s t u v w x y z { | } ~

Note: Of the special characters, ƀ is the symbol to denote a blank.

Reading Character Data

Reading characters is much different from reading numeric data. When using standard Pascal, the following features apply to reading data of type **char.**
   ```

1. Only one character can be read at a time.
2. Each blank is a separate character.
3. The ⟨RETURN⟩ character is read as a blank.
4. Each digit of a number is read as a separate character.

If you want to read in a student's initials followed by three test scores,

```
read (FirstInitial, MiddleInitial, LastInitial);
readln (Score1, Score2, Score3);
```

accomplishes this. When program execution is halted, you would type in something like

```
JDK 89 90 91
```

and press "return".

Some errors are caused by not being careful with character data. For example, suppose you want to enter three test scores followed by a student's initials. Appropriate program statements are

```
read (Score1, Score2, Score3);
readln (FirstInitial, MiddleInitial, LastInitial);
```

When program execution halts for expected input, suppose you enter

```
89 90 91 JDK
```

When you try to print these values using

```
writeln (Score1, Score2:5, Score3:5);
writeln (FirstInitial, MiddleInitial, LastInitial);
```

the output is

```
89    90    91
 JD
```

because the blank following 91 is read as a character when an attempt is made to read FirstInitial. Note that the first three characters following 91 are a blank followed by 'J' and 'D'. This problem can be avoided by entering the data as

```
89 90 91JDK
```

However, in actual practice, it probably would be better to enter the initials first and then the scores. This topic of reading character data is expanded when text files are introduced in Chapter 6.

STYLE TIP
■ ■ ■ ■ ■ ■ ■ ■ ■ ■ ■

A variable or expression may be used as a field width specifier. When running interactive programs, this idea can be used to control desired accuracy as follows:

```
writeln ('How many places of accuracy?');
readln (Places);
    .
    .
    .
writeln ('Result is ', Result:Places+2:Places);
```

Debugging writelns

A frequently used technique for debugging programs is inserting a **writeln** statement to print the values of variables. Once you have determined that the desired values are obtained, you can delete the **writeln** statements. For example, if your program segment is to read in three scores and three initials, you could write

```
readln (Score1, Score2, Score3);
writeln (Score1:5, Score2:5, Score3:5);   { for debugging }
readln (FirstInitial, MiddleInitial, LastInitial);
writeln (FirstInitial, MiddleInitial, LastInitial);
                                           { for debugging }
```

These debugging lines should be left in until the program has been sufficiently tested for input.

Reading Strings

Many current versions of Pascal—other than standard Pascal—permit reading textual data in strings in addition to one character at a time. These versions allow some string data type. For example, in Turbo Pascal, strings of up to 20 characters can be declared by

```
VAR
   Name : string [20];
```

With this declaration, string names can be entered by

```
writeln ('Enter your name and press <RETURN>.');
readln (Name);
```

A note of caution is in order. If you wish to enter a string and a numeric value, you must make sure that the number is not part of the string. For example, using the declaration for Name just given,

```
writeln ('Enter your name and age.  ');
readln (Name, Age);
```

Communication Skills Needed

Emphasis on communication has been increasing in almost every area of higher education. Evidence of this is the current trend toward "writing across the curriculum" programs implemented in many colleges and universities in the 1980s. Indications that this emphasis is shared among computer scientists was given by Paul M. Jackowitz, Richard M. Plishka, and James R. Sidbury, University of Scranton, when they stated, "Make it possible to write programs in English, and you will discover that programmers cannot write in English."

All computer science educators are painfully aware of the truth of this old joke. We want our students to be literate. We want them to have well-developed writing skills and the capacity to read technical journals in our area. But too often we produce skilled programmers whose communication skills are poor and who have almost no research skills. We must alleviate this problem. Since the organizational techniques used to write software are the same ones that should be used to write papers, computing science students should have excellent writing skills. We should exploit this similarity in skills to develop better writers.

Further, Janet Hartman of Illinois State University and Curt M. White of Indiana-Purdue University at Fort Wayne noted: "Students need to practice written and oral communication skills, both in communications classes and computer classes. Students should write system specifications, project specifications, memos, users' guides or anything else which requires them to communicate on both a nontechnical and technical level. They should do presentations in class and learn to augment their presentations with audiovisual aids."

On a more general note, the need for effective communication skills in computer science has been acknowledged in the 1991 curriculum guidelines of the Association for Computing Machinery, Inc. These guidelines state that "undergraduate programs should prepare students to apply their knowledge to specific, constrained problems and produce solutions. This includes the ability to . . . communicate that solution to colleagues, professionals in other fields, and the general public."

could result in the user entering

```
Joan Smith 23
```

and then pressing "return". Since the 23 is entered before column 20, it is considered part of the string of length 20. To avoid this problem, either enter the age first, enter data on separate lines, or enter the age starting after column 20.

Batch Input

Batch input refers to a program getting data from a file that has previously been created. The beginning of this text is written assuming the reader will use an interactive mode. Development of batch input is deferred until Chapter 6. If you are working in a batch mode, you should read Chapter 6 at this time and check with your instructor.

Exercises 2.3

1. Discuss the difference between using **read** and **readln** to get data for a program.

2. Assume a variable declaration section is

```
VAR
    Num1, Num2 : integer;
    Num3 : real;
    Ch : char;
```

and you wish to enter the data

```
15 65.3 -20
```

Explain what results from each statement. Also indicate what values are assigned to appropriate variables.

a. `readln (Num1, Num3, Num2);`
b. `readln (Num1, Num2, Num3);`
c. `readln (Num1, Num2, Ch, Num3);`
d. `readln (Num2, Num3, Ch, Num2);`
e. `readln (Num2, Num3, Ch, Ch, Num2);`
f. `readln (Num3, Num2);`
g. `readln (Num1, Num3);`
h. `readln (Num1, Ch, Num3);`
i. `read (Num1, Num3, Num2);`
j. `read (Num1, Num3, Ch, Num2);`
k. `read (Num1, Num3, Ch, Ch, Num2);`
l. `read (Num2, Num1, Ch, Num2);`

3. Write a program statement to be used to print a message to the screen directing the user to enter data in the form used for Exercise 2.

4. Write an appropriate program statement (or statements) to produce a screen message and write an appropriate input statement for each of the following.
   a. Desired input is number of hours worked and hourly pay rate.
   b. Desired input is three positive integers followed by −999.
   c. Desired input is price of an automobile and the state sales tax rate.
   d. Desired input is the game statistics for one basketball player (check with a coach to see what must be entered).
   e. Desired input is a student's initials, age, height, weight, and gender.

5. Assume variables are declared as in Exercise 2. If an input statement is

```
readln (Num1, Num2, Ch, Num3);
```

indicate which lines of data do not result in an error message. For those that do not, indicate the values of the variables. For those that produce an error, explain what the error is.
   a. 83 95 100
   b. 83 95.0 100
   c. 83 − 72 93.5
   d. 83 − 72   93.5
   e. 83.5
   f. 70 73 − 80.5
   g. 91 92 93 94
   h. − 76 − 81 − 16.5

6. Why is it a good idea to print out values of variables that have been read into a program?

7. Suppose Price is a variable of type **real** and you have the program statement

```
read (Price);
```

   a. What happens if you enter 17.95?
   b. How does this input statement compare to **readln** (Price)?

8. Write a complete program that will read your initials and five test scores. Your program should then compute your test average and print out all information in a reasonable form with suitable messages.

■ ■ ■ ■

■ 2.4
Using Constants

The word "constant" has several interpretations. In this section, it will refer to values defined in the **CONST** definition subsection of a program. Recall that a Pascal program consists of a program heading, a declaration section, and an executable section. The declaration section contains a variable declaration subsection, discussed in Section 1.4, and possibly a constant definition subsection. When both are used, the **CONST** subsection must precede the **VAR** subsection. We will now examine uses for constants defined in the **CONST** subsection.

Rationale for Uses

There are many reasons to use constants in a program. If a number is to be used frequently, the programmer may wish to give it a descriptive name in the **CONST** definition subsection and then use the descriptive name in the executable section, thus making the program easier to read. For example, if a program included a segment that computed a person's state income tax, and the state tax rate was 6.25 percent of taxable income, the **CONST** section might include:

```
CONST
    StateTaxRate = 0.0625;
```

This defines both the value and type for StateTaxRate. In the executable portion of the program, the statement

```
StateTax := Income * StateTaxRate;
```

computes the state tax owed. Or suppose you wanted a program to compute areas of circles. Depending upon the accuracy you desire, you could define pi "π" as

```
CONST
  Pi = 3.14159;
```

You could then have a statement in the executable section such as

```
Area := Pi * Radius * Radius;
```

where Area and Radius are appropriately declared variables.

Perhaps the most important use of constants is for values that are currently fixed but subject to change for subsequent runs of the program. If these are defined in the **CONST** section, they can be used throughout the program. If the value changes later, only one change need be made to keep the program current. This prevents the need to locate all uses of a constant in a program. Some examples might be

```
CONST
  MinimumWage = 4.25;
  SpeedLimit = 65;
  Price = 0.75;
  StateTaxRate = 0.0625;
```

Constants can also be used to name character strings that occur frequently in program output. Suppose a program needs to print two different company names. Instead of typing the names each time they are needed, the following definition could be used.

```
CONST
  Company1 = 'First National Bank of America';
  Company2 = 'Metropolitan Bank of New York';
```

Company1 and Company2 could then be used in **writeln** statements.

Another situation could call for a constant defined for later repeated use in making output more attractive. Included could be constants for underlining and for separating sections of output. Some definitions could be

```
CONST
  Underline = '----------------------------------';
  Splats = '**********************************';
```

To separate the output with asterisks, the statement

```
writeln (Splats, Splats);
```

A NOTE OF INTEREST

Defined Constants and Space Shuttle Computing

An excellent illustration of the utilization of defined constants in a program was given by J. F. ("Jack") Clemons, former manager of avionics flight software development and verification for the space shuttle on-board computers. In an interview with David Gifford, editor for *Communications of the ACM*, Clemons was asked: "Have you tried to restructure the software so that it can be changed easily?"

His response was, "By changing certain data constants, we can change relatively large portions of the software on a mission-to-mission basis. For example, we've designed the software so that characteristics like atmospheric conditions on launch day or different lift-off weights can be loaded as initial constants into the code. This is important when there are postponements or last-minute payload changes that invalidate the original inputs."

could be used. In a similar fashion

```
writeln (Underline);
```

could be used for underlining.

Software Engineering

The appropriate use of constants is consistent with principles of software engineering. Communication between teams of programmers is enhanced when program constants have been agreed upon. Each team should have a list of these constants for use as they work on their part of the system.

The maintenance phase of the software system life cycle is also aided by use of defined constants. Clearly, a large payroll system is dependent upon being able to perform computations that include deductions for federal tax, state tax, FICA, Medicare, health insurance, retirement options, and so on. If appropriate constants are defined for these deductions, system changes are easily made as necessary. For example, the current salary limit for deducting FICA taxes is $53,400. Since this amount changes regularly, one could define

```
CONST
  FICALimit = 53400.00
```

Program maintenance is then simplified by changing the value of this constant as the law changes.

Formatting Constants

Formatting numerical constants is identical to formatting reals and integers as discussed in Section 1.5. Real constants are formatted as reals and integer constants as integers. When character strings are defined as constants, a single positive integer can be used for formatting. This integer establishes the field width for the character string and right justifies the character string in the output field.

Exercises 2.4

1. One use of constants is for values that are used throughout a program but are subject to change over time (minimum wage, speed limit, and so on). List at least five items in this category that were not mentioned in this section.

2. Assume the **CONST** definition section of a program is

```
CONST
  CourseName = 'CPS 150';
  TotalPts = 100;
  Underline = '-------------------------------------------';
```

We want output as follows:

```
COURSE:            CPS 150      TEST #1
-------------------------------------------

TOTAL POINTS     100
```

Fill in the appropriate formatting positions in the following **writeln** statements to produce the indicated output.

```
writeln ('COURSE:':7, CourseName:    , 'TEST #1':13);
writeln (Underline:    );
writeln;
writeln ('TOTAL POINTS':12, TotalPts:    );
```

3. Using the same **CONST** definition section as in Exercise 2, what output is produced by the following segment of code?

```
writeln;
writeln (CourseName:10, 'TEST #2':20);
writeln (Underline);
writeln;
writeln ('Total points':15, TotalPts:14);
writeln ('My score':11, 93:18);
writeln ('Class average':16, 82.3:13:1);
```

4. Use the constant definition section to define appropriate constants for the following:

   a. Your name.

   b. Today's date.

   c. Your social security number.

   d. Your age.

   e. The name of your school.

   f. The number of students in your class.

   g. The average age of students in your class.

   h. The average hourly wage of steelworkers.

   i. The price of a new car.

■ ■ ■ ■

■ 2.5
Standard Functions

Some standard operations required by programmers are squaring numbers, finding square roots of numbers, rounding numbers, and truncating numbers. Because these operations are so basic, Pascal provides *standard (built-in) functions* for them. Different versions of Pascal and other programming languages have differing standard functions available, so you should always check which functions can be used. Appendix 2 sets forth those available in most versions of Pascal.

A function can be used in a program if it appears in the following form.

⟨function name⟩ (⟨argument⟩)

where *argument* is a value or variable with an assigned value. When a function is listed in this manner, it is said to be *called* or *invoked*. A function is invoked by using it in a program statement. If, for example, you want to square the integer 5,

   `sqr(5)`

produces the desired result.

The syntax diagram for this is

Many functions operate on numbers, starting with a given number and returning some associated value. Table 2.7 shows five standard functions, each with its argument type, data type of return, and an explanation of the value returned. A complete list of functions can be found in Appendix 2.

TABLE 2.7
Numeric function calls and return types

Function Call	Argument Type	Type of Return	Function Value
sqr(argument)	**real** or **integer**	Same as argument	Returns the square of the argument
sqrt(argument)	**real** or **integer** (nonnegative)	**real**	Returns the square root of the argument
abs(argument)	**real** or **integer**	Same as argument	Returns absolute value of the argument
round(argument)	**real**	**integer**	Returns value rounded to the nearest integer
trunc(argument)	**real**	**integer**	Returns value truncated to an integer

Several examples of specific function expressions together with the value returned by each expression are depicted in Table 2.8.

TABLE 2.8
Values of function expressions

Expression	Value
sqr(2)	4
sqr(2.0)	4.0
sqr(-3)	9
sqrt(25.0)	5.0
sqrt(25)	5.0
sqrt(0.0)	0.0
sqrt(-2.0)	Not permissible
abs(5.2)	5.2
abs(-3.4)	3.4
abs(-5)	5
round(3.78)	4
round(8.50)	9
round(-4.2)	−4
round(-4.7)	−5
trunc(3.78)	3
trunc(8.5)	8
trunc(-4.2)	−4
trunc(-4.7)	−4

Using Functions

When a function is invoked, it produces a value in much the same way that 3 + 3 produces 6. Thus, use of a function should be treated similarly to using constants or values of an expression. Since function calls are not complete Pascal statements, they must be used within some statement. Typical uses are in assignment statements,

```
X := sqrt(16.0);
```

output statements,

```
writeln (abs(-8):20);
```

or arithmetic expressions

```
X := round(3.78) + trunc(-4.1);
```

Arguments of functions can be expressions, variables, or constants. However, be sure the argument is always appropriate. For example,

```
A := 3.2;
X := sqrt(trunc(A));
```

is appropriate, but

```
A := -3.2;
X := sqrt(trunc(A));
```

produces an error since **trunc**(-3.2) has the value -3 and **sqrt**(-3) is not a valid expression.

The following example illustrates how functions can be used in expressions.

■ **EXAMPLE 2.3**

Find the value of the following expression:

```
4.2 + round(trunc(2.0 * 3.1) + 5.3) - sqrt(sqr(-4.1));
```

The solution is

```
4.2 + round(trunc(2.0 * 3.1) + 5.3) - sqrt(sqr(-4.1))
                        ↓                        ↓
4.2 +      round(trunc(6.2)     + 5.3) -   sqrt(16.81)
                  ↓                              ↓
4.2 +            round(6.0       + 5.3) -        4.1
                                 ↓
4.2 +                 round(11.3)       -        4.1
                          ↓
4.2 +                    11.0           -        4.1
         ↓
      15.2                                        4.1
                              ↓
                            11.1
```

■   ■

Character Functions

Ordering a character set requires associating an integer with each character. Data types ordered in some association with the integers are known as *ordinal data types*. Each integer is the ordinal of its associated character. Integers are therefore considered to be an ordinal data type. Character sets are also considered to be an ordinal data type, as shown in Table 2.9. In each case, the ordinal of the character appears to the left of the character.

Using ASCII, as shown in Table 2.9, the ordinal of a capital a ('A') is 65, the ordinal of the character representing the arabic number one ('1') is 49, the ordinal of a blank ('␢') is 32, and the ordinal of a lowercase a ('a') is 97.

Pascal provides several standard functions that have arguments of ordinal type. These are listed in Table 2.10 together with a related function **chr** that returns a character when called.

TABLE 2.9
ASCII ordering of a character set

Ordinal	Character	Ordinal	Character	Ordinal	Character
32	b	64	@	96	'
33	!	65	A	97	a
34	"	66	B	98	b
35	#	67	C	99	c
36	$	68	D	100	d
37	%	69	E	101	e
38	&	70	F	102	f
39	'	71	G	103	g
40	(	72	H	104	h
41	)	73	I	105	i
42	*	74	J	106	j
43	+	75	K	107	k
44	,	76	L	108	l
45	−	77	M	109	m
46	.	78	N	110	n
47	/	79	O	111	o
48	0	80	P	112	p
49	1	81	Q	113	q
50	2	82	R	114	r
51	3	83	S	115	s
52	4	84	T	116	t
53	5	85	U	117	u
54	6	86	V	118	v
55	7	87	W	119	w
56	8	88	X	120	x
57	9	89	Y	121	y
58	:	90	Z	122	z
59	;	91	[	123	{
60	<	92	\	124	|
61	=	93	]	125	}
62	>	94	^	126	~
63	?	95	—		

Note: Codes 00−31 and 127 are nonprintable control characters.

TABLE 2.10
Function calls with ordinal arguments or character values

Function Call	Argument Type	Type of Result	Function Value
ord(argument)	Any ordinal type	**integer**	Ordinal corresponding to argument
pred(argument)	Any ordinal type	Same as argument	Predecessor of the argument
succ(argument)	Any ordinal type	Same as argument	Successor of the argument
chr(argument)	**integer**	**char**	Character associated with the ordinal of the argument

Again using the ASCII collating sequence shown in Table 2.9, we can determine the value of these functions, as shown in Table 2.11.

TABLE 2.11
Values of character functions

Expression	Value
ord('E')	69
ord('9')	57
ord(9)	9
ord('>')	62
pred('N')	M
pred('A')	@
succ('(')	)
succ('!')	"
chr(74)	J
chr(32)	ƀ
chr(59)	;
chr(114)	r

Variables and variable expressions can be used as arguments for functions. For example, if Ch is a **char** variable and the assignment statement

```
Ch := 'D';
```

is made, then **ord**(Ch) has the value 68.

Let's now consider a short program that allows the use of standard functions **ord, pred, succ,** and **chr.**

```
PROGRAM FunctionTest (output);

VAR
  Ch : char;

BEGIN
  Ch := 'C';
  writeln ('Ord of C is', ord(Ch):5);
  writeln ('Succ of C is', succ(Ch):4);
  writeln ('Pred of C is', pred(Ch):4);
  writeln ('Chr of 67 is', chr(67):4)
END.
```

When this program is run, the output is

```
Ord of C is    67
Succ of C is   D
Pred of C is   B
Chr of 67 is   C
```

You should obtain a complete list of characters available and their respective ordinals for your local system. Note particular features such as when using EBCDIC, **succ**('R') is not 'S'; and when using ASCII, **chr**(n) is nonprintable for $n <$ 32 or $n >$ 126.

One of the uses for functions **chr** and **ord** is to convert between uppercase and lowercase letters. Closely related is the conversion of a digit (entered as a **char** value) to its integer value. In the next example, we show how to convert an uppercase letter to lowercase. Other conversions are deferred to the exercises.

Debugging or Sleuthing?

Investigating why programs don't work as expected requires ingenuity. The reason can be quite bizarre. To illustrate, consider two situations reported by Jon Bentley in *Communications of the ACM*.

1. "When a programmer used his new computer terminal, all was fine when he was sitting down, but he couldn't log in to the system when he was standing up. That behavior was 100 percent repeatable: he could always log in when sitting and never when standing."

2. "A banking system had worked for quite some time, but halted the first time it was used on international data. Programmers spent days scouring the code, but they couldn't find any stray command that would return control to the operating system."

What do you think are possible solutions? The answers are set forth in the programming problems for this chapter.

■ **EXAMPLE 2.4**

To show how functions **chr** and **ord** can be used to convert an uppercase letter to lowercase, let's assume that our task is to convert the letter 'H' into the letter 'h'. Using the ASCII chart shown in Table 2.9, we first note that the ordinal of 'H' is 72. We subtract the ordinal of 'A' from this to obtain

```
ord('H') - ord ('A')
```

which is

```
72 - 65 = 7
```

We now add the ordinal of 'a' to get

```
ord('H') - ord('A') + ord('a')
```

which yields

```
72 - 65 + 97 = 104
```

This is the ordinal of 'h'. It can be converted to the letter by using **chr**. Thus,

```
chr(ord('H') - ord('A') + ord('a'))
```

produces the letter 'h'.

In general, the following is sufficient for converting from uppercase to lowercase:

```
Lowercase := chr(ord(Uppercase) - ord('A') + ord('a'));
```

Note that if you always use the same ASCII ordering,

```
-ord('A') + ord('a')
```

could be replaced by the constant 32. If you choose to do this, it should be done in the **CONST** section. A typical definition is

```
CONST
   UpperToLowerShift = 32;
```

You would then write the Lowercase conversion as

```
Lowercase := chr(ord(Uppercase) + UpperToLowerShift);
```

■   ■

Exercises 2.5

1. Find the value of each of the following expressions:
   a. `abs(-11.2) + sqrt(round(15.51))`
   b. `trunc(abs(-14.2))`

    c. 4 * 11 MOD (trunc(trunc(8.9) / sqrt(16)))

    d. sqr(17 DIV 5 * 2)

    e. -5.0 + sqrt(5 * 5 - 4 * 6) / 2.0

    f. 3.1 * 0.2 - abs(-4.2 * 9.0 / 3.0)

2. Write a test program that illustrates what happens when an inappropriate argument is used with a function. Be sure to include something like **ord**(15.3).

3. Two standard algebraic problems come from the Pythagorean theorem and the quadratic formula. Assume variables *a*, *b*, and *c* have been declared in a program. Write Pascal expressions that allow you to evaluate

   a. the length of the hypotenuse of a right triangle

   $$(\sqrt{a^2 + b^2})$$

   b. both solutions to the quadratic formula

   $$\frac{-b \pm \sqrt{b^2 - 4ac}}{2a}$$

4. Indicate whether the following are valid or invalid expressions. Find the value of those that are valid; explain why the others are invalid.

   a. -6 MOD (sqrt(16))

   b. 8 DIV (trunc(sqrt(65)))

   c. sqrt(63 MOD (2))

   d. abs(-sqrt(sqr(3) + 7))

   e. sqrt(16 DIV (-3))

   f. sqrt(sqr(-4))

   g. round(14.38 * 10) / 10

5. The standard function **round** permits you to round to the nearest integer. Write an expression that permits you to round the real number X to the nearest tenth.

6. Using ASCII, find the values of each of the following expressions:

   a. ord(13 + 4 MOD 3)

   b. pred(succ('E'))

   c. succ(pred('E'))

   d. ord(5)

   e. ord('5')

   f. chr(ord('+'))

   g. ord(chr(40))

7. Assume the variable declaration section of a program is

   ```
   VAR
      X : real;
      A : integer;
      Ch : char;
   ```

   What output is produced by each of the following program fragments?

   a. X := -4.3;
      writeln (X:6:2, abs(X):6:2, trunc(X):6, round(X):6);

   b. X := -4.3;
      A := abs(round(X));
      writeln (ord(A));
      writeln (ord('A'));

   c. Ch := chr(76);
      writeln (Ch:5, pred(Ch):5, succ(Ch):5);

8. Write a complete program to print each uppercase letter of the alphabet and its ordinal in the collating sequence used by your machine's version of Pascal.

9. Using ASCII, show how each of the following conversions can be made.

   a. A lowercase letter converted into its uppercase equivalent.

   b. A digit entered as a **char** value into its indicated numeric value.

■ ■ ■ ■

Writing styles and suggestions are gathered for quick reference in the following style tip summary. These tips are intended to stimulate rather than terminate your imagination.

STYLE TIP
■ ■ ■ ■ ■ ■ ■ ■ ■ ■ ■ ■

1. Use descriptive identifiers. Words—Sum, Score, Average—are easier to understand than letters—A, B, C or X, Y, Z.

2. Constants can be used to create neat, attractive output. For example,

```
CONST
   Splats = '*******************************';
   Underline = '------------------------';
   Border = '*                           *';
```

3. Use the constant definition section to define an appropriately named blank and use it to control line spacing for output. Thus, you could have

```
CONST
   Skip = ' ';
   Indent = ' ';
```

and then output statements could be

```
writeln (Skip:20, <message>, Skip:10, <message>);
```

or

```
writeln (Indent:20, <message>, Skip:10, <message>);
```

4. As you write Pascal statements, use blanks for line spacing within the program. Spacing between words and expressions should resemble typical English usage. Thus,

```
PROGRAM EarlyBird (input, output);
```

is preferable to

```
PROGRAM   EarlyBird   (   input,   output   );
```

5. Output of a column of reals should have decimal points in a line.

```
  14.32
181.50
  93.63
```

6. Output can be made more attractive by using columns, left and right margins, underlining, and blank lines.

7. Extra **writelns** at the beginning and end of the executable section will separate desired output from other messages.

```
BEGIN
   writeln;
          .
          . (program body here)
          .
   writeln
END.
```

Complete programs are used to illustrate concepts developed throughout the text. In each case, a typical problem is stated. A solution is developed in pseudocode and illustrated with a structure chart. Module specifications are written for appropriate modules. Now, on to the problem for this chapter.

Write a complete program to find the unit price for a pizza. Input for the program consists of the price and size of the pizza. Size is the diameter of the pizza ordered. Output consists of the price per square inch. A first-level development is

1. Get the data
2. Perform the computations
3. Print the results

A structure chart for this problem is given in Figure 2.2.

FIGURE 2.2
Structure chart for the pizza problem

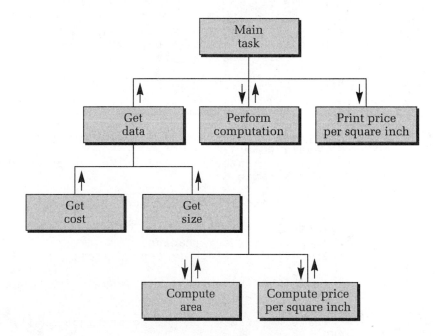

Module specifications for the main modules are

1. Get Data Module
   Data received: None
   Information returned: Price
                        Size
   Logic: Have the user enter price and size.

2. Perform Computation Module
   Data received: Price
                  Size
   Information returned: Price per square inch
   Logic: Given the diameter, find the radius.
          Compute the area using Area = Pi * Radius * Radius.
          Price per square inch is found by dividing Price by Area.

3. Print Results Module
   Data received: PricePerSquareInch
   Information returned: None
   Logic: Print the price per square inch.

A further refinement of the pseudocode produces

1. Get the data
   1.1 get price
   1.2 get size
2. Perform the computations
   2.1 compute area
   2.2 calculate unit price

Step 3 of the pseudocode, "Print the results" only requires printing the price per square inch, so no further development is required.

A complete program for this is

```
PROGRAM PizzaCost (input, output);

CONST
  Pi = 3.14;

VAR
  Size, Radius, Cost, Area,
  PricePerSquareInch : real;

BEGIN

  {  This module gets the data  }

  writeln ('Enter the pizza price and press <RETURN>.');
  readln (Cost);
  writeln ('Enter the pizza size and press <RETURN>.');
  readln (Size);

  {  This module computes the unit price  }

  Radius := Size / 2;
  Area := Pi * sqr (Radius);
  PricePerSquareInch := Cost / Area;

  {  This module prints the results  }

  writeln;
  writeln ('The price per square inch is $', PricePerSquareInch:4:2)
END.
```

A sample run of this program yields

```
Enter the pizza price and press <RETURN>.
?10.50
Enter the pizza size and press <RETURN>.
?16
The price per square inch is $0.05
```

■ Summary

Key Terms

argument
assignment statement
batch input
character set

collating sequence:
  ASCII, EBCDIC
constant
input

integer arithmetic
  operations: +, −,
  *, MOD, DIV
interactive input

invoke (call)
memory location
mixed-mode expression
ordinal data type
overflow
prompt

real arithmetic
  operations:
  +, −, *, /
self-documenting
  code

standard (built-in)
  function
underflow
user-friendly
variable

Keywords

abs	**pred**	**sqr**
chr	**read**	**sqrt**
DIV	**readln**	**succ**
MOD	**round**	**trunc**
ord		

Key Concepts

- Operations and priorities for data of type **integer** and **real** are summarized as follows:

Data Type	Operations	Priority
integer	*, **MOD, DIV**	1. Evaluate in order from left to right
	+, −,	2. Evaluate in order from left to right
real	*, /	1. Evaluate in order from left to right
	+, −	2. Evaluate in order from left to right

- Mixed-mode expressions return values of type **real.**
- Priority for order of operations on mixed-mode expressions is
  1. *, /, **MOD, DIV** in order from left to right
  2. +, − in order from left to right
- Overflow is caused by a value too large for computing on a particular machine.
- Underflow is caused by a value too small (close to zero) for computing. These numbers are automatically replaced by zero.
- A memory location can have a name which can be used to refer to the contents of the location.
- The name of a memory location is different from the contents of the memory location.
- Self-documenting code is code that is written using descriptive identifiers.
- Assignment statements are used to assign values to memory locations, for example

```
Sum := 30 + 60;
```

- Variables and variable expressions can be used in output statements.
- **read(ln)** is used to get data; correct form is
  read(ln) (⟨variable name⟩);
  read(ln) (⟨variable 1⟩, ⟨variable 2⟩, . . . , ⟨variable n⟩);
- **read(ln)** (⟨variable name⟩) causes a value to be transferred to the variable location.
- Interactive input expects data items to be entered from the keyboard at appropriate times during execution of the program.
- Data types for variables in a **read** or **readln** statement should match data items read as input.
- Appropriate uses for constants in the **CONST** definition section include frequently used numbers; current values subject to change over time, for example, (MinimumWage = 4.25); and character strings for output.

- Character strings are formatted using a single colon.
- Five standard numeric functions available in Pascal are **sqr, sqrt, abs, round,** and **trunc.**
- Functions can be used in assignment statements, for example

```
X := sqrt(16.0);
```

in output statements

```
writeln (abs(-8):20);
```

and in arithmetic expressions

```
X := round(3.78) + trunc(-4.1);
```

Four standard character functions available in Pascal are **ord, pred, succ,** and **chr.**

■ **Programming Problems and Projects**

Write a complete Pascal program for each of the following problems. Each program should use one or more **read** or **readln** statements to obtain necessary values. Each **read** or **readln** should be preceded by an appropriate prompting message.

1. Susan purchases a computer for $985. The sales tax on the purchase is 5.5 percent. Compute and print the total purchase price.

2. Find and print the area and perimeter of a rectangle that is 4.5 feet long and 2.3 feet wide. Print both rounded to the nearest tenth of a foot.

3. Compute and print the number of minutes in a year.

4. Light travels as $3*10^8$ meters per second. Compute and print the distance that a light beam would travel in one year. (This is called a light year.)

5. The 1927 New York Yankees won 110 games and lost 44. Compute their winning percentage and print it rounded to three decimal places.

6. A 10 kilogram object is traveling at 12 meters per second. Compute and print its momentum (momentum is mass times velocity).

7. Convert 98.0 degrees Fahrenheit to degrees Celsius.

8. Given a positive number, print its square and square root.

9. The Golden Sales Company pays its salespeople $.27 for each item they sell. Given the number of items sold by a salesperson, print the amount of pay due.

10. Given the length and width of a rectangle, print its area and perimeter.

11. The kinetic energy of a moving object is given by the formula:

$$KE = (1/2)mv^2$$

Given the mass (m) and the speed (v) of an object, find its kinetic energy.

12. Miss Lovelace wants a program to enable her to balance her checkbook. She wishes to enter a beginning balance, five letters for an abbreviation for the recipient of the check, and the amount of the check. Given this information, write a program that will find the new balance in her checkbook.

Debugging or Sleuthing: Answers

1. "The problem was in the terminal's keyboard: the tops of two keys were switched. When the programmer was seated, he was a touch-typist and the problem went unnoticed, but when he stood, he was led astray by hunting and pecking."

2. "When [the programmers] observed the behavior more closely, they found that the problem occurred as they entered data for the country of Ecuador: when the user typed the name of the capital city (Quito), the program interpreted that as a request to quit the run!"

13. A supermarket wants to install a computerized weighing system in its produce department. Input to this system will consist of a three-letter identifier for the type of produce, the weight of the produce purchase (in pounds), and the cost per pound of the produce. A typical input screen would be

```
Enter each of the following:

Description <RETURN>
?ABC
Weight <RETURN>
?2.0
Price/lb. <RETURN>
?1.98
```

Print a label showing the input information along with the total cost of the purchase. The label should appear as follows:

```
%%%%%%%%%%%%%%%%%%%%%%%%%%%%%%%%%%%%%%%%%%%%%%%

            Penny Spender Supermarket
               Produce Department

    ITEM      WEIGHT       COST/lb      COST
     ABC      2.0 lb        $1.98      $3.96

                    Thank you!

%%%%%%%%%%%%%%%%%%%%%%%%%%%%%%%%%%%%%%%%%%%%%%%
```

14. The New-Wave Computer Company sells its product, the NW-PC for $675. In addition, they sell memory expansion cards for $69.95, disk drives for $198.50, and software for $34.98 each. Given the number of memory cards, disk drives, and software packages desired by a customer purchasing an NW-PC, print out a bill of sale that appears as follows:

```
****************************
        New Wave Computers

    ITEM                COST
  1  NW-PC           $675.00
  2  Memory card      139.90
  1  Disk Drive       198.50
  4  Software          139.92
                      -------

        TOTAL        $1153.32
```

15. Write a test program that allows you to see the characters contained within the character set of your computer. Given a positive integer, you can use the **chr** function to determine the corresponding character. On most computers, only integers less than 255 are valid for this. Also, remember that most character sets contain some unprintable characters such as ASCII values less than 32. Print your output in the form:

```
Character number nnn is x.
```

16. Mr. Vigneault, a coach at Shepherd High School, is working on a program that can be used to assist cross-country runners in analyzing their times. As part of the program, a coach enters elapsed times for each runner given in units of minutes, seconds, and hundredths. In a 5000 meter (5K) race, elapsed times are entered at the one-mile and two-mile marks. These elapsed times are then used to compute "splits" for each part of the race; that is, how long did it take a runner to run each of the three race segments.

    Write a complete program that will accept as input three times given in units of minutes, seconds, and hundredths and then produce output that includes the split for each segment. Typical input would be

```
Runner number        234
Mile times:       1   5:34.22
                  2   11:21.67
Finish time:          17:46.85
```

Typical output would be

```
Runner number        234
Split one            5:34.22
Split two            5:47.45
Split three          6:25.18
Finish time          17:46.85
```

17. Many (but not all) instructors in beginning computer science courses encourage their students to use meaningful identifiers in writing code. It is natural to wonder to what extent this practice is followed outside the educational world. Investigate this issue by contacting several programmers who work for nearby companies. Prepare a complete written report of your conversations for distribution to class members. Include charts that summarize your findings.

CHAPTER

Great things are not done by impulse, but by a series of small things brought together.
Vincent van Gogh

Subprograms: Procedures and Functions for Problem Solving

Recall from Section 1.3 the process of solving a problem by stepwise refinement of tasks into subtasks. This top-down design method is especially suitable for writing Pascal programs to solve problems using *subprograms*.

The concept of a subprogram is not difficult to understand. It is a program within a program and is provided by most programming languages. Each subprogram should complete some task, the nature of which can range from simple to complex. You could have a subprogram that prints only a line of data, or you could rewrite an entire program as a subprogram. The main idea is to use a subprogram to perform some specific task.

■ 3.1
Program Design

Modularity

We have previously discussed and illustrated the process of solving a problem by top-down design. Using this method, we divide the main task into major subtasks, and then continue to divide the subtasks (stepwise refinement) into smaller subtasks until all subtasks can be easily performed. Once an algorithm for solving a problem has been developed using top-down design, the programmer then writes code to translate the general solution into a Pascal program.

As you have seen, code written to perform one well-defined subtask is referred to as a module. One should be able to design, code, and test each module in a program independently from the rest of the program. In this sense, a module is a subprogram containing all definitions and declarations needed to perform the indicated subtask. Everything required for the subtask (but not needed in other parts of the program) can be created in the subprogram. Consequently, the definitions and declarations have meaning only when the module is being used.

A program that has been created using modules to perform various tasks is said to possess *modularity*. In general, modular programs are easier to test, debug, and correct than programs that are not modular because each independent module can be tested by running it from a test driver. Then, once the modules are running correctly, they can become part of a longer program. This independent testing of modules is referred to as *bottom-up testing*.

Structured Programming

Structured programming is the process of developing a program where emphasis is placed on the communication between independent modules. Connections between these modules are specified in parameter lists and are usually controlled by the main program. Structured programming is especially suitable to large programs being worked on by teams. By carefully designing the modules and specifying what information is to be received by and returned from the module, a team of programmers can independently develop their module and then have it connect to the complete program.

The remainder of this chapter is devoted to seeing how subprograms can be written to accomplish specific tasks. There are two types of subprograms in standard Pascal: procedures and functions. We will first examine the writing and use of procedures. We will then learn how to write user-defined functions (we discussed built-in functions in Section 2.5).

■ **3.2**
Procedures As Subprograms

Procedures can be used as subprograms for a number of purposes. Two significant uses are to facilitate the top-down design philosophy of problem solving and to avoid having to write repeated segments of code.

A NOTE OF INTEREST

Structured Programming

From 1950 to the early 1970s programs were designed and written on a linear basis. A program written and designed on such a basis can be called an unstructured program. Structured programming, on the other hand, organizes a program around separate semi-independent modules that are linked together by a single sequence of simple commands.

In 1964, mathematicians Corrado Bohm and Guiseppe Jacopini proved that any program logic, regardless of complexity, can be expressed by using sequence, selection, and iteration. This result is termed the structure theorem. This result, combined with the efforts of Edger W. Dijkstra, led to a significant move toward structured programming and away from the use of **GOTO** statements.

In fact, in a letter to the editor of *Communications of the ACM* (Volume 11, March 1968), Dijkstra stated that the **GOTO** statement "should be abolished from all 'higher level' programming languages . . . . [The **GOTO** statement] is just too primitive; it is too much an invitation to make a mess of one's program."

The first time structured programming concepts were applied to a large-scale data processing application was the IBM Corporation's "New York Times Project" from 1969 to 1971. Using these techniques, programmers posted productivity figures from four to six times higher than those of the average programmer. In addition, the error rate was a phenomenally low 0.0004 per line of coding.

Procedures facilitate problem solving. Recall the Focus on Program Design problem in Chapter 2. In that problem, you were asked to compute the unit cost for a pizza. The main modules were

1.   Get the data
2.   Perform the computations
3.   Print the results

A procedure can be written for each of these tasks and the program can then call each procedure as needed. Thus, the main portion of the program would have the form

```
BEGIN {  Main program  }
  GetData ((parameter list));
  PerformComputations ((parameter list));
  PrintResults ((parameter list))
END.  {  of main program  }
```

This makes it easy to see and understand the main tasks of the program.

Before learning how to write procedures and the significance of the "parameter list" in the previous program segment, a few comments are in order. First, once you develop the ability to write and use subprograms, you will usually write programs by writing the main program first. Your main program should be written so it can be easily read by a nonprogrammer but still contain enough structure to enable a programmer to know what to do if asked to write code for the tasks. In this sense, it is not necessary for a person reading the main program to understand *how* a subprogram accomplishes its task; it need only be apparent *what* the subprogram does.

Second, we should briefly consider the problem of data flow. The most difficult aspect of learning to use subprograms is handling transmission of data. Recall from the structure charts used earlier that arrows were used to indicate if data were received by and/or sent from a module. Also, each module specification indicated if data were received by that module and if information was sent from it. Since a subprogram will be written to accomplish the task of each module, we must be able to transmit data as indicated. Once you have developed this ability, using procedures and functions becomes routine.

Form and Syntax

Procedures are placed in the declaration section of the main program. The form for a procedure is

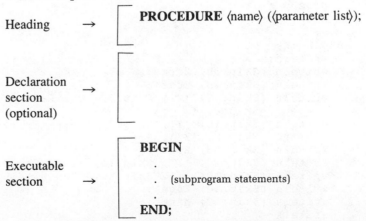

Heading   →   **PROCEDURE** ⟨name⟩ (⟨parameter list⟩);

Declaration
section   →
(optional)

                          BEGIN
                              .
Executable
section   →   .   (subprogram statements)
                              .
                          END;

The syntax diagram is

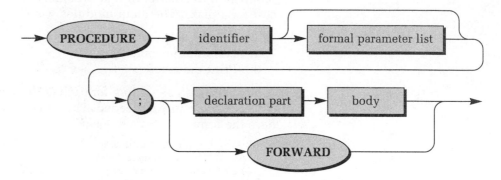

Procedures without Parameters

Some procedures are written without parameters because they require no data transmission to or from the main program or any other subprogram. Typically, these procedures print headings or closing messages for output. For example, suppose you are writing a program for Our Lady of Mercy Hospital and you wish the billing statement for each patient to have the heading

```
/////////////////////////////////////////
/                                         /
/          Our Lady of Mercy Hospital     /
/          --------------------------     /
/                                         /
/             1306 Central City           /
/             Phone (416) 333-5555         /
/                                         /
/////////////////////////////////////////
```

A procedure DisplayHeading can be written to print this message and you can then call it from the main program when needed by

```
DisplayHeading;
```

The procedure to perform this task is

```
PROCEDURE DisplayHeading;

   CONST
     Marks = '/////////////////////////////////////////';
     Edge  = '/                                         /';
     Skip  = ' ';

   BEGIN
     writeln;
     writeln (Skip:10, Marks);
     writeln (Skip:10, Edge);
     writeln (Skip:10, '/', Skip:7, 'Our Lady of Mercy Hospital',
              Skip:6, '/');
     writeln (Skip:10, '/', Skip:7, '--------------------------',
              Skip:6, '/');
     writeln (Skip:10, Edge);
     writeln (Skip:10, '/', Skip:11, '1306 Central City', Skip:11, '/');
     writeln (Skip:10, '/', Skip:10, 'Phone (416) 333-5555', Skip:9, '/');
     writeln (Skip:10, Edge);
     writeln (Skip:10, Marks);
     writeln
   END;    {  of PROCEDURE DisplayHeading  }
```

Parameters

Parameters are used so that values of variables may be transmitted, or passed, from the main program to the procedure and from the procedure to the main program. If values are to be passed only from the main program to the procedure, the parameters are called *value parameters.* If values are to be changed in the main program, the parameters are called *variable parameters.*

When using parameters with procedures, the following should be noted.

1. The number and order of parameters in the parameter list must match the number and order of variables or values used when calling the procedure from the main program.
2. The type of parameters must match the corresponding type of variables or values used when calling the procedure from the main program.
3. The parameter types are declared in the procedure heading.

Parameters contained in the procedure are *formal parameters.* Formal parameters can be thought of as blanks in the heading of the procedure waiting to receive values from actual parameters in a calling program. Parameters contained in the procedure call from the main program are *actual parameters.* Actual parameters are also referred to as arguments.

To illustrate formal and actual parameters used with procedures, consider the following complete program.

```
PROGRAM ProcDemo1 (output);

VAR
  Num1, Num2 : integer;
  Num3 : real;

{*******************************************}

PROCEDURE PrintNum (N1, N2 : integer;
                    N3 : real);
  BEGIN
    writeln;
    writeln ('Number 1 = ', N1:3);
    writeln ('Number 2 = ', N2:3);
    writeln ('Number 3 = ', N3:6:2)
  END;  {  of PROCEDURE PrintNum  }

{*******************************************}

BEGIN  {  Main program  }
  Num1 := 5;
  Num2 := 8;
  Num3 := Num2 / Num1;
  PrintNum (Num1, Num2, Num3)
END.  {  of main program  }
```

When this program is run, the output is

```
Number 1 =    5
Number 2 =    8
Number 3 =    1.60
```

In this program, N1, N2, and N3 are formal parameters; Num1, Num2, and Num3 are actual parameters. Let us now examine the relationship between the parameter list in the procedure

```
PROCEDURE PrintNum (N1, N2 : integer; N3 : real);
```

and the procedure call in the main program

```
PrintNum (Num1, Num2, Num3)
```

In this case, Num1 corresponds to N1, Num2 corresponds to N2, and Num3 corresponds to N3. Notice that both the number and type of variables in the parameter list correspond with the number and type of variables listed in the procedure call.

Value Parameters

The preceding procedure demonstrates the use of value parameters or of one-way transmission of values. Different memory areas have been set aside for the variables Num1, Num2, and Num3 and for N1, N2, and N3. Thus, initially we have

Main Program   Procedure

Num1   N1

Num2   N2

Num3   N3

The assignment statements

```
Num1 := 5;
Num2 := 8;
Num3 := Num2 / Num1;
```

produce

Main Program   Procedure

| 5 |
Num1   N1

| 8 |
Num2   N2

| 1.6 |
Num3   N3

When the procedure PrintNum is called from the main program by

```
PrintNum (Num1, Num2, Num3)
```

the values are transmitted to N1, N2, and N3, respectively, as follows:

Main Program   Procedure

| 5 | | 5 |
Num1   N1

| 8 | | 8 |
Num2   N2

| 1.6 | | 1.6 |
Num3   N3

At this stage, the procedure PrintNum can use N1, N2, and N3 in any appropriate manner.

These are value parameters because values are passed from the main program to the procedure only. If the procedure changes the value of N1, N2, or N3, the values of Num1, Num2, and Num3 will not be changed. For example, suppose the procedure is changed to

```
PROCEDURE PrintNum (N1, N2 : integer; N3 : real);
  BEGIN
    writeln;
    writeln (N1:10, N2:10, N3:10:2);
    N1 := 2 * N1;
    N2 := 2 * N2;
    N3 := 2 * N3;
    writeln (N1:10, N2:10, N3:10:2);
    writeln
  END;  { of PROCEDURE PrintNum  }
```

Furthermore, suppose the main program is changed to

```
BEGIN  {  Main program  }
  Num1 := 5;
  Num2 := 8;
  Num3 := Num2 / Num1;
  writeln;
  writeln (Num1:10, Num2:10, Num3:10:2);
  PrintNum (Num1, Num2, Num3);
  writeln (Num1:10, Num2:10, Num3:10:2);
  writeln
END.  {  of main program  }
```

When this program is run, the output is

```
     5          8       1.60        (from main program)
     5          8       1.60        (from procedure)
    10         16       3.20        (from procedure)
     5          8       1.60        (from main program)
```

The first line of this output is produced by the first

```
writeln (Num1:10, Num2:10, Num3:10:2);
```

of the main program. The next two lines of output come from the procedure. The last line of output is produced by the second

```
writeln (Num1:10, Num2:10, Num3:10:2);
```

of the main program. You should carefully note that although the procedure changes the values of N1, N2, and N3, the values of Num1, Num2, and Num3 have not been changed. Thus, we have

Main Program	Procedure
5	10
Num1	N1
8	16
Num2	N2
1.6	3.2
Num3	N3

Variable Parameters

You will frequently want a procedure to change values in the main program. This can be accomplished by using variable parameters in the parameter list. Variable parameters are declared by using the reserved word **VAR** to precede appropriate formal parameters in the procedure heading. This causes all of the formal parameters listed between **VAR** and the subsequent data type to be variable parameters. If value parameters of the same type are needed, they must be listed elsewhere. A separate **VAR** declaration is needed for each data type used when listing variable parameters. The use of **VAR** in a parameter list is a slightly different use than in the declaration of variables, yet it is the same reserved word.

When variable parameters are declared, transmission of values appears to be two-way rather than one-way. That is, values are sent from the main program to the procedure and from the procedure to the main program. Actually, when variable parameters are used, values are not transmitted at all. Variable parameters in the procedure heading are merely aliases for actual variables used in the main program. Thus, variables are said to be *passed by reference* rather than by value. When variable parameters are used, any change of values in the procedure produces a corresponding change of values in the main program.

To illustrate the declaration of variable parameters, consider the procedure heading

```
PROCEDURE PrintNum (VAR N1, N2 : integer; N3 : real);
```

In this case, N1 and N2 are variable parameters corresponding to integer variables in the main program. N3 is a value parameter corresponding to a real variable. This procedure can be called from the main program by

```
PrintNum (Num1, Num2, Num3);
```

To illustrate the passing of values, assume the procedure is

```
PROCEDURE PrintNum (VAR N1, N2 : integer; N3 : real);
  BEGIN
    writeln (N1, N2, N3:10:2);
    N1 := 2 * N1;
    N2 := 2 * N2;
    N3 := 2 * N3;
    writeln (N1, N2, N3:10:2)
  END;  {  of PROCEDURE PrintNum  }
```

If the corresponding variables in the main program are Num1, Num2, and Num3, respectively, initially we have

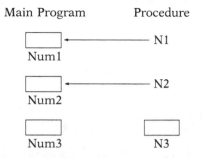

Technically, N1 and N2 do not exist as variables. They contain pointers to the same memory locations as Num1 and Num2 respectively. Thus, a statement in the procedure such as

```
N1 := 5;
```

causes the memory location reserved for Num1 to receive the value 5. That is, it causes the net action

```
Num1 := 5;
```

Thus, constants cannot be used when calling a procedure with variable parameters. For example,

```
PrintNum (3, 4, 5);
```

produces an error because 3 and 4 correspond to variable parameters.

If the main program makes the assignment statements

```
Num1 := 5;
Num2 := 8;
Num3 := Num2 / Num1;
```

we have

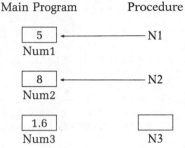

When the procedure is called by

```
PrintNum (Num1, Num2, Num3);
```

we have

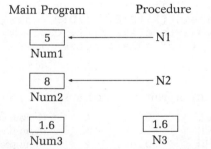

When the statements from the procedure,

```
N1 := 2 * N1;
N2 := 2 * N2;
N3 := 2 * N3;
```

are executed, we have

Main Program   Procedure

| 10 | ←————— N1
Num1

| 16 | ←————— N2
Num2

| 1.6 | | 3.2 |
Num3   N3

Notice that the variable parameters N1 and N2 produce changes in the corresponding variables in the main program, but the value parameter N3 does not.

Let us now consider a short, complete program that illustrates the difference between variable and value parameters. In this program (and through-

out the text), the graphic documentation that accompanies the program highlights the way in which parameters are passed between the main program
and the procedure.

```
PROGRAM ProcDemo2 (output);

VAR
  X, Y : real;
  Ch : char;

{*****************************************************}

PROCEDURE DemonstrateVAR (VAR X1 : real;
                              Y1 : real;
                          VAR Ch1 : char);
  BEGIN
    writeln (X1:10:2, Y1:10:2, Ch1:5);
    X1 := 2 * X1;
    Y1 := 2 * Y1;
    Ch1 := '*';
    writeln (X1:10:2, Y1:10:2, Ch1:5)
  END;  {  of PROCEDURE DemonstrateVAR  }

{*****************************************************}

BEGIN  {  Main program  }
  X := 3.6;
  Y := 5.2;
  Ch := 'A';
  writeln (X:10:2, Y:10:2, Ch:5);
  DemonstrateVAR (X, Y, Ch);
END.  {  of main program  }
```

The output from the program is

```
3.60        5.20      A      (from main program)
3.60        5.20      A      (from procedure)
7.20       10.40      *      (from procedure)
7.20        5.20      *      (from main program)
```

The variables can be depicted as

The assignment statements

```
X := 3.6;
Y := 5.2;
Ch := 'A';
```

produce

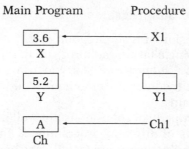

When the procedure is called by

```
DemonstrateVAR (X, Y, Ch);
```

the contents can be envisioned as

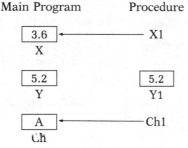

When the procedure assignment statements

```
X1 := 2 * X1;
Y1 := 2 * Y1;
Ch1 := '*';
```

are executed, the variables become

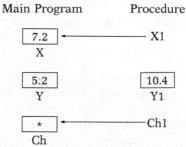

Notice that changes in the variable parameters X1 and Ch1 produce corresponding changes in X and Ch, but a change in the value parameter Y1 does not produce a change in Y.

Side Effects

A *side effect* is an unintentional change in a variable that is the result of some action taken in a program. A side effect is frequently caused by the misuse of variable parameters. Since any change in a variable parameter causes a change in the corresponding actual parameter in the calling program or procedure, you should use variable parameters only when your intent is to produce such changes. In all other cases, use value parameters.

Cohesive Subprograms

The cohesion of a subprogram is the degree to which the subprogram performs a single task. A subprogram that is developed in such a way is called a *cohesive subprogram*. As you use subprograms to implement a design based on modular development, you should always try to write cohesive subprograms.

The property of cohesion is not well defined. Subtask complexity varies in the minds of different programmers. In general, if the task is unclear, the corresponding subprogram will not be cohesive. When this happens, you should subdivide the task until a subsequent development allows cohesive subprograms.

To briefly illustrate the concept of cohesion, consider the first-level design of a problem to compute grades for a class. Step 3 of this design could be

3. Process grades for each student

Clearly, this is not a well-defined task. Thus, if you were to write a subprogram for this task, the subprogram would not be cohesive. When we look at the subsequent development

3.   Process grades for each student
    WHILE NOT eof DO
        3.1 get a line of data
        3.2 compute average
        3.3 compute letter grade
        3.4 print data
        3.5 compute totals

we see that procedures to accomplish subtasks 3.1, 3.2, 3.3, and 3.4 would be cohesive because each subtask consists of a single task. The final subtask, compute totals, may or may not result in a cohesive subprogram. More information is needed before you can decide what is to be done at this step.

Procedural Abstraction

The purpose of using procedures is to simplify reasoning. During the design stage, as a problem is subdivided into tasks, the problem solver (you) should have to consider only what a procedure is to do and not be concerned about details of the procedure. Instead, the procedure name and comments at the beginning of the procedure should be sufficient to inform the user as to what the procedure does. Developing procedures in this manner is referred to as *procedural abstraction.*

Procedural abstraction is the first step in designing and writing a procedure. The list of parameters and comments about the action of the procedure should precede writing the procedure body. This forces clarity of thought and aids design. Using this method might perhaps cause you to discover that your design is not sufficient to solve the task and that redesigning is necessary. Therefore, you could reduce design errors and save time when writing code.

Procedural abstraction becomes especially important when teams work on a project. Each member of the writing team should be able to understand the purpose and use of procedures written by other team members without having to analyze the body of each procedure. This is analogous to the situation in which you use a predefined function without really understanding how the function works.

Computer Ethics: Hacking and Other Intrusions

A famous sequence of computer intrusions was originally detailed by Clifford Stoll. The prime intruder came to Stoll's attention in August 1986, when he attempted to penetrate a computer at Lawrence Berkeley Laboratory (LBL). Instead of denying the intruder access, management at LBL went along with Stoll's recommendation that they attempt to unmask the intruder, even though the risk was substantial because the intruder had gained system-manager privileges.

Markus H., a member of a small group of West Germans, was an unusually persistent intruder, but no computer wizard. He made use of known deficiencies in the half-dozen or so operating systems, including UNIX, VMS, VM-TSO, and EMBOS, with which he was familiar, but he did not invent any new modes of entry. He penetrated 30 of the 450 computers then on the network system at LBL.

After Markus H. was successfully traced, efforts were instituted to make LBL's computers less vulnerable. To insure high security, it would have been necessary to change all passwords overnight and recertify each user. This and other demanding measures were deemed impractical. Instead, deletion of all expired passwords was instituted; shared accounts were eliminated; monitoring of incoming traffic was extended, with alarms set in key places; and education of users was attempted.

The episode was summed up by Stoll as a powerful learning experience for those involved in the detection process and for all those concerned about computer security. That the intruder was caught at all is a testimony to the ability of a large number of concerned professionals to keep the tracing effort secret.

In a later incident, an intruder left the following embarrassing message in the computer file assigned to Clifford Stoll: "The cuckoo has egg on his face." The reference is to Stoll's book, *The Cuckoo's Egg*, which tracks the intrusions of the West German hacker just described. The embarrassment was heightened by the fact that the computer, owned by Harvard University with which astronomer Stoll is now associated, is on the Internet network. The intruder, or intruders, who goes by the name of Dave, also attempted to break into dozens of other computers on the same network—and succeeded.

The "nom de guerre," Dave, was used by one or more of three Australians recently arrested by the federal police down under. The three, who at the time of their arrest were respectively 18, 20, and 21 years of age, successfully penetrated computers in both Australia and the United States.

The three Australians went beyond browsing to damage data in computers in their own nation and the United States. At the time they began their intrusions in 1988 (when the youngest was only 16), there was no law in Australia under which they could be prosecuted. It was not until legislation making such intrusions prosecutable was passed that the police began to take action.

Procedural abstraction is perhaps best formalized in terms of preconditions and postconditions. A *precondition* is a comment which states precisely what is true before a certain action is taken. A *postcondition* states what is true after the action has been taken. Carefully written preconditions and postconditions used with procedures enhance the concept of procedural abstraction. (Additional uses of preconditions and postconditions are discussed in Sections 4.6 and 5.4.)

In summary, procedural abstraction means that, when writing or using procedures, you should think of them as single, clearly understood units that each accomplishes a specific task.

Encapsulation

Encapsulation can be thought of as the process of hiding the implementation details of a subprogram. This is just what we do when we use a top-down design to solve a problem. We decide which tasks and subtasks are necessary to solve a problem without worrying about how the specific subtasks will be accomplished. In the sense of software engineering, encapsulation is what allows teams to work on a large system. It is only necessary to know what another team is doing, not how they are doing it.

Interface and Documentation

Independent subprograms (whether procedures or functions) need to communicate with the main program and other subprograms. A formal statement of how such communication occurs is called the *interface* of the subprogram. This usually consists of comments at the beginning of a subprogram and includes all the documentation the reader will need to use the subprogram. This information typically consists of

1. what is received by the subprogram when called
2. what task the subprogram performs
3. what is returned after the subprogram performs its task
4. how the subprogram is called

This information aids in debugging programs. In this text, our interface consists of the three-part documentation section

```
{  Given:   <Statement of information sent to the program>  }
{  Task:    <Statement of task(s) to be performed>          }
{  Return:  <Statement of value(s) to be returned>          }
```

The headings of subprograms in complete programs are given in this manner. When subprograms are separately developed and illustrated, this documentation will not be included; instead, text development immediately preceding the subprogram will serve the same purpose. How a subprogram is called is usually apparent from the identifiers listed in the subprogram heading.

Software Engineering

Perhaps the greatest difference between beginning students in computer science and "real world" programmers is how they perceive the need for documentation. Typically, beginning students want to make a program run; they view anything that delays this process as an impediment. Thus, some students consider using descriptive identifiers, writing variable dictionaries, describing a problem as part of program documentation, and using appropriate comments throughout a program as a nuisance.

In contrast, system designers and programmers who write code for a living often spend up to 50 percent of their time and effort on documentation. There are at least three reasons for this difference in perspective.

First, real programmers work on large, complex systems with highly developed logical paths. Without proper documentation, even the person who developed an algorithm will have difficulty following the logic six months later. Second, communication between and among teams is required as systems are developed. Complete, clear statements about what the problems are and how they are being solved is essential. And third, programmers know they can develop algorithms and write subsequent code. They are trained so that problems of searching, sorting, and file manipulation are routine. Knowing that they can solve a problem thus allows them to devote more time and energy to documenting how the solution has been achieved.

We close this section with a revision of the program from Chapter 2 that found the unit cost for a pizza. The structure chart is shown in Figure 3.1.

FIGURE 3.1
Structure chart for the pizza
problem

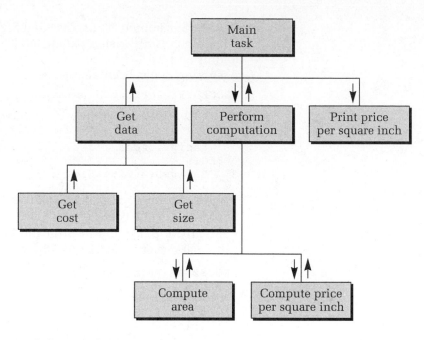

The module specifications are

1. GetData Module
   Data received: None
   Information returned: Cost
   　　　　　　　　　　　Size
   Logic: Have the user enter cost and size.

2. PerformComputation Module
   Data received: Cost
   　　　　　　　　　Size
   Information returned: Price per square inch
   Logic: Given the diameter, find the radius.
   　　　　Compute the area using Area = Pi * sqr(Radius).
   　　　　Price per square inch is found by dividing Cost by Area.

3. PrintResults Module
   Data received: PricePerSquareInch
   Information returned: None
   Logic: Print the price per square inch.

A procedure for getting the data requires two variable parameters, one for the size and one for the cost, since these values will be returned to the main program. This procedure would be

```
PROCEDURE GetData (VAR PizzaCost : real;
                   VAR PizzaSize : integer);
  BEGIN
    writeln ('Enter the pizza price and press <RETURN>.');
    readln (PizzaCost);
    writeln ('Enter the pizza size and press <RETURN>.');
    readln (PizzaSize)
  END; {  of PROCEDURE GetData  }
```

Let's now write a procedure for performing the desired computations. (Later we will learn how this task would be done with a function instead of a procedure.) This procedure receives the Cost and Size and then returns the

PricePerSquareInch. Thus, Cost and Size are value parameters and PricePer-SquareInch is a variable parameter. This procedure also requires variables Radius and Area to be declared in the declaration section of the procedure. Assuming Pi has been defined as a constant, the procedure is

```
PROCEDURE PerformComputations (PizzaCost : real;
                               PizzaSize : integer;
                               VAR PricePerSqInch : real);
  VAR
    Radius, Area : real;
  BEGIN
    Radius := PizzaSize / 2;
    Area := Pi * sqr(Radius);
    PricePerSqInch := PizzaCost / Area
  END;  { of PROCEDURE PerformComputations }
```

Finally, a procedure to print the results receives the unit cost. Thus, a value parameter is declared and the procedure is

```
PROCEDURE PrintResults (PricePerSqInch : real);
  BEGIN
    writeln;
    write ('The price per square inch is $');
    writeln (PricePerSqInch:6:2)
  END;  {  of PROCEDURE PrintResults  }
```

With these procedures written, the main program becomes

```
BEGIN  {  Main program  }
  GetData (Cost, Size);
  PerformComputations (Cost, Size, PricePerSquareInch);
  PrintResults (PricePerSquareInch)
END.  {  of main program  }
```

The complete program for this problem is as follows:

```
PROGRAM Pizza (input, output);

CONST
  Pi = 3.14159;

VAR
  Size : integer;
  Cost, PricePerSquareInch : real;


    {*************************************************************}


    PROCEDURE GetData (VAR PizzaCost : real;
                       VAR PizzaSize : integer);

      BEGIN
        writeln;
        writeln ('Enter the pizza price and press <RETURN>.');
        readln (PizzaCost);
        writeln ('Enter the pizza size and press <RETURN>.');
        readln (PizzaSize)
      END;  {  of PROCEDURE GetData  }


    {*************************************************************}


    PROCEDURE PerformComputations (PizzaCost : real;
                                   PizzaSize : integer;
                                   VAR PricePerSqInch : real);
```

1

```
VAR
  Radius, Area : real;

BEGIN
  Radius := PizzaSize / 2;
  Area := Pi * sqr(Radius);
  PricePerSqInch := PizzaCost / Area
END;  { of PROCEDURE PerformComputations  }
```

} 2

```
{*****************************************************************}

PROCEDURE PrintResults (PricePerSqInch : real);

  BEGIN
    writeln;
    write ('The price per square inch is $');
    writeln (PricePerSqInch:6:2)
  END;  { of PROCEDURE PrintResults  }

{*****************************************************************}

BEGIN  {  Main program  }
  GetData (Cost, Size);
```

} 3

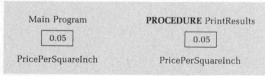

```
  PerformComputations (Cost, Size, PricePerSquareInch);
```

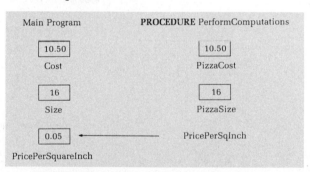

```
  PrintResults (PricePerSquareInch)
END.  { of main program  }
```

Sample runs of this program produce

```
Enter the pizza price and press <RETURN>.
?10.50
Enter the pizza size and press <RETURN>.
?16

The price per square inch is $  0.05

Enter the pizza price and press <RETURN>.
?8.75
Enter the pizza size and press <RETURN>.
?14

The price per square inch is $  0.06
```

Exercises 3.2

1. Explain the difference between value parameters and variable parameters, and between formal and actual parameters.

2. Write a test program to find what happens if the parameter lists do not match when a procedure is called from the main program. Investigate each of the following:

   a. correct number of parameters, wrong order
   b. incorrect number of parameters

3. Indicate which of the following parameters are value parameters and which are variable parameters.

   a. PROCEDURE Demo1 (VAR A, B : integer;
                       X : real);

   b. PROCEDURE Demo2 (VAR A : integer;
                       B : integer;
                       VAR X : real;
                       Ch : char);

   c. PROCEDURE Demo3 (A, B : integer;
                       VAR X, Y, Z : real;
                       Ch : char);

4. Indicate which of the following are appropriate procedure headings. Explain the problem with those that are inappropriate.

   a. PROCEDURE Prac1 (A : integer : Y : real);
   b. PROCEDURE Error? (Ch1, Ch2 : char);
   c. PROCEDURE Prac2 (A, VAR B : integer);
   d. PROCEDURE Prac3 (A, B, C : integer
                       VAR X, Y : real
                       Ch : char);
   e. PROCEDURE Prac4 (VAR A : integer,
                       X : real);

5. Indicate how each of the following procedures would be called from the main program.

   a. PROCEDURE Prob5 (A, B : integer;
                       Ch : char);
   b. PROCEDURE PrintHeader;
   c. PROCEDURE FindMax (N1, N2 : integer;
                         VAR NewMax : integer);
   d. PROCEDURE Switch (VAR X, Y : real);

6. Suppose a program contains the following procedure:

```
PROCEDURE Switch (VAR A, B : integer);
  VAR
    Temp : integer;
  BEGIN
    Temp := A;
    A := B;
    B := Temp
  END;  {  of PROCEDURE Switch  }
```

Indicate the output from each of the following fragments of code in the main program.

a. ```
   Num1 := 5;
   Num2 := 10;
   writeln (Num1, Num2);
   Switch (Num1, Num2);
   writeln (Num1, Num2);
   Switch (Num1, Num2);
   writeln (Num1, Num2);
   ```
b. ```
   N := 3;
   M := 20;
   Switch (M, N);
   writeln (M, N);
   Switch (N, M);
   writeln (N, M);
   ```

7. Write a procedure for each of the following and indicate how it would be called from the main program.

   a. Print the heading for the output.

      ```
      Acme National Electronics
         Board of Directors
            Annual Meeting
      ```

   b. Find the maximum and average of three reals. Both values are to be returned to the main program.

   c. Convert Fahrenheit temperature to Celsius.

8. Assume a program contains the variable declaration section

   ```
   VAR
      Num1, Num2 : integer;
      X, Y : real;
      Ch1, Ch2 : char;
   ```

   Furthermore, suppose the same program contains a procedure whose heading is

   ```
   PROCEDURE Demo (VAR N1, N2 : integer;
                       X1 : real;
                       Ch : char);
   ```

   Indicate which of the following are appropriate calls to the procedure Demo. Explain those that are inappropriate.

   a. `Demo (Num1, Num2);`

   b. `Demo (Num1, Num2, X);`

   c. `Demo (Num1, Num2, X, Ch1);`

   d. `Demo (X, Y, Num1, Ch2);`

   e. `Demo (Num2, X, Y, Ch1);`

   f. `Demo (Num1, Num2, Ch2);`

   g. `Demo;`

   h. `Demo (Num2, Num1, Y, Ch1);`

■ ■ ■ ■

■ 3.3
Scope of Identifiers

Global and Local Identifiers

Identifiers used to declare variables in the declaration section of a program can be used throughout the entire program. For purposes of this section, we will think of the program as a *block* and each subprogram as a *subblock* or block for the subprogram. Each block may contain a parameter list, a local declaration section, and the body of the block. A program block for **PROGRAM** ShowScope may be envisioned as in Figure 3.2. Furthermore, if X1 is a variable in ShowScope, we will indicate this as shown in Figure 3.3,

FIGURE 3.2
Program heading and
main block

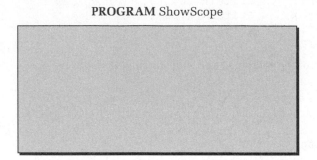

PROGRAM ShowScope

FIGURE 3.3
Variable location in main block

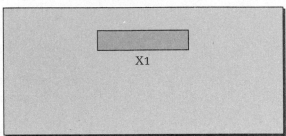

PROGRAM ShowScope

X1

where an area in memory has been set aside for X1. When a program contains a subprogram, a separate memory area within the memory area for the program is set aside for the subprogram to use while it executes. Thus, if ShowScope contains a procedure named Subprog1, we can envision this as shown in Figure 3.4. If Subprog1 contains the variable X2, we have the program shown in Figure 3.5. This could be indicated in the program by

```
PROGRAM ShowScope (input, output);

VAR
  X1 : real;

PROCEDURE Subprog1 (X2 : real);
```

FIGURE 3.4
Illustration of a subblock

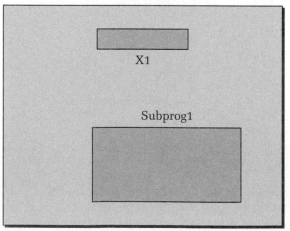

PROGRAM ShowScope

X1

Subprog1

FIGURE 3.5
Variable location within a
subblock

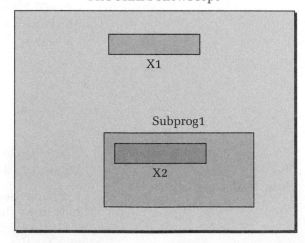

PROGRAM ShowScope

X1

Subprog1

X2

The *scope of an identifier* refers to the block in which it is declared or defined. When subprograms are used, each identifier is available to the block in which it is declared; this includes all subprograms contained within its block. Identifiers are not available outside their blocks.

Identifiers that are declared in the main block are called *global identifiers* (or *global variables*); identifiers that are restricted to use within a subblock are called *local identifiers* (or *local variables*).Variable X1 in Figure 3.5 can be used in the main program and in the procedure Subprog1; therefore it is a global identifier. On the other hand, X2 can only be used within the procedure where it is declared; it is a local identifier. Any attempt to reference X2 outside the procedure will result in an error.

Figure 3.6 is used to illustrate scope of identifiers. In this figure, the scope of X3 is **PROCEDURE** Inner, the scope of X2 is **PROCEDURE** Outer, and the scope of X1 is **PROGRAM** ShowScope. When procedures are nested like this, the scope of an identifier is the largest block in which it is declared.

FIGURE 3.6
Scope of identifiers

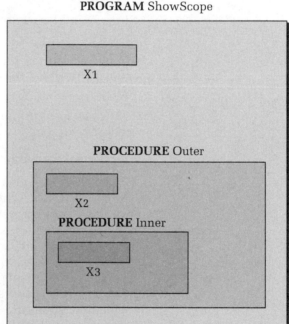

PROGRAM ShowScope

Let us now examine an illustration of local and global identifiers. Consider the program and procedure declaration

```
PROGRAM ScopePrac (output);

VAR
  A, B : integer;

PROCEDURE Subprog (A1 : integer);
  VAR
    X : real;
```

Blocks for this program can be envisioned as shown in Figure 3.7.

FIGURE 3.7
Relation of identifiers for
PROGRAM ScopePrac

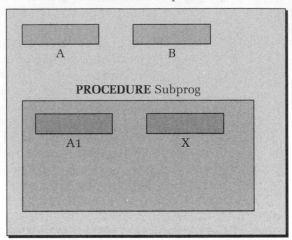

Since A and B are global, the statement

```
writeln (A, B, A1, X:10:2);
```

could be used in the procedure Subprog although A and B have not been specifically declared there. However,

```
writeln (A, B, A1, X:10:2);
```

could not be used in the main program because A1 and X are local to the procedure Subprog.

Using Global Variables and Constants

In general, it is not good practice to refer to global variables within procedures. Using locally defined variables helps to avoid unexpected side effects and protects your programs. In addition, locally defined variables facilitate debugging and top-down design and enhance the portability of procedures. This is especially important if a team is developing a program by having different people work on different procedures.

Using global constants is different. Since the values cannot be changed by a procedure, it is preferred that constants be defined in the **CONST** section of the main program and then be used whenever needed by any subprogram. This is especially important if the constant is subject to change over time, for example, StateTaxRate. When a change is necessary, one change in the main program is all that is needed to make all subprograms current. If a constant is used in only one procedure (or function), some programmers prefer to have it defined near the point of use. Thus, they would define it in the subprogram in which it is used.

Name of Identifiers

Since separate areas in memory are set aside when subprograms are used, it is possible to have identifiers with the same name in both the main program and a subprogram. Thus

```
PROGRAM Demo (input, output);

VAR
  Age : integer;

PROCEDURE Subprog (Age : integer);
```

can be envisioned as shown in Figure 3.8.

FIGURE 3.8
Using identifiers in subprograms

PROGRAM Demo

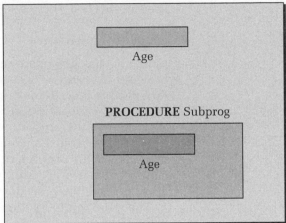

When the same name is used in this manner, any reference to this name results in action being taken as locally as possible. Thus, the assignment statement

```
Age := 20;
```

made in the procedure Subprog assigns 20 to Age in the procedure but not in the main program (see Figure 3.9).

FIGURE 3.9
Assigning values in subprograms

PROGRAM Demo

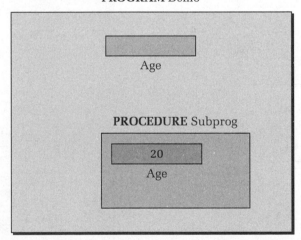

Now that you know you can use the same name for an identifier in a subprogram and the main program, the question is, "Should you?" There are two schools of thought regarding this issue. If you use the same name in the procedures, it facilitates matching parameter lists and independent development of procedures. However, this practice can be confusing when you first start working with subprograms. Thus, some instructors prefer using different, but related, identifiers. For example,

```
GetData (Score1, Score2);
```

in the main program could have a procedure heading of

```
PROCEDURE GetData (VAR Sc1, Sc2 : integer);
```

In this case, the use of Sc1 and Sc2 is obvious. Although this may facilitate better understanding in early work with subprograms, it is less conducive to portability and independent development of procedures. Both styles are used in this text.

Multiple Procedures

More than one procedure can be used in a program. When this occurs, all the previous uses and restrictions of identifiers apply to each procedure. Blocks for multiple procedures can be depicted as shown in Figure 3.10. Identifiers in the main program can be accessed by each procedure. However, local identifiers in the procedures cannot be accessed outside their blocks.

When a program contains several procedures, they can be called from the main part of the program in any order. However, if one procedure contains a call to another procedure (or function), the subprogram being called must appear before the procedure from which it is called.

The same names for identifiers can be used in different procedures. Thus, if the main program uses variables Wage and Hours, and both of these are used as arguments in calls to different procedures, you have the situation shown in Figure 3.11. Using the same names for identifiers in different

FIGURE 3.10
Blocks for multiple subprograms

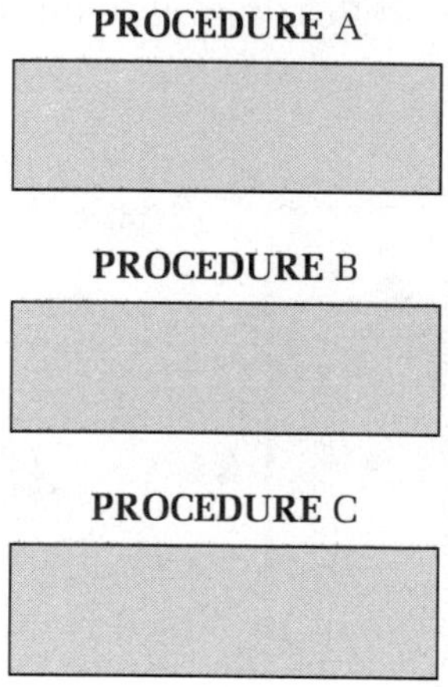

PROCEDURE A

PROCEDURE B

PROCEDURE C

FIGURE 3.11
Identifiers in multiple subprograms

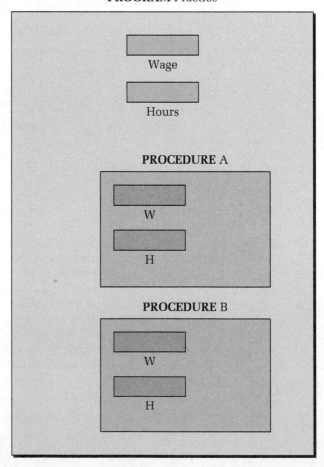

PROGRAM Practice

procedures makes it easier to keep track of the relationship between variables in the main program and their associated parameters in each subprogram.

Exercises 3.3

1. Explain the difference between local and global identifiers.

2. State the advantages of using local identifiers.

3. Discuss some appropriate uses for global identifiers. List several constants that would be appropriate global definitions.

4. What is meant by the scope of an identifier?

5. Write a test program that will enable you to see
   a. what happens when an attempt is made to access an identifier outside of its scope; and
   b. how the values change as a result of assignments in the subprogram and the main program when the same identifier is used in the main program and a procedure.

6. Review the following program:

```
PROGRAM Practice (input, output);

VAR
  A, B : integer;
  X : real;
  Ch : char;

PROCEDURE Sub1 (A1 : integer);
  VAR
    B1 : integer;
  BEGIN
    .
    .
    .
  END;  {  of PROCEDURE Sub1  }

PROCEDURE Sub2 (A1 : integer;
                VAR B1 : integer);
  VAR
    X1 : real;
    Ch1 : char;
  BEGIN
    .
    .
    .
  END;  {  of PROCEDURE Sub2  }
```

   a. List all global variables.
   b. List all local variables.
   c. Indicate the scope of each identifier.

7. Provide a schematic representation of the program and all subprograms and variables in Exercise 6.

8. Using the program with variables and subprograms as depicted in Figure 3.12, state the scope of each identifier.

FIGURE 3.12

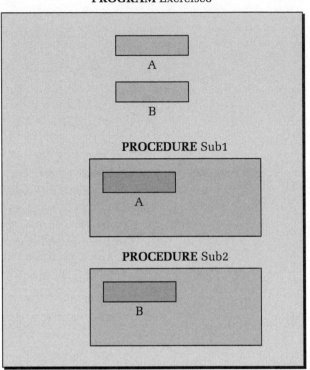

PROGRAM Exercise8

9. What is the output from the following program?

```
PROGRAM Exercise9 (output);

VAR
  A : integer;

PROCEDURE Sub1 (A : integer);
  BEGIN
    A := 20;
    writeln (A)
  END;  {  of PROCEDURE Sub1  }

PROCEDURE Sub2 (VAR A : integer);
  BEGIN
    A := 30;
    writeln (A)
  END;  {  of PROCEDURE Sub2  }

BEGIN  {  Main program  }
  A := 10;
  writeln (A);
  Sub1 (A);
  writeln (A);
```

```
   Sub2 (A);
   writeln (A)
END.  {  of main program  }
```

10. Review the following program.

```
PROGRAM ExerciseTen (output);

VAR
   Num1, Num2, : integer;

PROCEDURE Change (X : integer;
                        VAR Y : integer);
   VAR
     Num2 : integer;
   BEGIN
     Num2 := X;
     Y := Y + Num2;
     X := Y
   END;

BEGIN
   Num1 := 10;
   Num2 := 7;
   Change (Num1, Num2);
   writeln (Num1, Num2)
END.
```

a. What is the output of the program as written?
   Determine the output of the program if the following procedure headings are substituted.

b. `PROCEDURE Change (VAR X : integer; Y : integer);`

c. `PROCEDURE Change (X, Y : integer);`

d. `PROCEDURE Change (VAR X, Y : integer);`

11. Assume the variable declaration section of a program is

```
VAR
   Age, Hours : integer;
   Average : real;
   Initial : char;
```

Furthermore, assume that procedure headings and declaration sections for procedures in this program are as follows. Find all errors in each.

a. `PROCEDURE Average (Age1, Hrs : integer;`
   `                      VAR Aver : real);`

b. `PROCEDURE Sub1 (Hours : integer;`
   `                    VAR Average : real);`

```
      VAR
        Age : integer;
        Init : char;
```

c. `PROCEDURE Compute (Hrs : integer;`
   `                      VAR Aver : real);`

```
      VAR
        Age : real;
```

12. Write appropriate headings and declaration sections for the program and subprograms illustrated in Figure 3.13.

FIGURE 3.13

PROGRAM Exercise12

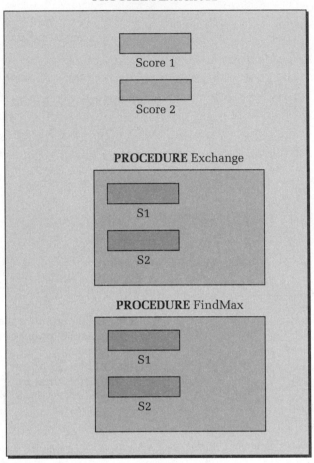

13. Find all errors in the following program.

```
PROGRAM Exercise13 (output);

VAR
  X, Y : real;

PROCEDURE Sub1 (VAR X1 : real);
  BEGIN
    writeln (X1:20:2);
    writeln (X:20:2);
    writeln (Y:20:2)
  END;  {  of PROCEDURE Sub1  }

BEGIN  {  Main program  }
  X := 10.0;
  Y := 2 * X;
  writeln (X:20:2, Y:20:2);
  Sub1 (X);
  writeln (X1:20:2);
  writeln (X:20:2);
  writeln (Y:20:2)
END.  {  of main program  }
```

14. Discuss the advantages and disadvantages of using the same names for identifiers in a subprogram and the main program.

■ ■ ■ ■

■ **3.4**
User-Defined Functions

The standard functions **sqr, sqrt, abs, round,** and **trunc** were introduced in Section 2.5. To briefly review, some concepts to note when using these functions are

1. An argument is required for each; thus, **sqrt**(Y) and **abs**(−21) are appropriate.
2. Standard functions can be used in expressions; for example,

    ```
    X := sqrt(Y) + sqrt(Z);
    ```

3. Standard functions can be used in output statements; for example,

    ```
    writeln (sqr(3):8);
    ```

Need for User-Defined Functions

It is relatively easy to envision the need for functions that are not on the list of standard functions available in Pascal. For example, if you must frequently cube numbers, it would be convenient to have a function Cube so you could make an assignment such as

```
X := Cube(Y);
```

Other examples from mathematics include an exponential function (x^Y), computing a factorial $(n!)$, computing a discriminant $(b^2 - 4ac)$, and finding roots of a quadratic equation

$$\left(\frac{-b \pm \sqrt{b^2 - 4ac}}{2a} \right)$$

In business, a motel might like to have available a function to determine a customer's bill given the number in the party, the length of stay, and any telephone charges. Similarly, a hospital might like a function to compute the room charge for a patient given the type of room (private, ward, and so on) and various other options, including telephone (yes or no) and television (yes or no). Functions such as these are not standard functions. However, in Pascal, we can create *user-defined functions* to perform these tasks.

Form for User-Defined Functions

A user-defined function is a subprogram and, as such, is part of the declaration section of the main (or calling) program. It has the components

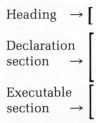

Heading →

Declaration section →

Executable section →

The general form for a function heading is

FUNCTION ⟨function name⟩ (⟨parameter list⟩) : ⟨return type⟩;

A syntax diagram for this is

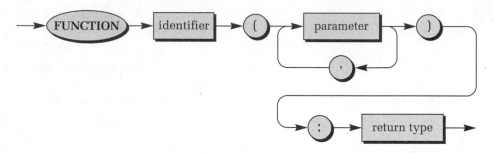

As with procedures, the formal parameter list (variables in the function heading) must match the number and corresponding types of actual parameters (variables in the function call) used when the function is called from the main program. Thus, if you are writing a function to compute the area of a rectangle and you want to call the function from the main program by

```
RectArea := Area(Width, Length);
```
the function Area might have

```
FUNCTION Area (W, L : integer) : integer;
```
as a heading. The two formal parameters, W and L, correspond to the actual parameters, Width and Length, assuming that Width and Length are of type **integer**. In general, you should make sure the formal parameter list and actual parameter list match up as indicated

```
(W, L : integer)
(Width, Length)
```
An exception to this is that an actual parameter of **integer** type may be associated with a formal parameter of **real** type.

A function to compute the cube of an integer could use the following as a heading:

```
FUNCTION Cube (X : integer) : integer;
```
Several additional comments on the general form for a function heading are now in order.

1. **FUNCTION** is a reserved word and must be used only as indicated.
2. The term "function name" is any valid identifier.
   a. The function name should be descriptive.
   b. Some value must be assigned to the function name in the executable section of the function. The last assigned value is the value returned to the main program; for example, in the function Cube, we have

   ```
   Cube := X * X * X;
   ```
   c. The function name can be used only on the left side of an assignment statement within the function. For example,

   ```
   Cube := Cube + 1;
   ```

produces an error. (An exception to this rule involves recursion and is discussed in Section 5.8.)

3. The term "return type" declares the data type for the function name. This indicates what type of value will be returned to the main program.

As in the main program, there does not have to be a declaration section for a function, but when there is one, only variables needed in the function are declared. Further, the section is usually not very elaborate because the purpose of a function is normally a small, single task.

Finally, the executable section for a function must perform the desired task, assign a value to the function name, terminate with a semicolon rather than a period, and have the general form

```
BEGIN
  .
  . (work of function here)
  .
END;
```

We will now illustrate user-defined functions with several examples.

■ **EXAMPLE 3.1**

Write a function to compute the cube of an integer. Since the actual parameter from the main program will be of **integer** type, we have

```
FUNCTION Cube (X : integer) : integer;
  BEGIN
    Cube := X * X * X
  END;
```

A typical call to this function from the main program is

```
A := Cube(5);
```

■

■ **EXAMPLE 3.2**

Let's write a function to perform the task of computing unit cost for pizza. (We did this with a procedure in Section 3.2.) Data sent to the function are size and cost. The function returns the unit cost. Formal parameters are Cost and Size. Using the function name PricePerSquareInch, we have

```
FUNCTION PricePerSquareInch (Cost, Size : real) : real;
  VAR
    Radius, Area : real;
  BEGIN
    Radius := Size / 2;
    Area := Pi * sqr(Radius);
    PricePerSquareInch := Cost / Area
  END; { of FUNCTION PricePerSquareInch }
```

This can be called from the main program by

```
UnitCost := PricePerSquareInch(Cost, Size);
```

■

■ **EXAMPLE 3.3**

Standard Pascal does not provide a power function comparable to BASIC's. (Some versions have a power operator built in, usually "**". Check your local system.) However, now that you know how to write a function, you can use the built-in functions **ln** and **exp** to write a power function. Before writing this, however, let's consider how these functions can be used to produce the desired result.

First, **exp** and **ln** are inverse functions in the sense that

$$\mathbf{exp}(\mathbf{ln}(X)) = X$$

for all positive X. Thus, we have

$$3^{2.5} = \mathbf{exp}(\mathbf{ln}(3^{2.5})).$$

Using properties of logarithms,

$$\mathbf{ln}(a^b) = b * \mathbf{ln}(a)$$

Hence,

$$\exp(\mathbf{ln}(3^{2.5})) = \mathbf{exp}(2.5 * \mathbf{ln}(3))$$

Since each of these operations can be performed in standard Pascal, we can compute $3^{2.5}$ by

$$3^{2.5} = \mathbf{exp}(2.5 * \mathbf{ln}(3))$$

or more generally,

$$A^X = \mathbf{exp}(X * \mathbf{ln}(A))$$

If we let Base denote the base A and Exponent denote the exponent X, we can now write a function Power as

```
FUNCTION Power (Base, Exponent : real) : real;
  BEGIN
    Power := exp(Exponent * ln(Base))
  END;  {  of FUNCTION Power  }
```

This can be called from the main program by

```
Base := 3;
Exponent := 2.5;
Num := Power(Base, Exponent);
```

■   ■

Use in a Program

Now that you have seen several examples of user-defined functions, let's consider their use in a program. Once they are written, they can be used in the same manner as standard functions. This usually means in one of the following forms.

1. Assignment statements

```
A := 5;
B := Cube(A);
```

2. Arithmetic expressions

```
A := 5;
B := 3 * Cube(A) + 2;
```

3. Output statements

```
A := 5;
writeln (Cube(A):17);
         .
         .
         .
```

Multiple Functions

Programs can contain more than one function. When several user-defined functions are needed in a program, each one should be developed and positioned in the program as previously indicated.

When a program calls several functions, they can generally be positioned above the main program body in any order. However, if one function contains a call to another function, the function being called must appear before the function from which it is called.

Exercises 3.4

1. Discuss the difference between a procedure and a function.

2. Write a test program to see what happens when the function name is used on the right side of an assignment statement. For example,

```
FUNCTION Total (OldSum, NewNum : integer) : integer;
  BEGIN
    Total := OldSum;
    Total := Total + NewNum
  END;
```

3. Indicate which of the following are valid function headings. Explain what is wrong with those that are invalid.

   a. `FUNCTION RoundTenth (X : real);`
   b. `FUNCTION MakeChange (X, Y) : real;`
   c. `FUNCTION Max (M1, M2, M3 : integer) : integer;`
   d. `FUNCTION Sign (Num : real) : char;`
   e. `FUNCTION Truth (Ch : char, Num : real) : boolean;`

4. Find all errors in each of the following functions.

   a. ```
      FUNCTION AvOf2 (N1, N2 : integer) : integer;
        BEGIN
          AvOf2 := (N1 + N2) / 2
        END;
      ```
   b. ```
      FUNCTION Total (L1, L2 : integer) : integer;
        VAR
          Sum : integer;
        BEGIN
          Total := 0;
          Sum := L1 + L2
        END;
      ```

5. Write a function for each of the following:

   a. Round a real to the nearest tenth.
   b. Round a real to the nearest hundredth.
   c. Convert degrees Fahrenheit to degrees Celsius.
   d. Compute the charge for cars at a parking lot; the rate is 75 cents per hour or fraction thereof.

6. Write a program that uses the function you wrote for Exercise 5d to print a ticket for a customer who parks in the parking lot. Assume the input is in minutes.

7. The factorial of a positive integer n is defined as
$n! = n * (n - 1) * \ldots * 2 * 1$ for $n > 1$.
Write a function (Factorial) that will compute and return $n!$.

8. Write a complete program using Cube and Factorial that will produce a table of the integers 1 to 10 together with their squares, cubes, and factorials.

9. Use the functions **sqr** and Cube to write a program to print a chart of the integers 1 to 5 together with their squares and cubes. Output from this program should be

Number	Number Squared	Number Cubed
1	1	1
2	4	8
3	9	27
4	16	64
5	25	125

10. Write a program that allows the user to enter a Base (a) and Exponent (x) and then have the program print the value of a^x.

11. Write a function (Arithmetic) that will receive a sign (+ or *) and two integers (N1, N2) and then compute and return either N1 + N2 or N1 * N2 depending on the sign received.

12. Algebra teachers often have students play "guess the rule." This consists of having the first person write down a rule (function) such as $y = x^2 + 1$. A second person then gives a value for x. The first person indicates the function value associated with the input. Thus, for $x = 3$, y would be 10 if $y = x^2 + 1$. The game continues until the second person guesses the rule.

   Write a program that allows you to play this game with another student. Write it in such a way that it can be easily modified to use different functions.

■ ■ ■ ■

■ 3.5
Using Subprograms

Use of subprograms facilitates writing programs for problems whose solutions have been developed using top-down design. A procedure or function can be written for each main task. Each subprogram can contain its own subprograms if needed.

How complex should a procedure or function be? In general, functions should be relatively short and perform a specific task. Procedures can be longer, but probably should not be more than one page of printout; some programmers prefer to limit procedures to no more than one full screen. If longer than a page or screen, possibly the task should be subdivided into smaller procedures or functions.

Functions Versus Procedures

When should you use a function rather than a procedure in a program? A general rule is to think of a function as a construct that returns only one

Niklaus Wirth

Niklaus Wirth began his work in the computing field by taking a course in numerical analysis at Laval University in Quebec, Canada. However, the computer (Alvac III E) was frequently out of order and the hexadecimal code programming exercises went untested. He received his doctorate from the University of California, Berkeley, in 1963.

After other early experiences in programming, it became apparent to Wirth that computers of the future had to be more effectively programmable. Consequently, he joined a research group that worked on developing a compiler for an IBM 704. This language was NELIAC, a dialect of ALGOL 58. In rapid succession, he developed or contributed to the development of Euler,

ALGOL W, and PL360. In 1967, he returned to Switzerland and established a team of three assistants with whom he developed and implemented the language Pascal.

Pascal was the first major programming language to implement the ideas and methodology of structured programming and was initially developed to teach programming concepts. It is particularly successful as a teaching language because it allows the teacher to focus on structures and concepts rather than features and peculiarities. However, it has rapidly expanded beyond its initial purpose and has found increasing acceptance in business and scientific applications.

value; thus, a function would be used when a single value is required in the main program. Variable parameters can be used with functions, but this is discouraged in good programming practices.

What Kind of Parameters Should Be Used?

Use variable parameters when information is going to be returned to the main program; otherwise, use value parameters. The choices will be apparent if you use data flow arrows or module specifications when designing the solution to the problem.

Using Stubs

As programs get longer and incorporate more subprograms, a technique frequently used to get the program running is *stub programming*. A stub program is a no-frills, simple version of what will be a final program. It does not contain details of output and full algorithm development. It does contain a rough version of each subprogram and all parameter lists. When the stub version runs, you know your logic is correct and values are appropriately being passed to and from subprograms. Then you can fill in necessary details to get a complete program.

Using Drivers

The main program is sometimes referred to as the *main driver*. When subprograms are used in a program, this driver can be modified to check subprograms in a sequential fashion. For example, suppose a main driver is

```
BEGIN { Main driver }
   Initialize (Sum, Count);
   GetData (Sum, Count);
   PerformComputation (Sum, Count);
   PrintResults (Sum, Count)
END. { of main driver }
```

Procedures can be checked by putting comment indicators around the remainder of the program and temporarily adding a statement to print values of variables. Thus, you could run the following version:

```
BEGIN  {  Main driver  }
  Initialize (Sum, Count);
  GetData (Sum, Count);
  writeln ('Sum is ', Sum; 'Count is ', Count);
{ PerformComputation (Sum, Count);
  PrintResults (Sum, Count)  }
END.  {  of main driver  }
```

Once you are sure a subprogram is running, you can remove the comment indicators and continue through the main driver to check successive subprograms.

FOCUS ON PROGRAM DESIGN

In order to encourage people to shop downtown, the Downtown Businesses Association partially subsidizes parking. They have established the E-Z Parking parking lot where customers are charged $0.75 for each full hour of parking. There is no charge for part of an hour. Thus, if someone has used the lot for less than an hour, there would be no charge.

The E-Z Parking parking lot is open from 9:00 A.M. until 11:00 P.M. When a vehicle enters, the driver is given a ticket with the entry time printed in military style. Thus, if a car entered the lot at 9:30 A.M., the ticket would read 0930. If a vehicle entered at 1:20 P.M., the ticket would read 1320. When the vehicle leaves, the driver presents the ticket to the attendant and the amount due is computed.

Let's now develop a solution and write a program to assist the attendant. Input consists of a starting and ending time. Output should be a statement to the customer indicating the input information, the total amount due, a heading, and a closing message. Sample output for the data 1050 (10:50 A.M.) and 1500 (3:00 P.M.) is

```
Please enter the time in and press <RETURN>.  1050
Please enter the time out and press <RETURN>.  1500


              E - Z Parking
              -------------

      Time in:   1050
      Time out:  1500

      Amount due     $  3.00

  Thank you for using E - Z Parking

              BUCKLE UP
                 and
              DRIVE SAFELY
```

A first-level development for this problem is

1. Get the data
2. Compute amount
3. Print results

A structure chart for this problem is given in Figure 3.14. (Recall, an arrow pointing into a module indicates data are being received while an arrow pointing out indicates data are being sent from the module.)

FIGURE 3.14
Structure chart for the parking lot program

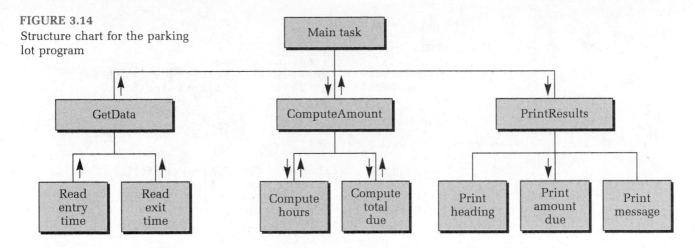

Module specifications for the three main modules are

1. GetData Module
   Data received: None
   Information returned: Entry time
                         Exit time
   Logic: Have the user enter information from the keyboard.

2. ComputeAmount Module
   Data received: Entry time
                   Exit time
   Information returned: Amount due
   Logic: Subtract the entry time from the exit time and use **DIV** 100 to
          get the number of full hours.

3. PrintResults Module
   Data received: Entry time
                   Exit time
                   Amount due
   Information returned: None
   Logic: Print the heading, entry time, exit time, amount due, and clos-
          ing message.

By examining the module specifications, we see that two variable parameters are needed for GetData. ComputeAmount needs two value parameters
and one variable parameter, and PrintResults needs three value parameters.

A second-level pseudocode development is

1. Get the data
    1.1 read time entered
    1.2 read time exited
2. Compute amount
    2.1 compute number of hours
    2.2 compute amount due
3. Print results
    3.1 print a heading
    3.2 print amount due
    3.3 print a closing message

The main driver is

```
BEGIN  {  Main program  }
  GetData (Entrytime, ExitTime);
  AmountDue := ComputeAmount(EntryTime, ExitTime);
  PrintResults (EntryTime, ExitTime, AmountDue)
END.  {  of main program  }
```

A complete program for this is

```
PROGRAM Parking (input, output);

{   This  program  prints statements for customers of the E-Z  }
{   Parking lot.  Interactive input consists of entry          }
{   time and exit time from the lot. Output consists of a      }
{   customer statement. Emphasis is placed on using            }
{   procedures and a function to develop the program.          }

CONST
  HourlyRate = 0.75;
  Indent = '  ';

VAR
  EntryTime,              {  Time of entry into parking lot     }
  ExitTime : integer;     {  Time of exit from parking lot      }
  AmountDue : real;       {  Cost of parking in lot             }

{********************************************************************** }

PROCEDURE GetData (VAR EntryTime, ExitTime : integer);

  {  Given:    Nothing                                             }
  {  Task:     Enter EntryTime and ExitTime from the keyboard      }
  {  Return:   EntryTime, ExitTime                                 }

  BEGIN
    writeln ('Please enter the time in and press <RETURN>.');
    readln (EntryTime);
    writeln ('Please enter the time out and press <RETURN>.');
    readln (ExitTime)
  END;  {  of PROCEDURE GetData  }

{********************************************************************** }

FUNCTION ComputeAmount (EntryTime, ExitTime : integer) : real;

  {  Given:    EntryTime and ExitTime                         }
  {  Task:     Find full hours and multiply by HourlyRate     }
  {  Return:   AmountDue                                      }

  VAR
    NumberOfHours : integer;

  BEGIN
    NumberOfHours := (ExitTime - EntryTime) DIV 100;
    ComputeAmount := NumberOfHours * HourlyRate
  END;  {  of FUNCTION ComputeAmount  }

{********************************************************************** }

PROCEDURE PrintHeading;

  {  Given:    Nothing                                         }
  {  Task:     Print a suitable heading for the ticket         }
  {  Return:   Nothing                                         }
```

1

2

```pascal
   BEGIN
      writeln;
      writeln (Indent:11, 'E - Z Parking');
      writeln (Indent:11, '-------------');
      writeln
   END; {  of PROCEDURE PrintHeading   }

{****************************************************************** }

PROCEDURE PrintMessage;
   {  Given:    Nothing                                            }
   {  Task:     Print a closing message for the ticket            }
   {  Return:   Nothing                                            }

   BEGIN
      writeln;
      writeln (Indent:1, 'Thank you for using E - Z Parking');
      writeln;
      writeln (Indent:13, 'BUCKLE UP');
      writeln (Indent:16, 'and');
      writeln (Indent:11, 'DRIVE SAFELY');
      writeln
   END; {  of PROCEDURE PrintMessage   }

{******************************************************************; }

PROCEDURE PrintResults (EntryTime, ExitTime : integer;
                        AmountDue : real);

   {  Given:    EntryTime, ExitTime, AmountDue                     }
   {  Task:     Print a customer receipt; calls both PrintHeading  }
   {            and PrintMessage                                    }
   {  Return:   Nothing                                            }

   BEGIN
      PrintHeading;
      writeln (Indent:4, 'Time in: ', EntryTime:6);
      writeln (Indent:4, 'Time out:', ExitTime:6);
      writeln;
      writeln (Indent:4, 'Amount due      $', AmountDue:6:2);
      PrintMessage
   END; {  of PROCEDURE PrintResults   }

{****************************************************************** }

BEGIN  {  Main program  }
   GetData (EntryTime, ExitTime);
   AmountDue := ComputeAmount(EntryTime, ExitTime);
   PrintResults (EntryTime, ExitTime, AmountDue)
END.  {  of main program   }
```

A sample run using the data 0930 as entry time and 1320 as exit time produces

```
      Please enter the time in and press <RETURN>.
      ?0930
      Please enter the time out and press <RETURN>.
      ?1320

                  E - Z Parking
                  -------------

          Time in:   0930
          Time out:  1320

          Amount due    $  2.25
```

```
            Thank you for using E - Z Parking

                      BUCKLE UP
                         and
                     DRIVE SAFELY
```

RUNNING AND DEBUGGING TIPS

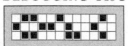

1. Each subprogram can be tested separately to see if it is producing the desired result. This is accomplished by a main program that calls and tests only the subprogram in question.

2. You can use related but not identical variable names in the parameter lists. For example,

```
PROCEDURE Compute (N1, N2 : integer;
                   VAR Av : real);
```

or

```
PROCEDURE Compute (Number1, Number2 : integer;
                   VAR Average : real);
```

could be called by

```
Compute (Number1, Number2, Average);
```

3. Be sure the type and order of actual parameters and formal parameters agree. You can do this by listing them one below the other. For example,

```
PROCEDURE GetData (VAR Init1,Init2:char; Sc:integer);
```

could be called by

```
        GetData (Initial1, Initial2, Score);
```

4. Carefully distinguish between value parameters and variable parameters. If a value is to be returned to the main program, it must be passed by reference using a variable parameter. This means it must be declared with **VAR** in the procedure heading.

■ Summary

Key Terms

actual parameter	main driver	structured programming
block	modularity	stub programming
bottom-up testing	passed by reference	subblock
cohesive subprogram	postcondition	subprogram
encapsulation	precondition	user-defined function
formal parameter	procedural abstraction	value parameter
global identifier (variable)	procedures	variable parameter
interface	scope of an identifier	
local identifier (variable)	side effect	

Keywords

FUNCTION   **PROCEDURE**   ln
                                                exp

Key Concepts

- A subprogram is a program within a program; procedures and functions are sub-programs.
- Subprograms can be utilized to perform specific tasks in a program. Procedures are often used to initialize variables (variable parameters), get data (variable parameters), print headings (no variables needed), perform computations (value and/or variable parameters), and print data (value parameters).
- The general form for a procedure heading is
  PROCEDURE ⟨name⟩ (⟨parameter list⟩);
- Value parameters are used when values are passed only from the main program to the procedure; a typical parameter list is

```
PROCEDURE PrintData (N1, N2 : integer;
                     X, Y : real);
```

- Variable parameters are used when values are to be returned to the main program; a typical parameter list is

```
PROCEDURE GetData (VAR Init1, Init2 : char;
                   VAR N1 : integer);
```

- A formal parameter is one listed in the subprogram heading; it is like a blank waiting to receive a value from the calling program.

```
                              formal parameters
                             ╱        │        ╲
PROCEDURE Arithmetic (Sym : char; N1, N2 : integer);
```

- An actual parameter is a variable listed in the subprogram call in the calling program.

```
                      actual parameters
                     ╱       │       │
Arithmetic (Symbol, Num1, Num2);
```

- The formal parameter list in the subprogram heading must match the number and types of actual parameters used in the main program when the subprogram is called.

```
PROCEDURE Arithmetic (Sym : char; N1, N2 : integer);
Arithmetic (Symbol, Num1, Num2);
```

- Global identifiers can be used by the main program and all subprograms.
- Local identifiers are available only to the subprogram in which they are declared.
- Each identifier is available to the block in which it is declared; this includes all subprograms contained within the block.
- Identifiers are not available outside their blocks.
- The scope of an identifier refers to the blocks in which the identifier is available.
- Understanding scope of identifiers is aided by graphic illustration of blocks in a program; thus,

```
PROGRAM Practice (input, output);
VAR
  X, Y, Z : real;
PROCEDURE Sub1 (X1 : real);
  VAR
    X2 : real;
  BEGIN
    .
    .
    .
  END; { of PROCEDURE Sub1 }
```

```
PROCEDURE Sub2 (X1 : real);
  VAR
    Z2 : real;
```

can be visualized as shown in Figure 3.15.

FIGURE 3.15

PROGRAM Practice

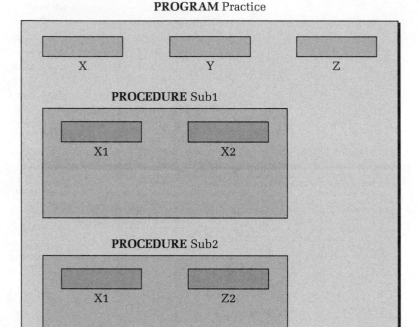

- A user-defined function is a subprogram that performs a specific task.
- The form for a user-defined function is

FUNCTION ⟨function name⟩ (⟨parameter list⟩) : ⟨return type⟩;
VAR
BEGIN

    .
    . (work of function here)
    .

END;

- An assignment must be made to the function name in the body of the function.
- Within a function, the function name can be used only on the left side of an assignment statement.

■ **Programming Problems and Projects**

The following programming problems will be run on a very limited set of data. In later chapters, as you build your programming skills, you will run these problems with larger data bases and subprograms for various parts. Problems marked with a box to the left of the number are referred to and used repeatedly; carefully choose the ones on which to work and then develop them completely.

1. Write a program to get the coefficients of a quadratic equation

   $$ax^2 + bx + c = 0$$

   from the keyboard and then print the value of the discriminant

   $$b^2 - 4ac$$

   A sample display for getting input is

   ```
   Enter coefficients a, b, and c for the quadratic equation
      ax² + bx + c = 0

   a = ?
   b = ?
   c = ?
   ```

   Run this program at least three times using test data that result in
   $b^2 - 4ac = 0$, $b^2 - 4ac > 0$, and $b^2 - 4ac < 0$.

2. Write a program to compute the cost for carpeting a room. Input
   should consist of the room length, room width, and carpet price per
   square yard. Use constants for the pad charge and installation charge.
   Include a heading as part of the output.

   A typical input screen would be:

   ```
   What is the room length in feet?  <RETURN>?
   What is the room width in feet?   <RETURN>?
   What is the carpet price/square yard? <RETURN>?
   ```

   Output for a sample run of this program (without a heading) could be

   ```
   Dimensions of the room (in feet) are 17 x 22.4
   The area to be carpeted is 41.6 square yards.
   The carpet price is $11.95 per yard.

      Room dimensions          17 x 22.5
      Carpet required          41.6 square yards
      Carpet price/yard        $11.95
      Pad price/yard           $ 2.95
      Installation cost/yard    $ .95
      Total cost/yard          $15.85
      Total cost               $659.36
   ```

3. Williamson's Paint and Papering store wants a computer program to
   help them determine how much paint is needed to paint a room. Assuming a room is to have four walls and the ceiling painted, input for
   the program should be the length, width, and height of the room. Use
   a constant for the wall height (usually eight feet). One gallon of paint
   should cover 250 square feet. Cost of paint for the walls and ceiling
   should be entered by the user. Output should be the amount and cost
   for each kind of paint, and the total cost.

4. The Fairfield College faculty recently signed a three-year contract that
   included salary increments of 7 percent, 6 percent, and 5 percent respectively for the next three years. Write a program that allows a user
   to enter the current salary and then prints out the compounded salary
   for each of the next three years.

5. Several instructors use various weights (percentage of the final grade)
   for test scores. Write a program that allows the user to enter three test
   scores and the weight for each score. Output should consist of the input data, the weighted score for each test, and the total score (sum of
   the weighted scores).

put data, the weighted score for each test, and the total score (sum of the weighted scores).

6. The Roll-Em Lanes bowling team would like to have a computer program to print the team results for one series of games. The team consists of four members whose names are Weber, Fazio, Martin, and Patterson. Each person on the team bowls three games during the series; thus, the input will contain three lines, each with four integer scores. Your output should include all input data, individual series totals, game average for each member, team series, and team average.

Sample output is

NAME	GAME 1	GAME 2	GAME 3	TOTAL	AVERAGE
Weber	212	220	190	622	207.3
Fazio	195	235	210	640	213.3
Martin	178	190	206	574	191.3
Patterson	195	215	210	620	206.7

Team Total: 2456

Team Average: 818.7

7. The Natural Pine Furniture Company has recently hired you to help them convert their antiquated payroll system to a computer-based model. They know you are still learning, so all they want right now is a program that will print a one-week pay report for three employees. You should use the constant definition section for the following:
   a. Federal withholding tax rate   18%
   b. State withholding tax rate   4.5%
   c. Hospitalization $25.65
   d. Union dues $7.85

Each line of input will contain the employee's initials, the number of hours worked, and the employee's hourly rate. Your output should include a report for each employee and a summary report for the company files.

A sample employee form follows:

```
Employee:      JIM
Hours Worked:  40.00
Hourly Rate:    9.75

    Total Wages:                            390.00

    Deductions:
        Federal Withholding      70.20
        State Withholding        17.55
        Hospitalization          26.65
        Union Dues                7.85
              Total Deductions   122.25

    Net Pay                               $267.75
```

Output for a summary report could be

Natural Pine Furniture Company
Weekly Summary

```
Gross Wages:

Deductions:
        Federal Withholding
        State Withholding
        Hospitalization
        Union Dues
                Total Deductions

Net Wages
```

■ 8. The Child-Growth Encyclopedia Company wants a computer program that will print a monthly sales chart. Products produced by the company, prices, and sales commissions for each are

a.	Basic encyclopedia	$325.00	22%
b.	Child educational supplement	$127.50	15%
c.	Annual update book	$ 18.95	20%

Monthly sales data for one region consist of a two-letter region identifier (such as MI) and three integers, representing the number of units sold for each product listed above. A typical input screen would be:

```
What is your sales region?
?MI
How many Basic Encyclopedia were sold?
?150
How many Child Supplements were sold?
?120
How many Annual Updates were sold?
?105
```

Write a program that will get the monthly sales data for two sales regions and produce the desired company chart. The prices may vary from month to month and should be defined in the constant definition section. The commissions are not subject to change. Typical output could be:

```
                    MONTHLY SALES CHART

                            Basic         Child        Annual
             Region      Encyclopedia   Supplement     Update

Units sold    MI            150            120           105
(by region)   TX            225            200           150
                          -----          -----         -----
Total units sold:           375            320           255

   Price/unit            $325.00        $127.50        $18.95

Gross Sales:         $121,875.00     $40,800.00     $4,832.25

   Commission rate        22%            15%           20%

Commissions paid:    $26,812.50      $6,120.00       $966.45
```

9. The Village Variety Store is having its annual Christmas sale. They would like you to write a program to produce a daily report for the store. Each item sold is identified by a code consisting of one letter followed by one digit. Your report should include data for three items. Each of the three lines of data will include item code, number of items sold, original item price, and reduction percentage. Your report

should include a chart with the input data, sale price per item, and total amount of sales per item. You should also print a daily summary. Sample input is

```
A1 13 5.95 15
A2 24 7.95 20
A3 80 3.95 50
```

Typical output form could be:

```
Item Code   # Sold   Original Price   Reductions   Sale Price   Income
---------   ------   --------------   ----------   ----------   ------
   A1         13         $5.95            15%         $5.06      $65.78

Daily Summary
-------------
   Gross Income:
```

10. The Holiday-Out Motel Company, Inc., wants a program that will print a statement for each overnight customer. Each line of input will contain room number (integer), number of nights (integer), room rate (real), telephone charges (real), and restaurant charges (real). You should use the constant definition section for the date and current tax rate. Each customer statement should include all input data, the date, tax rate and amount, total due, appropriate heading, and appropriate closing message. Test your program by running it for two customers. The tax rate applies only to the room cost. A typical input screen is

```
Room number?
?135
Room rate?
?39.95
Number of nights?
?3
Telephone charges?
?3.75
Meals?
?57.50
```

A customer statement form is

```
        Holiday-Out Motel Company, Inc.
        ------- ---- ----- -------- ---
Date: XX-XX-XX
Room #                      135
Room Rate:               $39.95
Number of Nights:             3

Room Cost:               $119.85
Tax:  XXX%                  4.79
     Subtotal:                    $124.64

Telephone:                         3.75
Meals:                            57.50

     TOTAL DUE                   $185.89

   Thank you for staying at Holiday-Out
               Drive safely
            Please come again
```

■ **11.** As a part-time job this semester, you are working for the Family Budget Assistance Center. Your boss has asked you to write and execute a program that will analyze data for a family. Input for each family will consist of

Family ID number	(**integer**)
Number in family	(**integer**)
Income	(**real**)
Total debts	(**real**)

Your program should output the following:

a. An appropriate header.
b. The family's identification number, number in family, income, and total debts.
c. Predicted family living expenses ($3000 times the size of the family).
d. The monthly payment necessary to pay off the debt in one year.
e. The amount the family should save (the family size times 2 percent of the income minus debt—Farm Size ∗ 0.02 (income − debt)).
f. Your service fee (.5 percent of the income).

Run your program for the following two families:

Identification Number	Size	Income	Debt
51	4	18000.00	2000.00
72	7	26000.00	4800.00

Output for the first family could be:

```
    Family Budget Assistance Center
            March 1989
        Telephone: (800)555-1234

Identification number            51
Family size                       4
Annual income            $ 18000.00
Total debt               $  2000.00
Expected living expenses $ 12000.00
Monthly payment          $    166.67
Savings                  $   1280.00
Service fee              $     90.00
```

■ **12.** The Caswell Catering and Convention Service has asked you to write a computer program to produce customers' bills. The program should read in the following data.

a. The number of adults to be served.
b. The number of children to be served.
c. The cost per adult meal.
d. The cost per child's meal (60 percent of the cost of the adult's meal).
e. The cost for dessert (same for adults and children).
f. The room fee (no room fee if catered at the person's home).
g. A percentage for tip and tax (not applied to the room fee).
h. Any deposit should be deducted from the bill.

Write a program and test it using data sets 2, 3, and 4.

Data Set	Child Count	Adult Count	Adult Cost	Dessert Cost	Room Rate	Tip/Tax	Deposit
1	7	23	12.75	1.00	45.00	18%	50.00
2	3	54	13.50	1.25	65.00	19%	40.00
3	15	24	12.00	0.00	45.00	18%	75.00
4	2	71	11.15	1.50	0.00	6%	0.00

Note that data set 1 was used to produce the following sample output.

```
          Caswell Catering and Convention Service
                        Final Bill

                    Number of adults:        23
                  Number of children:         7
     Cost per adult without dessert:    $    12.75
     Cost per child without dessert:    $     7.65
                   Cost per dessert:    $     1.00
                          Room fee:    $    45.00
                  Tip and tax rate:          0.18

         Total cost for adult meals:    $   293.25
         Total cost for child meals:    $    53.55
            Total cost for dessert:    $    30.00
                  Total food cost:    $   376.80
                Plus tip and tax:    $    67.82
                   Plus room fee:    $    45.00
                    Less deposit:    $    50.00

                       Balance due:    $   439.62
```

13. The Maripot Carpet Store has asked you to write a computer program to calculate the amount a customer should be charged. The president of the company has given you the following information to help in writing the program.

   a. The carpet charge is equal to the number of square yards purchased times the labor cost per square yard.

   b. The labor cost is equal to the number of square yards purchased times the cost per square yard. A fixed fee for floor preparation is added to some customers' bills.

   c. Large volume customers are given a percentage discount but the discount applies only to the carpet charge, not the labor costs.

   d. All customers are charged 4 percent sales tax on the carpet: there is no sales tax on the labor cost.

   Write the program and test it for customers 2, 3, and 4.

Customer	Sq. yds.	Cost per sq. yd.	Labor per sq. yd.	Prep. Cost	Discount
1	17	18.50	3.50	38.50	0.02
2	40	24.95	2.95	0.00	0.14
3	23	16.80	3.25	57.95	0.00
4	26	21.25	0.00	80.00	0.00

Note that the data for customer 1 were used to produce the following sample output.

```
Square yards purchased:         17
   Cost per square yard:  $   18.50
  Labor per square yard:  $    3.50
 Floor preparation cost:  $   38.50
        Cost for carpet:  $  314.50
         Cost for labor:  $   98.00
     Discount on carpet:  $    6.29
          Tax on carpet:  $   12.33
      Charge to customer: $  418.54
```

14. The manager of the Croswell Carpet Store has asked you to write a program to print customers' bill. The manager has given you the following information.

   - The store expresses the length and width of a room in terms of feet and tenths of a foot. For example, the length might be reported as 16.7 feet.
   - The amount of carpet purchased is expressed as square yards. It is found by dividing the area of the room (in square feet) by nine.
   - The store does not sell a fraction of a square yard. Thus, square yards must always be rounded up.
   - The carpet charge is equal to the number of square yards purchased times the carpet cost per square yard. Sales tax equal to 4 percent of the carpet cost must be added to the bill.
   - All customers are sold a carpet pad at $2.25 per square yard. Sales tax equal to 4 percent of the pad cost must be added to the bill.
   - The labor cost is equal to the number of square yards purchased times $2.40, which is the labor cost per square yard. No tax is charged on labor.
   - Large volume customers may be given a discount. The discount may apply only to the carpet cost (before sales tax is added), only to the pad cost (before sales tax is added), only to the labor cost, or to any combination of the three charges.
   - Each customer is identified by a five-digit number and that number should appear on the bill. The sample output follows:

```
Croswell Carpet Store
     Invoice

Customer number:       26817

     Carpet :       574.20
        Pad :        81.00
      Labor :        86.40

   Subtotal :       741.60
Less discount :       65.52

   Subtotal :       676.08
   Plus tax :        23.59
      Total :       699.67
```

Write the program and test it for the following three customers.
   a. Mr. Wilson (customer 81429) ordered carpet for his family room, which measures 25 feet long and 18 feet wide. The carpet sells for $12.95 per square yard and the manager agreed to give him a discount of 8 percent on the carpet and 6 percent on the labor.

    b. Mr. and Mrs. Adams (customer 04246) ordered carpet for their bedroom, which measures 16.5 feet by 15.4 feet. The carpet sells for $18.90 per square yard and the manager granted a discount of 12 percent of everything.

    c. Ms. Logan (customer 39050) ordered carpet that cost $8.95 per square yard for her daughter's bedroom. The room measures 13.1 by 12.5 feet. No discounts were given.

15. Each week Abduhl's Flying Carpets pays its salespeople a base salary plus a bonus for each carpet they sell. In addition, they pay a commission of 10 percent of the total sales by each salesperson.

    Write a program to compute a salesperson's salary for the month by inputting Base, Bonus, Quantity, and Sales, and making the necessary calculations. Use the following test data:

Salesperson	Base	Bonus	Quantity	Commission	Sales
1	250.00	15.00	20	10%	1543.69
2	280.00	19.50	36	10%	2375.90

The commission figure is 10 percent. Be sure you can change this easily if necessary. Sample output follows:

```
      Salesperson :      1
             Base :   250.00
            Bonus :    15.00
         Quantity :     20
      Total Bonus :   300.00
       Commission :     10%
            Sales :  1543.69
 Total Commission :    154.37
              Pay :    704.37
```

16. "Think Metric" is the preferred way of having members of a nonmetric society become familiar with the metric system. Unfortunately, during the transition, many people are forced to rely on converting from their present system to the metric system. Develop a solution and write a program to help people convert their height and weight from inches and pounds to centimeters and kilograms. The program should get input of a person's height (in feet and inches) and weight (rounded to the nearest pound) from a keyboard. Output should consist of the height and weight in metric units.

17. Discuss the issue of documenting subprograms with instructors of computer science, upper-level students majoring in computer science, and some of your classmates. Prepare a report for the class on this issue. Your report should contain information about different forms of documentation, the perceived need for documentation by various groups, significance of documenting data transmission, and so forth. If possible, use specific examples to illustrate good documentation of subprograms versus poor documentation of subprograms.

18. Reread the material in Section 3.2 concerning procedural abstraction. Then, from Problems 5, 7, 8, and 11, select one that you have not yet worked. Develop a structure chart and write module specifications for each module required for the problem you have chosen. Also, write a main driver for your program and write complete documentation for each subprogram including comments about all parameters.

C H A P T E R

What I tell you three times is true.

Lewis Carroll

Selection Statements

The previous chapters set the stage for using computers to solve problems. You have seen how programs in Pascal can be used to get data, perform computations, and print results. You should be able to write complete, short programs, so it is now time to examine other aspects of programming.

A major feature of a computer is its ability to make decisions. For example, a condition is examined and a decision is made as to which program statement is next executed. Statements that permit a computer to make decisions are called *selection statements*. Selection statements are examples of *control structures* because they allow the programmer to control the flow of execution of program statements.

■ 4.1
Boolean Expressions

Before looking at decision making, we need to examine the logical constructs in Pascal, which include a new data type called **boolean.** This data type allows you to represent something as true or false. Although this sounds relatively simple (and it is), this is a very significant feature of computers.

The boolean Data Type

Thus far we have used only the three data types **integer, real,** and **char;** a fourth data type is **boolean.** A typical declaration of a Boolean variable is

```
VAR
    Flag : boolean;
```

In general, Boolean variables are declared by

```
VAR
    ⟨variable 1⟩,
    ⟨variable 2⟩,
        .
        .
        .
    ⟨variable n⟩ : boolean;
```

There are only two values for variables of the **boolean** data type: **true** and **false.** These are both constant standard identifiers and can only be used as Boolean values. When these assignments are made, the contents of the designated memory locations will be the assigned values. For example, if the declaration

```
VAR
   Flag1, Flag2 : boolean;
```

is made,

```
Flag1 := true;
Flag2 := false;
```

produces

Flag1   Flag2

As with other data types, if two variables are of type **boolean,** the value of one variable can be assigned to another variable as

```
Flag1 := true;
Flag2 := Flag1;
```

and can be envisioned as

true		true

Flag1   Flag2

Note that quotation marks are not used when assigning the values **true** or **false** since these are Boolean constants, not strings.

The **boolean** data type is an ordinal type. Thus, there is an order relationship between **true** and **false: false < true.** Furthermore, the **ord** function can be applied to the **boolean** values: **ord(false)** = 0 and **ord(true)** = 1.

Output of boolean

In standard Pascal, Boolean variables can be used as arguments for **write** and **writeln.** Thus,

```
Flag := true;
writeln (Flag);
```

produces

```
true
```

However, some versions will not support output of Boolean variables.

The field width for Boolean output varies with the machine being used. It can be controlled by formatting with a colon followed by a positive integer to designate the field width. The Boolean value will appear right justified in the field.

Although Boolean variables and constants can be assigned and used in output statements, they cannot be used in input statements in standard Pascal. Thus, if Flag is a Boolean variable, a statement such as

```
read (Flag);
```

produces an error. Instead, one would typically read some value and then use this value to assign an appropriate Boolean value to a Boolean variable. This technique will be illustrated later.

Relational Operators and Simple Boolean Expressions

In arithmetic, integers and reals can be compared using equalities ($=$) and inequalities ($<$, $>$, $\neq$, and so on). Pascal also provides for the comparison of numbers or values of variables. The operators used for comparison are called *relational operators* and there are six of them. Their arithmetic notation, Pascal notation, and meaning are given in Table 4.1.

TABLE 4.1
Relational operators

Arithmetic Operation	Relational Operator	Meaning
=	=	Is equal to
<	<	Is less than
>	>	Is greater than
≤	<=	Is less than or equal to
≥	>=	Is greater than or equal to
≠	<>	Is not equal to

When two numbers or variable values are compared using a single relational operator, the expression is referred to as a *simple Boolean expression.* Each simple Boolean expression has the Boolean value **true** or **false** according to the arithmetic validity of the expression. In general, only data of the same type can be compared; thus, integers must be compared to integers, reals must be compared to reals, and characters must be compared to characters. The usual exception can be applied here; that is, reals can be compared to integers. When comparing reals, however, the computer representation of a real number might not be the exact real number intended.

Table 4.2 sets forth several Boolean expressions and their respective Boolean values, assuming the assignment statements A := 3 and B := 4 have been made.

TABLE 4.2
Values of simple Boolean expressions

Simple Boolean Expression	Boolean Value
7 = 7	**true**
-3.0 = 0.0	**false**
4.2 > 3.7	**true**
-18 < -15	**true**
13 < 100	**true**
13 <= 100	**true**
13 <= 13	**true**
0.012 > 0.013	**false**
-17.32 <> -17.32	**false**
A <= B	**true**
B > A	**true**

Arithmetic expressions can also be used in simple Boolean expressions. Thus,

```
4 < (3 + 2)
```

has the value **true.** When the computer evaluates this expression, the parentheses dictate that (3 + 2) be evaluated first and then the relational operator. Sequentially, this becomes

```
4 < (3 + 2)
4 <     5
true
```

What if the parentheses had not been used? Could the expression be evaluated? This type of expression necessitates a priority level for the relational operators and the arithmetic operators. A summary for the priority of these operations is

Expression	Priority
( )	1
*, /, **MOD, DIV**	2
+, −	3
=, <, >, <=, >=, <>	4

Thus, we see that the relational operators are evaluated last. As with arithmetic operators, these are evaluated in order from left to right. Thus, the expression

```
4 < 3 + 2
```

could be evaluated without parentheses and would have the same Boolean value.

The following example illustrates the evaluation of a somewhat more complex Boolean expression.

■ **EXAMPLE 4.1**

Indicate the successive steps in the evaluation of the Boolean expression

```
10 MOD 4 * 3 - 8 <= 18 + 30 DIV 4 - 20
```

The steps in this evaluation are

■

As shown in Example 4.1, even though parentheses are not required when using arithmetic expressions with relational operators, it is usually a good idea to use them to enhance the readability of the expression and to avoid using an incorrect expression.

Logical Operators and Compound Boolean Expressions

Boolean values may also be generated by using *logical operators* with simple Boolean expressions. The logical operators used by Pascal are **AND**, **OR**, and **NOT**. **AND** and **OR** are used to connect two Boolean expressions. **NOT** is used to negate the Boolean value of an expression; hence, it is sometimes referred to as *negation*. When these connectives or negation are used to generate Boolean values, the complete expression is referred to as a *compound Boolean expression*.

If **AND** is used to join two simple Boolean expressions, the resulting compound expression is **true** only when both simple expressions are **true**. If

OR is used, the result is **true** if either or both of the expressions are **true**. This is summarized as follows:

Expression 1 (E1)	Expression 2 (E2)	E1 AND E2	E1 OR E2
true	true	true	true
true	false	false	true
false	true	false	true
false	false	false	false

As previously indicated, **NOT** merely produces the logical complement of an expression as follows:

Expression (E)	NOT E
true	false
false	true

When using these operators with relational expressions, parentheses are required because logical operators are evaluated before relational operators. Illustrations of the Boolean values generated using logical operators are given in Table 4.3.

TABLE 4.3
Values of compound
Boolean expressions

Expression	Boolean Value
$(4.2 >= 5.0)$ **AND** $(8 = (3 + 5))$	**false**
$(4.2 >= 5.0)$ **OR** $(8 = (3 + 5))$	**true**
$(-2 < 0)$ **AND** $(18 >= 10)$	**true**
$(-2 < 0)$ **OR** $(18 >= 10)$	**true**
$(3 > 5)$ **AND** $(14.1 = 0.0)$	**false**
$(3 > 5)$ **OR** $(14.1 = 0.0)$	**false**
NOT $(18 = (10 + 8)$	**false**
NOT $(-4 > 0)$	**true**

Complex Boolean expressions can be generated by using several logical operators in an expression. The priority for evaluating these operators is

Operator	Priority
NOT	1
AND	2
OR	3

When complex expressions are being evaluated, the logical operators, arithmetic expressions, and relational operators are evaluated during successive passes through the expression. The priority list is now as follows:

Expression or Operation	Priority
( )	Evaluate from inside out
NOT	Evaluate from left to right
*, /, **MOD, DIV, AND**	Evaluate from left to right
+, −, **OR**	Evaluate from left to right
$<, <=, >, >=, =, <>$	Evaluate from left to right

George Boole

George Boole was born in 1815 in Lincoln, England. Boole was the son of a small shopkeeper and his family belonged to the lowest social class. In an attempt to rise above his station, Boole spent his early years teaching himself Latin and Greek. During this period, he also received elementary instruction in mathematics from his father.

At the age of 16, Boole worked as a teacher in an elementary school. He used most of his wages to help support his parents. At the age of 20 (after a brief, unsuccessful attempt to study for the clergy), he opened his own school. As part of his preparation for running his school, he had to learn more mathematics. This activity led to the development of some of the most significant mathematics of the nineteenth century.

Boole's major contributions were in the field of logic. An indication of his genius is given by the fact that his early work included the discovery of invariants. The mathematical significance of this is perhaps best explained by noting that the theory of relativity developed by Albert Einstein would not have been possible without the previous work on invariants.

Boole's first published contribution was *The Mathematical Analysis of Logic*, which appeared in 1848 while he was still working as an elementary teacher and the sole support for his parents. In 1849, he was appointed Professor of Mathematics at Queen's College in Cork, Ireland. The relative freedom from financial worry and time constraints the college appointment provided allowed him to pursue his work in mathematics. His masterpiece, *An Investigation of the Laws of Thought, on which Are Founded the Mathematical Theories of Logic and Probabilities*, was published in 1854. Boole was then 39, relatively old for such original work. According to Bertrand Russell, pure mathematics was discovered by Boole in this work.

The brilliance of Boole's work laid the foundation for what is currently studied as formal logic. The data type, Boolean, is named in honor of Boole because of his contribution to the development of logic as part of mathematics. Boole died in 1864. His early death resulted from pneumonia contracted by keeping a lecture engagement when he was soaked to the skin.

Thus, an expression like

```
0 < X AND X < 2
```

produces an error. It must be written as

```
(0 < X) AND (X < 2).
```

The following examples illustrate evaluation of some complex Boolean expressions.

■ **EXAMPLE 4.2**

```
(3 < 5) OR (21 <> 18) AND (-81 > 0)  ⎫
   ↓                                  ⎪
  TRUE OR (21 <> 18) AND (-81 > 0)    ⎬ first  pass
                ↓                     ⎪ (parentheses  first)
  true  OR    true   AND (-81 > 0)    ⎭
                              ↓
  true  OR    true   AND    false   ⎫ second pass
                       ↓
  true  OR              false       ⎬ third pass
         ↓
       true                         ⎭
```

■ EXAMPLE 4.3

```
NOT ((-5.0 >= -6.2)  OR  ((7 <> 3)  AND  (6 = (3 + 3))))
          ↓                    ↓                    ↓
NOT (     true       OR  (  true     AND  (6 =    6   )))
                                               ↓
NOT (     true       OR  (  true     AND  (true       ))
                                      ↓
NOT (     true       OR            true               )
                     ↓
NOT                  true
                     ↓
          false
```

■   ■

Exercises 4.1

1. Assume the variable declaration section of a program is

   ```
   VAR
      Flag1, Flag2 : boolean;
   ```

   What output is produced by the following segment of code?

   ```
   Flag1 := true;
   Flag2 := false;
   writeln (Flag1, true:6, Flag2:8);
   Flag1 := Flag2;
   writeln (Flag2:20);
   ```

2. Write a test program that illustrates what happens when Boolean expressions are not enclosed in parentheses. For example,

   ```
   3 < 5 AND 8.0 <> 4 * 3
   ```

3. Assume the variable declaration section of a program is

   ```
   VAR
      Ch : char;
      Flag : boolean;
   ```

   Indicate if the following assignment statements are valid or invalid.

   a. `Flag := !true';`   d. `Ch := Flag;`
   b. `Flag := T;`   e. `Ch := true;`
   c. `Flag := true;`   f. `Ch := 'T';`

4. Evaluate each of the following expressions:

   a. `(3 > 7) AND (2 < 0) OR (6 = 3 + 3)`
   b. `((3 > 7) AND (2 < 0)) OR (6 = 3 + 3)`
   c. `(3 > 7) AND ((2 < 0) OR (6 = 3 + 3))`
   d. `NOT ((-4.2 <> 3.0) AND (10 < 20))`
   e. `(NOT (-4.2 <> 3.0)) OR (NOT (10 < 20))`

5. For each of the following simple Boolean expressions, indicate whether it is **true, false,** or invalid.

   a. `-3.01 <= -3.001`
   b. `-3.0 = -3`
   c. `25 - 10 <> 3 * 5`
   d. `42 MOD 5 < 42 DIV 5`
   e. `-5 * (3 + 2) > 2 * (-10)`
   f. `10 / 5 < 1 + 1`
   g. `3 + 8 MOD 5 >= 6 - 12 MOD 2`

6. For each of the following expressions, indicate whether it is valid or invalid. Evaluate those that are valid.

   a. `3 < 4 OR 5 <> 6`

   b. `NOT 3.0 = 6 / 2`

   c. `NOT (true OR false)`

   d. `NOT true OR false`

   e. `NOT true OR NOT false`

   f. `NOT (18 < 25) AND OR (-3 < 0)`

   g. `8 * 3 < 20 + 10`

7. Assume the variable declaration section of a program is

   ```
   VAR
     Int1, Int2 : integer;
     Rl1, Rl2 : real;
     Flag1, Flag2 : boolean;
   ```

   and the values of the variables are

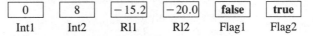

0	8	−15.2	−20.0	**false**	**true**
Int1	Int2	Rl1	Rl2	Flag1	Flag2

   Evaluate each of the following expressions:

   a. `(Int1 <= Int2) OR NOT (Rl2 = Rl1)`

   b. `NOT (Flag1) OR NOT (Flag2)`

   c. `NOT (Flag1 AND Flag2)`

   d. `((Rl1-Rl2) < 100/Int2) AND ((Int1 < 1) AND NOT (Flag2))`

   e. `NOT ((Int2 - 16 DIV 2) = Int1) AND Flag1`

8. DeMorgan's Laws state the following:

   a. **NOT** (A **OR** B) is equivalent to (**NOT** A) **AND** (**NOT** B)

   b. **NOT** (A **AND** B) is equivalent to (**NOT** A) **OR** (**NOT** B)

   Write a test program that demonstrates the validity of each of these equivalent statements.

   ■ ■ ■ ■

■ 4.2
IF . . . THEN Statements

The first decision-making statement we will examine is the **IF . . . THEN** statement. **IF . . . THEN** is used to make a program do something only when certain conditions are used. The form and syntax for an **IF . . . THEN** statement are

> **IF** ⟨Boolean expression⟩ **THEN**
>   ⟨statement⟩;

where ⟨statement⟩ represents any Pascal statement.

The Boolean expression can be any valid expression that is either **true** or **false** at the time of evaluation. If it is **true,** the statement following the reserved word **THEN** is executed. If it is **false,** control is transferred to the first program statement following the complete **IF . . . THEN** statement. In general, code would have the form

```
⟨statement 1⟩;
IF ⟨Boolean expression⟩ THEN
   ⟨statement 2⟩;
⟨statement 3⟩;
```

as illustrated in Figure 4.1.

FIGURE 4.1
IF . . . THEN flow diagram

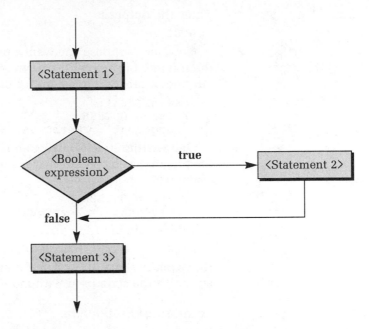

As a further illustration of how an **IF . . . THEN** statement works, consider the program fragment

```
Sum := 0.0;
read (Num);
IF Num > 0.0 THEN
   Sum := Sum + Num;
writeln (Sum:10:2);
```

If the value read is 75.85, prior to execution of the **IF . . . THEN** statement, the contents of Num and Sum are

75.85		0.0
Num		Sum

The Boolean expression Num > 0.0 is now evaluated and, since it is **true,** the statement

```
Sum := Sum + Num;
```

is executed and we have

75.85		75.85
Num		Sum

The next program statement is executed and produces the output

```
75.85
```

However, if the value read is -25.5, the variable values are

-25.5		0.0
Num		Sum

The Boolean expression Num > 0.0 is **false** and control is transferred to the line

```
writeln (Sum);
```

Thus, the output is

```
0.00
```

Now, let's suppose you want a program in which one objective is to count the number of zeros in the input. Assuming suitable initialization and declaration, a program fragment for this task could be

```
readln (Num);
IF Num = 0 THEN
   ZeroCount := ZeroCount + 1;
```

One writing style for using an **IF . . . THEN** statement calls for indenting the program statement to be executed if the Boolean expression is **true.** This, of course, is not required.

```
IF Num = 0 THEN
   ZeroCount := ZeroCount + 1;
```

could be written

```
IF Num = 0 THEN ZeroCount := Zerocount + 1;
```

However, the indenting style for simple **IF . . . THEN** statements is consistent with the style used with more elaborate conditional statements.

Compound Statements

The last concept needed before looking further at selection in Pascal is a *compound statement.* Simple statements conform to the syntax diagram for statements shown in Appendix 3. In a Pascal program, simple statements are separated by semicolons. Thus,

```
readln (A, B);
A := 3 * B;
writeln (A);
```

are three simple statements.

In some instances, it is necessary to perform several simple statements when some condition is true. For example, you may want the program to do certain things if a condition is true. In this situation, several simple statements that can be written as a single compound statement would be helpful. In general, there are several Pascal constructs that require compound statements. A compound statement is created by using the reserved words **BEGIN** and **END** at the beginning and end of a sequence of simple statements. Correct syntax for a compound statement is

```
BEGIN
   ⟨statement 1⟩;
   ⟨statement 2⟩;
        .
        .
        .
   ⟨statement n⟩
END;
```

Statements within a compound statement are separated by semicolons. The last statement before **END** does not require a semicolon, but if a semicolon is used here, it will not affect the program.

When a compound statement is executed within a program, the entire segment of code between **BEGIN** and **END** is treated as a single action. This is referred to as a *BEGIN . . . END block.* It is important that you develop a consistent, acceptable writing style for writing compound statements. What you use will vary according to your instructor's wishes and your personal preferences. Examples in this text will indent each simple statement within a compound statement two spaces. Thus,

```
BEGIN
  read (A, B);
  A := 3 * B;
  writeln (A)
END;
```

is a compound statement in a program; what it does is easily identified.

Using Compound Statements

As you might expect, compound statements can be (and frequently are) used as part of an **IF . . . THEN** statement. The form and syntax for this are

```
IF ⟨Boolean expression⟩ THEN
  BEGIN
    ⟨statement 1⟩;
    ⟨statement 2⟩;
        .
        .
        .
    ⟨statement n⟩
  END;
```

Program control is exactly as before depending on the value of the Boolean expression. For example, suppose you are writing a procedure to keep track of and compute fees for vehicles in a parking lot where separate records are kept for senior citizens. A segment of code in the procedure could be

```
IF Customer = 'S' THEN
  BEGIN
    SeniorCount := SeniorCount + 1;
    AmountDue := SeniorCitizenRate
  END;
```

IF . . . THEN Statements with Procedures

The next example designs a program to solve a problem using an **IF . . . THEN** statement with procedures.

■ **EXAMPLE 4.4**

Let's write a program that reads two integers and prints them in the order larger first, smaller second. The first-level pseudocode solution is

1. Read numbers
2. Determine larger
3. Print results

A structure chart for this is given in Figure 4.2.

FIGURE 4.2
Structure chart for
integer problem

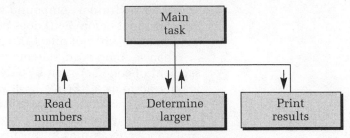

Procedures for ReadNumbers and PrintResults are similar to those used previously. Let's consider the module DetermineLarger. Data sent to this procedure will be two integers. Information returned will be the same two integers in the order larger, smaller. Code for this is

```
IF Num1 < Num2 THEN
  Switch (Num1, Num2);
```

where Switch is a procedure as follows:

```
PROCEDURE Switch (VAR Num1, Num2 : integer);
  VAR
    Temp : integer;
  BEGIN
    Temp := Num1;
    Num1 := Num2;
    Num2 := Temp
  END;  { of PROCEDURE Switch }
```

Note that an additional variable Temp is needed to temporarily hold the value of Num1. This type of exchange is used frequently throughout the text.
The main program for this is

```
BEGIN {  Main program  }
  ReadNumbers (Num1, Num2);
  IF Num1 < Num2 THEN
    Switch (Num1, Num2);
  PrintResults (Num1, Num2)
END.  { of main program  }
```

A complete program for this is

```
PROGRAM UseIFTHEN (input, output);

{  This short program illustrates using an IF...THEN statement; }
{  two numbers are read, then printed in order, larger first.   }

CONST
  Skip = ' ';

VAR
  Num1, Num2 : integer;            {  Two numbers to be arranged   }

{*****************************************************************}

PROCEDURE ReadNumbers (VAR Num1, Num2 : integer);

  {  Given:   Nothing                                            }
  {  Task:    Read two numbers entered from the keyboard         }
  {  Return:  Two integers                                       }

  BEGIN
    writeln;
    writeln ('Enter two integers and press <RETURN>.');
    readln (Num1, Num2)
  END;  { of PROCEDURE ReadNumbers  }
```

1

```
{*************************************************************}

PROCEDURE Switch (VAR Num1, Num2 : integer);

  {  Given:    Two integers, Num1 and Num2              }
  {  Task:     Use variable parameters to switch values  }
  {  Return:   Two integers, Num1 and Num2, with values  }
  {            switched, if in wrong order               }

  VAR
    Temp : integer;

  BEGIN
    Temp := Num1;
    Num1 := Num2;
    Num2 := Temp
  END;  {  of PROCEDURE Switch  }


{*************************************************************}

PROCEDURE PrintResults (Num1, Num2 : integer);

  {  Given:    Two integers                             }
  {  Task:     Print the integers with a suitable heading }
  {  Return:   Nothing                                   }

  BEGIN
    writeln;
    writeln (Skip:19, 'Larger number', Skip:10, 'Smaller number');
    writeln (Skip:19, '-------------', Skip:10, '--------------');
    writeln;
    writeln (Num1:26, Num2:23)
  END;  {  of PROCEDURE PrintResults  }

{*************************************************************}

BEGIN  {  Main program  }
  ReadNumbers (Num1, Num2);
  IF Num1 < Num2 THEN
    Switch (Num1, Num2);
  PrintResults (Num1, Num2)
END.  {  of main program  }
```

(brace spanning PROCEDURE Switch block) **2**

(brace spanning PROCEDURE PrintResults block) **3**

Sample runs of this program produce

```
                Enter two integers and press <RETURN>.
                ?35 115


                             Larger number        Smaller number
                             -------------         --------------

                                  115                    35

                Enter two integers and press <RETURN>.
                ?85 26


                             Larger number        Smaller number
                             -------------         --------------

                                   85                    26
```

Note that two runs of this program are required to test the logic of the **IF . . . THEN** statement.

Exercises 4.2

1. What is the output from each of the following program fragments? Assume the following assignment statements precede each fragment:

```
A := 10;
B := 5;
```

a.
```
IF A <= B THEN
    B := A;
writeln (A, B);
```

b.
```
IF A <= B THEN
    BEGIN
        B := A;
        writeln (A, B)
    END;
```

c.
```
IF A < B THEN
    Temp := A;
A := B;
B := Temp;
writeln (A, B);
```

d.
```
IF A < B THEN
    BEGIN
        Temp := A;
        A := B;
        B := Temp
    END;
writeln (A, B);
```

e.
```
IF (A < B) OR (B - A < 0) THEN
    BEGIN
        A := A + B;
        B := B - 1;
        writeln (A, B)
    END;
writeln (A, B);
```

f.
```
IF (A < B) AND (B - A < 0) THEN
    BEGIN
        A := A + B;
        B := B - 1;
        writeln (A, B)
    END;
writeln (A, B);
```

2. Write a test program to illustrate what happens when a semicolon is inadvertently inserted after **THEN** in an **IF . . . THEN** statement. For example,

```
IF A > 0 THEN;
    Sum := Sum + A;
```

3. Find and explain the errors in each of the following program fragments. You may assume all variables have been suitably declared.

a.
```
IF A := 10 THEN
    writeln (A);
```

b.
```
X := 7;
IF 3 < X < 10 THEN
    BEGIN
        X := X + 1;
        writeln (X)
    END;
```

c.
```
Count := 0;
Sum := 0;
A := 50;
IF A > 0 THEN
    Count := Count + 1;
    Sum := Sum + A;
```

d.
```
read (Ch);
IF Ch = 'A' OR 'B' THEN
    writeln (Ch:10);
```

4. What is the output from each of the following program fragments? Assume variables have been suitably declared.

   a.
   ```
   J := 18;
   IF J MOD 5 = 0 THEN
     writeln (J);
   ```

   b.
   ```
   A := 5;
   B := 90;
   B := B DIV A - 5;
   IF B > A THEN
     B := A * 30;
   writeln (A, B);
   ```

5. Can a simple statement be written using a **BEGIN . . . END** block? Write a short program that allows you to verify your answer.

6. Discuss the differences in the following programs. Predict the output for each program using sample values for Num.

   a.
   ```
   PROGRAM Exercise6a (input, output);
   VAR
     Num : integer;
   BEGIN
     writeln ('Enter an integer and press <RETURN>.');
     readln (Num);
     IF Num > 0 THEN
       writeln;
       writeln ('The number is':22, Num:6);
       writeln;
       writeln ('The number squared is':30, Num *
                Num:6);
       writeln ('The number cubed is':28, Num * Num *
                Num:6);
       writeln
   END.
   ```

   b.
   ```
   PROGRAM Exercise6b (input, output);
   VAR
     Num : integer;
   BEGIN  {  Main program  }
     writeln ('Enter an integer and press <RETURN>.');
     readln (Num);
     IF Num > 0 THEN
       BEGIN  {  Start output  }
         writeln;
         writeln ('The number is':22, Num:6);
         writeln;
         writeln ('The number squared is':30, Num * Num:6);
         writeln ('The number cubed is':28, Num * Num *
                  Num:6);
         writeln
       END  {  output for one number  }
   END.
   ```

7. Discuss writing style and readability of compound statements.

8. Find all errors in the following compound statements.

   a.
   ```
   BEGIN
     read (A)
     writeln (A)
   END;
   ```

```
b. BEGIN
      Sum := Sum + Num
   END;
c. BEGIN
      read (Size1, Size2);
      writeln (Size1:8, Size2:8)
   END.
d. BEGIN
      readln (Age, Weight);
      TotalAge := TotalAge + Age;
      TotalWeight := TotalWeight + Weight;
      writeln (Age:8, Weight:8)
```

9. Write a single compound statement that will:
   a. Read three integers from the keyboard.
   b. Add them to a previous total.
   c. Print the numbers on one line.
   d. Skip a line (output).
   e. Print the new total.

10. Write a program fragment that reads three reals, counts the number of positive reals, and accumulates the sum of positive reals.

11. Write a program fragment that reads three characters and then prints them only if they have been read in alphabetical order (for example, print "boy" but do not print "dog").

12. Given two integers, A and B, A is a divisor of B if B **MOD** A = 0. Write a complete program that reads two positive integers A and B and then, if A is a divisor of B,
    a. Print A.
    b. Print B.
    c. Print the result of B divided by A.

    For example, the output could be

```
A is 14
B is 42
B divided by A is 3
```

■ ■ ■ ■

■ 4.3
IF . . . THEN . . . ELSE Statements

Form and Syntax

The previous section discussed the one-way selection statement **IF . . . THEN**. The second selection statement we will examine is the two-way selection statement **IF . . . THEN . . . ELSE**. Correct form and syntax for **IF . . . THEN . . . ELSE** are

> **IF** ⟨Boolean expression⟩ **THEN**
>   ⟨statement⟩
> **ELSE**
>   ⟨statement⟩;

Flow of control when using an **IF . . . THEN . . . ELSE** statement is as follows:

1. The Boolean expression is evaluated.
2. If the Boolean expression is **true,** the statement following **THEN** is executed and control is transferred to the first program statement following the complete **IF . . . THEN . . . ELSE** statement.
3. If the Boolean expression is **false,** the statement following **ELSE** is executed and control is transferred to the first program statement following the **IF . . . THEN . . . ELSE** statement.

A flow diagram is given in Figure 4.3.

FIGURE 4.3
IF . . . THEN . . . ELSE
flow diagram

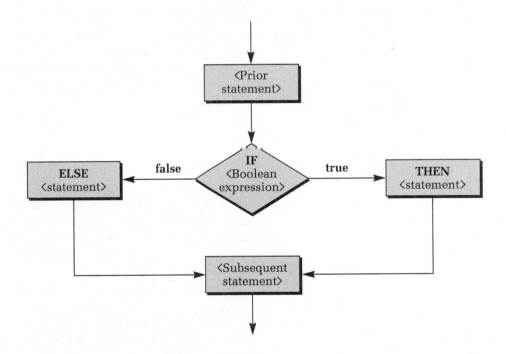

A few points to remember concerning **IF . . . THEN . . . ELSE** statements are:

1. The Boolean expression can be any valid expression having a value of **true** or **false** at the time it is evaluated.
2. The complete **IF . . . THEN . . . ELSE** statement is one program statement and is separated from other complete statements by a semicolon whenever appropriate.
3. There is no semicolon preceding the reserved word **ELSE**. A semicolon preceding the reserved word **ELSE** causes the compiler to treat the **IF . . . THEN** portion as a complete program statement and the **ELSE** portion as a separate statement. This produces an error message indicating that **ELSE** is being used without an **IF . . . THEN.**
4. Writing style should include indenting within the **ELSE** option in a manner consistent with indenting in the **IF . . . THEN** option.

■ EXAMPLE 4.5

Let's write a program fragment to keep separate counts of the negative and nonnegative numbers entered as data. Assuming all variables have been suitably declared and initialized, an **IF . . . THEN . . . ELSE** statement could be used as follows:

```
writeln ('Please enter a number and press <RETURN>.');
readln (Num);
IF Num < 0 THEN
  NegCount := NegCount + 1
ELSE
  NonNegCount := NonNegCount + 1;
```

■   ■

Using Compound Statements

Program statements in both the **IF . . . THEN** option and the **ELSE** option can be compound statements. When using compound statements in these options, you should use a consistent, readable indenting style; remember to use **BEGIN . . . END** for each compound statement; and do not put a semicolon before **ELSE**.

■ EXAMPLE 4.6

Suppose you want a program to read a number, count it as negative or nonnegative, and print it in either a column of nonnegative numbers or a column of negative numbers. Assuming all variables have been suitably declared and initialized, the fragment might be

```
writeln ('Please enter a number and press <RETURN>.');
readln (Num);
IF Num < 0 THEN
  BEGIN
    NegCount := NegCount + 1;
    writeln (Num:15)
  END  { of IF...THEN option  }
ELSE
  BEGIN
    NonNegCount := NonNegCount + 1;
    writeln (Num:30)
  END; { of ELSE option  }
```

■   ■

We next consider an example of a program fragment that requires the use of compound statements within an **IF . . . THEN . . . ELSE** statement.

■ EXAMPLE 4.7

Let's write a function that computes gross wages for an employee of the Florida OJ Canning Company. Input includes hours worked and the hourly rate. Overtime (more than 40 hours) pay is computed as time-and-a-half. A function would be

```
FUNCTION ComputeWages (Hours, PayRate : real) : real;
  VAR
    Overtime : real;
  BEGIN
    IF Hours <= 40.0 THEN
      ComputeWages := Hours * PayRate
    ELSE
      BEGIN
        Overtime := 1.5 * (Hours - 40.0) * PayRate;
        ComputeWages := 40 * PayRate + Overtime
      END
  END;  { of FUNCTION ComputeWages }
```

Robust Programs

If a program is completely protected against all possible crashes from bad data and unexpected values, it is said to be *robust.* The preceding examples have all assumed that desired data would be accurately entered from the keyboard. In actual practice, this is seldom the case. **IF . . . THEN . . . ELSE** statements can be used to guard against bad data entries. For example, if a program is designed to use positive numbers, you could guard against negatives and zero by

```
writeln ('Enter a positive number and press <RETURN>.');
readln (Number);
IF Number <= 0 THEN
  writeln ('You entered a nonpositive number.');
ELSE
  .
  .    (code for expected action here)
  .
```

This program protection can be used anywhere in a program. For example, if you are finding square roots of numbers, you could avoid a program crash by

```
IF Num < 0 THEN
  writeln ('The number ', Num, ' is negative.')
ELSE
  .
  .    (rest of action here)
  .
```

In actual practice, students need to balance robustness against amount of code and efficiency. An overemphasis on making a program robust can detract from time spent learning new programming concepts. You should discuss this with your instructor and decide what is best for your situation. Generally, there should be an agreement between the programmer and the customer regarding the level of robustness required. For most programs and examples in this text, it is assumed that valid data are entered when requested.

Guarding against Overflow

As we discussed in Chapter 2, integer overflow occurs when the absolute value of an integer exceeds **maxint** and real overflow occurs when a value is obtained that is too large to be stored in a memory location. Both of these

Artificial Intelligence

Artificial intelligence (AI) research seeks to understand the principles of human intelligence and apply those principles to the creation of smarter computer programs. The original goal of AI research was to create programs with humanlike intelligence and capabilities, yet after many years of research, little progress has been made toward this goal.

In recent years, however, AI researchers have pursued much more modest goals with much greater success. Programs based on AI techniques are playing increasingly important roles in such down-to-earth areas as medicine, education, recreation, business, and industry. Such programs come nowhere near to achieving human levels of intelligence, but they often have capabilities that are not easily achieved with non-AI programs.

The main principles of AI can be summarized as follows:

Search: a method whereby the computer solves a problem by searching through all logically possible solutions.

Rules: knowledge about what actions to take in particular circumstances is stored as rules; each rule has the form

IF ⟨situation⟩ **THEN** ⟨action or conclusion⟩

Reasoning: programs can use reasoning to draw conclusions from the facts and rules available to the program.

Planning: the control program plans the actions that must be taken to accomplish a particular goal, then modifies the plan if unexpected obstacles are encountered; this is most widely used in robot control.

Pattern recognition: important for rule-based systems, the **IF** part of a rule specifies a particular pattern of facts; the rule is to be applied when that pattern is recognized in the facts known to the program.

Knowledge bases: storage of the facts and rules that govern the operation of an AI program.

values vary according to the complier being used. The maximum value of an integer is stored in **maxint**. Unfortunately, there is no convenient analogue for reals. You will need to check your system manual to determine how large a real can be. Typically, this limit will be given in the form $9999 * 10^x$. Both the number of nines and the integer x will vary.

One method that is used to guard against integer overflow is based on the principle of checking a number against some function of **maxint**. Thus, if you want to multiply a number by 10, you would first compare it to **maxint DIV** 10. A typical segment of code could be

```
IF Num > maxint DIV 10 THEN
   .
   .    (overflow message)
   .
ELSE
   BEGIN
     Num := Num * 10;
       .
       .   (rest of action)
       .
   END;
```

We can now use this same idea with a **boolean** valued function. For example, consider the function

```
FUNCTION NearOverflow (Num : integer) : boolean;
   BEGIN
     NearOverflow := (Num > maxint DIV 10)
   END;
```

This could be used in the following manner:

```
IF NearOverflow (Num) THEN
   .
   .  (overflow message)
   .
ELSE
   BEGIN
     Num := Num * 10;
        .
        .  (rest of action)
        .
   END;
```

Exercises 4.3

1. What output is produced from each of the following program fragments? Assume all variables have been suitably declared.

   a.
   ```
   A := -14;
   B := 0;
   IF A < B THEN
      writeln (A, abs(A))
   ELSE
      writeln (A * B);
   ```

   b.
   ```
   A := 50;
   B := 25;
   Count := 0;
   Sum := 0;
   IF A = B THEN
      writeln (A, B)
   ELSE
      BEGIN
        Count := Count + 1;
        Sum := Sum + A + B;
        writeln (A, B)
      END;
   writeln (Count, Sum);
   ```

   c.
   ```
   Temp := 0;
   A := 10;
   B := 5;
   IF A > B THEN
      writeln (A, B)
   ELSE
      Temp := A;
      A := B;
      B := Temp;
   writeln (A, B);
   ```

2. Write a test program that illustrates what error message occurs when a semicolon precedes **ELSE** in an **IF . . . THEN . . . ELSE** statement. For example,

   ```
   PROGRAM SyntaxError (output);
   VAR
     A, B : integer;
   BEGIN
     A := 10;
     B := 5;
     IF A < B THEN
        writeln (A);
     ELSE
        writeln (B)
   END.
   ```

3. Find all errors in the following program fragments.

a.
```
IF Ch <> ' .' THEN
    CharCount := CharCount + 1;
    writeln (Ch)
ELSE
    PeriodCount := PeriodCount + 1;
```

b.
```
IF Age < 20 THEN
    BEGIN
        YoungCount := YoungCount + 1;
        YoungAge := YoungAge + Age
    END;
ELSE
    BEGIN
        OldCount := OldCount + 1;
        OldAge := OldAge + Age
    END;
```

c.
```
IF Age < 20 THEN
    BEGIN
        YoungCount := YoungCount + 1;
        YoungAge := YoungAge + Age
    END
ELSE
    OldCount := OldCount + 1;
    OldAge := OldAge + Age;
```

4. Write a program to balance your checkbook. Your program should get an entry from the keyboard, keep track of the number of deposits and checks, and keep a running balance. The data consist of a character, D (deposit) or C (check), followed by an amount.

■ ■ ■ ■

■ 4.4
Nested and Extended IF Statements

Multiway Selection

Sections 4.2 and 4.3 examined one-way (**IF . . . THEN**) and two-way (**IF . . . THEN . . . ELSE**) selection. Since each of these is a single Pascal statement, either can be used as part of a selection statement to achieve multiple selection. In this case, the multiple selection statement is referred to as a *nested IF statement*. These nested statements can be any combination of **IF . . . THEN** or **IF . . . THEN . . . ELSE** statements.

To illustrate, let's write a program fragment to issue interim progress reports for students in a class. If a student's score is below 50, the student is failing. If the score is between 50 and 69 inclusive, the progress is unsatisfactory. If the score is 70 or above, the progress is satisfactory. The first decision to be made is based on whether the score is below 50 or not; the design is

```
IF Score >= 50 THEN
    .
    .   (progress report here)
    .
ELSE
    writeln ('You are currently failing.':34);
```

We now use a nested **IF . . . THEN . . . ELSE** statement for the progress report for students who are not failing. The complete fragment is

```
IF Score >= 50 THEN
   IF Score > 69 THEN
      writeln ('Your progress is satisfactory.':38)
   ELSE
      writeln ('Your progress is unsatisfactory.':40)
ELSE
   writeln ('You are currently failing.':34);
```

One particular instance of nesting selection statements requires special development. When additional **IF . . . THEN . . . ELSE** statements are used in the **ELSE** option, we call this an *extended IF statement* and use the following form:

IF ⟨condition 1⟩ **THEN**

    .

    .   (action 1 here)

    .

ELSE IF ⟨condition 2⟩ **THEN**

    .

    .   (action 2 here)

    .

ELSE IF ⟨condition 3⟩ **THEN**

    .

    .   (action 3 here)

    .

ELSE

    .

    .   (action 4 here)

    .

Using this form, we could redesign the previous fragment that printed progress reports as follows:

```
IF Score > 69 THEN
   writeln ('Your progress is satisfactory.':38)
ELSE IF Score > 50 THEN
   writeln ('Your progress is unsatisfactory.':40)
ELSE
   writeln ('You are currently failing.':34);
```

If you trace through both fragments with scores of 40, 60, and 80, you will see they produce identical output.

Another method of writing the nested fragment is to use sequential selection statements as follows:

```
IF Score > 69 THEN
   writeln ('Your progress is satisfactory.':38);
IF (Score <= 69) AND (Score >= 50) THEN
   writeln ('Your progress is unsatisfactory.':40);
IF Score < 50 THEN
   writeln ('You are currently failing.':34);
```

However, this is less efficient because each **IF . . . THEN** statement is executed each time through the program. You should generally avoid using sequential **IF . . . THEN** statements if a nested statement can be used; this reduces execution time for a program.

Tracing the flow of logic through nested or extended **IF** statements can be tedious. However, it is essential that you develop this ability. For practice, let's trace through the following example.

Consider the nested statement

```
IF A > 0 THEN
  IF A MOD 2 = 0 THEN
    Sum1 := Sum1 + A
  ELSE
    Sum2 := Sum2 + A
ELSE IF A = 0 THEN
  writeln ('A is zero':18)
ELSE
  NegSum := NegSum + A;
writeln ('All done':17);
```

We will trace through this statement and discover what action is taken when A is assigned 20, 15, 0, and −30, respectively. For A := 20, the statement A > 0 is **true,** hence

```
A MOD 2 = 0
```

is evaluated. This is **true,** so

```
Sum1 := Sum1 + A
```

is executed and control is transferred to

```
writeln ('All done':17);
```

For A := 15, A > 0 is **true** and

```
A MOD 2 = 0
```

is evaluated. This is **false,** so

```
Sum2 := Sum2 + A
```

is executed and control is again transferred out of the nested statement to

```
writeln ('All done':17);
```

For A := 0, A > 0 is **false,** thus

```
A = 0
```

is evaluated. Since this is **true,** the statement

```
writeln ('A is zero':18)
```

is executed and control is transferred to

```
writeln ('All done':17);
```

Finally, for A := −30, A > 0 is **false,** thus

```
A = 0
```

is evaluated. This is **false,** so

```
NegSum := NegSum + A;
```

is executed and then control is transferred to

```
writeln ('All done':17);
```

■   ■

Note that this example traces through all possibilities involved in the nested statement. This is essential to guarantee your statement is properly constructed.

Designing solutions to problems that require multiway selection can be difficult. A few guidelines can help. If a decision has two courses of action and one is complex and the other is fairly simple, nest the complex part in the **IF . . . THEN** option and the simple part in the **ELSE** option. This method is frequently used to check for bad data. An example of the program design for this could be:

```
    .
    .  (get the data)
    .
IF DataOK THEN
    .
    .  (complex action here)
    .
ELSE
(message about bad data)
```

This method could also be used to guard against dividing by zero in computation. For instance, we could have

```
Divisor := <value>;
IF Divisor <> 0 THEN
    .
    .  (proceed with action)
    .
ELSE
  writeln ('Division by zero');
```

When there are several courses of action that can be considered sequentially, an extended **IF ... THEN ... ELSE** should be used. To illustrate, consider the program fragment of Example 4.9.

■ **EXAMPLE 4.9**

Let's write a program fragment that allows you to assign letter grades based on students' semester averages. Grades are to be assigned according to the scale

$100 >/ X >/ 90$	A
$90 > X >/ 80$	B
$80 > X >/ 70$	C
$70 > X >/ 55$	D
$55 > X$	E

Extended **IF**s can be used to accomplish this as follows:

```
IF Average >= 90 THEN
  Grade := 'A'
ELSE IF Average >= 80 THEN
  Grade := 'B'
ELSE IF Average >= 70 THEN
  Grade := 'C'
ELSE IF Average >= 55 THEN
  Grade := 'D'
ELSE
  Grade := 'E';
```

Since any Average over 100 or less than zero would be a sign of some data or program error, this example could be protected with a statement as follows:

```
IF (Average <= 100) AND (Average >= 0) THEN
    .
    .  (compute letter grade)
    .
ELSE
  writeln ('There is an error. Average is':38,
           Average:8:2);
```

■   ■

Protecting parts of a program in this manner will help you avoid unexpected results or program crashes. It also allows you to identify the source of an error.

Form and Syntax

The rule for matching **ELSE**s in nested selection statements is:

> *When an **ELSE** is encountered, it is matched with the most recent **THEN** that has not yet been matched.*

Matching **IF . . . THEN**s with **ELSE**s is a common source of errors. When designing programs, you should be very careful to match them correctly.

A situation that can lead to an error is an **IF . . . THEN . . . ELSE** statement such as

```
IF ⟨condition 1⟩ THEN
   .
   . ⟨action 1⟩
   .
ELSE
   .
   . ⟨action 2⟩
   .
```

where action 1 consists of an **IF . . . THEN** statement. Specifically, suppose you want a fragment of code to read a list of positive integers and print those that are perfect squares. A method of protecting against negative integers and zero could be:

```
readln (Num);
IF Num > 0 THEN
   .
   . (action 1 here)
   .
ELSE
  writeln (Num, ' is not positive.');
```

If we now develop action 1 so that it prints only those positive integers that are perfect squares, it is

```
IF sqrt(Num) = trunc(sqrt(Num)) THEN
   writeln (Num)
```

Nesting this selection statement in our design, we have

```
readln (Num);
IF Num > 0 THEN
  IF sqrt(Num) = trunc(sqrt(Num)) THEN
    writeln (Num)
ELSE
  writeln (Num, ' is not positive,');
```

If you now use this segment with input of 20 for Num, the output is

```
20 is not positive.
```

Thus, this fragment is not correct to solve the problem. The indenting is consistent with our intent, but the actual execution of the fragment treated the code as

```
readln (Num);
IF Num > 0 THEN
IF sqrt(Num) = trunc(sqrt(Num)) THEN
  writeln (Num)
ELSE
  writeln (Num, ' is not positive.');
```

because the **ELSE** is matched with the most recent **THEN**. This problem can be resolved two ways. First, you could use an **ELSE** option with an *empty (null) statement*. Thus, you would have

```
readln (Num);
IF Num > 0 THEN
  IF sqrt(Num) = trunc(sqrt(Num)) THEN
    writeln (Num)
  ELSE  {  Do nothing  }
ELSE
  writeln (Num, ' is not positive.');
```

Or you could redesign the fragment as follows:

```
readln (Num);
IF Num <= 0 THEN
  writeln (Num,' is not positive.');
ELSE IF sqrt(Num) = trunc(sqrt(Num)) THEN
  writeln (Num);
```

STYLE TIP

■ ■ ■ ■ ■ ■ ■ ■ ■ ■ ■ ■

It is very important to use a consistent, readable writing style when using nested or extended **IF** statements. The style used here for nested **IF** statements is to indent each nested statement two spaces. Also, each **ELSE** of an **IF . . . THEN . . . ELSE** statement is in the same column as the **IF** of that statement. This allows you to see at a glance where the **ELSE**s match with the **IF . . . THEN**s. For example,

IF . . . THEN
  IF . . . THEN
  ELSE
ELSE

An extended **IF** statement has all the **ELSE**s on the same indenting level as the first **IF**. This reinforces the concept of extended **IF**. For example,

IF . . . THEN
ELSE IF . . . THEN
ELSE IF . . . THEN
ELSE

We conclude this section with an example that uses nested **IF** statements.

■ **EXAMPLE 4.10**

Write a program that computes the gross pay for an employee of the Clean Products Corporation of America. The corporation produces three products: A, B, and C. Supervisors earn a commission of 7 percent of sales and representatives earn 5 percent. Bonuses of $100 are paid to supervisors whose commission exceeds $300 and to representatives whose commission exceeds $200. Input is in the form

S 18 15 10

where the first position contains an 'S' or 'R' for supervisor or representative, respectively. The next three integers include the number of units of each of the products sold. Since product prices may vary over time, the constant definition section will be used to indicate the current prices. The section for this problem will be

```
CONST
  SuperRate = 0.07;
  RepRate = 0.05;
  APrice = 13.95;
  BPrice = 17.95;
  CPrice = 29.95;
```

A first-level pseudocode development for this problem is

1. Get the data
2. Compute commission and bonus
3. Print heading
4. Print results

The structure chart for this is given in Figure 4.4.

FIGURE 4.4
Structure chart for the Clean Products Corporation of America problem

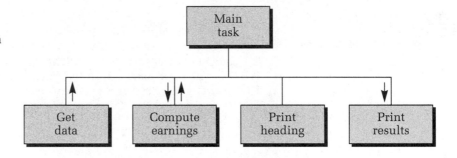

Module specifications for each of the main modules are

1. <u>GetData Module</u>
   Data received: None
   Information returned: Employee classification
   　　　　　　　　　　　　　　　Sales of products A, B, and C
   Logic: Read input data from the keyboard.

2. <u>ComputeCommAndBonus Module</u>
   Data received: Classification
   　　　　　　　　　　　ASales
   　　　　　　　　　　　BSales
   　　　　　　　　　　　CSales
   Information returned: ACommission
   　　　　　　　　　　　　　　　BCommission
   　　　　　　　　　　　　　　　CCommission
   　　　　　　　　　　　　　　　TotalCommission
   　　　　　　　　　　　　　　　Bonus
   Logic: **IF** a supervisor **THEN**
   　　　　　compute total commission
   　　　　　compute bonus

   　　　　ELSE
   　　　　　compute total commission
   　　　　　compute bonus

3. PrintHeading Module
   Data received: None
   Information returned: None
   Logic: Use **writeln** statements to print a heading for the report.

4. PrintResults Module
   Data received: Classification
                   ASales
                   BSales
                   CSales
                   ACommission
                   BCommission
                   CCommission
                   TotalCommission
                   Bonus
   Information returned: None
   Logic: Use **writeln** statements to print the employee's report.

Modules for GetData, PrintHeading, and PrintResults are similar to those previously developed. The module ComputeCommAndBonus requires some development. Step 2 of the pseudocode, "Compute commission and bonus" becomes

2.   Compute commission and bonus
    2.1 **IF** employee is supervisor **THEN**
          compute supervisor's earnings
       ELSE
          compute representative's earnings

where "compute supervisor's earnings" is refined to

    2.1.1   compute commission from sales of A
    2.1.2   compute commission from sales of B
    2.1.3   compute commission from sales of C
    2.1.4   compute total commission
    2.1.5   compute supervisor's bonus
          2.1.5.1 **IF** total commission > 300 **THEN**
                  bonus is 100.00
              ELSE
                  bonus is 0.00

A similar development follows for computing a representative's earnings. Step 3 will be an appropriate procedure to print a heading. Step 4 will contain whatever you feel is appropriate for output. It should include at least the number of sales, amount of sales, commissions, bonuses, and total compensation.

The main program for this problem is

```
BEGIN  { Main program  }
  GetData (Classification, ASales, BSales, CSales);
  ComputeCommAndBonus (Classification, ASales, BSales, CSales,
                   AComm, BComm, CComm, TotalCommission,
                   Bonus);
  PrintHeading;
  PrintResults (Classification, ASales, BSales, CSales,
             AComm, BComm, CComm, TotalCommission, Bonus)
END.  { of main program  }
```

A complete program for this is

```
PROGRAM ComputeEarnings (input, output);

{  This program computes gross pay for an employee. Note the    }
{  use of constants and selection.                              }

CONST
   CompanyName = 'Clean Products Corporation of America';
   Line = '-------------------------------------';
   SuperRate = 0.07;
   RepRate = 0.05;
   APrice = 13.95;
   BPrice = 17.95;
   CPrice = 29.95;
   Month = 'June';
   Skip = ' ';

VAR
   ASales, BSales, CSales : integer; { Sales of Products A, B, C }
   AComm, BComm, CComm,         { Commission on sales of A, B, C   }
   Bonus,                       { Bonus, if earned                 }
   TotalCommission : real;      { Commission on all products       }
   Classification : char;       { S-Supervisor or R-Representative }

{*******************************************************************}

PROCEDURE GetData (VAR Classification : char;
                   VAR ASales, BSales, CSales : integer);

{  Given:    Nothing                                              }
{  Task:     Have classification and sales amounts entered        }
{                   from the keyboard                             }
{  Return:   Classification, ASales, BSales, and CSales           }

   BEGIN
     writeln ('Enter S or R for classification.');
     readln (Classification);
     writeln ('Enter ASales, BSales, CSales');
     readln (ASales, BSales, CSales)
   END;   { of PROCEDURE GetData }

{*******************************************************************}

PROCEDURE ComputeCommAndBonus (Classification : char;
                               ASales, BSales, CSales : integer;
                               VAR AComm, BComm, CComm,
                               TotalCommission, Bonus : real);

   {  Given:    Employee classification and sales for products A,  }
   {                   B, and C                                    }
   {  Task:     Compute commission and bonus                       }
   {  Return:   Commission for each of products A, B, and C;       }
   {                   TotalCommission; and Bonus                  }

   BEGIN
     IF Classification = 'S' THEN              { Supervisor }
       BEGIN
         AComm := ASales * APrice * SuperRate;
         BComm := BSales * BPrice * SuperRate;
         CComm := CSales * CPrice * SuperRate;
         TotalCommission := AComm + BComm + CComm;
         IF TotalCommission > 300.0 THEN
           Bonus := 100.0
         ELSE
           Bonus := 0.0
       END
```

1

2

```
      ELSE                                    { Representative }
        BEGIN
          AComm := ASales * APrice * RepRate;
          BComm := BSales * BPrice * RepRate;
          CComm := CSales * CPrice * RepRate;
          TotalCommission := AComm + BComm + CComm;
          IF TotalCommission > 200.0 THEN
            Bonus := 100.0
          ELSE
            Bonus := 0.0
        END   { of ELSE option  }
    END;  { of PROCEDURE ComputeCommAndBonus }

{*****************************************************************}

PROCEDURE PrintHeading;
  { Given:   Nothing                                            }
  { Task:    Print a heading for the output                     }
  { Return:  Nothing                                            }

  BEGIN
    writeln;
    writeln (Skip:10, CompanyName);
    writeln (Skip:10, Line);
    writeln;
    writeln (Skip:10, 'Sales Report for', Month:10);
    writeln;
    write (Skip:10, 'Classification');
    IF Classification = 'S' THEN
      writeln (Skip:12, 'Supervisor')
    ELSE
      writeln (Skip:12, 'Representative');
    writeln;
    writeln (Skip:12, 'Product     Sales      Commission');
    writeln (Skip:12, '-------     -----      ----------');
    writeln
  END;  { of PROCEDURE PrintHeading }

{*****************************************************************}

PROCEDURE PrintResults (Classification : char;
                        ASales, BSales, CSales, : integer;
                        AComm, BComm, CComm,
                        TotalCommission, Bonus : real);

  { Given:   Employee classification; sales of products A, B,   }
  {          and C; commissions for products A, B, and C;       }
  {          total commission; and bonus                        }
  { Task:    Print the results in a readable form               }
  { Return:  Nothing                                            }

  BEGIN
    writeln (Skip:15, 'A', ASales:13, AComm:14:2);
    writeln (Skip:15, 'B', BSales:13, BComm:14:2);
    writeln (Skip:15, 'C', CSales:13, CComm:14:2);
    writeln;
    writeln ('Subtotal':31, '$':3, TotalCommission:9:2);
    writeln;
    writeln ('Your bonus is:':31, '$':3, Bonus:9:2)
    writeln ('------':43);
    writeln;
    writeln ('Total Due':31, '$':3, (TotalCommission + Bonus):9:2)
  END;  { of PROCEDURE PrintResults }

{*****************************************************************}
```

3

4

```
      BEGIN  { Main program }
        GetData (Classification, ASales, BSales, CSales);
        ComputeCommAndBonus (Classification, ASales, BSales, CSales,
                        AComm, BComm, CComm, TotalCommission, Bonus);
        PrintHeading;
        PrintResults (Classification, ASales, BSales, CSales, AComm,
                     BComm, CComm, TotalCommission, Bonus)
      END.  { of main program }
```

A sample run produces

```
      Enter R or S for classification.
      ?S
      Enter ASales, BSales, CSales
      ?1100 990 510


                     Clean Products Corporation of America
                     -------------------------------------

                     Sales Report for          June

                     Classification            Supervisor

                        Product      Sales     Commission
                        -------      -----     ----------

                          A          1100        1074.15
                          B           990        1243.93
                          C           510        1069.21

                                   Subtotal  $   3387.30

                             Your bonus is:  $    100.00
                                                 ------

                                  Total Due  $   3487.30
```

■   ■

Program Testing

In actual practice, a great deal of time is spent testing programs in an attempt to make them run properly when they are installed for some specific purpose. Formal program verification is discussed in Section 4.6 and is developed more fully in subsequent course work. However, examining the issue of which data are minimally necessary for program testing is appropriate when working with selection statements.

As you might expect, test data should include information that tests every logical branch in a program. Whenever a program contains an **IF . . . THEN . . . ELSE** statement of the form

```
IF ⟨condition⟩ THEN
   (action 1 here)
ELSE
   (action 2 here)
```

the test data should guarantee that both the **IF . . . THEN** and the **ELSE** option are executed.

Nesting and use of extended **IF** statements require a bit more care when selecting test data. In general, a single **IF . . . THEN . . . ELSE** statement requires at least two data items for testing. If an **IF . . . THEN . . . ELSE** statement is nested within the **IF . . . THEN** option, at least two more data items are required to test the nested selection statement.

For purposes of illustration, let's reexamine **PROCEDURE** ComputeComm AndBonus from Example 4.10. This procedure contains the logic

```
IF Classification = 'S' THEN
    .
    .
    .
   IF TotalCommission > 300.00 THEN
      .
      .
      .
   ELSE
      .
      .
      .
ELSE
   .
   .
   .
   IF TotalCommission > 200.00 THEN
      .
      .
      .
   ELSE
      .
      .
      .
```

To see what data should minimally be used to test this procedure, consider the following table:

Classification	Total Commission
'S'	400.00
'S'	250.00
'R'	250.00
'R'	150.00

It is a good idea to also include boundary conditions in the test data. Thus, the previous table could also have listed 300.00 as the total commission for 'S' and 200.00 as the total commission for 'R'.

In summary, you should always make sure every logical branch is executed when running the program with test data.

Exercises 4.4

1. Consider the program fragment

```
IF X >= 0.0 THEN
  IF X < 1000.00 THEN
    BEGIN
      Y := 2 * X;
      IF X <= 500 THEN
        X := X / 10
    END
  ELSE
    Y := 3 * X
ELSE
  Y := abs(X);
```

Indicate the values of X and Y after this fragment is executed for each of the following initial values of X.

a. X := 381.5;

b. X := -21.0;

c. X := 600.0;

d. X := 3000.0;

2. Write and run a test program that illustrates the checking of all branches of nested **IF** ... **THEN** ... **ELSE** statements.

3. Rewrite each of the following fragments using nested or extended **IF**s without compound conditions.

a.
```
IF (Ch = 'M') AND (Sum > 1000) THEN
   X := X + 1;
IF (Ch = 'M') AND (Sum <= 1000) THEN
   X := X + 2;
IF (Ch = 'F') AND (Sum > 1000) THEN
   X := X + 3;
IF (Ch = 'F') AND (Sum <= 1000) THEN
   X := X + 4;
```

b.
```
read (Num);
IF (Num > 0) AND (Num <= 10000) THEN
  BEGIN
    Count := Count + 1;
    Sum := Sum + Num
  END
ELSE
  writeln ('Value out of range':27);
```

c.
```
IF (A > 0) AND (B > 0) THEN
  writeln ('Both positive':22)
ELSE
  writeln ('Some negative':22);
```

d.
```
IF ((A > 0) AND (B > 0)) OR (C > 0) THEN
  writeln ('Option one':19)
ELSE
  writeln ('Option two':19);
```

4. Consider each of the following program fragments.

a.
```
IF A < 0 THEN
   IF B < 0 THEN
      A := B
ELSE
   A := B + 10;
writeln (A, B);
```

b.
```
IF A < 0 THEN
   BEGIN
      IF B < 0 THEN
         A := B
   END
ELSE
   A := B + 10;
writeln (A, B);
```

c.
```
IF A >= 0 THEN
   A := B + 10
ELSE IF B < 0 THEN
   A := B;
writeln (A, B);
```

```
d. IF A >= 0 THEN
      A := B + 10;
   IF B < 0 THEN
      A := B;
   writeln (A, B);
```

Indicate the output of each fragment for each of the following assignment statements.

```
 i. A := -5;
    B := 5;

 ii. A := -5;
     B := -3;

iii. A := 10;
     B := 8;

 iv. A := 10;
     B := -4;
```

5. Look back to Example 4.9, in which we assigned grades to students, and rewrite the grade assignment fragment using a different nesting. Could you rewrite it without using any nesting? Should you?

6. Many nationally based tests report scores and indicate in which quartile the score lies. Assuming the following quartile designation,

Score	Quartile
100–75	1
74–50	2
49–25	3
24–0	4

write a program to read a score from the keyboard and report in which quartile the score lies.

7. What are the values of A, B, and C after the following program fragment is executed?

```
A := -8;
B := 21;
C := A + B;
IF A > B THEN
   BEGIN
      A := B;
      C := A * B
   END
ELSE IF A < 0 THEN
   BEGIN
      A := abs(A);
      B := B - A;
      C := A * B
   END
ELSE
   C := 0;
```

8. Create minimal sets of test data for each part of Exercise 4 and for Exercise 7. Explain why each data item has been included.

9. Discuss a technique that could be used as a debugging aid to guarantee that all possible logical paths of a program have been used.

■ ■ ■ ■ ■

■ 4.5
CASE Statements

Thus far, this chapter has examined one-way selection, two-way selection, and multiway selection. Section 4.4 illustrated how multiple selection can be achieved using nested and extended **IF** statements. Since multiple selection can sometimes be difficult to follow, Pascal provides an alternative method of handling this concept, the **CASE** statement.

Form and Syntax

CASE statements can often be used when there are several options that depend on the value of a single variable or expression. The general structure for a **CASE** statement is

```
CASE ⟨selector⟩ OF
    ⟨label list 1⟩ : ⟨statement 1⟩;
    ⟨label list 2⟩ : ⟨statement 2⟩;
            .                .
            .                .
            .                .
    ⟨label list n⟩ : ⟨statement n⟩
END;
```

and is shown graphically in Figure 4.5.

FIGURE 4.5
CASE flow diagram

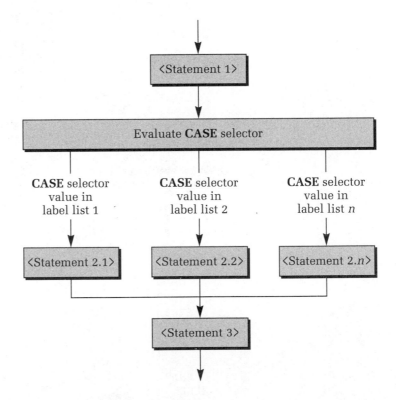

The selector can be any variable or expression whose value is any data type we have studied previously except for **real** (only ordinal data types can be used). Values of the selector constitute the label list. Thus, if Age is an integer variable whose values are restricted to 18, 19, and 20, we could have

```
CASE Age OF
  18 : ⟨statement 1⟩;
  19 : ⟨statement 2⟩;
  20 : ⟨statement 3⟩
END;
```

When this program statement is executed, the value of Age will determine to which statement control is transferred. More specifically, the program fragment

```
Age := 19;
CASE Age OF
  18 : writeln ('I just became a legal voter.');
  19 : writeln ('This is my second year to vote.');
  20 : writeln ('I am almost twenty-one.')
END;
```

produces the output

```
This is my second year to vote.
```

Before considering more examples, several comments are in order.

1. The flow of logic within a **CASE** statement is as follows:
   a. The value of the selector is determined
   b. The value is found in the label list
   c. The statement following the value in the list is executed
   d. Control is transferred to the first program statement following the **CASE** statement **END**
2. The selector can have a value of any type previously studied except **real**. Only ordinal data types may be used.
3. Several values, separated by commas, may appear on one line. For example, if Age could have any integer value from 15 to 25 inclusive, the **CASE** statement could appear as

```
CASE Age OF
  15, 16, 17     : ⟨statement 1⟩;
  18, 19, 20, 21 : ⟨statement 2⟩;
  22, 23, 24     : ⟨statement 3⟩;
  25             : ⟨statement 4⟩
END;
```

4. All possible values of the **CASE** selector do not have to be listed. However, if a value that is not listed is used, most versions of Pascal produce a run-time error message and execution is terminated. Consequently, it is preferable to list all values of the **CASE** selector. If certain values require no action, list them on the same option with a null statement; for example,

```
CASE Age OF
  18 : ⟨statement 1⟩;
  19 : ;  {  Do nothing  }
  20 : ⟨statement 2⟩
END;
```

5. Values for the selector can appear only once in the list. Thus,

```
CASE Age OF
  18        : ⟨statement 1⟩;
  18, 19    : ⟨statement 2⟩;  {  error  }
  20        : ⟨statement 3⟩
END;
```

produces an error since it is not clear which statement should be executed when the value of Age is 18.

6. Proper syntax for using **CASE** statements includes
   a. a colon separates each label from its respective statement;
   b. a semicolon follows each statement option except the statement preceding **END**;
   c. commas are placed between labels on the same option.
7. **END** is used without a **BEGIN.** This is our first instance of this happening. An appropriate program comment should indicate the end of a **CASE** statement. Therefore, our examples will include

```
END;  {  of CASE  }
```

8. Statements for each option can be compound; if they are, they must be in a **BEGIN . . . END** block.

STYLE TIP

Writing style for a **CASE** statement should be consistent with your previously developed style. The lines containing options should be indented, the colons should be lined up, and **END** should start in the same column as **CASE.** Thus, a typical **CASE** statement is

```
CASE Score OF
  10, 9, 8     : writeln ('Excellent');
  7, 6, 5      : writeln ('Fair');
  4, 3, 2, 1, 0 : writeln ('Failing')
END;  {  of CASE Score  }
```

At this stage, let's consider several examples that illustrate various uses of **CASE** statements. Since our purpose is for illustration, the examples will be somewhat contrived. Later examples will serve to illustrate how these statements are used in solving problems.

■ EXAMPLE 4.11

The selector can have a value of type **char,** and the ordinal of the character determines the option. Thus, the label list must contain the appropriate characters in single quotation marks. If Grade has values 'A', 'B', 'C', 'D', or 'E', a **CASE** statement could be

```
CASE Grade OF
  'A' : Points := 4.0;
  'B' : Points := 3.0;
  'C' : Points := 2.0;
  'D' : Points := 1.0;
  'E' : Points := 0.0
END;  {  of CASE Grade  }
```

■ **EXAMPLE 4.12**

To avoid inappropriate values for the **CASE** selector, the entire **CASE** statement may be protected by using an **IF . . . THEN . . . ELSE** statement. For example, suppose you are using a **CASE** statement for number of days worked. You expect the values to be 1, 2, 3, 4, or 5, so you could protect the statement by

```
IF (NumDays > 0) AND (NumDays < 6) THEN
  CASE NumDays OF
    1 : ⟨statement 1⟩;
    2 : ⟨statement 2⟩;
    3 : ⟨statement 3⟩;
    4 : ⟨statement 4⟩;
    5 : ⟨statement 5⟩
  END  {  of CASE NumDays  }
ELSE
  writeln ('Value of NumDays', NumDays, 'is out of range.');
```

A good debugging technique is to print the value of the selector in your **ELSE** statement.

■

■

■ **EXAMPLE 4.13**

Compound statements can be used with any or all of the options in the following form.

```
CASE Age OF
  18 : BEGIN
          .
          .
          .
       END;
  19 : BEGIN
          .
          .
          .
       END;
  20 : BEGIN
          .
          .
          .
       END
END;  {  of CASE Age  }
```

■

■

OTHERWISE Option

T Some versions of Pascal provide an additional reserved word and option, **OTHERWISE,** which can be used with **CASE** statements. The general structure for this option is

```
CASE ⟨selector⟩ OF
  ⟨label 1⟩ : ⟨statement 1⟩;
            .
            .
            .
  ⟨label n⟩ : ⟨statement n⟩
OTHERWISE
  ⟨statement 1⟩;
  ⟨statement 2⟩;
            .
            .
            .
  ⟨statement n⟩
END;    {      of CASE      }
```

This option can be used if the same action is to be taken for several values of the **CASE** selector. It can also be used to protect against a **CASE** selector that is out of range. Note that the statements following **OTHERWISE** are executed sequentially and do not have to be in a **BEGIN** . . . **END** block. You should check your version of Pascal to see if this option is available to you.

Equivalent of Extended IFs

As previously indicated, **CASE** statements can sometimes (ordinal data types) be used instead of extended **IFs** when multiple selection is required for solving a problem. The following example illustrates this use.

■ **EXAMPLE 4.14**

Let us rewrite the following program fragment using a **CASE** statement.

```
IF (Score = 10) OR (Score = 9) THEN
   Grade := 'A'
ELSE IF (Score = 8) OR (Score = 7) THEN
   Grade := 'B'
ELSE IF (Score = 6) OR (Score = 5) THEN
   Grade := 'C'
ELSE
   Grade := 'E';
```

If we assume Score is an integer variable with values 0, 1, 2, . . . , 10, we could use a **CASE** statement as follows:

```
CASE Score OF
  10, 9        : Grade := 'A';
   8, 7        : Grade := 'B';
   6, 5        : Grade := 'C';
   4, 3, 2, 1, 0 : Grade := 'E'
END; {  of CASE Score  }
```

■   ■

Use in Problems

CASE statements should not be used for relational tests involving large ranges of values. For example, if one wanted to examine a range from 0 to 100 to determine test scores, nested selection would be better than a **CASE** state-

A NOTE OF INTEREST

A Software Glitch

The software glitch that disrupted AT&T's long-distance telephone service for nine hours in January 1990, dramatically demonstrates what can go wrong even in the most reliable and scrupulously tested systems. Of the roughly 100 million telephone calls placed with AT&T during that period, only about half got through. The breakdown cost the company more than $60 million in lost revenues and caused considerable inconvenience and irritation for telephone-dependent customers.

The trouble began at a "switch"—one of 114 interconnected, computer-operated electronic switching systems scattered across the United States. These sophisticated systems, each a maze of electronic equipment housed in a large room, form the backbone of the AT&T long-distance telephone network.

When a local exchange delivers a telephone call to the network, it arrives at one of these switching centers, which can handle up to 700,000 calls an hour. The switch immediately springs into action. It scans a list of 14 different routes it can use to complete the call, and at the same time hands off the telephone number to a parallel, signaling network, invisible to any caller. This private data network allows computers to scout the possible routes and to determine whether the switch at the other end can deliver the call to the local company it serves.

If the answer is no, the call is stopped at the original switch to keep it from tying up a line, and the caller gets a busy signal. If the answer is yes, a signaling-network computer makes a reservation at the destination switch and orders the original switch to pass along the waiting call—after that switch makes a final check to ensure that the chosen line is functioning properly. The whole process of passing a call down the network takes 4 to 6 seconds. Because the switches must keep in constant touch with the signaling network and its computers, each switch has a computer program that handles all the necessary communications between the switch and the signaling network.

AT&T's first indication that something might be amiss appeared on a giant video display at the company's network control center in Bedminster, N.J. At 2:25 P.M. on Monday, January 15, 1990, network managers saw an alarming increase in the number of red warning signals appearing on many of the 75 video screens showing the status of various parts of AT&T's world-wide network. The warnings signaled a serious collapse in the network's ability to complete calls within the United States.

To bring the network back up to speed, AT&T engineers first tried a number of standard procedures that had worked in the past. This time, the methods failed. The engineers realized they had a problem never seen before. Nonetheless, within a few hours, they managed to stabilize the network by temporarily cutting back on the number of messages moving through the signaling network. They cleared the last defective link at 11:30 that night.

Meanwhile, a team of more than 100 telephone technicians tried frantically to track down the fault. Because the problem involved the signaling network and seemed to bounce from one switch to another, they zeroed in on the software that permitted each switch to communicate with the signaling-network computers.

The day after the slowdown, AT&T personnel removed the apparently faulty software from each switch, temporarily replacing it with an earlier version of the communications program. A close examination of the flawed software turned up a single error in one line of the program. Just one month earlier, network technicians had changed the software to speed the processing of certain messages, and the change had inadvertently introduced a flaw into the system.

From that finding, AT&T could reconstruct what had happened.

ment. We close this section with some examples that illustrate how **CASE** statements can be used in solving problems.

■ **EXAMPLE 4.15**

Suppose you are writing a program for a gasoline station owner who sells four grades of gasoline: regular, premium, unleaded and super unleaded. Your program reads a character (R, P, U, S) that designates which kind of gasoline was purchased and then takes subsequent action. The outline for this fragment is

```
      readln (GasType);
      CASE GasType OF
        'R' : ⟨action for regular⟩;
        'P' : ⟨action for premium⟩;
        'U' : ⟨action for unleaded⟩;
        'S' : ⟨action for super unleaded⟩

      END;  {  of CASE GasType  }
```

■ EXAMPLE 4.16

An alternative method of assigning letter grades based on integer scores between 0 and 100 inclusive is to divide the score by 10 and assign grades according to some scale. This idea could be used in conjunction with a **CASE** statement as follows:

```
      NewScore := Score DIV 10;
      CASE NewScore OF
        10, 9          : Grade := 'A';
        8              : Grade := 'B';
        7              : Grade := 'C';
        6, 5           : Grade := 'D';
        4, 3, 2, 1, 0 : Grade := 'E'
      END;  {  of CASE NewScore  }
```

Exercises 4.5

1. Discuss the need for program protection when using a **CASE** statement.

2. Write a test program to see whether or not the **OTHERWISE** option is available on your system.

3. Show how the following **CASE** statement could be protected against unexpected values.

```
      CASE Age DIV 10 OF
        10,9,8,7 : writeln ('These are retirement years':40);
           6,5,4 : writeln ('These are middle age years':40);
             3,2 : writeln ('These are mobile years':40);
               1 : writeln ('These are school years':40)
      END;  {  of CASE Age  }
```

4. Find all errors in the following statements.

```
      a. CASE A OF
           1        :  ;
           2        : A := 2 * A
           3        ; A := 3 * A;
           4; 5; 6 : A := 4 * A
         END;  {  of CASE A  }
```

```
      b. CASE Num OF
           5              : Num := Num + 5;
           6, 7           ; Num := Num + 6;
           7, 8, 9, 10 : Num := Num + 10
         END;  {  of CASE Num  }
```

```
      c. CASE Age OF
           15, 16, 17 : YCount := YCount + 1;
                        writeln (Age, YCount);
           18, 19, 20 : MCount := MCount + 1;
           21         : writeln (Age)
         END;  {  of CASE Age  }
```

```
 d. CASE Ch OF
      A : Points := 4.0;
      B : Points := 3.0;
      C : Points := 2.0;
      D : Points := 1.0;
      E : Points := 0.0
    END;  { of CASE Ch  }
```

```
 e. CASE Score OF
      5        : Grade := 'A';
      4        : Grade := 'B';
      3        : Grade := 'C';
      2, 1, 0 : Grade := 'E';
```

```
 f. CASE Num / 10 OF
      1 : Num := Num + 1;
      2 : Num := Num + 2;
      3 : Num := Num + 3
    END;  { of CASE Num  }
```

5. What is the output from each of the following program fragments?

```
 a. A := 5;
    Power := 3;
    CASE Power OF
      0 : B := 1;
      1 : B := A;
      2 : B := A * A;
      3 : B := A * A * A
    END;  { of CASE Power  }
    writeln (A, Power, B);
```

```
 b. GasType := 'S';
    write ('You have purchased ');
    CASE GasType OF
      'R' : write ('Regular');
      'P' : write ('Premium');
      'U' : write ('Unleaded');
      'S' : write ('Super Unleaded')
    END;  { of CASE GasType  }
    writeln (' gasoline');
```

```
 c. A := 6;
    B := -3;
    CASE A OF
      10, 9, 8 : CASE B OF
                   -3, -4, -5 : A := A * B;
                    0, -1, -2 : A := A + B
                 END;
       7, 6, 5 : CASE B OF
                   -5, -4 : A := A * B;
                   -3, -2 : A := A + B;
                   -1,  0 : A := A - B
                 END
    END;  { of CASE A  }
    writeln (A, B);
```

```
 d. Symbol := '-';
    A := 5;
    B := 10;
    CASE Symbol OF
      '+' : Num := A + B;
      '-' : Num := A - B;
```

```
      '*' : Num := A * B
    END;  {  of CASE Symbol  }
    writeln (A, B, Num);
```

6. Rewrite each of the following program fragments using a **CASE** statement.

   a.
```
IF Power = 1 THEN
   Num := A;
IF Power = 2 THEN
   Num := A * A;
IF Power = 3 THEN
   Num := A * A * A;
```

   b. Assume Score is an integer between 0 and 10.

```
IF Score > 9 THEN
   Grade := 'A'
ELSE IF Score > 8 THEN
   Grade := 'B'
ELSE IF Score > 7 THEN
   Grade := 'C'
ELSE IF Score > 5 THEN
   Grade := 'D'
ELSE
   Grade := 'E';
```

   c. Assume Measurement is either M or N.

```
IF Measurement = 'M' THEN
   BEGIN
     writeln ('This is a metric measurement.':37);
     writeln ('It will be converted to nonmetric.':42);
     Length := Num * CMToInches
   END
ELSE
   BEGIN
     writeln ('This is a nonmetric measurement.':40);
     writeln ('It will be converted to metric.':39);
     Length := Num * InchesToCM
   END;
```

7. Show how a **CASE** statement could be used in a program to compute college tuition fees. Assume there are different fee rates for each of undergraduates (U), graduates (G), foreign students (F), and special students (S).

8. Use nested **CASE** statements to design a program fragment to compute postage for domestic (nonforeign) mail. The design should provide for four weight categories for both letters and packages. Each can be sent first, second, third, or fourth class.

■ ■ ■ ■

■ 4.6
Assertions
(Optional)

An *assertion* is a program comment in the form of a statement about what we expect to be true at the point in the program where the assertion is placed. For example, if you wish to compute a test average by dividing the SumOfScores by NumberOfStudents, you could use an assertion in the following manner:

```
{  Assertion: NumberOfStudents <> 0  }
ClassAverage := SumOfScores / NumberOfStudents;
```

Assertions are usually **boolean**-valued expressions and typically concern program action. Assertions frequently come in pairs: one preceding program action and one following the action. In this format, the first assertion is a precondition and the second is a postcondition.

To illustrate preconditions and postconditions, consider the following segment of code:

```
IF Num1 < Num2 THEN
   BEGIN
     Temp := Num1;
     Num1 := Num2;
     Num2 := Temp
   END;
```

The intent of this code is to have Num1 be greater than or equal to Num2. If we intend for both Num1 and Num2 to be positive, we can write

```
{  Assertion: Num1 >= 0 AND Num2 >= 0  }  ←——Precondition

IF NUM1 < Num2 THEN
   BEGIN
     Temp := Num1;
     Num1 := Num2;
     Num2 := Temp
   END;

{  Assertion: Num1 >= Num2 >= 0  }          ←—— Postcondition
```

In practice, you may choose to label preconditions and postconditions as the following comments illustrate.

```
{  Precondition: Num1 >= 0 and Num2 >= 0  }

IF Num1 < Num2 THEN
   BEGIN
     Temp := Num1;
     Num1 := Num2;
     Num2 := Temp
   END;

{  Postcondition: Num1 >= Num2 >= 0  }
```

As a second example, consider a **CASE** statement used to assign grades based on quiz scores.

```
CASE Score OF
   10            : Grade := 'A';
   9, 8          : Grade := 'B';
   7, 6          : Grade := 'C';
   5, 4          : Grade := 'D';
   3, 2, 1, 0 : Grade := 'E'
END;  {  of CASE Score  }
```

Assertions can be used as preconditions and postconditions in the following manner.

```
{  Precondition:  Score is an integer between 0 and 10
                  inclusive  }

CASE Score OF
   10        : Grade := 'A';
   9,8       : Grade := 'B';
   7,6       : Grade := 'C';
   5,4       : Grade := 'D';
   3,2,1,0 : Grade := 'E'
END;  {  of CASE Score  }
```

```
{  Postcondition:  Grade has been assigned a letter grade
                   according to the scale
              10       ── A
              8,9      ── B
              6,7      ── C
              4,5      ── D
              0,1,2,3 ── E   }
```

Assertions can be used in *program proofs*. Simply put, a program proof is an analysis of a program that attempts to verify the correctness of program results. A detailed study of program proofs is beyond the scope of this text. If, however, you use assertions as preconditions and postconditions now, you will better understand them in subsequent courses. If you do choose to use assertions in this manner, be aware that the postcondition of one action is the precondition of the next action.

FOCUS ON PROGRAM DESIGN

The Gas-N-Clean Service Station sells gasoline and has a car wash. Fees for the car wash are $1.25 with a gasoline purchase of $10.00 or more and $3.00 otherwise. Three kinds of gasoline are available: regular at $1.149, unleaded at $1.199, and super unleaded at $1.289 per gallon. Write a program that prints a statement for a customer. Input consists of number of gallons purchased, kind of gasoline purchased (R, U, S, or, for no purchase, N), and car wash desired (Y or N). Use the constant definition section for gasoline prices. Your output should include appropriate messages. Sample output for this data is

```
Enter number of gallons and press <RETURN>.
?9.7
Enter gas type (R, U, S, or N) and press <RETURN>.
?R
Enter Y or N for car wash and press <RETURN>.
?Y


              *******************************************
              *                                         *
              *      Gas-N-Clean Service Station        *
              *                                         *
              *          July 25, 1992                  *
              *                                         *
              *******************************************

        Amount of gasoline purchased         9.700 Gallons
        Price per gallon                 $   1.149
        Total gasoline cost              $  11.15
        Car wash cost                    $   1.25
                                            ------
                    Total due            $  12.40

                   Thank you for stopping

                    Please come again

            Remember to buckle up and drive safely
```

A first-level pseudocode development is

1. Get data
2. Compute charges
3. Print results

A structure chart for this problem is given in Figure 4.6.

FIGURE 4.6
Structure chart for the Gas-N-
Clean Service Station problem

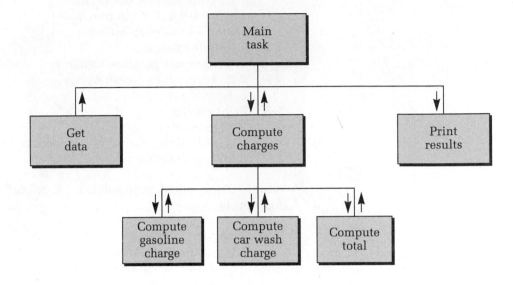

Module specifications for the main modules are

1. GetData Module
   Data received: None
   Information returned: Number of gallons purchased
                        Type of gasoline
                        A choice as to whether or not a car wash is
                            desired
   Logic: Get information interactively from the keyboard.

2. ComputeCharges Module
   Data received: NumGallons
                  GasType
                  WashOption
   Information returned: GasCost
                         WashCost
                         TotalCost
   Logic: Use a **CASE** statement to compute the GasCost.
          Use nested selection to determine the WashCost.
          Sum GasCost and WashCost to get TotalCost.

3. PrintResults Module
   Data received: NumGallons
                  GasType
                  WashOption
                  GasCost
                  WashCost
                  TotalCost
   Information returned: None
   Logic: Use a procedure for the heading.
          Use several **writeln** statements.

Further refinement of the pseudocode produces

1. Get data
    1.1   read number of gallons
    1.2   read kind of gas purchased
    1.3   read car wash option
2. Compute charges
    2.1   compute gasoline charge
    2.2   compute car wash charge
    2.3   compute total
3. Print results
    3.1   print heading
    3.2   print information in transaction
    3.3   print closing message

Module 2 consists of three subtasks. A refined pseudocode development of this step is

2. Compute charges
    2.1   compute gasoline charge
          2.1.1 **CASE** GasType **OF**
                  'R'
                  'U'
                  'S'
                  'N'
    2.2   compute car wash charge
          2.2.1 **IF** WashOption is yes **THEN**
                  compute charge
              ELSE
                  charge is 0.0
    2.3   compute total
          2.3.1 Total is GasCost plus WashCost

A Pascal program for this problem follows.

```
PROGRAM GasNClean (input, output);

{  This program is used to compute the amount due from a        }
{  customer of the Gas-N-Clean Service Station.  Constants      }
{  are used for gasoline prices.  Note  the use of  nested      }
{  selection to compute cost of the car wash.                   }

CONST
  Skip = ' ';
  Date = 'July 25, 1992';
  RegularPrice = 1.149;
  UnleadedPrice = 1.199;
  SuperUnleadedPrice = 1.289;

VAR
  GasType,                { Type of gasoline purchased (R,U,S,N)  }
  WashOption : char;      { Character designating option (Y,N)    }
  NumGallons,             { Number of gallons purchased           }
  GasCost,                { Computed cost for gasoline            }
  WashCost,               { Car wash cost                         }
  TotalCost : real;       { Total amount due                      }

{********************************************************************* }
```

```
PROCEDURE GetData (VAR NumGallons : real;
                   VAR GasType, WashOption : char);

  {  Given:    Nothing                                             }
  {  Task:     Have NumGallons, GasType, and WashOption entered    }
  {               from the keyboard                                }
  {  Return:   NumGallons, GasType, and WashOption                 }

  BEGIN
    writeln ('Enter number of gallons and press <RETURN>.');
    readln (NumGallons);
    writeln ('Enter gas type (R, U, S, or N) and press <RETURN>.');
    readln (GasType);
    writeln ('Enter Y or N for car wash and press <RETURN>.');
    readln (WashOption)
  END;  {  of PROCEDURE GetData  }

{***************************************************************** }

PROCEDURE ComputeCharges (VAR GasCost, WashCost, TotalCost : real;
                          NumGallons : real;
                          GasType, WashOption : char);

  {  Given:    NumGallons, GasType, and WashOption                 }
  {  Task:     Compute GasCost, WashCost, and TotalCost            }
  {  Return:   GasCost, WashCost, and TotalCost                    }

  BEGIN

  {  Compute gas cost  }
    CASE GasType OF
      'R'  :  GasCost := NumGallons * RegularPrice;
      'U'  :  GasCost := NumGallons * UnleadedPrice;
      'S'  :  GasCost := NumGallons * SuperUnleadedPrice;
      'N'  :  GasCost := 0.0
    END;  {  of CASE GasType  }

  {  Compute car wash cost  }
    IF WashOption = 'Y' THEN
      IF GasCost >= 10.0 THEN
        WashCost := 1.25
      ELSE
        WashCost := 3.0
    ELSE
      WashCost := 0.0;
    TotalCost := GasCost + WashCost
  END;  {  of PROCEDURE ComputeCharges  }

{***************************************************************** }

PROCEDURE PrintHeading;

  {  Given:    Nothing                                             }
  {  Task:     Print a heading for the output                      }
  {  Return:   Nothing                                             }

  BEGIN
    writeln;
    writeln (Skip:20, '*******************************************');
    writeln (Skip:20, '*                                         *');
    writeln (Skip:20, '*      Gas-N-Clean Service Station        *');
    writeln (Skip:20, '*                                         *');
    writeln (Skip:20, '*', Skip:12, Date, Skip:13,                '*');
    writeln (Skip:20, '*                                         *');
    writeln (Skip:20, '*******************************************');
```

```
          writeln
     END.  { of PROCEDURE PrintHeading }

{********************************************************************}

PROCEDURE PrintMessage;

  { Given:    Nothing                                               }
  { Task:     Print an appropriate closing message                 }
  { Return:   Nothing                                              }

  BEGIN
    writeln;
    writeln (Skip:28, 'Thank you for stopping');
    writeln;
    writeln (Skip:30, 'Please come again');
    writeln;
    writeln (Skip:20, 'Remember to buckle up and drive safely');
    writeln
  END; { of PROCEDURE PrintMessage }

{********************************************************************}

PROCEDURE PrintResults (NumGallons: real;
                        GasType, WashOption : char;
                        GasCost, WashCost, TotalCost : real);

  { Given:    NumGallons, GasType, WashOption, computed costs      }
  {               for GasCost, WashCost, and TotalCost             }
  { Task:     Print customer statement                            }
  { Return:   Nothing                                             }

  BEGIN
    PrintHeading;

    writeln (Skip:10, 'Amount of gasoline purchased', Skip:12,
             NumGallons:6:3, ' Gallons');
    write (Skip:10, 'Price per gallon', Skip:22, '$');

    CASE GasType OF
      'R'  :   writeln (RegularPrice:7:3);
      'U'  :   writeln (UnleadedPrice:7:3);
      'S'  :   writeln (SuperUnleadedPrice:7:3);
      'N'  :   writeln (0.0:7:3)
    END;  { of CASE GasType  }

    writeln (Skip:10, 'Total gasoline cost', Skip:19, '$', GasCost:6:2);
    IF WashCost > 0 THEN
      writeln (Skip:10, 'Car wash cost', Skip:25, '$', WashCost:6:2);
    writeln (Skip:48,'-------');
    writeln (Skip:25, 'Total due', Skip:14, '$', TotalCost:6:2);

    PrintMessage
  END;  { of PROCEDURE PrintResults  }

{********************************************************************}

BEGIN  { Main program }
  GetData (NumGallons, GasType, WashOption);
  ComputeCharges (GasCost, WashCost, TotalCost, NumGallons,
                  GasType, WashOption);
  PrintResults (NumGallons, GasType, WashOption, GasCost,
                WashCost, TotalCost)
END.  { of main program  }
```

A sample run of this program produces

```
Enter number of gallons and press <RETURN>.
?11.3
Enter gas type (R, U, S, or N) and press <RETURN>.
?S
Enter Y or N for car wash and press <RETURN>.
?N
```

```
        *******************************************
        *                                         *
        *       Gas-N-Clean Service Station        *
        *                                         *
        *            July 25, 1992                 *
        *                                         *
        *******************************************


   Amount of gasoline purchased            11.300 Gallons
   Price per gallon                     $   1.289
   Total gasoline cost                  $  14.57
                                           -------
                      Total due          $  14.57

                   Thank you for stopping

                   Please come again

          Remember to buckle up and drive safely
```

RUNNING AND DEBUGGING TIPS

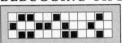

1. **IF** . . . **THEN** . . . **ELSE** is a single statement in Pascal. Thus, a semicolon before the **ELSE** creates an **IF** . . . **THEN** statement and **ELSE** appears incorrectly as a reserved word.

2. A misplaced semicolon used with an **IF** . . . **THEN** statement can also be a problem. For example,

   Incorrect

   ```
   IF A > 0 THEN;
      writeln (A);
   ```

   Correct

   ```
   IF A > 0 THEN
      writeln (A);
   ```

3. Be careful with compound statements as options in an **IF** . . . **THEN** . . . **ELSE** statement. They must be in a **BEGIN** . . . **END** block.

   Incorrect

   ```
   IF A >= 0 THEN
      writeln (A);
      A := A + 10
   ELSE
      writeln ('A is negative');
   ```

   Correct

   ```
   IF A >= 0 THEN
      BEGIN
         writeln (A);
         A := A + 10
      END
   ELSE
      writeln ('A is negative');
   ```

4. Your test data should include values that will check both options of an **IF** . . . **THEN** . . . **ELSE** statement.

5. **IF. . . THEN . . . ELSE** can be used to check for other program errors. In particular,
   a. Check for bad data by
      read (⟨data⟩);
      IF ⟨bad data⟩ **THEN**
      .
      .   (error message)
      .

      ELSE
      .
      .   (proceed with program)
      .

   b. Check for reasonable computed values by
      IF ⟨unreasonable values⟩ **THEN**
      .
      .   (error message)
      .

      ELSE
      .
      .   (proceed with program)
      .

      For example, if you were computing a student's test average, you could have
      IF (TestAverage > 100) **OR** (TestAverage < 0) **THEN**
      .
      .   (error message)
      .

      ELSE
      .
      .   (proceed with program)
      .

6. Be careful with Boolean expressions. You should always keep expressions reasonably simple, use parentheses, and minimize use of **NOT**.

7. Be careful to properly match **ELSE**s with **IF**s in nested **IF** . . . **THEN** . . . **ELSE** statements. Indenting levels for writing code are very helpful.
   IF ⟨condition 1⟩ **THEN**
      IF ⟨condition 2⟩ **THEN**
      .
      .   (action here)
      .

      ELSE
      .
      .   (action here)
      .

   ELSE
      .
      .   (action here)
      .

8. The form for using extended **IF** statements is
   IF ⟨condition 1⟩ **THEN**
      .
      .   (action 1 here)
      .

   ELSE IF ⟨condition 2⟩ **THEN**
      .
      .   (action 2 here)
      .

ELSE

.
.   (final option here)
.

9. Be sure to include the **END** of a **CASE** Statement.

■ **Summary**

Key Terms

BEGIN . . . END block	empty (null) statement	nested **IF** statement
compound Boolean expression	extended **IF** statement	relational operator
compound statement	logical operators: **AND, OR, NOT**	robust
control structure	negation	selection statement
		simple Boolean expression

Key Terms (optional)

assertion	program proof

Keywords

AND	**false**	**OR**
boolean	**IF**	**OTHERWISE**
CASE	**NOT**	(non-standard)
ELSE	**OF**	**THEN**
		true

Key Concepts

- Relational operators are $=, >, <, >=, <=, <>$.
- Priority for evaluating relational operators is last.
- Logical operators **AND, OR,** and **NOT** are used as operators on Boolean expressions.
- Variables of type **boolean** may only have values **true** or **false.**
- A complete priority listing of arithmetic operators, relational operators, and logical operators is

Expression or Operation	Priority
( )	1. Evaluate from inside out
NOT	2. Evaluate from left to right
*, /, **MOD, DIV, AND**	3. Evaluate from left to right
+, −, **OR**	4. Evaluate from left to right
$<, <=, >, >=, =, <>$	5. Evaluate from left to right

- A selection statement is a program statement that transfers control to various branches of the program.
- A compound statement is sometimes referred to as a **BEGIN . . . END** block; when it is executed, the entire segment of code between the **BEGIN** and **END** is treated like a single statement.
- **IF . . . THEN . . . ELSE** is a two-way selection statement.
- A semicolon should not precede the **ELSE** portion of an **IF . . . THEN . . . ELSE** statement.
- If the Boolean expression in an **IF . . . THEN . . . ELSE** statement is **true,** the command following **THEN** is executed; if the expression is **false,** the command following **ELSE** is executed.
- Multiple selections can be achieved by using decision statements within decision statements; this is termed multiway selection.

- An extended **IF** statement is a statement of the form

  IF ⟨condition 1⟩ **THEN**

  .
  . (action 1 here)
  .

  ELSE IF ⟨condition 2⟩ **THEN**

  .
  . (action 2 here)
  .

  ELSE IF ⟨condition 3⟩ **THEN**

  .
  . (action 3 here)
  .

  ELSE

  .
  . (action 4 here)
  .

- Program protection can be achieved by using selection statements to guard against unexpected results.
- **CASE** statements sometimes can be used as alternatives to multiple selection.
- **CASE** statements use an **END** without any **BEGIN.**
- **OTHERWISE,** a reserved word in some versions of Pascal, can be used to handle values not listed in the **CASE** statement.

■ Programming Problems and Projects

The first 13 problems listed here are relatively short, but to complete them you must use concepts presented in this chapter.

Some of the remaining programming problems are used as the basis for writing programs for subsequent chapters as well as for this chapter. In this chapter, each program is run on a very limited set of data. Material in later chapters permits us to run the programs on larger data bases. Since the problems marked by a color square are referred to and used repeatedly, carefully choose which ones you work on and then develop them completely.

1. A three-minute telephone call to Scio, N.Y., costs $1.15. Each additional minute costs $0.26. Given the total length of a call in minutes, print the cost.

2. When you first learned to divide, you expressed answers using a quotient and a remainder rather than a fraction or decimal quotient. For example, if you divided 7 by 2, your answers would have been given as 3 r. 1. Given two integers, divide the larger by the smaller and print the answer in this form. Do not assume that the numbers are entered in any order.

3. Revise Problem 2 so that, if there is no remainder, you print only the quotient without a remainder or the letter r.

4. Given the coordinates of two points on a graph, find and print the slope of a line passing through them. Remember that the slope of a line can be undefined.

■ 5. Dr. Lae Z. Programmer wishes to computerize his grading system. He gives five tests, then averages only the four highest scores. An average of 90 or better earns a grade of A, 80–89 a grade of B, and so on. Write a program that accepts five test scores and prints the average and grade according to this method.

6. Given the lengths of three sides of a triangle, print whether the triangle is scalene, isosceles, or equilateral.

7. Given the lengths of three sides of a triangle, determine whether or not the triangle is a right triangle using the Pythagorean theorem. Do not assume that the sides are entered in any order.

8. Given three integers, print only the largest.

9. The island nation of Babbage charges its citizens an income tax each year. The tax rate is based upon the following table:

Income	Tax Rate
$ 0 - 5,000	0
5,000 - 10,000	3%
10,001 - 20,000	5.5%
20,001 - 40,000	10.8%
over $40,000	23.7%

Write a program that, when given a person's income, prints the tax owed rounded to the nearest dollar.

10. Many states base the cost of car registration on the weight of the vehicle. Suppose the fees are as follows:

Weight	Cost
up to 1,500 pounds	$23.75
1,500 to 2,500 pounds	27.95
2,500 to 3,000 pounds	30.25
over 3,000 pounds	37.00

Given the weight of a car, find and print the cost of registration.

11. The Mapes Railroad Corporation pays an annual bonus as a part of its profit sharing plan. This year all employees who have been with the company for ten years or more receive a bonus of 12 percent of their annual salary, and those who have worked at Mapes between five and nine years receive a bonus of 5.75 percent. Those who have been with the company less than five years receive no bonus.

Given the initials of an employee, the employee's annual salary, and the number of years employed with the company, find and print the bonus. All bonuses are rounded to the nearest dollar. Output should be in the following form.

```
MAPES RAILROAD CORP.

Employee xxx    Years of service nn
     Bonus earned: $ yyyy
```

12. A substance floats in water if its density (mass/volume) is less than 1 g/cc. It sinks if it is 1 or more. Given the mass and volume of an object, print whether it will sink or float.

13. Mr. Arthur Einstein, your high school physics teacher, wants a program for English-to-metric conversions. You are given a letter indicating whether the measurement is in pounds (P), feet (F), or miles (M). Such measures are to be converted to newtons, meters, and kilometers

respectively. (There are 4.9 newtons in a pound, 3.28 feet in a meter, and 1.61 kilometers in a mile.)

Given an appropriate identifying letter and the size of the measurement, convert it to metric units. Print the answer in the following form.

```
3.0 miles = 4.83 kilometers.
```

■ 14. The Caswell Catering and Convention Service (Chapter 3, Problem 12) has decided to revise its billing practices and is in need of a new program to prepare bills. The changes Caswell wishes to make follow.

a. For adults, the deluxe meals will cost $15.80 per person and the standard meals will cost $11.75 per person, dessert included. Children's meals will cost 60 percent of adult meals. Everyone within a given party must be served the same meal type.

b. There are five banquet halls. Room A rents for $55.00, room B rents for $75.00, room C rents for $85.00, room D rents for $100.00, and room E rents for $130.00. The Caswells are considering increasing the room fees in about six months and this should be taken into account.

c. A surcharge, currently 7 percent, is added to the total bill if the catering is to be done on the weekend (Friday, Saturday, or Sunday).

d. All customers will be charged the same rate for tip and tax, currently 18 percent. It is applied only to the cost of food.

e. To induce customers to pay promptly, a discount is offered if payment is made within ten days. This discount depends on the amount of the total bill. If the bill is less than $100.00, the discount is .5 percent; if the bill is at least $100.00 but less than $200.00, the discount is 1.5 percent; if the bill is at least $200.00 but less than $400.00, the discount is 3 percent; if the bill is at least $400.00 but less than $800.00, the discount is 4 percent; and, if the bill is at least $800.00, the discount is 5 percent.

Test your program on each of the following three customers.

Customer A: this customer is using room C on Tuesday night. The party includes 80 adults and 6 children. The standard meal is being served. The customer paid a $60.00 deposit.
Customer B: this customer is using room A on Saturday night. Deluxe meals are being served to 15 adults. A deposit of $50.00 was paid.
Customer C: this customer is using room D on Sunday afternoon. The party includes 30 children and 2 adults, all of whom are served the standard meal.

Output should be in the same form as that for Problem 12, Chapter 3.

■ 15. State University charges $90.00 for each semester hour of credit, $200.00 per semester for a regular room, $250.00 per semester for an air-conditioned room, and $400.00 per semester for food. All students are charged a $30.00 matriculation fee. Graduating students must also pay a $35.00 diploma fee. Write a program to compute the fees that must be paid by a student. Your program should include an appropriate warning message if a student in taking more than 21 credit hours or fewer than 12 credit hours. A typical line of data for one student would include room type (R or A), student number (in four digits), credit hours, and graduating (T or F).

16. Write a program to determine the day of the week a person was born given his or her birth date. Following are the steps you should use to find the day of the week corresponding to any date in this century.
   a. Divide the last two digits of the birth year by 4. Put the quotient (ignoring the remainder) in Total. For example, if the person was born in 1983, divide 83 by 4 and store 20 in Total.
   b. Add the last two digits of the birth year to Total.
   c. Add the last two digits of the birth date to Total.
   d. Using the following table, find the "month number" and add it to Total.
   January = 1
   February = 4 .
   March = 4
   April = 0
   May = 2
   June = 5
   July = 0
   August = 3
   September = 6
   October = 1
   November = 4
   December = 6
   e. If the year is a leap year and, if the month you are working with is either January or February, then subtract 1 from the Total.
   f. Find the remainder when Total is divided by 7. Look up the remainder in the following table to determine the day of the week the person was born. Note that you should not use this procedure if the person's year of birth is earlier than 1900.
   1 = Sunday
   2 = Monday
   3 = Tuesday
   4 = Wednesday
   5 = Thursday
   6 = Friday
   0 = Saturday

Typical input is

   5 – 15 78

where the first entry (5 – 15) represents the birthdate (May 15) and the second entry (78) represents the birth year. An appropriate error message should be printed if a person's year of birth is before 1900.

■ 17. Community Hospital needs a program to compute and print a statement for each patient. Charges for each day are as follows:
   a. room charges
      i. private room—$125.00
      ii. semiprivate room—$95.00
      iii. ward—$75.00
   b. telephone charge—$1.75
   c. television charge—$3.50

Write a program to get a line of data from the keyboard, compute the patient's bill, and print an appropriate statement. Typical input is

```
5PNY
```

where "5" indicates the number of days spent in the hospital, "P" represents the room type (P, S, or W), "N" represents the telephone option (Y or N), and "Y" represents the television option (Y or N). A statement for the data given follows.

```
            Community Hospital

         Patient Billing Statement

Number of days in hospital:      5
Type of room:               Private

Room charge              $625.00
Telephone charge         $  0.00
Television charge        $ 17.50
                         -------

     TOTAL DUE           $642.50
```

18. Write a program that converts degrees Fahrenheit to degrees Celsius and degrees Celsius to degrees Fahrenheit. In the input the temperature is followed by a designator (F or C) indicating whether the given temperature is Fahrenheit or Celsius.

■ 19. The city of Mt. Pleasant bills its residents for sewage, water, and sanitation every three months. The sewer and water charge is figured according to how much water is used by the resident. The scale is

Amount (gallons)	Rate (per gallon)
Less than 1,000	$0.03
1,000 to 2,000	$30 + $0.02 for each gallon over 1,000
Greater than 2,000	$50 + $0.015 for each gallon over 2,000

The sanitation charge is $7.50 per month.

Write a program to read the number of months for which a resident is being billed (1, 2, or 3) and how much water was used; then print out a statement with appropriate charges and messages. Use the constant definition section for all rates and include an error check for incorrect number of months. Typical input is

```
3 2175
```

■ 20. Al Derrick, owner of the Lucky Wildcat Well Corporation, wants a program to help him decide whether or not a well is making money. Data for a well will consist of one or two lines. The first line contains a single character (D for a dry well, O for oil found, and G for gas found) followed by a real number for the cost of the well. If an "O" or "G" is detected, the cost will be followed by an integer indicating the volume of oil or gas found. In this case, there will also be a second line containing an "N" or "S" indicating whether or not sulfur is present. If there is sulfur, the "S" will be followed by the percentage of sulfur present in the oil or gas.

Unit prices are $5.50 for oil and $2.20 for gas. These should be defined as constants. Your program should compute the total revenue for a well (reduce output for sulfur present) and print out all pertinent information with an appropriate message to Mr. Derrick. A gusher is defined as a well with profit in excess of $50,000. Typical input is

```
G 8000.00 20000
S 0.15
```

21. The Mathematical Association of America hosts an annual summer meeting. Each state sends one official delegate to the section officer's meeting at this summer session. The national organization reimburses the official state delegates according to the following scale:

Round-trip Mileage	Rate
Up to 500 miles	15 cents per mile
500 to 1,000 miles	$75.00 plus 12 cents for each mile over 500
1,000 to 1,500 miles	$135.00 plus 10 cents for each mile over 1,000
1,500 to 2,000 miles	$185.00 plus 8 cents for each mile over 1,500
2,000 to 3,000 miles	$225.00 plus 6 cents for each mile over 2,000
Over 3,000 miles	$285.00 plus 5 cents for each mile over 3,000

Write a program that will accept as input the number of round-trip miles for a delegate and compute the amount of reimbursement.

■ 22. Dr. Lae Z. Programmer (Problem 5) wants you to write a program to compute and print out the grade for a student in his class. The grade is based on three examinations (worth a possible 100 points each), five quizzes (10 points each), and a 200-point final examination. Your output should include all scores, the percentage grade, and the letter grade. The grading scale is

```
90 <= average <= 100    A
80 <= average <  90     B
70 <= average <  80     C
60 <= average <  70     D
 0 <= average <  60     E
```

Typical input is

```
80 93 85 (examination scores)
 9 10 8 7 10 (quiz scores)
175 (final examination)
```

■ 23. Dr. Lae Z. Programmer now wants you to modify Problem 22 by adding a check for bad data. Any time an unexpected score occurs, you are to print an appropriate error message and terminate the program.

24. A quadratic equation is one of the form

$$ax^2 + bx + c = 0$$

where $a \neq 0$. Solutions to this equation are given by

$$x = \frac{-b \pm \sqrt{b^2 - 4ac}}{2a}$$

where the quantity $(b^2 - 4ac)$ is referred to as the discriminant of the equation. Write a program to read three integers as the respective coefficients (*a*, *b*, and *c*), compute the discriminant, and print out the solutions. Use the following rules:

a. discriminant $= 0 \rightarrow$ single root.

b. discriminant $< 0 \rightarrow$ no real number solution.

c. discriminant $> 0 \rightarrow$ two distinct real solutions.

25. Write a program that gets as input the lengths of three sides of a triangle. Output should first identify the triangle as scalene, isosceles, or equilateral. The program should use the Pythagorean theorem to determine whether or not scalene or isoceles triangles are right triangles. An appropriate message should be part of the output.

■ 26. The sign on the attendant's booth at the Pentagon parking lot is

PENTAGON VISITOR PARKING

Cars:

First 2 hours	Free
Next 3 hours	0.50/hour
Next 10 hours	0.25/hour

Trucks:

First 1 hour	Free
Next 2 hours	1.00/hour
Next 12 hours	0.75/hour
Senior Citizens:	no charge

Write a program that will accept as input a one-character designator (C, T, or S) followed by the number of minutes a vehicle has been in the lot. The program should then compute the appropriate charge and print a ticket for the customer. Any part of an hour is to be counted as a full hour.

27. Milt Walker, the chief of advertising for the Isabella Potato Industry, wants you to write a program to compute an itemized bill and total cost of his "This Spud's for You!" ad campaign. The standard black and white full-page ads have base prices as follows:

Drillers' News (code N)	$ 400
Playperson (code P)	$2,000
Outdoors (code O)	$ 900
Independent News (code I)	$1,200

Each ad is allowed 15 lines of print with a rate of $20.00 for each line in excess of 15 lines. Each ad is either black and white (code B) and subject to the base prices, or is in color (code C) and subject to the following rates:

| Three color (code T) | 40 percent increase over base |
| Full color (code F) | 60 percent increase over base |

Write a program to input Milt's choice of magazine (N, P, O, or I), the number of lines of print (integer), and either black and white (B) or color (C) with a choice of three colors (T) or full color (F). Output should include an appropriate title, all the information and costs used to compute the price of an ad, the total price of the ad, and finally the total price of all ads.

28. Write a program that will add, subtract, multiply, and divide fractions. Input will consist of a single line representing a fraction arithmetic problem as follows:

integer/integer operation integer/integer

For example, a line of input might be

`2/3 + 1/2`

Your program should
a. check for division by zero.
b. check for proper operation symbols.
c. print the problem in its original form.
d. print the answer.
e. print all fractions in horizontal form.

Your answer need not be in lowest terms. For the sample input

`2/3 + 1/2`

sample output is

$$\frac{2}{3} + \frac{1}{2} = \frac{7}{6}$$

29. Write an interactive program that permits the user to print various recipes. Write a procedure for each recipe. After the user enters a one-letter identifier for the desired recipe, a **CASE** statement should be used to call the appropriate procedure. Part of the code could be

```
readln (Selection);
CASE Selection OF
   'J'  :  Jambalaya;
   'S'  :  Spaghetti;
   'T'  :  Tacos
END;  {  of CASE Selection  }
```

30. The force of gravity is different for each of the nine planets in our solar system. For example, on Mercury it is only 0.38 times as strong as on Earth. Thus, if you weigh 100 pounds (on Earth), you would weigh only 38 pounds on Mercury. Write an interactive program that allows you to enter your (Earth) weight and your choice of planet to which you would like your weight converted. Output should be your weight on the desired planet together with the planet name. The screen message for input should include a menu for planet choice. Use a **CASE** statement in the program for computation and output. The relative forces of gravity are

Earth	1.00
Jupiter	2.65
Mars	0.39
Mercury	0.38
Neptune	1.23
Pluto	0.05
Saturn	1.17
Uranus	1.05
Venus	0.78

■ 31. Cramer's Rule is a method for solving a system of linear equations. If you have two equations with variables x and y written as

$$ax + by = c$$
$$dx + ey = f$$

then the solution for x and y can be given as

$$x = \frac{\begin{vmatrix} c & b \\ f & e \end{vmatrix}}{\begin{vmatrix} a & b \\ d & e \end{vmatrix}} \qquad y = \frac{\begin{vmatrix} a & c \\ d & f \end{vmatrix}}{\begin{vmatrix} a & b \\ d & e \end{vmatrix}}$$

Using this notation,

$$\begin{vmatrix} a & b \\ d & e \end{vmatrix}$$

is the determinant of the matrix

$$\begin{bmatrix} a & b \\ d & e \end{bmatrix}$$

and is equal to $ae - bd$.

Write a complete program that will solve a system of two equations using Cramer's Rule. Input will be all coefficients and constants in the system. Output will be the solution to the system. Typical output is

```
For the system of equations

      x  +  2y  =  5
     2x  -   y  =  0

we have the solution

      x  =  1
      y  =  2
```

Use an **IF . . . THEN . . . ELSE** statement to guard against division by zero.

32. Contact a programmer and discuss the concept of robustness in a program. Prepare a report of your conversation for class. Your report should include a list of specific instances of how programmers make programs robust.

33. Conduct an unscientific survey of at least two people from each of the following groups: students in upper-level computer science courses, instructors of computer science, and programmers working in industry. Your survey should attempt to ascertain the importance of and use of robustness at each level. Discuss the similarities and differences of your findings with those of other class members.

34. Selecting appropriate test data for a program that uses nested selection is a nontrivial task. Create diagrams that allow you to trace the flow of logic when nested selection is used. Use your diagrams to draw conclusions about minimal test data required to test all branches of a program that uses nested selection to various levels.

"Can you do Addition?" the White Queen asked. "What's one and one and one and one and one and one and one and one and one and one?"

"I don't know," said Alice, "I lost count."

Lewis Carroll

Methods of Controlling Repetition

The previous chapter on selection introduced you to a programming concept that takes advantage of a computer's ability to select. A second major concept utilizing the speed of a computer is repetition. Many problems require a process to be repeated. When this is the case, some form of controlled repetition is needed.

This chapter examines the different methods Pascal permits for performing some process repeatedly. For example, as yet we cannot conveniently write a program that solves the simple problem of adding the integers from 1 to 100 or processing the grades of 30 students in a class. By the end of this chapter, you will be able to solve these problems three different ways. The three forms of repetition (loops) are

1. **FOR . . . TO . . . DO**
2. **WHILE . . . DO**
3. **REPEAT . . . UNTIL**

Each of these three loops contains the basic constructs necessary for repetition: a variable is assigned some value, the variable value changes at some point in the loop, and repetition continues until the value reaches some predetermined value. When the predetermined value (or **boolean** condition) is reached, repetition is terminated and program control moves to the next executable statement.

■ 5.1 Classifying Loops

Pretest and Posttest Loops

A loop that uses a condition to control whether or not the body of the loop is executed before going through the loop is a *pretest* or *entrance controlled loop*. The testing condition is the *pretest condition*. If the condition is **true**, the body of the loop is executed. If the condition is **false**, the program skips to the first line of code following the loop. The **FOR** loops and the **WHILE** . . . **DO** loop are pretest loops.

A loop that examines a **boolean** expression after the loop body is executed is a *posttest* or *exit controlled loop*. This is the **REPEAT . . . UNTIL** loop.

Fixed Repetition versus Variable Condition Loops

Fixed repetition (iterated) loops are used when it can be determined in advance how often a segment of code needs to be repeated. For instance, you might have a predetermined number of repetitions of a segment of code for: (1) a program to add the integers from 1 to 100; or (2) programs using a fixed number of data lines, for example, game statistics for a team of 12 basketball players. The number of repetitions need not be constant. For example, a user might enter information during execution of a program that would determine how often a segment should be repeated. **FOR** loops are fixed repetition loops.

Variable condition loops are needed to solve problems where conditions change within the body of the loop. These conditions involve sentinel values, Boolean flags, arithmetic expressions or end-of-line and end-of-file markers (see Chapter 6). A variable condition loop uses a control feature that provides more power than what is available in many old languages such as BASIC and FORTRAN. **WHILE . . . DO** and **REPEAT . . . UNTIL** are variable condition loops.

■ 5.2
FOR Loops

There are two kinds of **FOR** loops, the **FOR . . . TO . . . DO** loop and the **FOR . . . DOWNTO . . . DO** loop. These loops are pretest and fixed repetition loops.

FOR . . . TO . . . DO . . . Loops

The form necessary for using a **FOR . . . TO . . . DO** loop is

```
        FOR ⟨index⟩ : = ⟨initial value⟩ TO ⟨final value⟩ DO
          ⟨statement⟩;
or
        FOR ⟨index⟩ := ⟨initial value⟩ TO ⟨final value⟩ DO
        BEGIN
          ⟨statement 1⟩;
          ⟨statement 2⟩;
               .
               .
               .
          ⟨statement n⟩
        END;
```

A **FOR . . . TO . . . DO** loop is considered to be a single executable statement. The actions performed in the loop are referred to as the body of the loop. The internal logic of a **FOR . . . TO . . . DO** loop is

1. The *index* is assigned the initial value.
2. The index value is compared to the final value.

3. If the index value is less than or equal to the final value
   a. the body of the loop is executed,
   b. the index value is incremented by one, and
   c. another check with the final value is made.
4. If the index value exceeds the final value
   a. the index may revert to an unassigned status, and
   b. control of the program is transferred to the first statement following the loop.

A flow diagram is given in Figure 5.1.

FOR J := ⟨initial value⟩ **TO** ⟨final value⟩ **DO**

FIGURE 5.1
FOR . . . TO . . . DO
flow diagram

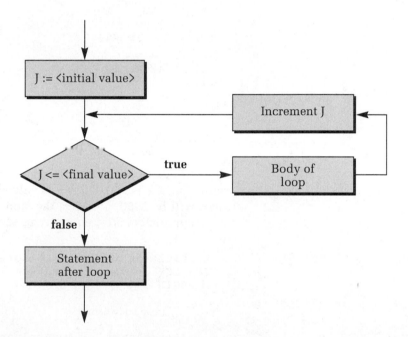

Accumulators

The problem of adding the integers from 1 to 100 needs only one statement in the body of the loop. This problem can be solved by code that constructs an *accumulator*. An accumulator merely sums values of some variable. In the following code, the index variable, LCV (loop control variable), successively assumes the values 1, 2, 3, . . . , 100.

```
Sum:= 0;
FOR LCV := 1 To 100 DO
   Sum := Sum + LCV;
```

LCV	Sum	
1	0	— Initial value
2	1	— Values on successive
3	3	passes through loop
4	6	
5	10	
.	.	
.	.	
.	.	

This program segment contains an example of graphic documentation. Throughout the text, these insets will be used to help illustrate what the code is actually doing. The insets are not part of the program; they merely show what some specific code is trying to accomplish.

To see how Sum accumulates these values, let's trace through the code for several values of LCV. Initially, Sum is set to zero by

```
Sum := 0;
```

When LCV is assigned the value 1,

```
Sum := Sum + LCV;
```

produces

1		Ø 1
LCV		Sum

For LCV = 2, we get

2		1̸ 3
LCV		Sum

LCV = 3 yields

3		3̸ 6
LCV		Sum

Note that Sum has been assigned a value equal to 1 + 2 + 3. The final value for LCV is 100. Once this value has been assigned to Sum, the value of Sum will be 5050, which is the sum 1 + 2 + 3 + ... + 100.

Accumulators are frequently used in loops. The general form for this use is

```
Accumulator := 0;  {  before loop  }
FOR LCV := <initial value> TO <final value> DO
  BEGIN
    .
    .  (loop body here)
    .
    Accumulator := Accumulator + <new value>
  END;  {  of FOR loop  }
```

Some comments concerning the syntax and form of **FOR ... TO ... DO** loops are now necessary.

1. The words **FOR, TO,** and **DO** are reserved and must be used only in the order **FOR ... TO ... DO.**
2. The index must be declared as a variable. Although it can be any ordinal data type, we will use mostly integer examples.
3. The index variable can be any valid identifier.
4. The index can be used within the loop just as any other variable except that the value of the index variable cannot be changed by the statements in the body of the loop.
5. The initial and final values may be constants or variable expressions with appropriate values.
6. The loop will be repeated for each value of the index in the range indicated by the initial and final values.
7. The index may not retain the last value it had during the last time through the loop. When the loop is finished, the index variable may revert to a state of having no assigned value.

At this point you might try writing some test programs to see what happens if you don't follow these rules. Then consider the following examples, which illustrate the features of **FOR . . . TO . . . DO** loops.

■ **EXAMPLE 5.1**

Write a segment of code to list the integers from 1 to 10 together with their squares and cubes. This can be done by

```
FOR J := 1 TO 10 DO
   writeln (J, J * J, J * J * J);
```

This segment produces

```
 1          1          1
 2          4          8
 3          9         27
 4         16         64
 5         25        125
 6         36        216
 7         49        343
 8         64        512
 9         81        729
10        100       1000
```

■ **EXAMPLE 5.2**

Write a **FOR . . . TO . . . DO** loop to produce the following design.

```
        **
       *  *
      *    *
     *      *
    *        *
```

Assuming the first asterisk is in column 20, the following loop will produce the desired result. Note carefully how the output is formatted.

```
FOR J := 1 TO 5 DO
   writeln ('*':21-J, '*':2*J-1);
```

■ **EXAMPLE 5.3**

When computing compound interest, it is necessary to evaluate the quantity $(1 + R)^N$ where R is the interest rate for one time period and N is the number of time periods. A **FOR . . . TO . . . DO** loop can be used to perform this computation. If we declare a variable Base, this can be solved by

```
{ Initialize Base }

Base := 1;
FOR J := 1 TO N DO
   Base := Base * (1 + R);
```

Base

$\boxed{1}$ ←—— Initial value

$(1 + R)^1$ ←— Value after successive
$(1 + R)^2$ passes through loop
$(1 + R)^3$

.
.
.

$(1 + R)^N$

FOR . . . DOWNTO . . . DO Loops

A second pretest, fixed repetition loop is the **FOR . . . DOWNTO . . . DO** loop. This loop does exactly what you expect; it is identical to a **FOR . . . TO . . . DO** loop except the index variable is decreased by one instead of increased by one each time through the loop. This is referred to as a *decrement*. The test is index value $>=$ final value. The loop terminates when the index value is less than the final value. Proper form and syntax for a loop of this type are

```
        FOR ⟨index⟩ := ⟨initial value⟩ DOWNTO ⟨final value⟩ DO
           ⟨statement⟩;
  or
        FOR ⟨index⟩ := ⟨initial value⟩ DOWNTO ⟨final value⟩ DO
        BEGIN
           ⟨statement 1⟩;
           ⟨statement 2⟩;
                .
                .
                .
           ⟨statement n⟩
        END;
```

The conditions for **FOR . . . DOWNTO . . . DO** loops are the same as **FOR . . . TO . . . DO** loops. We will now consider an example of a **FOR . . . DOWNTO . . . DO** loop.

■ **EXAMPLE 5.4**

Illustrate the index values of a **FOR . . . DOWNTO . . . DO** loop by writing the index value during each pass through the loop. The segment of code for this could be

```
FOR K := 20 DOWNTO 15 DO
   writeln ('K =', K:4);
```

and the output is

```
K =   20
K =   19
K =   18
K =   17
K =   16
K =   15
```

From this point on, both **FOR . . . TO . . . DO** and **FOR . . . DOWNTO . . . DO** loops will be referred to as **FOR** loops. The form intended should be clear from the context.

Writing Style for Loops

As you can see, writing style is an important consideration when writing code using loops. There are three features to consider. First, the body of the loop should be indented. Compare the following:

```
FOR J := 1 TO 10 DO
  BEGIN
    read (Num, Amt);
    Total1 := Total1 + Amt;
    Total2 := Total2 + Num;
    writeln ('The number is', Num:6)
  END;
writeln ('The total amount is', Total1:8:2);
Average := Total2 / 10;


FOR J := 1 TO 10 DO
BEGIN
read (Num, Amt);
Total1 := Total1 + Amt;
Total2 := Total2 + Num;
writeln ('The number is', Num:6)
END;
writeln ('The total amount is', Total1:8:2);
Average := Total2 / 10;
```

The indenting in the first segment makes it easier to determine what is contained in the body of the loop than it is in the second segment, without any indenting.

Second, blank lines can be used before and after a loop for better readability. Compare the following:

```
readln (X, Y);
writeln (X:6:2, Y:6:2);
writeln;

FOR J := -3 TO 5 DO
  writeln (J:3, '*':5);

Sum := Sum + X;
writeln (Sum:10:2);


readln (X, Y);
writeln (X:6:2, Y:6:2);
writeln;
FOR J := -3 TO 5 DO
  writeln (J:3, '*':5);
Sum := Sum + X;
writeln (Sum:10:2);
```

Again, the first segment is a bit more clear because it emphasizes that the entire loop is a single executable statement and makes it easy to locate the loop.

Third, comments within loops make them more readable. In particular, a comment should always accompany the **END** of a compound statement that is the body of a loop. The general form for this is

```
{ Get a test score }
FOR J := 1 TO 50 DO
  BEGIN
     .
     . (body of the loop)
     .
  END;  {  of FOR loop  }
```

We close this section with an example that uses a **FOR** loop to solve a problem.

STYLE TIP

There are three features you may wish to incorporate as you work with **FOR** loops. First, loop limits can be defined as constants or declared as variables and then have assigned values. Thus, you could have

```
CONST
  LoopLimit = 50;
```

Second, the loop control variable could be declared as

```
VAR
  LCV : integer;
```

The loop could then be written as

```
FOR LCV := 1 TO LoopLimit DO
    .
    . (body of the loop here)
    .
```

Third, a loop limit could be declared as a variable and then have the user enter a value during execution.

```
VAR
  LoopLimit : integer;
    .
    .
    .
  writeln ('How many entries?');
  readln (LoopLimit);
  FOR LCV := 1 TO LoopLimit DO
    .
    .
    .
```

■ EXAMPLE 5.5

Suppose you have been asked to write a segment of code to compute the test average for each of 30 students in a class and the overall class average. Data for each student consist of the student's initials and four test scores.

A first-level pseudocode development is

1. Print a heading
2. Initialize Total
3. Process data for each of 30 students
4. Compute class average
5. Print a summary

A **FOR** loop could be used to implement step 3. The step could first be refined to

3. Process data for each of 30 students
   3.1   get data for a student
   3.2   compute average
   3.3   add to Total
   3.4   print student data

Charles Babbage

The first person to propose the concept of the modern computer was Charles Babbage (1791–1871), a man truly ahead of his time. Babbage was a professor of mathematics at Cambridge University, as well as an inventor. As a mathematician, he realized the time-consuming and boring nature of constructing mathematical tables (squares, logarithms, sines, cosines, and so on). Since the calculators developed by Pascal and Leibniz could not provide the calculations required for these more complex tables, Babbage proposed the idea of building a machine that could compute the various properties of numbers, accurate to twenty digits.

With a grant from the British government, he designed and partially built a simple model of the difference engine. However, the lack of technology in the 1800s prevented him from making a working model. Discouraged by his inability to materialize his ideas, Babbage imagined a better version, which would be a general-purpose, problem-solving machine—the analytical engine.

The similarities between the analytical engine and the modern computer are amazing. Babbage's analytical engine, which was intended to be a steam-powered device, had four components:

1. A "mill" that manipulated and computed the data;

2. a "store" that held the data;
3. an "operator" of the system that carried out instructions; and
4. a separate device that entered data and received processed information via punched cards.

After spending many years sketching variations and improvements for this new model, Babbage received some assistance in 1842 from Ada Augusta Byron (see the next Note of Interest).

The code for this step is

```
FOR LCV := 1 TO ClassSize DO
  BEGIN
    writeln ('Enter three initials and press <RETURN>.');
    readln (Init1, Init2, Init3);
    writeln ('Enter four test scores and press <RETURN>.');
    readln (Score1, Score2, Score3, Score4);
    Average := (Score1 + Score2 + Score3 + Score4) / 4;
    Total := Total + Average;
    writeln;
    write (Init1:4; Init2, Init3);
    write (Score1:6, Score2:6, Score3:6, Score4:6);
    writeln (Average:10:2)
  END;
```

Exercises 5.2

1. What is the output from each of the following segments of code?

   a. ```
      FOR K := 3 TO 8 DO
         writeln ('*':K);
      ```

   b. ```
      FOR J := 1 TO 10 DO
         writeln (J:4, ' :', (10-J):5);
      ```

   c. ```
      A := 2;
      FOR J := (3 * 2 - 4) TO 10 * A DO
         writeln ('**', J:4);
      ```

   d. ```
      FOR J := 50 DOWNTO 30 DO
         writeln (51 - J:5);
      ```

2. Write a test program for each of the following:

   a. Illustrate what happens when the loop control variable is assigned a value inside the loop.

   b. Demonstrate how an accumulator works. For this test program, sum the integers from 1 to 10. Your output should show each partial sum as it is assigned to the accumulator.

3. Write segments of code using **FOR . . . TO . . . DO** or **FOR . . . DOWNTO . . . DO** loops to produce the following designs. Start each design in column 2.

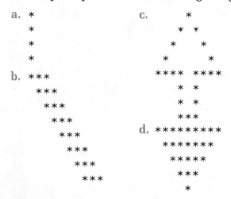

4. Which of the following segments of code do you think accomplish their intended task? For those that do not, what changes would you suggest?

   a. ```
      FOR K := 1 TO 5 DO;
         writeln (K);
      ```

   b. ```
      Sum := 0;
      FOR J := 1 TO 10 DO
         read (A);
         Sum := Sum + A;
      writeln (Sum:15);
      ```

   c. ```
      Sum := 0;
      FOR J = -3 TO 3 DO
         Sum := Sum + J;
      ```

   d. ```
      A := 0;
      FOR K := 1 TO 10 DO
         BEGIN
            A := A + K;
            writeln (K:5, A:5, A + K:5)
         END;
      writeln (K:5, A:5, A + K:5);
      ```

5. Produce each of the following outputs using both a **FOR . . . TO . . . DO** loop and a **FOR . . . DOWNTO . . . DO** loop.

   a. 1   2   3   4   5

   b. ```
      *
       *
        *
         *
          *
      ```
      ```

6. Rewrite the following segment of code using a **FOR . . . DOWNTO . . . DO** loop to produce the same result.

```
Sum := 0;
FOR K := 1 TO 4 DO
   BEGIN
      writeln ('*':21+K);
      Sum := Sum + K
   END;
```

7. Rewrite the following segment of code using a **FOR . . . TO . . . DO** loop to produce the same result.

```
FOR J := 10 DOWNTO 2 DO
   writeln (J:J);
```

8. Write a complete program that produces a table showing the temperature equivalents in degrees Fahrenheit and degrees Celsius. Let the user enter the starting and ending values. Use the formula

   CelsTemp = 5/9 ∗ (FarenTemp − 32)

9. Write a complete program to produce a chart consisting of the multiples of 5 from −50 to 50 together with the squares and cubes of these numbers. Use a procedure to print a suitable heading and user-defined functions for square and cube.

10. The formula $A = P(1 + R)^N$ can be used to compute the amount due (A) when a principal (P) has been borrowed at a monthly rate (R) for a period of N months. Write a complete program that will read in the principal, annual interest rate (divide by 12 for monthly rate), and number of months and then produce a chart that shows how much will be due at the end of each month.

■ ■ ■ ■

■ 5.3
WHILE . . . DO LOOPS

FOR loops, loops in which the body of the loop is repeated a fixed number of times, were presented in Section 5.2. There are problems in which this loop is inappropriate, since a segment of code may need to be repeated an unknown number of times. The condition controlling the loop must be variable rather than constant. Recall, Pascal provides two repetition statements with variable control conditions, one with a pretest condition and one with a posttest condition.

The pretest loop with variable conditions in Pascal is the **WHILE . . . DO** loop. The condition controlling the loop is a Boolean expression written between the reserved words **WHILE** and **DO.** Correct form and syntax for such a loop are

> **WHILE** ⟨Boolean expression⟩ **DO**
>   ⟨statement⟩;
> or
> **WHILE** ⟨Boolean expression⟩ **DO**
>   **BEGIN**
>   ⟨statement 1⟩;
>   ⟨statement 2⟩;
>   .
>   .
>   .
>   ⟨statement n⟩
>   **END;**

The flow diagram for a **WHILE . . . DO** loop is given in Figure 5.2.

FIGURE 5.2
WHILE . . . DO flow diagram

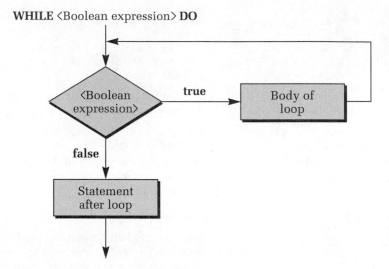

Program control, when using a **WHILE . . . DO** loop, is in order as follows:

1. The loop condition is examined.
2. If the loop condition is **true,** the entire body of the loop is executed before another check is made.
3. If the loop condition is **false,** control is transferred to the first line following the loop. For example,

```
A := 1;
WHILE A < 0 DO
  BEGIN
    Num := 5;
    writeln (Num);
    A := A + 10
  END;
writeln (A);
```

produces the single line of output

```
1
```

Before analyzing the components of the **WHILE . . . DO** statement, let's consider a short example.

■ **EXAMPLE 5.6**

This example prints some powers of two.

```
Power2 := 1;
WHILE Power2 < 100 DO
  BEGIN
    writeln (Power2);
    Power2 := Power2 * 2
  END;
```

Power2

1 ← Initial value
2^1 ← Value on successive
2^2 passes through loop
2^3 .
2^4 .
2^5 .
2^6
2^7 ← **WHILE** condition no longer **true**

The output from this segment of code is

```
1
2
4
8
16
32
64
```

With this example in mind, let's examine the general form for using a **WHILE . . . DO** loop.

1. The Boolean expression can be any expression that has Boolean values. Standard examples include relational operators and Boolean variables; thus, each of the following would be appropriate.

```
WHILE J < 10 DO
WHILE A <> B DO
WHILE Flag = true DO
WHILE Flag DO
```

2. The Boolean expression must have a value prior to entering the loop.
3. The body of the loop can be a single statement or a compound statement.
4. Provision must be made for appropriately changing the loop control condition in the body of the loop. If no such changes are made, the following could happen.

   a. If the loop condition is **true** and no changes are made, a condition called an *infinite loop* is caused. For example,

   ```
   A := 1;
   WHILE A > 0 DO
     BEGIN
       Num := 5;
       writeln (Num)
     END;
   writeln (A);
   ```

   The condition A > 0 is **true,** the body is executed, and the condition is retested. However, since the condition is not changed within the loop body, it will always be **true** and will cause an infinite loop. It will not produce a compilation error but, when you run the program, the output will be a list of 5s.

   b. If the loop condition is **true** and changes are made, but the condition never becomes **false,** you again have an infinite loop. An example of this is

   ```
   Power3 := 1;
   WHILE Power3 <> 100 DO
     BEGIN
       writeln (Power3);
       Power3 := Power3 * 3
     END;
   ```

   Since the variable Power3 never is assigned the value 100, the condition Power3 <> 100 is always **true** and you never get out of the loop.

Sentinel Values

The Boolean expression of a variable control loop is frequently controlled by a *sentinel value.* For example, a program might require the user to enter numeric data. When there are no more data, the user will be instructed to enter a special (sentinel) value. This then signifies the end of the process. Example 5.7 illustrates the use of such a sentinel.

■ **EXAMPLE 5.7**

Let's write a segment of code that allows the user to enter a set of test scores and then print the average score.

```
NumScores := 0;
Sum := 0;
writeln ('Enter a score and press <RETURN>, -999 to quit.');
readln (Score);
WHILE Score <> -999 DO
  BEGIN
    NumScores := NumScores + 1;
    Sum := Sum + Score;
    writeln ('Enter a score and press <RETURN>, -999 to quit.');
    readln (Score)
  END;
IF NumScores > 0 THEN
  Average := Sum / NumScores;
  writeln;
  writeln ('The average of ', NumScores:4, ' scores is ',
           Average:6:2);
```
■   ■

Writing Style

Writing style for **WHILE . . . DO** loops should be similar to that adopted for **FOR** loops; that is, indenting, skipping lines, and comments should all be used to enhance readability.

Using Counters

Since **WHILE . . . DO** loops may be repeated a variable number of times, it is a common practice to count the number of times the loop body is executed. This is accomplished by declaring an appropriately named integer variable, initializing it to zero before the loop, and then incrementing it by one each time through the loop. For example, if you use Count for your variable name, Example 5.6 (in which we printed some powers of two) could be modified to

```
Count := 0;
Power2 := 1;

WHILE Power2 < 100 DO
  BEGIN
    writeln (Power2);
    Power2 := Power2 * 2;
    Count := Count + 1
  END;  {  of WHILE...DO  }

writeln ('There are', Count:4,
          ' powers of 2 less than 100.');
```

The output from this segment of code is

```
        1
        2
        4
        8
       16
       32
       64
There are   7 powers of 2 less than 100.
```

Although the process is tedious, it is instructive to trace the values of variables through a loop where a *counter* is used. Therefore, let us consider the segment of code we have just seen. Before the loop is entered, we have

0		1
Count		Power2

The loop control is Power2 < 100 (1 < 100). Since this is **true,** the loop body is executed and the new values become

1		2
Count		Power2

Prior to each successive time through the loop, the condition Power2 < 100 is checked. Thus, the loop produces the sequence of values

Count	Power2
1	2
2	4
3	8
4	16
5	32
6	64
7	128

Although Power2 is 128, the remainder of the loop is executed before checking the loop condition. Once a loop is entered, it is executed completely before the loop control condition is reexamined. Since 128 < 100 is **false,** control is transferred to the statement following the loop.

Compound Conditions

All previous examples and illustrations of **WHILE . . . DO** loops have used simple Boolean expressions. However, since any Boolean expression can be used as a loop control condition, compound Boolean expressions can also be used. For example,

```
read (A, B);
WHILE (A < 0) AND (B < 0) DO
  BEGIN
    writeln (A, B);
    A := A - 5;
    B := B - 3
  END;
```

will go through the body of the loop only when the Boolean expression (A > 0) **AND** (B > 0) is **true.** Thus, if the values of A and B obtained from the keyboard are

17 8

the output from this segment of code is

```
17        8
12        5
 7        2
```

Compound Boolean expressions can be as complex as you wish to make them. However, if several conditions are involved, the program can become difficult to read and debug; therefore, you may wish to redesign your solution to avoid this problem.

Ada Augusta Byron

Ada Augusta Byron, Countess of Lovelace (1815–1852), became interested in Charles Babbage's efforts when she was translating a paper on the analytical engine from French to English. Upon meeting Babbage, she began the task of writing an original paper. Through the process, she documented Babbage's ideas and made it possible to understand Babbage's original intentions. Over time, she became a full collaborator on the project, correcting some errors and suggesting the use of the binary system of storage rather than the decimal.

Lady Lovelace's most important contribution was her concept of a loop. She observed that a repetition of a sequence of instructions often was necessary to perform a single calculation. Thus, she discovered that by using a single set of cards and a conditional jump facility, the calculation could be performed with a fraction of the effort. This idea has earned her the distinction of being the first programmer.

In honor of her role as the first computer programmer, the United States Department of Defense named its newly-designed computer language Ada.

Exercises 5.3

1. Compare and contrast **FOR** loops with **WHILE . . . DO** loops.

2. Write a test program that illustrates what happens when you have an infinite loop.

3. What is the output from each of the following segments of code?

a.
```
K := 1;
WHILE K <= 10 DO
  BEGIN
    writeln (K);
    K := K + 1        Arbitrary Semicolon?
  END;
```
b.
```
A := 1;
WHILE 17 MOD A <> 5 DO
  BEGIN
    writeln (A, 17 MOD A);
    A := A + 1
  END;
```
c.
```
A := 2;
B := 50;
WHILE A < B DO
  A := A * 3;
writeln (A, B);
```
d.
```
Count := 0;
Sum := 0;
WHILE Count < 5 DO
  BEGIN
    Count := Count + 1;
    Sum := Sum + Count;
    writeln ('The partial sum is', Sum:4)
  END;
writeln ('The count is', Count:4);
```
e.
```
X := 3.0;
Y := 2.0;
WHILE X * Y < 100 DO
  X := X * Y;
writeln (X:10:2, Y:10:2);
```

4. Indicate which of the following are infinite loops and explain why they are infinite.

   a.
   ```
   J := 1;
   WHILE J < 10 DO
      writeln (J);
      J := J + 1;
   ```

   b.
   ```
   A := 2;
   WHILE A < 20 DO
      BEGIN
         writeln (A);
         A := A * 2
      END;
   ```

   c.
   ```
   A := 2;
   WHILE A <> 20 DO
      BEGIN
         writeln (A);
         A := A * 2
      END;
   ```

   d.
   ```
   B := 15;
   WHILE B DIV 3 = 5 DO
      BEGIN
         writeln (B, B DIV 5);
         B := B - 1
      END;
   ```

5. Write a **WHILE . . . DO** loop for each of the following tasks.

   a. Print a positive real number, Num, and then print successive values where each value is 0.5 less than the previous value. The list should continue as long as values to be printed are positive.

   b. Print a list of squares of positive integers as long as the difference between consecutive squares is less than 50.

6. Write a segment of code that reads a positive integer and prints a list of powers of the integer that are less than 10,000.

■ ■ ■ ■

■ 5.4
REPEAT . . . UNTIL
Loops

The previous two sections discussed two kinds of repetition. We looked at fixed repetition using **FOR** loops and variable repetition using **WHILE . . . DO** loops. Pascal provides a second form of variable repetition, a **REPEAT . . . UNTIL** loop, which is a *posttest* or *exit controlled loop*.

The basic form and syntax for a **REPEAT . . . UNTIL** loop is

```
REPEAT
   ⟨statement 1⟩;
   ⟨statement 2⟩;
        .
        .
        .
   ⟨statement n⟩
UNTIL ⟨Boolean expression⟩;
```

A flow diagram for a **REPEAT . . . UNTIL** loop is given in Figure 5.3.

FIGURE 5.3
REPEAT . . . UNTIL
flow diagram

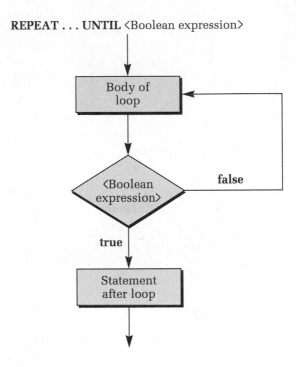

REPEAT . . . UNTIL ⟨Boolean expression⟩

Prior to examining this form, let us consider the fragment of code

```
Count := 0;
REPEAT
  Count := Count + 1;
  writeln (Count)
UNTIL Count = 5;
writeln ('All done':10);
```

The output for this fragment is

```
        1
        2
        3
        4
        5
All done
```

With this example in mind, the following comments concerning the use of a **REPEAT . . . UNTIL** loop are in order.

1. The program statements between **REPEAT** and **UNTIL** are executed in order as they appear. Thus, a **BEGIN . . . END** block is not necessary.
2. A semicolon is not required between the last statement in the body of the loop and the reserved word **UNTIL**.
3. The Boolean expression must have a value before it is used at the end of the loop.
4. The loop must be entered at least once because the Boolean expression is not evaluated until after the loop body has been executed.

5. When the Boolean expression is evaluated, if it is **false,** control is transferred back to the top of the loop; if it is **true,** control is transferred to the next program statement.

6. Provision must be made for changing values inside the loop so that the Boolean expression used to control the loop will eventually be **true.** If this is not done, you will have an infinite loop, as shown.

```
J := 0;
REPEAT
  J := J + 2;
  writeln (J)
UNTIL J = 5;
```

7. Writing style for using **REPEAT . . . UNTIL** loops should be consistent with your style for using other loop structures.

There are two important differences between **WHILE . . . DO** and **REPEAT . . . UNTIL** loops. First, a **REPEAT . . . UNTIL** loop must be executed at least once, but a **WHILE . . . DO** loop can be skipped if the initial value of the Boolean expression is **false.** Because of this, **REPEAT . . . UNTIL** loops are generally used less frequently than **WHILE . . . DO** loops.

The second difference is that a **REPEAT . . . UNTIL** loop is repeated until the Boolean expression becomes **true;** in a **WHILE . . . DO** loop, repetition continues until the Boolean expression becomes **false.**

■ **EXAMPLE 5.8**

An early method of approximating square roots was the Newton-Raphson method. This method consisted of starting with an approximation and then getting successively better approximations until the desired degree of accuracy was achieved.

Writing code for this method, each NewGuess is defined to be

```
NewGuess := 1/2 * (OldGuess + Number / OldGuess)
```

Thus, if the number entered was 34 and the first approximation was 5, the second approximation would be

```
1/2 * (5 + 34 / 5)        (5.9)
```

and the third approximation would be

```
1/2 * (5.9 + 34 / 5.9)        (5.83135593)
```

Let's see how a **REPEAT . . . UNTIL** loop can be used to obtain successively better approximations until a desired degree of accuracy is reached.

Assume Number contains the number whose square root we wish to approximate, OldGuess contains a first approximation, and DesiredAccuracy is a defined constant. A loop used in the solution of this problem is

```
writeln (NewGuess:12:8);
REPEAT
  OldGuess := NewGuess;
  NewGuess := 1/2 * (OldGuess + Number / OldGuess);
  writeln (NewGuess:12:8)
UNTIL abs(NewGuess - OldGuess) < DesiredAccuracy;
```

If DesiredAccuracy is 0.0001, Number is 34, and NewGuess is originally 5, the output from this segment is

```
5.00000000
5.90000000
5.83135593
5.83095191
5.83095189
```

■ EXAMPLE 5.9

Interactive programming frequently requires the use of a menu to give the user a choice of options. For example, suppose you want a menu to be

```
Which of the following recipes do you wish to see?

    (T)acos
    (J)ambalaya
    (G)umbo
    (Q)uit

Enter the first letter and press ⟨RETURN⟩.
```

This screen message could then be written as a procedure menu and the main program could use a **REPEAT . . . UNTIL** loop as follows:

```
REPEAT
  Menu;
  readln (Selection);
  CASE Selection OF
    'T' : Tacos;
    'J' : Jambalaya;
    'G' : Gumbo;
    'Q' : GoodbyeMessage
  END  {  of CASE Selection  }
UNTIL Selection = 'Q';
```

where Tacos, Jambalaya, Gumbo, and GoodbyeMessage are each separate procedures with appropriate messages.

Compound Conditions

The Boolean expression used with a **REPEAT . . . UNTIL** loop can be as complex as you choose to make it. However, as with **WHILE . . . DO** loops, if the expression gets too complicated, you might enhance program readability and design by redesigning the algorithm to use simpler expressions.

Choosing the Correct Loop

"Which loop should I use?" is a question often faced by programmers. A partial answer is easy. If a loop is to be repeated a predetermined number of times during execution, a **FOR** loop is preferable. If the number of repetitions is not known, one of the variable control loops should be used.

The more difficult part of the answer is deciding which variable control loop is appropriate. Simply stated, if a control check is needed before the loop is executed, use a **WHILE . . . DO** loop. If the check is needed at the end of the loop, use a **REPEAT . . . UNTIL** loop. Remember, however, a **REPEAT**

. . . **UNTIL** loop must always be executed at least once. Therefore, if there is a possibility that the loop will never be executed, a **WHILE . . . DO** loop must be used. For example, when reading data (especially from files, see Chapter 10), if there is a possibility of no data, a **WHILE . . . DO** loop must be used with a prompting read or other control check prior to the loop. Thus, you could have

```
writeln ('Enter a score, -999 to quit.');
readln (Score);
MoreData := (Score <> -999);
WHILE MoreData DO
  BEGIN
    .
    .  (process data)
    .
    writeln ('Enter a score, -999 to quit.');
    readln (Score);
    MoreData := (Score <> -999)
  END;  {  of WHILE loop  }
```

If the three lines of code required to get a score were written as a procedure, this would appear as

```
GetData (Score, MoreData);
WHILE MoreData DO
  BEGIN
    .
    .  (process data)
    .
    GetData (Score, MoreData)
  END;  {  of WHILE loop  }
```

In the event either variable control loop can be used, the problem itself might help with the decision. Does the process need to be repeated until something happens, or does the process continue as long as (while) some condition is true? If either of these is apparent, use the code that most accurately reflects the solution to the problem.

Data Validation

Variable condition loops can be used to make programs more robust. In particular, suppose you are writing an interactive program that expects positive integers to be entered from the keyboard, with a sentinel value of -999 to be entered when you wish to quit. You can guard against bad data by using the following:

```
REPEAT
  writeln ('Enter a positive integer; <-999> to quit.');
  readln (Num)
UNTIL (Num > 0) OR (Num = -999);
```

This process of examining data prior to its use in a program is referred to as *data validation*, and loops are useful for such validation. A second example of using a loop for this purpose follows.

■ **EXAMPLE 5.10**

One problem associated with interactive programs is guarding against typing errors. This example illustrates how a **REPEAT . . . UNTIL** loop can be used to avoid having something entered other than the anticipated responses.

Specifically, suppose users of an interactive program are asked to indicate whether or not they wish to continue by entering either a 'Y' or 'N'. The screen message could be

```
Do you wish to continue? <Y or N>
?
```

You wish to allow any of 'Y', 'y', 'N', or 'n' to be used as an appropriate response. Any other entry is considered an error. This can be accomplished by the following:

```
REPEAT
  writeln ('Do you wish to continue? <Y or N>');
  readln (Response);
  GoodResponse := (Response = 'Y') OR (Response = 'y') OR
                  (Response = 'N') OR (Response = 'n')
UNTIL GoodResponse;
```

Any response other than those permitted as good data (Y, y, N, n) results in GoodResponse being **false** and the loop being executed again.

Exercises 5.4

1. Explain the difference between a pretest loop and a posttest loop.

2. Write a test program that illustrates what happens when the initial condition for a **REPEAT . . . UNTIL** loop is **false.** Compare this with a similar condition for a **WHILE . . . DO** loop.

3. Indicate what the output will be from each of the following.

   a.
   ```
   A := 0;
   B := 10;
   REPEAT
     A := A + 1;
     B := B - 1;
     writeln (A, B)
   UNTIL A > B;
   ```

   b.
   ```
   Power := 1;
   REPEAT
     Power := Power * 2;
     writeln (Power)
   UNTIL Power > 100;
   ```

   c.
   ```
   J := 1;
   REPEAT
     writeln (J);
     J := J + 1
   UNTIL J > 10;
   ```

   d.
   ```
   A := 1;
   REPEAT
     writeln (A, 17 MOD A);
     A := A + 1
   UNTIL 17 MOD A = 5;
   ```

4. Indicate which of the following are infinite loops and explain why.

   a.
   ```
   J := 1;
   REPEAT
     writeln (J)
   UNTIL J > 10;
   J := J + 1;
   ```

```
b. A := 2;
   REPEAT
     writeln (A);
     A := A * 2
   UNTIL A > 20;
c. A := 2;
   REPEAT
     writeln (A);
     A := A * 2
   UNTIL A = 20;
d. B := 15;
   REPEAT
     writeln (B, B DIV 5);
     B := B - 1
   UNTIL B DIV 3 <> 5;
```

5. Write a **REPEAT . . . UNTIL** loop for each of the following tasks.

   a. Print a positive real number, Num, and then print successive values where each value is 0.5 less than the previous value. The list should continue as long as values to be printed are positive.

   b. Print a list of squares of positive integers as long as the difference between consecutive squares is less than 50.

6. Discuss whether or not a priming read is needed before a **REPEAT . . . UNTIL** loop that is used to get data?

7. Give an example of a situation that would require a predetermined number of repetitions.

8. In mathematics and science, many applications require a certain level or degree of accuracy obtained by successive approximations. Explain how the process of reaching the desired level of accuracy would relate to loops in Pascal.

9. Write a program that utilizes the algorithm for approximating a square root as shown in Example 5.8. Let the defined accuracy be 0.0001. Input should consist of a number whose square root is desired. Your program should guard against bad data entries (negatives and zero). Output should include a list of approximations and a check of your final approximation.

10. Compare and contrast the three repetition structures previously discussed in this chapter.

■ ■ ■ ■

■ 5.5
Loop Verification
(Optional)

Loop verification is the process of guaranteeing that a loop performs its intended task. Such verification is part of program testing and correctness to which we referred in Chapter 4.

Some work has been done on constructing formal proofs that loops are "correct." We now examine a modified version of loop verification; a complete treatment of the issue will be the topic of subsequent course work.

Preconditions and Postconditions with Loops

Preconditions and postconditions can be used with loops. Loop preconditions are referred to as *input assertions*. They are comments that indicate what can be expected to be true before the loop is entered. Loop postconditions are referred to as *output assertions*. They are comments that indicate what can be expected to be true when the loop is exited.

To illustrate input and output assertions, let's consider the mathematical problem of summing the proper divisors of a positive integer. For example, we have

Integer	Proper Divisors	Sum
6	1, 2, 3	6
9	1, 3	4
12	1, 2, 3, 4, 6	16

As part of a program that will have a positive integer as input, and as output, will have a determination of whether the integer is perfect (Sum = integer), abundant (Sum > integer), or deficient (Sum < integer), it is necessary to sum the divisors. A loop to perform this task is

```
DivisorSum := 0;
FOR TrialDivisor := 1 TO Num DIV 2 DO
   IF Num MOD TrialDivisor = 0 THEN
      DivisorSum := DivisorSum + TrialDivisor;
```

An input assertion for this loop is

```
{  Precondition: 1. Num is a positive integer.        }
{                2. DivisorSum = 0.                    }
```

An output assertion is

```
{  Postcondition: DivisorSum is the sum of all proper  }
{                 divisors of Num.                     }
```

When these are placed with the previous code, we have

```
DivisorSum := 0;
 {  Precondition: 1. Num is a positive integer.        }
 {                2. DivisorSum = 0.                    }

FOR TrialDivisor := 1 TO Num DIV 2 DO
   IF Num MOD TrialDivisor = 0 THEN
      DivisorSum := DivisorSum + TrialDivisor;

 {  Postcondition: DivisorSum is the sum of all proper }
 {                 divisors of Num.                     }
```

Invariant and Variant Assertions

A *loop invariant* is an assertion that expresses a relationship between variables that remains constant throughout all iterations of the loop. In other words, it is a statement that is true both before the loop is entered and after each pass through the loop. An invariant assertion for the preceding code segment could be

```
{  DivisorSum is the sum of proper divisors of Num that  }
{  are less than or equal to TrialDivisor.               }
```

A *loop variant* is an assertion whose truth changes between the first and final execution of the loop. The loop variant expression should be stated in such a way that it guarantees the loop is exited. Thus, it contains some statement about the loop variable being incremented (or decremented) during execution of the loop. In the preceding code, we could have

```
{  TrialDivisor is incremented by 1 each time through the  }
{  loop. It eventually exceeds the value Num DIV 2, at     }
{  which point the loop is exited.                         }
```

Variant and invariant assertions usually occur in pairs.

We now use four kinds of assertions—input, output, variant, and invariant—to produce the formally verified loop which follows.

```
DivisorSum := 0;

{  Precondition: 1. Num is a positive integer.  }   (input
{                2. DivisorSum = 0.              }   assertion)

FOR TrialDivisor := 1 TO Num DIV 2 DO

{  TrialDivisor is incremented by 1 each time    }   (variant
{  through the loop. It eventually exceeds the   }   assertion)
{  value Num DIV 2, at which point the loop is   }
{  exited.                                       }

  IF Num MOD TrialDivisor = 0 THEN
    DivisorSum := DivisorSum + TrialDivisor;

{  DivisorSum is the sum of proper divisors of   }   (invariant
{  Num that are less than or equal to            }   assertion)
{  TrialDivisor.                                 }

{  Postcondition: DivisorSum is the sum of       }   (output
{  all proper divisors of Num.                   }   assertion)
```

In general, code that is presented in this text does not include formal verification of the loops. This issue is similar to that of robustness. In an introductory course, a decision must be made on the trade-off between learning new concepts and writing robust programs with formal verification of loops. We encourage the practice, but space and time considerations make it inconvenient to include such documentation at this level. We close this discussion with another example illustrating loop verification.

■ **EXAMPLE 5.11**

Consider the problem of finding the greatest common divisor (GCD) of two positive integers. To illustrate, we have

Num1	Num2	GCD (Num 1, Num2)
8	12	4
20	10	10
15	32	1
70	40	10

A segment of code to produce the GCD of two positive integers after they have been ordered as Small, Large, is

```
TrialGCD := Small;
GCDFound := false;
WHILE NOT GCDFound DO
  IF (Large MOD TrialGCD = 0) AND
     (Small MOD TrialGCD = 0) THEN
```

```
   BEGIN
      GCD := TrialGCD:
      GCDFound := true
   END
 ELSE
   TrialGCD := TrialGCD - 1;
```

Using assertions as previously indicated, this code would appear as

```
TrialGCD := Small;
GCDFound := false;

{  Precondition: 1. Small <= Large                          }
{               2. TrialGCD (Small) is the first           }
{                  candidate for GCD                        }
{               3. GCDFound is false                        }

WHILE NOT GCDFound DO

{  TrialGCD assumes integer values ranging from Small       }
{  to 1. It is decremented by 1 each time through the       }
{  loop. When TrialGCD divides both Small and Large,        }
{  the loop is exited. Exit is guaranteed since 1           }
{  divides both Small and Large.                            }

IF (Large MOD TrialGCD = 0) AND
   (Small MOD TrialGCD = 0) THEN
   BEGIN

      {  When TrialGCD divides both Large and Small,        }
      {  then GCD is assigned that value.                   }

      GCD := TrialGCD;
      GCDFound := true
   END
ELSE
 TrialGCD := TrialGCD - 1;

{  Postcondition: GCD is the greatest common divisor        }
{          of Small and Large.                              }
```

Exercises 5.5 (Optional)

1. Write appropriate input assertions and output assertions for each of the following loops.

   a.
   ```
   readln (Score);
   WHILE Score <> -999 DO
      BEGIN
         NumScores := NumScores + 1;
         Sum := Sum + Score;
         writeln ('Enter a score; -999 to quit.');
         readln (Score)
      END;
   ```

   b.
   ```
   Count := 0;
   Power2 := 1;
   WHILE Power2 < 100 DO
      BEGIN
         writeln (Power2);
         Power2 := Power2 * 2;
         Count := Count + 1
      END;
   ```

c. (From Example 5.8)

```
REPEAT
  OldGuess := NewGuess;
  NewGuess := 1/2 * (OldGuess + Number / OldGuess);
  writeln (NewGuess:12:8)
UNTIL abs(NewGuess - OldGuess) < DesiredAccuracy;
```

2. Write appropriate loop invariant and loop variant assertions for each of the loops in Exercise 1.

3. The following loop comes from a program called HiLo. The user enters a number, Guess, and the computer then displays a message indicating whether the guess is correct, too high, or too low. Add appropriate input assertions, output assertions, loop invariant assertions, and loop variant assertions to the following code.

```
Correct := false;
Count := 0;
WHILE (Count < MaxTries) AND (NOT Correct) DO
  BEGIN
    Count := Count + 1;
    writeln ('Enter choice number ', Count);
    readln (Guess);
    IF Guess = Choice THEN
      BEGIN
        Correct := true;
        writeln ('Congratulations!')
      END
    ELSE IF Guess < Choice THEN
      writeln ('Your guess is too low')
    ELSE
      writeln ('Your guess is too high')
  END;
```

■ 5.6
Nested Loops

In this chapter, we have examined three loop structures. Each of them has been discussed with respect to syntax, semantics, form, writing style, and use in programs. But remember that each loop is treated as a single Pascal statement. In this sense, it is possible to have a loop as one of the statements in the body of another loop. When this happens, the loops are said to be *nested*.

Loops can be nested to any depth; that is; a loop can be within a loop within a loop, and so on. Also, any of the three types of loops can be nested within any loop. However, a programmer should be careful not to design a program with nesting that is too complex. If program logic becomes too difficult to follow, you might better redesign the program. For example, you could split off the inner logic into a separate subprogram.

Flow of Control

As a first example of using a loop within a loop, consider

```
FOR K := 1 TO 5 DO
  FOR J := 1 TO 3 DO
    writeln (K + J);
```

When this fragment is executed, the following happens:

1. K is assigned a value.
2. For each value of K, the following loop is executed.

```
FOR J := 1 TO 3 DO
   writeln (K + J);
```

Thus, for K := 1, the "inside" or nested loop produces the output

```
2
3
4
```

At this point, K := 2 and the next portion of the output produced by the nested loop is

```
3
4
5
```

The complete output from these nested loops is

```
2 ⎫
3 ⎬ from K := 1
4 ⎭
3 ⎫
4 ⎬ from K := 2
5 ⎭
4 ⎫
5 ⎬ from K := 3
6 ⎭
5 ⎫
6 ⎬ from K := 4
7 ⎭
6 ⎫
7 ⎬ from K := 5
8 ⎭
```

As you can see, for each value assigned to the index of the outside loop, the inside loop is executed completely. Suppose you want the output to be printed in the form of a chart as follows:

```
2    3    4
3    4    5
4    5    6
5    6    7
6    7    8
```

The pseudocode design to produce this output is

1. **FOR** K := 1 **TO** 5 **DO**
produce a line

A refinement of this is

1. **FOR** K:= 1 **TO** 5 **DO**
   1.1 print on one line
   1.2 advance the printer

The Pascal code for this development becomes

```
FOR K := 1 TO 5 DO
   BEGIN
     FOR J := 1 TO 3 DO
        write ((K + J):4);
     writeln
   END;
```

Our next example shows how nested loops can be used to produce a design.

■ **EXAMPLE 5.12**

Use nested **FOR** loops to produce the output

```
*
**
***
****
*****
```

where the left asterisks are in column 10.

The first-level pseudocode to solve this problem could be

1. **FOR** K := 1 **TO** 5 **DO**
    produce a line

A refinement of this could be

1. **FOR** K := 1 **TO** 5 **DO**
    1.1 print on one line
    1.2 advance the printer

Step 1.1 is not yet sufficiently refined, so our next level could be

1. **FOR** K := 1 **TO** 5 **DO**
    1.1 print on one line
        1.1.1 put a blank in column 9
        1.1.2 print K asterisks
    1.2 advance the printer

We can now write a program fragment to produce the desired output as follows:

```
FOR K := 1 TO 5 DO
  BEGIN
    write (' ':9);
    FOR J := 1 TO K DO
      write ('*');
    writeln
  END;  { of outer loop }
```

A significant feature has been added to this program fragment. Note that the loop control for the inner loop is the index of the outer loop.

■   ■

STYLE TIP

■ ■ ■ ■ ■ ■ ■ ■ ■ ■ ■

When working with nested loops, use line comments to indicate the effect of each loop control variable. For example,

```
FOR K := 1 TO 5 DO  {  Each value produces a line  }
  BEGIN
    write (' ':9);
    FOR J := 1 TO K DO  {  This moves across one line  }
      write ('*');
    writeln
  END;  { of outer loop }
```

Thus far, nested loops have been used only with **FOR** loops, but any of the loop structures may be used in nesting. Our next example illustrates a **REPEAT . . . UNTIL** loop nested within a **WHILE . . . DO** loop.

■ **EXAMPLE 5.13**

Trace the flow of control and indicate the output for the following program fragment.

```
A := 10;
B := 0;
WHILE A > B DO
  BEGIN
    writeln (A:5);
    REPEAT
      writeln (A:5, B:5, (A + B):5);
      A := A - 2
    UNTIL A <= 6;
    B := B + 2
  END;  {  of WHILE...DO  }
writeln;
writeln ('All done':20);
```

The assignment statements produce

10		0
A		B

and A > B is **true;** thus, the **WHILE . . . DO** loop is entered. The first time through this loop the **REPEAT . . . UNTIL** loop is used. Output for the first pass is

```
10
10    0   10
```

and the values for A and B are

8		0
A		B

The Boolean expression A <= 6 is **false** and the **REPEAT . . . UNTIL** loop is executed again to produce the next line of output

```
 8    0    8
```

and the values for A and B become

6		0
A		B

At this point, A <= 6 is **true** and control transfers to the line of code

```
B := B + 2;
```

Thus, the variable values are

6		2
A		B

and the Boolean expression A > B is **true.** This means the **WHILE . . . DO** loop will be repeated. The output for the second time through this loop is

```
6
6    2    8
```

and the values for the variables are

A   B

Now A > B is **false** and control is transferred to the line following the
WHILE . . . DO loop. Output for the complete fragment is

```
10
10       0    10
 8       0     8
 6
 6       2     8

        All done
```

■   ■

Example 5.13 is a bit contrived and tracing the flow of control somewhat
tedious. However, it is important for you to be able to follow the logic
involved in using nested loops.

Writing Style

As usual, you should be aware of the significance of using a consistent,
readable style of writing when using nested loops. There are at least three
features you should consider.

1. **Indenting.** Each loop should have its own level of indenting. This
   makes it easier to identify the body of the loop. If the loop body
   consists of a compound statement, the **BEGIN** and **END** should start
   in the same column. Using our previous indenting style, a typical
   nesting might be

```
FOR K := 1 TO 10 DO
  BEGIN
    WHILE A > 0 DO
      BEGIN
        REPEAT
           .
           .
           .
        UNTIL <condition>;  {  end of REPEAT loop  }
        <statement>
      END;  {  of WHILE...DO loop  }
    <statement>
  END;  {  of FOR loop  }
```

   If the body of a loop becomes very long, it is sometimes difficult to
   match the **BEGIN**s with the proper **END**s. In this case, you should
   either redesign the program (for example, write a separate subprogram) or be especially careful.
2. **Using comments.** Comments can precede a loop and explain what the
   loop will do, or they can be used with statements inside the loop to
   explain what the statement does. They should be used to indicate the
   end of a loop where the loop body is a compound statement.
3. **Skipping lines.** This is an effective way of isolating loops within a
   program and making nested loops easier to identify.

A note of caution is in order with respect to writing style. Program documentation is important; however, excessive use of comments and skipped lines can detract from readability. You should develop a happy medium.

Statement Execution in Nested Loops

Using nested loops can significantly increase the number of times statements get executed in a program. To illustrate, suppose a program contains a **REPEAT . . . UNTIL** loop that gets executed six times before it is exited. This is illustrated by

```
          ┌ REPEAT
          │    .
6 times   │    .         (action here)
          │    .
          └ UNTIL <condition 1>;
```

If one of the statements inside this loop is another loop, the inner loop will be executed six times. Suppose this inner loop is repeated five times whenever it is entered. This means each statement within the inner loop will be executed $6 \times 5 = 30$ times when the program is run. This is illustrated by

```
          ┌ REPEAT
          │    .
          │    .            (action here)
          │    .
          │    WHILE <condition 2> DO                      ┐
          │       BEGIN                                    │
6 times  ─┤          <statement>┐─────── 30 times          ├─ 5 times
          │       END; {  of WHILE . . . DO  }             ┘
          │    .
          │    .
          │    .
          └ UNTIL <condition 1>;
```

When a third level of nesting is used, the number of times a statement is executed can be determined by the product of three factors, $n_1 * n_2 * n_3$, where n_1 represents the number of repetitions of the outside loop, n_2 represents the number of repetitions for the first level of nesting, and n_3 represents the number of repetitions for the innermost loop.

We close this section with an example of a program that uses nested loops to print a multiplication table.

■ EXAMPLE 5.14

This example presents a complete program whose output is the multiplication table from 1×1 to 10×10. A suitable heading is part of the output.

```
PROGRAM MultTable (input, output);

CONST
   Indent = ' ';
```

```
{*************************************************************}


PROCEDURE PrintHeading;

  { Given:   Nothing                                          }
  { Task:    Print a heading for the multiplication table     }
  { Return:  Nothing                                          }

  BEGIN
    writeln;
    writeln (Indent:17, 'Multiplication Table');
    writeln (Indent:17, '--------------------');
    writeln (Indent:10, '( Generated by nested FOR loops )');
    writeln
  END;  { of PROCEDURE PrintHeading  }


{*************************************************************}


PROCEDURE PrintTable;

  { Given:   Nothing                                          }
  { Task:    Use nested loops to print a multiplication table }
  { Return:  Nothing                                          }

  VAR
    Row, Column : integer;

  BEGIN

    { Print the column heads  }
    writeln (Indent:11, '   1   2   3   4   5   6   7   8   9  10');
    writeln (Indent:8, '---!-------------------------------------');

    { Now start the loop  }
    FOR Row := 1 TO 10 DO
      BEGIN  { print one row  }
        write (Row:10, ' !');
        FOR Column := 1 TO 10 DO
          write (Row * Column:4);
        writeln;
        writeln (Indent:11,'!')
      END;  { of each row  }
    writeln
  END;  { of PROCEDURE PrintTable  }


{*************************************************************}


BEGIN  { Main program  }
  PrintHeading;
  PrintTable
END.  { of main program  }
```

The output from this program is

```
                Multiplication Table
                --------------------
          ( Generated by nested FOR loops )

           1    2    3    4    5    6    7    8    9   10
    ---!-----------------------------------------------------
     1 !    1    2    3    4    5    6    7    8    9   10
       !
     2 !    2    4    6    8   10   12   14   16   18   20
       !
     3 !    3    6    9   12   15   18   21   24   27   30
       !
     4 !    4    8   12   16   20   24   28   32   36   40
       !
     5 !    5   10   15   20   25   30   35   40   45   50
       !
     6 !    6   12   18   24   30   36   42   48   54   60
       !
     7 !    7   14   21   28   35   42   49   56   63   70
       !
     8 !    8   16   24   32   40   48   56   64   72   80
       !
     9 !    9   18   27   36   45   54   63   72   81   90
       !
    10 !   10   20   30   40   50   60   70   80   90  100
       !
```

A NOTE OF INTEREST

A Digital Matter of Life and Death

The radiation-therapy machine, a Therac 25 linear accelerator, was designed to send a penetrating X-ray or electron beam deep into a cancer patient's body to destroy embedded tumors without injuring skin tissue. But in three separate instances in 1985 and 1986, the machine failed. Instead of delivering a safe level of radiation, the Therac 25 administered a dose that was more than 100 times larger than the typical treatment dose. Two patients died and a third was severely burned.

The malfunction was caused by an error in the computer program controlling the machine. It was a subtle error that no one had picked up during the extensive testing the machine had undergone. The error surfaced only when a technician happened to use a specific, unusual combination of keystrokes to instruct the machine.

The Therac incidents and other cases of medical device failures caused by computer errors have focused attention on the increasingly important role played by computers in medical applications. Computers or machines with built-in microprocessors perform functions that range from keeping track of patients to diagnosing ailments and providing treatments.

"The impact of computers on medical care and the medical community is the most significant factor that we have to face," says Frank E. Samuel Jr., president of the Health Industry Manufacturers Association (HIMA), based in Washington, D.C. "Health care will change more dramatically in the next 10 years because of software-driven products than for any other single cause." Samuel made his remarks at a recent HIMA-sponsored conference on the regulation of medical software.

At the same time, reports of medical devices with computer-related problems are appearing more and more frequently. In 1985, the Food and Drug Administration (FDA) reported that recalls of medical devices because of computer faults had roughly doubled over the previous five years. Since then, the number of such complaints has risen further.

The FDA, in its mandated role as guardian of public health and safety, is now preparing to regulate the software component of medical devices. The agency's effort has already raised questions about what kinds of products, software and information systems should be regulated.

Exercises 5.6

1. Write a program fragment that uses nested loops to produce each of the following designs.

```
a. *****          b.      *          c. ***
   ****                  ***            ***
   ***                  *****           ***
   **                 *******           ***
   *                   *****         ******
                        ***          ******
                         *           ******
```

2. What is the output from each of the following fragments?

```
a. FOR K := 2 TO 6 DO
     BEGIN
       FOR J := 5 TO 10 DO
         write (K + J);
         writeln
     END;
b. FOR K := 2 TO 6 DO
     BEGIN
       FOR J := 5 TO 10 DO
         write (K * J);
         writeln
     END;
c. Sum := 0;
   A := 7;
   WHILE A < 10 DO
     BEGIN
       FOR K := A TO 10 DO
         Sum := Sum + K;
       A := A + 1
     END;
   writeln (Sum);
d. Sum := 0;
   FOR K := 1 TO 10 DO
     FOR J := (10*K-9) TO (10*K) DO
       Sum := Sum + J;
   writeln (Sum);
```

3. What output is produced from the following segment of code?

```
A := 4;
B := 7;
REPEAT
  Num := A;
  WHILE Num <= B DO
    BEGIN
      FOR K := A TO B DO
        write (Num:4);
      writeln;
      Num := Num + 1
    END;  { of WHILE...DO }
  writeln;
  A := A + 1
UNTIL A = B;  { end of REPEAT...UNTIL loop }
```

4. Write a program fragment that uses nested loops to produce the output

```
2    4    6    8   10
3    6    9   12   15
4    8   12   16   20
5   10   15   20   25
```

■ ■ ■ ■

■ 5.7
Repetition and Selection

Selection within Repetition (Loops)

In Chapter 4 we discussed the use of selection statements. In this chapter we have discussed the use of three different types of loops. It is now time to see how they are used together. We will first examine selection statements contained within the body of a loop.

■ **EXAMPLE 5.15**

Write a program fragment that computes gross wages for employees of the Florida OJ Canning Company. The data consist of three initials, the total hours worked, and the hourly rate; for example,

　　JHA 44.5 12.75

Overtime (more than 40 hours) is computed as time-and-a-half. The output should include all input data and a column of gross wages.

A first-level pseudocode development for this program is

1. **WHILE** MoreEmployees **DO**
　1.1　process one employee
　1.2　print results

This could be refined to

1. **WHILE** MoreEmployees **DO**
　1.1　process one employee
　　　1.1.1　get data
　　　1.1.2　compute wage
　1.2　print results

Step 1.1.2 can be refined to

　1.1.2　compute wage
　　　1.1.2.1　**IF** Hours <= 40.0 **THEN**
　　　　　　compute regular time
　　　　　ELSE
　　　　　　compute time-and-a-half

and the final algorithm for the fragment is

1. **WHILE** MoreEmployees **DO**
　1.1　process one employee
　　　1.1.1　get data
　　　1.1.2　compute wage
　　　　　1.1.2.1　**IF** Hours <= 40.0 **THEN**
　　　　　　　　compute regular time
　　　　　　　ELSE
　　　　　　　　compute time-and-a-half
　1.2　print results

The code for this fragment is

```
writeln ('Any employees?   <Y> or <N>');
readln (Choice);
MoreEmployees := (Choice = 'Y') OR (Choice = 'y');
WHILE MoreEmployees DO
```

```
        BEGIN
          writeln;
          writeln ('Enter initials, hours, and payrate.');
          readln (Init1, Init2, Init3, Hours, PayRate);
          IF Hours <= 40.0 THEN
            TotalWage := Hours * PayRate
          ELSE
            BEGIN
              Overtime := 1.5 * (Hours - 40.0) * PayRate;
              TotalWage := 40 * PayRate + Overtime
            END;  {  of ELSE option  }
          writeln;
          write (Init1:5, Init2, Init3);
          write (Hours:10:2, PayRate:10:2);
          writeln ('$':10, TotalWage:7:2);
          writeln;
          writeln ('Any more employees?  <Y> or <N>');
          readln (Choice);
          MoreEmployees := (Choice = 'Y') OR (Choice = 'y')
        END;  {  of WHILE...DO  }
```

Repetition (Loops) within Selection

The next example illustrates the use of a loop within an **IF . . . THEN** statement.

■ **EXAMPLE 5.16**

Write a program fragment that allows you to read an integer from the keyboard. If the integer is between 0 and 50, you are to print a chart containing all positive integers less than the integer, their squares and cubes. Thus, if 4 is read, the chart is

```
1       1       1
2       4       8
3       9       27
```

The design for this problem has a first-level pseudocode development of

1. **readln** Num
2. **IF** (Num > 0) **AND** (Num < 50) **THEN**
   2.1   print the chart

Step 2.1 can be refined to

    2.1   print the chart
        2.1.1   **FOR** K := 1 **TO** Num − 1 **DO**
            2.1.1.1   print each line

We can now write the code for this fragment as follows:

```
readln (Num);
IF (Num > 0) AND (Num < 50) THEN
  FOR K := 1 TO Num - 1 DO
    writeln (K, K * K, K * K * K);
```

Exercises 5.7

1. Find and explain the errors in each of the following program fragments. You may assume all variables have been suitably declared.

  a.
```
A := 25;
Flag := true;
WHILE Flag = true DO
  IF A >= 100 THEN
    BEGIN
      writeln (A);
      Flag := false
    END;
```

  b.
```
FOR K := 1 TO 10 DO
    writeln (K, K * K);
    IF K MOD 3 = 0 THEN
      BEGIN
        write (K);
        writeln (' is a multiple of three')
      END;
```

2. What is the output from each of the following program fragments? Assume variables have been suitably declared.

  a.
```
FOR K := 1 TO 100 DO
    IF K MOD 5 = 0 THEN
      writeln (K);
```

  b.
```
J := 20;
IF J MOD 5 = 0 THEN
    FOR K := 1 TO 100 DO
      writeln (K);
```

  c.
```
A := 5;
B := 90;
REPEAT
  B := B DIV A - 5;
  IF B > A THEN
    B := A + 30
UNTIL B < 0;
writeln (A, B);
```

  d.
```
Count := 0;
FOR K := -5 TO 5 DO
  IF K MOD 3 = 0 THEN
    BEGIN
      write ('K = ', K:4, '  output ');
      WHILE Count < 10 DO
        BEGIN
          Count := Count + 1;
          writeln (Count:4)
        END;
      Count := 0;
      writeln
    END;
```

  e.
```
A := 5;
B := 2;
IF A < B THEN
    FOR K := A TO B DO
      writeln (K)
ELSE
    FOR K := A DOWNTO B DO
      writeln (K);
```

```
f. FOR K := -5 TO 5 DO
     BEGIN
       write ('K = ', K:4, '  output ');
       A := K;
       IF K < 0 THEN           {  K = -5, -4, -3, -2, -1  }
         REPEAT
           writeln (-2 * A:5);
           A := A + 1
         UNTIL A > 0
       ELSE                    {  K = 0, 1, 2, 3, 4, 5  }
         WHILE (A MOD 2 = 0) DO
           BEGIN
             writeln (A);
             A := A + 1
           END;  {  of IF...THEN...ELSE  }
       writeln
     END;  {  of FOR loop  }
```

3. Write a program fragment that reads reals from the keyboard, counts the number of positive reals, and accumulates their sum.

4. Given two integers, A and B, A is a divisor of B if B **MOD** A = 0. Write a complete program that reads a positive integer B and then prints all the positive divisors of B.

■ ■ ■ ■

■ 5.8
Recursion

OBJECTIVES

- to understand how recursion can be used to control the iteration of a process
- to be able to use recursion to solve problems that could also be solved using **FOR, WHILE,** and **REPEAT** loops
- to be able to use recursion to solve a problem that could not easily be solved using the other iterative control structures of this chapter
- to understand what happens in memory when recursion is used

In your previous work with subprograms, you have seen instances in which one subprogram calls another. So far in this chapter, you have seen how to control iterative processes by Pascal's **FOR, WHILE,** and **REPEAT** statements. Let's now consider how we can use a subprogram that calls itself to control an iterative process.

Recursive Processes

Many problems can be solved by having a subtask call itself as part of the solution. This process is called *recursion;* subprograms that call themselves are *recursive subprograms*. Recursion is frequently used in mathematics. Consider, for example, the definition of $n!$ (n factorial) for a nonnegative integer n. This is defined by

$0! = 1$
$1! = 1$
for $n > 1$, $n! = n * (n - 1)!$
Thus, $6! = 6 * 5!$
$= 6 * 5 * 4!$
$= 6 * 5 * 4 * 3!$
$= 6 * 5 * 4 * 3 * 2!$
$= 6 * 5 * 4 * 3 * 2 * 1$

Another well-known mathematical example is the Fibonacci sequence. In this sequence, the first term is 1, the second term is 1, and each successive term is defined to be the sum of the previous two. More precisely, the Fibonacci sequence

$a_1, a_2, a_3, \ldots, a_n$

is defined by

$a_1 = 1$
$a_2 = 1$
$a_n = a_{n-1} + a_{n-2}$ for $n > 2$

This generates the sequence

1, 1, 2, 3, 5, 8, 13, 21, . . .

In both examples, note that the general term was defined by using the previous term or terms.

What applications does recursion have for computing? In many instances, a procedure or function can be written to accomplish a recursive task. If the language allows a subprogram to call itself (Pascal does, FORTRAN does not), it is sometimes easier to solve a problem by this process.

■ **EXAMPLE 5.17**

As an example of a recursive function, consider the sigma function— denoted by $\sum\limits_{i=1}^{n} i$ —which is used to compute the sum of integers from 1 to n.

```
FUNCTION Sigma (N : integer) : integer;
  BEGIN
    IF N <= 1 THEN
      Sigma := N
    ELSE
      Sigma := N + Sigma(N-1)
  END;  {  of FUNCTION Sigma  }
```

To illustrate how this recursive function works, suppose it is called from the main program by a statement such as

```
Sum := Sigma(5);
```

In the **ELSE** portion of the function, we first have

```
Sigma := 5 + Sigma(4)
```

At this stage, note that Sigma(4) must be computed. This call produces

```
Sigma := 4 + Sigma(3)
```

If we envision these recursive calls as occurring on levels, we have

```
1.  Sigma := 5 + Sigma(4)
   2.  Sigma := 4 + Sigma(3)
      3.  Sigma := 3 + Sigma(2)
         4.  Sigma := 2 + Sigma(1)
            5.  Sigma := 1
```

Now the end of the recursion has been reached and the steps are reversed for assigning values. Thus, we have

```
      5. Sigma := 1
     4. Sigma := 2 + 1
    3. Sigma := 3 + 3
   2. Sigma := 4 + 6
  1. Sigma := 5 + 10
```

Thus, Sigma is assigned the value 15.

■   ■

Before analyzing what happens in memory when recursive subprograms are used, some comments about recursion are in order.

1. The recursive process must have a well-defined termination. This termination is referred to as a *stopping state*. In Example 5.17, the stopping state was

```
IF N <= 1 THEN
   Sigma := N
```

2. The recursive process must have well-defined steps that lead to the stopping state. These steps are usually called *recursive steps*. In Example 5.17, these steps were

```
Sigma := N + Sigma(N-1)
```

Note that, in the recursive call, the parameter is simplified toward the stopping state.

What Really Happens?

What really happens when a subprogram calls itself? First, we need to examine the idea of a *stack*. Imagine a stack as a pile of cafeteria trays: the last one put on the stack is the first one taken off the stack. This is what occurs in memory when a recursive subprogram is used. Each call to the subprogram can be thought of as adding a tray to the stack. In the previous function, the first call creates a level of recursion that contains the partially complete assignment statement

```
Sigma := 5 + Sigma(4)
```

This corresponds to the first tray in the stack. In reality, this is an area in memory waiting to receive a value for 5 + Sigma(4). At this level, operation is temporarily suspended until a value is returned for Sigma(4). However, the call Sigma(4) produces

```
Sigma := 4 + Sigma(3)
```

This corresponds to the second tray on the stack. As before, operation is temporarily suspended until Sigma(3) is computed. This process is repeated until finally the last call, Sigma(1), returns a value.

At this stage, the stack may be envisioned as illustrated in Figure 5.4. Since different areas of memory are used for each successive call to Sigma, each variable Sigma represents a different memory location.

FIGURE 5.4
Stack for **FUNCTION** Sigma

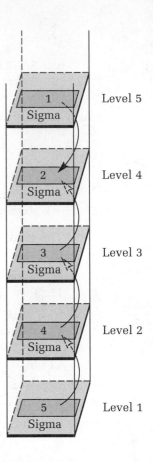

The levels of recursion that have been temporarily suspended can now be completed in reverse order. Thus, since the assignment

```
Sigma(1) := 1
```

has been made, then

```
Sigma(2) := 2 + Sigma(1)
```

becomes

```
Sigma(2) := 2 + 1
```

This then permits

```
Sigma(3) := 3 + Sigma(2)
```

to become

```
Sigma(3) := 3 + 3
```

Continuing until the first level of recursion has been reached, we obtain

```
Sigma := 5 + 10
```

This "unstacking" is illustrated in Figure 5.5.

FIGURE 5.5
"Unstacking" **FUNCTION** Sigma

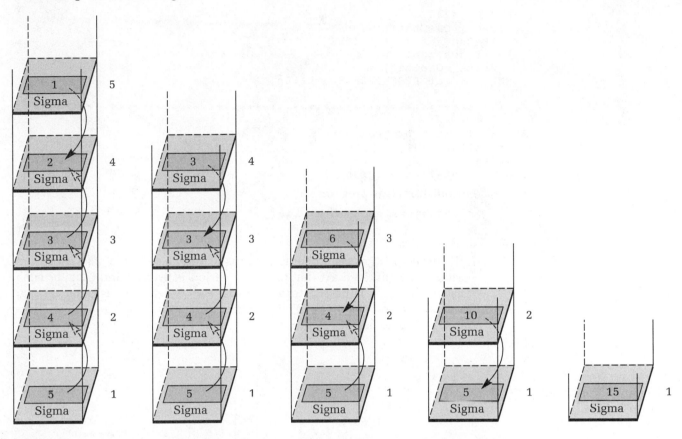

■ **EXAMPLE 5.18**

Let's now consider a second example of recursion. In this example, a procedure is used recursively to print a line of text in reverse order. Assume the line of text has only one period (and this is at the end of the line); the stopping state is when the character read is a period. Using the data line

> This is a short sentence. ▌

a complete program is

```
PROGRAM LineInReverse (input, output);

{   This program uses a procedure recursively to print a line    }
{   of text in reverse.                                          }

{****************************************************************  }

PROCEDURE StackItUp;

  { Given:   Nothing                                              }
  { Task:    Read one character; if a period, print it;  if not, }
  {                call this same procedure                       }
  { Return:  Nothing                                              }
```

```
      VAR
        OneChar : char;

      BEGIN
        read (OneChar);
        IF OneChar <> '.' THEN
          StackItUp;
        write (OneChar)
      END;  {  of PROCEDURE StackItUp  }


{ ********************************************************************* }

BEGIN  {  Main program  }
  StackItUp;
  writeln
END.  {  of main program  }
```

Output from this program is

.ecnetnes trohs a si sihT

In Example 5.18, as each character is read, it is placed on a stack until the period is encountered. At that time, the period is printed and then, as each level in the stack is passed through in reverse order, the character on that level is printed. The stack created while this program is running is illustrated in Figure 5.6.

FIGURE 5.6
Stack created by **PROCEDURE**
StackItUp

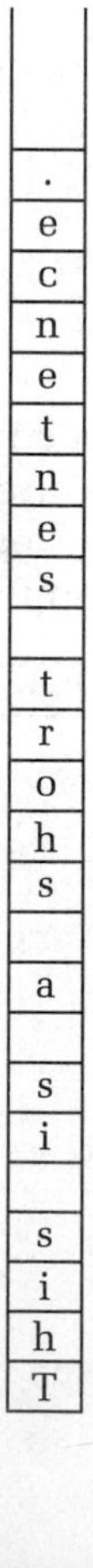

Let's now consider another example of a recursive function. Recall, the factorial of a nonnegative integer, n, is defined to be

$$1 * 2 * 3 * \ldots * (n - 1) * n$$

and is denoted by $n!$. Thus,

$$4! = 1 * 2 * 3 * 4$$

For the sake of completing this definition, $1! = 1$ and $0! = 1$. A recursive function to compute $n!$ is

```
FUNCTION Factorial (N : integer) : integer;
  BEGIN
    IF N = 0 THEN
      Factorial := 1
    ELSE
      Factorial := N * Factorial(N-1)
  END;  {  of FUNCTION Factorial  }
```

If this function is called from the main program by a statement such as

```
Product := Factorial(4);
```

we envision the levels of recursion as

```
1. Factorial := 4 * Factorial(3)
  2. Factorial := 3 * Factorial(2)
    3. Factorial := 2 * Factorial(1)
      4. Factorial := 1 * Factorial(0)
        5. Factorial(0) := 1
```

Successive values would then be assigned in reverse order to produce

```
        5. Factorial(0) := 1
      4. Factorial := 1 * 1
    3. Factorial := 2 * 1
  2. Factorial := 3 * 2
1. Factorial := 4 * 6
```

■

Why Use Recursion?

You may have noticed that the previous recursive functions Sigma and Factorial could have been written using other iterative control structures. For example, we could write

```
FUNCTION NonRecursiveSigma (N : integer) : integer;

  VAR
    J, Sum : integer;

  BEGIN
    Sum := 0;
    FOR J := 1 TO N DO
      Sum := Sum + J;
    NonRecursiveSigma := Sum
  END;  {  of FUNCTION NonRecursiveSigma  }
```

It is not coincidental that the recursive function Sigma can be rewritten using the function NonRecursiveSigma. In principal, any recursive subprogram can be rewritten in a nonrecursive manner. Furthermore, recursion generally requires more memory than equivalent nonrecursive iteration and is usually difficult for beginning programmers to comprehend. Why then do we use recursion? There are several reasons. First, a recursive thought process may be the best way to think about solving the problem. If so, it naturally leads to using recursion in a program. A classical example of this is the Towers of Hanoi problem, which requires a sequence of moving disks on pegs. This problem is fully developed as our next example.

Second, some recursive solutions can be very short compared to other iterative solutions. Such nonrecursive solutions may require an explicit stack and unusual coding. In some instances, use of a recursive algorithm can be very simple, and some programmers consider recursive solutions elegant because of this simplicity. The Towers of Hanoi problem provides an example of such elegance.

Third and finally, subsequent work in Pascal can be aided by recursion. For example, one of the fastest sorting algorithms available, the quick sort, uses recursion (see Chapter 19). Also, recursion is a valuable tool when working with dynamic data structures (Chapters 15, 16, and 18).

Having now seen several reasons why recursion should be used, let's consider when recursion should not be used. If a solution to a problem is easier to obtain using nonrecursive methods, it is usually preferable to use them. A nonrecursive solution may require less execution time and use memory more efficiently. Using the previous examples, the recursive function Factorial should probably be written using nonrecursive iteration, but reversing a line of text would typically be done using recursion because a nonrecursive solution is difficult to write.

In summary, recursion is a powerful and necessary programming technique. You should therefore become familiar with using recursive subprograms, be able to recognize when a recursive algorithm is appropriate, and be able to implement a recursive subprogram. We will return to a more in-depth treatment of recursion in Chapter 17.

■ **EXAMPLE 5.20**

A classic problem called the Towers of Hanoi problem involves three pegs and disks as depicted in Figure 5.7.

FIGURE 5.7
Towers of Hanoi problem

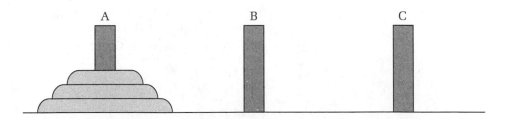

The object is to move the disks from peg A to peg C. The rules are that only one disk may be moved at a time and a larger disk can never be placed on a smaller disk. (Legend has it that this problem—but with 64 disks—was given to monks in an ancient monastery. The world was to come to an end when all 64 disks were in order on peg C.)

To see how this problem can be solved, let's start with a one-disk problem. In this case, merely move the disk from peg A to peg C. The two-disk problem is almost as easy. Move disk 1 to peg B, disk 2 to peg C, and use the solution to the one-disk problem to move disk 1 to peg C. (Note the reference to the previous solution.)

Things get a little more interesting with a three-disk problem. First, use the two-disk solution to get the top two disks in order on peg B. Then move disk 3 to peg C. Finally, use a two-disk solution to move the two disks from peg B to peg C. Again, notice how a reference was made to the previous solution. By now you should begin to see the pattern for solving the problem. However, before generalizing, let's first look at the four-disk problem. As expected, the solution is to

1. use the three-disk solution to move three disks to peg B.
2. move disk four to peg C.
3. use the three-disk solution to move the three disks from peg B to peg C.

This process can be generalized as a solution to the problem for n disks.

1. use the $(n - 1)$-disk solution to move $(n - 1)$ disks to peg B.
2. move disk n to peg C.
3. use the $(n - 1)$-disk solution to move $(n - 1)$ disks from peg B to peg C.

This general solution is recursive in nature because each particular solution depends on a solution for the previous number of disks. This process continues until there is only one disk to move. This corresponds to the stopping state when a recursive program is written to solve the problem. A complete interactive program that prints out each step in the solution to this problem is

```
PROGRAM TowersOfHanoi (input, output);

{   This program uses recursion to solve the classic  Towers      }
{   of Hanoi problem.                                             }

VAR
  NumDisks : integer;

{******************************************************************* }

PROCEDURE ListTheMoves (NumDisks : integer;
                        StartPeg, LastPeg, SparePeg : char);

  {  Given:   The number of disks to move, the initial peg          }
  {                 StartPeg, the working peg SparePeg, and         }
  {                 the destination peg LastPeg                      }
  {  Task:    Move NumDisks from StartPeg to LastPeg using          }
  {                 SparePeg; involves recursive calls              }
  {  Return:  Nothing                                               }

BEGIN
  IF NumDisks = 1 THEN
    writeln ('Move a disk from ', StartPeg, ' to ', LastPeg)
  ELSE
    BEGIN
      ListTheMoves (NumDisks-1, StartPeg, SparePeg, LastPeg);
      writeln ('Move a disk from ', StartPeg, ' to ', LastPeg);
      ListTheMoves (NumDisks-1, SparePeg, LastPeg, StartPeg)
```

```
        END  {  of ELSE option  }
      END;  {  of PROCEDURE ListTheMove  }

  {************************************************************* }

  BEGIN  {  Main program  }
    write ('How many disks in this game?  ');
    readln (NumDisks);
    writeln;
    writeln ('Start with ', NumDisks, ' disks on Peg A');
    writeln;
    writeln ('Then proceed as follows:');
    writeln;
    ListTheMoves (NumDisks, 'A', 'C', 'B')
  END.  {  of main program  }
```

Sample runs for three-disk and four-disk problems produce the following:

```
How many disks in this game?  3

Start with 3 disks on Peg A

Then proceed as follows:

Move a disk from A to C
Move a disk from A to B
Move a disk from C to B
Move a disk from A to C
Move a disk from B to A
Move a disk from B to C
Move a disk from A to C

How many disks in this game?  4

Start with 4 disks on Peg A

Then proceed as follows:

Move a disk from A to B
Move a disk form A to C
Move a disk from B to C
Move a disk from A to B
Move a disk from C to A
Move a disk from C to B
Move a disk from A to B
Move a disk from A to C
Move a disk from B to C
Move a disk from B to A
Move a disk from C to A
Move a disk from B to C
Move a disk from A to B
Move a disk from A to C
Move a disk from B to C
```

Exercises 5.8

1. Explain what is wrong with the following recursive function:

```
FUNCTION Recur (X : real) : real;
  BEGIN
    Recur := Recur(X / 2)
  END;
```

2. Write a recursive function that reverses the digits of a positive integer. If the integer used as input is 1234, output should be 4321.

3. Consider the following recursive function:

```
FUNCTION A (X : real;
            N : integer) : real;
  BEGIN
    IF N = 0 THEN
      A := 1.0
    ELSE
      A := X * A(X, N-1)
  END; { of FUNCTION A }
```

a. What would the value of Y be for each of

   i. Y := A(3.0, 2);

   ii. Y := A(2.0, 3);

   iii. Y := A(4.0, 4);

   iv. Y := A(1.0, 6);

b. Explain what standard computation is performed by **FUNCTION** A.

c. Rewrite **FUNCTION** A using iteration rather than recursion.

4. Recall the Fibonacci sequence
1, 1, 2, 3, 5, 8, 13, 21, . . .
where for $n > 2$ the nth term is the sum of the previous two. Write a recursive function to compute the nth term in the Fibonacci sequence.

5. Write a function that uses nonrecursive iteration to compute $n!$.

■ ■ ■ ■

| FOCUS ON PROGRAM DESIGN | This program illustrates the combined use of repetition and selection statements. The problem statement is: |

Write a program that allows positive integers to be entered from the keyboard and, for each such entry, list all primes less than or equal to the number. The program should include a check for bad data and use of a sentinel value to terminate the process.

Typical output for the integer 17 is

```
Enter a positive integer; <-999> to quit.
?17
            -------------------------------------------------
                        The number is 17.  The prime numbers
                        less than or equal to 17 are:

                                    2
                                    3
                                    5
                                    7
                                   11
                                   13
                                   17

Enter a positive integer; <-999> to quit.
?-999
```

You should note the mathematical property that a number K is prime if it has no divisors other than 1 and itself. This definition tells us that, when we check for divisors, numbers between 2 and K − 1 must be examined. (Actually, we don't need to examine nearly that many, but we shall use this straightforward approach now and consider refinements of the algorithm in Chapter 12.) Also note that 1 is not prime by definition.

A first-level pseudocode development for this problem is

1. Get a number
WHILE MoreData **Do**
    2. Examine the number
    3. Get a number

A structure chart for this problem is shown in Figure 5.8.

FIGURE 5.8
Structure chart for
PROGRAM ListPrimes

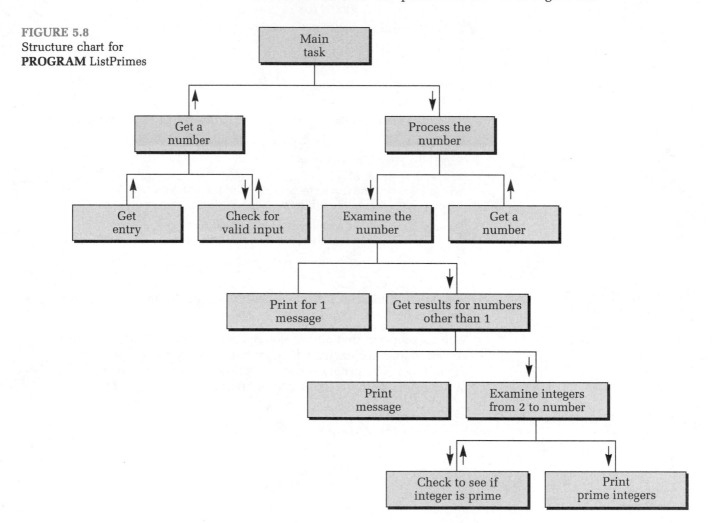

The module specifications for the main modules are

1. GetANumber Module
    Data received: None
    Information returned: Number
                          Boolean flag MoreData
    Logic: Get an entry from the keyboard.
          Make sure it is a valid entry or the sentinel
            value for terminating the process.
          If it is the sentinel value, set the
            boolean variable MoreData to **false**.

2. <u>ExamineTheNumber Module</u>
   Data received: The integer read
   Information returned: None
   Logic: **IF** the number is 1 **THEN** print a message
        ELSE
          Print a heading.
          FOR K := 2 **TO** Number **DO**
            Check K for a prime number.
              IF K is prime **THEN** print it.

A second-level development is

1. Get a number
   1.1 Get entry from the keyboard
   1.2 Check for valid entry
WHILE MoreData **DO**
2. Examine the number
   IF Number is 1 **THEN**
       2.1 print a message for one
   ELSE list the primes
       2.2 print a message
       2.3 check for primes less than or equal to Number
3. Get a number
   3.1 Get entry from the keyboard
   3.2 Check for valid entry

Step 2.3 can be refined to

    2.3 check for primes less than or equal to Number
       FOR K := 2 **TO** Number **DO**
         2.3.1 check to see if K is prime
         2.3.2 **IF** K is prime **THEN**
             print K in list of primes

Thus, the complete pseudocode development is

1. Get a number
   1.1 Get entry from the keyboard
   1.2 Check for valid entry

WHILE MoreData **DO**
2. Examine the number
   IF Number is 1 **THEN**
       2.1 print a message for one
   ELSE list the primes
       2.2 print a message
       2.3 check for primes less than or equal to Number
          FOR K := 2 **TO** Number **DO**
            2.3.1 check to see if K is prime
            2.3.2 **IF** K is prime **THEN**
                print K in a list of primes
3. Get a number
   3.1 Get entry from the keyboard
   3.2 Check for valid entry

With this pseudocode development, the main program would be

```
BEGIN  {  Main program  }
  GetANumber (Num, MoreData);
  WHILE MoreData DO
    BEGIN
      ExamineTheNumber (Num);
      GetANumber (Num, MoreData)
    END {  of WHILE loop  }
END.  {  of main program  }
```

A complete program for this problem is

```
PROGRAM ListPrimes (input, output);

CONST
  Skip = ' ';
  Dashes = '----------------------------------------------------';

VAR
  Number : integer;
  MoreData : boolean;

{*******************************************************************}

PROCEDURE GetANumber  (VAR Number : integer;
                       VAR MoreData : boolean);

  {  Given:    Nothing                                              }
  {  Task:     Read an integer entered from the keyboard            }
  {  Return:   The integer read                                     }

  BEGIN
    REPEAT
      writeln;
      writeln ('Enter a positive integer; <-999> to quit.');
      readln (Number);
      MoreData := Number <> -999
    UNTIL (Number > 0) OR (Number = -999)  {  assumes valid data  }
  END;  {  of PROCEDURE GetANumber  }

{*******************************************************************}

PROCEDURE PrintOneMessage;

  {  Given:    Nothing                                              }
  {  Task:     Print a message for 1                                }
  {  Return:   Nothing                                              }

  BEGIN
    writeln;
    writeln (Skip:10, Dashes);
    writeln;
    writeln (Skip:20, '1 is not prime by definition.')
  END;  {  of PROCEDURE PrintOneMessage  }

{*******************************************************************}

PROCEDURE PrintMessage (Number : integer);

  {  Given:    The integer read                                     }
  {  Task:     Print a heading for the output                       }
  {  Return:   Nothing                                              }
```

1

```
      BEGIN
        writeln;
        writeln (Skip:10, Dashes);
        writeln;
        writeln (Skip:20, 'The number is ', Number,
                 '.  The prime numbers');
        writeln (Skip:20, 'less than or equal to ', Number,  ' are:');
        writeln
      END;  {  of PROCEDURE PrintMessage  }

{*****************************************************************}

PROCEDURE ListAllPrimes (Number : integer);

   {  Given:    The integer read                                   }
   {  Task:     List all primes less than or equal to the integer  }
   {                    read                                       }
   {  Return:   Nothing                                            }

   VAR
     Prime : boolean;
     Candidate, Divisor : integer;
     LimitForCheck : real;

   BEGIN
     FOR Candidate := 2 TO Number DO
       BEGIN
         Prime := true;
         Divisor := 2;
         LimitForCheck := Candidate - 1;
         WHILE (Divisor <= LimitForCheck) AND Prime DO
           IF Candidate MOD Divisor = 0 THEN
             Prime := false          {  Candidate has a divisor  }
           ELSE
             Divisor := Divisor + 1;
         IF Prime THEN               {  Print in list of primes  }
           writeln (Candidate:35)
       END  {  of FOR loop  }
   END;  {  of PROCEDURE ListAllPrimes  }

{*****************************************************************}

PROCEDURE ExamineTheNumber (Number : integer);

   {  Given:    The integer read (Number)                    }
   {  Task:     Print primes less than or equal to Number    }
   {  Return:   Nothing                                      }

   BEGIN
     IF Number = 1 THEN
       PrintOneMessage
     ELSE
       BEGIN
         PrintMessage (Number);
         ListAllPrimes (Number)
       END  {  of ELSE option  }
   END;  {  of PROCEDURE ExamineTheNumber  }

{*****************************************************************}

BEGIN  {  Main program  }
  GetANumber (Number, MoreData);
  WHILE MoreData DO
```

2

```
    BEGIN
      ExamineTheNumber (Number);
      GetANumber (Number, MoreData)
    END {  of WHILE loop  }
  END. {  of  main program  }
```

Sample runs of this program produce the output

```
Enter a positive integer; <-999> to quit.
?10

------------------------------------------------

                        The number is 10.  The prime numbers
                        less than or equal to 10 are:

                                      2
                                      3
                                      5
                                      7

Enter a positive integer; <-999> to quit.
?17

------------------------------------------------

                        The number is 17.  The prime numbers
                        less than or equal to 17 are:

                                      2
                                      3
                                      5
                                      7
                                      11
                                      13
                                      17

Enter a positive integer; <-999> to quit.
?1
------------------------------------------------

                        1 is not prime by definition.

Enter a positive integer; <-999> to quit.
?25
------------------------------------------------

                        The number is 25.  The prime numbers
                        less than or equal to 25 are:

                                      2
                                      3
                                      5
                                      7
                                      11
                                      13
                                      17
                                      19
                                      23

Enter a positive integer; <-999> to quit.
?-3
Enter a positive integer; <-999> to quit.
?2
------------------------------------------------
```

```
The number is 2.  The prime numbers
less than or equal to 2 are:

                    2

Enter a positive integer; <-999> to quit.
?-999
```

More efficient algorithms than what we used here do exist. However, the purpose of this program was to see how loops can be used to solve a problem.

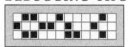

RUNNING AND DEBUGGING TIPS

1. Most errors involving loops are not compilation errors. Thus, you will not be able to detect most errors until you try to run the program.
2. A syntax error that will not be detected by the compiler is a semicolon after a **WHILE . . . DO.** The fragment

```
WHILE MoreData DO;
  BEGIN
    readln (A);
    writeln (A)
  END;
```

   is incorrect and will not get past

```
WHILE MoreData DO;
```

   Note that this is an infinite loop.
3. Carefully check entry conditions for each loop.
4. Carefully check exit conditions for each loop. Make sure the loop is exited (not infinite) and that you have the correct number of repetitions.
5. Loop entry, execution, and exit can be checked by
   a. pencil and paper check on initial and final values
   b. count of the number of repetitions
   c. use of debugging **writeln**s
      i. Boolean condition prior to loop
      ii. variables inside loop
      iii. values of the counter in loop
      iv. Boolean values inside the loop
      v. values after loop is exited

■ Summary

Key Terms

accumulator	infinite loop	pretest condition
counter	nested loop	pretest (entrance
data validation	posttest (exit controlled)	controlled) loop
decrement	loop	sentinel value
fixed repetition		variable condition loop
(iterated) loop		
index		

Key Terms (optional)

input assertion	loop verification
loop invariant	output assertion
loop variant	

Keywords

DO	TO	UNTIL
DOWNTO	REPEAT	WHILE
FOR		

Key Concepts

- The following table provides a comparison summary of the three repetition structures discussed in this chapter.

Traits of Loops	FOR . . . TO . . . DO Loop	WHILE . . . DO Loop	REPEAT . . . UNTIL Loop
Pretest loop	yes	yes	no
Posttest loop	no	no	yes
BEGIN . . . END for compound statements	required	required	not required
Repetition	fixed	variable	variable
Loop index	yes	no	no
Index automatically incremented	yes	no	no
Boolean expression used	no	yes	yes

- A fixed repetition loop (**FOR . . . TO . . . DO**) is to be used when you know exactly how many times something is to be repeated. The basic form for a **FOR . . . TO . . . DO** loop is

```
FOR J := 1 TO 5 DO
   <statement>;
or

FOR J := 1 TO 5 DO
   BEGIN
     <statement 1>;
     <statement 2>;
            .
            .
            .
     <statement n>
   END;
```

After the loop is finished, the value of the index variable may become unassigned and program control is transferred to the first executable statement following the loop.

- A **WHILE . . . DO** loop is a pretest loop that can have a variable loop control; a typical loop is

```
Score := 0;
Sum  := 0;
MoreData := true;
WHILE MoreData DO
   BEGIN
     Sum := Sum + Score;
     writeln ('Enter a score; -999 to quit.');
     readln (Score);
     MoreData := (Score <> -999)
   END;
```

- A counter is a variable whose purpose is to indicate how often the body of a loop is executed.

- An accumulator is a variable whose purpose is to sum values.
- An infinite **WHILE . . . DO** loop is caused by having a **true** loop control condition that is never changed to **false.**
- A posttest loop has a Boolean condition checked after the loop body has been completed.
- A **REPEAT . . . UNTIL** loop is a posttest loop; a typical loop is

```
REPEAT
   writeln ('Enter a positive integer;  <-999> to quit .');
   readln (Num)
UNTIL (Num < 0) OR (Num = -999);
```

- **REPEAT . . . UNTIL** and **WHILE . . . DO** are variable control loops; **FOR** is a fixed control loop.
- **WHILE . . . DO** and **FOR** are pretest loops; **REPEAT . . . UNTIL** is a posttest loop.
- Any one of these loops can be nested within any other of the loops.
- Indenting each loop is important for program readability.
- Several levels of nesting make the logic of a program difficult to follow.
- Loops and conditionals are frequently used together. Careful program design will facilitate writing code in which these concepts are integrated; typical forms are

```
WHILE <condition1> DO
   BEGIN
      .
      .
      .
      IF <condition2> THEN
         .
         .
         .
      ELSE
         .
         .
         .
      .
      .
   END;  {  of WHILE...DO  }

and

IF <condition> THEN
   BEGIN
      .
      .
      .
      FOR J := <value1> TO <valueN> DO
         BEGIN
            .
            .
            END;  {  of FOR loop  }
         .
         .
         .
   END  {  of IF...THEN  }
ELSE
   .
   .
   .
```

■ **Programming Problems and Projects**

■ 1. The Caswell Catering and Convention Service (Problem 12, Chapter 3 and Problem 14, Chapter 4) wants you to upgrade their program so they can use it for all of their customers.

2. Modify your program for a service station owner (Focus on Program Design, Chapter 4) so that it can be used for an unknown number of customers. Your output should include the number of customers and all other pertinent items in a daily summary.

3. Modify the Community Hospital program (Problem 17, Chapter 4) so that it can be run for all patients leaving the hospital in one day. Include appropriate bad data checks and daily summary items.

4. The greatest common divisor (GCD) of two integers a and b is a positive integer c such that c divides a, c divides b, and for any other common divisor d of a and b, d is less than or equal to c. (For example, the GCD of 18 and 45 is 9.)

   One method of finding the GCD of two positive integers (a, b) is to begin with the smaller (a) and see if it is a divisor of the larger (b). If it is, then the smaller is the GCD. If not, find the next largest divisor of a and see if it is a divisor of b. Continue this process until you find a divisor of both a and b. This is the GCD of a and b.

   Write an interactive program that will accept two positive integers as input and then print out their GCD. Enchance your output by printing all divisors of a that do not divide b. A sample run could produce

```
Enter two positive integers.
?42 72

The divisors of 42 that do not divide 72 are:

      42
      21
      14
       7

The GCD of 42 and 72 is 6.
```

5. The least common multiple (LCM) of two positive integers a and b is a positive integer c such that c is a multiple of both a and b and for any other multiple m of a and b, c is a divisor of m. (For example, the LCM of 12 and 8 is 24.

   Write a program that allows the user to enter two positive integers and then print the LCM. The program should guard against bad data and should allow the user the option of "trying another pair" or quitting.

6. A perfect number is a positive integer such that the sum of the proper divisors equals the number. Thus, $28 = 1 + 2 + 4 + 7 + 14$ is a perfect number. If the sum of the divisors is less than the number, it is deficient. If the sum exceeds the number, it is abundant.

   a. Write a program that allows the user to enter a positive integer and then displays the result indicating whether the number entered is perfect, deficient, or abundant.

   b. Write another program that allows the user to enter a positive integer N and then displays all perfect numbers less than or equal to N.

Your programs should guard against bad data and should allow the user the option of entering another integer or quitting.

7. In these days of increased awareness of automobile mileage, more motorists are computing their miles per gallon (mpg) than ever before. Write a program that will perform these computations for a traveler. Data for the program will be entered as indicated by the following table.

Odometer Reading	Gallons of Fuel Purchased
18828(start)	—
19240	9.7
19616	10.2
19944	8.8
20329	10.1
20769(finish)	10.3

The program should compute the mpg for each tank and the cumulative mpg each time the tank is filled up. Your output should produce a chart with the following headings:

Odometer (begin)	Odometer (end)	Fuel (tank)	Miles (tank)	Fuel (trip)	Miles (trip)	Mpg (tank)	Mpg (trip)

8. Parkside's Other Triangle is generated from two positive integers, one for the size and one for the seed. For example,

Size 6, Seed 1

```
1 2 4 7 2 7
  3 5 8 3 8
    6 9 4 9
      1 5 1
        6 2
          3
```

Size 5, Seed 3

```
3 4 6 9 4
  5 7 1 5
    8 2 6
      3 7
        8
```

The size gives the number of columns. Seed specifies the starting value for column 1. Column n contains n values. The successive values are obtained by adding 1 to the previous value. When 9 is reached, the next value becomes 1.

Write a program that reads pairs of positive integers and produces Parkside's Other Triangle for each pair. The check for bad data should include checking for seeds between 1 and 9 inclusive.

9. Modify the sewage, water, and sanitation problem (Problem 19, Chapter 4) so that it can be used with data containing appropriate information for all residents of the community.

■ 10. Modify the program for the Lucky Wildcat Well Corporation (Problem 20, Chapter 4) so that it can be run with data containing information about all of Al Derrick's wells.

11. Modify the program concerning the Mathematical Association of America (Problem 21, Chapter 4). There will be 50 official state delegates attending the next summer national meeting. The new data file

will contain the two-letter state abbreviation for each delegate. Output should include one column with the state abbreviation and another with the amount reimbursed.

12. In Fibonacci's sequence,

$0, 1, 1, 2, 3, 5, 8, 13, \ldots$

the first two terms are 0 and 1 and each successive term is formed by adding the previous two terms. Write a program that will read positive integers and then print the number of terms indicated by each integer read. Be sure to test your program with data that includes the integers 1 and 2.

■ 13. Dr. Lae Z. Programmer is at it again. Now that you have written a program to compute the grade for one student in his class (Problems 5, 22, and 23, Chapter 4), he wants you to modify this program so it can be used for the entire class. He will help you by making the first entry be a positive integer representing the number of students in the class. Your new version should compute an overall class average and the number of students receiving each letter grade.

■ 14. Modify the Pentagon Parking Lot problem (Problem 26, Chapter 4) so that it can be used for all customers in one day. In the new program, time should be entered in military style as a four-digit integer. The lot opens at 0600 (6:00 A.M.) and closes at 2200 (10:00 P.M.). Your program should include appropriate summary information.

15. The Natural Pine Furniture Company (Problem 7, Chapter 3) now wants you to refine your program so that it will print a one-week pay report for each employee. You do not know how many employees there are, but you do know that all information for each employee is on a separate line. Each line of input will contain the employee's initials, the number of hours worked, and the hourly rate. You are to use the constant definition section for the following:

federal withholding tax rate	18%
state withholding tax rate	4.5%
hospitalization	$25.65
union dues	$ 7.85

Your output should include a report for each employee and a summary report for the company files.

16. Orlando Tree Service, Incorporated, offers the following services and rates to its customers:

a. tree removal	$500 per tree
b. tree trimming	$80 per hour
c. stump grinding	$25 plus $2 per inch for each stump whose diameter exceeds ten inches. The $2 charge is only for the diameter inches in excess of ten.

Write a complete program to allow the manager, Mr. Sorwind, to provide an estimate when he bids on a job. Your output should include a listing of each separate charge and a total. A 10 percent discount is given for any job whose total exceeds $1000.

Typical data for one customer are

```
R 7
T 6.5
G 8
8 10 12 14 15 15 20 25
```

where "R," "T," and "G" are codes for removal, trimming, and grinding, respectively. The integer following "G" represents the number of stumps to be ground. The next line of integers represents the diameters of stumps to be ground.

17. A standard science experiment is to drop a ball and see how high it bounces. Once the "bounciness" of the ball has been determined, the ratio gives a bounciness index. For example, if a ball dropped from a height of ten feet bounces six feet high, the index is 0.6 and the total distance traveled by the ball is 16 feet after one bounce. If the ball were to continue bouncing, the distance after two bounces would be 10 ft. + 6 ft. + 6 ft. + 3.6 ft. = 25.6 ft. Note that distance traveled for each successive bounce is the distance to the floor plus 0.6 of that distance as the ball comes back up.

    Write a program that lets the user enter the initial height of the ball and the number of times the ball is allowed to continue bouncing. Output should be the total distance traveled by the ball. At some point in this process, the distance traveled by the ball becomes negligible. Use the **CONST** section to define a "negligible" distance (for example, 0.00001 inches). Terminate the computing when the distance becomes negligible. When this stage is reached, include the number of bounces as part of the output.

18. Write a program that prints a calendar for one month. Input consists of an integer specifying the first day of the month (1 = Sunday) and an integer specifying how many days are in a month.

■ 19. An amortization table shows the rate at which a loan is paid off. It contains monthly entries showing the interest paid that month, the principal paid, and the remaining balance. Given the amount of money borrowed (the principal), the annual interest rate, and the amount the person wishes to repay each month, print an amortization table. (Be certain that the payment desired is larger than the first month's interest.) Your table should stop when the loan is paid off, and should be printed with the following heads.

    ```
    MONTH NUMBER   INTEREST PAID   PRINCIPAL PAID   BALANCE
    ```

20. Computers work in the binary system, which is based upon powers of 2. Write a program that prints out the first 15 powers of 2 beginning with 2 to the zero power. Print your output in headed columns.

21. Print a list of the positive integers less than 500 that are divisible by either 5 or 7. When the list is complete, print a count of the number of integers that were found.

22. Write a program that reads in 20 real numbers, then prints the average of the positive numbers and the average of the negative numbers.

■ 23. In 1626, the Dutch settlers purchased Manhattan Island from the Indians. According to legend, the purchase price was $24. Suppose that the

Indians had invested this amount at 3 percent annual interest compounded quarterly. If the money had earned interest from the start of 1626 to the end of last year, how much money would the Indians have in the bank today? (*Hint:* use nested loops for the compounding.)

24. Write a program to print the sum of the odd integers from 1 to 99.

25. The theory of relativity holds that as an object moves, it gets smaller. The new length of the object can be determined from the formula:

    New Length = Original Length $* \sqrt{1 - B^2}$

    B^2 is the percentage of the speed of light at which the object is moving, entered in decimal form. Given the length of an object, print its new length for speeds ranging from 0 to 99 percent of the speed of light. Print the output in the following columns:

    ```
    Percent of Light Speed   Length
    ------- -- ----- -----   ------
    ```

■ 26. Mr. Christian uses a 90 percent, 80 percent, 70 percent, 60 percent grading scale on his tests. Given a list of test scores, print out the number of As, Bs, Cs, Ds, and Fs on the test. Terminate the list of scores with a sentinel value.

27. The mathematician Gottfried Leibniz determined a formula for estimating the value of pi.

    $$\frac{pi}{4} = 1 - \frac{1}{3} + \frac{1}{5} - \frac{1}{7} + \frac{1}{9} - \frac{1}{11} + \cdots$$

    Evaluate the first 200 terms of this formula and print its approximation of pi.

28. In a biology experiment, Carey finds that a sample of an organism doubles in population every 12 hours. If she starts with one thousand organisms, in how many hours will she have one million?

29. Pascal does not have a mathematical operator that permits raising a number to a power. We can easily write a program to perform this function, however. Given an integer to represent the base number and a positive integer to represent the power desired, write a program that prints the number raised to that power.

30. Mr. Thomas has negotiated a salary schedule for his new job. He will be paid one cent the first day, with the daily rate doubling each day. Write a program that will find his total earnings for 30 days. Print your results in a table set up as follows:

Day Number	Daily Salary	Total Earned
1	.01	.01
2	.02	.03
3	.	.
.	.	.
.	.	.
.		
30		

31. Write a program to print the perimeter and area of rectangles using all combinations of lengths and widths running from 1 foot to 10 feet in increments of 1 foot. Print the output in headed columns.

32. Teachers in most school districts are paid on a salary schedule that provides a salary based on their number of years of teaching experience. Suppose that a beginning teacher in the Babbage School District is paid $19,000 the first year. For each year of experience after this up to 12 years, a 4 percent increase over the preceding value is received. Write a program that prints a salary schedule for teachers in this district. The output should appear as follows:

```
Years Experience          Salary
----------------          ------
        0                $19,000
        1                $19,760
        2                $20,550
        3                $21,372
        .                    .
        .                    .
        .                    .
       12
```

(Actually, most teacher's salary schedules are more complex than this. As an additional problem, you might like to find out how the salary schedule is determined in your school district and write a program to print the salary schedule.)

33. The Euclidean Algorithm can be used to find the greatest common divisor (GCD) of two positive integers (n_1, n_2). For example, suppose $n_1 = 72$ and $n_2 = 42$; you can use this algorithm in the following manner:
    1. Divide the larger by the smaller as

       $72 = 42 * 1 + 30$

    2. Divide the divisor (42) by the remainder (30)

       $42 = 30 * 1 + 12$

    3. Repeat this process until you get a remainder of zero

       $30 = 12 * 2 + 6$
       $12 = 6 * 2 + 0$

    The last nonzero remainder is the GCD of n_1 and n_2.
       Write a program that lets the user enter two integers and then prints out each step in the process of using the Euclidean Algorithm to find their GCD.

34. Cramer's Rule for solving a system of equations was given in Problem 31, Chapter 4. Add an enhancement to your program by using a loop to guarantee that the coefficients and constants entered by the user are precisely those that were intended.

35. Gaussian Elimination is another method used to solve systems of equations. To illustrate, if the system is

    $x - 2y = 1$
    $2x + y = 7$

    Gaussian Elimination would start with the augmented matrix

    $$\begin{bmatrix} 1 & -2 & \vdots & 1 \\ 2 & 1 & \vdots & 7 \end{bmatrix}$$

and proceed to produce the identity matrix on the left side

$$\begin{bmatrix} 1 & 0 & \vdots & 3 \\ 0 & 1 & \vdots & 1 \end{bmatrix}$$

At this stage, the solution to the system is seen to be $x = 3$ and $y = 1$.

Write a program in which the user enters coefficients for a system of two equations containing two variables. The program should then solve the system and display the answer. Your program should include the following:

a. a check for bad data.
b. a solvable system check.
c. a display of partial results as the matrix operations are performed.

36. A Pythagorean triple consists of three integers A, B, and C such that $A^2 + B^2 = C^2$. For example, 3, 4, 5 is such a triple because $3^2 + 4^2 = 5^2$. These triples can be generated by positive integers m, n, ($m > n$) where $a = m^1 - n^2$, $b = 2mn$, and $c = m^2 + n^2$. These triples will be primitive (no common factors) if m and n have no common factors and are not both odd. Write a program that allows the user to enter a value for m and then prints out all possible primitive Pythagorean triples such that $m > n$. Use one function to find the greatest common factor of m and n, another to see if m and n are both odd, and another to guard against overflow. For the input value of $m = 5$, typical output would be

m	n	a	b	c	a²	b²	c²
2	1	3	4	5	9	16	25
3	2	5	12	13	25	144	169
4	1	15	8	17	225	64	289
4	3	7	24	25	49	576	625
5	2	21	20	29	441	400	841
5	4	9	40	41	81	1600	1681

37. This chapter's Focus on Program Design problem determined whether or not an integer was prime by checking for divisors less than or equal to the number minus 1. The check started with 2 and incremented trial divisors by 1 each time as seen by the code

```
Prime := true;
Divisor := 2;
LimitForCheck := Candidate - 1;
WHILE (Divisor <= LimitForCheck) AND Prime DO
  IF Candidate MOD Divisor = 0 THEN
    Prime := false
  ELSE
    Divisor := Divisor + 1;
```

Other methods can be used to determine whether or not an integer N is prime. For example, you may
a. check divisors from 2 to $(N - 1)/2$ incrementing by 1.
b. check divisors from 2 to sqrt(N) incrementing by 1.
c. check divisor 2, 3, 5, . . . $(N - 1)/2$ incrementing by 2.
d. check divisor 2, 3, 5, . . . sqrt(N) incrementing by 2.

Write a program that allows the user to choose between these options in order to compare relative efficiency of different algorithms. Use a function for each option.

38. The prime factorization of a positive integer is the positive integer written as the product of primes. For example, the prime factorization of 72 is

    ```
    72 = 2 * 3 * 3 * 4
    ```

    Write a program that allows the user to enter a positive integer and then displays the prime factorization of the integer. A minimal main program could be

    ```
    BEGIN  {  Main program  }
      GetANumber (Num);
      NumberIsPrime := PrimeCheck(Num);
      IF NumberIsPrime THEN
        writeln (Num, ' is prime.')
      ELSE
        PrintFactorization(Num)
    END.  {  of main program  }
    ```

    Enhancements to this program could include an error trap for bad data and a loop for repeated trials.

39. As you might expect, instructors of computer science do not agree on whether a **REPEAT . . . UNTIL** loop or a **WHILE . . . DO** loop is the preferred variable control loop in Pascal. Interview several computer science instructors at your institution to determine what preference (if any) they have regarding these two forms of repetition. Prepare a class report based on your interviews. Include advantages and disadvantages of each form of repetition.

40. Examine the repetition constructs of at least five other programming languages. Prepare a report that compares and contrasts repetition in each of the languages. Be sure to include information such as which languages provide for both fixed and variable repetition and which languages have more than one kind of variable repetition. Which language appears to have the most desirable form of repetition? Include your rationale for this decision in your report.

41. Examine some old computer science texts and talk to some computer science instructors who worked with the early languages to see how repetition was achieved in the "early days." Prepare a brief chronological chart for class display that depicts the various stages in developing repetition.

42. The greatest common divisor of two positive integers a and b, GCD (a,b), is the largest positive integer that divides both a and b. Thus, GCD(102, 30) = 6. This can be fund using the division algorithm as follows:

    ```
    102 = 30 * 3 + 12
     30 = 12 * 2 + 6
     12 = 6 * 2 + 0
    ```

    Note that

    $$GCD(102,30) = GCD(30, 12)$$
    $$= GCD(12,6)$$
    $$= 6$$

In each case, the remainder is used for the next step. The process terminates when a remainder of zero is obtained. Write a recursive function that returns the GCD of two positive integers.

43. A palindrome is a number or word that is the same when read either forwards or backwards. For example, *12321* and *mom* are palindromes. Write a recursive function that can be used to determine whether or not an integer is a palindrome. Use this function in a complete program that reads a list of integers and then displays the list with an asterisk following each palindrome.

44. Recall the Fibonacci sequence discussed at the beginning of Section 5.8. Write a recursive function that returns the nth Fibonacci number. Input for a call to the function will be a positive integer.

45 Probability courses often contain problems which require students to compute the number of ways k items can be chosen from a set of n objects. It is shown that there are

$$C(n, k) = \frac{n!}{k! \, (n - k)!}$$

such choices. This is sometimes referred to as "n choose k". To illustrate, if you wish to select three items from a total of five possible objects, there are

$$C(5, 3) = \frac{5!}{3! \, (5 - 3)!} = \frac{5 * 4 * 3 * 2 * 1}{(3 * 2 * 1) \, (2 * 1)} = 10$$

such possibilities.

In mathematics, the number of $C(n,k)$ is a binomial coefficient because, for appropriate values of n and k, it produces coefficients in the expansion of $(x = y)^n$. Thus,

$$(x + y)^4 = C(4,0)x^4 + C(4,1)x^3y + C(4,2)xy^2 + C(4,3)xy^3 + C(4,4)y^4$$

a. Write a function that returns the value $C(n,k)$. Arguments for a function call will be integers n,k such that $n > k \geq 0$. (*Hint:* Simplify the expression $\frac{n!}{k! \, (n - k)!}$ before computing.)

b. Write an interactive program that receives as input the power to which a binomial is to be raised. Output should be the expanded binomial.

CHAPTER

6

There are 350 varieties of shark, not counting loan and pool.

L. M. Boyd

Text Files and Enumerated Data Types

Having now completed five chapters, you've made a significant step in the process of learning to use a programming language for the purpose of solving problems. We have covered the essential elements of arithmetic, variables, input/output, selection, repetition, and subprograms and are now ready to look at a somewhat different area of Pascal.

Thus far, you have been unable to work with large amounts of data. In order to write programs that solve problems using large data bases, it is necessary to be able to store, retrieve, and manage the data. In this chapter, we first look at storage and retrieval of data (text files) and then study a feature of Pascal (enumerated data types) that facilitates handling the data.

These topics are not closely related but, since both are essential for working with data structures which are presented in Chapter 7, we present them together. As you study this material, remember that we are "setting the stage" for working with large amounts of data.

■ 6.1
Text Files

The implementation of concepts presented in this section depends on the computer you are using; it is very system dependent. It will probably be necessary for your instructor to supplement this material with examples and explanations suitable for your particular environment. At the very least, you should be able to use the manual for your system for reference.

Consider the relatively simple problem of using a computer to compute and print water bills for a community of 30,000 customers. If the data needed consist of a customer name, address, and amount of water used, you can imagine that entering this information interactively every billing period would involve an enormous amount of time. In addition to saving that time, it is often desirable to save information between runs of a program for later use.

To avoid these problems, we can store data in some secondary storage device, usually magnetic tapes or disks. Data can be created separately from a program, stored on these devices, and then accessed by programs when necessary. It is also possible to modify and save this information for other runs of the same program or for running another program using this same data. For now we will store all data in *text files* (other kinds of files are examined in Chapter 10).

Text files can be created by a text editor or by a program. Often the editor you use to create your program can be used to create a text file. The use of text editors varies significantly and you should consult your instructor and/ or manual to use this method. This, however, is how your instructor may create data files for you to use with subsequent programming problems.

Each line in a data file has an *end-of-line (eoln) marker,* which has an ASCII representation. For text writing purposes, we use the symbol ▌ to represent this. Thus, two lines of integer data could be envisioned as

```
18 26 17 21 ▌
19 23 18 22 ▌
```

Each data file has an *end-of-file (eof) marker* after the last end-of-line marker. As with the end-of-line marker, an end-of-file marker also has an ASCII representation. For text writing purposes, we use the symbol ▪ to represent end-of-file. To illustrate, suppose a text file is used to store data for students in a class. If each line consists of an identification number for each student followed by three scores, a, typical file can be envisioned as

```
00723 85 93 100 ▌
00131 78 91 85 ▌
00458 82 75 86 ▌ ▪
```

Technically these lines are stored as one continuous stream with end-of-line markers used to differentiate between lines and the end-of-file marker to signify the end of one file.

```
00723 85 93 100 ▌ 00131 78 91 85 ▌ 00458 82 75 86 ▌ ▪
```

However, we frequently use separate lines to illustrate lines in a text file. Both end-of-line and end-of-file markers are appropriately placed by the computer at the time a file is created. When characters are read, **eoln** markers are read as blanks. Later in this text, we see how special functions can be used to detect when end-of-line and end-of-file symbols have been reached when reading data from a data file.

When a text file in secondary storage is to be used by a program, a file variable (or symbolic file name) must be included in the file list along with the standard files **input** and **output** as part of the program heading. Thus, if ClassList is the file variable, a heading might be

```
PROGRAM ClassRecordBook (input, output, ClassList);
```

This file variable must be declared in the variable declaration section and is of type **text.** Thus, the declaration section would be

```
VAR
   ClassList : text;
```

The file variable ClassList must be associated with the text file, which is stored externally. This may be done with a procedure file prior to compiling and running the program. It may also be accomplished within the program; for example, in Turbo Pascal, an **assign** statement is used for this purpose. Thus, if the data needed in a program are stored on a disk under the name Data1, the statement

```
assign (ClassList, 'Data1');
```

establishes the desired relationship between the file variable ClassList and the data stored externally in the text file, Data1.

Reading from a Text File

Before data can be read from a file, the file must be *opened for reading*. This is done by the statement

```
reset (<file variable>);
```

This statement moves a data pointer to the first position of the first line of the data file to be read. Thus,

```
reset (ClassList);
```

positions the pointer as follows:

| 00723 85 93 100 | 00131 78 91 85 | 00458 82 75 86 | ■ |

↑
pointer here

Reading from a text file is very similar to getting input interactively or reading from a standard input file. Standard procedures **read** and **readln** are used with appropriate variables as arguments in either format as shown.

> **read** (⟨file variable⟩, ⟨input list⟩);
> or
> **readln** (⟨file variable⟩, ⟨input list⟩);

If the file variable is not specified, the standard file **input** is assumed. Thus, data from one line of the file of student test scores, ClassList, can be obtained by

```
readln (ClassList, IDNumber, Score1, Score2, Score3);
```

As data items are read using **readln,** values are stored in the designated variables and the pointer is moved to the first position past the end-of-line marker. Thus,

```
reset (ClassList);
readln (ClassList, IDNumber, Score1, Score2, Score3);
```

results in

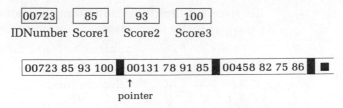

It is not necessary to read all values in a line of data. If only some values are read, a **readln** statement still causes the pointer to move to the first position past the end-of-line marker. Thus,

```
reset (ClassList);
readln (ClassList, IDNumber, Score1);
```

results in

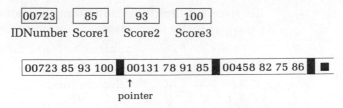

However, when data items are read using **read,** the pointer moves to the first position past the last data item read. Thus, the statement

```
read (ClassList, IDNumber, Score1);
```

results in the following:

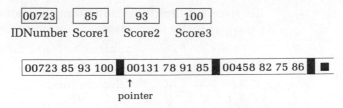

Variables in the variable list of **read** and **readln** can be listed one at a time or in any combination that does not result in a type conflict. For example,

```
readln (ClassList, IDNumber, Score1);
```

can be replaced by

```
read (ClassList, IDNumber);
readln (ClassList, Score1);
```

Pascal has two Boolean-valued functions that may be used when working with text files: **eoln** (for end-of-line) and **eof** (for end-of-file). Only if the data pointer is at an end-of-line or end-of-file marker is the Boolean function **eoln** (⟨file variable⟩) true. Similarly, **eof** (⟨file variable⟩) is true only when the data pointer is positioned at the end-of-file marker. This allows both **eoln** (⟨file variable⟩) and **eof** (⟨file variable⟩) to be used as Boolean conditions when designing problem solutions. Thus, part of a solution might be

```
WHILE NOT eof(<file variable>) DO
    process a line of data
```

In this loop, data from one line of the text file would typically be read by a **readln** statement. This allows the end-of-file condition to become **true** after the last data line has been read.

Text files can contain any character available in the character set being used. When numeric data are stored, the system converts a number to an appropriate character representation. When this number is retrieved from the file, another conversion takes place to change the character representation to a number.

■ **EXAMPLE 6.1**

Let's now write a short program that uses the text file ClassList and the end-of-file (**eof**) condition. If the problem is to print a listing of student identification numbers, test scores, and test averages, a first-level pseudocode development is

1. Open the file
2. Print a heading
3. **WHILE NOT eof** (⟨file variable⟩) **DO**
   3.1 process a line of data

Step 3.1 can be refined to

   3.1 process a line of data
        3.1.1 get the data
        3.1.2 compute test average
        3.1.3 print the data

A short program to accomplish this task is

```
PROGRAM ClassRecordBook (input, output, ClassList);

{   This program uses data from a text file.  Data for each     }
{   student are on a separate line in the file.  Lines  are     }
{   processed until there are no more lines.                    }

VAR
  Score1, Score2, Score3,        { Test scores                  }
  IDNumber : integer;            { Student number               }
  TestAverage : real;            { Average of three tests       }
  ClassList : text;              { Text file                    }

{**************************************************************** }

FUNCTION Average (Score1, Score2, Score3 : integer) : real;

  { Given:    Three integers                                     }
  { Task:     Compute their average                              }
  { Return:   The average of three integers                      }

  BEGIN
    Average := (Score1 + Score2 + Score3) / 3
  END;  { of FUNCTION Average  }

{**************************************************************** }

PROCEDURE PrintHeading;

  { Given:    Nothing                                            }
  { Task:     Print the heading                                  }
  { Return:   Nothing                                            }
```

```
    CONST
      Skip = ' ';

    BEGIN
      writeln;
      writeln ('Identification Number', Skip:5, 'Test Scores',
              Skip:5, 'Average');
      writeln ('--------------------', Skip:5, '-----------',
              Skip:5, '-------');
      writeln
    END;   {  of PROCEDURE PrintHeading  }

{************************************************************* }

BEGIN  {  Main program  }
  reset (ClassList);
  PrintHeading;
  WHILE NOT eof(ClassList) DO
    BEGIN
      readln (ClassList, IDNumber, Score1, Score2, Score3);
      TestAverage := Average(Score1, Score2, Score3);
      writeln (IDNumber:10, Score1:19, Score2:4, Score3:4,
              TestAverage:11:2)
    END  {  of WHILE NOT eof DO loop  }
END.  {  of main program  }
```

When this program is run using the text file ClassList with values

```
00123 85 93 100 | 00131 78 91 85 | 00458 82 75 86 | ▪
```

the output produced is

```
Identification Number            Test Scores     Average
--------------------             -----------     -------

              123                85  93 100       92.67
              131                78  91  85       84.67
              458                82  75  86       81.00
```

A note of caution is in order. Any attempt to **read** beyond the end of a file results in an error. To illustrate, if

```
read (ClassList, IDNumber, Score1, Score2, Score3);
```

had been used in the previous example instead of

```
readln (ClassList, IDNumber, Score1, Score2, Score3);
```

an error would have occurred because, when **read** is used with the last line of data, the data pointer is positioned as

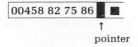

```
00458 82 75 86 | ▪
               ↑
             pointer
```

At this point, even though **eoln** (ClassList) is **true**, **eof** (ClassList) is still **false** and the loop for processing a line of data would be entered one more time. Using **readln,** however, positions the data pointer as

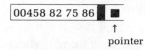

↑
pointer

and this causes the end-of-file condition to be **true** when expected.

Writing to a Text File

It is also possible to write to a text file. If you want the file saved for later use, a file variable must be included in the file list as part of the program heading just as is done when reading from files. The file variable must also be declared to be of type **text**. Before writing to a file, it must be *opened for writing* by

```
rewrite (<file variable>);
```

This standard procedure creates an empty file with the specified name. If there were any values previously in the file, they are erased by this statement. Data are then written to the file by using standard procedures **write** and **writeln.** The general form is

> **write** (⟨file variable⟩, ⟨list of values⟩);
> or
> **writeln** (⟨file variable⟩, ⟨list of values⟩);

These both cause the list of values to be written on one line in the file. The difference is that **writeln** causes an end-of-line marker to be placed after the last data item. Using **write** allows you to continue entering data items on the same line with subsequent **write** or **writeln** statements. If you wish,

```
writeln (<file variable>);
```

can be used to place an end-of-line marker at the end of a data line.

Formatting can be used to control spacing of data items in a line of text. For example, since numeric items must be separated, you might choose to put test scores in a file by

```
writeln (ClassList, Score1:4, Score2:4, Score3:4);
```

If the scores are 85, 72, and 95, the line of data created is

```
85  72  95
```

and each integer is allotted four columns. Let's now illustrate writing to a file with an example.

EXAMPLE 6.2

Let's write a program that allows you to create a text file containing data for students in a class. Each line in the file is to contain a student identification number followed by three test scores. A first-level pseudocode development is

1. Open the file
2. **WHILE** more data **DO**
   2.1 process a line

Step 2.1 can be refined to

> 2.1   process a line
>> 2.1.1   get data from keyboard
>> 2.1.2   write data to text file

A complete program for this is

```
PROGRAM CreateFile (input, output, ClassList);

{   This program creates a text file.  Each line of the file   }
{   contains data for one student.  Data are entered  inter-   }
{   actively from the keyboard and then written to the file.   }

VAR
   Score1, Score2, Score3,      {  Scores for three tests     }
   IDNumber : integer;          {  Student number             }
   Response : char;             {  Indicator for continuation }
   MoreData : boolean;          {  Loop control variable      }
   ClassList : text;            {  External text file         }


{*********************************************************************}


PROCEDURE GetStudentData (VAR IDNumber, Score1, Score2,
                          Score3 : integer);

   {  Given:    Nothing                                        }
   {  Task:     Get IDNumber and three test scores from the    }
   {               keyboard                                    }
   {  Return:   IDNumber, Score1, Score2, and Score3           }

   BEGIN
     write ('Please enter a student ID number');
     writeln (' and three test scores.');
     writeln ('Separate entries by a space.');
     writeln;
     readln (IDNumber, Score1, Score2, Score3)
   END;  {  of PROCEDURE GetStudentData  }


{*********************************************************************}


BEGIN  {  Main program  }
  rewrite (ClassList);                        {  Open for writing  }
  MoreData := true;
  WHILE MoreData DO
    BEGIN
      GetStudentData (IDNumber, Score1, Score2, Score3);
      writeln (ClassList, IDNumber, Score1:4, Score2:4, Score3:4);

      {  Check for more data  }

      writeln;
      writeln ('Any more students? Y or N');
      readln (Response);
      IF (Response = 'N') OR (Response = 'n') THEN
        MoreData := false
    END  {  of WHILE...DO loop  }
END.  {  of main program  }
```

External and Internal Files

Files used thus far have been *external files,* files that are stored in secondary memory and are external to main memory. If a program is to use an external file, a file variable must be included in the file list portion of the program heading. The file variable must then be declared in the variable declaration section as type **text.**

On some occasions, it is desirable to use a file only while the program is running and it is not necessary to save the contents for later use. In this case, an *internal file* (also called a *temporary* or *scratch file*) can be created by declaring a file variable of type **text** in the variable declaration section, but it should not be included in the file list of the program heading. Internal files are normally used during file processing when it is desirable to temporarily save the contents of a file that is being altered. Our next example illustrates use of an internal file.

■ **EXAMPLE 6.3**

Let's write a program that allows you to update the text file ClassList by adding one more test score to each line of data. We need two text files in this program: ClassList (external) and TempFile (internal). With these two files, we can create new lines in TempFile by reading a line from ClassList and getting a score from the keyboard. When all lines have been updated, we copy TempFile to ClassList.

A first-level pseudocode solution for this problem is

1. Open files (**reset** ClassList, **rewrite** TempFile)
2. **WHILE NOT eof** (ClassList) **DO**
   2.1 read one line
   2.2 get new score
   2.3 write one line to TempFile
3. Open files (**reset** TempFile, **rewrite** ClassList)
4. Update file
   WHILE NOT eof (TempFile) **DO**
   4.1 read one line from TempFile
   4.2 write one line to ClassList

A complete program for this problem is

```
PROGRAM UpdateClassList (input, output, ClassList);

{   This program updates an existing text  file.  The   process   }
{   requires a second file.  Contents of the external file are    }
{   copied to a temporary internal file and the external   file   }
{   is then updated one line at a time.                           }

VAR
   Score1, Score2,                      {  Scores for four tests  }
   Score3, Score4,
   IDNumber : integer;                  {  Student number         }
   ClassList, TempFile : text;          {  Text files             }

BEGIN  {  Main program  }
   reset (ClassList);                                {  Open files  }
   rewrite (TempFile);
```

```
      WHILE NOT eof(ClassList) DO                  { Copy to TempFile    }
        BEGIN
          readln (ClassList, IDNumber, Score1, Score2, Score3);
          writeln ('Enter a new test score for student ', IDNumber);
          readln (Score4);
          writeln (TempFile, IDNumber, Score1:4, Score2:4,
                  Score3:4, Score4:4)
        END;  { of lines in ClassList  }
      reset (TempFile);                                 { Open files     }
      rewrite (ClassList); { Note: contents of old ClassList erased }
      WHILE NOT eof(TempFile) DO                    { Copy to ClassList  }
        BEGIN
          readln (TempFile, IDNumber, Score1, Score2, Score3, Score4);
          writeln (ClassList, IDNumber, Score1:4, Score2:4, Score3:4,
                  Score4:4)
        END  { of copying TempFile to ClassList  }
    END.  { of main program  }
```

■ **EXAMPLE 6.4**

As an illustration of using **eoln,** let's write a program that replaces all blanks in a text file with asterisks. Output is directed to the monitor and a new text file is created for the purpose of saving the altered form of the original text file. Note that reading a character advances the data pointer only one character position unless **readln** is used.

A first-level pseudocode development is

1. Open the files
WHILE NOT eof (FileWithBlanks) **DO**
2. Process one line
3. Prepare for the next line

A second-level pseudocode development is

1. Open the files
   1.1 Open FileWithBlanks
   1.2 Open FileWithoutBlanks
WHILE NOT eof (FileWithBlanks) **DO**
2. Process one line
   2.1 Read a character
   2.2 **IF** character is a blank **THEN**
      2.2.1   replace with an asterisk
   2.3 Write character to FileWithoutBlanks
   2.4 Write character to the screen
3. Prepare for the next line
   3.1 Insert end-of-line in FileWithoutBlanks
   3.2 End-of-line to screen
   3.3 Advance pointer in FileWithBlanks

A complete program for this is

```
PROGRAM DeleteBlanks (input, output, FileWithBlanks,
                      FileWithoutBlanks);

{ This  program illustrates  using eof  and eoln  with a text }
{ file.  It replaces blanks with asterisks.                   }
```

```
VAR
  FileWithBlanks,                       {  Existing text file       }
  FileWithoutBlanks : text;             {  Altered text file        }
  Ch : char;                            {  Used for reading characters }

BEGIN
  reset (FileWithBlanks);                         {  Open the files     }
  rewrite (FileWithoutBlanks);
  WHILE NOT eof(FileWithBlanks) DO
    BEGIN                                         {  Process one line   }
      WHILE NOT eoln(FileWithBlanks) DO
        BEGIN
          read (FileWithBlanks, Ch);
          IF Ch = ' ' THEN
            Ch := '*';
          write (FileWithoutBlanks, Ch);
          write (Ch)                              {  Write to the screen }
        END;   {  of reading one line  }
      writeln (FileWithoutBlanks);          {  Insert end-of-line  }
      writeln;
      readln (FileWithBlanks)             {  Advance the pointer  }
    END {  of lines in text file  }
END. {  of main program  }
```

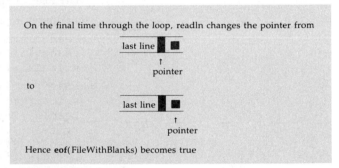

On the final time through the loop, readln changes the pointer from

last line

↑
pointer

to

last line

↑
pointer

Hence **eof**(FileWithBlanks) becomes true

When this is run using the text file

```
This is a text file with normal blanks.
After it has been processed by
PROGRAM DeleteBlanks, every blank will
be replaced with an asterisk "*".
```

the output to the screen is

```
This*is*a*text*file*with*normal*blanks.
After*it*has*been*processed*by
PROGRAM*DeleteBlanks,*every*blank*will
be*replaced*with*an*asterisk*"*".
```

The external text file FileWithoutBlanks also contains the version shown as output.

■   ■

The material in this section allows us to make a substantial change in our approach to writing programs. We are no longer dependent upon an interactive mode and we can now proceed assuming data files exist for a program. This somewhat simplifies program design and also allows us to design programs for large sets of data. Consequently, most programs developed in the remainder of this text use text files for input. If you wish to continue with interactive programs, you should be able to make appropriate modifications.

Exercises 6.1

1. Explain the difference between an external file and an internal file. Give appropriate uses for each.

2. Write a test program that allows you to print a line of text from a file to the output file.

3. Explain what is wrong with using

   ```
   writeln (ClassList, Score1, Score2, Score3);
   ```

   if you want to write three scores to the text file ClassList.

4. Write a program that allows you to display a text file line by line.

5. Assume that a text file, InFile, is as illustrated.

   | 18 | 19M | − 14.3 | JO | 142.1F | ■ |

   For each question, the pointer is positioned at the beginning of the file and the variable declaration section of a program is

   ```
   VAR
     A, B : integer:
     X, Y : real;
     Ch : char;
     InFile : text;
   ```

   What output is produced from each segment of code?

   a. ```
   read (InFile, A);
   read (Infile, B, Ch);
   writeln (A:5, B:5, Ch:5);
   ```

   b. ```
   read (Infile, Ch);
   write (Ch:10);
   readln (InFile, Ch);
   writeln (Ch);
   read (InFile, Ch);
   writeln (Ch:10);
   ```

   c. ```
   read (InFile, A, B, Ch, X);
   writeln (A, B, Ch, X);
   writeln (A:5, B:5, Ch:5, X:10:2);
   read (InFile, Ch);
   writeln (Ch:5);
   ```

   d. ```
   readln (InFile);
   read (InFile, Ch, Ch);
   readln (InFile, Y);
   writeln (Ch:5, Y:10:2);
   ```

6. Using the same text file and variable declaration section in Exercise 5, indicate the contents of each variable location and the position of the pointer after the segment of code is executed. Assume the pointer is positioned at the beginning for each problem.

   a. ```
   read (InFile, Ch, A);
   ```

   b. ```
   readln (InFile, Ch, A);
   ```

   c. ```
   readln (InFile);
   ```

   d. ```
   readln (InFile);
   readln (InFile);
   ```

   e. ```
   readln (InFile, A, B, Ch, X);
   ```

   f. ```
   read (InFile, A, B, Ch, Y);
   ```

g. ```
readln (InFile, A, Ch);
readln (Infile, Ch, Ch, B);
```

h. ```
read (InFile, A, B, Ch, X, Ch);
```

7. Again use the same text file and variable declaration section as in Exercise 5. For each of the following segments of code, indicate if the exercise produces an error and, if so, explain why an error occurs.

   a. ```
read (InFile, X, Y);
```

   b. ```
readln (InFile, A);
read (InFile, B);
```

   c. ```
readln (InFile, Ch);
readln (InFile, Ch);
readln (InFile, Ch);
```

   d. ```
read (InFile, X, A, Ch, B, Ch);
```

   e. ```
readln (InFile);
read (InFile, Ch, Ch, A, Ch, B);
```

8. Write a complete Pascal program that reads your (three) initials and five test scores from a text file. Your program should then compute your test average and print out all information in a reasonable form with suitable messages.

9. Write a program that allows you to create a text file that contains your name, address, social security number, and age. Reset the file and have the information printed as output. Save the file in secondary storage for later use.

10. Show what output is produced from the following program. Also indicate the contents of each file after the program is run.

```pascal
PROGRAM Exercise10 (input, output, F2);
VAR
   Ch : char;
   F1, F2 : text;
BEGIN
   rewrite (F1);
   rewrite (F2);
   writeln (F1, 'This is a test.');
   writeln (F1, 'This is another line.');
   reset (F1);
   WHILE NOT eof(F1) DO
     BEGIN
       WHILE NOT eoln(F1) DO
         BEGIN
           read (F1, Ch);
           IF Ch = ' ' THEN
             writeln ('*')
           ELSE
             write (F2, Ch)
         END;
         readln (F1)
     END
END.
```

11. Write a program that deletes all blanks from a text file. Your program should save the revised file for later use.

12. Write a program using a **CASE** statement to scramble a text file by replacing all blanks with an asterisk (*), and interchanging all A's with U's and E's with I's. Your program should print out the scrambled file and save it for subsequent use.
```

13. Write a program to update a text file by numbering the lines consecutively as 1, 2, 3, ...

14. Write a program to count the number of words in a text file. Assume that each word is followed by a blank or a period.

15. Write a program to find the longest word in a text file. Output should include the word and its length.

16. Write a program to compute the average length of words in a text file.

■ ■ ■ ■

■ 6.2
TYPE Definitions in Pascal

Ordinal Data Types

Of the data types we have previously used, **integer, char,** and **boolean** are called ordinal data types. A data type is ordinal if values of that type have an immediate predecessor and an immediate successor. The exception is that the first listed element has only a successor and the last listed element has only a predecessor. Data of type **integer** are ordinal and can be listed as $-$**maxint,** . . ., $-1, 0, 1, 2, . . .,$ + **maxint.** Boolean values **false** and **true,** and data of type **char** are listed according to the collating sequence shown in Appendix 4. Data of type **real** are not ordinal because a given real has neither an immediate predecessor nor an immediate successor. Permissible values for data of these three ordinal data types are summarized as follows:

Data Type	Values
integer	−maxint to maxint
char	Character set in a collating sequence
boolean	true, false

The four data types **integer, char, boolean,** and **real** used thus far are standard data types. We are now ready to see how Pascal allows us to define other data types called *enumerated data types.*

Simple Enumerated Data Types

The declaration section of a program may contain a **TYPE** definition section that can be used to define a data type. For example,

```
TYPE
    Weekday = (Mon, Tues, Wed, Thur, Fri);
```

After such a definition has been made, the variable declaration section can contain identifiers of the type Weekday. Thus, we could have

```
VAR
    Day : Weekday;
```

Values in an enumerated data type can be any legal identifier. Several comments are now in order concerning the **TYPE** definition.

1. Simple enumerated types are also referred to as *user-defined data types.* (Other user-defined data types include subranges and structured data types, which will be studied later.)

2. This defined type will be an ordinal data type with the first defined constant having ordinal zero. Ordinal values increase by one in order from left to right. Every constant except the first has a predecessor and every constant except the last has a successor. Using the previously defined **TYPE** Weekday, we have

```
Mon        Tues        Wed        Thurs        Fri
 ↕          ↕           ↕           ↕            ↕
 0          1           2           3            4
```

3. Variables can be declared to be of the new type.
4. The values defined in the **TYPE** definition section are constants that can be used in the program. These values must be valid identifiers.
5. No identifier can belong to more than one enumerated data type.
6. Identifiers that are defined values cannot be used as operands in arithmetic expressions.
7. Enumerated data types are for internal use only; you cannot **read** or **write** values of these variables.

Thus, given the previous **TYPE** definition of Weekday and the variable declaration of Day, each of the following would be an appropriate program statement.

```
a. Day := Tues;
b. Day := pred(Day);
c. IF Day = Mon THEN
      .
      .
      .
   ELSE
      .
      .
      .
d. FOR Day := Mon TO Fri DO
      BEGIN
         .
         .
         .
      END;
```

Having seen an example of an enumerated data type and some typical related program statements, let us look at a more formal method of definition. In general, we have

```
TYPE
   ⟨type identifier⟩ = (⟨constant1⟩, ⟨constant2⟩, . . . ⟨constantn⟩);
VAR
   ⟨identifier⟩ : ⟨type identifier⟩;
```

The **TYPE** definition section is part of the declaration section of a program. It follows the constant definition section (**CONST**) and precedes the variable declaration section (**VAR**) as shown in Figure 6.1.

FIGURE 6.1
Placement of **TYPE** definition
section

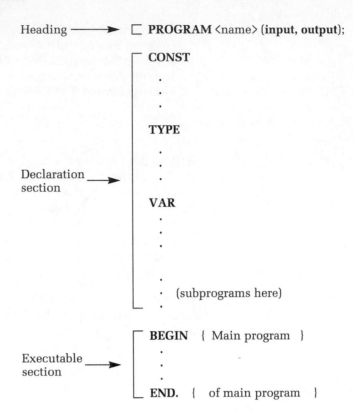

The following short program illustrates the placement and use of enumerated data types.

```
PROGRAM TypePrac (output);

CONST
  Skip = ' ';

TYPE
  Weekday = (Mon, Tues, Wed, Thur, Fri);

VAR
  Day : Weekday;

BEGIN
  Day := Wed;
  IF Day < Fri THEN
    writeln (Skip:20, 'Not near the weekend.')
  ELSE
    writeln (Skip:20, 'The weekend starts tomorrow.')
END.
```

The output from this program is

```
Not near the weekend.
```

Reasons for Using Enumerated Data Types

At first it may seem like a lot of trouble to define new types for use in a Pascal program, but there are several reasons for using them. In fact, being able to create enumerated data types is one of the advantages of using Pascal as a programming language. Why? With enumerated data types, you can express clearly the logical structure of data, enhance the readability of your program, provide program protection against bad data values, and declare parameters in subprograms.

Suppose you are working on a program to count the number of days in the month of a certain year. Enumerated data types allow you to use the following definition and subsequent declaration.

```
TYPE
   AllMonths = (Jan, Feb, March, April, May, June, July,
                Aug, Sept, Oct, Nov, Dec);
VAR
   Month : AllMonths;
```

With this definition it is easier to understand what the code does. It could contain statements such as

```
FOR Month := Jan TO April DO
   .
   .
   .
```

or

```
IF (Month = Feb) AND (Year MOD 4 = 0) THEN
   NumDays := 29;
```

This second segment of code clearly indicates that you are counting the extra day in February for a leap year. (This is an over-simplification of checking for a leap year. See Exercise 7 at the end of this section.)

Enumerated data types may be used in **CASE** statements. For example, movie ticket prices are frequently broken into three categories: youth, adult, and senior citizen. If the following definition and declaration were made,

```
TYPE
   Categories = (Youth, Adult, Senior);
VAR
   Patron : Categories;
```

a program statement could be something like

```
CASE Patron OF
   Youth  : Price := YouthPrice;
   Adult  : Price := AdultPrice;
   Senior : Price := Senior Price
END;  { of CASE Patron }
```

Once an enumerated data type has been defined at the global level, it is available to all subprograms. Thus, if you have a function for counting the days, a typical function heading might be

```
FUNCTION NumDays (Month : AllMonths;
                  Year : integer) : integer;
```

This aspect of user-defined data types will become more significant when we examine structured data types, including arrays and records.

Recall the limitation imposed on variables that are of an enumerated type: they are for internal use only; you cannot **read** or **write** values of these variables. Thus, in the earlier example using months of the year, you could have the following statement:

```
Month := June;
```

but not

```
writeln (Month);
```

However (as we saw in Section 4.5), use of a **CASE** statement allows translation procedures to be written with relative ease.

We close this section with some typical definitions for enumerated data types. These are intended to improve program readability. You are encouraged to incorporate enumerated data types in your subsequent programs. In general, you are limited only by your imagination.

```
TYPE
   SoftDrinks = (Pepsi, Coke, SevenUp, Orange, RootBeer);
   Seasons = (Winter, Spring, Summer, Fall);
   Colors = (Red, Orange, Yellow, Green, Blue, Indigo, Violet);
   ClassStanding = (Freshman, Sophomore, Junior, Senior);
   Fruits = (Apple, Orange, Banana);
   Vegetables = (Corn, Peas, Broccoli, Spinach);
```

With these type definitions, each of the following would be a reasonable variable declaration:

```
VAR
   Pop, Soda : SoftDrinks;
   Season : Seasons;
   Hue : Colors;
   Class : ClassStanding;
   Appetizer : Fruits;
   SideDish : Vegetables;
```

Exercises 6.2

1. Explain what is meant by ordinal data type.

2. Write a test program to see what happens in each of the following instances.

   a. Try to **write** the value of a variable that is an enumerated data type.

   b. Try to find the predecessor (**pred**) of a defined constant whose ordinal is zero in an enumerated type.

3. Find all errors in the following definitions.

   a.
   ```
   TYPE
      Names = (John, Joe, Mary, Jane);
      People = (Henry, Sue, Jane, Bill);
   ```

b. ```
TYPE
   Colors = (Red, Blue, Red, Orange);
```
**c.** ```
TYPE
   Letters = A, C, E;
```

4. Assume the **TYPE** definition

```
TYPE
   Colors = (Red, Orange, Yellow, Blue, Green);
```

has been given. Indicate whether each of the following is **true** or **false**.

a. ```
Orange < Blue
```
**b.** ```
(Green <> Red) AND (Blue > Green)
```
c. ```
(Yellow < Orange) OR (Blue >= Red)
```

5. Assume the **TYPE** definition and variable declaration

```
TYPE
   AllDays = (Sun, Mon, Tues, Wed, Thur, Fri, Sat);
VAR
   Day, Weekday, Weekend : AllDays;
```

have been given. Indicate which of the following are valid program statements. For those that are not, give an explanation.

a. ```
Day := Tues;
```
**b.** ```
Day := Tues + Wed;
```
c. ```
Weekday := Sun;
```
**d.** ```
IF Day = Sat THEN
   writeln ('Clean the garage.':30);
```
e. ```
IF (Day < Sat) AND (Day > Sun) THEN
   writeln ('It is a workday.':30)
ELSE
   writeln ('It is the weekend.':30);
```
**f.** ```
FOR Day := Mon TO Fri DO
   writeln (Day);
```
g. ```
read (Day);
IF Day < Sat THEN
   Weekday := Day;
```
**h.** ```
Wed := Tues + 1;
```

6. Assume the following definitions and declarations have been made in a program.

```
TYPE
   Cloth = (Flannel, Cotton, Rayon, Orlon);
VAR
   Material : Cloth;
   NumberOfYards, Price : real;
```

What would be the output from the following segment of code?

```
Material := Cotton;
NumberOfYards := 3.5;
IF (Material = Rayon) OR (Material = Orlon) THEN
   Price := NumberOfYards * 4.5
ELSE IF Material = Cotton THEN
   Price := NumberOfYards * 2.75
ELSE
   Price := NumberOfYards * 2.5;
writeln (Price:30:2);
```
```

7. Find the complete definition of a leap year in the Gregorian calendar. Define appropriate data types and write a segment of code that would indicate whether or not a given year was a leap year.

■ ■ ■ ■

■ **6.3**

Subrange as a Data Type

Defining Subranges

In the previous section, we learned how to define new data types using the **TYPE** definition section. Now we will investigate another way to define new data types.

A *subrange* of an existing ordinal data type may be defined as a data type by

> **TYPE**
> ⟨identifier⟩ = ⟨initial value⟩. .⟨final value⟩;

where the initial value and final value are separated by two periods. For example, we could have a subrange of the integers defined by

```
TYPE
    USYears = 1776..1992;
```

When defining a subrange, the following items should be noted.

1. The original data type must be an ordinal type.
2. Any valid identifier may be used for the name of the type.
3. The initial and final values must be of the original data type.
4. Since the underlying data type is ordinal, it is ordered. In this ordering, the initial value of a defined subrange must occur before the final value.
5. Only values in the indicated subrange (endpoints included) may be assigned to a variable of the type defined by the subrange.
6. The same value may appear in different subranges.

We illustrate some of these points in the following example.

■ **EXAMPLE 6.5**

Consider the subranges Weekdays and Midweek of the enumerated ordinal Days.

```
TYPE
    Days = (Sun, Mon, Tues, Wed, Thur, Fri, Sat);    {  Enumerated  }
    Weekdays = Mon..Fri;                             {  Subrange    }
    Midweek = Tues..Thur;                            {  Subrange    }
VAR
    SchoolDay : Weekdays;
    Workday : Midweek;
```

In this case, Days is defined first and we can then define appropriate subranges. With the variable SchoolDay declared as of type Weekdays, you can use any of the values Mon, Tues, Wed, Thur, or Fri with SchoolDay. However, you cannot assign either Sat or Sun to SchoolDay.

Notice that Tues, Wed, and Thur are values that appear in different type definitions. However, since they appear in subranges, this will not produce an error. Furthermore,

```
Workday := Tues;
SchoolDay := Workday;
```

are both acceptable statements.

Some other subrange definitions are

```
TYPE
  Grades = 'A'..'E';
  Alphabet = 'A'..'Z';
  ScoreRange = 0..100;
  Months = (Jan, Feb, Mar, Apr, May, June, July, Aug, Sept,
            Oct, Nov, Dec);
  Year = Jan..Dec;
  Summer = June..Aug;
```

Months is not a subrange here. However, once defined, an appropriate subrange such as Summer may be defined. With these subranges defined, each of the following declarations would be appropriate.

```
VAR
  FinalGrade : Grades;
  Letter : Alphabet;
  TestScore : ScoreRange;
  SumMonth : Summer;
```

Compatible and Identical Types

Now that we know how to define subranges of existing ordinal data types, we need to look carefully at compatibility of variables. Variables are of *compatible type* if they have the same base type. Thus, in

```
TYPE
  AgeRange = 0..110;
VAR
  Age : AgeRange;
  Year : integer;
```

the variables Age and Year are compatible because they both have **integer** as the base type (AgeRange is a subrange of integers). If variables are compatible, assignments may be made between them or they may be manipulated in any manner that variables of that base type may be manipulated.

Even when variables are compatible, you should exercise caution when making assignment statements. To illustrate, using Age and Year as previously declared, consider the statements

```
Age := Year;
Year := Age;
```

Since Age is of type AgeRange and AgeRange is a subrange of **integer,** any value in Age is acceptable as a value that can be assigned to Year. Thus,

```
Year := Age;
```

is permissible. However, since values for Age are restricted to the defined subrange, it is possible that

```
Age := Year;
```

will produce a run-time error. Since they are compatible, there will not be a compilation error, but consider

```
Year := 150;
Age := Year;
```

Since 150 is not in the subrange for Age, execution would be halted and an error message printed.

Two variables are said to be of *identical type* if—and only if—they are declared with the same type identifier. It is important to distinguish between compatible and identical types for variables when using subprograms. A value parameter and its argument must be of compatible type; a variable parameter and its argument must be of identical type. A type compatibility error will be generated if these rules are not followed. To illustrate, consider

```
TYPE
   GoodScore = 60..100;
VAR
   Score1, Score2 : GoodScore;
PROCEDURE Compute (HS1 : integer;
                   VAR HS2 : GoodScore);
```

This procedure may be called by

```
Compute (Score1, Score2);
```

Note that HS1 is a value parameter and need only be compatible with Score1. HS2 is a variable parameter and must be identical in type to Score2.

When used as data types for parameters, **TYPE** definitions must be defined in the main program since they cannot be defined in a subprogram heading. You may, however, define **TYPE**s internally for subprograms.

Using Subranges

T There are several good reasons for using subranges, in particular, for batch programs. Although they require extra time and thought when you are writing a program, the long-range benefits far outweigh these minor inconveniences. One of the more obvious benefits is program protection. By carefully defining subranges, you avoid the possibility of working with bad data or data out of the expected range. Although such data will not be detected during compilation, an inappropriate assignment will halt execution in most versions of Pascal. This makes it easier to locate the source of an error. It also avoids the possibility of producing incorrect results. If, for example, a data entry operator inadvertently types in 400 rather than 40 for the hours worked by an employee, a definition and declaration such as

```
TYPE
   TotalHours = 0..60;
VAR
   Hours : TotalHours;
```

would cause execution to be stopped with the statement

```
read (Hours);
```

since 400 is not in the defined subrange. This is not necessarily the best way to avoid bad data with an interactive program, but it is better than allowing bad data to go undetected.

Another alternative for interactive programs is to use a conditional **IF . . . THEN . . . ELSE** or a **REPEAT . . . UNTIL** loop to guarantee that the data are in the appropriate range. This approach prevents program crashes and makes a program more user-friendly. For example, if you wanted to guarantee the number of hours entered is between 0 and 60, you could use a validation loop as follows:

```
REPEAT
  writeln ('Enter hours worked <0..60> or <-999 to quit>.');
  readln (Hours)
UNTIL (Hours >= 0) AND (Hours <= 60) OR (Hours = -999);
```

If you had a longer interactive example where the user could choose whether or not to repeat some process you could use

```
REPEAT
  .
  .  (    action here    )
  .
  writeln ('Do you wish to continue? <Y> or <N>');
  readln (Ch);
  Continue := (Ch = 'Y') OR (Ch = 'y')
UNTIL NOT Continue;
```

STYLE TIP

■ ■ ■ ■ ■ ■ ■ ■ ■ ■ ■

The **CONST** and **TYPE** definition sections can be used together to enhance readability and facilitate program design. For example, rather than use the subrange

```
TYPE
  USYears = 1776..1992;
```

you could define an ending constant and then use it as indicated.

```
CONST
  CurrentYear = 1992;
TYPE
  USYears = 1776..CurrentYear;
```

Software Engineering

Enumerated types and subranges are features of Pascal that are consistent with principles of software engineering. As has been previously stated, communication, readability, and maintenance are essential in developing large systems. Use of enumerated types and subranges is important for all of these areas. To illustrate, suppose a program includes working with a chemical reaction that normally occurs around 180 degrees Fahrenheit. If the definition section includes

```
TYPE
  ReactionRange = 150..210;
```

subsequent modules could use a variable such as

```
VAR
  ReactionTemp : ReactionRange;
```

As we progress into the next chapter, you will see how use of enumerated or user-defined data types becomes even more essential to maintaining principles of software engineering. Specifically, defining data structures becomes an important design consideration.

Exercises 6.3

1. Indicate whether the following **TYPE** definitions, subsequent declarations, and uses are valid or invalid. Explain what is wrong with those that are invalid.

   a. TYPE
        Reverse = 10..1;

```
      b. TYPE
            Bases = (Home, First, Second, Third);
            Double = Home..Second;
            Score = Second..Home;

      c. TYPE
            Colors = (Red, White, Blue);
            Stripes = Red..White;
         VAR
            Hue : Stripes;
         BEGIN
            Hue := Blue;

      d. TYPE
            Weekdays = Mon..Fri;
            Days = (Sun, Mon, Tues, Wed, Thur, Fri, Sat);

      e. TYPE
            ScoreRange = 0..100;
            HighScores = 70..100;
            Midscores = 50..70;
            LowScores = 20..60;
         VAR
            Score1 : Midscores;
            Score2 : HighScores;
         BEGIN
            Score1 := 60;
            Score2 := Score1 + 5;
```

2. Write a test program to see what happens when you try to use (assign, read, and so on) a value for a variable that is not in the defined subrange.

3. Explain why each of the following subrange definitions might be used in a program.

   a. `Dependents = 0..20;` c. `QuizScores = 0..10;`

   b. `HoursWorked = 0..60;` d. `TotalPoints = 0..700;`

4. Indicate reasonable subranges for each of the following. Explain your answers.

   a. `TwentiethCentury =`

   b. `Digits =`

   c. `JuneTemp =`

   d. `WinterRange =`

   e. `Colors = (Black, Brown, Red, Pink, Yellow, White);`
      `LightColors =`

5. Assume the declaration section of a program contains

```
TYPE
   ChessPieces = (Pawn, Knight, Bishop, Rook, King, Queen);
   Expendable = Pawn..Rook;
   Valuable = King..Queen;
   LowRange = 0..20;
   Midrange = 40..80;
VAR
   Piece1 : Valuable;
   Piece2 : Expendable;
   Piece3 : ChessPieces;
   Score1 : LowRange;
   Score2 : Midrange;
   Score3 : integer;
```

Indicate which of the following pairs of variables are of compatible type.

a. `Piece1` and `Piece2`

b. `Piece2` and `Piece3`

c. `Piece3` and `Score1`

d. `Score1` and `Score2`

e. `Score1` and `Score3`

f. `Piece2` and `Score3`

6. Assume the declaration section of a program contains the following:

```
TYPE
   PointRange = 400..700;
   FlowerList = (Rose, Iris, Tulip, Begonia);
   Sublist = Rose..Tulip;
VAR
   TotalPts : PointRange;
   Total : integer;
   Flower : Sublist;
   OldFlower : FlowerList;
```

The procedure heading is

```
PROCEDURE TypePrac (A : PointRange;
                    VAR B : integer;
                    Fl : Sublist);
```

Indicate which of the following are valid calls to this procedure.

a. `TypePrac (TotalPts, Total, Flower);`

b. `TypePrac (Total, TotalPts, Flower);`

c. `TypePrac (TotalPts, Total, OldFlower);`

d. `TypePrac (Total, Total, Flower);`

e. `TypePrac (Total, Total, OldFlower);`

■ ■ ■ ■

■ 6.4
Operations on Ordinal Data Types

Functions for Ordinal Data Types

Earlier we characterized ordinal data types as those in which there was a first and last listed element and each element other than the first and last had an immediate predecessor and an immediate successor. Of the standard data types, only **real** is not ordinal. Since the enumerated data types are all ordinal, the functions **ord, pred,** and **succ** may be used on them. Thus, if we have the definition

```
TYPE
   Days = (Sun, Mon, Tues, Wed, Thur, Fri, Sat);
   Weekdays = Mon..Fri;
```

the following function calls have the indicated values.

Function Call	Value
ord(Sun)	0
ord(Wed)	3
pred(Thur)	Wed
succ(Fri)	Sat
ord(**pred**(Fri))	4

When using functions on enumerated ordinals, the following should be noted.

1. The first-listed identifier has ordinal zero.
2. Successive ordinals are determined by the order in which identifiers are listed.
3. You cannot use **pred** on the first identifier or **succ** on the final identifier.
4. If a subrange data type is defined, the functions return values consistent with the underlying base type; for example, **ord**(Wed) = 3.

Using Ordinal Values of Enumerated Data Types

Now that you have some familiarity with ordinal data types and functions that use them as arguments, let us consider some ways they could be incorporated into programs. One typical use is in Boolean expressions. Suppose you are writing a program to compute the payroll for a company that pays time-and-a-half for working on Saturday. Assume the definition and declaration

```
TYPE
   Workdays = (Mon, Tues, Wed, Thur, Fri, Sat);
VAR
   Day : Workdays;
```

have been made. A typical segment of code is

```
Day := <some value>;
IF Day = Sat THEN
   ComputeOvertime(<calculation>)
ELSE
   ComputeRegularPay(<calculation>)
```

A second use is with **CASE** statements. As previously explained, one limitation of enumerated data types is that they have no external representation (that is, you cannot **read** or **write** their values). However, you can circumvent this limitation by appropriate use of a **CASE** statement. For example, suppose we have the definition and declaration

```
TYPE
   Colors = (Red, White, Blue);
VAR
   Hue : Colors;
```

If you wish to print the value of Hue, you could do so by

```
CASE Hue OF
   Red   : writeln ('Red':20);
   White : writeln ('White':20);
   Blue  : writeln ('Blue':20)
END; { of CASE Hue }
```

since most versions of Pascal do not permit

```
writeln (Hue:20);
```

A third use is as a loop index. For example, consider

```
TYPE
   AllDays = (Sun, Mon, Tues, Wed, Thur, Fri, Sat);
VAR
   Day : AllDays;
```

A NOTE OF INTEREST

Computer Ethics: Viruses

Tiny programs that deliberately cause mischief are epidemic among computers and are causing nervousness among those who monitor them.

Written by malicious programmers, the "computer viruses" are sneaked into computer systems by piggybacking them on legitimate programs and messages. There, they may be passed along or instructed to wait until a prearranged moment to burst forth and destroy data.

At NASA headquarters in Washington, several hundred computers had to be resuscitated after being infected. NASA officials have taken extra precautions and reminded their machines' users to follow routine computer hygiene: Don't trust foreign data or strange machines.

Viruses have the eerie ability to perch disguised among legitimate data just as biological viruses hide among genes in human cells, then spring out unexpectedly, multiplying and causing damage. Experts say that even when they try to study viruses in controlled conditions, the programs can get out of control and erase everything in a computer. The viruses can be virtually impossible to stop if their creators are determined enough.

"The only way to protect every body against them is to do something much worse than the viruses: Stop talking to one another with computers," say William H. Murray, an information-security specialist at Ernst and Whinney financial consultants in Hartford, Conn.

Hundreds of programs and files have been destroyed by the viruses, and thousands of hours of repair or prevention time have been logged. Programmers have quickly produced antidote programs with such titles as "Vaccine," "Flu Shot," "Data Physician" and "Syringe."

Experts say known damage is minimal compared with the huge, destructive potential. They express the hope that the attacks will persuade computer users to minimize access to programming and data.

Viruses are the newest of evolving methods of computer mayhem. One type of virus is the "Trojan horse": it looks and acts like a normal program but contains hidden commands that eventually take effect, ordering mischief. The "time bomb" explodes at a set time; the "logic bomb" goes off when the computer arrives at a certain result during normal computation. The "salami attack" executes barely noticeable small acts, such as shaving a penny from thousands of accounts.

A virus typically is written as perhaps only a few hundred characters in a program containing tens of thousands of characters. When the computer reads legitimate instructions, it encounters the virus, which instructs the computer to suspend normal operations for a fraction of a second.

During that time, the virus instructs the computer to check for other copies of itself and, if none is found, to make and hide copies. Instruction to commit damage may be included.

Is Your Machine at Risk?

1. Computer viruses are actually miniature computer programs. Most were written by malicious programmers intent on destroying information in computers for fun.
2. Those who write virus programs often conceal them on floppy disks that are inserted in the computer.
3. A malicious programmer makes the disk available to others, saying it contains a useful program or game. These programs can be lent to others or put onto computerized "bulletin boards" where anyone can copy them for personal use.
4. A computer receiving the programs will "read" the disk and the tiny virus program at the same time. The virus may then order the computer to do a number of things:
   - Tell it to read the virus and follow instructions.
   - Tell it to make a copy of the virus and place it on any disk inserted in the machine today.
   - Tell it to check the computer's clock, and on a certain date destroy all information that tells where data is stored on any disk: if an operator has no way of retrieving information, it is destroyed.
   - Tell it not to list the virus programs when the computer is asked for an index of programs.
5. In this way, the computer will copy the virus onto many disks—perhaps all or nearly all the disks used in the infected machine. The virus may also be passed over the telephone, when one computer sends or receives data from another.
6. Ultimately hundreds or thousands of people may have infected disks and potential time bombs in their systems.

Each of the following would be an appropriate loop.

```
1. FOR Day := Mon TO Fri DO
     BEGIN
       .
       .
       .
     END;
2. Day := Mon;
   WHILE Day < Sat DO
     BEGIN
       Day := succ(Day);
         .
         .
         .
     END;
3. Day := Sun;
   REPEAT
     Day := succ(Day);
       .
       .
       .
   UNTIL Day = Fri;
```

The loop control in a **FOR** loop is based on the ordinals of the values of the loop index. Thus, the statement

```
FOR Day := Mon TO Fri DO
```

is treated like the statement

```
FOR J := 1 TO 5 DO
```

because **ord**(Mon) is 1 and **ord**(Fri) is 5.

In the **WHILE . . . DO** and **REPEAT . . . UNTIL** loops, you must be sure to increment—increase the ordinal of—the variable. One method of doing this is to use the function **succ**.

Exercises 6.4

1. Suppose the following **TYPE** definition is given.

```
TYPE
  Trees = (Oak, Ash, Maple, Pine);
  SlackType = (Denim, Cotton, Polyester);
```

Give the value of each of the following expressions. Indicate any expression that is invalid.

a. pred(Ash)
b. succ(Denim)
c. ord(Polyester)
d. ord(pred(Oak))
e. ord(succ(Maple))
f. succ(Polyester)
g. ord(pred(succ(Oak)))

2. Write a test program that lists the ordinals of values in a subrange of an enumerated data type.

3. The character set for some computers is such that **ord**('A') = 1 and **ord**('Z') = 26. Assuming such a sequence, what is the value of each of the following? Indicate any expressions that are invalid.

a. `chr(ord('D'))`   d. `ord(chr(10 MOD 3) + chr(20))`

b. `ord(chr(10))`   e. `ord(pred('K') + 3)`

c. `chr(3 * ord('E'))`   f. `succ(chr(ord('Z') - 1))`

4. Write a program that will list the letters of the alphabet and their respective ordinals for the character set used with your machine.

5. Assume the **TYPE** definition and variable declaration

```
TYPE
   AllDays = (Sun, Mon, Tues, Wed, Thur, Fri, Sat);
VAR
   Day : AllDays;
```

are made.

a. What would be the output from the following **REPEAT . . . UNTIL** loop?

```
Day := Sun;
REPEAT
  CASE Day OF
    Sat, Sun                  : writeln ('Weekend':20);
    Mon, Tues, Wed, Thur, Fri : writeln ('Weekday':20)
  END; {  of CASE Day  }
  Day := succ(Day)
UNTIL Day = Sat;
```

b. Rewrite the previous loop as both a **WHILE . . . DO** loop and a **FOR** loop.

c. Find another method to control the loop variable (for example, replace

```
Day := succ(Day)
```

and make any other necessary changes).

d. Revise the loop so that all seven days are considered.

6. A standard programming problem is to convert an integer character to its corresponding numerical value, for example, the character '2' to the number 2. Since the digits are listed sequentially in every character set, this could be accomplished by

```
ord('2') - ord('0');
```

a. Write a function to convert a single character digit ('0', '1', . . ., '9') to its corresponding numerical value.

b. Write a function to convert a two-digit number read as consecutive characters into the corresponding numerical value.

7. Suppose you are working with a program that reads an integer representing a month of the year (Jan = 1). Write a function to convert the integer into the appropriate month.

■ ■ ■ ■

**FOCUS ON
PROGRAM DESIGN**

The summary program for this chapter computes the number of days in your birth year from your birthday to the end of the year. Sample input (if you were born on March 16, 1971) would be

```
3 16 71
```

We want the output to be

```
During your birth year,  1971,
you were alive  291 days.
```

Features of this program include enumerated data types and subranges. In particular, note the data type

```
AllMonths = (Jan, Feb, March, April, May, June,
             July, Aug, Sept, Oct, Nov, Dec);
```

A reasonable first-level pseudocode design for this program is

1. Get data
2. Assign month
3. Compute days
4. Print results

A structure chart for this is given in Figure 6.2.

FIGURE 6.2
Structure chart for
PROGRAM Birthday

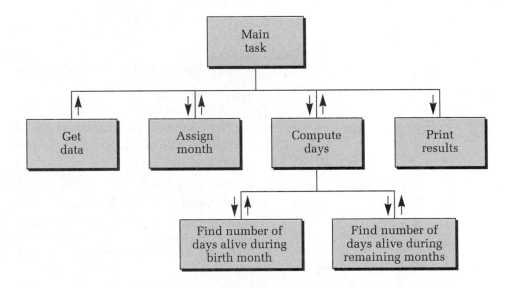

Module specifications for this problem are

1. <u>GetData Module</u>
   Data received: None
   Information returned: Day
                        Month
                        Year of birth
   Logic: Have the user enter his/her birth date.

2. <u>AssignMonth Module</u>
   Data received: A numerical equivalent of the birth month
   Information returned: The name of the birth month
   Logic: A **CASE** statement assigns the name of the birth month to
          BirthMonth, which is an enumerated data type.

3. <u>ComputeDays Module</u>
   Data received: Month
                  Day
                  Year of birth
   Information returned: The number of days alive during the year of
                        birth

Logic: Compute the number of days alive during the month of birth.
Compute the number of days in the remaining months.

4. PrintResults Module
   Data received: Number of days alive during the year of birth
                  Year of birth
   Information returned: None
   Logic: Use **write(ln)** statements to print the results in a readable
          form.

GetData merely consists of a **readln** statement; AssignMonth is a procedure using a **CASE** statement (a function could be used here instead), and Print-Results prints the information in a readable form. A function for computing the number of days is further developed as

3. Compute days
   3.1 compute days alive during birth month
   3.2 compute total of days in remaining months

This could be refined to

3. Compute days
   3.1 compute days alive during birth month
       3.1.1 compute for months with 31 days
       3.1.2 compute for months with 30 days
       3.1.3 compute for February
             IF leap year **THEN** use 29 days
             ELSE use 28 days
   3.2 compute total of days in remaining months
       IF NOT December **THEN**
           FOR rest of months **DO**
               add number of days in month

The complete program to solve this problem is

```
PROGRAM Birthday (input, output);

{  This program determines how many days you were alive during  }
{  your  birth year.  Input is your  birth  date.  Later,  you  }
{  can use this  program as the basis for a biorhythm program.  }
{  Pay special attention to the use of enumerated data types    }
{  and subranges.                                               }

TYPE
  AllMonths = (Jan, Feb, March, April, May, June,
               July, Aug, Sept, Oct, Nov, Dec);
  DayRange = 1..31;
  MonthRange = 1..12;
  YearRange = 0..99;

VAR
  BirthMonth : AllMonths;      { Literal form of birth month  }
  DayNum : DayRange;           { The day you were born        }
  Month : MonthRange;          { Birth month                  }
  TotalDays : integer;         { Days alive in birth year     }
  Year : YearRange;            { Representation of birth year  }

{*************************************************************** }
```

```
PROCEDURE GetData (VAR Month : MonthRange;
                   VAR Day : DayRange;
                   VAR Year : YearRange);

  {  Given:    Nothing                                      }
  {  Task:     Enter your birthdate in the form 3 16 71     }
  {  Return:   Month, day, and year of birth                }

  BEGIN
    writeln ('Please enter your birth date in the form 3 16 71.');
    writeln ('Press <RETURN> when finished.');
    readln (Month, Day, Year)
  END;  {  of PROCEDURE GetData  }
```

> 1

```
{*************************************************************** }
```

```
PROCEDURE AssignMonth (Month : MonthRange;
                       VAR BirthMonth : AllMonths);

  {  Given:    A numerical equivalent of the birth month     }
  {  Task:     Convert to literal BirthMonth                 }
  {  Return:   Literal BirthMonth                            }

  BEGIN
    CASE Month OF
       1 : BirthMonth := Jan;
       2 : BirthMonth := Feb;
       3 : BirthMonth := March;
       4 : BirthMonth := April;
       5 : BirthMonth := May;
       6 : BirthMonth := June;
       7 : BirthMonth := July;
       8 : BirthMonth := Aug;
       9 : BirthMonth := Sept;
      10 : BirthMonth := Oct;
      11 : BirthMonth := Nov;
      12 : BirthMonth := Dec
    END  {  of CASE Month  }
  END;  {  of PROCEDURE AssignMonth  }
```

> 2

```
{*************************************************************** }
```

```
FUNCTION ComputeDays (BirthMonth : AllMonths;
                      DayNum : DayRange;
                      Year : YearRange) : integer;

  {  Given:    The month, day, and year of birth             }
  {  Task:     Compute the days alive during the year of birth }
  {  Return:   Number of days alive during the year of birth  }

  VAR
    Days : integer;
    Mon : AllMonths;

  BEGIN

    {  Compute days alive in birth month  }
```

```
      CASE BirthMonth OF
        Jan, March, May, July, Aug, Oct, Dec : Days := 31-DayNum+1;
        April, June, Sept, Nov                : Days := 30-DayNum+1;
        Feb                                   : IF Year MOD 4 = 0 THEN
                                                   Days := 29-DayNum+1
                                                ELSE
                                                   Days := 28-DayNum+1
      END;  { of CASE BirthMonth }

      { Now compute days in remaining months }

      IF BirthMonth <> Dec THEN
        FOR Mon := succ(BirthMonth) TO Dec DO
          CASE Mon OF
            Jan, March, May, July, Aug, Oct, Dec : Days := Days+31;
            April, June, Sept, Nov                : Days := Days+30;
            Feb                                   : IF Year MOD 4 = 0 THEN
                                                       Days := Days+29
                                                    ELSE
                                                       Days := Days+28

          END; { of CASE Mon }

      { Assign total days to function's name }

      ComputeDays := Days

    END;    { of FUNCTION ComputeDays }

{***************************************************************** }

PROCEDURE PrintResults (TotalDays : integer;
                        Year : YearRange);

  { Given:   Birth year and total days alive during that year  }
  { Task:    Print a message indicating the year of birth and   }
  {          number of days alive during that year              }
  { Return:  Nothing                                            }

  BEGIN
    writeln ('During your birth year,', (Year+1900):6, ',');
    writeln ('you were alive', TotalDays:5, ' days.');
    writeln
  END;  { of PROCEDURE PrintResults }

{****************************************************************** }

BEGIN  { Main program }
  GetData (Month, DayNum, Year);
  AssignMonth (Month, BirthMonth);
  TotalDays := ComputeDays(BirthMonth, DayNum, Year);
  PrintResults (TotalDays, Year)
END.  { of main program }
```

A sample run of this program produces

```
Please enter your birthdate in the form 3 16 71.
Press <RETURN> when finished.
3 16 71
During your birth year, 1971,
you were alive  291 days.
```

RUNNING AND DEBUGGING TIPS

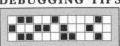

1. An end-of-line marker is read as a blank. When reading numeric data, this is not a problem. However, when reading data of type **char,** you may forget to advance the pointer to the next line.

2. Permanent text files must be listed in the program heading file list as well as in the variable declaration section.

3. Be aware of the possibility of extra blanks at the beginning or end of lines in a text file. Some implementations cause these to be inserted when creating a text file.

4. The end-of-line marker is read as a blank. Thus, when working with character data in a text file, it may appear that extra blanks are in the file. However, the **eoln** function still returns **true** when the pointer is positioned at an end-of-line marker.

5. Subranges should be used if the bounds of a variable are known.

6. Enumerated data types should be used to enhance readability.

7. Be careful not to use **pred** on the first element in a list or **succ** on the last element.

8. Make sure variable parameters passed to subprograms are of identical type. For example, using the following declaration

```
TYPE
   Weekdays = (Mon, Tues, Wed, Thur, Fri);
VAR
   Day : Weekdays;
```

if a procedure call was

```
PrintChart (Day);
```

a procedure heading could be

```
PROCEDURE PrintChart (VAR Wkday : Weekdays);
```

9. A value parameter and its argument must be of compatible type.

■ Summary

Key Terms

compatible type	external file	scratch file
end-of-file (**eof**) marker	identical type	subrange
end-of-line (**eoln**) marker	internal file	temporary file
	opened for reading	text file
enumerated data type	opened for writing	user-defined data type

Keywords

assign	**reset**	**text**
eof	**rewrite**	**TYPE**
eoln		

Key Concepts

- Text files can be used to store data between runs of a program.
- An end-of-line marker (■) is placed at the end of each line in a text file.
- An end of file marker (■) is placed after the last character in a text file.
- A text file can be declared by

```
VAR
   <file name> : text;
```

- An external file exists outside the program block in secondary storage. When used, it must be included in the file list as part of the program heading.
- An internal file exists within the program block. Values stored there will be lost when the program is no longer running.

- Text files must be opened before they can be written to or read from. Before reading from a file, it can be opened by

  reset (⟨file variable⟩);

  Before writing to a file, it can be opened by

  rewrite (⟨file variable⟩);

- Reading from a text file can be accomplished by

  read (⟨file variable⟩, ⟨list of variables⟩);
  or
  readln (⟨file variable⟩, ⟨list of variables⟩);

  If no file variable is given, the procedures apply to the standard file **input**.

- Writing to a text file can be accomplished by

  write (⟨file variable⟩, ⟨list of values⟩);
  or
  writeln (⟨file variable⟩, ⟨list of values⟩);

  If no file variable is given, the procedures apply to the standard file **output**.

- A data type is ordinal if data of that type have a first and last listed element and each element other than the first and last has an immediate predecessor and an immediate successor.
- Enumerated data types can be defined by using the **TYPE** definition section; typical syntax and form are

```
TYPE
   Weekdays = (Mon, Tue, Wed, Thur, Fri);
```

- When a simple enumerated data type has been defined,
  1. The newly defined type will be an ordinal data type.
  2. Variables can be declared to be of the new type.
  3. The identifiers declared in the **TYPE** definition section are constants that can be used in the program.
  4. No identifier can belong to more than one data type.
  5. Identifiers that are defined values cannot be used as operands in expressions.
- You cannot **read** or **write** values of an enumerated data type.
- A subrange of an existing ordinal data type can be defined by

  TYPE
      ⟨identifier⟩ = ⟨initial value⟩..⟨final value⟩;

  For example:

```
TYPE
   ScoreRange = 0..100;
   Alphabet = 'A'..'Z';
```

- Type compatible variables must have the same base type.
- Type identical variables must have the same type identifier.
- Two significant reasons for using subranges are program protection and program readability.
- The functions **pred, succ,** and **ord** can be used on enumerated data types and subranges of existing ordinal data types.
- When one of the functions **pred, succ,** or **ord** is used with an argument whose value is in a subrange, reference is to the base data type, not the subrange; thus, in

```
TYPE
   Letters = 'J'..'O';
```

  ord('J') does not have the value 0. Rather, it yields the appropriate ordinal for the collating sequence being used. In the ASCII collating sequence, **ord**('J') yields 74 and in EBCDIC it yields 209.

■ **Programming Problems and Projects**

1. Write a program to compute the payroll for a company. Data for each employee will be on two lines. Line 1 contains an employee number followed by the hourly wage rate. Line 2 contains seven integer entries indicating the hours worked each day. Wages are to be computed at time-and-a-half for anything over eight hours on a weekday and double time for any weekend work. Deductions should be withheld as follows:
   a. state income tax   4.6%
   b. federal income tax   21.0%
   c. social security (FICA)   6.2%
   d. Medicare tax   1.45%

   Employee numbers are the subrange 0001 . . 9999. You should define and use a data type for the days of the week.

2. The Caswell Catering and Convention Service (Problem 12, Chapter 3; Problem 14, Chapter 4; and Problem 1, Chapter 5) wants to upgrade their existing computer program. Use the **TYPE** definition section for each of the following and revise the program you developed previously as appropriate.
   a. The room names have been changed to a color-coded scheme as follows:
      Room A   RedRoom
      Room B   BlueRoom
      Room C   YellowRoom
      Room D   GreenRoom
      Room E   BrownRoom
   b. Use a subrange for the room rents.
   c. Use defined constants for the low value and high value of the room rents.

■ 3. State University (Problem 15, Chapter 4) wants you to upgrade their computer program by using the **TYPE** definition section for each of the following:
   a. The room types will be Regular or AirConditioned.
   b. Students' numbers will be between 0001 and 9999 (use **CONST** for end values).
   c. Credit hours taken must be between 1 and 25.
   d. The GoodRange for credit hours is 12 to 21.

   Your new version should be able to be used on a data file with several students' information.

4. Al Derrick (Problem 20, Chapter 4, and Problem 10, Chapter 5) wants you to revise his program by using the **TYPE** definition section to enhance readability and ensure protection against bad data. Your new version should run for several wells and include: types of wells (Dry, Oil, and Gas), volume for gas (between 10,000 and 100,000), and volume for oil (between 2,000 and 50,000).

■ 5. Dr. Lae Z. Programmer is relentless. He wants you to modify your latest version of the grading program (Problem 5, 22, and 23, Chapter 4; Problem 13, Chapter 5) by using the **TYPE** definition section. Your new version should include a range for test scores (from 0 to 100), a range for quiz scores (from 0 to 10), and a range for the final examination (from 0 to 200).

■ 6. Upgrade your most recent version of the Pentagon Parking Lot program (Problem 26, Chapter 4; Problem 14, Chapter 5) by using the **TYPE** definition section. Time in and time out will be between 0600 and 2200 (6:00 A.M. and 10:00 P.M.). Vehicle type should be denoted by Car, Truck, or Senior.

7. Read a text file containing a paragraph of text. Count the number of words in the paragraph. Assume that consecutive words are separated by at least one blank.

8. Write a program to print the contents of a text file omitting any occurrences of the letter "e" from the output.

9. A text file contains a list of integers in order from lowest to highest. Write a program to read and print the text file with all duplications eliminated.

10. Mr. John Napier, Professor at Lancaster Community College wants a program to compute grade point averages. Each line of a text file contains three initials followed by an unknown number of letter grades. These grades are A, B, C, D, or E. Write a program that reads the file and prints a list of the students' initials and their grade point averages. (Assume an A is 4 points, a B is 3 points, and so on.) Print an asterisk next to any grade point average that is greater than 3.75.

11. An amortization table (Problem 19, Chapter 5) shows the rate at which a loan is paid off. It contains monthly entries showing the interest paid that month, the principal paid, and the remaining balance. Given the amount of money borrowed (the principal), the annual interest rate, and the amount the person wishes to repay each month, print an amortization table. (The payment desired must be larger than the first month's interest.) Your table should stop when the loan is paid off, and should be printed with the following heads:

```
MONTH NUMBER   INTEREST PAID   PRINCIPAL PAID   BALANCE
```

Create an enumerated data type for the month number. Limit this to require that the loan be paid back within 60 months.

12. In 1626, the Dutch settlers purchased Manhattan Island from the Indians (Problem 23, Chapter 5). According to legend, the purchase price was $24. Suppose the Indians had invested this amount at 3 percent annual interest compounded quarterly. If the money had earned interest from the start of 1626 to the end of last year, how much money would the Indians have in the bank today? (*Hint:* Use nested loops for the compounding.) Create an enumerated data type for the range of years (1626 to last year) that will be used.

13. Mr. Christian (Problem 26, Chapter 5) uses a 90 percent, 80 percent, 70 percent, 60 percent grading scale on his tests. Given a list of test scores, print the number of A's, B's, C's, D's, and E's on the test. Terminate the list of scores with a sentinel value. Use a subrange of the integers for the input grades.

14. Write a program to print the perimeter and area of rectangles using all combinations of lengths and widths running from 1 foot to 10 feet in increments of 1 foot. Print the output in headed columns. Use a subrange to restrict the lengths and widths from 1 to 10.

15. Contact a programmer, graduate student, or upper-division major in computer sciences and discuss the issue of using enumerated and other user-defined data types. Among other things, find how often (or even if) that person uses such data types, how important he or she considers such data types as part of a programming language, and some specific examples of how he or she uses enumerated data types. Give an oral report of your findings to your class.

16. It was reported in this chapter that enumerated and other user-defined data types are one of the advantages of Pascal as a programming language. Examine several other programming languages to see if they include a comparable feature. Prepare a chart that summarizes your findings.

17. Using a team of three or four students, contact businesses and offices that use computers for data storage. Find exactly how they enter, store, and retrieve data. Discuss with them methods by which they use their databases and how large the databases are. Discuss what they like and dislike about data entry and retrieval. Ask if they have suggestions for modifying any aspect of working with their databases. Prepare a report for class that summarizes your team's findings.

CHAPTER

7

*They may say what they like,
everything is organized
matter.*

Napoleon Bonaparte

One-Dimensional Arrays

This chapter begins a significant new stage of programming. Prior to now, we have been unable to manipulate and store large amounts of data in a convenient way. For example, if we wanted to work with a long list of numbers or names, we had to declare a separate variable for each number or name. Fortunately, Pascal (and all other programming languages) provides several structured variables to facilitate solving problems that require working with large amounts of data. Simply put, a structured variable uses one identifier to reserve a large amount of memory. This memory is capable of holding several individual values. Structured variables included in this text are arrays, records, files, and sets.

Arrays, the topic of this chapter, are designed to handle large amounts of data of the same type in an organized manner. They are used whenever there is a need to store data for subsequent use in a program. Using arrays permits us to set aside a group of memory locations that we can then manipulate as a single entity or have direct access to any component. Some very standard applications for array variables include creating tabular output (tables), alphabetizing a list of names, analyzing a list of test scores, manipulating character data, and keeping an inventory.

■ 7.1
Arrays

Basic Idea and Notation

As previously mentioned, there are many instances in which several variables of the same data type are required. Let us at this point work with a list of five integers: 18, 17, 21, 18, and 19. Prior to this chapter, we would have declared five variables—A, B, C, D, and E—and assigned them appropriate values, or read them from an input file. This would have produced five values in memory each accessed by a separate identifier.

18	17	21	18	19
A	B	C	D	E

If the list was very long, this would be an inefficient way to work with these data; an alternative is to use an array. In Pascal, we declare a variable as an array variable using either of the following methods:

a. `VAR`
   `List : ARRAY [1..5] OF integer;`
b. `TYPE`
   `Numbers = ARRAY [1..5] OF integer;`
   `VAR`
   `List : Numbers;`

With either of these declarations, we now have five integer variables with which to work. They are denoted by

List[1]	List[2]	List[3]	List[4]	List[5]

and each is referred to as a *component* (or *element*) *of the array*. A good method of visualizing these variables is to assume that memory locations are aligned in a column on top of each other and the name of the column is List. If we then assign the five values of our list to these five variables, we have the following in memory.

List

18	List[1]
17	List[2]
21	List[3]
18	List[4]
19	List[5]

The components of an array are referred to by their relative position in the array. This relative position is called the *index* or *subscript* of the component. In the array of our five values, the component List[3] has an index of 3 and value of 21.

For the sake of convenience, you may choose to depict an array by listing only the index beside its appropriate component. Thus, List could be shown as

List

	1
	2
	3
	4
	5

If you choose this method, remember that the array elements are referenced by the array name and the index; for example, List[3] for the third component. Whichever method you use, it is important to remember that each array component is a variable and can be treated exactly as any other declared variable of that base type in the program.

Declaring an Array

An array type can be defined as a user-defined type and then an appropriate variable can be declared to be of this type. An earlier declaration was

```
TYPE
   Numbers = ARRAY [1..5] OF integer;
VAR
   List : Numbers;
```

Let us now examine this declaration more closely. Several comments are in order.

1. "Numbers" is a user-defined data type.
2. "**ARRAY**" is a reserved word and is used to indicate that an array type is being defined.
3. "[1 . . 5]" is the syntax that indicates the array consists of five memory locations accessed by specifying each of the numbers, 1, 2, 3, 4, and 5. We frequently say the array is of length five. The information inside the brackets is the *index type* and is used to refer to components of an array. This index type can be any ordinal data type that specifies a beginning value and an ending value. However, subranges of integer data type are the most easily read and frequently used index types.
4. The reserved word **OF** refers to the data type for the components of the array.
5. The key word **integer** indicates the data type for the components. This can, of course, be any valid data type.
6. "List" can be any valid identifier. As always, it is good practice to use descriptive names to enhance readability.

The general form for defining an array type is

```
TYPE
   ⟨name⟩ = ARRAY [⟨index type⟩] OF ⟨component type⟩;
```

where "name" is any valid identifier, "index type" is any ordinal data type that specifies both an initial value and a final value, and "component type" is any predefined or user-defined data type (except files). The syntax diagram for this is

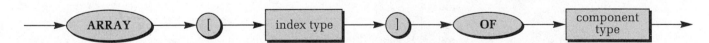

The following example illustrates another declaration of an array variable.

■ EXAMPLE 7.1

Suppose you want to create a list of ten integer variables for the hours worked by ten employees as follows:

Employee Number	Hours Worked
1	35
2	40
3	20
4	38
5	25
6	40
7	25
8	40
9	20
10	45

Declare an array that has ten components of type **integer** and show how it can be visualized. A descriptive name could be Hours. There are ten items, so we will use **ARRAY** [1 . . 10] in the definition. Since the data consist of integers, the component type will be **integer**. An appropriate definition and subsequent declaration could be

```
TYPE
   HourList = ARRAY [1..10] OF integer;
VAR
   Hours : HourList;
```

At this stage, the components can be visualized as

Hours

	Hours[1]
	Hours[2]
	Hours[3]
	Hours[4]
	Hours[5]
	Hours[6]
	Hours[7]
	Hours[8]
	Hours[9]
	Hours[10]

After making appropriate assignment statements, Hours can be visualized as

Hours

35	Hours[1]
40	Hours[2]
20	Hours[3]
38	Hours[4]
25	Hours[5]
40	Hours[6]
25	Hours[7]
40	Hours[8]
20	Hours[9]
45	Hours[10]

Other Indices and Data Types

The previous two arrays used index types that were subranges of the **integer** data type. Although this is a common method of specifying the index to an array, one could use subranges of any ordinal type for this declaration. The following examples illustrate some array definitions with other indices and data types.

■ EXAMPLE 7.2

Declare an array to allow you to store the hourly price for a share of IBM stock. A descriptive name could be StockPrice. A price is quoted at each hour from 9:00 A.M. to 3:00 P.M., so we will use **ARRAY** [9 . . 15] in the declaration section. Since the data consist of reals, the data type must be **real**. A possible declaration could be

```
TYPE
   StockPriceList = ARRAY [9..15] OF real;
VAR
   StockPrice : StockPriceList;
```

This would then allow us to store the 9:00 A.M. price in StockPrice[9], the 1:00 P.M. price in StockPrice[13], and so on.

■

■ EXAMPLE 7.3

The declaration

```
TYPE
   AlphaList = ARRAY [-2..3] OF char;
VAR
   Alpha : AlphaList;
```

will reserve components, which can be depicted as

Alpha

	Alpha[−2]
	Alpha[−1]
	Alpha[0]
	Alpha[1]
	Alpha[2]
	Alpha[3]

Each component is a character variable.

■

■ EXAMPLE 7.4

The declaration

```
TYPE
   TotalHoursList = ARRAY ['A'..'E'] OF integer;
VAR
   TotalHours : TotalHoursList;
```

will reserve components, which can be depicted as

	'A'
	'B'
	'C'
	'D'
	'E'

Components of this array are integer variables.

■   ■

■ **EXAMPLE 7.5**

The declaration

```
TYPE
  FlagValues = ARRAY [1..4] OF boolean;
VAR
  Flag : FlagValues;
```

will produce an array whose components are **boolean** variables.

■   ■

It is important to note that in each example, the array components will have no values assigned until the program specifically makes some kind of assignment. Declaring an array does not assign values to any of the components.

Two additional array definitions and subsequent declarations follow.

```
1. TYPE
     Days = (Mon, Tues, Wed, Thur, Fri, Sat, Sun);
     Workdays = ARRAY [Mon..Fri] OF real;
   VAR
     HoursWorked : Workdays;
2. TYPE
     List50 = ARRAY [1..50] OF real;
     List25 = ARRAY [1..25] OF integer;
     String20 = ARRAY [1..20] OF char;
   VAR
     PhoneCharge : List50;
     Score : List25;
     Word : String20;
     A, B, C, D : List50;
```

A more efficient method of manipulating character data than the strings just used will be presented in Section 7.5 when we discuss packed arrays.

STYLE TIP

■ ■ ■ ■ ■ ■ ■ ■ ■ ■ ■

Descriptive constants and type identifiers should be utilized when working with arrays. For example, if you are working with an array of test scores for a class of 35 students, you could have

```
CONST
  ClassSize = 35;
TYPE
  TestScores = 0..100;
  ScoreList = ARRAY [1..ClassSize] OF TestScores;
VAR
  Score : ScoreList;
```

Assignment Statements

Suppose we have declared an array

```
A : ARRAY [1..5] OF integer;
```

and we want to put the values 1, 4, 9, 16, and 25 into the respective components. We can accomplish this with the assignment statements

```
A[1] := 1;
A[2] := 4;
A[3] := 9;
A[4] := 16;
A[5] := 25;
```

If variables B and C of type **integer** are declared in the program, then the following are also appropriate assignment statements.

```
A[3] := B;
C := A[2];
A[2] := A[5];
```

If you want to interchange values of two components (for example, exchange A[2] with A[3]), you could use a third integer variable.

```
B := A[2];
A[2] := A[3];
A[3] := B;
```

This exchange is frequently used in sorting algorithms, so let us examine it more closely. Assume B contains no previously assigned value, and A[2] and A[3] contain 4 and 9, respectively.

The assignment statement

```
B := A[2];
```

produces

The assignment statement

```
A[2] := A[3];
```

produces

and finally the assignment statement

```
A[3] := B;
```

produces

in which the original values of A[2] and A[3] have been interchanged.

The next example illustrates the use of a **TYPE** definition and a subsequent assignment statement.

Given the following definitions,

```
TYPE
    Seasons = (Fall, Winter, Spring, Summer);
    TemperatureList = ARRAY [Seasons] OF real;
VAR
    AvTemp : TemperatureList;
```

an assignment statement such as

```
    AvTemp[Fall] := 53.2;
```

would be appropriate. The array would then be

AvTemp

53.2	Fall
	Winter
	Spring
	Summer

Arithmetic

Components of an array can also be used in any appropriate arithmetic operation. For example, suppose A is the array of integers

A

1	A[1]
4	A[2]
9	A[3]
16	A[4]
25	A[5]

and the values of the components of the array are to be added. This could be accomplished by the statement

```
Sum := A[1] + A[2] + A[3] + A[4] + A[5];
```

Each of the following would also be a valid use of an array component.

```
B := 3 * A[2];
C := A[4] MOD 3;
D := A[2] * A[5];
```

For the array A given, these assignment statements produce

55	12	1	100
Sum	B	C	D

Some invalid assignment statements and the reasons they are invalid follow.

```
A[0] := 7;        (0 is not a valid subscript.)
A[2] := 3.5;      (Component A[2] is not of type real.)
A[2.0] := 3;      (A subscript of type real is not allowed.)
```

Monolithic Idea: Invention of the Integrated Circuit

One of the most significant breakthroughs in the history of technology occurred in the late 1950s. Prior to 1958, computer circuitry was limited because transistors, diodes, resistors and capacitors were separate units that had to be wired together and soldered by hand. Although designers could design intricate computer supercircuits using 500,000 transistors, they were almost impossible to build because of the extensive handwork involved. For example, a circuit with 100,000 components could require over 1,000,000 soldered connections. It was virtually impossible to assemble that many components without human error. Thus, the electronics industry was faced with an apparently insurmountable limit.

About this time, Jack St. Clair Kilby developed what has come to be known as the Monolithic Idea. He decided you could put the components of an entire circuit in a monolithic block of silicon. The idea, together with Robert Noyce's work on interconnecting circuits, allowed electronics engineers to overcome the obstacle presented by separate components. Kilby and Noyce's work resulted in the integrated circuit, the most important new product in the history of electronics. For their efforts, both men were awarded the National Medal of Science.

Reading and Writing

Since array components are names for variables, they can be used with **read, readln, write,** and **writeln**. For example, if Score is an array of five integers and you want to input the scores 65, 43, 98, 75, and 83 from a data file, you could use the code

```
readln (Data, Score[1], Score[2], Score[3],
           Score[4], Score[5]);
```

This would produce the array

Score

65	Score[1]
43	Score[2]
98	Score[3]
75	Score[4]
83	Score[5]

If you want to print the scores above 80, you could use the code

```
writeln (Score[3]:10, Score[5]:10);
```

to produce

```
        98          83
```

It is important to note that you cannot **read** or **write** values into or from an entire array by a reference to the array name (an exception will be explained in Section 7.5). Statements such as

```
read(A);
writeln(A);
```

are invalid if A is an array.

Be careful to avoid out-of-range array references. For example, if the array A has index values 1 . . 5, a reference to A[6] or A[0] would then produce an error. This becomes more of a problem when you start processing arrays with loops in the next section.

Exercises 7.1

1. Using descriptive names, define an array type and declare subsequent variables for each of the following:

   a. A list of 35 test scores

   b. The prices of 20 automobiles

   c. The answers to 50 true or false questions

   d. A list of letter grades for the classes you are taking this semester

2. Write a test program in which you declare an array of three components, read values into each component, sum the components, and print out the sum and value of each component.

3. Find all errors in the following definitions of array types.

   a. ```
      TYPE
          Time = ARRAY [1..12] OF Hours;
      ```

   b. ```
      TYPE
          Scores = ARRAY [1..30] OF integer;
      ```

   c. ```
      TYPE
          Alphabet = ARRAY OF char;
      ```

   d. ```
      TYPE
          List = ARRAY [1 TO 10] OF real;
      ```

   e. ```
      TYPE
          Answers = ARRAY [OF boolean];
      ```

   f. ```
      TYPE
          X = ARRAY [1...5] OF real;
      ```

4. Assume the array List is declared as

   ```
   TYPE
      Scores = ARRAY [1..100] OF integer;
   VAR
      List : Scores;
   ```

   and that all other variables have been appropriately declared. Label the following as valid or invalid. Include an explanation for any that are invalid.

   a. `read (List[3]);`

   b. `A := List[3] + List[4];`

   c. `writeln (List);`

   d. `List[10] := 3.2;`

   e. `Max := List[50];`

   f. `Average := (List[1] + List[8]) / 2;`

   g. `write (List[25, 50, 75, 100]);`

   h. `write ((List[10] + List[90]):25);`

   i. ```
      FOR J := 1 TO 100 DO
         read (List);
      ```

   j. `List[36] := List[102];`

   k. `Scores[47] := 92;`

   l. `List[40] := List[41] / 2;`

5. Change each of the following so that the **TYPE** definition section is used to define the array type.

   a. ```
      VAR
          LetterList : ARRAY [1..100] OF 'A'..'Z';
      ```

   b. ```
      VAR
          CompanyName : ARRAY [1..30] OF char;
      ```
      ```

c. VAR
```
   ScoreList : ARRAY [30..59] OF real;
```

6. Consider the array declared by
```
TYPE
   ListOfSizes = ARRAY [1..5] OF integer;
VAR
   WaistSize : ListOfSizes;
```
   a. Sketch how the array should be envisioned in memory.
   b. After assignments
```
   WaistSize[1] := 34;
   WaistSize[3] := 36;
   WaistSize[5] := 32;
   WaistSize[2] := 2 * 15;
   WaistSize[4] := (WaistSize[1] + WaistSize[3]) DIV 2;
```
   have been made, sketch the array and indicate the contents of each component.

7. Let the array Money be declared by
```
TYPE
   List3 = ARRAY [1..3] OF real;
VAR
   Money : List3;
```
   Let Temp, X, and Y be real variables and assume Money has the indicated values

   Money

19.26	Money[1]
10.04	Money[2]
17.32	Money[3]

   Assuming Money contains the values indicated before each segment is executed, indicate what the array would contain after each section of code.

   a.
```
Temp := 173.21;
X := Temp + Money[2];
Money[1] := X;
```
   b.
```
IF Money[2] < Money[1] THEN
   BEGIN
      Temp := Money[2];
      Money[2] := Money[1];
      Money[1] := Temp
   END;
```
   c.
```
Money[3] := 20 - Money[3];
```

8. Let the array List be declared by
```
TYPE
   Scores = ARRAY [1..5] OF real;
VAR
   List : Scores;
```
   Write a program segment to initialize all components of List to 0.0.

■ ■ ■ ■

Loops for Input and Output

One advantage of using arrays is the small amount of code needed when loops are used to manipulate array components. For example, suppose a list of 100 scores stored in a data file is to be used in a program. If an array is declared by

```
TYPE
   List100 = ARRAY [1..100] OF integer;
VAR
   Score : List100;
   J : integer;
Data : text;
```

the values in file Data can be read into the array using a **FOR** loop as follows:

```
FOR J := 1 TO 100 DO
   read (Data, Score[J]);
```

Remember, a statement such as **read** (Data, Score) is invalid. You may only read data into individual components of the array.

Loops can be similarly used to produce output of array components. For example, if the array of test scores just given is to be printed in a column,

```
FOR J := 1 TO 100 DO
   writeln (Score[J]);
```

will accomplish this. If the components of Score contain the values

Score

78	Score[1]
93	Score[2]
.	.
.	.
.	.
82	Score[100]

the loop for writing produces

```
78
93
 .
 .
 .
82
```

Note that you cannot cause the array components to be printed by a statement such as **write** (Score) or **writeln** (Score). These are invalid. You must refer to the individual components.

Loops for output are seldom this simple. Usually we are required to format the output in some manner. For example, suppose the array Score is as declared and we wish to print these scores ten to a line, each with a field width of five spaces. The following segment of code would accomplish this.

```
FOR J := 1 TO 100 DO
   BEGIN
      write (Score[J]:5);
      IF J MOD 10 = 0 THEN
         writeln
   END;
```

Loops for Assigning

Loops can also be used to assign values to array components. In certain instances, you might wish to have an array contain values that are not read from an input file. The following examples show how loops can be used to solve such instances.

■ EXAMPLE 7.7

Recall the array A in Section 7.1 in which we made the following assignments.

```
A[1] := 1;
A[2] := 4;
A[3] := 9;
A[4] := 16;
A[5] := 25;
```

These assignments could have been made with the loop

```
FOR J := 1 TO 5 DO
   A[J] := J * J;
```

■

■ EXAMPLE 7.8

Suppose an array is needed whose components contain the letters of the alphabet in order from A to Z. Assuming you are using the ASCII character set, the desired array could be declared by

```
TYPE
   Letters = ARRAY [1..26] OF char;
VAR
   Alphabet : Letters;
```

The array Alphabet could then be assigned the desired characters by the statement

```
FOR J := 1 TO 26 DO
   Alphabet[J] := chr(J-1 + ord('A'));
```

If

```
J := 1;
```

we have

```
Alphabet[1] := chr(ord('A'));
```

Thus,

```
Alphabet[1] := 'A';
```

Similarly, for

```
J := 2;
```

we have

```
Alphabet[2] := chr(1 + ord('A'));
```

Eventually we obtain

Alphabet

'A'	Alphabet[1]
'B'	Alphabet[2]
'C'	Alphabet[3]
.	.
.	.
.	.
'Z'	Alphabet[26]

■

Assignment of values from components of one array to corresponding components of another array is a frequently encountered problem. For example, suppose the arrays A and B are declared as

```
TYPE
   List50 = ARRAY [1..50] OF real;
VAR
   A, B : List50;
```

If B has been assigned values and you want to put the contents of B into A component by component, you could use the loop

```
FOR J := 1 TO 50 DO
   A[J] := B[J];
```

However, for problems of this type, Pascal allows the entire array to be assigned by

```
A := B;
```

This aggregate assignment actually causes 50 assignments to be made at the component level. The arrays must be of the same type to do this.

Processing with Loops

Loops are especially suitable for reading, writing, and assigning array components, and can be used in conjunction with arrays to process data. For example, suppose A and B are declared as

```
TYPE
   List100 = ARRAY [1..100] OF real;
VAR
   A, B : List100;
```

and you want to add the values of components of B to the respective values of components of A. You could use the loop

```
FOR J := 1 TO 100 DO
   A[J] := A[J] + B[J];
```

It would appear that since

```
A := B;
```

is valid,

```
A := A + B;
```

would accomplish this. Not true. Pascal does not allow the aggregate addition of A + B where A and B are arrays.

The following examples illustrate additional uses of loops for processing data contained in array variables.

■ **EXAMPLE 7.9**

Recall the problem earlier in this section in which we read 100 test scores into an array. Assume the scores have been read and you now wish to find the average score and the largest score. Assume variables Sum, Max, and Average have been appropriately declared. The following segment will compute the average.

```
Sum := 0;
FOR J := 1 TO 100 DO
  Sum := Sum + Score[J];
Average := Sum / 100;
```

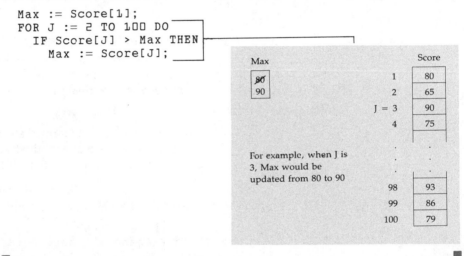

The maximum score can be found by using the following segment of code.

```
Max := Score[1];
FOR J := 2 TO 100 DO
  IF Score[J] > Max THEN
    Max := Score[J];
```

Write a segment of code to find the smallest value of array A and the index of the smallest value. Assume the variables have been declared as

```
TYPE
  Column100 = ARRAY [1..100] OF real;
VAR
  A : Column100;
  Min : real;
  Index : integer;
```

and the values have been read into components of A. The following algorithm will solve the problem.

1. Assign 1 to Index
2. **FOR** J := 2 **TO** 100 **DO**
      IF A[J] < A[Index] **THEN** assign J to Index
3. Assign A[Index] to Min

The segment of code is

```
Index := 1;
FOR J := 2 TO 100 DO
  IF A[J] < A[Index] THEN
      Index := J;
Min := A[Index];
```

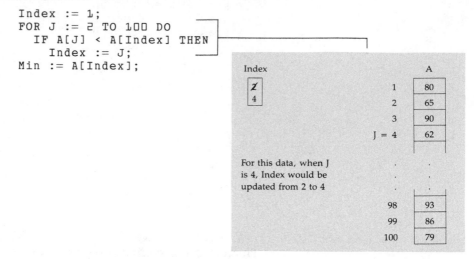

A very standard problem encountered when working with arrays is, what do you do when you don't know exactly how many components of an array will be needed? You must decide some upper limit for the length of the array. A standard procedure is to declare a reasonable limit, keeping two points in mind.

1. The length must be sufficient to store all the data.
2. The amount of storage space must not be excessive; do not set aside excessive amounts of space that will not be used.

To guard against the possibility of not reading all the data into array elements, an **IF . . . THEN** statement, such as

```
IF NOT eof(Data) THEN
    writeln ('There are more data.');
```

could be included in the procedure used to get data from the data file. These points are illustrated in Example 7.11. The array will be partially filled when the number of checks is less than the array length. This information can be retained by including a program statement such as

```
NumberOfChecks := J;
```

after the loop is exited.

■ **EXAMPLE 7.11**

Suppose an input file contains an unknown number of dollar amounts from personal checks. Write a segment of code to read them into an array and output the number of checks. Since the data are in dollars, we use real components and the identifier Check.

```
TYPE
  List = ARRAY [1..?] OF real;
VAR
  Check : List;
```

If we think there are fewer than 50 checks, we could define a constant by

```
CONST
  MaxChecks = 50;
```

and then define List by

```
List = ARRAY [1..MaxChecks] OF real;
```

The data could then be accessed using a **WHILE . . . DO** loop.

```
J := 0;
WHILE NOT eof(Data) AND (J < MaxChecks) DO
  BEGIN
    J := J + 1;
    readln (Data, Check[J])
  END;
IF NOT eof(Data) THEN
  writeln ('There are more data.');
  NumberOfChecks := J;
```

Now we have the data in the array, we know the number of data items, and NumberOfChecks can be used as a loop limit. Then the loop

```
FOR J := 1 TO NumberOfChecks DO
  BEGIN
    writeln;
    writeln ('Check number':20, J:4, '$':5, Checks[J]:7:2)
  END;
```

will print the checks on every other line.

■   ■

We close this section with a final example using more elaborate **TYPE** definitions, loops, and arrays.

■ **EXAMPLE 7.12**

```
PROGRAM Economy (input, output, Data);

{   This program illustrates the use of TYPE definitions, loops, and   }
{   arrays. Values are read into an array and the maximum and average  }
{   are found. The array contents, maximum, and average are printed.   }

CONST
  StartYear = 1982;
  LastYear = 1990;

TYPE
  RecentYears = StartYear..LastYear;
  EconIndicator = ARRAY [RecentYears] OF real;

VAR
  GrossNatlProd : EconIndicator;   { Array of gross national product  }
  Max : real;                      { Maximum value in the array       }
  Sum : real;                      { Total of values in the array     }
  Average : real;                  { Average of values in the array   }
  NumYears : integer;              { Number of years used             }
  Year : RecentYears;              { Years from StartYear to LastYear  }
  Data : text;                     { File of GNPs                     }

BEGIN   { Main program }

  { Get the data }
```

```
        reset (Data);
        Sum := 0;
        FOR Year := StartYear TO LastYear DO
          BEGIN
            readln (Data, GrossNatlProd[Year]);
            Sum := Sum + GrossNatlProd[Year]
          END;

        {  Find the maximum  }

        Max := GrossNatlProd[StartYear];              {  Get initial value         }
        FOR Year := StartYear + 1 TO LastYear DO
          IF GrossNatlProd[Year] > Max THEN           {  Check for larger value  }
            Max := GrossNatlProd[Year];

        {  Find the average  }

        NumYears := LastYear - StartYear + 1;
        Average := Sum / NumYears;

        {  Now display all data  }

        writeln ('Year', 'Gross National Product':30);
        writeln ('(in billions}':29);
        writeln ('----', '----------------------':30);
        writeln;
        FOR Year := StartYear TO LastYear DO
          writeln (Year, GrossNatlProd[Year]:20:1);

        {  Now display the maximum and average  }

        writeln;
        writeln ('The greatest GNP in recent years was',
                 Max:10:2,' billion dollars.');
        writeln ('The average GNP for ', NumYears, ' years was',
                 Average:10:2, ' billion dollars.');
        writeln

END.  {  of main program  }
```

The output for this program is

```
    Year          Gross National Product
                       (in billions)
    ----          ----------------------

    1982               3160.0
    1983               3405.7
    1984               3772.2
    1985               4014.9
    1986               4231.6
    1987               4524.3
    1988               4880.6
    1989               5200.8
    1990               5463.6

The greatest GNP in recent years was   5463.60 billion dollars.
The average GNP for 9 years was   4294.86 billion dollars.
```

STYLE TIP

■ ■ ■ ■ ■ ■ ■ ■ ■ ■ ■

Indices with semantic meaning can be useful when working with arrays. For example, suppose you are writing a program that includes the inventory for shoe styles in a shoe store. If the styles are docksider, high pump, loafer, low pump, plain tie, and wing tip, you would define

```
TYPE
  Style = (Docksider, HighPump, Loafer
          LowPump, PlainTie, WingTip);
  ShoeInventory = ARRAY [Docksider..WingTip] OF
                                        integer;

VAR
  Stock : ShoeInventory;
  ShoeType : Style;
```

Typical program statements could be

```
Stock[WingTip] := 25;
Stock[Loafer] := Stock[Loafer] - 3;
FOR ShoeType := Docksider TO WingTip DO
  writeln (Stock[ShoeType]);
```

Exercises 7.2

1. Assume the following array declarations.

```
TYPE
  NumList = ARRAY [1..5] OF integer;
  AnswerList = ARRAY [1..10] OF boolean;
  NameList = ARRAY [1..20] OF char;
VAR
  List, Score : NumList;
  Answer : AnswerList;
  Name : NameList;
```

Indicate the contents of the arrays after each segment of code.

a. ```
FOR J := 1 TO 5 DO
   List[J] := J DIV 3;
```

b. ```
FOR J := 2 TO 6 DO
   BEGIN
     List[J-1] := J + 3;
     Score[J-1] := List[J-1] DIV 3
   END;
```

c. ```
FOR J := 1 TO 10 DO
   IF J MOD 2 = 0 THEN
     Answer[J] := true
   ELSE
     Answer[J] := false;
```

d. ```
FOR J := 1 TO 20 DO
   Name[J] := chr(J + 64);
```

2. Write a test program to illustrate what happens when you try to use an index that is not in the defined subrange for an array; for example, try to use the loop

```
FOR J := 1 TO 10 DO
  read (Data, A[J]);
```

when A has been declared as

```
TYPE
  NumList = ARRAY [1..5] OF integer;
VAR
  A : NumList;
```

3. Let the array Best be declared by

```
TYPE
  List30 = ARRAY [1..30] OF integer;
VAR
  Best : List30;
```

and assume that test scores have been read into Best. What does the following section of code do?

```
Count := 0;
FOR J := 1 TO 30 DO
  IF Best[J] > 90 THEN
    Count := Count + 1;
```

4. Declare an array and write a segment of code to

   a. Read 20 integer test scores into the array.

   b. Count the number of scores greater than or equal to 55.

5. Declare an array using the **TYPE** definition section and write a section of code to read a name of 20 characters from a line of input.

6. Let the array List be declared by

```
TYPE
  Numbers = ARRAY [11..17] OF integer;
VAR
  List : Numbers;
```

and assume the components have values of

List

−2	List[11]
3	List[12]
0	List[13]
−8	List[14]
20	List[15]
14	List[16]
−121	List[17]

Show what the array components would be after the following program segment is executed.

```
FOR J := 11 TO 17 DO
  IF List[J] < 0 THEN
    List[J] := 0;
```

7. Assume the array A is declared as

```
TYPE
  List100 = ARRAY [1..100] OF real;
VAR
  A : List100;
```

Write a segment of code that uses a loop to initialize all components to zero.

8. The following can be used to input the values in Example 7.11. Discuss how it is different.

```
FOR J := 1 TO 50 DO
  IF NOT eof(Data) THEN
    readln (Data, Check[J]);
```

9. Let the array N be declared as

```
TYPE
  String10 = ARRAY [1..10] OF char;
VAR
  N : String10;
```

and assume the array components have been assigned the values

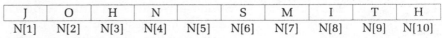

	J	O	H	N		S	M	I	T	H
	N[1]	N[2]	N[3]	N[4]	N[5]	N[6]	N[7]	N[8]	N[9]	N[10]

What output is produced by the following?

a.
```
FOR J := 1 TO 10 DO
   write (N[J]);
writeln;
```

b.
```
FOR J := 1 TO 5 DO
   write (N[J+5]);
write (', ');
FOR J := 1 TO 4 DO
   write (N[J]);
writeln;
```

c.
```
FOR J := 10 DOWNTO 1 DO
   write (N[J]);
```

10. Let arrays A, B, and C be declared as

```
TYPE
   FirstList = ARRAY [21..40] OF real;
   SecondList = ARRAY [-4..15] OF real;
VAR
   A, B : FirstList;
   C : SecondlList;
```

Indicate if the following are valid or invalid. Include an explanation for those that are invalid.

a.
```
FOR J := 21 TO 40 DO
   A[J] := C[J-25];
```

b.
```
A := B;
```

c.
```
A := C;
```

d.
```
FOR J := 1 TO 10 DO
   B[J+20] := C[J+10];
```

e.
```
FOR J := 11 TO 20 DO
   B[J+20] := A[J+20];
```

11. Assume an array has been declared as

```
TYPE
   List50 = ARRAY [1..50] OF integer;
VAR
   TestScore : List50;
```

Write a segment of code to print a suitable heading (assume this is a list of test scores) and then output a numbered list of the array components.

12. Write a program segment to read 100 real numbers from a data file, compute the average, and find both the largest and smallest values.

■ ■ ■ ■

■ 7.3
Selection and Bubble Sorts

A common problem involving arrays is sorting the components of the array in either ascending or descending order. Other sorting algorithms are given in Chapter 12 and 19, but let us here consider two of the easier methods, the *selection sort* and the *bubble sort*.

Selection Sort

Suppose we have an array A of five integers that we wish to sort from smallest to largest. The values currently in A are as depicted on the left; we wish to end up with values as on the right.

A			A	
6	A[1]		1	A[1]
4	A[2]		4	A[2]
8	A[3]		6	A[3]
10	A[4]		8	A[4]
1	A[5]		10	A[5]

The basic idea of a selection sort is

1. Find the smallest number in the array and exchange it with A[1].
2. Find the smallest number among A[2] through A[5] and exchange it with A[2].
3. Continue this process until the array is sorted.

The first step produces

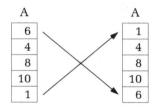

The second, third, and fourth steps produce

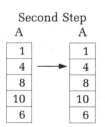
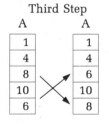
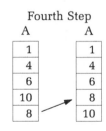

Notice that in the second step, since the second smallest number was already in place, we need not exchange anything. Before writing the algorithm for this sorting procedure, note the following:

1. If the array is of length n, we need $n - 1$ steps.
2. We must be able to find the smallest number.
3. We need to exchange appropriate array components.

If two or more values in the list are equal, an exchange would not be made when finding the smallest number. Thus, rather than find the smallest numbers, we must be able to find one of the remaining smallest numbers.

When the code is written for this sort, note that strict inequality ($<$) rather than weak inequality ($<=$) is used when looking for the smallest remaining value. The algorithm to sort by selection is

A NOTE OF INTEREST

Too Few Women in the Computer Science Pipeline?

Studies show that women in computer science programs in U.S. universities terminate their training earlier than men do. Between 1983 and 1986 (the latest year for which we have such figures) the percentage of bachelor's degrees in computer science awarded to women was in the range 36–37 percent and the percentage of master's degrees was in the range of 28–30 percent. During the same time span, the percentage of doctoral degrees awarded to women was in the range of only 10–12 percent, and it has remained at that level, with the exception of a slight increase in 1989.

If we look at the people who are training the future computer scientists, we may find a clue as to why this discrepancy exists. Women currently hold only 6.5 percent of the faculty positions in the computer science and computer engineering departments in the 158 Ph.D-granting institutions included in the 1988–1989 Taulbee Survey. In fact, a third of these departments have no female faculty members at all. This pattern of decreasing representation is often described as pipeline shrinkage: as women move along the academic pipeline, their percentages continue to shrink.

The ACM Committee on the Status of Women has made a number of recommendations to promote change. These recommendations include:

Ensure equal access to computers for young girls and boys and develop educational software appealing to both.

Establish programs (such as science fairs, scouting programs, and conferences in which women speak about their careers in science and engineering) to encourage high school girls to continue with math and science.

Develop programs to pair undergraduate women with women graduate students or faculty members who serve as role models, providing encouragement and advice.

Provide women with opportunities for successful professional experiences (such as involvement in research projects) beginning as early as the undergraduate years.

Establish programs that make women computer scientists visible to undergraduates and graduate students. Women can be invited to campuses to give talks or to serve as visiting faculty members (as, for example, in the National Science Foundation's Visiting Professorships for Women).

Encourage men and women to serve as mentors for young women in the field.

Maintain lists of qualified women computer scientists to increase the participation of women in influential positions such as program committees, editorial boards, and policy boards.

Establish more reentry programs that enable women who have stopped their scientific training prematurely to retrain as computer scientists.

Increase awareness of, and sensitivity to, subtle discrimination and its effects.

Develop and enforce safety procedures on campus. Provide safe access at all hours to public terminal areas, well-lit routes from offices to parking lots, and services to escort those walking on campus after dark.

Provide affordable, quality childcare.

1. **FOR** J := 1 **TO** N − 1
   1.1   find the smallest value among A[J], A[J + 1], . . . A[N] and store the index of the smallest value in Index
   1.2   exchange the values of A[J] and A[Index], if necessary

In Section 7.2 (Example 7.10) we saw a segment of code required to find the smallest value of array A. With suitable changes, we will incorporate this in the segment of code for a selection sort.

```
Index := 1;
FOR J := 2 TO ArrayLength DO
  IF A[J] < A[Index] THEN
    Index := J;
```

Let A be an array of length n and assume all variables have been appropriately declared. Then the following will sort A from low to high.

```
FOR J := 1 TO N-1 DO        {  Find the minimum N-1 times  }
  BEGIN
    Index := J;
    FOR K := J + 1 TO N DO
      IF A[K] < A[Index] THEN
        Index := K;  {  Find index of smallest number  }
    IF Index <> J THEN
      BEGIN
        Temp := A[Index];
        A[Index] := A[J];
        A[J] := Temp
      END  {  of exchange  }
END;  {  of FOR J loop  }
```

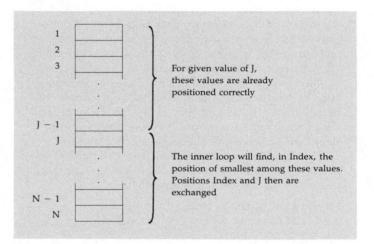

Let us now trace this sort for the five integers in the array we sorted in the beginning of this section.

A

6	A[1]
4	A[2]
8	A[3]
10	A[4]
1	A[5]

For J := 1, Index := 1, and this produces

1

Index

For the loop **FOR** K := 2 **TO** 5, we get successive assignments

K	Index
2	2
3	2
4	2
5	5

The statements

```
Temp := A[Index];
A[Index] := A[J];
A[J] := Temp;
```

produce the partially sorted array

A

1	A[1]
4	A[2]
8	A[3]
10	A[4]
6	A[5]

Each successive J value continues to partially sort the array until J := 4. This pass produces a completely sorted array.

■ **EXAMPLE 7.13**

Our concluding example:

1. Inputs real numbers from a data file.
2. Echo prints the numbers in a column of width six with two places to the right of the decimal (:6:2).
3. Sorts the array from low to high.
4. Prints the sorted array using the same output format.

An expanded pseudocode development for this is

1. Print header—prints a suitable explanation of the program and includes a heading for the unsorted list
2. Get data (echo print)—uses a **WHILE** loop to read the data and print it in the same order in which it is read
3. Sort list—uses the selection sort to sort the array from low to high
4. Output sorted list—uses a **FOR** loop to output the sorted list

```
PROGRAM ArraySample (input, output, DataFile);

{   This program illustrates the use of a sorting algorithm        }
{   with an array of reals.  Output includes data in both an       }
{   unsorted and a sorted list.  The data are formatted  and       }
{   numbered to enhance readability.                               }

CONST
  Skip = ' ';
  ListMax = 20;

TYPE
  NumList = ARRAY [1..ListMax] OF real;

VAR
  Index : integer;       { Stores position of an element          }
  J, K : integer;        { Indices                                }
  NumReals : integer;    { Length of the list                     }
  Temp : real;           { Temporary storage for array elements   }
  List : NumList;        { Array of reals                         }
  DataFile : text;       { File of data                           }

{ ***************************************************************** }
```

```
PROCEDURE PrintHeading;

   {  Given:    Nothing                                            }
   {  Task:     Print a heading for the output  }                  }
   {  Return:   Nothing                                            }

   BEGIN
     writeln;
     writeln (Skip:10, 'This sample program does the following:');
     writeln;
     writeln (Skip:12, '<1> Gets reals from a data file.');
     writeln (Skip:12, '<2> Echo prints the data.');
     writeln (Skip:12, '<3> Sorts the data from low to high.');
     writeln (Skip:12, '<4> Prints a sorted list of the data.');
     writeln
   END;  {  of PROCEDURE PrintHeading  }

{*********************************************************************}

BEGIN {  Main program  }

   {  Print the heading  }

   PrintHeading;

   {  Get the data and echo print it  }

   writeln (Skip:10, 'The original data are as follows:');
   writeln;
   NumReals := 0;
   reset (DataFile);
   WHILE NOT eof(DataFile) AND (NumReals < ListMax) DO
     BEGIN
       NumReals := NumReals + 1;
       readln (DataFile, List[NumReals]);
       writeln (Skip:12, '<', NumReals:2, '>', List[NumReals]:6:2)
     END;  {  of WHILE NOT loop  }
   IF NOT eof(DataFile) THEN
     writeln ('There are more data.');

   {  Now sort the list  }

   FOR J := 1 TO NumReals - 1 DO
     BEGIN
       Index := J;
       FOR K := J + 1 TO NumReals DO
         IF List[K] < List[Index] THEN
           Index := K;
       IF Index <> J THEN
         BEGIN
           Temp := List[Index];
           List[Index] := List[J];
           List[J] := Temp
         END  {  of exchange  }
     END;  {  of FOR loop (selection sort)  }

   {  Now print the sorted list  }

   writeln;
   writeln (Skip:10, 'The sorted list is as follows:');
   writeln;
   FOR J := 1 TO NumReals DO
     writeln (Skip:12, '<' J:2 '>', List[J]:6:2)

END.  {  of main program  }
```

The output for this program is

```
This sample program does the following:

    <1> Gets reals from a data file.
    <2> Echo prints the data.
    <3> Sorts the data from low to high.
    <4> Prints a sorted list of the data.

The original data are as follows:

    < 1> 34.56
    < 2> 78.21
    < 3> 23.30
    < 4> 89.90
    < 5> 45.00
    < 6> 56.80
    < 7> 39.01
    < 8> 45.56
    < 9> 34.40
    <10> 45.10
    <11> 98.20
    <12>  5.60
    <13>  8.00
    <14> 45.00
    <15> 99.00
    <16> 56.78
    <17> 56.78
    <18> 45.00

The sorted list is as follows:

    < 1>  5.60
    < 2>  8.00
    < 3> 23.30
    < 4> 34.40
    < 5> 34.56
    < 6> 39.01
    < 7> 45.00
    < 8> 45.00
    < 9> 45.00
    <10> 45.10
    <11> 45.56
    <12> 56.78
    <13> 56.78
    <14> 56.80
    <15> 78.21
    <16> 89.90
    <17> 98.20
    <18> 99.00
```

Bubble Sort

The sorting algorithm commonly referred to as a bubble sort rearranges the elements of an array until they are in either ascending or descending order. Like the selection sort, an extra array is not used. Basically, a bubble sort starts at the beginning of an array and compares two consecutive elements of the array. If they are in the correct order, the next pair of elements is compared. If they are not in the correct order, they are switched and the next pair compared. When this has been done for the entire array, the correct element will be in the last position.

Starting at the top (the beginning) each time, successive passes through the array are made until the array is sorted. Two items should be noted here.

1. A flag is needed to indicate whether or not an exchange was made during a given pass through the array. If none was made, the array is sorted.
2. Since each pass filters the largest (or smallest) element to the bottom, the length of what remains to be sorted can be decreased by one after each pass.

To illustrate how this algorithm works, assume the array is

```
   A
 ┌────┐
 │ 12 │
 ├────┤
 │  0 │
 ├────┤
 │  3 │
 ├────┤
 │  2 │
 ├────┤
 │  8 │
 └────┘
```

The first pass through the array produces

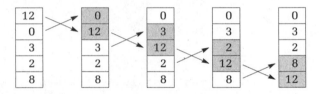

Since an exchange was made, we need to make at least one more pass through the array. However, the length is decreased by one because there is no need to compare the last two elements since the largest element is in its correct position. A second pass produces

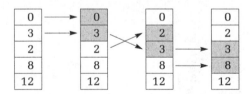

At this stage, the array is sorted, but since an exchange was made, the length is decreased by one and another pass is made. Since no exchange is made during this third pass, the sorting process is terminated.

Assuming the variable declaration section includes

```
VAR
  ExchangeMade : boolean;
  J, Length, Last, Temp : integer;
```

values to be sorted are in the array A, and Length has been assigned a value, an algorithm for a bubble sort could be as follows:

```
Last := Length - 1;
REPEAT
  ExchangeMade := false;
  FOR J := 1 TO Last DO
    IF A[J] > A[J+1] THEN
```

```
        BEGIN          {  Exchange values  }
           Temp := A[J];
           A[J] := A[J+1];
           A[J+1] := Temp;
           ExchangeMade := true
        END;
     Last := Last - 1         {  Decrement length  }
  UNTIL (NOT ExchangeMade) OR (Length = 1);
```

Exercises 7.3

1. Assume the array Column is to be sorted from low to high using the selection sort.

   Column

−20
10
0
10
8
30
−2

   a. Sketch the contents of the array after each of the first two passes.

   b. How many exchanges are made during the sort?

2. Write a test program that prints the partially sorted arrays after each pass during a selection sort.

3. Change the code for the selection sort so it sorts an array from high to low.

4. Write a complete program to

   a. Read ten reals into an array from an input file.

   b. If the first real is positive, sort the array from high to low; if it is negative, sort the array from low to high.

   c. Print a numbered column containing the sorted reals with the format :10:2.

5. The array

17
0
3
2
8

   requires five exchanges of elements when sorted using a bubble sort. Since each exchange requires three assignment statements, there are 15 assignments for elements in the array. Sort the same array using the selection sort and determine the number of assignments made.

6. Modify the selection sort by including a counter that counts the number of assignments of array elements made during a sort.

7. Using the modification in Exercise 6, sort lists of differing lengths that contain randomly generated numbers. Display the results of how many assignments were made for each sort on a graph similar to that shown here. Use lists whose lengths are multiples of ten.

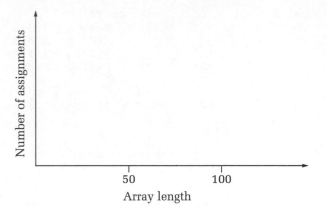

8. Modify the bubble sort to include a counter for the number of assignments made during a sort.

9. Use the modified versions of both sorts to examine their relative efficiency; that is, run them on arrays of varying lengths and plot the results on a graph. What are your conclusions?

10. Modify the bubble sort to sort from high to low rather than low to high.

11. Sorting parallel arrays is a common practice (for example, an array of names and a corresponding array of scores on test). Modify both sorts so that you can sort a list of initials and associated test scores.

■ ■ ■ ■

■ 7.4
Arrays and Subprograms

Procedures and functions should be used with arrays to maintain the structured design philosophy. Before we look at specific examples, let us examine the method and syntax necessary for passing an array to a procedure. Recall that to pass either a value or variable parameter to a procedure, we must declare an actual parameter of exactly the same type as the formal parameter in the procedure heading. In addition, if more than one parameter is passed, there must be a one-for-one ordered matching of the actual parameters with the formal parameters in the heading of the procedure. Consider, for example, the following program that reads two integer test scores, computes their average in a procedure called CalcMean, and outputs the results.

■ **EXAMPLE 7.14**

```
PROGRAM AverageOfTwo (input, output);

VAR
  Num1, Num2 : integer;
  Ave : real;

{*******************************************************************}

PROCEDURE CalcMean (Num1, Num2 : integer;
                    VAR Ave : real);

  { Given:    Two integers                            }
  { Task:     Compute their average                   }
  { Return:   Average of the two integers             }
```

```
    VAR
      Sum : integer;

    BEGIN
      Sum := Num1 + Num2;
      Ave := Sum / 2.0
    END;   {  of PROCEDURE CalcMean  }

{**********************************************************************}

BEGIN  {  Main program  }
  readln (Num1, Num2);
  CalcMean (Num1, Num2, Ave);
  writeln ('The average of ', Num1:5, ' and ', Num2:5, ' is ',
           Ave:6:2)
END.   {  of main program  }
```

The procedure call

```
    CalcMean (Num1, Num2, Ave);
```

and the procedure heading

```
    PROCEDURE CalcMean (Num1, Num2 : integer;
                        VAR Ave : real);
```

have the desired matching of variables.

■   ■

Let us now modify the program so it will determine the average of 100 test scores in the array Scores. The procedure call in the program will be

```
    CalcMean (Scores, Ave);
```

and the procedure heading will have to match these variables. If Scores also is the variable name to be used in the procedure heading, we have

```
    PROCEDURE CalcMean (Scores : ???;
                        VAR Ave : real);
```

Pascal requires that a **TYPE** definition be given. For example, if we have

```
    CONST
      MaxLength = 100;
    TYPE
      List = ARRAY [1..MaxLength] OF integer;
    VAR
      Scores : List;
```

the procedure heading could be

```
    PROCEDURE CalcMean (Scores : List;
                        VAR Ave : real);
```

This is consistent with allowing only identifiers of identical or compatible types to be associated. A common mistake is to attempt to build a data type inside the procedure heading. This will not work. The statement

```
  PROCEDURE CalcMean (Scores : ARRAY [1..MaxLength] OF integer;
                      VAR Ave : real);
```

produces an error message because Pascal compilers check for name equivalence rather than structure equivalence. To illustrate, you could have two arrays

```
    Position : ARRAY [1..3] OF real;
    Nutrition : ARRAY [1..3] OF real;
```

where Position is used to represent coordinates of a point in space and Nutrition is used to represent the volume, weight, and caloric content of a serving of food. Although Position and Nutrition have the same structure, they have significantly different meanings. Thus, by insisting on name equivalence, the chances of inadvertent or meaningless uses of structured variables are decreased. Also, compiler implementation of name equivalence is easier than compiler implementation of structure equivalence.

We can now write a revised version of the program in Example 7.14 to find the average and include a procedure that requires passing an array variable.

■ **EXAMPLE 7.15**

```
PROGRAM Average (input, output, ScoreFile);

CONST
  MaxLength = 100;

TYPE
  List = ARRAY [1..MaxLength] OF integer;

VAR
  Scores : List;
  Ave : real;
  J, Length : integer;
  ScoreFile : text;

{****************************************************************** }

PROCEDURE CalcMean (Scores : List;
                    VAR Ave : real;
                    Length : integer);

  {  Given:    An array of scores and number of scores in the    }
  {                array                                          }
  {  Task:     Compute the average of scores in the array        }
  {  Return:   The average score                                 }

  VAR
    J, Sum : integer;

  BEGIN
    Sum := 0;
    FOR J := 1 TO Length DO
      Sum := Sum + Scores[J];
    Ave := Sum / Length
  END;  {  of PROCEDURE CalcMean  }

{****************************************************************** }

BEGIN  {  Main program  }
  reset (ScoreFile);
  Length := 0;
  WHILE NOT eof(ScoreFile) AND (Length < MaxLength) DO
    BEGIN
      Length := Length + 1;
      readln (ScoreFile, Scores[Length])
    END;  {  of WHILE NOT eof  }
  CalcMean (Scores, Ave, Length);
  writeln ('The average of':20);
```

```
   writeln;
   FOR J := 1 TO Length DO
      writeln (Scores[J]:12);
   writeln;
   writeln ('is':10, Ave:8:2)
END.  {  of main program  }
```

Before we consider more procedures with arrays, we restate a rule: To pass an array to a procedure or function, the array must be declared with an identifier that uses a **TYPE** identifier; the matching variable in the procedure must use the same **TYPE** identifier.

Now that we know how to pass an array, let's rewrite our last example using a completely modular development. In this version, CalcMean is a function instead of a procedure. The first-level pseudocode development is

1. Get the scores (**PROCEDURE** GetData)
2. Compute the average (**FUNCTION** CalcMean)
3. Print a header (**PROCEDURE** PrintHeader)
4. Print the results (**PROCEDURE** PrintResults)

The procedure to get the scores requires a **VAR** declaration in the procedure heading for the array. If List is defined as a data type, we have

```
PROCEDURE GetData (VAR Scores : List;
                     VAR Length : integer);
   BEGIN
     Length := 0;
     WHILE NOT eof(ScoreFile) AND (Length < MaxLength) DO
       BEGIN
         Length := Length + 1;
         readln (ScoreFile, Scores[Length])
       END
   END;  {  of PROCEDURE GetData  }
```

The average score could be computed by the function CalcMean.

```
FUNCTION CalcMean (Scores : List;
                     Length : integer) : real;
   VAR
     J, Sum : integer;
   BEGIN
     Sum := 0;
     FOR J := 1 TO Length DO
       Sum := Sum + Scores[J];
     CalcMean := Sum / Length
   END;  {  of FUNCTION CalcMean  }
```

A procedure to print a heading would be written in a manner similar to that we have used previously. If we want the output to be

```
Test Scores
---- ------

    99
    98
    97
    96
    95

The average score on this test was 97.00.
```

the procedure for the heading could be

```
PROCEDURE PrintHeader;
  BEGIN
    writeln;
    writeln ('Test Scores');
    writeln ('---- ------');
    writeln
  END;  {  of PROCEDURE PrintHeader  }
```

A procedure to print the results could be

```
PROCEDURE PrintResults (Scores : List;
                        Ave : real;
                        Length : integer);
  VAR
    J : integer;
  BEGIN
    FOR J := 1 TO Length DO
      writeln (Scores[J]:5);
    writeln;
    writeln ('The average score on this test was',
             Ave:6:2, '.')
  END;  {  of PROCEDURE PrintResults  }
```

This procedure could be called by

```
PrintResults (Scores, Ave, Length);
```

where Ave is found by

```
Ave := CalcMean(Scores, Length);
```

The following example is a complete program for this development.

■ EXAMPLE 7.16

```
PROGRAM TestScores (input, output ScoreFile);

CONST
  MaxLength = 100;

TYPE
  List = ARRAY [1..MaxLength] OF integer;

VAR
  Scores : List;
  Ave : real;
  Length : integer;
  ScoreFile : text;

{*************************************************************** }

PROCEDURE GetData (VAR Scores : List;
                   VAR Length : integer);

  {  Given:   Nothing                                          }
  {  Task:    Read scores from a data file into an array       }
  {  Return:  Array of scores (with length)                    }

  BEGIN
    IF NOT eof(ScoreFile) THEN
      BEGIN
```

```
                      Length := 0;
                      WHILE NOT eof(ScoreFile) AND (Length < MaxLength) DO
                        BEGIN
                          Length := Length + 1;
                          readln (ScoreFile, Scores[Length])
                        END {  of WHILE NOT eof  }
               END  {  of IF NOT eof  }
             ELSE
               writeln ('ScoreFile is empty')
           END; {  of PROCEDURE GetData  }


{********************************************************************** }

FUNCTION CalcMean (Scores : List;
                          Length : integer) : real;

   {  Given:    A list of scores                                      }
   {  Task:     Compute the average score                             }
   {  Return:   The average score                                     }

   VAR
     J, Sum : integer;

   BEGIN
     Sum := 0;
     FOR J := 1 TO Length DO
       Sum := Sum + Scores[J];
     CalcMean := Sum / Length
   END; (  of FUNCTION CalcMean  )


{********************************************************************** }

PROCEDURE PrintHeader;

   {  Given:    Nothing                                               }
   {  Task:     Print a heading for the output                        }
   {  Return:   Nothing                                               }

   BEGIN
     writeln;
     writeln ('Test Scores');
     writeln ('---- ------');
     writeln
   END; {  of PROCEDURE PrintHeader  }


{********************************************************************** }

PROCEDURE PrintResults  (Scores : List;
                          Ave : real;
                          Length : integer);

   {  Given:    Array of scores and average score                    }
   {  Task:     Print the scores in a list and print the average     }
   {                 score                                            }
   {  Return:   Nothing                                              }

   VAR
     J : integer;

   BEGIN
     FOR J := 1 TO Length DO
       writeln (Scores[J]:5);
```

```
         writeln;
         writeln ('The average score on this test was', Ave:6:2, '.')
      END;  (  of PROCEDURE PrintResults  )

  {*********************************************************************** }

  BEGIN  {  Main program  }
    reset (ScoreFile);
    GetData (Scores, Length);
    Ave := CalcMean(Scores, Length);
    PrintHeader;
    PrintResults (Scores, Ave, Length)
  END.  {  of main program  }
```

As previously mentioned, sorting arrays is a standard problem for programmers. Now that we can pass arrays to procedures and functions, let us consider a problem in which an unknown number of reals are to be read from an input file and a sorted list (high to low) is to be printed as output. A first-level pseudocode design is

1. Get data (**PROCEDURE** GetData)
2. Sort list (**PROCEDURE** Sort)
3. Print header (**PROCEDURE** PrintHeader)
4. Print sorted list (**PROCEDURE** PrintData)

Since the number of data items is unknown, we will have to declare an array that is of sufficient length to store all the data but that does not use an unreasonable amount of memory. The nature of the problem will provide sufficient information for this declaration. For now, assume we know there are at most 50 data items. Then the following declaration will be sufficient.

```
  CONST
    MaxLength = 50;
  TYPE
    NumList = ARRAY [1..MaxLength] OF real;
  VAR
    List : NumList;
    Length : integer;
```

The procedure to sort the array uses a version of the selection sort from Section 7.3. Both the array and the number of data items need to be passed to the procedure. An appropriate procedure is

```
  PROCEDURE Sort (VAR List : NumList;
                      Length : integer);
    VAR
      J, K, Index : integer;
      Temp : real;
    BEGIN
      FOR J := 1 TO Length-1 DO
        BEGIN
          Index := J;
          FOR K := J + 1 TO Length DO
            IF List[K] > List[Index] THEN
              Index := K;
          IF Index <> J THEN
            BEGIN
              Temp := List[Index];
              List[Index] := List[J];
              List[J] := Temp
            END  {  of exchange  }
```

```
        END  {  of FOR J loop  }
      END;  {  of PROCEDURE Sort  }
```

This procedure could be called by the statement

```
  Sort (List, Length);
```

After suitable procedures are written for getting the data, printing a header, and printing the data, the main body of the program could be

```
  BEGIN  {  Main program  }
    GetData (List, Length);
    Sort (List, Length);
    PrintHeader;
    PrintData (List, Length)
  END.  {  of main program  }
```

Arrays and Variable Parameters

Let's now reconsider the issue of value parameters and variable parameters used with arrays. Because value parameters require separate memory of approximately the same size as that used by actual parameters in the main program, value parameters that are array types can require a great deal of memory. Thus, many programmers use only variable parameters when they work with arrays. This saves memory and speeds execution. Since most of your programs are relatively short and process small data files, this will not be a major problem. However, as data bases become larger and you use more elaborate structures, you may wish to consider using variable parameters even when changes are not made in the variables.

Software Engineering

Passing arrays is a software engineering concern. Passing arrays by reference results in a significant savings of memory. The problem this creates when several modules (teams) use the same array is that inadvertent changes made in an array within a specific module now become changes in the array used by other modules. These side effects would not occur if the array was passed as a value parameter.

How do designers solve this problem? There is no clear solution. If the arrays are fairly small and memory allocation is not a problem, arrays should be passed as value parameters when possible. When conditions require arrays to be passed by reference, it is extremely important to guarantee that no unwanted changes are made. This necessity increases the need for careful and thorough documentation.

Data Abstraction

Now that you are somewhat comfortable with the concept of an array as a data structure, it is time to take a broader look at how data relate to structures used to store and manipulate data. When designing the solution to a problem, it is not important to be initially concerned about the specifics of how data will be manipulated. These are implementation details that can (and should) be dealt with at a fairly low level in a modular development. The properties of a data structure will, however, be part of the design at a fairly high level.

The separation between the conceptual definition of a data structure and its eventual implementation is called *data abstraction*. This process of deferring details to the lowest possible level parallels the method of designing algorithms; that is, design first and do implementation details last.

Data abstraction is not a well-defined process, but we attempt to illustrate data abstraction with the following. Suppose you are designing a program that will be required to work with a list of names and an associated list of numbers (student names and test scores). Reasonable tasks would be to

1. Get the data
2. Sort the lists by name or number
3. Print the lists

In your design, you might have procedures such as

```
GetNames (<procedure here>);
GetScores (<procedure here>);
SortByName (<procedure here>);
SortByScore (<procedure here>);
PrintNamesAndScores (<procedure here>);
```

Even though you have not yet worked with implementation details required to write the procedures, you could use data structure properties in a design. For example, at this point, you probably could design a problem solution using some of the previously mentioned procedures that work with an array of names and/or an array of associated test scores.

Abstract Data Types

Two abstraction concepts have been previously discussed: procedural abstraction and data abstraction. A third form of abstraction arises from the use of defined types. Specifically, an *abstract data type* (*ADT*) consists of a class of objects, a defined set of properties of these objects, and a set of operations for processing the objects.

Our work thus far is fairly limited in terms of what could be considered an abstract data type. However, it is possible to think of an array as a list. The class of objects would then be lists. Some properties of these lists include identical element type, order, varying lengths, and direct access of individual components. Operations for processing the lists include searching for an element, sorting in ascending or descending order, inserting an element, and deleting an element.

As before, it is not necessary that you be overly concerned about specific implementation details at this point. But your growth as a computer scientist will be enhanced if you develop a perspective of abstract data types and use this perspective in the design of problem solutions.

Much of the remainder of this book is devoted to developing properties of data structures and operations for processing the structures. As you progress through the material on higher-dimensional arrays, records, files, and sets, try to analyze each structure with related properties and operations as an abstract data type.

Exercises 7.4

1. Assume the following declarations have been made in a program.

```
TYPE
  Row = ARRAY [1..10] OF integer;
  Column = ARRAY [1..30] OF real;
```

```
    String20 = ARRAY [1..20] OF char;
    Week = (Sun, Mon, Tues, Wed, Thur, Fri, Sat);
VAR
    List1, List2 : Row;
    Aray : Column;
    Name1, Name2 : String20;
    Day : Week;
    A, B : ARRAY [1..10] OF integer;
```

Indicate which of the following are valid **PROCEDURE** declarations. Write an appropriate line of code that will call each of those that are valid. Include an explanation for those that are invalid.

a. `PROCEDURE NewList (X : Row; Y : Column);`

b. `PROCEDURE NewList (VAR X : Row : VAR Y : Column);`

c. `PROCEDURE NewList (X : ARRAY [1..10] OF integer);`

d. `PROCEDURE NewList (VAR X, Y : Row);`

e. `PROCEDURE NewList (VAR Column : Column);`

f. `PROCEDURE WorkWeek (Days : ARRAY [Mon..Fri] OF Week);`

g. `PROCEDURE Surname (X : Name);`

h. `PROCEDURE Surnames (X, Y : String20);`

i. `PROCEDURE GetData (X : Week; VAR Y : Name);`

j. `PROCEDURE Table (VAR X : Row; VAR Y : Row);`

2. Write a test program that illustrates what happens when you define an array structure in a procedure heading. For example,

`PROCEDURE Sort (List : ARRAY [1..20] OF real);`

3. When possible, use the **TYPE** and **VAR** declaration sections of Exercise 1 to write **PROCEDURE** declarations so that each of the following statements in the main program is an appropriate call to a procedure. Explain any inappropriate calls.

a. `OldList (List1, Aray);`

b. `ChangeList (List1, Name1, Day);`

c. `Scores (A, B);`

d. `Surname (String20);`

4. Write an appropriate **PROCEDURE** declaration and a line of code to call the procedure for each of the following.

a. A procedure to **read** 20 test scores into an array and save them for later use.

b. A procedure to count the number of occurrences of the letter A in an array of 50 characters.

c. A procedure to take two arrays of 10 integers each and produce a sorted array of 20 integers for later use.

d. A procedure to **read** integer test scores from a data file, count the number of scores, count the number of scores greater than or equal to 90, and save this information for later use.

5. Assume the following declarations have been made.

```
TYPE
    Column10 = ARRAY [1..10] OF integer;
VAR
    List1, List2 : Column10;
    K : integer;
```

Indicate the contents of each array after the call to the corresponding procedure.

```
a. PROCEDURE Sample (VAR List1 : Column10;
                          List2 : Column10);
   VAR
     J : integer;
   BEGIN
     FOR J := 1 TO 10 DO
       BEGIN
         List1[J] := J * J;
         List2[J] := List1[J] MOD 2
       END
   END;  {  of PROCEDURE Sample  }
   BEGIN  {  Main program  }
     .
     .

     .
     FOR K := 1 TO 10 DO
       BEGIN
         List1[K] := 0;
         List2[K] := 0
       END;
     Sample (List1, List2);
```

b. Replace the procedure call with

```
Sample (List2, List1);
```

c. Replace the procedure call with consecutive calls

```
Sample (List1, List2);
Sample (List2, List1);
```

6. For the following, declare appropriate variables, write the indicated procedures, and call the procedures from the main program.

   a. Read a line of text from an input file that contains 30 characters.

   b. Count the number of blanks in the line of text.

   c. Print the line of text in reverse order and print the number of blanks.

7. Write a procedure to examine an array of integers and then return the maximum value, minimum value, and number of negative values to the main program.

8. Write **PROCEDURE** BubbleSort for the bubble sort of Section 7.3. Show how it would be called from the main program.

9. Write **PROCEDURE** Exchange for the bubble sort that will exchange values of array components. Then rewrite the bubbles sort using **PROCEDURE** Exchange.

10. Discuss some of the implementation details you would need in order to read a list of names into an array.

11. Suppose you have an array of student names and an array of these students' test scores. How would the array of names be affected if you sorted the test scores from high to low?

■ ■ ■ ■

■ 7.5
Packed Arrays

One weakness of standard Pascal is the absence of a *string data type*. Since this text is written assuming standard Pascal is being used, this section shows how arrays can be used to simulate a string data type. Most nonstandard versions of Pascal do, however, have such a type. If your version of Pascal has the string data type available, you may wish to skip this section.

Basic Idea and Notation

Arrays, as you recall, are useful for handling large amounts of data. One of the disadvantages of using arrays, however, is that they require large amounts of memory. In particular, arrays of character data use much more memory than is necessary. To illustrate, let us take a closer look at an array declared by

```
VAR
   Examine : ARRAY [1..5] OF char;
```

When this structured variable is declared, the following variables are reserved.

Examine

	Examine[1]
	Examine[2]
	Examine[3]
	Examine[4]
	Examine[5]

Each component of the array Examine is one *word* in memory and each word consists of several *bytes*. Let us consider the array Examine in which each word consists of four bytes. The array would be pictured as

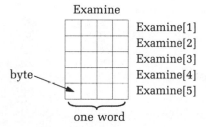

We could assign the word "HELLO" to the array Examine by either

```
Examine[1] := 'H';
Examine[2] := 'E';
Examine[3] := 'L';
Examine[4] := 'L';
Examine[5] := 'O';
```

or

```
Examine := 'HELLO'
```

depending on which version of Pascal is being used. In either case, after the assignment, the array would look like

Examine

H				Examine[1]
E				Examine[2]
L				Examine[3]
L				Examine[4]
O				Examine[5]

because a byte is the unit of storage necessary for storing a character variable.

As you can see, 20 bytes of storage have been reserved, but only 5 have been used. Pascal provides a more efficient way of defining arrays that does not use unnecessary amounts of storage space. Instead of declaring a variable

Ⓣ as an array, we can declare a variable as a *packed array*. With this declaration, the computer then packs the data in consecutive bytes.

Packed arrays can be used with any data type (**char, real, integer, boolean,** and so on). However, it is not always wise to do so because it takes longer to access individual components of a packed array than it does to access individual components of an array that has not been declared as packed. Storage space is saved, but time may be lost. For more information on using arrays that are packed and those that are not (*unpacked arrays*), see Appendix 8.

Let us now consider the declaration

```
TYPE
   String5 = PACKED ARRAY [1..5] OF char;
VAR
   Examine : String5;
```

and the assignment of the word "HELLO" as before. Using a packed array, we then have the following in memory.

Examine

| H | E | L | L | O | | | |

Notice that less than two words (5 bytes) are used to store what previously required five words (20 bytes). We can still access the individual components as before. For example,

```
writeln (Examine[2]);
```

produces

E

as a line of output.

Character Strings

Every programming language needs to be able to handle character data. Names, words, phrases, and sentences are frequently used as part of some information that must be analyzed. In standard Pascal, character strings are formed by declaring packed arrays of character variables. For example, if the first 20 spaces of an input line are reserved for a customer's name, an appropriate character string could be declared by

```
TYPE
   String20 = PACKED ARRAY [1..20] OF char;
VAR
   Name : String20;
   DataFile : text;
```

If the line of input is

| Smith John A.   * ▮

↑
position 21

we could read the name into the packed array by the code

```
FOR J := 1 TO 20 DO
   read (DataFile, Name[J]);
```

Now when we refer to the array Name, we can envision the string

```
'Smith John A.'
```

But since we declared a fixed length string, the actual string is

```
'Smith John A.         '
```

There are at least three important uses for string variables.

1. String variables of the same length can be compared (Boolean values); this permits alphabetizing.
2. String variables can be written using a single **write** or **writeln** statement; they cannot be read using a single **read** statement.
3. A single assignment statement can assign text to a string variable.

Let's examine each use individually.

Comparing String Variables. Strings of the same length can be compared using the standard relational operators: "$=$, $<$, $>$, $<>$, $<=$, and $>=$." For example, if 'Smith' and 'Jones' are strings, then 'Smith' $<$ 'Jones', 'Smith' $<>$ 'Jones', and so on are all valid Boolean expressions. The Boolean value is determined by the collating sequence. Using the collating sequence for the ASCII character set, the following comparisons yield the indicated values.

Comparison	Boolean Value
'Smith' $<$ 'Jones'	**false**
'Jake' $<$ 'John'	**true**
'ABC' $=$ 'ABA'	**false**
'Smith Doug' $<$ 'Smith John'	**true**

What would happen if you wanted to evaluate 'William Joe' $<$ 'Williams Bo'? Since a character-by-character comparison is implemented by the computer, no decision is made until the blank following the *m* of William is compared to the *s* of Williams. Using the full ASCII character code, this Boolean expression is **true,** which is how these strings are alphabetized.

Writing String Variables. Recall the declaration

```
TYPE
   String20 = PACKED ARRAY [1..20] OF char;
VAR
   Name : String20;
```

When data are read from an input file, a loop is used to get the data one character at a time.

```
FOR J := 1 TO 20 DO
   read (DataFile, Name[J]);
```

If we now wish to write the string Name, we could use a similar loop and write it one character at a time.

```
FOR J := 1 TO 20 DO
   write (Name[J]);
```

However, Pascal provides a more convenient method for writing strings. The write loop could be replaced by

```
write (Name);
```

Assigning Text to a String. The third feature of string variables is that a single assignment can be used to assign text to a string. If Name is a string of length 20, then

```
Name := 'Smith John A.          ';
```

is a valid statement. Note that there must be exactly 20 characters in the text string in order for this assignment to be valid. The statements

```
Name := 'Smith John A.';
Name := 'Theodore Allen Washington';
```

are both invalid because the text strings are not exactly 20 characters long.

There are some standard problems that will be encountered when trying to read data into a packed array. First, assume we have to read a line of data that consists of a company name. Furthermore, assume we do not know the length of the name. The input line could be

```
Prudent Investors Company
```

or

```
Com Mfg. Co.
```

If we know the company name will be no more than 30 characters, we can declare a fixed length array in the following manner.

```
TYPE
   String30 = PACKED ARRAY [1..30] OF char;
VAR
   CompanyName : String30;
```

and then read the name with the segment of code

```
StringLength := 0;
WHILE NOT eoln(DataFile) AND (StringLength < 30) DO
  BEGIN
    StringLength := StringLength + 1;
    read (DataFile, CompanyName[StringLength])
  END;  {  of WHILE NOT eoln DO  }
readln (DataFile);
FOR J := (StringLength + 1) TO 30 DO
  CompanyName[J] := ' ' {  blank fills the rest of name  }
```

This will read the name as desired and then fill the array with blanks to the desired length. Applied to the two data lines just mentioned, this segment of code would produce the following character strings.

```
'Prudent Investors Company     '
'Com Mfg. Co.                   '
```

Second, we may want to read data from a data file in which a field of fixed length is used for some character data. For example, suppose the first 30 columns of a data line are reserved for the company name and then some other information is on the same line. We could have

Prudent Investors Company   1905 South Drive

↑
column 31

This data could be accessed by the loop

```
FOR J := 1 TO 30 DO
  read (DataFile, CompanyName[J]);
```

Although the second format for an input file is easier to use, it is sometimes difficult to obtain data in such a precise format. Hence, we must be able to read data both ways.

We are now ready to write a short program using packed arrays. Suppose the problem is to get two names from a data file, arrange them alphabetically, and then print the alphabetized list. Assume the names are in a field of fixed length 25 on two adjacent lines. A first-level pseudocode development is

1. Get the data (**PROCEDURE** GetData)
2. Arrange alphabetically (**PROCEDURE** Alphabetize)
3. Print the data (**PROCEDURE** PrintData)

A procedure to get one line of data is

```
PROCEDURE GetData (VAR Name : String25);
  VAR
    J, StringLength : integer;
  BEGIN
    StringLength := 0;
    WHILE NOT eoln(DataFile) AND (StringLength < 25) DO
      BEGIN
        StringLength := StringLength + 1;
        read (DataFile, Name[StringLength])
      END;  {  of WHILE NOT eoln DO  }
    readln (DataFile);
    FOR J := (StringLength + 1) TO 25 DO
      Name[J] := ' ' {   blank fills the rest of name  }
  END;  {  of PROCEDURE GetData  }
```

After the two names have been read from the input file, they could be arranged alphabetically by

```
PROCEDURE Alphabetize (VAR Name1, Name2 : String25);
  VAR
    Temp : String25;
  BEGIN
    IF Name2 < Name1 THEN
      BEGIN  {  Exchange when necessary  }
        Temp := Name1;
        Name1 := Name2;
        Name2 := Temp
      END {  of IF...THEN  }
  END;  {  of PROCEDURE Alphabetize  }
```

The procedure for printing the name should include some header and some formatting of the names. For example, suppose you want to say

```
The alphabetized list is below.
--- ------------ ---- -- -----
```

and then print the list indented ten spaces after skipping two lines. A procedure to do this is

```
PROCEDURE PrintData (Name1, Name2 : String25);
  BEGIN
    writeln;
    writeln (Skip:10, 'The alphabetized list is below.');
    writeln (Skip:10, '--- ------------ ---- -- -----');
    writeln;
    writeln (Skip:20, Name1);
    writeln (Skip:20, Name2)
  END;  {  of PROCEDURE PrintData  }
```

We can now write the complete program.

```
PROGRAM SampleNames (input, output, DataFile);

CONST
  Skip = ' ';
```

```
TYPE
  String25 = PACKED ARRAY [1..25] OF char;

VAR
  Name1, Name2 : String25;
  DataFile : text;

{****************************************************************** }

PROCEDURE GetData (VAR Name : String25);

  {  Given:    Nothing                                            }
  {  Task:     Read a name from the data file                     }
  {  Return:   One name (string of 25 characters)                 }

  VAR
    J, StringLength : integer;

  BEGIN
    StringLength := 0;
    WHILE NOT eoln(DataFile) AND (StringLength < 25) DO
      BEGIN
        StringLength := StringLength + 1;
        read (DataFile, Name[StringLength])
      END;
    readln (DataFile);
    FOR J := (StringLength + 1) TO 25 DO
      Name[J] := ' '          {  Blank fills the remainder of Name }
  END; {  of PROCEDURE GetData  }

{****************************************************************** }

PROCEDURE Alphabetize  (VAR Name1, Name2 : String25);

  {  Given:    Two names                                          }
  {  Task:     Sort the names alphabetically                      }
  {  Return:   The names in sorted order                          }

  VAR
    Temp : String25;

  BEGIN
    IF Name2 < Name1 THEN
      BEGIN                            {  Exchange when necessary  }
        Temp := Name1;
        Name1 := Name2;
        Name2 := Temp
      END {  of IF...THEN  }
  END; {  of PROCEDURE Alphabetize  }

{****************************************************************** }

PROCEDURE PrintData (Name1, Name2 : String25);

  {  Given:    Names in alphabetical order                        }
  {  Task:     Print the names                                    }
  {  Return:   Nothing                                            }

  BEGIN
    writeln;
    writeln (Skip:10, 'The alphabetized list is below.');
    writeln (Skip:10, '--- ------------ ---- -- ------;);
    writeln;
```

```
         writeln (Skip:20, Name1);
         writeln (Skip:20, Name2)
    END;  {  of PROCEDURE PrintData  }


{************************************************************** }

    BEGIN  {  Main program  }
      reset (DataFile);
      GetData (Name1);
      GetData (Name2);
      Alphabetize (Name1, Name2);
      PrintData (Name1, Name2)
    END.  {  of main program  }
```

Exercises 7.5

1. Indicate which of the following string comparisons are valid. For those that are, indicate whether they are **true** or **false** using the full ASCII character set.

   a. `'Mathematics' <> 'CompScience'`

   b. `'Jefferson' < 'Jeffersonian'`

   c. `'Smith Karen' < 'Smithsonian'`

   d. `'#45' <= '$45'`

   e. `'Hoof in mouth' = 'Foot in door'`

   f. `'453012' > '200000'`

2. Write a test program that allows you to examine the Boolean expression

   `'William Joe' < 'Williams Bo'`

3. Suppose Message is declared as

```
TYPE
   String50 = PACKED ARRAY [1..50] OF char;
VAR
   Message : String50;
```

   and the input file consists of the line

   `To err is human. Computers do not forgive.`

   What output is produced by each of the following segments?

```
a. FOR J := 1 TO 50 DO
     IF NOT eoln(Data) THEN
       read (Data, Message[J])
     ELSE
       Message[J] := ' ';
   writeln (Message);
```

```
b. FOR J := 1 TO 50 DO
     IF NOT eoln(Data) THEN
       read (Data, Message[J])
     ELSE
       Message[J] := ' ';
   Count := 0;
   FOR J := 1 TO 50 DO
     IF Message[J] := ' ' THEN
       Count := Count + 1;
   writeln (Message);
   writeln ('There are', Count:3, 'blanks.':8);
```

```
c. FOR J := 1 TO 20 DO
     read (Data, Message[2+J]);
   FOR J := 21 TO 40 DO
     Message[J] := ' ';
```

```
                FOR J := 41 TO 50 DO
                  Message[J] := '*';
                writeln (Message);
            d. FOR J := 1 TO 50 DO
                  IF NOT eoln(Data) THEN
                    read (Data, Message[J])
                  ELSE
                    Message[J] := ' ';
                writeln (Message);
                FOR J := 50 DOWNTO 1 DO
                  write (Message[J]);
```

4. Assume the following declarations.
   ```
   TYPE
     String10 = PACKED ARRAY [1..10] OF char;
     String20 = PACKED ARRAY [1..20] OF char;
   VAR
     A, B : String10;
     C : String20;
   ```
   a. Indicate whether the following are valid or invalid.

      i. `A := B;`

      ii. `C := A + B;`

      iii.
      ```
      FOR J := 1 TO 20 DO
        C[J] := A[J] + B[J];
      ```

      iv.
      ```
      FOR J := 1 TO 20 DO
        IF J <= 10 THEN
          A[J] := C[J]
        ELSE
          B[J-10] := C[J];
      ```

   b. Write a segment of code that will make the string C consist of the strings A and B where the lesser (alphabetically) of A and B is the first half of C.

5. Assume a packed array Message of length 100 has been declared and data have been read into it from an input file. Write a segment of the code to count the number of occurrences of the letter M in the string Message.

6. Write a test program to see what happens if you try to read in an entire packed array with one **read** or **readln** statement.

■ ■ ■ ■

■ 7.6
Searching Algorithms

The need to search an array for a value is a common problem. For example, you might wish to replace a test score for a student, delete a name from a directory or mailing list, or upgrade the pay scale for certain employees. These and other problems require you to be able to examine elements in some list until the desired value is located. When it is found, some action is taken. The lists, of course, could be either arrays or files. In this section, we assume all lists are nonempty.

Sequential Search

The first searching algorithm we will examine is the most common method, a *sequential (linear) search*. This process is accomplished by examining the first element in some list and then proceeding to examine the elements in the order they appear until a match is found. Variations of this basic process include searching a sorted list for the first occurrence of a value, searching a sorted list for all occurrences of a value, and searching an unsorted list for the first occurrence of a value.

To illustrate a sequential search, suppose you have an array A of integers and you want to find the first occurrence of some particular value (Num). As you search the array, if the desired value is located, you want to print its position. If the value is not in the array, an appropriate message should be printed. The code for such a search is

```
Index := 1;
WHILE (Num <> A[Index]) AND (Index < Length) DO
  Index := Index + 1;
```

A reasonable message for output is

```
IF Num = A[Index] THEN
  writeln (Num, ' is in position', Index:5)
ELSE
  writeln (Num, ' is not in the list.')
```

Let's now consider some variations of this problem. Our code works for both a sorted and an unsorted list. However, if we are searching a sorted list, the algorithm can be improved. For example, if the array components are sorted from low to high, we need to continue the search only until the value in an array component exceeds the value of Num. At that point, there is no need to examine the remaining components. The only change required in the loop for searching is to replace

```
Num <> A[Index]
```

with

```
Num > A[Index]
```

Thus, we have

```
Index := 1;
WHILE (Num > A[Index]) AND (Index < Length) DO
  Index := Index + 1;
```

A relatively easy modification of the sequential search is to examine a list for all occurrences of some value. If searching an array, you would generally print the positions and values when a match is found. To illustrate, if A is an array of integers and Num has an integer value, we can search A for the number of occurrences of Num by

```
Count := 0;
FOR Index := 1 TO Length DO
  IF Num = A[Index] THEN
    BEGIN
      Count := Count + 1;
      writeln (Num, ' is in position', Index:5)
    END;
```

This code works for an unsorted list. A modification of the code for working with a sorted list is included as an exercise.

Binary Search

Searching relatively small lists sequentially does not require much computer time. However, when the lists get longer (as, for example, telephone directories and lists of credit card customers), sequential searches are inefficient. In a sense, they correspond to looking up a word in the dictionary by starting at the first word and proceeding word-by-word until the desired word is found. Since extra computer time means considerably extra expense for most companies where large amounts of data must be frequently searched, a more efficient way of searching is needed.

If the list to be searched has been sorted, it can be searched for a particular value by a method referred to as a *binary search*. Essentially, a binary search consists of examining a middle value of an array to see which half contains the desired value. The middle value of this half is then examined to see which half of the half contains the value in question. This halving process is continued until the value is located or it is determined that the value is not in the list. (Remember, however, in order to use a binary search, the list must be sorted and the sorting process has its own costs which should be evaluated, but this subject is outside the scope of this text.)

The code for this process is relatively short. If A is the array to be searched for Num, and First, Mid, and Last are integer variables such that First contains the index of the first possible position to be searched and Last contains the index of the last possible position, the code for a list in ascending order is

```
Found := false;
WHILE NOT Found AND (First <= Last) DO
   BEGIN
      Mid := (First + Last) DIV 2;
      IF Num < A[Mid] THEN
         Last := Mid - 1
```

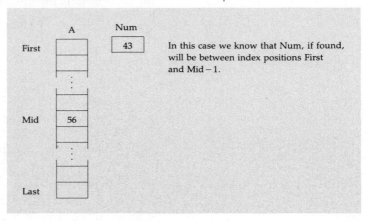

In this case we know that Num, if found, will be between index positions First and Mid − 1.

```
      ELSE IF Num > A[Mid] THEN
         First := Mid + 1
      ELSE
         Found := true
END;
```

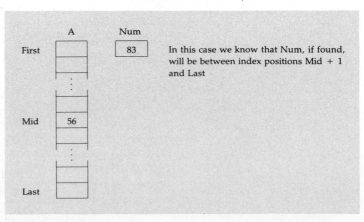

In this case we know that Num, if found, will be between index positions Mid + 1 and Last

When this loop is executed, it is exited when the value is located or it is determined that the value is not in the list. Depending on what you want done with the value being looked for, you can modify action at the bottom of the loop or use the values in Found and Mid outside the loop. For example, if you just want to know where the value is, you can change

```
Found := true
```

to

```
BEGIN
  Found := true;
  writeln (Num, ' is in position', Mid:5)
END;
```

Before continuing, let's walk through this search to better understand how it works. Assume A is the array

4	7	19	25	36	37	50	100	101	205	220	271	306	321

A[1]   A[14]

with values as indicated. Furthermore, assume Num contains the value 25. Then initially, First, Last, and Num have the values

1		14		25

First   Last   Num

A listing of values by each pass through the loop produces

	First	Last	Mid	A[Mid]	Found
Before loop	1	14	Undefined	Undefined	**false**
After first pass	1	6	7	50	**false**
After second pass	4	6	3	19	**false**
After third pass	4	4	5	36	**false**
After fourth pass	4	4	4	25	**true**

To illustrate what happens when the value being looked for is not in the array, suppose Num contains 210. The listing of values then produces

	First	Last	Mid	A[Mid]	Found
Before loop	1	14	Undefined	Undefined	**false**
After first pass	8	14	7	50	**false**
After second pass	8	10	11	220	**false**
After third pass	10	10	9	101	**false**
After fourth pass	11	10	10	205	**false**

At this stage, First > Last and the loop is exited.

Inserting and Deleting in a Sorted Array

Arrays are typically searched because you want to either insert an element into the array or delete an element from the array. To illustrate, let's consider the array A

2	5	8	10	10	12	15	18	21	30

A[1] A[2]   A[10]

If we wish to remove the element 12 from the array, we would end up with

2	5	8	10	10	15	18	21	30

A[1] A[2]   A[9]

Note that 12 has been deleted from the array and then elements listed "after" 12 in the array have been "advanced" one position.

To illustrate what happens when an element is to be inserted into an array, again consider the array A

2	5	8	10	10	12	15	18	21	30

A[1] A[2]   A[10]

If we want to insert 17 into the sorted array, we would first determine that it belongs between 15 and 18. We would then reassign elements 18, 21, and 30 to produce

2	5	8	10	10	12	15		18	21	30

A[1] A[2]   ↑   A[11]

17 goes here

17 is then assigned to the appropriate array component to produce the array

2	5	8	10	10	12	15	17	18	21	30

A[1] A[2]   A[11]

Writing the code for inserting and deleting in a sorted array is deferred to the Exercises.

Relative Efficiency of Searches

Let's now examine briefly the efficiency of a binary search compared to a sequential search. For purposes of this discussion, assume a sequential search on a list of 15 items requires at most 15 microseconds. The nature of a sequential search is such that every time you double the list length, the maximum searching time is also doubled; Figure 7.1 illustrates this increase.

FIGURE 7.1
Sequential search

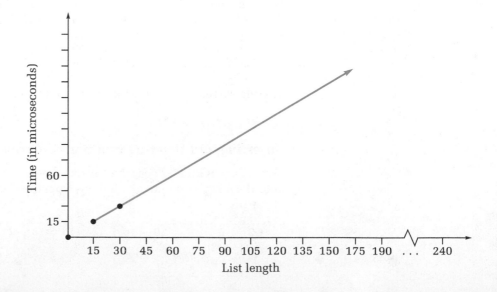

Next, assume a list of 15 items requires a maximum of 60 microseconds when searched by a binary search. Since this process consists of successively halving the list, at most four passes will be required to locate the value. This means each pass uses 15 microseconds. When the list length is doubled, it requires only one more pass. Thus, a list of 30 items requires 75 microseconds and a list of 60 items requires 90 microseconds. This is shown graphically in Figure 7.2. The comparison of these two searches is shown on the same graph in Figure 7.3.

FIGURE 7.2
Binary search

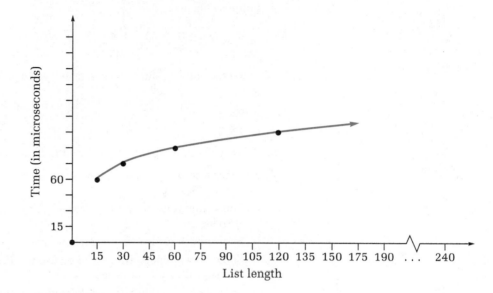

FIGURE 7.3
Sequential search versus binary search

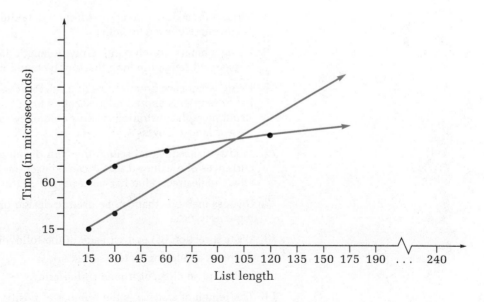

Exercises 7.6

1. Write a sequential search using a **FOR** loop to locate and print all occurrences of the same value.

2. Write a procedure for the sequential search and show how it can be called from the main program.

3. Modify the sequential search by putting a counter in the loop to count how many passes are made when searching a sorted array for a value. Write and run a program that uses this version on lists of length 15, 30, 60, 120, and 240. In each case, search for a value as follows and plot your results on a graph.

   a. In the first half

   b. In the second half

   c. That is not there

4. Repeat Exercise 3 for a binary search.

5. Suppose the array A is

18	25	37	92	104

   A[1]   A[5]

   Trace the values using a binary search to look for

   a. 18

   b. 92

   c. 76

6. Write a procedure to search a sorted list and remove all duplicates.

7. Suppose a sorted list of social security numbers is in secondary storage in a file named StudentNum.

   a. Show how this file can be searched for a certain number using a sequential search.

   b. Show how this file can be searched for a certain number using a binary search.

   c. Show how a binary search can be used to indicate where a new number can be inserted in proper order.

   d. Show how a number can be deleted from the file.

8. Write a procedure to read text from a data file and determine the number of occurrences of each vowel.

9. Using a binary search on an array of length 35, what is the maximum number of passes through the loop that can be made when searching for a value?

10. Using worst-case possibilities of 3 microseconds for a sequential search of a list of ten items and 25 microseconds for a binary search of the same list, construct a graph illustrating relative efficiency for these two methods applied to lists of longer lengths.

11. Modify the sequential search that you developed in Exercise 1 to list all occurrences of a value so that it can be used on a sorted list. That is, have it stop after the desired value has been passed in the list.

12. Discuss methods that can be used to design programs to guard against searching empty lists.

13. Write a section of code for each of the following:

    a. Insert an element into a sorted array.

    b. Delete an element from a sorted array.

14. The length of a string is the number of positions from the first nonblank character to the last nonblank character. Thus, the packed array

T	h	i	s		i	s		a		s	t	r	i	n	g	.													

    would have length = 17. Write a function that receives a packed array of type [1 . . 30] of **char** and returns the length of the string.

■ ■ ■ ■ ■

**FOCUS ON
PROGRAM DESIGN**

The sample program for this chapter features the use of arrays and subprograms. Since sorting an array is a common practice, it has been included as part of the program. Specifically, suppose the Home Sales Realty Company, Inc. wants to print a list containing the amount of all sales for a month. Each sale amount is recorded on a separate line of input and the number of homes sold is less than 20. Write a program to do the following:

1. Read the data from the input file.
2. Print the data in the order in which it is read with a suitable header and format.
3. Print a sorted list (high to low) of sales with a suitable header and format.
4. Print the total number of sales for the month, the total amount of sales, the average sale price, and the company commission (7 percent).

Sample input would be

```
85000
76234
115100
98200
121750
76700
```

where each line represents the sale price of a home. Typical output would include an unsorted list of sales, a sorted list of sales, and appropriate summary data.

A first-level pseudocode development is

1. Get data (**PROCEDURE** GetData)
2. Print header (**PROCEDURE** PrintH1)
3. Print unsorted list (**PROCEDURE** PrintList)
4. Sort list (**PROCEDURE** Sort)
5. Print header (**PROCEDURE** PrintH2)
6. Print sorted list (**PROCEDURE** PrintList)
7. Compute data (**FUNCTION** Total and **PROCEDURE** Compute)
8. Print results (**PROCEDURE** PrintResults)

Notice that **PROCEDURE** PrintList is called twice and **PROCEDURE** PrintResults includes output for number of sales, total of sales, average sale price, and company commission. These are printed with suitable headings.

A structure chart for this is given in Figure 7.4.

FIGURE 7.4
Structure chart for Home Sales
Realty Company, Inc. program

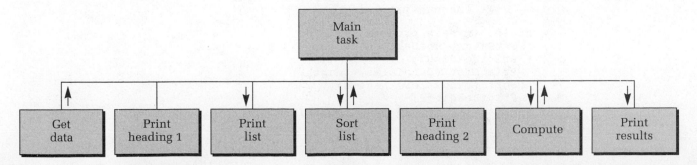

Module specifications for the main modules are

1. GetData Module
   Data received: None
   Information returned: Sales for a month
                         Number of sales
   Logic: Use a **WHILE** loop to read entries into an array.

2. PrintHeading1 Module
   Data received: None
   Information returned: None
   Logic: Use **writeln** statements to print a suitable heading for an un-
           sorted list.

3. PrintList Module
   Data received: Array of sales with number of sales
   Information returned: None
   Logic: Use a **FOR** loop with the array length as a loop control variable
           to print the list of sales for a month.

4. Sort Module
   Data received: Unsorted array of sales
                   Number of sales
   Information returned: Sorted array of sales
   Logic: Use a selection sort to sort the array.

5. PrintHeading2 Module
   Data received: None
   Information returned: None
   Logic: Use **writeln** statements to print a suitable heading for the sorted
           list.

6. Compute Module
   Data received: Array of sales with number of sales
   Information returned: Total sales
                         Average sale
                         Company commission
   Logic: Use a function to compute the total sales.
           Use a procedure to compute the average sale.
           Compute company commission by using a defined constant,
           CommissionRate.

7. PrintResults Module
   Data received: Number of sales
                   Total sales
                   Average sales
                   Company commission
   Information returned: None
   Logic: Use **writeln** statements to print a summary report.

The main program is

```
BEGIN  {  Main program  }
  GetData (JuneSales, Length);
  PrintHeading1;
  PrintList (JuneSales, Length);
  Sort (JuneSales, Length);
  PrintHeading2;
  PrintList (JuneSales, Length);
```

```
      Compute (TotalSales, AverageSale, CompanyCom, JuneSales, Length);
      PrintResults (TotalSales, AverageSale, CompanyCom, Length)
END.  {  of main program  }
```

The complete program for this problem is

```
PROGRAM MonthlyList (input, output, SalesList);

{  This program illustrates the use of arrays with procedures    }
{  and  functions.  Note the  use of both  value and variable    }
{  parameters.  Also note  that a procedure  is  used to sort     }
{  the array.                                                     }

CONST
  Skip = ' ';
  CommissionRate = 0.07;
  MaxLength = 20;

TYPE
  List = ARRAY [1..MaxLength] OF real;

VAR
  JuneSales : List;                {  Number of June sales         }
  TotalSales,                      {  Total of June sales          }
  AverageSale,                     {  Amount of average sale       }
  CompanyCom : real;               {  Commission for the company   }
  Length : integer;                {  Array length of values       }
  SalesList : text;                {  Data file of sales           }

{******************************************************************** }

PROCEDURE GetData (VAR JuneSales : List;
                   VAR Length : integer);

  {  Given:   Nothing                                               }
  {  Task:    Read selling prices into array JuneSales              }
  {  Return:  Array of JuneSales and array length                  }

  BEGIN
    Length := 0;
    WHILE NOT eof(SalesList) AND (Length < MaxLength) DO
      BEGIN
        Length := Length + 1;
        readln (SalesList, JuneSales[Length])
      END  {  of WHILE NOT eof  }
  END;  {  of PROCEDURE GetData  }

{********************************************************************}

PROCEDURE PrintHeading1;

  {  Given:   Nothing                                               }
  {  Task:    Print a heading for the unsorted list of sales        }
  {  Return:  Nothing                                               }

  BEGIN
    writeln;
    writeln (Skip:10, 'An unsorted list of sales for the');
    writeln (Skip:10, 'month of June is as follows:');
    writeln (Skip:10, '---------------------------------');
    writeln
  END;  {  of PROCEDURE PrintHeading1  }
```

1

2

```
{********************************************************************* }

PROCEDURE PrintList (JuneSales : List;
                     Length : integer);

  { Given:    An unsorted array (with length) of Sales for June   }
  { Task:     Print the list                                      }
  { Return:   Nothing                                             }

  VAR
    J : integer;

  BEGIN
    FOR J := 1 TO Length DO
      writeln (Skip:14, '<', J:2, '>', '$':2, JuneSales[J]:11:2)
  END;  (  of PROCEDURE PrintList  )

{********************************************************************* }

PROCEDURE Sort (VAR JuneSales : List;
                Length : integer);

  { Given:    An unsorted array (with length) of sales for June   }
  { Task:     Use a selection sort to sort the list              }
  { Return:   A sorted list of sales for June                    }

  VAR
    J, K, Index : integer;
    Temp : real;

  BEGIN
    FOR J := 1 TO Length - 1 DO
      BEGIN
        Index := J;
        FOR K := J + 1 TO Length DO
          IF JuneSales[K] > JuneSales[Index] THEN
            Index := K;
        IF Index <> J THEN
          BEGIN
            Temp := JuneSales[Index];
            JuneSales[Index] := JuneSales[J];
            JuneSales[J] := Temp
          END  { of exchange  }
      END  { of FOR J loop  }
  END;  { of PROCEDURE Sort  }

{********************************************************************* }

PROCEDURE PrintHeading2;

  { Given:    Nothing                                             }
  { Task:     Print a heading for the sorted list of sales        }
  { Return:   Nothing                                             }

  BEGIN
    writeln;
    writeln (Skip:10, 'Sales for the month of June');
    writeln (Skip:10, 'sorted from high to low are:');
    writeln (Skip:10, '---------------------------');
    writeln
  END;  { of PROCEDURE PrintHeading2  }

{********************************************************************* }
```

3

4

5

```
FUNCTION Total (JuneSales : List;
                Length : integer) : real;

  { Given:    An array (with length) of June sales          }
  { Task:     Sum the array components                      }
  { Return:   Total of sales for June                       }

  VAR
    J : integer;
    Sum : real;

  BEGIN
    Sum := 0;
    FOR J := 1 TO Length DO
      Sum := Sum + JuneSales[J];
    Total := Sum
  END; {  of FUNCTION Total  }
```

⎱
⎰ 6

```
{******************************************************************* }

PROCEDURE Compute (VAR TotalSales, AverageSale, CompanyCom : real;
                   VAR JuneSales : List;
                   Length : integer);

  { Given:    An array (with length) of June sales          }
  { Task:     Compute TotalSales, AverageSale, and CompanyCom }
  {                   for the month of June                 }
  { Return:   TotalSales, AverageSale, and CompanyCom       }

  BEGIN
    TotalSales := Total(JuneSales, Length);
    AverageSale := TotalSales / Length;
    CompanyCom := TotalSales * CommissionRate
  END; {  of PROCEDURE Compute  }

{******************************************************************* }

PROCEDURE PrintResults (TotalSales, AverageSale, CompanyCom : real;
                        Length : integer);

  { Given:    TotalSales, AverageSale, CompanyCom, and number }
  {                   of sales (Length) for June            }
  { Task:     Print summary information for the month       }
  { Return:   Nothing                                       }

  BEGIN
    writeln;
    writeln (Skip:10, 'There were', Length:3 ' sales during June.');
    writeln;
    writeln (Skip:10 'The total sales were', '$':2, TotalSales:12:2);
    writeln;
    writeln (Skip:10, 'The average sale was', '$':2, AverageSale:12:2);
    writeln;
    writeln (Skip:10, 'The company commission was', '$':2,
             CompanyCom:11:2);
    writeln
  END; {  of PROCEDURE PrintResults  }

{*******************************************************************}

BEGIN  {  Main program  }
  reset (SalesList);
  GetData (JuneSales, Length);
```

⎱
⎰ 7

```
        PrintHeading1;
        PrintList (JuneSales, Length);
        Sort (JuneSales, Length);
        PrintHeading2;
        PrintList (JuneSales, Length);
        Compute (TotalSales, AverageSale, CompanyCom, JuneSales, Length);
        PrintResults (TotalSales, AverageSale, CompanyCom, Length)
    END.  { of main program  }
```

The output for this program is

```
An unsorted list of sales for the
month of June is as follows:
---------------------------------

          < 1> $     85000.00
          < 2> $     78234.00
          < 3> $    115100.00
          < 4> $     98200.00
          < 5> $    121750.00
          < 6> $     76700.00


Sales for the month of June
sorted from high to low are:
----------------------------

          < 1> $    121750.00
          < 2> $    115100.00
          < 3> $     98200.00
          < 4> $     85000.00
          < 5> $     76700.00
          < 6> $     76234.00


There were 6 sales during June.

The total sales were $    572984.00

The average sale was $     95497.33

The company commission was $     40108.88
```

RUNNING AND DEBUGGING TIPS

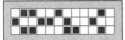

1. Be careful not to misuse type identifiers. For example, in

```
TYPE
   String = PACKED ARRAY [1..10] OF char;
VAR
   Word : String;
```

String is a data type; hence, a reference such as String := 'First name' is incorrect.

2. Do not attempt to use a subscript that is out of range. Suppose we have

```
VAR
   List : ARRAY [1..6] OF integer;
```

An inadvertent reference such as

```
FOR J := 1 TO 10 DO
   writeln (List[J]);
```

may produce an error message indicating that the subscript is out of range.

3. Counters are frequently used with loops and arrays. Be careful to make the final value the correct value. For example,

```
Count := 1;
WHILE NOT eof(<file name>) DO
   BEGIN
```

```
      readln (<file name>), (A[Count]);
      Count := Count + 1
   END;
```

used on the data file

```
18  21  33  ■
```

will have a value of 4 in Count when this loop is exited. This could be corrected by rewriting the segment as

```
Count := 0;
WHILE NOT eof(<file name>) DO
  BEGIN
    Count := Count + 1;
    readln (<file name>), (A[Count])
  END;
```

4. Comparing array components to each other can lead to errors in using subscripts. Two common misuses are shown.
   a. Attempting to compare A[J] to A[J + 1]. If this does not stop at array length $-$ 1, then J + 1 will be out of range.
   b. Attempting to compare A[J $-$ 1] to A[J]. This presents the same problem at the beginning of an array. Remember, J $-$ 1 cannot have a value less than the initial index value.

5. Make sure the array index is correctly initialized. For example,

```
J := 0;
WHILE NOT eof(<file name>) DO
  BEGIN
    J := J + 1;
    readln (<file name>), (A[J])
  END;
```

Note that the first value is then read into A[1].

6. After using a sequential search, make sure you check to see if the value has been found. For example, if Num contains the value 3 and A is the array

```
1  4  5  10
```
       A

the search

```
Index := 1;
WHILE (Num <> A[Index]) AND (Index < Length) DO
  Index := Index + 1;
```

yields values

```
  3        4        10
Num     Index    A[Index]
```

Depending on program use, you should check for Num = A[Index] or use a Boolean flag to indicate if a match has been found.

■ **Summary**

Key Terms

abstract data type (ADT)	data abstraction	selection sort
array	index (subscript)	sequential (linear) search
binary search	index type	string data type
bubble sort	packed array	unpacked array
byte		word
component (element) of an array		

Keywords

ARRAY   PACKED   string

Key Concepts

- An array is a structured variable; a single declaration can reserve several variables.
- It is good practice to define array types in the **TYPE** declaration section and then declare a variable of that type; for example,

```
TYPE
   List10 = ARRAY [1..10] OF real;
VAR
   X : List10;
```

- Arrays can be visualized as lists; thus, the previous array could be envisioned as

```
X
        1
        2
        3
        4
        5
        6
        7
        8
        9
        10
```

- Each component of an array is a variable of the declared type and can be used the same as any other variable of that type.
- Loops can be used to read data into arrays; for example,

```
J := 0;
WHILE NOT eof(<file name>) AND (J < MaxLength) DO
   BEGIN
      J := J + 1;
      readln (<file name>), (List[J])
   END;
```

- Loops can be used to print data from arrays; for example, if Score is an array of 20 test scores, they can be printed by

```
FOR J := 1 TO 20 DO
   writeln (Score[J]);
```

- Manipulating components of an array is generally accomplished by using the index as a loop variable; for example, assuming the previous Score, to find the smallest value in the array we can use

```
Small := Score[1];
FOR J := 2 TO 20 DO
   IF Score[J] < Small THEN
      Small := Score[J];
```

- A selection sort is one method of sorting elements in an array from high to low or low to high; for example, if A is an array of length n, a low-to-high sort is

```
FOR J := 1 TO N - 1 DO
   BEGIN
      Index := J;
      FOR K := J + 1 TO N DO
         IF A[K] < A[Index] THEN
            Index := K;
```

```
          IF Index <> J THEN
            BEGIN
              Temp := A[Index];
              A[Index] := A[J];
              A[J] := Temp
            END  {  of exchange  }
     END;  {  of selection sort  }
```

- A bubble sort sorts an array by comparing consecutive elements in the array and exchanging them if they are out of order; several passes through the array are made until the list is sorted.
- When arrays are to be passed to subprograms, the type should be defined in the **TYPE** section; thus, we could have

```
TYPE
  List200 = ARRAY [1..200] OF real;

PROCEDURE Practice (X : List200);
```

- If the array being passed is a variable parameter, it should be declared accordingly; for example,

```
PROCEDURE GetData (VAR X : List200);
```

- Sorting arrays is conveniently done using procedures; such procedures facilitate program design.
- Data abstraction is the process of separating a conceptual definition of a data structure from its implementation details.
- An abstract data type (ADT) consists of a class of objects, a defined set of properties for these objects, and a set of operations for processing the objects.
- Packed arrays are used for character strings to reduce memory required for string storage and manipulation; a typical packed array declaration is

```
TYPE
  String20 - PACKED ARRAY [1..20] OF char;
VAR
  Name : String20;
```

- Character strings (packed arrays of characters) can be compared; this facilitates alphabetizing a list of names.
- Character strings can be printed using a single **write** or **writeln** statement; thus, if Name is a packed array of characters, it can be printed by

```
writeln (Name:30);
```

- Packed arrays of characters must still be read one character at a time.
- A single assignment statement can be used to assign a string to a packed array of the same length; for example,

```
Name := 'Smith John';
```

- A sequential search of a list consists of examining the first item in a list and then proceeding through the list in sequence until the desired value is found or the end of the list is reached; code for this search is

```
Index := 1;
WHILE (Num <> A[Index] AND (Index < Length) DO
  Index := Index + 1;
```

- A binary search of a list consists of deciding which half of the list contains the value in question and then which half of that half, and so on; code for this search is

```
Found := false;
WHILE NOT Found AND (First <= Last) DO
  BEGIN
    Mid := (First + Last) DIV 2;
```

```
          IF Num < A[Mid] THEN
            Last := Mid - 1
          ELSE IF Num > A[Mid] THEN
            First := Mid + 1
          ELSE
            Found := true
        END;
```

■ **Programming Problems and Projects**

1. Write a program to read an unknown number of integer test scores from an input file (assume at most 150 scores). Print out the original list of scores, the scores sorted from low to high, the scores sorted from high to low, the highest score, the lowest score, and the average score.

2. Write a program to help you balance your checkbook. The input consists of the beginning balance and then a sequence of transactions, each followed by a transaction code. Deposits are followed by a "D" and withdrawals are followed by a "W." The output should consist of a list of transactions, a running balance, an ending balance, the number of withdrawals, and the number of deposits. Include an appropriate message for overdrawn accounts.

3. Write a program to read a line of text as input. Print out the original line of text, the line of text in reverse order, and the number of vowels contained in the line.

4. Write a program that sorts data of type **real** as it is read from the input file. Do this by putting the first data item in the first component of an array and then inserting each subsequent number in the array in order from high to low. Print out the sorted array. Assume there are at most 25 numbers.

5. A palindrome is a word (or number) that is the same forwards and backwards. Write a program to read several lines of text as input. Inspect each word to see if it is a palindrome. The output should list all palindromes and a count of the number of palindromes in the message.

6. One of the problems faced by designers of word processors is that of printing text without separating a word at the end of a line. Write a program to read several lines of text as input. Then print the message with each line starting in column 10 and no line exceeding column 70. No word should be separated at the end of a line.

7. Your local state university has to raise funds for an art center. As a first step, they are going to approach 20 previously identified donors and ask for additional donations. Because the donors wish to remain anonymous, only the respective totals of their previous donations are listed in a data file. After they are contacted, the additional donations are listed at the end of the data file in the same order as the first 20 entries. Write a computer program to read the first 20 entries into one array and the second 20 entries into a second array. Compute the previous total donations and the new donations for the art center. Print the following:
   a. The list of previous donations
   b. The list of new donations
   c. An unsorted list of total donations

    d. A sorted list of total donations

    e. Total donations before the fund drive

    f. Total donations for the art center

    g. The maximum donation for the art center

8. Write a program that can be used as a text analyzer. Your program should be capable of reading an input file and keeping track of the frequency of occurrence of each letter of the alphabet. There should also be a count of all characters (including blanks) encountered that are not in the alphabet. Your output should be the data file printed line-by-line followed by a histogram reflecting the frequency of occurrence of each letter in the alphabet. For example, the following histogram indicates five occurrences of a, two of b, and three of c.

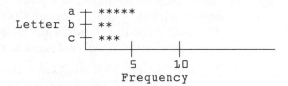

9. The Third Interdenominational Church has on file a list of all of its benefactors (a maximum of 20 names, each up to 30 characters) along with an unknown number of amounts that each has donated to the church. You have been asked to write a program that does the following:

    a. Print the name of each donor and the amount (in descending order) of any donations given by each.

    b. Print the total amounts in ascending order.

    c. Print the grand total of all donations.

    d. Print the largest single amount donated and the name of the benefactor who made this donation.

10. Read in a list of 50 integers from the data file NumberList. Place the even numbers into an array called Even, the odd numbers into an array called Odd, and the negatives into an array called Negative. Print all three arrays after all numbers have been read.

11. Read in 300 real numbers. Print the average of the numbers followed by all the numbers that are greater than the average.

12. Read in the names of five candidates in a class election and the number of votes received by each. Print the list of candidates, the number of votes they received, and the percentage of the total vote they received sorted into order from the winner to the person with the fewest votes. You may assume that all names are 20 characters in length.

13. In many sports events, contestants are rated by judges with an average score being determined by discarding the highest and lowest scores and averaging the remaining scores. Write a program in which eight scores are entered, computing the average score for the contestant.

14. Given a list of 20 test scores (integers), print the score that is nearest to the average.

15. The Game of Nim is played with three piles of stones. There are three stones in the first pile, five stones in the second, and eight stones in the third. Two players alternate taking as many stones as they like from any one pile. Play continues until someone is forced to take the

last stone. The person taking the last stone loses. Write a program which permits two people to play the game of Nim using an array to keep track of the number of stones in each pile.

16. There is an effective strategy that can virtually guarantee victory in the game of Nim. Devise a strategy and modify the program in Problem 15 so that the computer plays against a person. Your program should be virtually unbeatable if the proper strategy is developed.

17. The median of a set of numbers is the value in the middle of the set if the set is arranged in order. The mode is the number listed most often. Given a list of 21 numbers, print the median and mode of the list.

18. Rewrite Problem 17 to permit the use of any length list of numbers.

19. The standard deviation is a statistic frequently used in education measurement. Write a program that, given a list of test scores, will find and print the standard deviation of the numbers. The standard deviation formula can be found in most statistics books.

20. Revise Problem 19 so that after the standard deviation is printed, you can print a list of test scores that are more than one standard deviation below the average and a list of the scores more than one standard deviation above the average.

21. The z-score is defined as the score earned on a test divided by the standard deviation. Given a data file containing an unknown number of test scores (maximum of 100), print a list showing each test score (from highest to lowest) and the corresponding z-score.

22. Salespeople for the Wellsville Wholesale Company earn a commission based on their sales. The commission rates are as follows:

Sales	Commission
$0–1000	3%
1001–5000	4.5%
5001–10000	5.25%
over 10000	6%

In addition, any salesperson who sells above the average of all salespeople receive a $50 bonus, and the top salesperson receives an additional $75 bonus.

Given the names and amounts sold by each of 20 salespeople, write a program that prints a table showing the salesperson's name, the amount sold, the commission rate, and the total amount earned. The average sales should also be printed.

23. Ms. Alicia Citizen, your school's Student Government advisor, has come to you for help. She wants a program to total votes for the next Student Government election. Fifteen candidates will be in the election with five positions to be filled. Each person can vote for up to five candidates. The five highest vote getters will be the winners.

A data file called VoteList contains a list of candidates (by candidate number) voted for by each student. Any line of the file may contain up to five numbers, but if it contains more than five numbers, it is discarded as a void ballot. Write a program to read the file and print a list of the total votes received by each candidate. Also, print the five highest vote getters in order from highest to lowest vote totals.

24. The data file InstructorList contains a list of the instructors in your school along with the room number to which each is assigned. Write a program that, given the name of the instructor, does a linear search to find and print the room to which the instructor is assigned.

25. Rewrite Problem 24 so that when given a room number, the name of the instructor assigned to that room is found using a binary search. Assume the file is arranged in order of room numbers.

26. Write a language translation program that permits the entry of a word in English, with the corresponding word of another language being printed. The dictionary words can be stored in parallel arrays, with the English array being sorted into alphabetical order prior to the first entry of a word. Your program should first sort the dictionary words.

27. Elementary and middle school students are often given the task of converting numbers from one base to another. For example, 19 in base 10 is 103 in base 4 ($1 \times 4^2 + 0 \times 4^1 + 3 \times 4^0$). Conversely, 123 in base 4 is 27 in base 10. Write an interactive program that allows the user to choose from the following:

```
<1>  Convert from base 10 to base A
<2>  Convert from base A to base 10
<3>  Quit
```

If options 1 or 2 are chosen, the user should then enter the intended base and the number to be converted. A sample run of the program would produce the output:

```
This program allows you to convert between bases.  Which of the
following would you like?

     <1>  Convert from base 10 to base A
     <2>  Convert from base A to base 10
     <3>  Quit

Enter your choice and press <RETURN>.
?1

Enter the number in base 10 and press <RETURN>.
?237

Enter the new base and press <RETURN>.
?4

The number 237 in base 4 is:   3231

Press <RETURN> to continue

This program allows you to convert between bases. Which of the
following would you like?

     <1>  Convert from base 10 to base A
     <2>  Convert from base A to Base 10
     <3>  Quit

Enter your choice and press <RETURN>.
?2

What number would you like to have converted?
?2332
```

```
Converting to base 10, we get:

2 *     1 =            2
3 *     4 =           12
3 *    16 =           48
2 *    64 =          128
                    -----
The base 10 value is    190

Press <RETURN> to continue

This program allows you to convert between bases. Which of the
following would you like?

    <1>   Convert from base 10 to base A
    <2>   Convert from base A to base 10
    <3>   Quit

Enter your choice and press <RETURN>.
?3
```

28. One of the principles underlying the concept of data abstraction is that implementation details of data structures should be deferred to the lowest possible level. To illustrate, consider the high-level design to which we referred in our previous discussion of data abstraction. Our program required you to work with a list of names and an associated list of numbers (student names and test scores). The following first-level design was suggested:

    1. GetNames (⟨procedure here⟩);
    2. GetScores (⟨procedure here⟩);
    3. SortByName (⟨procedure here⟩);
    4. PrintNamesAndScores (⟨procedure here⟩);
    5. SortByScore (⟨procedure here⟩);

    Write complete documentation for each of these modules, including a description of all parameters and data structures required.

    Present your documentation to the class. Ask if your classmates have questions about the number or type of parameters, the data structures required, and/or the main tasks to be performed by each module.

29. Contact programmers at your university and/or some businesses and discuss with them the use of lists as a data type. Ask what kinds of programming problems require the use of a list, how the programmers handle data entry (list length), and what operations they perform on the list (search, sort, and so on).

    Give an oral report of your findings to the class.

30. Select a programming problem from this chapter that you have not yet worked. Construct a structure chart and write all documentary information necessary for the problem you have chosen. Do not write code. When you are finished, have a classmate read your documentation to see if precisely what is to be done is clear.

CHAPTER

Why don't we notice all these extra dimensions, if they are really there?

Stephen W. Hawking

Arrays of More Than One Dimension

Chapter 7 illustrated the significance and uses of one-dimensional arrays. There are, however, several kinds of problems that require arrays of more than one dimension. For example, if you want to work with a table that has both rows and columns, a one-dimensional array will not suffice. Other programming problems require the use of a list of names; these are not conveniently written as one-dimensional arrays. Such problems can be solved using arrays of more than one dimension.

■ 8.1
Two-Dimensional Arrays

Basic Idea and Notation

One-dimensional arrays are very useful when working with a row or column of numbers. However, suppose we want to work with data that are best represented in tabular form. For example, box scores in baseball are reported with one player name listed for each row and one statistic listed for each column. Another example is an instructor's grade book in which a student name is listed for each row and test and/or quiz scores are listed for each column. In both cases, a multiple reference is needed for a single data item.

Pascal accomplishes multiple reference by using *two-dimensional arrays*. In these arrays, the row subrange always precedes the column subrange and they are separated by commas. To illustrate, suppose we want to print the table

```
1    2    3    4
2    4    6    8
3    6    9    12
```

where we need to access both the row and column for a single data entry. This table could be produced by either of the following declarations.

369

1. `VAR`
    `Table : ARRAY [1..3, 1..4] OF integer;`
2. `TYPE`
    `Matrix = ARRAY [1..3, 1..4] OF integer;`
`VAR`
    `Table : Matrix;`

It is the index—[1 .. 3, 1 .. 4]—of each of these declarations that differs from one-dimensional arrays. These declarations reserve memory that can be visualized as three rows, each of which holds four variables. Thus, 12 variable locations have been reserved as shown.

Table

As a second illustration of the use of two-dimensional arrays, suppose we want to print the batting statistics for a softball team of 15 players. If the statistics consist of at bats (AB), hits (H), runs (R), and runs batted in (RBI) for each player, we naturally choose to work with a 15 × 4 table. Hence, a reasonable variable declaration is

```
TYPE
   Table15X4 = ARRAY [1..15, 1..4] OF integer;
VAR
   Stats : Table15X4;
```

The reserved memory area can be visualized as

Stats

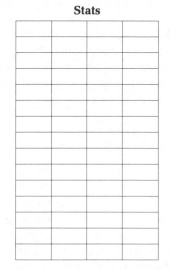

with 60 variable locations reserved.

Before proceeding further, let's examine another method of declaring two-dimensional arrays. Our 3 × 4 table could be thought of as three arrays each of length four, as follows:

Hence, we have a list of arrays and we could have declared the table by

```
TYPE
   Row = ARRAY [1..4] OF integer;
   Matrix = ARRAY [1..3] OF Row;
VAR
   Table : Matrix;
```

The softball statistics could be declared by

```
CONST
   NumberOfStats = 4;
   RosterSize = 15;
TYPE
   PlayerStats = ARRAY [1..NumberOfStats] OF integer;
   TeamTable = ARRAY [1..RosterSize] OF PlayerStats;
VAR
   Stats : TeamTable;
```

Semantic indices could be utilized by

```
TYPE
   Stat = (AtBat, Hits, Runs, RBI);
   StatChart = ARRAY [1..RosterSize, Stat] OF integer;
VAR
   Player : StatChart;
```

In this case, a typical entry is

```
Player[5, Hits] := 2;
```

In general, a two-dimensional array can be defined by

ARRAY [⟨row index⟩, ⟨column index⟩] **OF** ⟨element type⟩;

or

TYPE
   RowType = **ARRAY** [⟨column index⟩] **OF** ⟨element type⟩;
   Matrix = **ARRAY** [⟨row index⟩] **OF** RowType;

Whichever method of declaration is used, the problem now becomes one of accessing individual components of the two-dimensional array. For example, in the table

```
1     2     3     4
2     4     6     8
3     6     9    12
```

the "8" is in row two and column four. Note that both the row and column position of an element must be indicated. Therefore, in order to put an "8" in this position, we use an assignment statement such as

```
Table[2,4] := 8;
```

This assignment statement would be used for either of the declaration forms mentioned earlier.

Next let's assign the values just given to the appropriate variables in Table by 12 assignment statements as follows:

```
Table[1,1] := 1;
Table[1,2] := 2;
Table[1,3] := 3;
Table[1,4] := 4;
Table[2,1] := 2;
```

STYLE TIP
■ ■ ■ ■ ■ ■ ■ ■ ■ ■ ■

When working with charts or tables of a fixed grid size (say 15 × 4), descriptive identifiers could be

```
Chart15X4
```

or

```
Table15X4
```

If the number of rows and columns vary for different runs of the program (for example, the number of players on a team could vary from year to year), you could define a type by

```
CONST
  NumRows = 15;
  NumColumns = 4;
TYPE
  RowRange = 1..NumRows;
  ColumnRange = 1..NumColumns;
  Table = ARRAY [RowRange, ColumnRange] OF integer;
VAR
  Stats : Table;
```

```
Table[2,2] := 4;
Table[2,3] := 6;
Table[2,4] := 8;
Table[3,1] := 3;
Table[3,2] := 6;
Table[3,3] := 9;
Table[3,4] := 12;
```

As you can see, this is extremely tedious. Instead, we can note the relationship between the indices and the assigned values and make the row index Row and the column index Column. The values to be assigned are then Row * Column and we can use nested loops to perform these assignments as follows:

```
FOR Row := 1 TO 3 DO
  FOR Column := 1 TO 4 DO
    Table[Row, Column] := Row * Column;
```

Since two-dimensional arrays frequently require working with nested loops, let us examine more closely what this segment of code does. When Row := 1, the loop

```
FOR Column := 1 TO 4 DO
  Table[1, Column] := 1 * Column;
```

is executed. This performs the four assignments

```
Table[1,1] := 1 * 1;
Table[1,2] := 1 * 2;
Table[1,3] := 1 * 3;
Table[1,4] := 1 * 4;
```

and we have the memory area

Table

1	2	3	4

Similar results hold for Row := 2 and Row := 3 and we produce a two-dimensional array that can be visualized as

Table

1	2	3	4
2	4	6	8
3	6	9	12

The following examples will help you learn to work with and understand the notation for two-dimensional arrays.

■ **EXAMPLE 8.1**

Assume the declaration

```
TYPE
  Table5X4 = ARRAY [1..5, 1..4] OF integer;
VAR
  Table : Table5X4;
```

has been made and consider the segment of code

```
FOR Row := 1 TO 5 DO
  FOR Column := 1 TO 4 DO
    Table[Row, Column] := Row DIV Column;
```

When Row := 1, the loop

```
FOR Column := 1 TO 4 DO
  Table[1, Column] := 1 DIV Column;
```

is executed. This causes the assignment statements

```
Table[1,1] := 1 DIV 1;
Table[1,2] := 1 DIV 2;
Table[1,3] := 1 DIV 3;
Table[1,4] := 1 DIV 4;
```

The contents of the memory area after that first pass through the loop are

Table

1	0	0	0

When Row := 2, the assignments are

```
Table[2,1] := 2 DIV 1;
Table[2,2] := 2 DIV 2;
Table[2,3] := 2 DIV 3;
Table[2,4] := 2 DIV 4;
```

Table now has values as follows:

Table

1	0	0	0
2	1	0	0

The contents of Table after the entire outside loop has been executed are

Table

1	0	0	0
2	1	0	0
3	1	1	0
4	2	1	1
5	2	1	1

■

■ **EXAMPLE 8.2**

Declare a two-dimensional array and write a segment of code to produce the memory area and contents depicted as follows:

2	3	4	5	6	7	8
3	4	5	6	7	8	9
4	5	6	7	8	9	10
5	6	7	8	9	10	11

An appropriate definition is

```
TYPE
   Table4X7 = ARRAY [1..4, 1..7] OF integer;
```

or

```
TYPE
   Table4X7 = ARRAY [1..4] OF
               ARRAY [1..7] OF integer;
VAR
   Table : Table4X7;
```

and a segment of code to produce the desired contents is

```
FOR Row := 1 TO 4 DO
   FOR Column := 1 TO 7 DO
      Table[Row, Column] := Row + Column;
```

■   ■

Reading and Writing

Most problems using two-dimensional arrays require reading data from an input file into the array and writing values from the array to create some tabular form of output. For example, suppose we have our two-dimensional array for softball statistics.

```
TYPE
   Table15X4 = ARRAY [1..15, 1..4] OF integer;
VAR
   Stats : Table15X4;
```

If the data file consists of 15 lines and each line contains statistics for one player as follows,

```
AB  H  R  RBI
┌──┬──┬──┬──┐
│4 │2 │1 │1 │█   (player #1)
└──┴──┴──┴──┘

┌──┬──┬──┬──┐
│3 │1 │0 │1 │█   (player #2)
└──┴──┴──┴──┘
         .        .
         .        .
         .        .
┌──┬──┬──┬──┐
│0 │0 │0 │0 │█   (player #15)
└──┴──┴──┴──┘
```

we can get the data from the file by reading it one line at a time for 15 lines. This is done using nested loops as follows:

```
FOR Row := 1 TO 15 DO
  BEGIN
    FOR Column := 1 TO 4 DO
      read (Stats[Row, Column]);
    readln
  END;
```

When Row := 1, the loop

```
FOR Column := 1 TO 4 DO
  read (Stats[Row, Column]);
```

reads the first line of data. In a similar manner, as Row assumes the values 2 through 15, the lines 2 through 15 would be read. After reading the data into an array, some operations and/or updating will be performed and we will output the data in tabular form. For example, suppose we want to print the softball statistics in the 15 × 4 table using only three spaces for each column. We note the following:

1. Three spaces per column can be controlled by formatting the output.
2. One line of output can be generated by a **FOR** loop containing a **write** statement; for example,

```
FOR Column := 1 TO 4 DO
  write (Stats[Row, Column]:3);
```

3. The output buffer will be dumped to the printer after each **write** loop by using **writeln**.
4. We do this for 15 lines by another loop

```
FOR Row := 1 TO 15 DO
  BEGIN
    FOR Column := 1 TO 4 DO
      write (Stats[Row, Column]:3);
    writeln
  END;
```

This last segment of code produces the desired output.

In actual practice, we will also be concerned with headings for our tables and controlling where the data occur on the page. For example, suppose we want to identify the columns of softball statistics as AB, H, R, and RBI; underline the headings; and start the output (AB) in column 25. The following segment of code accomplishes our objectives.

```
writeln (Skip:24,'AB H  R RBI');
writeln (Skip:24,'-----------');
writeln;
```

```
FOR Row := 1 TO 15 DO
  BEGIN
    write (Skip:22);  {  Set the left margin  }
    FOR Column := 1 TO 4 DO
      write (Stats[Row, Column]:3);
    writeln  {  Advance to next line  }
  END;
```

The data file used earlier for our ballplayers causes an output of

```
AB H  R RBI
----------

4  2  1  1
3  1  0  0
   .
   .
   .
0  0  0  0
```

Manipulating Two-Dimensional Array Components

Often we want to work with some but not all of the components of an array. For example, suppose we have a two-dimensional array of test scores for students in a class. If there are 20 students with five scores each, an appropriate two-dimensional array could be declared as

```
TYPE
  Table20X5 = ARRAY [1..20, 1..5] OF integer;
VAR
  Score : Table20X5;
```

After scores have been read into the array Score, we can envision the memory area as follows:

Score

98	86	100	76	95	(student #1)
72	68	65	74	81	(student #2)
85	81	91	84	83	(student #3)
					.
					.
					.
					.
					.
					.
					.
					.
					.
					.
					.
					.
					.
					.
76	81	72	87	80	(student #20)

When printing a table with test scores, one would normally compute several items, including total points for each student, percentage grade for each student, and average score for each test. Let's examine what is required for each of these computations. First, to get the total points for each student, we declare a one-dimensional array to store these values, so assume the declaration

```
TYPE
   List20 = ARRAY [1..20] OF integer;
VAR
   TotalPoints : List20;
```

Since the first student's test scores are in the first row, we could write

```
TotalPoints[1] := Score[1,1] + Score[1,2] +
                  Score[1,3] + Score[1,4] +
                  Score[1,5];
```

To compute this total for each student, we could use the loop

```
FOR Student := 1 TO 20 DO
   TotalPoints[Student] := Score[Student, 1] +
                           Score[Student, 2] +
                           Score[Student, 3] +
                           Score[Student, 4] +
                           Score[Student, 5];
```

and this would produce the array of totals

TotalPoints

455	TotalPoints[1]
360	TotalPoints[2]
424	TotalPoints[3]
.	.
.	.
.	.
396	TotalPoints[20]

If the two-dimensional array has several columns, we can use a loop to sum an array of numbers. We can, for instance, write a loop to sum the five test scores for the first student in our table.

```
TotalPoints[1] := 0;
FOR Test := 1 TO 5 DO
   TotalPoints[1] := TotalPoints[1] + Score[1, Test];
```

To do this for each student, we use a second loop.

```
FOR Student := 1 TO 20 DO
   BEGIN
      TotalPoints[Student] := 0;
      FOR Test := 1 TO 5 DO
         TotalPoints[Student] := TotalPoints[Student] +
                                 Score[Student, Test]
   END;
```

The second task in our problem is to compute the percentage grade for each student. If we want to save these percentages, we can declare an array as follows:

```
TYPE
   Column20 = ARRAY [1..20] OF real;
VAR
   Percent : Column20;
```

and include a segment of code

```
FOR Student := 1 TO 20 DO
   Percent[Student] := TotalPoints[Student] / 5;
```

The third task is to find the average score for each test. To find these numbers, we need to add all 20 scores for each test and divide the respective total by 20. We first have to find the sum of each column and we need to declare an array in which to store the averages. The declaration could be

```
TYPE
   List5 = Array [1..5] OF real;
VAR
   TestAv: List5;
```

We now need a loop to find the total of each column. Assuming we have an integer variable Sum declared, we can sum column one by

```
Sum := 0;
FOR Student := 1 TO 20 DO
   Sum := Sum + Score[Student, 1];
```

TestAv[1] can now be found by

```
TestAv[1] := Sum / 20;
```

To do this for each column, we use a second loop as follows:

```
FOR Test := 1 TO 5 DO              {  Test is the column subscript  }
   BEGIN
      Sum := 0;
      FOR Student := 1 TO 20 DO    {  Student is the row subscript  }
         Sum := Sum + Score[Student, Test];
      TestAv[Test] := Sum / 20
   END;
```

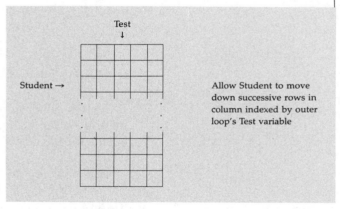

Allow Student to move down successive rows in column indexed by outer loop's Test variable

As a concluding example of manipulating elements of two-dimensional arrays, consider the following.

■ **EXAMPLE 8.3**

Assume we have the declarations

```
CONST
   NumRows = 20;
   NumColumns = 50;
TYPE
   TableSize = ARRAY [1..NumRows,
                      1..NumColumns] OF integer;
   List = ARRAY [1..NumRows] OF integer;
VAR
   Table : TableSize;
   Max : List;
```

and values have been read into the two-dimensional array from an input file. Let's write a segment of code to find the maximum value in each row and then store this value in the array Max. To find the maximum of row one, we can write

```
Max[1] := Table[1,1];
FOR Column := 2 TO NumColumns DO
  IF Table[1, Column] > Max[1] THEN
    Max[1] := Table[1, Column];
```

To do this for each of the rows, we use a second loop as follows:

```
FOR Row := 1 TO NumRows DO
  BEGIN
    Max[Row] := Table[Row, 1];
    FOR Column := 2 TO NumColumns DO
      IF Table[Row, Column] > Max[Row] THEN
        Max[Row] := Table[Row, Column]
  END;
```

Procedures and Two-Dimensional Arrays

When we start writing programs with two-dimensional arrays, we will use procedures as before to maintain the top-down design philosophy. As with one-dimensional arrays, there are three relatively standard uses of procedures in most problems: to get the data, to manipulate the data, and to display the data.

When using procedures with data that require an array as a data structure, the array type must be defined in the **TYPE** section. The actual parameters and formal parameters can then be of the defined array type. As with one-dimensional arrays, we pass two-dimensional arrays by reference to conserve memory allocation.

■ **EXAMPLE 8.4**

Western Jeans, Inc. wants a program to help them keep track of their inventory of jeans. The jeans are coded by waist size and inseam. The waist sizes are the integer values from 24 to 46 and the inseams are the integer values from 26 to 40. Thus, there are 23 waist sizes and 15 inseams for each waist size. The first 23 lines of the data file contain the starting inventory. Each line corresponds to a waist size and contains 15 integers, one for each inseam. The next 23 lines of the data file contain the sales information for a day. Let's write a program to find and print the closing inventory.

A first-level pseudocode development for this program is

1. Get starting inventory
2. Get new sales
3. Update inventory
4. Print heading
5. Print closing inventory

Each of these steps uses a procedure.

Since there are 23 waist sizes and 15 inseams, we use definitions as follows:

```
CONST
  FirstWaist = 24;
  LastWaist = 46;
  FirstInseam = 26;
  LastInseam = 40;
```

```
TYPE
  WaistSizes = FirstWaist..LastWaist;
  InseamSizes = FirstInseam..LastInseam;
  Table = ARRAY [WaistSizes, InseamSizes] OF integer;
```

We use variables declared as follows:

```
VAR
  Inventory : Table;
  Sales : Table;
```

Assuming variables have been declared as needed, let's now write a procedure to get the starting inventory.

```
PROCEDURE GetData (VAR Matrix : Table);
  VAR
    Row, Column : integer;
  BEGIN
    FOR Row := FirstWaist TO LastWaist DO
      BEGIN
        FOR Column := FirstInseam TO LastInseam DO
          read (Data, Matrix[Row, Column]);
        readln (Data)
      END
  END;
```

Note that **VAR** is used because the new data will be needed later in the program. This procedure will be called from the main program by

```
GetData (Inventory);
```

The next task is to get the sales for a day. Since this merely requires reading the next 23 lines from the data file, we do not need to write a new procedure. We call GetData again by

```
GetData (Sales);
```

We now need a procedure to update the starting inventory. This updating can be accomplished by sending both two-dimensional arrays to a procedure and then finding the respective differences of components.

```
PROCEDURE Update (VAR Inventory : Table;
                  VAR Sales : Table);
  VAR
    Row, Column : integer;
  BEGIN
    FOR Row := FirstWaist TO LastWaist DO
      FOR Column := FirstInseam TO LastInseam DO
        Inventory[Row, Column] := Inventory[Row, Column] -
                                  Sales[Row, Column]
  END;
```

This is called by the statement

```
Update (Inventory, Sales);
```

The procedure for the heading is as before, so we need not write it here. Let's assume the arrays have been assigned the necessary values. The output procedure will be

```
PROCEDURE PrintData (VAR Inventory : Table);
  CONST
    Mark = ' !';
  VAR
    Row, Column : integer;
```

```
          BEGIN
            FOR Row := FirstWaist TO LastWaist DO
              BEGIN
                write (Row:6, Mark);
                FOR Column := FirstInseam TO LastInseam DO
                  write (Inventory[Row, Column]:4);
                writeln;
                writeln (Mark:6)
              END {  of printing one row  }
          END;
```

This procedure could be called from the main program by

```
    PrintData (Inventory);
```

Once these procedures have been written, the main program becomes

```
    BEGIN
      reset (Data);
      GetData (Inventory);
      GetData (Sales);
      Update (Inventory, Sales);
      PrintHeading;
      PrintData (Inventory)
    END. {  of main program  }
```

The Next Decade: What the Future Holds

Daniel E. Kinnaman has addressed the issue of technology-literate classrooms in the 1990s. He visited several top research and development programs in search of the most promising projects, products, and ideas for technology's future role in the classroom. A partial list of projects, project directors, and summary comments regarding programs follows.

The Technical Education Research Centers (TERC) and Dr. Robert Tinker. They are developing programs designed to involve students and teachers from around the world in conducting global ecology research with full-time scientists.

The Massachusetts Institute of Technology and Dr. Seymour Papert. They are working on a project involving the development of robotic kits that allow children to build computer intelligence into a robot.

Harvard's Educational Technology Center (ETC) and Dr. Judah Schwartz. They are working on software whose purpose is to teach children how to think. One current project is a series called *Visualizing Algebra*.

Institute for Research on Learning (IRL). They are working on "Dynagrams," a project that allows students to interact with dynamic diagrams on a computer screen.

In summarizing what these and other educational leaders had to say, Kinneman stated:

Many of these thinkers hold similar perspectives on the uses of technology in schools, perspectives that strongly influence their development efforts. These common beliefs include the following:

All of education, from the physical organization of schools to instructional methods and assessment, needs to be open to review and change.

Inquiry-centered, process-oriented learning environments in which students are active participants on an academic adventure are heavily favored over the traditional classroom setting.

There is a decided emphasis, at least presently, on improving math and science education.

In the 1990s, schools will look to technology more than ever before for educational solutions.

Although computer power will continue to increase at astounding rates, technology is still just a vehicle. It isn't a destination. It can be a critical ingredient of successful school experience for children, but its usefulness is dependent upon the context in which it is used.

Exercises 8.1

1. Define a two-dimensional array type for each of the following using both the **ARRAY** [. . , . .] and **ARRAY** [. .] **OF ARRAY** [. .] forms.

   a. A table with real number entries that shows the prices for four different drugs charged by five drug stores.

   b. A table with character entries that shows the grades earned by 20 students in six courses.

   c. A table with integer entries that shows the 12 quiz scores earned by 30 students in a class.

2. Write a test program to read integers into a 3 × 5 array and then print out the array components together with each row sum and each column sum.

3. For each of the following declarations, sketch what is reserved in memory. In each case, state how many variables are available to the programmer.

   a. TYPE
   ```
        ShippingCostTable = ARRAY [1..10] OF
                                 ARRAY [1..4] OF real;
        GradeBookTable = ARRAY [1..35, 1..6] OF integer;
   VAR
        ShippingCost : ShippingCostTable;
        GradeBook : GradeBookTable;
   ```

   b. TYPE
   ```
        Matrix = ARRAY [1..3, 2..6] OF integer;
   VAR
        A : Matrix;
   ```

   c. TYPE
   ```
        Weekdays = (Mon, Tues, Wed, Thur, Fri);
        Chores = (Wash, Iron, Clean, Mow, Sweep);
        ScheduleTable = ARRAY [Weekdays, Chores] OF boolean;
   VAR
        Schedule : ScheduleTable;
   ```

   d. TYPE
   ```
        Questions = 1..50;
        Answers = 1..5;
        Table = ARRAY [Questions, Answers] OF char;
   VAR
        AnswerSheet : Table;
   ```

4. Assume the array A has been declared as
   ```
   TYPE
     Table3X5 = ARRAY [1..3, 1..5] OF integer;
   VAR
     A : Table3X5;
   ```
   Indicate the array contents produced by each of the following:

   a.
   ```
   FOR J := 1 TO 3 DO
       FOR K := 1 TO 5 DO
           A[J,K] := J - K;
   ```
   c.
   ```
   FOR K := 1 TO 5 DO
       FOR J := 1 TO 3 DO
           A[J,K] := J;
   ```
   b.
   ```
   FOR J := 1 TO 3 DO
       FOR K := 1 TO 5 DO
           A[J,K] := J;
   ```
   d.
   ```
   FOR J := 3 DOWNTO 1 DO
       FOR K := 1 TO 5 DO
           A[J,K] := J MOD K;
   ```

5. Let the two-dimensional array A be declared by
   ```
   TYPE
     Table3X6 = ARRAY [1..3, 1..6] OF integer;
   VAR
     A : Table3X6;
   ```

Write nested loops that causes the following values to be stored in A:

a.

A

3	4	5	6	7	8
5	6	7	8	9	10
7	8	9	10	11	12

b.

A

0	0	0	0	0	0
0	0	0	0	0	0
0	0	0	0	0	0

c.

A

2	2	2	2	2	2
4	4	4	4	4	4
6	6	6	6	6	6

6. Declare a two-dimensional array and write a segment of code that reads the following input file into the array.

```
13.2 15.1 10.3 8.2 43.6 ▮
```

```
37.2 25.6 34.1 17.0 15.2 ▮
```

7. Suppose an input file contains 50 lines of data and the first 20 spaces of each line are reserved for a customer's name. The rest of the line contains other information. Declare a two-dimensional array to hold the names and write a segment of code to read the names into the array. A sample line of input is

```
Smith John O          268-14-1801 ▮
```
↑
position 21

8. Assume the declaration

```
TYPE
   Table4X5 = ARRAY [1..4, 1..5] OF real;
VAR
   Table : Table4X5;
```

has been made and values have been read into Table as follows:

Table

−2.0	3.0	0.0	8.0	10.0
0.0	−4.0	3.0	1.0	2.0
1.0	2.0	3.0	8.0	−6.0
−4.0	1.0	4.0	6.0	82.0

Indicate what the components of Table would be after each of the following segments of code is executed.

```
a. FOR J := 1 TO 4 DO
     FOR K := 1 TO 5 DO
       IF J MOD K = 0 THEN
         A[J,K] := 0.0
       ELSE
         A[J,K] := -1.0;
b. FOR J := 1 TO 4 DO
     IF A[J,1] <> 0.0 THEN
       FOR K := 1 TO 5 DO
         A[J,K] := A[J,K] / A[J,1];
```

```
c. FOR K := 1 TO 5 DO
     IF A[1,K] = 0.0 THEN
       FOR J := 1 TO 4 DO
         A[J,K] := 0.0;
```

9. Let the two-dimensional array Table be declared as in Exercise 8. Declare additional arrays as needed and write segments of code for each of the following:

   a. Find and save the minimum of each row.

   b. Find and save the maximum of each column.

   c. Find the total of all the components.

10. Example 8.4 illustrates the use of procedures with two-dimensional arrays. For actual use, you would also need a list indicating what to order to maintain the inventory. Write a procedure (assuming all declarations have been made) to print a table indicating which sizes of jeans have a supply fewer than four. Do this by putting an '*' in the cell if the supply is low or a ' ' if the supply is adequate.

11. Suppose you want to work with a table that has three rows and eight columns of integers.

    a. Declare an appropriate two-dimensional array that can be used with procedures.

    b. Write a procedure to replace all negative numbers with zero.

    c. Show what is needed to call this procedure from the main program.

12. If A and B are matrices of size $m \times n$, their sum A + B is defined by A + B = $[a+b]_{ij}$, where a and b are corresponding components in A and B. Write a program to

    a. Read values into two matrices of size $m \times n$.

    b. Compute the sum.

    c. Print out the matrices together with the sum.

13. If A and B are matrices of sizes $m \times n$ and $n \times p$, their product is defined to be the $m \times p$ matrix AB where

$$AB = [c_{ik}], c_{ik} = \sum_{j=1}^{n} a_{ij}b_{jk}$$

Write a program that will

a. Read values into two matrices whose product is defined.

b. Compute their product.

c. Print out the matrices together with their product.

■ ■ ■ ■

■ 8.2
Arrays of String Variables

T

Basic Idea and Notation

Recall from Section 7.5 that we defined string variables as packed arrays of characters. At that time, we learned that strings of the same length can be compared and strings can be printed using a single **write** or **writeln** command. A typical declaration for a name 20 characters in length is

```
TYPE
  String20 = PACKED ARRAY [1..20] OF char;
```

```
VAR
  Name : String20;
```

Thus, Name could be envisioned as

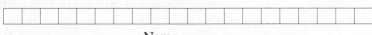

Name

It is a natural extension to next consider the problem of working with an array of strings. For example, if we need a data structure for 50 names, this can be declared by

```
TYPE
  String20 = PACKED ARRAY [1..20] OF char;
  NameList = ARRAY [1..50] OF String20;
VAR
  Name : NameList;
```

Name can then be envisioned as

Name

	Name[1]
	Name[2]
	Name[3]
. .	.
.	.
.	.
	Name[50]

where each component of Name is a packed array.

Alphabetizing a List of Names

One standard problem faced by programmers is that of alphabetizing a list of names. For example, programs that work with class lists, bank statements, magazine subscriptions, names in a telephone book, credit card customers, and so on require alphabetizing. As indicated, Pascal provides the facility for using an array of packed arrays as a data structure for such lists.

Problems that require alphabetizing names contain at least three main tasks: get the data, alphabetize the list, and print the list. Prior to writing procedures for each of these tasks, let's consider some associated problems. When getting the data, you will usually encounter one of two formats. First, data may be entered with a constant field width for each name. Each name would typically be followed by some additional data item. Thus, if each name uses 20 character positions and position 21 contains the start of numeric data, the data file might be

Smith John 18	Jones Harriet 19
↑	↑
position 21	position 21

In this case, the name can be read into the appropriate component by a fixed loop. The first name can be accessed by

```
FOR K := 1 TO 20 DO
  read (Data, Name[1,K]);
```

and the second name by

```
FOR K := 1 TO 20 DO
  read (Data, Name[2,K]);
```

A second form for entering data is to use some symbol to indicate the end of a name. When the data are in this form, you must be able to recognize the symbol and fill the remaining positions with blanks. Thus, the data file could be

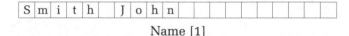

In this case, the first name can be obtained by

```
K := 0;
read (Data, Ch);
WHILE (Ch <> '*') AND (K < 20) DO
  BEGIN
    K := K + 1;
    Name[1,K] := Ch;
    read (Data, Ch)
  END;
FOR J := K + 1 TO 20 DO
  Name[1,J] := ' ';
```

This process will fill the remaining positions in the name with blanks. Thus, Name[1] would be

| S | m | i | t | h | | J | o | h | n | | | | | | | | | | |

Name [1]

The second name in the data file would be similarly read. The only change is from Name[1,K] to Name[2,K].

The next problem in getting data is determining how many lines are available. If the number of lines is known, you can use a **FOR** loop. More realistically, however, there will be an unknown number of lines and you will need the **eof** condition in a variable control loop and a counter to determine the number of names. To illustrate, assume there are an unknown number of data lines where each line contains a name in the first 20 positions. If the declaration section of a program is

```
TYPE
  String20 = PACKED ARRAY [1..20] OF char;
  NameList = ARRAY [1..50] OF String20;
VAR
  Name: NameList;
  Length : integer;
  Data : text;
```

a procedure to get the data is

```
PROCEDURE GetData (VAR Name : NameList;
                   VAR Length : integer);
  VAR
    K : integer;
  BEGIN
    reset (Data);
    Length := 0;
    WHILE NOT eof(Data) AND (Length < 50) DO
      BEGIN
        Length := Length + 1                 {  Increment counter    }
        FOR K := 1 TO 20 DO
          read (Data, Name[Length, K]);      {  Get a name           }
        readln (Data)                        {  Advance the pointer  }
      END;
```

```
      IF NOT eof(Data) THEN
        writeln ('There are more data.')
END;   {  of PROCEDURE GetData  }
```

This procedure is called from the main program by

```
GetData (Name, Length);
```

Let's now consider the problem of alphabetizing a list of names. If we assume the same data structure we've just seen and let Length represent the number of names, a procedure to sort the list alphabetically (using the selection sort discussed in Section 7.3) is

```
PROCEDURE SelectionSort (VAR Name : NameList;
                             Length : integer);
  VAR
    J, K, Index : integer;
    Temp : String20;
  BEGIN
    FOR J := 1 TO Length - 1 DO
      BEGIN
        Index := J;
        FOR K := J + 1 TO Length DO
          IF Name[K] < Name[Index] THEN
            Index := K;
        IF Index <> J THEN
          BEGIN
            Temp := Name[Index];
            Name[Index] := Name[J];
            Name[J] := Temp
          END { of exchange }
      END { of sort }
END; { of PROCEDURE SelectionSort }
```

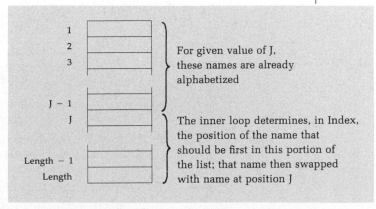

This procedure could be called from the main program by

```
SelectionSort (Name, Length);
```

Once the list of names has been sorted, you usually want to print the sorted list. A procedure to do this is

```
PROCEDURE PrintData (VAR Name : NameList;
                         Length : integer);
  VAR
    J : integer;
  BEGIN
    FOR J := 1 TO Length DO
      writeln (Name[J]:50)
END; { of PROCEDURE PrintData }
```

This could be called from the main program by

```
        PrintData (Name, Length);
```

We can now use the procedures in a simple program that gets the names, sorts them, and prints them as follows:

```
BEGIN  {  Main program  }
  GetData (Name, Length);
  SelectionSort (Name, Length);
  PrintData (Name, Length)
END.  {  of main program  }
```

Exercises 8.2

1. Assume the declarations and definitions

```
TYPE
  String20 = PACKED ARRAY [1..20] OF char;
  StateList = ARRAY [1..50] OF String20;
VAR
  State : StateList;
```

have been made and an alphabetical listing of the 50 states of the United States of America is contained in the data structure State. Furthermore, assume that each state name begins in position one of each component. Indicate the output for each of the following:

a.
```
FOR J := 1 TO 50 DO
  IF State[J,1] = 'O' THEN
    writeln (State[J]:35);
```

b.
```
FOR J := 50 DOWNTO 1 DO
  IF J MOD 5 = 0 THEN
    writeln (State[J]:35);
```

c.
```
FOR J := 1 TO 50 DO
  writeln (State[J,1]:10, State[J,2]);
```

d.
```
CountA := 0;
FOR J := 1 TO 50 DO
  FOR K := 1 TO 20 DO
    IF State[J,K] = 'A' THEN
      CountA := CountA + 1;
writeln (CountA:20);
```

2. Assume you have a sorted list of names. Write a fragment of code to inspect the list of names and print the full name of each Smith on the list.

3. The procedure in this section to get names from a data file assumed the names in the data file were of fixed length and that there were an unknown number of data lines. Modify the procedure for each of the following situations.

   a. Variable length names followed by an '*' and a known number of data lines

   b. Variable length names followed by an '*' and an unknown number of data lines

   c. Fixed length names (20 characters) and a known number of data lines

   d. Names are entered in the form first name, space, last name and you want to sort by last name.

4. If each line of a data file contains a name followed by an age, for example,

the data will be put into two arrays, one for the names and one for the ages. Show how the sorting procedure can be modified so that the array of ages will keep the same order as the array of names.

5. Write a complete program to read ten names from an input file (where each line contains one name of 20 characters), sort the names in reverse alphabetical order, and print the sorted list.

■ ■ ■ ■

■ **8.3**
Parallel Arrays

There are many practical situations in which more than one type of array is required to handle the data. For example, you may wish to keep a record of names of people and their donations to a charitable organization. You could accomplish this by using a packed array of names and an equal length array of donations—of **real** or **integer**. Programs for these situations can use *parallel arrays,* a term used for arrays of the same length, where elements in each array must be in the same relative positions. These arrays have the same index type. However, most uses of parallel arrays have the added condition of different data types for the array components. Otherwise, a two-dimensional array would suffice. Generally, situations that call for two or more arrays of the same length but of different data types are situations in which parallel arrays can be used. Later we will see that this situation can also be handled as a single array of records.

Using Parallel Arrays

Let's look at a typical problem that requires working with both a list of names and a list of numbers. Suppose the input file consists of 30 lines and each line contains a name in the first 20 spaces and an integer starting in space 21 that is the amount of a donation. We are to read all data into appropriate arrays, alphabetize the names, print the alphabetized list with the amount of each donation, and find the total of all donations.

This problem can be solved using parallel arrays for the list of names and the list of donations. Appropriate declarations are

```
CONST
  NumberOfDonors = 30;
TYPE
  String20 = PACKED ARRAY [1..20] OF char;
  IndexType = 1..NumberOfDonors;
  NameList = ARRAY [IndexType] OF String20;
  AmountList = ARRAY [IndexType] OF integer;
VAR
  Donor : NameList;
  Amount : AmountList;
```

A procedure to read the data from an input file is

```
PROCEDURE GetData (VAR Donor : NameList;
                        VAR Amount : AmountList);
  VAR
    J, K : integer;
  BEGIN
    FOR J := 1 TO NumberOfDonors DO
      BEGIN
        FOR K := 1 TO 20 DO
          read (Data, Donor[J,K]);
        readln (Data, Amount[J])
      END
  END;  { of PROCEDURE GetData  }
```

STYLE TIP

Since parallel arrays use the same index type, definitions could have the form

```
CONST
  NumberOfDonors = 30;
TYPE
  String20 = PACKED ARRAY [1..20] OF char;
  IndexType = 1..NumberOfDonors;
  NameList = ARRAY [IndexType] OF String20;
  AmountList = ARRAY [IndexType] OF integer;
```

This procedure could be called by

```
GetData (Donor, Amount);
```

After this procedure has been called from the main program, the parallel arrays could be envisioned as

	Donor	Amount	
Donor[1]	Smith John	100	Amount[1]
Donor[2]	Jones Jerry	250	Amount[2]
.	.	.	
.	.	.	
.	.	.	
Donor[30]	Generous George	525	Amount[30]

The next task is to alphabetize the names. However, we must be careful to keep the amount donated with the name of the donor. This can be accomplished by passing both the list of names and the list of donations to the sorting procedure and modifying the code to include exchanging the amount of donation whenever the names are exchanged. Since NumberOfDonors is defined in the constant section, a Length argument is not needed. Using the procedure heading

```
PROCEDURE Sort (VAR Donor : NameList;
                VAR Amount : AmountList);
```

the code for sorting would be changed in order to interchange both a name and an amount. Thus,

```
Temp := Donor[Index];
Donor[Index] := Donor[J];
Donor[J] := Temp;
```

would become

```
Temp := Donor[Index];
TempAmount := Amount[Index];
Donor[Index] := Donor[J];
Amount[Index] := Amount[J];
Donor[J] := Temp;
Amount[J] := TempAmount;
```

The procedure for sorting the list of names and rearranging the list of donations accordingly is called by

```
Sort (Donor, Amount);
```

Our next task is to print the alphabetized list together with the donations. If Donor and Amount have been sorted appropriately, we can use the following procedure to produce the desired output.

Computer Ethics: Worms

In *The Shockwave Rider* (1975), J. Brunner developed the notion of an omnipotent "tapeworm" program running loose through a network of computers—an idea that then seemed rather disturbing, but which was then well beyond our capabilities. The basic model, however, was a very provocative one: a program or a computation that can move from machine to machine, harnessing resources as needed, and replicating itself when necessary.

On November 2, 1988, Cornell computer science graduate student Robert Morris released a worm program into the ARPANET. Over an eight-hour period it invaded between 2,500 and 3,000 VAX and Sun computers running the Berkeley UNIX operating system. The worm program disabled virtually all of the computers by replicating rampantly and clogging them with many copies. Many of the computers had to be disconnected from the network until all copies of the worm could be expurgated and until the security loopholes that the worm used to gain entry could be plugged. Most computers were fully operational within two or three days. No files were damaged on any of the computers invaded by the worm.

This incident gained much public attention and produced a widespread outcry in the computing community, perhaps because so many people saw that they had been within a hair's breadth of losing valuable files. After an investigation, Cornell suspended Morris and decried his action as irresponsible. In July 1989, a grand jury brought an indictment against Morris for violation of the Federal Computer Privacy Act of 1986. He was tried and convicted in January 1990.

```
PROCEDURE PrintData (VAR Donor : NameList;
                     VAR Amount : AmountList);
  VAR
    J : integer;
  BEGIN
    FOR J := 1 TO NumberOfDonors DO
      BEGIN
        write (Donor[J]:40);
        writeln ('$':3, Amount[J]:5)
      END
  END;  {  of PROCEDURE PrintData  }
```

This would be called by

```
PrintData (Donor, Amount);
```

The last task this program requires is to find the total of all donations. The following function could perform this task.

```
FUNCTION Total (Amount : AmountList) : integer;
  VAR
    Sum, J : integer;
  BEGIN
    Sum := 0;
    FOR J := 1 TO NumberOfDonors DO
      Sum := Sum + Amount[J];
    Total := Sum
  END;  {  of FUNCTION Total  }
```

This function could be called by

```
TotalDonations := Total(Amount);
```

where TotalDonations has been declared as an **integer** variable. A complete program for this problem is as follows:

```
PROGRAM Donations (input, output, Data);

{   This program reads data from an input file where each line   }
{   consists of a donor name followed by the  amount  donated.   }
```

```
{    Output consists of an alphabetically sorted list  together  }
{    with the amount of each donation.  This is accomplished by  }
{    using parallel arrays.  The  total amount  donated is also  }
{    listed.                                                     }

CONST
  NumberOfDonors = 30;

TYPE
  String20 = PACKED ARRAY [1..20] OF char;
  IndexType = 1..NumberOfDonors;
  NameList = ARRAY [IndexType] OF String20;
  AmountList = ARRAY [IndexType] OF integer;

VAR
  Amount : AmountList;            {    An array for amounts donated }
  Donor : NameList;               {    An array for donor names     }
  TotalDonations : integer;       {    Total amount donated         }
  Data : text;                    {    Names and amounts donated    }

{*************************************************************** }

PROCEDURE GetData (VAR Donor : NameList;
                   VAR Amount : AmountList);

  {  Given:    Nothing                                          }
  {  Task:     Read names and donations into respective arrays  }
  {  Return:   Parallel arrays of names and donations           }

  VAR
    J, K : integer;

  BEGIN
    FOR J := 1 TO NumberOFDonors DO
      BEGIN
        FOR K := 1 TO 20 DO
          read (Data, Donor[J,K]);
        readln (Data, Amount[J])
      END
  END;  {  of PROCEDURE GetData  }

{*************************************************************** }

PROCEDURE SelectionSort (VAR Donor : NameList;
                         VAR Amount : AmountList);

  {  Given:    Unsorted parallel arrays of names and donations  }
  {  Task:     Sort alphabetically                              }
  {  Return:   An alphabetically sorted list of names with      }
  {                      respective donations                   }

  VAR
    TempDonor : String20;
    TempAmount : integer;
    J, K, Index : integer;

  BEGIN
    FOR J := 1 TO NumberOfDonors - 1 DO
      BEGIN
        Index := J;
        FOR K := J + 1 TO NumberOfDonors DO
```

```
            IF Donor[K] < Donor[Index] THEN
               Index := K;
            IF Index <> J THEN      { Exchange if necessary  }
              BEGIN
                TempDonor := Donor[Index];
                TempAmount := Amount[Index];
                Donor[Index] := Donor[J];
                Amount[Index] := Amount[J];
                Donor[J] := TempDonor;
                Amount[J] := TempAmount
              END  {  of exchange   }
        END  {  of one pass  }
  END;  {  of PROCEDURE SelectionSort   }


{********************************************************************** }


FUNCTION Total (Amount : AmountList) : integer;

  {  Given:    An array of amounts                                     }
  {  Task:     Sum the components of the array                         }
  {  Return:   The total of array components                           }

  VAR
    Sum, J : integer;

  BEGIN
    SUM := 0;
    FOR J := 1 TO NumberOfDonors DO
      Sum := Sum + Amount[J];
    Total := Sum
  END;  {  of FUNCTION Total   }


{********************************************************************** }


PROCEDURE PrintHeading;

  {  Given:    Nothing                                                 }
  {  Task:     Print a heading for the output                          }
  {  Return:   Nothing                                                 }

  BEGIN
    writeln;
    writeln ('Donor Name':33, 'Donation':17);
    writeln ('----------':33, '--------':17);
    writeln
  END;  {  of PROCEDURE PrintHeading   }


{********************************************************************** }


PROCEDURE PrintData (VAR Donor : NameList;
                     VAR Amount : AmountList;
                     TotalDonations : integer);

  {  Given:    Parallel arrays of names and donations and total        }
  {                donations                                           }
  {  Task:     Print a list of names and amounts donated; end          }
  {                with the total of all donations                     }
  {  Return:   Nothing                                                 }

  VAR
    J : integer;
```

```
      BEGIN
        FOR J := 1 TO NumberOfDonors DO
          BEGIN
            write (Donor[J]:40);
            writeln ('$':3, Amount[J]:5)
          END;  {  of FOR J loop  }
        writeln ('------':49);
        writeln ('Total':40, '$':3, TotalDonations:5);
        writeln
      END;  {  of PROCEDURE PrintData  }


{************************************************************* }


BEGIN  {  Main program  }
  reset (Data);
  GetData (Donor, Amount);
  SelectionSort (Donor, Amount);
  TotalDonations := Total(Amount);
  PrintHeading;
  PrintData (Donor, Amount, TotalDonations)
END.  {  of main program  }
```

Output created from an input file of 30 lines is

```
        Donor Name           Donation
        ----------           --------

        Alexander Candy      $   300
        Anderson Tony        $   375
        Banks Marj           $   375
        Born Patty           $   100
        Brown Ron            $   200
        Darnell Linda        $   275
        Erickson Thomas      $   100
        Fox William          $   300
        Francis Denise       $   350
        Generous George      $   525
        Gillette Mike        $   350
        Hancock Kirk         $   500
        Higgins Sam          $   300
        Janson Kevin         $   200
        Johnson Ed           $   350
        Johnson Martha       $   400
        Jones Jerry          $   250
        Kelly Marvin         $   475
        Kneff Susan          $   300
        Lasher John          $   175
        Lyon Elizabeth       $   425
        Moore Robert         $   100
        Muller Marjorie      $   250
        Smith John           $   100
        Trost Frostie        $    50
        Trudo Rosemary       $   200
        Weber Sharon         $   150
        Williams Art         $   350
        Williams Jane        $   175
        Wilson Mary          $   275
                             ------
                    Total $ 8275
```

Exercises 8.3

1. Which of the following are appropriate declarations for parallel arrays? Explain.

   a. TYPE
   ```
        String15 = PACKED ARRAY [1..15] OF char;
        List15 = ARRAY [1..15] OF real;
   ```

```
VAR
    Names : ARRAY [1..10] OF String15;
    Amounts : List15;
b. TYPE
    Chart = ARRAY [1..12, 1..10] OF integer;
    String10 = PACKED ARRAY [1..10] OF char;
    List = ARRAY [1..12] OF String10;
VAR
    Table : Chart;
    Names : List;
```

2. Write a test program to read names and amounts from a data file. Your program should print out both lists and the total of the amounts. Assume each line of data is similar to

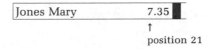

position 21

3. Parallel arrays could be used when working with a list of student names and the grades the students receive in a class.

   a. Define array types and declare subsequent arrays that could be used in such a program.

   b. Write a function that counts the number of occurrences for each letter grade A, B, C, D, and E.

4. Declare appropriate arrays and write a procedure to read data from an input file where there are an unknown number of lines (but less than 100) and each line contains a name (20 spaces), an age (integer), a marital status (character), and an income (real). A typical data line is

Smith John   35M 28502.16

5. Modify the code of Exercise 4 to accommodate data entered in the data file in the following format:

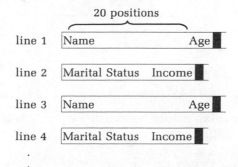

6. Write a procedure to sort the arrays of Exercise 4 according to income.

■ ■ ■ ■

■ 8.4
Higher-Dimensional
Arrays

Thus far we have worked with arrays of one and two dimensions. Arrays of three, four, or higher dimensions can also be declared and used. Pascal places no limitation on the number of dimensions of an array.

Declarations of Higher-Dimensional Arrays

Declarations of *higher-dimensional arrays* usually assume one of two basic forms. First, a three-dimensional array type can be defined using the form

---

ARRAY [1 . . 3, 1 . . 4, 1 . . 5] **OF** ⟨data type⟩;

Each dimension can vary in any of the ways used for arrays of one or two dimensions and the data type can be any standard or user-defined ordinal data type. Second, a three-dimensional array can be defined as an array of two-dimensional arrays using the form

---

ARRAY [1 . . 3] **OF ARRAY** [1 . . 4, 1 . . 5] **OF integer**;

Each of these declarations will reserve 60 locations in memory. This can be visualized as shown in Figure 8.1.

FIGURE 8.1
Three-dimensional array with components A[I,J,K]

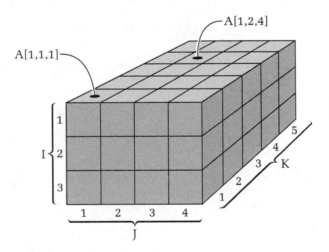

An array of dimension n can be defined by

$\quad$ **ARRAY** [1 . . a_1, 1 . . a_2, . . . , 1 . . a_n] **OF** ⟨data type⟩;

which would reserve $a_1 * a_2 * . . . * a_n$ locations in memory. A general definition is

---

ARRAY [a_1 . . b_1, a_2 . . b_2, . . . , a_n . . b_n] **OF** ⟨data type⟩;

---

where $a_i \leq b_i$, for $1 \leq i \leq n$.

$\quad$ Declarations and uses of higher-dimensional arrays are usually facilitated by descriptive names and user-defined data types. For example, suppose we want to declare a three-dimensional array to hold the contents of a book of tables. If there are 50 pages and each page contains a table of 15 rows and 10 columns, a reasonable declaration is

```
TYPE
  Page = 1..50;
  Row = 1..15;
  Column = 1..10;
  Book = ARRAY [Page, Row, Column] OF integer;
VAR
  Item : Book;
```

When this declaration is compared to

```
TYPE
  Book = ARRAY [1..50, 1..15, 1..10] OF integer;
VAR
  Item : Book;
```

we realize that both arrays are identical in structure, but, in the first declaration, it is easier to see what the dimensions represent.

Accessing Components

Elements in higher-dimensional arrays are accessed and used in a manner similar to two-dimensional arrays. The difference is that in a three-dimensional array, each element needs three indices for reference. A similar result holds for other dimensions. To illustrate using this notation, recall the declaration

```
TYPE
  Page = 1..50;
  Row = 1..15;
  Column = 1..10;
  Book = ARRAY [Page, Row, Column] OF integer;
VAR
  Item : Book;
```

If you want to assign a ten to the item on page three, row five, column seven, the statement

```
Item[3,5,7] := 10;
```

accomplishes this. Similarly, this item can be printed by

```
write (Item[3,5,7]);
```

Using this same declaration, we can

1. Print the fourth row of page 21 with the following segment of code.

```
FOR K := 1 TO 10 DO
  write (Item[21,4,K]:5);
writeln;
```

2. Print the top row of every page with

```
FOR I := 1 TO 50 DO
  BEGIN
    FOR K := 1 TO 10 DO
      write (Item[I,1,K]:5);
    writeln
  END;
```

3. Print page 35 with

```
FOR J := 1 TO 15 DO
  BEGIN
    FOR K := 1 TO 10 DO
      write (Item[35,J,K]:5);
    writeln
  END;
```

4. Print every page that does not have a zero in the first row and the first column with

```
FOR I := 1 TO 50 DO
  IF Item[I,1,1] <> 0 THEN
    FOR J := 1 TO 15 DO
      BEGIN
        FOR K := 1 TO 10 DO
          write (Item[I,J,K]:5);
        writeln
      END;
```

As another illustration of the use of higher-dimensional arrays, consider the situation where the manager of a high-rise office complex wants a program to assist in keeping track of the tenants in each office. Suppose there are 20 floors, each with the floor plan shown in Figure 8.2. Each wing contains five rooms.

Figure 8.2
High-rise floor plan

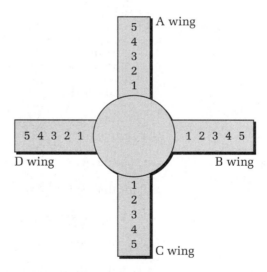

Let's first declare an appropriate array where the tenant's name can be stored (assume each name consists of 20 characters). This can be accomplished by

```
TYPE
  Floors = 1..20;
  Wings = 'A'..'D';
  Offices = 1..5;
  Name = PACKED ARRAY [1..20] OF char;
  Occupant = ARRAY [Floors, Wings, Offices] OF Name;
VAR
  Tenant : Occupant;
  Floor : Floors;
  Wing : Wings;
  Office : Offices;
```

Note that this is really a four-dimensional array, since the data type Name is **PACKED ARRAY.**

Now let's write a segment of code to print a list of names of all tenants on the top floor. To get the names of all tenants of the twentieth floor, we need to print the names for each office in each wing. Assuming a field width of 30 columns, the following code completes the desired task.

```
FOR Wing := 'A' TO 'D' DO
  FOR Office := 1 TO 5 DO
    writeln (Tenant[20, Wing, Office]:30);
```

How would we write a segment of code to read the name of the new tenant on the third floor, B wing, room 5 from the data file? Recall that character strings must be read one character at a time. Tenant [3,'B',5] is the variable name. Since this is a packed array, the code for reading is

```
FOR L := 1 TO 20 DO
  read (Tenant[3,'B',5,L]);
```

Assume the string 'Unoccupied   ' has been entered for each vacant office and we are to write a segment of code to list all vacant offices. This problem requires us to examine every name and print the location of the unoccupied offices.

Hence, when we encounter the name 'Unoccupied   ', we want to print the respective indices. This is accomplished by

```
FOR Floor := 1 TO 20 DO
  FOR Wing := 'A' TO 'D' DO
    FOR Office := 1 TO 5 DO
      IF Tenant[Floor, Wing, Office] = 'Unoccupied
        THEN writeln (Floor:5, Wing:5, Office:5);
```

As you can see, working with higher-dimensional arrays requires very careful handling of the indices. Nested loops are frequently used for processing array elements and proper formatting of output is critical.

Exercises 8.4

1. How many memory locations are reserved in each of the following declarations?

   a.
   ```
   TYPE
     Block = ARRAY [1..2, 1..3, 1..10] OF char;
   VAR
     A : Block;
   ```

   b.
   ```
   TYPE
     Block = ARRAY [-2..3] OF ARRAY [2..4, 3..6] OF real;
   VAR
     A : Block;
   ```

   c.
   ```
   TYPE
     Color = (Red, Black, White);
     Size = (Small, Large);
     Year = 1950..1960;
     Specifications = ARRAY [Color, Size, Year];
   VAR
     A : Specifications;
   ```

   d.
   ```
   TYPE
     String15 = PACKED ARRAY [1..15] OF char;
     List10 = ARRAY [1..10] OF String15;
     NameTable = ARRAY [1..4] OF List10;
   VAR
     A : NameTable;
   ```

2. Write a test program to read values into an array of size 3 × 4 × 5. Assuming this represents three pages, each of which contains a 4 × 5 table, print out the table for each page together with a page number.

3. Declare a three-dimensional array that a hospital could use to keep track of the types of rooms available: private (P), semiprivate (S), and ward (W). The hospital has four floors, five wings, and 20 rooms in each wing.

4. Consider the declaration

```
TYPE
  Pages = 1..50;
  Rows = 1..15;
  Columns = 1..10;
  Book = ARRAY [Pages, Rows, Columns] OF integer;
VAR
  Page : Pages;
  Row : Rows;
  Column : Columns;
  Item : Book;
```

a. Write a segment of code to do each of the following:

i. Print the fourth column of page 3.

ii. Print the top seven rows of page 46.

iii. Create a new page 30 by adding the corresponding elements of page 31 to page 30.

b. What is a general description of the output produced by the following segments of code?

i.
```
FOR Page := 1 TO 15 DO
   BEGIN
     FOR Column := 1 TO 10 DO
       write (Item[Page, Page, Column]:4);
     writeln
   END;
```

ii.
```
For Page := 1 TO 50 DO
   FOR Column := 1 TO 10 DO
     writeln (Item[Page, Column, Column]:(Column+4));
```

Use the following problem statement, definitions, and declarations for Exercises 5–8.

An athletic conference consisting of ten universities wishes to have a program to keep track of the number of athletic grants-in-aid for each team at each institution. The conference programmer has defined the following structure:

```
CONST
  MaxGrants = 90;

TYPE
  Schools = 'A'..'J';
  Sports = (Baseball, Basketball, CrossCountry,
            FieldHockey, Football, Golf, Gymnastics,
            Swimming, Tennis, Track, Volleyball, Wrestling);
  Sex = (Male, Female);
  NumberOfGrants = 0..MaxGrants;
  GrantChart = ARRAY [Schools, Sports, Sex] OF NumberOfGrants;
```

```
VAR
  NumGrants : integer;
  Grants : GrantChart;
  School : Schools;
  Sport : Sports;
  Gender : Sex;
```

5. How many memory locations are reserved in the array Grants?

6. Explain what tasks are performed by each of the following segments of code.

a.
```
NumGrants := 0;
FOR School := 'A' TO 'J' DO
  FOR Sport := Baseball TO Wrestling DO
    NumGrants := NumGrants + Grants[School, Sport, Female];
```

b.
```
   Sum := 0;
   FOR School := 'A' TO 'J' DO
     FOR Sport := Baseball TO Wrestling DO
       FOR Gender := Male TO Female DO
         IF Grants[School, Sport, Gender] = 0 THEN
           Sum := Sum + 1;
```

7. Write a segment of code for each of the following tasks.

a. Find the total number of grants for each university.

b. Find the total number of grants for each sport.

c. List all schools that have ten or more grants in field hockey.

8. Explain how a **CASE** statement can be used to help display all sports (indicate male or female) and the number of grants in each sport for school 'D'.

■ ■ ■ ■

FOCUS ON
PROGRAM DESIGN

This program simulates the solution to a problem that could be posed by a small airline. Mountain-Air Commuters, Inc., is a small airline commuter service. Each of their planes is a 30-passenger plane with a floor plan as follows:

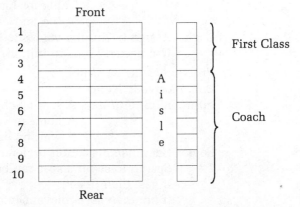

The first three rows are designated as first class because the seats are wider and there is more leg room. (In reality, most commuter planes do not have a first class section. However, rather than include the large data base needed for larger planes, we simulate the problem using a seating plan with only ten rows.)

Write a program that assigns seats to passengers on a first-come, first-served basis according to the following rules:

1. First class and coach requests must be honored; if seats in the requested sections are all full, the customer's name should go on a waiting list for the next flight.
2. Specific seat requests should be honored next; if a requested seat is occupied, the person should be placed in the same row, if possible.
3. If a requested row is filled, the passenger should be seated as far forward as possible.
4. If all seats are filled, the passenger's name is put on a waiting list for the next flight.

Output should include a seating chart with passenger names appropriately printed and a waiting list for the next flight. Each data line (input) contains the passenger's name, first class (F) or coach (C) designation, and seat request indicating the row and column desired.

A typical line of data would be

```
Smith John              C 5 2
```

where C represents a coach choice, 5 is a request for row five, and 2 represents the preferred seat.

A first-level pseudocode development for this problem is

1. Initialize variables
2. **WHILE NOT eof DO** process a name
3. Print a seating chart
4. **IF** there is a waiting list **THEN** print the list

A complete structure chart for this problem is given in Figure 8.3. Module specifications for the main modules are

1. Initialize Module
   Data received: None
   Information returned: Value for WaitCount
                        Value for EmptyWaitingList
                        Value for SeatPlan
   Logic: Assign beginning values to the parameters.
          Use nested loops to initialize the array SeatPlan.

2. ProcessAName Module
   Data received: None
   Information returned: A seating chart
                        A **boolean** value for extra passengers
                        A waiting list for the next flight
   Logic: Get a name, section preference, and seat choice.
          Search to see if a seat can be found.
          If yes, then ticket.
          If no, then save relevant information.

3. PrintSeatingChart Module
   Data received: A two-dimensional array of names of ticketed passengers.
   Information returned: None
   Logic: Print the seating plan indicating row, seat, and section choice for each passenger.

FIGURE 8.3
Structure chart for Mountain-
Air Commuters, Inc. problem

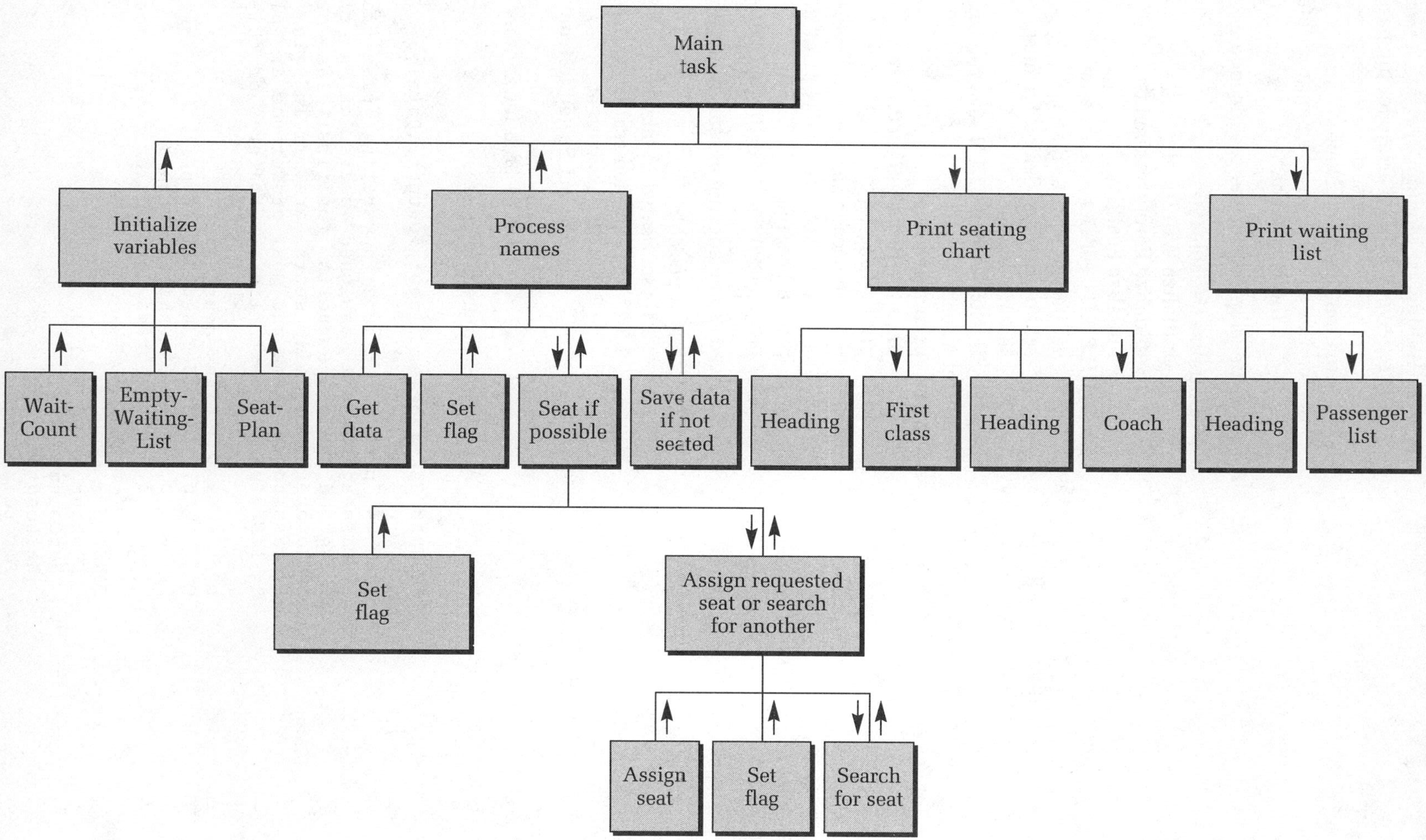

4. <u>PrintWaitingList Module</u>
Data received: Parallel arrays for the passenger's name, section choice, and seat preference
Information returned: None
Logic: Use a loop to print an appropriately titled list of passengers for the next flight.

A further development of the pseudocode is

1. Initialize variables
   1.1 initialize WaitCount
   1.2 initialize EmptyWaitingList
   1.3 initialize SeatPlan
2. **WHILE NOT eof DO** process a name
   2.1 get passenger information
   2.2 set **boolean** flag Seated for **false**
   2.3 seat if possible
   2.4 **IF NOT** seated **THEN** save relevant information
3. Print a seating chart
   3.1 print a heading
   3.2 print the first class section
   3.3 print a heading
   3.4 print the coach section
4. **IF** there is a waiting list **THEN** print the list
   4.1 print a heading
   4.2 print passenger list with four columns

Step 2.3 needs some additional refinement. Further development yields

   2.3 seat if possible
      2.3.1 set Seated to **false**
      2.3.2 **IF** requested seat is available **THEN**
         2.3.2.1 assign seat
         2.3.2.2 set Seated to **true**
         ELSE
         2.3.2.3 search for another seat

A complete program for this is

```
PROGRAM SeatingPlan (input, output, Data);

{ This  program  prints  a  seating  plan  for  an  airline.  }
{ Passengers  are  assigned  seats  on  a  first-come, first-  }
{ served basis.  Requests  for first class or  coach must be   }
{ honored.  If  all  seats  are  filled  in  a  section,  the  }
{ passenger's name and seat preference are placed on a waiting }
{ list for the next flight.  Features of this program include  }
{                                                              }
{      a.  defined constants                                   }
{      b.  user-defined data types                             }
{      c.  multidimensional arrays                             }
{      d.  subprograms for modular development                 }

CONST
  NumRows = 10;
  NumColumns = 3;
  MaxLength = 50;
  FirstClassBegin = 1;
  FirstClassEnd = 3;
```

```
            CoachBegin = 4;
            CoachEnd = 10;
            EmptyString = '                    ';
            Skip = ' ';

         TYPE
            String20 = PACKED ARRAY [1..20] OF char;
            SeatingPlan = ARRAY [1..NumRows, 1..NumColumns] OF String20;
            NotSeatedList = ARRAY [1..MaxLength] OF String20;
            SectionOptionList = ARRAY [1..MaxLength] OF char;
            SeatChoiceList = ARRAY [1..MaxLength, 1..2] OF integer;

         VAR
            Seated : boolean;                      { Indicator for seat found }
            WaitingList : NotSeatedList;           { Name list for next flight}
            WaitCount : integer;                   { Counter for waiting list }
            EmptyWaitingList : boolean;            { Indicator for empty list }
            Seat : SeatingPlan;                    { 2-dim array of seats     }
            Name : String20;                       { String for names         }
            SectionChoice : char;                  { First class or coach     }
            RowChoice, ColumnChoice : integer;     { Seat preference          }
            SectionOption : SectionOptionList;     { Array of section options }
            SeatChoice : SeatChoiceList;           { Array of seat choices    }
            Data : text;                           { Names,section-seat choice}

{***************************************************************** }

PROCEDURE Initialize (VAR Seat : SeatingPlan);

   { Given:    A two-dimensional array of strings                 }
   { Task:     Initialize all cells to an empty string            }
   { Return:   An initialized two-dimensional array               }

   VAR
      J, K : integer;

   BEGIN
      FOR J := 1 TO NumRows DO
         FOR K := 1 TO NumColumns DO
            Seat[J,K] := EmptyString
   END;   { of PROCEDURE Initialize   }

{***************************************************************** }

PROCEDURE GetAName (VAR Name : String20;
                    VAR SectionChoice : char;
                    VAR RowChoice,
                    ColumnChoice : integer);

   { Given:    Nothing                                            }
   { Task:     Read a name, section option, and seat preference   }
   {                 from the input file                          }
   { Return:   Passenger name, section and seat preference        }

   VAR
      J : integer;

   BEGIN
      FOR J := 1 TO 20 DO
         read (Data, Name[J]);
      readln (Data, SectionChoice, RowChoice, ColumnChoice)
   END;   { of PROCEDURE GetAName   }

{***************************************************************** }
```

1

```
PROCEDURE SeatIfPossible (Name : String20;
                          VAR Seat : SeatingPlan;
                          RowChoice,
                          ColumnChoice : integer;
                          SectionChoice : char;
                          VAR Seated : boolean);

{ Given:    Passenger name, section and seat preference     }
{ Task:     If requested seat is available, assign seat     }
{           If not available, use Search to check for an    }
{               alternate seat                              }
{ Return:   Seat assignment if one has been made            }
{           Boolean flag to indicate if seat was found      }

PROCEDURE Search (Name : String20;
                  VAR Seat : SeatingPlan;
                  VAR Seated : boolean;
                  FirstRow,
                  LastRow : integer);

  { Given:    Passenger name, current seating chart, row      }
  {               designators for first class and coach        }
  {               sections                                      }
  { Task:     Search indicated rows to see if an alternate     }
  {               seat is available; if yes, assign            }
  {               passenger to it                              }
  { Return:   Updated seating plan and Boolean flag indica-    }
  {               ting whether or not a seat was found         }

  VAR
    Row, Column : integer;

  BEGIN  { PROCEDURE Search }
    Seated := false;
    Row := FirstRow;
    REPEAT
      Column := 1;                          { Start searching rows }
      REPEAT                                { Search one row        }
        IF Seat[Row, Column] = EmptyString THEN
          BEGIN
            Seat[Row, Column] := Name;
            Seated := true
          END
        ELSE
          Column := Column + 1
      UNTIL Seated OR (Column > NumColumns);
      Row := Row + 1                        { Search next row       }
    UNTIL Seated OR (Row > LastRow)
  END; { of PROCEDURE Search }

BEGIN  { PROCEDURE SeatIfPossible }
  Seated := false;
  IF Seat[RowChoice, ColumnChoice] = EmptyString THEN
    BEGIN
      Seat[RowChoice, ColumnChoice] := Name;
      Seated := true
    END
  ELSE
    CASE SectionChoice OF
      'F' :  Search (Name, Seat, Seated,
                     FirstClassBegin, FirstClassEnd);
      'C' :  Search (Name, Seat, Seated,
                     CoachBegin, CoachEnd)
```

2

```
            END  {  of CASE SectionChoice  }
        END;  {  of PROCEDURE SeatIfPossible  }


{****************************************************************** }


PROCEDURE PrintSeatingChart (VAR Seat : SeatingPlan);

    {  Given:    The seating chart, a two-dimensional array of       }
    {                     names                                      }
    {  Task:     Print the passenger names in rows and columns       }
    {                     according to their assigned seats          }
    {  Return:   Nothing                                             }

    VAR
      J, K : integer;

    BEGIN
      writeln;
      writeln (Skip:10, 'MOUNTAIN-AIR COMMUTERS');
      writeln (Skip:15, 'Seating Chart');
      writeln;
      writeln ('First Class section');
      writeln ('-------------------');
      writeln;
      FOR J := 1 TO FirstClassEnd DO
        BEGIN
          FOR K := 1 TO NumColumns DO
            write (Seat[J,K]:22);
          writeln
        END;  {  of FOR J loop  }
      writeln;
      writeln ('Coach section');
      writeln ('-------------');
      writeln;
      FOR J := CoachBegin TO CoachEnd DO
        BEGIN
          FOR K := 1 TO NumColumns DO
            write (Seat[J,K]:22);
          writeln
        END;  {  of FOR K loop  }
      writeln
    END;  {  of PROCEDURE PrintSeatingChart  }


{****************************************************************** }


PROCEDURE PrintWaitingList  (VAR WaitingList : NotSeatedList;
                             VAR SectionOption : SectionOptionList;
                             VAR SeatChoice : SeatChoiceList;
                             WaitCount : integer);

    {  Given:    An array of names of passengers not seated, the     }
    {                     section choice and seat preference for each }
    {  Task:     Print a waiting list for the next flight            }
    {  Return:   Nothing                                             }

    VAR
      J : integer;

    BEGIN
      writeln;
      writeln (Skip:10, 'Waiting list for next flight');
      writeln;
```

```
                writeln ('NAME':10, 'SECTION CHOICE':27,
                         'ROW NUMBER':15, 'COLUMN NUMBER':15);
                write ('-----------------------------------');
                writeln ('-----------------------------------');
                writeln;
                FOR J := 1 TO WaitCount DO
                    writeln ('<', J:2, '>', WaitingList[J]:22, SectionOption[J]:4,
                             SeatChoice[J,1]:15, SeatChoice[J,2]:15)
                END;  {  of PROCEDURE PrintWaitingList  }


    {************************************************************** }

    BEGIN  {  Main program  }
      WaitCount := 0;
      EmptyWaitingList := true;
      Initialize (Seat);
      reset (Data);
      WHILE NOT eof(Data) DO
        BEGIN
          GetAName (Name, SectionChoice, RowChoice, ColumnChoice);
          Seated := false;
          SeatIfPossible (Name, Seat, RowChoice, ColumnChoice,
                          SectionChoice, Seated);
          IF NOT Seated THEN   {  Save information for waiting list  }
            BEGIN
              WaitCount := WaitCount + 1;
              WaitingList[WaitCount] := Name;
              SectionOption[WaitCount] := SectionChoice;
              SeatChoice[WaitCount, 1] := RowChoice;
              SeatChoice[WaitCount, 2] := ColumnChoice;
              EmptyWaitingList := false
            END {  of IF NOT Seated  }
        END;  {  of WHILE NOT eof  }
      PrintSeatingChart (Seat);
      IF NOT EmptyWaitingList THEN
        PrintWaitingList (WaitingList, SectionOption, SeatChoice,
                          WaitCount)
    END.  {  of main program  }
```

Using the data file

```
            Smith John          F 3 2
            Alexander Joe       C 9 3
            Allen Darcy         F 3 2
            Jones Mary          C 8 1
            Humphrey H          C 8 2
            Johnson M           F 3 1
            Eastman Ken         F 1 1
            Winston Sam         C 8 3
            Smythe Susan        C 9 1
            Hendricks J B       C 9 2
            Hanson Cynthia      C 9 3
            Zoranson Steve      C 10 1
            Radamacher Joe      C 10 3
            Borack Bill         C 10 2
            Seracki Don         C 9 2
            Henry John          F 1 2
            Steveson Enghart    F 1 3
            Johansen Mary       F 2 1
            Smith Martha        F 2 2
            Jones Martha        F 2 3
            Rinehart Jim        F 3 3
            Rinehart Jane       F 3 2
```

```
               Swenson Cecil       C 4 1
               Swenson Carol       C 4 2
               Byes Nikoline       C 4 3
               Byes Jennifer       C 5 3
               Harris John         C 5 2
               Harris Judy         C 5 1
               Hartman F G         C 6 1
               Hartman D T         C 6 2
               Lakes William       C 6 3
               Lampton George      C 7 1
               Hayes Woodrow       C 7 2
               Champion M G        C 7 3
               Thomas Lynda        C 8 1
               Sisler Susan        C 8 2
               Stowers Steve       C 8 3
               Banks M J           C 5 3
               Banks H W           C 5 2
               Brown Susan         C 3 1
               Wince Ann           C 8 2
               Wince Joanne        C 8 1
```

sample output is

```
            MOUNTAIN-AIR COMMUTERS
                Seating Chart

    First class section
    -------------------

        Allen Darcy         Eastman Ken         Henry John
        Steveson Enghart    Johansen Mary       Smith Martha
        Johnson M           Smith John          Jones Martha


    Coach section
    -------------

        Hanson Cynthia      Seracki Don         Swenson Cecil
        Swenson Carol       Byes Nikoline       Byes Jennifer
        Harris John         Harris Judy         Hartman F G
        Hartman D T         Lakes William       Lampton George
        Jones Mary          Humphrey H          Winston Sam
        Smythe Susan        Hendricks J B       Alexander Joe
        Zoranson Steve      Borack Bill         Radamacher Joe


             Waiting list for next flight
```

	NAME	SECTION CHOICE	ROW NUMBER	COLUMN NUMBER
< 1>	Rinehart Jim	F	3	3
< 2>	Rinehart Jane	F	3	2
< 3>	Hayes Woodrow	C	7	2
< 4>	Champion M G	C	7	3
< 5>	Thomas Lynda	C	8	1
< 6>	Sisler Susan	C	8	2
< 7>	Stowers Steve	C	8	3
< 8>	Banks M J	C	5	3
< 9>	Banks H W	C	5	2
<10>	Brown Susan	C	3	1
<11>	Wince Ann	C	8	2
<12>	Wince Joanne	C	8	1

**RUNNING AND
DEBUGGING TIPS**

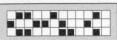

1. Use subrange types with descriptive identifiers for specifying index ranges. For example,

```
TYPE
   Page = 1..50;
   Row = 1..15;
   Column = 1..10;
   Book = ARRAY [Page, Row, Column] OF real;
```

2. Develop and maintain a systematic method of processing nested loops. For example, students with mathematical backgrounds will often use I, J, and K as index variables for three-dimensional arrays.

3. Be careful to properly subscript multidimensional array components.

4. When using an array of packed arrays as a list of strings, remember that in standard Pascal, strings must be read in one character at a time. However, strings can be written by a single **writeln** command.

5. When sorting one array in a program that uses parallel arrays, remember to make similar component exchanges in all arrays.

6. Define all data structures in the **TYPE** definition section.

■ **Summary**

Key Terms

higher-dimensional
   array

parallel array

two-dimensional array

Key Concepts

▪ Two-dimensional arrays can be declared in several ways; one descriptive method is

```
TYPE
   Chart4X6 = ARRAY [1..4, 1..6] OF real;
VAR
   Table : Chart4X6;
```

▪ Nested loops are frequently used to **read** and **write** values in two-dimensional arrays; for example, data can be read by

```
FOR Row := 1 TO 4 DO
   FOR Column := 1 TO 6 DO
     read (Table[Row, Column]);
```

▪ When processing the components of a single row or single column, leave the appropriate row or column index fixed and let the other index vary as a loop index; for example, to sum row 3, use

```
Sum := 0;
FOR Column := 1 TO NumOfColumns DO
   Sum := Sum + A[3, Column];
```

To sum column 3, use

```
Sum := 0;
FOR Row := 1 TO NumOfRows DO
   Sum := Sum + A[Row, 3];
```

▪ An array of strings in Pascal is a special case of a two-dimensional array; the data structure is an array of packed arrays and can be declared by

```
TYPE
   String20 = PACKED ARRAY [1..20] OF char;
   NameList = ARRAY [1..50] OF String20;
```

```
VAR
   Name : NameList;
```

- Arrays of strings (packed arrays of characters) can be alphabetized by using the selection sort.
- Three standard procedures used in programs that work with arrays of strings are (1) get the data, (2) alphabetize the array, and (3) print the alphabetized list.
- Parallel arrays may be used to solve problems that require arrays of the same index type but of different data types.
- A typical problem in which one would use parallel arrays involves working with a list of names and an associated list of numbers (for example, test scores). In the next chapter, we will see that this can also be done with a single array of records.
- A typical data structure declaration for using names and scores is

```
TYPE
   String20 = PACKED ARRAY [1..20] OF char;
   NameList = ARRAY [1..30] OF String20;
   ScoreList = ARRAY [1..30] OF integer;
VAR
   Name : NameList;
   Score : ScoreList;
```

- Data structures for solving problems can require arrays of three or more dimensions.
- A typical declaration for an array of three dimensions is

```
TYPE
   Dim1 = 1..10;
   Dim2 = 1..20;
   Dim3 = 1..30;
   Block = ARRAY [Dim1, Dim2, Dim3] OF real;
VAR
   Item : Block;
```

In this array, a typical component is accessed by

```
Item[I,J,K]
```

- Nested loops are frequently used when working with higher-dimensional arrays; for example, all values on the first level of array Item as just declared can be printed by

```
FOR J := 1 TO 20 DO
   BEGIN
      FOR K := 1 TO 30 DO
         BEGIN
            write (Item[1,J,K]:5:2);
            writeln
         END;  {  of 1 line  }
      writeln
   END;  {  of 20 lines  }
```

- When working with subprograms, array variables are usually passed by reference.

■ Programming Problems and Projects

■ 1. The local high school sports boosters are conducting a fund drive to help raise money for the athletic program. As each donation is received, the person's name and amount of donation are entered on one line in a data file. Write a program to

   a. Print an alphabetized list of all donors together with their corresponding donation.

   b. Print a list of donations from high to low together with the donors' names.

   c. Compute and print the average and total of all donations.

2. Due to not meeting the original goal, your local high school sports boosters (Problem 1) are at it again. For their second effort, each donor's name and donation are added as a separate line at the end of the previously sorted list. Write a program to produce lists, sum, and average as in Problem 1. No donor's name should appear more than once in a list.

3. Dr. Lae Z. Programmer (Problem 5, 22, and 23, Chapter 4; Problem 13, Chapter 5; and Problem 5, Chapter 6) now expects you to write a program to do all record keeping for the class. For each student, consecutive lines of the data file contain the student's name, ten quiz scores, six program scores, and three examination scores. Your output should include
   a. An alphabetized list together with
       i. quiz total
      ii. program total
     iii. examination total
      iv. total points
       v. percentage grade
      vi. letter grade
   b. The overall class average
   c. A histogram depicting the grade distribution

4. The All Metro Basketball Conference consists of ten teams. The conference commissioner has created a data file in which each line contains one school's name, location, and nickname for the school team. You are to write a program to read this data and then produce three lists, each of which contains all information about the school. All lists are to be sorted alphabetically, the first by school name, the second by school location, and the third by nickname.

5. Upgrade the program for Mountain-Air Commuters, Inc. (Focus on Program Design) so it can be used for each of five daily flights. Passengers on a waiting list must be processed first. Print a seating chart for each flight.

6. Add yet another upgrade to the Mountain-Air Commuters, Inc. program. Write an interactive version to consider the possibility of seating passengers who wish to be seated together in the same row. If no such seating is possible, they should then be given a choice of alternate seating (if possible) or taking a later flight.

7. Salespersons at McHenry Tool Corporation are given a monthly commission check. The commission is computed by multiplying the salesperson's gross monthly sales by the person's commission rate.

   Write a program to compute a salesperson's monthly commission computed to the nearest penny. The program should prepare a list of all salespersons in descending order based on monthly commission earned (the person earning the highest commission on top). Each salesperson's commission should be printed next to his or her name. At the bottom of the list, indicate the total monthly commission (summed across all salespersons) and the average commission per salesperson. McHenry never employs more than 60 salespersons.

   Any names of persons who have invalid data should be printed out separately. Data are invalid if the commission rate is not between 0.01 and 0.50, or if the gross monthly sales figure is negative.

8. In order to reduce their costs, the McHenry Tool Corporation (Problem 7) is switching from monthly to biannual commission checks. The commission is now computed by multiplying a person's commission rate by the sum of his or her gross monthly sales for a six-month period.

   The McHenry Tool Corporation has asked that you develop the necessary computer program. The program should differ from Problem 7 in the following ways:

   a. Each name on the output should be followed by the six figures for gross monthly sales. The columns should be labeled "January" through "June." Total six-month gross sales should be given next, followed by rate of commission, and amount of six-month commission check to the nearest penny.

   b. Commission rates are based on gross six-month sales. If sales are less than $20,000, the commission rate is 3 percent. If sales are at least $20,000 but less than $40,000, the commission rate is 5 percent. If sales are at least $40,000 but less than $60,000, the commission rate is 5.5 percent. If sales are at least $60,000 but less than $80,000, the commission rate is 6 percent. If sales are at least $80,000 but less than $90,000, the commission rate is 6.5 percent. If sales are at least $90,000, the commission rate is 8 percent.

   c. At the bottom of each column, the program should provide the total and the mean for that column (the column for commission rates does not require a total, only a mean).

9. The dean of a small undergraduate college (enrollment less than 2,000) has asked you to write a program to figure grade point averages for an unknown number of students.

   The output should be an alphabetized roster showing the sex, identification number (social security number), grade point average (rounded to three decimal places), and class status (freshman, sophomore, junior, or senior) for each student.

   The data provide the name, sex (M or F), social security number (ID), and number of semesters completed. Also provided are the number of courses taken and the letter grade and number of credits for each course. The possible letter grades are A (4 points), B (3 points), C (2 points), D (1 point), and E (0 points). Class status is determined by the number of credits as follows:

1–25 credits	Freshman
26–55 credits	Sophomore
56–85 credits	Junior
86 or more credits	Senior

10. You have just started work for the Michigan Association of Automobile Manufacturers and have been asked to analyze sales data on five subcompact cars for the last six months. Your analysis should be in table form and should include the name of each make and model, a model's sales volume for each month, a model's total and average sales volume for six months, a model's total sales revenue for six months, and the total and average sales volume for each month. In addition, your output should include the total and average sales volume of all models for the entire six months and the make and model name of the car with the largest total sales revenue and the amount of that revenue.

11. You have been asked to write a program to assist with the inventory and ordering for Tite-Jeans, Inc. They manufacture three styles: straight, flair, and peg. In each style, waist sizes vary by integer values from 24 to 46 and inseams vary by integer values from 26 to 40. Write a program to
    a. Read in the starting inventory.
    b. Read in daily sales.
    c. Print the ending inventory for each style.
    d. Print order charts for each style that is low in stock (fewer than three).
    e. Print an emergency order list for those that are out of stock.

12. You have been asked to write a program that will grade results of a True-False quiz and display the results in tabular form. The quiz consists of ten questions. The data file for this problem consists of
    a. correct responses (answer key) on line one; and
    b. a four-digit student identification number followed by that student's ten responses on each successive line.

    Thus, the data file would be

    | TFFTFTTFTT |

    | 0461 TTFTTFTFTT |

    | 3218 TFFTTTTFTT |

    ·

    ·

    ·

    Your program should read the key and store it in an array. It should then read the remaining lines, storing the student identification numbers in one array and the number of correct responses in a parallel array. Output should consist of a table with three columns: one for the student identification number, one for the number of correct responses, and one for the quiz grade. Grades are assigned as follows:

10	A
9	B
8, 7	C
6, 5	D
4 or less	E

    Your output should also include the quiz average for the entire class.

13. A few members (total unknown, but no more than 25) at Oakland Mountain Country Club want to computerize their golf scores. Each member plays 20 games, some 18 holes and some 9 holes. Each member's name (no more than 20 characters) is written on a data card, followed on a second card by the 20 scores. Each score is immediately followed by an 'E' or an 'N', indicating 18 or 9 holes, respectively.

Write a program to read all the names and scores into two parallel two-dimensional arrays. Calculate everyone's 18-hole average. (Double the 9-hole scores before you store them in the array and treat as 18-hole scores.) Calculate how much each average is over or under par (par is 72 and should be declared as a constant). Output should be each name, average, difference from par, and scores.

14. Write a program to keep statistics for a basketball team consisting of 15 players. Statistics for each player should include shots attempted, shots made, and shooting percentage; free throws attempted, free throws made, and free throw percentage; offensive rebounds and defensive rebounds; assists; turnovers; and total points. Appropriate team totals should be listed as part of the output.

15. A magic square is a square array of positive integers such that the sum of each row, column, and diagonal is the same constant. For example,

16	3	2	13
5	10	11	8
9	6	7	12
4	15	14	1

is a magic square whose constant is 34.

Write a program to have as input four lines of four positive integers. The program should then determine whether or not the square is a magic square.

16. Pascal's Triangle can be used to recognize coefficients of a quantity raised to a power. The rules for forming this triangle of integers are such that each row must start and end with a 1, and each entry in a row is the sum of the two values diagonally above the new entry. Thus, four rows of Pascal's Triangle are

```
      1
    1   1
  1   2   1
1   3   3   1
```

This triangle can be used as a convenient way to get the coefficients of a quantity of two terms raised to a power (binomial coefficients). For example,

$(a + b)^3 = 1a^3 + 3a^2b + 3ab^2 + 1b^3$

where the coefficients 1, 3, 3, and 1 come from the fourth row of Pascal's Triangle.

Write a complete program to print out Pascal's Triangle for ten rows.

17. Your former high school principal has come to you for help. He wants you to develop a program to maintain a list of the 20 students in the school with the highest scores on the SAT test. Input is from a text file containing the name (20 characters), and the total SAT score (verbal plus mathematical). Write a program that, when all data have been read, prints out a list of the 20 highest scores from highest to lowest,

and the students' names. You may assume that no two students have the same score.

18. The transpose of a matrix (table) is a new matrix with the row and column positions reversed. That is, the transpose of matrix *A*, an *M* by *N* matrix is an *N* by *M* matrix, with each element, $A[m,n]$ stored in $B[n,m]$. Given a 3 × 5 matrix of integers, create a matrix that is its transpose. Print both the original matrix and the new matrix.

■ 19. Mr. Laven, a mathematics instructor at your college, wants you to write a program to help him keep his students' grades. He wants to keep track of up to 30 grades for each of up to 35 students. Your program should read grades and names from a text file, and then print the following:
   a. A table showing the names in alphabetical order and grades received by each student.
   b. An alphabetical list of students with their total points and average score.
   c. A list of averages from highest to lowest with corresponding students' names.

20. Write a program in which a person can enter data into a 5 × 7 matrix. Print the original matrix along with the average of each row and column.

21. Matrix *M* is symmetric if it has the same number of rows as columns, and if each element $M[x,y]$ is equal to $M[y,x]$. Write a program to check a matrix entered by the user to see if it is symmetric or not.

■ 22. The following table shows the total sales for salespeople of the Falcon Manufacturing Company.

Salesperson	Week 1	Week 2	Week 3	Week 4
Anna, Michael	30	25	45	18
Henderson, Marge	22	30	32	35
Johnson, Fred	12	17	19	15
Striker, Nancy	32	30	33	31
Ryan, Renee	22	17	28	16

The price of the product being sold is $1,985.95. Write a program that permits the input of the previous data, and prints both a replica of the original table and a table showing the dollar value of sales for each individual during each week along with their total sales. Also, print the total sales for each week and the total sales for the company.

23. The computer science office wants a computerized system for finding telephone numbers of students. The program should read a list of up to 20 students and their telephone numbers from a text file. It should permit the entry of a student's name, and then print the name and telephone number. (A binary search could be used for this.) If the name is not found, an appropriate message should be printed.

24. Write a program to permit two people to play the game of Battleship. Your program should record the ship positions, hits, misses, and ship sinkings for each player.

25. Rewrite the Battleship program (Problem 24) to have a person play against the computer.

26. Arrange a visit with a travel agent or an airlines reservation agent. Discuss with the agent the information each requests from prospective passengers. If possible, have the agent set up a mock booking using the computerized reservation system. Examine the screen displays.

    Prepare a report of your visit for the class. Be sure to discuss how the designers of the reservation system may have used multidimensional arrays.

27. Contact someone who routinely uses a spreadsheet as part of his or her daily work. Have the person show you several usual operations with the spreadsheet. In particular, see how to adjust the size of the spreadsheet, sum rows, sum columns, and use functions to define entries for specific locations.

    Give an oral report of your discussion to your class. Explain how the various spreadsheet operations relate to what you have studied about two-dimensional arrays.

28. Select an unworked problem from the previously listed programming problems for this chapter. Construct a structure chart and write all documentary information necessary for the problem you have chosen. Do not write code. When you are finished, have a classmate read your documentation to see if precisely what is to be done is clear.

CHAPTER

9

As every man goes through life, he fills in a number of forms for the record, each containing a number of questions. There are thus hundreds of little threads radiating from each man, millions of threads in all. If these threads were suddenly visible, people would lose all ability to move.

Alexander I. Solzhenitsyn

Records

The previous two chapters dealt extensively with the concept of the structured data type **ARRAY.** Recall that when you declare an array, you reserve a predetermined number of memory locations. The variables representing these memory locations are of the same base type and can be accessed by reference to the index of an array element.

All components of an array must be of the same data type; this is a serious limitation since there are many situations in which this is not possible; for example, a bank may wish to keep a record of the name, address, telephone number, marital status, social security number, annual salary, total assets, and total liabilities of each customer. Fortunately, Pascal provides another structured data type, **RECORD,** which allows heterogeneous information to be stored, accessed, and manipulated. A record contains fields, which can be of different data types. This chapter shows you how to declare records, how to access the various fields within a record, and how to work with arrays of records.

■ 9.1
Record Definitions

Record As a Structured Data Type

A *record* is a collection of *fields* that may be treated as a whole or individually. To illustrate, a record that contains fields for a customer's name, age, and annual income could be visualized as shown in Figure 9.1.

FIGURE 9.1
Fields in a record

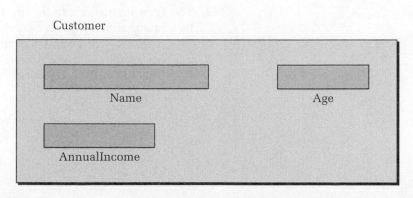

Customer

Name   Age

AnnualIncome

This schematic representation may help you understand why a record is considered a structured data type and familiarize you with the idea of using fields in a record.

Declaring a RECORD

Let's now consider our first example of a formally declared record. Assume we want a record to contain a customer's name, age, and annual income. The following definition and subsequent declaration can be made.

```
TYPE
  CustomerInfo = RECORD
                   Name : PACKED ARRAY [1..30] OF char;
                   Age : integer;
                   AnnualIncome : real
                 END;  {  of RECORD CustomerInfo  }
VAR
  Customer : CustomerInfo;
```

Components of a record are called fields and each field has an associated data type. The general form for defining a record data type using the **TYPE** definition section is

---

TYPE
  ⟨type identifier⟩ = **RECORD**
                        ⟨field identifier 1⟩ : ⟨data type 1⟩;
                        ⟨field identifier 2⟩ : ⟨data type 2⟩;
                              .
                              .
                              .
                        ⟨field identifier n⟩ : ⟨data type n⟩
                        END;   {   of **RECORD** definition   }

The syntax diagram for this is

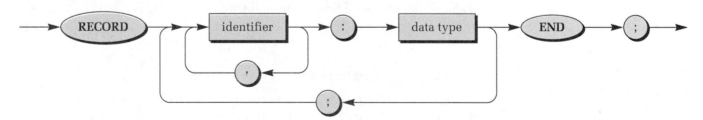

The following comments are in order concerning this form.

1. The type identifier can be any valid identifier. It should be descriptive to enhance program readability.
2. The reserved word **RECORD** must precede the field identifiers.
3. Each field identifier within a record must be unique. However, field identifiers in different records may use the same name. Thus,

```
FirstRecord = RECORD
                Name : PACKED ARRAY [1..30] OF char;
                Age : integer
              END; {  of RECORD FirstRecord  }
```

and

```
SecondRecord = RECORD
                 Name : PACKED ARRAY [1..30] OF char;
                 Age : integer;
                 IQ : integer
               END; { of RECORD SecondRecord }
```

can both be defined in the same program.

4. Data types for fields can be user-defined. Thus, our earlier definitions could have been

```
TYPE
   String30 = PACKED ARRAY [1..30] OF char;
   CustomerInfo = RECORD
                    Name : String30;
                    Age : integer;
                    AnnualIncome : real
                  END; { of RECORD CustomerInfo }
VAR
   Customer : CustomerInfo;
```

5. **END;** is required to signify the end of a **RECORD** definition. This is the second instance (remember **CASE**?) in which **END** is used without a **BEGIN.**

6. Fields of the same base type can be declared together. Thus,

```
Info = RECORD
         Name : String30;
         Age, IQ : integer
       END; { of RECORD Info }
```

is appropriate. However, you are encouraged to list each field separately to enhance readability and reinforce the concept of fields in a record. The following example defines another record.

■ EXAMPLE 9.1

Suppose you want to keep a record for a college student. The record is to contain a field for each of the following: student's name (Smith Jane), social security number (111-22-3333), class status (Fr, So, Jr, or Sr), previous credit hours earned (56), credit hours being taken (17), and grade point average (3.27). We can define a record and declare an appropriate variable as follows:

```
TYPE
   String30 = PACKED ARRAY [1..30] OF char;
   String11 = PACKED ARRAY [1..11] OF char;
   Class = (Fr, So, Jr, Sr);
   StudentInfo = RECORD
                   Name : String30;
                   SSN : String11;
                   Status : Class;
                   HoursEarned : 0..999;
                   HoursTaking : 0..30;
                   GPA : real
                 END; { of RECORD StudentInfo }
VAR
   Student : StudentInfo;
```

STYLE TIP

■ ■ ■ ■ ■ ■ ■ ■ ■ ■ ■ ■

Use descriptive field names, appropriate subranges, and a descriptive variable name when defining records. For example, if you want a record with fields for a student's name, age, gender, and class status, you can use

```
TYPE
   String20 = PACKED ARRAY [1..20] OF char;
   StudentRecord = RECORD
                      Name : String20;
                      Age : 0..99;
                      Gender : (Male, Female);
                      ClassStatus : (Fr, So, Jr, Sr)
                   END;  {  of RECORD StudentRecord  }
VAR
   Student : StudentRecord;
```

The fields would then be

```
Student.Name
Student.Age
Student.Gender
Student.ClassStatus
```

and you can use program statements such as

```
IF Student.Gender = Male THEN
```

or

```
IF Student.Age < 21 THEN
```

Fields in a Record

Now that you know how to define a record, you need to examine how to access fields in a record. For our discussion, let us consider a record defined by

```
TYPE
   String30 = PACKED ARRAY [1..30] OF char;
   Employee = RECORD
                 Name : String30;
                 Age : integer;
                 MaritalStatus : char;
                 Wage : real
              END;  {  of RECORD Employee  }
VAR
   Programmer : Employee;
```

Programmer can be visualized as in Figure 9.2.

FIGURE 9.2
Defined fields in Programmer

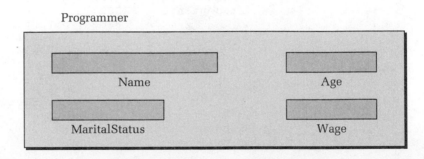

Each field within a record is a variable and can be uniquely identified by

⟨record name⟩ . ⟨field name⟩

where a period separates the record name from the field name. Thus, the four field variables are

```
Programmer.Name
Programmer.Age
Programmer.MaritalStatus
Programmer.Wage
```

Each of these variables may be used in any manner consistent with the defined base type. To illustrate, suppose Programmer.Name and Programmer.Age have been assigned values and you wish to print the names of those employees under 30 years of age. You could have a fragment of code such as

```
IF Programmer.Age < 30 THEN
    writeln (Programmer.Name:40);
```

If you wish to compute gross salary, you might have

```
read (Hours);
Gross := Hours * Programmer.Wage;
```

Other Fields

Thus far, our fields have been declared in a relatively direct fashion. This is not always the case. Sometimes, when establishing the structure of a record, the data type of a field needs more development. For example, suppose you wish to declare a record for each student in a class and the record is to contain student name, class name, four test scores, ten quiz scores, final average, and letter grade. This can be visualized as shown in Figure 9.3.

FIGURE 9.3
Fields in Student

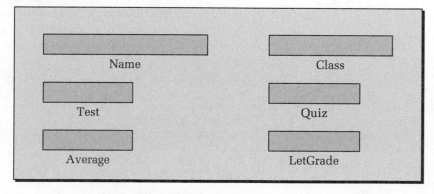

In this case, Test and Quiz are both arrays. Thus, a subsequent development is shown in Figure 9.4.

FIGURE 9.4
Arrays as fields in a record

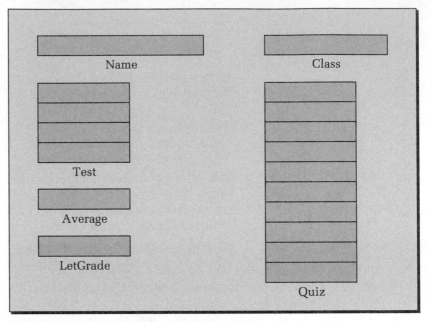

This record can now be formally defined by

```
TYPE
    String30 = PACKED ARRAY [1..30] OF char;
    String10 = PACKED ARRAY [1..10] OF char;
    TestScores = ARRAY [1..4] OF integer;
    QuizScores = ARRAY [1..10] OF integer;
    StudentInfo = RECORD
                    Name : String30;
                    Class : String10;
                    Test : TestScores;
                    Quiz : QuizScores;
                    Average : real;
                    LetGrade : char
                  END;  {  of RECORD StudentInfo  }
VAR
    Student : StudentInfo;
```

If the student associated with this record earned an 89 on the first test and a 9 (out of 10) on the first quiz, this information could be entered by reading the values or by assigning them appropriately. Thus, either of the following would suffice.

```
read (Student.Test[1], Student.Quiz[1]);
```

or

```
Student.Test[1] := 89;
Student.Quiz[1] := 9;
```

Exercises 9.1

1. Explain why records are structured data types.

2. Write a test program to
    a. Define a **RECORD** type in which the record contains fields for your name and your age.
    b. Declare a record variable to be of this type.
    c. Read in your name and age from a data file.
    d. Print out your name and age.

3. Discuss the similarities and differences between arrays and records as structured data types.

4. Use the **TYPE** definition section to define a record for each record illustrated in Figure 9.5(a), (b), and (c), respectively. In each case, also declare a record variable to be of the defined type.

FIGURE 9.5
Records with fields illustrated

(a)   TeamMember

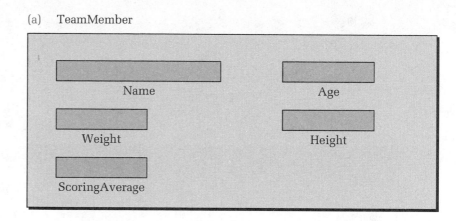

(b)   Book

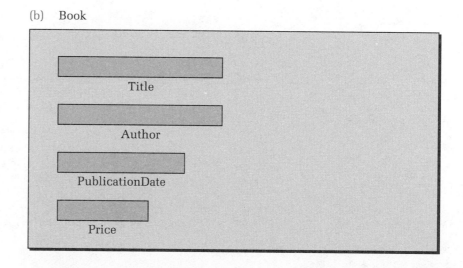

(c)   Student

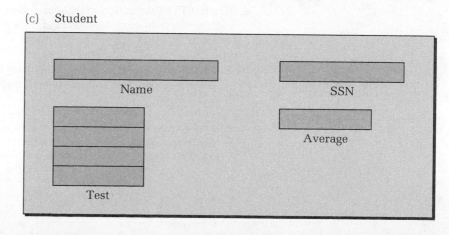

5. Draw a schematic representation of each of the following record definitions.

a.
```
TYPE
   String30 = PACKED ARRAY [1..30] OF char;
   String11 = PACKED ARRAY [1..11] OF char;
   EmployeeInfo = RECORD
                     Name : String30;
                     SSN : String11;
                     NumOfDep : integer;
                     HourlyWage : real
                  END;
VAR
   Employee : EmployeeInfo;
```

b.
```
TYPE
   HouseInfo = RECORD
                  Location : PACKED ARRAY [1..20]
                                OF char;
                  Age : integer;
                  NumRooms : integer;
                  NumBaths : integer;
                  BuildingType : (Brick, Frame);
                  Taxes : real;
                  Price : real
               END;
VAR
   House : HouseInfo;
```

c.
```
TYPE
   String20 = PACKED ARRAY [1..20] OF char;
   String30 = PACKED ARRAY [1..30] OF char;
   String8 = PACKED ARRAY [1..8] OF char;
   PhoneBook = RECORD
                  Name : String30;
                  Address : ARRAY [1..4]
                               OF String20;
                  PhoneNum : String8
               END;
VAR
   PhoneListing : PhoneBook;
```

6. Use the **TYPE** definition section to define an appropriate **RECORD** type for each of the following. In each case, also declare an appropriate record variable.

a. Families in your former school district: each record should contain the last name, parents' first and last names, address, number of children, and the ages of children.

b. Students in a school system: each record should contain the student's name, identification number, classification (Fr, So, Jr, or Sr), courses being taken (at most six), and grade point average.

7. Find all errors in each of the following definitions or declarations.

    a. ```
    TYPE
       Info : RECORD
                 Name = PACKED ARRAY [1..30] OF char;
                 Age : 0..100
              END;
    ```

    b. ```
    TYPE
       Member = RECORD
                   Age : integer;
                   IQ : integer
                END;
    VAR
       Member : Member;
    ```

    c. ```
    VAR
       Member = RECORD
                   Name : PACKED ARRAY [1..30] OF char;
                   Age : 0..100;
                   IQ = 50..200
                END;
    ```

8. Given the record defined by

    ```
    TYPE
       String30 = PACKED ARRAY [1..30] OF char;
       Weekdays = (Mon, Tues, Wed, Thur, Fri);
       ListOfScores = ARRAY [1..5] OF integer;
       Info = RECORD
                 Name : String30;
                 Day : Weekdays;
                 Score : ListOfScores;
                 Average : real
              END;
    VAR
       Contestant : Info;
       Sum : integer;
    ```

    assume values have been assigned as indicated in Figure 9.6. Indicate which of the following are valid and, if invalid, explain why.

    a. `Day := Wed;`

    b. `Contestant.Day := Wed;`

    c. `Score := 70;`

    d. `Score[3] := 70;`

    e. `Contestant.Score[3] := 70;`

    f. `Contestant[3].Score := 70;`

    g. ```
    FOR J := 1 TO 5 DO
       Sum := Sum + Contestant.Score[J];
    ```

    h. `Contestant.Score[3] := Score[2];`

    i. `Contestant.Score[3] := Contestant.Score[2] + 3;`

    j. `Average := (Score[1] + Score[2] + Score[3]) / 3;`

    k. ```
    IF Contestant.Day < Wed THEN
       Contestant.Average := Contestant.Score[1] +
                             Contestant.Score[2];
    ```

    l. `writeln (Contestant.Name:40, Contestant.Average:10:2);`
    ```

FIGURE 9.6
Values in fields of Contestant

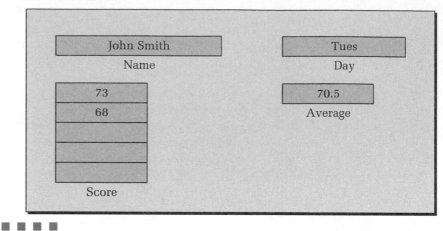

Contestant

■ ■ ■ ■

■ 9.2
Using Records

The previous section introduced you to the concept of **RECORD** as a structured data type. At this stage, you should be comfortable with this concept and be able to use the **TYPE** definition section to define such a data type. In this section, we will examine methods of working with records.

WITH . . . DO Using Records

Let's consider a record that contains fields for a student's name, three test scores, and test average. It could be defined by

```
TYPE
   String20 = PACKED ARRAY [1..20] OF char;
   List3 = ARRAY [1..3] OF integer;
   StudentRecord = RECORD
                     Name : String20;
                     Score : List3;
                     Average : real
                  END;  {  of RECORD StudentRecord  }
VAR
   Student : StudentRecord;
```

and envisioned as shown in Figure 9.7.

FIGURE 9.7
Fields in Student

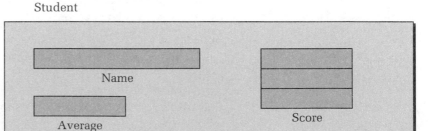

Student

To use this record, we need to assign or read data into appropriate fields. Therefore, assume a line of data is

Washington Joe   79 83 94

T   This data can be read by the fragment of code

```
FOR J := 1 TO 20 DO
   read (DataFile, Student.Name[J]);
FOR J := 1 TO 3 DO
   read (DataFile, Student.Score[J]);
readln (DataFile);
```

The average can be computed by

```
Student.Average := (Student.Score[1] +
                    Student.Score[2] +
                    Student.Score[3]) / 3;
```

Notice that each field identifier includes the record name. Fortunately, when working with fields of a record, Pascal provides a more convenient method of referring to these fields: a **WITH . . . DO** statement. Using this option, the previous fragment can be rewritten as

```
WITH Student DO
   BEGIN
     FOR J := 1 TO 20 DO
        read ((DataFile, Name[J]);
     FOR J := 1 TO 3 DO
        read (DataFile, Score[J]);
     readln (DataFile);
     Average := (Score[1] + Score[2] + Score[3]) / 3
   END;  {  of WITH...DO  }
```

Formally, a **WITH . . . DO** statement has the form

```
WITH ⟨record name⟩ DO
   BEGIN
     ⟨statement 1⟩;
     ⟨statement 2⟩;
          .
          .
          .
     ⟨statement n⟩
   END;
```

where the statements used may refer to the field identifiers but do not include the record name as part of the field identifier. This eliminates use of the period following the record name. Thus, instead of Student.Score[J], you can use Score[J].

As a second illustration, suppose you have a record defined as

```
TYPE
   String20 = PACKED ARRAY [1..20] OF char;
   PatientInfo = RECORD
                    Name : String20;
                    Age : integer;
                    Height : integer;
                    Weight : integer;
                    Gender : char
                 END;  {  of RECORD PatientInfo  }
VAR
   Patient : PatientInfo;
```

Values can be assigned to the various fields specifically by

```
Patient.Name := 'Jones Connie      ';
Patient.Age := 19;
Patient.Height := 67;
Patient.Weight := 125;
Patient.Gender := 'F';
```

or by

```
WITH Patient DO
  BEGIN
    Name := 'Jones Connie      ';
    Age := 19;
    Height := 67;
    Weight := 125;
    Gender := 'F'
  END;  {  of WITH...DO  }
```

A single **WITH . . . DO** statement can be used with more than one record. For example, using the previous two record definitions, it is possible to write

```
WITH Student, Patient DO
  BEGIN
    Average := (Score[1] + Score[2] + Score[3]) / 3;
    Age := 19
  END;  {  of WITH...DO  }
```

This is equivalent to the nested use of **WITH . . . DO,** as follows:

```
WITH Student DO
  WITH Patient DO
    BEGIN
      Average := (Score[1] + Score[2] + Score[3]) / 3;
      Age := 19
    END;
```

In this nesting, the record identifier is associated with each field defined in that record. Thus,

```
Age := 19
```

can be thought of as

```
Patient.Age := 19
```

Since Average is not a field in Patient, it will not be associated with the record identifier Patient. It will, however, be associated with the record identifier Student.

When using more than one record in a single **WITH . . . DO** statement, each field identifier should have a unique reference to exactly one of the listed records. If a field identifier is used in more than one of the records, the reference may be ambiguous and a logic error may result. Thus,

```
WITH Student, Patient DO
  writeln (Name);
```

is incorrect and could produce a result different from what you expect; it is not clear whether the reference is to Student.Name or Patient.Name. In some versions of Pascal, this is a compilation error. In others, it is a logic error and does not produce either a run-time error or a compilation error. Thus, while you might want to print Student.Name, you would print Patient.Name instead. This is because successive identifiers used as we just have are treated as if they are nested.

Copying Records

How can information contained in one record be transferred to another record? For example, we need to do this when we want to sort an array of records. To illustrate how records can be copied, consider the following definitions and declarations.

```
TYPE
  InfoA = RECORD
            Field1 : integer;
            Field2 : real;
            Field3 : char
          END;  {  of RECORD InfoA  }
  InfoB = RECORD
            Field1 : integer;
            Field2 : real;
            Field3 : char
          END;  {  of RECORD InfoB  }
VAR
  Rec1, Rec2 : InfoA;
  Rec3 : InfoB;
```

The three records declared can be envisioned as shown in Figure 9.8.

FIGURE 9.8
Copying records

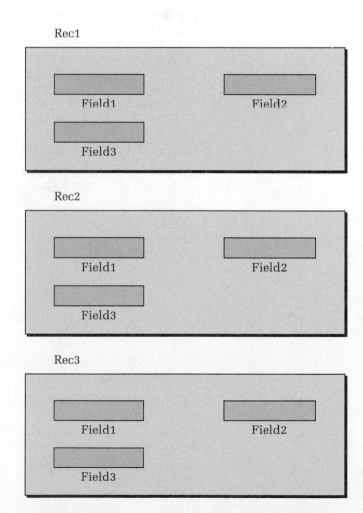

Rec1

Field1   Field2

Field3

Rec2

Field1   Field2

Field3

Rec3

Field1   Field2

Field3

Now, suppose data have been assigned to Rec1 by

```
WITH Rec1 DO
  BEGIN
    Field1 := 25;
    Field2 := 89.5;
    Field3 := 'M'
  END;  {  of WITH...DO  }
```

These data can be copied to the corresponding fields of Rec2 by

```
Rec2 := Rec1;
```

This single assignment statement accomplishes all the following:

```
Rec2.Field1 := Rec1.Field1;
Rec2.Field2 := Rec1.Field2;
Rec2.Field3 := Rec1.Field3;
```

It is important to note that such an assignment can only be made when the records are of identical type. For example, notice that InfoA and InfoB have the same structure but have been defined as different types. In this case, if you wish to assign the values in the fields of Rec1 to the corresponding fields of Rec3, the statement

```
Rec3 := Rec1;
```

produces a compilation error. Although Rec1 and Rec3 have the same structure, they are not of identical type. In this case, the information can be transferred by

```
WITH Rec3 DO
  BEGIN
    Field1 := Rec1.Field1;
    Field2 := Rec1.Field2;
    Field3 := Rec1.Field3
  END;  {  of WITH...DO  }
```

Reading Data into a Record

Once a record has been defined for a program, one task is to get data into the record. This is usually accomplished by reading from a data file. To illustrate, assume we have a record defined by

```
TYPE
  String20 = PACKED ARRAY [1..20] OF char;
  PatientInfo = RECORD
                  Name : String20;
                  Age : integer;
                  Height : integer;
                  Weight : integer;
                  Gender : char
                END;  {  of RECORD PatientInfo  }
VAR
  Patient : PatientInfo;
```

and a line of data is

```
Smith Mary            21 67 125F
```

One method of getting the data is to use a **WITH ... DO** statement in the main body of a program such as

```
BEGIN  {  Main program  }
reset (DataFile);
  WITH Patient DO
```

```
      BEGIN
        FOR J := 1 TO 20 DO
          read (DataFile, Name[J]);
        readln (DataFile, Age, Height, Weight, Gender)
      END;  { of WITH...DO  }
```

However, good program design would have us use a procedure for this task. Therefore, in order to use a procedure, we must be careful to use the user-defined data type PatientInfo and a variable parameter in the procedure heading. With these two considerations, an appropriate procedure is

```
PROCEDURE GetData (VAR Patient : PatientInfo);
  VAR
    J : integer;
  BEGIN
    WITH Patient DO
      BEGIN
        FOR J := 1 TO 20 DO
          read (DataFile, Name[J]);
        readln (DataFile, Age, Height, Weight, Gender)
      END  { of WITH...DO  }
  END;  { of PROCEDURE GetData  }
```

This is called from the main program by

```
GetData (Patient);
```

As a second example of getting data for a record, suppose you are writing a program to be used to compute grades of students in a class. As part of the program, a record type can be declared as

```
CONST
  NumQuizzes = 10;
  NumTest = 4;
TYPE
  String20 = PACKED ARRAY [1..20] OF char;
  QuizList = ARRAY [1..NumQuizzes] OF integer;
  TestList = ARRAY [1..NumTests] OF integer;
  StudentRecord = RECORD
                    Name : String20;
                    Quiz : QuizList;
                    Test : TestList;
                    QuizTotal : integer;
                    TestAverage : real;
                    LetterGrade : 'A'..'E'
                  END;  { of RECORD StudentRecord  }
VAR
  Student : StudentRecord;
```

If each line of data contains a student's name, ten quiz scores, and four test scores and looks like

| Smith Mary J. | 9 8 10 7 10 9 8 10 9 4 | 89 92 85 97 |
| Name | Quiz scores | Test scores |

a procedure to get this data could be

```
PROCEDURE GetData (VAR Student : StudentRecord);
  VAR
    J : integer;
  BEGIN
    WITH Student DO
      BEGIN
        FOR J := 1 TO 20 DO
          read (DataFile, Name[J]);
```

```
                    FOR J := 1 TO NumQuizzes DO
                       read (DataFile, Quiz[J]);
                    FOR J := 1 TO NumTests DO
                       read (DataFile, Test[J])
                 END;  {  of WITH...DO  }
              readln (DataFile)
            END;  {  of PROCEDURE GetData  }
```

It would be called from the main program by

```
    GetData (Student);
```

Let's now continue this example by writing a function to compute the test average for a student. Since this average is found by using the four test scores in the record, such a function could be

```
    FUNCTION TestAv (Test : TestList) : real;
      VAR
        J : integer;
        Sum : integer;
      BEGIN
        Sum := 0;
        FOR J := 1 TO NumTests DO
          Sum := Sum + Test[J];
        TestAv := Sum / NumTests
      END;  {  of FUNCTION TestAv  }
```

Since the array of test scores was the only parameter sent to the function and the average would normally be stored in the field TestAverage, this function could be called by

```
    Student.TestAverage := TestAv(Student.Test);
```

Printing Data from a Record

After information has been assigned or read from a data file and appropriate calculations have been made, you will want to print information from the record. Since this is frequently done in a procedure, let us assume the previous record for a student has the values illustrated in Figure 9.9.

FIGURE 9.9
Fields with values

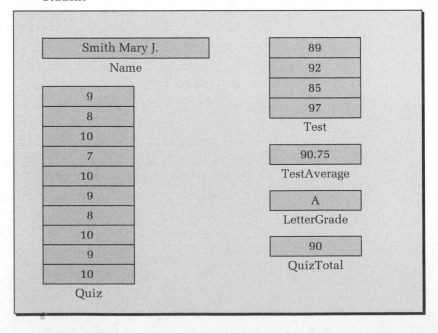

Using Key Fields in Records

The need to search records by certain key fields is a basic and very important process. To illustrate, consider how Ted Celentino, a former director of PARS applications for the on-line reservation system of TWA, responded to the question: "How are reservations indexed?" He said: "By the passenger's name, flight number, and departure date. All three are needed. If a passenger forgets his or her flight number, the agent can try to find a record of it by looking through all flights to the appropriate destination at that particular travel time. It's rare that a passenger doesn't know at least a couple of pieces of information that lead to his or her record."

If you want the output for a student to be

```
Name:           Smith Mary J.
Quiz Scores:    9 8 10 7 10 9 8 10 9 10
Quiz Total:     90
Test Scores:    89 92 85 97
Test Average:   90.75
Letter Grade:   A
```

a procedure for producing this is

```
PROCEDURE PrintData (Student : StudentRecord);
  CONST
    Skip = ' ';
  VAR
    J : integer;

  BEGIN
    writeln;
    WITH Student DO
      BEGIN
        writeln (Skip:10, 'Name:', Name:29);
        write (Skip:10, 'Quiz Scores:');
        FOR J := 1 TO NumQuizzes DO
          write (Quiz[J]:3);
        writeln;
        writeln (Skip:10, 'Quiz Total:', QuizTotal:5);
        write (Skip:10, 'Test Scores:');
        FOR J := 1 TO NumTests DO
          write (Test[J]:4);
        writeln;
        writeln (Skip:10, 'Test Average:', TestAverage:6:2);
        writeln (Skip:10, 'Letter Grade:', LetterGrade:2)
      END  {  of WITH...DO  }
  END;  {  of PROCEDURE PrintData  }
```

This procedure would be called from the main program by

```
PrintData (Student);
```

■ **EXAMPLE 9.2**

As a concluding example, let's consider a short interactive program that uses records and procedures to perform the arithmetic operation of multiplying two fractions. The fractions should be entered in the form

```
1/2
```

The program declares a record for each fraction and uses procedures to get the data, multiply the fractions, and print the results.

Before writing this program, let's examine appropriate record definitions and a procedure for computing the product. A definition is

```
TYPE
   RationalNumber = RECORD
                      Numerator : integer;
                      Denominator : integer
                    END;  {  of RECORD RationalNumber  }
VAR
   X, Y, Product : RationalNumber;
```

A procedure for computing the product is

```
PROCEDURE ComputeProduct (X, Y : RationalNumber;
                          VAR Product : RationalNumber);
   BEGIN
     WITH Product DO
       BEGIN
         Numerator := X.Numerator * Y.Numerator;
         Denominator := X.Denominator * Y.Denominator
       END  {  of WITH...DO  }
   END;  {  of PROCEDURE ComputeProduct  }
```

This procedure is called from the main program by

```
ComputeProduct (X, Y, Product);
```

A complete program for this problem follows.

```
PROGRAM Fractions (input, output);

{  This program illustrates the use of records with procedures.  }
{  In particular, procedures are used to                         }
{                                                                }
{      1.  get the data                                          }
{      2.  perform computations                                  }
{      3.  print the results                                     }
{                                                                }
{  The specific task is to compute the product of two rational   }
{  numbers.                                                       }

TYPE
   RationalNumber = RECORD
                      Numerator : integer;
                      Denominator : integer
                    END;  {  of RECORD RationalNumber  }

VAR
   X, Y, Product : RationalNumber;
   MoreData : boolean;
   Response : char;

{*************************************************************** }
```

```
PROCEDURE GetData (VAR X, Y : RationalNumber);

   {  Given:    Nothing                                          }
   {  Task:     Have entered from the keyboard the numerator and }
   {               denominator of two fractions                  }
   {  Return:   Two records, each containing a field for the     }
   {               numerator and denominator of a fraction       }

   VAR
     Slash : char;

   BEGIN
     WITH X DO
       BEGIN
         write ('Enter a fraction in the form a/b.  ');
         readln (Numerator, Slash, Denominator)
       END;  {  of WITH X DO  }
     WITH Y DO
       BEGIN
         write ('Enter a fraction in the form a/b.  ');
         readln (Numerator, Slash, Denominator)
       END  {  of WITH Y DO  }
   END;  {  of PROCEDURE GetData  }

{***************************************************************** }

PROCEDURE ComputeProduct (X, Y : RationalNumber;
                          VAR Product : RationalNumber);

   {  Given:    Records for two fractions                        }
   {  Task:     Compute the product and store result             }
   {  Return:   Product of the fraction                          }

   BEGIN
     WITH Product DO
       BEGIN
         Numerator := X.Numerator * Y.Numerator;
         Denominator := X.Denominator * Y.Denominator
       END  {  of WITH...DO  }
   END;  {  of PROCEDURE ComputeProduct  }

{***************************************************************** }

PROCEDURE PrintResults (X, Y, Product : RationalNumber);

   {  Given:    Records for each of two given fractions and their }
   {               product                                        }
   {  Task:     Print an equation stating the problem and answer; }
   {               standard fraction form should be used as       }
   {               output                                         }
   {  Return:   Nothing                                           }

   BEGIN
     writeln;
     writeln (X.Numerator:13, Y.Numerator:6, Product.Numerator:6);
     writeln ('--- * --- = ---':25);
     writeln (X.Denominator:13, Y.Denominator:6, Product.Denominator:6);
     writeln
   END;  {  of PROCEDURE PrintResults  }

{***************************************************************** }
```

```
BEGIN  {  Main program  }
  MoreData := true;
  WHILE MoreData DO
    BEGIN
      GetData (X, Y);
      ComputeProduct (X, Y, Product);
      PrintResults (X, Y, Product);
      write ('Do you wish to see another problem?  <Y> or <N>  ');
      readln (Response);
      Moredata := (Response = 'Y') OR (Response = 'y');
      writeln
    END  {  of WHILE...DO  }
END.  {  of main program  }
```

With input from the keyboard of

```
3/4 1/2
3/2 7/10
2/3 4/5
```

sample output is

```
Enter a fraction in the form a/b.  3/4
Enter a fraction in the form a/b.  1/2


       3     1     3
      --- * --- = ---
       4     2     8


Do you wish to see another problem?  <Y> or <N>   Y

Enter a fraction in the form a/b.  3/2
Enter a fraction in the form a/b.  7/10


       3     7    21
      --- * --- = ---
       2    10    20


Do you wish to see another problem?  <Y> or <N>   Y

Enter a fraction in the form a/b.  2/3
Enter a fraction in the form a/b.  4/5


       2     4     8
      --- * --- = ---
       3     5    15


Do you wish to see another problem?  <Y> or <N>   N
```

Exercises 9.2

1. Assume a program contains the following **TYPE** definition and **VAR** declaration sections.

```
TYPE
  Info1 = RECORD
             Initial : char;
             Age : integer
          END;
  Info2 = RECORD
             Initial : char;
             Age : integer
          END;
```

```
VAR
   Cust1, Cust2 : Info1;
   Cust3, Cust4 : Info2;
```

Indicate which of the following statements are valid. Give an explanation for those that are invalid.

a. `Cust1 := Cust2;`

b. `Cust2 := Cust3;`

c. `Cust3 := Cust4;`

d.
```
WITH Cust1 DO
   BEGIN
      Initial := 'W';
      Age := 21
   END;
```

e.
```
WITH Cust1, Cust2 DO
   BEGIN
      Initial := 'W';
      Age := 21
   END;
```

2. Write a test program to see what happens when two different records with the same field name are used in a single **WITH . . . DO** statement. Use the declarations and **TYPE** definitions in Exercise 1. For example,

```
WITH Student1, Student2 DO
   Age := 21;
writeln (Student1.Age);
writeln (Student2.Age);
```

3. Assume the **TYPE** and **VAR** sections of a program include

```
TYPE
   String11 = PACKED ARRAY [1..11] OF char;
   String20 = PACKED ARRAY [1..20] OF char;
   Info = RECORD
            Name : String20;
            SSN : String11;
            Age : integer;
            HourlyWage : real;
            HoursWorked : real;
            Volunteer : boolean
          END;
VAR
   Employee1, Employee2 : Info;
```

a. Show three different methods of transferring all information from the record for Employee1 to the record for Employee2.

b. Suppose you wished to transfer all information from the record for Employee1 to the record for Employee2 except HoursWorked. Discuss different methods for doing this. Which do you feel is the most efficient?

4. Assume the **TYPE** and **VAR** sections of a program are the same as in Exercise 3. Write a procedure to be used to read information into such a record from a data file. A typical line of data is

| Smith Jane M. | 111-22-3333 25 10.50 41.5Y ▮ |

where 'Y' indicates the worker is a volunteer (**true**) and 'N' indicates the worker is not a volunteer (**false**).

5. Assume a record has been declared by

```
TYPE
  String20 = PACKED ARRAY [1..20] OF char;
  StudentInfo = RECORD
                  Name : String20;
                  TotalPts : 0..500;
                  LetterGrade : char
                END;
VAR
  Student : StudentInfo;
```

Write a function to compute the student's letter grade based on cutoff levels of 90 percent, 80 percent, 70 percent, and 60 percent. Show how this function is used in a program to assign the appropriate letter grade to the appropriate field of a student's record.

6. Review Example 9.2, in which two fractions were multiplied. In a similar fashion, write procedures for

a. Dividing two fractions (watch out for zero).

b. Adding two fractions.

c. Subtracting two fractions.

7. Some instructors throw out the lowest test score for each student when computing the student's test average. Assume a record Student of type StudentRecord has been declared and data have been read into appropriate fields.

a. Write a function to compute the test average using the best three scores.

b. Show how a constant in the **CONST** section can be used to generalize this to finding the best $n - 1$ of n scores.

c. Rewrite the function using a sort to sort the array of scores from high to low and then add the first three from the array.

d. Must the entire array be sorted in order to find the three highest scores? Explain.

8. Show how the program Fractions in Example 9.2 can be modified to check for nonzero denominators.

■ ■ ■ ■

■ 9.3
Data Structures with Records

Nested Records

The first concept to be examined in this section is that of *nested record*. A nested record is a record which is a field in another record. For example, suppose you are working on a program to be used by a biology department and part of your work is to declare a record for a faculty member. This record is to contain fields for the person's name, office number, telephone number, and supply order. Let us assume that the supply order information is to contain the company name, a description of the item ordered, its price, and the quantity ordered. The record for each faculty member, with SupplyOrder as a record within a record, can be visualized as shown in Figure 9.10.

FIGURE 9.10
Illustration of a nested record

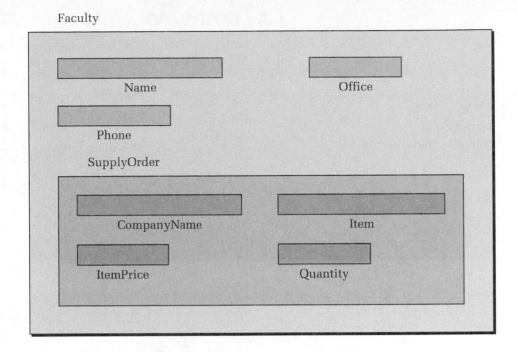

Let's now look at how such a record can be declared. One possible method is

```
TYPE
   String20 = PACKED ARRAY [1..20] OF char;
   String12 = PACKED ARRAY [1..12] OF char;
   OrderInfo = RECORD
                  CompanyName : String20;
                  Item : String20;
                  ItemPrice : real;
                  Quantity : integer
               END;  {  of RECORD OrderInfo  }
   FacultyInfo = RECORD
                  Name : String20;
                  Office : integer;
                  Phone : String12;
                  SupplyOrder : OrderInfo
               END;  {  of RECORD FacultyInfo  }
VAR
   Faculty : FacultyInfo;
```

We must now consider how to access fields in the nested record. We do this by continuing our notation for field designators. Thus,

```
Faculty.Name
Faculty.Office
Faculty.Phone
```

refer to the first three fields of Faculty, and

```
Faculty.SupplyOrder.CompanyName
Faculty.SupplyOrder.Item
Faculty.SupplyOrder.ItemPrice
Faculty.SupplyOrder.Quantity
```

are used to access fields of the nested record

```
Faculty.SupplyOrder
```

Using WITH . . . DO

As expected, **WITH . . . DO** can be used with nested records. Let us consider the problem of assigning data to the various fields of Faculty as previously declared. If we wish to have values assigned as in Figure 9.11, we can use the following assignment statements.

FIGURE 9.11
Values in fields of a nested record

Faculty

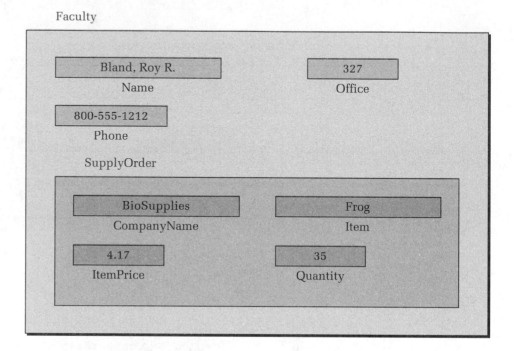

```
WITH Faculty DO
  BEGIN
    Name := 'Bland Roy R.          ';
    Office := 327;
    Phone := '800-555-1212';
    SupplyOrder.CompanyName := 'BioSupplies          ';
    SupplyOrder.Item := 'Frog                  ';
    SupplyOrder.ItemPrice := 4.17;
    SupplyOrder.Quantity := 35
  END;
```

Note that the last four assignment statements all used fields in the record SupplyOrder. Thus, a **WITH . . . DO** statement can be used there in the following manner:

```
WITH Faculty DO
  BEGIN
    Name := 'Bland Roy R.          ';
    Office := 327;
    Phone := '800-555-1212';
    WITH SupplyOrder DO
      BEGIN
        CompanyName := 'BioSupplies          ';
        Item := 'Frog                  ';
        ItemPrice := 4.17;
        Quantity := 35
      END  {  of WITH SupplyOrder DO  }
  END;  {  of WITH Faculty DO  }
```

There is yet a third way to accomplish our task. **WITH ... DO** can be used with both the main record name and the nested record name as follows:

```
WITH Faculty, SupplyOrder DO
   BEGIN
     Name := 'Bland Roy R.          ';
     Office := 327;
     Phone := '800-555-1212';
     CompanyName := 'BioSupplies          ';
     Item := 'Frog                  ';
     ItemPrice := 4.17;
     Quantity := 35
   END;  {  WITH...DO  }
```

Since SupplyOrder is nested within Faculty, each reference is distinctly identified and the fragment accomplishes our objective. When using nested records, you must be careful to identify fields distinctly. To illustrate, suppose Faculty1 and Faculty2 are also of type FacultyInfo. Then each of the following is valid.

```
Faculty1.Name := Faculty2.Name;
Faculty1.SupplyOrder.Item := Faculty2.SupplyOrder.Item;
Faculty1.SupplyOrder := Faculty2.SupplyOrder;
```

Note that in the third statement, you are transferring the contents of an entire record. This statement is valid because both records are of type OrderInfo.

To illustrate some attempts to use inappropriate designators, assume Faculty, Faculty1, and Faculty2 are of type FacultyInfo. Consider the following inappropriate references.

```
Faculty.Item := 'Frog                  '; { Incorrect }
```

In this designator, the intermediate descriptor is missing. Thus, something like

```
Faculty.SupplyOrder.Item
```

is needed. In

```
SupplyOrder.Quantity := 35; { Incorrect }
```

no reference is made to which record is being accessed. A record name must be stated, such as

```
Faculty1.SupplyOrder.Quantity
```

As our final example of working with nested records, let's write a procedure to get data from a data file for a record of type FacultyInfo with the following definitions and declarations.

```
TYPE
   String20 = PACKED ARRAY [1..20] OF char;
   String12 = PACKED ARRAY [1..12] OF char;
   OrderInfo = RECORD
                  CompanyName : String20;
                  Item : String20;
                  ItemPrice : real;
                  Quantity : integer
               END;  { of RECORD OrderInfo  }
   FacultyInfo = RECORD
                   Name : String20;
                   Office : 100..399;
                   Phone : String12;
                   SupplyOrder : OrderInfo
                 END;  { of RECORD FacultyInfo  }
VAR
   Faculty : FacultyInfo;
```

Impact of Computers on Art

Dana J. Lamb recently discussed the impact of computers on the arts in an article appearing in *Academic Computing*. Among other things, she reported part of a conversation held with Alice Jones, a freelance graphic designer, who was a member of a summer arts program studying developments in full-color graphics on personal computers. When Jones was asked about the use of computers in her professional pursuits, she indicated her study led her to believe that the time required to produce a typical paste-up could be reduced by as much as 75 percent, depending on the proficiency of the graphic artist. She pointed out that the traditional means of production art required the teamwork of a graphic artist, typesetter, copy camera operator, photographer, and/or illustrator. The logistics of even the simplest paste-up with a few black and white photographs often required days in transit as copy was typeset at one location; photos and illustrations created, then reduced or enlarged at two other locations; and all traveling from each place of business to another while the graphic designer sits waiting. Jones observed that this dispersion of design components has been suddenly unified and put into the hands of the designer.

Later in the article, Lamb addressed the issue of how artists perceive the computer. According to Lamb, the opinions of those in the art world can be divided into three major groups:

1. those who deny that the computer has any legitimate place in the creation of art;
2. those who believe that the computer should be included in the realm of traditional and/or nontraditional tools in the creation of art; and
3. those who believe that the computer, together with its fundamental structure, is an art medium unto itself.

Lamb concluded her article with the following paragraph:

It is easy to forget that we are witnessing the infancy of this medium in relationship to the arts because of its phenomenal growth in eight years. Artists have been using computers since the 1950s but up to the last decade were viewed as oddities with few arenas to exhibit or share their work. Those days are over, and as the image of these machines becomes less a philosophical issue and simply another tool in the creative process, we can move on to develop the "clear path" between the visual concept and final product espoused.

If we assume the data for a faculty member are on two lines of the data file as

(line 1) | Bland Roy R.   327 800-555-1212 |

(line 2) | BioSupplies   Frog   4.17 35 |

a procedure to obtain this data is

```
PROCEDURE GetData (VAR Faculty : FacultyInfo);
   VAR
      J : integer;
      Blank : char;
   BEGIN
      WITH Faculty, SupplyOrder DO
        BEGIN
          FOR J := 1 TO 20 DO
            read (Data, Name[J]);
          read (Data, Office);
          read (Data, Blank);   {  Move the pointer  }
          FOR J := 1 TO 12 DO
            read (Data, Phone[J]);
          readln (Data);  {  Go to beginning of the next line  }

     {  Now read the second line  }
```

```
       FOR J := 1 TO 20 DO
          read (Data, CompanyName[J]);
       FOR J := 1 TO 20 DO
          read (Data, Item[J]);
       readln (Data, ItemPrice, Quantity)
    END  {  of WITH Faculty, SupplyOrder DO  }
END;  {  of PROCEDURE GetData  }
```

This procedure is called from the main program by

```
  GetData (Faculty);
```

Array of Records

Next we will use structured data types to look at an *array of records*. It is easy to imagine needing to make a list of information about several people, events, or items. Furthermore, it is not unusual for the information about a particular person, event, or item to consist of several different data items. When this situation occurs, a record can be defined for each person, event, or item and an array of these records can be used to achieve the desired result. In such situations, you can frequently use an array of records rather than a parallel array.

For example, suppose the local high school sports boosters want you to write a program to enable them to keep track of the names and donations of its members. Assume there is a maximum of 50 members making a donation. This problem was solved in Chapter 8 using parallel arrays; it can now be solved by using an array of records. Each record will have two fields: the donor's name and the amount donated. The record could be visualized as shown in Figure 9.12.

FIGURE 9.12
Fields in TempDonor

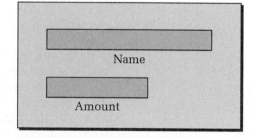

We will now declare an array of these records to produce the arrangement shown in Figure 9.13.

The definitions and declarations needed are

```
CONST
  ClubSize = 50;
TYPE
  String20 = PACKED ARRAY [1..20] OF char;
  MemberInfo = RECORD
                 Name : String20;
                 Amount : real
               END; {  of RECORD MemberInfo  }
  DonorList = ARRAY  [1..ClubSize] OF MemberInfo;
VAR
  Donor : DonorList;
  TempDonor : MemberInfo;
  Count : integer;
```

FIGURE 9.13
Illustration of an array of
records

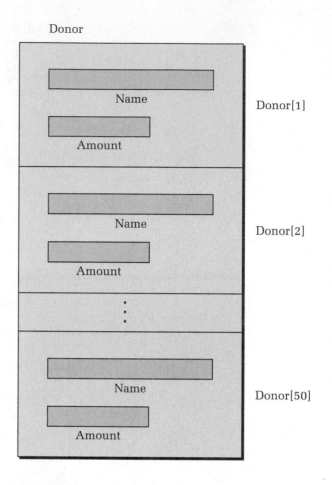

Before proceeding, note the following:

1. Structures are built in the **TYPE** definition section to facilitate later work with procedures and functions.

2. Each record is now an array element and can be accessed by a reference to the index. Thus, if the third member's name is Tom Jones and he donates $100.00, you can write

```
Donor[3].Name := 'Jones Tom            ';
Donor[3].Amount := 100.0;
```

Better still, you can use **WITH . . . DO** to get

```
WITH Donor[3] DO
  BEGIN
    Name := 'Jones Tom            ';
    Amount := 100.0
  END;   {  of WITH...DO  }
```

3. Since all records in an array are of identical type, contents of two records can be interchanged by

```
TempDonor := Donor[J];
Donor[J] := Donor[K];
Donor[K] := TempDonor;
```

This is needed if records are to be sorted by one of their fields.

4. Be careful with syntax when using an array of records or an array as a field within a record. For example, if an array of five scores has

been defined as a field in an array of records as shown in Figure 9.14, note the following distinctions:

a. `Student[2].Average`   (Average for student 2)
b. `Student[2].Score[4]`   (Score on test 4 for student 2)
c. `Student.Score[2]`   (Not defined; student is an array)

FIGURE 9.14
Array of records

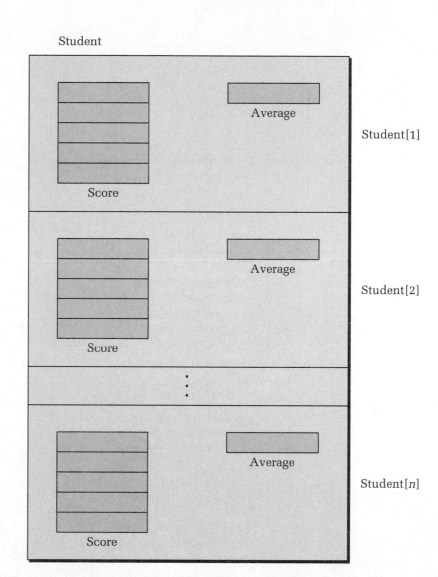

Student

Student[1]

Student[2]

Student[n]

Let's now return to the problem posed by the sports boosters. A first-level pseudocode design is

1. Get the data
2. Sort alphabetically by name
3. Print the sorted list

If we assume each line of the data file is of the form

| Jones Tom | 100.0 |

a procedure to get the data is not difficult. We have to remember, however, to count the actual number of donors read. Such a procedure is

```
PROCEDURE GetData (VAR Donor : DonorList;
                   VAR Count : integer);
  VAR
    J : integer;
  BEGIN
    Count := 0;
    WHILE NOT eof (DataFile) AND (Count < ClubSize) DO
      BEGIN
        Count := Count + 1;
        WITH Donor[Count] DO
          BEGIN
            FOR J := 1 TO 20 DO
              read (DataFile, Name[J]);
            readln (DataFile, Amount)
          END  {  of WITH Donor[Count] DO  }
      END  {  of WHILE NOT eof  }
  END;  {  of PROCEDURE GetData  }
```

This procedure is called from the main program by

```
GetData (Donor, Count);
```

and Count will contain the actual number of donors after the procedure is called.

The next procedure in this problem will require a sort. A sort that actually exchanges entire records is not very efficient. When working with an array of records, it is more efficient to use an *index sort*, which essentially uses a separate array to reorder the indices in the desired order. However, the formal development of this sorting technique is not covered here; it is deferred to a subsequent course. Therefore, for now, recall the selection sort developed in Chapter 7 as follows:

```
FOR J := 1 TO N-1 DO                 {  Find the minimum N-1 times  }
  BEGIN
    Index := J;
    FOR K := J + 1 TO N DO
      IF A[K] < A[Index] THEN        {  Find smallest number         }
        Index := K;
      IF Index <> J THEN
        BEGIN
          Temp := A[Index];
          A[Index] := A[J];
          A[J] := Temp
        END  {  of exchange  }
  END;  {  of one pass  }
```

With suitable changes, the array of records can be sorted alphabetically by

```
PROCEDURE Sort (VAR Donor : DonorList;
                Count : integer);
  VAR
    J, K, Index : integer;
    Temp : MemberInfo;
  BEGIN
    FOR J := 1 TO Count-1 DO
      BEGIN
        Index := J;
        FOR K := J + 1 TO Count DO
          IF Donor[K].Name < Donor[Index].Name THEN
            Index := K;
```

```
            IF Index <> J THEN
               BEGIN
                 Temp := Donor[Index];
                 Donor[Index] := Donor[J];
                 Donor[J] := Temp
               END {  of exchange  }
          END {  of FOR loop  }
        END; {  of PROCEDURE Sort  }
```

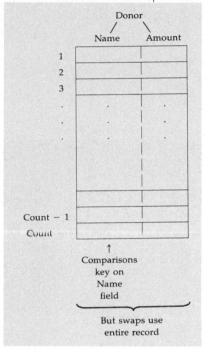

This procedure would be called from the main program by

```
    Sort (Donor, Count);
```

In this procedure, note that the sort is by only one field in the record, specifically, the donor's name

```
    IF Donor[K].Name < Donor[Index].Name THEN
```

However, when the names are to be exchanged, contents of the entire record are exchanged by

```
    Temp := Donor[Index];
```

We conclude this example by writing a procedure to print the results. If we want the output to be

```
             Local Sports Boosters
                 Donation List
-----------------------------------------

      Name                    Amount
      ----                    ------

Anerice Sue                   150.00
Compton John                  125.00
      .                          .
      .                          .
      .                          .
```

a procedure to produce this is

```
PROCEDURE PrintList (VAR Donor : DonorList;
                         Count : integer);
  CONST
    Skip = ' ' ;
  VAR
    J : integer;
  BEGIN
    writeln;
    writeln (Skip:20, 'Local Sports Boosters');
    writeln (Skip:24, 'Donation List');
    writeln (Skip:10, '----------------------------------------');
    writeln;
    writeln (Skip:13, 'Name', Skip:27, 'Amount');
    writeln (Skip:13, '----', Skip:27, '------');
    writeln;

  {  Now print the list  }

    FOR J := 1 TO Count DO
      WITH Donor[J] DO
        writeln (Skip:10, Name, Amount:20:2);
    writeln
  END;  {  of PROCEDURE PrintList  }
```

With these three procedures available, the main program is then

```
BEGIN  {  Main program  }
  reset (DataFile);
  GetData (Donor, Count);
  Sort (Donor, Count);
  PrintList (Donor, Count)
END.  {  of main program  }
```

This example is less involved than many of your problems will be, but it does illustrate an array of records, appropriate notation for fields in an array of records, sorting an array of records by using one field of the records, and using procedures with an array of records.

Exercises 9.3

1. Consider the declaration

```
TYPE
  B = RECORD
        C : real;
        D : integer
      END;
  A = RECORD
        E : boolean;
        F : B
      END;
VAR
  G : A;
```

a. Give a schematic representation of the record G.

b. Indicate which of the following are valid references.

i. G.E	vi. A.F.C
ii. G.C	vii. A.E
iii. G.F.D	viii. WITH G DO
iv. F.D	ix. WITH G, F DO
v. G.A	x. G.F.C

c. Why would it be incorrect to define record A before record B?

2. Write a test program that illustrates the difference between an array of records and a record with an array component.

3. Give an appropriate definition and declaration for a record that will contain fields for a person's name, address, social security number, annual income, and family information. Address is a record with fields for street address, city, state abbreviation, and zip code. Family information is a record with fields for marital status (S, M, W, or D) and number of children.

4. Consider the following definitions and subsequent declarations.

```
TYPE
   String20 = PACKED ARRAY [1..20] OF char;
   Mood = (Quiet, Bright, Surly);
   CurrentHealth = (Poor, Average, Good);
   PatientStatus = RECORD
                      Mental : Mood;
                      Physical : CurrentHealth
                   END;  { of RECORD PatientStatus  }
   PatientInfo = RECORD
                    Name : String20;
                    Status : PatientStatus;
                    PastDue : boolean
                 END;  { of RECORD PatientInfo  }
VAR
   Patient1, Patient2 : PatientInfo;
```

   a. Give a schematic representation for Patient1.

   b. Show how a single letter (Q, B, or S) can be read from a data file and then have the appropriate value assigned to Patient1.Status.Mental.

   c. Write a procedure to read a line of data and assign (if necessary) appropriate values to the various fields. A typical data line is

Smith Sue   BAF

   and indicates that Sue Smith's mood is bright, her health is average, and her account is not past due.

5. Declare an array of records to be used for 15 players on a basketball team. The following information is needed for each player: name, age, height, weight, scoring average, and rebounding average.

6. Declare an array of records to be used for students in a classroom (at most 40 students). Each record should contain fields for a student's name, social security number, ten quiz scores, three test scores, overall average, and letter grade.

7. Consider the following declaration of an array of records.

```
CONST
   ClassSize = 35;
TYPE
   String20 = PACKED ARRAY [1..20] OF char;
   Attendance = (Excellent, Average, Poor);
   TestList = ARRAY [1..4] OF integer;
   StudentInfo = RECORD
                    Name : String20;
                    Atten : Attendance;
                    Test : TestList;
                    Aver : real
                 END;
   StudentList = ARRAY [1..ClassSize] OF StudentInfo;
VAR
   Student : StudentList;
```

   a. Give a schematic representation for Student.

   b. Explain what the following function accomplishes.

```
FUNCTION GuessWhat (Test : TestList) : real;
  VAR
    K, Sum : integer;
  BEGIN
    Sum := 0;
    FOR K := 1 TO 4 DO
      Sum := Sum + Test[K];
    GuessWhat := Sum / 4
  END;
```

   c. Write a procedure to print out the information for one student. In this procedure, the entire word describing attendance is to be printed.

8. Reconsider the problem in this section that kept a record of the name and amount donated for each member of the local high school boosters club. Expanding on that problem, write a procedure or function for each of the following.

   a. Find the maximum donation and print out the amount together with the donor's name.

   b. Find the sum of all donations.

   c. Find the average of all donations.

   d. Sort the array according to size of the donation, largest first.

■ ■ ■ ■

■ 9.4
Record Variants

You should have noticed by now that when records are defined, each record has certain fixed fields. Since it is sometimes desirable to use a record structure in which the number and type of fields vary, Pascal allows records to be defined with a *variant part*. For example, a real estate company might want the records for their customers to contain different information depending on whether the property for sale is a house or a business. For houses, the number of bedrooms, bathrooms, and whether or not there is a fireplace could be indicated; for businesses, the number of offices and amount of possible rental income could be listed.

Defining a Variant Part

In order to define the variant part of a record, we use a form of the **CASE** statement to specify which fields should be included. Then, depending on the value of the identifier in the **CASE** part of the definition, the desired fields are listed. In the real estate example, we could have

```
TYPE
  PropertyType = (House, Business);
  Listing = RECORD
              CASE Kind : PropertyType OF
                House    : (NumBedrms : integer;
                            NumBaths : integer;
                            Fireplace : boolean);
                Business : (NumOffices : integer;
                            RentalIncome : integer)
            END;  { of RECORD Listing }
VAR
  Property : Listing;
```

Now Property is a record with a variant part. Kind is not a reserved word and is called the *tag field*. Depending on the value assigned to Kind, the appropriate fields are available. If the assignment

```
Property.Kind := House;
```

is made, the record can be envisioned as shown in Figure 9.15(a). If the assignment

```
Property.Kind := Business;
```

is made, we have the record illustrated in Figure 9.15(b).

FIGURE 9.15
Fields in a variant record

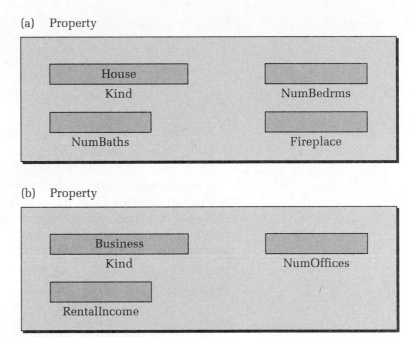

(a) Property

House
Kind

NumBedrms

NumBaths

Fireplace

(b) Property

Business
Kind

NumOffices

RentalIncome

In actual practice, records with variant parts usually have fixed parts also. Suppose the address and price of each property listed for sale should be included. Since fields for these would be defined for every record, these fields would be referred to as the *fixed part*. A complete definition is

```
TYPE
   PropertyType = (House, Business);
   String30 = PACKED ARRAY [1..30] OF char;
   Listing = RECORD
              Address : String30;              } fixed
              Price : integer;                 } part
              CASE Kind : PropertyType OF
                 House    : (NumBedrms : integer;
                             NumBaths : integer;    } variant
                             Fireplace : boolean);  } part
                 Business : (NumOffices : integer;
                             RentalIncome : integer)
              END;  { of RECORD Listing }
VAR
   Property : Listing;
```

The following points concerning variant parts should now be made.

1. The variant part of a record must be listed after the fixed part.
2. Only one variant part can be defined in a record.
3. The data type for the tag field must be ordinal.
4. Only one **END** is used to terminate the definition. This terminates both **CASE** and **RECORD**.

Records with variant parts are defined by a form as follows:

⟨record name⟩ = **RECORD**
        ⟨field 1⟩ : ⟨type⟩;
        ⟨field 2⟩ : ⟨type⟩;   ⎫
           .   ⎬ fixed
           .   ⎪ part
           .
        ⟨field *n*⟩ : ⟨type⟩;   ⎭
        CASE ⟨tag field⟩ : ⟨tag type⟩ **OF**
           ⟨value 1⟩ : (⟨field list⟩);   ⎫
           ⟨value 2⟩ : (⟨field list⟩);   ⎬ variant
               .   ⎪   part
               .
               .
        ⟨value *m*⟩ : (⟨field list⟩)   ⎭
      END;

It is possible to completely avoid the use of variant parts of a record. One can list all possible fields in the fixed part and then use them appropriately. However, this usually means that more storage is required. To illustrate, let's consider how memory is allocated. For each field in the fixed part of the previous example, an area in memory is reserved as:

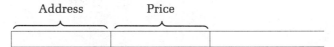

For the variant part of the record, a single area is reserved that will subsequently be utilized by whichever fields are determined by the value of the tag field. In this sense, they overlap as indicated.

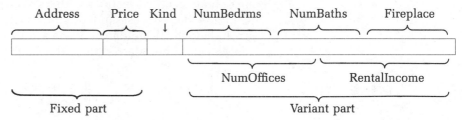

A note of caution is in order for those who include variant records as part of programs. Careful programming is needed to properly initialize the variant part or unexpected results may be obtained. For example, using the previous illustration, suppose Kind is first House with values for NumBedrms, NumBaths, and Fireplace. If a subsequent value of Kind is Business and no new data are read or assigned, the value of NumOffices may in fact be NumBedrms.

We close this section with an example that illustrates a definition and subsequent use of a record with a variant part.

■ **EXAMPLE 9.3**

Define a record to be used when working with plane geometric figures. The record should have fixed fields for the type of figure (a single character designator) and area. The variant part should have fields for information needed to compute the area. After the record is defined, write a procedure to get data from a line of the data file. Then write a function that can be used to compute the area of the plane figure.

To complete the definition of the record, let's assume we are working with at most the geometric figures circle, square, and triangle (C, S, and T, respectively). An appropriate definition is

```
TYPE
   FigureShape = (Circle, Square, Triangle);
   FigureInfo = RECORD
                   Object : char;
                   Area : real;
                   CASE Shape : FigureShape OF
                      Circle   : (Radius : real);
                      Square   : (Side : real);
                      Triangle : (Base, Height : real)
                 END;  {  of RECORD FigureInfo  }
VAR
   Figure : FigureInfo;
```

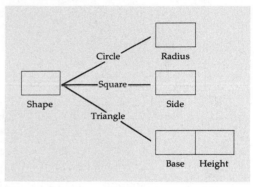

Each data line has a single character designating the kind of figure followed by appropriate information needed to compute the area. For example,

```
T 6.0 8.0
```

represents a triangle with base 6.0 and height 8.0. A procedure to get a line of data is

```
PROCEDURE GetData (VAR Figure : FigureInfo);
   BEGIN
      WITH Figure DO
        BEGIN
          read (Data, Object);
          CASE Object OF
            'C' : BEGIN
                    Shape := Circle;
                    readln (Data, Radius)
                  END;
            'S' : BEGIN
                    Shape := Square;
                    readln (Data, Side)
                  END;
            'T' : BEGIN
                    Shape := Triangle;
                    readln (Data, Base, Height)
                  END
          END  {  of CASE Object  }
        END  {  of WITH...DO  }
   END; {  of PROCEDURE GetData  }
```

This is called from the main program by

```
GetData (Figure);
```

Finally, a function to compute the area is

```
FUNCTION ComputeArea (Figure : FigureInfo) : real;
  CONST
    Pi = 3.14159;
  BEGIN
    WITH Figure DO
      BEGIN
        CASE Shape OF
           Circle   : ComputeArea := Pi * Radius * Radius;
           Square   : ComputeArea := Side * Side;
           Triangle : ComputeArea := 0.5 * Base * Height
        END  {  of CASE Shape  }
      END    {of WITH...DO  }
  END;  {  of FUNCTION ComputeArea  }
```

This function is called by

```
Figure.Area := ComputeArea(Figure);
```

Exercises 9.4

1. Explain how memory may be saved when records with variant parts are declared.

2. Assume a record is defined by

```
TYPE
  TagType = (One, Two);
  Info = RECORD
              Fixed : integer;
              CASE Tag : TagType OF
                One : (A, B : integer);
                Two : (X : real;
                          Ch : char)
           END;
```

and the variable declaration section of a program includes

```
VAR
  RecordCheck : Info;
```

What is the output from the following fragment of code?

```
WITH RecordCheck DO
  BEGIN
    Fixed := 1000;
    Tag := One;
    A := 100;
    B := 500;
    writeln (Fixed:15, A:15, B:15);
    Tag := Two;
    X := 10.5;
    Ch := 'Y';
    writeln (Fixed:15, X:15.2, Ch:15);
    writeln (A:15, B:15, X:15:2, Ch:15)
  END;
```

Artist of Interface

Millions of people encounter the graphic art of Susan Kare every day, and many more will experience her unusual work in the months ahead. Her carefully crafted images have won a place among the cultural symbols of our age, yet few people have any idea who she is or where her work can be seen.

Only a handful of industry insiders know that Kare is the artist responsible for the graphic appearance of some of the country's best-known computer software. Based in San Francisco, she designed most of the distinctive icons, typefaces and other graphic elements that gave the original Macintosh computer its characteristic—and widely emulated—appearance. Many consider her to be the mother of the famous Macintosh trash can.

Since then, Kare has parlayed her initial work for Apple Computer Inc. into a full-time business, designing graphical user interfaces, or GUIs, for computer companies and software developers. The user interface is the software that allows an operator to control a personal computer and direct its functions. A decade ago, most interfaces forced the user to type cryptic commands in a blank space on the display.

With the introduction of the Macintosh in 1984, Apple pushed the world toward the graphic interface, which provides greater ease of use. A graphic interface allows an operator to control the computer by manipulating symbols displayed on its monitor, usually with a mouse or trackball.

The growing demand for graphical user interfaces has forced Kare to turn down work. She has rejected potential clients in part because she refuses to hire people to share the work load. "I do every job myself because I think of it as an art," she said. She works almost entirely on a computer, shunning traditional artist's tools for their electronic successors. "Anything that's bound for the screen, I do on the screen," she said. If there is a secret to her work, it is simplicity, restraint and common sense.

3. Find all errors in the following definitions.

a.
```
TYPE
    Info = RECORD
               A : real;
               CASE Tag : TagType OF
                  B : (X, Y : real);
                  C : (Z : boolean)
           END;
```

b.
```
TYPE
    TagType = (A, B, C);
    Info = RECORD
               D : integer;
               Flag : boolean;
               CASE Tag : TagType OF
                  A : (X, Y : real);
                  B : (Z : real)
           END;
```

c.
```
TYPE
    TagType = (A, B, C);
    Info = RECORD
               D : integer;
               Flag : boolean
               CASE Tag OF
                  A : (X : real);
                  B : (Y : real);
                  C : (Z : real)
           END;
```

d. TYPE
```
      TagType = (A, B, C);
      Info = RECORD
                   D : integer;
                   CASE Tag1 : TagType OF
                     A : (X : real);
                     B : (Y : real);
                     C : (Z : real)
                   END;  {  of CASE  }
                   CASE Tag2 : TagType OF
                     A : (X1 : real);
                     B : (Y1 : real);
                     C : (Z1 : real)
                 END;  {  of RECORD Info  }
```

4. Redefine the following record without using a variant part.

```
TYPE
  Shapes = (Circle, Square, Triangle);
  FigureInfo = RECORD
                    Object : char;
                    Area : real;
                    CASE Shape : Shapes OF
                       Circle   : (Radius : real);
                       Square   : (Side : real);
                       Triangle : (Base, Height : real)
                 END;
VAR
  Figure : FigureInfo;
```

5. Using the record defined in Exercise 4, indicate the names of the fields available and provide an illustration of these fields after each of the following assignments is made.

   a. Shape := Circle;

   b. Shape := Square;

   c. Shape := Triangle;

6. Redefine the record of Exercise 4 to include rectangles and parallelograms.

7. Define a record with a variant part to be used for working with various publications. For each record, there should be fields for the author, title, and date. If the publication is a book, there should be fields for the publisher and city. If the publication is an article, there should be fields for the journal name and volume number.

■ ■ ■ ■

FOCUS ON PROGRAM DESIGN	

FOCUS ON PROGRAM DESIGN

The sample program for this chapter features working with an array of records. The array is first sorted using the field containing a name. It is then sorted using the field containing a real number.

Let's write a program to help your local high school sports boosters keep records of donors and amounts donated. The data file consists of a name (first 20 positions) and an amount donated (starting in position 21) on each line. For example,

```
Jones Jerry         250
```

Your program should get the data from the data file and read it into a record for each donor. Output should consist of two lists as follows:

1. an alphabetical listing together with the amount donated.
2. a listing sorted according to the amount donated.

A first-level pseudocode development for this problem is

1.   Get the data
2.   Sort by name
3.   Print the first list
4.   Sort by amount
5.   Print the second list

Module specifications for the main modules are

1. GetData Module
   Data received: None
   Information returned: Array of records containing names, amounts,
                          and array length
   Logic: Use a **WHILE NOT eof** loop with a counter to read the data file.

2. SortByName Module
   Data received: Unsorted array of records containing names and
                    amounts with the list length
   Information returned: An alphabetized list of names with associated
                          amounts
   Logic: Use a selection sort to sort the array of records.

3. PrintList Module
   Data received: Array of records
                    Array length
   Information returned: None
   Logic: Call procedure PrintHeading.
           Use a loop to print the names and amounts.

4. SortByAmount Module
   Data received: Array of records sorted alphabetically
                    List length
   Information returned: Array of records sorted by size of donation
   Logic: Use a selection sort to sort the list of donations.

A refinement of the pseudocode yields

1.   Get the data
     WHILE NOT eof DO
     1.1   get a name
     1.2   get the amount
2.   Sort by name (use selection sort)
3.   Print the first list
     3.1   print a heading
     3.2   print the names and amounts
4.   Sort by amount (use selection sort)
5.   Print the second list
     5.1   print a heading
     5.2   print the names and amounts

A complete structure chart is given in Figure 9.16.

FIGURE 9.16
Structure chart for boosters
problem

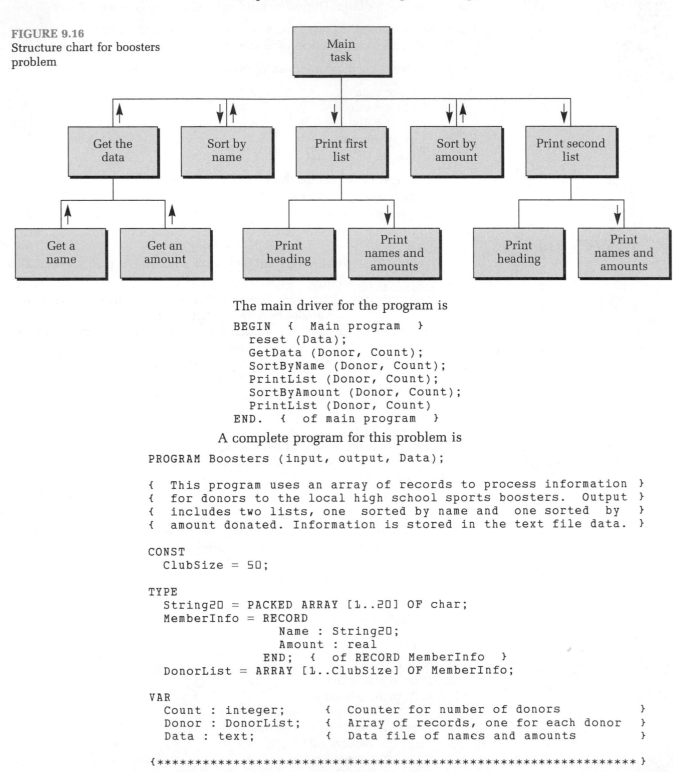

The main driver for the program is

```
BEGIN  { Main program  }
  reset (Data);
  GetData (Donor, Count);
  SortByName (Donor, Count);
  PrintList (Donor, Count);
  SortByAmount (Donor, Count);
  PrintList (Donor, Count)
END.  { of main program  }
```

A complete program for this problem is

```
PROGRAM Boosters (input, output, Data);

{  This program uses an array of records to process information }
{  for donors to the local high school sports boosters.  Output }
{  includes two lists, one  sorted by name and  one sorted  by  }
{  amount donated. Information is stored in the text file data.  }

CONST
  ClubSize = 50;

TYPE
  String20 = PACKED ARRAY [1..20] OF char;
  MemberInfo = RECORD
                 Name : String20;
                 Amount : real
               END; { of RECORD MemberInfo  }
  DonorList = ARRAY [1..ClubSize] OF MemberInfo;

VAR
  Count : integer;      { Counter for number of donors          }
  Donor : DonorList;    { Array of records, one for each donor  }
  Data : text;          { Data file of names and amounts        }

{***************************************************************** }
```

```
PROCEDURE GetData (VAR Donor : DonorList;
                   VAR Count : integer);

  {  Given:    Nothing                                       }
  {  Task:     Read donor names and amounts from the text file, }
  {                 Data, into an array of records           }
  {  Return:   An array of records and number of donors      }

  VAR
    J : integer;

  BEGIN
    Count := 0;
    WHILE NOT eof(Data) AND (Count < ClubSize) DO
      BEGIN
        Count := Count + 1;
        WITH Donor[Count] DO
          BEGIN
            FOR J := 1 TO 20 DO
              read (Data, Name[J]);
            readln (Data, Amount)
          END  {  of WITH...DO  }
      END;  {  of WHILE NOT eof  }
    IF NOT eof(Data) THEN
      writeln ('Not all data read.')
  END;  {  of PROCEDURE GetData  }
```

1

```
{****************************************************************** }
```

```
PROCEDURE SortByName (VAR Donor : DonorList;
                      Count : integer);

  {  Given:    An array of records and number of records     }
  {  Task:     Sort alphabetically by the field Donor[J].Name }
  {  Return:   An alphabetized array of records               }

  VAR
    J, K, Index : integer;
    Temp : MemberInfo;

  BEGIN
    FOR J := 1 TO Count - 1 DO
      BEGIN
        Index := J;
        FOR K := J + 1 TO Count DO
          IF Donor[K].Name < Donor[Index].Name THEN
            Index := K;
        IF Index <> J THEN
          BEGIN
            Temp := Donor[Index];
            Donor[Index] := Donor[J];
            Donor[J] := Temp
          END  {  of exchange  }
      END  {  of FOR J loop  }
  END;  {  of PROCEDURE SortByName  }
```

2

```
{    ****************************************************************************** }
```

```
PROCEDURE SortByAmount (VAR Donor : DonorList;
                            Count : integer);

  {  Given:    An array of records and number of records        }
  {  Task:     Sort by amount donated, Donor[J].Amount          }
  {  Return:   An array of records sorted by amount donated      }

  VAR
    J, K, Index : integer;
    Temp : MemberInfo;

  BEGIN
    FOR J := 1 TO Count - 1 DO
      BEGIN
        Index := J;
        FOR K := J + 1 TO Count DO
          IF Donor[K].Amount > Donor[Index].Amount THEN
            Index := K;
        IF Index <> J THEN
          BEGIN
            Temp := Donor[Index];
            Donor[Index] := Donor[J];
            Donor[J] := Temp
          END { of exchange }
      END { of FOR J loop }
  END; { of PROCEDURE SortByAmount }
```

4

```
{*****************************************************************}

PROCEDURE PrintHeading;

  {  Given:    Nothing                                          }
  {  Task:     Print a heading for the output                   }
  {  Return:   Nothing                                          }

  CONST
    Skip = ' ';

  BEGIN
    writeln;
    writeln (Skip:20, 'Local Sports Boosters');
    writeln (Skip:24, 'Donation List');
    writeln (Skip:10, '------------------------------------------')
    writeln;
    writeln (Skip:13, 'Name', Skip:21, 'Amount');
    writeln (Skip:13, '----', Skip:21, '------');
    writeln
  END; { of PROCEDURE PrintHeading }

{*****************************************************************}

PROCEDURE PrintList (VAR Donor : DonorList;
                       Count : integer);

  {  Given:    An array of records and number of records        }
  {  Task:     Print a list containing one column for the name  }
  {            and one column for the amount donated            }
  {  Return:   Nothing                                          }

  CONST
    Skip = ' ';
```

3

```
VAR
  J : integer;

BEGIN
  PrintHeading;
  FOR J := 1 TO Count DO
    WITH Donor[J] DO
      writeln (Skip:10, Name, Amount:14:2);
  writeln
END;  { of PROCEDURE PrintList  }

{********************************************************************

BEGIN  {  Main program  }
  Reset (Data);
  GetData (Donor, Count);
  SortByName (Donor, Count);
  PrintList (Donor, Count);
  SortByAmount (Donor, Count);
  PrintList (Donor, Count)
END.  { of main program  }
```

The output from this program is

```
                    Local Sports Boosters
                       Donation List
          ------------------------------------------------

             Name                        Amount
             ----                        ------

          Alexander Candy             300.00
          Anderson Tony               375.00
          Banks Marj                  375.00
          Born Patty                  100.00
          Brown Ron                   200.00
          Darnell Linda               275.00
          Erickson Thomas             100.00
          Fox William                 300.00
          Francis Denise              350.00
          Generous George             525.00
          Gillette Mike               350.00
          Hancock Kirk                500.00
          Higgins Sam                 300.00
          Janson Kevin                200.00
          Johnson Ed                  350.00
          Johnson Martha              400.00
          Jones Jerry                 250.00
          Kelly Marvin                475.00
          Kneff Susan                 300.00
          Lasher John                 175.00
          Lyon Elizabeth              425.00
          Moore Robert                100.00
          Muller Marjorie             250.00
          Smith John                  100.00
          Trost Frostie                50.00
          Trudo Rosemary              200.00
          Weber Sharon                150.00
          Williams Art                350.00
          Williams Jane               175.00
          Wilson Mary                 275.00
```

```
                 Local Sports Boosters
                    Donation List
         ---------------------------------------------

              Name                    Amount
              ----                    ------

         Generous George             525.00
         Hancock Kirk                500.00
         Kelly Marvin                475.00
         Lyon Elizabeth              425.00
         Johnson Martha              400.00
         Anderson Tony               375.00
         Banks Marj                  375.00
         Francis Denise              350.00
         Gillette Mike               350.00
         Johnson Ed                  350.00
         Williams Art                350.00
         Higgins Sam                 300.00
         Alexander Candy             300.00
         Kneff Susan                 300.00
         Fox William                 300.00
         Darnell Linda               275.00
         Wilson Mary                 275.00
         Muller Marjorie             250.00
         Jones Jerry                 250.00
         Trudo Rosemary              200.00
         Brown Ron                   200.00
         Janson Kevin                200.00
         Lasher John                 175.00
         Williams Jane               175.00
         Weber Sharon                150.00
         Erickson Thomas             100.00
         Born Patty                  100.00
         Smith John                  100.00
         Moore Robert                100.00
         Trost Frostie                50.00
```

RUNNING AND DEBUGGING TIPS

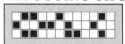

1. Be sure to use the full field name when working with fields in a record. You may only leave off the record name when using **WITH . . . DO**.
2. Terminate each record definition with an **END**. This is an instance when **END** is used without a **BEGIN**.
3. Although field names in different record types can be the same, you are encouraged to use distinct names. This enhances readability and reduces the chances of making errors.
4. Be careful with syntax when using an array of records or an array as a field within a record. For example, be able to distinguish between Student[K].Average, Student.Score[J], and Student[K].Score[J].

■ Summary

Key Terms

array of records	index sort	tag field
field	nested records	variant part
fixed part	record	

Keywords

RECORD   **WITH**

Key Concepts

- A **RECORD** is a structured data type that is a collection of fields; the fields may be treated as a whole or individually.
- Fields in a record can be of different data types.
- Records can be declared or defined by

⟨record name⟩ = **RECORD**
            ⟨field identifier 1⟩ : ⟨data type 1⟩;
            ⟨field identifier 2⟩ : ⟨data type 2⟩;
                        .
                        .
                        .
            ⟨field identifier *n*⟩ : ⟨data type *n*⟩
        END;   {   of **RECORD** definition   }

- Fields can be accessed as variables by
⟨record name⟩.⟨field identifier⟩
- Records can be schematically represented as in Figure 9.17.

FIGURE 9.17
Fields in a record

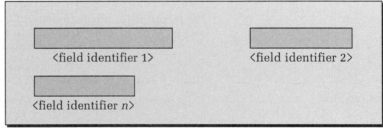

⟨record name⟩

⟨field identifier 1⟩

⟨field identifier 2⟩

⟨field identifier *n*⟩

- **WITH** ⟨record name⟩ **DO** can be used instead of a specific reference to the record name with each field of a record; thus, you could have

```
WITH Student DO
  BEGIN
    Name := 'Smith John          ';
    Average := 93.4;
    Grade := 'A'
  END;
```

instead of

```
Student.Name := 'Smith John          ';
Student.Average := 93.4;
Student.Grade := 'A';
```

- If two records, A and B, are of identical type, contents of all fields of one may be assigned to corresponding fields of the other by a single assignment statement such as

```
A := B;
```

- Either entire records or fields within a record can be passed to appropriate subprograms.
- A record may be used as a field in another record.
- A **WITH** . . . **DO** statement may be used to access fields of nested records.

- Records may be used as components of an array.
- An array of records may be sorted by one of the fields in each record.
- Records with variant parts list all fixed fields (if any) first and then list the variant fields using a **CASE** statement; for example,

```
TYPE
    MaritalStatus = (Married, Single, Divorced);
    String20 = PACKED ARRAY [1..20] OF char;
    Info = RECORD
               Name : String20;
               CASE Status : MaritalStatus OF
                   Married  : (SpouseName : String20;
                               NumKids : integer);
                   Single   : (Gender : char;
                               Age : integer);
                   Divorced : (NumKids : integer;
                               Age : integer;
                               Gender : char;
                               LivesAlone : boolean)
           END;  { of RECORD Info }
VAR
    Customer : Info;
```

- After a value has been assigned to a tag field, the remaining record fields are the ones listed in the **CASE** part of the definition; for example, if we use the previous definition and we have

```
Customer.Status := Divorced;
```

the record fields are as shown in Figure 9.18.

FIGURE 9.18
Value of a tag field

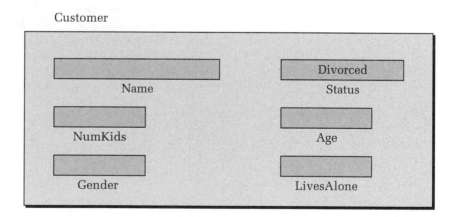

- **Programming Problems and Projects**

1. Write a program to be used by the registrar of a university. The program should get information from a data file and the data for each student should include student name, student number, classification (1 for freshman, 2 for sophomore, 3 for junior, 4 for senior, or 7 for special student), hours completed, hours taking, and grade point average.

    Output should include an alphabetical listing of all students, an alphabetical listing of students in each class, and a listing of all students ordered by grade point average.

2. Robert Day, basketball coach at Indiana College, wants you to write a program to help him analyze information about his basketball team. He wants a record for each player containing the player's name, position played, high school graduated from, height, scoring average, rebounding average, grade point average, and seasons of eligibility remaining.

   The program should read the information for each player from a data file. The output should include an alphabetized list of names together with other pertinent information, a list sorted according to scoring average, an alphabetized list of all players with a grade point average above 3.0, and an alphabetized list of high schools together with an alphabetized list of players who graduated from each school.

■ 3. Final grades in Dr. Lae Z. Programmer's (Problems 5, 22, and 23, Chapter 4; Problem 13, Chapter 5; Problem 5, Chapter 6; and Problem 3, Chapter 8) computer science class are to be computed using the following course requirements.

Requirement	Possible Points
1. Quiz scores (ten points each and the best 10 out of 12 are counted)	100 points
2. Two hourly tests	200 points
3. Eight programming assignments (25 points each)	200 points
4. Test program assignments (two at 50 points each)	100 points
5. Final examination	100 points
Total	700 points

Cutoff percentages for the grades of A, B, C, D, and E are 90 percent, 80 percent, 70 percent, and 55 percent, respectively.

Write a program to keep a record of each student's name, social security number, quiz scores (all 12), hourly examination scores, programming assignment scores, test program scores, and final examination score.

Your program should read data from a data file, compute total points for each student, calculate the letter grade, and output results. The output should be sorted by total points from high to low and include all raw data, the ten best quiz scores, total points and percentage score, and letter grade. Use procedures and functions where appropriate.

4. Write a program to input an unknown number of pairs of fractions with an operation (either +, −, *, or /) between the fractions. The program should perform the operation on the fractions or indicate that the operation is impossible. Answers should be reduced to lowest terms.

Sample Input	Sample Output

```
                3       5      19
3/4 + 5/6      ---  +  ---  =  ---
                4       6      12


                4       1       5
4/9 - 1/6      ---  -  ---  =  ---
                9       6      18


                4       0
4/5 / 0/2      ---  /  ---  =  Impossible
                5       2


                4       7
4/3 + 7/0      ---  +  ---  =  Impossible
                3       0


                6      20       8
6/5 * 20/3     ---  *  ---  =  ---
                5       3       1
```

5. Complex numbers are numbers of the form $a + bi$ where a and b are real and i represents $\sqrt{-1}$. Complex number arithmetic is defined by

Sum	$(a + bi) + (c + di) = (a + c) + (b + d)i$
Difference	$(a + bi) - (c + di) = (a - c) + (b - d)i$
Product	$(a + bi)(c + di) = (ac - bd) + (ad + bc)i$
Quotient	$(a + bi)/(c + di) = \dfrac{ac+bd}{c^2+d^2} + \dfrac{bc - ad}{c^2 + d^2} i$

Write a program to be used to perform these calculations on two complex numbers. Each line of data consists of a single character designator (S, D, P, or Q) followed by four reals representing two complex numbers. For example, $(2 + 3i) + (5 - 2i)$ are represented by

```
S2 3 5 -2
```

A record should be used for each complex number. The output should be in the form $a + bi$.

■ 6. The Readmore Public Library wants a program to keep track of the books checked out. Information for each book should be kept in a record and the fields should include the author's name, a nonfiction designator (**boolean**), the title, the library catalog number, and the copyright date. Each customer can check out at most ten books.

Your program should read information from a data file and print two lists alphabetized by author name, one for nonfiction and the other for fiction. A typical data line is

```
Kidder Tracy    T Soul of a New Machine    81.6044 1982
                ↑                           ↑
           position 21                 position 52
```

■ 7. Modify Problem 6 so that a daily printout is available that contains a summary of the day's transactions at the Readmore Public Library. You will need a record for each customer containing the customer's name and library card number. Be sure to make provision for books that are returned.

8. Write a program to be used to keep track of bank accounts. Define a record that includes each customer's name, account number, starting balance, transaction record, and ending balance.

   The transaction record should list all deposits and withdrawals. A special message should be printed whenever there are insufficient funds for a withdrawal. When a name is read from the data file, all previous records should be searched to see if you are processing a new account. The final output for each customer should look like a typical bank statement.

9. Write a program that uses records to analyze poker hands. Each hand consists of five records (cards). Each record should have one field for the suit and one for the value. Rankings for the hands from high to low are

   straight flush
   four of a kind
   full house
   flush
   straight
   three of a kind
   two pair
   one pair
   none of the above

   Your program should read data for five cards from a data file, evaluate the hand, and print out the hand together with a message indicating its value.

10. Problem 9 can be modified several ways. A first modification is to compare two different hands using only the ranking indicated. A second (more difficult) modification is to also compare hands that have the same ranking. For example, a pair of 8s is better than a pair of 7s. Extend Problem 9 to incorporate some of these modifications.

11. Divers at the Olympics are judged by seven judges. Points for each dive are awarded according to the following procedure.

   a. Each judge assigns a score between 0.0 and 10.0 inclusive.
   b. The high score and low score are eliminated.
   c. The five remaining scores are summed and this total is multiplied by 0.6. This result is then multiplied by the degree of difficulty of the dive (0.0 to 3.0).

   The first level of competition consists of 24 divers each making ten dives. Divers with the 12 highest totals advance to the finals.

   Write a program to keep a record for each diver. Each record should contain information for all ten dives, the diver's name, and the total score. One round of competition consists of each diver making one dive. A typical line of data consists of the diver's name, degree of difficulty for the dive, and seven judges' scores. Part of your output should include a list of divers who advance to the finals.

12. The University Biology Department has a Conservation Club that works with the state Department of Natural Resources. Their project for the semester is to help capture and tag migratory birds. You have been asked to write a computer program to help them store information. In general, the program must have information for each bird tagged entered interactively into an array of records and then stored in a text file for subsequent use. For each bird tagged, you need a field for the tag number, tagging site, sex, bird type, date, and name of the DNR officer doing the tagging. After all data have been entered, the program should print one list sorted by tag number and one sorted by bird type.

■ 13. Mrs. Crown, your computer science instructor, wishes to keep track of the maintenance record of her computers and has turned to you for help. She wants to keep track of the type of machine, its serial number (up to ten characters), the year of purchase, and a **boolean** variable indicating whether the machine is under service contract.

Write a program that permits the entry of records, then prints a list of the machines that are under warranty and a list of those not under warranty. Both lists should be arranged in order of serial number.

14. Most microcomputer owners soon develop a large, often unorganized, library of software on several floppy disks. This is your chance to help them. Define a record containing the disk number of each disk, and a list of up to 30 program titles on each disk. Write a program to read a text file containing the information for a disk and then print an alphabetized listing of the program titles on that disk.

15. Revise the program in Problem 14 to permit the user of the program to enter the program name desired, and have the program print the number of the disk(s) containing the program.

16. Write a program to read records containing the name, address, telephone number, and class of some of your friends. Print a list of the names of the students in the file who are in your class.

■ 17. The Falcon Manufacturing Company (Problem 22, Chapter 8) wishes to keep computerized records of its telephone-order customers. They want the name, street address, city, state, and zip code for each customer. They include either a "T" if the customer is a business, or an "F" if the customer is an individual. A 30-character description of each business is also included. An individual's credit limit is in the record.

Write a program to read the information for the customer from a text file and print a list of the information for businesses and a separate list of the information for individuals. There are no more than 50 records in the file.

18. Visit your local registrar and discuss how records of students are processed. Discover what data are kept in each record, how the data are

entered, and what the fields of each record are. Have the registrar explain what operations are used with a student's record. Specifically, how is information added to or deleted from a record? Discuss the issue of sorting records. What kinds of lists must the registrar produce for those within the system who need information about students?

Prepare a written report of your visit for the class. Be sure to include a graphic that shows a student's record can be envisioned.

19. Select an unworked problem from the previously listed programming problems for this chapter. Construct a structure chart and write all documentary information necessary for this problem. Do not write code. When finished, have a classmate read your documentation to see if precisely what is to be done is clear.

CHAPTER

*The volume of paper expands
to fill the available briefcases.*
Edmund "Jerry" Brown

More about Files

[T] Chapter 6 introduced the concept of text files that are used to provide data for a program and to store data between runs of a program. All data in a text file are stored as a sequence of characters of type **char.** We are now ready to examine these files in more detail.

But first, a note of caution is in order. File manipulation is extremely system dependent. This is especially true with microcomputers. Since it is likely that your system has some differences from standard Pascal, you are encouraged to consult your system manual.

■ 10.1
File Definition

Basic Idea and Notation

You can save information between runs of a program by using secondary storage devices such as tapes or disks (personal computers use floppy or hard disks). As a beginning programmer, you need not normally be concerned with the actual physical construct of these storage devices, but you do need to know how to work with them. To oversimplify, you need to be able to get data into a program, manipulate these data, and save the data (and results) for later use. For example, if you write a program that computes grades for students in a class, you need to periodically enter data for processing. Pascal solves this problem with a structured data type **FILE.** A *file* is a data structure that consists of a sequence of components all of the same type. A **FILE** data type is defined by

```
TYPE
    ⟨file identifier⟩ = FILE OF ⟨data type⟩;
VAR
    ⟨file name⟩ : ⟨file identifier⟩;
```

Thus, if you wish to work with a file of integers, you define

```
TYPE
   FileOfInt = FILE OF integer;
VAR
   File1 : FileOfInt;
```

In this case, File1 is the desired file. Several comments are now in order.

1. Data entries in a file are called *components of the file.*
2. All components of a file must be of the same data type.
3. The only data type not permitted as a component of a file is another file type. This differs from arrays in that

ARRAY [ ] OF ARRAY [ ] OF ⟨data type⟩;

is permitted, but

FILE OF FILE OF ⟨data type⟩;

is not permitted.

Each of the following is a valid definition of a file type.

```
TYPE
   Identifier1 = FILE OF real;
   Identifier2 = FILE OF ARRAY [1..20] OF integer;
   Identifier3 = FILE OF boolean;
```

Files of records are frequently used in programs. Thus, to keep a record for each student in a class, you could have the definition

```
TYPE
   String20 = PACKED ARRAY [1..20] OF char;
   ExamScores = ARRAY [1..4] OF integer;
   QuizScores = ARRAY [1..10] OF integer;
   StudentInfo = RECORD
                    Name : String20;
                    IDNumber : 0..999;
                    Exam : ExamScores;
                    Quiz : QuizScores;
                    Average : real;
                    Grade : char
                 END;  {  of RECORD StudentInfo  }
   StudentFile = FILE OF StudentInfo;
VAR
   Student : StudentFile;
```

There is a difference between a text file and a file of characters. Although a text file consists of a sequence of characters, it also has "lines" separated by end-of-line markers. A file of characters, which is of the type **FILE OF char,** does not have line separators.

Comparison to Arrays

Files and one-dimensional arrays have some similarities: both are structured data types and components must be of the same type. There are, however, some important differences.

1. Files permit you to store and retrieve information between runs of a program.
2. Only one component of a file is available at a time.
3. In standard versions of Pascal, files must be sequentially accessed; that is, when working with files, you start at the beginning and process the components in sequence. It is not possible (as with arrays) to access some component directly without first having somehow moved through the previous components.

4. Files do not have a defined length. Once a file has been defined, the number of components is limited only by the amount of storage available. However, this is usually so large you could think of it as unbounded.

5. Files are stored in secondary storage; arrays are only stored in memory.

File Window and Buffer Variables

Before we get to specific work with files, we need to examine the concepts of a *file window* and a *buffer variable*. A file can be visualized as a sequence of components as follows:

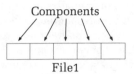

Components

File1

Only one of these components can be "seen" at a time. An imaginary window is associated with a file and values can be transferred to (or from) a component of the file only through this window. Thus, the window must be properly positioned before attempting to transmit data to or from a component.

This imaginary window, which is called a file window, has no name in Pascal. However, there is a related concept, called a buffer variable, that is the actual vehicle through which values are passed to or from the file component. When a file is declared in a program, a buffer variable is automatically declared and therefore available to the programmer. To illustrate, given the following declaration of FileA,

```
TYPE
   FileInfo = FILE OF integer;
VAR
   FileA : FileInfo;
```

the buffer variable (FileA^ or FileA↑) can be used in the program. The buffer variable is always the file name followed by a caret (^) or an up arrow (↑). Historically, the phrase "up arrow" has been used when referring to buffer variables. However, we will use the caret symbol when designating buffer variables because it is available on computer keyboards (above the 6).

The buffer variable is not declared in the variable declaration section. In general, we have

Declaration	Buffer Variable
VAR	
⟨file name⟩ : **FILE OF** ⟨data type⟩;	⟨file name⟩^

The buffer variable is of the same data type as one component of the file. It allows us to access data at the position of the file marker or pointer that was used when illustrating text files. Although its use is intended for passing values to and from a file, it can be used very much like a regularly declared variable of that type. Specifically, from FileA, FileA^ is a variable of type **integer** and statements such as

```
FileA^ := 21;
Age := FileA^;
GetData (FileA^);   (where GetData is a procedure)
```

are appropriate.

Relational Databases

One advance in data management that has gained tremendously in popularity, and in fact is revolutionizing system development practices, is the increased use of the database management system, known as DBMS. An especially important development in database technology is the relational database.

The relational DBMS is based on the concept of multiple "flat files" that are "related" via common fields. A flat file is essentially a two-dimensional matrix of columns and rows where columns represent the fields contained in a record and rows contain different records. A simple example of the flat file concept is a spreadsheet such as Lotus 1-2-3, although the analogy is somewhat misleading since spreadsheets are most commonly used for purposes other than database management.

In a relational database there are usually several flat files, each of which is used to store information about a different "entity" in the world. The objectives of relational technology are to ensure that each file in the database contains information about only the entity with which it is associated, and to provide linkages between files that represent the relationships between those entities that exist in the real world.

Let's look at a simple example of a relational database that is used to process customer orders. Such a relational database would contain at least two files, one for customer data and one for order data. The customer file would contain information (that is, fields) such as the customer's account number, name, address, and phone number; the order file would contain fields such as product number, product name, order quantity, unit cost, and total order cost. To enable the system to match an order to the customer who placed it, the customer's account number would also be contained in the order file. Thus, when the user needs combined order and customer information (as, for example, to prepare and mail an invoice), the two files can be temporarily "joined" together based on common values in each file's respective customer account number fields.

At the mainframe level of computing, the relational DBMS is one of several types of database management systems, along with other types such as hierarchical and network. At the microcomputer level, however, DBMS software is almost exclusively relational. Common packages such as dBASE III, RBase System V, and SQLBase are all relational and provide essentially the same basic structures and capabilities, even though they require different syntax to accomplish similar activities.

Exercises 10.1

1. Discuss the similarities between arrays and files.

2. Discuss the differences between arrays and files.

3. Indicate which of the following are valid declarations of files. Give an explanation for those that are invalid. State what the component type is for those that are valid.

    a. ```
    TYPE
        FileOfAges = FILE OF 0..120;
    VAR
        AgeFile : FileOfAges;
    ```
    b. ```
    TYPE
        String20 = PACKED ARRAY [1..20] OF char;
        FileOfNames = ARRAY [1..100] OF String20;
    VAR
        NameFile : FileOfNames;
    ```
    c. ```
    TYPE
        FileA = FILE OF real;
        FileB = FILE OF FileA;
    VAR
        RealFile : FileB;
    ```
    d. ```
    TYPE
        FileOfInt = FILE [1..100] OF integer;
    VAR
        File1 : FileOfInt;
    ```

e. ```
TYPE
   IntFile = FILE OF integer;
VAR
   OldFile, NewFile, TempFile : IntFile;
```

4. Assume a program contains definition and declaration sections as listed. State which buffer variables are available and the data type of each.

```
TYPE
   FileOfAges = FILE OF 0..120;
   IntFile = FILE OF integer;
   RealFile = FILE OF real;
   TruthFile = FILE OF boolean;
   List20 = ARRAY [1..20] OF real;
   ListFile = FILE OF List20;
   StudentInfo = RECORD
                    Name : PACKED ARRAY [1..20] OF char;
                    Age : 0..120
                 END;
   StudentFile = FILE OF StudentInfo;
VAR
   File1, File2 : FileOfAges;
   OldFile : StudentFile;
   NewFile : ListFile;
   TempFile : RealFile;
   TransFile : TruthFile;
   A, B, C : IntFile;
```

5. Define a file type and then declare a file to be used with records of patients for a physician. Information should include the name, address, height, weight, age, gender, and insurance company of each patient.

■ ■ ■ ■

■ 10.2
Working with Files

Now that we have examined the concepts of files, file windows, and buffer variables, we need to see how values are transmitted to and from file components. Let's first examine the process of putting data into a file.

Creating a File

[T] Once a file has been declared in a program, entering data to the file is referred to as *writing to the file*. Before writing to a file, the file window must be positioned at the beginning of the file, by using the standard procedure **rewrite**. This is referred to as *opening a file*. Thus, if FileA is declared by

```
TYPE
   IntFile = FILE OF integer;
VAR
   FileA : IntFile;
```

then

```
rewrite (FileA);
```

opens FileA for receiving values of type **integer**. At this stage, the window is positioned at the beginning of FileA; FileA is ready to have any previous information overwritten, thus any previous values in FileA are no longer available; and values may now be stored in successive components of FileA (each value transferred is appended to the previous list of values).

[T] Most versions of Pascal allow values to be transferred (written) to a file by assigning the desired value to the buffer variable and using the standard
```

procedure **put** with the buffer variable as an argument. We can, for instance, store the values 10, 20, and 30 in FileA by

```
rewrite (FileA);  {  Open for writing  }
FileA^ := 10;
put (FileA);
FileA^ := 20;
put (FileA);
FileA^ := 30;
put (FileA);
```

The **put** procedure has the effect of transferring the value of the buffer variable to the component in the window and then advancing the window to the next component. After **put** is called, the buffer variable becomes unassigned; this sequence is illustrated in Table 10.1.

TABLE 10.1
Using **put** to write to a file

Pascal Statement	Buffer	Effect
rewrite (FileA);	FileA^	window — FileA
FileA^ := 10;	10 — FileA^	window — FileA
put (FileA);	FileA^	10 — FileA — window
FileA^ := 20;	20 — FileA^	10 — FileA — window
put (FileA);	FileA^	10 20 — FileA — window
FileA^ := 30;	30 — FileA^	10 20 — FileA — window
put (FileA);	FileA^	10 20 30 — FileA — window

Standard Pascal also allows values to be written to a file using the procedure **write.** When this is used, the arguments for **write** are the file name followed by one argument. Thus, the previous fragment could be

```
rewrite (FileA);  {  Open for writing  }
write (FileA, 10);
write (FileA, 20);
write (FileA, 30);
```

The procedure **writeln** can only be used with files of type **text.**

The Standard Function eof

The Boolean function **eof** can be used on all files much the same as it is used on text files. When a file is opened for writing, an end-of-file marker is placed at the beginning of the file. This can be thought of as the window being positioned at the end-of-file marker. When a value is transferred by **put** or **write,** the end-of-file marker is advanced to the same component position to which the window moves. The reason for this is relatively obvious. When retrieving data from a file, we need to know when we have reached the end of the file. The function **eof** is used with the file name for an argument. As expected, **eof** (⟨file name⟩) is **true** when the window is positioned at the end-of-file marker. When writing to a file, **eof** (⟨file name⟩) is always **true.**

Retrieving File Data

The process of retrieving data from a file is referred to as *reading from a file.* In order to retrieve data from a file, you must first open the file for reading. This is accomplished by using the standard procedure

    reset (⟨file name⟩);

This has the effect of repositioning the window at the beginning of the file. Furthermore, when a file is open for reading, the value of the file component in the window is automatically assigned to the buffer variable. The window can be advanced to the next file component by a call to the standard procedure

    get (⟨file name⟩);

Using the previous example of FileA with values as depicted

```
10 20 30 ■
     FileA
```

we could transfer values to the main program by

```
reset (FileA);
N1 := FileA^;
get (FileA);
N2 := FileA^;
get (FileA);
N3 := FileA^;
```

Positioning of the window and transferring of values for this segment of code is illustrated in Table 10.2.

This example of retrieving data is a bit contrived since we know there are exactly three components before the end-of-file marker. A more realistic retrieval would use the **eof** function; for example,

```
reset (FileA);
WHILE NOT eof(FileA) DO
  BEGIN
    .
    .     (process FileA^)
    .
    get (FileA)
  END;
```

The standard procedure **read** can also be used to transfer data from a file. After the file has been opened for reading, **read** can be used with the file

TABLE 10.2
Using **get** to read from a file

Pascal Statement	Buffer	Effect

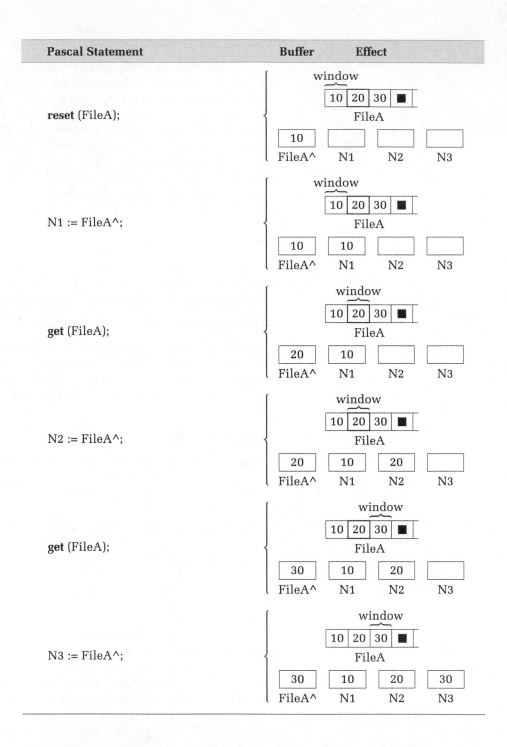

name and variable names as arguments. Thus, the following could replace the previous code fragment.

```
reset (FileA);
read (FileA, N1);
read (FileA, N2);
read (FileA, N3);
```

The previous code using **get** is helpful in understanding the function of a buffer. However, many students find **read** easier to use.

Opening Files

A file cannot be opened for writing and reading at the same time. When a file is opened for writing, it remains open for receiving values that will be appended to the file until the window is repositioned by **rewrite** or **reset,** or until the program is terminated. Thus, you may create a file and then, later in the program, add to the file without reopening it. In a similar fashion, before you first read from a file, it must be opened by **reset** (⟨file name⟩). You can then transfer values from the file using either **read** or **get.**

Let's now consider a short example in which we do something with each component of a file.

■ **EXAMPLE 10.1**

Suppose we have a file of reals and we want to create another file by subtracting 5.0 from each component. Assume the following definitions and declarations.

```
TYPE
  RealFile = FILE OF real;
VAR
  OldFile : RealFile;
  NewFile : RealFile;
```

We can accomplish our objective by

```
reset (OldFile);  {  Open OldFile  }
rewrite (NewFile);  {  Open NewFile  }
WHILE NOT eof(OldFile) DO
  BEGIN
    NewFile^ := OldFile^ - 5.0;
    put (NewFile);
    get (OldFile)
  END;
```

■   ■

Procedures and Files

Much of the work of processing files is accomplished by using procedures. Thus, you should continue using the **TYPE** definition section for defining file types. Files can be used as arguments in a procedure call, but in the procedure heading, files must be listed as variable parameters. This requirement is implicit in the fact that you cannot assign a file variable all at once (as you can a value parameter).

■ **EXAMPLE 10.2**

Let's write a procedure to accomplish the task of Example 10.1.

```
PROCEDURE Subtract5 (VAR OldFile, NewFile : RealFile);
  BEGIN
    reset (OldFile);
    rewrite (NewFile);
    WHILE NOT eof(OldFile) DO
      BEGIN
        NewFile^ := OldFile^ - 5.0;
        put (NewFile);
        get (OldFile)
      END  {  of WHILE...DO  }
  END;  {  of PROCEDURE Subtract5  }
```

This procedure is called from the main program by

```
Subtract5 (OldFile, NewFile);
```

Note that even though no changes are made in OldFile, it is passed as a variable parameter.

◼   ◼

Internal and External Files

Recall from Chapter 8, files used to store data in secondary storage between runs of a program are called external files, and files that are used for processing only and are not saved in secondary storage are internal files. External files must be listed in the program heading in the following form:

> **PROGRAM** ⟨name⟩ (**input, output,** ⟨external file name⟩);

They are declared in the variable declaration section. Internal files are not listed in the program heading but are declared in the variable declaration section.

Typically, a programming problem has some external file in secondary storage that is to be updated in some form. This requires some temporary internal files to be declared for use in the program. When the program is exited, all external files are saved in secondary storage while the internal files are no longer available.

Processing Files

Before looking at a specific problem for processing files, let's consider the general problem of updating an external file. Since we eventually will **rewrite** the external file, we must be careful not to erase the original contents before they have been saved and/or processed in some temporary internal file. In our early work with files, we accomplish this by copying external files to temporary files and then working with the temporary files until the desired tasks are completed. At this point, we then copy the appropriate temporary file to the external file. In reality, this method may prove to be inefficient but, until you become more experienced in file manipulation, it is good practice to avoid working directly with external files.

Let's now consider a relatively short example of updating a file of test scores for students in a class. In the last section of this chapter, we will see a detailed treatment of processing files.

◼ **EXAMPLE 10.3**

Assume we have an external file consisting of total points for each student in a class. Furthermore, assume the data file **(input)** contains test scores that are to be added (in the same order) to the previous totals to obtain new totals. A first-level pseudocode solution to this problem is

1. Copy the totals to a temporary file from the external file
2. Process the temporary file
3. Copy the temporary file to the external file

Assume the program heading is

```
PROGRAM Grades (input, output, TotalPts);
```

and the definitions and declarations are

```
TYPE
  IntFile = FILE OF integer;
VAR
  TotalPts : IntFile;
  Temp1File : IntFile;
  Temp2File : IntFile;
```

A procedure to copy the contents from one file to another is

```
PROCEDURE Copy (VAR OldFile, NewFile : IntFile);
  BEGIN
    reset (OldFile);
    rewrite (NewFile);
    WHILE NOT eof(OldFile) DO
      BEGIN
        NewFile^ := OldFile^;
        put (NewFile);
        get (OldFile)
      END {  of WHILE...DO  }
  END; {  of PROCEDURE Copy  }
```

This is called from the main program by

```
Copy (TotalPts, Temp1File);
```

We can now process Temp1File by adding corresponding scores from the data file. A procedure for this is

```
PROCEDURE AddScores (VAR OldFile, NewFile : IntFile);
  VAR
    NewScore : integer;
  BEGIN
    reset (OldFile);
    rewrite (NewFile);
    WHILE NOT eof(OldFile) DO
      BEGIN
        read (NewScore); {  Get score from data file  }
        NewFile^ := NewScore + OldFile^;
        put (NewFile);
        get (OldFile)
      END {  of WHILE...DO  }
  END; {  of PROCEDURE AddScores  }
```

This procedure could be called from the main program by

```
AddScores (Temp1File, Temp2File);
```

At this stage, the updated scores are in Temp2File and they need to be stored in the external file TotalPts before the program is exited. This is done by another call to Copy in the main program. Thus,

```
Copy (Temp2File, TotalPts);
```

achieves the desired results. The main program is then

```
BEGIN {  Main program  }
  Copy (TotalPts, Temp1File);
  AddScores (Temp1File, Temp2File);
  Copy (Temp2File, TotalPts)
END. {  of main program  }
```

A NOTE OF INTEREST

Backup and Recovery of Data

The need for organizational backup and recovery procedures to prevent loss of data is due to two types of events; in particular, natural disasters and simple human errors. Natural disasters, although infrequent, are typically large-scale emergencies that can completely shut down, if not ruin, an organization's computer facilities. Examples are such potentially catastrophic events as fires, floods, and earthquakes. Human errors, on the other hand, are the most frequent cause of computer problems (has anyone NEVER erased the wrong file by mistake?), but may not be as crippling as natural disasters. Although they may not result in catastrophic loss, human errors are, at the least, a nuisance to affected individuals.

Organizations have developed a variety of backup and recovery procedures to cope with system failures

and to reduce resultant losses. To reduce losses from natural disasters, some organizations have prepared contingency plans covering backup computer locations, off-site program and data storage, and emergency staffing requirements. These contingency plans can usually be put into effect quickly and with minimal disruption of computer services. To minimize human errors (accidents can never be eliminated), organizations typically try to provide sound user-training programs and user-based physical backup measures.

A more recent problem regarding backup and recovery of data has emerged. Specifically, as storage and retrieval technology changes, old data storage can become difficult to access. As an illustration, see the next Note of Interest.

This example obviously overlooks some significant points; for example, how do we know the scores match up, that each student's new score is added to that student's previous total? We will address these issues later in the chapter. Let's now see how one file can be appended to an existing file.

■ **EXAMPLE 10.4**

Assume the files are named OldFile and NewFile and the task is to append NewFile to OldFile. We will use a temporary file, TempFile, for completing this task. A first-level pseudocode development for this problem is

1. Reset OldFile and NewFile
2. Open TempFile for writing
3. **WHILE NOT eof** (OldFile) **DO**
   3.1   write elements to TempFile
4. **WHILE NOT eof** (NewFile) **DO**
   4.1   write elements to TempFile
5. Copy TempFile to OldFile

Step 3 can be refined to

3. **WHILE NOT eof** (OldFile) **DO**
   3.1   write elements to TempFile
        3.1.1   assign OldFile buffer value to TempFile buffer
        3.1.2   write value to TempFile
        3.1.3   advance window of OldFile

The code for this step is

```
WHILE NOT eof(OldFile) DO
  BEGIN
    TempFile^ := OldFile^;
    put (TempFile);
    get (OldFile)
  END;  {  of WHILE NOT eof  }
```

The complete code for this example is left as an exercise.

■   ■

Exercises 10.2

1. Review the difference between internal files and external files.

2. Write test programs that illustrate the following.
   a. What happens when you try to write to a file that has not been opened for writing.
   b. What happens when you try to get data from a file that has not been reset.
   c. What happens when a procedure uses a file as a value parameter.

3. Declare an appropriate file and store the positive multiples of 7 that are less than 100.

4. Explain how the file of Exercise 3 can be saved for another program to use.

5. Consider the file with integer components as shown.

   FivesFile

   Write a segment of code that would assign the values respectively to variables A, B, C, and D. Use both **get** and **read.**

6. Consider the following file with component values as illustrated.

```
TYPE
   RealFile = FILE OF real;
VAR
   Prices : RealFile;
```

| 15.95 | 17.99 | 21.95 | 19.99 | ■ | |

   Prices

   a. Declare a new file and put values in the components that are 15 percent less than the values in components of Prices.
   b. Update the values in Prices so that each value is increased by 10 percent.

7. Discuss the difference between **reset** and **rewrite.**

8. You have been asked to write a program to examine a file of integers and replace every negative number with zero. Assume IntFile has been appropriately declared and contains five integer values. Why will the following segment of code not work?

```
rewrite (IntFile);
FOR J := 1 TO 5 DO
  BEGIN
    get (IntFile);
    IF IntFile^ < 0 THEN
      IntFile^ := 0;
    put (IntFile)
  END;
```

9. Consider the files declared by

```
TYPE
   FileOfInt = FILE OF integer;
VAR
   File1, File2 : FileOfInt;
```

   Find all errors in each of the following.

```
a. reset (File1);
   FOR J := 1 TO 5 DO
     BEGIN
       File1^ := 10 * J;
       put (File1)
     END;
```

```
b. rewrite (File1);
   FOR J := 1 TO 5 DO
     BEGIN
       File1^ := 10 * J;
       put (File1)
     END;
c. rewrite (File1);
   FOR J := 1 TO 5 DO
     BEGIN
       File1 := 10 * J;
       put (File1)
     END;
d. rewrite (File1);
   FOR J := 1 TO 5 DO
     File1^ := J * 10;
e. reset (File2);
   WHILE NOT eof(File1) DO
     BEGIN
       File2^ := File1^;
       put (File2);
       get (File1)
     END;
f. reset (File2);
   rewrite (File1);
   WHILE NOT eof(File2) DO
     BEGIN
       File1^ := File2^;
       put (File1);
       get (File2)
     END;
```

10. Assume the files OldFile and NewFile are declared as

```
TYPE
   IntFile = FILE OF integer;
VAR
   OldFile, NewFile : IntFile;
```

Furthermore, for each of the following, assume OldFile has component values as illustrated.

-2	-1	0	1	2	■	

OldFile

Indicate the values in components of both OldFile and NewFile after each of the following segments of code.

```
a. reset (OldFile);
   rewrite (NewFile);
   WHILE NOT eof(OldFile) DO
     BEGIN
       IF OldFile^ > 0 THEN
         BEGIN
           NewFile^ := OldFile^;
           put (NewFile)
         END;
       get (OldFile)
     END;
```

```
b. rewrite (OldFile);
   rewrite (NewFile);
   WHILE NOT eof(OldFile) DO
     BEGIN
       IF OldFile^ > 0 THEN
         BEGIN
           NewFile^ := OldFile^;
           put (NewFile)
         END
     END;
c. reset (OldFile);
   rewrite (NewFile);
   WHILE NOT eof(OldFile) DO
     BEGIN
       NewFile^ := abs(OldFile^);
       put (NewFile);
       get (OldFile)
     END;
   rewrite (OldFile);
   reset (NewFile);
   WHILE NOT eof(NewFile) DO
     BEGIN
       OldFile^ := NewFile^;
       put (OldFile);
       get (NewFile)
     END;
```

11. Assume OldFile and NewFile are as declared in Exercise 10. Furthermore, assume OldFile contains the values

8	−17	0	−4	21	■

OldFile

Indicate the output from the following segment of code and the values of the components in OldFile and NewFile.

```
reset (OldFile);
rewrite (NewFile);
WHILE NOT eof(OldFile) DO
  BEGIN
    NewFile^ := OldFile^;
    IF NewFile^ < 0 THEN
      writeln (NewFile^)
    ELSE
      put (NewFile);
      get (OldFile)
  END;
```

12. Assume you have declared three files (File1, File2, and File3) in a program such that the component type for each file is **real.** Furthermore, assume that both File1 and File2 contain an unknown number of values. Write a segment of code to transfer the corresponding sum of components from File1 and File2 into File3. Since File1 and File2 may have a different number of components, after one end-of-file is reached, you should add zeros until the next end-of-file is reached. Thus, your segment produces

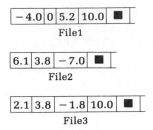

13. Write a complete program that finishes the work started in Example 10.4. Your program should print out the contents of each file used and of the final file.

■ 10.3
Files with Structured Components

In actual practice, components of files are frequently some structured data type. A program might use a file of arrays or a file of records and when such a file is desired, you declare it as an external file and then create components from a text file. Once the data have been thus converted, you can access an entire array or record rather than accessing individual fields or components. The data are also saved in structured form between runs of a program. When data have been stored in structured components, it is relatively easy to update and work with these files. For example, a doctor might have a file of records for patients and wish to insert or delete records of the patients, choose to examine the individual fields of each record, print an alphabetical list, or print a list of patients with unpaid bills.

Let's now examine a typical declaration. Suppose you are writing a program to use a file of records. Each record contains information about a student in a computer science class: in particular, the student's name, three test scores (in an array), identification number, and test average. A declaration for such a file could be

```
TYPE
   String20 = PACKED ARRAY [1..20] OF char;
   Scores = ARRAY [1..3] OF 0..100;
   StudentInfo = RECORD
                     Name : String20;
                     Score : Scores;
                     IDNumber : 0..999;
                     Average : real
                  END; { of RECORD StudentInfo }
   StudentFile = FILE OF StudentInfo;
VAR
   Student : StudentFile;
```

FIGURE 10.1
File Student

Student is a file of records that can be illustrated as shown in Figure 10.1.

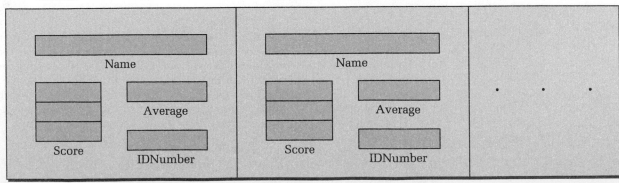

After Student has been properly opened for reading by **reset** (Student), the statement

```
get (Student);
```

causes the contents of a record to be transferred to Student^. The field identifiers are

```
Student^.Name
Student^.IDNumber
Student^.Score
Student^.Average
```

Student^.Score is an array. Components of this array are

```
Student^.Score[1]
Student^.Score[2]
Student^.Score[3]
```

If you wish to compute the average for a student whose record is in the buffer, you can write

```
Sum := 0;
WITH Student^ DO
  BEGIN
    FOR J := 1 TO 3 DO
      Sum := Sum + Score[J];
    Average := Sum / 3
  END;
```

At this stage, you may want to save this computed average for later use. Unfortunately, **put** (Student) will not work because the file is open for reading rather than writing. We will solve this and other problems in the remainder of this section as we investigate methods of manipulating files.

Creating a File of Records

One of the first problems to be solved when working with files whose components are structured variables is to transfer data from some text file (usually **input**) into the appropriate file of structured components. Once the new file with structured components has been created, it can be saved in secondary storage by declaring it as an external file. To illustrate the process of creating a file of records, let's continue the example of records for students in a computer science class. Recall the definitions and subsequent declaration

```
TYPE
  String20 = PACKED ARRAY [1..20] OF char;
  Scores = ARRAY [1..3] OF 0..100;
  StudentInfo = RECORD
                  Name : String20;
                  IDNumber : 0..999;
                  Score : Scores;
                  Average : real
                END; { of RECORD StudentInfo }
  StudentFile = FILE OF StudentInfo;
VAR
  Student : StudentFile;
```

Before we can create the file of records, we need to know how data were entered in the text file (assume **input**). For purposes of this example, assume data for each student are contained on a single line, 20 positions are used for the name, and an identification number is followed by three test scores. Thus, the data file could be

| Smith John | 065 89 92 76 ▪ | Jones Mary | 021 93 97 85 ▪ ▪ |

A procedure to create the file of records is

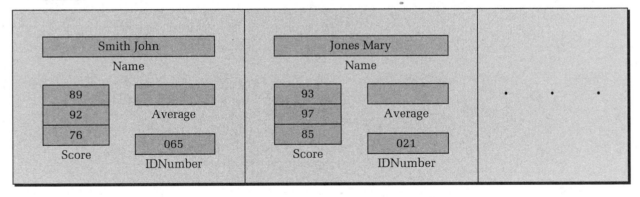

```
PROCEDURE CreateFile (VAR Student : StudentFile);
  VAR
    J : integer;
  BEGIN
    rewrite (Student);  {  Open for writing  }
    WHILE NOT eof(input) DO
      BEGIN  {  Get data for one record  }
        WITH Student^ DO
          BEGIN
            FOR J := 1 TO 20 DO
              read (Name[J]);
            read (IDNumber);
            readln (Score[1], Score[2], Score[3])
          END;
        put (Student)  {  Put buffer contents in file  }
      END
  END;  {  of PROCEDURE CreateFile  }
```

This procedure is called from the main program by

```
CreateFile (Student);
```

After it is executed, we have the records shown in Figure 10.2.

FIGURE 10.2
File Student with values

Student

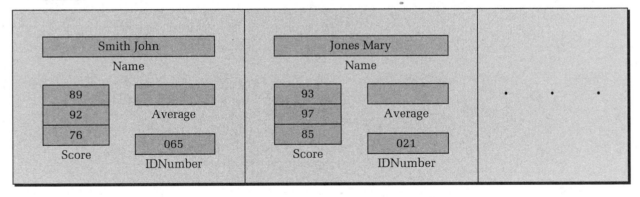

Storing Structured Files

Structured files may be stored in secondary memory for subsequent use. When files other than those of type **text** are stored, they are stored as binary files. In this form, the data may be accessed by a program. However, an attempt to "look at" such a file by using a text editor or some other system command usually results in a display of gibberish characters.

Programmers need not worry about the form of data being stored. The change in representation is performed by the operating system. Even though you cannot "see" components of a file that has been saved in secondary memory, you should use files of structured components for the following reasons:

1. Values of structured file types can be read from or written to nontext files. For example, you can read or write an entire record.
2. The information in structured file types can be transferred more rapidly than with files of type **text** since the operating system does not do as much encoding and decoding.
3. Data are usually stored more compactly when saved as part of a structured file type.

A common error for beginning programmers is to create a text file that "looks like" a structured file and then attempt to use it as a structured file. For example, a text file of data may be arranged to look like a file of records by using a text editor. However, an attempt to read a record from this file results in an error. You must first create a file of records as discussed previously.

File Manipulation

Several problems are typically involved with manipulating files and file components. Generally, a program starts with an existing file, revises it in some fashion, and then saves the revised file. Because files in standard Pascal must be accessed sequentially, this usually necessitates copying the existing external file to a temporary internal file, revising the temporary file, and copying the revised file to the external file. The existing external file is often referred to as the *master file*. The file containing changes to be made in the master file is called the *transaction file*.

To illustrate a simple update problem, let's consider again the problem using the file containing records for students in a computer science class. Assume that the external file has been named Student. Now suppose we wish to delete a record from Student (master file) because some student moved to Australia. This problem can be solved by searching Student sequentially for the record in question. As the name in each record is examined, if the record is to be kept, it is put in a temporary file. The desired record is not transferred, thus accomplishing the update. Finally, Student is rewritten by copying the contents of the temporary file to Student.

A first-level pseudocode development is

1. Get the name to be deleted
2. Search Student for a match copying each nonmatch to TempFile
3. Copy the remainder of Student to TempFile
4. Copy TempFile to Student

Using the previous declarations and assuming that the name of the student whose record is to be deleted has been read into MovedAway, step 2 can be solved by

```
reset (Student);  {  Open the files  }
rewrite (TempFile);
Found := false;
WHILE NOT eof(Student) AND NOT Found DO
  BEGIN
    IF Student^.Name = MovedAway THEN
      Found := true
    ELSE
      BEGIN
        TempFile^ := Student^;
        put (TempFile)
      END;
    get (Student)
  END;  {  of search for a student name  }

{  Now copy the rest of student file  }

WHILE NOT eof(Student) DO
  BEGIN
    TempFile^ := Student^;
    put (TempFile);
    get (Student)
  END;
```

We now need to copy TempFile to Student so that the revised master file is saved as an external file. A procedure for this was developed in Section 10.2; it is called from the main program by

```
Copy (TempFile, Student);
```

As a second illustration of file manipulation, let's consider the standard problem of merging two sorted files. For example, suppose the master file is a file of records and each record contains a field for the name of a customer. Furthermore, assume this file has been sorted alphabetically by name. Now suppose an alphabetical listing of new customers is to be merged with the old file to produce a current file containing records for all customers sorted alphabetically by name.

As before, we use a temporary file to hold the full sorted list and then copy the temporary file to the master file. This can be envisioned as illustrated in Figure 10.3.

FIGURE 10.3
Merging files

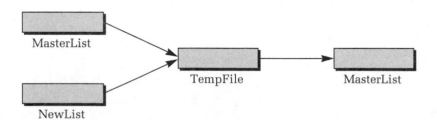

MasterList

NewList

TempFile

MasterList

An algorithm for the merge is not too difficult. All files are first opened. Then the initial records from MasterList and NewList are compared. The record containing the name that comes first alphabetically is transferred to TempFile and, as shown in the graphic documentation for the following program segment, the next record is obtained from the file containing the record that was transferred.

This process continues until the end of one file is reached. At that time, the remainder of the other file is copied into TempFile.

Assuming that each record has a field identified by Name, which is of type String30, and that FileType has been defined as the type for files being used, a procedure for merging is

```
PROCEDURE Merge (VAR Master, NewFile : FileType);
VAR
   TempFile : FileType;
BEGIN
   reset (Master);
   reset (NewFile);
   rewrite (TempFile);

{  Compare top records until an eof of one of the   }
{    input files is reached                         }

   WHILE NOT eof(Master) AND NOT eof(NewFile) DO
     BEGIN
       IF Master^.Name < NewFile^.Name THEN
         BEGIN
           TempFile^ := Master^;
           get (Master)
         END
       ELSE
         BEGIN
           TempFile^ := NewFile^;
           get (NewFile)
         END;
       put (TempFile)
     END;
```

Current Last Record

Current Record → Master

Current Record → NewFile

TempFile

The smaller of these two records must be transferred to the end of TempFile. Then advance within the file from which that record was taken.

```
{  Now copy the remaining names   }

   WHILE NOT eof(Master) DO
     BEGIN
       TempFile^ := Master^;
       put (TempFile);
       get (Master)
     END;
```

```
WHILE NOT eof(NewFile) DO
  BEGIN
    TempFile^ := NewFile^;
    put (TempFile);
    get (NewFile)
  END;

{ Now copy back to Master }

  rewrite (Master);
  reset (TempFile);
  WHILE NOT eof(TempFile) DO
    BEGIN
      Master^ := TempFile^;
      put (Master);
      get (TempFile)
    END

END; { of PROCEDURE Merge }
```

This procedure can be called from the main program by

```
Merge (Master, NewFile);
```

History Stuck on Old Computer Tapes

A slice of recent U.S. history has become as unreadable as Egyptian hieroglyphics before the discovery of the Rosetta stone. And more historic, scientific, and business data is in danger of dissolving into a meaningless jumble of letters, numbers, and computer symbols.

Paying millions to preserve the information is part of the price for the country's embrace of more and more powerful computers. Much information from the past 30 years is stranded on computer tape from primitive or discarded systems—it's unintelligible or soon to be so.

Hundreds of thousands of Americans researching family history—the largest use of the National Archives—will find records of their relatives beyond reach. Detection of diseases, environmental threats or shifts in social class could be delayed because data was lost before researchers even knew which questions to ask.

"The ability to read our nation's historical records is threatened by the complexity of modern computers," said Representative Bob Wise, chairman of a House information subcommittee that wants the government to start buying computers to preserve data for future researchers. A number of records already are lost or out of reach:

Two hundred reels of 17-year-old Public Health Service computer tapes were destroyed because no one could find out what the names and numbers on them meant.

The government's Agent Orange Task Force, asked to determine whether Vietnam soldiers were sickened by exposure to the herbicide, was unable to decode Pentagon computer tapes containing the date, site, and size of every U.S. herbicide bombing during the war.

The most extensive record of Americans who served in World War II exists only on 1,600 reels of microfilm of computer punch cards. No staff, money, or machine is available to return the data to a computer so citizens could trace the war history of their relatives.

Census data from the 1960s and NASA's early scientific observations of the earth and planets exist on thousands of reels of old tape. Some may have decomposed; others may fall apart if run through the balky equipment that survives from that era.

A final comment is in order. It is frequently necessary to work with files of records that have been sorted according to a field of the record. Since you might want to work with the records sorted by some other field, you must first be able to sort an unsorted file. In general, this is done by transferring the file components to array components, sorting the array, and transferring the sorted array components back to the file. This means that you must have some idea of how many components are in the file and declare the array length accordingly. The physical setting of a problem usually provides this information. For example, physicians will have some idea of how many patients (100, 200, or 1,000) they see.

Exercises 10.3

1. Declare appropriate files for each of the following. Fields for each record are indicated.
   a. Flight information for an airplane; include flight number, airline, arrival time, arriving from, departure time, and destination.
   b. Bookstore inventory; include author, title, stock number, price, and quantity.
   c. Records for a magazine subscription agency; include name and address, indicating street number, street name, city, state, and zip code.

2. Write a test program that allows you to declare a file of records, read data into the file, and print information from selected records according to the value in some key field.

3. Suppose data in a text file contains information for students in a class. Each student's information will use three data lines as illustrated.

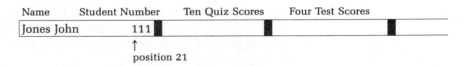

a. Declare a file of records to be used to store this data.
b. Write a procedure to create a file of records containing appropriate information from the text file.
c. Write a procedure to sort the file alphabetically.

4. Illustrate the values of components and fields in Student and Student∧ during the first pass through the loop in **PROCEDURE** CreateFile.

5. Consider the file Student declared by

```
TYPE
   String20 = PACKED ARRAY [1..20] OF char;
   Scores = ARRAY [1..3] OF 0..100;
   StudentInfo = RECORD
                    Name : String20;
                    IDNumber : 0..999;
                    Score : Scores;
                    Average : real
                 END;
   StudentFile = FILE OF StudentInfo;
VAR
   Student : StudentInfo;
```

Write a procedure for each of the following tasks. In each case, show how the procedure is called from the main program. (You may assume the file has been alphabetized.)

a. Add one record in alphabetical order.

b. Add one record to the bottom of the file.

c. Update the record of 'Smith Jane   ' by changing her score on the second test from an 82 to an 89.

d. The scores from test three have just been entered into a data file. Each line contains an identification number followed by three integer scores. Update Student to include these scores (the first two scores have already been transferred to the appropriate student records).

e. Assume all test scores have been entered. Update Student by computing the test average for each student.

f. Print a list containing each student's name and test average; the list should be sorted by test average from high to low.

■ ■ ■ ■

FOCUS ON PROGRAM DESIGN

The chapter summary program for this chapter is an elementary version that could be expanded to a comprehensive programming project. Suppose the registrar at your institution wants a program to allow updating a file of student records. A master file of student records currently exists; it is sorted alphabetically. Each record contains a field for the student's name, ID number, grade point average, and total hours completed. This file is to be updated by information contained in a transaction file. Each line in the transaction file contains a student number, letter grade for a course taken, and number of credit hours for the course. A typical data line would be

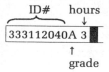

```
     ID#    hours
             ↓
 333112040A 3
          ↑
       grade
```

For each data line in the transaction file, your program should search the contents of the master file for a match. If a match is found, appropriate changes should be made in grade point average and total hours completed. If no match is found, the information should be printed in an Exception Report. After all transactions are completed, an alphabetized list should be printed and the master file should be updated.

A first-level pseudocode development for this is

1. Open the files
2. Copy contents of MasterFile to an array
3. Update the records
4. Print the list
5. Update MasterFile

A complete structure diagram for this program is given in Figure 10.4.

FIGURE 10.4
Structure chart for the file update program

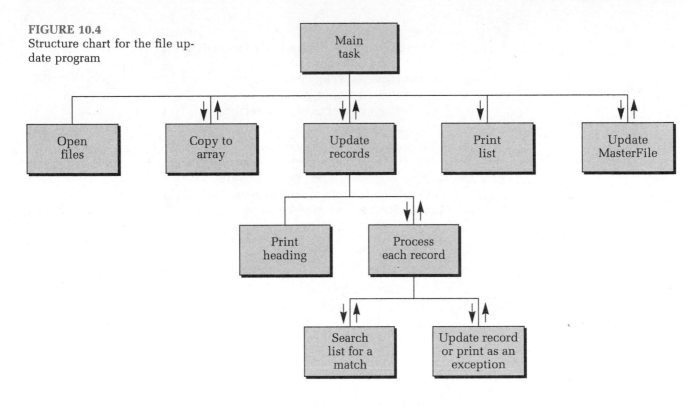

Module specifications for the main modules are

1. <u>OpenFiles Module</u>
    Data received: None
    Information returned: None
    Logic: Use **reset** to prepare files for reading.

2. <u>LoadArray Module</u>
    Data received: File of records
    Information returned: Array of records
                           Number of records
    Logic: Copy contents of each record in MasterFile to a record in
           Student.
           Count the number of records in the array.

3. <u>UpdateRecords Module</u>
    Data received: An array of records
                   Length of the array
                   A transaction file
    Information returned: An updated array of records
    Logic: For each data line in TransactionFile, search for a match in the
           array.
           IF a match is found, **THEN**
             update the record
           ELSE
             print out an Exception Report

4. <u>PrintList Module</u>
Data received: A sorted array of records
     Length of the array
Information returned: None
Logic: Print a heading.
   Print contents of each record.

5. <u>UpdateMasterFile Module</u>
Data received: An array of records
     Length of the array
     MasterFile of records
Information returned: An updated MasterFile
Logic: For each record in Student, copy contents into a record in
   MasterFile

Further pseudocode development is

1. Open the files
  1.1 **reset** MasterFile
  1.2 **reset** TransactionFile
2. Copy contents of MasterFile to an array
  2.1 set counter to zero
  2.2 **REPEAT**
    2.2.1 increment counter
    2.2.2 copy contents of one record
    UNTIL eof (MasterFile)
3. Update the records
  3.1 print Exception Report heading
  3.2 **WHILE NOT eof** (TransactionFile) **DO**
    3.2.1 search for a match
    3.2.2 **IF NOT** Found **THEN**
       print as part of Exception Report
      ELSE
       update the record
4. Print the list
  4.1 print a heading
  4.2 print an alphabetized list
5. Update the MasterFile
  5.1 **rewrite** MasterFile
  5.2 **FOR** each record in the array **DO**
    copy contents to a record in MasterFile

Step 3.2.1 is a sequential search of the array. If a match is found, the array position is returned. If not, a zero is returned. The portion of step 3.2.2 designed to update the record consists of incrementing the grade point average. A **CASE** statement is used to direct action for grades of 'A', 'B', 'C', 'D', 'E', 'W', 'I'. This program assumes valid data are contained in Transaction-File. A complete program for this problem is

```
PROGRAM FileUpdate (input, output, MasterFile, TransactionFile);

{  This program updates a file of student records. Transactions }
{  are   stored in the text  file  TransactionFile.  Each  line }
{  consists of a student number, grade for a course taken,  and }
{  credit hours for the course.  The file of records is  copied }
{  to  an  array  of  records  for  processing.  This  facilitates }
```

```
{  searching for matches of student numbers.  It is assumed the  }
{  master file is alphabetized.  If it is not, one could add  a  }
{  procedure to sort the array before rewriting the master file. }

CONST
  MaxLength = 200;

TYPE
  String9 = PACKED ARRAY [1..9] OF char;
  String20 = PACKED ARRAY [1..20] OF char;
  StudentRecord = RECORD
                    Name : String20;
                    IDNumber : String9;
                    GPA : real;
                    Hours : integer
                  END;  {  of RECORD StudentRecord  }
  StudentList = ARRAY [1..MaxLength] OF StudentRecord;
  RecordsFile = FILE OF StudentRecord;

VAR
  NumberOfRecords : integer; {  Number of records read        }
  Student : StudentList;     {  Array of student records      }
  MasterFile : RecordsFile;  {  Master file of student records }
  TransactionFile : text;    {  Transaction file for updating  }

{****************************************************************** }

PROCEDURE OpenFiles (VAR MasterFile : RecordsFile;
                     VAR TransactionFile : text);

{  Given:   Nothing                                            }
{  Task:    Open the files for reading                         }
{  Return:  MasterFile and TransactionFile ready to be read    }

BEGIN
  reset (MasterFile);
  reset (TransactionFile)
END;  {  of PROCEDURE OpenFiles  }

{****************************************************************** }

PROCEDURE LoadArray (VAR MasterFile : RecordsFile;
                     VAR Student : StudentList;
                     VAR NumberOfRecords : integer);

  {  Given:   Master file containing data for each student    }
  {  Task:    Create an array of student records from MasterFile }
  {  Return:  Array of student records and number of records  }

  BEGIN
    NumberOfRecords := 0;
    get (MasterFile);
    WHILE NOT eof(MasterFile) AND (NumberOfRecords < MaxLength) DO
      BEGIN
        NumberOfRecords := NumberOfRecords + 1;
        Student[NumberOfRecords] := MasterFile^;
        get (MasterFile)
      END;  {  of WHILE...DO  }
    IF NOT eof(MasterFile) THEN
      writeln ('There are more data.')
  END;  {  of PROCEDURE LoadArray  }

{****************************************************************** }
```

1

2

```
FUNCTION NewGPA (Hours, CourseHours : integer;
                GPA, HonorPoints : real) : real;

  {  Given:    Total hours accumulated, credit hours for the     }
  {                 course completed, current GPA, HonorPoints    }
  {                 corresponding to the letter grade received    }
  {  Task:     Compute the new grade point average               }
  {  Return:   New grade point average                           }

  VAR
    OldHours : integer;

  BEGIN
    OldHours := Hours;
    Hours := Hours + CourseHours;
    NewGPA := (OldHours * GPA + CourseHours * HonorPoints) / Hours
  END;  {  of FUNCTION NewGPA   }

{*********************************************************************** }

FUNCTION SeqSearch (Student : StudentList;
                    IDNumber : String9;
                    NumberOfRecords : integer) : integer;

  {  Given:    An array of student records, a student ID number,   }
  {                 and the number of records                      }
  {  Task:     Sequentially search the array to find a match for   }
  {                 the ID number                                  }
  {  Return:   The index of the record where a match was found;    }
  {                 return 0 if not match                          }

  VAR
    Found : boolean;
    LCV : integer;

  BEGIN
    SeqSearch := 0;
    Found := false;
    LCV := 0;
    WHILE (LCV < NumberOfRecords) AND (NOT Found) DO
      BEGIN
        LCV := LCV + 1;
        IF Student[LCV].IDNumber = IDNumber THEN
          BEGIN
            SeqSearch := LCV;
            Found := true
          END  {  of IF...THEN   }
      END  {  of WHILE loop   }
  END;  {  of FUNCTION SeqSearch   }

{*********************************************************************** }

PROCEDURE UpdateRecords (VAR TransactionFile : text;
                         VAR Student : StudentList;
                         NumberOfRecords : integer);

  {  Given:    A transaction file for updating records, an array   }
  {                 of student records, and the number of student  }
  {                 records                                        }
  {  Task:     Read a line from the transaction file; search array }
  {                 Student for a match of IDNumber; IF match THEN  }
  {                 update hours and GPA; ELSE print as part of     }
```

```
{                    Exception Report                            }
{  Return:  An updated array of student records                  }

CONST
  Skip = ' ';

VAR
  J, Index, CourseHours : integer;
  IDNumber : String9;
  Grade : char;
  MatchFound : boolean;

BEGIN

  {  Print heading for the Exception Report  }

  writeln ('EXCEPTION REPORT':35);
  writeln ('ID NUMBER':20, 'GRADE':12, 'HOURS':10);
  writeln (Skip:10, '-------------------------------');
  writeln;

{  Now read the transaction file  }

WHILE NOT eof(TransactionFile) DO
  BEGIN
    FOR J := 1 TO 9 DO
      read (TransactionFile, IDNumber[J]);
    readln (TransactionFile, Grade, CourseHours);
    Index := SeqSearch(Student, IDNumber, NumberOfRecords);
    MatchFound := Index <> 0;
    IF MatchFound THEN              {  Update student record  }
      WITH Student[Index] DO
        CASE Grade OF
          'A'  :  BEGIN
                    GPA := NewGPA(Hours, CourseHours, GPA, 4.0);
                    Hours := Hours + CourseHours
                  END;
          'B'  :  BEGIN
                    GPA := NewGPA(Hours, CourseHours, GPA, 3.0);
                    Hours := Hours + CourseHours
                  END;
          'C'  :  BEGIN
                    GPA := NewGPA(Hours, CourseHours, GPA, 2.0);
                    Hours := Hours + CourseHours
                  END;
          'D'  :  BEGIN
                    GPA := NewGPA(Hours, CourseHours, GPA, 1.0);
                    Hours := Hours + CourseHours
                  END;
          'E'  :  BEGIN
                    GPA := NewGPA(Hours, CourseHours, GPA, 0.0);
                    Hours := Hours + CourseHours
                  END;
          'W', 'I'  :                           {  do nothing  }
        END  {  of CASE Grade  }
      ELSE             {  Print as part of Exception Report  }
        writeln (IDNumber:20, Grade:10, CourseHours:10)
  END  {  of WHILE NOT eof(TransactionFile)  }
END; {  of PROCEDURE UpdateRecords  }

{**************************************************************** }
```

```
PROCEDURE PrintList (VAR Student : StudentList;
                     NumberOfRecords : integer);

  { Given:   An array of student records and number of records  }
  { Task:    Print a list of records with appropriate heading   }
  { Return:  Nothing                                            }

  VAR
    J : integer;

  BEGIN

    { Print a heading for the revised list  }

    writeln;
    writeln ('UPDATED REPORT':30);
    writeln ('STUDENT FILE LISTING':34);
    writeln;
    writeln ('NAME':10, 'ID NUMBER':25, 'GPA':8, 'CREDITS':10);
    writeln ('-------------------------------------------------------');
    writeln;

    { Now print the list  }

    FOR J := 1 TO NumberOfRecords DO
      WITH Student[J] DO
        writeln (Name:20, IDNumber:15, GPA:8:2, Hours:8)
  END;  { of PROCEDURE PrintList  }

{*****************************************************************  }

PROCEDURE UpdateMasterFile (VAR MasterFile : RecordsFile;
                            VAR Student : StudentList;
                            NumberOfRecords : integer);

  { Given:   An array of student records and the array length  }
  { Task:    Copy the records into MasterFile for storage       }
  { Return:  A file of student records                          }

  VAR
    J : integer;

  BEGIN
    rewrite (MasterFile);
    FOR J := 1 TO NumberOfRecords DO
      BEGIN
        MasterFile^ := Student[J];
        put (MasterFile)
      END { of FOR loop  }
  END;  { of PROCEDURE UpdateMasterFile  }

{*****************************************************************  }

BEGIN  { Main program  }
  OpenFiles (MasterFile, TransactionFile);
  LoadArray (MasterFile, Student, NumberOfRecords);
  UpdateRecords (TransactionFile, Student, NumberOfRecords);
  PrintList (Student, NumberOfRecords);
  UpdateMasterFile (MasterFile, Student, NumberOfRecords)
END.  { of main program  }
```

If you use data in MasterFile as

```
BARRETT RODA        345678901 3.67 23
BORGNINE ERNIST     369325263 4.12 14
CADABRA ABRA        123450987 3.33 23
DJIKSTRA EDGAR      345998765 3.90 33
GARZELONI RANDY     444226666 2.20 18
GLUTZ AGATHA        320678230 3.00 22
HOLBRUCK HALL       321908765 3.50 29
HUNTER MICHAEL      234098112 2.50 22
JOHNSON ROSALYN     345123690 3.25 20
LOCKLEAR HEATHER    369426163 4.00 30
MCMANN ABAGAIL      333112040 3.97 41
MILDEW MORRIS       234812057 3.67 34
MORSE SAMUEL        334558778 3.00 28
NOVAK JAMES         348524598 1.50 13
OHERLAHE TERRY      333662222 2.75 21
RACKHAM HORACE      345878643 4.00 30
SNYDER JUDITH       356913580 2.75 24
VANDERSYS RALPH     367120987 3.23 22
VAUGHN SARAH        238498765 3.00 24
WIDGET WENDELL      444113333 1.25 10
WILSON PHILIP       345719642 3.00 25
WITWERTH JANUARY    367138302 2.10 20
WORDEN JACK         359241234 3.33 25
WOURTHY CONSTANCE   342092834 3.50 32
```

and data in TransactionFile as

```
333112040A 3
333112040A 4
333112040A 4
444113333A 3
444113333A 4
444113333A 3
444113333A 2
238498765A 3
238498765A 3
238498765A 4
238498766A 4
369325263A 3
369325263A 3
369325263A 4
369325263C 4
320678230A 5
320678230A 3
320678230A 3
320678230A 4
444226666A 3
444226666A 4
444226666A 3
444226667A 4
367138302A 3
367138302A 3
367138302A 3
367138302B 3
367120987A 4
367120987A 4
367120987A 3
367120987I 3
367120987A 3
```

```
369426163A 4
369426163A 3
345678901A 3
345678901A 4
345678901A 3
345678900A 4
123450987A 3
123450987A 3
123450987A 4
123450987E 3
234098112A 3
234098112A 3
444226666D 3
367138302D 3
123450987C 4
123450987D 3
123450987A 2
333112040D 4
333112040A 3
444113333D 4
444113333A 3
369235263D 4
369235263A 3
320678230D 3
320678230D 4
320678230W 3
334229023D 4
```

output for this program is

```
                     EXCEPTION REPORT
          ID NUMBER        GRADE      HOURS
          --------------------------------------

          238498766          A          4
          444226667          A          4
          345678900          A          4
          369235263          D          4
          369235263          A          3
          334229023          D          4
```

```
                     UPDATED REPORT
                 STUDENT FILE LISTING


          NAME                ID NUMBER      GPA     CREDITS
          -----------------------------------------------------

          BARRETT RODA        345678901     3.77       33
          BORGNINE ERNIST     369325263     3.77       28
          CADABRA ABRA        123450987     3.01       45
          DJIKSTRA EDGAR      345998765     3.90       33
          GARZELONI RANDY     444226666     2.66       31
          GLUTZ AGATHA        320678230     3.02       44
          HOLBRUCK HALL       321908765     3.50       29
          HUNTER MICHAEL      234098112     2.82       28
          JOHNSON ROSALYN     345123690     3.25       20
          LOCKLEAR HEATHER    369426163     4.00       37
          MCMANN ABAGAIL      333112040     3.78       59
          MILDEW MORRIS       234812057     3.67       34
          MORSE SAMUEL        334558778     3.00       28
          NOVAK JAMES         348524598     1.50       13
          OHERLAHE TERRY      333662222     2.75       21
          RACKHAM HORACE      345878643     4.00       30
          SNYDER JUDITH       356913580     2.75       24
```

```
VANDERSYS RALPH          367120987    3.53    36
VAUGHN SARAH             238498765    3.29    34
WIDGET WENDELL           444113333    2.64    29
WILSON PHILIP            345719642    3.00    25
WITWERTH JANUARY         367138302    2.53    32
WORDEN JACK              359241234    3.33    25
WOURTHY CONSTANCE        342092834    3.50    32
```

RUNNING AND DEBUGGING TIPS

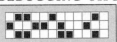

1. Be sure all files (except **input** and **output**) are properly opened for reading and writing. Remember, you must **reset** before reading from a file and **rewrite** before writing to a file.
2. Don't try to read past the end-of-file marker. This is a common error that occurs when trying to **read** without a sufficient check for **eof.**
3. Be careful to use file names as arguments correctly when using **read, readln, write, writeln, and eof.**
4. List all external files in the program heading and then be sure to declare them in the variable declaration section.
5. All files listed in a procedure heading must be variable parameters.
6. Protect against working with empty files or empty lines of a text file.
7. Remember, the file buffer is undefined when **eof** (⟨file name⟩) is **true.**

■ Summary

Key Terms

buffer variable	file window	reading from a file
component of a file	master file	transaction file
file	opening a file	writing to a file

Keywords

FILE	put
get	

Key Concepts

■ A file is a sequence of components all of the same data type; a typical declaration is

```
TYPE
   RealFile = FILE OF real;
VAR
   FileA : RealFile;
```

■ In standard implementations of Pascal, files must be accessed sequentially.
■ File window is a phrase commonly used to describe which component of the file is available for having data passed to or from it.
■ A buffer variable is an undeclared variable that is used to transfer data to or from a file component; if the file name is FileA, then the identifier for the buffer variable is FileA^.
■ Before transferring values to a file—writing to a file—the file must be opened for writing by **rewrite** (⟨file name⟩); values can then be transferred from the file buffer using **put** or **write** (⟨file name⟩, ⟨value⟩); for example,

```
rewrite (NewFile);
NewFile^ := 10;
put (NewFile);
```

or

```
rewrite (NewFile);
write (NewFile, 10);
```

- Before transferring values from a file—reading from a file—the file must be opened for reading by **reset** (⟨file name⟩); values can then be transferred from the file by assignments from the file buffer and by using **get** (⟨file name⟩) or **read** (⟨file name⟩, ⟨variable name⟩); for example,

```
reset (NewFile);
A := NewFile^;
get (NewFile);
```

or

```
reset (NewFile);
read (NewFile, A );
```

- An end-of-file marker is automatically placed at the end of the file—**eof** (⟨file name⟩)—when a file is created.
- A file cannot be opened for reading and writing at the same time.
- When a file is declared as a parameter in a procedure heading, it must be listed as a variable parameter; for example,

```
PROCEDURE Update (VAR OldFile, NewFile : ⟨file type⟩);
```

- Components of a file can be arrays; the declaration

```
VAR
   F : FILE OF ARRAY [1..10] OF real;
```

can be depicted as shown in Figure 10.5, where F^ is an array and array components are denoted by F^[J].

FIGURE 10.5
File of arrays

F

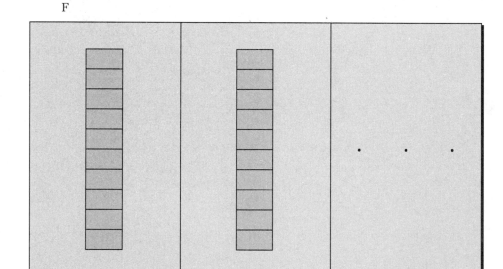

- File components can also be records and can be declared by

```
TYPE
   RecType = RECORD
                Name : PACKED ARRAY [1..20] OF char;
                Age : 0..120;
                Gender : char
             END;   {  of RECORD RecType  }
VAR
   F : FILE OF RecType;
```

and depicted as shown in Figure 10.6. In this case, the buffer variable F^ is a record and fields can be denoted by

FIGURE 10.6
File of records

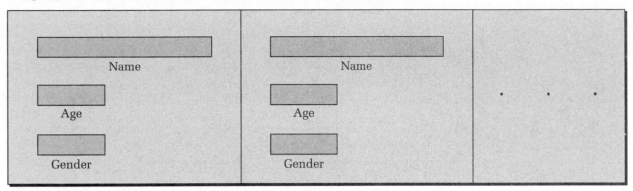

```
F^.Name
F^.Age
F^.Gender
```

- Files with structured components frequently have to be processed and/or up-dated; for a file of records, you might insert or delete a record, sort the file by a field, merge two files, update each record, or produce a printed list according to some field.
- When updating or otherwise processing a file, changes are normally made in a transaction (temporary) file and then copied back into the master (permanent) file.
- Since input data are generally in a text file, you need to create a file of struc-tured components from the text file; you can then use **get** and **put** to transfer en-tire structures at one time.

■ Programming Problems and Projects

1. *The Pentagon* is a mathematics magazine published by Kappa Mu Ep-silon, a mathematics honorary society. Write a program to be used by the business manager for the purpose of generating mailing labels. The subscribers' information should be read into a file of records. Each record should contain the subscriber's name; address, including street and street number, apartment number (if any), city, two-letter abbreviation for the state, and the zip code; expiration information, including month and year.

   Your program should create an alphabetically sorted master file, print an alphabetical list for the office, print a mailing list sorted by zip code for bulk mailing, and denote all last issues by a special symbol.

2. The relentless Dr. Lae Z. Programmer (Problems 5, 22, and 23; Chap-ter 4; Problem 13, Chapter 5; Problem 5, Chapter 6; Problem 3, Chap-ter 8; and Problem 3, Chapter 9) now wants you to create a file of records for students in his computer science course. You should pro-vide fields for the student's name, ten quiz scores, six program scores, and three examination scores. Your program should
   a. Read in the names from a text file.
   b. Include procedures for updating quiz scores, program scores, and examination scores.
   c. Be able to update the file by adding or deleting a record.
   d. Print an alphabetized list of the data base at any given time.

3. Write a program to do part of the work of a word processor. Your program should read a text file and print it in paragraph form. The left margin should be in column 10 and the right margin in column 72. In the input file, periods will designate the end of sentences and the "*" symbol will denote a new paragraph. No word should be split between lines. Your program should save the edited file in a file of type **text**.

4. Slow-pitch softball is rapidly becoming a popular summer pastime. Assume your local community is to have a new ladies' league this year consisting of eight teams, with 15 players each. This league gets the field one night per week for four games. They will play a double round-robin (each team plays every other team twice, resulting in 14 games). Write a program to
   a. Create a file of records (one record for each team) in which the team name is included.
   b. Print a schedule.
   c. List the teams alphabetically by team name.
   d. Print a list of players for each team.

5. The registrar at State University (Problem 15, Chapter 4; Problem 3, Chapter 6) wants you to write an interactive program to assist with record keeping. Your program should create a file of records. The record for each student should contain the student's name, identification number, credit hours completed, the number of credit hours in which currently enrolled, and grade point average. Your program should also contain a procedure for each of the following updates.
   a. Semester-end data of hours completed and grade point average for the semester.
   b. Insert a record.
   c. Delete a record.
   d. Print a list sorted alphabetically.
   e. Print a list sorted by grade point average.

6. The local high school sports boosters (Problems 1 and 2, Chapter 8) need more help. They want you to write a program to create a file of records in which each record contains the parents' names, the children's first names (at most ten children), and the names of the sports in which the children participated.

   A typical record is shown in Figure 10.7. Your program should create a file from a text file and save it for later use, print an alphabetical list of parents' names, and print a list of the names of parents of football players.

FIGURE 10.7
Typical values for fields in a record

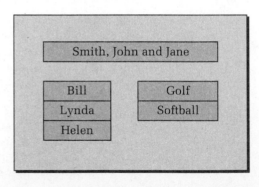

7. A popular use of text files is for teachers to create a bank of test items and then use them to generate quizzes using some form of random generation. Write a program to allow you to create files of type **text** that contain questions for each of three chapters. Second, generate two quizzes of three questions for each of the three chapters.

8. Public service departments must always be on the lookout for those who try to abuse the system by accepting assistance from similar agencies in different geographic areas. Write a program to compare names from one county with those from another county and print all names that are on both lists.

9. Write a program to be used by flight agents at an airport (see Exercise 1a, Section 10.3). Your program should use a file of records where the record for each flight contains flight number, airline, arrival time, arriving from, departure time, and destination. Your program should list incoming flights sorted by time, list departing flights sorted by time, add flights, and delete flights.

10. Congratulations! You have just been asked to write a program that will assign dates for the Valentine's Day dance. Each student record will contain the student's name, age, gender (M or F), and the names of three date preferences (ranked). Your program should
   a. Create a master file from the input file.
   b. Create and save alphabetically sorted files of males and females.
   c. Print a list of couples for the dance. The genders must be opposite and the age difference may be no more than three years. Dating preferences should be in the following form.

	CAN'T MISS!	
First request	Matches	First request
	GOOD BET!	
First request	Matches	Second request
Second request	Matches	First request
	GOOD LUCK!	
	Any other matches	
	OUT OF LUCK!	
	You are not on any list	

It's obvious (isn't it?) that a person can have at most one date for the dance.

11. A data file consists of an unknown number of real numbers. Write a program to read the file and print the highest value, lowest value, and average of the numbers in the file.

■ 12. The Falcon Manufacturing Company (Problem 22, Chapter 8 and Problem 17, Chapter 9) wants you to write an inventory file program. The file should contain a 30-character part name, an integer part number, the quantity on hand, and the price of an item. The program should permit the entry of new items into the file and the deletion of existing items. The items to be changed will be entered from the keyboard.

■ 13. Write a program for the Falcon Manufacturing Company (Problem 12) to allow a secretary to enter an item number and a quantity, and whether it is to be added to or deleted from the stock. The program should prepare a new data file with the updated information. If the user requests to remove more items than are on hand, an appropriate warning message should be issued.

■ 14. Write a program to read the inventory file of the Falcon Manufacturing Company (Problems 12 and 13) and then print a listing of the inventory. The program should print an asterisk (*) next to the quantity of any item of which there are fewer than 50 on hand.

■ 15. Revise the program that you wrote in answer to Problem 22 in Chapter 8 to permit the sales figures of the Falcon Manufacturing Company to be read from a file. Also revise the program so that the information on the total dollar amount of sales for each product by each salesperson is written to a file for later use.

■ 16. Write a program to read the total dollars sales file from Problem 15 for last month and the corresponding file for this month and print out a table showing the total sales by each salesperson for each product during the two-month period.

17. A data file contains an alphabetized list of the secondary students in your former high school, and another contains an alphabetized list of the elementary students. Write a program to merge these two files and print an alphabetized list of all students in your former school.

18. The Andover Telephone Company (whose motto is "We send your messages of Andover.") wants a computerized directory information system. The data file should contain the customer names and telephone numbers. Your program should permit:
    a. The entry of new customers' names and telephone numbers.
    b. The deletion of existing customers' names and telephone numbers.
    c. The printing of all customers' names and their telephone numbers.
    d. The entry from the keyboard of a customer's name with the program then printing the telephone number (if found).

Whenever customers' names and numbers are to be added or deleted, the file should be updated accordingly. You may assume there are no more than 50 customers.

19. Revise the program written to keep the grades of Mr. Laven's students (Problem 19, Chapter 8) to read the grades entered previously from a file and, when the program is complete, print the updated list of grades.

20. Recognizing your talents as a programmer, the principal of the local high school wants you to write a program to work with a data file containing the names of the students who were absent at the start of the school day. These names are kept as 30-character packed arrays. The program should permit the principal to enter the name of a student later in the day to check to see if the student was absent at the start of the day.

21. Revise Problem 13 from Chapter 9 to permit Mrs. Crown's computer maintenance records to be kept in a file. Your program should allow the data on a machine to be changed and new machines to be added.

22. Contact a programmer at your university or some company or corporation to discuss data structures. Find out how much (if any) he or she uses arrays, records, and files. If the programmer does use arrays, records, or files, what kinds of programming problems require their use? Find out what kinds of operations are used with these data struc-

tures. What limitations do these structures possess for the problems that need to be solved?

Write a complete report summarizing your discussion.

23. Problems involving data management are routinely addressed in non-programming courses taught in schools of business. These courses may be taught in departments such as Management Information Systems (MIS) or Business Information Systems (BIS). Contact an instructor of such a course and discuss the issue of using data structures to manage information. How are data structures presented to the classes? What are some typical real-world problems?

    Give an oral report of your discussion to your class. Compare and contrast the instructor's presentations with those provided in your own class. Use charts with transparencies as part of your presentation.

24. Select an unworked problem from the previously listed programming problems for this chapter. Construct a structure chart and write all documentary information necessary for this problem. Do not write code. When finished, have a classmate read your documentation to see if precisely what is to be done is clear.

CHAPTER

By a "set" we shall
understand any collection
into a whole . . . of definite,
distinguishable objects . . . of
our intuition and thought.
Georg Cantor

Sets

We have thus far investigated the structured variables, arrays, records, and files. These are structured because, when declared, a certain structure is reserved to subsequently hold values. In an array, a predetermined number of elements all of the same type can be held. A record contains a predetermined number of fields that can hold elements of different types. A file is somewhat like an array but the length is not predetermined and elements must be accessed sequentially.

Another structured data type available in Pascal is a *set*. Since the implementation of sets varies greatly from system to system, you need to check statements and examples in this chapter on your system.

The goal of this chapter is to enable you to use sets when writing programs to solve problems. One fairly common use for sets is to guard against an inadvertent keystroke when users are working with interactive programs. But before you can use sets in a program, you must understand certain fundamentals. In particular, you must be able to properly define sets and use set operations.

■ 11.1
Declarations and Terms

Basic Idea and Notation

A set in Pascal is a structured data type consisting of a collection of distinct elements from an indicated base type (which must be ordinal type). Sets in Pascal are defined and used in a manner consistent with the use of sets in mathematics. A set type is defined by

```
TYPE
    ⟨type name⟩ = SET OF ⟨base type⟩;
```

A set variable is then declared by

```
VAR
    ⟨variable name⟩ : ⟨type name⟩;
```

In a program working with characters of the alphabet, you might have

```
TYPE
  Alphabet = SET OF 'A'..'Z';
VAR
  Vowels, Consonants : Alphabet;
```

In a similar fashion, if your program analyzes digits and arithmetic symbols, you might have

```
TYPE
  Units = SET OF 0..9;
  Symbols = SET OF '*'..'/';  {  Arithmetic symbols  }
VAR
  Digits : Units;
  ArithSym : Symbols;
```

In these examples, Alphabet, Units, and Symbols are set types. Vowels, Consonants, Digits, and ArithSym are set variables.

A set can contain elements; these elements must be of the defined base type, which must be an ordinal data type. Most implementations of Pascal limit the maximum size of the base type of a set. This limit is such that a base type of **integer** is not allowed. Often the limit is at least **128** so base types of **char** and subranges of **integer** within 0..127 can usually be used.

Assignments to Sets

Once a set variable has been declared, it is undefined until an assignment of values is made. The syntax for assigning is

⟨set name⟩ := [⟨values⟩];

For example, we can have

```
Vowels := ['A', 'E', 'I', 'O', 'U'];
Consonants := ['B'..'D', 'F'..'H', 'J'..'N',
               'P'..'T','V'..'Z'];
Digits := [0..9];
ArithSym := ['+', '-', '*', '/'];
```

Notice that the assigned values must be included in brackets and must be of the defined base type. Appropriate values depend on the character set being used. Also, subranges of the base type can be used; thus,

```
Consonants := ['B'..'D'];
```

is the same as

```
Consonants := ['B', 'C', 'D'];
```

It is also possible to have set constants. Just as 4, 'H', and −56.20 are constants, [2,4,6] is a constant. In the previous example, this could have been caused by

```
Digits := [2,4,6];
```

As mentioned, sets are structured data types because, in a sense, they can be thought of as containing a list of elements. However, in listing the elements, note that each element can be listed only once and order makes no difference; thus, [2,4,6] is the same as [4,2,6].

Fractal Geometry and Benoit Mandelbrot

Fractal geometry as a serious mathematical endeavor began [in about 1975] with the pioneering work of Benoit B. Mandelbrot, a Fellow of the Thomas J. Watson Research Center, IBM Corporation. Fractal geometry is a theory of geometric forms so complex they defy analysis and classification by traditional Euclidean means. Yet fractal shapes occur universally in the natural world. Mandelbrot has recognized them not only in coastlines, landscapes, lungs, and turbulent water flow but also in the chaotic fluctuation of prices on the Chicago commodity exchange.

Though Mandelbrot's first comprehensive publication of fractal theory took place in 1975, mathematicians were aware of some of the basic elements during the period from 1875 to 1925. However, because mathematicians at that time thought such knowledge of "fractal dimension" deserved little attention, their discoveries were left as unrelated odds and ends. Also, the creation of fractal illustrations—a laborious and nearly impossible task at the turn of the twentieth century— can now be done quickly and precisely using computer graphics. (Even personal computers can now be used to generate fractal patterns with relative ease.)

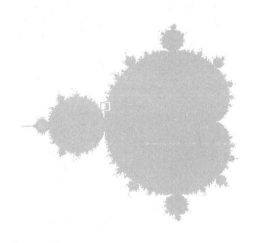

The picture on the left shows an enlargement of the area of the Mandelbrot set shown as a rectangle in the picture on the right.

Source: From *For All Practical Purposes: Introduction to Contemporary Mathematics.* By Consortium for Mathematics and Its Applications. Copyright © 1991 by COMAP, Inc. Reprinted by permission of W.H. Freeman and Company.

Other Terminology

Once a value of the base type has been assigned to a set, it is an *element of the set*. Thus, if we have

```
Digits := [2,4,6];
```

2, 4, and 6 are elements of Digits. Testing membership in a set is discussed in the next section.

As in mathematics, any set that contains all possible values of the base type is called the *universal set*. In

```
Digits := [0..9];
```

Digits is a universal set. It is also possible to consider a set constant as a universal set. Thus, ['A' . . 'Z'] is a universal set if the **TYPE** definition section contains

```
⟨type name⟩= SET OF 'A'..'Z';
```

If A and B have been declared as sets of the same type and all of the elements of A are also contained in B, A is a *subset* of B. If we have

```
VAR
   A, B : Units;
```

and the assignments

```
A := [1,2,3,4,5];
B := [0..6];
```

have been made, A is a subset of B. Note, however, that B is not a subset of A since B contains two elements (0 and 6) that are not contained in A.

The *empty set,* or *null set,* is the set containing no elements. It is denoted by [ ].

Note that these definitions allow for set theory results of mathematics to hold in Pascal. Some of these follow.

1. The empty set is a subset of every set.
2. If A is a subset of B and B is a subset of C, then A is a subset of C.
3. Every set (of the base type) is a subset of the universal set.

Exercises 11.1

1. Find all errors in the following definitions and declarations. Explain your answers.
   a. ```
      TYPE
         Numbers = SET OF real;
      ```
   b. ```
      TYPE
         Numbers = SET OF integer;
      ```
   c. ```
      TYPE
         Alphabet : SET OF 'A'..'Z';
      ```
   d. ```
      TYPE
         Alphabet = SET OF ['A'..'Z'];
      ```
   e. ```
      TYPE
         Conditions = (Sunny, Mild, Rainy, Windy);
         Weather = SET OF Conditions;
      VAR
         TodaysWeather : Weather;
      ```

2. Write a test program to
   a. Discover if **char** is a permissible base type for a set.
   b. Determine the limitation on the size of the base type for a set.

3. Suppose a set A is declared by
   ```
   TYPE
     Letters = SET OF 'A'..'Z';
   VAR
     A : Letters;
   ```
   a. Show how A can be made to contain the letters of your name.
   b. Assign the letters of the word *PASCAL* to A.
   ```

  c. Assuming the assignment

```
A := ['T', 'O', 'Y'];
```

    list all elements and subsets of A.

4. Let the sets A, B, and U be declared by

```
TYPE
   Alphabet = SET OF 'A'..'Z';
VAR
   A, B, U : Alphabet;
```

and the assignments

```
A := ['B', 'F', 'J'..'T'];
B := ['O'..'S'];
U := ['A'..'Z'];
```

be made. Indicate whether each of the following is **true** or **false**.

  a. [ ] is a subset of B   e. 'B' is a subset of A

  b. B is an element of A   f. A is a subset of U

  c. B is a subset of A   g. 'O' is an element of A

  d. 'B' is an element of A

5. Assume A, B, and U are declared as in Exercise 4. Find and explain all errors in the following assignment statements.

  a. `A := 'J'..'O';`   d. `A := ['E', 'I', 'E', 'I', 'O'];`

  b. `U := [];`   e. `[] := ['D'];`

  c. `B := [A..Z];`   f. `B := ['A'..'T', 'S'];`

6. Let A be a set declared by

```
TYPE
   NumRange = 0..100;
VAR
   A : SET OF NumRange;
   M, N : integer;
```

Indicate if the following are valid or invalid. For those that are valid, list the elements of A. For those that are invalid, explain why.

  a. `A := [19];`

  b. `A := 19;`

  c. `M := 80;`
     `N := 40;`
     `A := [M + N, M MOD N, M DIV N];`

  d. `M := 10;`
     `N := 2;`
     `A := [M, M * N, M / N];`

7. Define a set type and declare a set variable to be used for each of the following.

  a. Set values consist of colors of the rainbow.

  b. Set values consist of class in school (Freshman, Sophomore, Junior, or Senior).

  c. Set values consist of fruits.

  d. Set values consist of grades for a class.

8. Explain why **SET** is not an enumerated type.

■ ■ ■ ■

■ 11.2
Set Operations and Relational Operators

Set Operations

Pascal provides for the set operations *union, intersection,* and *difference* where, in each case, two sets are combined to produce a single set. If A and B are sets of the same type, these operations are defined as follows:

- The union of A and B is A + B where A + B contains any element that is in A or that is in B.
- The intersection of A and B is A * B where A * B contains the elements that are in both A and B.
- The difference of A and B is A − B where A − B contains the elements that are in A but not in B.

To illustrate, suppose A and B are sets that contain integer values and the assignment statements

```
A := [1..5];
B := [3..9];
```

are made. The values produced by set operations follow.

Set Operation	Values
A + B	[1..9]
A * B	[3,4,5]
A − B	[1,2]
B − A	[6..9]

Multiple operations can be performed with sets and, when such an expression is encountered, the same operator priority exists as with priorities for evaluating arithmetic expressions. Thus, if A and B contain the values previously indicated,

```
A + B - A * B
```

produces

```
[1..5] + [3..9]  -  [1..5] * [3..9]
                              ↓
[1..5] + [3..9]  -       [3,4,5]
          ↓
      [1..9]      -       [3,4,5]
                     ↓
           [1,2,6..9]
```

Relational Operators

Relational operators can also be used with sets in Pascal. These operators correspond to the normal set operators equal, not equal, subset, and superset. In each case, a Boolean value is produced. If A and B are sets, these operators are defined as shown in Table 11.1.

Boolean values associated with some set expressions follow.

Set Expression	Boolean Value
[1,2,3] <= [0..10]	true
[0..10] <= [1,2,3]	false
[0..10] = [0..5, 6..10]	true
[] = ([1,2] - [0..10])	true
[1..5] <> [1..3, 4, 5]	false
[] <= [1,2,3]	true

TABLE 11.1
Set operations

Operator	Relational Expression	Definition
= (Equal)	A = B	A equals B; that is, every element in A is contained in B and every element in B is contained in A.
<> (Not equal)	A <> B	A does not equal B; that is, either A or B contains an element that is not contained in the other set.
<= (Subset)	A <= B	A is a subset of B; that is, every element of A is also contained in B.
>= (Superset)	A >= B	A is a superset of B (B is a subset of A); that is, every element of B is contained in A.

Set Membership

Membership in a set is indicated in Pascal by the reserved word **IN**. The general form is

⟨element⟩ **IN** ⟨set⟩

This returns a value of **true** if the element is in the set and a value of **false** if it is not. To illustrate, suppose A and B are sets and the assignments

```
A := [0..20];
B := [5..10];
```

are made. The values of expressions using **IN** follow.

Expression	Boolean Value
10 IN A	true
5 IN (A − B)	false
20 IN B	false
7 IN (A * B)	true
80 DIV 20 IN A * B	?

Note that the last expression cannot be evaluated until priorities are assigned to the operators. Fortunately, these priorities are identical to those used for arithmetic expressions with **IN** on the same level as relational operators. They are shown in Table 11.2.

TABLE 11.2
Operator priorities including set operations

Priority Level	Operators
1	( )
2	**NOT**
3	*, /, **MOD, DIV, AND**
4	+, −, **OR**
5	<, >, <=, >=, =, <>, **IN**

Operations at each level are performed in order from left to right as they appear in an expression. Thus, the expression

```
80 DIV 20 IN A * B
```

produces

```
80 DIV 20 IN A * B
    ↓
    4      IN A * B
               ↓
    4      IN [5..10]
             ↓
           false
```

Exercises 11.2

1. When using sets in Pascal, is $>=$ the logical complement of $<=$? Give an example to illustrate your answer.

2. Let A and B be sets defined such that A := [0 . . 10] and B := [2,4,6,8,10] are valid. Write a test program to show that
   a. A + B = A
   b. A * B = B
   c. A − B = [0,1,3,5,7,9]

3. For each of the following sets A and B, find A + B, A * B, A − B, and B − A.
   a. A := [−3 . . 2,8,10], B := [0 . . 4,7 . . 10]
   b. A := [0,1,5 . . 10,20], B := [2,4,6,7 . . 11]
   c. A := [ ], B := [1 . . 15]
   d. A := [0 . . 5, 10, 14 . . 20], B := [3,10,15]

4. Given the following sets
   A := [0,2,4,6,8,10];
   B := [1,3,5,7,9];
   C := [0 . . 5];
   indicate the values in each of the following sets.
   a. A * B − C   e. A − B * C
   b. A * (B − C)   f. A − (B − (A − B))
   c. A * (B + C)   g. A * (B * C)
   d. A * B + A * C   h. (A * B) * C

5. Using sets A, B, and C with values assigned as in Exercise 4, indicate whether each of the following is **true** or **false**.
   a. A * B = [ ]   d. A + B <> C
   b. C <= A + B   e. A − B >= [ ]
   c. [5] <= B   f. (A + B = C) **OR** ([ ] <= B − C)

6. In mathematics, when X is an element of a set A, this is denoted by X ∈ A. If X is not in A, we write X ∉ A. Let B be a set declared by

   ```
   VAR
     B : SET OF 0..10;
   ```

   Examine the following for validity and decide how Pascal handles the concept of not-an-element-of.
   a. 4 NOT IN B   d. NOT (4 IN B)
   b. 4 NOT (IN B)   e. 4 IN NOT B
   c. NOT 4 IN B   f. 4 IN (NOT B)

7. Write a short program to count the number of uppercase vowels in a text file. Your program should include the set type

```
TYPE
   AlphaUppercase = SET OF 'A'..'Z';
```

and set variable VowelsUppercase declared by

```
VAR
   VowelsUppercase : AlphaUppercase;
```

■ ■ ■ ■

Uses for Sets

Now that we know how to declare sets, assign values to sets, and operate with sets, we need to examine some uses of sets in programs. First, however, we need to note an important limitation of sets: as with other structured variables, sets cannot be read or written directly. However, the two processes—generating a set and printing the elements of a set—are not difficult to code. To illustrate generating a set, suppose you wish to create a set and have it contain all the characters in the alphabet in a line of text. (For this example we assume that the text file does not contain lowercase letters.) You can declare this set with

```
TYPE
   AlphaSymbols = 'A'..'Z';
   Symbols = SET OF AlphaSymbols;
VAR
   Alphabet : Symbols;
   SentenceChar : Symbols;
   Ch : char;
```

Code to generate the set SentenceChar is

```
Alphabet := ['A'..'Z'];
SentenceChar := [];
WHILE NOT eoln(Data) DO
   BEGIN
      read (Data, Ch);
      IF Ch IN Alphabet THEN
         SentenceChar := SentenceChar + [Ch]
   END;
```

For many examples we assume the text file does not contain lowercase letters. As you will see in the Focus on Program Design section, a slight modification can be made to accommodate both uppercase and lowercase letters. For example, you could use both uppercase and lowercase letters by changing the set definitions to

```
TYPE
   Symbols = SET OF char;
VAR
   UppercaseAlphabet : Symbols;
   LowercaseAlphabet : Symbols;
   Alphabet: Symbols;
```

Alphabet could then be formed in the program by

```
UppercaseAlphabet := ['A'..'Z'];
LowercaseAlphabet := ['a'..'z'];
Alphabet := UppercaseAlphabet + LowercaseAlphabet;
```

or

```
Alphabet := ['A'..'Z', 'a'..'z']
```

The general procedure of getting values into a set is to initialize the set by assigning the empty set and use set union to add elements to the set.

The process of printing values of elements in a set is equally short. Assuming you know the data type of elements in the set, a loop can be used where the loop control variable ranges over values of this data type. Whenever a value is in the set, it is printed. To illustrate, assume the set Sentence-Char now contains all the alphabetical characters from a line of text and you wish to print these characters. Since we know the data type for elements of SentenceChar will be characters in 'A' . . 'Z', we can print the contained values by

```
FOR Ch := 'A' TO 'Z' DO
  IF Ch IN SentenceChar THEN
    write (Ch:2);
writeln;
```

If these two fragments of code are applied to the line of text

```
THIS LINE (OBVIOUSLY MADE UP!) DOESN'T MAKE MUCH SENSE.
```

the output is

```
A B C D E H I K L M N O P S T U V Y
```

Now that you are familiar with how to generate elements in a set and subsequently print contents of a set, let's examine some uses for sets in programs. Specifically, let's look at using sets to replace complex Boolean expressions, protect a program against bad data, protect against invalid **CASE** statements, and aid in interactive programming.

Suppose you are writing a program to analyze responses to questions on a standard machine-scored form. If you want a certain action to take place for every response of A, B, or C, instead of

```
IF (Response='A') OR (Response='B') OR (Response='C') THEN
```

you could have

```
IF Response IN ['A', 'B', 'C'] THEN
       .
       .
       .
```

STYLE TIP

Sets with appropriate names are particularly useful for checking data. For example, a typical problem when working with dynamic variables is to examine an arithmetic expression for correct form. Thus, 3 + 4 is a valid expression but 3 + * 4 is not. As part of a program that analyzes such expressions, you might choose to define the following sets.

```
TYPE
  ValidDigits = SET OF '0'..'9';
  Symbols = SET OF char;
VAR
  Digits : ValidDigits;
  ValidOperator : Symbols;
  LeftSymbol, RightSymbol : Symbols;
```

These sets can now be assigned values such as

```
Digits := ['0'..'9'];
ValidOperator := ['+', '*', '-', '/'];
LeftSymbol := ['(', '[', '{'];
RightSymbol := [')', ']', '}'];
```

To demonstrate protecting a program against bad data, suppose you are writing a program to use a relatively large data file. Furthermore, suppose that the data are entered by operators in such a fashion that the first entry on the first line for each customer is a single-digit code. This is followed by appropriate data for the customer. To make sure the code is properly entered, you can define a set ValidSym and assign it all appropriate symbols. Your program design can be

```
read (Data, Sym);
IF Sym IN ValidSym THEN
   BEGIN
      .
      .    (action here)
      .
   END
ELSE
   (error message here)
```

Specifically, a program for printing mailing labels might require a 3, 4, or 5 to indicate the number of lines for the name and address that follow. If you are writing a program that also partially edits the data file, you can have

```
read (NumLines);
IF NumLines IN [3,4,5] THEN
   BEGIN
      .
      .    (process number of lines)
      .
   END
ELSE
   (error message here)
```

The third use of sets is to protect against invalid **CASE** statements. To illustrate, suppose you are working with a program that uses a **CASE** statement where the selector is a letter grade assigned to students. Without sets, the statement is

```
CASE LetGrade OF
   'A' : ...
   'B' : ...
   'C' : ...
   'D' : ...
   'E' : ...
END;  {  of CASE LetGrade  }
```

To protect against the possibility of LetGrade being assigned a value not in the **CASE** selector list, sets can be used as follows:

```
IF LetGrade IN ['A'..'E'] THEN
   CASE LetGrade OF
      'A' : ...
      'B' : ...
      'C' : ...
      'D' : ...
      'E' : ...
   END  {  of CASE LetGrade  }
ELSE
   (error message here)
```

A fourth use of sets is as an aid in writing interactive programs. Frequently a user will be asked to respond by pressing a certain key or keys. For example, a message such as the following may be given:

```
Do you wish to continue?
<Y> or <N> and press <RETURN>.
```

In such cases, two problems may occur. First, the user might use uppercase or lowercase letters for a correct response. Second, the user might inadvertently strike the wrong key. To make this part of the program correct and guard against bad data, you could have a set declared and initialized as

```
GoodResponse := ['Y', 'y', 'N', 'n'];
```

and then use a **REPEAT . . . UNTIL** loop as follows:

```
REPEAT
  writeln ('Do you wish to continue?');
  writeln ('<Y> or <N> and press <RETURN>.');
  readln (Response)
UNTIL Response IN GoodResponse;
```

You could then use a **boolean** variable Continue by first assigning it a value **false** and then follow the **REPEAT . . . UNTIL** loop with

```
Continue := Response IN ['Y', 'y'];
```

Sets with Functions

Sets can be used with subprograms. In general, set types can be used as parameters in much the same way that arrays, records, and files are used. However, when working with functions, sets cannot be returned as values of a function because functions cannot return structured types.

To illustrate using sets with functions, let's consider two examples.

■ **EXAMPLE 11.1**

Let's write a function to determine the cardinality (size or number of elements) of a set. Assuming appropriate **TYPE** definitions, such a function can be

```
FUNCTION Cardinality (S : <set type>) : integer;
  VAR
    Ct : integer;
    X : <base type for set>;
  BEGIN
    Ct := 0;
    FOR X := <initial value> TO <final value> DO
      IF X IN S THEN
        Ct := Ct + 1;
    ,Cardinality := Ct
  END;
```

initial   . . .   final
value   value

If given X in set S,
increase cardinality counter

S

This is called from the main program by

```
SetSize := Cardinality(<set name>);
```

A NOTE OF INTEREST

Time Is Cure for Computerphobia

Looking back on an article published in 1985, we see the then-prevalent attitude toward computers. What can make an otherwise stalwart manager break into a cold sweat, reel with dizziness, and suffer waves of nausea? The answer is not the latest version of the flu. It's the computer! As reported in the *Executive Action Series,* published by the Bureau of Business Practice, Waterford, Connecticut, a surprising number of managers fear, distrust, and even hate the computer, some in phobic proportions.

Is there a cure for this phobia that has such a destructive effect on productivity? Time is the answer, say the experts. It takes time to overcome computerphobia. A gradual introduction to computer technology is essential. Companies that provide both private instruction to managers and the time to master simple programming have more personnel regularly using their terminals. Confidence and motivation grow as managers successfully master simple computer tasks.

Computerphobia may be slowly decreasing over the years. There is now a growing interest in the concept of Executive Information Systems (EIS), systems designed specifically to meet the unique needs of high-level managers. They focus on communications, unstructured decision-making situations, and related areas that are part of executives' jobs. As these technologies develop, managerial computerphobia decreases and use of technology increases.

■ EXAMPLE 11.2

For our second example, let's consider a function to find the maximum (largest ordinal) element of a set. This would typically be applied to a set whose elements are in some subrange of the integers. If not, however, you can easily modify the function by considering the ordinals of set elements.

```
FUNCTION MaxElement (S : <set type>) : <base type>;
  VAR
    Temp : <base type>;
    X : <base type>;
  BEGIN
    IF S = [] THEN
      BEGIN
        writeln ('You are working with an empty set!':40);
        MaxElement := <initial value>
      END
    ELSE
      BEGIN
        Temp := <initial value>;
        FOR X := <initial value> TO <final value> DO
          IF (X IN S) AND (X > Temp) THEN
            Temp := X;
          MaxElement := Temp
      END  {  of ELSE option  }
  END;  {  of FUNCTION MaxElement  }
```

initial   . . .   final
value   ↖   value
Any new value of X which is
also in S causes Temp to be
adjusted
                                    ↘
                                    S

This is called from the main program by

```
Largest := MaxElement(<set name>);
```

Sets with Procedures

As you recall, sets cannot be returned as values of a function. However, when a program requires a set to be returned from a subprogram, the set can be used as a variable parameter with a procedure. In this manner, sets can either be generated or modified with subprograms. The Focus on Program Design section at the end of this chapter illustrates such a use.

Exercises 11.3

1. Modify the function MaxElement used in Example 11.2 to find the character in a line of text that is latest in the alphabet. Use this function with the Focus on Program Design code presented at the end of this chapter.

2. Write a test program to create a set containing all the consonants from a line of text. Your program should also print all elements in the set.

3. Write a short program to reproduce a text file where every vowel is replaced by an asterisk.

4. Modify the code used to find all the alphabet characters in a line of text so that a complete text file can be analyzed rather than just one line.

5. Write a program to simulate arithmetic indicated in a text file. The arithmetic expression should always be of the form digit-symbol-digit (9 + 8) where all digits and symbols are given as data of type **char**. Your program should protect against bad operation symbols, bad digits (actually nondigits), and division by zero.

6. To illustrate how sets can be used to protect against invalid values for **CASE** selectors, write a short program that uses a **CASE** statement. Run it with an invalid **CASE** selector value. Change the program so the **CASE** statement is protected by using a set. Rerun the program with the same invalid selector.

7. Write a Boolean function to analyze an integer between $-9,999$ and $9,999$ which returns the value **true** if the integer contains only odd digits (1,731) and **false** otherwise.

8. Write a function that returns the length of a string passed to the function as a packed array. Punctuation marks and internal blanks should add to the string length. Blanks at the beginning or end should not.

■ ■ ■ ■

**FOCUS ON
PROGRAM DESIGN**

The sample program for this chapter illustrates a use of sets. In particular, a set is used as a variable parameter in a procedure. The specific problem is to write a program to determine the alphabetical characters used in a line of text. Output from the program is an echo print of the text line, a list of letters in the text, and the number of distinct letters used in the line.

A first-level pseudocode development for this problem is

1. Get the characters
2. Print the characters
3. Determine the cardinality of the set
4. Print a closing message

A structure chart for this program is given in Figure 11.1.

FIGURE 11.1
Structure chart for **PROGRAM**
SymbolCheck

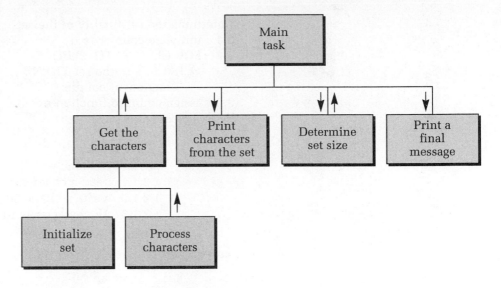

Module specifications for the main modules are

1. GetLetters Module
   Data received: None
   Information returned: A set of letters from a sentence
   Logic: Initialize the set.
          Add (union) distinct letters from a line of text.

2. PrintSet Module
   Data received: A set of letters
   Information returned: None
   Logic: Use a **FOR** loop to scan the alphabet and print the letters contained in the set.

3. Cardinality Module
   Data received: A set of letters
   Information returned: The cardinality of the set
   Logic: Use a function to count the number of distinct elements in a set.

4. PrintMessage Module
   Data received: Cardinality of the set
   Information returned: None
   Logic: Print a message indicating the set size.

A refinement of the pseudocode produces

1.   Get the characters
       1.1   initialize set
       1.2   **WHILE NOT eoln DO**
            1.2.1   process a character
2.   Print the characters
       2.1   **FOR** Ch := 'A' **TO** 'z' **DO**
             IF Ch is in the set **THEN**
               print Ch

    3. Determine the cardinality of the set
       3.1   initialize counter to 0
       3.2   **FOR** Ch := 'A' **TO** 'z' **DO**
               IF Ch is in the set **THEN**
                  increment counter
       3.3   assign count to function name
    4. Print a closing message

Step 1.2.1 could be refined to

    1.2.1   process a character
         1.2.1.1   read a character
         1.2.1.2   write a character (echo print)
         1.2.1.3   **IF** character is in the alphabet **THEN**
                         add it to the set of characters

The main program is

```
BEGIN  {  Main program  }
  reset (Data);
  GetLetters (SentenceChar);
  PrintSet (SentenceChar);
  SetSize := Cardinality(SentenceChar);
  PrintMessage (SetSize)
END.  {  of main program  }
```

A complete program for this is

```
PROGRAM SymbolCheck (input, output, Data);

{  This program illustrates working with sets.  It reads a line  }
{  of text and  determines the  number of  distinct letters in   }
{  that line.  Output  includes  the  distinct letters  and the  }
{  set cardinality.  Information for this program is stored in    }
{  the text file Data.                                           }

CONST
  Skip = ' ';

TYPE
  AlphaSymbols = SET OF char;

VAR
  SentenceChar : AlphaSymbols;       {  Set of possible letters  }
  SetSize : integer;                 {  Cardinality of the set   }
  Data : text;                       {  Data file                }

{*************************************************************** }

PROCEDURE GetLetters (VAR SentenceChar : AlphaSymbols);

  {  Given:   Nothing                                            }
  {  Task:    Read characters from the text file, Data; echo     }
  {           print them; store the alphabetical                 }
  {           characters in a set                                }
  {  Return:  The set of letters contained in the line of        }
  {           text                                               }

  VAR
    Ch : char;
    Alphabet : AlphaSymbols;
```

```
      BEGIN
        SentenceChar := [];
        Alphabet := ['A'..'Z'] + ['a'..'z'];
        writeln (Skip:10, 'The line of text is below:');
        writeln; write (Skip:10);
        WHILE NOT eoln(Data) DO
          BEGIN
            read (Data, Ch);
            write (Ch);                              {  echo print  }
            IF Ch IN Alphabet THEN
              SentenceChar := SentenceChar + [Ch]
          END;  {  of WHILE NOT eoln(Data)  }        {  of one line  }
        writeln
      END;  {  of PROCEDURE GetLetters  }

{*************************************************************** }

PROCEDURE PrintSet (SentenceChar : AlphaSymbols);

  {  Given:   A set of characters                              }
  {  Task:    Print all characters in the set                  }
  {  Return:  Nothing                                          }

  VAR
    Ch : char;

  BEGIN
    writeln (Skip:10, 'The letters in this line are:');
    writeln; write (Skip:10);
    FOR Ch := 'A' TO 'z' DO
      IF Ch IN SentenceChar THEN
        write (Ch:2);
    writeln
  END;  {  of PROCEDURE PrintSet  }

{*************************************************************** }

FUNCTION Cardinality (SentenceChar : AlphaSymbols) : integer;

  {  Given:   A set of characters                              }
  {  Task:    Determine the number of characters in the set    }
  {  Return:  The set size (cardinality)                       }

  VAR
    Ct : integer;
    X : char;

  BEGIN
    Ct := 0;
    FOR X := 'A' TO 'z' DO
      IF X IN SentenceChar THEN
        Ct := Ct + 1;
    Cardinality := Ct
  END;  {  of FUNCTION Cardinality  }

{*************************************************************** }

PROCEDURE PrintMessage (SetSize : integer);

  {  Given:    The cardinality of the set                      }
  {  Task:     Print a closing message                         }
  {  Return:   Nothing                                         }
```

```
      BEGIN
        write (Skip:10);
        writeln ('There are', SetSize:3, ' letters in this sentence.')
      END;  {  of PROCEDURE PrintMessage  }
```

```
{*********************************************************** }
```

```
BEGIN  {  Main program  }
  reset (Data);
  GetLetters (SentenceChar);
  PrintSet (SentenceChar);
  SetSize := Cardinality(SentenceChar);
  PrintMessage (SetSize)
END.  {  of main program  }
```

When this program is run on the line of text

```
The numbers -2, 5, 20 and symbols '?', ':' should be ignored.
```

The output is

```
The line of text is below:
```

```
The numbers -2, 5, 20 and symbols '?', ':' should be ignored.
```

```
The letters in this line are:
```

```
 T a b d e g h i l m n o r s u y
```

```
There are   16 letters in this sentence.
```

RUNNING AND DEBUGGING TIPS

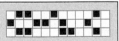

1. When defining a set type, do not use brackets in the definition; thus, the following is incorrect

   ```
   TYPE
     Alphabet = SET OF ['A'..'Z'];
   ```

   The correct form is

   ```
   TYPE
     Alphabet = SET OF 'A'..'Z';
   ```

2. Remember to initialize a set before using it in the program. Declaring a set does not give it a value. If your declaration is

   ```
   VAR
     Vowels : Alphabet;
   ```

   the program should contain

   ```
   Vowels := ['A', 'E', 'I', 'O', 'U'];
   ```

3. Attempting to add an element to a set rather than a set to a set is a common error. If you wish to add 'D' to the set ['A', 'B', 'C'], you should write

   ```
   ['A', 'B', 'C'] + ['D']
   ```

   rather than

   ```
   ['A', 'B', 'C'] + 'D'
   ```

   This is especially a problem when the value of a variable is to be added to a set.

   ```
   ['A', 'B', 'C'] + Ch;
   ```

   should be

   ```
   ['A', 'B', 'C'] + [Ch];
   ```

4. Avoid confusing arrays and array notation with sets and set notation.

5. Certain operators (+, −, and ∗) have different meanings when used with sets.

■ **Summary**

Key Terms

difference	intersection	union
element of a set	set	universal set
empty (null) set	subset	

Keywords

IN	**SET**

Key Concepts

- A **SET** in Pascal is a structured data type that consists of distinct elements from an indicated base type; sets can be declared by

```
TYPE
   Alphabet = SET OF char;
VAR
   Vowels : Alphabet;
   GoodResponse : Alphabet;
```

In this definition and declaration, Alphabet is a **SET** type and Vowels and Good-Response are set variables.

- Values must be assigned to a set; thus, we could have

```
Vowels := ['A', 'E', 'I', 'O', 'U'];
GoodResponse := ['Y', 'y', 'N', 'n'];
```

- When listing elements in a set, order makes no difference and each element may be listed only once.

- Standard set operations in Pascal are defined to be consistent with set operations of mathematics; to illustrate, if

```
A := [1,2,3,4];
```

and

```
B := [3,4,5];
```

the union, intersection, and difference of these sets are as follows:

Term	Expression	Value
Union	A + B	[1..5]
Intersection	A ∗ B	[3,4]
Difference	A − B	[1,2]
	B − A	[5]

- Set membership is denoted by using the reserved word **IN**. Such an expression returns a Boolean value; thus, if

```
A := [1,2,3,4];
```

we have

Expression	Value
2 IN A	**true**
6 IN A	**false**

■ The relational operators ($<=$, $>=$, $<>$, and $=$) can be used with sets forming Boolean expressions and returning values consistent with expected subset and set equality relationships; to illustrate, if

```
A := [1,2,3];
B := [0..5];
C := [2,4];
```

we have

Expression	Value
A <= B	**true**
B <= C	**false**
B >= C	**true**
A = B	**false**
B <> C	**true**

■ Priority levels for set operations are consistent with those used for arithmetic expressions; they are

Priority Level	Operation
1	( )
2	**NOT**
3	$*$, /, **MOD, DIV, AND**
4	$+$, $-$, **OR**
5	$<$, $>$, $<=$, $>=$, $<>$, $=$, **IN**

■ Sets cannot be used with **read** or **write**; however, you can generate a set by initializing the set, assigning the empty set, and using set union to add elements to the set. For example, a set of characters in a text line can be generated by

```
S := [];
WHILE NOT eoln(Data) DO
  BEGIN
    read (Data, Ch);
    S := S + [Ch]
  END;
```

This set can be printed by

```
FOR Ch := <initial value> TO <final value> DO
  IF Ch IN S THEN
    write (Ch:2);
```

■ Four uses for sets in programs are to replace complex Boolean expressions, to protect a program (or segment) from bad data, to protect against invalid **CASE** statements, and to aid in interactive programming.
■ Sets can be used as parameters with subprograms.
■ Sets cannot be returned as the value of a function.
■ Sets can be generated or modified through subprograms by using variable parameters with procedures.

■ Programming Problems and Projects

Each of the following programming problems can be solved with a program using sets. Hints are provided to indicate some of the uses; you may, of course, find others.

1. Write a program to be used to simulate a medical diagnosis. Assume the following symptoms are coded as indicated.

Symptom	Code
Headache	1
Fever	2
Sore throat	3
Cough	4
Sneeze	5
Stomach pain	6
Heart pain	7
Muscle pain	8
Nausea	9
Back pain	10
Exhaustion	11
Jaundice	12
High blood pressure	13

Furthermore, assume each of the following diseases is characterized by the symptoms as indicated.

Disease	Symptoms
Cold	1,2,3,4,5
Flu	1,2,6,8,9
Migraine	1,9
Mononucleosis	2,3,11,12
Ulcer	6,9
Arteriosclerosis	7,10,11,13
Appendicitis	2,6

Your program should accept as input a person's name and symptoms (coded) and provide a preliminary diagnosis. Sets can be used for
a. Bad data check
b. Symptoms = 1 . . 13;
   Disease = **SET OF** Symptoms;
c. Cold, Flu, Migraine, Mononucleosis, Ulcer, Arteriosclerosis, Appendicitis : Disease;

2. Write a program to serve as a simple text analyzer. Input is any text file. Output should be three histograms: one each for vowel frequency, consonant frequency, and other symbol frequency. Your program should use a set for vowels, one for consonants, and a third for other symbols.

3. Typists often complain that the standard QWERTY keyboard

$$Q\ W\ E\ R\ T\ Y\ U\ I\ O\ P$$
$$A\ S\ D\ F\ G\ H\ J\ K\ L\ ;$$
$$Z\ X\ C\ V\ B\ N\ M\ ,\ .\ /$$
space bar

is not efficient. As you can see, many frequently used letters (E, T, N, R, and I) are not on the middle row. A new keyboard, the Maltron keyboard, has been proposed. Its design is

Q P Y C B V M U Z L
A N I S F E D T H O R ; : .
J G W K X
space bar

Write a program to analyze a text file to see how many jumps are required by each keyboard. For purposes of this program, a jump will be any valid symbol not on the middle row. Output should include the number of valid symbols read and the number of jumps for each keyboard.

4. Write a program to serve as a simple compiler for a Pascal program. Your compiler should work on a program that uses only single-letter identifiers. Your compiler should create a set of identifiers, make sure identifiers are not declared twice, make sure all identifiers on the left of an assignment are declared, and make sure there are no type mismatch errors. For purposes of your compiler program, assume as follows:

   a. Variables are declared between **VAR** and **BEGIN**; for example,

   ```
   VAR
     X, Y : real;
     A, B, C : integer;
     M : char;
   BEGIN
   ```

   b. Each program line is a complete Pascal statement.
   c. The only assignments are of the form X := Y;. Output should include the program line number and an appropriate error message for each error. Run your compiler with several short Pascal programs as text files. Compare your error list with that given in Appendix 5.

5. A number in exponential notation preceded by a plus or minus sign may have the form

Sign	Positive integer	Decimal	Positive integer	E	Sign	Exponent (three digits)

   For example, $-45.302E+002$ is the number -4530.2. If the number is in standard form, it will have exactly one digit on the left side of the decimal ($-4.5302E+003$).

   Write a program to read numbers in exponential form from a text file, one number per line. Your program should check to see if each number is in proper form. For those that are, print out the number as given and the number in standard form.

6. Write a program to analyze a text file for words of differing length. Your program should keep a list of all words of length one, two, . . ., ten. It should also count the number of words whose length exceeds ten.

   A word ends when one alphabetical character is followed by a character not in the alphabet or when an end-of-line is reached. All words start with letters (7UP is not a word). Your output should be an alphabetized list for each word length. It should also include the number of words whose length exceeds ten characters. An apostrophe does not add to the length of a word.

7. The Falcon Manufacturing Company (Problem 22, Chapter 8; Problem 17, Chapter 9; Problems 12–16, Chapter 10) wants a computerized system to check if a customer is approved for credit. A customer number should be entered from the keyboard, with the program printing the credit limit for the customer if credit has been approved, and "No credit" if it has not. Each line of a text file contains a customer number and the credit limit. Valid customer numbers range from 100 to 999, and credit limits are $100, $300, $500, $1000, and unlimited credit.

8. Write a program in which you read a text file and print out the number of times a character in the file matches a character in your name.

9. The Court Survey Corporation wishes to conduct a poll by sending questionnaires to men and women between 25 and 30 years of age living in your state or any state adjacent to it. A text file containing names, street addresses, cities, states, zip codes, and ages is to be read, with the program printing the names and addresses of those persons matching the criteria.

10. Write a program to test your ESP and that of a friend. Each of you should secretly enter ten integers between 1 and 100. Have the program check each list and print the values that are in both lists and the number of values that are in both lists.

11. Modify Problem 22 from Chapter 7 (the Wellsville Wholesale Company commission problem) to define the sales ranges as sets. Use these sets to verify input and determine the proper commission rate.

12. The Ohio Programmers' Association offices are in a large building with five wings lettered A through E. The office numbers in the wings are as follows:

Wing	Rooms
A	100–150 and 281–300
B	151–190 and 205–220
C	10–50 and 191–204
D	1–9 and 51–99
E	221–280 and 301–319

Write a program for the receptionist, Miss Lovelace, so that she can enter an office number from the keyboard and then have the computer print the wing in which the office is located.

13. Not all programming languages include sets as a data structure. Examine several other languages to determine what data structures they include. Prepare a chart that compares and contrasts the data structures of Pascal (arrays, records, files, and sets) with the data structures of other languages. Give an oral presentation of your results to the class.

14. Select an unworked problem from the programming problems previously listed for this chapter. Construct a structure chart and write all documentary information necessary for the problem. Do not write code. When you are finished, have a classmate read your documentation to see if precisely what is to be done is clear.

*Nothing puzzles me more
than time and space.*
Charles Lamb 1775–1834

Algorithm Analysis—Space and Time Considerations

In this chapter, we will introduce a technique for analyzing the efficiency of algorithms. We can then use this technique, known as *big-O analysis,* to categorize algorithms with respect to the length of time and the amount of storage they require for their execution. In Sections 12.2 and 12.3, we will use big-O analysis to examine the time efficiency of some simple sorting algorithms. In Section 12.4, we will use big-O analysis to describe the interplay between the time and storage requirements of an algorithm. In Section 12.5, we will analyze the time efficiency of simple *search algorithms.* Finally, in the Focus on Program Design section, we will discuss a scheme for developing programs to measure empirically the efficiency of an algorithm.

■ 12.1
Designing Programs—A Look Back and a Look Ahead

OBJECTIVES

- to develop a prespective on the study of computer science beyond the learning of a particular programming language, such as Pascal
- to be able to identify criteria by which complex software is evaluated

This chapter marks an important step in your exploration of computer science. Up to this point, it has been difficult to divorce your study of computer science from the learning of Pascal. You have developed problem-solving skills, but the problems we have encountered have been very focused. That is, the problems were chosen specifically to illustrate a particular feature of Pascal. This is the way that problem-solving skills must be developed: starting with small problems and working toward large ones.

By now you know almost all features of the Pascal programming language. You are ready to direct your attention toward larger, more complex problems that require integrating many of the particular skills you have developed. Now our attention will be directed more toward issues of software design and less toward describing Pascal. If we need a particular feature of Pascal that has not yet been discussed, we will introduce it when appropriate. But our primary objective is to study more complex problems and the software design issues that arise out of them. From here on, we view Pascal primarily as the vehicle to implement, test, and experiment with our solutions to problems. The techniques of software design we are about to explore will enable us to write programs that are

- Large. Actually our programs could properly be called systems since they typically involve numerous modules that interact to solve one complex problem.
- Reliable. The measure of the reliability of a system is that it anticipate and handle all types of exceptional circumstances.
- Flexible. The system should be easily modified to handle circumstances that may change in the future.
- Expandable. If the system is successful, it will frequently spawn new computing needs. We should be able to incorporate solutions to these new needs into the original system with relative ease.
- Efficient. The system should make optimal use of time and space resources.
- Structured. The system should be divided into compact modules, each of which is responsible for a specific, well-defined task.
- User-friendly. The system should be clearly documented so that it is easy to use.

In designing software to meet these criteria, one of the key skills you must develop is the ability to choose the appropriate tools for the job. You should not have to rediscover algorithms and techniques for information storage and retrieval each time you write a new program. As a computer scientist, you must have a detailed knowledge of algorithms and data storage techniques at your fingertips and be able to apply this knowledge when designing software to solve a variety of problems. You should be able to look into your storehouse of algorithms and data storage strategies, choose the most appropriate methods, and then tailor them to the application at hand.

As you expand your knowledge of computer science, you will find that a given problem frequently lends itself to more than one method of solution. Hence, in addition to knowing the individual principles, you must also be able to evaluate them comparatively. This comparative evaluation must be conducted in as systematic and quantitative a fashion as possible. That is, you must be able to justify your choice of a method by presenting cogent arguments based on facts and figures pertinent to the problem. Given this perspective on computer science, we must turn our attention to a twofold task:

1. Stocking our algorithmic toolbox with methods that have become standards in computer science.
2. Developing criteria for knowing which tool to choose in a particular situation.

To begin this task, we reach back to the sorting and searching algorithms that we first saw in Chapter 10. We also consider some new techniques for sorting and searching. We then evaluate these techniques for their efficiency in terms of execution time and use of space (memory) resources. To conduct such a time/space analysis, we introduce what has come to be known as big-O notation. In effect, big-O notation is the mathematical measuring stick by which computer scientists quantitatively evaluate algorithms. It allows us to place algorithms into categories based on their efficiency. Such categorization helps us determine whether or not a proposed solution is practical in terms of the real world requirements and constraints dictated by the problem.

■ 12.2
Simple Sorting Algorithms

Our discussion in this section will use an array of records that we want to sort in ascending order according to a given field within each record. The field on which the sort is based is known as the key field. For instance, we may wish to arrange a list of student records in alphabetical order according to student last name or a list of inventory records in order according to product identification numbers. Hence the following Pascal declarations provide a suitable setting for our coming discussion of the sorting problem.

```
CONST
  MaxIndex = 100;        {  Easily adjusted  }

TYPE
  SortRecord = RECORD
                 Key : KeyType;  {  Any type that can be ordered  }
                 OtherData : WhateverType {  Data associated with the Key  }
               END;
  SortArray = ARRAY [1..MaxIndex] OF SortRecord;
```

We wish to write a sort procedure that meets the following specifications:

```
PROCEDURE Sort (N : integer; VAR List : SortArray);

{  Given:   Array List containing entries in locations 1 through N.    }
{  Task:    Apply appropriate sorting algorithm to these entries.      }
{  Return:  Array List with first N entries arranged in ascending order. }
```

Two aspects of these declarations are worth noting. First, the fashion in which we have made our **CONST** and **TYPE** declarations allows this procedure to eventually sort an array of any size and base type provided that the definitions of MaxIndex, KeyType, WhateverType, and SortRecord are appropriately altered. This method of declaration represents an attempt to make the Pascal procedure abstract: it embodies an algorithm that can sort a variety of data types. In this sense, it represents a more general sorting procedure than that introduced in Chapter 10.

Second, the measure of an algorithm's run-time efficiency is in direct proportion to the number of elementary machine operations that must be performed as the algorithm is executed. With sorting algorithms, these elementary machine operations compare and interchange two data items. Depending upon the amount of data in the OtherData field in the preceding declarations, it is entirely possible that interchanging two data items could be considerably more costly in machine time than comparing two items. Why? An interchange of large data items will generate a loop that moves a significant number of bytes at the machine language level.

Our analysis of run-time efficiency should take this into account. It may well be more important to minimize data interchanges at the expense of comparisons. This complication did not enter into our earlier discussion of sorting because, at that stage, we were concerned with sorting arrays of simple, unstructured data items only.

OBJECTIVES

- to develop a procedural interface that can be used with a variety of sorting algorithms
- to understand the potential difference in efficiency between the computer operations of comparing data items and interchanging them
- to be able to trace in detail the comparisons and interchanges of data items that occur during execution of the bubble sort algorithm
- to be able to trace in detail the comparisons and interchanges of data items that occur during execution of the selection sort algorithm
- to be able to trace in detail the comparisons and interchanges of data items that occur during execution of the insertion sort algorithm

■ **EXAMPLE 12.1**

Given arrays A and B of type NameList as follows,

```
TYPE
   NameData = PACKED ARRAY [1..40] OF char;
   NameList = ARRAY [1..1000] OF NameData;
```

consider the following two code fragments that act upon them.

Fragment 1

```
StartWithX := 0;
FOR J := 1 TO 1000 DO
   IF A[J,1] = 'X' THEN
      StartWithX := StartWithX + 1;
```

Fragment 2

```
B := A;
```

In this instance, an assignment statement can be misleading in its efficiency. The assignment statement in Fragment 2 results in 1,000 names being copied from A to B. Moreover, each name consists of 40 characters, so 40,000 elementary machine operations may be involved. In Fragment 1, each of the 1,000 comparisons and the potential incrementing of StartWithX represents a faster sequence of operations than the internal copying of 40 characters from one location to another. Hence Fragment 1 illustrates how repeated comparisons can be considerably less costly than seemingly simple assignment statements that manipulate large data aggregates.

■   ■

Bubble Sort

The *bubble sort* represents an alternative to the selection sort algorithm discussed in Section 10.3. Given a list of data records stored in an array, pass through the array and compare adjacent pairs of keys. Whenever two keys are out of order with respect to each other, interchange the associated records. The effect of such a pass through a list of names is traced in Figure 12.1, where a "snapshot" of the array after each comparison is given. Notice that after such a pass, we are assured that the list will have the name that comes last in alphabetical order in the final array position. That is, the last name will "sink" to the bottom of the array, and preceding names will gradually "percolate" to the top.

If one pass through an array of N records can guarantee that the record with the key that comes last in order is in the appropriate position, then slicing off the last element and passing through the remaining $N - 1$ entries using the same logic will guarantee that the record with the key second to last in order is in its appropriate position. Repeating the process for a total of $N - 1$ passes eventually insures that all records are in their appropriate positions. In general, on the Kth pass through the array, $N - K$ comparisons of pairs must be made.

Thus, the bubble sort algorithm involves two nested loops. The outer loop controls the number of (successively smaller) passes through the array. The inner loop controls the pairs of adjacent entries being compared.

FIGURE 12.1
Trace of bubble sort on an array with four names

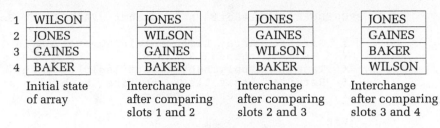

1	WILSON	JONES	JONES
2	JONES	WILSON	GAINES
3	GAINES	GAINES	WILSON
4	BAKER	BAKER	BAKER

Initial state of array | Interchange after comparing slots 1 and 2 | Interchange after comparing slots 2 and 3 | Interchange after comparing slots 3 and 4

First pass through array

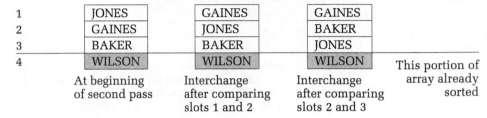

1	JONES	GAINES	GAINES
2	GAINES	JONES	BAKER
3	BAKER	BAKER	JONES
4	WILSON	WILSON	WILSON

At beginning of second pass | Interchange after comparing slots 1 and 2 | Interchange after comparing slots 2 and 3 | This portion of array already sorted

Second pass through array

GAINES	BAKER
BAKER	GAINES
JONES	JONES
WILSON	WILSON

At beginning of third pass | Interchange after comparing slots 1 and 2 | This portion of array already sorted

Third pass through array

If we ever make a complete pass through the inner loop without having to make an interchange, we can declare the array sorted and avoid all future passes through the array. A top-level pseudocode development of the algorithm is

1. Initialize counter K to zero.
2. Initialize Boolean ExchangeMade to **true.**
3. **WHILE** (K < N − 1) **AND** ExchangeMade
    3.1. set ExchangeMade to **false**
    3.2. increment counter K
    3.3. **FOR** J := 1 **TO** N − K
        3.3.1. **IF** Key field of entry in Jth slot > Key field of entry in (J + 1)st slot **THEN**
            3.3.1.1. exchange these entries
            3.3.1.2. set ExchangeMade to **true**

The complete Pascal procedure to implement this algorithm for an arbitrary array of records follows. The procedure assumes the existence of appropriate **CONST** and **TYPE** declarations.

```
PROCEDURE BubbleSort (N : integer; VAR List : SortArray);

{  Given:   Array List containing entries in locations 1    }
{           through N.                                       }
{  Task:    Apply bubble sort logic to List.                 }
{  Return:  Array List with first N entries arranged in      }
{           ascending order.                                 }

VAR
  K, J : integer;
  ExchangeMade : boolean;
  Temp : SortRecord;

BEGIN
  K := 0;
  ExchangeMade := true;
  { Make up to N - 1 passes through array, exit early if no exchanges }
  { are made on previous pass.                                        }
  WHILE (K < N - 1) AND ExchangeMade DO { K  counts passes  }
    BEGIN
      ExchangeMade := false;
      K := K + 1;
      { Compare N - K adjacent pairs of array entries.                }
      FOR J := 1 TO N - K DO {  Number of comparisons on Kth pass  }
        IF List[J].Key > List[J + 1].Key THEN {  Must interchange  }
          BEGIN
            Temp := List[J];
            List[J] := List[J+1];
            List[J+1] := Temp;
            ExchangeMade := true
          END
    END
END; {  of PROCEDURE BubbleSort  }
```

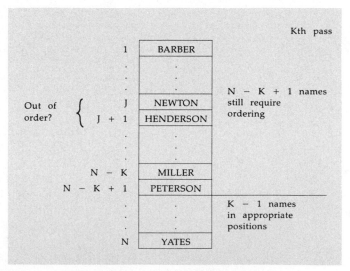

■ EXAMPLE 12.2

Trace the action of the **PROCEDURE** BubbleSort if N is 5 and the array List initially contains

First pass through array

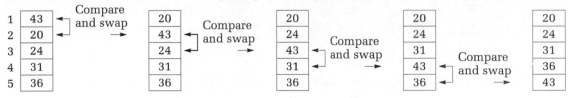

Second pass through array

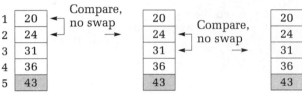

ExchangeMade remained false throughout inner loop, so algorithm is done.
∎   ∎

In the next section we analyze in detail the run-time efficiency of the bubble sort. But we should first consider two other sorting algorithms to which the efficiency of bubble sort may be compared: *selection sort* and *insertion sort*.

Selection Sort Revisited

Since its introduction in Chapter 10, we have used the selection sort algorithm to sort arrays of records on a key field. Now let's compare it to the bubble sort algorithm.

The motivation of the bubble sort is to place the (current) largest array value in the (current) last array slot, then seal off that slot from future consideration, and repeat the process. The selection sort algorithm is somewhat similarly motivated, but it attempts to avoid the multitude of interchanges of adjacent entries. To do this, on the Kth pass through the array, it determines the position of the smallest entry among

```
List[K].Key, List[K+1].Key, ..., List[N].Key
```

Then this smallest entry is swapped with the Kth entry, K is incremented by 1, and the process is repeated. Figure 12.2 illustrates how this algorithm works on repeated passes through an array with six entries. Asterisks are used to indicate the successively smallest (alphabetically) entries as they are being correctly located in the array.

As we see next, the Pascal procedure for selection sort uses, as its inner loop, a simple algorithm to find the minimum entry and store its position in a variable MinPosition. This inner loop avoids the potentially frequent interchange of array elements that is necessary in the inner loop of BubbleSort.

FIGURE 12.2
Trace of selection sort logic

Original order of Keys	K = 1	K = 2	K = 3	K = 4	K = 5
DAVE	ARON*	ARON*	ARON*	ARON*	ARON*
TOM	TOM	BEV*	BEV*	BEV*	BEV*
PAM	PAM	PAM	DAVE*	DAVE*	DAVE*
ARON	DAVE	DAVE	PAM	PAM*	PAM*
BEV	BEV	TOM	TOM	TOM	SAM*
SAM	SAM	SAM	SAM	SAM	TOM*

```
PROCEDURE SelectionSort (N : integer; VAR List : SortArray);

{  Given:    Array List containing entries in locations 1    }
{            through N.                                       }
{  Task:     Apply selection sort logic to List.             }
{  Return:   Array List with first N entries arranged in     }
{            ascending order.                                 }

VAR
  K, J, MinPosition : integer;
  Temp : SortRecord;

BEGIN
  { Make N - 1 passes through successively smaller segments  }
  { of the array.                                             }
  FOR K := 1 TO N - 1 DO {  Number of passes  }
    BEGIN
      { The following loop will find the position of the     }
      { Kth smallest array entry.                            }
      MinPosition := K; {  Initially assume Kth is smallest  }
      FOR J := K + 1 TO N DO  {  Test previous smallest  }
        IF List[J].Key < List[MinPosition].Key THEN
          MinPosition := J;
          {  Note index, not array element, assigned here.  }
      Temp := List[K];  {  Now swap smallest outside the inner loop  }
      List[K] := List[MinPosition];
      List[MinPosition] := Temp
    END
END; {  of PROCEDURE SelectionSort  }
```

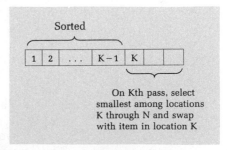

Sorted

| 1 | 2 | ... | K−1 | K | | |

On Kth pass, select smallest among locations K through N and swap with item in location K

Example 12.3 indicates that the selection sort algorithm swaps no data values until exiting the inner loop. This apparently reduces the number of data interchanges and makes the selection sort more efficient than the bubble sort. Is this a significant improvement? Or have other subtle inefficiencies been introduced to offset this apparent gain? These are difficult questions to answer unless we have a better grasp of how to measure program efficiency. We'll explore efficiency in the next section; but first, let's see one more sorting algorithm for comparison purposes.

■ EXAMPLE 12.3

Trace the action of the **PROCEDURE** SelectionSort if N is 5 and the array List initially contains

1 | 30
2 | 39
3 | 22
4 | 19
5 | 34

First pass through array

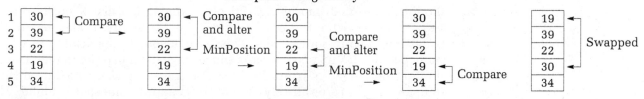

Second pass through array

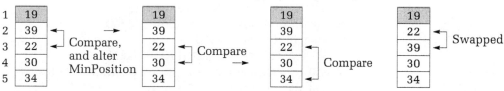

Third pass through array

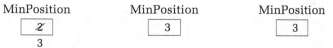

Fourth pass through array

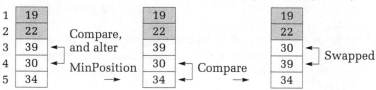

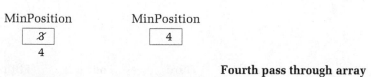

Insertion Sort

Although it reduces the number of data interchanges, the selection sort apparently will not allow an effective—and automatic—loop exit if the array becomes ordered during an early pass. In this regard, bubble sort is more efficient than selection sort for an array that is nearly ordered to begin with. However, even with just one entry out of order, bubble sort's early loop exit can fail to reduce the number of comparisons that are made.

The insertion sort attempts to take greater advantage of an array's partial ordering. The goal is that on the Kth pass through, the Kth element among

```
List[1].Key, List[2].Key, ... List[K].Key
```

should be inserted into its rightful place among the first K entries in the array. Thus, after the Kth pass (K starting at 2), the first K elements of the array should be in sorted order. This is analogous to the fashion in which many people pick up playing cards and arrange them in order in their hands. Holding the first (K − 1) cards in order, a person will pick up the Kth card and compare it with cards already held until its appropriate spot is found. The following steps will achieve this logic:

1. **FOR** K := 2 **TO** N {   K index of array element to insert   }
   1.1   ItemToInsert := List[K].Key
   1.2   J := K − 1 {   J starts at K − 1 and is decremented until
                                   insertion position is found   }
   1.3   **WHILE** (insertion position not found) **AND**
              (not beginning of array) **DO**
          1.3.1   **IF** ItemToInsert < List[J].Key **THEN**
                     1.3.1.1   Move List[J] to index position J + 1
                     1.3.1.2   Reduce J by 1
          1.3.2   **ELSE**
                     1.3.2.1   The insertion position has been found
   1.4   ItemToInsert should be positioned at index J + 1

In effect, for each pass, the index J begins at the (K − 1)st element and moves that element to position J + 1 until we find the insertion point for what was originally the Kth element.

Insertion sort for each value of K is traced in Figure 12.3. In each column of this diagram the data items are sorted in alphabetical order relative to each other above the item with the asterisk; below this item the data are not affected.

FIGURE 12.3
Trace of repeated passes from insertion sort

Original order of Keys	First pass K = 2	Second pass K = 3	Third pass K = 4	Fourth pass K = 5	Fifth pass K = 6
PAM	PAM	DAVE	ARON	ARON	ARON
SAM	SAM*	PAM	DAVE	DAVE	BEV
DAVE	DAVE	SAM*	PAM	PAM	DAVE
ARON	ARON	ARON	SAM*	SAM	PAM
TOM	TOM	TOM	TOM	TOM*	SAM
BEV	BEV	BEV	BEV	BEV	TOM*

To implement the insertion sort algorithm in Pascal we have the following code:

```
PROCEDURE  InsertionSort (N : integer; VAR List : SortArray);

  { Given:    Array List with entries in locations 1       }
  {           through N.                                    }
  { Task:     Apply insertion sort logic to List.          }
  { Return:   Array List with first N entries arranged in  }
  {           ascending order.                              }

  VAR K, J : integer;
      ItemToInsert : SortRecord;
      StillLooking : boolean;

  BEGIN
    { On the Kth pass, insert item K into its correct position among  }
    { the first K entries in array.                                   }
    FOR K := 2 TO N DO
      BEGIN
        { Walk backwards through list, looking for slot to insert A[K] }
        ItemToInsert := List[K];
        J := K - 1;
        StillLooking := true;
        WHILE (J >= 1) AND StillLooking DO
          { ItemToInsert is compared to List[J] }
          IF ItemToInsert.Key < List[J].Key THEN
            BEGIN
              List[J + 1] := List[J];
              J := J - 1
            END
          ELSE
            StillLooking := false;
        { Upon leaving loop, J + 1 is the index where ItemToInsert belongs }
        List[J + 1] := ItemToInsert
      END  { FOR }
  END;  { of PROCEDURE InsertionSort }
```

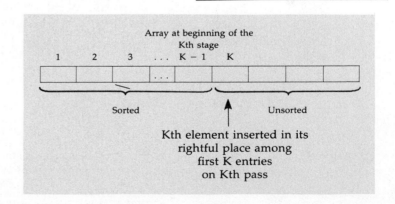

■ **EXAMPLE 12.4**

Trace the action of the **PROCEDURE** InsertionSort if N is 5 and the array List initially contains

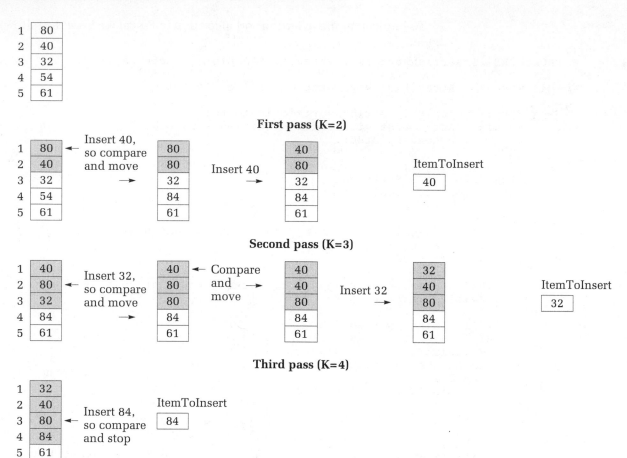

First pass (K=2)

Second pass (K=3)

Third pass (K=4)

Fourth pass (K=5)

Exercises 12.2

1. Which of the sorting methods studied in this section allows a possible early exit from its inner loop? What is the potential advantage in using this early exit?

2. Which of the sorting methods studied in this section allows a possible early exit from its outer loop? What is the potential advantage in using this early exit?

3. Which of the sorting methods studied in this section does not allow the possibility of an early exit from its inner or outer loops? What potential advantage does this method have over the other two methods that were presented?

4. Suppose that, intially, an array contains seven integer entries arranged in the following order:

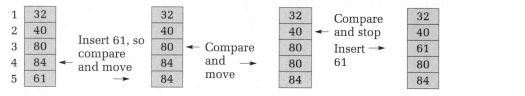

1	43
2	40
3	18
4	24
5	39
6	60
7	12

Trace the order of the array entries after each successive pass of the bubble sort.

5. Repeat Exercise 4 for the selection sort.

6. Repeat Exercise 4 for the insertion sort.

7. Consider the following sort algorithm. Which of the methods studied in this section does this new algorithm most closely resemble? In what ways is it different from that method? Trace the action of this new sort algorithm on the array from Exercise 4.

```
PROCEDURE Sort (N : integer; VAR List : SortArray);

  { Given:    Array List containing entries in locations 1      }
  {                  through N.                                  }
  { Task:     Apply sort logic to List.                         }
  { Return:   Array List with first N entries arranged in       }
  {                  ascending order.                           }

  VAR
    K, J : integer;
    ExchangeMade : boolean;
    Temp : SortRecord;

  BEGIN
    K := 0;
    ExchangeMade := true;
    WHILE (K < N - 1) AND ExchangeMade DO
      BEGIN
        ExchangeMade := false;
        K := K + 1;
        FOR J := N DOWNTO K + 1  DO
          IF List[J].Key < List[J - 1].Key THEN
            BEGIN
              Temp := List[J];
              List[J] := List[J - 1];
              List[J - 1] := Temp;
              ExchangeMade := true
            END
      END
  END; { of PROCEDURE Sort }
```

8. Consider the following sort algorithm. Which of the methods studied in this section does this new algorithm most closely resemble? In what ways is it different from that method? Trace the action of this new sort algorithm on the array from Exercise 4.

```
PROCEDURE Sort (N : integer; VAR List : SortArray);

  { Given:    Array List containing entries in locations 1      }
  {                  through N.                                  }
  { Task:     Apply sort logic to List.                         }
  { Return:   Array List with first N entries arranged in       }
  {                  ascending order.                           }
```

```
                      VAR
                        K, J, Position : integer;
                        Temp :  SortRecord;

                      BEGIN
                        FOR K := 1 TO N - 1 DO
                          BEGIN
                            Position := 1;
                            FOR J := 2 TO N - K + 1 DO
                              IF List[J].Key > List[Position].Key THEN
                                Position := J;
                            Temp := List[N - K + 1];
                            List[N - K + 1] := List[Position];
                            List[Position] := Temp
                          END
                      END; { of PROCEDURE Sort }
```

9. Consider the following sort algorithm. Which of the methods studied in this section does this new algorithm most closely resemble? In what ways is it different from that method? Trace the action of this new sort algorithm on the array from Exercise 4.

```
PROCEDURE  Sort (N : integer; VAR List : SortArray);

  {  Given:    Array List with entries in locations 1       }
  {            through N.                                    }
  {  Task:     Apply sort logic to List.                    }
  {  Return:   Array List with first N entries arranged in  }
  {            ascending order.                             }

  VAR
    K, J : integer;
    Done : boolean;
    Temp : SortRecord;

  BEGIN
    FOR K := N - 1 DOWNTO 1 DO
      BEGIN
        J := K;
        Done := false;
        WHILE (J <= N - 1) AND NOT Done DO
          IF List[J].Key > List[J + 1].Key THEN
            BEGIN
              Temp := List[J];
              List[J] := List[J + 1];
              List[J + 1] := Temp;
              J := J + 1
            END
          ELSE
            Done := true
      END { of FOR loop }
  END; { of PROCEDURE Sort }
```

10. Devise sample data sets to demonstrate the *best-case* and *worst-case* behavior of the bubble sort, insertion sort, and selection sort. That is, for each sorting algorithm, construct data sets that illustrate the minimum and maximum number of comparisons required for that particular algorithm.

11. Construct a data set in which just one value is out of order and yet the Boolean test of the ExchangeMode variable never allows an early exit from the outer loop of bubble sort. How does the insertion sort perform on this same data set? Better, worse, or the same? Explain why.

12. Modify the sorting algorithms of this section so that they receive an additional argument indicating whether the sort should be in ascending or descending order.

13. The inner loop of an insertion sort can be modified to merely find the appropriate position for the Kth array entry instead of actually shifting items to make room for this entry. The shifting of items and placement of the original Kth entry can then be achieved in a separate loop. Write a new insertion sort procedure that implements this modification. Intuitively, is your new version more or less efficient than the old version? Why?

14. Modify all of the sorting algorithms presented in this chapter to include counters for the number of comparisons and data interchanges that are made. Then run those sorting algorithms on a variety of data sets, maintaining a chart of the counters for each algorithm. Prepare a written statement to summarize your conclusions about the relative efficiencies of the algorithms.

■ ■ ■ ■

■ 12.3
Which Sort Is Best? A Big-O Analysis

OBJECTIVES

- to understand the formal definition of big-O notation
- to be able to use big-O notation in classifying the time efficiency of algorithms involving nonrecursive, iterative control constructs
- to see the relationship between an algorithm's big-O classification and its expected run-time on a computer
- to recognize often-used big-O categories
- to apply big-O notation in analyzing the time efficiencies of the bubble sort, selection sort, and insertion sort algorithms

Computers do their work in terms of certain fundamental operations: comparing two numbers, moving the contents of one memory word to another, and so on. It should come as no surprise to you that a simple instruction in a high-level language such as Pascal may be translated (via a compiler) into many of these fundamental machine-level instructions. On most modern computers the speeds of these fundamental operations are measured in microseconds—that is, millionths of a second—although some larger supercomputers are beginning to break the nanosecond (billionth of a second) barrier. Let's assume, for the sake of argument, that we are working with a hypothetical computer that requires one microsecond to perform one of its fundamental operations.

With execution speeds of this kind, it makes little sense to analyze the efficiency of those portions of a program that perform only initializations and final reporting of summary results. The key to analyzing a procedure's efficiency is to scrutinize its loops and, even more importantly, its nested loops. Consider the following two examples of nested loops intended to sum each of the rows of an N × N two-dimensional array A, storing the row sums in a one-dimensional array Sum and the overall total in GrandTotal.

■ EXAMPLE 12.5

```
GrandTotal := 0;
FOR K := 1 TO N DO
  BEGIN
    Sum[K] := 0;
    FOR J := 1 TO N DO
      BEGIN
        Sum[K] := Sum[K] + A[K,J];
        GrandTotal := GrandTotal + A[K,J]
      END
  END
```

■ **EXAMPLE 12.6**

```
GrandTotal := 0;
FOR K := 1 TO N DO
  BEGIN
    Sum[K] := 0;
    FOR J := 1 TO N DO
      Sum[K] := Sum[K] + A[K,J];
    Grandtotal := GrandTotal + Sum[K]
  END
```

■   ■

If we analyze the number of addition operations required by these two examples, it should be immediately obvious that Example 12.6 is better in this respect. Because Example 12.5 incorporates the accumulating of GrandTotal into its inner loop, it requires $2N^2$ additions. That is, the additions Sum[K] + A[K,J] and GrandTotal + A[K,J] are each executed N^2 times, for a total of $2N^2$. Example 12.6, on the other hand, accumulates GrandTotal after the inner loop; hence it requires only $N^2 + N$ additions, which is less than $2N^2$ for any N after 1. Example 12.6 is seemingly guaranteed to execute faster than Example 12.5 for any nontrivial value of N.

But note that "faster" here may not have much significance in the real world of computing. Assuming that our hypothetical computer allows us to declare an array that is 1,000 by 1,000, Example 12.5 would require two seconds to perform its additions; Example 12.6 would require just over one second. On a larger 100,000 by 100,000 array, Example 12.5 would crunch numbers for slightly under six hours and Example 12.6 would take about three hours.

Although Example 12.6 is certainly better from an aesthetic perspective, it is not good enough to be appreciably different from a user's perspective. That is, in situations where one version will respond within seconds, so will the other. Conversely, when one is annoyingly slow, the other will be also. In terms of the *order of magnitude* of run-time involved, these versions should not be considered significantly different. For the 1,000 by 1,000 array, both versions would be fast enough to allow their use in an interactive environment. For the 100,000 by 100,000 array, both versions would dictate an overnight run in batch mode since an interactive user will be no more willing to wait three hours than six hours for a response.

Thus, because of the phenomenal execution speeds and very large amounts of available memory on modern computers, proportionally small differences between algorithms often have little practical impact. Such considerations have led computer scientists toward devising a method of algorithm classification that makes more precise the notion of order of magnitude as it applies to time and space considerations. This method of classification, typically referred to as *big-O notation* (in reference to "on the order of"), hinges on the following definition:

> **Big-O notation.** Suppose there exists a function $f(n)$ defined on the nonnegative integers such that the number of operations required by an algorithm for an input of size n is less than some constant C times $f(n)$ for all but finitely many n. That is, the number of operations is *proportional* to $f(n)$ for all large values of n. Such an algorithm is said to be an $O(f(n))$ algorithm relative to the number of operations it requires to execute. Similarly, we could classify an algorithm as $O(f(n))$ relative to the number of memory locations it requires to execute.

Figure 12.4 provides a graphical aid to understanding this formal definition of big-O notation. In general, we expect an algorithm's run-time to increase as it must manipulate an increasing number of data items, that is, as n increases. This increasing run-time is depicted by the somewhat irregular, wavy curve in Figure 12.4. Now compare the wavy curve representing actual run-time to the smoother curve of $C*f(n)$. Note that, for some small values of n, the actual number of operations for the algorithm may exceed $C*f(n)$.

FIGURE 12.4
Graphical representation of
$O(f(n))$

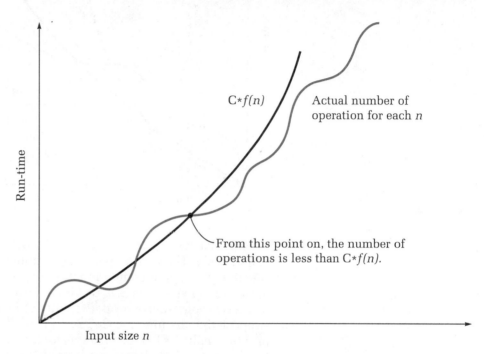

However, the graph indicates that there is a point on the horizontal axis beyond which $C*f(n)$ is always greater than the number of operations required for n data items. This is precisely the criterion that defines an algorithm's being $O(f(n))$.

To say that an algorithm is $O(f(n))$ thus indicates that the function $f(n)$ may be useful in characterizing how the algorithm is performing for large n. For such n, we are assured that the operations required by the algorithm will be bounded by a constant times $f(n)$. The phrasing "for all large values of n" in the definition highlights the fact that there is little difference in the choice of an algorithm if n is reasonably small. For example, almost any sorting algorithm would sort 100 integers instantly.

We should also note that a given algorithm may be $O(f(n))$ for many different functions f. As Figure 12.5 depicts, any algorithm that is $O(n^2)$ will also be $O(n^3)$.

Our main interest in classifying an algorithm with big-O notation is to find a relatively simple function $f(n)$ such that $C*f(n)$ parallels the number of operations as closely as possible. Hence, saying that an algorithm is $O(n^2)$ is considered a better characterization of its efficiency than saying it is $O(n^3)$.

The importance of the constant C, known as the constant of proportionality, lies in comparing algorithms that share the same function $f(n)$; it makes almost no difference in the comparison of algorithms for which $f(n)$ is of different magnitude. It is therefore appropriate to say that the function $f(n)$ dominates the run-time performance of an algorithm and characterizes it in its big-O analysis. The following example should help clarify this situation.

FIGURE 12.5
Any algorithm which is $O(n^2)$ is
also $O(n^3)$

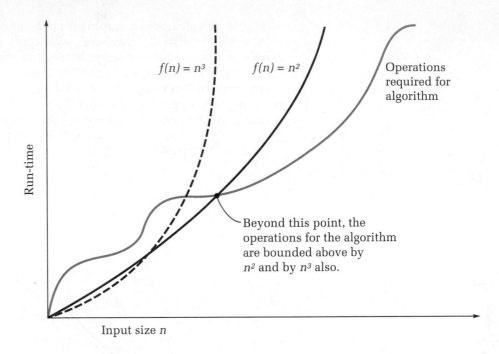

$f(n) = n^3$ $f(n) = n^2$ Operations required for algorithm

Beyond this point, the operations for the algorithm are bounded above by n^2 and by n^3 also.

Run-time

Input size n

Consider two algorithms L_1 and L_2 with run-times equal to $2n^2$ and n^2 respectively. The constants of proportionality of L_1 and L_2 are 2 and 1 respectively. The dominating function $f(n)$ for both of these algorithms is n^2, but L_2 runs twice as fast as L_1 for a data set of n values. The different sizes of the two constants of proportionality indicate that L_2 is faster than L_1. Now suppose that the function $f(n)$ for L_2 is n^3. Then, even though its constant of proportionality is half of what it is for L_1, L_2 will be frustratingly slower than L_1 for large n. This latter comparison is shown in Figure 12.6.

FIGURE 12.6
Graphical comparison of two
run-times

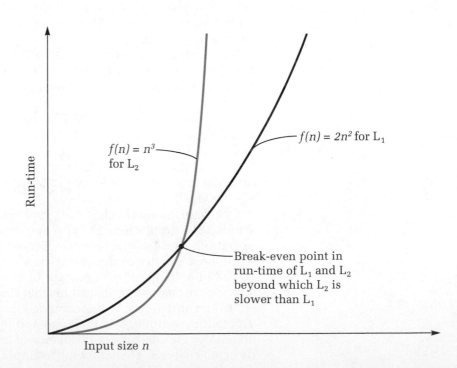

$f(n) = n^3$ for L_2 $f(n) = 2n^2$ for L_1

Break-even point in run-time of L_1 and L_2 beyond which L_2 is slower than L_1

Run-time

Input size n

■ **EXAMPLE 12.7**

Use big-O analysis to characterize the two code segments from Examples 12.5 and 12.6 respectively.

Because the algorithm of Example 12.5 performs $2N^2$ additions, it is characterized as $O(N^2)$ with 2 as a constant of proportionality. We previously determined that the code of Example 12.6 performs $N^2 + N$ additions. However, $N^2 + N \leq 1.1N^2$ for any $N \geq 10$. Hence, we can characterize Example 12.6 as an $O(N^2)$ algorithm using 1.1 as a constant of proportionality. These two characterizations demonstrate that, although Example 12.6 is almost twice as fast as Example 12.5, they are in the same big-O category. Coupled with our earlier analysis of these two examples, this is an indication that algorithms in the same big-O category may be expected to have the same orders of magnitude in their run-time.

■   ■

How Well Does the Big-O Notation Provide a Way of Classifying Algorithms from a Real World Perspective? To answer this question, consider Table 12.1. This table presents some typical $f(n)$ functions we will use to classify algorithms and their order of magnitude run-time for inputs of various sizes on a hypothetical computer. From this table, we can see that an $O(n^2)$ algorithm will take hours to execute for an input of size 10^5. How many hours is dependent upon the constant of proportionality in the definition of the big-O notation.

TABLE 12.1

Some typical $f(n)$ functions and associated run-times

Assuming proportionality constant K = 1 and one operation per microsecond, approximate run-times for input of size			
$f(n)$	10^3	10^5	10^6
$log_2 n$	0.000010 seconds	0.000017 seconds	0.000020 seconds
n	0.001 seconds	0.1 seconds	1 second
$n\ log_2 n$	0.01 seconds	1.7 seconds	20 seconds
n^2	1 second	3 hours	12 days
n^3	17 minutes	32 centuries	3×10^4 centuries
2^n	10^{285} centuries	10^{10^4} years	10^{10^5} years

Regardless of the value of this constant of proportionality, a categorization of an algorithm as an $O(n^2)$ algorithm has thus achieved a very practical goal. We now know that, for an input of size 10^5, we cannot expect an immediate response for such an algorithm. Moreover, we also know that, for a reasonably small constant of proportionality, we have an algorithm for which submission as an overnight job would not be impractical. That is, unlike an $O(n^3)$ algorithm, we could expect the computer to finish executing our algorithm in a time frame that would be acceptable if it could be scheduled to not interfere with other uses of the machine. On the other hand, an $O(n^3)$ algorithm applied to a data set of this size would be completely impractical.

How Does One Determine the Function $f(n)$ That Categorizes a Particular Algorithm? We give an overview of that process here and illustrate it by doing actual analyses for our three sorting algorithms. It is generally the case that, by analyzing the loop structure of an algorithm, we can estimate the number of run-time operations (or amount of memory units) required by the algorithm as a sum of several terms, each dependent on n, the number of items being processed by the algorithm. That is, typically we are able to express the number of run-time operations (or amount of memory) as a sum of the form

$$f_1(n) + f_2(n) + \ldots f_k(n)$$

Moreover, it is also typical that we identify one of the terms in this expression as the *dominant term*. A dominant term is one which, for bigger values of n, becomes so large that it allows us to ignore all the other terms from a big-O perspective. For instance, suppose that we had an expression involving two terms such as

$$n^2 + 6n$$

Here, the n^2 term dominates the $6n$ term since, for $n \geq 6$, we have

$$n^2 + 6n \leq n^2 + n^2 = 2n^2$$

Thus, $n^2 + 6n$ would lead to an $O(n^2)$ categorization because of the dominance of the n^2 term.

In general, the problem of big-O categorization reduces to finding the dominant term in an expression representing the number of operations or amount of memory required by an algorithm.

■ **EXAMPLE 12.8**

Use big-O notation to analyze the time efficiency of the following fragment of Pascal code.

```
FOR K := 1 TO N DIV 2 DO
   BEGIN
   .
   .
   .
      FOR J := 1 TO N * N DO
         BEGIN
         .
         .
         .
         END;
   .
   .
   .
   END;
```

Since these loops are nested, the number of times statements within the innermost loop are executed is the product of the number of repetitions of the two individual loops. Hence the efficiency is $N^3/2$, or $O(N^3)$ in big-O terms, with a constant of proportionality equal to ½.

Note that the important principle illustrated by this example is that, for two loops with $O(f_1(n))$ and $O(f_2(n))$ efficiencies, the efficiency of the nesting of these two loops (in any order) is $O(f_1(n) * f_2(n))$.

■   ■

■ **EXAMPLE 12.9**

Use big-O notation to analyze the time efficiency of the following fragment of Pascal code.

```
FOR K := 1 TO N DIV 2 DO
   BEGIN
      .
      .
      .
   END;
FOR J := 1 TO N * N DO
   BEGIN
      .
      .
      .
   END;
```

Since one loop follows the other the number of operations executed by both of them is the sum of the individual loop efficiencies. Hence the efficiency is N/2 + N^2, or O(N^2) in big-O terms.

The important principle illustrated by Example 12.9 is that, for two loops with O($f_1(n)$) and O($f_2(n)$) efficiencies, the efficiency of the sequencing of these two loops (in any order) is O($f_D(n)$) where $f_D(n)$ is the dominant of the functions $f_1(n)$ and $f_2(n)$.

■

■ EXAMPLE 12.10

Use big-O notation to analyze the time efficiency of the following fragment of Pascal code.

```
K := N;
WHILE K > 1 DO
   BEGIN
      .
      .
      .
      K := K DIV 2
   END;
```

Since the loop control variable is cut in half each time through the loop, the number of times that statements inside the loop will be executed is log$_2$N. Note that the halving of a loop is central to the binary search algorithm, which was introduced in Section 10.6 and which will be explored further in Section 12.5.

The principle emerging from Example 12.10 is that an algorithm that halves the data remaining to be processed on each iteration of a loop will be an O(log$_2 n$) algorithm.

■

Table 12.2, which lists frequently occurring dominant terms, will prove helpful in our future big-O analyses of algorithms.

TABLE 12.2
Common dominant terms in expressions for algorithmic efficiency based on the variable n

n dominates $\log_a n$, a is often 2
$n \log_a n$ dominates n, a is often 2
n^2 dominates $n \log_a n$
n^m dominates n^k when $m > k$
a^n dominates n^m for any $a > 1$ and $m \geq 0$

It is worthwhile to briefly characterize some of the classes of algorithms that arise due to the dominant terms listed in Table 12.2. Algorithms whose efficiency is dominated by a $\log_a n$ term (and hence are categorized as

$O(\log_a n))$ are often called *logarithmic algorithms*. Since $\log_a n$ will increase much more slowly than n itself, logarithmic algorithms are generally very efficient.

Algorithms whose efficiency can be expressed in terms of a polynomial of the form

$$a_m n^m + a_{m-1} n^{m-1} + \ldots + a_2 n^2 + a_1 n + a_0$$

are called *polynomial algorithms*. Since the highest power of n will dominate such a polynomial, such algorithms are $O(n^m)$. The only polynomial algorithms we will discuss in this book have $m = 1, 2,$ or 3; they are called *linear, quadratic,* or *cubic algorithms* respectively.

Algorithms with efficiency dominated by a term of the form a^n are called *exponential algorithms*. Exponential algorithms are of more theoretical than practical interest because they cannot reasonably be run on typical computers for moderate values of n. (However, to see why this last statement may have to change in the future, be sure to read this section's Note of Interest, which discusses *parallel processing*.)

Big-O Analysis of Bubble Sort

We are now ready to carry out some real comparisons between the three sorting methods we have discussed so far—bubble, insertion, and selection. To do so, we must determine functions $f(n)$ that allow us to make statements like "Sorting algorithm X requires $O(f(n))$ comparisons." If it turns out that all three sorts share the same $f(n)$ function, then we can conclude that the differences between them are not approaching an order of magnitude scale. Rather, they would be more subtle distinctions, which would not appear as dramatic run-time differences.

We also realize that the key to doing a big-O analysis is to focus our attention on the loops in the algorithm. We do that first for the bubble sort. Recall the loop structure of the bubble sort.

```
K := 0;
ExchangeMade := true;
WHILE (K < N - 1) AND ExchangeMade DO
  BEGIN
    ExchangeMade := false;
    K   := K + 1;
    FOR J := 1 TO N - K DO
      IF List[J].Key > List[J+1].Key THEN      Inner
      .                                          Loop
      . {Swap}
      .
```

(Outer Loop)

Assume that we have a worst case possible for bubble sort, in which the ExchangeMade variable is always set to **true** so that an early exit is never made from the outer loop. If we then consider the comparison at the top of the inner loop, we note that it will be executed first $n - 1$ times, then $n - 2$ times, and so on down to one time for the final execution of the inner loop. Hence, the number of comparisons will be the sum of the sequence of numbers

$n - 1$
$n - 2$
.
.
.

A NOTE OF INTEREST

Artificial Intelligence, the Complexity of Algorithms, and Parallel Processing

Perhaps no area of computer science demands as much in terms of efficient algorithms as does *artificial intelligence* (AI). Those engaged in research in this field are concerned with writing programs that have the computer mimic intelligent human behavior in limited domains such as natural language understanding, theorem proving, and game playing. Why is efficiency so important in such programs? Typically the strategy behind such a system is to have the computer search an enormous number of possibilities for the solution to the problem it is given. These possibilities comprise what is typically called the *state space* for the problem. For instance, for a computer program that plays a game like checkers or chess, the state space would be a suitable representation of all game board configurations that could eventually be generated from the current state of the game. The computer's goal is to search through the state space, looking for a state in which it would win the game. The state space determined by the initial configuration of a chess game has been computed to be about 10^{120} different possible moves. The time required for a computer to examine each of these different moves, assuming it could examine one every microsecond, would be 10^{95} years. Even for a simpler game such as checkers, the time required for a computer to search all states in the game would require 10^{23} years.

The reason for these extraordinarily large and impractical time frames is that a "brute force" strategy of searching all states in such AI applications leads to exponential algorithms. To avoid exponential algorithms, researchers in artificial intelligence have attempted to follow the lead of human reasoning. That is, the human mind seems able to eliminate many of the possibilities in a search space without ever examining them. Similarly AI programmers attempt to weed out large sections of the state space to be searched using what are known as *heuristics*. Heuristics are rules of thumb that enable one to rule out a vast number of possible states by doing some relatively simple computations. For instance, in a game like checkers or chess, a heuristic might involve a mathematical formula that attached a positive or negative weight to a particular state of the game. Those states for which the heuristic value indicates a probable lack of success in future searching are simply eliminated from the state space. Since a heuristic is the computational equivalent of an educated guess, it runs the risk of making an error. However, it is often viewed as a worthwhile risk if it can enhance the efficiency of the search algorithm to a category that is no longer exponential.

In addition to the use of heuristics to increase algorithmic efficiency, there is another ray of hope on the horizon for those presently working in AI research and other fields where exponential algorithms are often encountered. That ray of hope is *parallel processing*. A parallel processing computer has a network of processors that allow many operations (such as those involved in searching a state space) to be performed simultaneously, that is, in parallel. From a theoretical perspective, if a sufficient number of processors can be linked into such a parallel processing network and if the logic of a particular algorithm allows many operations to be performed in parallel, then it is conceivable that—in the future—some exponential algorithms may run in a reasonable time frame on larger data sets than can be accommodated on single-processor machines.

The success or failure of parallel processing computers will definitely play an instrumental role in the future of artificial intelligence and other areas of computer science in which exponential algorithms are frequently encountered. If parallel processing succeeds, we may find ourselves in the exciting position of having to reconsider what makes an algorithm practical or impractical.

A formula from algebra will show this sum to be

$$n(n - 1) / 2$$

Thus we conclude that the bubble sort is an $O(n^2)$ algorithm in those situations for which the ExchangeMade test does not allow an early loop exit.

Big-O Analysis of Insertion Sort

Recall that the loop structure of the insertion sort is given by

```
FOR K := 2 TO N DO
  BEGIN
    ItemToInsert := List[K];
    J := K - 1;
    StillLooking := true;
    WHILE (J >= 1) AND StillLooking Do
      IF ItemToInsert.Key < List[J].Key THEN
        BEGIN
          .
          .  { Move List[J]  }
          .
          J := J - 1
        END
      ELSE
        StillLooking := false
          .
          .
          .
```

Here, if the inner loop is never short-circuited by Done, the comparison appearing as its first statement will be executed once for the first execution of the outer loop, then twice, and so on, reaching $n - 1$ executions on the final pass. We have a situation virtually identical to our preliminary analysis of the bubble sort. That is, the number of comparisons can be bounded by $n^2/2$ and the algorithm is therefore $O(n^2)$. Of course, with the insertion sort, the hope is that setting the Boolean variable Done in the **ELSE** clause can reduce the number of comparisons made by the inner loop. However, it is clear that we can concoct many data sets for which this will have little or no effect. So, as with bubble sort, we are forced into concluding that insertion sort cannot guarantee better than $O(n^2)$ comparisons.

Big-O Analysis of Selection Sort

The loop structure of this algorithm was given by

```
FOR K := 1 TO N - 1 DO
  BEGIN
    MinPosition := K;
    FOR J := K + 1 TO N DO
      IF List[J].Key < List[MinPosition].Key THEN
        MinPosition := J;
          .
          .
          .
```

A little investigation uncovers a familiar pattern to the nested loops of the selection sort. Observe that the first time the inner loop is executed, the comparison in the **IF** statement will be made $n - 1$ times. Then it will be made $n - 2$ times; $n - 3$ times; . . . ; and finally, just one time. This is precisely the way the **IF** statement in the bubble sort was executed in repeated passes. Thus, like the bubble and insertion sorts, the selection sort is an $O(n^2)$ algorithm in terms of number of comparisons. The area in which the selection sort potentially offers better efficiency is that the number of interchanges of data in array locations is guaranteed to be $O(n)$ because the swap in selection sort occurs in the outer loop. In both of the other sorts, the swap occurs in the inner loop but is subject to a conditional test. This means that, in their worst cases, both of the other algorithms require $O(n^2)$ swaps as well as $O(n^2)$ comparisons.

Despite the fact that selection sort will usually fare better in the number of data interchanges required to sort an array, it has a drawback not found in the other two. It is apparently impossible to short-circuit either of the nested loops in selection sort when it is given a list in nearly sorted order. So, for such data sets, the selection sort may be an order of magnitude worse than the other two. This is initially rather disheartening news. It seems as if it is impossible to declare any sort a decisive winner. Indeed, our big-O analyses indicate that there is little to choose from the bubble, insertion, and selection algorithms.

The fact that we were able to reach such a conclusion, systematically however, is significant. It reveals the value of a big-O analysis. After all, even knowledge of a negative variety can be valuable in choosing appropriate algorithms under certain circumstances. For instance, if a particular application usually involved adding a small amount of data at the end of an already sorted list and then re-sorting, we now know to avoid selection sort. Moreover, when we study more powerful sorting techniques in the next section (and again in Chapter 18), we will see that it is indeed possible to break the $O(n^2)$ barrier limiting each of our three methods.

Exercises 12.3

1. Do a big-O analysis for those statements inside each of the following nested loop constructs.

   a.
   ```
   FOR K := 1 TO N DO
       FOR J := 6 TO M DO
           .
           .
           .
   ```

   b.
   ```
   FOR K := 1 TO N DO
       BEGIN
           J := N;
           WHILE J > 0 DO
               BEGIN
                   .
                   .
                   .
                   J := J DIV 2
               END
       END
   ```

   c.
   ```
   K := 1;
   REPEAT
       J :- 1;
       REPEAT
           .
           .
           .
           J := 2 * J
       UNTIL J >= N;
       K := K + 1
   UNTIL K >= N
   ```

2. Suppose we have an algorithm that requires precisely

   $$6 * \log_2 n + 34 * n^2 + 12$$

   operations for an input of n data items. Indicate which of the following are valid big-O classifications of the algorithm.

   a. $O(n^3)$ e. $O(n * \log_2 n)$

   b. $O(n^2)$ f. $O(\log_2 n)$

   c. $O(n)$ g. $O(1)$

   d. $O(n^2 * \log_2 n)$

   Of those that you have indicated are valid, which is the best big-O classification? Why?

3. A certain algorithm always requires 32 operations, regardless of the amount of data input. Provide a big-O classification of the algorithm that reflects the efficiency of the algorithm as accurately as possible.

4. An algorithm has an efficiency $O(n^2 \sin(n))$. Is it any better than $O(n^2)$ for large integer n?

5. Suppose that each of the following expressions represents the number of logical operations in an algorithm as a function of n, the size of the list being manipulated. For each expression, determine the dominant term and then classify the algorithm in big-O terms.

   a. $n^3 + n^2 \log_2 n + n^3 \log_2 n$

   b. $n + 4n^2 + 4^n$

   c. $48n^4 + 16n^2 + \log_8 n + 2^n$

6. Consider the following nested loop construct. Categorize its efficiency in terms of the variable N using big-O notation. Finally, suppose the statements indicated by the ellipses required four main memory accesses (each requiring one microsecond) and two disk file accesses (each requiring one millisecond). Express in milliseconds the amount of time this construct would require to execute if N were 1,000.

```
X := 1;
REPEAT
  Y := N;
  WHILE Y > 0 DO
    BEGIN
      .
      .
      .
      Y := Y - 1
    END;
  X := X + X
UNTIL X > N * N;
```

7. Look back to the data set you constructed for Exercise 11 in Section 12.2. Evaluate the performance of insertion sort on that data set in terms of a big-O analysis.

8. You and a friend are engaged in an argument. She claims that a certain algorithm is $O(n^2 * \log_2 n)$ in its efficiency. You claim that it is $O(n^2)$. Consider and answer the following questions.

   a. Are there circumstances under which both of you could be correct? If so, explain what such circumstances are.

   b. Are there circumstances under which both of you could be wrong? If so, explain what such circumstances are.

   c. Are there circumstances under which she could be right and you could be wrong? If so, explain what such circumstances are.

   d. Are there circumstances under which she could be wrong and you could be right? If so, explain what such circumstances are.

9. You and your friend are engaged in another argument. She claims that a certain algorithm is $O(n^2 + \log_2 n)$ in its efficiency. You claim that it is $O(n^2)$. Consider and answer the following questions.

   a. Are there circumstances under which both of you could be correct? If so, explain what such circumstances are.

   b. Are there circumstances under which both of you could be wrong? If so, explain what such circumstances are.

   c. Are there circumstances under which she could be right and you could be wrong? If so, explain what such circumstances are.

d. Are there circumstances under which she could be wrong and you could be right? If so, explain what such circumstances are.

10. Is an $O(n^2)$ algorithm also an $O(n^3)$ algorithm? Justify your answer in a carefully written paragraph.

■ ■ ■ ■

■ 12.4
The Space/Time Trade-off: Pointer Sort and Radix Sort

OBJECTIVES

- to understand the concept of a pointer
- to understand the difference between physically sorting and logically sorting
- to be able to apply pointers in logically sorting an array without interchanging data items
- to understand what is meant by the time/space trade-off
- to understand the radix sort algorithm and be able to trace its action on appropriate data sets
- to analyze the time and space efficiency of the radix sort algorithm
- to understand why the radix sort algorithm is not as generally applicable as other sorting algorithms we have studied

Early in our discussion of efficiency considerations, we noted that true runtime efficiency was best measured in fundamental machine operations and that one instruction in a high-level language may actually translate into many such primitive operations. To illustrate this, suppose that the data being sorted by one of our algorithms are records, each of which require 100 bytes of internal storage. Then, depending on your computer, it is entirely conceivable that one comparison or assignment statement in a high-level language could generate a machine language loop with 100 repetitions of such fundamental operations: one for each of the bytes that must be swapped. Those seemingly innocent portions of code, which swap two records using a temporary storage location, actually lead to the movement of 300 bytes inside the machine.

The first question we address in this section is whether, in such a situation, we can replace this large-scale internal transfer of entire records with the much swifter operation of swapping two integers. Although the solution we discuss does not achieve an order of magnitude speed increase in the big-O sense, it nonetheless reduces the number of actual machine-level swaps by a factor proportional to the record length involved, a factor that could produce a noticeable improvement in the procedure's run-time.

Bubble Sort Implemented with Pointers

So far our algorithms to sort data have implicitly assumed that the data are to be *physically sorted,* that is, the data are to be arranged in order within the array being sorted. Hence, the data in the first index of our List array are the data that come first in order according to the Key field; the data in the second index, second in order; and so on. However, if we are only interested in processing the data of List in order by Key field, is it really necessary that the data be arranged in physically ordered fashion in computer memory? No. It is possible to step logically through the data in order by Key without physically arranging it that way in memory. To do so we must use another array of *pointers.*

> **Pointer.** A pointer is a memory location in which we store the location of a data item as opposed to the data item itself.

Pointers can keep track of the *logical order* of the data without requiring it to be physically moved. At the end of our sorting routine, Pointer[1] tells us the location of the data that should come first in our alphabetical listing; Pointer[2] contains the location of the data that should come second; and so on. The sorting algorithm itself uses the logic of the bubble sort to interchange pointers instead of interchanging actual data. The actual data never move, remaining precisely where they were stored upon initial input. Instead of the expensive, time-consuming swapping of potentially large records, we are able to swap integer pointers quickly.

A Pascal procedure to implement this *pointer sort* technique follows. In addition to the declarations we have already been using in this chapter, this procedure assumes an external declaration of the form

```
TYPE
  .
  .
  .
  PointerArray = ARRAY [1..MaxIndex] OF integer;
```

Besides the List array, the procedure receives an array Pointer of type PointerArray. The procedure initializes the Pointer array to the state pictured in the "Before" snapshot of Figure 12.7. Then, via repeated swaps of integer pointers, the array is returned as shown in the "After" snapshot.

FIGURE 12.7
"Before" (left) and "After" (right) snapshots of pointer sort

	Key field of List	Pointer		Key field of List	Pointer
1	MAXWELL	1		MAXWELL	4
2	BUCKNER	2		BUCKNER	2
3	LANIER	3		LANIER	3
4	AARON	4		AARON	1

Snapshot of List and Pointer immediately after initializaion

Snapshot of List and Pointer returned by PointerBubbleSort

As the figure indicates, the List array itself is never altered.

```
PROCEDURE  PointerBubbleSort (N : integer;
                             List : SortArray;
                             VAR Pointer : PointerArray);

{  Given:    Array List containing entries in locations 1   }
{            through N.                                      }
{  Task:     Use bubble sort logic to arrange an array of   }
{            pointers that yield logical ordering of List.  }
{  Return:   Appropriately arranged Pointer array.          }

VAR
  K, J, Temp : integer;
  ExchangeMade : boolean;

BEGIN
  {  Begin by initializing Pointer array  }
  FOR K := 1 TO N DO
    Pointer[K] := K;
  K := 0;
  ExchangeMade := true;
  { Make up to N - 1 passes through array, exit early if no exchanges }
  { are made on previous pass.                                        }
  WHILE (K < N - 1) AND ExchangeMade DO
    BEGIN
      K := K + 1;
      ExchangeMade := false;
      { Via pointers, compare N - K adjacent pairs of array entries. }
      FOR J := 1 TO N - K DO
        {  Compare values referenced by Pointer  }
        IF List[Pointer[J]].Key > List[Pointer[J+1]].Key THEN
          {  If necessary, swap pointers but not data  }
```

```
              BEGIN
                Temp := Pointer[J];
                Pointer[J] := Pointer[J+1];
                Pointer[J+1] := Temp;
                ExchangeMade :=  true
              END
         END {  of WHILE  }
     END; {  of PROCEDURE PointerBubbleSort  }
```

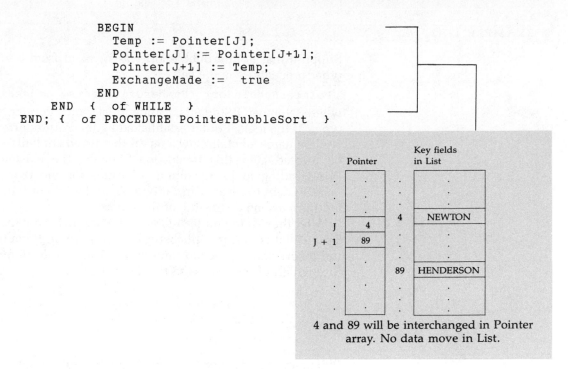

4 and 89 will be interchanged in Pointer array. No data move in List.

■ **EXAMPLE 12.11**

Given the physically ordered List of Figure 12.7, trace the action of **PROCEDURE** PointerBubbleSort on the array of pointers during each pass through the algorithm.

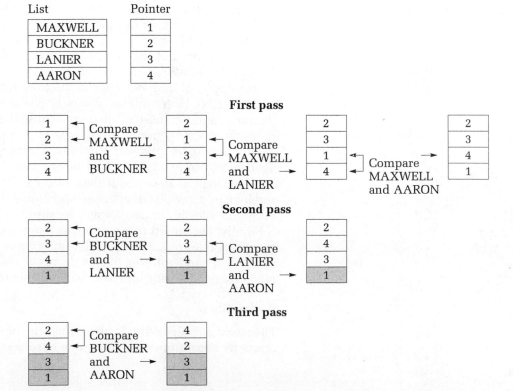

■ **EXAMPLE 12.12**

Suppose that PointerBubbleSort was invoked from a main program or another procedure via the call

```
PointerBubbleSort (NumberOfStudents, StudentList, Pointer);
```

where NumberOfStudents, StudentList, and Pointer are of appropriate types. If the logical order established by the Pointer array is alphabetical by student name, explain how a report that listed students alphabetically could be printed after this invocation. Assume the existence of a procedure PrintHeading to print column headings for the report and a procedure PrintStudent to receive an individual student record and print it in formatted form as one detail line of the report.

After the call to PointerBubbleSort, Pointer[1] contains the position of the record that is first in alphabetical order, Pointer[2] contains the position of the record that is second, and so on. Hence the following loop will step through all of the entries in the desired order.

```
PrintHeading;
FOR K := 1 TO NumberOfStudents DO
  PrintStudent (StudentList[Pointer[K]]);
```

■   ■

Efficiency Analysis for Sorts Implemented with Pointers. The pointer technique illustrated here for the bubble sort may also be used with the insertion and selection algorithms. In any of these cases, the mere introduction of the pointer strategy will not reduce the big-O categorization of the sort. However, in cases where the data items being sorted use enough internal storage to substantially slow down swapping times, the pointer sort can attain a considerable savings in run-time.

Is this run-time savings achieved without any sacrifice? An old saying that has been passed down by computer people since the days of the early vacuum tube machines is "You get nothing for nothing." We have not escaped the consequences of that adage by using pointers to increase run-time efficiency. The pointers store *data about data;* this requires additional memory. If your application is not approaching the limits of memory, this cost may not be crucial. In certain situations, however, it could be the last straw for a program running short of memory. Thus, the pointer sort is essentially a trade-off; by using more memory, we get a program that runs faster.

This *time/space trade-off* continually recurs in the analysis of computer algorithms. Many sophisticated techniques to increase speed will need to store substantial data about data to do so. Those algorithms that solve a problem in a fashion that saves space *and* decreases run-time are indeed worthy of special praise. We will be sure to note them.

Finally, the notion of a pointer, as defined and introduced here, plays an important role in our study of data structures beginning in Chapter 15. The time you spend exploring the details of the pointer sort technique will prove very valuable in your understanding of this topic in the future.

Radix Sort

The *radix sort* algorithm is also called the *bin sort,* a name derived from its origin as a technique used on (now obsolete) machines called card sorters.

Computer Graphics, Visualization, and Virtual Reality

In *computer graphics,* the efficiency of algorithms and the speed of processing hardware are of vital importance. Recent hardware developments now enable scientists to transform numeric data into computer images approaching the quality of photographs in their realism. The essential principle behind such graphics is to develop a numerical model of a physical phenomenon and then, via sophisticated mathematical algorithms, transform the model into a picture on the screen of a high-resolution graphics workstation. With faster computers and algorithms, more considerations of physical laws can be built into such models. The result of being able to incorporate more such laws is to produce images that appear very realistic.

The computational cost of such photorealism remains steep, however, progress is being made. Each year the Association of Computing Machinery's Special Interest Group on Computer Graphics (ACM SIGGRAPH) sponsors an art show at their annual meeting. The best of the digital imagery displayed at these shows is typically highlighted in the July issue of *Communications of the ACM.* For example, "Digital Image— Digital Cinema" (*Communications of the ACM* 33, No. 7 (July 1990): 30–39) and "Art & Design & Computer Graphics Technology" (*Communications of the ACM* 34, No. 7 (July 1991): 30–39) present full-color portfolios that demonstrate the degree to which the computer is influencing art and graphic design.

Who knows? Might we someday achieve the situation described by Robert Heinlein in his science-fiction novel *The Moon Is a Harsh Mistress.* In this story the president of the United States, Adam Selene, appears only on television, never in person. Why? Because he is not a human being, but solely the product of computer-generated graphic images. Such animation may soon be possible as faster hardware merges with the more efficient rendering algorithms that experts in computer graphics are now developing. Such techniques are giving rise to a new area of research known as virtual reality, in which the computer is used to view ideas without having to build a physical model.

Though it's unlikely that virtual reality will create a simulated president such as Adam Selene, it is already having a dramatic effect in design-intensive fields such as architecture. Donald Greenberg of Cornell University described such virtual reality systems in "Computers and Architecture" (*Scientific American* 264, No. 8 (February 1991). According to Greenberg, "advanced modeling and rendering algorithms allow designers and clients to walk visually through buildings long before construction . . . seeing results of their design decisions immediately and revising them interactively."

These machines would sort a deck of keypunched cards by shuffling the cards into small bins, then collecting the cards from the bins into a newly arranged deck, and repeating this shuffling-collection process until the deck was magically sorted. There was, as we shall see, a very clever algorithm behind this rapid shuffling.

For integer data, the repeated passes of radix sort focus first on the ones digit of each number, then on the tens digit, the hundreds digit, and so on until the highest order digit of the largest number is reached. For string data, the first pass hinges on the rightmost character in each string with successive passes always shifting their attention one character position to the left. To illustrate the algorithm, we will trace it on the following list of nine integers:

459 254 472 534 649 239 432 654 477

On each pass through this data, radix sort will arrange it into ten sublists (bins)—one sublist for each of the digits 0 through 9. Hence, on the first pass, all the numbers with ones digit equal to zero are grouped in one sublist, all those with ones digit equal to one are grouped in another sublist, and so on. The resulting sublists follow.

First pass of
radix sort

Digit	Sublist		
0			
1			
2	472	432	
3			
4	254	534	654
5			
6			
7	477		
8			
9	459	649	239

The sublists are then collected into one large list with the numbers in the sublist for 0 coming first, then those in the sublist for 1, and so on up to the sublist for 9. Hence we would have a newly arranged list:

472 432 254 534 654 477 459 649 239

This new list is again partitioned into sublists, this time keying on the tens digit. The result is shown below.

Second pass of
radix sort

Digit	Sublist		
0			
1			
2			
3	432	534	239
4	649		
5	654	254	459
6			
7	472	477	
8			
9			

Note that in each sublist the data are arranged in order relative to their last two digits. The sublists would now be collected into a new master list:

432 534 239 649 654 254 459 472 477

Now, focusing on the hundreds digit, the master list would be classified into ten sublists one more time. These final sublists are shown below. When the sublists are collected from this final partitioning, the data are arranged in ascending order.

Third (final) pass of
radix sort

Digit	Sublist			
0				
1				
2	239	254		
3				
4	432	459	472	477
5	534			
6	649	654		
7				
8				
9				

A pseudocode statement of the radix sort algorithm follows.

1. Begin with the current digit as the one's digit
2. **WHILE** there is still a digit on which to classify data **DO**
   2.1 **FOR** each number in the master list **DO**
       2.1.1 add that number to appropriate sublist, keying on current digit
   2.2 **FOR** each sublist (from 0 through 9) **DO**
       2.2.1 append that sublist to a newly arranged master list
   2.3 Advance the current digit one place to the left

If the radix sort is being applied to character strings instead of integers, this algorithm would have to proceed from the rightmost character to the leftmost character instead of from the ones digit to the highest order digit.

Efficiency of Radix Sort. An analysis of the loop structure in the preceding pseudocode for radix sort indicates that, for each pass through the outer **WHILE** loop, $O(n)$ operations must be performed. These $O(n)$ operations consist of the arithmetic necessary to isolate a particular digit within a number, appending that number to the proper sublist, and then collecting it again into a new master list. Since the outer **WHILE** loop will only be executed C times—where C is the number of digits (or characters) in the integer (or string)—the radix sort is an $O(n)$ sorting algorithm.

Although the radix sort is significantly faster than the other $O(n^2)$ algorithms we have studied in this chapter, there are again trade-off factors to consider. It is potentially much less space efficient than the other sorting algorithms we have studied. This is due to the need for storing sublists for each of the possible digits in the number or characters in the string. Using arrays to store the sublists and without any prior knowledge about the distribution of the data, we would be forced to allocate an additional $10n$ storage locations when sorting an array of n integers and $27n$ storage locations when sorting n strings of letters and blanks. We shall alleviate this memory crunch somewhat when we study linked lists in Chapter 15, but even then the radix sort will remain a space inefficient algorithm compared to other sorting algorithms. Other criteria negating the very good time efficiency of the radix sort are its inflexibility for data of varying size and the fact that, although $O(n)$ in time, its constant of proportionality in this regard is often large enough to often make it less time efficient than the more sophisticated sorting algorithms we will study in Chapter 19.

■ **EXAMPLE 12.13**

Assume the existence of the following declarations and procedure to perform radix sort on an array of four-digit numbers.

```
CONST
  MaxIndex = 100;
TYPE
  SingleDigit = 0..9;
  FourDigitNumbers = 0..9999;
  SortArray = ARRAY [1..MaxIndex] OF FourDigitNumbers;
  BinStructure = ARRAY [SingleDigit] OF SortArray;
  BinCounters = ARRAY [SingleDigit] OF integer;
  .
  .
  .
FUNCTION Digit(Number, K : integer) : SingleDigit;
```

```
{  Given:    Integers Number and K.                              }
{  Task:     Determine Kth digit in Number, with one's digit being }
{            viewed as first.                                     }
{  Return:   The Kth digit in Number.                            }
 .
 .
 .

PROCEDURE InitializeCtrs (VAR S : BinCounters);

{  Given:    S, an array of bin counters.                        }
{  Task:     Initialize all counters in array to zero.           }
{  Return:   The array initialized to zero.                      }
 .
 .
 .

PROCEDURE AddToBin (VAR Bins : BinStructure;
                    VAR S : BinCounters;
                    Number, Place : integer);

{  Given:    Bins, an array of bins, along with counters         }
{            indicating number of values currently in each       }
{            individual bin.                                     }
{  Task:     Insert Number in bin indicated by Place.            }
{  Return:   Bins with Number added and updated counter array S. }
 .
 .
 .

PROCEDURE CollectBins (VAR A : SortArray;
                       Bins : BinStructure;
                       S : BinCounters);

{  Given:    Bins, with each bin containing number of values     }
{            indicated by BinCounter array S.                    }
{  Task:     Append Bins to each other starting with bin indexed }
{            by zero.                                            }
{  Return:   Appended Bins in array A.                           }
```

Then the Pascal code for radix sort would be

```
PROCEDURE RadixSort (N : integer; VAR List : SortArray);

{  Given:    Array List containing entries in locations 1 through N. }
{  Task:     Apply radix sort algorithm.                         }
{  Return:   Array List with first N entries arranged in ascending }
{            order.                                              }

  VAR
    K, J : integer;
    Bins : BinStructure;
    BinCtr : BinCounters;

  BEGIN
    InitializeCtrs (BinCtr);
    {  For K loop controls digit used to classify data.  }
    FOR K := 1 TO 4 DO
      BEGIN
        {  For J loop iterates through all numbers, putting them into }
        {  bin determined by Kth digit.                   }
        FOR J := 1 TO N DO
          AddToBin (Bins, BinCtr, List[J], Digit(List[J], K));
        CollectBins (List, Bins, BinCtr);
        InitializeCtrs(BinCtr)
      END
  END;  {  of PROCEDURE RadixSort  }
```

Exercises 12.4

1. Suppose that you are given the following list of keys

1	9438
2	3216
3	416
4	9021
5	1142
6	3316
7	94

   Show what the contents of the Pointer array would be after each pass through the outer loop of **PROCEDURE** PointerBubbleSort discussed in this section.

2. Consider again the data set given in Exercise 1. How many passes would be made through the outer loop of the radix sort algorithm for this data? Trace the contents of the array after each of these passes.

3. Consider the following list of strings:

1	CHOCOLATE
2	VANILLA
3	CARAMEL
4	PEACH
5	STRAWBERRY
6	CHERRY

   How many passes would be made through the outer loop of the radix sort algorithm for these data? Trace the contents of the list after each of these passes.

4. Explain the difference between physical and logical ordering.

5. Cite an application in which the mere logical ordering of data, as achieved by the pointer sort technique, would not be sufficient; that is, give an application in which physical ordering of data is required.

6. What is the time/space trade-off? Define and discuss various contexts in which it may arise.

7. When the bubble sort was modified with an array of pointers, did it improve its $O(n^2)$ run-time efficiency in a significant sense? Under what circumstances would you call the improvement in efficiency significant? Provide your answer to this question in a short essay in which you define "significant" and then explain why the circumstance you describe would lead to a significant improvement.

8. The bubble, insertion, and selection sort algorithms are all $O(n)$ in their space requirements. That is, each algorithm requires memory proportional to n to sort the items in an array of n items. From a big-O perspective, what are the space requirements of these algorithms when the pointer sort technique is incorporated into their logic?

9. Would you expect that the pointer strategy would have least effect on the run-time efficiency of bubble, selection, or insertion sort? Provide a rationale for your answer in a short essay.

10. Suppose you have 1,000 records to be sorted. Would the run-time efficiency of the pointer sort increase significantly if the 1,000 records were broken into four groups, each group sorted, and then merged together as one large sorted array as compared to sorting the initial unsegmented array? Why or why not?

11. Incorporate the pointer sort technique into the selection sort algorithm.

12. Incorporate the pointer sort technique into the insertion sort algorithm.

13. Write the procedures and functions assumed to exist in the version of RadixSort given in Example 12.13.

14. Write a radix sort procedure to sort an arbitrary array of integers. Analyze the space efficiency of your procedure.

15. Write a radix sort procedure to sort an array of strings. Analyze the space efficiency of your procedure. Be sure to carefully state the assumptions you make about strings in performing your analysis of space efficiency.

16. Describe the complications in implementing the radix sort algorithm for an array of real numbers. Discuss a strategy that could be used to overcome these complications.

■ ■ ■ ■

■ 12.5
Simple Search Algorithms

OBJECTIVES

- to formalize a context in which search algorithms may be applied
- to understand the logic of the sequential search algorithm
- to analyze the efficiency of the sequential search algorithm
- to understand the logic of the binary search algorithm
- to recognize situations in which a key-to-address transformation may be used as an O(1) search method.

Many programs extensively employ algorithms that find a particular data item in a large collection of such items. Such algorithms, typically called *search algorithms,* are given the value of a key field that identifies the item being sought; they then return either all the data associated with that particular key or a flag indicating that it could not be found. You saw search algorithms in Section 10.6 when we described some operations that were frequently required in processing arrays. We now explore search algorithms and subject them to an efficiency analysis using the big-O notation we have developed.

The general setup for the search algorithms we discuss in this chapter is given by the following skeletal declarations:

```
CONST
   MaxIndex = 100; {  Easily adjusted  }
   .
   .
   .
TYPE
   KeyType = {  Appropriate data type for key field in record  };
   DataRec = RECORD
                Key : KeyType;
                OtherData : {  Appropriate Type  }
             END;
   DataArray = ARRAY [1..MaxIndex] OF DataRec;
   .
   .
   .
PROCEDURE    Search (Target : KeyType;
                SearchList : DataArray;
                VAR InfoWanted : DataRec;
                VAR Found : boolean);

   {  Given:    A collection of records in SearchList and Target storing key  }
   {            value of record being sought.                                 }
   {  Task:     Find the record associated with Target.                       }
   {  Return:   All data associated with Target in InfoWanted and Found set   }
   {            to true or false indicating whether or not the search         }
   {            was successful.                                               }
```

Figure 12.8 graphically portrays this setup. Specific search algorithms may require some additional information for their implementation; for example,

FIGURE 12.8
General setup for search algorithm

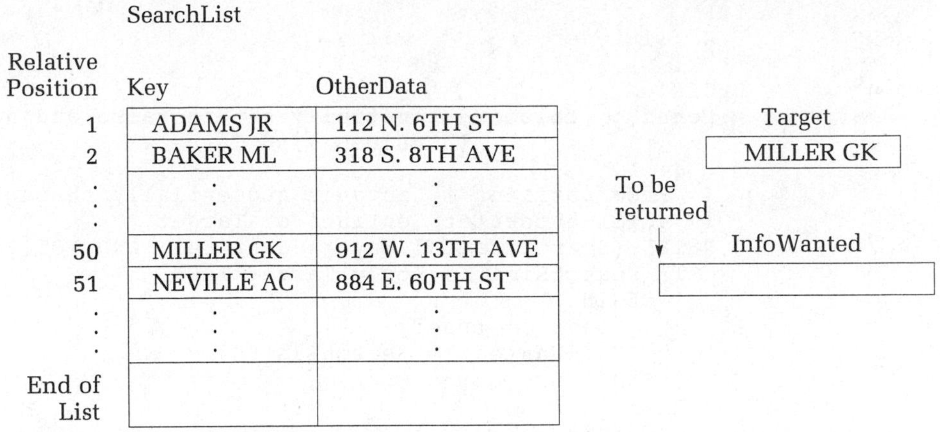

SearchList

Relative
Position   Key   OtherData

Relative Position	Key	OtherData
1	ADAMS JR	112 N. 6TH ST
2	BAKER ML	318 S. 8TH AVE
.	.	.
.	.	.
.	.	.
50	MILLER GK	912 W. 13TH AVE
51	NEVILLE AC	884 E. 60TH ST
.	.	.
.	.	.
End of List		

Target

MILLER GK

To be
returned

↓ InfoWanted

a particular sentinel value that marks the end of the list or knowledge of the number of entries in the list. We will discuss these particulars with the individual algorithms themselves.

Sequential Search Algorithm

The task of a computer scientist working with search algorithms may be compared to that of a librarian. Just as the librarian must devise a method of storing books on shelves in a fashion that allows patrons to easily find the books they want, so must a computer scientist devise methods of organizing large collections of electronic data so that records within that data can always be quickly found. Imagine the plight of the librarian who just throws books upon shelves as they are unpacked from shipping boxes, without any consideration toward organizing the chaos! Unless the library had an artificially small collection, it would take patrons an impractical length of time to find their reading material. Because of the lack of any organizational order imposed on the books, the only search strategy available would be to pull books from the shelves in some arbitrary sequence until the desired book was found.

As a programmer given a completely unordered set of data, this is the same strategy you would have to follow. The logic of such a *sequential search* strategy is extremely simple and appears in the following **PROCEDURE** SequentialSearch. This procedure assumes that the final record in the list is flagged by a special Sentinel value in its Key field.

```
PROCEDURE SequentialSearch  (Target : KeyType;
                             Sentinel : KeyType;
                             SearchList : DataArray;
                             VAR InfoWanted : DataRec;
                             VAR Found : boolean);

{ Given:   List of records in SearchList, Target storing  }
{          key value being sought, and Sentinel value     }
{          marking end of list.                           }
{ Task:    Sequentially pass through SearchList seeking    }
{          Target.                                        }
{ Return:  DataRec associated with Target in InfoWanted.  }
{          If not found, return false in boolean          }
{          variable Found.                                }
```

```
VAR
  K : integer;

BEGIN
  Found := false; {  Initially set to false and not changed  }
                  {  unless find Target.                      }
  K := 1;
  {  From position 1, advance sequentially through SearchList  }
  {  until encounter Sentinel or Target.                       }
  WHILE (SearchList[K].Key <> Sentinel) AND NOT Found DO
    IF SearchList[K].Key = Target THEN
      BEGIN
        Found := true;
        InfoWanted := SearchList[K]
      END
    ELSE
      K := K + 1
END; {  of PROCEDURE SequentialSearch  }
```

Efficiency of Sequential Search. Unfortunately, the simplicity of the sequential search is offset by its inefficiency as a search strategy. Obviously, the average number of probes into the list before the target key is found will be $n/2$, where n is the number of records in the list. For unsuccessful invocations of the procedure, all n records must be checked before we can conclude failure. Thus, in terms of a big-O classification, the method is clearly $O(n)$. This may not seem bad when compared to the $O(n^2)$ efficiency of our sorting methods, but searching is conceptually a much simpler operation than sorting: it should be significantly faster. Moreover, though $O(n)$ may seem fast enough at microsecond speeds, there are many applications where an $O(n)$ time factor can be unacceptably slow.

For instance, when a compiler processes your source program in Pascal, it must continually search a list of identifiers that have been previously declared. (This list is typically called a *symbol table*.) Hence, in such an application, the search operation merely represents the inner loop within a much more complex outer loop that is repeating until it reaches the end of your source file: an inner loop which, repeated at $O(n)$ speeds, would make your compiler intolerably slow.

Another situation in which $O(n)$ is not good enough for searching occurs when the list being searched is stored in a *disk file* instead of a main memory array. Now, because accessing data on disk is a much slower operation than accessing data in main memory, each probe into the list might conceivably require approximately one millisecond (one-thousandth of a second) instead of a microsecond. Searching such a list of one million records at $O(n)$ speed would hence require one thousand seconds instead of just one second. That long a wait for one record is certain to generate angry users. We conclude that, although the sequential search may be fast enough for small and infrequently accessed lists stored in main memory, we need something that is better by an order of magnitude for many practical applications.

Binary Search Algorithm

By paying what may initially seem like a small price, we can dramatically increase the efficiency of our search effort using the *binary search* described in Section 10.6. The price we must pay is threefold.

1. The list of records with keys must be maintained in physically sorted order unless we are willing to use an additional list of pointers similar to that used in the PointerBubbleSort algorithm. (See the Exercises at the end of this section.)
2. The number of records in the list must be maintained in a separate variable.
3. We must be able to randomly access, by relative position, records in the list. This is the type of access you have in Pascal arrays, but which is lacking in standard Pascal files.

For instance, suppose that the list of integer keys appearing in Figure 12.9 has the access facility of the third point just cited and that we wish to locate

FIGURE 12.9

Physically ordered random access list of keys for binary search

Position	Key
1	1119
2	1203
3	1212
4	1519
5	1604
6	1649
7	1821
8	2312
9	2409
10	3612

Number of Records $n = 10$
Target = 1649

the randomly accessible data associated with the Target key 1649. The strategy of the binary search is to begin the search in the middle of the list. In the case of Figure 12.9, this would mean beginning the search with the key found at position 5. Since the Target we are seeking is greater than the key found at position 5, we are able to conclude that the key we want will be found among positions 6 through 10—if at all.

We will split those positions that remain viable candidates for finding the Target by accessing the middle position:

$$(6 + 10) / 2 = 8$$

Since the key at position 8 is greater than Target, we are able to conclude that the key being sought will be found in positions 6 or 7—if it is to be found at all. Notice that, after only two accesses into the list, our list of remaining viable candidates for a match has shrunk to 2. (Compare this figure to a sequential search after two accesses into the same list.) We now split the distance between positions 6 and 7, arriving (by integer arithmetic) at position 6. Here we find the key being sought after a mere three probes into the list.

Crucial to the entire binary search algorithm are two pointers, Low and High, to the bottom and top respectively of the current list of viable candidates. We must repeatedly compute the Middle index of that portion of the list between Low and High and compare the data at that Middle index to the Target using the following logic.

```
                    IF Target < SearchList[Middle].Key THEN
                       High must be reduced to Middle - 1
                    ELSE IF Target > SearchList[Middle].Key THEN
                       Low must be increased to Middle + 1
                    ELSE
                       Search is done
                       Target has been found in SearchList
```

Should these pointers ever cross, that is, if High were to become less than Low, we would conclude that the Target does not appear in the list. The entire algorithm is formalized in the following Pascal procedure:

```
PROCEDURE  BinarySearch (Target : KeyType;
                         N : integer;
                         SearchList : DataArray;
                         VAR InfoWanted : DataRec;
                         VAR Found : boolean);

   {  Given:    List of sorted records in SearchList, Target   }
   {            storing key value being sought, and N storing   }
   {            number of records in the list.                  }
   {  Task:     Apply binary search algorithm.                  }
   {  Return:   DataRec associated with Target in InfoWanted.   }
   {            If not found, return false in Boolean            }
   {            variable Found.                                  }

VAR
   High, Low, Middle : integer;

BEGIN
   Found := false;
   Low := 1;
   High := N;
   {  Indices between Low and High inclusive represent positions   }
   {  where Target could possibly located.                        }
   WHILE NOT Found AND (Low <= High) DO
      BEGIN
         Middle := (Low + High) DIV 2;
         IF Target < SearchList[Middle].Key THEN {  Work with low end  }
            High := Middle - 1
```

	Key	
1	102	Initial Low
2	183	
.	219	
.	264	If Target > 351, then
Middle	351	Low must be reset to
.	499	point at 499
.	506	
	530	
N	642	Initial High

	Key	
1	102	Initial Low
2	183	
.	219	
.	264	If Target < 351, then
Middle	351	High must be reset to
.	499	point at 264
.	506	
	530	
N	642	Initial High

```
         ELSE IF Target > SearchList[Middle].Key THEN {  Work with high end  }
            Low := Middle + 1
         ELSE {  Success!  }
            BEGIN
               Found := true;
               InfoWanted := SearchList[Middle]
            END
      END
END; {  of PROCEDURE BinarySearch  }
```

■ **EXAMPLE 12.14**

Trace the action of **PROCEDURE** BinarySearch as it locates the record associated with Target 1519 in the array of Figure 12.9.

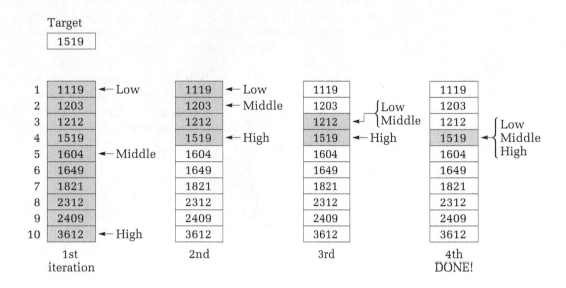

■ **EXAMPLE 12.15**

Trace the action of **PROCEDURE** BinarySearch as it reports that target 2392 cannot be found in the array of Figure 12.9.

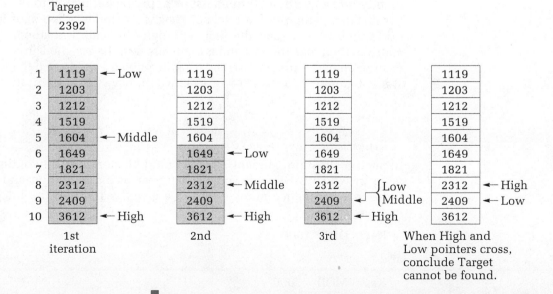

Efficiency of Binary Search.   As indicated by the shaded portions of the lists in the preceding examples, the binary search continually halves the size of the list that must still be searched. This continual halving is critical to the effectiveness of the algorithm. When applied to the list of keys in Figure 12.9, the method in the worst case would require four different accesses. For an ordered list of 50,000 keys, the worst-case efficiency is a mere sixteen different accesses. (In case you do not believe this dramatic increase in efficiency as the list gets larger, try plugging 50,000 into a handheld calculator and count how many times you must halve the displayed number to reduce it to 1.) The same list of 1,000,000 records stored on disk that would require approximately 1,000 seconds to search sequentially will result in a virtually instantaneous response with the binary search strategy.

More formally, for a list of n items, the maximum number of times we would cut the list in half before finding the target item or declaring the search unsuccessful is

$$(\log_2 n) + 1$$

Thus, the binary search is the first $O(\log_2 n)$ algorithm we have studied. (See Example 12.10.) In terms of the categorizations discussed in Section 12.3, it is a logarithmic algorithm. Expressions involving a $\log_2 n$ factor will arise frequently as we analyze other algorithms. They are extremely fast when compared to $O(n)$ algorithms, particularly for large values of n.

The drawback of the binary search lies not in any consideration of its processing speed but rather in a reexamination of the price that must be paid for being able to use it. For a volatile list (that is, one undergoing frequent additions and deletions), the requirement of maintaining the list in physical order can be quite costly. For large lists, it makes the operations of adding and deleting records so inefficient that the very fast search speed is all but negated. We will analyze this problem of list maintenance more deeply in future chapters.

Key-to-Address Transformations

A search technique so simple that it is often overlooked presents itself in certain situations where a record's key value can be transformed conveniently into a position within a list by applying a function to the key value. For instance, suppose that a school assigns its students five-digit identification numbers in which the first two digits indicate the student's year of matriculation and the last three digits are simply assigned in a sequential fashion among students matriculating in a given year. Hence the fourteenth student admitted in the class of 1992 would have the identification number

$$\underbrace{9 \quad 2}_{\substack{\text{year of} \\ \text{matriculation}}} \quad \underbrace{0 \quad 1 \quad 4}_{\substack{\text{sequence number} \\ \text{within that year}}}$$

In such a situation, student records could be stored in a two-dimensional table in which rows were indexed by year of matriculation and columns indexed by sequence number within a given year. Then the integer arithmetic operations

Key   **DIV**   1000

and

Key   **MOD**   1000

would yield a given student's row and column index respectively. The address of a student's record could therefore be obtained from the student's identification number using a mere two operations.

In such situations, the search efficiency to locate a student's record is O(1) in its big-O classification. The apparent restriction that must apply for this technique to work is that the transformation applied to a key to yield an address cannot yield the same address for two different students. As we shall see in Chapter 20, even this restriction can be relaxed somewhat if slightly more sophisticated search techniques are employed. Another drawback of the key-to-address transformation technique is its potentially inefficient use of space. You will perform such a space analysis for this strategy in this section's Exercises.

Exercises 12.5

1. Suppose that an array contains key values

   18 40 46 50 52 58 63 70 77 90

   in index locations 1 through 10. Trace the index values for the Low, High, and Middle pointers in the binary search algorithm if the Target 43 is being sought. Repeat for Target values 40 and 90.

2. In Exercise 10 of Section 12.2 we defined the notions of best-case and worst-case behavior of an algorithm. Devise sample data sets to demonstrate the best-case and worst-case behavior of the binary search algorithm.

3. What is a compiler symbol table? Explain why a sequential search applied to such a table is not a practical strategy.

4. Explain the difference in run-time efficiency considerations for a program that manipulates data in a main memory array versus one that accesses data stored in a disk file.

5. How many times would the **WHILE** loop in **PROCEDURE** BinarySearch be executed if $n = 1,000,000$?

6. Consider the following modified version of the binary search algorithm. (Modifications are indicated by a comment highlighted by asterisks.) Will this new version of the binary search algorithm work correctly for all data? If not, specify a situation in which this version will fail.

```
PROCEDURE  BinarySearch (Target : KeyType;
                         N : integer;
                         SearchList : DataArray;
                         VAR InfoWanted : DataRec;
                         VAR Found : boolean);

{ Given:   List of sorted records in SearchList, Target  }
{          storing key value being sought, and N storing  }
{          number of records in the list.                 }
{ Task:    Apply binary search algorithm.                 }
{ Return:  DataRec associated with Target in InfoWanted.  }
{          If not found, return false in Boolean          }
{          variable Found.                                }

VAR
  High, Low, Middle : integer;

BEGIN
  Found := false;
  Low := 1;
  High := N;
  WHILE NOT Found AND (Low <= High) DO
```

```
        BEGIN
          Middle := (Low + High) DIV 2;
          IF Target < SearchList[Middle].Key THEN {  Work with low end  }
            High := Middle    { ****** Modification here ****** }
          ELSE IF Target > SearchList[Middle].Key THEN {  Work with high end  }
            Low := Middle       { ****** Modification here ****** }
          ELSE {  Success!  }
            BEGIN
              Found := true;
              InfoWanted := SearchList[Middle]
            END
      END
    END; {  of PROCEDURE BinarySearch  }
```

7. Consider the following modified version of the binary search algorithm. (Modifications are indicated by a comment highlighted by asterisks.) Will this new version of the binary search algorithm work correctly for all data? If not, specify a situation in which this version will fail.

```
PROCEDURE  BinarySearch (Target : KeyType;
                         N : integer;
                         SearchList : DataArray;
                         VAR InfoWanted : DataRec;
                         VAR Found : boolean);
{  Given:   List of sorted records in SearchList, Target    }
{           storing key value being sought, and N storing    }
{           number of records in the list.                   }
{  Task:    Apply binary search algorithm.                   }
{  Return:  DataRec associated with Target in InfoWanted.    }
{           If not found, return false in Boolean            }
{           variable Found.                                  }

VAR
  High, Low, Middle : integer;

BEGIN
  Found := false;
  Low := 1;
  High := N;
  REPEAT    { ***** Use REPEAT instead of WHILE ***** }
    Middle := (Low + High) DIV 2;
    IF Target < SearchList[Middle].Key THEN {  Work with low end  }
      High := Middle - 1
    ELSE IF Target > SearchList[Middle].Key THEN {  Work with high end  }
      Low := Middle + 1
    ELSE {  Success!  }
      BEGIN
        Found := true;
        InfoWanted := SearchList[Middle]
      END
  UNTIL Found OR ( Low > High )   { ****** Loop exit condition ****** }
END; {  of PROCEDURE BinarySearch  }
```

8. Consider the example of a key-to-address transformation for student identification numbers given in this section. Discuss the space efficiency of this strategy. Upon what factor is the space efficiency dependent?

9. Devise a key-to-address transformation to locate records in a data structure for employees of the East Publishing Company. Departments in the company are identified by a one-letter code A–Z. An employee's payroll identification number consists of a department code followed by another one-letter code representing the employee's pay rate classification, and a two-digit number assigned in sequential fashion to employees within a given department. Hence, the identification number DX40 is assigned to the 40th employee in department D; the X indicates the employee's pay rate category.

10. The requirement for the binary search that the data in an array be physically ordered can actually be circumvented by keeping track of the logical order of the data via a pointer array analogous to that used in the pointer sort. Rewrite the binary search algorithm under such an assumption. Explain why it might be advantageous to use this technique.

11. Implement the following modification to the sequential search algorithm. Temporarily insert the key for which you are searching at the end of the list. Search sequentially until you find this key; then examine the position where you found it to determine whether or not the search was successful. Note that this strategy requires your knowing the number of items in the list rather than a sentinel value stored at the end of the list. Comment on the run-time efficiency of this new strategy versus the sequential search algorithm discussed in this chapter.

12. Modify the insertion sort algorithm of Section 12.2 so that it finds the insertion point for the next array entry using an appropriate modification of the halving strategy employed by the binary search algorithm. Once this insertion point is determined, other array entries must be moved accordingly to make room for the entry being inserted. After completing this modified version of the insertion sort, perform a big-O analysis of its efficiency.

13. In a search procedure such as sequential or binary search, the array to be searched is passed as a value parameter to the procedure because we do not want the array altered during execution of the procedure. Write a short essay in which you explain why, from a time efficiency perspective, it would be wiser to pass large arrays as **VAR** parameters to such procedure—even though this violates dictates of program style that we have previously established. *Remember:* Your answer to this question should be based on efficiency rather than on style considerations. Check with your instructor about whether you should incorporate such a change in philosophy into future programming efforts. *Hint:* Think about what must be done by a compiler to provide a procedure with a copy of a data item passed as a value parameter. Compare this to what must be done when a parameter is passed by reference.

14. Imagine that you have been hired to write an information retrieval program for a company or organization. You must interview people within the organization to determine exactly what their information retrieval needs are. Construct questions that you could ask in such an interview to enable you to determine which search strategy would be most appropriate for the program you must write. Then, in an essay explain how answers to these questions would dictate your choice of search strategy.

■ ■ ■ ■

FOCUS ON PROGRAM DESIGN

Rather than present a complete program as we have done in previous Focus on Program Design sections, we will use this chapter's Focus section to examine how we can augment a program to help us analyze its own efficiency. This technique, known as *profiling,* consists of inserting counters that accumulate the total number of times that certain critical operations are performed as an algorithm executes.

To illustrate the technique, we return to the program developed in the Focus on Program Design section for Chapter 5. Recall that the central ListAllPrimes procedure of this program determined all primes less than or equal to a specified positive integer Number. Portions of this original program are presented here, along with new additions (indicated by shading) that illustrate the profiling technique.

Before discussing these additions, however, we will turn our attention to trying to analyze the time efficiency of the ListAllPrimes procedure. The nested loop structure of this procedure is given by the following schematic

```
FOR Candidate := 2 TO Number
   ⋮
     WHILE                    Inner WHILE        Outer FOR loop
       ⋮                      loop executed      executed Number − 1
                              Candidate - 2 or   times
                              fewer times
```

Certainly the schematic indicates that we are safe in saying that **PROCEDURE** ListAllPrimes is $O(Number^2)$ in its time efficiency. However, the early exit condition from the inner loop will be reached quite often. This leads us to believe that the algorithm may actually be substantially faster then $O(Number^2)$.

Unfortunately, determining how much faster it is than $O(Number^2)$ by using a purely mathematical analysis may be impossible or at least require a knowledge of mathematical number theory beyond our present means. We propose instead to use the computer to help us analyze the algorithm from an empirical perspective. An examination of the shaded code in the partial listing given here indicates that profiling the ListAllPrimes algorithm is achieved by

- Declaring a global Boolean constant that is set to **true** to "turn on" profiling. All executable statements related to profiling are conditionally qualified by

  `IF Profile THEN . . .`

  Thus, to turn off profiling in the program, you would merely set this constant to **false**.
- A global variable ProfiledOperations is initialized to zero upon entry to ListAllPrimes and then increased by 1 each time an addition or **MOD** operation is performed.
- A ProfileReport procedure is called conditionally by the main program to report a comparison between N^2 and the actual number of operations performed during execution of the algorithm.

We should justify the use of globally declared data within the procedure ListAllPrimes. The alternative would be to add extra parameters to the formal parameter list of ListAllPrimes—parameters that are concerned with profiling instead of the actual algorithm implemented by ListAllPrimes. That is, the profiling data items are completely extraneous to the logic of the procedure; they are there only to measure empirically the performance of the algorithm. As such, adding them to the formal parameter list would make the interface to the procedure considerably more confusing than necessary.

We emphasize that the use of globals in such profiling applications is an exceptional circumstance. In general, the maxim that procedures and functions should only use locally declared data remains true.

A partial program listing follows. The results of sample runs are discussed after the listing.

```
PROGRAM ListPrimes (input, output);

CONST
  Skip = ' ';
  Dashes = '----------------------------------------------------';
  Profile = true;
```

```
VAR
  Number : integer;
  MoreData : boolean;
  ProfiledOperations : integer;
     .
     .
     .


{*******************************************************************}


PROCEDURE ListAllPrimes (Number : integer);

  {  Given:    The integer read                                    }
  {  Task:     List all primes less than or equal to the integer   }
  {            read                                                 }
  {  Return:   Nothing                                             }

  VAR
    Prime : boolean;
    Candidate, Divisor, LimitForCheck : integer;

  BEGIN
    FOR Candidate := 2 TO Number DO
      BEGIN
        Prime := true;
        Divisor := 2;
        LimitForCheck := Candidate - 1
        WHILE (Divisor <= LimitForCheck) AND Prime DO
          BEGIN
            IF Candidate MOD Divisor = 0 THEN
              Prime := false        {  Candidate has a divisor  }
            ELSE
              Divisor := Divisor + 1;
            IF Profile THEN
              ProfiledOperations := ProfiledOperations + 1
          END
        IF Prime THEN               {  Print in list of primes  }
          writeln (Candidate:35)
      END   {  of FOR loop  }
  END;  {  of PROCEDURE ListAllPrimes  }


{********************************************************************* }


PROCEDURE ProfileReport (Number : integer);

  {  Given:    The count of profiled operations (global)            }
  {            and Number being profiled                            }
  {  Task:     Report a comparison of the number of profiled        }
  {            operations to O(N^2)                                 }

  BEGIN
  writeln;
  writeln('   For N: ', Number : 3);
  writeln('   Number of profiled operations: ', ProfiledOperations : 6);
  writeln('   Compare to O(N^2):               ', Number * Number : 6);
  writeln
END;  { of PROCEDURE ProfileReport }


{********************************************************************* }
```

```
PROCEDURE ExamineTheNumber (Number : integer);

  { Given:   The integer read (Number)                              }
  { Task:    Print primes less than or equal to Number              }
  { Return:  Nothing                                                }

  BEGIN
    IF Number = 1 THEN
      PrintOneMessage
    ELSE
      BEGIN
        PrintMessage (Number);
        ListAllPrimes (Number);
        IF Profile THEN
          ProfileReport (Number)
      END { of ELSE option  }
  END; { of PROCEDURE ExamineTheNumber  }


{***************************************************************** }

BEGIN { Main program  }
  GetANumber (Number, MoreData);
  WHILE MoreData DO
    BEGIN
      ExamineTheNumber (Number);
      GetANumber (Number, MoreData)
    END { of WHILE loop  }
  END. { of  main program  }
```

Here are a few sample runs, with profiling output only.

```
        Enter a positive integer, <-999> to quit.    17

            .
            . (primes listed here)
            .

        For N:  17
        Number of profiled operations:      55
        Compare to O(N^2):                 289

        Enter a positive integer, <-999> to quit.    45

            .
            . (primes listed here)
            .

        For N:  45
        Number of profiled operations:     296
        Compare to O(N^2):                2025

        Enter a positive integer, <-999> to quit.   100

            .
            . (primes listed here)
            .

        For N: 100
        Number of profiled operations:    1133
        Compare to O(N^2):               10000

        Enter a positive integer, <-999> to quit.   150

            .
            . (primes listed here)
            .

        For N: 150
        Number of profiled operations:    2414
        Compare to O(N^2):               22500

        Enter a positive integer, <-999> to quit.  -999
```

What have we learned from the runs of this profiled program? The observed number of operations that are reported by the program offer empirical evidence that we are well within the bounds of an $O(N^2)$ algorithm. They indicate that we can perhaps even place the algorithm into a more efficient big-O category. What category? This could be explored by fine-tuning the ProfileReport procedure to compare the actual number of performed operations with N^r for values of r less than 2 or with $N * \log_2 N$.

At the time we introduced the ListAllPrimes algorithm in Chapter 5, we commented that it was not necessarily the best way to perform this task. We can now suggest a number of ways to improve the algorithm and evaluate the efficiency of each succeeding version of the algorithm by a combination of formal big-O analysis and empirical profiling. Our series of refinements is illustrative of a process that can often be applied to the first version of an algorithm. That is, reflection upon how a given algorithm works can often lead to a new algorithm, which achieves the same end in a much more efficient manner.

Observation 1
The greatest divisor of a number, other than itself, cannot exceed one-half of the number.

Observation 2
Divisors of a number come in pairs. For instance, 36 is divided evenly by 4 since 4 * 9 = 36. Here the divisor 4 is paired with the divisor 9. The search for divisors in the inner loop of our algorithm need not consider the larger value in such a divisor pair. Why? Because it cannot find such a larger divisor without first finding the smaller value in the divisor pair.

Observation 3
The Greek mathematician Eratosthenes devised a "sieve" technique for finding all prime numbers between 2 and Num. The *sieve of Eratosthenes* can be viewed as a Boolean array indexed from 2 to Num and initialized to **true** in all of its locations. Successive array indices that are

Multiples of 2 greater than 2 are set to false.
Multiples of 3 greater than 3 are set to false.
Multiples of 4 can be ignored. Why?
Multiples of 5 greater than 5 are set to false.
Multiples of 6 can be ignored. Why?
Multiples of 7 greater than 7 are set to false.

and so on. The prime numbers are those array indices where a true value remains.

You will be asked to continue exploration of such prime number algorithms in the problems. Profiling can be a valuable aide in such exploration. It provides statistical evidence of an algorithm's performance in cases where pure mathematical analysis may be inconclusive.

RUNNING AND DEBUGGING TIPS

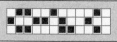

1. Procedures with an array as a value parameter in their formal parameter list will run faster if the array parameter is converted into a **VAR** parameter. Making such a change will eliminate the machine instructions involved in copying an actual parameter that is passed to the procedure. However, making such a change for the sake of efficiency should be carefully weighed against the consideration that the procedure's actual parameter list will now not reflect whether the role of an array parameter is to serve only as input to the procedure.

2. When profiling an algorithm, use a Boolean constant that can be set to **true** or **false** to turn profiling on or off respectively.

3. When using integer counters in profiling a program, be careful that the number of operations executed by the algorithm does not overflow the capacity of integer storage. Most Pascal implementations offer additional integer data types that can accommodate values too large for standard integers. Consult local system reference materials to find out what your version of Pascal may offer in this regard.

■ Summary

Key Terms

artificial intelligence
best case
big-O analysis
big-O notation
binary search
bin sort
bubble sort
compiler symbol table
computer graphics
cubic algorithm
data about data
disk file
dominant term
exponential algorithm

heuristics
insertion sort
linear algorithm
logarithmic algorithm
logical order
$\log_2 n$ search algorithm
order of magnitude
parallel processing
permutation
physically sorted
pointers
pointer sort
polynomial algorithm

profile
proportional
quadratic algorithm
radix sort
search algorithm
selection sort
sequential search
shaker sort
sieve of Eratosthenes
state space
symbol table
time/space trade-off
worst case

Key Concepts

■ An integral part of designing efficient software is the selection of appropriate algorithms to perform the task at hand.
■ Two of the criteria used in selecting algorithms for a given task are time and space efficiency. An algorithm's time efficiency determines how long it requires to run. An algorithm's space efficiency is a measure of how much primary and secondary memory it consumes.
■ Three simple sorting algorithms are the bubble sort, insertion sort, and selection sort. The latter minimizes the number of data interchanges that must be made at the expense of not being more efficient for data that are already partially ordered.
■ Pointer sort and radix sort are techniques to enhance the time efficiency of a sort at the expense of increased space requirements.
■ Three simple search algorithms are the sequential search, binary search, and key-to-address transformation technique.
■ Profiling is an empirical technique that can be used to measure an algorithm's efficiency when a big-O analysis is inconclusive.
■ Big-O analyses of sort and search algorithms discussed in this chapter are summarized in the following table, which is continued on the next page.

Algorithms	Time Efficiency	Additional Comments
Bubble sort	$O(n^2)$ comparisons and interchanges in worst case	Can be faster if input data already almost sorted.
Insertion sort	$O(n^2)$ comparisons and interchanges in worst case	Also can be faster if input data already almost sorted.
Selection sort	$O(n^2)$ comparisons, $O(n)$ interchanges in worst case	Not significantly faster if input data already almost sorted.

Algorithms	Time Efficiency	Additional Comments
Pointer sort	Reflects number of comparisons of method upon which it is layered	Though number of interchanges not reduced, amount of data swapped for each interchange is potentially less. Drawback is the additional memory required for pointers.
Radix sort	$O(n)$ comparisons and interchanges	Limited in the types of data upon which it works. Though $O(n)$, may have a large constant of proportionality, which can make the $O(n)$ rating a misleading one. For arrays, a large space requirement for storing sublists.
Sequential search	$O(n)$ probes into list in worst case	Most inefficient of search algorithms we will study, but still appropriate for small lists stored in main memory.
Binary search	$O(\log_2 n)$ probes in worst case	Drawbacks are that we must continually maintain a count of number of records in list and that the list must be maintained in sorted order.
Key-to-address transformation	$O(1)$ list probes	Not applicable for many types of keys. Potential space inefficiencies.

■ **Programming Problems and Projects**

1. Incorporate each of the observations cited in the Focus on Program Design section into the ListAllPrimes algorithm. For each successive modification to the algorithm, run a series of tests in which you use profiling to measure the efficiency of the resulting algorithm. Write up the results of your experimentation, addressing such issues as:
   a. Which technique produces the fastest runs?
   b. Does any technique appear to be an order of magnitude better in its time efficiency? Cite results from profiling to back up your claims in this regard.
   c. What trade-offs are involved in using these techniques to achieve a faster run-time?

2. Suppose that you know the keys in a list are arranged in increasing order. How could the sequential search algorithm presented in this chapter be improved with this knowledge? Rewrite the Pascal procedure to incorporate this improvement and then test your new procedure in a complete program.

3. Rewrite the binary search algorithm presented in this chapter with a splitting strategy other than halving. One possibility would be to use an interpolation strategy that would examine the target's distance from the current low and high pointers. This is more analogous to the way in which we look up names in a phone book. That is, for a name beginning with *S,* we do not open the phone book to the middle page but rather to a point approximately two-thirds of the way from the beginning of the book. Test run your program against a pure binary search and, through tracing the performance of each algorithm, determine whether there is any significant difference between the two techniques.

4. Repeat Problem 3, but change your algorithm so that, after the initial interpolative guess as to the location of the target, data locations are examined sequentially in an appropriate direction until the key is found or until it can be determined that the key is not in the list.

5. Consider a list of records for students at a university. The list includes fields for student name, credits taken, credits earned, and total grade points. Write a program that, based upon a user's request, will sort the list of records in ascending or descending order keying on one of the four fields within the record. For instance, the user might specify that the sort should proceed in descending order according to credits earned. As much as possible, try to refrain from having to write a separate sort procedure for each particular ordering and field. Experiment by developing different procedures based on each of the five sorting strategies discussed in this chapter.

6. Consider the same list of records as in Problem 5. Now write a procedure to sort the records in descending order by credits earned. Records having the same number of credits earned should be arranged in descending order by total grade points. Those with the same number of credits earned and total grade points should be arranged alphabetically by name. Incorporate this procedure into the complete program that you wrote for Problem 5. Experiment by developing different procedures based on each of the five sorting strategies discussed in this chapter.

7. Rewrite the pointer sort with the pointer array as a local variable instead of as a global variable. How would this affect a higher level procedure that calls upon the pointer sort? Illustrate by calling your new version of the pointer sort from a sample main program.

8. Merge the segmenting strategy described in Exercise 10 from Section 12.4 with the insertion sort, bubble sort, and selection sort algorithms. Empirically test how this affects the run-time of the sort on a file of 1,000 records. Does altering the number of segments affect the run-time?

9. Implement the binary search algorithm for a disk file containing approximately 1,000 records of the structure described in Problem 5.

10. Design a complete program to load information into the data base for employees of East Publishing Company described in Exercise 9 of Section 12.5. Then repeatedly call on a search procedure to retrieve the information associated with a given employee's identification key.

11. A *permutation* of the integers from 1 to N is an arrangement of these integers in which no repetition occurs. For example,

    3 1 4 5 2
    and
    5 3 2 4 1

    are two permutations of the integers from 1 to 5.

    Write a procedure to load an array indexed from 1 . . N with a randomly generated permutation of the integers from 1 to N. (If your version of Pascal does not have a random number generator, see Appendix 9, in which an algorithm for generating random numbers in standard Pascal is discussed.) This procedure should be an O(N) algorithm.

    Once you have written this procedure, use it to repeatedly load an array that is then passed to a sorting algorithm such as bubble, selection, or insertion sort. Add profiling counters to the sort algorithm to keep track of the number of comparisons and data interchanges performed by the algorithm. Average out these profiling counters over repeated invocations of the sort procedure and describe how these averages fit into the big-O analyses that were done in this chapter. Do you observe any discrepancies between your averages and the predictions of the big-O analyses? If so, attempt to explain them.

For any or all of Problems 12–16, design a program to answer the question posed. Then analyze the time efficiency of your program by using an appropriate combination of big-O analysis and profiling. Run your program to try to see the relationship between big-O classification and actual run-time as measured by a clock. Finally, for each program you implement, attempt to refine its run-time efficiency by making observations similar to those described in the Focus on Program Design section for this chapter.

12. In the first century A.D. the numbers were separated into "abundant" (such as 12, whose divisors have a sum greater than 12), "deficient" (such as 9, whose divisors have a sum less than 9), and "perfect" (such as 6, whose divisors add up to 6).

    In all cases, you do not include the number itself. For example, the only numbers that divide evenly into 6 are 1, 2, 3, and 6, and 6 = 1 + 2 + 3.

    Write a program to list all numbers between 2 and N and classify each as abundant, deficient, or perfect and keep track of the numbers in each class.

13. In the first century A.D., Nicomachus wrote a book entitled *Introduction Arithmetica*. In it, the question "How can the cubes be represented in terms of the natural numbers?" was answered by the statement that "Cubical numbers are always equal to the sum of successive odd numbers and can be represented this way." For example,

$$1^3 = 1 = 1$$
$$2^3 = 8 = 3 + 5$$
$$3^3 = 27 = 7 + 9 + 11$$
$$4^3 = 64 = 13 + 15 + 17 + 19$$

Write a program to find the successive odd numbers whose sum equals K^3 for K having the values from 1 to N.

14. A conjecture, first made by the mathematician Goldbach, whose proof has defied all attempts, is that "every even number larger than two can be written as the sum of two prime numbers." For example,

$$4 = 2 + 2$$
$$6 = 3 + 3$$
$$8 = 3 + 5$$
$$10 = 3 + 7$$
$$100 = 89 + 11$$

Write a program that determines for every even integer N with $2 \leq N$ two prime numbers P and Q such that N = P + Q.

15. A pair of numbers M and N are called "friendly" (or they are referred to as an "amicable pair") if the sum of all the divisors of M (excluding M) is equal to the number N and the sum of all the divisors of the number N (excluding N) is equal to M (M ≠ N). For example, the numbers 220 and 284 are an amicable pair because the only numbers that divide evenly into 220 (1, 2, 4, 5, 10, 11, 20, 22, 44, 55, and 110) add up to 284, and the only numbers that divide evenly into 284 (1, 2, 4, 71, and 142) add up to 220.

Write a program to find at least one other pair of amicable numbers. Be prepared to let your program search for some time.

16. A consequence of a famous theorem (of the mathematician Fermat) is the fact that

$$2^{(P-1)} \text{ MOD } P = 1$$

for every odd prime number P. An odd positive integer K satisfying

$$2^{(K-1)} \text{ MOD } K = 1$$

is called a pseudoprime. Write a program to determine a table of pseudoprimes and primes between 2 and N. How many pseudoprimes occur that are not prime numbers?

17. The importance of communication skills in "selling" a program to those who will eventually use it should not be underestimated. Keeping this in mind, write a user's guide for the program you developed in Problem 5. You should assume that the user is able to log-on to (or boot) the system, but beyond that has no other knowledge of how to run this or any other program. Remember that unless the user's guide is very, very clear *and* very, very concise, it will probably be thrown in a file drawer—and your program never used.

18. (For the mathematically inclined) In this chapter's Note of Interest on "Artificial Intelligence, the Complexity of Algorithms, and Parallel Processing," the claim is made that parallel processing may allow some exponential algorithms to run "in a reasonable time frame on larger data sets than can be accommodated on single-processor machines." Note that no claim is made that exponential algorithms will, *in general,* become practical on parallel processing machines.

Provide a carefully constructed argument in which you show that adding more processors to a machine can never result in an exponential algorithm's becoming practical for a wide variety of data sets. Your argument should explain the relationship between the number of processors used and the size of the data set that can be accommodated in reasonable time by the exponential algorithm. In essay form, justify the claim that the only real mathematical answer to solving a problem with an exponential algorithm in reasonable time is to discover a non-exponential algorithm that solves the same problem.

19. One of the drawbacks to the bubble sort algorithm is that a data set with just one item out of order can lead to worst-case performance for the algorithm. First, explain how this can happen.

    Because of this phenomenon, a variation on the bubble sort called a *shaker sort* will, on alternative passes through the array, put the largest entry into the last index and then the smallest entry into the first index. Explain how this idea can eliminate the worst-case performance of bubble sort on an array with just one item out of order. Then implement the shaker sort algorithm. Profile the number of comparisons and data interchanges in both the shaker sort and the bubble sort for a variety of data sets. Keep track of the empirical results you obtain from profiling these two algorithms. Finally, in a written report, compare the performance of these two algorithms based upon your empirical data. Be sure that your report addresses situations in which the shaker sort will actually perform worse than the plain bubble sort.

CHAPTER

13

Our life is frittered away by detail . . . Simplify, simplify.
Henry David Thoreau
1817–1862

Data: From Abstraction to Implementation

In the early chapters of this book, we discussed the control structures typically used in developing algorithms. We introduced techniques to describe such control structures before we wrote them in Pascal. For instance, we have used pseudocode to depict iterative and decisional considerations involved in algorithms. We've used modular structure charts to model the stepwise refinement process that subdivides a complex problem into smaller, more manageable problems.

We have not as yet developed similar techniques to conceptualize the data being manipulated by our algorithms. Although we have introduced increasingly complex structured data types such as arrays, records, and sets, these data types have been described directly by their declarations in Pascal. In this respect, our perspective on structured data has been somewhat restricted by considerations of what Pascal conveniently provides for us. We now wish to consider the problem of data (and particularly data structures) from a more abstract, conceptual perspective.

In Section 13.1, we discuss the importance of building abstract models of data and draw analogies to the model-building often done by engineers. In Section 13.2, we introduce the notion of an *abstract data type,* using strings as our initial example. The two-dimensional table and keyed list abstract data types are discussed in Sections 13.3 and 13.4 respectively. Each of these abstract data types is presented first as a conceptual object, equipped with formal properties and operations; various implementations of these abstractions are also discussed and evaluated. As we pursue our study of data structures in later chapters, the three abstract data types introduced in this chapter will continue to appear in applications.

Recall the goals that we have set for ourselves in Section 12.1: designing software systems that are large, reliable, flexible, expandable, and efficient.

■ 13.1
The Computer Scientist as a Builder of Models

Clearly, these are nontrivial. How can we have a reasonable chance of attaining them? The evolution of the answer to this question is an indication of how far the young discipline of computer science has progressed. In the late 1950s and early 1960s, there was a widely held belief that designing effective software systems was something akin to an occult art. That is, those who succeeded in designing such systems did so for a variety of mysterious reasons that could not be discerned. Their success, as opposed to the high percentage of software designers who failed, was somewhat mystical—similar to the spark of unfathomable inspiration that separates a great painter from a doodler.

Software Engineering

This view of successful software designers began to change in the latter part of the 1960s. As we saw in Chapter 1 (in Section 1.3), their methodology is typical of an engineer's approach to problem solving. What characterizes this engineering approach? To answer the question, consider the various phases involved in the successful development of a complex structure such as a bridge. First, the engineer gets together with the (often nontechnical) people who want the bridge built to learn about the function of the bridge: is it to be part of a heavily traveled urban freeway or a one-lane country road? From such meetings, the engineer develops a conceptual picture of the bridge. This picture exists as an abstract entity in the engineer's mind and perhaps in very rough form as an initial drawing. At this stage the engineer is working with ideas and ignoring most physical construction details; that is, the engineer is working with *abstractions*.

The next steps allow the engineer to come successively closer to the tangible implementation of the bridge as a physical structure. A miniature prototype of the bridge will be built. This model will allow the engineer to come face-to-face with many potential construction problems. It also provides a way to check whether the bridge will serve the needs specified by those who originally wanted the bridge built. This prototype will be followed by the development of detailed plans in blueprint form. Again this represents a step away from the purely abstract view of the bridge toward its actual implementation. These blueprints provide the essential details to the contractor who will eventually build the bridge. This contractor completes the entire process by implementing the engineer's plans in the physical structure of the bridge.

As we review the engineering approach, two important points should be made.

1. The entire process that culminates in the building of the bridge is a series of refinements from an abstract view of the bridge to its very tangible implementation. This process parallels very closely the phases in the development of a successful software system, beginning with a purely conceptual view of the problem to be solved and culminating with the implementation of a solution to that problem in (Pascal) program code.

2. This engineering approach truly places the emphasis on design issues. The design process is a very creative endeavor. Typically, during the design process, engineers will want to try out various combinations of possible options and will frequently change their minds about many significant aspects of the overall design. The time for such experimentation is when the design exists only in abstract form. That is when such creative considerations are possible—even encouraged—because of the openness of the conceptual model. As

the model draws nearer to actual implementation, a myriad of details specific to the chosen implementation make similar "what-if" reasoning expensive and often impossible for all practical purposes.

As early software developers analyzed frequent programming failures, they looked to the already established field of engineering for a paradigm. The engineering methodology of successively refining abstract models toward an eventual implementation made sense as an approach to developing programs also. A system designer who moves too quickly into the detailed coding phase of a programming project is analogous to an engineer who allows construction of a bridge to begin before adequate planning has been done. Both are heading for final results that are inelegant and riddled with serious flaws. However, because of the more rigorous design methodology embedded for years in their profession, engineers did not find themselves in this predicament as often as did programmers.

The solution seemed obvious: attempt to embed a similarly rigorous methodology into the discipline of computer science. Hence software engineering has developed into an important area of study within computer science. It represents an attempt to apply the structured methods of engineering to

A NOTE OF INTEREST

FORTRAN 53, 66, 77, 90: Keeping Pace with the Trends

In 1953 John Backus, now a fellow at the IBM Almaden Research Center and a winner of the prestigious Turing Award, invented FORTRAN (FORmula TRANslation), the first high-level programming language. It is interesting that, in an industry whose products typically become obsolete in three to five years, FORTRAN still remains the most widely used language for scientific and engineering applications. Part of the reason for this longevity is FORTRAN's reputation for generating extremely efficient machine code. Another ingredient is the fact that so much is invested in already written and optimized FORTRAN code; it would cost a fortune to redo all that work in another language.

Another important factor in the continuing saga of FORTRAN is its ability to keep pace with current trends in programming methodology. For instance, the first standards document for FORTRAN was written in 1966. The so-called FORTRAN 66 language emphasized modular program development by providing a fairly comprehensive facility for developing subroutines with parameter lists. Those subroutines could be compiled separately and then linked into a variety of applications. This led to the development of a large number of well-designed FORTRAN libraries for number-crunching tasks; these libraries are still used by a large core of programmers.

The trade press began to sound the death knell for FORTRAN when the structured programming "revolution" occurred in the late 1960s and early 1970s. FORTRAN 66 did not provide the necessary decisional and iterative control constructs to perform truly structured programming. The reaction of the FORTRAN community was to develop a new set of standards: FORTRAN 77.

FORTRAN 77 remained upward compatible with FORTRAN 66, thereby ensuring that existing programs would continue to work in the new language. However, it also introduced a variety of structured control constructs to answer its critics. The results? Most scientists and engineers chose to stick with FORTRAN instead of converting to upstart languages such as Pascal and C.

In the 1980s, data abstraction replaced structured programming as the computer science trend of the decade. As early as 1979, those who defined FORTRAN standards had begun to react. After 13 years of bitter negotiations, the new standard—FORTRAN 90—has emerged. Among the features of FORTRAN 90 are

IN and OUT subroutine parameters, a device that encourages the definition of an algorithm by formal preconditions and postconditions.

Modules that allow PUBLIC and PRIVATE access to data types. In particular, implementors may use these access facilities to hide the details of the data structures they are implementing in a module.

Recursive procedures.

New data types, including pointers.

Computer scientists (including the authors of this text) may continue to look upon FORTRAN with disdain, but that doesn't mean the language won't continue to be a survivor in the faddish computer industry. Though FORTRAN may not be a trendsetter, those who define this language have shown a knack for recognizing which trends will endure and then building these trends into the next set of standards for the language.

software development. At the same time, it fosters creativity by freeing the system designer from the details of program code and allowing work at a higher level of abstraction. Its goal is to assure that software is produced in a way that is cost-effective and reliable enough to deserve the increasing trust we are placing in it. We will follow its dictates as we begin our excursion into more advanced programming methodology.

Exercises 13.1

1. What are the characteristics of the software engineering approach to system development?

2. From a software design perspective, explain why it is less costly to consider changes in design when the system is being modeled abstractly instead of when it is being implemented. Be sure to specify what factors enter into your consideration of the term *costly*.

3. You are working on a large software project as part of a development team. Another member of the team maintains that doing a conceptual design for the software will only result in getting a late start in writing Pascal code and will make the project fall behind schedule. Write a tactful memorandum to this team member in which you provide a convincing argument against the team member's position.

■ ■ ■ ■

■ 13.2
The String Abstract Data Type

OBJECTIVES

- to understand what is involved in defining an abstract data type (ADT)
- to understand what is meant by data abstraction
- to see how ADTs facilitate conceptual model-building
- to understand what is meant by the implementation of an ADT
- to formally define and be able to use the string ADT
- to compare and contrast several implementations of the string ADT
- to see the motivation for three guidelines that govern the definition and implementation of all ADTs: the encapsulation principle, the ADT use rule, and the ADT implementation rule

The best way to clarify the conceptual, model-building approach is to provide an example. We wish to write a program to solve the problem involving strings that is presented in Example 13.1. (Look back to Section 7.5 to refresh your memory of strings.)

The high-level solution presented in Example 13.1 is totally independent of considerations regarding how the strings will be declared in Pascal. Such considerations are details of the eventual implementation of strings and must be completely avoided at this early stage of design. To consider them now would place severe restrictions on the design endeavor.

Instead, the high-level pseudocode takes the perspective that strings are abstract entities that are manipulated by abstract operations such as search, length, and delete. As we begin to refine this pseudocode, it is necessary to pin down exactly what we mean by these abstractions. That is, we must define the notion of a string precisely enough to insure that our pseudocode algorithm is unambiguous. Yet, our definition must be entirely conceptual: it must be free from specifics about how a string will be implemented in a programming language. Such a definition will allow us to refine our algorithm without worrying about details of how a string will eventually be declared.

To define a string, or any other data type, at such a conceptual level is to define it as an abstract data type (ADT).

> **Abstract data type (ADT).** An ADT is a collection of data objects that share a defined set of properties and operations for processing the objects.

In providing a definition for an ADT such as a string, we must specify both the properties and operations shared by all strings. Typically the properties are specified by describing the individual elements composing an object *and* the relationships among those individual elements. The operations may be specified using preconditions and postconditions. Similar to the way in which we defined a loop precondition in Section 4.6, a precondition for an

ADT operation must indicate what can be expected to be true before the operation is performed. A postcondition indicates what can be expected to be true after the operation is performed.

■ **EXAMPLE 13.1**

The program will read pairs of strings. The first string in a pair is designated the master string; the second is the target string. All occurrences of the target string in the master string should be removed from the master string, and the modified master string should then be written out. Thus, if the master string were "BAA-BAA BLACK SHEEP" and the target string were "BAA", the modified master string should be "- BLACK SHEEP".

We begin to design our solution to this problem by describing an algorithm in high-level pseudocode.

1. Read the MasterString
2. Read the TargetString
3. Search the MasterString from its beginning for an occurrence of the TargetString
4. **WHILE** an occurrence of TargetString is found
   4.1 Delete characters from the MasterString, beginning at the position where TargetString was found. Delete as many characters from the MasterString as there are characters in the length of TargetString
   4.2 Search the MasterString for an occurrence of the TargetString beginning at the position where the last match occurred
5. Write the (modified) MasterString

To illustrate defining ADTs, here is a definition of the string ADT. You will find Table 13.1 helpful in visualizing the effects of the operations described in the definition.

> **String.** A string is a finite sequence of characters excluding a specially-designated null character. (Hence non-null characters are the individual elements in a string.) By *sequence,* we mean that the characters in a string are related in linear fashion with an identifiable first element, second element, and so on. The *null character* is the character whose ordinal value is zero.

The operations associated with the string ADT are

Create operation	
Preconditions:	S is an arbitrary string in an unknown state.
Postconditions:	S is an initialized empty string.
ReadAString operation	
Preconditions:	S is a previously created string.
Postconditions:	S contains a sequence of characters read from standard input.
WriteAString operation	
Preconditions:	S is a previously created string with arbitrary contents.
Postconditions:	S is unchanged and its contents have been written to standard output.

Assign operation
  Preconditions: *Source* and *Destination* are previously created strings with arbitrary contents.
  Postconditions: *Destination* contains a copy of the string in *Source*.

Length operation
  Preconditions: *S* is a previously created string with arbitrary contents.
  Postconditions: *Length* returns the number of characters in *S*.

Concatenate operation
  Preconditions: *S* and *T* are two arbitrary, previously created strings.
  Postconditions: *S* has contents of *T* appended to it. *T* is left unchanged.

Substring operation
  Preconditions: *S* is an arbitrary, previously created string. *Start* and *Stop* represent positions within *S*, with *Start* <= *Stop*.
  Postconditions: *T* contains a copy of that portion of *S* beginning at *Start* and ending at *Stop*. If *Stop* > *Length*(*S*), then *T* terminates with the last character in *S*. If *Start* > *Length*(*S*), then *T* is empty.

Search operation
  Preconditions: *Master* and *Target* are two previously created strings with *Target* potentially contained in *Master*. *Start* represents a character position in *Master*.
  Postconditions: *Search* returns the position of the first occurrence of *Target* in *Master* at position *Start* or after. Zero is returned if *Target* is not found in this portion of *Master*.

Insert operation
  Preconditions: *S* and *T* are two arbitrary, previously created strings. *Place* represents the position where a copy of *T* is to be inserted in *S*.
  Postconditions: *S* has a copy of *T* inserted at position *Place*. If *Place* is greater than *Length*(*S*), *S* is not altered.

Delete operation
  Preconditions: *S* is an arbitrary, previously created string. *Start* and *Number* represent a starting position in *S* and a number of characters to delete from *S*, beginning at that position.
  Postconditions: *S* is returned with the designated characters removed. If the number of characters specified extends beyond the length of *S*, delete only through the end of the string.

Equal operation
  Preconditions: *S* and *T* are two arbitrary, previously created strings.
  Postconditions: *Equal* returns true if *S* and *T* match, character for character; otherwise it returns false.

LessThan operation
  Preconditions: *S* and *T* are two arbitrary, previously created strings.
  Postconditions: *LessThan* returns true if *S* precedes *T* in lexicographic order. Otherwise it returns false.

GreaterThan operation
  Preconditions: *S* and *T* are two arbitrary, previously created strings.
  Postconditions: *GreaterThan* returns true if *S* follows *T* in lexicographic order; otherwise false is returned.

Several comments are now in order. First, note that a string is described from a completely conceptual perspective: there is no hint of a realization of strings in a particular programming language. Second, the Create operation will be a standard operation for every ADT we discuss. It represents an initialization process which any object must undergo before it can be reliably acted upon by other operations. We have tried to emphasize this point in the definition of the string ADT by frequently mentioning the need for a "previously created" string in the precondition for an operation. In future ADT definitions we shall frequently leave this unsaid. Remember that the assumption is that no object is ever acted upon by any operation until it has been created.

Table 13.1 provides visual examples of the effect of the various string operations. You should study this table carefully before proceeding. Use it to make sure that you have a precise understanding of each string operation. To make this real; you may find it helps to think of operations you typically perform on text when editing with your favorite word processor.

TABLE 13.1
Examples of string operations

Create					
S		yields →	S		
???			"" (An empty string)		
Assign					
Source	Destination	yields →	Source	Destination	
"BIRD"	"DOG"		"BIRD"	"BIRD"	
Length					
S		yields →			
"BIRDS OF A FEATHER"			18		
Concatenate					
S	T	yields →	S		
"BIRD"	"DOG"		"BIRDDOG"		
Substring					
S	Start	Stop	yields →	T	
"TALE OF TWO CITIES"	4	7		"E OF"	
Search					
Master		Target	yields →		
"MODERN BASEBALL HISTORY"		"BASEBALL"		8	
Insert					
S	T	Place	yields →	S	
"SALT PEPPER"	" AND"	5		"SALT AND PEPPER"	
Delete					
S	Start	Number	yields →	S	
"SALT AND PEPPER"	5	9		"SALTER"	

TABLE 13.1
Examples of string operations (*continued*)

Equal

S	T	yields	
"WIG"	"WAG"	→	**false** since S and T differ in second position

LessThan

S	T	yields	
"WIG"	"WAG"	→	**true** since S precedes T in lexicographic ordering

GreaterThan

S	T	yields	
"WIG"	"WAG"	→	**false**

The separation of an ADT's specification from declarations and instructions that implement the data type in a particular language is called *data abstraction*. It turns out that some abstract data types will have very easy implementations in Pascal. The Pascal implementations of other abstract data types will be much less direct. At early stages of problem analysis, we don't want language considerations to influence our solution to the problem. Such considerations should come later, after we have accurately described the problem.

An abstract data type may be viewed as a formal description of data elements and relationships that are envisioned by the software engineer; it is thus a conceptual model. Ultimately, however, this model will be implemented in an appropriate computer language via declarations for the elements and relationships and instructions (often in the form of procedure/function calls) for the operations. At an even deeper level, the implementation of the abstract data type in a computer language is translated by the compiler into a physical, electronic representation on a particular computer.

This hierarchy of levels of abstraction is illustrated in Figure 13.1.

FIGURE 13.1
Levels of abstraction in specifying data

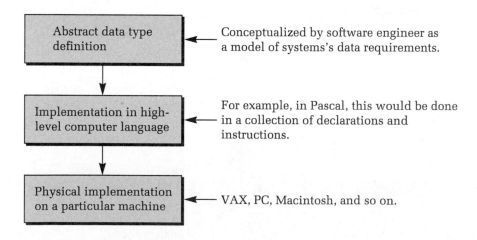

T **Pascal Interface for String Operations**

The first step in moving toward an implementation of an ADT in a particular computer language such as Pascal is to restate the operations that act on ADT objects as procedure and function headers. We shall call such a collection of procedure and function headers the Pascal *interface for an ADT*. Such an interface for the string ADT is given here. The

```
{ Given:                                              }
{ Task:                                               }
{ Return:                                             }
```

style of documentation that we have used throughout the text is used to describe the preconditions and postconditions of each operation.

```
PROCEDURE Create (VAR S : String);

  { Given:    An arbitrary string variable S in an unknown state   }
  { Task:     Initialize S                                         }
  { Return:   S as an initialized empty string.                   }

PROCEDURE ReadAString (VAR S : String);

  { Given:    A previously created string S with arbitrary contents }
  { Task:     Read a line of characters from the standard input source }
  {           into S                                               }
  { Return:   S contains the characters read from standard input.  }

PROCEDURE WriteAString (S : String);

  { Given:    A previously created string S with arbitrary contents }
  { Task:     Write the contents of S to standard output           }
  { Return:   Nothing.                                             }

PROCEDURE Assign (Source : String;
                  VAR Destination : String);

  { Given:    Source, a string with arbitrary contents            }
  { Task:     Copy the contents of Source to Destination          }
  { Return:   Destination contains copy of Source.                }

FUNCTION Length (S : String) : integer;

  { Given:    An arbitrary string S                               }
  { Task:     Count the number of non-null characters in S        }
  { Return:   The counted number of characters in S.              }

PROCEDURE Concatenate (VAR S : String;
                       T : String);

  { Given:    S and T, two arbitrary strings                      }
  { Task:     Append the contents of T to S                       }
  { Return:   S, with T appended to it.                           }

PROCEDURE Substring (S : String;
                     Start, Stop : integer;
                     VAR T : String);

  { Given:    S -- an arbitrary string                            }
  {           Start and Stop representing positions within S      }
  {           Assume Start <= Stop                                }
  { Task:     Copy the characters between positions Start and Stop in S }
  {           into T                                              }
  { Return:   T contains that portion of S beginning at Start and }
  {           ending at Stop.  If Stop > Length(S), then stop at last }
  {           character in S.  If Start > Length(S), then T is empty. }
```

```
FUNCTION Search (Master, Target : String;
                 Start : integer) : integer;

   { Given:    Master, Target --  two strings with Target potentially     }
   {           contained in Master                                         }
   {           Start -- representing a character position in Master        }
   { Task:     Master is to be searched for Target from the Start          }
   {           position onward                                             }
   { Return:   The position of the first occurrence of Target in           }
   {           Master at position Start or after.  Zero returned           }
   {           if Target is not found in this portion of Master.           }

PROCEDURE Insert (VAR S : String;
                  Place : integer;
                  T : String);

   { Given:    S and T -- two arbitrary strings                           }
   {           Place -- the position where T is to be inserted in S       }
   { Task:     Insert T into S                                            }
   { Return:   S with T inserted at position Place.  If Place is greater  }
   {           than Length(S), S is not altered.                          }

PROCEDURE Delete (VAR S : String;
                  Start, Number : integer);

   { Given:    S --  an arbitrary string                                  }
   {           Start, Number -- a starting position in S and a number     }
   {           of characters to delete from S, beginning at that position }
   { Task:     Delete the designated characters from S                    }
   { Return:   S with the designated characters removed.  If the number of}
   {           characters specified extends beyond Length(S), delete only }
   {           through the end of the string.                             }

FUNCTION Equal (S, T : String) : boolean;

   { Given:    S and T -- two arbitrary strings                           }
   { Task:     Test the two strings for equality                          }
   { Return:   True if S and T match, character for character;            }
   {           false otherwise.                                           }

FUNCTION LessThan (S, T : String) : boolean;

   { Given:    S and T -- two arbitrary strings                           }
   { Task:     Test if S precedes T in alphabetical order                 }
   { Return:   True if S precedes T in alphabetical order;                }
   {           false otherwise.                                           }

FUNCTION GreaterThan (S, T : String) : boolean;

   { Given:    S and T, two arbitrary strings                            }
   { Task:     Test if S follows T in alphabetical order                  }
   { Return:   True if S follows T in alphabetical order;                 }
   {           false otherwise.                                           }
```

The interface for an ADT provides the means by which we are allowed to use an ADT when programming in a particular language. The interface should parallel the formal operations of an ADT as closely as the programming language will allow. It is the view of the ADT given to those who want to use it. The implementor of an ADT must provide a package of procedures and functions that adheres to the interface.

Note that neither our definition nor our Pascal interface provides any clue about how the string ADT will be implemented. (You may be thinking that strings are packed arrays of characters. We will soon see that there are more efficient alternatives.) In effect both the definition and the interface tell us *what* a string is and *what* we can do with strings, but shield us from the detail of *how* the various operations are actually achieved. Drawing a distinction between *what* and *how* is a critical test of a good ADT definition and an interface to that ADT in a particular language. Both the definition and interface should be crystal clear in regard to the former and offer no insight with respect to the latter.

■ **EXAMPLE 13.2**

Refine the high-level pseudocode of Example 13.1 into a Pascal main program to remove all occurrences of a target string from a substring. Use only the operations provided by the Pascal interface for the string ADT; assume nothing about how strings will be implemented.

```
TYPE
  String = { The hidden implementation of string is put here };

VAR
  MasterString, TargetString : String;
  Continue : char;
  Pos : integer;
  .
  :
BEGIN { Main program }
  { Remember to "create" all strings before using them }
  Create (MasterString);
  Create (TargetString);
  { Allow user to run until 'N' is entered }
  REPEAT
    writeln ('Enter master string');
    ReadAString (MasterString);
    writeln ('Enter target string');
    ReadAString (TargetString);
    { Pos is index of first occurrence of Target in Master }
    Pos := Search (MasterString, TargetString, 1);
    WHILE Pos <> 0 DO
      BEGIN
        Delete (MasterString, Pos, Length (TargetString));
        { Set Pos to index of next occurrence }
        Pos := Search (MasterString, TargetString, Pos)
      END;
    { Pos is 0 when there are no more occurrences of Target in Master }
    WriteAString (MasterString);
    writeln;
    write ('Again? ');
    readln (Continue)
  UNTIL (Continue = 'N') OR (Continue = 'n')
END.
```

■   ■

Example 13.2 indicates that an algorithm that manipulates strings will not necessarily use all string operations. This is because an ADT is intended to be a general, reusable component. The string operations we have defined can be used in a wide variety of applications. Our goal in implementing the string ADT will be to insure this high degree of generality. If we can do that, we will no longer need to reinvent code for strings each time we need them in an application. This is the power of abstraction.

Implementations of the String ADT

We already have developed a main program that uses the string ADT at a high level of abstraction. We are now ready to switch gears, move to a lower level, and discuss how to implement this abstraction. It is critically important that our implementation does not force any change upon the logic at the higher level of abstraction.

Packed Array Implementation of the String ADT. Based upon our less formal study of strings in Section 7.5, our early inclination may be to declare the type string as a packed array of **char.**

```
CONST
   MaxStringLength = 132;    { Or other appropriate size limit }
TYPE
   String = PACKED ARRAY [1..MaxStringLength] of char;
```

If the length of a given string is less than MaxStringLength, then the null character **chr**(0) can be used to fill an array location marking the end of the string. Under this implementation, a string cannot have more than MaxString-Length characters; this recognizes the fact that implementations of ADTs may introduce limitations due to a particular programming language construct.

Given this **TYPE** declaration, we must now provide complete procedures or functions for each of the string operations. As illustrated in the following examples, the implementations must adhere precisely to the Pascal interface we have specified in our ADT definition.

■ **EXAMPLE 13.3**

Implement the Create operation for the packed array implementation of the string ADT.

```
PROCEDURE Create (VAR S : String);

  { Given:   An arbitrary string variable S in an unknown state        }
  { Task:    Initialize S                                              }
  { Return:  S as an initialized empty string                         }

  VAR
    K : integer;

  BEGIN
    { Since Length will rely on a null character at the end of a string  }
    { that is less than MaxStringLength characters, we will initialize   }
    { S[1] to chr(0).                                                   }
    S[1] := chr(0)
  END; { of PROCEDURE Create }
```

Implement the ReadAString operation for the packed array implementation of the string ADT.

```
PROCEDURE ReadAString (VAR S : String);

  { Given:    A previously created string S with arbitrary contents   }
  { Task:     Read a line of characters from the standard input source }
  {           into S                                                    }
  { Return:   S contains the characters read from standard input       }

  VAR
    K, L : integer;

BEGIN
  K := 0;
  WHILE NOT eoln AND ( K < MaxStringLength ) DO
    BEGIN
      K := K + 1;
      { K references the position to store the next character }
      read (S[K])
    END;
  readln;
  { Now put a null character at the end of a string containing less than }
  { MaxStringLength characters.                                          }
  IF K < MaxStringLength THEN
    S[K + 1] := chr(0)
END;  { of PROCEDURE ReadAString }
```

Implement the Length operation for the packed array implementation of the string ADT.

```
FUNCTION Length (S : String) : integer;

  { Given:    An arbitrary string S                              }
  { Task:     Count the number of characters in S                }
  { Return:   The counted number of characters in S              }

  VAR
    K : integer;
    FoundNull : boolean;

  BEGIN
    { Search through the string until encounter null character or reach }
    { MaxStringLength                                                    }
    K := 1;
    FoundNull := false;
    { Initially, K references first character in the string              }
    WHILE (K <= MaxStringLength) AND NOT FoundNull DO
      IF S[K] = chr(0) THEN
        FoundNull := true
      ELSE
        K := K + 1;
    { If null character encountered, K is 1 more than length of string   }
    IF FoundNull THEN
      Length := K - 1
    ELSE
      Length := MaxStringLength
  END; { of FUNCTION Length }
```

In this implementation of the Length operation, it is tempting to try to control the **WHILE** loop with a condition that doesn't require a Boolean:

```
WHILE (K <= MaxStringLength) AND (S[K] <> chr(0)) DO
```

Unfortunately, this fails in Pascal when K reaches (MaxStringLength + 1). Instead of exiting the loop, the (S[K] <> chr(0)) test will generate an "index out of range" error.

■   ■

■ **EXAMPLE 13.6**

Implement the Search operation for the packed array implementation of the string ADT.

The logic of this algorithm is somewhat more difficult than that of the operations we have implemented in earlier examples. It can be described in skeletal pseudocode as follows.

1. Initially, align the Target string against the leftmost portion of the Master string
2. **WHILE** a match can still be found **AND** a match has not yet been found **DO**
   2.1 Do a character-by-character comparison of Target against Master until you can conclude match or no match;
   2.2 **IF** no match **THEN**
       realign Target one position to the right against new portion of Master

Figure 13.2 depicts how this search would proceed for a particular example. In the first snapshot of that figure, we see the three-character string "KOM" aligned against the first three characters of "KOKOMO" with a mismatch occurring in position 3. In the second snapshot (the next time through the **WHILE** loop), "KOM" is aligned against "OKO" in "KOKOMO"; a mismatch occurs immediately. On the next iteration of the **WHILE** loop, a match is found, starting at position 3.

FIGURE 13.2
Trace of Search ("KOKOMO", "KOM", 1)

			1 2 3 4 5 6
Snapshot 1	Master	:	K O K O M O
	Target	:	K O M
			↑
			Mismatch in position 3
			1 2 3 4 5 6
Snapshot 2	Master	:	K O K O M O
	Target	:	K O M
			↑
			Mismatch in position 2
			1 2 3 4 5 6
Snapshot 3	Master	:	K O K O M O
	Target	:	K O M
			Successful match, return position 3

The refinement of the pseudocode into a full Pascal implementation yields the following function.

```
FUNCTION Search (Master, Target : String;
                 Start : integer) : integer;

   {  Given:    Master, Target --  two strings with Target potentially    }
   {            contained in Master                                        }
   {            Start -- representing a character position in Master       }
   {  Task:     Master is to be searched for Target from the Start         }
   {            position onward                                            }
   {  Return:   The position of the first occurrence of Target in          }
   {            Master at position Start or after.  Zero returned          }
   {            if Target is not found in this portion of Master.          }

   VAR
     M, T : integer;

   BEGIN
     { M references position in Master, T in Target }
     M := Start;
     T := 1;
     WHILE (T <= Length(Target)) AND
           (Length(Target) <= Length(Master) - Start  + 1) DO
       IF Master[M] = Target[T] THEN  {  Current characters match }
         BEGIN
           M := M + 1;
           T := T + 1
         END
       ELSE                           { No match, so realign }
         BEGIN
           Start := Start + 1;
           M := Start;
           T := 1
         END;
```

Upon mismatch at M, increment Start and realign to:

```
     { If T incremented beyond Length(Target), a match was found. }
     IF T > Length(Target) THEN
       Search := Start
     ELSE
       Search := 0
   END; { of FUNCTION Search }
```

The average performance of the implementation of the Search operation in Example 13.6 is worth analyzing. It is highly dependent on the nature of the text being processed. In normal English text, we would not expect to proceed very far into Target before determining that realignment is necessary. In the worst case, however, we may have to proceed all the way up to the last character of Target before determining that realignment is necessary. In such a case, the efficiency of Search deteriorates to O(Length(Master) * Length-(Target)). This worst case is illustrated in Figures 13.3 and 13.4.

FIGURE 13.3
Worst case for Search

```
Master   :   AAAAAAAAAAAH
Target   :   AAAAAAH
```

We must repeatedly compare characters
all the way up to H before realigning

FIGURE 13.4
Action of Search for data of Figure 13.3

```
Snapshot 1     Master   :   AAAAAAAAAAAH

               Target   :   AAAAAAH
                                  ↑
```
The first pass through Target ends here
with a mismatch of A and H

```
Snapshot 2     Master   :   AAAAAAAAAAAH

               Target   :   AAAAAAH
                              ↑
```
The second pass through Target starts here

```
Snapshot 3     Master   :   AAAAAAAAAAAH

               Target   :   AAAAAAH
                                   ↑
```
The second pass ends here after 6
matches of the A character followed by
a mismatch of A and H

■ **EXAMPLE 13.7**

Implement the Delete operation for the packed array implementation of the string ADT.

```
PROCEDURE Delete (VAR S : String;
                  Start, Number : integer);

{   Given:    S --  an arbitrary string                              }
{             Start, Number -- a starting position in S and a number  }
{             of characters to delete from S, beginning at that position }
{   Task:     Delete the designated characters from S                }
{   Return:   S with the designated characters removed.  If the number of }
{             characters specified extends beyond Length(S), delete only  }
{             through the end of the string.                          }

VAR
   J, EndOfString : integer;

BEGIN
   EndOfString := Length (S);
   IF (Number > 0) AND (Start <= EndOfString) THEN  { there is something to do }
      BEGIN
         { Adjust Number in case it takes us beyond end of string }
         IF Start + Number > EndOfString THEN
            Number := EndOfString - Start + 1;
         { First, shift text at end of string }
         FOR J := Start + Number TO EndOfString DO
            S[J - Number] := S[J];
         { Then, add the null character to mark end of string }
         S[EndOfString - Number + 1] := chr(0)
      END
END; { of PROCEDURE Delete }
```

Examples 13.3 – 13.7 have provided a start toward a full implementation of the string ADT using a **PACKED ARRAY OF char.** Notice how all of these procedures and functions must be coordinated with each other. Also notice that the limit on a string's length imposed by the constant MaxStringLength keeps this implementation from being a perfect model of the ADT. When you complete the implementation in the Exercises, you will have to be careful to point out how this limitation can affect the result of certain operations.

Now, consider efficiency. Why might the packed array implementation of strings not be appropriate for certain applications? The Length operation in this implementation is $O(\text{MaxStringLength})$. This means that higher-level applications that repeatedly invoke the Length function (such as that in Example 13.2) might be slowed considerably by using this implementation. We will now examine another implementation of strings that can provide $O(1)$ efficiency for the Length operation.

Embedded Length Implementation of the String ADT. Our strategy in this implementation will be to associate an integer with each packed array of **char.** The integer will be used to maintain the current length of the string. Thus, a string will now be implemented as two data items: an **integer** length and a **PACKED ARRAY OF char.** However, it is imperative that high-level logic using the string ADT still be able to view a string as a single abstract entity. Toward this end, we will encapsulate the data items comprising a string into a record.

```
CONST
  MaxStringLength = 132;
TYPE
  String = RECORD
              StringText : PACKED ARRAY [1..MaxStringLength] OF char;
              Length     : integer
           END;
```

Such encapsulation is relatively simple and is extremely important to programming with abstract data types. Without it, high-level procedures would not be able to identify the ADT as a single, unified entity. To stress the critical role played by encapsulation of ADTs, we formalize it in the following principle.

Encapsulation principle. Whenever the implementation of an ADT involves several data items, these data items should be grouped into a record by which the ADT is identified to high-level logic.

Adhering to this principle, we can now carry out this new implementation of the string ADT. Implementations of five operations are provided in Examples 13.8–13.12; the rest are left for you in the Exercises.

■ EXAMPLE 13.8

Implement the Create operation for the embedded length implementation of the string ADT.

```
PROCEDURE Create (VAR S : String);

   {  Given:    An arbitrary string variable S in an unknown state     }
   {  Task:     Initialize S                                           }
   {  Return:   S as an initialized empty string.                      }

   BEGIN
     S.Length := 0
   END;  { of PROCEDURE Create  }
```

■

■ EXAMPLE 13.9

Implement the ReadAString operation for the embedded length implementation of the string ADT.

```
PROCEDURE ReadAString (VAR S : String);

   {  Given:    A previously created string S with arbitrary contents    }
   {  Task:     Read a line of characters from the standard input source }
   {            into S                                                   }
   {  Return:   S contains the characters read from standard input.      }

   VAR
     K : integer;
```

```
BEGIN
  K := 0;
  WHILE NOT eoln AND (K < MaxStringLength) DO
    BEGIN
      K := K + 1;
      { K references the position to store the next character }
      read (S.StringText[K])
    END;
  { K has recorded the length of the string }
  readln;
  S.Length := K
END;  { of PROCEDURE ReadAString }
```

■   ■

■ **EXAMPLE 13.10**

Implement the Length operation for the embedded length implementation of the string ADT.

```
FUNCTION Length (S : String) : integer;

  { Given:    An arbitrary string S                                    }
  { Task:     Count the number of characters in S, up to and including }
  {           the last nonblank character                              }
  { Return:   The counted number of characters in S.                   }

  BEGIN
    Length := S.Length
  END;  { of FUNCTION Length  }
```

It is particularly noteworthy that the embedded length implementation achieves an $O(1)$ efficiency for this operation. Compare this to the efficiency of Example 13.5, in which a packed array implementation was used.

■   ■

■ **EXAMPLE 13.11**

Implement the Search operation for the embedded length implementation of the string ADT.

```
FUNCTION Search (Master, Target : String;
                 Start : integer) : integer;

  { Given:    Master, Target --  two strings with Target potentially   }
  {           contained in Master                                      }
  {           Start -- representing a character position in Master      }
  { Task:     Master is to be searched for Target from the Start        }
  {           position onward                                          }
  { Return:   The position of the first occurrence of Target in         }
  {           Master at position Start or after.  Zero returned         }
  {           if Target is not found in this portion of Master.        }

  VAR
    M, T : integer;
```

```
BEGIN
  {M references position in Master, T in Target }
  M := Start;
  T := 1;
  WHILE (T <= Target.Length) AND
        (Target.Length <= Master.Length - Start  + 1) DO
    IF Master.StringText[M] = Target.StringText[T] THEN { Current characters
                                                          match }
      BEGIN
        M := M + 1;
        T := T + 1
      END
    ELSE                         { No match, so realign }
      BEGIN
        Start := Start + 1;
        M := Start;
        T := 1
      END;
  { If T is incremented beyond Length(Target), a match was found }
  IF T > Target.Length THEN
    Search := Start
  ELSE
    Search := 0
END; { of FUNCTION Search }
```

■

■ EXAMPLE 13.12

Implement the Delete operation for the embedded length implementation of the string ADT.

```
PROCEDURE Delete (VAR S : String;
                  Start, Number : integer);

{  Given:    S --  an arbitrary string                              }
{            Start, Number -- a starting position in S and a number  }
{            of characters to delete from S, beginning at that position }
{  Task:     Delete the designated characters from S                }
{  Return:   S with the designated characters removed.  If the number of }
{            characters specified extends beyond Length(S), delete only  }
{            through the end of the string.                         }

VAR
  J  : integer;

BEGIN
  IF (Number > 0) AND (Start <= S.Length) THEN { there is something to do }
    BEGIN
      { Adjust Number in case it takes us beyond end of string }
      IF Start + Number > S.Length THEN
        Number := S.Length - Start + 1;
      { Shift text at end of string }
      FOR J := Start + Number TO S.Length DO
        S.StringText[J - Number] := S.StringText[J];
      { Compute the new length }
      S.Length := S.Length - Number
    END
END; { of PROCEDURE Delete }
```

■

Compare the collection of operations implemented in Examples 13.8–13.12 to the corresponding operations implemented for the packed array string implementation in Examples 13.3–13.7. It should be apparent that the embedded length implementation offers greater overall elegance and time efficiency—at the expense of the space associated with the embedded integer length field.

Observations on ADTs and Their Implementations

We can now make some observations about the relationship between ADTs and their various implementations. These observations represent general conclusions that may be applied to all of the ADTs we will study. Here, we illustrate them with the string ADT and its two implementations.

First, high-level logic, such as that presented in Example 13.2, cannot distinguish between different implementations of an ADT. We should be able to plug any implementation of an ADT into high-level logic without changing that logic. This shielding of high-level logic from any implementation details is summarized in the following two rules.

> **ADT use rule.** Algorithms that use an abstract data type should only access variables of that ADT through the operations provided in the ADT definition.

> **ADT implementation rule.** An implementation of an abstract data type must provide an interface that is entirely consistent with the operations specified in the ADT's definition.

T If users and implementors of ADTs comply fully with these rules, all high-level logic will be plug-compatible with all possible implementations of an ADT. The implementation is said to exhibit *information hiding:* it hides information from higher level logic. This is the ideal. In some situations, the syntax of Pascal will force us into compromising the ideal. We will be careful to point those out and hold such compromises to a minimum.

Second, if high-level logic cannot tell the difference between two implementations, then why would we ever want more than one implementation of an ADT? Part of the answer lies in the different time and space efficiencies that various implementations provide. For instance, the high-level logic of Example 13.2 iteratively calls the string Length function. Because this function has $O(1)$ time efficiency in the embedded length implementation and $O(\text{MaxStringLength})$ time efficiency in the packed array implementation, the former implementation represents a more efficient choice for this application.

Another aspect of the answer to this question is the limitations that an implementation may impose as it attempts to model an abstraction. For instance, both the packed array and embedded length implementations of the string ADT impose a maximum string length limitation. When we study linked lists in Chapter 15, we will be able to provide an implementation of the string ADT that does not have this maximum length restriction. You may also explore a more flexible implementation of strings, the *workspace-index method,* in the problems at the end of the chapter.

The availability of different implementations of an ADT—all compatible from their outward interface—gives rise to some very exciting prospects for the software design endeavor we have been describing in this chapter. The implication is that, at a high level, we design complex software by constructing a model that operates only on abstract data types. Once we have a high-level model with which we are satisfied, we can plug in the best implementation of the ADT for our particular application.

If formalized big-O analysis is inconclusive about which is the best implementation, it is relatively painless to experiment with several implementations. Different implementations can be plugged in, we can empirically profile their performance, and then choose the best. With the ADT approach, all this experimentation can be done without any modification of the high-level model.

Exercises 13.2

1. Using only the operations provided by the string ADT, write a high-level algorithm in Pascal to scan a master string and replace all occurrences of a given target string by a specified replacement string. For example, if the master string is

   "MARY MARY QUITE CONTRARY"

   and the target and replacement string are "ARY" and "ARTHA", then the resulting master string would be

   "MARTHA MARTHA QUITE CONTRARTHA"

2. Consider the following version of the Pascal code that appeared in Example 13.2. The shaded line has been modified. From an ADT perspective, what is wrong with this version of the code?

```
TYPE
  String = { The hidden implementation of string is put here };

VAR
  MasterString, TargetString: String;
  Continue: char;
  Pos: integer;
  .
  .
  .

BEGIN { Main program }
  Create (MasterString);
  Create (TargetString);
  REPEAT
    writeln ('Enter master string');
    ReadAString (MasterString);
    writeln ('Enter target string');
    ReadAString (TargetString);
    Pos := Search (MasterString, TargetString, 1);
    WHILE Pos <> 0 DO
      BEGIN
        Delete (MasterString, Pos, TargetString.Length);
        Pos := Search (MasterString, TargetString, Pos)
      END;
    WriteAString (MasterString);
    writeln;
    write ('Again? ');
    readln (Continue)
  UNTIL (Continue = 'N') OR (Continue = 'n')
END.
```

3. The algorithm of Example 13.2 will work for both the packed array and embedded length implementations of the string ADT without the two initial calls

to the Create operation. Why shouldn't we remove these calls from the algorithm?

4. Examples 13.3–13.7 provided implementations for five string operations under the packed array implementation. Write implementations of the remaining operations that are consistent with the implementations provided in these examples. If the implementation of a particular operation is limited by the imposition of a maximum string length, be sure that your documentation for that operation specifies precisely what will happen in all circumstances.

5. Analyze the efficiency of each of the operations that you implemented in Exercise 4.

6. Examples 13.8–13.12 provided implementation for five string operations under the embedded length implementation. Write implementations of the remaining operations that are consistent with the implementations provided in these examples. If the implementation of a particular operation is limited by the imposition of a maximum string length, be sure that your documentation for that operation specifies precisely what will happen in all circumstances.

7. Analyze the efficiency of each of the operations that you implemented in Exercise 6.

8. What is the big-O efficiency of the algorithm in Example 13.2? Assume that the packed array implementation of strings is used. Does your answer change if the embedded length implementation is used?

9. Suppose that the type CharSet is defined to be **SET OF char.** Consider the following interface as an addition to those operations that we have already defined for the string ADT.

```
PROCEDURE ExtractWord (N : integer;
                       S : String;
                       WordDelims : CharSet;
                       VAR NthWord : String);

{ Given:    S, an arbitrary string, to be viewed as composed of individual  }
{           words;                                                           }
{           N, designating the Nth word in S;                               }
{           WordDelims, the set of characters that determine where words     }
{           begin and end in the string.                                     }
{ Task:     Scan S for the Nth word in it.                                   }
{ Return:   NthWord contains the Nth word in S.  If S contains fewer than    }
{           N words, the NthWord is the empty string.                        }
```

For example, if S is "For score and seven years ago, our forefathers", then ExtractWord (6, S, [' ', ',', '.'], NthWord) should return "ago" in the NthWord parameter. (Note what what may look to you like a line of apostrophes and commas is actually the Pascal notation for a blank (' '), a comma (','), and a period ('.').)

   a. Write an implementation of this operation using the packed array implementation of strings.
   b. Write an implementation of this operation using the embedded length implementation of strings.
   c. Analyze the efficiency of each of the implementations you've written in this exercise.

10. In the implementations of the string Search operation (Examples 13.6 and 13.11), the Length operation is repeatedly called. Rewrite each of these implementations in a fashion that does not unnecessarily call the Length operation. Then, in a brief essay, discuss how these changes affect the time efficiency of each example.

■ ■ ■ ■

■ 13.3
The Two-Dimensional Table Abstract Data Type

The model-building approach described in the first two sections of this chapter is critical when you design software to solve problems that are not initially well-defined in terms of the data type required. You might argue that as authors, we should pose only well-defined problems. But remember that real programs are not meant to solve textbook problems; they are meant to solve real problems. Typically these problems are posed by people who may have little knowledge of computers and programming; their statements of the problem are not likely to be as specific as "Use a two-dimensional array to . . .". The inherent vagueness of many initial problems makes it imperative that you be able to model data at an abstract level.

To illustrate, suppose that you are computer operations manager for Wing-and-a-Prayer Airlines. In that role, you receive the following important memorandum:

MEMORANDUM
Wing-and-a-Prayer-Airlines

TO: Computer Operations Manager
FROM: Vice President in Charge of Scheduling
DATE: August 28, 1994
RE: Matching flights and pilots

As you know, we presently have 1,500 flights (with identification numbers 3000 to 4499) and employ 1,400 pilots (with identification numbers 1000–2399) to fly them. However, because of factors such as type of airplane, amount of pilot experience, pilot geographic locations, and FAA regulations, each of our pilots qualifies to fly on only a relatively small percentage of flights. To help our schedulers, we frequently need to answer questions such as the following:

1. Given a flight, what are identification numbers of the pilots qualified to fly it?
2. Given a pilot number, what are the flight numbers that pilot is qualified to fly?
3. Given a flight number and a pilot number, do we have a match? In other words, is the pilot specified qualified for the particular flight?

Right now our schedulers attempt to answer such questions by time-consuming manual methods. I'm sure that you can easily computerize this task for them. Thanks in advance for your help in this matter.

Faced with this charge, one abstract conceptualization you might consider is that of the table pictured in Table 13.2. Here a **true** entry in a particular row and column indicates the pilot is qualified for the corresponding flight; **false** indicates the pilot is not qualified.

■ EXAMPLE 13.13

Given the two-dimensional table of Table 13.2 as a model of the pilot/flight data for Wing-and-a-Prayer, formulate a high-level algorithm to respond to the three types of queries posed in the memo.

TABLE 13.2
Flight/pilot data base for Wing-and-a-Prayer Airlines

Pilot Number	Flight Number					
	3000	3001	3002	...	4498	4499
1000	true	false	false	...	true	false
1001	false	false	false	...	true	true
1002	true	true	false	...	false	false
.	.	.	.	...	.	.
.	.	.	.	...	.	.
.	.	.	.	...	.	.
2398	false	true	false	...	false	false
2399	false	false	true	...	false	true

1. Initialize the table to all **false**s
2. Load the table by reading pairs of numbers representing a pilot and a flight for which the pilot is qualified. Assign **true** to these locations.
3. **REPEAT**
   3.1 Read a Query
   3.2 **CASE** Query **OF**
       3.2.1   Query is a flight number:
           3.2.1.1 Travel along corresponding column, writing out number of each qualified pilot
       3.2.2   Query is a pilot number
           3.2.2.1 Travel along corresponding row, writing out each flight for which the pilot is qualified
       3.2.3   Query is flight and pilot number
           3.2.3.1 Access information at that row and column
           3.2.3.2 **IF true THEN**
                 write ('QUALIFIED')
                ELSE
                 write ('NOT QUALIFIED')

To refine the algorithm presented in Example 13.13, we must provide a formal definition for the two-dimensional table ADT.

Two-dimensional table. A two-dimensional table is a collection of data of the same type arranged as a rectangular grid. Any entry in the grid may be specified by giving its row and column position. The rows and columns themselves are each indexed by a separate contiguous range of some ordinal data type, such as the integers.

The operations performed on a table are

Create operation
   Preconditions: *T* is a two-dimensional table in an unreliable state.
   Postconditions: *T* is a two-dimensional table with all row and column entries initialized to a designated default value.

Retrieve operation

Preconditions:	*T* is an arbitrary two-dimensional table that has been previously created. *R* is a particular row index within the contiguous range of valid row indices for the table. *C* is similarly a particular column index.
Postconditions:	Retrieve returns the value stored in row *R*, column *C* of table *T* without affecting the table at all.

Assign operation

Preconditions:	*T* is a previously created two-dimensional table. *R* and *C* are row and column indices respectively for table *T*. *V* is a value of the type stored at each table location.
Postconditions:	The value *V* is stored at row *R*, column *C* of table *T*.

The effect of each of these operations may be illustrated using the pilot-flight table of Table 13.2. Here the data at each grid location is Boolean. The Create operation for this table returns a table with all **false** entries—the default value for a particular pilot and flight. The Assign operation is then used to place the value **true** at specified table locations. The Assign operation also can be used to place a **false** value in a particular row and column of the table. Finally, the Retrieve operation returns the Boolean value stored at a given location in the grid. For instance, Retrieve for row index 1001 and column index 4498 yields **true** in Table 13.2. For row 2398 and column 3000 this operation yields **false.**

Although Table 13.2 illustrates a two-dimensional table with Boolean data stored at each grid location, you should recognize that not all two-dimensional tables will store Boolean data. The only requirements are that data items at each grid location in a given table are of the same type and that there is a well-defined default value to which all grid locations are set as a result of the Create operation.

To move toward an implementation of the two-dimensional table ADT in Pascal we must translate the precondition and postcondition specifications for table operations into Pascal procedure and function headers. Such a Pascal interface for the two-dimensional table ADT is provided next.

Pascal Interface for Two-Dimensional Table

```
PROCEDURE Create (VAR T: TwoDTable);

  { Given:   T, a two-dimensional table in an unreliable state      }
  { Task:    Initialize the table to the default value for table entries }
  { Return:  T, an initialized table                                }

FUNCTION Retrieve (T : TwoDTable;
                   R, C : integer) : TableData;

  { Given:   T, an arbitrary two-dimensional table, which as been   }
  {          previously created                                     }
  { Task:    Retrieve the value at row R and column C of the table  }
  { Return:  The value retrieved                                    }
```

```
      PROCEDURE Assign (VAR T : TwoDTable;
                            R, C : integer;
                            V : TableData);

      {  Given:    T, an arbitrary two-dimensional table, which has been    }
      {            previously created                                       }
      {  Task:     Assign value V to row R, column C of the table           }
      {  Return:   T, with value V assigned to the designated row and column }
```

■ **EXAMPLE 13.14**

Given this formal definition and Pascal interface for the two-dimensional table ADT, refine the algorithm of Example 13.13 into a Pascal main program. Be sure to follow the ADT use rule.

```
CONST
   LowFlight = 3000;
   HighFlight = 4499;
   LowPilot = 1000;
   HighPilot = 2399;

TYPE
   FlightRange = LowFlight..HighFlight;
   PilotRange = LowPilot..HightPilot;
   TableData = boolean;
   TwoDTable = { The hidden implementation of two-dimensional table would
                 appear here }

VAR
   Pilot : PilotRange;
   Flight : FlightRange;
   PFInfo : TwoDTable;
   Query : Char;
   PFFile : text;

BEGIN { Main program }
   Create (PFInfo);
   reset(PFFile);

   { The next loop reads in all pilot/flight pairs from the file and "loads"
     them in the table by calling on the Assign operation. }

   WHILE NOT eof(PFData) DO
      BEGIN
         readln(PFFile, Pilot, Flight);
         Assign(PFInfo, Pilot, Flight, true)
      END;

   { Then enter the loop that fields the three types of queries.  Note that
     the Retrieve operation is used extensively to process these queries }

   REPEAT
      write('Query type [F]light, [P]ilot, [B]oth, or [Q]uit-->');
      readln(Query);
      CASE Query OF
         'F', 'f':
            BEGIN
               write('Enter flight number-->');
               readln(Flight);
               writeln('Qualified pilots are:');
```

```
            FOR Pilot := LowPilot TO HighPilot DO
              IF Retrieve (PFInfo, Pilot, Flight) THEN
                writeln(Pilot)
          END;
       'P', 'p':
          BEGIN
            write('Enter pilot number-->');
            readln(Pilot);
            writeln('(S)he may pilot flights');
            FOR Flight := LowFlight TO HighFlight DO
              IF Retrieve (PFInfo, Pilot, Flight) THEN
                writeln(Flight)
          END;
       'B', 'b':
          BEGIN
            write('Enter pilot and flight number-->');
            readln(Pilot, Flight);
            IF Retrieve (PFInfo, Pilot, Flight) THEN
              writeln('QUALIFIED')
            ELSE
              writeln('NOT QUALIFIED')
          END;
       'Q', 'q':
          BEGIN
          END { Quit Option }
      END { Case }
   UNTIL (Query = 'Q') OR (Query = 'q')
END.
```

Implementations of the Two-Dimensional Table ADT

Example 13.14 has provided a complete main program that makes no assumptions about the implementation of the underlying ADT. Only after completing such high-level logic is it appropriate to begin thinking about implementation details. In the case of the two-dimensional table ADT, it is tempting to use the implementation that is provided directly by Pascal arrays. In particular, the following declarations would be suitable for Table 13.2.

```
CONST
  LowFlight = 3000;
  HighFlight = 4499;
  LowPilot = 1000;
  HighPilot = 2399;
    .
    .
    .

TYPE
  FlightRange = LowFlight..HighFlight;
  PilotRange = LowPilot..HighPilot;
  TwoDTable = ARRAY [PilotRange,FlightRange] OF boolean;
    .
    .
    .

VAR
  PFInfo : TwoDTable;
```

We wish to discuss two issues with respect to this implementation of Wing-and-a-Prayer's table. First, when Pascal provides an obvious and direct implementation of the abstract data type, how does Pascal itself implement your declarations? The designers of your Pascal compiler must translate the declarations and instructions in your Pascal programs into a suitable representation in the internal machine code of your computer. Recall that this deeper level implementation issue was alluded to in Figure 13.1 though not discussed in detail. We now more fully realize that the designers of a compiler are concerned with implementing abstractions from a perspective that is different than that of the users of the compiler. In the case of a two-dimensional table, the implementation issue facing designers of a compiler is how to represent a two-dimensional structure on a machine in which units of computer memory are inevitably arranged as a one-dimensional sequence of cells.

Second, after discussing the compiler's implementation of your declaration for a two-dimensional table, we will want to evaluate that implementation. How efficient is the compiler's implementation of your structure with respect to time and space considerations? This is a particularly important question for exceedingly large tables such as the one we need in our current Wing-and-a-Prayer application. We will see that the compiler's implementation of a two-dimensional table may be, at best, inefficient and, at worst, totally impractical for our application.

Row-Major Implementation of Two-Dimensional Arrays

To simplify the discussion that follows, instead of working with the huge amount of information in Table 13.2, let's work with the following more manageable declaration:

```
VAR
    Numbers : ARRAY [1..6,1..5] OF integer;
```

A sample assignment of values to the table Numbers is pictured in Figure 13.5.

FIGURE 13.5
Values in the ARRAY Numbers

	Column				
	1	2	3	4	5
1	10	18	42	6	14
2	13	19	8	1	44
Row 3	63	80	12	90	51
4	16	13	9	8	4
5	12	11	12	14	83
6	1	4	18	99	90

From the perspective of the compiler writer, a two-dimensional array declaration represents a level of abstraction because internally computer memory is not arranged as a rectangular grid. Instead, computer memory locations are arranged in a linear sequence beginning with location 1, and then 2, 3, 4, and so on. Because of this, there must be manipulations behind the scenes when a program requests the entry in the 5th row and 4th column of a two-dimensional array (as highlighted in Figure 13.5). Essentially, the coordinates of the 5th row and the 4th column must be transformed into an address within this linear sequence of memory locations. The nature of the transformation is dependent upon how the designers of the compiler have chosen to implement the application programmer's mental image of rows and columns within the linear sequence of memory locations.

Suppose that our compiler has chosen to store the 30 entries in the two-dimensional array Numbers as indicated in Figure 13.6.

FIGURE 13.6
Linear storage of data from Figure 13.5

| 10 | 18 | 42 | 6 | 14 | 13 | 19 | 8 | 1 | 44 | 63 | 80 | 12 | 90 | 51 | 16 | 13 | 9 | 8 | 4 | 12 | 11 | 12 | 14 | 83 | 1 | 4 | 18 | 99 | 90 |

According to this arrangement, the first row would take up the first five locations in the list allocated for the array; the second row, the second five locations; and so on. The entry in the 5th row and 4th column would in fact be located in the 24th position within the list.

In this array the Kth row and the Jth column must be transformed into the

$$(5 * (K - 1) + J)\text{th}$$

position in the list. In even more general terms, if NCol is the number of columns in the array, then the entry in the Kth row and Jth column is given as the

$$(NCol * (K - 1) + J)\text{th}$$

entry in the linear list corresponding to the two-dimensional array. Most high-level computer languages implement two-dimensional arrays (and higher) in such a *row-major* fashion and do so in a way that is largely hidden from the applications programmer. However, all programmers should be aware that multidimensional arrays are inherently less efficient than one-dimensional arrays because of the computations required by the transformation from row/column coordinates to linear address each time an entry in the array is accessed. Such a transformation is often called a *mapping function*.

If you've programmed in FORTRAN, you will recall that, when initializing a two-dimensional array via a data statement, the entries for the array must be listed by column; that is, first column, second column, and so on. This is because FORTRAN is one of the few high-level languages to store a multidimensional array in *column-major* order, as indicated in Figure 13.7.

FIGURE 13.7
Column-major storage of data from Figure 13.5

| 10 | 13 | 63 | 16 | 12 | 1 | 18 | 19 | 80 | 13 | 11 | 4 | 42 | 8 | 12 | 9 | 12 | 18 | 6 | 1 | 90 | 8 | 14 | 99 | 14 | 44 | 51 | 4 | 83 | 90 |

To access the entry in the Kth row and the Jth column of a two-dimensional array stored in column-major order, the transformation

$$NRow * (J - 1) + K$$

is required; NRow represents the number of rows in the array. The fact that this transformation requires the number of rows but not the number of columns also explains why many FORTRAN compilers insist that a subroutine be informed of the number of rows in an array passed down from a calling program but not the number of columns.

The Sparse Table Problem

From what has been said about the compiler's possible implementation strategy for a two-dimensional array, it should be clear that we might be paying a very high price in memory for the flight-pilot table of Wing-and-a-Prayer Airlines. In general, for a two-dimensional table with NRow rows and NCol columns, the space efficiency of a row-major implementation is O(NRow * NCol).

In particular, we would be charged for 2,100,000 (1,500 × 1,400) Boolean memory locations if our Pascal compiler implemented the array in row-major fashion. Since many Pascal compilers allocate one byte of storage for each Boolean location, your seemingly simple declaration of a two-dimensional table may require over two megabytes (two million bytes) of memory. Depending on your computer, this is quite likely to exceed the amount of memory a program is allowed to consume. Thus, we have a real space-efficiency problem. Our Pascal declarations for the Wing-and-a-Prayer table may be nothing more than a wishful pipe dream that is not remotely realizable on our machine.

Does this mean that you cannot implement the conceptual flight/pilot table? For the sake of your job (as computer operations manager), we hope not! Rather, this illustrates that designers must be acutely aware of how the compiler may "automatically" implement certain concepts for them and then they must be prepared to implement them differently when the compiler's strategy fails. In this instance, we propose to take advantage of an additional fact given to us in the specifications. That is, any given pilot qualifies to fly on only a relatively small percentage of flights. This means that relatively few entries in Table 13.2 will be **true.** A table such as this, in which a high percentage of the data storage locations will be one uniform value (**false** in this case), is called a *sparse table*. We can use the sparseness of **true** values in the table to implement it by strategies other than row-major or column-major form (and hence save your job). However, note that, regardless of the implementation we choose, we are still working with a table at the abstract level.

An Alternative Implementation for a Sparse Table

We are seeking an implementation that will conserve memory by not actually storing the high percentage of **false** entries that appear in the conceptual table. One possibility is simply to store a list of ordered pairs of integers: the first entry in the pair is a pilot number and the second is a flight number. One of those pairs is on the list for each **true** entry in the conceptual table. Conversely, a **false** entry in the conceptual table does not get a (pilot, flight) pair on the ordered list. Hence, a probe into the Kth row and the Jth column of the conceptual table returns **true** if an appropriate search algorithm can find the pair (K, J) on the list implementation of the table; it returns **false** otherwise.

What have we gained? For each **true** value in the conceptual table, we now must store two integers—so there is actually a loss in this regard. However, for the much higher percentage of **false** values, we now store absolutely nothing on the list.

The Example, Exercises, and Problems that follow have you explore this suggested implementation for a sparse table. In designing a system based on this implementation, you will discover certain run-time inefficiencies that can be at least partially overcome by using the more sophisticated implementation strategies to be introduced in Chapters 15 and 20.

Sparse Tables and Language Compilers

Two-dimensional tables play a crucial role in many language compilers. To see why, consider a problem substantially easier than writing a compiler. Suppose that you are reading a stream of characters intended to identify one of the twelve months. You are to read these characters until you have read enough to uniquely identify a month or until you can conclude that the stream of characters will not identify any month. Thus, upon reading 'D', you could declare the month to be DECEMBER. However, you would have to read the three characters 'JUL' before you could declare the month to be JULY. Moreover, if you read the three characters 'JUK', you could declare that the input stream cannot possibly identify any month. (Note that the problem we are de-

1. state := start
2. **REPEAT**
   2.1 read(c)
   2.2 state := table [state,c]
3. **UNTIL eoln**
      OR state = error
      OR state is one of months jan..dec

Why is our month-recognition algorithm a relevant issue with respect to the topics we have discussed in this chapter? First note that our two-dimensional table clearly embodies the sparse table concept. In this particular sparse table, the vast majority of entries are the error state. Hence, our algorithm to recognize a month

State	Letter																									
	A	B	C	D	E	F	G	H	I	J	K	L	M	N	O	P	Q	R	S	T	U	V	W	X	Y	Z
start	a			dec		feb				j			m	nov	oct				sep							
j	jan																				ju					
m	ma																									
a															apr						aug					
ju												jul	jun													
ma																		mar							may	

scribing does not demand that the input stream be a completely correct spelling of some month, only that the input stream begin with characters that uniquely define a month. Thus, both 'DECEMBER' and 'DIZZY' would be viewed as input streams that uniquely identify the month DECEMBER because you could quit processing characters as soon as the leading 'D' is read.)

The driving force behind an algorithm that would allow you to process an input stream in the fashion just described is a two-dimensional table such as that pictured here. The columns of this table are indexed by the letters of the alphabet, and the rows are indexed by the various "frames of mind" (officially called states) in which you may find yourself after having read a portion of the input stream. For instance, this table indicates that, if you begin processing characters in the *start* state and read the character 'J', then you switch to the *j* state. One in the *j* state, you expect to encounter either 'A' or 'U' as the next character, which will respectively cause you to switch to the *jan* state or the *ju* State. In addition to the states that index the rows of this table, we also have the states

jan, feb, mar, apr, may, jun, jul, aug, sept, oct, nov, dec

which correspond to your having recognized a uniquely defined month. The state *error* is indicated by the vacant entries in the table.

Given this table, the algorithm to recognize a month is extremely compact. It follows in pseudocode form.

from an incoming stream of characters is dependent on our ability to implement a sparse table.

Second, this particular example is representative, on a small scale, of an entire class of algorithms for recognizing a valid sequence of symbols arriving on an input stream. In fact, this is precisely what must be done by a compiler for a high-level language such as Pascal. That is, it must successfully read the symbols in the source program that serves as its input stream and declare the sequence of symbols valid or invalid according to the rules of the language. Many compilers are actually driven by a table similar to the one we used for our month recognition algorithm. One of the major differences in such a compiler table is the increased size of the table due to the relative complexity of the language (versus our simple month recognition example). Hence, an efficient representation of a sparse matrix can be crucial to determining whether or not a compiler can process source programs at a reasonable rate of speed.

Algorithms that are driven by a table such as the one we have discussed here are known as finite state machines, or finite state automata. We will examine another application of finite state machines in Chapter 14. For a more general treatment, we encourage you to consult Chapter 10 of *Discrete Mathematics* (second edition) by Richard Johnsonbaugh (New York: Macmillan, 1990).

■ **EXAMPLE 13.15**

The following declarations would provide a suitable basis for implementing Wing-and-a-Prayer's sparse pilot/flight table in the fashion just discussed.

```
CONST
   LowFlight = 3000;
   HighFlight = 4499;
   LowPilot = 1000;
   HighPilot = 2399;
   MaxPairs = 6000;        { Or other appropriate constant indicating the  }
                           { maximum overall number of pilot/flight        }
                           { qualification pairs.                          }

   HighPilotPlus1 = 2400;  { Used as sentinel.  }

TYPE
   FlightRange = LowFlight .. HighFlight;
   PilotRange = LowPilot .. HighPilot;
   PilotRangePlus1 = LowPilot .. HighPilotPlus1;
   PFSparseTableRec = RECORD
                         PilotNum : PilotRangePlus1;
                         FlightNum : FlightRange
                      END;
   TwoDTable = ARRAY [1..MaxPairs] OF PFSparseTableRec;
   TableData = boolean;
```

The following function could be used to implement the retrieve operation for the sparse table.

```
FUNCTION Retrieve (T : TwoDTable;
                   R, C : integer) : TableData;

{ Given:    T, an arbitrary two-dimensional table                          }
{ Task:     Retrieve the value at row R and column C of the table          }
{ Return:   The value retrieved                                            }

{ In this implementation of TwoDTable for the Wing-and-a-Prayer pilot-     }
{ flight data base, an array of (pilot, flight) pairs with HighPilotPlus1  }
{ in the PilotNum field of the last record of the array is used to         }
{ implement the conceptual table of boolean values.                       }

VAR
   K : integer;
   Found : boolean;

BEGIN
   Found := false;
   K := 1;
   WHILE NOT Found AND (T[K].PilotNum <> HighPilotPlus1) DO
      { K proceeds sequentially through the list of pilot/flight pairs }
      IF (T[K].PilotNum = R) AND (T[K].FlightNum = C) THEN
         Found := true
      ELSE
         K := K + 1;
   { If loop exited because T[K].PilotNum = HighPilotPlus1, Found will be false }
   Retrieve := Found
END;  { of FUNCTION Retrieve }
```

■   ■

In Section 12.4, we introduced the notion of the time/space trade-off. The Retrieve operation implemented in Example 13.15 clearly illustrates this trade-off. To avoid storage of a multitude of default **false** values, we are paying the price of a sequential search each time the Retrieve operation is invoked. In the Exercises, you will use big-O notation to analyze more formally the efficiency of the two-dimensional table implementation we have suggested here. You will also explore using the binary search as an alternate means of searching the list of pilot/flight pairs used in this implementation. More efficient implementations will be presented in future chapters as we examine more sophisticated data structures.

Exercises 13.3

1. Show by an example how the row-major and column-major implementations for a two-dimensional array would differ.

2. What would the mapping function be for a three-dimensional table implemented in row-major form? Can you generalize this to tables of even higher dimensions?

3. Give some examples (besides the flight/pilot data base) of applications that, at the abstract level, call for a sparse table.

4. Is a two-dimensional M by M array more or less efficient than a one-dimensional array of extent M^2? Explain your answer.

5. Many languages, such as Pascal, allow subscripts for an arbitrary range of ordinal values, not necessarily always integers starting at 1. Specify how this would affect the mapping functions discussed in this chapter to translate two-dimensional table coordinates into linear list positions.

6. The two-dimensional array in Pascal is an obvious, built-in implementation of the two-dimensional table ADT. Write full versions of the Create, Retrieve, and Assign operations for this implementation. Assume that TableData is of **TYPE** integer with a default value of zero. Be sure that you follow the dictates of the ADT implementation rule introduced in Section 13.2.

Exercises 7–12 refer to the alternate implementation for a sparse table discussed at the end of this section and in Example 13.15.

7. Given the declarations and implementation of the Retrieve operation in Example 13.15, write the **PROCEDURE** for the corresponding Create operation.

8. Given the declarations and implementation of the Retrieve operation in Example 13.15, write the **PROCEDURE** for the corresponding Assign operation.

9. Rewrite the implementation of the retrieve operation in Example 13.15 to use a modified version of the binary search algorithm. How must your answers to Exercises 7 and 8 change to accommodate this?

10. Using big-O notation, analyze the time efficiency of the retrieve and assign operations you have implemented in Exercise 9.

11. Analyze the space efficiency of the sparse table implementation you have provided in your answers to Exercise 9 versus a row-major implementation of the same table. What percentage of values would have to be false for your implementation to be more space efficient than a row-major implementation?

12. Discuss why the binary search technique you employed in Exercise 9 would be a poor strategy for a two-dimensional table that is frequently changed by the Assign operation. Compare and contrast the effectiveness of the binary search strategy versus the sequential search strategy used in Example 13.15. Which of the strategies would you use for the pilot/flight table needed by Wing-and-a-Prayer Airlines? Defend you choice in a short essay.

13. Implementations of ADTs may not achieve a perfect representation of the abstraction they embody. The definition of a two-dimensional table ADT por-

trays a rectangular grid with no inherent limit on the number of rows and number of columns. In what sense are the implementations of the two-dimensional table ADT discussed in this section (row-major, column-major, and Example 13.15) imperfect representations of this concept?

14. How would the sparse table implementation discussed at the end of this section have to be adjusted for non-Boolean data?

15. In what sense does the radix sort algorithm discussed in Section 15.4 require a sparse table?

16. In the Pascal interface for a two-dimensional table, the table T is given as a value parameter. From an efficiency perspective, explain why it would be better to have T be a **VAR** parameter. What are the arguments against T being a **VAR** parameter?

■ ■ ■ ■

■ 13.4
The Keyed List Abstract Data Type

OBJECTIVES

- to understand and be able to use the definition of the keyed list ADT
- to understand how procedures can be used as parameters to other procedures
- to consider several different implementations of the keyed list ADT
- to recognize the shortcomings of each of these implementations and recognize the need for more sophisticated implementations to be studied in future chapters.

In Chapter 12, we approached sorting and searching from the perspective of manipulating an array of records, each of which had a designated key field. So many data processing activities organize records by key fields that it would seem worth our while to view a list of such records from an abstract perspective. Doing so may allow us to bring the power of abstraction to bear in a variety of applications. Toward that end, we introduce the following definition of the *keyed list* ADT.

Keyed list. A keyed list is a collection of records, each of which is the same type. The records in the list are organized around a designated key field in each record. This key field must take on a unique value for each record and have a well-defined ordering in the sense that, for two different values a and b, we can determine whether $a < b$ or $a > b$. Clearly, data types such as integer, real, and string meet this ordering criterion. The records are to be viewed as arranged in logical order by this key field.

The operations for a keyed list are

Create operation	
Preconditions:	L is an arbitrary keyed list in an unreliable state.
Postconditions:	L is initialized to the empty list.
Add operation	
Preconditions:	L is a keyed list. *Item* is a record to be inserted in L. *Success* is a Boolean variable.
Postconditions:	If possible, L has *Item* inserted with respect to the ordering on the key field. *Success* is returned as **true** to signal this insertion. If *Item* cannot be inserted in L, *Success* is returned as **false,** and the list is left unchanged.

Delete operation
Preconditions: *L* is a keyed list. *Target* is a key value associated with a record to be removed from the list *L*. *Success* is a Boolean variable.

Postconditions: If the record with the *Target* key can be found in *L*, it is removed from *L* and *Success* is set to **true.** Otherwise, *Success* is set to **false** and *L* is left unchanged.

Retrieve operation
Preconditions: *L* is a keyed list, *Target* is a key value to be found in *L*, *Success* is a Boolean variable.

Postconditions: If the *Target* can be found in *L*, then *Item* contains the record associated with *Target* and *Success* is set to **true.** Otherwise, *Success* is set to **false,** and *Item's* contents are unreliable. In either case, the keyed list *L* is left unchanged.

TraverseInOrder operation
Preconditions: *L* is a keyed list and *ProcessNode* is an algorithmic process which can be applied to each data node on the list *L*.

Postconditions: Each data node in *L* is visited in the order determined by the key field. As each node is visited, *ProcessNode* is applied to it.

The effect of each list operation is highlighted in Figure 13.8 for a list in which the key field is a string representing a last name. For such a keyed list, the natural ordering would be alphabetical by last name. Note from the figure that all list operations preserve this order. It is also apparent from this figure that the TraverseInOrder operation is a bit different than other ADT opera-

FIGURE 13.8
Keyed List Operations

Key	OtherData
ALLEN	4.32
CARSON	6.19
SMITH	3.00
WILSON	7.38

Add MICHAEL
(as logical third entry in list)

Key	OtherData
ALLEN	4.32
CARSON	6.19
MICHAEL	5.64
SMITH	3.00
WILSON	7.38

ALLEN	4.32
CARSON	6.19
SMITH	3.00
WILSON	7.38

Retrieve SMITH

SMITH	3.00

SMITH's record is found and returned in specified variable.

ALLEN	4.32
CARSON	6.19
SMITH	3.00
WILSON	7.38

Delete SMITH

ALLEN	4.32
CARSON	6.19
WILSON	7.38

ALLEN	4.32
CARSON	6.19
SMITH	3.00
WILSON	7.38

TransversInOrder,
applying ProcessNode which adds 1 to OtherData

ALLEN	5.32
CARSON	7.19
SMITH	4.00
WILSON	8.38

tions we have discussed. Not only is this operation given a data structure to act upon, but it is also given a process that acts upon each node in the data structure. In the figure, this process adds 1 to the OtherData field in each list node. If, however, we wanted an alphabetical listing of each record in the list, we could also achieve this by using the TraverseInOrder operation — providing it with a ProcessNode algorithm that printed each record in an appropriate format.

Pascal Interface for Keyed List ADT

The ability of the TraverseInOrder operation to receive not only data in the form of a keyed list but also an algorithmic process that can be applied to each node in the list will complicate the translation of keyed list operations into Pascal procedure headers. This complication is reflected in the following Pascal interface. The **PROCEDURE** TraverseInOrder in this interface must have a parameter which is itself a procedure. The syntax for doing this in Pascal is discussed after the interface.

```
TYPE
    KeyType = { An appropriate type for the key field in list records    }
    OtherDataType = { An appropriate type for the other data associated with  }
                    { each key field                                      }
    ListNode = RECORD
                    Key : KeyType;
                    OtherData : OtherDataType
               END;
    KeyedList = { The hidden implementation }

PROCEDURE Create(VAR L : KeyedList);

    {  Given:    An arbitrary keyed list variable L          }
    {  Task:     Initialize the list                         }
    {  Return:   L initialized to the empty list.            }

PROCEDURE Add (VAR L : KeyedList;
                   Item : ListNode;
                   VAR Success : boolean);

    {  Given:    A keyed list L ordered by Key field         }
    {            and an Item to be inserted in that list     }
    {  Task:     Insert the item into the list               }
    {  Return:   L with Item inserted with respect to the    }
    {            ordering on the key field.  If L cannot be  }
    {            inserted, Success is returned as false, and }
    {            the list is left unchanged.  Otherwise,     }
    {            Success returned as true.                   }

PROCEDURE Delete (VAR L : KeyedList;
                      Target : KeyType;
                      VAR Success : boolean);

    {  Given:    A keyed list L ordered by Key field          }
    {            and a Target key to be removed from          }
    {            that list                                    }
    {  Task:     Remove the record with key field matching    }
    {            Target from the list                         }
    {  Return:   L with the Target key removed.  If the Target }
    {            cannot be found, Success is returned as       }
    {            false.  Otherwise, it is returned as true.    }
```

```
PROCEDURE Retrieve (L : KeyedList;
                    Target : KeyType;
                    VAR Item : ListNode;
                    VAR Success : boolean);

{  Given:    A keyed list L ordered by Key field         }
{            and a Target key to be found in that list.   }
{  Task:     Find the record with key field matching      }
{            Target's value                               }
{  Return:   The data associated with Target in Item.  If }
{            the Target cannot be found, then Success is   }
{            returned as false; otherwise true.           }

PROCEDURE TraverseInOrder (VAR L : KeyedList;
                           PROCEDURE ProcessNode (VAR Item : ListNode));

{  Given:    Keyed list L                                 }
{  Task:     Traverse the list in the order determined by }
{            the key field, applying the procedure        }
{            ProcessNode to each record in the list       }
{  Return:   L with each node affected by ProcessNode.    }
```

Procedures and Functions as Parameters

[T] The TraverseInOrder operation in the preceding interface employs a Pascal technique that we have not seen before. Notice that one of the formal parameters in the interface for **PROCEDURE** TraverseInOrder is a procedure. The formal parameter

```
PROCEDURE ProcessNode(VAR Item: ListNode)
```

will allow us to pass to TraverseInOrder an actual parameter which is itself a procedure. This actual parameter is the one that is applied to each item in the keyed list L. By passing in different procedures in this parameter slot, we may have different processes applied to each item in the list. The following example should help clarify this usage.

■ **EXAMPLE 13.16**

Write procedures to print an item in a keyed list and add 1 to a real Other-Data field in a keyed list. Then pass these procedures to the TraverseInOrder operation to print each item in a list, add 1 to the OtherData field of each item, and finally print each item again with its updated OtherData field.

```
CONST
   StringLength = 15;

TYPE
   String = PACKED ARRAY [1..StringLength] OF char;
   KeyType = String;
   OtherDataType = real;
   ListNode = RECORD
                 Key : KeyType;
                 OtherData : OtherDataType
              END;
   KeyedList = { The hidden implementation }

VAR
   L : KeyedList;
```

```
PROCEDURE PrintNode (VAR Item : ListNode);

   { Given:   One node's data to be printed  }
   { Return:  The node with its data printed }

   BEGIN
     writeln (Item.Key:20, Item.OtherData:5)
   END;

PROCEDURE AddOne (VAR Item : ListNode);

   { Given:   One node in a keyed list       }
   { Task:    Add one to the OtherData field }
   {          in that node                   }
   { Return:  The list node with an updated  }
   {          OtherData field                }

   BEGIN
     Item.OtherData := Item.OtherData + 1.0
   END;
            .
            .
            .
   { In main program }
   TraverseInOrder (L, PrintNode);
   TraverseInOrder (L, AddOne);
   TraverseInOrder (L, PrintNode);
```

A procedure passed as a parameter to another procedure must have a formal parameter list that matches, in number and type of arguments, the declaration in the formal parameter list of the receiving procedure. For instance, in Example 13.16, the formal parameter lists of PrintNode and Add-One must match that of the formal procedure parameter ProcessNode.

Judicious use of procedural parameters can enhance a procedure's ability to be of general use. For instance, the procedural parameter in the Traverse-InOrder operation allows this single procedure to perform a variety of actions on each item in a keyed list. Which action is invoked on a particular call to TraverseInOrder is determined by the actual parameter passed in the ProcessNode slot.

Example 13.16 illustrated how you call a procedure with another procedure as parameter, but it did not show the details of writing the procedure that is invoked. These details are uncovered in the next example.

■ EXAMPLE 13.17

Write a sorting procedure that makes its comparison using a general Precedes relationship passed in as a parameter. No specific < or > comparison should appear in the sort procedure's definition. Then use this procedure in a program to sort an array of integers first in descending order and then in ascending order.

```
PROGRAM ProcedureParameter(input,output);

   { Demonstrate the use of procedure parameters in Pascal.        }
   { A sort procedure is written which sorts values in the order   }
   { determined by a function parameter passed to the Sort procedure. }
```

```
CONST
  IndexLimit = 100;

TYPE
  ElementType = integer;
  SortArray = ARRAY [1..IndexLimit] of ElementType;

VAR
  Size, J : integer;
  Data : SortArray;

FUNCTION GreaterThan (A, B : ElementType) : boolean;
  { Used as the actual parameter for Precedes }

  { Given:    Two values to compare                           }
  { Task:     Compare the two values using a "greater than"    }
  {           relation appropriate for ElementType            }
  { Return:   True if A is greater than B and false otherwise }

  BEGIN
    GreaterThan := (A > B)
  END; { of FUNCTION GreaterThan  }

FUNCTION LessThan (A, B : ElementType) : boolean;
  { Used as the actual parameter for Precedes }

  { Given:    Two values to compare                           }
  { Task:     Compare the two values using a "less than"       }
  {           relation appropriate for ElementType            }
  { Return:   True if A is less than B and false otherwise    }

  BEGIN
    LessThan := (A < B)
  END; { of FUNCTION LessThan  }

{ Insertion sort algorithm }
PROCEDURE Sort ( VAR A : SortArray;
                 N : integer;
                 Precedes : FUNCTION (A, B: ElementType) : boolean );

  { Given:    Array of values to be returned in order        }
  {           according to Precedes relation and N, the       }
  {           number of values in array                       }
  { Task:     Sort the array using the insertion sort         }
  {           algorithm                                       }
  { Return:   The array arranged in order by the Precedes      }
  {           relation that is passed in as a parameter       }

  VAR
    K, J : integer;
    ItemToInsert : ElementType;
    StillLooking : boolean;

  BEGIN  { Sort }
    FOR K := 2 TO N DO
      BEGIN
        { Walk backwards through list, looking for slot to insert A[K] }
        ItemToInsert := A[K];
        J := K - 1;
        StillLooking := true;
        WHILE (J >= 1) AND StillLooking DO
          { ItemToInsert is compared to A[J] }
          IF Precedes(ItemToInsert, A[J]) THEN   { Here use Precedes parameter }
```

```
            BEGIN
              A[J + 1] := A[J];
              J := J - 1
            END
          ELSE
            StillLooking := false;
        { Upon leaving loop, J + 1 is the index where ItemToInsert belongs }
        A[J + 1] := ItemToInsert
      END { FOR }
  END; { of PROCEDURE Sort }

BEGIN { Main program to demonstrate procedure call to sort in descending order }
  write('How many values to sort? ');
  readln(Size);
  FOR J := 1 TO Size DO
    read(Data[J]);
  readln;
  { Sample call to produce a sort of integers in descending order }
  Sort (Data, Size, GreaterThan);
  writeln ('Descending Order');
  FOR J := 1 TO Size DO
    writeln(Data[J]:6);
  { Sample call to produce a sort of integers in ascending order }
  Sort (Data, Size, LessThan);
  writeln ('Ascending Order');
  FOR J := 1 TO Size DO
    writeln(Data[J]:6)
END.
```

The shaded lines in the previous code indicate how the function parameter is used in the definition of **PROCEDURE** Sort and, then, how Sort is invoked with actual GreaterThan and LessThan relationships.

A sample run of this program would appear as:

```
How many values to sort?  4
12
70
34
88
Descending Order
    88
    70
    34
    12
Ascending Order
    12
    34
    70
    88
```

Don't underestimate the generality of the Sort procedure in Example 13.17. It can be used for much more than merely sorting integers in ascending or descending order. For instance, if ElementType were a more complex record structure, we could define suitable actual parameters for the Precedes relationship to sort an array of records in ascending order based on one field and in descending order based on another field. You will explore these more general uses on the Sort procedure in the Exercises.

Implementations of the Keyed List ADT

We needed the preceding digression on procedure and function parameters because of the operations presented in the definition of the keyed list ADT. Now that we understand the use of such parameters, it is time to again direct our attention to this ADT and its implementations. We will consider two implementations in this section; each will have major shortcomings from an efficiency perspective. In future chapters, we will explore more sophisticated implementations that can improve these inefficiencies.

Implementation 1: Physically Ordered Array with Binary Search. The strategy of this implementation is to maintain an array of records in physical order by key field. Bundled with the array is a count of the number of records in the structure. Hence, the declaration for the encapsulated implementation of the keyed list is

```
CONST
   MaxListSize =  {  An appropriate choice for the maximum number of records
                     that can be stored in the list at any one time  }

TYPE
   KeyType =  {  An appropriate type for the key field in list records  }
   OtherDataType =  {  An appropriate type for the other data associated with
                       each key field  }
   ListNode = RECORD
                 Key : KeyType;
                 OtherData : OtherDataType
              END;
   KeyedList = RECORD
                 DataRec : ARRAY [1..MaxListSize] OF ListNode;
                 NumberRec : integer
               END;
```

A keyed list L with four records in it is depicted in Figure 13.9.

FIGURE 13.9

Implementation of keyed list by physically ordered array

KeyedList

NumberRec		DataRec	
4		Key	OtherData
	1	BAKER	4.32
	2	DOWNING	6.82
	3	,MILLER	10.49
	4	SMITH	7.33
	5		
	6		
	7		
	8		
	9		
MaxListSize = 10			

To add a record to the list in this figure, we must

1. Search for the first record in the list that has a key field value greater than that of the item we are adding.

2. Then, beginning with that record, move all records down one slot in the array.
3. Finally, insert the new item into the array slot that has been vacated and increase by 1 the number of records.

These actions are highlighted in Figure 13.10. Carefully study that figure in conjunction with examining the code in Example 13.18.

FIGURE 13.10
Add PATRICK to list of Figure 13.9

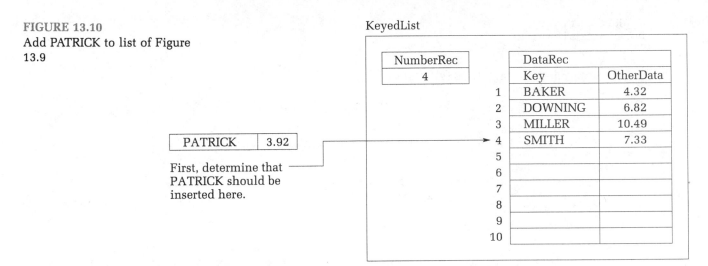

First, determine that PATRICK should be inserted here.

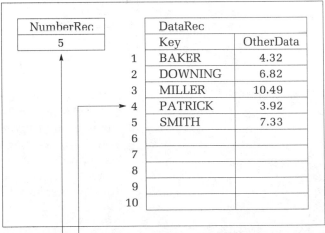

Vacate the slot by physically moving records down.

Complete insertion of PATRICK and update counter.

■ EXAMPLE 13.18

Write complete Pascal code for the Add operation. Be sure to follow the ADT implementation rule.

```
PROCEDURE Add (VAR L : KeyedList;
               Item : ListNode;
               VAR Success : boolean);
```

```
{  Given:     A keyed list L ordered by Key field         }
{             and an Item to be inserted in that list      }
{  Task:      Insert the item into the list                }
{  Return:    L with Item inserted with respect to the     }
{             ordering on the key field.  If L cannot be   }
{             inserted, Success is returned as false, and  }
{             the list is left unchanged.  Otherwise,      }
{             Success returned as true.                    }

VAR
  J, K : integer;
  Done : boolean;

BEGIN
  IF L.NumberRec = MaxListSize THEN
    Success := false
  ELSE
    BEGIN
      Success := true;
      { Find insertion slot for Item in physically ordered list }
      K := 1;
      Done := false;
      WHILE (K <= L.NumberRec) AND NOT Done DO
        { Compare Item's Key to that at index K }
        IF L.DataRec[K].Key > Item.Key THEN
          Done := true   { K is insertion slot }
        ELSE
          K := K + 1;
      { From insertion slot down, each record must be moved down one slot }
      FOR J := L.NumberRec DOWNTO K DO
        L.DataRec[J + 1] := L.DataRec[J];
      L.DataRec[K] := Item;
      L.NumberRec := L.NumberRec + 1
    END
END; { of PROCEDURE Add }
```

Because the implementation of Add always maintains the array in physical order by key field, the Retrieve operation can be implemented using the binary search algorithm. (Note that a variation of the binary search algorithm could also be used to find the insertion slot in **PROCEDURE** Add; you will develop this variation in the Exercises.)

We complete our discussion of this implementation by illustrating how the TraverseInOrder procedure would use its procedure parameter.

■ EXAMPLE 13.19

Write complete Pascal code for the TraverseInOrder operation. Be sure to obey the ADT implementation rule.

```
PROCEDURE TraverseInOrder (VAR L : KeyedList;
                           PROCEDURE ProcessNode (VAR Item : List-
                             Node));
  {  Given:   Keyed list L                              }
  {  Task:    Traverse the list in the order determined by  }
  {           the key field, applying the procedure        }
  {           ProcessNode to each record in the list       }
  {  Return:  L with each node affected by ProcessNode     }

  VAR
    J : integer;
```

```
BEGIN
  FOR J := 1 TO L.NumberRec DO
    ProcessNode (L.DataRec[J])
END; { of PROCEDURE TraverseInOrder }
```

Implementation 2: Unordered Array with Sequential Search and Pointer Sort. Our second implementation attempts to eliminate the inefficiency involved in moving a potentially large number of records each time an Add or Delete is performed. The encapsulation of the keyed list ADT still includes an array of records and a counter. However, now when a record is added, it is merely added at the end of the list. Figure 13.11 illustrates this strategy.

FIGURE 13.11
Addition of records using unordered array implementation

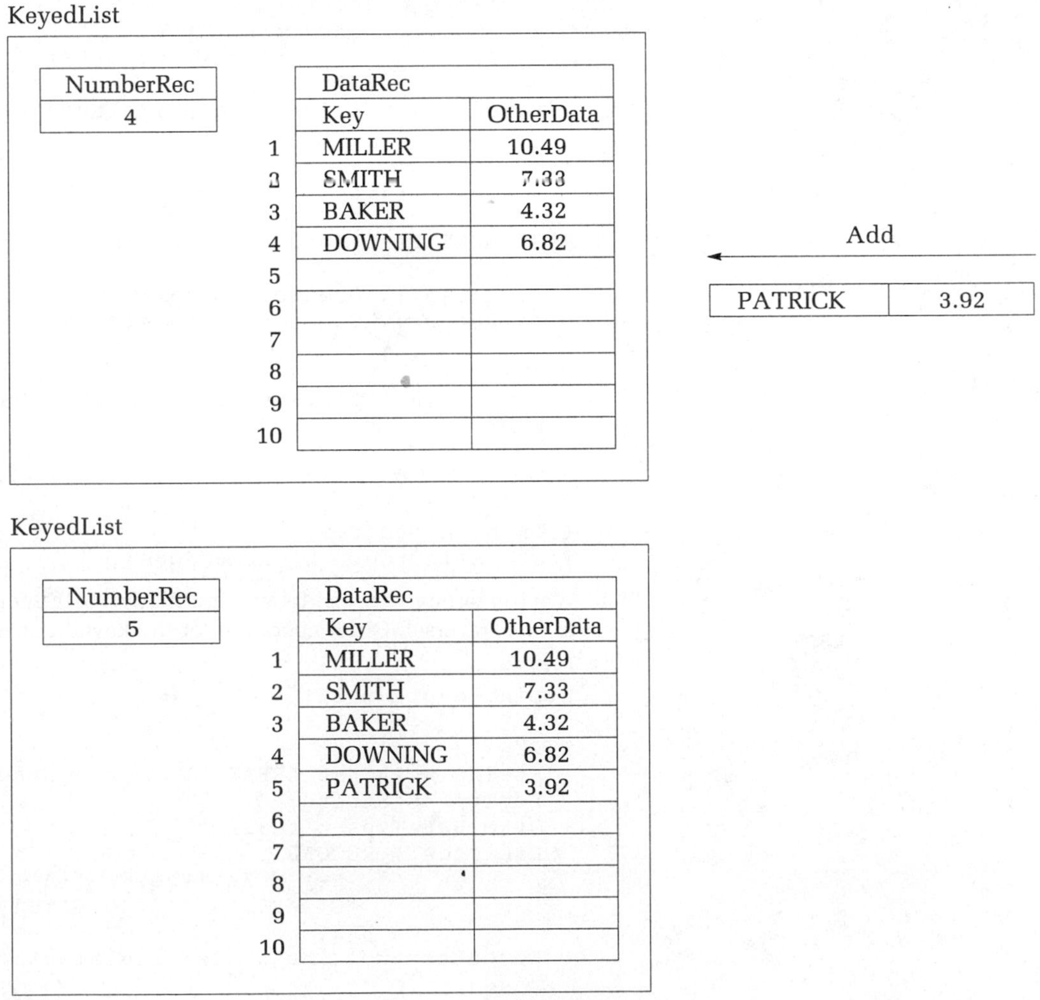

KeyedList

	NumberRec		DataRec	
	4		Key	OtherData
		1	MILLER	10.49
		2	SMITH	7.33
		3	BAKER	4.32
		4	DOWNING	6.82
		5		
		6		
		7		
		8		
		9		
		10		

Add

PATRICK	3.92

KeyedList

	NumberRec		DataRec	
	5		Key	OtherData
		1	MILLER	10.49
		2	SMITH	7.33
		3	BAKER	4.32
		4	DOWNING	6.82
		5	PATRICK	3.92
		6		
		7		
		8		
		9		
		10		

As you can see, the increase in efficiency of the Add operation is being bargained for a decrease in efficiency for other operations. For instance, the Retrieve operation would now require a sequential search. Also, implementation of the TraverseInOrder operation would require initially performing a pointer sort (Section 12.4) so that the list could be accessed in order by key field. The details of this implementation are left for you in the Exercises.

These trade-offs in efficiency for various operations are what make the keyed list ADT a particularly interesting one to study. We will return to it often in future chapters.

Exercises 13.4

1. What is wrong with the following **PROCEDURE** PrintNode and its use in a call to the TraverseInOrder operation for the keyed list ADT?

```
CONST
StringLength = 15;

TYPE
  String = PACKED ARRAY [1..StringLength] OF char;
  KeyType = String;
  OtherDataType = real;
  ListNode = RECORD
                  Key : KeyType;
                  OtherData : OtherDataType
               END;
  KeyedList = { The hidden implementation }

VAR
  L : KeyedList;

PROCEDURE PrintNode (Item : ListNode);

  { Given:   One node's data to be printed   }
  { Return:  The node with its data printed. }

  BEGIN
    writeln (Item.Key:20, Item.OtherData:5)
  END;
  .
  .
  .
{ In main program }
TraverseInOrder (L, PrintNode);
```

2. What is wrong with the following **PROCEDURE** Increase and its use in a call to the TraverseInOrder operation for the keyed list ADT?

```
CONST
StringLength = 15;

TYPE
  String = PACKED ARRAY [1..StringLength] OF char;
  KeyType = String;
  OtherDataType = real;
  ListNode = RECORD
                  Key : KeyType;
                  OtherData : OtherDataType;
               END;
  KeyedList = { The hidden implementation }

VAR
  L : KeyedList;

PROCEDURE Increase (VAR Item : ListNode
                         X : real);
```

```
{  Given:     One node in a keyed list,         }
{             and a value to add to the         }
{             OtherData field in that node      }
{  Task:      Add X to the OtherData field      }
{             in that node                      }
{  Return:    The list node with an updated     }
{             OtherData field.                  }

BEGIN
  Item.OtherData := Item.OtherData + X
END;
         .
         .
         .
{ In main program }
TraverseInOrder (L, Increase (Item, 3.0) );
```

3. Given the following declaration for the data nodes in a keyed list,

```
CONST
StringLength = 15;

TYPE
  String = PACKED ARRAY [1..StringLength] OF char;
  KeyType = String;
  OtherDataType = real;
  ListNode = RECORD
                Key : KeyType;
                OtherData : OtherDataType;
             END;
  KeyedList = {  The hidden implementation  }
```

write a procedure that can be used as an actual parameter passed to the TraverseInOrder operation. This procedure should change to zero the OtherData field in those nodes that have a negative OtherData field; other nodes should be left unchanged. Finally indicate how you would call on TraverseInOrder using the procedure you have written.

4. Consider the problem given in Example 13.17. Suppose that ElementType in this program was not integer but instead defined by the following declaration.

```
TYPE
  ElementType = RECORD
                   Field1 : PACKED ARRAY [1..20] OF char;
                   Field2 : real
                END;
```

Define procedures that may be passed as actual parameters for the Precedes argument in **PROCEDURE** Sort to achieve the following orderings:

a. Array arranged alphabetically by Field1.
b. Array arranged in descending order by Field2.
c. Array arranged in descending order by Field2; those array elements which have the same value for Field2 should be arranged alphabetically.

Then indicate how you would invoke Sort with each of these procedures to achieve the desired ordering.

Exercises 5−8 refer to Implementation 1 of a keyed list, that is, physically ordered array with binary search to retrieve data.

5. Consider the following modification to the **FOR** loop to move records down in the code for the Add operation of Example 13.18.

```
{  From insertion slot down, each record must be moved down one slot  }
FOR J := K TO L.NumberRec DO
  L.DataRec[J + 1] := L.DataRec[J];
```

Will the procedure still work with this change to the loop? If not, describe what will go wrong.

6. Complete the implementation of the keyed list by developing code for the Create, Delete, and Retrieve operations. Be sure to obey the ADT implementation rule.

7. Given the implementations of operations in Examples 13.18, 13.19, and Exercise 6, provide a big-O efficiency analysis of each operation. You should consider both the number of comparisons and data interchanges in this analysis.

8. Modify the implementation of the Add operation in Example 13.18 so that a variation of the binary search algorithm is used to find the insertion slot. How does this new implementation affect your efficiency analysis from Exercise 7?

Exercises 9–10 refer to Implementation 2 of a keyed list, that is, an unordered array with sequential search to retrieve data and pointer sort to traverse in order.

9. Write data declarations and Pascal code for all keyed list operations under this implementation.

10. Given the implementations of operations in Exercise 9, provide a big-O efficiency analysis of each operation. You should consider both the number of comparisons and data interchanges in this analysis.

11. You have been assigned the task of developing an application that uses a keyed list in which the key field is a postal zip code. There is to be a record in the list for each zip code in the United States. Given this list, users of the application you develop will often want to see the information associated with a particular zip code and print reports in zip code order.

    Which of the two implementations of a keyed list that were presented in this section would you choose for your application? Write a memo to your supervisor defending your choice.

12. In the keyed list ADT, there is no operation that allows changing a record's key field. Show how one could, however, change a record's key field by using the Delete and Add operations.

13. In a written statement discuss various reasons why the Success Boolean parameter for the Add operation might return a **false** value.

■ ■ ■ ■

FOCUS ON PROGRAM DESIGN

To illustrate how approaching a design at an abstract level can make a hard problem easier, consider the task specified in the following memorandum.

Approaching a solution to this problem from an abstract data type perspective means that we essentially need not worry about how to handle an individual transaction on the keyed list of employees. This keyed list will be the computer embodiment of the stack of index cards presently maintained by the payroll director. These individual transactions are viewed as provided operations. Our logic is instead focused at a higher level, reflected in the modularstructure chart of Figure 13.12.

Similarly the module specifications need not specify details of the list because we will access the list only through the allowable, defined operations.

1. LoadEmployeeList Module
   Data received: None
   Information returned: A keyed list of employee records is read in from a text file

MEMORANDUM
FlyByNight Credit Card Company

TO: Computer Operations Manager
FROM: Director of Payroll
DATE: November 18, 1996
RE: Hourly employee payroll system

The number of hourly employees we have is growing so fast that we *must* computerize record keeping for them *immediately.* Here is a description of the process as we presently do it by hand. As much as possible, the essence of this process should be preserved in the automated system you will develop.

A record for each employee is kept on an index card. There are two items of information on that index card: an employee's name (in "lastname, firstname" form) and hourly pay rate. These index cards are kept in alphabetical order by employee name.

Each Friday, I go through the stack of index cards and perform three tasks. First, I add cards (in alphabetical order, of course) of new employees. Second, I go through the entire stack and write a paycheck for each employee. The information on this paycheck consists of the employee's name and salary. The salary is determined by multiplying the employee's hourly rate times the number of hours worked during that week. Finally, after all paychecks have been produced, I remove from the stack the index cards belonging to those employees who have been released or who have quit.

FIGURE 13.12

Modular structure chart for Fly-ByNight payroll processing

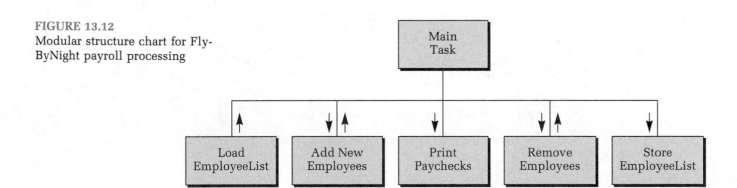

Logic: Repeatedly get a record from the text file and Add it to the employee list

2. AddNewEmployee Module
   Data received: List of previous employees
   Information returned: List of previous employees augmented with records of new employees
   Logic: While there is a new employee to add, obtain information on new employee and Add record to employee list

3. PrintPaychecks Module
   Data received: List of Employees
   Information returned: None
   Logic: Traverse the list, applying to each record a procedure that obtains the hours worked for a given employee and then prints a paycheck for that employee

   4. RemoveEmployees Module
      Data received: List of employees
      Information returned: List with departing employees removed
      Logic: While there is another departing employee, obtain the employee's name and delete that record

   5. StoreEmployeeList Module
      Data received: List of employees
      Information returned: None
      Logic: Traverse the List, applying to each record a procedure that writes the record to a text file

The program itself is derived immediately from these specifications. Since we are assuming the basic operations on keyed lists, those procedures and the details of their implementation are omitted in the following listing. Any implementation of the keyed list data type could be plugged into this program, and it would function correctly. By providing an abstract definition of a data type that may be used in this and other applications, we have been able to separate our solution to this problem from the details of implementing that data type.

```
PROGRAM FlyByNightPayroll (input, output, EmployeeFile, NewEmployeeFile);

   { The following is a partial program to solve the problem posed in the     }
   { memo from FlyByNight's payroll director.  The implementations of the     }
   { keyed list are hidden.  Also, the implementations of the operations on   }
   { the keyed list ADT are not provided.  The portion of the program that    }
   { is given accesses the keyed list ADT only through its abstract           }
   { definition.                                                              }

CONST
  NameLength = 30;  { Maximum length for name }

TYPE
  KeyType = PACKED ARRAY [1..NameLength] of char;  { Employee name }
  OtherDataType = real;  { Hourly salary rate }
  ListNode = RECORD
               Key : KeyType;
               OtherData : OtherDataType
             END;
  KeyedList =           { The hidden implementation }

VAR
  EmployeeFile, NewEmployeeFile : text;
  EmployeeList : KeyedList;

  { The implementation of keyed list operations would appear here in         }
  { complete program.                                                        }

PROCEDURE LoadEmployeeList (VAR EmployeeList : KeyedList);

   { Given:   An empty keyed list                                            }
   { Task:    Load list from text file EmployeeFile                          }
   { Return:  EmployeeList containing data on all employees in file.  If data }
   {          on all employees in file will not fit in EmployeeList,          }
   {          EmployeeList contains as many records as possible.              }

  VAR
    K : integer;
    Item : ListNode;
    Success : boolean;
```

```
        BEGIN
          reset (EmployeeFile);
          Success := true;
          { Read until end of file or cannot add more to list }
          WHILE (NOT eof (EmployeeFile)) AND Success DO
            BEGIN
              FOR K := 1 TO NameLength DO
                read (EmployeeFile, Item.Key[K]);
              readln (EmployeeFile, Item.OtherData);
              Add (EmployeeList, Item, Success)
            END;
          { If Success is false, could not add all records from file }
          IF NOT Success THEN
            writeln ('Warning -- not able to load entire file');
          close (EmployeeFile)
        END; { of PROCEDURE LoadEmployeeList }


PROCEDURE ReadAKey (VAR Name : KeyType);

  { Given:   Nothing                                                       }
  { Task:    Read an employee name from standard input                     }
  { Return:  Employee name in Name, with spaces appended in character      }
  {          positions beyond end of name.                                 }

  VAR
    K, L : integer;

  BEGIN
    K := 0;
    WHILE NOT eoln DO
      BEGIN
        K := K + 1;
        read (Name[K])
      END;
    readln;
    { Pad with spaces from index K + 1 onward }
    FOR L := K + 1 TO NameLength DO
      Name[L] := ' '
  END; { of PROCEDURE ReadAKey }


PROCEDURE AddNewEmployees (VAR EmployeeList : KeyedList);

  { Given:   List of previous employees                                    }
  { Task:    Add records of new employees to the list                      }
  { Return:  Original list augmented by new employees.  If no room in      }
  {          list for new employee, warn user and quit.                    }

  VAR
    Item : ListNode;
    Success : boolean;

  BEGIN
    write ('Enter new employee name (* to quit) ');
    ReadAKey (Item.Key);
    Success := true;
    { Continue adding new employees until * entered or Success returned as false }
    WHILE (Item.Key[1] <> '*') AND Success DO
      BEGIN
        write ('Enter pay rate ');
        readln (Item.OtherData);
        Add (EmployeeList, Item, Success);
        IF Success THEN
```

```
                 BEGIN
                   write ('Enter employee name (* to quit) ');
                   ReadAKey (Item.Key)
                 END
               ELSE
                 writeln ('Warning -- unable to add this record')
           END
     END; { of PROCEDURE AddNewEmployees }


PROCEDURE PrintPayChecks (EmployeeList : KeyedList);

   { Given:   List of all employee records                              }
   { Task:    Print paycheck for each employee                          }
   { Return:  Employee list unchanged.                                  }

   PROCEDURE PrintOneCheck (VAR Item : ListNode); { Used as procedure para- }
                                         { meter to TraverseInOrder        }

   {  Given:   Data on one employee in Item                             }
   {  Task:    Inquire about that employee's hours worked, and use this }
   {           information to print paycheck for employee               }
   {  Return:  Employee's data unchanged.                               }

      VAR
        HrsWorked : integer;

      BEGIN
        writeln;
        write ('Hours worked for ',Item.Key);
        readln (HrsWorked);
        writeln;
        writeln ('***************************************************************')
        writeln ('           FlyByNight Credit Co. Payroll');
        writeln (Item.Key);
        writeln ('Pay is: ', Item.OtherData * HrsWorked : 10 : 2);
        writeln ('***************************************************************')
      END; { of PROCEDURE PrintOneCheck }

   BEGIN
     TraverseInOrder (EmployeeList, PrintOneCheck)
   END; { of PROCEDURE PrintPayChecks }


PROCEDURE RemoveEmployees (VAR EmployeeList : KeyedList);

   {  Given:   Keyed list of employee records                           }
   {  Task:    Determine which records must be removed and delete them  }
   {  Return:  EmployeeList with those records deleted                  }

   VAR
     Target : KeyType;
     Success : boolean;

   BEGIN
     write ('Enter employee name to delete (* to quit) ');
     ReadAKey (Target);
     WHILE Target[1] <> '*' DO
       BEGIN
         Delete (EmployeeList, Target, Success);
         IF NOT Success THEN
           writeln ('Warning -- cannot find ', Target);
         write ('Enter employee name to delete (* to quit) ');
         ReadAKey (Target)
       END
   END; { of PROCEDURE RemoveEmployees }
```

```
PROCEDURE StoreEmployeeList (EmployeeList : KeyedList);

   { Given:    Keyed list of employee records                           }
   { Task:     Write those records, alphabetically, to new employee file }
   { Return:   Permanent file with all employee records.                 }

   PROCEDURE StoreOneRecord (VAR Item : ListNode);   { Used as procedure  }
                                                     { parameter to       }
                                                     { TraverseInOrder    }

      { Given:    One employee record                                    }
      { Task:     Write those records, alphabetically, to new employee file }
      { Return:   Permanent file with all employee records.              }

      BEGIN
        writeln (NewEmployeeFile, Item.Key, Item.OtherData : 8 : 2)
      END; { of PROCEDURE StoreOneRecord }

   BEGIN
     rewrite (NewEmployeeFile);
     TraverseInOrder (EmployeeList, StoreOneRecord);
     close (NewEmployeeFile)
   END; { of PROCEDURE StoreEmployeeList }

BEGIN  { main program                                                     }
  Create (EmployeeList);
  LoadEmployeeList (EmployeeList);
  AddNewEmployees (EmployeeList);
  PrintPayChecks (EmployeeList);
  RemoveEmployees (EmployeeList);
  StoreEmployeeList (EmployeeList)
END.


Sample input file:
BENTON,GRACE              6.92
HARRISON,DAVID            5.98
TAYLOR,EDNA               7.23

Sample run
Enter new employee name (* to quit) MILLER,JAMES
Enter pay rate 9.10
Enter employee name (* to quit) *

Hours worked for BENTON,GRACE                 40
****************************************************************
          FlyByNight Credit Co. Payroll
BENTON,GRACE
Pay is:    276.80
****************************************************************

Hours worked for HARRISON,DAVID               10
****************************************************************
          FlyByNight Credit Co. Payroll
HARRISON,DAVID
Pay is:     59.80
****************************************************************

Hours worked for MILLER,JAMES                 25
****************************************************************
          FlyByNight Credit Co. Payroll
MILLER,JAMES
Pay is:    227.50
****************************************************************
```

```
Hours worked for TAYLOR,EDNA                          50
**************************************************************
            FlyByNight Credit Co. Payroll
TAYLOR,EDNA
Pay is:     361.50
**************************************************************
Enter employee name to delete (* to quit) HARRISON,DAVID
Enter employee name to delete (* to quit) *

The new employee file created by this run is

BENTON,GRACE                      6.92
MILLER,JAMES                      9.10
TAYLOR,EDNA                       7.23
```

RUNNING AND DEBUGGING TIPS

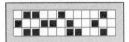

1. When accessing an ADT, be sure that you only use those operations specified in the ADT definition. This is the ADT use rule. For instance, it would be wrong to access a record in a keyed list by referring to its array index. This would be assuming that the implementor of the ADT is storing data in an array. Such an assumption is not warranted according to the definition of this ADT.

2. When writing the implementation of an ADT, be sure that the procedures and functions you develop obey the interface established by the ADT's definition. This is the ADT implementation rule. For instance, if you, as implementor, need a counter to keep track of the number of records in a keyed list, don't add the counter as an extra parameter in procedure calls. Instead, encapsulate it in a record containing all data items needed for the implementation.

3. When providing the implementation of an ADT, be sure that each individual operation is thoroughly tested and debugged before it is used by higher level logic. Then if errors occur when higher level modules execute, you can be assured that these errors are the result of the algorithms that use the ADT and are not in the implementation of the ADT.

4. The importance of the Create operation for an ADT should not be underestimated. From the implementor's perspective, here is where crucial initializations occur that will insure the smooth functioning of other operations. From the prospective of the user of the ADT, you must be sure to call the Create operation for each instance of a variable of that type. Failing to do so will usually lead to very bizarre program behavior.

■ Summary

Key Terms

abstract data type
abstraction
ADT implementation rule
ADT use rule
column major
data abstraction
embedded length implementation
encapsulation principle

implementation
information hiding
interface for an ADT
keyed list
mapping function
packed array implementation
physically ordered array implementation

row major
sparse table
string ADT
two-dimensional table
unordered array implementation
workspace-index method

Key Concepts

- Computer scientists engage in a modeling process as they develop software to satisfy users' needs. In this respect, the way in which a computer scientist works parallels the engineering profession. Consequently, this systematic approach towards the development of successful software is often called software engineering.

- Abstract data types are defined apart from considerations of their implementation in a particular programming language. A complete definition for an abstract data type must include a description of the individual elements, the relationship between these individual elements, and the operations that can be performed upon them. These operations are conveniently specified as procedure and function interfaces.

- The string is an example of an abstract data type. Two implementations for this ADT are the packed array implementation and the embedded length implementation.

- The encapsulation principle, the ADT use rule, and the ADT implementation rule are guidelines governing the relationship between implementations of an ADT and higher level algorithms using that implementation.

- We must often determine which of a variety of implementations is best in terms of time and space efficiency for a particular application.

- Another abstract data type, the two-dimensional table, can consume a large amount of memory.

- When most entries in a two-dimensional table are the same value, the table is said to be sparse. We must often devise implementations for sparse tables that are more space efficient than the row-major implementation used by most Pascal compilers.

- The keyed list is an ADT characterized by operations that add, retrieve, delete, and traverse in order. All of these operations are performed relative to a particular key field.

- A physically ordered array with binary search and an unordered array with pointer sort are two ways of implementing a keyed list.

■ Programming Problems and Projects

Many of the problems in this chapter require that you write the implementation for an ADT and then use that ADT in a program. It is often interesting to work on such a problem with a classmate. One of you provides the implementation of the ADT; the other writes the higher level algorithm that uses the ADT. If you both obey the ADT use implementation rules, you should be able to work independently of each other and develop an elegant solution to the problem.

In other Problems (5, 6, 7, 10, and 11) you are asked to write an ADT definition as part of your answer to the problem. Your definition should be presented first in formal precondition and postcondition form and then translated into an appropriate Pascal interface. Be sure you are not ambiguous in your presentation of the definition and interface. This aspect of these problems will serve to test the precision with which you write and document.

1. Complete the program in the Focus on Program Design section by providing an implementation of the keyed list ADT.

2. Write a small-scale text editor system by loading lines of text from a file into an array of strings.
   a. Allow the user of your program to appropriately modify the text in this array of strings. These modifications should be performed by accessing the strings in the array only through string ADT operations.
   b. Once the text has been modified, write the array of strings out to a new text file.

c. Test your text editor by using it to create and then modify a modest Pascal program, which you then provide as input to your compiler.

3. Write a program to solve Problem 6 of Chapter 7. Unlike the program you may have written when studying Chapter 7, your new program should only access the strings it manipulates by calling on appropriate string ADT operations. Do you need to define any new operations for the string ADT to solve this problem? If so, be sure to document their interfaces very carefully.

4. Write a program to solve Problem 18 of Chapter 8. Unlike the program you may have written when studying Chapter 8, your new program should access the matrix only through defined operations on the two-dimensional table ADT. Then, provide an implementation of the two-dimensional table other than the standard row-major implementation provided by Pascal. Use this new implementation in your program.

5. Consider a rational number as an abstract data type. (Recall that a rational number is one that can be expressed as the quotient of two integers.) Write a definition for this ADT that includes operations such as

- Add two rational numbers.
- Subtract two rational numbers.
- Multiply two rational numbers.
- Divide two rational numbers.
- Reduce a rational number to lowest terms.

Finally, by using an implementation of your defined ADT, develop a program to solve Problem 28 of Chapter 4; however, now be sure that you access the fractions manipulated in that program only by provided ADT operations.

6. Begin this problem by providing a definition of a complex number as an abstract data type. (See Problem 5 in Chapter 9.) Next provide an implementation for your definition of the complex number ADT. Finally, use your implementation to write a main program to solve Problem 5 of Chapter 9. Be sure that you access the complex number ADT only through the provided operations.

7. If you are now familiar with the notion of a set from your previous work in mathematics, formalize the definition of a set as an abstract data type. Be sure to minimally include the following operations in your definition:

- Given a value V and a set S, determine whether or not V is **IN** S.
- Given two sets S_1 and S_2, determine whether or not S_1 is equal to S_2.
- Given two sets S_1 and S_2, determine whether or not S_1 is a subset of S_2.
- Given a value V and a set S, add the value V to the set S.
- Given a value V and a set S, remove the value V from the set S.
- Given two sets S_1 and S_2, return their set intersection.
- Given two sets S_1 and S_2, return their set difference.
- Given two sets S_1 and S_2, return their union.

Pascal offers its users a predefined set type. Browse in your local reference material and find out how your version of Pascal implements sets. What are the limitations of this particular implementation? Give some examples of applications where this compiler-provided implementation would be insufficient. Develop your own implementation for the set ADT that you have defined.

One idea for such an implementation is to use a Boolean array indexed by the values that could be in a set. Then you can determine whether or not a value X is in a set by examining the Boolean value stored in index position X of the associated array. If this Boolean value is **true,** view X as being in the set. Otherwise X is not considered a member of the set.

Finally, use your implementation of sets in a program to solve Problem 3 or Problem 12 in Chapter 11. Be sure that your program obeys the ADT use rule.

8. Invented by mathematician John H. Conway (*Scientific American,* October 1970, p. 120), The Game of Life models the growth and changes in a complex collection of living organisms. The model can be interpreted as applying to a collection of microorganisms, an ecologically closed system of animals or plants, or an urban development.

   Start with a checkerboard of size N by N on which "markers" are to be placed. Each location that is not on a border has eight neighbors. The markers are born, survive, or die during a "generation" according to the following rules:

   - *Survival:* Markers with two or three neighboring markers survive to the next generation.
   - *Death:* Markers with four or more neighbors die from overcrowding and are removed for the next generation. Markers with zero or one neighbors die from isolation and are removed for the next generation.
   - *Birth:* Each empty location that has exactly three markers in the eight neighboring locations is a birth location. A marker is placed in the location for the next generation.

   For example, on a 6 $\times$ 6 space the following pattern

		X			
	X	X			
				X	
	X			X	

   would look as follows in the next generation:

	X	X			
	X	X	X		
	X	X	X		

Certain patterns are stable; for example,

Other patterns repeat a sequence:

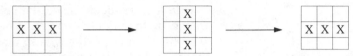

Because, conceptually, two N × N matrices are required to implement The Game of Life, it is clear that memory limitations could easily become a problem for a large N.

After initializing the first generation, print it out. Then calculate the next generation in another array and print this too. Repeat for a specified number of generations. Your output should be an "X" for live cells and a blank otherwise.

Develop the high-level logic of your program by employing the fundamental Assign/Retrieve operations for matrices. First use your compiler's implementation of these operations. Then, switch to the implementation of sparse matrices described in Section 13.3. Your high-level logic should not need to change at all. In a written statement, describe the performance differences you observe with these two implementations. Explain why these differences occur.

9. Though the packed array and embedded length method for strings are very easy to implement, they lead to two potential problems. First, what about the string longer than MaxStringLength characters? These methods simply cannot accommodate such a string. Second, since most strings will be considerably shorter than MaxStringLength characters, these methods will waste a sizable amount of memory. This memory waste is shown in Figure 13.13.

FIGURE 13.13
Memory wasted by fixed length implementations of string

```
1  2  3  4  5  6  7  8  9  ...  39  40 = MaxStringLength
```

| S | M | I | T | H | | J | O | E | | | |

Approximately 75 percent wasted

We'll look at another possible implementation for strings in the next chapter when we discuss linked lists. The alternate implementation method we propose here is known as the *workspace-index method*. The idea behind the workspace-index method is that one large memory workspace is allocated to storing all strings. Additionally an index table of records with two fields for each string is maintained. One field in the record for a string contains the address in the workspace at which that particular string starts, and the other contains the length of each string. This principle is illustrated in Figure 13.14.

FIGURE 13.14
Workspace-index method of handling strings

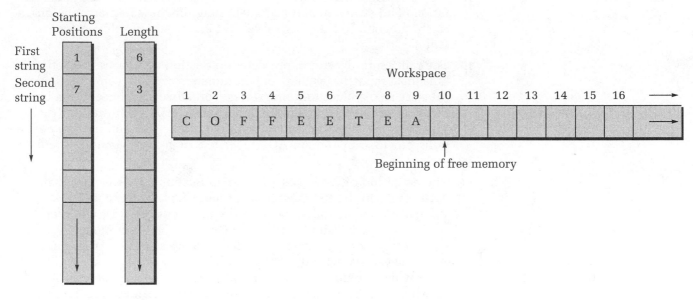

Suppose now that we were to add a third string to the collection in Figure 13.14. All that we need to know is where the free portion of the workspace begins (in this case it begins at location 10). We place the string starting at that location, add appropriate entries to our index table, and adjust the pointer to the beginning of the free memory. This threefold process is illustrated in Figure 13.15 for the addition of the string 'CREAM'.

FIGURE 13.15
String 'CREAM' added to workspace-index storage of Figure 13.14

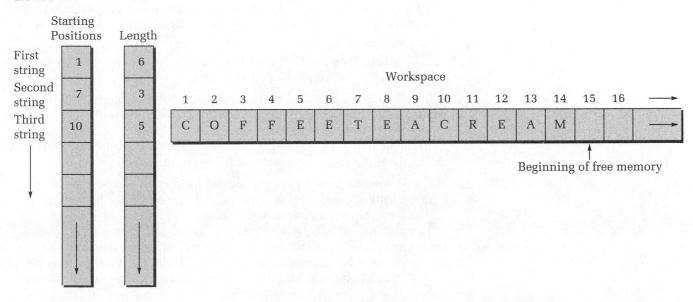

The storage advantages of the workspace-index method should be evident. By associating two indexing integers with each string, we are trading off the storage required for two integers against the potentially large number of wasted characters that pad strings in the fixed length method. Moreover, the only restraint on maximum string length is the amount of storage left in the workspace.

Begin your work on this problem by a workspace-index implementation of all string operations. Then, plug this new implementation into a program like the high-level text editor you developed for Problem 2.

10. The radix sort algorithm, presented in Section 12.4, uses the notion of bins: data repositories that contain numbers or strings in a particular category as the algorithm progresses. Formalize the concept of a bin for the radix sort algorithm by providing an ADT definition for it. Then provide an implementation for your bin ADT and use the operations provided by the bin ADT to write a high-level version of radix sort.

11. The definition of the keyed list ADT in Section 13.4 specifies that each record in the list must have a unique key value, that is, a key value shared by no other value in the list. Consider a variation on this ADT in which we allow multiple records to share the same key value (for example, several people may have identical names). Call this ADT a keyed list with duplicate keys.
   a. Provide a complete definition for this ADT. Be very precise about what happens for each of the Add, Delete, Retrieve, and Traverse-InOrder operations. Do you need to add any new operations because of the possibility of duplicate keys?
   b. Translate your definition from Part **a** into a Pascal interface for a keyed list with duplicate keys.
   c. Develop an implementation for this ADT. Discuss in a written statement any limitations of your implementation relative to the definition and interface of Parts **a** and **b**.
   d. Test your implementation by plugging it into a program like that of this chapter's Focus on Program Design section. In a program such as this one, how can you distinguish between employees who have the same name?

Before working Problems 12 and 13, reread the Note of Interest on Sparse Tables and Language Compilers in Section 13.3.

12. Write a program that will appropriately recognize a month from an input stream of characters. Implement that sparse two-dimensional table as a Pascal function that uses **CASE** and/or **IF . . . THEN . . . ELSE** statements. This function should receive a current state and a character and return the next state given by that table.

13. (This problem is especially appropriate for a class of 15 or more students.) Write a program that appropriately recognizes a first name of a member of your computer science class.

Use the following strategy. Obtain a list of first names of all class members; discard any duplicates from this list. Then develop a two-dimensional table analogous to the table developed for month names in the Note of Interest. The same algorithm (used to recognize month names in the Note of Interest section) may now be used to recognize names from members of your class. Implement the sparse two-dimensional table needed for this algorithm as a Pascal function that uses **CASE** and/or **IF . . . THEN . . . ELSE** statements. This function should receive a current state and a character and return the next state given by the table.

CHAPTER

14

*I believe in Michelangelo,
Velázquez, and Rembrandt; in
the might of design.*
George Bernard Shaw
(1856–1950)

Software Engineering and the System Life Cycle

In Chapter 13 and in earlier chapters, we discussed a philosophy of software design called **software engineering**. This philosophy emphasizes an evolutionary progression from the building of a conceptual model of the system to the eventual implementation of that model in a programming language such as Pascal. At the heart of this progression lies the abstract data type as a means of conceptualizing the data needs of the system before considering how those needs are to be implemented.

In Chapter 12, we described some relatively simple algorithms to perform operations on arrays and illustrated how to evaluate such algorithms using big-O notation. The purpose of this description was twofold. First, as software designers, we need to be aware of the variety of algorithms available to perform a particular task such as sorting or searching. Chapter 12 began to equip us with this knowledge in a systematic, organized fashion. Second, along with an understanding of various algorithms, we must be able to evaluate and select the best of all possible algorithms for a particular application. Big-O analysis provides us with a guide for such evaluation and selection.

It is now time to put the methods described in the preceding chapters into the context of large-scale systems development. In so doing, we will describe a series of phases known as the software system life cycle. As we walk through these phases, we hope you begin to appreciate the enormous complexity involved in the development of successful software systems. It is not uncommon that a problem which appears simple spawns a variety of complications. Handling such complications in a graceful and efficient fashion is an essential ingredient to succeeding in computer science.

In Section 14.1, we examine the initial analysis phase of the system life cycle. This phase is followed by the design and implementation phases, as described in Section 14.2. Section 14.3 treats the testing, maintenance, and obsolescence stages. Section 14.4 touches upon the pragmatic issues of file

653

processing. We examine its importance in certain types of software systems and discuss the inadequacies of standard Pascal for such systems.

Sections 14.5 and 14.6 provide a brief glimpse of some future directions in software engineering. In Section 14.5, we discuss formal verification as an alternative to testing. In Section 14.6, we investigate a programming paradigm called *object-oriented programming*.

■ 14.1
The Analysis Phase of the System Life Cycle

OBJECTIVES

- to understand what is done during the analysis phase of systems development
- to be able to define the responsibilities of a systems analyst
- to gain additional familiarity with the use of data flow diagrams as a tool for modeling user needs
- to recognize the importance of oral and written communication skills in the analysis phase

It has been said that the only simple problems in computing are those defined in textbooks. Perhaps a key to the truth of this statement is its use of the word *defined*. Once a problem is specifically defined, the most difficult obstacle to solving that problem effectively may well have been surmounted. In the analysis phase you must define in detail the problem that you are charged with solving.

It is important to remember that in trying to provide such a definition, you are typically working with a problem originally posed by someone other than yourself. We have tried to emphasize this fact in the preceding chapter by introducing problems in the form of memoranda from computer users. This is done to emphasize that programs are written not for computer scientists but for computer users, users who often know virtually nothing about the computer other than a vague (and often inaccurate) notion that it can magically take care of all of their recordkeeping and computational needs. Bridging the gap between potentially naive users and the computer-oriented people who eventually are responsible for implementing the software system constitutes the first phase of the system life cycle.

Though many people are aware that *systems analysts* work with computers in some way, few know specifically what a systems analyst does. More than anything else, the systems analyst is responsible for the *analysis* phase of the system life cycle. A systems analyst talks to the users who initally request the system to learn exactly what these users need. This is done not only by talking to users, but also by studying in detail what these users do. For instance, a systems analyst working for a bank on an automated teller system would have to become an expert on the various duties and responsibilities of a teller. Having learned what the automated system is supposed to do, the systems analyst must then develop formal specifications describing the system and its requirements. The technical people who design and code the software will work from these specifications.

FIGURE 14.1
Data flow diagram for payroll department

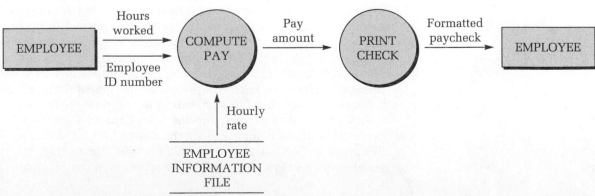

Using Data Flow Diagrams

A *data flow diagram* is a graphic specification technique often used by systems analysts to provide a clear picture of a user's requirements. On the surface, a data flow diagram could be viewed as a collection of circular "bubbles" joined together by strings. (In fact, data flow diagrams are sometimes referred to as bubble diagrams.) The strings connecting the bubbles are officially called data flows and are named in a way that reflects the information they carry. The circular bubbles represent processes that transform incoming data flows into outgoing data flows, which may in turn be acted upon by another process.

Figure 14.1 depicts a portion of a data flow diagram that describes how a payroll department might operate. Rectangular boxes in a data flow diagram indicate initial sources and final destinations of data flows. In Figure 14.1, the EMPLOYEE is both an initial source (of hours worked and ID number) and a final destination (of a formatted paycheck). Parallel lines highlight a data base that must be accessed to do the required processing. For instance, in Figure 14.1, the hourly rate must be retrieved from the EMPLOYEE INFORMATION FILE by the COMPUTE PAY process.

■ **EXAMPLE 14.1**

You receive the following memorandum from the registrar at the University of Hard Knocks. In it she requests the automation of the university's recordkeeping on its students. Provide a data flow diagram to depict the information processing done by the registrar.

MEMORANDUM
University of Hard Knocks

TO: Director of Data Processing
FROM: Head Registrar
DATE: July 29, 1995
RE: Automation of recordkeeping on students

As you know, we presently maintain our student records by manual methods. We believe the time has come to computerize this operation and request that you do so for us.

Here is what we need. Each student's record consists of his or her name, the number of credits that student has taken, the number of credits earned, and the total grade points for that student. We maintain these records by student's last name. Of course, at numerous times, we must add new students to our records and remove those who have graduated or withdrawn from school. Students often come into our office and request to see their current record, so we must be able to quickly find that information. At the end of each semester we print a grade report for each student. This report consists of the four items cited plus the student's GPA. At the end of the year, the Dean of Students requests two lists of graduating seniors. One of these lists is to be printed in alphabetical order by student name. The other is printed in order by student grade point average.

Certainly the situation described in this memo is an oversimplification of any real college registrar's office. However, even this relatively unsophisticated situation can offer us some interesting food for thought. For one thing, the memo demonstrates the fact that your first contact with a user requesting the system will often leave gaps in your knowledge about the system she wants. The head registrar's memo leaves unanswered the following questions.

1. What is the university's definition of grade points?
2. When grade reports are printed for each student, is it important that they be printed in any particular order?
3. Since grade reports are printed at the end of each semester, do you need some means of updating a student's record at the end of a semester?
4. What is the method used to compute a student's GPA?
5. What separates seniors who graduate from those seniors who don't graduate?
6. Is the list printed in order by student GPA arranged from best student to worst student or vice versa?

You would have to communicate those questions to the registrar before the specifics of the system could be modeled in a data flow diagram. Suppose that you do that and receive the following reply.

MEMORANDUM
University of Hard Knocks

TO: Director of Data Processing
FROM: Head Registrar
DATE: August 2, 1995
RE: Responses to your questions

Question 1: Four grade points are assigned for a one-credit A grade, three for a B, two for a C, one for a D, and zero for an F. Courses worth more than one credit have their corresponding grade points multiplied accordingly.

Question 2: Grade reports should be printed in alphabetical order by student last name.

Question 3: At the end of each semester, faculty turn in grades for each class they teach. We use the grades on these class rosters to update a student's academic information before printing a grade report.

Question 4: GPA is computed as the quotient of total grade points divided by credits taken.

Question 5: A graduating senior must have earned at least 120 credits.

Question 6: The list is to be printed from best student to worst student.

This sort of diaglogue with the registrar allows you, a systems analyst, to generate the data flow diagram in Figure 14.2. In this figure, the process PrintGradeReport transforms a student academic record into an appropri-

FIGURE 14.2
Data flow diagram of information to be processed in registrar's system

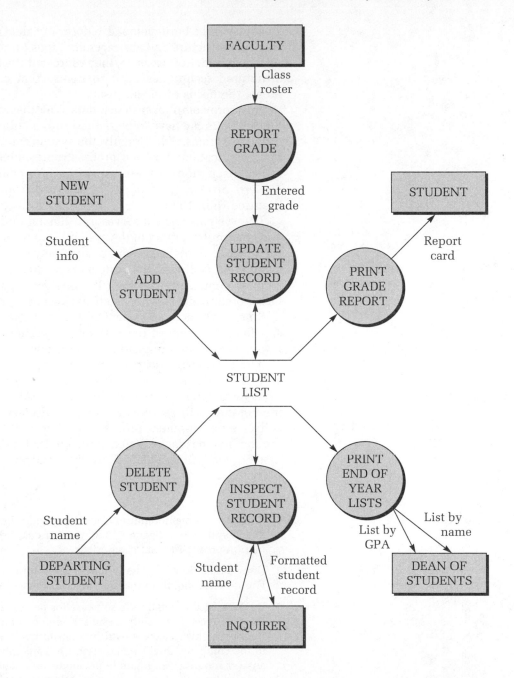

ately formatted report card. Similarly, the process ChangeStudent transforms newly reported grades for a student into an appropriately updated student record in the StudentList data base.

■   ■

Perfecting the Model

The role of the data flow diagram in the various phases of modeling that occur in the development of a system is to provide an initial overview of the fashion in which a user processes information. Data flow diagrams for a system would be developed before any decisions are made regarding the modular structure and abstract data types upon which the eventual program will be based. In this sense, they represent the first step in the progression of structured techniques used to insure that a software system adequately meets the needs of its end users.

For more complex systems, data flow diagrams such as that appearing in Figure 14.2 may have to be refined into a collection of more detailed subordinate diagrams. Additionally, the systems analyst may have to provide written specifications for each process represented in the diagram. A more detailed discussion of these aspects of the analysis phase may be found in *Modern Structured Analysis* by Edward Yourdon (Englewood Cliffs, N.J.: Prentice-Hall, 1989).

The systems analyst serves as a liaison and translator between the users and the implementors of the system. Depending on the size and structure of the organization, the systems analyst may or may not become involved in the design and coding of the system. Typically, such involvement will occur in smaller organizations where the analyst may wear many hats, but not in larger organizations where staff sizes allow a greater degree of specialization.

Since an exact assessment of the end user's needs is vital for the most satisfactory design of the system, the systems analyst must have excellent interpersonal communication skills as well as a strong computer background.

It is beyond the scope of this text to present any detailed treatment of systems analysis strategies. Instead, we will occasionally present specifications for programs in the form of memoranda from hypothetical users. These memoranda will serve as realistic reminders of the role of the user in the software development process. Yet they will be simplistic enough to avoid the massive headaches often connected with the analysis phase of a project. Instead, we will concentrate on the next phases of the software system life cycle.

Exercises 14.1

1. Consider the memorandum from Wing-and-a-Prayer's vice president in charge of scheduling (see Section 13.3). Draw a data flow diagram to model the information processing that it describes.

2. Draw a data flow diagram to model the information processing activities that you do each month in maintaining your checking account at a local bank.

3. BugFree Incorporated sells software for personal computers. Most orders that BugFree receives come from subscribers to computer magazines who respond to BugFree's advertisement by filling out forms in the ads and then mailing them to the company. BugFree also uses a toll-free phone number to accept orders, answer inquiries, and handle payments and cancellations of orders. Software ordered from BugFree is either sent directly to the customer or to local computer stores, which then distribute the product to the customer. This rapidly expanding business must keep records on its customers, product inventory, and billing information. Draw a data flow diagram to depict the flow of information at BugFree.

4. Develop a data flow diagram to depict the flow of information described in the memorandum that accompanied the Focus on Program Design section in Chapter 13.

5. For this task, you'll work with another student. Each of you should develop a memorandum to specify what you view as the information-processing needs of an administrative office at your school (or any other office environment with which you may be familiar). Your memorandum should provide information

similar to that provided by the registrar at the University of Hard Knocks (see Example 14.1).

Exchange your memoranda and draw a data flow diagram to model the activity described in the other person's memo. Then get together with the other person to resolve any questions you might have and to critique the accuracy and completeness of the other's data flow diagram.

6. Consider the following memorandum from the registrar at the renowned American Basket Weaving University—one of the main competitors of the University of Hard Knocks.

MEMORANDUM
American Basket Weaving University

 TO: Director of Data Processing
FROM: Head Registrar
DATE: July 29, 1996
 RE: Automation of record keeping on students

Records for students at our school consist of a University identification number, a last name, a first name, a middle initial, a Social Security number, a list of courses the student has taken along with the grade received in each course, and a list of extracurricular activities in which the student has indicated an interest. A university identification number for a student consists of a six-digit number: the first two digits represent the year a student entered the university. The remaining four digits are simply assigned on a sequential basis as students are admitted to the school. For instance, the student with ID number 930023 is the 23rd student admitted in the class that entered A.B.W.U. in 1993.

Given this data base, we frequently need to work with it in the following ways:

- Find and display all data for a particular student, as identified by university ID number.
- Add and delete student records from the data base.
- Print records for all students in Social Security number order, starting with the most recent class and working backwards.
- Add, change, or delete the information on a course for a particular student. For instance, change the grade received by student 930023 in CompSci2 from C to B.
- Find all students with an extracurricular interest that matches a particular target interest. Students' extracurricular interests are viewed as arbitrarily long strings. These strings are entered into our records directly from information provided by students on their registration forms. For instance, a given student may have indicated PLAYING BASKETBALL and GOING TO PLAYS as her two interests. We would want to be able to find this student (as well as students who indicated an interest such as WATCHING BASKETBALL or SHOOTING BASKETBALLS) if we were to search our data base for students who had an interest matching BASKETBALL.

Develop a data flow diagram to model the information processing that occurs in the registrar's office at A.B.W.U.

7. Write an essay in which you defend or attack the following position: To prepare for a career as a systems analyst, it is more important to develop interpersonal communication skills than it is to acquire a mass of technical knowledge about specific computer systems.

■ **14.2**
The Design and Implementation Phases of the System Life Cycle

Given specifications for the user's requirements, the next phase in the system's development is the construction of a relatively detailed design plan. This will guide future work on the implementation of the system. Note that, during the design phase, emphasis switches from understanding and specifying user needs to specifying how we will develop a software system to meet those needs. As such, we begin to consider, from a technical perspective, the data structures that will be needed to process information in the system. This processing of information must be achieved in a fashion consistent with the data flow diagrams and other documents produced during the analysis phase.

Design

The key feature of design plan is that it must effectively divide the overall problem into a collection of smaller, more manageable problems. Each of these smaller units will be handled by a separate program module in the implementation phase. These modules should be tested, verified, and debugged individually before being integrated into the entire system.

We can draw certain analogies between this modular structuring of a program and the boss-worker relationships that typically exist in any large corporation. Just as any effective boss must be able to delegate responsibilities, program modules that control the major logical decisions in a software system must be able to rely on lower level modules to reliably preform subordinate tasks.

Modular structure charts, which we have been using throughout this text, represent one of the most important graphic tools used by software designers to reflect the relationships between the modules comprising the entire software system. Given a comprehensive data flow diagram from the analysis phase, the software designer can transform this into an initial structure chart by roughly equating each process in the data flow diagram with a module in the structure chart (see Figure 14.3). This initial structure chart can then be refined into a more detailed design by establishing hierarchical relationships between modules and by adding lower level modules.

FIGURE 14.3
Modular structure chart for three-module system

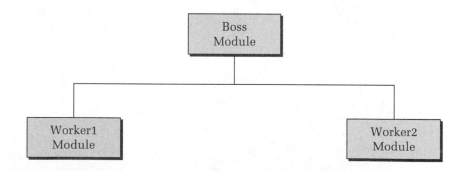

What distinguishes a good modular structure from a poor one? To answer this question we may again draw some apt comparisons between software structure and corporate boss-worker relationships. First, we note that such a structure should be developed in a *top-down* fashion. The overriding principle of top-down design is that we make decisions about the responsibilities of top-level bosses before deciding what the lower-level workers are to do. If such decisions are made in a way which progresses downward on a level-by-level basis in the structure chart, we find that boss modules truly will control the major logic of a program, just as corporate bosses should be in control of the most important aspects of their company's policy.

To proceed in an opposite, bottom-up fashion is to court organizational disaster. That is, if we decide what worker modules are to do before considering the responsibilities of boss modules, we frequently run into situations where a boss module is forced into some very clumsy program logic. By proceeding bottom-up, we are not able to see the full range of subordinate tasks that a boss may require. The end result is that the boss will have to take care of minor details—a situation comparable to a corporate executive's having to momentarily leave his or her desk to go out on the assembly line and fasten a bolt that everyone else had forgotten. Such distraction can only result in the boss's doing a poorer job in more important areas of responsibility.

A second criterion to be used in judging the modular structure of a system is the degree to which individual modules are *functionally cohesive*. That is, each module should focus on achieving one particular predefined task without having unexpected side effects on the performance of other modules in the same system. For instance, a module responsible for formatting an output line in a report should not also be updating a field within a customer's record. This could potentially cause great confusion for the module whose assigned task was to guarantee updating of the entire customer record. Thus, as a system designer, you must insure that you break down the system into its component modules following the "natural" lines of decomposition. The case studies presented in our Focus on Program Design sections will help you develop a feel for what such natural lines are. This talent will be further honed as you take more advanced courses in software engineering.

A third criterion used to evaluate the modular structure of a system is the way in which the modules within the system interact with each other. This interface between a pair of modules is often referred to as *coupling*. In drawing modular structure charts, we have used unlabeled arrows to indicate whether a given module receives data from its calling module, returns information to its calling module, or both. These data flow arrows have thus given some sense of the coupling between two modules.

Ideally, a given module in a system works independently of the others. Yet we can never attain this ideal because modules must interact with each other in any meaningful system. Hence the goal is to hold this interaction to a minimum. That is, there should be no more coupling between modules than necessary to allow them to perform their respective tasks within the framework of the overall system.

Consider the following example of a situation in which an excess of coupling could exist between two modules. Suppose we have a module to update a customer record for a business. One of the tasks subordinate to updating this record is to read new transactions in which the customer has taken part and update the balance owed field within the customer record. Schematically, the relationship between these two modules is given in Figure 14.4.

The coupling question that arises from this figure is: How do the data flow arrows between the modules UpdateCustomerRecord and UpdateBalanceOwed eventually resolve themselves as parameters? One possibility would

FIGURE 14.4
Portion of modular structure
chart for coupling example

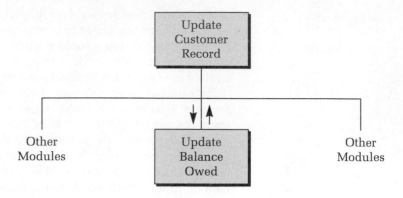

be for UpdateCustomerRecord to pass the entire customer record to Update-BalanceOwed as a **VAR** parameter. A second possibility is for UpdateCustomerRecord to merely pass the balance owed field within the customer record to UpdateBalanceOwed. From a data coupling perspective, the second alternative is much better. In the first alternative, more coupling than necessary exists between the modules because UpdateBalanceOwed is given access to more than it requires to do its specific task. A careless error in UpdateBalanceOwed could inadvertently alter another field such as an address or name within the customer record. Hence, the UpdateBalanceOwed module could have erroneous side effects which might corrupt the entire system. The second alternative, on the other hand, completely eliminates the chance of this happening by simply not allowing UpdateBalanceOwed to access fields it does not specifically need. Thus, minimizing coupling has guarded the system against any inadvertent side effects of a low-level module.

Having generated a structure chart in which modules are functionally cohesive and minimally coupled, the designer must then describe the general data structures to be manipulated by the system and the logic to be followed by each module. In an ideal world, the former could be done simply by specifying the abstract data types that the system will need. This ideal situation occurred in the Focus on Program Design section of Chapter 13. There we had a payroll application for which the keyed list ADT provided a perfect fit.

In more complex situations, an ADT may provide only a starting point in describing the data structures required by the system. For example, we may need the operations provided by the keyed list ADT plus a few more operations that are not included in the ADT's definition. This situation occurs in the registrar's system we analyzed in Example 14.1. This application requires everything offered by the keyed list ADT plus:

- The ability to alter a record that already exists in the list
- The ability to traverse the list in decreasing GPA order as well as alphabetically by name

Because applications frequently require variations upon off-the-shelf ADTs, it is not inappropriate for the designer to give some indication of how such variations might be accomplished. This is illustrated in the following example.

■ **EXAMPLE 14.2**

Design a modular structure chart along with the data structures for the registrar's system analyzed in Example 14.1.

As a designer presented with a data flow diagram from the analysis phase (Figure 14.2), your task is to transform it into an appropriate modular structure chart for the system. To a certain extent, the processes specified in the data flow diagram have already provided an initial breakdown of the problem facing the registrar. This initial breakdown can be represented in what is frequently called a first-cut (or first-level) structure chart, an early, relatively rough modular structure for a system. It's called first-cut because we intend to modify and expand upon its structure as we go through a stepwise refinement of the system's design.

The first-cut structure chart for the registrar's system is presented in Figure 14.5.

FIGURE 14.5
First-cut structure chart for registrar's system

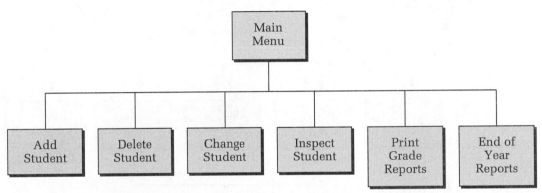

Transforming this first-cut structure chart into a final modular structure that completely specifies the system's design will require careful consideration of such issues as the user interface presented by our program and the implementation of data structures needed by the system. First, we want our top-level program to interact with users through a menu of choices. We want the user to be able to select a particular operation; the program should then dispatch processing to the appropriate subordinate module. Hence, we will need a GetSelection module assigned the task of handling this interface between the user and the menu of choices. Second, we must begin to consider the pertinent data structures, their implementation, and the subordinate modules necessary to access these data structures.

For the registrar's system, the crucial data structure is the keyed list of student records. As we have already indicated, the keyed list used in this system must be extended to allow for changes to records and traversing in GPA order. In this design of the registrar's system, we will use an array implementation of the list. We will maintain the array in physical order using student name as a key, hence allowing a binary search of the list when we wish to inspect a student by name. We therefore need to add the following modules to the system's design:

- A FindStudent module to implement the binary search so that records can be inspected, changed, and deleted.
- A FindSlot module to determine the position where a new student record will be added.
- Modules to produce formatted lists in name order and GPA order. Since the list is being maintained in name order, producing a list in GPA order will require a subordinate sorting algorithm. The pointer sort algorithm discussed in Section 12.4 will be ideal for this GPA sort since it will not disturb the physical order of the records.

With these considerations taken into account, a refined structure chart emerges. This final structure chart (Figure 14.6) now provides us with a detailed blueprint of the system's design.

FIGURE 14.6
Modular structure for registrar's system

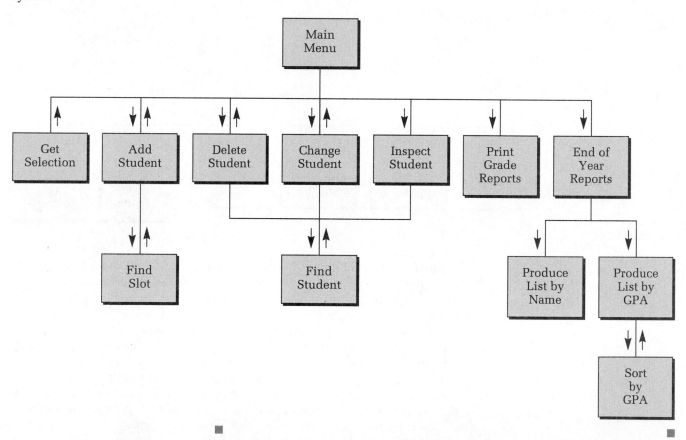

Two comments are in order regarding the design that evolved in Example 14.2. First, what are the ramifications of our having to extend the notion of a keyed list by adding ChangeStudent and SortByGPA operations? Conceptually, this is a fairly simple extension. However, from a coding perspective, it means that we will not be able to plug directly into a provided implementation of the keyed list ADT. Instead, we will have to tinker with the code of such an implementation, in effect reinventing and then extending the wheel.

This will be a nuisance, but it is a nuisance necessitated by Pascal language syntax—not by any flaw in the design process. A newer class of languages, called object-oriented languages, offer features that make it much easier for programmers to extend ADTs to meet the needs of a particular implementation. We will briefly discuss object-oriented languages in Section 14.6.

Second, in Example 14.2, we made the design decision that we would maintain an array in physical order by student name to allow use of the binary search algorithm when a particular student's record is being retrieved. Like many design decisions, this carries with it a trade-off. The price we will pay for being able to use the binary search algorithm in the Inspect-Student module will be a potentially excessive amount of data movement in the AddStudent and DeleteStudent modules. To see why this excessive data movement will occur, consider the add situation pictured in Figure 14.7.

FIGURE 14.7
Possible add situation for array implementation of student list

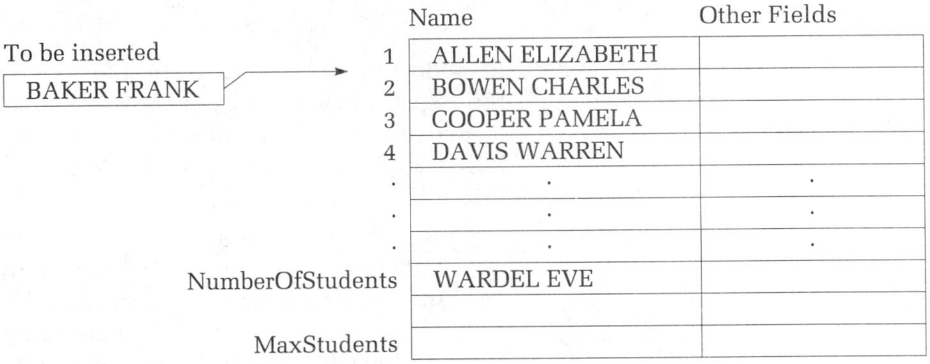

NumberOfStudents = current number of students
MaxStudents = maximum students possible

Here the addition of BAKER FRANK will force all records beginning at the second index to be moved down one slot. In a realistic situation where the school may have 10,000 students, each with a record consisting of 500 bytes, this will mean shuffling 5,000,000 bytes of data around in computer storage. If the storage involved is a magnetic disk instead of primary memory, this "pushing down" of all records starting with the second one could well leave the system in a loop that would require several minutes to execute.

An analogous problem occurs when a record near the top of the list is deleted. All the records below it must rise one slot to maintain the list in physical order. Thus, the design proposed in Example 14.2 will not fare particularly well with respect to add and delete performance. Nonetheless, in this chapter, we will live with these inefficiencies so that we may illustrate an actual implementation with the techniques we presently know. As we develop more powerful methods later in the text, we'll consider implementation strategies that circumvent these problems.

After determining the modular structure chart and major data structures for a system, the final step in the design process is to develop logic specifications for each module in the system. There are a variety of techniques for doing this; our preference is to follow the three-step approach we have used consistently throughout the text.

1. Specify the data received by the module. This serves to specify the preconditions for the module; that is, what we know to be true upon entry to the module.
2. Specify the information returned from the module. This serves to specify the postconditions for the module; that is, what we know to be true upon leaving the module.
3. Specify the logic to be followed by the module. Pseudocode is a convenient vehicle for doing this. The amount of detail given in the specifications is dependent on the degree to which you view the design of the system as dictating the implementation phase that follows. For instance, if you as designer have a great deal of confidence in the programmers who will implement the system, you will not need to specify logic in minute detail.

EXAMPLE 14.3

Provide a modular specification for the AddStudent module in the design of the registrar's system from Example 14.2.

Because that design specified a physically ordered array as an implementation technique for the student list, our modular specification should take this into account.

AddStudent Module
Data Received: List of students (with encapsulated number of students)
Information Returned: Transformed list with appropriate addition
                       Updated number of students
Logic: Obtain data for new student.
       Call on FindSlot module to find array location to insert student.
       Roll down all entries in array below this location.
       Insert new student at vacated location.
       Update total number of students.

EXAMPLE 14.4

Provide a modular logic specification for the FindStudent module in the design of the registrar's system from Example 14.2.

Here, because a well-known algorithm (binary search) is to be used, we may choose to provide minimal logical detail. Our assumption is that the eventual implementor of this module will be familiar with the code for the binary search.

FindStudent Module
Data Received: List of students (with encapsulated number of students)
              Target name
Information Returned: Record containing data associated with target
                 name
                 Array location of that record
                 Boolean flag indicating whether record found
Logic: Binary search algorithm.

In summary, the design phase of the system life cycle includes developing specifications for

1. The modular structure of the program.
2. The major data structures to be used by the program.
3. The logic needed by individual modules.

The system designer thus produces a set of documents that are then used by programmers who begin the actual coding of the system in an appropriate computer language. As we shall see, an effective design will facilitate this coding effort and will lead to a rather natural way of testing and verifying the correctness of the software that is written.

Implementation

In the implementation phase, you must churn out the Pascal code (or other appropriate language) necessary to put into effect the blueprint developed in the design phase. Although the terminology "churn out" may seem a bit degrading considering the amount of effort that must go into the writing of a program, we use it to stress the importance of the design phase. Given an appropriate set of formal specifications from the design phase, coding the programs really can be an easy task. The completeness of the design phase is the key to determining how easy coding is. Time spent in the design phase will be more than repaid by time gained in coding. This point cannot be overemphasized! The most common mistake made by most beginning programmers is jumping almost immediately into the *coding phase,* thereby digging themselves into holes they could have avoided by more thorough consideration of design issues.

A side issue of the coding phase is *documentation:* the insertion of explanatory remarks into your program so that it makes sense when read by someone else (or by yourself at some time in the distant future). Few computer scientists like to do documentation. However, that does not eliminate the absolute necessity of doing it.

In the real world, programs are worked on by teams of programmers, not just one individual. In such an environment, you must explain what your code is doing to the other people who will have to work with it. Moreover, should your code have to undergo revisions in the future (often termed *program maintenance*), your documentation will be vitally important. Without it, those programmers doing the revisions will have to waste days or even weeks trying to decipher logic that the passage of time has made cryptic. Computer lore is filled with horror stories of programmers who were assigned the unenviable task of maintaining poorly documented code. Edward Yourdon has presented this problem by saying,

> *Virtually every major organization that began computerizing 20 years ago is now faced with 20-year-old systems whose implementation is a mystery, and, far worse, whose user requirements are a mystery. The only solution to this crisis in the future is to maintain accurate, up-to-date documentation for as long as the system itself survives* (Modern Structured Analysis *(Englewood Cliffs, N.J.: Prentice-Hall, 1989), 448*).

Minimally, each module you write should include documentation stating its general purpose, identifying all parameters and major local variables, and clarifying any obscure code segments. So, get into the habit of documenting all procedures via the "Given:, Task:, Return:" style that we have been using throughout the text. When combined with other written specifications from the analysis and design phases, well-documented code will help insure that your software system has a long and productive lifetime.

Exercises 14.2

1. What is meant by the term *functionally cohesive* in reference to modular structure charts?

2. What is meant by the term *coupling* in reference to modular structure charts?

3. Explain why the following portion of a modular structure chart for a payroll system is not functionally cohesive.

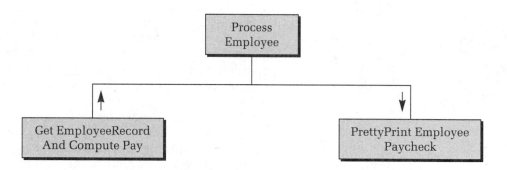

Correct the modular structure to make it more functionally cohesive.

4. Suppose that we have a search module that receives a customer identification key and then searches for that customer's record in a list of records, returning it to the calling module. Suppose also that this search module prints a "CANNOT FIND CUSTOMER" message if the record associated with this key cannot be located. From the perspective of functional cohesion, why is the printing of this message a poor strategy?

5. Explain why using global variables is a poor strategy from a data coupling perspective.

6. Suppose that a student record at the University of Hard Knocks contains information about the student's grades in courses the student has taken and about the tuition that the student owes the university. Why should a module that computes a student's grade point average not be passed the entire student record as a parameter?

7. Data flow diagrams and modular structure charts are graphic modeling tools related to the development cycle of a software system. Discuss similarities and differences between these two tools.

8. In Exercise 6 of Section 14.1 you analyzed a system requested by the registrar at American Basket Weaving University. Now follow up this analysis by doing a design for the system. Include a complete set of module specifications in your design.

■ ■ ■ ■

■ 14.3
Testing, Maintenance, and Obsolescence Phases of the System Life Cycle

A program's usefulness is ultimately demonstrated in the final three phases—testing, maintenance, and obsolescence—of the system life cycle.

Testing

An endeavor far more creative than coding and documentation is the testing that must be coordinated with a system's implementation. This chapter's Notes of Interest will attest to the importance of software reliability; it has become a moral and ethical issue as well as a technical one. Given this importance, how do we systematically verify the correctness of the software we develop?

First, we must realize that testing and verification is a critical and full-fledged phase of the system life cycle. As such, time must be allocated for it. A common mistake beginning programmers make is to assume the correctness of their program after one or two successful test runs. Though you should feel confident that your software will be error-free if it has been carefully designed, even well-designed systems must be thoroughly tested and verified before being released to users.

As an example, consider the following statistics, which summarize the percentages of total project time (not including maintenance) devoted to testing in several computerized systems developed for Air Force space missions.

SAGE	47%
NAVAL TACTICAL DATA SYSTEM	50%
GEMINI	47%
SATURN V	49%

(See R. W. Jensen and C. C. Tonies, *Software Engineering* (Englewood Cliffs, N.J.: Prentice-Hall, 1979), 330.)

Such statistics are amazingly consistent across a wide variety of large system development projects. "In examining conventionally scheduled projects," Frederick P. Brooks "found few that allowed one-half of the projected schedule for testing, but that most did indeed spend half of the actual schedule for that purpose. Many of these were on schedule until and except in system testing" (*The Mythical Man-Month* (Reading, Mass.: Addison-Wesley, 1982)).

The general rule of thumb is that the *testing phase* of a large project can (and should) consume roughly half of the time scheduled for the project. Of course, assignments in a programming course may not be of the same magnitude as an Air Force space mission, but the message is clear. If you fail to schedule a considerable amount of time to verify the correctness of your program, your users (or instructor) will inevitably find bugs in it.

How exactly does one verify the correctness of a large program? One way is to construct formal mathematical proofs of your algorithm's correctness. Though progress is being made in applying this type of formal mathematical approach (see Section 14.5), the complex problems of most real-world systems do not allow this method to be used efficiently. Consequently, the most often employed method of verifying a program's correctness is to test it thoroughly.

Modular Testing. If testing is important enough to take 50 percent of your time, it must clearly require more than a haphazard approach. Hence, we

Software Reliability and Defense Systems

The issue of software testing takes on great importance as we begin to increasingly rely on the computer as an aide in the decision-making process.

In "Computer System Reliability and Nuclear War" (*Communications of the ACM* 30, No. 2 (February 1987): 112–131), Alan Borning of the University of Washington evaluates the problems of software testing for the Strategic Defense Initiative, popularly known as Star Wars:

> *The SDI envisions a multilayer defense against nuclear ballistic missiles. The computer software to run such a defense would be the most complex ever built. A report by the Defensive Technologies Study Team, commissioned by the Department of Defense to study the feasibility of such a system, estimates a system with 6–10 million lines of code. Enemy missiles would first be attacked in their boost phase, requiring action within 90 seconds or so of a detected launch. This time interval is so short that the human role in the system could be minimal at best, with virtually no possibility of decision making by national leaders. Although pieces of the system could be tested and simulation tests performed, it would be impossible to test the entire system under actual battle conditions short of fighting a nuclear war. It has been the universal experience in large computer systems that there is no substitute for testing under actual conditions of use. The SDI is the most extreme example so far of an untestable system.*

Such systems are somewhat unique in that (we hope) many of them will never actually be used. If they ever are used, it may be too late to engage in the repair of minor flaws that normally arise in the maintenance phase of the system life cycle. It is not an understatement to say that the future of the human race may be riding on the thoroughness with which the systems have been tested. Is there any testing strategy that can be convincing enough under these circumstances? The apparent success of American Patriot missiles in destroying Iraqi Scud missiles in the Persian Gulf War has refueled speculation about the role of computer-controlled defense systems. Of the 43 Scud missiles launched against coalition forces in Saudi Arabia and Kuwait, Patriot systems intercepted 29, while 11 others were allowed to land in the ocean or remote areas of the desert. However, mere numbers can be somewhat deceiving. In his article "Lessons from the Patriot Missile Software Effort" (*IEEE Software* 8, No. 3 (May 1991): 105–108), Galen Gruman points out:

> *In one case, an Iraqi missile intercepted by a Patriot system stationed in Israel was merely knocked off target. In several other cases, debris from the intercepted Scuds damaged homes and injured people. Tougher for any interceptor are missiles that fall apart in flight, since the Patriot at best will hit only one piece, which may not be the warhead. For example, of the Scuds launched against Saudi Arabia and Kuwait, seven (including some that were allowed to fall) broke up during flight and could not be targeted—including one missile whose debris fell on a military barracks near Dhahran, Saudi Arabia, killing 28 soldiers. The Scuds fell apart because they were apparently old and poorly maintained, but both the U.S. and Soviet Union have multiple-warhead missiles designed just to avoid total destruction by antimissile systems.*

counsel against strategies such as creating your test data "on the fly" or creating test data by random techniques. Testing must be planned to be convincing. The plan that we shall briefly describe here begins with *modular testing*. Modular testing is the natural outgrowth of the principles of modular design.

The key to modular testing is to test each individual module as it is developed. Do not wait until the entire system has been coded to begin your testing. Thus, testing on the modular level involves

1. Developing short *driver modules* that artificially call the modules you have written and report the values returned by these modules.
2. Developing short *stub modules* that (again artificially) are called by the modules you have written. Such stubs should report the intermediate values they are sent and return appropriate values so that the module being tested can continue execution.
3. Designing *test cases* that exercise all the logical possibilities the module may encounter. Be aware that such test cases consist of more

than just strategically chosen input data. Each set of input data must also include its expected result (sometimes called the *test oracle*) if it is truly to convince anyone of the module's correctness.

We have already discussed techniques for writing drivers and stubs in Chapter 3. It is the third point about testing on the modular level to which we must turn our attention.

In designing test cases, programmers begin to mix methods of science and art. Every mathematician knows that we can never actually prove anything by testing examples (that is, input data). So, how can we verify a module's correctness by merely concocting examples? One proposed answer is to classify input data according to possible testing conditions. Hence, a finite set of well-chosen equivalence classes of test cases can be sufficient to cover an infinite number of possible inputs. Deciding what such equivalence classes should be is the point at which the process becomes more of an art than a science.

■ **EXAMPLE 14.5**

To illustrate these principles, consider the fee structure at the E-Z Park parking lot. Parking fees for vehicles are based on the following rules:

The module is given two data items: a character, which may be 'C' or 'T' indicating whether the vehicle is a car or truck; and an integer number indicating the number of hours the vehicle spent in the parking lot. Cars are charged $1.00 for each of the first three hours they are in the lot and $0.50 for each hour after that. Trucks are charged $2.00 for each of the first four hours they are in the lot and $0.75 per hour thereafter.

After computing the appropriate charge, a new module (ComputeParking-Fee) is to call on another new module (PrettyPrintTicket), which appropriately formats a parking fee ticket showing the vehicle type, hours parked, and resulting fee. The ComputeParkingFee module is given here.

```
PROCEDURE ComputeParkingFee (VehicleCategory : char;
                            Hours : integer);

  { Given:   Vehicle type in VehicleCategory and time spent in lot in Hours.   }
  {          Assume both parameters checked for validity outside this module.  }
  { Task:    Compute charge for parking and call on PrettyPrintTicket          }
  {          to output ticket.                                                 }
  { Return:  Nothing.                                                          }

VAR
  Charge : real;

BEGIN
  CASE VehicleCategory OF
    'C' : IF Hours <= 3 THEN
            Charge := Hours
          ELSE
            Charge := 3 + (Hours - 3) * 0.5;
    'T' : IF Hours <= 4 THEN
            Charge := Hours * 2
          ELSE
            Charge := 8 + (Hours - 4) * 0.75
  END; { of CASE VehicleCategory  }
  PrettyPrintTicket (VehicleCategory, Hours, Charge)
END; { of PROCEDURE ComputeParkingFee  }
```

An appropriate driver main program would simply allow us to repeatedly send data to the ComputeParkingFee module to check its behavior in a variety of situations. An appropriate stub for the call to PrettyPrintTicket would merely inform us that we reached this subordinate module and print the values received so that we could be sure they had been transmitted correctly. At this stage, the stub need not concern itself with detailed, formatted output; we are at the moment interested only in testing ComputeParkingFee.

In testing this module, we can begin by identifying the following six *equivalence classes:*

1. A car in the lot less than three hours.
2. A car in the lot exactly three hours.
3. A car in the lot more than three hours.
4. A truck in the lot less than four hours.
5. A truck in the lot exactly four hours.
6. A truck in the lot more than four hours.

Choosing one test case for each equivalence class, we arrive at the following set of test cases.

VehicleCategory	Hours	Expected Results
'C'	2	Charge = 2.00
'C'	3	Charge = 3.00
'C'	5	Charge = 4.00
'T'	3	Charge = 6.00
'T'	4	Charge = 8.00
'T'	8	Charge = 11.00

The test cases for exactly three hours for a car and exactly four hours for a truck are particularly important since they represent *boundary conditions* at which a carelessly constructed conditional check could easily produce a wrong result.

■   ■

This parking lot example, though illustrative of the method we wish to employ, is artificially simple. The next example presents a more complex testing situation.

■ **EXAMPLE 14.6**

Consider developing a strategy to test the sorting algorithms we discussed in Chapter 12. Recall that each of these algorithms—bubble sort, insertion sort, and selection sort—received an array of physical size MaxIndex and an integer N to indicate the logical size of the array, that is, the number of items currently stored in the array.

Our criterion for choosing equivalence classes of test data for such a sorting algorithm is based on two factors:

1. The size of N: the number of items to be sorted.
2. The ordering of the original data.

The following table presents a partitioning of test data into equivalence classes for this example.

Size of N	Order of Original Data	Expected Results
N = 1	Not applicable	
N = 2	Ascending	
N = 2	Descending	
N midsize and even	Descending	
N midsize and even	Ascending	Array to be
N midsize and even	Randomized	arranged in
N midsize and odd	Ascending	ascending order
N midsize and odd	Descending	for all cases.
N midsize and odd	Randomized	
N = physical array size	Ascending	
N = physical array size	Descending	
N = physical array size	Randomized	

The module should be run for a minimum of 12 cases, one for each of the classes dictated by our table. Ideally, a few subcases should be run for each of the randomized cases. We cannot overemphasize the importance of testing seemingly trivial cases such as N = 1 and N = 2. These lower boundary conditions are typical examples of data that may cause an otherwise perfectly functioning loop to be incorrectly skipped. Similarly, it is important to test the upper boundary condition in which N reaches the physical array size.

■   ■

Testing for Robustness. Yet another issue in modular testing is the question of how a module will react when it receives invalid data. For instance, in our current version of the ComputeParkingFee module in Example 14.5, there is a potentially disastrous side effect that occurs when the module receives a vehicle type other than 'C' or 'T.' (What is it?)

Similar reasoning dictates that the sort test data of Example 14.6 should perhaps contain test cases for N = 0 and N greater than the physical array size even though such cases should not arise in normal use of the sort module. A *robust* module is one that guards against harmful side effects when it receives invalid or unexpected data.

It is particularly critical that any modules with which the user is to interact be robust. Inadvertent wrong keystrokes by a user can crash a program or, even worse, result in a program performing its computations with incorrect data. Robustness may be so critical in some systems that you may have to improve upon the interaction capabilities provided by your programming language. Consider, for instance, what your version of Pascal will do when a user enters

`1.l5` (first character is a lowercase L)

instead of

`1.15`

in response to **read** (X) where X is a real. The accidentally typed lowercase 'l' can crash the **read** procedure offered by many versions of Pascal.

One way to avoid these problems is to write your own procedure to read a real number. In this procedure, read the input a character at a time and convert the incoming stream of characters to its corresponding real value. Because you are reading characters instead of reals, nothing the user types can crash your procedure. If a character that is not expected as part of a real is read, your procedure can take corrective action and warn the user of the problem.

A paradigm known as a *finite state machine* is often used by software engineers to perform such robustness checks on user input. (See the Note of Interest in Chapter 13 entitled "Sparse Tables and Language Compilers.") A finite state machine is best described by a diagram referred to as a *state-transition diagram*. A state-transition diagram for the problem of reading a real number entered in decimal form appears in Figure 14.8.

Interpret the circles in this diagram as the states of the machine. Hence the machine of Figure 14.8 can be in a LeadingSpaces state, a LeftOfDecimal state, a RightOfDecimal state, a Done state, or an Error state. In a particular state, the machine is expecting certain characters as valid input for that state.

The arrows leading from the states are called *transitions*. Transitions indicate what the machine will do when it encounters a particular character in its current state. Each transition is labeled with one or more characters and, potentially, an action to take upon reading such a character. For instance, when the machine of Figure 14.8 is in the LeadingSpaces state and it reads a space, it remains in the LeadingSpaces state. Consistent with Pascal syntax for entering a real in decimal form, the machine must read a ' + ', ' − ', or digit before it can begin the accumulation of a real value and switch to the Left-OfDecimal state. Any other character read in the LeadingSpaces state results in an error.

While in the LeftOfDecimal state, the machine reads digits on a character-by-character basis. As each digit is read, its value must be added to a running total that will be returned from the procedure. The only valid transitions

FIGURE 14.8
State-transition diagram for reading a real number in decimal form

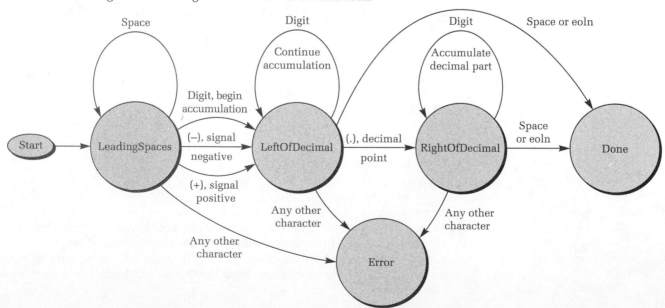

from the LeftOfDecimal state occur when a space, **eoln,** or decimal point is encountered. In a similar fashion, the RightOfDecimal state must read characters until the machine reaches the Done or Error state. You should trace the action of the machine in Figure 14.8 on a variety of input sequences to convince yourself that it correctly handles all possibilities.

The following example illustrates that using Pascal's enumerated type makes it relatively easy to translate a finite state machine into a Pascal procedure.

■ **EXAMPLE 14.7**

Write a robust Pascal procedure to read a real number employing the logic of the finite state machine in Figure 14.8.

The strategy of the procedure is to repeatedly read a character which is then analyzed in a **CASE** statement driven by the current state of the machine.

```
PROCEDURE ReadReal(VAR Val : real);

   { Given:    Nothing                                               }
   { Task:     Read one real value in decimal form from the current }
   {           line of input characters.  Assume at least one digit }
   {           to the left of a decimal point. If the current line of }
   {           input characters  does not constitute a valid real,  }
   {           force the user to  retype the offending sequence of  }
   {           characters.                                          }
   { Return:   The real value read in Val.                          }

   TYPE
     { This enumerated type captures the states of Figure 14.8      }
     Possibilities = (LeadingSpaces, LeftOfDecimal, RightOfDecimal, Error,
                   Done);

   VAR
     Ch : char;
     State : Possibilities;
     Negative : boolean; { To signal negative numbers }
     Multiplier : real; { For digits to right of decimal }

   BEGIN
     REPEAT { Stay in the outer REPEAT until read a valid real }
       { The inner loop embodies the logic of the finite state machine  }
       { in Figure 14.8                                                 }
       Negative := false; { Initially assume positive, toggle to signal negative }
       Multiplier := 0.1;
       Val := 0;
       State := LeadingSpaces; { Initial state to consume any leading spaces }
       REPEAT
         READ(Ch);
         CASE State OF
           LeadingSpaces:
             IF ('0' <= Ch) AND (Ch <= '9') THEN { Have read a digit }
               BEGIN
                 State := LeftOfDecimal;
                 Val := 10 * Val + (ord(Ch) - ord('0')) { Use ord to convert   }
                                                        { character to number }
               END
             ELSE IF Ch = '-' THEN { Signal negative number }
               BEGIN
                 Negative := true;
```

```
                State := LeftOfDecimal
              END
            ELSE IF Ch = '+' THEN { Leading positive sign }
              State := LeftOfDecimal
            ELSE IF Ch <> ' ' THEN
              State := Error;
          LeftOfDecimal:
            IF ('0' <= Ch) AND (Ch <= '9') THEN { Have read a digit }
              Val := 10 * Val + (ord(Ch) - ord('0'))
            ELSE IF Ch = '.' THEN { Decimal point }
              State := RightOfDecimal
            ELSE IF (Ch = ' ') THEN { End of current number }
              State := Done
            ELSE
              State := Error;
          RightOfDecimal:
            IF ('0' <= Ch) AND (Ch <= '9') THEN { Have read a digit }
              BEGIN
                Val := Val + Multiplier * (ord(Ch) - ord('0'));
                Multiplier := Multiplier * 0.1
              END
            ELSE IF (Ch = ' ') THEN { End of current number }
              State := Done
            ELSE
              State := Error
        END {CASE}
    UNTIL (State = Error) OR (State = Done) OR eoln;
    { If there was bad input, force the user to reenter until get valid real }
    IF State = Error THEN
      BEGIN
        writeln ('Bad Number - Please reenter this number ');
        readln
      END
    ELSE IF Negative THEN
      Val := - Val
  UNTIL (State = Done) OR eoln
END; { ReadReal }
```

To illustrate the use of the **PROCEDURE** ReadReal, consider the following driver program and the results of the sample run.

```
BEGIN {  Driver program  }
  REPEAT
    ReadReal (Number);
    IF eoln THEN
      readln;
    writeln (Number : 10 : 2)
  UNTIL Number = 0.0
END.
```

A sample run is as follows:

```
45.61
        45.61
11.2 34.8
        11.20
        34.80
19.6                    ◄──── Note that lowercase L typed instead of digit 1
Bad Number - Please reenter this number
19.6
        19.60
0.0
        0.00
```

It is probably safe to say that no module of reasonable complexity can be guaranteed to be 100 percent robust. For each safeguard against invalid data, a user will no doubt find some way of inadvertently bypassing that safeguard. How robust an individual module must be is a reflection of how it fits into the overall modular structure of the system. It is not reasonable to expect every module in a system to guard itself against every potential kind of invalid data. Such a strategy would have the vast majority of modules more preoccupied with this issue than with their assigned responsibility within the system. A better strategy is to have a few modules whose only responsibility is to screen incoming data against invalid values. In this way we can assure that other modules will be called only when we have valid data to give them. The degree to which an individual module should be robust is thus intimately tied to the overall system design and should be stated as part of the specifications for that module.

White Box/Black Box Testing. One factor that can influence the design of test cases is the knowledge you have of the design and implementation of the module being tested. If you have detailed knowledge of the design and implementation, you can engage in *white box testing*. That is, the module represents a "white box" because you are aware of the internal logic and data structure implementations in the module. In white box testing, test cases can be partitioned into equivalence classes which specifically exercise each logical path through a module. In *black box testing,* the module is approached without knowledge of its internal structure. You know what the module is supposed to do but not how it does it.

For instance, in Examples 14.2 and 14.4, we made the design decision to implement the list of students in the registrar's system with an array maintained in physical order by student name. This decision allowed us to use the binary search algorithm in the specifications for the FindStudent module. We'll work with this module again in the next examples.

■ **EXAMPLE 14.8**

Provide Pascal code for implementing the list of students and the FindStudent module described in Examples 14.2 and 14.4.

```
CONST
  MaxStudents  = 10;   { Small for testing purposes }
  StringLength = 40;

TYPE
  StudentRec = RECORD
                 Name : String;  { Assume appropriate implementation of  }
                                 { the String ADT                        }
                 CredTaken : integer;
                 CredEarned : integer;
                 TotalGradePts : integer
               END;
  StudentList = RECORD   { Encapsulated list }
                  List : ARRAY [1..MaxStudents] OF StudentRec;
                  NumberOfStudents : integer
                END;
  .
  .
  .
```

```
PROCEDURE FindStudent (Target : String;
                       Students : StudentList;
                       VAR InfoWanted : StudentRec;
                       VAR Mid : integer;
                       VAR Found : boolean);

{   Given:    List of student records, each identified by a unique Name field. }
{             A name to search for in Target.                                  }
{   Task:     Apply binary search algorithm to find Target.                    }
{   Return:   If Target found, return associated record in InfoWanted,         }
{             associated position in Mid, and Found as true.                   }
{             Otherwise return Found as false.                                 }

VAR
  High, Low : integer;

BEGIN
  Found := false;
  Low := 1;
  High := Students.NumberOfStudents;
  WHILE NOT Found AND (Low <= High) DO
    BEGIN
      Mid := (Low + High) DIV 2;
      IF LessThan (Target, Students.List[Mid].Name) THEN
        High := Mid - 1
      ELSE IF GreaterThan (Target, Students.List[Mid].Name) THEN
        Low := Mid + 1
      ELSE
        BEGIN
          Found := true;
          InfoWanted := Students.List[Mid]
        END
    END
END; {  of PROCEDURE FindStudent  }
```

■

■ EXAMPLE 14.9

To design a complete set of test cases for **PROCEDURE** FindStudent in Example 14.8, we use the following table. The seven cases presented in the table exercise all logical paths through the binary search algorithm.

Test Case	NumberOf-Students	List	Target	Expected Results	Rationale
I	10	ALLEN BAKER DAVIS GREEN HUFF MILLER NOLAN PAYTON SMITH TAYLOR	Try each name in the Students list	Found **true**. InfoWanted contains associated record. Mid contains associated position	Can we find everything in the full list?

Test Case	NumberOf-Students	List	Target	Expected Results	Rationale
II	10	Same as test case I	Try AARON, NATHAN, ZEBRA	Found **false**.	Is Found correctly returned as **False** for Target data items that precede all list elements, follow all list elements, and are interspersed in the middle of the list? This case tests the full list.
III	5	ALLEN DAVIS HUFF NOLAN SMITH	Same as test case I	Same as test case I	Can we find everything in a mid-sized list?
IV	5	Same as test case III	Same as test case II	Same as test case II	Same as test case II but for mid-sized list.
V	1	HUFF	HUFF	Same as test case I	Can we handle successful search in a one-element list?
VI	1	HUFF	Same as test case II	Same as test case II	Can we handle unsuccessful searches in a one-element list?
VII	0		HUFF	Same as test case II	Robustness check. What if we call on FindStudent with the empty list?

Note that, in Example 14.9, our test cases are sure to exercise the situation in which the array is completely full. This represents a boundary condition for the algorithm; we are aware of this condition because we are testing from a white box perspective. Were we testing instead from a black box perspective, it might not be possible to exercise all such boundary conditions.

System and Acceptance Testing. In practice, testing at the modular level tends to be white box testing since a well-designed module will be compact and focused. Hence it is relatively easy to explore the internal structure of a module and create test cases geared toward that internal structure. As modules merge together into a full-fledged software system, the testing of the entire system takes on more of a black box perspective.

In *system testing,* you exercise the interfaces between modules instead of the logic of a particular module. System testing should not occur until each module has been individually tested by white box methods. In larger systems you may find it advantageous to test related subcollections of modules before jumping to a test of the entire system. This will allow you more easily to localize the location of any errors that are found.

Ultimately, the system is tested not only by technical people but by the end users who must work with the system on a regular basis. This final phase of *acceptance testing* carried out by end users is totally black box in nature. Typically end users neither want nor need detailed knowledge of *how* a system is implemented; instead, they have a very substantial interest in *what* the system does. Does it successfully meet the specifications that were described very early in the analysis phase of the project? Consequently, end users will test and ultimately accept or reject the system based upon how it meets these specifications.

Debugging Errors Found During Testing. The main goal of all testing we have discussed is to find errors. Though at first glance this statement may seem counterproductive, remember that it is better for errors to be detected at the testing stage than when the software is in use (or when your instructor is assigning a grade). Given this negative premise of testing, you must also know how to debug your programs when testing achieves its goal of finding errors. If testing can be categorized as an art, debugging could facetiously be described as bordering on the occult.

The following general guidelines apply to the debugging of all programs.

1. Typing is no substitute for thinking. Don't be too quick to make changes in your source program. Instead, when an error occurs, take your test cases and trace them by hand through the logic currently present in your module. Here the advantage of modular testing becomes apparent. Such hand tracing is nearly impossible if you are working with an entire system; with merely one module it is quite manageable.

2. Make use of the various debugging tools provided with most compilers. These tools allow you to scatter tracer output (to display the value of key variables at various stages of an algorithm) and breakpoints (to halt program execution at a key step so that you can examine the values contained in variables) throughout your program in a conveniently interactive fashion. The time you spend learning how to use such tools will be repaid many times over.

3. Don't assume that once you've repaired your program for the test case which generated the error, all previous tests cases will still work correctly. You now have a new program, and all of your carefully designed test cases need to be applied again.

4. Leave time to debug. This avoids "band-aid" corrections (often called patches) and encourages alternatives that may actually improve the design of your program. There is nothing wrong with completely scrapping an approach that has been shown, by testing, to be ill-conceived. Indeed, to try to make such an approach work by installing repeated and intricate fixes can only lead to a system doomed to a very short life.

5. Keep your test cases in a file so that as you make future modifications you can use them again conveniently.

The (Lack of) Responsibility of Software Developers

If you have ever purchased software such as a word processor or spreadsheet for a microcomputer you have probably signed a license agreement in which you agree not to copy the software except for your own backup protection. The fineprint in such software licenses also typically contains disclaimers about the responsibility of the software developer should you eventually do something such as underpay your income tax because of a bug in the spreadsheet you used to keep your tax records.

For instance, the second page of the user's guide of a popular spreadsheet program provides the following disclaimer of warranties. The actual company name (designated here as *X*) is not given. This disclaimer is typical of that used by virtually all software companies.

The software and user manuals are provided "as is" and without express or limited warranty of any kind by either X or anyone who has been involved in the creation, production, or distribution of the software, including, but not limited to, the implied warranties of merchantability and fitness for a particular purpose.

The entire risk as to the quality and performance of the software and user manuals is with you. Should the software and user manuals prove defective, you (and not X or anyone else who has been involved in the creation, production, or distribution of the software) assume the entire cost of all necessary servicing, repair or correction.

Compare such a disclaimer to the claims that appear in the software ads that adorn all popular computing magazines and you will see a real contradiction. Products that profess to do virtually everything guarantee absolutely nothing.

Perhaps the reservations that software developers have about guaranteeing the reliability of their products should not be surprising given what we have learned about the software system life cycle. The complexity of software design and testing makes it virtually impossible to develop software that is 100 percent free of bugs. To customers in the software marketplace, the message is clear: Caveat emptor (Let the buyer beware)!

Maintenance

What follows acceptance testing of your system? Once your program has been thoroughly tested, it is ready to be released to the users who originally requested it. In theory, you are done; these users will live happily ever after using the program that you so painstakingly developed. In practice, unfortunately, it rarely works out this way. Instead, users begin to find flaws with your program. (Nobody is perfect!) These flaws typically are due to such factors as

- Your misunderstanding the users' exact needs during the analysis phase.
- Your system's slow performance when it encounters large volumes of user data.
- User needs that have changed since you initially did your analysis.
- Changes in computer hardware and operating system software.

When flaws like these arise, you must maintain your system. That is, you must make the necessary changes to correct the flaws. Here is where good program design and documentation pay off again. It is absolutely essential that you (or someone else assigned to *maintenance*) be able to understand your code after months or perhaps years away from it. Moreover, if your modules are functionally cohesive and minimally coupled, then you should be able to make the appropriate changes in them without causing problems in other modules of the system. That a program must be maintained is not an indication of poor design; it is rather a fact of the software life cycle. That a program can be easily maintained is actually an indication that it was soundly designed from its conception.

Obsolescence

As we saw in Chapter 1, despite all your best efforts, your program may become obsolete in time. At that point, the system life cycle must begin anew. You may then be asked to develop a new program to meet the changed needs of the user and to make use of any expanded software capabilities.

Dynamic Nature of the System Life Cycle

Let us recap the phases of the system life cycle: analysis, design, implementation (coding), testing and verification, maintenance, and obsolescence. Though we have discussed each as a separate entity, they are all interwoven into a dynamic, iterative process. The process is dynamic because the dividing lines between the phases are always changing. That is, as you are doing analysis, you are probably already beginning to consider many design and coding issues. The process is iterative in that, from one phase, you may frequently have to return to an earlier phase. For instance, though you may be designing your system, if a question arises about what the user wants, you will have to temporarily return to analysis before completing the design. Similarly, during implementation, you may find it necessary to alter certain design considerations. The fact that many people are usually involved in the system life cycle—users, analysts, designers, and programmers—also contributes to the volatile nature of systems development.

Perhaps one of the worst misconceptions about those of us who work in the computer field is that we deal with problems that have very rigid, well-defined solutions. We hope our discussion of the system life cycle has convinced you that nothing could be further from the truth. To truly contribute over the span of the entire life cycle, you must be skilled at communicating with people, thinking abstractly, and then following through on the details of a plan. The effective computer scientist must truly be a person for all seasons.

Exercises 14.3

1. Summarize what is involved in each of the phases of the system life cycle. If you were to specialize your career in one of these phases, which one would it be? Why? Provide your answer in essay form.

2. What is meant by the term *boundary conditions* for an algorithm?

3. What is a robust module? Should every module in a system be completely robust? Justify your answer in a written essay.

4. Consider the ComputeParkingFee procedure discussed in this section (Example 14.5). Is it robust? What does it do if it does not receive a 'C' or 'T' for its Category parameter? Rewrite this module to make it more robust.

5. Employees at the University of Hard Knocks are paid by the following rules.
   - Employees who sign a contract for a total annual wage are paid 1/52 of that amount each week.
   - Hourly employees receive a paycheck based on the number of hours they work in a given week and their hourly rate. They are paid this hourly rate for each of the first 40 hours they work. After 40 hours, they are paid time-and-a-half for each additional hour of work. Moreover, work on a holiday is a special case for hourly employees. They get paid double-time for all holiday work.

   Write a procedure to compute the pay for an employee of the University of Hard Knocks and then dispatch the appropriate information to a check printing module. Completely test the procedure you write by integrating it with appropriate driver and stub modules and by designing a complete set of test data for the module.

6. Develop test data for the AddStudent module of Example 14.3.

7. Design test data for **PROCEDURE** ReadReal of Example 14.7. Remember that robustness is a high priority for this module, so your test data should be designed with that in mind. If your test data detect any flaws in the algorithm, fix them.

8. Extend the finite state machine of Figure 14.8 to accept reals entered with Pascal's "E" exponential notation. Then incorporate this extended finite state machine into the **PROCEDURE** ReadReal of Example 14.7. Finally, design test data for the extended procedure.

9. Extend the **PROCEDURE** ReadReal of Example 14.7 so that it rejects any number outside of a certain range (to be specified by additional parameters). Illustrate the use of your new procedure in a driver program.

10. Develop modular test data for the implementation of each string operation defined in Section 13.2. Then carry out system testing for the main program of Example 13.2.

11. Each type of computer has its own particular syntax for what it allows as a valid file name. Often such a file name may include an optional disk and directory specifier. Along the lines of Figure 14.8, develop a finite state machine to validate an input stream of characters intended to represent a file name on the computer system you use. Then translate your finite state machine into a robust procedure which returns in a string a file name entered by a user. Design test data for this procedure and create a driver program to test it.

12. This section has presented modular testing as the design of equivalence classes of test cases that exercise all the logical possibilities a module may encounter. You are working on a software system with a friend who claims that such comprehensive testing is impossible. As evidence, the friend cites a module she has written with 20 **IF . . . THEN . . . ELSE** statements in it. Your friend points out that there are approximately 2^{20} logical paths through this module, and that comprehensive modular testing is therefore impossible. In a written essay, refute your friend's claim. (*Hint:* Consider the cohesion of the module used as an example by your friend.)

■ 14.4
Pragmatics: Random Access File Implementations of Lists (Optional)

In the Focus on Program Design section of Chapter 13, we used an array as a means of implementing a keyed list. In Example 14.2, the array again emerged as a strategy for implementing an extended form of the keyed list ADT to be used by a university registrar. In both of these situations, an array does not represent a realistic solution to the problem posed. Why? Array storage is not permanent; when we quit a program, data in an array are lost.

We can try to overcome this limitation by loading the array from a text file at the beginning of a program and then writing it out to another text file when we quit the program. This is the strategy we used in Chapter 13's Focus on Program Design section. However, then we often run into another problem: the limited amount of main memory storage that an array may claim. Since arrays reside in main memory, the amount of data they may contain at any one time is dependent on the amount of memory available on your computer system. In many practical situations, loading an entire employee payroll list or student registration list into an array for processing isn't remotely possible. The size of the list exceeds by far the main memory at your disposal. In such situations, there is no choice but to store and process the data using a file.

We have used files in previous chapters. For example, Chapter 10 provided you with an introduction to the sequential processing of files with structured components (*sequential access files*). For instance, the declarations

```
TYPE
    .
    .
    .
    StudentRec = RECORD
                     Name : String;
                     CredTaken : integer;
                     CredEarned : integer;
                     TotalGradePts : integer
                 END;
    StudentList = FILE OF StudentRec;
    .
    .
    .
VAR
    .
    .
    .
    NextStudent : StudentRec;
    Students : StudentList;
```

allow you to process records in the disk file Students via Pascal's caret notation, Students^, which accesses the contents of the *file buffer*. Essentially, the buffer for the file Students is an area in main memory capable of storing precisely one record from the file (which may have arbitrarily many records stored on a permanent basis). The standard Pascal statement

```
NextStudent := Students^;
```

assigns the contents of the buffer to the record variable NextStudent. Similarly

```
Students^ := NextStudent;
```

copies the contents of NextStudent into the buffer. The standard Pascal statement **put**(Students) transfers the contents of the buffer to the currently accessed record in the file Students, whereas **get**(Students) moves data in the opposite direction, that is, from the currently accessed file record to the buffer. These Pascal file concepts are highlighted in Figure 14.9.

Figure 14.9
File operations in standard Pascal

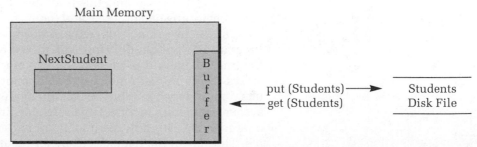

■ **EXAMPLE 14.10**

A typical loop to process every record in an already existing Students file is

```
reset (Students);
WHILE NOT eof (Students) DO
  BEGIN
    NextStudent := Students^;
    ProcessRecord (NextStudent);  {  Assume procedure exists  }
    get (Students)
  END;
```

Note that **reset** retrieves the first record into the buffer; hence the **get** appears at the end of the loop.

■   ■

■ **EXAMPLE 14.11**

To create a file, the following loop is used.

```
rewrite (Students);
CreateRecord (NextStudent);  {  Assume procedure exists  }
WHILE  {  NextStudent to be added to file  }  DO
  BEGIN
    Student^ := NextStudent;
    put (Students);
    CreateRecord (NextStudent)
  END;
```

■   ■

In practice, most Pascal implementations also allow **read** and **write** to access files that are not text files. In such implementations, the single statement

```
read (Students, NextStudent);
```

is equivalent to the two statements

```
NextStudent := Students^;
get (Students);
```

Similarly, the single statement

```
write (Students, NextStudent);
```

is equivalent to

```
Students^ := NextStudent;
put (Students);
```

T Turbo Pascal supports only **read** and **write** in this fashion, hence eliminating the standard **get** and **put** from its repertoire.

The problem with the Pascal file processing statements we have reviewed is that they perform only sequential file processing, that is, processing in which the records in a file are accessed in the order first record, second record, third record, and so on. Hence, to access the 40th record, you first have to access records 1 through 39. This type of processing is simply not suitable if we are to use a permanent disk file to implement a keyed list.

List operations and algorithms such as the binary search require that we be able to randomly access any record by specifying its relative position in the list. One approach to overcoming this limitation is to load all the components of a file into an array at the beginning of a program and then write out the (perhaps updated) components to a new file when the program terminates. This strategy will work with small files, but it is not adequate for large files since such files typically consume too much space if loaded entirely into an array in main memory.

[T]   Although random file processing is not part of standard Pascal, it is so essential to file processing algorithms that most Pascal compilers include nonstandard extensions that allow you to perform direct access file operations. For instance, using the Turbo Pascal compiler, the statements

```
seek (Students, K);
read (Students, NewStudent);
```

will directly retrieve the Kth file record into the record variable NewStudent, with the first file record referenced by K = 0. Similarly, the statements

```
seek (Students, K);
write (Students, NewStudent);
```

will send the contents of the record variable NewStudent to the Kth record position in the file Students.

If you are not using Turbo Pascal, you should consult local system documentation to find out what nonstandard statements will perform similar *random access file* operations for your compiler. (Appendix 10 provides a summary of such statements for many popular Pascal compilers.) The point is that, as long as your version of Pascal supports random file access, our array implementation of a list can be easily converted to a random access file implementation. For instance, again using Turbo Pascal for illustration purposes, the array-based statement

```
Students[K] := NewStudent;
```

becomes

```
seek (Students, K);
write (Students, NewStudent);
```

in a file-based implementation. You will be asked to convert the registrar's system to such a random access file implementation in the Problems at the end of the chapter.

The practical importance of file-oriented implementations of abstract data types versus array implementations cannot be overstated. The permanent nature of data stored in files makes such implementations essential in many data processing applications. Files have the additional advantage of being almost limitless in size (arrays are bounded by the restraints of main memory). Of course, what we already have learned about the trade-off computer scientists often face should warn you that these advantages do not come without a price. With random access files, that price is slower access. Whereas array entries can be accessed at microsecond speeds, random file access is at millisecond speed: slower by a factor of 1,000. This becomes crucial in the more powerful search algorithms we'll discuss in later chapters.

Despite the importance of random access files, the case studies we present in this text will typically be written using arrays. We do this for two main reasons. First, the code for arrays tends to be cleaner, usually involving fewer statements to get the same conceptual operation done. Second, the system-dependent aspect of random access file processing in Pascal tends to make such presentations less worthwhile for those of you using different versions of Pascal than we are. However, given what we have already said about the conceptual similarities between arrays and random access files, conversion from the former to the latter should always be a relatively easy matter.

Exercises 14.4

1. Discuss the advantages and disadvantages of an array implementation of a list versus an implementation using a random access file.

2. Using Appendix 10 or local system reference material, determine the statements used for random access file processing in the version of Pascal you use. Use the statements to write instruction sequences that will

    a. Assign to a main memory variable the Kth component of a random access file.

    b. Assign to the Kth component of a random access file the contents of a main memory variable of the same type as a file component.

3. Discuss how the instruction sequences you developed for Exercise 2 could be used to convert an array implementation of a list into a random file implementation.

4. Explain why a pointer sort that uses an array of pointers in main memory would be particularly appropriate for a list implemented via a random access file.

5. In Section 10.3 you discovered that altering just one component of a sequential file would require copying all the records in the file into a new file. Explain why this is not practical for many applications and how random access files provide a more efficient means of updating an individual component of the file. Illustrate by using appropriate random file instructions from your version of Pascal.

6. Explain why loading a sequential file into an array at the beginning of a program and then writing the array to a sequential file at the end of a program is often not a viable alternative to random file processing. Under what conditions would it be a viable alternative?

7. You are implementing a keyed list (Section 13.4) as a physically ordered random access file with the binary search algorithm used for the Retrieve operation. From an efficiency perspective, discuss the implications of this implementation strategy with respect to the Add and Delete operations.

■ ■ ■ ■

■ 14.5
Formal Verification (Optional)

The approach we have taken in Section 14.3 to insuring software reliability is to emphasize the construction of thorough and convincing test data as a means of verifying program/module correctness. However, this strategy of verification cannot be construed as a formal proof of the algorithm's correctness. We have attempted to show that an algorithm is correct by showing that it works for a comprehensive set of examples. But, from a mathematical perspective, a theorem cannot be proven by example. This is because there are infinitely many possibilities for such examples, hence making it impossible to test every one. Instead of testing, a formal approach to algorithm verification demands an airtight proof using the basic axioms and principles of logic.

Formal Algorithm Verification by the Method of Inductive Assertions

Some work has been done in this area of formal algorithm verification. We shall attempt to summarize one of the more frequently used techniques, known as the *method of inductive assertions,* by formally proving the correctness of the following algorithm. The algorithm is to compute N^M for N a real and M a nonnegative integer. Our correctness proof will use the principle of mathematical induction. (This principle is covered extensively in most discrete mathematics texts; be sure to review it before proceeding if you are not familiar with it.)

```
PROCEDURE Power (N : real;
                 M : integer;
                 VAR R : real);

{ Given:    N, a real number, and M, a nonnegative integer.  }
{ Task:     Compute N raised to power M.                      }
{ Return:   The computed value in R.                          }

BEGIN
  R := 1;
  WHILE M > 0 DO
    BEGIN
      R := R * N;
      M := M - 1
    END
END; { of PROCEDURE Power }
```

A formal proof of such an algorithm involves appropriately identifying the input assertions, output assertions, and loop invariants of the algorithm. (See Chapter 4, Section 4.6 and Chapter 5, Section 5.3.) All three of these are statements about the algorithm expressed in formal mathematical terms. The input assertions represent all necessary input conditions to the algorithm. For our example, the input assertions would be

$N \in$ reals

$M \in$ integers

$M \geq 0$

The output assertions represent in formal terms the desired result. Here we would have

$R = N^M$

as the lone output assertion for our algorithm.

Finally, we must identify the loop invariants of our algorithm. A loop invariant may be thought of as a special type of assertion that expresses a relationship between variables and remains constant through all iterations of a loop. Note that it is not the variables that remain fixed but rather the relationship between them. This is a key distinction to make. As we shall see, correctly identifying loop invariants is often the most crucial and difficult step in setting the stage for a proof (by induction) of an algorithm's correctness.

For the Power algorithm under consideration, let R_k and M_k be the respective values of R and M after k times through the **WHILE** loop. Both R and

M change each time the loop is executed while N remains fixed throughout the algorithm. The loop invariant relationship we wish to prove is then given by

$$R_k \times N^{M_k} = N^M$$

If we can prove this loop invariant, then it follows immediately that the algorithm is correct. Why? If the looping ends after j times through the loop, M_j will be zero because of the conditional test in the **WHILE.** Hence, because of the loop invariant relationship, we will have

$$R_j \times N^{M_j} = N^M$$
$$\downarrow$$
$$R_j \times N^0 = N^M$$
$$\downarrow$$
$$R_j = N^M$$

Therefore, when the loop terminates after j iterations, R will contain the value N^M and thereby satisfy the output assertion. The entire problem of proving the algorithm's correctness has thus been reduced to achieving an inductive proof of the loop invariant relationship.

Inductive Proof

Now we will work through the inductive proof of

$$R_k \times N^{M_k} = N^M$$

Basis Step with $k = 0$. Before looping begins, $R_0 = 1$ and $M_0 = M$ since these are the values of the variable established by the input assertions. Hence the loop invariant relationship for $k = 0$ becomes

$$1 \times N^M = N^M$$

which is trivially true.

Inductive Step. By the standard inductive assumption, we assume

$$R_k \times N^{M_k} = N^M$$

and attempt to show

$$R_{k+1} \times N^{M_{k+1}} = N^M$$

In going from the kth pass through the **WHILE** loop to the $(k + 1)$st pass through the loop we have

$$R_{k+1} = R_k \times N$$

and

$$M_{k+1} = M_k - 1$$

Hence

$$R_{k+1} \times N^{M_{k+1}}$$
$$= (R_k \times N) \times N^{(M_k - 1)}$$
$$= R_k \times N^{M_k}$$
$$= N^M$$

by the inductive assumption.

The inductive step thus completes the formal proof of the algorithm's correctness. Note how the pivotal point in the entire proof was the determination of the loop invariant. This determination drives the rest of the proof. We can summarize the steps involved in the overall proof as follows:

1. Specification of input assertions.
2. Specification of output assertions.
3. Specification of loop invariants, from which the output assertions follows.
4. Proof (via induction) of the loop invariants.

What Do Proofs Really Prove?

One of the valid criticisms of our proof is that it proves correct an algorithm which is obviously correct to start with. This criticism can often be made of formal correctness proofs as they presently stand. That is, the present state of the art in *formal verification* methods has not advanced to the point where they are of value in most realistically complex situations. Other criticisms of the method include:

1. The proof method assumes the correctness of the input and output assertions. If they are wrong, a proof of the program could be done but the program could still contain errors.
2. The proof method says nothing about how the program will act when exceptional conditions occur which deviate from the input assertions.
3. The proof method focuses only on the logic within an individual module. It verifies nothing with respect to how the modules of a system will interact.
4. The proof method relies upon a completely accurate interpretation of the action dictated by a given algorithmic statement. This action is often called the *semantics* of the statement. If our interpretation of a statement's semantics does not match what actually happens when the program runs, the program may result in an error even though it has been proved correct.
5. Practical machine limitations such as round-off and overflow are usually not considered in formal correctness proofs.
6. Proof techniques ignore the problem of unwanted side effects caused by an algorithm. Such side effects may result in an error in the overall system even though each module has been proved correct.
7. Proofs of nonnumerical algorithms such as searching and sorting are much more difficult than proofs of numerical algorithms. (These criticisms are set forth in more expanded form in Glenford Myer, *Software Reliability* (New York: Wiley & Sons, 1976), 319–320.)

Formal correctness proofs must currently be considered as a technique that is mostly of theoretical importance. They simply are not sophisticated enough to find practical application in programs that solve realistically complex problems. However, a technique should not be rejected because it presently has little practical value. Many useful methods in computer science had their roots in pure theory. Perhaps the ultimate hope for the formal correctness methods we have discussed is that they can be automated. That is, in the future we may have software that receives input/output assertions as its input, generates the code to satisfy these assertions, and then proves the correctness of the code. Though it is obviously a long way from happening, such automatic program synthesis does not seem to be impossible in principle. (The potential of formal methods in algorithm verification is the feature topic in the September 1990 issues of *IEEE Computer* and *IEEE Software*.)

A NOTE OF INTEREST

Program Verification: Possible or Not?

According to mathematical logician Jon Barwise, an article by University of Minnesota, Duluth philosopher James Fetzer has touched off a debate that could be "just as exciting and just as acrimonious" as the debates about the nature of mathematics that raged in the early twentieth century. Fetzer's article, entitled "Program Verification: The Very Idea" appears in the September, 1988 issue of the *Communications of the ACM* (Vol. 31, No. 8: 1048–1063). In it, Fetzer argues that computer programs, as "encodings of algorithms that can be compiled and executed by a machine," defy formal proofs of correctness in the sense discussed in Section 14.5 of this text. Arguing from the premise that "the function of a program is to satisfy the constraints imposed by an abstract machine for which there is an intended interpretation with respect to a physical system," Fetzer argues that "the behavior of that system cannot be subject to conclusive absolute verification but requires instead empirical inductive investigation to support inconclusive relative verifications."

To a degree, Fetzer's article can be viewed as an attack upon much of the research being done in formally proving the correctness of programs. As such, it has been the subject of heated criticism from many computer scientists. For instance, one letter of response signed by 10 computer scientists from institutions including the University of Maryland, Cornell University, and Stanford University blasted the *Communications* for even publishing Fetzer's article:

However, by publishing the ill-informed, irresponsible, and dangerous article by Fetzer, the editors of Communications *have abrogated their responsibility, to both the ACM membership and to the public at large, to engage in serious enquiry into techniques that may justify the practice of computer science as a socially responsible engineering endeavor. The article is ill-informed and irresponsible because it attacks a parody of both the intent and the practice of formal verification. It is dangerous because its pretentious and ponderous style may lead the uninformed to take it seriously* (Communications of the ACM 32, No. 3 (March 1989): 287–288).

The war of letters and responses over Fetzer's article raged on in the April, 1989 *Communications of the ACM*. At issue appears to be the role of abstract reasoning about algorithms in ensuring the correctness of software that runs on real-world machines. Like many philosophical questions, those raised by Fetzer will probably never be answered to the satisfaction of everyone involved in the debate. Nonetheless, as pointed out by Michael Evangelist, a senior researcher in software technology at MCC in Austin, Texas, "Fetzer has helped to draw the distinction better between reasoning about physical objects and about abstractions of those objects."

Exercises 14.5

1. Use the method of inductive assertions to prove the correctness of the following algorithm.

```
PROCEDURE Difference (X, Y : integer;
                            VAR Z : integer);

  { Given:    Integers X and Y.                }
  { Task:     Compute the difference X - Y.  }
  { Return:   Computed difference in Z.       }

  VAR W : integer;

  BEGIN
    Z := X;
    W := Y;
    WHILE W > 0 DO
      BEGIN
        Z := Z - 1;
        W := W - 1
      END
  END; { of PROCEDURE Difference }
```

2. Use the method of inductive assertions to prove the correctness of the following algorithm.

```
PROCEDURE Cube (X : integer;
                     VAR Z : integer);

  { Given:    Integer X.                  }
  { Task:     Compute X cubed.            }
  { Return:   The computed value in Z.    }

  VAR A, B, C : integer;

  BEGIN
    A := 1;
    B := 0;
    C := X;
    Z := 0;
    WHILE C > 0 DO
      BEGIN
        Z := Z + A + B;
        B := B + 2 * A + 1;
        A := A + 3;
        C := C - 1
      END
  END; { of PROCEDURE Cube }
```

3. Could an algorithm that has been proven correct by formal verification methods still produce a "wrong answer" when it is implemented in a particular programming language on a particular machine? Provide a written rationale for your answer.

■ ■ ■ ■

■ **14.6**
Object-Oriented Programming (Optional)

In Chapter 13 we introduced the notion of abstract data types. That chapter's Focus on Program Design section illustrated that using abstract data types by invoking their operations without making assumptions about their implementations can be a powerful aide in controlling the complexity of a program. Then, in Example 14.2, we carried out a system design which illustrated a shortcoming of abstract data types. In that example, we needed a data structure that resembled a keyed list ADT but that required a bit more. The rigidity of the ADT's definition makes it difficult for the code resulting from that design (see this chapter's Focus on Program Design) to plug directly into the operations provided with the keyed list. Instead, we are forced to reinvent the wheel: we can borrow many ideas from the keyed list ADT but must start our coding efforts from scratch. We have lost the timesaving advantage of being able to reuse code provided by an ADT's implementation.

System developers using the ADT approach frequently found themselves restricted in this fashion by the inflexibility of ADT definitions. They needed a way of making an ADT's definition more malleable. This would allow a developer to redefine certain ADT operations, extend the ADT by defining new operations, and yet still reuse much of an ADT's implementation. What has emerged from this need to fine-tune ADTs to particular applications is a new paradigm called *object-oriented programming*.

A detailed discussion of object-oriented programming is certainly beyond the scope of this text, in part because the Pascal language does not support this paradigm. Object-oriented programming will, however, certainly play a major role in the future of software engineering. Many implementors of Pascal compilers, aware of this coming trend, are beginning to offer object-oriented extensions to their versions of Pascal. Other languages, such as Smalltalk and C++, have incorporated object-oriented features as part of their standards. To provide you with a base of information, we will provide a brief description of some of the key components of the object-oriented paradigm.

Object-Oriented Encapsulation

The object-oriented paradigm carries encapsulation one step further than we were able to do in Chapter 13 by bundling both the data fields and the operations for an ADT into the ADT's declaration. Such a ADT declaration creates what is called a *class object*. Think of it as a "super" **TYPE** declaration. Using a hypothetical Pascal-like syntax, the declaration of a class object for the keyed list ADT might appear as follows.

```
TYPE
  KeyType = { An appropriate type for the key field in list records }
  OtherDataType = { An appropriate type for the other data associated with }
                  { each key field                                         }
  ListNode = RECORD
                Key : KeyType;
                OtherData : OtherDataType
             END;
  KeyedList = OBJECT { Hypothetical syntax only }
                { The next two items are data fields used for an array }
                { implementation                                       }
                List : ARRAY [1..MaxListSize] OF ListNode;
                NumberOfNodes : integer;
                { Then come the operations owned by an object of       }
                { type KeyedList                                       }
                PROCEDURE Create;
                PROCEDURE Add (Item : ListNode;
                              VAR Success : Boolean);
                PROCEDURE Delete (Target : KeyType;
                                 VAR Success : boolean);
                PROCEDURE Retrieve (Target : KeyType;
                                   VAR Item : ListNode;
                                   VAR Success : boolean);
                PROCEDURE TraverseInOrder (PROCEDURE ProcessNode
                                          (VAR Item : ListNode))
              END; { of definition of class object KeyedList }
```

We could then declare *instances* of the class KeyedList. Instances are themselves objects that could be thought of as variables of **TYPE** KeyedList.

```
VAR  {  Hypothetical syntax only  }
  List1, List2 : KeyedList;
```

Because the operations have been encapsulated within the definition of the KeyedList class, the instances List1 and List2 are viewed as owning these operations. Hence we invoke an operation not by passing List1 or List2 as an argument to the operation but rather by "telling" List1 or List2 to perform that operation. For example, again using a hypothetical Pascal-like syntax, we would have

```
List1.Create;  { Tell List1 to create itself }
readln (Item);
List1.Add (Item,Success);  { Tell List1 to add Item to itself }
```

One interesting perspective that emerges from object-oriented encapsulation is called *programming by personification*. Objects take on a person-like quality, and we invoke operations by telling an object to perform an operation that is part of its encapsulation. Object-oriented disciples often use the term *message-passing*; for example, "send the Create message to object List1."

Clearly, object-oriented programming requires a slightly different view of algorithms and data structures. Feeling at ease with that view only comes with much experience. Our intent here is not to provide that experience, but only to present an overview of what the object-oriented paradigm has to offer.

Object-Oriented Inheritance

One of the key features of object-oriented programming is the ability to extend previously defined class objects. Such extension is termed *inheritance*. The newly defined class object automatically inherits everything the original class had, but it also can provide new operations specific to a particular application. Recall this was exactly the obstacle we faced in designing the student list for the registrar's system in Example 14.2. An object-oriented language allows us to define a new class object StudentList by inheriting from and extending the KeyedList class object.

```
TYPE
  .
  .
  .
  StudentList = OBJECT (KeyedList)   { Hypothetical inheritance syntax }
            GPAPointerArray : ARRAY [1..MaxListSize] OF integer;
                              {used to apply pointer sort algorithm
                               for ordering by GPA }
            PROCEDURE PrintGPAOrderedList
          END;
  .
  .
  .
VAR
  Students : StudentList;
```

In this sample code, Students is a KeyedList because it is an instance of a class object that inherits KeyedList. Hence, we could invoke all the operations that come with KeyedList. For instance,

```
Students.Create;
ReadNewStudent (Item);
Students.Add (Item,Success);
```

However, we also have the ability to define operations beyond a plain KeyedList. In our sample code segment, we could provide our own implementation of operation PrintGPAOrderedList and invoke it by

```
Students.PrintGPAOrderedList
```

Inheritance is thus a powerful, object-oriented mechanism. It allows you to reuse code already developed for a class object and yet extend the capabilities of that original class in ways particularly suited to your needs.

Object-Oriented Polymorphism

Polymorphism (which is Greek for "many shapes") is a feature of object-oriented programming that allows one operation to have different meaning for different kinds of objects. For instance, continuing from the previous sample code, suppose that the Create operation had to perform different tasks for objects belonging to class StudentList than it did for objects belonging to class KeyedList. Then, we could add an overriding definition of the Create operation to the declaration of class StudentList.

```
TYPD
  .
  .
  .
  StudentList = OBJECT (KeyedList)    { Hypothetical inheritance syntax }
                  PROCEDURE Create;   { Overrides KeyedList Create }
                  GPA PointerArray : ARRAY [1..MaxListSize] OF integer;
                                        { used to apply pointer sort algorithm }
                                        { for ordering by GPA                  }
                  PROCEDURE PrintGPAOrderedList
                END;
  .
  .
  .
VAR
  PlainList : KeyedList;
  Students : StudentList;
```

Polymorphism now implies that an object-oriented language would use KeyedList's Create when PlainList.Create is invoked and StudentList's Create when Students.Create is called. Our simple example belies the importance of polymorphism in developing large object-oriented systems. It allows the design of complex hierarchies of object classes, many of which inherit behavior from other classes. Polymorphism eliminates name clashes among the operations that may be defined for these various classes. In effect, it allows one name to take "many shapes" in the form of operations appropriate to differing data types.

We hope this brief excursion into object-oriented programming has whetted your appetite. There seems little doubt that the next decade will find this paradigm playing an increasingly active role in accelerating the software system life cycle. An excellent source to continue your exploration of this topic is *Object-Oriented Programming: An Evolutionary Approach* by Brad J. Cox (Reading, Mass.: Addison-Wesley, 1986).

IBM and Apple = Pinstripes and T-Shirts

After signing the Treaty of Amiens in 1802, Napoleon said, "What a beautiful fix we are in now; peace has been declared." In July 1991, representatives of IBM and Apple announced an alliance that similarly shocked many industry analysts. IBM has long been positioned in the mainstream of the computer industry, gaining its reputation more from selling the reliability of its corporate image than from technological innovation. Apple, on the other hand, has based its claim to fame on bold new technologies developed by computer enthusiasts with a distinct bent toward "hacking." For instance, the window-based environment of the first Apple Macintosh in 1983 established a new and exciting mode of human-computer interaction. When IBM and Microsoft later "copied" the "look and feel" of the Mac environment to an IBM-compatible operating system, Apple promptly took them to court in a case whose effects on the software industry are still being debated.

Small wonder that eyebrows have been raised by the agreement between these two corporate antagonists. What are the underlying reasons for the move? According to joint press releases, the companies will cooperate on four fronts:

1. IBM will take steps to better integrate the Mac into IBM-based computer networks.

2. Apple will build future machines using IBM's RISC architecture chip technology.
3. The companies will work together on developing data standards for multimedia.
4. There will be a joint endeavor to produce a new, object-oriented operating system that will eventually be marketed for both IBM and Apple computers.

The last of these ventures is the one that seems to be generating the most excitement on an industry-wide basis. The two companies had been working individually on object-oriented operating systems. Apple had been calling their exploratory system Pink; IBM had called theirs Metaphor. It now appears that the Pink and Metaphor research groups will combine their efforts, with the long-range goal that users and third-party software developers will only have to deal with one common interface for a variety of different machines from the two companies. By taking advantage of the abstraction emphasized by the object-oriented approach, the details of the particular machine will be completely hidden.

It all sounds good in theory, but can researchers from two such historically different companies really define a common set of goals? If they can, will it destroy their own individual initiatives? Only time will tell.

Exercises 14.6

1. Consult local reference documents for the version of Pascal that you are using to see if it offers object-oriented extensions to the standard. If it does, use these extensions to develop an object-oriented, encapsulated implementation of the string or keyed list ADT. Then incorporate your implementation into a higher level algorithm that uses this ADT. See the Problems at the end of Chapter 13 for some ideas regarding such higher level algorithms.

2. Read the first chapter of the text by Cox cited at the end of this section. Then, in your own words, explain how the object-oriented approach can often eliminate complex **CASE** constructs from a program.

■ ■ ■ ■

FOCUS ON PROGRAM DESIGN

In this section, we complete the design of the registrar's system as begun in Example 14.2. In particular, we must develop modular specifications for the structure chart of Figure 14.6. Once we complete this design, we will code the system, using an array physically ordered by student name to implement the list of student records. The program presented here assumes an appropriate implementation of the string ADT that we defined in Chapter 13. Testing and fine-tuning the robustness of the system is left for you to carry out in the Problems.

1. MainMenu Module
   Data Received: None
   Information Returned: None
   Logic: Perform necessary initializations.
          Repeatedly call on GetSelection module to obtain user choice
            of operation and dispatch to appropriate subordinate
            module.

2. GetSelection Module
   Data Received: None
   Information Returned: User choice of operation in form of character
   Logic: Print menu of possible operations.
          Read user choice from terminal.

3. AddStudent Module
   Data Received: List of students (with encapsulated number of students)
   Information Returned: Transformed list with appropriate addition
            Updated number of students
   Logic: Obtain data for new student.
          Call on FindSlot module to find array location to insert student.
          Roll down all entries in array below this location.
          Insert new student at vacated location.
          Update total number of students.

4. FindSlot Module
   Data Received: List of students (with encapsulated number of students)
            Name of student to add
   Information Returned: Array location to insert student
   Logic: Repeatedly examine array location beginning with first until
          we encounter a student whose name alphabetically follows
          that of new student.

5. DeleteStudent Module
   Data Received: List of students (with encapsulated number of students)
   Information Returned: Transformed list with appropriate deletion
            Updated number of students
   Logic: Obtain name of student to be deleted.
          Call on FindStudent module to get the array location of this
           student.
          Provided that the student was found in the array, move all
           students following the one to be deleted up one slot in the
           array, hence destroying data for deleted student.
          Update total number of students.

6. ChangeStudent Module
   Data Received: List of students (with encapsulated number of students)
   Information Returned: Transformed list with appropriate record change
   Logic: Obtain name of student whose records are to be altered.
          Call on FindStudent module to get array location of this student.

Provided that the student was found in the list, determine field to be changed and assign the appropriate new value to that field in the located record.

7. InspectStudent Module

Data Received: List of students (with encapsulated number of students)

Information Returned: None

Logic: Obtain name of student to inspect.

Call on FindStudent module to return that student's complete record.

Provided the student was found, display the record in an appropriate format.

8. FindStudent Module

Data Received: List of students (with encapsulated number of students)

Target name

Information Returned: Record containing data associated with target name

Array location of that record

Boolean flag indicating whether record found

Logic: Binary search algorithm.

9. PrintGradeReports Module

Data Received: List of students (with encapsulated number of students)

Information Returned: None

Logic: For each student, access record in list and print out appropriately formatted report card including grade point average

10. EndOfYearReports Module

Data Received: List of students (with encapsulated number of students)

Information Returned: None

Logic: Print appropriate headings for report in alphabetical order by name.

Call on PrintListByName module to print detail lines in appropriate order.

Print appropriate headings for report in order by GPA.

Call on PrintListByGPA module to print detail lines in appropriate order.

11. PrintListByName Module

Data Received: List of students (with encapsulated number of students)

Information Returned: None

Logic: Proceed through list in the physical order in which it has been maintained, printing out each student's record in appropriate format.

12. PrintListByGPA Module

Data Received: List of students (with encapsulated number of students)

Information Returned: None

Logic: Call on SortByGPA to establish pointers that will lead through list in descending GPA order.

Use these pointers to proceed through list in logical order, printing each record in appropriate format.

13. <u>SortByGPA Module</u>
   Data Received: List of students (with encapsulated number of students)
   Information Returned: Array of pointers to lead through list in descending GPA order
   Logic: Pointer bubble sort algorithm.

```pascal
PROGRAM RegistrarSystem (input, output);

  {  Array implementation of registrar's system at U. of Hard    }
  {  Knocks.  Allows all needed list operations, including grade }
  {  reports and end of year reports sorted by name and end of   }
  {  year reports sorted by grade point average.                 }

  CONST
    MaxStudents = 10;     {  Maximum number of students           }
    CredToGrad = 120;     {  Credits to graduate                  }

  TYPE
    StudentRec = RECORD
                   Name : String;  { Assume appropriate implementation of the
                                     string ADT }
                   CredTaken : integer;
                   CredEarned : integer;
                   TotalGradePts : integer
                 END;
    StudentList = RECORD   {  Encapsulated implementation of list }
                    List : ARRAY [1..MaxStudents] OF StudentRec;
                    NumberOfStudents : integer   { Current number of students }
                  END;

  VAR
    Choice : char;              {  User's choice of menu option }
    Students : StudentList;     {  Array implementation of list }

{*****************************************************************}

  PROCEDURE GetSelection (VAR Choice : char);

    {  Given:    Nothing.                                       }
    {  Task:     Print menu and read user's response.           }
    {  Return:   User's response in Choice.                     }

    BEGIN
      writeln;
      writeln ('A)dd Student');
      writeln ('C)hange Student Record');
      writeln ('I)nspect Student Record');
      writeln ('D)elete Student Record');
      writeln ('G)rade Reports');
      writeln ('E)nd of Year Reports');
      writeln ('Q)uit');
      write ('Choose by entering first letter of selection-->');
      readln (Choice)
    END;  {  of PROCEDURE GetSelection  }

{*****************************************************************}

  PROCEDURE CreateStudentList (VAR Students : StudentList);

    {  Given:    Uninitialized list of students                 }
    {  Task:     Initialize the list to the empty list          }
    {  Return:   Students initialized to the empty list         }

    VAR K : integer;
```

```
      BEGIN
        Students.NumberOfStudents := 0;
        { Initialize all strings in the list  }
        FOR K := 1 TO MaxStudents DO
          Create (Students.List[K].Name)
      END;

{******************************************************************}

   PROCEDURE AddStudent (VAR Students : StudentList);

      {  Given:   List of students.                              }
      {  Task:    Prompt user for student to add, find           }
      {           appropriate slot for that student, and insert  }
      {           new student in that slot.                      }
      {  Return:  List and NumberOfStudents in updated form.     }

      VAR
        NewStudent : StudentRec;
        K, LocationOfAdd : integer;

      PROCEDURE FindSlot (Students : StudentList;
                          NewName : String;
                          VAR LocationOfAdd : integer);

         {  Given:   List of student records in Students and name  }
         {           of student to add in NewStudent.              }
         {  Task:    Search Students sequentially for slot to      }
         {           locate NewName.                               }
         {  Return:  Index location for NewName in LocationOfAdd.  }

         VAR
           Found : boolean;

         BEGIN {  PROCEDURE FindSlot  }
           LocationOfAdd := 1;
           Found := false;
           WHILE (LocationOfAdd <= Students.NumberOfStudents) AND NOT Found DO
             IF GreaterThan (Students.List[LocationOfAdd].Name, NewName) THEN
               Found := true
             ELSE
               LocationOfAdd := LocationOfAdd + 1
         END; {  of PROCEDURE FindSlot  }

      BEGIN {  PROCEDURE AddStudent  }
        WITH NewStudent DO

          BEGIN
            Create (Name);
            write ('Enter new student name-->');
            ReadAString (Name);
            write ('Enter credits taken, earned, and total grade points-->');
            readln (CredTaken, CredEarned, TotalGradePts);
            { Find slot where new student belongs  }
            FindSlot (Students, Name, LocationOfAdd)
          END;

        { From that slot on, move down rest of records  }
        FOR K := Students.NumberOfStudents DOWNTO LocationOfAdd DO
          Students.List[K + 1] := Students.List[K];
        Students.NumberOfStudents := Students.NumberOfStudents + 1;
        Students.List[LocationOfAdd] := NewStudent
      END; {  of PROCEDURE AddStudent  }

{******************************************************************}
```

```
      PROCEDURE FindStudent(Target : String;
                            Students : StudentList;
                            VAR InfoWanted : StudentRec;
                            VAR Mid : integer;
                            VAR Found : boolean);

        { Given:   List of student records in Students and   }
        {          to search for in Target.                  }
        { Task:    Apply binary search algorithm to find Target. }
        { Return:  If Target found, return associated record in }
        {          InfoWanted, associated position in Mid, and }
        {          Found as true.  Otherwise return Found as  }
        {          false.                                     }

        VAR
          High, Low : integer;

        BEGIN
          Found := false;
          Low := 1;
          High := Students.NumberOfStudents;
          WHILE NOT Found AND (Low <= High) DO
            BEGIN
              Mid := (Low + High) DIV 2;
              IF LessThan (Target, Students.List[Mid].Name) THEN
                High := Mid - 1
              ELSE IF GreaterThan (Target, Students.List[Mid].Name) THEN
                Low := Mid + 1
              ELSE
                BEGIN
                  Found := true;
                  InfoWanted := Students.List[Mid]
                END
          END
      END; { of PROCEDURE FindStudent  }

{******************************************************************}

    PROCEDURE DeleteStudent (VAR Students : StudentList);

        { Given:   List of student records in Students.      }
        { Task:    Prompts user for name to delete.  If this name }
        {          is in list, remove it.  Otherwise print error }
        {          message.                                  }
        { Return:  Updated List and NumberOfStudents  if name }
        {          is found.                                 }

        VAR
          DeleteName : String;
          K, LocationOfDelete : integer;
          Found : boolean;
          DeleteRec : StudentRec;

        BEGIN
          Create (DeleteName);
          write ('Student to delete-->');
          ReadAString (DeleteName);

          { Call on binary search to locate student  }
          FindStudent (DeleteName, Students, DeleteRec,
                       LocationOfDelete, Found);
          IF NOT Found THEN
            writeln ('Error in delete')
          ELSE
            BEGIN
```

```
                  {  Move up all records below delete location  }
                  FOR K := LocationOfDelete TO Students.NumberOfStudents - 1 DO
                     Students.List[K] := Students.List[K + 1];
                  Students.NumberOfStudents := Students.NumberOfStudents - 1
               END
       END;  {  of PROCEDURE DeleteStudent  }



{******************************************************************}


   PROCEDURE ChangeStudent(VAR Students : StudentList);

      {  Given:   List of student records in Students.            }
      {  Task:    Prompt user for change desired if record can be  }
      {           found, make appropriate change.  Otherwise,      }
      {           print error message.                             }
      {  Return:  Students list with updated record.               }

      VAR
        ChangeName : String;
        ChangeField : integer;
        Found : boolean;
        ChangeRec : StudentRec;
        ChangeLoc : integer;

      BEGIN
        Create(ChangeName);
        writeln ('Enter name of student to change-->');
        ReadAString (ChangeName);

        {  Call on binary search to find record wanted  }
        FindStudent (ChangeName, Students, ChangeRec,
                     ChangeLoc, Found);
        IF NOT Found THEN
           BEGIN
             WriteAString (ChangeName);
             writeln (' not found.')
           END
        ELSE
           BEGIN
             write ('Field to change--> 1-Taken,2-Earned,3-Points');
             readln (ChangeField);

             {  Obtain new value for appropriate field  }
             WITH Students.List[ChangeLoc] DO
               CASE ChangeField OF
                 1 : BEGIN
                       write ('New value for credits taken-->');
                       readln (CredTaken)
                     END;
                 2 : BEGIN
                       write('New value for credits earned-->');
                       readln(CredEarned)
                     END;
                 3 : BEGIN
                       write('New value for total grade points-->');
                       readln(TotalGradePts)
                     END
               END   {  of CASE ChangeField  }
           END   {  of ELSE statement  }
       END;  {  of PROCEDURE ChangeStudent  }


{******************************************************************}
```

```
PROCEDURE InspectStudent (Students : StudentList);

  {  Given:    List of student records in Students and current  }
  {            number of students in NumberOfStudents.          }
  {  Task:     Prompts user for name to inspect and calls on    }
  {            binary search to find it.                        }
  {  Return:   Nothing.                                         }

  CONST
    Skip = ' ';

  VAR
    InspectName : String;
    InspectLoc : integer;
    InspectRec : StudentRec;
    Found : boolean;

  BEGIN
    Create(InspectName);
    write ('Name of student to inspect-->');
    ReadAString (InspectName);

    {  Call on binary search to obtain desired record  }
    FindStudent (InspectName, Students, InspectRec,
                 InspectLoc, Found);
    IF NOT Found THEN
      BEGIN
        WriteAString (InspectName);
        writeln (' not found.')
      END
    ELSE
      WITH InspectRec DO
        BEGIN
          WriteAString (Name);
          writeln (Skip:2, CredTaken, CredEarned, TotalGradePts)
        END
  END;  {  of PROCEDURE InspectStudent  }

{******************************************************************}

  PROCEDURE PrintGradeReports (Students : StudentList);

  {  Given:    List of student records in Students.             }
  {  Task:     Proceed sequentially through list, computing     }
  {            and printing report card for each student.       }
  {  Return:   Nothing.                                         }

  VAR
    K : integer;
    GPA : real;

  BEGIN
    FOR K := 1 TO Students.NumberOfStudents DO
      WITH Students.List[K] DO
        BEGIN
          GPA := TotalGradePts / CredTaken;
          write ('Student ');
          WriteAString (Name);
          writeln;
          writeln ('Taken ', CredTaken : 10 );
          writeln ('Earned ', CredEarned : 9 );
          writeln ('GPA ', GPA: 6 : 2);
          writeln
        END {of WITH...DO }
  END;  {  of PROCEDURE PrintGradeReports  }
```

```
{*******************************************************************}

   PROCEDURE EndOfYearReports (Students : StudentList);

      { Given:   List of student records in Students.          }
      { Task:    Oversees printing of end of year reports for  }
      {          graduating seniors.                            }
      { Return:  Nothing.                                       }

   CONST
     Skip = '';

   PROCEDURE PrintListByName (Students : StudentList);

      { Given:   List of student records in Students.          }
      { Task:    Sequentially print detail lines in            }
      {          alphabetical order by name, which is also the }
      {          physical order of the list.                   }
      { Return:  Nothing.                                       }

      VAR
        K : integer;

      BEGIN { PROCEDURE PrintListByName }
        FOR K := 1 TO Students.NumberOfStudents DO
          WITH Students.List[K] DO
            IF CredEarned >= CredToGrad THEN
              BEGIN
                WriteAString (Name);
                writeln (Skip : 40 - Length (Name), CredTaken : 10, CredEarned : 10,
                         TotalGradePts : 10)
              END
      END; { of PROCEDURE PrintListByName }

   PROCEDURE PrintListByGPA (Students : StudentList);

      { Given:   List of student records in Students.          }
      { Task:    Establishes GPA order in Pointer array and    }
      {          then prints detail lines in this GPA order.   }
      { Return:  Nothing.                                       }

      TYPE
        PointerArray = ARRAY [1..MaxStudents] OF integer;

      VAR
        K : integer;
        GPA : real;
        Pointer : PointerArray;

      PROCEDURE SortByGPA (Students : StudentList;
                           VAR Pointer : PointerArray);

         { Given:   List of student records in Students.          }
         { Task:    Apply pointer bubble sort algorithm to        }
         {          determine GPA descending order.               }
         { Return:  Pointer array indicating GPA order.           }

         VAR
           K, J, Temp : integer;
           ExchangeMade : boolean;

         BEGIN { PROCEDURE SortByGPA }
           FOR K := 1 TO Students.NumberOfStudents DO
             Pointer[K] := K;
```

```
            K := 0;
            ExchangeMade := true;
            WHILE (K <= Students.NumberOfStudents - 1) AND ExchangeMade DO
               BEGIN
                  ExchangeMade := false;
                  K := K + 1;
                  FOR J := 1 TO Students.NumberOfStudents - K DO

                     { Sort algorithm keys on grade point average  }
                     IF Students.List[Pointer[J]].TotalGradePts /
                        Students.List[Pointer[J]].CredTaken <
                        Students.List[Pointer[J + 1]].TotalGradePts /
                        Students.List[Pointer[J + 1]].CredTaken THEN
                        BEGIN
                           Temp := Pointer[J];
                           Pointer[J] := Pointer[J + 1];
                           Pointer[J + 1] := Temp;
                           ExchangeMade := true
                        END { of IF...THEN  }
               END { of WHILE }
         END; { of PROCEDURE SortByGPA  }

      BEGIN  { PROCEDURE PrintListByGPA  }
         SortByGPA (Students, Pointer);
         FOR K := 1 TO Students.NumberOfStudents DO
            WITH Students.List[Pointer[K]] DO
               IF CredEarned >= CredToGrad THEN
                  BEGIN
                     GPA := TotalGradePts / CredTaken;
                     WriteAString (Name);
                     writeln (Skip: 40 - Length (Name), CredTaken: 10, CredEarned: 10,
                           GPA: 10: 2)
                  END { of IF...THEN  }
      END; { of PROCEDURE PrintListByGPA  }

   BEGIN  { PROCEDURE EndOfYearReports  }
      writeln ('                       REPORT BY NAME ');
      writeln ('NAME', Skip : 36, 'TAKEN': 10, 'EARNED': 10, 'POINTS': 10);
      PrintListByName (Students);
      writeln;
      writeln ('                       REPORT BY GPA ');
      writeln ('NAME', Skip : 36, 'TAKEN': 10, 'EARNED': 10, 'GPA': 10);
      PrintListByGPA (Students);
   END; { of PROCEDURE EndOfYearReports  }


{*********************************************************************}


   BEGIN  { Main  }
      writeln ('Welcome to Registrar System at U. of Hard Knocks');
      CreateStudentList (Students);
      REPEAT
         GetSelection (Choice);
         CASE Choice OF
            'A': AddStudent(Students);
            'C': ChangeStudent(Students);
            'I': InspectStudent(Students);
            'D': DeleteStudent(Students);
            'G': PrintGradeReports(Students);
            'E': EndOfYearReports(Students);
            'Q': BEGIN END
         END { of CASE Choice }
      UNTIL Choice = 'Q' { Q is quit option  }
   END. { of main program  }
```

Sample runs for a few of the menu options follow. These are included to give you a feel for the functioning of the system once all the pieces have been tied together. However, these sample runs should by no means be considered complete in terms of testing the system. In the Problems, you will develop a testing strategy for this system.

```
Welcome to Registrar System at U. of Hard Knocks

A)dd Student
C)hange Student Record
I)nspect Student Record
D)elete Student Record
G)rade Reports
E)nd of Year Reports
Q)uit
Choose by entering first letter of selection-->A
Enter new student name-->SMART, LES
Enter credits taken, earned, and total grade points-->80 60 120

A)dd Student
C)hange Student Record
I)nspect Student Record
D)elete Student Record
G)rade Reports
E)nd of Year Reports
Q)uit
Choose by entering first letter of selection-->A
Enter new student name-->WOOD, HOLLY
Enter credits taken, earned, and total grade points-->123 120 357

A)dd Student
C)hange Student Record
I)nspect Student Record
D)elete Student Record
G)rade Reports
E)nd of Year Reports
Q)uit
Choose by entering first letter of selection-->A
Enter new student name-->AVREG, JOE
Enter credits taken, earned, and total grade points-->96 93 208

A)dd Student
C)hange Student Record
I)nspect Student Record
D)elete Student Record
G)rade Reports
E)nd of Year Reports
Q)uit
Choose by entering first letter of selection-->A

Enter new student name-->CLEAR, BEA
Enter credits taken, earned, and total grade points-->120 120 436

A)dd Student
C)hange Student Record
I)nspect Student Record
D)elete Student Record
G)rade Reports
E)nd of Year Reports
Q)uit
Choose by entering first letter of selection-->G
```

```
Student AVREG, JOE
Taken        96
Earned       93
GPA        2.17

Student CLEAR, BEA
Taken       120
Earned      120
GPA        3.63

Student SMART, LES
Taken        80
Earned       60
GPA        1.50

Student WOOD, HOLLY
Taken       123
Earned      120
GPA        2.90

A)dd Student
C)hange Student Record
I)nspect Student Record
D)elete Student Record
G)rade Reports
E)nd of Year Reports
Q)uit
Choose by entering first letter of selection-->E
                REPORT BY NAME
NAME                            TAKEN     EARNED     POINTS
CLEAR, BEA                       120        120        436
WOOD, HOLLY                      123        120        357
                REPORT BY GPA
NAME                            TAKEN     EARNED     POINTS
CLEAR, BEA                       120        120       3.63
WOOD, HOLLY                      123        120       2.90

A)dd Student
C)hange Student Record
I)nspect Student Record
D)elete Student Record
G)rade Reports
E)nd of Year Reports
Q)uit
Choose by entering first letter of selection-->Q
```

RUNNING AND DEBUGGING TIPS

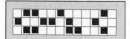

1. When testing a large program, always test modules individually before testing the entire system.

2. When developing test cases, keep them in a file so that they can be used again easily after fixing errors.

3. The finite state machine paradigm is a systematic way of insuring that users enter valid input to your program.

4. Be sure to design test data that exercises the boundary conditions of a module: this is where an error is most likely to occur.

■ Summary

Key Terms

acceptance testing	equivalence classes	structured English
analysis	finite state machine	stub module
black box testing	fixed length method	systems analyst
boundary conditions	functionally cohesive	system testing
coding phase	maintenance	test cases
coupling	modular specification	testing phase
data flow diagram	modular testing	test oracle
documentation	robust	transitions
driver module	state-transition diagram	white box testing
encapsulation	strings	

Key Terms (Optional)

class object	message-passing	programming by
file buffer	method of inductive	personification
formal verification	assertions	random access file
inheritance	object-oriented	semantics
instances	programming	sequential access files
inductive assertions	polymorphism	
loop invariant		

Key Concepts

- During the analysis phase of the software system life cycle you must determine the users' requirements. Typically, this involves considerable interaction between the systems analyst and end users. A data flow diagram is one example of a document that would be developed during this phase. Ultimately, the users' requirements must be described in a form suitable to pass on to the design phase.
- During the design phase, the users' requirements are examined, and the system that will ultimately meet these requirements begins to take shape. Software designers must turn out a blueprint of the eventual software system that can then be translated into program code. Typical of the documents produced during the design phase are modular structure charts, layout of data structures, and modular logic specifications.
- A good design is developed in a top-down fashion. Individual modules within the design should be functionally cohesive: they should focus on one particular task. Modules within the design should be minimally coupled; they should not transfer more information than necessary between themselves. This avoids the possibility of one module's inadvertently affecting data being used by another.
- Testing and verification can consume up to 50 percent of the time spent in developing a software system. Each module should be tested as it is finished. Use drivers to feed inputs into the module and stubs to check the module's interactions with subordinate modules.
- System and acceptance testing follows modular testing.
- The maintenance phase of a system follows its release to users. During this phase, adjustments must be made to the system in response to bugs and changes in user requirements.
- Obsolescence is the sixth, and ultimately inevitable, phase of the software system life cycle.

Key Concepts (Optional)

- Though not part of standard Pascal, random access files provide a useful means of implementing a list in situations where the data must be stored permanently. The price one pays for this permanent storage is a longer time to access one list entry.

- Formal algorithm verification by such methods as inductive assertions is of theoretical interest now and offers promise of more reliable software in the future.
- Object-oriented programming allows systems developers to reuse and extend implementations of ADTs in a more flexible fashion than traditional languages.

■ Programming Problems and Projects

1. Design a complete set of modular test cases for the system in the Focus on Program Design section. Be as thorough as possible in your testing; pay particular attention to robustness issues. Wherever your testing locates an error, modify the code to fix it. (An interesting class experiment for this program is to turn it into a contest. The student who finds and fixes the most errors wins.)

2. If your instructor assigned Section 14.4, modify the program in the Focus on Program Design so that the student list is implemented with a random access file.

3. Invite the registrar of your university to your class to discuss the type of data processing operations in which the registrar's office is typically engaged. After this discussion (which should no doubt include time for questions), describe the data involved in the operations of your registrar's office in terms of abstract data types. Develop a data flow diagram to picture the way in which the registrar's office processes information.

4. Consider the following data declaration and function header.

```
TYPE
   KindOfTriangle = (Scalene, Isosceles, Equilateral, Impossible);
   .
   .
   .

FUNCTION TriangleType (Side1, Side2, Side3 : Integer) : KindOfTriangle;

{ This function receives three positive integers representing the    }
{ length of sides of a possible triangle. It is to return the        }
{ type of triangle with those lengths as sides:                      }
{                                                                     }
{           Equilateral--all sides equal                             }
{           Isosceles--two sides equal                               }
{           Scalene--no sides equal                                  }
{                                                                     }
{ Additionally, the function should return the value Impossible if    }
{ the three positive integers do not constitute a valid set of       }
{ triangle sides.                                                     }
```

For this problem, work with another student. Each of you should develop independently, first, a robust version of the function just described and, second, a complete set of test data (including robustness checks) for the function. Next, jointly develop a driver program and test your functions. Have your partner use his or her test data on the function you developed. Then use your test data on your partner's function. The winner is the one whose function fails for the fewer number of test cases.

5. In Exercise 8 of Section 14.2 you designed a system for the registrar at American Basket Weaving University. Implement and fully test that system.

6. In Exercise 11 of Section 14.3 you developed and tested a module to read strings that are valid file names on your particular computer sys-

tem. Incorporate this module into a larger program that could be used to backup text files. The user should enter two file names: a source file and a destination file. Your program should then copy from the source to the destination. If your file name module does its job correctly, your program should never crash because it tries to access an "invalid file name."

7. For Problem 5 of Chapter 13, you developed a program that allowed its user to enter rational numbers and then perform operations upon them. Now make your program more user-friendly and robust by reading all rational numbers entered by the user in a module ReadRational. The logic of this module should be driven by a finite-state machine that filters out erroneous input. Submit a diagram of the finite-state machine as part of the documentation accompanying your program.

8. For Problem 6 of Chapter 13, you developed a program that allowed its user to enter complex numbers and then perform operations upon them. Now make your program more user-friendly and robust by reading all complex numbers entered by the user in a module ReadComplex. The logic of this module should be driven by a finite-state machine that filters out erroneous input. Submit a diagram of the finite-state machine as part of the documentation accompanying your program.

9. Assume that you would like to make some extra cash by writing a program to facilitate some activity for a particular business, organization, or school. Write a proposal that clearly explains what your program will do, how much it would cost, why the purchase of this program would be beneficial to the institution, and how soon you could complete this project. Be sure to limit your project so that it does not exceed your ability as a programmer.

10. Research the topic of formal methods in algorithm verification, using the September 1990 issues of *IEEE Computer* and *IEEE Software* as initial references. Then write a paper in which you discuss the role that formal algorithm verification may play in future software development. Your paper should address such issues as how formal verification can reduce the amount of time spent in testing software and how it can be used to insure a degree of software reliability exceeding what can be achieved by testing alone. Be sure to respond to the criticisms of formal verification summarized in Section 14.5.

11. Interview a systems analyst at a local company or organization. Then, write a paper or prepare a presentation in which you describe the techniques used by that systems analyst to determine user needs and to document these user needs in written or diagrammatic form.

12. The September 1990 issue of *Communications of the ACM* was dedicated to the topic of object-oriented programming. Using the articles in this issue as a starting point, write a research paper in which you describe how software development will be affected by the object-oriented paradigm. Your paper should discuss such issues as building software libraries that are usable in a variety of contexts and building software systems that are easily extended when the need to do so arises.

These are the ties which, though light as air, are strong as links of iron.

Edmund Burke
1729–1797

Linked Lists and Pointers

In the previous chapters we discovered that an array implementation (with binary search) of a keyed list requires $O(n)$ data interchanges for the add and delete operations. Attempting to maintain such an array-implemented list in order parallels the dynamics of waiting in a long line. When someone cuts into the middle of the line, there is a domino-like effect that forces everyone behind that person to move back. When someone in the middle of the line decides to leave the line, the reverse effect occurs; everyone behind the departed person is able to move ahead one slot. It is possible to draw an analogy between people waiting in a line and data items stored next to each other in computer memory. If the data items are arranged in some type of order and it becomes necessary to insert into or delete from the middle of the line, a considerable amount of data movement is involved. This data movement requires computer time and decreases program efficiency. The central motivation behind the linked list data structure is to eliminate the data movement associated with insertions into and deletions from the middle of the list. Of course, by now we might suspect that efficiency in eliminating such data movement can only come by trading off other efficiency factors. One of the crucial questions to ask yourself as we study linked lists is "What price are we paying to handle additions and deletions effectively?"

One way of conceptually picturing a linked list is to think of a game some parents use to make the opening of holiday gifts particularly exciting for their children. One feature of the game that helps to build children's anticipation insures that minor gifts are opened first, gradually building up to the most substantial gift. (Recall from your own childhood experience the partial letdown that occurred when you opened a gift package containing a mere pair of socks after having already unwrapped something significantly more exciting such as a baseball glove or new doll.) Thus, the premises of this gift-giving game are that gifts may be ranked according to their desirability and that the game is more fun when the most desirable gifts are opened last.

To achieve this end, parents will hide their child's wrapped gifts at various locations throughout the home. For instance, let us suppose a scenario in which parents have the following four gifts for their child, ranked and hidden as indicated.

Ranking	Gift	Hiding Place
Least desirable	Pair of socks	Under Bed
↓	Box of candy	Kitchen drawer
	Video game	Basement cabinet
Most desirable	Bicycle	Garage

The parents will then tell the child *only* the location of the least desirable gift; here, for instance, they would give instructions to look under a bed for the first gift. Upon opening that gift, the child will find the uninspiring pair of socks *plus* a more intriguing note with the information that the child's next gift will be in a kitchen drawer. The pattern should now be obvious. From the box of candy, the child follows an informational pointer to a basement cabinet, where the video game is discovered along with a similar informational link to the garage as a location where something bigger and better may be found. Here the now-eager child will uncover a bike along with a final (and no doubt disappointing) note indicating that the end of the chain of gifts has been reached.

A conceptual picture of this chain of gifts is presented in Figure 15.1.

FIGURE 15.1
A linked chain of gifts

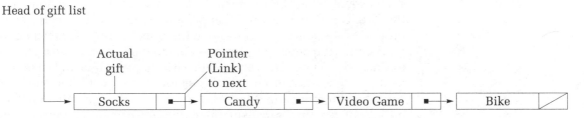

This same conceptual picture applies to the *linked list* abstract data structure we are about to study. In this figure, the arrows connecting packages represent the informational note in each package which tells us the location of the next package. Conceptually, the form taken by this informational pointer is not important. However, it is crucial that we have a reliable *pointer* to the leading gift (often called a *head pointer*) and, thereafter, a reliable pointer in each package (often called a *node*) to the next package. Should any pointer be flawed, the remaining gifts on the chain become essentially inaccessible (much to the dismay of the child who wanted that bike so desperately).

In addition to introducing us to much of the vernacular that comes with linked lists, this review of a simple childhood game can also give us a hint of the ease with which such a linked chain of nodes can handle additions and deletions. For instance, suppose that a sudden windfall allows the parents of the child in our example to buy a baseball glove in addition to the four gifts they had already purchased. Assuming that this new gift is ranked between the video game and the bicycle in desirability, consider what must be done to link it into the gift chain. We must do as follows:

1. Find a place to hide it; for example, the attic.
2. Take the informational linking note from the video game package and put it in the baseball glove package. (Why?)
3. Insert a new informational pointer in the video game package, indicating the attic as the location of the next node. (Why?)

Figure 15.2 portrays such an addition with circled numbers corresponding to the three steps just described. The important aspect to note in this series of moves is that no gift that was already in place had to be moved to accommodate adding the new gift. From a conceptual perspective, this is why linked lists will be able to avoid the movement of data that was associated with an insertion into an array-implemented list.

FIGURE 15.2
Adding a baseball glove to the
chain of Figure 15.1

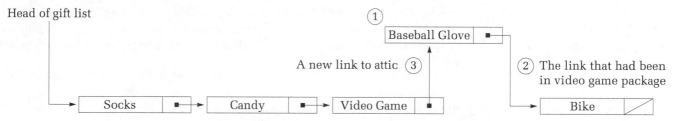

Along the same lines, let us now suppose that our shameless parents devour all of their child's candy before the holiday arrives. Clearly they must remove this package from the chain to hide this disgusting behavior from their child. Using Figure 15.3, convince yourself that the following steps will accomplish this deletion:

1. Remove the now-empty candy package from the kitchen drawer.
2. Before throwing away the empty package, remove the linking note from it and put this note in the package containing the socks.
3. Dispose of the incriminating candy container and the linking note that originally was in the package with the socks.

FIGURE 15.3
Removing candy from the chain
of Figure 15.2

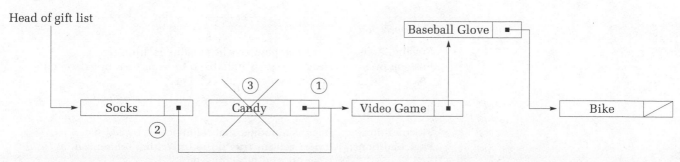

It is important to note again that no package remaining on the chain had to be physically moved to a new location: a situation much different from what happened when we removed a name from an array-implemented list in the last chapter.

Have we strayed too far from computer science in using such a nontechnical, elementary example to introduce our chapter on linked lists? Not at all! In fact, we've achieved two very important goals. First, if you understand all the details of the gift-giving game, then you essentially understand the important concepts involved in the linked list data structure. Second, this is just another illustration of the fact that computer techniques are often just formalizations in a logic machine of the way we, as human beings, have been doing things for many years. Consequently, you should never feel intimidated by such a computer technique; merely try to relate it to an analogous—and familiar—manual method. Doing this will help give substance to the more formal computer science method.

■ 15.1
The Linked List as an Abstract Data Type

OBJECTIVES

- to formalize the notion of a linked list as an ADT
- to understand, at an abstract level, why a linked list allows additions and deletions of nodes with minimal data movement
- to realize, at an abstract level, the price paid in search efficiency for the efficiency gained in adding and deleting nodes.
- to realize that, although a linked list may be viewed as an ADT, it is also a data structure that can be used to implement other ADTs, such as keyed lists

Recall from Chapter 13 that to formally specify an abstract data type (ADT), we must describe the individual elements of the structure, the relationship(s) between these elements, and the logical operations to be performed on the structure.

A formalization for the intuitive notion of a linked list follows. This formalization uses the terminology *linear ordering*. By linear ordering, we mean any ordering of data in which there is an identifiable first element, second element, and so forth. For instance, a string could be viewed as a linear ordering of characters. Also, a keyed list has a linear ordering determined by its key field. It is important to realize that linear ordering is a logical concept; it need not coincide with physical ordering of data.

Linked list. A linked list is a collection of elements called nodes. Each node contains a data portion and a pointer. The data portions in all nodes are of the same type. The pointer in a given node contains the location of the node that follows the given node in the linear ordering of the list. The entire list is referenced by a separate head pointer to the first element in the linear ordering. The head pointer is simply the location of this first element. It is not a linked list node and hence has no data associated with it. A special value designated as *Null* is assigned to a pointer that references an empty linked list.

The operations that can be performed on a linked list are:

Create operation

Preconditions: *Head* is a pointer whose value is arbitrary.
Postconditions: *Head* pointer is initialized to *Null*, thereby referencing the empty list.

Empty operation

Preconditions: *Head* is a pointer that references a linked list.
Postconditions: *Empty* returns **true** if the linked list referenced by *Head* is empty and **false** otherwise.

Next operation

Preconditions:	*P* is a pointer to a node in a linked list. Assume that *P* is not *Null*.
Postconditions:	*Next* returns a pointer to the node following that referenced by *P*. If no node follows *P* in the list, then *Next* returns *Null*.

InsertNode operation

Preconditions:	*Head* pointer references a linked list. *P* and *Prev* are also pointers. *P* references a node to be inserted in the linked list after the list node referenced by *Prev*. *Prev* is equal to *Null* if the insertion is to occur at the front of the list.
Postconditions:	Node referenced by *P* is inserted into list referenced by *Head* after the node referenced by *Prev*.

DeleteNode operation

Preconditions:	*Head* pointer references a linked list. *P* and *Prev* are also pointers. *P* references a node to be deleted from the linked list. *Prev* references the list node preceding that referenced by *P*. *Prev* is equal to *Null* if *P* references the first node in the list.
Postconditions:	Node referenced by *P* is removed from the list referenced by *Head*.

LinkedTraverse operation

Preconditions:	*Head* is a pointer referencing a linked list, and *ProcessNode* is an algorithmic process which can be applied to the data portion of each node on the list.
Postconditions:	Each node in the list referenced by *Head* is visited in the linear order determined by the pointers in the list. As each node is visited, *ProcessNode* is applied to it.

Figure 15.4 depicts the action of the Create, Next, InsertNode, DeleteNode, and LinkedTraverse operations on a linked list of integers. Study this figure carefully and observe that every linked list will have one *Null* pointer associated with it. After the Create operation, the Head pointer for the resulting empty list is *Null*. For a non-empty list, the pointer in the final node on the list is *Null*. Note the distinction between a pointer that is *Null* and a pointer that is undefined. The former reliably indicates a reference to an empty structure through a specific flagging value. The latter is completely unreliable in terms of what it references.

The figure also indicates that insertion into and deletion from a linked list require a pointer to the node to be acted upon and a pointer to the node which precedes this node in the linear ordering of the list. For both of these operations, the pointer to the preceding node is necessary since the pointer within that node must be altered as part of the operation. For example, in Figure 15.4, when we insert 46 after the node containing 19, the node containing 19 is altered by having its pointer reference the node containing 46 instead of the node containing 63. This alteration of the node containing 19 requires that we have a pointer (*Prev*) that references it. In the event that the insertion or deletion occurs at the front of the list, the *Prev* pointer is set to *Null* to signal this special condition.

Finally, Figure 15.4 illustrates that the linear ordering of the linked list may not necessarily coincide with the natural ordering of data in the list. In this figure, the linear ordering of the list is not in correspondence with either ascending or descending order by integer value. What defines the linear ordering will vary from application to application.

FIGURE 15.4
Actions of some linked list operations

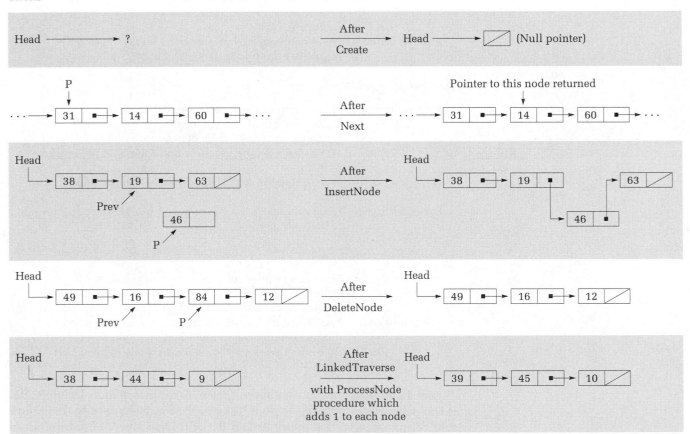

One application we can immediately envision is to use a linked list as an implementation technique for the keyed list ADT. The linear ordering established by the links would mirror the order determined by the key fields in the nodes. For instance, Figure 15.5 depicts a linked list in which the links establish an alphabetical ordering according to key field.

FIGURE 15.5
Alphabetically ordered linked list with four nodes

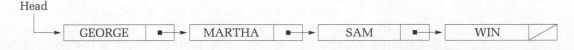

The operations of adding a node and deleting a node from such a list may also be conveniently represented in such a schematic form. In fact, you will soon discover that the best way to conceive algorithms that manipulate linked lists is to draw what you want to happen via such logical pictures. Such a picture of a linked list is completely at the abstract level; it implies nothing about how the linked list will finally be implemented. Once you understand the concept from such a graphic representation, it is usually a straightforward matter to actually implement it.

For instance, we now wish to add a node containing PRIM to the list shown in Figure 15.5; then all we need to do is to store PRIM in an available memory location outside of the list, such as the one pointed to by P in Figure 15.6. We then reset the pointer link of the node containing MARTHA to point to the node containing PRIM, and the pointer link of the node containing PRIM to point to the node containing SAM. This logically maintains the alphabetical order of the data in the nodes without physically moving any of the existing nodes.

FIGURE 15.6
Insertion of node containing
PRIM into linked list of Figure
15.5

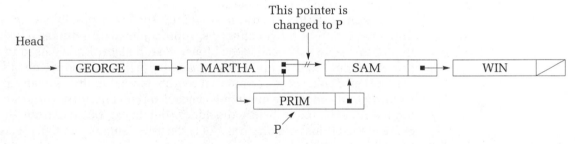

Similarly, should you then wish to delete an existing node from the linked list, a graphic representation of the list can again indicate how the pointers should be altered to reflect such a change. For example, given the list of Figure 15.6, the diagram of Figure 15.7 pictorially outlines what must be done if we want to delete the node containing MARTHA. Notice in this figure that, as was the case for insertion, only pointers must be changed to delete a node. Again, no movement of data occurs.

FIGURE 15.7
Deletion of node containing
MARTHA from linked list of
Figure 15.6

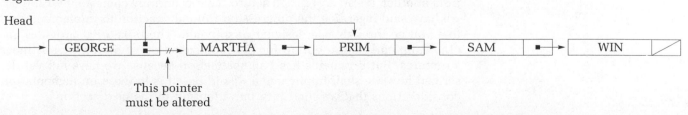

Efficiency Considerations for Linked Lists

These addition/deletion considerations may make a linked list an attractive alternative to an array implementation of a keyed list. The diagrams of Figures 15.6 and 15.7 indicate that adds and deletes merely require the exchange of two pointers. Since pointers are merely locations of other nodes, this means that we are usually manipulating mere integers or similarly simple data in doing such pointer operations. Hence, both additions and deletions would appear to be O(1) operations in terms of data movement for linked lists. This compares very favorably to the massive movement of entire records which was forced by an addition or deletion on an array implementation of a list. In general, such insertion and removal operations will be O(n) in terms of data movement in an array implementation of a list.

Despite this substantive advantage, you should proceed cautiously and not be too quick to adopt the linked list as a cure for all the ills involved with list-oriented systems. The experience you have already gained should make you suspicious that there has to be a trade-off involved to get this superior efficiency for add and delete operations. Here the price we pay is to give up random access on the nodes in the list. For example, to access the fourth node, we must follow the head pointer to the first node, the first node's pointer to the second, and so on, until we reach the fourth node. Hence, any operation that requires finding a particular node on the list will essentially have to invoke a sequential search algorithm.

The superb O($\log_2 n$) search efficiency that was possible with an array implementation of a list cannot be approached with a linked implementation of the same list because the binary search algorithm we used to achieve this efficiency requires random access into the list. Instead we must settle for the O(n) efficiency of the sequential search. Note that this is even a deterring factor in add and delete operations because, typically, an appropriate spot in the list must be found before the add or delete can occur. Although the add or delete itself may require only O(1) data movements, an O(n) search must usually precede it.

Despite this search inefficiency, linked lists can be used to tremendous advantage when implementing lists that are highly *volatile;* that is, frequently undergoing insertions and deletions. If the percentage of these operations is sufficiently high in relation to requests for finding and inspecting nodes, then the linked implementation will probably pay off.

Before proceeding, we should clarify one point regarding linked lists as an ADT. That is, although a linked list may be viewed from this abstract perspective, it also represents an implementation strategy for more general linear structures such as the keyed list ADT. In that sense, we can compare the linked list to the array implementation of a keyed list, which we have already studied, and to several other list implementation schemes, which we will present in future chapters.

Thus, a linked list is, from one perspective, an implementation strategy; from another, it's an abstract structure. This is entirely consistent with what we have said regarding the progression from abstraction to implementation that you go through as a designer of software. The linked list provides another implementation option for the representation of more general linear structures. But it remains itself an abstraction because we have not yet described how we shall implement a linked list. It is to these implementation considerations that we shall turn our attention in the next section.

Pascal Interface for the Linked List ADT

To develop an implementation of the linked list ADT, we must establish a **PROCEDURE** and **FUNCTION** interfaces for the operations we have defined.

```
CONST
  Null =  { A special flagging value for the TYPE Pointer below.  A pointer  }
          { with the value Null is to be viewed as pointing at an            }
          { empty linked list.  This is significantly different from         }
          { a pointer's being undefined, in which case it may be            }
          { unreliably pointing at "garbage."                               }

TYPE
  Pointer = { Still an abstract notion, to be regarded as capable of          }
            { storing the location in memory of a linked list node           }
  LinkedListNode = RECORD
                     Data : LinkedListData { Any appropriate type   };
                     Link : Pointer
                   END;

PROCEDURE Create (VAR Head : Pointer);

  { Given:   A pointer Head whose value is arbitrary        }
  { Task:    Initialize linked list referenced by Head      }
  {          to the empty list                              }
  { Return:  Head pointer referencing the empty list.       }

FUNCTION Empty (Head : Pointer) : boolean;

  { Given:   A linked list referenced by the pointer Head   }
  { Task:    Determine if the linked list is empty          }
  { Return:  True if the linked list is empty and           }
  {          false otherwise.                               }

FUNCTION Next (P : Pointer) : Pointer;

  { Given:   A pointer P to a node in a linked list.        }
  {          Assume that P is not Null.                     }
  { Task:    Determine the node which follows the node      }
  {          referenced by P                                }
  { Return:  A pointer to the node following that           }
  {          referenced by P. If no node follows P, then    }
  {          return Null.                                   }

PROCEDURE InsertNode (VAR Head : Pointer;
                          P, Prev : Pointer);

  { Given:   Linked list referenced by Head pointer.        }
  {          Node referenced by P to be inserted in the     }
  {          list after node referenced by Prev, with       }
  {          Prev equal to Null if insertion is to          }
  {          occur at front of list.                        }
  { Task:    Set pointers to link node P into list          }
  { Return:  Appropriately updated linked list.             }

PROCEDURE DeleteNode (VAR Head : Pointer;
                          P, Prev : Pointer);

  { Given:   Linked list referenced by pointer Head.        }
  {          Pointer P to node to be removed from this      }
  {          list and pointer Prev to node preceding P.     }
  {          Prev is Null if node referenced by P is at     }
```

```
{               front of list.                                    }
{  Task:        Remove node P from list                           }
{  Return:      Appropriately altered list.                       }

PROCEDURE LinkedTraverse (VAR Head : Pointer;
                    PROCEDURE ProcessNode (VAR Item : LinkedListData));

{  Given:       Linked list referenced by Head pointer            }
{  Task:        Traverse the list in the linear order             }
{               determined by the links, applying the             }
{               procedure ProcessNode to each record              }
{               in the list                                       }
{  Return:      The list referenced by Head with each node        }
{               affected by ProcessNode.                          }
```

Exercises 15.1

1. In what way is the data structure involved with the PointerSort in Chapter 12 not a linked list?

2. What are the advantages and the disadvantages of a linked list implementation of a keyed list compared to a physically ordered array implementation?

3. What are the advantages and disadvantages of a linked list implementation of a keyed list compared to an implementation that uses an unordered array with sequential search?

For Exercises 4–6, use the Pascal interface to the linked list ADT to write appropriate program segments.

4. Given that the **TYPE** LinkedListData is **char**, use LinkedTraverse with a ProcessNode parameter that will print the **ord** value of each character in a linked list.

5. Given that the **TYPE** LinkedListData is **real**, use LinkedTraverse with a ProcessNode parameter that will print the value of each positive number in a linked list. Numbers in the list that are not positive should not be printed.

6. Given that the **TYPE** LinkedListData is **integer**, write a loop that starts at the beginning of a linked list and returns a pointer to the first list node with the value zero in its Data field. If no such node exists in the list, a Null pointer should be returned. (*Hint*: Use the Next operation.)

■ ■ ■ ■

■ 15.2 Array Implementation of a Linked List

OBJECTIVES

- to reiterate that a linked list is an ADT which may itself be used to implement more general linear ADTs such as a keyed list
- to develop an implementation of the linked list ADT in which linked list nodes are embedded in an array
- to develop a scheme for efficiently managing the nodes that are inserted into and deleted from linked lists

Objectives continued.

Our previous remarks on the layers between pure abstraction and pure implementation should be heeded here so that you do not confuse the previously presented array implementations of a keyed list (Section 13.4) with the array implementation of a linked list which we are about to describe. Figure 15.8 makes this distinction more apparent. By using an array to now implement a linked list, we will be providing a different implementation of a keyed list than the straightforward array schemes presented in Section 13.4. This different implementation will carry with it all of the advantages and disadvantages that come with using linked lists; that is, efficient additions and deletions but slow sequential searching.

The technique for implementing a linked list using an array should already be evident from our earlier discussion of the chain of gifts. We merely need to declare an array of records—each with an appropriate Data field and a Link field—to serve as a pointer to the next record on the list. Since the location of this next record can be specified as an array position, it is clear

■ to be able to write programs that use the linked list ADT in a fashion consistent with the ADT use rule; that is, in a fashion that is shielded from the underlying implementation

that this Link field need only be an ordinary integer. Figure 15.9 portrays such an array implementation of a simple linked list of five alphabetically ordered names.

In order to implement a procedure for inserting a node into such a linked list, we must first consider where such nodes are to come from. That is, we need a procedure that supplies an unused node from the pool of available unused locations. We call this procedure GetNode. Similarly, when a node in the linked list is deleted, we should be able to return it to the pool of available nodes. ReturnNode will be our procedure to do this.

FIGURE 15.8
Levels of abstraction in implementing lists

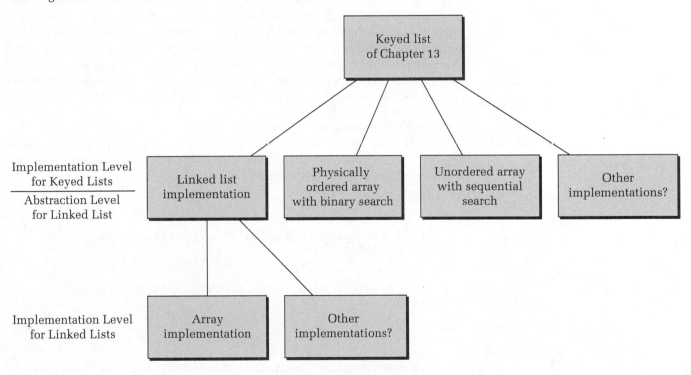

FIGURE 15.9
Logical representation versus array implementation

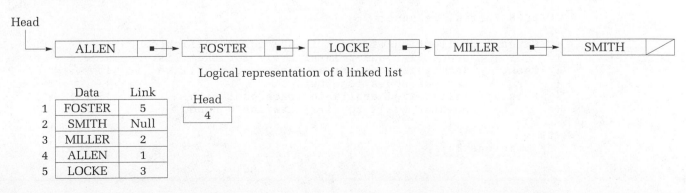

Logical representation of a linked list

	Data	Link
1	FOSTER	5
2	SMITH	Null
3	MILLER	2
4	ALLEN	1
5	LOCKE	3

Head
4

The most convenient way of viewing this available pool of nodes is as a special linked list with its own head pointer, Avail, which is woven into the same array used by the active nodes on other lists. Because the order of nodes is not important in this available space list, all insertions and deletions can occur at its head.

■ EXAMPLE 15.1

Write a package of procedures to manage the pool of available nodes that are accessed by linked list operations.

We will call these procedures InitializeSpace, GetNode, and ReturnNode. The pool of available nodes is identified by the global variable Space. Because this pool is used by all linked list operations, we will access it as a global variable when implementing these operations. The less attractive alternative is to include it as an extra parameter for all operations. This latter alternative would force users of the linked list ADT to include an additional Space parameter whenever they invoke a linked list operation. That additional parameter would *decrease* the degree to which the linked list's implementation was hidden from users.

The InitializeSpace procedure activates the available space list by intially linking all array locations into the available chain. The graphic documentation that accompanies the procedures highlights how this available node list is then manipulated by GetNode and ReturnNode.

```
{  Global declarations   }

CONST
  TotalSpace = {  Set to the number of nodes in available space pool };
  Null = 0;    {  To flag end of list                                 }

TYPE
  Pointer = integer;  { Pointers will just reference array indices }
  LinkedListNode = RECORD
                    Data : LinkedListData;
                    Link : Pointer
                  END;
  SpaceStructure = RECORD
                    Nodes : ARRAY [1..TotalSpace] OF LinkedListNode;
                    Avail : Pointer  { References first available node }
                  END;

VAR
  Space : SpaceStructure;  { The global pool of available nodes }

PROCEDURE InitializeSpace;

  {  Given:   Collection of nodes in Space for available    }
  {           space list and pointer Avail for that list.   }
  {  Task:    Set Avail to point at first one and link      }
  {           rest of nodes together.                       }
  {  Return:  Initialized available space pool with         }
  {           pointer Avail to first available node.        }

  VAR
    K : integer;
```

```
BEGIN
  WITH Space DO
    BEGIN
      { Initially, a node in available space is linked to  }
      { node in the immediately adjacent array position.   }
      FOR K := 1 TO TotalSpace - 1 DO
        Nodes[K].Link := K + 1;
      Nodes[TotalSpace].Link := Null;
      Avail := 1
    END
END; { of PROCEDURE Initialize }
```

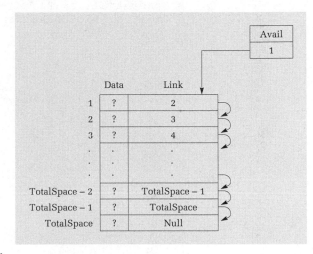

```
PROCEDURE GetNode (VAR P : Pointer);

  { Given:   Global list of available nodes in Space with  }
  {          pointer Avail to first available node.         }
  { Task:    Determine first available node.                }
  { Return:  Pointer P to that available node and new       }
  {          available space list with that node removed.   }

  BEGIN
    WITH Space DO
      IF Avail = Null THEN
        writeln ('No space available.')
      ELSE
        BEGIN
          P := Avail;
          Avail := Nodes[Avail].Link
        END
END; { of PROCEDURE GetNode }
```

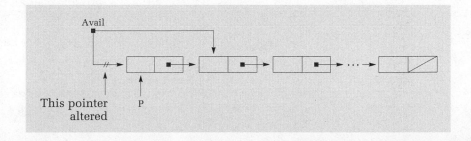

```
PROCEDURE ReturnNode (P :  Pointer);

   {  Given:   Global list of available nodes in Space with    }
   {           pointer Avail to first available node, and a     }
   {           pointer P to a node to be returned to            }
   {           available space.                                 }
   {  Task:    Return node referenced by P to list of           }
   {           available nodes.                                 }
   {  Return:  Appropriately updated list of available nodes.   }

  BEGIN
    Space.Nodes[P].Link := Space.Avail;
    Space.Avail := P
  END; {  of PROCEDURE ReturnNode  }
```

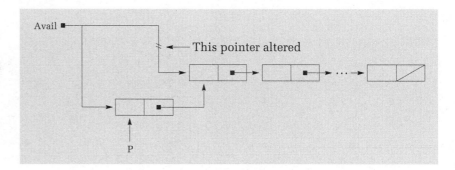

We are now ready to implement the Create, Next, and InsertNode operations for the linked list ADT. The linked lists that these operations manipulate are assumed to reside in the global structure Space defined in Example 15.1.

■ **EXAMPLE 15.2**

Implement the Create operation for the linked list ADT.

```
   {  Assume global declarations from Example 15.1  }

   PROCEDURE Create (VAR Head : Pointer);

      {  Given:   A pointer Head whose value is arbitrary     }
      {  Task:    Initialize linked list referenced by Head   }
      {           to the empty list                           }
      {  Return:  Head pointer referencing the empty list.    }

      BEGIN
        Head := Null
      END; {  of PROCEDURE Create  }
```

■ EXAMPLE 15.3

Implement the Next operation for the linked list ADT.

```
FUNCTION Next (P : Pointer) : Pointer;

    {  Given:   A pointer P to a node in a linked list.      }
    {           Assume that P is not Null.                   }
    {  Task:    Determined the node that follows the node    }
    {           referenced by P.                             }
    {  Return:  A pointer to the node following that         }
    {           referenced by P. If no node follows P, then  }
    {           return Null.                                 }

    BEGIN
      Next := Space.Nodes[P].Link
    END;
```

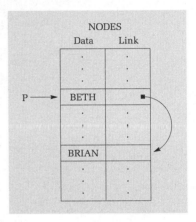

Although the code for the Next operation is only one instruction, it is not trivial. You should ponder it and the accompanying graphic documentation until you are convinced of its correctness. It may well be one of the most powerful single-line procedures you will ever see.

■ EXAMPLE 15.4

Implement the InsertNode operation for the linked list ADT.

```
PROCEDURE InsertNode (VAR Head : Pointer;
                      P, Prev : Pointer);

    {  Given:   Linked list referenced by Head pointer.      }
    {           Node referenced by P to be inserted in the   }
    {           list after node referenced by Prev, with     }
    {           Prev equal to Null if insertion is to        }
    {           occur at front of list.                      }
    {  Task:    Set pointers to link node P into list.       }
    {  Return:  Appropriately updated linked list.           }
```

```
BEGIN
  WITH Space DO
    IF Prev = Null THEN {  Insert at front  }
      BEGIN
        Nodes[P].Link := Head;
        Head := P
      END
    ELSE
      BEGIN
        Nodes[P].Link := Nodes[Prev].Link;
        Nodes[Prev].Link := P
      END { IF }
END; { of PROCEDURE InsertNode }
```

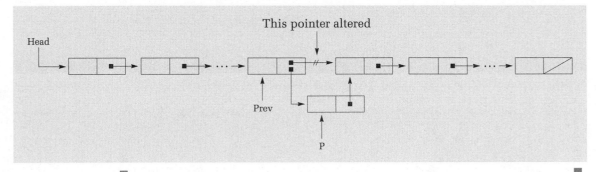

As with code for the Next operation in Example 15.3, the brevity of In-sertNode's implementation in Example 15.4 belies its complexity. You should convince yourself that the present version of InsertNode is sufficient to handle all cases: insertion in an empty list and insertion at the front, middle, and end of a nonempty list. The best way to do this is to draw an abstract picture of the list for each of these conditions and trace the action of the procedure's statements on that picture. (See Figure 15.10.)

FIGURE 15.10
Tracing of four possibilities in InsertNode procedure

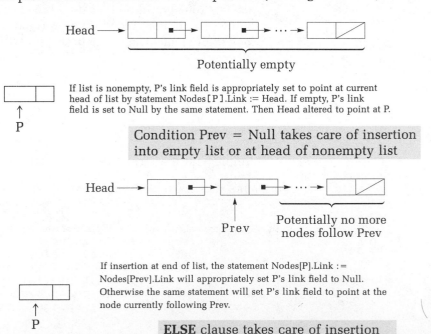

The InsertNode operation alone is not sufficient to load data into a meaningful linked list. First, InsertNode assumes that the pointer P, which references the node to be inserted, has already been obtained via a call to Get-Node and filled with appropriate data. Thus, InsertNode is concerned only with the pointer manipulations that link the node into the list, not with finding the insertion point. Second, InsertNode assumes that the location in the list where the insertion is to occur has already been found and stored in Prev.

We now consider how to find the pointer Prev that InsertNode requires. For this discussion, we assume that the list is to be maintained in ascending order. To determine Prev, we must therefore compare the data in the node referenced by P (the node to be inserted) to the data in successive nodes along the list. We know that we have found the spot to insert the node referenced by P when we come to the first node on the list containing data greater than (or equal to) that in P. That is, a loop to find the node that should follow P may be roughly given as

```
Start pointer Q at head of list
WHILE (data referenced by P > data referenced by Q)
    AND NOT at end of list DO
        Advance Q to next node
```

Unfortunately this loop will not find the node after which P belongs but rather the node before which it belongs. This can be easily remedied by adding Prev as a "tag-along" pointer in the loop.

```
Start Prev at Null
Start Q at head of list
WHILE (data referenced by P > data referenced by Q)
    AND NOT at end of list DO
        Set Prev to Q {  Prev tagging along  }
        Advance Q to next node
```

■ **EXAMPLE 15.5**

Provide a Pascal implementation of the logic described in the preceding pseudocode.

```
{  Assume same global declarations used in Example 15.1 }

PROCEDURE  FindInsertionSlot (Head, P : Pointer;
                             VAR Prev : Pointer);

{  Given:   Linked list referenced by Head and node to be  }
{           inserted referenced by P.  Assume that the     }
{           linear order of the list matches ascending     }
{           order by Data field.                           }
{  Task:    Find node in list after which node referenced  }
{           by P is to be located.                         }
{  Return:  Pointer Prev to that node.  Prev is Null if    }
{           node referenced by P belongs at front of list. }

VAR  Q : Pointer; {  Pointer used to advance through loop  }
     SlotFound : boolean;

BEGIN
  Prev := Null;
  Q := Head;
  SlotFound := false;
```

```
{  Q advances until end of list is reached or until data referenced  }
{  by Q is greater than or equal to that referenced by P.            }
WHILE (Q <> Null) AND NOT SlotFound DO
   IF Space.Nodes[P].Data > Space.Nodes[Q].Data THEN
      BEGIN
         Prev := Q; {  Prev tags along behind Q  }
         Q := Next (Q) {  Q advances  }
      END
   ELSE
      SlotFound := true
END; {  of PROCEDURE FindInsertionSlot  }
```

■   ■

The Boolean variable SlotFound is required in FindInsertionSlot because of the way in which Pascal may determine the Boolean result of an **AND** conditional. It is tempting to try to avoid using this Boolean and instead rewrite the **WHILE** condition as

```
WHILE (Q <> Null) AND (Space.Nodes[P].Data > Space.Nodes[Q].Data) DO
   BEGIN
      Prev := Q;
      Q := Next (Q)
   END;
```

This will work fine as long as the node referenced by P does not belong at the end of the list. However, when P does belong at the end of the list, the conditional test

```
Space.Nodes[P].Data > Space.Nodes[Q].Data
```

may result in a run-time "Index out of range" error because Q is Null. Thus, the SlotFound Boolean variable is necessary to avoid Q's becoming an invalid index reference for the Space array.

With the procedures InsertNode and FindInsertionSlot that we have developed, it is now clear how we could build up a linked list. Assuming appropriate variable declarations, the following sequence will create a linked list referenced by Head and then successively add nodes to it until SentinelValue is entered.

```
InitializeSpace; {  Initialize available space.  }
Create (Head);   {  Initialize linked list referenced by Head.  }
GetNode (P);
ReadInData (Space.Nodes[P].Data); {  Call procedure which fills  }
                                  {  data portion of node.       }

WHILE Space.Nodes[P].Data <> SentinelValue DO
   BEGIN
      FindInsertionSlot (Head, P, Prev);
      InsertNode (Head, P, Prev);
      GetNode (P);
      ReadInData (Space.Nodes[P].Data)
   END;
ReturnNode (P); {  Return last node entered since  }
                {  it was not linked into list.    }
```

■ **EXAMPLE 15.6**

Given the Initialize, GetNode, and insertion procedures we have discussed, trace the status of the Data and Link fields in the Nodes array and the Avail and Head pointers as the following items arrive for insertion into an alphabetically arranged linked list.

> *WAGNER*
> *ELLIS*
> *GORDON*
> *NIEMAN*
> *HILLER*

Before first insertion

	Data	Link
1		2
2		3
3		4
4		5
5		6
6		7
7		8
8		Null	TotalSpace

Avail	Head
1	Null

After first insertion

	Data	Link
1	WAGNER	Null
2		3
3		4
4		5
5		6
6		7
7		8
8		Null	TotalSpace

Avail	Head
2	1

After second insertion

	Data	Link
1	WAGNER	Null
2	ELLIS	1
3		4
4		5
5		6
6		7
7		8
8		Null	TotalSpace

Avail	Head
3	2

After third insertion

	Data	Link
1	WAGNER	Null
2	ELLIS	3
3	GORDON	1
4		5
5		6
6		7
7		8
8		Null	TotalSpace

Avail	Head
4	2

After fourth insertion

	Data	Link
1	WAGNER	Null
2	ELLIS	3
3	GORDON	4
4	NIEMAN	1
5		6
6		7
7		8
8		Null

TotalSpace

Avail
5

Head
2

After fifth insertion

	Data	Link
1	WAGNER	Null
2	ELLIS	3
3	GORDON	5
4	NIEMAN	1
5	HILLER	4
6		7
7		8
8		Null

TotalSpace

Avail
6

Head
2

The DeleteNode operation can be implemented in a fashion similar to InsertNode. Using the logic outlined in Figure 15.7, the node is first unchained from the list. Then a call to ReturnNode restores this node to the pool of available nodes. As in the InsertNode procedure, DeleteNode presupposes that P and Prev have been determined. This determination could be done in a FindNodeToDelete procedure similar to (though slightly different from) the FindInsertionSlot procedure we developed.

■ **EXAMPLE 15.7**

Implement the DeleteNode operation.

```
{ Assume same global declarations used for Example 15.1 }

PROCEDURE DeleteNode (VAR Head: Pointer;
                          P, Prev : Pointer);

  { Given:    Linked list referenced by pointer Head.        }
  {           Pointer P to node  to be removed from this     }
  {           list and pointer Prev to node preceding P.     }
  {           Prev is Null  if node referenced by P is at    }
  {           front of list.                                 }
  { Task:     Remove node P from list.                       }
  { Return:   Appropriately altered list.                    }
```

```
BEGIN
  IF Prev = Null THEN  {  Delete first node  }
    Head := Space.Nodes[Head].Link
  ELSE
    Space.Nodes[Prev].Link := Space.Nodes[P].Link;
  ReturnNode (P)   {  Return the deleted node  }
END;  {  of PROCEDURE DeleteNode  }
```

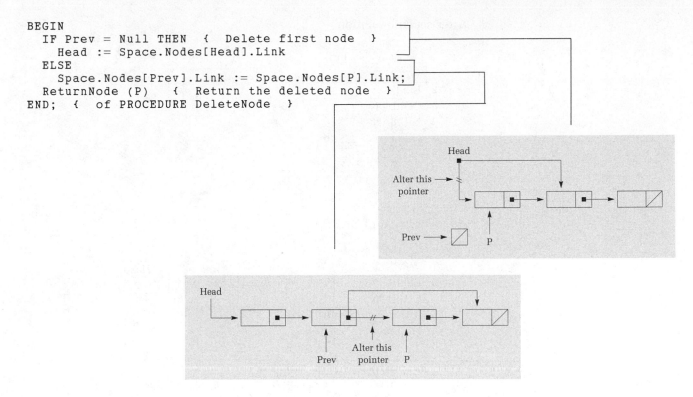

Assume that the following operations occur in sequence on the list developed in Example 15.6.

Delete WAGNER
Delete NIEMAN
Insert ZARDA

Trace the status of the Space array and the Avail and Head pointers as these operations occur.

After first deletion

	Data	Link
1	WAGNER	6
2	ELLIS	3
3	GORDON	5
4	NIEMAN	Null
5	HILLER	4
6		7
7		8
8		Null	TotalSpace

Avail	Head
1	2

After second deletion

	Data	Link
1	WAGNER	6
2	ELLIS	3
3	GORDON	5
4	NIEMAN	1
5	HILLER	Null
6		7
7		8
8		Null

TotalSpace

Avail	Head
4	2

After insertion of ZARDA

	Data	Link
1	WAGNER	6
2	ELLIS	3
3	GORDON	5
4	ZARDA	Null
5	HILLER	4
6		7
7		8
8		Null

TotalSpace

Avail	Head
1	2

Note that data contained in nodes that are returned to the available space pool are not actually destroyed until the nodes are reused via a call to GetNode.

We have begun to develop a package of procedures that may be used to process linked lists implemented by arrays. These procedures are low-level in the sense that they would appear deep in the modular structure chart of a software system that used linked lists. They represent essential linked list operations. Note that more such primitive procedures would need to be developed to complete a linked list package; for example, finding a particular node and traversing the list in a specified order. You will be developing these additional procedures in the Exercises. The following example indicates how this package of procedures could be used to maintain a list of strings in alphabetical order.

■ **EXAMPLE 15.9**

Use a linked list implemented by an array to maintain a list of strings in alphabetical order. The modular structure chart for such a program is given by Modular specifications are not given here because logic for most of the mod-

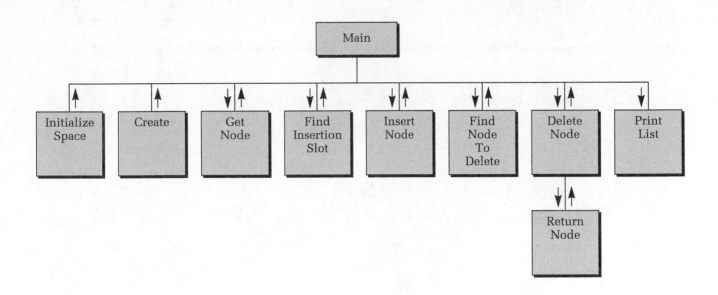

ules has already been developed in the preceding discussion. Rather, the following main program indicates how these individual modules may be used in concert with each other. To avoid a name conflict between the Create operations for linked lists and strings, the program uses a call of the form CreateString for the string ADT.

```
PROGRAM ArrayImpOfLinkedList (input, output);

{  Demonstrate use of essential operations for array              }
{  implementation of a linked list by maintaining a list          }
{  of strings in alphabetical order.                              }

{  Global declarations of Example 15.1 augmented for the particular }
{  needs of this program.                                         }

CONST
  TotalSpace = 100;
  Null = 0;    {  to flag end of list  }

TYPE
  Pointer = integer;  { Since pointers will just reference array indices }
  LinkedListData = String;  { Assume appropriate implementation of string ADT }
  LinkedListNode = RECORD
                     Data : LinkedListData;
                     Link : Pointer
                   END;
  SpaceStructure = RECORD
                     Nodes : ARRAY [1..TotalSpace] OF LinkedListNode;
                     Avail : Pointer  { References first available node }
                   END;

VAR
  Space : SpaceStructure;  { The global pool of available nodes }
  Head, P : Pointer;
```

```
      DeleteData : LinkedListData;
      Command : char;

      .
      .  { Procedures for linked list and string operations here }
      .


  { PrintOneNode is passed as parameter to LinkedTraverse }
  PROCEDURE PrintOneNode (VAR Item : LinkedListData);

      {  Given:     Item, one data item on a linked list        }
      {  Task:      Print the item                              }
      {  Return:    Nothing                                     }

      BEGIN
        WriteAString (Item);
        writeln
      END; { of PROCEDURE PrintOneNode }

  BEGIN {  Main program  }
    InitializeSpace;
    Create (Head);
    REPEAT
      write('[A]dd node, [D]elete node, [P]rint list, or [Q]uit --> ');
      readln(Command);
      CASE Command OF
        'A', 'a':
          BEGIN
            GetNode (P);
            write ('Enter data --> ');
            CreateString (Space.Nodes[P].Data);  {  Create for string  }
            ReadAString (Space.Nodes[P].Data);
            FindInsertionSlot(Head, P, Prev);
            InsertNode(Head, P, Prev)
          END;
        'D', 'd':
          BEGIN
            write ('Enter node to delete --> ');
            CreateString (DeleteData);  {  Create for string  }
            ReadAString (DeleteData);
            FindNodeToDelete (Head, P, Prev, DeleteData, Found);
            IF Found THEN
              DeleteNode(Head, P, Prev)
            ELSE
              BEGIN
                WriteAString (DeleteData);
                writeln (' not found')
              END
          END;
        'P', 'p':
          LinkedTraverse (Head, PrintOneNode)
        'Q', 'q':
          BEGIN
          END
        END {  CASE  }
    UNTIL (Command = 'q') OR (Command = 'Q')
  END.
```

A sample run of this program would appear as

```
      [A]dd node, [D]elete node, [P]rint list, or [Q]uit --> A
      Enter data --> SMITH
      [A]dd node, [D]elete node, [P]rint list, or [Q]uit --> A
      Enter data --> JONES
```

```
[A]dd node, [D]elete node, [P]rint list; or [Q]uit --> A
Enter data > MILLER
[A]dd node, [D]elete node, [P]rint list, or [Q]uit --> P
JONES
MILLER
SMITH
[A]dd node, [D]elete node, [P]rint list, or [Q]uit --> D
Enter node to delete --> MILLER
[A]dd node, [D]elete node, [P]rint list, or [Q]uit --> P
JONES
SMITH
[A]dd node, [D]elete node, [P]rint list, or [Q]uit --> Q
```

The particular package we have started upon here represents only one of two possible implementation strategies we will discuss for linked lists. In the next section we shall describe a similar package of procedures for an alternate strategy using a special feature of Pascal called a pointer variable. These two implementation strategies will prove to be interchangeable to a degree. Since you've learned the details of the array implementation, understanding how Pascal pointer variables are manipulated should be relatively easy. As you'll see, each implementation has inherent advantages and disadvantages. We'll contrast these advantages and disadvantages as we present the pointer variable scheme.

Exercises 15.2

1. Suppose that you are given the following initial state of an array implementation of a linked list.

	Data	Link
1	47	3
2	89	5
3	66	7
4	100	2
5	13	10
6	55	2
7	112	4
8	178	0
9	79	6
10	19	8

a. Indicate the nodes on the list if the head pointer is 9 and 0 is used to indicate the Null pointer.

b. Indicate the final state of the Data and Link fields after the following program segment is executed.

```
WITH Space DO
  BEGIN
    J := 4;
    Nodes[J].Data := 883;
    J := Nodes[J].Link;
    WHILE Nodes[J].Link <> 0 DO
      BEGIN
        J := Nodes[J].Link;
        Nodes[J].Data := 912
      END
  END;
```

2. Consider the array implementation of a linked list of names that appears in Figure 15.9. Suppose that the physical order of the five names in that list was given by

Data	Link		
LOCKE	?		Head
MILLER	?		?
SMITH	?		
FOSTER	?		
ALLEN	?		

Fill in the Head and Link fields so that the list could be traversed in logical alphabetical order.

3. Indicate the changes in the Link and Head fields from Exercise 2 if MILLER is deleted from the list.

4. Indicate the changes in the Link and Head fields from Exercise 2 if ALLEN is deleted from the list.

5. Consider an array implementation of a linked list of names which is to be maintained in alphabetical order. Trace the status of the Data and Link fields and the Head and Avail pointers as the following operations are performed on the list:

> *Insert JAMES*
> *Insert CHILTON*
> *Insert SEFTON*
> *Insert LEE*
> *Delete CHILTON*
> *Insert WAGNER*
> *Delete JAMES*
> *Insert AARON*

6. Consider the following slightly modified version of **PROCEDURE** InsertNode.

```
PROCEDURE InsertNode (VAR Head : Pointer;
                      P, Prev : Pointer);

{ Given:    Linked list referenced by Head pointer.       }
{           Node referenced by P to be inserted in the     }
{           list after node referenced by Prev, with       }
{           Prev equal to Null if insertion is to           }
{           occur at front of list.                         }
{ Task:     Set pointers to link node P into list.          }
{ Return:   Appropriately updated linked list.              }

BEGIN
  WITH Space DO
    IF Prev = Null THEN {  Insert at front  }
      BEGIN
        Nodes[P].Link := Head;
        Head := P
      END
    ELSE
      BEGIN
        Nodes[Prev].Link := P;
        Nodes[P].Link := Nodes[Prev].Link
      END {  IF  }
END;  {  of PROCEDURE InsertNode  }
```

Will this version of the procedure still perform the InsertNode operation correctly? If not, explain what it will do to a linked list when called; use diagrams of a linked list before and after the procedure is called to clarify your explanation.

7. Assuming an array implementation of a linked list, write **PROCEDURE** LinkedTraverse as specified in the definition of the linked list ADT in Section 15.1.

8. Assuming an array implementation of a linked list, write **FUNCTION** Empty as specified in the definition of the linked list ADT in Section 15.1.

9. Write the **PROCEDURE** FindNodeToDelete that is invoked in the main program of Example 15.9.

10. The main program of Example 15.9 doesn't completely obey the ADT use rule in that it fails to hide completely the array implementation of a linked list that it is using. How does it fail in this regard? How would you correct it? (*Hint*: Think about adding an operation to our definition of the linked list ADT in Section 15.1.)

11. Use an array implementation of a linked list to develop implementations of each of the keyed list ADT operations specified in Section 13.4.

12. Write a procedure to reverse a linked list referenced by the pointer Head.

13. Suppose you sort a list of input values by reading them in one at a time and inserting them into a linked list arranged in ascending order. Clearly, after you have read all of the input values you will have a sorted list. Let's call this algorithm the *linked list sort*. Analyze the time efficiency of this algorithm in terms of number of comparisons and number of data interchanges. Compare its efficiency to that of the other sort algorithms we have studied—insertion, bubble, selection and radix sort.

14. Your friend claims that nodes in the available space list are always linked to nodes in the next physical array location; that is, an available node at location P is always linked to the node at location P + 1. Is your friend right or wrong? If your friend is wrong, write a statement explaining the error in your friend's logic.

■ ■ ■ ■

■ 15.3
Pascal Pointer Variable Implementation of a Linked List: Dynamic Memory Management in Pascal

OBJECTIVES

- to realize the static limitations of the array implementation of a linked list
- to gain familiarity with the syntax of Pascal pointer variables
- to understand the use of Pascal's **new** and **dispose** procedures in managing that segment of memory known as the heap
- to be able to develop an implementation of the linked list ADT using Pascal pointer variables
Objectives continued.

Perhaps the biggest drawback of the array method of implementing a linked list is the static nature of the memory storage associated with an array. Suppose, for example, we declare an array Nodes of size 100. Then the storage in the Space structure is static in the sense that it is allocated at the time the program is compiled, not when it actually runs. Because of this, we are charged for 100 locations whether or not they are all used. When we have only 50 records to process in the array, 50 percent of the memory allocation is being wasted. Even more serious is the limitation that, if we have over 100 records to process, we must edit and recompile the program using a larger array size.

Pascal pointer variables, on the other hand, are an example of a technique known as *dynamic memory management*. A feature that is not available in many older languages such as FORTRAN, COBOL, and BASIC, dynamic memory management is used by Pascal to allow the programmer to claim only that amount of memory which is actually needed at run-time.

To understand dynamic memory management, we must first understand the configuration of memory when your program is loaded into it from an external file. As indicated in Figure 15.11, there are memory costs that must

- to understand the difference between static and dynamic memory management
- to compare the two implementations of linked list we have studied—array and pointer variables

be paid in addition to the storage space required for the object code of your program. In particular, memory must have room to accommodate:

- Various operating system requirements.
- A stack used by the operating system for procedure and function processing (to be explained in Chapter 16).
- The object code of your program; that is, the machine-language version of your program's instructions.
- Static data areas; that is, the globally declared variables in your program.

FIGURE 15.11

Computer memory configuration for typical program

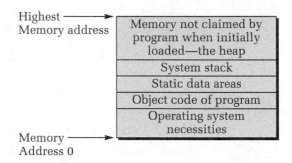

Notice that the four memory components listed generally will not consume all of the available computer memory. What remains is called the *heap*. Unless you have already used the dynamic memory allocation scheme of a language like Pascal, your programs have never been able to get at the heap and take advantage of it. With Pascal's pointer variables, all this changes.

Suppose we have a record declaration, such as that for LinkedListNode in our definition of the linked list ADT. Then, by using a caret (^) character, we can declare a **TYPE** for variables that are pointers to such a record. Syntactically, the declarations would appear as

```
TYPE
     .
     .
     .
  Pointer = ^LinkedListNode;
  LinkedListNode = RECORD
                   Data : LinkedListData {  Any appropriate type  };
                   Link : Pointer
                 END;
     .
     .
     .
VAR
  P : Pointer;
```

These declarations establish P as a variable of user-defined **TYPE** Pointer. A variable of **TYPE** Pointer references ("points at") records of **TYPE** LinkedListNode. Note there is a hint of circularity here in that Pointer uses LinkedListNode in its declaration, and there is a field of **TYPE** Pointer in the declaration of LinkedListNode. Syntactically, Pascal requires the declaration of the **TYPE** Pointer before the declaration of a record (or other structure) that incorporates elements of **TYPE** Pointer.

With Pascal pointer variables, you are able to call upon Pascal's memory management system—a high-powered parallel to the GetNode and Return-Node operations that we developed in Section 15.2. The key is a supplied

Storage of Disk Files and Computer Security

Operating systems typically grant their users disk storage in units called blocks. On the magnetic disk itself, a block is a contiguous area capable of storing a fixed amount of data. For example, a block in DEC's well-known VAX/VMS time-sharing system is 512 bytes. As a user enters data into a disk file, the system must grant additional blocks of storage as they are needed. In such a time-sharing environment, although each block represents a physically contiguous storage area on the disk, it may not be possible for the operating system to give a user blocks that are physically next to each other. Instead, when a user needs an additional storage block, the operating system may put information into the current block about where the next block is located. In effect, a link is established from the current block to the next block. By the time a naive user has completed entering a four-block file, it may be scattered over the entire disk surface, as indicated in the following diagram:

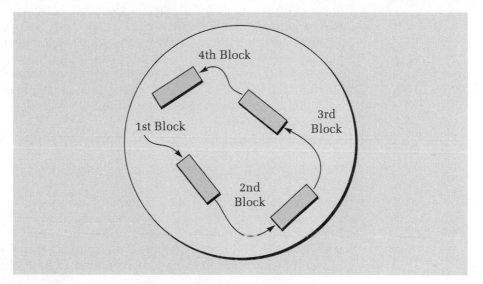

Although this may seem like an ingenious way of extending files indefinitely, one pays in several ways for such scattered blocks. Namely, the read-write head that seeks and puts data on the disk surface is forced to move greater distances, thereby slowing system performance. To combat such inefficiencies, shrewd users can often take advantage of options that allow them to pre-allocate the contiguous disk storage that will be required for a file. Moreover, system managers may occasionally shut down the entire system to rebuild disks, a process that entails copying all files that are presently scattered over the disk onto a new disk in physically contiguous form.

Yet another more serious price which may be paid for storing disk files in this fashion revolves around the issue of data security and what the operating system does with blocks that are no longer needed by a user. From what we have discussed in this chapter, it is clear that the disk blocks used to store a file are returned to some type of available block list when a user deletes that file from his or her directory. When these blocks are returned to that available space list, the data in them may remain intact until another user's request to extend a file results in the blocks' being reallocated to that new user. This means that, if clever users ("hackers") know how to access the available space list, they may be able to scavenge through data that other users once owned and then released (assuming it was destroyed upon being released).

One of the authors was actually involved in an incident in which such a clever student was able to "find" old versions of a test that a professor had typed in on the computer and then discarded into this available block list. Needless to say, the professor whose tests were being explored by the student was somewhat alarmed upon discovering what had happened. As a protection against this type of scavenging, many operating systems will, by default or as an option, actually destroy data that is returned to the available block list.

procedure **new**, which takes as its only argument a pointer variable such as P and returns in P a pointer; that is, a memory address indicating the location within the heap where the heap manager has allocated space for the currently requested record. Thus, **new** is essentially a Pascal-supplied dynamic version of the GetNode procedure which we developed ourselves for the array implementation of a linked list.

Several facts about the **new** procedure should be emphasized at this point.

- **new** is a run-time request for memory. Unlike an array, you are not charged for the memory requested until you actually have something to store in it. Moreover, unlike static array declarations, you are not charged for an excess of memory that you may not even need for this particular run of the program.
- After a call to **new**(P) for a suitably declared pointer variable P, P is a memory address. As such, its actual value is of little concern to you. Suffice it to say that it is an address somewhere in the heap. How the heap manager was able to arrive at such an address involves a system-dependent, more sophisticated version of our own GetNode algorithm. Note that, as a memory address, P's actual value is not important. In fact, Pascal won't even let you see what it is since a statement like **write**(P) will result in a syntax error.
- However, Pascal will allow you to manipulate pointer variables in the ways necessary to implement a variety of data structures, including linked lists. For instance, the contents of one pointer variable may be assigned to another.
- Pascal also lets you get at the contents of records that are stored at an address "pointed to" by a pointer variable such as P. To access the contents of such a dynamically allocated record, the caret (^) notation (also referred to as the up-arrow notation) is again used. Hence P^ refers to the contents of the record at the address pointed to by P. That is, P^ is the actual data and P is where the data are stored. Figure 15.12 illustrates this crucial difference between the adress stored in a pointer variable P and the contents of the record stored at that address. Given P, fields within such a record may be examined by the usual dot qualification; for example, P^.Name or P^.Address. (In this figure, P itself is 22706, a memory address. P^ is the contents of the record at address 22706. Hence P^.Name is BURTON JB and P^.Address is 194 E MAPLE ST. NY NY.)
- Should you request space from the heap manager when none is available, a run-time error will result.

FIGURE 15.12
The difference between P and P^

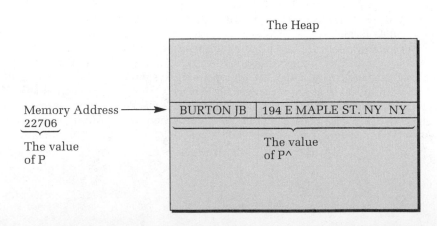

The Heap

Memory Address ⟶ 22706

The value of P

BURTON JB | 194 E MAPLE ST. NY NY

The value of P^

Just as **new** provides an alternative to the GetNode procedure from our earlier array implementation, Pascal also provides a **dispose** procedure as a dynamic alternative to our ReturnNode procedure. If P is appropriately declared as a pointer variable, then the statement

```
dispose (P)
```

will return the memory space being referenced by P to the Pascal memory management system for later use. The amount of space obtained by **new**(P) or returned by **dispose**(P) is always equal to the size of the record associated with P.

Pascal uses the reserved word **NIL** as a special flagging value for pointer variables. **NIL** is essentially the analogue of the defined constant Null in our array-based implementation. When a pointer variable in Pascal has the value **NIL**, it is well-defined, but it is not pointing to any node in memory. Thus, it is valid to check whether P = **NIL**, but it is not valid to refer to P^ when P is **NIL**. The latter type of reference will usually cause a run-time error. Typically the **NIL** value is assigned to the Head pointer before any nodes are added to the list and to the link field pointer in the last node on the list.

Consider now some sample statements that could be used to manipulate variables of the **TYPE** Pointer we defined in our previous declarations. To assign a value to the Data field, of a node referenced by P, a statement of the form

```
P^.Data := X
```

would suffice where X is of the appropriate type. The Link field in the node referenced by P could be "aimed at" another node referenced by a pointer Q via the statement

```
P^.Link := Q
```

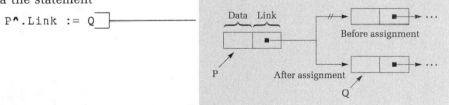

Finally, if the node referenced by P has been appropriately chained into an existing linked list, then P can be advanced to the next node on the list by the statement

```
P := P^.Link
```

Note that this statement is the direct analogue of the statement

```
P := Space.Nodes[P].Link
```

from our array implementation of a linked list.

Some additional examples will serve to clarify the logic involving pointer variables.

■ **EXAMPLE 15.10**

Suppose we have a pointer type established by the following declarations:

```
TYPE
  PtrToNode = ^Node;
  Node = RECORD
            Info : integer;
            FollowedBy : PtrToNode
          END;
```

```
VAR
   P, Q, : PtrToNode;
```

Describe the effect of the following sequence of instructions:

```
new(P);                    {1}
new(Q);                    {2}
P^.Info := 5;              {3}
Q^.Info := 3;              {4}
P^.FollowedBy := Q;        {5}
Q^.FollowedBy := NIL;      {6}
```

The easiest way to describe such code is to visualize its effect. Consequently, we provide an answer in the form of a series of snapshots, identified by the bracketed number that marks each line of code.

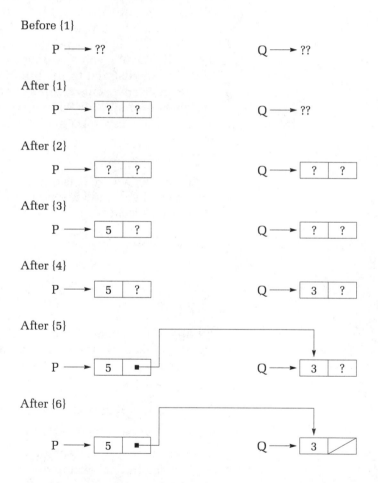

■ **EXAMPLE 15.11**

Given the declarations of Example 15.10, write a code segment specifically designed to add a node containing Info value 12 to the following list referenced by P:

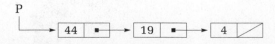

```
new(Q);                                          {  Grab a node in the heap   }
Q^.Info := 12;                                   {  Assign its Info value      }
Q^.FollowedBy := NIL;                            {  Q will be at end of list   }
P^.FollowedBy^.FollowedBy^.FollowedBy := Q; {  Chain it into list at end  }
```
■   ■

Clearly, programming with Pascal pointer variables requires your having an accurate mental image of the effects of each instruction. You can never actually grasp the value of the pointer itself—as you can with array-based pointers. In one sense, this allows Pascal pointer variables to be dynamic and hence more powerful than their array-based counterparts. However, because you cannot effectively trace the value of a Pascal pointer variable, you must exercise extreme care when programming with them. The debugging technique of inserting tracer **writeln** instructions no longer will allow you to examine the value of an unreliable pointer variable. Faced with a bug, you must carefully draw linked list pictures and manually execute your code against those pictures until you find the instruction that is going awry.

Implementing the Linked List ADT with Pascal Pointer Variables

Now that we have covered the syntax of Pascal pointer variables, we are ready to use them to provide an alternate implementation for the linked list ADT. Doing so will be relatively easy because the detailed logic of each operation parallels exactly what we have already done for the array implementation. In the following four examples, we provide Pascal pointer variable versions of the Create, Next, InsertNode, and DeleteNode operations. You should compare them to their array-based analogues in Examples 15.2, 15.3, 15.4, and 15.7 respectively.

■ **EXAMPLE 15.12**

Consider the following **TYPE** declarations for a Pascal pointer variable implementation of the linked list ADT.

```
TYPE
   Pointer = ^LinkedListNode;
   LinkedListNode = RECORD
                         Data : LinkedListData;
                         Link : Pointer
                    END;
```

Using these declarations, implement the Create operation for the linked list ADT.

```
PROCEDURE Create (VAR Head : Pointer);

   { Given:  A pointer Head whose value is arbitrary    }
   { Task:   Initialize linked list referenced by Head  }
   {            to the empty list                        }
   { Return: Head pointer referencing the empty list     }

   BEGIN
      Head := NIL
   END; {  of PROCEDURE Create  }
```
■   ■

Implement the Next operation for the Pascal pointer version of the linked list ADT.

```
FUNCTION Next (P : Pointer) : Pointer;

  {  Given:   A pointer P to a node in a linked list.   }
  {           Assume that P is not NIL.                  }
  {  Task:    Determine the Node which follows the node  }
  {           referenced by P.                           }
  {  Return:  A pointer to the node following that       }
  {           referenced by P. If no node follows P, then }
  {           return NIL.                                }

BEGIN
  Next := P^.Link  {  Note that a function may return a pointer type  }
END;
```

Implement the InsertNode operation for a Pascal pointer linked list.

```
PROCEDURE InsertNode (VAR Head : Pointer;
                      P, Prev : Pointer);

  {  Given:   Linked list referenced by Head pointer.    }
  {           Node referenced by P to be inserted in the }
  {           list after node referenced by Prev, with   }
  {           Prev equal to NIL if insertion is to        }
  {           occur at front of list.                    }
  {  Task:    Set pointers to link node P into list.     }
  {  Return:  Appropriately updated linked list.         }

BEGIN
  IF Prev = NIL THEN {  Insert at front  }
    BEGIN
      P^.Link := Head;
      Head := P
    END
  ELSE
    BEGIN
      P^.Link := Prev^.Link;
      Prev^.Link := P
    END {  IF  }
END; {  of PROCEDURE InsertNode  }
```

Implement the DeleteNode operation for a Pascal pointer variable implementation.

```
PROCEDURE DeleteNode (VAR Head : Pointer;
                      P, Prev : Pointer);

  {  Given:   Linked list referenced by pointer Head.    }
  {           Pointer P to node to be removed from this  }
  {           list and pointer Prev to node preceding P. }
```

```
{              Prev is NIL if node referenced by P is at      }
{              front of list.                                 }
{  Task:       Remove node P from list.                       }
{  Return:     Appropriately altered list.                    }

BEGIN
  IF Prev = NIL THEN  {  Delete first node  }
    Head := Head^.Link
  ELSE
    Prev^.Link := P^.Link;
  dispose (P)  {  Return the deleted node  }
END;  {  of PROCEDURE DeleteNode  }
```

Since both the InsertNode and DeleteNode procedures assume that the pointers P and Prev have been appropriately set prior to calling, we should describe how this would be done for a pointer variable implementation. The following procedure, FindNodeToDelete, is based on a pointer variable implementation. You should carefully compare it to the FindInsertionSlot procedure we developed for an array implementation in Example 15.5. Note the similarities in the way the procedures' loops are controlled. Just as we had to use a Boolean variable to avoid a potential Null index reference in the array procedure, so must we use a Boolean variable to avoid a potential reference through a **NIL**-valued pointer in the pointer variable version.

■ **EXAMPLE 15.16**

Develop a procedure that could be called prior to DeleteNode to find the node to remove from a linked list and establish the P and Prev parameters for DeleteNode.

```
{  Assume same declarations used in previous examples }

PROCEDURE  FindNodeToDelete (Head : Pointer;
                             VAR P, Prev : Pointer;
                             Target : LinkListData;
                             VAR Found : boolean);

{  Given:      Linked list referenced by pointer variable     }
{              Head and Target data to be found in that list.  }
{  Task:       Search list for Target.                         }
{  Return:     Pointers P and Prev to node containing Target   }
{              data and the preceding node respectively.       }
{              Prev set to NIL if Target occurs at the front   }
{              of the list.  Found set to true or false        }
{              depending upon whether or not Target was found. }

BEGIN
  Prev := NIL;
  P := Head;
  Found := false;
  {  P advances until end of list or Target value is           }
  {  reached.                                                  }
  WHILE (P <> NIL) AND NOT Found DO
    IF P^.Data = Target THEN
      Found := true
    ELSE { Still looking }
```

```
                         BEGIN
                           Prev := P;  {  Prev tags along  }
                           P := P^.Link {   P advances   }
                         END
              END;  {  of PROCEDURE FindNodeToDelete  }
                  ■                                              ■
```

■ **EXAMPLE 15.17**

In Example 15.9 we provided a complete main program to maintain a list of strings in alphabetical order using an array implementation of a linked list. Here we change the underlying implementation of the linked list structure in that program to a Pascal pointer variable implementation. Other than that change, the design and logic of the program parallels exactly that of Example 15.9.

```
PROGRAM PointerVarImpOfLinkedList (input, output);

{  Demonstrate use of essential operations for Pascal pointer      }
{  implementation of a linked list by maintaining a list           }
{  of strings in alphabetical order.                               }

TYPE
  Pointer = ^LinkedListNode;
  LinkedListData = String;   { Assume appropriate implementation of string ADT }
  LinkedListNode = RECORD
                     Data : LinkedListData;
                     Link : Pointer
                   END;

VAR
  Head, P : Pointer;
  DeleteData : LinkedListData;
  Command : char;


    .
    .  { Procedures for linked list and string operations here }
    .


{ PrintOneNode is passed as parameter to LinkedTraverse }
PROCEDURE PrintOneNode (VAR Item : LinkedListData);

  {  Given:    Item, one data item on a linked list         }
  {  Task:     Print the item                               }
  {  Return:   Nothing                                      }

  BEGIN
    WriteAString (Item);
    writeln
  END; { of PROCEDURE PrintOneNode }

BEGIN {  Main program  }
  Create (Head);
  REPEAT
    write('[A]dd node, [D]elete node, [P]rint list, or [Q]uit --> ');
    readln(Command);
    CASE Command OF
      'A', 'a':
        BEGIN
          new (P);
          write ('Enter data --> ');
          CreateString (P^.Data);  {  Create for String  }
```

```
            ReadAString (P^.Data);
            FindInsertionSlot(Head, P, Prev);
            InsertNode(Head, P, Prev)
         END;
      'D', 'd':
         BEGIN
            write ('Enter node to delete --> ');
            CreateString (DeleteData);  { Create for string }
            ReadAString (DeleteData);
            FindNodeToDelete (Head, P, Prev, DeleteData, Found);
            IF Found THEN
               DeleteNode(Head, P, Prev)
            ELSE
               BEGIN
                  WriteAString (DeleteData);
                  writeln (' not found')
               END
         END;
      'P', 'p':
         LinkedTraverse (Head, PrintOneNode)
      'Q', 'q':
         BEGIN
         END
      END {  CASE  }
   UNTIL (Command = 'q') OR (Command = 'Q')
END.
```

The sample run for this program would appear *exactly* as that given in Example 15.9. This is not surprising since we have changed only the underlying implementation of the list structure. At the user level, this change should be completely hidden. Also note that the main programs of the two examples are nearly identical. You will consider how to make them identical in the Exercises.

Now let's compare the two linked list implementations we have discussed. From an efficiency perspective, there is little difference because the algorithms behind Pascal's **new** and **dispose** procedures mirror very closely the logic of their counterparts GetNode and ReturnNode in the array implementation. The array implementation has the advantage of not being specifically tied to Pascal or a similar language that directly supports dynamic memory management. Moreover, the array implementation can be directly converted to a random access file implementation using the strategy we discussed in Chapter 14.

The array implementation also allows for easier program tracing when debugging is needed since the values of the links may be directly printed via **write** statements. However, this advantage is somewhat tempered by the fact that most Pascal compilers come with debugging tools that allow you to actually see the values of pointer variables even though Pascal itself will not let you **write** them.

From a convenience perspective, pointer variables emerge a clear winner—totally eliminating your worries about managing available nodes. Pascal's dynamic memory management also allows your linked list (or other data structure) to expand into all of the memory available at run-time. Array implementations, on the other hand, are bounded by the size of an array declared at compile time. In this book, we tend to use pointer variable implementations for data structures where possible because of the convenience. However, in certain situations where a concept can be more clearly illustrated by giving some tangible numbers for pointer values, we occasionally resort to array implementations.

Exercises 15.3

Exercises 1–6 refer to the following **TYPE** and **VAR** declarations:

```
TYPE
  Ptr = ^Node;
  Node = RECORD
              Num : integer;
              Next : Ptr
          END;

VAR
  A, B, C : Ptr;
```

1. Specify which of the following statements are syntactically correct. For those that are wrong, explain why they are wrong.

   a. `A := B;`

   b. `A := A^.Num;`

   c. `A := A^.Ptr;`

   d. `dispose (B^);`

   e. `dispose (B^.Num);`

   f. `dispose (B);`

   g. `writeln (B);`

   h. `writeln (B^);`

   i. `writeln (B^.Num);`

2. Show how the schematic

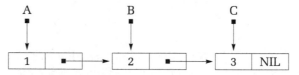

   would be changed by each of the following:

   a. `A := A^.Next;`

   b. `B := A;`

   c. `C := A^.Next;`

   d. `B^.Num := C^.Num;`

   e. `A^.Num := B^.Next^.Num;`

   f. `C^.Next := A;`

3. Write one statement to change

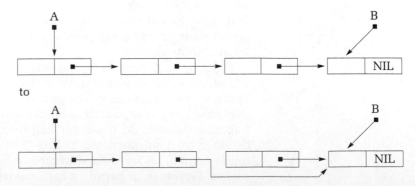

   to

4. Consider the list

Write code to create a new linked list element with value 12 and insert it at the beginning of the list headed by A.

5. Consider the list

Write code to remove the element at the head of the list and then add this element at the end of the list.

6. Indicate the output for each of the following:

a. ```
new (A);
new (B);
A^.Num := 10;
B^.Num := 20;
B := A;
A^.Num := 5;
writeln (A^.Num, B^.Num);
```

b. ```
new (C);
C^.Num := 100;
new (B);
B^.Num := C^.Num MOD 8;
new (A);
A^.Num := B^.Num + C^.Num;
writeln (A^.Num, B^.Num, C^.Num);
```

c. ```
new (A);
new (B);
A^.Num := 10;
A^.Next := B;
A^.Next^.Num := 100;
writeln (A^.Num, B^.Num);
```

7. The statement

```
P := P + 1
```

advances a pointer to the next node for an array implementation of a keyed list. What corresponding statement advances a pointer to the next node for an array implementation of a linked list? For a pointer variable implementation of a linked list? Qualify your answers by providing the record description from which you are working.

8. Implement the LinkedTraverse operation for a Pascal pointer linked list.

9. Write a procedure to reverse a linked list referenced by a Pascal pointer variable.

10. Write a function Sum to sum the integers in a linked list of integers. Show how it is called from the main program.

11. Write a procedure to dispose of all nodes in a linked list referenced by the Pascal pointer variable Head. Why can't it be done by simply passing the **dispose** procedure as an actual parameter to the LinkedTraverse operation?

12. Write a procedure that receives head pointers to two linked lists arranged in ascending order. Your procedure should merge these two lists into a single list, also arranged in ascending order. A head pointer to the merged list should be returned.
```

13. In what ways are the main programs of Examples 15.9 and 15.17 not identical? How would you adjust the definition of the LinkedList ADT so that the two programs could be identical?

14. Discuss ways in which Pascal's **new** and **dispose** are more powerful than the GetNode and ReturnNode operations that were developed in Section 15.2.

15. Suppose that you have a program that manipulates a dynamic structure using Pascal pointer variables. At the end of this program you wish to save this data structure to a file so that it may be reloaded upon the next run of the program. One strategy is to simply traverse the data structure, writing each node (including its pointer values) to a disk file. Although this approach is legal in Pascal, it will not work. Explain why. Then describe an alternate strategy that will allow saving a data structure from one run of the program to the next.

16. You are writing a program that requires two linked lists, each with a different data type in its nodes. Would you use array implementations for the linked lists or Pascal pointer variable implementations? Explain why.

■ ■ ■ ■

■ 15.4
Variations on
Linked List
Structures

Linked lists provide a tremendously useful tool in situations where a highly volatile general list must be maintained in some prescribed logical order. Their widespread use has led to the development of several "tricks of the trade" particularly suitable in certain applications. These are ways of fine-tuning the basic linked list structure to tailor it to the needs of particular situations. Four such variations on the linked list are presented in this section: dummy headers, circular lists, doubly linked lists, and multilinked lists.

Dummy Headers

A *dummy header* node in the list before the first actual data node can often contain useful information about the structure (for example, the number of nodes). If such information is of a different type than other list nodes, a record variant can be used to store it (see Section 11.4). A query algorithm can then determine the status of the list by examining the contents of the dummy header node without having to traverse the entire list. This amounts to adding one more node to the list. Figure 15.13 illustrates this concept. Additions to and deletions from the list require changing this information-keeping field in the dummy header node of the list.

FIGURE 15.13
Linked list with dummy header
indicating the length of the list

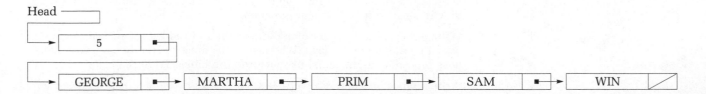

There is another distinct advantage of the dummy header node. If the list becomes empty and a dummy header node is not used, then the Head pointer for the list must be made **NIL**. But if the dummy header node is present, then the Head pointer never needs to be changed to **NIL** because it always points to this dummy header. That is, the empty list is only empty in a logical sense. Physically, it still contains the dummy header. This convention can serve to simplify the coding involved in procedures InsertNode and DeleteNode by removing the special handling previously required for inserts and deletes at the beginning of the list. (You will write these simplified procedures as an exercise at the end of this section.) This convenience factor alone provides substantial practical motivation for always using dummy headers.

Circular Linked Lists

Although linked lists are as we have described them are satisfactory in many instances, some applications must continuously cycle through the data in a list. After completing one cycle through the list, another is immediately begun. For such applications, the existence of a **NIL** pointer in the final node of a list represents an inconvenience. It would be desirable to be able to enter the list anywhere and process it efficiently independent of the entry point. In other words, we need a linked list that has no beginning or end.

Circular linked lists are precisely such data structures. A singly linked circular list is a linked list in which the last node of the list points to the first node in the list. Notice that in circular list structures, there are no **NIL** links. Figure 15.14 depicts a singly linked circular list.

FIGURE 15.14
Singly linked circular list

Head

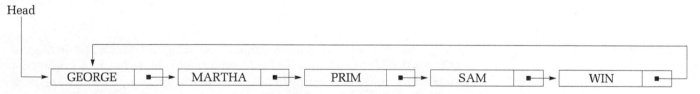

As an example of the utility of such a circular list in the area of operating systems, suppose the nodes in Figure 15.14 represent current users on a time-sharing computer. In such an environment, the operating system schedules each user for a small time slice on the central processing unit (CPU) and then proceeds to devote its momentary attention to the next user. When the final user has completed his or her time slice, ownership of the CPU must again revert to the first user, and the scheduling cycle starts again. Because of the speed of the CPU, this cyclic scheduling creates the illusion for each user that the computer is dedicated to his or her particular process. Clearly, a circular linked list is made to order for this type of scheduling. The circularity insures no unnecessary interruptions in restarting the scheduling cycle when the end of the user list is reached. The linked nature of the structure enables the operating system to quickly process new users who log on and users who then complete their work and log off.

Doubly Linked Circular Lists

In the previously developed procedures InsertNode and DeleteNode, we had prior knowledge about where in the list insertions and deletions were to be performed. In general, this information may have to be determined through a routine that searches the entire list. Because search algorithms require time proportional to the length of the list, run-time can be substantial if the list is very long. As an example, suppose we have a singly linked list in which we wish to insert a node A pointed to by Point1 just before a node B pointed to by Point2. We can change the link field of A to point to B, but we do not know the address of (that is, a pointer to) the node preceding B. If we are to depend upon the current structure of the list, then we must search the list for B—an inefficient procedure we wish to avoid. In other words, even in situations where we may be able to locate B by other means (such as a hashing strategy to be studied in Chapter 20), we must traverse the list up to B to find the previous node.

Inserting node A before node B is shown in Figure 15.15. In a singly linked structure, time-consuming sequential searching is required to determine the address of the node preceding B.

FIGURE 15.15
Inserting node A before node B

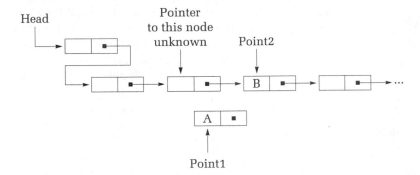

A satisfactory way of getting around the difficulty presented in Figure 15.15 is a *doubly linked circular list* in which each node has two pointers: a forward link and a backward link. The forward link is a pointer to the next node in the list; the backward link points to the preceding node. The circular nature of the list, along with a special dummy header node, can be used to conveniently avoid special conditional checking when adding to or deleting from the beginning or end of the list.

Figure 15.16 illustrates a doubly linked circular list. This list has five nodes (plus a dummy header), each having a forward link (FLink) and a backward link (BLink). FLink points to the successor node, whereas BLink points to the predecessor node. Because the list is circular, BLink of the first node must point to the last node, and FLink of the last node must point to the first node.

FIGURE 15.16
Doubly linked circular list

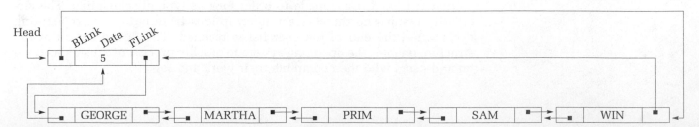

Inserting a node into a doubly linked list, or deleting one from it, is potentially a much easier task because we do not need a separate pointer to a preceding node. Hence we may be able to avoid the time inefficiency inherent in finding such a pointer in situations where the insertion or deletion point can be found by means faster than traversing the list.

■ **EXAMPLE 15.18**

Develop a procedure to insert a node into a doubly linked circular list with a dummy header. As with the InsertNode operation for singly linked lists, assume that the point for insertion has already been found according to criteria suitable for the particular list.

```
{  Global declarations  }

TYPE
  Pointer = ^LinkedListNode;
  LinkedListNode = RECORD
                Data  : LinkedListData;
                FLink : Pointer;
                BLink : Pointer
              END;

PROCEDURE InsertNodeDouble (Point1, Point2 : Pointer);

  {  Given:   Doubly linked circular list with a dummy header  }
  {           and a node within that list referenced by        }
  {           Point2. Point1 referencing a node to be          }
  {           inserted in that list prior to node referenced    }
  {           by Point2.                                        }
  {  Task:    Adjust pointers to link node referenced by       }
  {           Point1 into the list.                            }
  {  Return:  Appropriately altered list.                      }

  VAR
    Prev : Pointer;

  BEGIN
    Prev := Point2^.BLink;
    Point1^.FLink := Point2;
    Point1^.BLink := Prev;
    Prev^.FLink := Point1;
    Point2^.BLink := Point1
  END; {  of PROCEDURE InsertNodeDouble  }
```

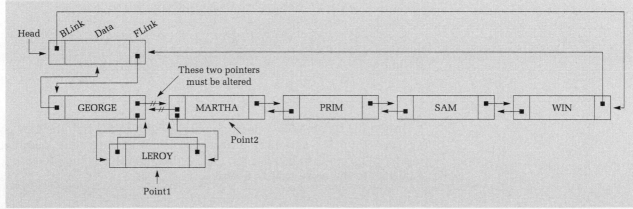

Note that the procedure InsertNodeDouble illustrates how streamlined insert and delete procedures become when a dummy header is used. In particular, because the empty list appears as

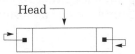

the procedure works without any awkward checking of whether the list is empty or whether the insertion is being made at the front of the list. Clearly a dummy header simplifies procedures in this situation.

■

■ **EXAMPLE 15.19**

Develop a procedure to delete a node from a doubly linked list consistent with the declarations in Example 15.18.

```
PROCEDURE DeleteNodeDouble (Point1 : Pointer);

   {  Given:    Node referenced by Point1 in a circular   }
   {            doubly linked list with a dummy header.    }
   {  Task:     Adjust pointers to remove node Point1 from }
   {            the list.                                   }
   {  Return:   Appropriately altered list with Point1     }
   {            removed.                                    }

VAR
  Save : Pointer;

  BEGIN
  Save := Point1^.Blink;
  Save^.Flink := Point1^.Flink;
  Save := Point1^.Flink;
  Save^.Blink := Point1^.Blink;
  dispose (Point1)
END; {  of PROCEDURE DeleteNodeDouble  }
```

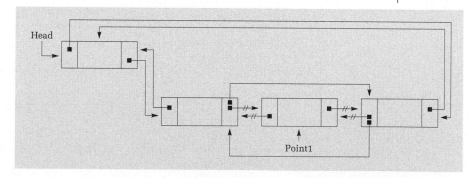

Unlike the DeleteNode operation for a singly linked list, the corresponding procedure for a doubly linked list requires only one parameter—a pointer to the node to be removed. The critical pointer to the preceding node is built into the node that is deleted.

■

Computer Viruses

Many computer installations are now confronted with a threat akin to germ warfare, which could disable their largest machines. A computer "virus" attacks a computer system in essentially the same way a biological virus attacks the human body.

A computer virus is actually a small undetected program that, over time, infects other programs and eventually disables the entire system. A typical virus in a host program might contain the following instructions:

1. Temporarily suspend execution of host program
2. Search the computer's memory for other likely uninfected programs.
3. If found, insert a copy of these instructions.
4. Return control of computer back to host program.

This virus would take less than a second to execute, would be virtually undetected, and could attack indefinetely. It can even spread to other computers, when an infected program is swapped or copied for another user.

Adding to the problem is the fact that the saboteur can add instructions to delay the signal for the virus to attack. As researcher Fred Cohen explains, a disgruntled employee instructed the program to remain dormant until his personal password was removed from the system. Once the employee was fired, and his password removed, the virus shut down the entire system.

The Pentagon addresses this problem by isolating its top-secret computers. The military's most sensitive computers are kept in electronically shielded rooms and, when necessary, connected with wire that runs through pipes filled with gas under pressure. The gas pressure would drop if someone attempted to penetrate the pipes to tap into the wires. Marvin Shaefer, chief scientist at the Pentagon computer security center, admits that computers without good access controls are vulnerable to virus attacks.

Computer scientists differ as to whether or not public discussion of computer viruses should even be encouraged. Jerry Lobel, manager of computer security at Honeywell International in Phoenix expresses concern because "it only takes a half-way decent programmer about half a day of thinking to figure out how to do it. If you tell enough people about it there's going to be one crazy out there who's going to try."

Cohen disagrees, insisting that ignorance is always more dangerous than knowledge. "It's better to have somebody friendly do the experiments, tell you how bad it is, show you how it works, and help you counteract it, than to have somebody vicious come along and do it." If you wait, it might be too late.

If your curiosity is aroused, you can find more detailed accounts of the evolution of the computer virus problem in "Attack of the Computer Virus" by Lee Dembart (*Discover*, November 1984), "Is Your Computer Infected?" by William D. Marbach (*Newsweek*, February 1, 1988), and *Computer Viruses, Worms, Data Diddlers, Killer Programs, and Other Threats to Your System* by John McAfee and Colin Haynes (New York, N.Y.: St. Martin's Press, 1989).

Multilinked Lists

We shall end this discussion of variations on the linked list theme by noting that a doubly linked list is a special case of a structure known as a *multilinked list*. Because each link field determines an order in which the nodes of a list are to be processed, we can in fact establish a different link field for every different order in which we wish to process the nodes in a list. Figure 15.17 illustrates such a multilinked list. By following the IDLink fields, we traverse the list in IDNumber order; by following the NameLink fields, we traverse the list in alphabetical order by Name.

FIGURE 15.17
Link fields for processing nodes

	IDHead	NameHead
	4	3

	Name	IDNumber	NameLink	IDLink
1	SAM	8316	4	Null
2	MARTHA	4212	5	5
3	GEORGE	6490	2	1
4	WIN	1330	Null	2
5	PRIM	5560	1	3

Multilink List

In the problems at the end of the chapter, you will consider how a multilinked list could have been used as an alternative implementation for the list of student records in Chapter 14's Focus on Program Design section.

Exercises 15.4

1. Repeat Exercise 5 from Section 15.2, this time using a linked list with a dummy header.

2. Repeat Exercise 5 from Section 15.2 with a circular linked list and a dummy header.

3. Repeat Exercise 5 from Section 15.2 for a doubly linked circular list with a dummy header.

4. Suppose that we also wish to be able to go through the list of Exercise 5 from Section 15.2 in zip code order where:

   > JAMES has zip code 54952
   > CHILTON has zip code 48649
   > SEFTON has zip code 22111
   > LEE has zip code 84682
   > WAGNER has zip code 11843
   > AARON has zip code 99218

   Trace the status of all fields (including headers and available space pointer) in an array-based, multilinked implementation of this list of names and zip codes.

5. In Examples 15.18 and 15.19 we provided procedures for insertion into and deletion from a doubly linked circular list with dummy header. Each of those procedures used a locally declared pointer variable. Rewrite each of those procedures without using such a locally declared pointer.

6. Examples 15.18 and 15.19 provided implementations for the Insert and Delete operations for a doubly linked list. Complete the implementation of a package of operations for this data structure by writing procedures/functions for the Create, Empty, Next, and LinkedTraverse operations. Be sure that your implementations of these operations are consistent with those presented in Examples 15.18 and 15.19.

7. Rewrite the InsertNodeDouble and DeleteNodeDouble procedures of Example 15.18 and 15.19 under the assumption that the doubly linked list is *not* circular and does *not* have a dummy header. (Doing this should make you appreciate the elegance of dummy headers.)

8. Write a package of procedures and functions to implement the Create, Next, Empty, InsertNode, DeleteNode, and Linked Traverse operations for a singly linked list with a dummy header. Be sure that your LinkedTraverse procedure doesn't process the dummy header.

9. Write a package of procedures and functions to implement the Create, Next, Empty, InsertNode, DeleteNode, and LinkedTraverse operations for a singly linked circular list with no dummy header. Be sure that your LinkedTraverse procedure does not loop infinitely.

10. Write a package of procedures to implement the Create, Next, Empty, InsertNode, DeleteNode, FindInsertionSlot (see Example 15.5), and FindNodeToDelete (see Example 15.16) for a multilinked list that maintains a list in alphabetical order by name (a string) and also in order by integer identification number (like the list in Figure 15.17). Finally, develop traversal operations for each possible ordering of the list.

■ ■ ■ ■

■ 15.5
An Implementation of Strings Using Linked Lists

OBJECTIVES

- to understand how linked lists could be used to implement the string ADT
- to be able to write implementations of string operations using linked lists of characters
- to analyze the efficiency of using linked lists of characters to implement strings, particularly from a space perspective
- to see how character clusters can enhance the space efficiency of a linked list implementation of strings

Thus far our discussion of linked lists has focused upon their application as an implementation technique for the keyed list ADT. However, linked lists provide means of implementing a wide variety of higher-level ADTs. In this section, we shall give some indication of how linked lists could be used to implement the string ADT introduced in Section 13.2.

Recall that we have already presented two implementation strategies for strings: the **PACKED ARRAY** and embedded length implementations. Both of these strategies imposed a static limit on the maximum length of a string. This static limit poses a twofold disadvantage. First, short strings waste much of the static array storage. Second, strings longer than the statically declared maximum length simply cannot be accommodated. Yet another drawback of both of these implementation techniques is that a tremendous amount of data movement would occur if the Insert and Delete operations for strings are frequently invoked.

Linked lists of characters stored in the heap (*linked list implementations of strings*) could improve upon these inefficiencies. The virtually "infinite" size of the heap would allow strings to attain arbitrary length, and the Insert and Delete operations would be handled swiftly by pointer manipulations. By using a doubly linked circular list, we would even have a conveniently accessible pointer to the last character in the string. This pointer will prove necessary in implementing the Insert and Delete operations. Under this implementation, the three strings 'COFFEE', 'TEA', and 'CREAM' would appear as depicted in Figure 15.18.

FIGURE 15.18
'COFFEE', 'TEA', and 'CREAM', each in a circular doubly linked list

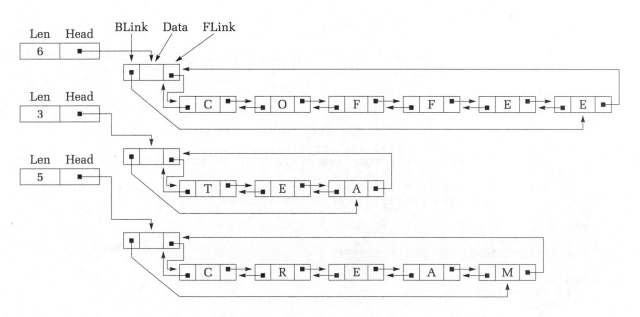

A Pascal declaration to match the snapshots in Figure 15.18 declares a string in the following fashion:

```
TYPE
   StringPtr  = ^StringNode;
   StringNode = RECORD
                   BLink : StringPtr;
                   Data  : char;
                   FLink : StringPtr
                END;
   String     = RECORD
                   Head : StringPtr;
                   Len  : integer
                END
```

Thus, the String type is an encapsulation of a head pointer to a doubly linked list of characters and a length field. Including the latter field will make the Length operation O(1) in its efficiency. Although this field could be avoided by using the dummy header as a record variant, there are reasons for not doing so in this particular application. You will discover these reasons in the Exercises.

Let us consider how some of the string operations we have specified would be performed in such an implementation. The assignment of one string to another could be achieved in very slick and efficient (though perhaps somewhat deceptive) fashion. That is, instead of physically creating two identical strings, we will simply have two separate Head pointers referencing the same string. This particular strategy does have some potential repercussions which might have to be avoided in certain applications (as we'll see in the Exercises). The Search operation for strings presents no real problem and is examined in an exercise at the end of the chapter. The Substring operation does present a problem and will be discussed in greater detail later in this section. Insertion, deletion, and concatenation (which may be viewed as a special case of insertion) can be handled elegantly and efficiently using the linked list method, as the following example indicates.

■ **EXAMPLE 15.20**

Implement the Insert operation for strings using the encapsulation of the preceding declarations.

```
PROCEDURE Insert (VAR S : String;
                  Place : integer;
                  T : String);

  { Given:      S and T--two arbitrary strings                      }
  {             Place--the position where T is to be inserted in S  }
  { Task:       Insert T into S                                     }
  { Return:     S with T inserted at position Place.  If Place is greater }
  {             than Length(S), S is not altered.                   }

  VAR
    K : integer;
    FirstInT, LastInT, P : StringPtr;

  BEGIN
    IF Place <= S.Len THEN
      BEGIN
        P := S.Head;
        {    First find position by traversing list  }
        FOR K := 1 TO Place DO
          P := P^.FLink;
```

```
    {  Now link it in  }
    FirstInT := T.Head^.FLink;
    LastInT := T.Head^.BLink;
    FirstInT^.BLink := P^.BLink;
    LastInT^.FLink := P;
    P^.BLink^.FLink := FirstInT;
    P^.BLink := LastInT;
    {  Finally update length  }
    S.Len := S.Len + T.Len
   END
END; {  of PROCEDURE Insert  }
```

Note that this procedure is doing a task slightly more complicated than our previous insertion algorithm for a linked list. Earlier, we were concerned only with inserting one node. Here we are inserting an entire collection of nodes; we are inserting one linked list within another (see Figure 15.19). This is done with relative ease because our implementation of a doubly linked list gives us convenient pointers to both the first and last nodes in the list. Hence, our linked list implementation of strings has provided a rather neat illustration of the utility of double linking.

FIGURE 15.19
Two strings from Figure 15.18
after Insert (S, 4, T)

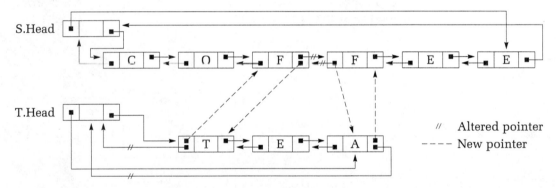

Efficiency Considerations for the Linked List Method

In this string-handling application we have seen that the linked list method allows both dynamic string allocation with no practical limit on string length and extremely efficient insertion and deletion operations. However, there are also some potentially steep costs in using this method.

Three general problem areas exist. First, you may have already noticed that, although the procedure Insert achieves a very efficient insertion, it renders string T thereafter inaccessible as a separate entity. This is because the pointers within string T had to be altered to chain it into string S. (See Figure 15.19).

Second, consider an application in which operating with substrings is of more importance than insertion and deletion. With both the **PACKED AR-RAY** and embedded length, the substring consisting of the Jth through the Kth characters could be directly accessed because the characters within any given string are physically next to each other. Accessing the same substring via the linked list implementation requires beginning at the initial character in the string and traversing the entire string until the Jth character is reached. Our implementation of a string as a doubly linked list allows this process to be made somewhat more efficient. In particular, the length of the string from which we want to extract a substring could be checked to determine if the substring occurs in the front or back half. If it is in the back half, the pointer to the last character in the string could be used to begin a traversal from the rear of the list until we reach the desired substring. However, this would still require a sequential processing of the list until the desired substring is found. Hence, for substring operations, the linked list method does not stack up to either of the other two methods.

A third problem arises in the efficiency of memory utilization for the linked list method as we have described it here. If the data portion of a node in the linked list contains only one character, then the two pointers associated with that node could require four to eight times more memory than the data. That is, only 11 to 20 percent of memory is being utilized to store the data in which we are really interested; the rest of the memory is storing data about data.

This memory utilization problem may be somewhat alleviated by making the data portion of a node a *cluster* of characters. Suppose, for instance, we choose a cluster size of four characters. Then the same strings given in Figure 15.18 would appear as shown in Figure 15.20. Here we have used the symbol (~) to represent a null character, that is, a character that is always ignored when the string is processed.

FIGURE 15.20
Strings from Figure 15.18 with a cluster size of four

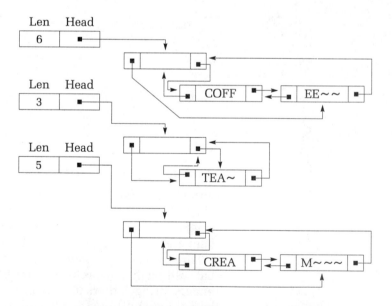

Notice that, although this technique has enabled us to devote a greater percentage of memory for storage of data, a significant complication has been added: our code must now always account for null characters. For example, if we wish to insert the second string from Figure 15.19 in the first string beginning at position 4, the scheme pictured in Figure 15.21 emerges.

FIGURE 15.21
After insertion of T into S beginning at position 4

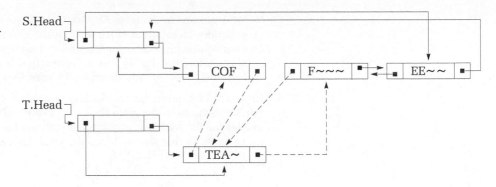

Here the node containing 'COFF' had to be split into the two nodes 'COF~' and 'F~~~' to achieve an effective insertion. As you might expect, we have had to trade-off one feature for another. To gain more effective memory utilization, we have had to make our program code more cumbersome and less efficient in its execution time.

Exercises 15.5

1. Discuss some of the potential unsuspected results that might occur if the string assignment strategy discussed in this section were actually used. In particular, consider what might happen in the following situation:

```
Create (S1);
Create (S2);
ReadAString (S1);
Assign (S1, S2);    {  ADT operation for S2 := S1  }
ReadAString (S1);
WriteAString (S2);
```

Now suppose that a user enters the string 'COFFEE' for the first ReadAString and 'TEA' for the second ReadAString. What's the output?

2. Hou would you correct the problem identified in Exercise 1? Implement this correction by providing code for the Assign operation.

3. Write implementations for each operation of the string ADT using the doubly linked list method described in this section. Then analyze the time efficiency of each implemented operation.

4. Repeat Exercise 3 except now use a singly linked list of characters with a head pointer and no dummy header.

5. Exercises 3 and 4 provide two alternative linked list methods of implementing strings.

   a. For each method, develop a formula that expresses the percentage of memory devoted to storing overhead data (as opposed to actual character data). Each of these formulas should be expressed as a function of the following general parameters:

   P—The number of bytes to store a pointer/integer.
   S—The number of bytes to store one character (usually S = 1).
   C—The cluster size.
   A—The average string length in your application.

   For each formula you develop, explain how you derive it.

b. Your answer to Exercise 5a should indicate that the singly linked method is generally more space efficient than the doubly linked list. However, suppose your application calls for frequently inserting one string in another. For this application, the doubly linked list method is more time efficient. Explain why. If it will help, include diagrams in your explanation.

6. How would you rewrite the declarations for the doubly linked list implementation of string to incorporate the storage of a string's length into the dummy header for the list? Would your declarations be more or less space efficient than those given in this section? Explain your answer.

■ ■ ■ ■

■ 15.6
A Linked List Implementation of a Sparse Table

OBJECTIVES

■ to understand how linked lists could be used to implement a sparse table
■ to be able to write implementations of sparse table operations using linked lists
■ to analyze the efficiency of linked lists as an implementation technique for sparse tables

In previous sections we have seen how a linked list or variation thereof may be used to efficiently implement keyed lists and strings. To further emphasize the utility of linked lists, we will now show how linked lists may be used to implement a two-dimensional sparse table (as defined in Chapter 13); we call this a *linked list implementation of a sparse table*.

Consider the sparse table of integers pictured in Table 15.1. In Section 13.3, we described a strategy for implementing such a table which would have us store a list of those row and column coordinates that do not resolve to zero. Along with each such coordinate pair we would store its associated nontrivial value. The drawback of this approach stems from the implementation of the list of nonzero coordinates via an array. The array implementation will result in a solution that is extremely inefficient for any volatile table of data. The reasons for this inefficiency parallel those that often make an array implementation of the keyed list ADT inadequate. That is, if we somehow order the data to enable use of the binary search, adds and deletes (in this case assigning a nonzero value to a location which was previously zero or vice versa) will involve the shifting of large amounts of data. Conversely, if we neglect to order the data, adding new nonzero values can be done efficiently but search efficiency will deteriorate.

TABLE 15.1
Sparse table of integer data

	1	2	3	4	5	6	7	8	9	10	11	12	13	14
1	0	83	19	40	0	0	0	0	0	0	0	0	0	0
2	0	0	0	91	0	42	12	0	0	0	0	0	0	0
3	0	0	0	0	0	18	4	0	0	0	0	0	0	0
4	0	0	0	0	0	0	0	0	71	64	0	13	0	0
5	0	0	0	0	0	0	0	0	0	0	0	0	21	40

The implementation method we now propose uses linked lists to insure no data shifting occurs when a zero value is changed to nonzero (or vice versa). Moreover, by employing many linked lists (one for each row), it reduces the length of sequential searches to the number of nonzero column coordinates in a particular targeted row instead of all nonzero row-column coordinates for the entire table. The method requires an array of pointers, each leading to a linked list storing the nonzero data in a given row of the sparse table. Each node in one of these linked lists would need to contain not only an entry from the table but also an indication of which column within that particular row is occupied by the data in this node. We further stipulate that, for efficiency in processing, each linked list be arranged in ascending order of column numbers within that row. Given these conventions, the 5 × 14 table from Table 15.1 would be represented by Figure 15.22.

FIGURE 15.22
Linked list representation of sparse table from Table 15.1

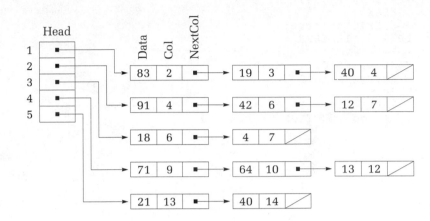

■ **EXAMPLE 15.21**

Given the implementation scheme depicted in Figure 15.22, provide declarations for the two-dimensional table ADT. Then write code for the Retrieve operation (see Section 13.3).

```
CONST
   NumberRows = { This constant sets number of rows in the sparse table. }
                { There is no limit on number of columns in this          }
                { implementation.                                         }

TYPE
   SparsePointer = ^SparseNode;
   SparseNode = RECORD
                   Data : TableData;  { Any appropriate numeric type }
                   Col : integer;
                   NextCol : SparsePointer
                END;
   TwoDTable = ARRAY [1..NumberRows] OF SparsePointer;

FUNCTION Retrieve (T : TwoDTable;
                   R, C : integer) : TableData;

   { Given:      T, an arbitrary two-dimensional table                   }
   { Task:       Retrieve the value at row R and column C of the table   }
   { Return:     The value retrieved                                     }

   { A limitation--R must not be greater than NumberRows.  We will later }
   { discuss a way of overcoming this limitation.                        }

VAR
   P : SparsePointer;
   Exit : boolean;
```

```
BEGIN
  Exit := false;
  P := T[R];
  { P advances through list, searching for column index greater than or    }
  { equal to C.                                                             }
  WHILE (P <> NIL) AND NOT Exit DO
    IF P^.Col < C THEN
        P := P^.NextCol
    ELSE
        Exit := true;
  IF P = NIL THEN
      Retrieve := 0
  ELSE IF P^.Col > C THEN
      Retrieve := 0
  ELSE
      Retrieve := P^.Data
END; { of FUNCTION Retrieve }
```

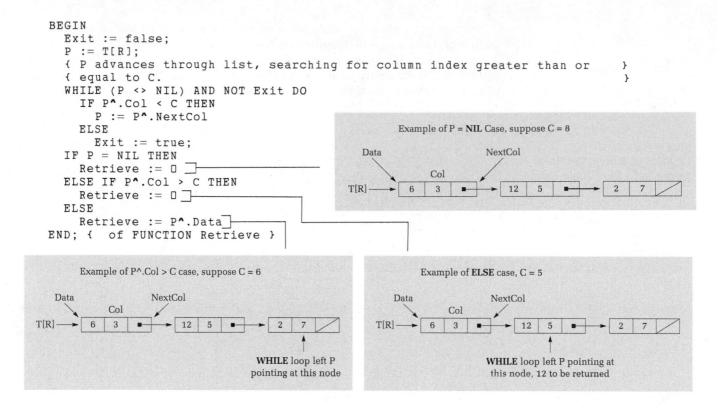

Example of P = **NIL** Case, suppose C = 8

Data   NextCol
Col
T[R] → | 6 | 3 | ■ | → | 12 | 5 | ■ | → | 2 | 7 | ⧄ |

Example of P^.Col > C case, suppose C = 6

Data   NextCol
Col
T[R] → | 6 | 3 | ■ | → | 12 | 5 | ■ | → | 2 | 7 | ⧄ |

WHILE loop left P pointing at this node

Example of **ELSE** case, C = 5

Data   NextCol
Col
T[R] → | 6 | 3 | ■ | → | 12 | 5 | ■ | → | 2 | 7 | ⧄ |

WHILE loop left P pointing at this node, 12 to be returned

Efficiency Considerations for the Sparse Table

Our comments preceding Example 15.21 indicated that, with respect to run-time, the efficiency of this implementation of a sparse table will require no wholesale data movement when values are assigned to the array. Moreover, since accessing a particular value in the table requires a sequential search along one of the many linked lists which contain a row, we essentially have a retrieval time of O(NumberOfColumns).

Since the main motivation for an implementation of a sparse table is to save memory space, a more important efficiency consideration is exactly how much space we have saved. To determine this, we define the efficiency ratio of a sparse table implementation by the fraction

$$\frac{\text{Number of storage locations used by particular sparse table implementation method}}{\text{Number of storage locations used by standard row-major form}}$$

Clearly, the smaller we can make this ratio, the better our implementation is with respect to memory utilization. Moreover, this ratio must drop below 1 before a particular method can even begin to surpass standard row-major form. In the case of Table 15.1, if we assume that a pointer takes as much memory as one integer, the *efficiency ratio* of our linked list method is given by

5 locations for head-of-list pointers
3 locations for each of 13 nonzero values

This yields a total of 44 storage locations, compared to 70 for a row-major implementation, hence giving a desirable efficiency ratio of 44/70.

However, our simple example of a 5 × 14 table is so small that it is hardly worth considering. A more interesting question is attempting to determine, in general, when a linked list implementation as described here achieves a savings in memory over the standard row-major method. We claim that, assuming that the data in a sparse table are of integer type, the efficiency ratio for this linked list implementation of a sparse matrix drops below 1 only when the number of nonzero locations in the table is less than

NRow * (NCol − 1) / 3

where NRow is the number of rows in the original table and NCol is the number of columns. To see this, note that each nonzero matrix entry requires three integers to represent it in the linked list implementation. Moreover, each row requires an integer head pointer. Thus the total number of integers required to store N nonzero entries via the linked list method is

NRow + N * 3

Since we want to force the efficiency ratio

$$\frac{NRow + N * 3}{NRow * NCol}$$

to be less than 1, we conclude that

NRow + N * 3 < NRow * NCol
    N * 3 < NRow * NCol − NRow
      N < NRow * (NCol − 1) / 3

Similar types of efficiency analyses can be carried out for different base data types and implementation schemes.

Two limitations of the implementation that we have devised in Example 15.21 should be noted. First, from a conceptual standpoint, there sould be no static limit on the number of rows or number of colums in a two-dimensional table. The declarations in Example 15.21, however, place such a static limit on the number of rows because an array of head pointers is used. Using a linked list of row head pointers would remove this limitation, as indicated in Figure 15.23. You will analyze the cost of removing it in the Exercises.

FIGURE 15.23

A linked list implementation of a two-dimensional table with no limitation on the number of rows or number of columns

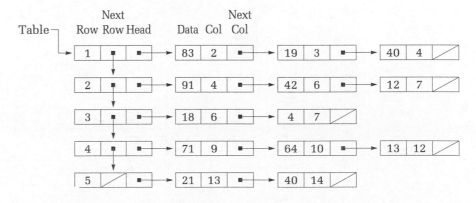

Second, for many higher-level algorithms that manipulate two-dimensional tables, it is important to traverse a row or column of the table, applying a certain process to each element along that row or column. The high-level algorithm expressed in Example 13.14 provided an illustration of

the need for such row and column traversals. In such applications, it would be convenient to extend the basic operations on a two-dimensional table with the two additional operations defined by

```
PROCEDURE TraverseRow (VAR T : TwoDTable;
                        R : integer;
                        PROCEDURE ProcessElement (VAR Element : TableData) );

  { Given:    A two-dimensional table T, R representing a row within the   }
  {           table, and a procedure that can be applied to any data       }
  {           element in the table                                         }
  { Task:     Apply procedure ProcessElement to each table element in row R }
  { Return:   Table T with each element in row R affected by ProcessNode   }

PROCEDURE TraverseColumn (VAR T : TwoDTable;
                           C : integer;
                           PROCEDURE ProcessElement (VAR Element : TableData) );

  { Given:    A two-dimensional table T, C representing a column within    }
  {           that table, and a procedure that can be applied to any data  }
  {           element in the table                                         }
  { Task:     Apply procedure ProcessElement to each table element in      }
  {           column C                                                     }
  { Return:   Table T with each element in column C affected by ProcessNode }
```

The representations suggested by Figures 15.22 and 15.23 will provide a very efficient means of implementing the TraverseRow operation but will bog down in TraverseColumn. This is because, to move from table position T[J, K] to T[J, K + 1] we need only follow one link in Figures 15.22 and 15.23. However, to move from T[J, K] to T[J + 1,K] we must potentially search the entire linked list representing row J + 1.

FIGURE 15.24
Multilinked implementation allowing row or column access

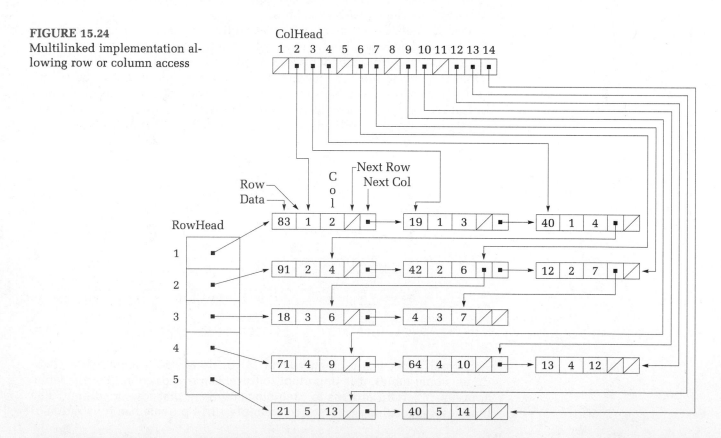

By employing a multilinked representation, we can eliminate this bias toward row traversals in our representation schemes. That is, not only must we link the nodes representing nontrivial data along a given row, but also along each column. The picture of such a structure that emerges from Table 15.1 is given in Figure 15.24.

Exercises 15.6

1. Complete the implementation of the two-dimensional table that was begun in Example 15.21. That is, provide code for the Create and Assign operations consistent with the Retrieve operation in that example.

2. Analyze the time efficiency of the Assign operation that you wrote for Exercise 1.

3. Implement the Create, Assign, and Retrieve operations for the representation of a two-dimensional table suggested by Figure 15.23.

4. Analyze the efficiency of each operation you implemented in Exercise 3.

5. Look back to the high-level algorithm that appeared in Example 13.14. Rewrite this algorithm using the TraverseRow and TraverseColumn operations introduced in Section 15.6.

6. Extend your implementation of the two-dimensional table from Exercise 3 by coding the TraverseRow and TaverseColumn operations. What are the respective time efficiencies of each of these operations?

7. Implement the two-dimensional table operations, including TraverseRow and TraverseColumn, using the representation suggested by Figure 15.24. Analyze the efficiencies of the two traversal operations, and compare those efficiencies to your results from Exercise 6.

8. In this section we carried out a space efficiency analysis for the two-dimensional table representation suggested by Figure 15.22. We found that, for a table with integer data, this scheme become space efficient when

$$N < NRow * (NCol - 1) / 3$$

where N is the number of nontrivial values in a sparse table. Carry out a similar space efficiency analysis for the representation of Figure 15.23.

9. Repeat Exercise 8 for the two-dimensional table implementation suggested by Figure 15.24. In a written statement, discuss the price that is paid for the faster column access allowed by this representation.

■ ■ ■ ■

FOCUS ON PROGRAM DESIGN

Although we can define the linked list as an ADT, a key theme of this chapter has been that the linked list is of great value when viewed as an implementation technique for other higher-level ADTs and their logic. We have seen linked lists used to implement the keyed list, string, and two-dimensional table ADTs.

Now, in this section, we will use the linked list to implement a very space-efficient version of the radix sort algorithm (see Section 12.4). Moreover, this will be one of those rare instances in which a space-efficient version is also more time-efficient. To achieve this, we will specify that the sort algorithm receive a linked list of integers to be sorted, rather than an array. A top-level pseudocode description of radix sort is then given by

1. Set NumberOfDigits to the number of digits in largest number in the list

2. **FOR** K := 1 **TO** NumberOfDigits **DO**
   2.1 **WHILE** the list to sort is not empty **DO**
      2.1.1 Transfer the first number in the sort list to the appropriate bin, keying on the Kth digit (1 corresponding to ones digit, 2 to tens digit, and so forth).
   2.2 **FOR** J := 0 **TO** 9 **DO**
      2.2.1 Append the numbers in Jth bin to the list to sort

In our discussion of the radix sort in Section 12.4, we were somewhat shackled by approaches that employed static allocation of the bins used to classify numbers. For instance, we determined that sorting n numbers by this algorithm would require $11n$ storage locations—n for the numbers being sorted and an additional $10n$ locations for the bins associated with the 10 possible digits.

Pascal pointer variables provide a new implementation strategy for the bins needed by radix sort. The dynamic allocation associated with these pointer variables will allow each bin to claim only the storage that it needs as the algorithm runs. We propose the following implementation for bins.

```
TYPE
  BinPointer = ^BinNode;
  BinNode = RECORD
              Data : integer;  {  or other data type for sorting  }
              Link : BinPointer
            END;

  Bin = RECORD
          Head : BinPointer;
          Tail : BinPointer
        END;
  BinStructure = ARRAY [0..9] OF Bin;

VAR
  Bins : BinStructure;
```

Unlike other instances of linked lists we have studied in this chapter, a list of **TYPE** Bin will include a Tail pointer to the last node on the list as well as a Head pointer to the first node. This additional pointer will enable us to be particularly efficient during that phase of the algorithm that collects the bins associated with particular digits into a new master bin. Figure 15.25 depicts how this efficiency can be achieved. To append Bins[K] (the Kth bin in a BinStructure) to the ListToSort, we must:

1. Aim the Link field in the last node of the ListToSort at the first node in Bins[K]. See 1 in Figure 15.25.
2. Aim the Tail pointer for the ListToSort at the last node in Bins[K]. See 2 in Figure 15.25.

FIGURE 15.25
Appending one bin to another

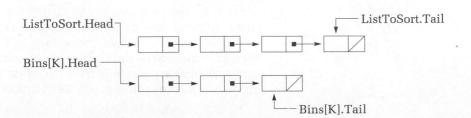

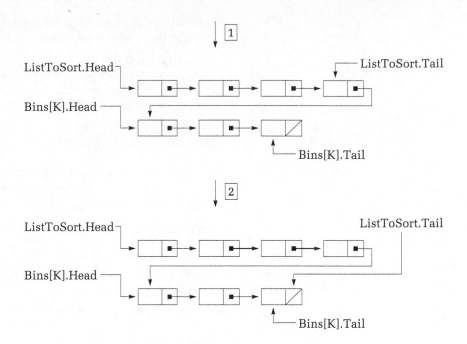

The entire process of appending one bin to the list to sort is thus achieved by resetting two pointers. Compare this to our implementation of bins by arrays in Section 12.4. There the process of appending a bin required physically moving each item in the bin to the array being sorted.

We can now refine our high-level pseudocode for this new version of radix sort. It will require the subordinate modules indicated in the structure chart shown in Figure 15.26.

FIGURE 15.26
Structure chart for RadixSort

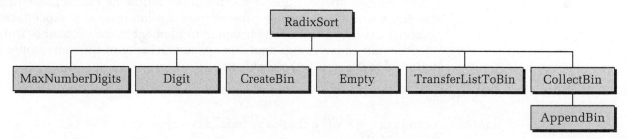

The specifications for each subordinate module are

1. MaxNumberDigits Module
    Data Received: List of integers (assumed to be non-negative)
    Information Returned: The number of digits in the largest integer in
    list
    Logic: Make one pass through list to determine largest
2. Digit module
    Data Received: Nonnegative integer Number
    K representing a digit position in Number, with
    K = 1 corresponding to ones digit, 2 to tens digit,
    and so on

Information return: Digit in position K of Number
Logic: Use modular arithmetic functions of Pascal

3. Createbin Module
   Data Received: One list of type Bin in arbitrary state
   Information Returned: Bin intialized to emtpy list
   Logic: Set Head and Tail pointers appropriately

4. TransferListToBin Module
   Data Received: List to sort
             A bin
   Information Returned: First number in list to sort has been removed
             and appended to bin
   Logic: Only involves pointer exchanges

5. Empty Module
   Data Received: List of type Bin
   Information Returned: **true** if list empty, **false** otherwise
   Logic: Check head and tail pointers

6. CollectBins Module
   Data Received: BinStructure Array
             List to sort (empty when received)
   Information Returned: Sublists in BinStructure have been succes-
             sively
             appended to sort list
   Logic: Order of appending runs from bin 0 to bin 9
             Repeatedly call on AppendBin

7. AppendBin Module
   Data Received: List to sort
             A bin
   Information Returned: List to sort has bin appended to it
   Logic: See Figure 15.25

These module specifications give rise to the following Pascal procedure for the radix sort algorithm. We present only the top-level sort procedure; the subordinate modules are left for you to implement in the problems. You will also formally analyze the time and space efficiency of this new implementation of radix sort in the problems.

```
TYPE
  BinPointer = ^BinNode;
  BinNode = RECORD
              Data : integer;    { or other appropriate type }
              Link : BinPointer
            END;
  Bin = RECORD
          Head : BinPointer;
          Tail : BinPointer
        END;

PROCEDURE RadixSort (VAR List : Bin);

  { Given:    List containing entries to sort          }
  { Task:     Apply radix sort algorithm to list       }
  { Return:   List with entries arranged in            }
  {           ascending order.                         }

  TYPE BinStructure = ARRAY [0..9] OF Bin; { index subrange must change if }
                                           { sorting data other than       }
                                           { integers                      }
```

```
VAR
   K, J, NumberOfDigits, WhichBin : integer;
   Bins : BinStructure;


.
.   { Subordinate procedures would appear here }
.
BEGIN
   NumberOfDigits := MaxNumberDigits (List);
   FOR K := 1 TO NumberOfDigits DO
      BEGIN
         FOR J := 0 TO 9 DO
            Create (Bins[J]);
         { Go through the list to sort, continuially removing the first     }
         { number in the list and transferring it to the appropriate bin.   }
         WHILE NOT Empty (List) DO
            BEGIN
               WhichBin := Digit (List.Head^.Data, K); { Which bin to transfer to? }
               TransferListToBin (List, Bins[WhichBin])
            END;
         CollectBins (List, Bins)
      END
END; { of PROCEDURE RadixSort }
```

RUNNING AND DEBUGGING TIPS

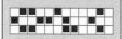

1. You must be very careful when programming with pointers; one misplaced pointer can "lose" an entire data structure. Consequently, modular testing is more important than ever. Test the reliability of each module before releasing it for use in a large program.

2. Be sure that you consider the boundary conditions when developing linked list algorithms. Are you sure that your logic covers the empty list, the first node on the list, the last node on the list? For instance, if your insertion algorithm works for all lists but the empty list, it might as well not work at all since you'll never be able to get any data on the list.

3. Never reference P^ when P is a **NIL** pointer. The following loop control structure

   `WHILE (P <> NIL) AND (P^.Data <> Target) DO`

   is asking for trouble because when P is **NIL**, the reference to P^.Data may cause a run-time error before the loop is exited. The test for (P^.Data <> Target) should be in the loop body and flagged with a Boolean variable.

4. Programming with pointers is programming with logical pictures of linked lists. Draw a picture of what you want to do with a pointer and then write the code to make it happen. When debugging, verify and trace your code by drawing pictures of what it does with your data. For instance, an assignment to a pointer in your code corresponds to aiming an arrow somewhere in your corresponding snapshot of the data structure.

5. An array implementation of linked lists will allow you to insert tracer **writeln**s to see the actual values of pointers. Design your algorithms so that an array implementation can be conveniently plugged in. Then, if you're in deep enough trouble, you can always resort to tracing pointers values via the array implementation.

6. If your Pascal compiler comes with a software debugger, learn how to use it. Most compilers do, and most debuggers will allow you to step through your program one instruction at a time, actually examining the contents of pointer variables that may have gone astray. The hour you spend learning how to use the debugger will be repaid many times over in the time you save debugging this and future programs involving pointers.

■ Summary

Key Terms

circular linked list
cluster
concatenation
data movement
doubly linked circular
  list
dummy header
dynamic memory
  management

efficiency ratio
head pointer
heap
linear ordering
link
linked list
linked list
  implementation of
  sparse table

linked list
  implementation of
  strings
list traversal
multilinked list
node
Pascal pointer variable
pointer
volatile list

Keywords

dispose   **new**   **NIL**

Key Concepts

- The linked list structure is especially convenient for implementing a variety of higher-level list ADTs in situations where add and delete operations dominate search operations.
- The linked list allows adds and deletes to occur by mere pointer manipulation instead of large-scale data movement. The price paid for this gain is the inefficiency of a sequential search strategy.
- An overview of the advantages and disadvantages of a linked list versus an array implementation of a keyed list is given in the following table.

	Implementation of keyed list using array maintained in physical order so that binary search may be used	Implementation of keyed list using linked list
Add	$O(\log_2 n)$ comparisons to find location where addition should occur. $O(n)$ data interchanges to rearrange list.	$O(n)$ comparisons to find location where addition should occur. $O(1)$ pointer interchanges to rearrange list.
Retrieve	$O(\log_2 n)$ comparisons to find data item.	$O(n)$ comparisons to find data item.
Delete	$O(\log_2 n)$ comparisons to find data item to delete. $O(n)$ data interchanges to rearrange list.	$O(n)$ comparisons to find data item to delete. $O(1)$ pointer interchanges to rearrange list.
TraverseInOrder	Immediate if the logical order of the traversal matches the physical order of the list. Otherwise a pointer sort algorithm must be used.	If more than one logical ordering desired, a multilinked list must be used. That is, a series of links for each ordering must be maintained.
Other considerations	Number of items in list must be maintained. Size of list is bounded by physical size of array.	If Pascal pointers are used to implement, size of list is bounded only by available space in heap.

- A linked list can be implemented by an array or by Pascal pointer variables. The following table summarizes the advantages and disadvantages of each implementation strategy.

	Dynamic versus static	Ease of use	Random access file applicability	Debugging	Other languages
Array implementation of linked list	Static. Size of array declared at compile time and limits number of linked list nodes.	Must write your own available space routines.	Easily generalized to random access files.	Values of pointers are merely integers and thus can be easily traced.	Easily adaptable to any languages that have arrays.
Pascal pointer variable implementation	Dynamic. Request memory as needed from Pascal heap.	Pascal's **new** and **dispose** take care of heap management for you.	Pascal's pointer variables exist only in main memory.	Pascal will not let you see, via **write** statements, the values of pointers. You can examine only the contents of what the pointer variables are referencing.	Not available in older languages such as BASIC, FORTRAN, and COBOL.

- Four variations on the basic linked list structure are dummy headers, circular linking, double linking, and multilinking.
- Dummy headers are used to store special information about a list (such as number of nodes) and to simplify the logic of insertion and deletion algorithms.
- Double linking avoids the necessity of having a tag-along pointer to the node prior to the one to be deleted. This is particularly important if we can find a node for deletion by means other than sequential searching of the list.
- Multilinking allows traversal of the list in logical order according to more than one key field.

■ Programming Problems and Projects

1. Complete the development of a linked list radix sort (see the Focus on Program Design section) in stages.
   a. Write the necessary subordinate modules.
   b. Write a main program so that you can thoroughly test the algorithm.
   c. Design test data that are sure to exercise the various boundary conditions of the subordinate modules.
   d. Do a big-O analysis of the time and space requirements of this version of radix sort. If you also implemented an array version of radix sort in Chapter 12, profile both versions by counting the number of operations that each must perform (see the Focus on Program Design section in Chapter 12). Prepare a written report in which you compare the empirical performance of both versions.

2. Wing-and-a-Prayer Airlines maintains four scheduled flights per day which they identify by the numbers 1, 2, 3, and 4. For each of these flights, they keep an alphabetized list of passengers. The data base for the entire airline could hence be viewed as four linked lists. Write a program that sets up and maintains this data base by handling commands of the following form:

Command→Add
Flight number→3
Passenger name→BROWN

Command→Delete
From flight number→1
Passenger name→JONES

Command→ List
Flight number→2
(List alphabetically all passengers for the specified flight)

Use an appropriate string storage strategy for the passenger names.

3. In order to take care of their growing business, the Fly-by-Night credit card company would like to update their customer data file. Write a program in a high-level language that sets up a doubly linked list into which a record is
   a. Inserted into the list in the correct place, sorted according to the social security number of the customer.
   b. Updated if the customer record exists.
   c. Deleted if the customer no longer wishes to patronize the company.

In the preceding data manipulation activities, the list should always remain in order sorted by the social security number.

4. As a struggling professional football team, the Bay Area Brawlers have a highly volatile player roster. Write a program that allows the team to maintain its roster as a linked list in alphabetical order by player last name. Other data items stored for each player are

   - Height
   - Weight
   - Age
   - University affiliation

As an added option, allow your program to access players in descending order of weight and age.

5. Develop a line-oriented text editor that assigns a number to each line of text and then maintains the lines in a linked list by line number order (similar to the fashion in which BASIC programs are maintained on many systems). Your program should be able to process the following commands:

   I-line number 'text'
     (instruction to insert text at specified line number)
   L-line1-line2
     (instruction to list line1 through line2)
   D-line1-line2
     (Instruction to delete line1 through line2)

If you feel really ambitious, incorporate into your program a string storage strategy which will allow the user to perform editing operations such as inserting and deleting characters within a given line.

6. Write a program that, given a file of text, will add to an index those words in the text that are marked by special delimiting brackets []. The words in the index will be printed after the text itself has been formatted and printed. Words in this index should be listed in alphabetical order with a page number reference for each page of text on which they are delimited by the special brackets. Note that this program would be part of a word processing system an author could use when developing a book with an index of terms.

7. Write a program that allows input of an arbitrary number of polynomials as coefficient and exponent pairs. Store each polynomial as a linked list of coefficient-exponent pairs arranged in descending order by exponent. Note that the coefficient-exponent pairs need not be input in descending order; it is the responsibility of your program to put them in that order. Your program should then be able to evaluate each of the polynomials for an arbitrary argument X and be able to output each of the polynomials in the appropriate descending exponent order. Be sure that your program works for all "unusual" polynomials such as the zero polynomial, polynomials of degree one, and constant polynomials.

8. Implement the registrar's system (see the Focus on Program Design section of Chapter 14) using a multilinked list structure.

9. Develop a sparse table solution for Wing-and-a-Prayer's pilot/flight data base (see Section 13.3) using a multilinked list to implement the sparse table.

10. Redo Problem 3 from Chapter 13, except now use linked lists to implement the string ADT required in that program.

11. Redo Problem 4 from Chapter 13, except now use linked lists to implement the two-dimensional table ADT.

12. Redo Problem 7 from Chapter 13, except now use linked lists to implement the set ADT that you defined for that problem.

13. Redo the Game of Life program that you developed for Problem 8 in Chapter 13, except now use linked lists to implement the two-dimensional table ADT.

14. Use a linked list implementation of a keyed list to compete the partial program presented in the Focus on Program Design in Chapter 13.

15. Redo Problem 5 of Chapter 14, for the registrar of American Basket Weaving University, except now use linked lists to implement the ADTs that you designed for that program.

16. In Example 15.17, we developed main program to maintain a list of strings in alphabetical order. Now extend that main program to a multilinked list structure in which you maintain records in alphabetical order by a string field and in descending order by another integer field. Besides allowing additions and deletions, your program should provide traversals based on the string or integer field.

17. Consider the following problem, often referred to as the Josephus problem. Imagine that N people have decided to commit mass suicide by arranging themselves in a circle and killing the Mth person around the circle, with the size of the circle being reduced by one each time a person is killed. The problem is to find out which person is the last to die, or more generally, to find the order in which the people are executed. For example, if $N = 9$ and $M = 5$, then the people are killed in the order 5, 1, 7, 4, 3, 6, 9, 2, and 8.

   To solve the Josephus problem, write a program that inserts people 1 through N into a list and then appropriately deletes people from the list until only one is left.

18. Computers can store and do arithmetic only with integers of limited size. When integers surpass that limiting value, overflow occurs and the results will either be unreliable or cause your program to die with a run-time error. However, by altering the implementation of an integer, you can develop algorithms to do virtually limitless integer arithmetic. The basis of such an implementation is to store each digit of an integer in a list. That is, represent an integer as a list of digits. Then develop algorithms to do integer arithmetic operations on a digit-by-digit basis, taking carries, borrows, and so forth into account as you do when performing these operations by hand.

   After carefully considering which list implementation best suits the problem, develop procedures to perform extended integer addition, subtraction, multiplication, and division (quotient and remainder). As one test case, add the following integers and print the sum.

   ```
     5643127821
   + 9276577159
   ──────────────
   ```

19. By consulting reference manuals for your version of Pascal and by writing a variety of experimental programs, attempt to discover the details of how your Pascal compiler manages the allocation of memory in the heap. Prepare a written report in which you describe your findings. Be sure to compare the array-based implementation of pointers presented in Section 15.2 of this chapter with the techniques used by your Pascal compiler.

20. Your friend offers the following criticism of linked lists: "The problem with linked lists is that they cannot be used with large data bases stored in files since pointers represent locations in main memory."

   Explain the fallacy in your friend's criticism. Then, in a detailed statement, discuss how linked lists could be implemented for data stored in random access files.

Stacks and Queues

In the last chapter we introduced the linked list as a data structure designed to handle conveniently the insertion and deletion of entries in a linearly ordered list. In this chapter we shall study two special types of linearly ordered lists: the stack and the queue. These lists are special because of the restrictions imposed upon the way in which entries may be inserted and removed. Both structures may be implemented by arrays or dynamically allocated linked lists.

The linear order of a stack is often described as *last-in, first-out (LIFO)*. Consider, for example, the order in which a smart traveler will pack a suitcase. To minimize shuffling, the last item packed should be the first worn. Another familiar example of such a storage strategy is that of the pop-up mechanism used to store trays for a cafeteria line. The first trays loaded into the mechanism may well have a long wait before they escape to a passing diner.

A list of data items processed via a last-in, first-out scheduling strategy is called a *stack*. As we shall see in this and later chapters, stacks are an extremely useful data structure. They find extensive applications in the processing of subroutine calls, the syntactical checking and translation of programming languages by compilers, and the powerful programming technique of recursion (see Chapter 17).

In contrast to the linear order of a stack, a *queue* is a *first-in, first-out (FIFO)* list. This latter name comes close to completely characterizing the restricted types of adds and deletes that can be performed on a queue. Insertions are limited to one end of the list, whereas deletions may occur only at the other end. The conceptual picture that emerges from the notion of a queue is that of a waiting line; for example, jobs waiting to be serviced by a computer, or cars forming a long line at a busy toll booth.

■ 16.1
The Stack Abstract Data Type and Its Implementation

The last-in, first-out nature of the stack implies that all additions and deletions occur at one designated end of the stack. That designated end is called the *top*, and the operations of adding to or deleting from the stack are referred to as *pushing* and *popping* respectively. More formally, we define the stack ADT as follows.

> **Stack.** A stack is a restricted list in which entries are added to and removed from one designated end called the top.

The operations to be performed on a stack are specified by the following pre- and postconditions.

Create operation
    Preconditions: S is an arbitrary stack in an unknown state.
    Postconditions: S is initialized to the empty stack.

Empty operation
    Preconditions: S is a previously created stack.
    Postconditions: *Empty* returns **true** if S is empty, **false** otherwise.

Full operation
    Preconditions: S is a previously created stack.
    Postconditions: *Full* returns **true** if S is full, **false** otherwise.

Push operation
    Preconditions: S is a previously created stack. *Item* is a value to be added to the top of the stack.
    Postconditions: S is returned with *Item* added to the top of the stack. If S is full, it is left unchanged.

Pop operation
    Preconditions: S is a previously created stack.
    Postconditions: S has its top value removed. *Item* contains the value that was on the top of the stack S. If S is empty, contents of *Item* are unreliable and S is unchanged.

OnTop operation
    Preconditions: S is a previously created stack.
    Postconditions: *OnTop* returns the value on the top of the stack S. Unlike *Pop*, the stack is left unchanged. If the stack S is empty, the value returned by *OnTop* is unreliable.

Figure 16.1 depicts the critical push and pop operations for the stack ADT. Conceptually, it is easiest to develop a mental image of the push and pop operations if you picture a stack as a vertical list with the first entry at the bottom and the last at the top. Then, as indicated in Figure 16.1, adding to the stack—that is, pushing—essentially makes this stack become taller, and removing from the stack—that is, popping—results in a shorter stack.

Stacks and Procedure Calls

Before we discuss methods of implementing a stack, we shall give some hint of their importance in the processing of procedure (and function) calls. Of key importance to the processing of procedures in any language is that the return from a procedure must be to the instruction immediately following the call that originally transferred control to the procedure. For example, in the partial coding that follows:

```
PROGRAM Main;
     .
     .
     .
```

FIGURE 16.1
Pushing onto and popping from
the stack

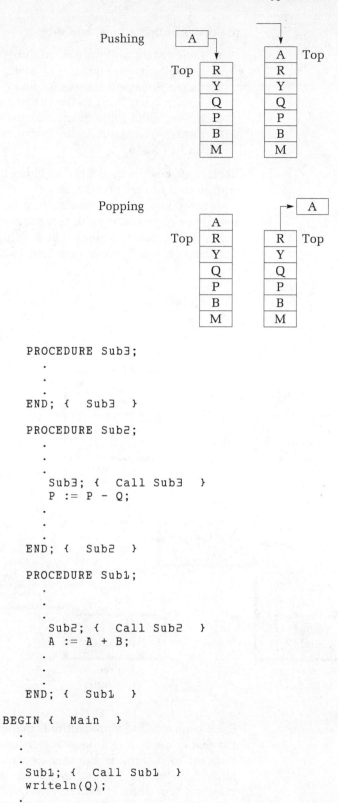

```
PROCEDURE Sub3;
  .
  .
  .
END; {  Sub3  }

PROCEDURE Sub2;
  .
  .
  .
    Sub3; {  Call Sub3  }
    P := P - Q;
  .
  .
  .
END; {  Sub2  }

PROCEDURE Sub1;
  .
  .
  .
    Sub2; {  Call Sub2  }
    A := A + B;
  .
  .
  .
END; {  Sub1  }

BEGIN {  Main  }
  .
  .
  .
    Sub1; {  Call Sub1  }
    writeln(Q);
  .
  .
  .
END. {  Main  }
```

the order of operations would be

1. Leave Main and transfer to Sub1.
2. Leave Sub1 and transfer to Sub2.
3. Leave Sub2 and transfer to Sub3.
4. Return from Sub3 to the instruction P := P − Q in Sub2.
5. Return from Sub2 to the instruction A := A + B in Sub1.
6. Return from Sub1 to the instruction writeln(Q) in Main.
7. End of Main.

Each time a call is made, the machine must remember where to return upon completion of that procedure.

A stack is precisely the structure capable of storing the data necessary to handle calls and returns in this sequence. Hence the preceding partial coding would generate a stack that develops as illustrated in Figure 16.2. (The numbers in the figure correspond to the order of operations just shown.)

FIGURE 16.2
Memory stack generated by previous partial coding

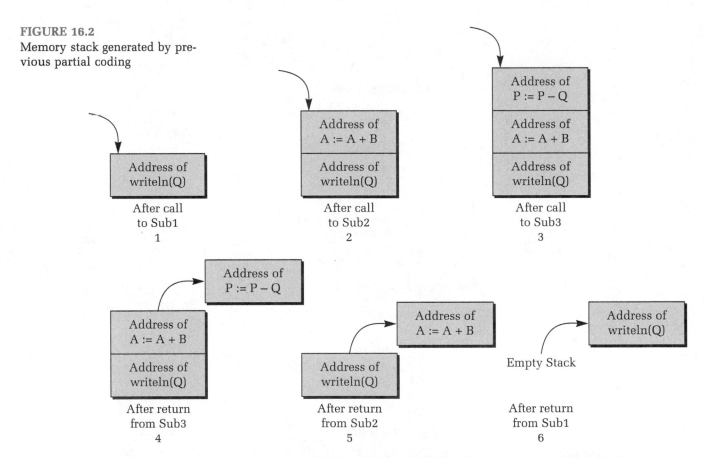

Each time a call to a procedure is made, a return address is pushed on top of the stack. Each time a procedure is completed, the top item on the stack is popped to determine the memory address to which the return operation should be made. The nature of the leave-return sequence for procedures makes it crucial that the first return address accessed be the last one that was remembered by the computer. Because there is only one point, the top, at which data may enter or exit a stack, it is the ideal data structure to be used for this "last-stored, first-recalled" type of operation.

This description of the method by which a compiler actually implements procedure calls is just one illustration of the utility of stacks. In Chapter 17, we'll discuss a different type of procedure usage called recursion, and examine in detail the role of the stack in handling such a recursive call.

Pascal Interface for the Stack Abstract Data Type

The transition from defining a stack as an ADT to implementing this structure in a computer language requires, as usual, an interface to the ADT's operations. A Pascal interface for the stack ADT follows.

```
TYPE
  StackData = {  The type of each data item in the stack  };

PROCEDURE Create (VAR S : Stack);

  {  Given:   An arbitrary stack variable S in unknown state.       }
  {  Task:    Initialize S to the empty stack.                      }
  {  Return:  S initialized to the empty stack.                     }

FUNCTION Empty (S : Stack) : boolean;

  {  Given:   A previously created stack S.                         }
  {  Task:    Check if S is empty.                                  }
  {  Return:  True if S is empty, false otherwise.                  }

FUNCTION Full (S : Stack) : boolean;

  {  Given:   A previously created stack S.                         }
  {  Task:    Check if S is full.                                   }
  {  Return:  True if S is full, false otherwise.                   }

PROCEDURE Push (VAR S : Stack;
                    Item : StackData);

  {  Given:   A previously created stack S.  An item to be added to }
  {           the top of the stack.                                 }
  {  Task:    Add the item to the stack if possible.                }
  {  Return:  S with Item added to the top of the stack.  If S is   }
  {           full, it is left unchanged.                           }

PROCEDURE Pop (VAR S : Stack;
                   VAR Item : StackData);

  {  Given:   A previously created stack S.                         }
  {  Task:    Remove the item from the top of the stack if possible. }
  {  Return:  S with its top value removed.  Item contains the value }
  {           that was on the top of the stack S.  If S is empty,   }
  {           contents of Item are unreliable and S is unchanged.   }

FUNCTION OnTop (S : Stack) : StackData;  { Only valid if StackData is  }
                                         { a valid return value for    }
                                         { a function.                 }

  {  Given:   A previously created stack S.                         }
  {  Task:    Determine the value on top of the stack without changing }
  {           the stack.                                            }
  {  Return:  The value on the top of the stack.  Unlike Pop,       }
  {           the stack is left unchanged.  If the stack S is       }
  {           empty, the value returned by OnTop is unreliable.     }
```

We will discuss two implementations of these procedural interfaces in Pascal. The first uses an array and, consequently, limits the size to which a stack may grow. The second employs a linked list with pointer variables, thereby allowing the stack to become as large as the free space in the Pascal heap.

Array Implementation of a Stack

Using an array to implement a stack is relatively straightforward. Because insertions and deletions occur at the same end of a stack, only one pointer will be needed. We call that pointer Top. In Figure 16.3, we trace it through the procedure example from Figure 16.2.

FIGURE 16.3
Array implementation of stack from Figure 16.2

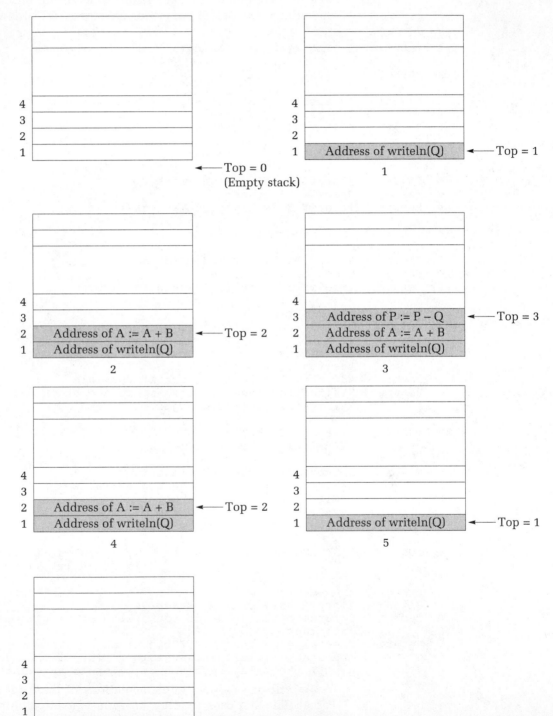

As in Figure 16.2, the numbers below each array correspond to the operations performed in our previous sequence of procedure calls and returns. The empty stack is signaled by the condition Top = 0. If we think of Top as pointing to the last entry pushed, then the two instructions

```
Top := Top + 1;
S[Top] := Item;
```

will push the contents of Item onto the stack. Popping an entry from the stack into Item requires

```
Item := S[Top];
Top := Top - 1;
```

Complete procedures for the Push and Pop operations follow in Example 16.1. These procedures use a record to encapsulate the top pointer and data array into one unified Stack type. These procedures also assume the existence of Empty and Full functions to test for these special boundary conditions. You will be asked to write these functions in the Exercises at the end of this section.

■ **EXAMPLE 16.1**

Implement the Push and Pop operations for an array implementation of a stack.

```
CONST
   StackSize = { Maximum number of elements allowed in stack at any time };

TYPE
   StackData = { The type of each data item in the stack };
   Stack = RECORD
             List : ARRAY [1..StackSize] OF StackData;
             Top : integer
           END;

PROCEDURE Push (VAR S : Stack;
                Item : StackData);

{  Given:   A previously created stack S.  An item to be added to     }
{           the top of the stack.                                     }
{  Task:    Add the item to the stack if possible.                    }
{  Return:  S with Item added to the top of the stack.  If S is       }
{           full, it is left unchanged.                               }

BEGIN
  IF NOT Full (S) THEN
    BEGIN
      S.Top := S.Top + 1;
      S.List[S.Top] := Item
    END
END;  { of PROCEDURE Push }
```

```
PROCEDURE Pop (VAR S : Stack;
               VAR Item : StackData);

{ Given:    A previously created stack S.                         }
{ Task:     Remove the item from the top of the stack if possible. }
{ Return:   S with its top value removed.  Item contains the value }
{           that was on the top of the stack S.  If S is empty,    }
{           contents of Item are unreliable and S is unchanged.    }

BEGIN
  IF NOT Empty (S) THEN
    BEGIN
      Item := S.List[S.Top];
      S.Top := S.Top - 1
    END
END;  { of PROCEDURE Pop }
```

Linked List Implementation of a Stack

When we choose a linked list implementation of a stack, we are paying the price of a relatively small amount of memory space needed to maintain linking pointers for the dynamic allocation of stack space. Assuming that we do not use a dummy header for the linked list, a stack with the three integer entries 18, 40, and 31 would appear as follows:

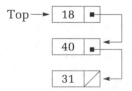

The Top pointer must be initialized to **NIL,** and, thereafter, the condition

```
Top = NIL
```

could be used to test for an empty stack. A full stack occurs only when Pascal's **new** procedure reports that there is no available space—a condition that standard Pascal does not allow you to check.

Full procedures to push and pop the stack now become nothing more than insertions to and deletions from the beginning of a linked list. As such, they are special cases of the procedures already developed in Chapter 15. You will write them as exercises at the end of this section.

■ **EXAMPLE 16.2**

To illustrate the use of stack operations in a program, let's consider a program that will check an arithmetic expression to make sure that parentheses are correctly matched (nested). Our program considers

(3 + 4 ∗ (5 **MOD** 3))

to make sure that each left parenthesis is paired with a following right parenthesis in the expression.

A first-level pseudocode for this problem is

1. **WHILE NOT eoln DO**
   1.1 Read a character
   1.2 **IF** it is a "(" **THEN**
            Push it onto the stack
   1.3 **IF** it is a ")" **THEN**
            Check for empty stack before popping previous "("
2. Check for empty stack

The growing and shrinking of the stack is illustrated in Figure 16.4.

FIGURE 16.4
Using a stack to check for balanced parentheses

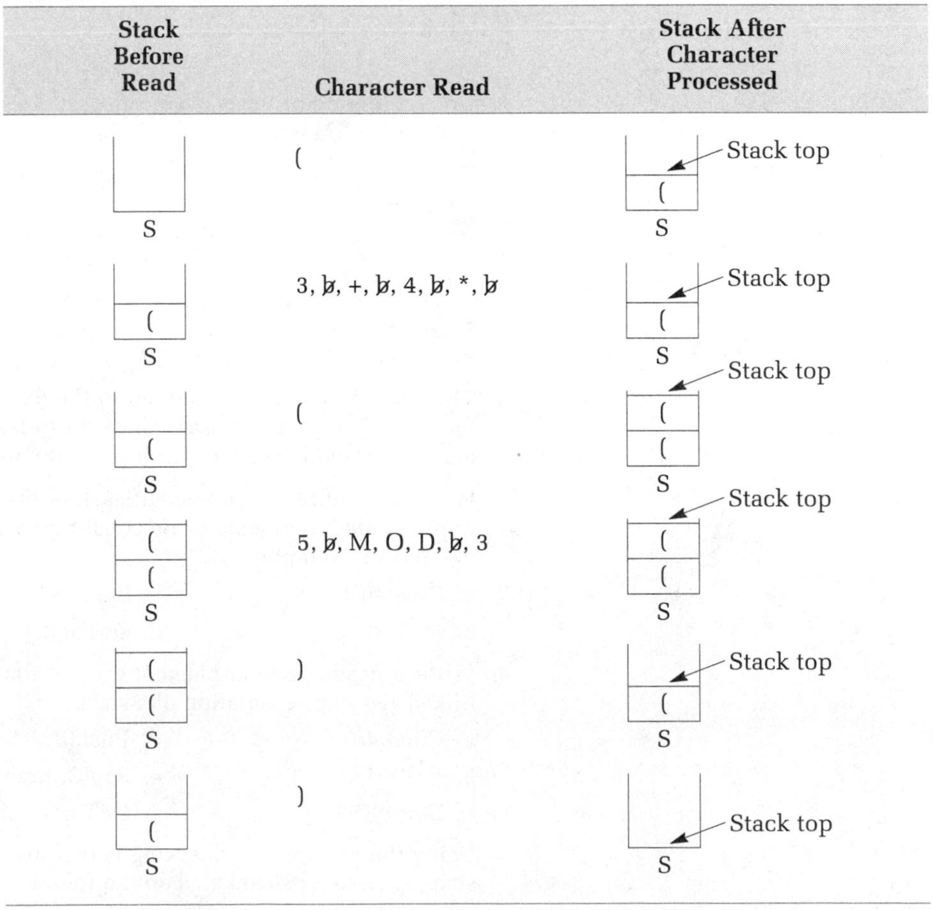

Stack Before Read	Character Read	Stack After Character Processed
	(	(← Stack top
(	3, ҍ, +, ҍ, 4, ҍ, ∗, ҍ	(← Stack top
(	(	((← Stack top
((	5, ҍ, M, O, D, ҍ, 3	((← Stack top
((	)	(← Stack top
(	)	← Stack top

*ҍ represents a blank space

Assuming the existence of procedures and functions for the basic stack operations, the main body of a program that examines an expression for correct use of parenthesis is

```
BEGIN  {  Main program  }
  Create (S);
  WHILE not eoln DO
    BEGIN
      read (Symbol);
      IF Symbol = '(' THEN
        Push (S, Symbol)
      ELSE IF Symbol = ')' THEN
        IF Empty (S) THEN
          writeln ('The parentheses are not correct.')
        ELSE
          Pop (S, Symbol)
    END; {  of WHILE  }

  {  Now check for empty stack  }
  IF NOT Empty (S) THEN
    writeln ('The parentheses are not correct.'
END.  {  of main program  }
```

This program will print an error message for an invalid expression and nothing for a valid expression. Several modifications of this short program are available and are suggested in the Exercises at the end of this section.

■   ■

Exercises 16.1

1. Draw a picture of the stack of integers S after each one of the following operations is performed:

```
Create (S);
Pus (S, 4);
Push (S, 10);
Push (S, 12);
Pop (S, Item);
Push (S, 3*Item);
Item := OnTop (S);
Push (S, 3*Item);
```

2. The OnTop operation described in the definition of the stack as an abstract data type is actually unnecessary since it can be defined in terms of other stack operations. Provide such a definition of the OnTop operation.

3. Write procedures to implement each of the following operations for an array implementation of a stack. Be consistent with the operations already implemented in Example 16.1.

   a. Create(S)   c. Empty(S)
   b. Full(S)   d. OnTop(S)

4. Write procedures to implement each of the following stack operations for a linked list implementation of a stack.

   a. Create(S)   d. Push(S, Item)
   b. Full(S)   e. Pop(S, Item)
   c. Empty(S)   f. OnTop(S)

5. Using the program for checking parentheses (Example 16.2), illustrate how the stack grows and shrinks when the following expression is examined.

```
(5/(3 - 2 * (4 + 3) - (8 DIV 2)))
```

6. Modify the program in Example 16.2 so that several expressions may be examined. Also provide more descriptive error messages.

7. Write a program that utilizes a stack to print a line of text in reverse order.

8. Consider an additional stack operation called Destroy. Destroy is the opposite of Create. That is, it disposes of a stack and recovers whatever memory space can be recovered.

   a. Write a formal Pascal interface for the Destroy operation. Be sure the interface is completely documented.

   b. For which of the stack implementations discussed in Section 16.1 would this operation have no real effect? Explain why.

   c. Develop a complete version of the Destroy operation for the stack implementation that you did not identify as your answer to (b).

■ ■ ■ ■

■ 16.2
An Application of Stacks: Parsing and Evaluating Arithmetic Expressions

OBJECTIVES

- to understand the differences between infix, postfix, and prefix forms of algebraic expressions
- to see why the postfix and prefix forms of expressions never need parentheses to override operator hierarchy
- to be able to convert infix expressions to their postfix and prefix equivalents using manual methods
- to understand the computer algorithm that relies on a stack to convert infix expressions to their postfix equivalents
- to be aware of the role of infix and in-stack priority functions in driving the algorithm to convert infix expressions to postfix
- to understand the algorithm that uses a stack to evaluate a postfix expression

Often the logic of problems for which stacks are a suitable data structure involves the necessity to backtrack, to return to a previous state. For instance, consider the problem of finding your way out of a maze. One approach to take would be to probe a given path in the maze as deeply as possible. Upon finding a dead end, you would need to backtrack to previously visited maze locations in order to try other paths. Such backtracking would require recalling these previous locations in the reverse order from which you visited them.

Not many of us need to find our way out of a maze. However, the designers of compilers are faced with an analogous backtracking situation in the evaluation of arithmetic expressions. As you scan the expression

A + B/C + D

in left-to-right order, it is impossible to tell upon initially encountering the plus sign whether or not you should apply the indicated addition operation to A and the immediately following operand. Instead, you must probe further into the expression to determine whether an operation with a higher priority occurs. While you undertake this probing of the expression, you must stack previously encountered operation symbols until you are certain of the operands to which they can be applied.

Compounding the backtracking problem just described, there are often many different ways of representing the same algebraic expression. For example, the assignment statements

Z := A * B/C + D;
Z := (A * B)/C + D;
Z := ((A * B)/C) + D;

should all result in the same order of arithmetic operations even though the expressions involved are written in distinctly different form. The process of checking the syntax of such an expression and representing it in one unique form is called *parsing* the expression. One frequently used method of parsing relies heavily upon stacks.

Infix, Postfix, and Prefix Notation

Usual algebraic notation is often termed *infix* notation; the arithmetic operator appears between the two operands to which it is being applied. Infix notation may require parentheses to specify a desired order of operations.

For example, in the expression A/B + C, the division will occur first. If we want the addition to occur first, the expression must be parenthesized as A/(B + C).

Using *postfix* notation (also called reverse Polish notation after the nationality of its originator, the Polish logician Jan Lukasiewicz), the need for parentheses is eliminated because the operator is placed directly after the two operands to which it applies. Hence, A/B + C would be written as AB/C+ in postfix form. This says:

1. Apply the division operator to A and B.
2. To that result, add C.

The infix expression A/(B + C) would be written as ABC+/ in postfix notation. Reading this postfix expression from left to right, we are told to

1. Apply the addition operator to B and C.
2. Then divide that result into A.

Although relatively short expressions such as the preceding ones can be converted from infix to postfix via an intuitive process, a more systematic method is required for complicated expressions. We propose the following algorithm for humans (and will soon consider a different one for computers):

1. Completely parenthesize the infix expression to specify the order of all operations.
2. Move each operator to the space held by its corresponding right parenthesis.
3. Remove all parentheses.

Consider this three-step method as it applies to the following expression in which ^ is used to indicate exponentiation:

A/B^C + D∗E − A∗C

Completely parenthesizing this expression yields

(((A/(B^C)) + (D∗E)) − (A∗C))

Moving each operator to its corresponding right parenthesis, we obtain

(((A/(B^C)) + (D∗E)) − (A∗C))

Removing all parentheses, we are left with

ABC^/DE∗ + AC∗ −

Had we started out with

A/B^C − (D∗E − A∗C)

our three-step procedure would have resulted in

((A/(B^C)) − ((D∗E) − (A∗C)))

Removing the parentheses would then yield

ABC^/DE∗AC∗ − −

In a similar way, an expression can be converted into *prefix* form, in which an operator immediately precedes its two operands. The conversion algorithm for infix to prefix specifies that, after completely parenthesizing the infix expression according to order of priority, we move each operator to its corresponding left parenthesis. Applying the method to

$$A/B{\wedge}C + D*E - A*C$$

gives us

$$(\ (A/(B{\wedge}C) \ ) + (\ (D*E) - (A*C) \ ) \ )$$

and finally the prefix form

$$+/A{\wedge}BC - *DE*AC$$

The importance of postfix and prefix notation in parsing arithmetic expressions is that these notations are completely free of parentheses. Consequently, an expression in postfix (or prefix) form is in unique form. In the design of compilers, this parsing of an expression into postfix form is crucial because having a unique form for an expression greatly simplifies its eventual evaluation. Thus, in handling an expression, a compiler must

1. Parse into postfix form.
2. Apply an evaluation algorithm to the postfix form.

We limit our discussion here to postfix notation. The techniques we cover are easily adaptable to the functionally equivalent prefix form.

Converting Infix Expressions to Postfix

First consider the problem of parsing an expression from infix to postfix form. Our three-step procedure is not easily adaptable to machine coding. Instead, we will use an algorithm that has as its essential data structures:

1. A stream of characters containing the infix expression and terminated by the special delimiter '#'.
2. A stack OpStack which may contain
   a. Arithmetic operators: '+', '−', '*', and '/'
   b. The left parenthesis '('. The right parenthesis ')' is processed by the algorithm but never stored in the stack.
   c. The special delimiter: '#'
3. A string Postfix containing the final postfix expression.

To eliminate details that would only clutter the main logic of the algorithm, we will assume that the string representing the infix expression contains *tokens* (that is, incoming symbols) consisting only of the arithmetic operators '+', '−', '*', and '/'; parentheses; the delimiting character '#'; and operands that each consist of a single uppercase alphabetic character. We will also assume that these tokens may be read from a line without any intervening spaces. Later, we will consider some of the complications introduced by tokens of varying size and type and by the exponentiation operator '^'. Thus, for the present, the algorithm we discuss will convert infix expressions of the form

$$A*B + (C - D/E)$$

into their corresponding postfix notation.
  The description of the algorithm is as follows:

1. Define a function InfixPriority, which takes an operator, parenthesis, or # as its argument and returns an integer as

Character	*	/	+	−	(	)	#
Returned Value	2	2	1	1	3	0	0

This function reflects the relative position of an operator in the arithmetic hierarchy and is used with the function StackPriority (defined in step 2) to determine how long an operator waits in the stack before being appended to the postfix string.

2. Define another function StackPriority, which takes the same possibilities for an argument and returns an integer as

Character	*	/	+	−	(	)	#
Returned Value	2	2	1	1	0	undefined	0

This function applies to operators in the operator stack as their priority in the arithmetic hierarchy is compared to that of incoming operators from the infix string. The result of this comparison determines whether or not an operator waits in the stack or is appended to the postfix string.

3. Initialize OpStack by pushing #.
4. Read the next character Ch from the infix expression.
5. Test Ch and
   5.1 If Ch is an operand, append it to the Postfix string.
   5.2 If Ch is a right parenthesis, then pop entries from stack and append them to Postfix until a left parenthesis is popped. Doing this insures that operators within a parenthesized portion of an infix expression will be applied first, regardless of their priority in the usual arithmetic hierarchy. Discard both left and right parentheses.
   5.3 If Ch is a #, pop all entries that remain on the stack and append them to Postfix string.
   5.4 Otherwise, pop from the stack and append to the Postfix string operators whose StackPriority is greater than or equal to the InfixPriority of Ch. Stop this series of popping operations when you reach a stack element whose StackPriority is less than the InfixPriority of Ch. This comparison, keying on the priority of Ch from the infix string and operators that have previously been pushed onto the operator stack, insures that operators are applied in the right order in the resulting postfix string. After popping these operators, push Ch.
6. Repeat steps 4 and 5 until Ch is the delimiter #.

The key to the algorithm is the use of the stack to hold operators from the infix expression that appear to the left of another given operator even though that latter operator must be applied first. The defined functions InfixPriority and StackPriority are used to specify this priority of operators and the asso-

A NOTE OF INTEREST

Hypertext

The recent introduction of HyperCard software by Apple Computer Company has enabled thousands of microcomputer users to have at their fingertips a medium known as hypertext. Apple's description of the Hyper-Card software revolves around the notion of a stack of computerized cards on which almost any type of information may be stored in a very free format. However, this stack of hypertext cards differs somewhat from the formal stack data structure that we are studying in this chapter.

A stack of hypertext cards may be viewed as a collection of data nodes through which one may browse, normally in sequence from top card to bottom card. One difference between hypertext nodes and conventional documents is that, in addition to text and computer graphics, hypertext nodes may consist of sound, video sequences, and animation. Moreover, hypertext stacks are associative. That is, at any card in the stack, the user is allowed to follow a variety of links which may lead to other stacks. For instance, a card that was playing a Beethoven symphony could allow us to follow a link to a musical history stack where the importance of that symphony from a historical perspective could be explored.

According to John B. Smith and Stephen F. Weiss (in "Hypertext," *Communications of the ACM* 31, No. 7 (July 1988)), this unrestricted associativity between hypertext stacks parallels the flexibility of human memory. Smith and Weiss cite the following quotation from Vannevar Bush, a well-known electrical engineer who speculated as early as the 1940s about the way in which humans think:

The human mind . . . operates by association. With one item in its grasp, it snaps instantly to the next that is suggested by the association of thoughts, in accordance with some intricate web of trails carried by the cells of the brain.

Selection by association, rather than indexing may yet be mechanized. One cannot hope . . . to equal the speed and flexibility with which the mind follows an associative trail, but it should be possible to beat the mind decisively in regard to the permanence and clarity of the items resurrected from storage.

If the notion of electronic hypertext intrigues you, consult the *Communications of the ACM* issue cited here and *Communications of the ACM* 33, No. 3 (March 1990). Both of these issues are dedicated to this revolutionary and rapidly growing field.

ciated pushing and popping operations. This entire process is best understood by carefully tracing through an example.

■ **EXAMPLE 16.3**

Parse the infix expression

    A*B + (C − D / E)#

into its equivalent postfix form. Trace the contents of the operator stack and the postfix string as each character is read.

The solution to this problem is presented in Table 16.1. In this table, the parenthesized numbers in the "Commentary" column refer to subcases of step 5 in the preceding algorithm.

■

The following Pascal procedure implements our algorithm for converting infix expressions of the form we have specified. You should study and thoroughly understand this algorithm before moving on to this chapter's Focus on Program Design section. There, the infix-to-postfix algorithm will be the focal point for an entire program that works with expressions of a slightly more complicated form.

TABLE 16.1
Parsing of infix expression
A∗B + (C − D/E)#

Ch	OpStack	Postfix	Commentary
	#		Push #
A			Read Ch
		A	Append Ch to Postfix (5.1)
∗			Read Ch
	∗ #		Push Ch (5.4)
B			Read Ch
		AB	Append Ch to Postfix (5.1)
+			Read Ch
	+ #	AB∗	Pop ∗, append ∗ to Postfix, push Ch (5.4)
(			Read Ch
	(+ #		Push Ch (5.4)
C			Read Ch
		AB∗C	Append Ch to Postfix (5.1)
−			Read Ch
	− (+ #		Push Ch (5.4)
D			Read Ch
		AB∗CD	Append Ch to Postfix (5.1)
/			Read Ch
	/ − (+ #		Push Ch (5.4)
E			Read Ch
		AB∗CDE	Append Ch to Postfix (5.1)
)			Read Ch
	+ #	AB∗CDE/−	Pop and append to Postfix until (reached (5.2)
#			Read Ch
		AB∗CDE/− +#	Pop and append rest of stack to Postfix (5.3)

```
TYPE
   PostfixString = { Assume a suitable implementation of the string ADT, }
                    { augmented by an Append operation.  Append (S, C) is }
                    { invoked to append a character C to the end of a     }
                    { string S.                                           }
   StackData = char;
   Stack = { Assume a suitable ADT implementation }

PROCEDURE Convert (VAR Postfix : PostFixString);

   { Given:    Infix expression being read from standard input.    }
   {           The expression consists of single-letter variable   }
   {           names; operators +, *, -, /; parentheses; and the   }
   {           special end token #.  Assume that no spaces are     }
   {           embedded in expression.                             }
   { Task:     Convert this input into postfix expression.         }
   { Return:   The postfix expression in Postfix.                  }

   VAR
      Item, Ch : char;
      OpStack : Stack;

   BEGIN {  Convert  }
      CreateString (Postfix);   { CreateString avoids name clash with }
                                { Create operation for stack          }
      Create (OpStack);
      Push (OpStack,'#');
      { Read character tokens until eoln encountered               }
      REPEAT
        read (Ch);
        IF ('A' <= Ch) AND (Ch <= 'Z') THEN
           {  Single character operand  }
           Append (Postfix, Ch)
        ELSE IF Ch = ')' THEN
          BEGIN
             Pop (OpStack, Item);
             WHILE Item <> '(' DO
                BEGIN
                   Append (Postfix, Item);
                   Pop (Opstack, Item)
                END
          END
        ELSE IF Ch = '#'
          BEGIN
             WHILE NOT Empty (OpStack) DO
                BEGIN
                   Pop(Opstack, Item);
                   Append (Postfix, Item)
                END
          END
```

"A" < = Ch AND Ch < = "Z"

In this case, transfer Ch to Postfix.

Ch = ")"

In this case, pop stack until encounter matching left parenthesis.

Ch = "#"

In this case, pop rest of stack to Postfix.

```
            ELSE { Operator +, -, *, / or left parenthesis }
               BEGIN
                 Pop (OpStack, Item);
                 WHILE StackPriority (Item) >= InfixPriority (Ch) DO
                    BEGIN
                      Append (Postfix, Item);
                      Pop (OpStack, Item)
                    END;
                 Push (Opstack, Item);
                 Push (Opstack, Ch)
               END
       UNTIL Ch = '#';
       readln    { So standard input is ready for next call to Convert }
   END; {  of PROCEDURE Convert  }
```

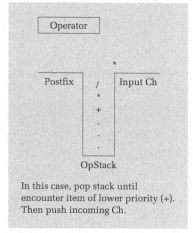

In this case, pop stack until encounter item of lower priority (+). Then push incoming Ch.

Evaluating Postfix Expressions

Once an expression has been parsed and represented in postfix form, another stack plays an essential role in its final evaluation. To evaluate a postfix expression, we repeatedly read characters from the postfix expression. If the character read is an operand, push the value associated with it onto the stack. If it is an operator, pop two values from the stack, apply the operator to them, and push the result back onto the stack. After the last operand in the postfix expression has been processed, the value of the expression is the one entry on the stack. The technique is illustrated in the following example.

■ **EXAMPLE 16.4**

Consider the postfix expression from Example 16.3.

$$AB*CDE/-+\#$$

Let us suppose that the symbols A, B, C, D, and E had associated with them the following values:

Symbol	Value
A	5
B	3
C	6
D	8
E	2

The evaluation of the expression under this assignment of values proceeds as indicated in Figure 16.5.

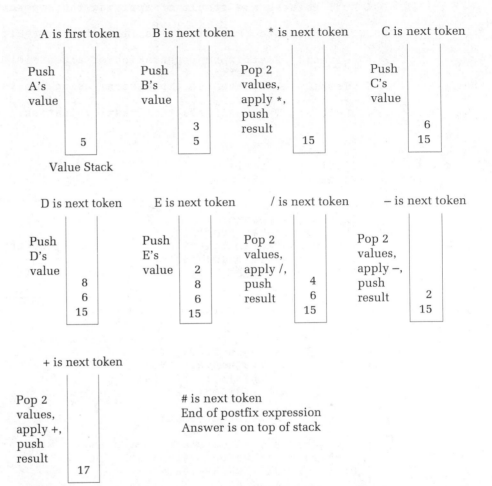

FIGURE 16.5
Evaluation of AB*CDE/− + #

Assuming functions ValueOf, which will return the value associated with a particular symbol; Eval, which will return the result of applying an operator to two values; and NextToken, which will return the next token to be read from the postfix expression, the Pascal function to evaluate a postfix expression is given by

```
TYPE
   PostfixString = { Assume a suitable implementation of the string ADT, }
                   { augmented by a NextToken operation.  NextToken (S) }
                   { is a function which returns successive characters  }
                   { from a string S.  That is, the first time it is    }
                   { called it returns the first character in S, then   }
                   { the second character in S, and so forth.           }
   StackData = real;
   Stack = { Assume a suitable ADT implementation }

   { Also we assume the existence of a function ValueOf which associates }
   { a character with its real value--similar to the fashion in which    }
   { each variable in a program is associated with a value.  Since our   }
```

```
{ tokens are only single characters, an easy way of implementing   }
{ ValueOf would be to use an array of reals indexed by the subrange }
{ 'A' .. 'Z'.  In effect, this would create a mini, 26-location     }
{ "memory."  Finally, we assume the existence of an Eval function   }
{ which receives two real operands and the operator to apply to them. }
{ Eval returns the result of applying that operator to the operands.  }

FUNCTION Evaluate (Postfix : PostfixString) : real;

{   Given:    Postfix representation of algebraic expression        }
{             in Postfix.                                           }
{   Task:     Evaluate the expression, using the value of each      }
{             token.                                               }
{   Return:   The real result of that evaluation.                  }

VAR
  Ch : char;
  V, V1, V2 : real;
  ValueStack : Stack;

BEGIN
  Create (ValueStack);
  Ch := NextToken (Postfix);
  { Read character tokens from Postfix string until               }
  { delimiter is encountered.                                     }
  WHILE Ch <> '#' {  the ending delimiter  } DO
    BEGIN
      IF ('A' <= Ch) AND (Ch <= 'Z') THEN {Operand}
        Push (ValueStack, ValueOf (Ch))
      ELSE
        BEGIN
          Pop (ValueStack, V2);
          Pop (ValueStack, V1);
          V := Eval(V1, V2, Ch);
          Push (ValueStack, V)
        END;
      Ch := NextToken (Postfix)
    END;
  {  What's left on stack is the answer we want  }
  Evaluate := OnTop (ValueStack)
END; {  of FUNCTION Evaluate  }
```

Exercises 16.2

1. What are the infix, postfix, and prefix forms of the expression

   A + B * (C − D)/(P − R)?

2. Trace the contents of the stack as the postfix form of the expression in Exercise 1 is evaluated. Assume the following assignment of values: A = 6, B = 4, C = 3, D = 1, P = 12, and R = 11.

3. Consider the expression with the infix notation

   P + (Q − F)/Y

   Using the algorithm discussed in this section to transform this into a postfix expression, trace the state of both the operator stack and postfix string as each character of the infix expression is processed. Conduct your trace following the style of Table 16.1.

4. Using the postfix expression you have obtained in Exercise 3, trace the stack of real values that would develop as the postfix expression is evaluated. You should indicate the numeric values on the stack as each character in the postfix expression is processed. Assume the values F = 4, P = 10, Q = 18, and Y = 2.

5. Parse the infix expression

    P * (Q/Y) + A − B + D * Y#

    using the following definitions of InfixPriority and StackPriority:

Priority	*	/	+	−	(	)	#
Infix	2	2	4	4	5	0	0
Stack	1	1	3	3	0	undefined	0

    Trace this parsing operation following the style of Table 16.1.

6. Using the postfix string you have obtained in Exercise 5, trace the stack of real numeric values that would develop as the postfix expression is evaluated. You should indicate the values on the stack as each character in the postfix expression is processed. Assume the values A = 4, B = 3, D = 2, P = 1, Q = 4, and Y = 2.

7. Write an implementation of the Append operation suitable for use with postfix strings in this section's Convert procedure.

8. Write implementations of the NextToken, Value, and Eval operations suitable for this section's Evaluate function.

9. Explain how the relationship between the stack priorities and infix priorities of (,), *, /, +, −, and # controls the parsing of the infix expression. Then explain how you would extend the definition of the stack and infix priority functions of this section to include an exponentiation operator ^. The exponentiation operator should be right associative; that is, in an expression such as A^B^C, the exponentiations should occur in right-to-left order.

10. How would the functions InfixPriority and StackPriority be extended to include the Boolean operators <, >, <=, >=, =, < >, **AND, OR,** and **NOT**? Justify your choices of priority values for these Boolean operators.

■ ■ ■ ■

■ 16.3
The Queue Abstract Data Type: Its Use and Implementations

OBJECTIVES

- to understand the definition of the queue ADT
- to understand what is meant by a computer simulation
- to be able to use the queue ADT in a simulation program
- to examine three implementations of the queue ADT: array, circular array, and linked list

The stack ADT that we have studied in the first two sections of this chapter is a last-in, first-out list. The next type of restricted list that we will examine, the queue, is a first-in, first-out list. All additions to a queue occur at one end, which we will designate as the rear of the queue. Items that enter the queue at the rear must move up to the front of the queue before they can be removed.

The operations on a queue thus parallel the dynamics of a waiting line. The linear order underlying a queue is determined by the length of time an item has been in the queue. This concept is depicted in Figure 16.6. The analogy of a waiting line makes a queue the obvious ADT to use in many applications concerned with scheduling. Before we explore such applications, however, we must formally define a queue as an ADT.

> **Queue.** A queue is merely a restricted form of a list. In particular, the restrictions upon a queue are that all additions to the queue occur at one end, the rear, and all removals from the queue occur at the other end, the front. The effect of these restrictions is to insure that the earlier an item enters a queue, the earlier it will leave the queue. That is, items are processed on a first-in, first-out basis.

FIGURE 16.6
Abstract data type queue as
computer embodiment of waiting line

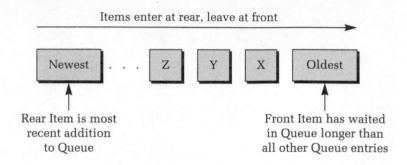

The five basic operations on a queue are specified by the following pre-
and postconditions.

Create operation
  Preconditions: Q is an arbitrary queue in unknown state.
  Postconditions: Q is initialized to the empty queue.

Empty operation
  Preconditions: Q is a previously created queue.
  Postconditions: *Empty* returns **true** if Q is empty, **false** otherwise.

Full operation
  Preconditions: Q is a previously created queue.
  Postconditions: *Full* returns **true** if Q is full, **false** otherwise.

Enqueue operation
  Preconditions: Q is a previously created queue. *Item* is a value to be
                  added to the rear of the queue.
  Postconditions: Q is returned with *Item* added to the rear of the
                  queue. If Q is full, it is left unchanged.

Dequeue operation
  Preconditions: Q is a previously created queue.
  Postconditions: Q has its front value removed.
                  Item contains the value that was at the front of Q. If
                  Q is empty, contents of *Item* are unreliable.

■ **EXAMPLE 16.5**

To help conceptualize queue operations, consider the following sequence of
actions on a queue of integers.

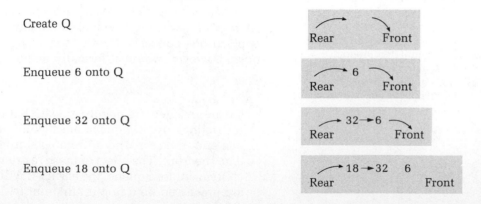

Create Q

Enqueue 6 onto Q

Enqueue 32 onto Q

Enqueue 18 onto Q

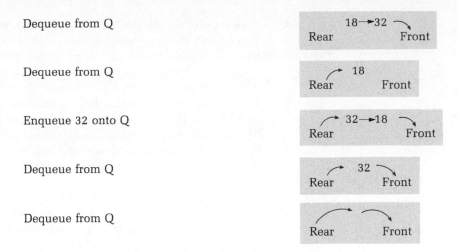

Dequeue from Q	18→32 Rear / Front
Dequeue from Q	18 Rear Front
Enqueue 32 onto Q	32→18 Rear / Front
Dequeue from Q	32 Rear / Front
Dequeue from Q	Rear Front

Application of a Queue in Computer Simulation

Before discussing implementations of a queue, we will examine how this ADT can be used in an application known as computer *simulation*. To introduce the notion of a simulation, consider the following question.

> *The star car washing team at Octopus Car Wash requires precisely four minutes to wash a car. On the average, a car arrives at Octopus every four minutes. In a typical 10-hour day at Octopus, how long does a car have to wait between its arrival and beginning its wash?*

It's tempting to answer this question by reasoning that the combination of four minutes to wash a car and four minutes between arrivals implies that no car should wait at all. However, such reasoning would not reflect the reality that cars arrive sporadically. Such sporadic arrival patterns are what can cause dreadful waiting lines.

That cars arrive, on the average, every four minutes really means that, in any given minute, there is a 25 percent chance that a car will arrive. We wish to reflect the notion of "chance" in a program that models the operation of Octopus Car Wash during a typical day. A computer simulation is a program that models a real-life event. To incorporate chance into simulations, a special function known as a *random number generator* is used.

A random number generator is a function that returns an unpredictable numerical value each time it is called. For our purposes, the value returned from a random number generator will be a real value greater than or equal to zero but less than 1. We will approach a random number generator as a "black box" function. That is, we will not worry about the internal logic of how such numbers are generated. Many versions of Pascal supply a random number generator; if yours doesn't, you might use the one given in Appendix 9. Our only concern in using a random number generator is that if we call on the **FUNCTION** Random in a loop such as the following

```
FOR K := 1 TO 100 DO
   BEGIN
      X := Random  {  A parameterless function  }
   END;
```

then we should see 100 values that obey statistical properties of randomness. Essentially these properties require that no pattern of values tends to recur and that values are evenly spread over the interval from 0.0 to 1.0.

How will a random number generator be used to reflect the "reality" of cars arriving at Octopus Car Wash? We will view each iteration through a loop as one minute in the daily operation of Octopus. On each iteration, we will call on Random to generate a random number. If it is less than or equal to 0.25 (corresponding to the 25 percent chance of an arrival), our program will interpret that as a car arriving during that minute. If the random number is greater than 0.25, the program decides that no car arrived during that minute.

When a car does arrive, it will be added to the waiting queue of cars. So that we may accumulate some statistical results, the car will be time-stamped with the time that it entered the queue. This time stamp will allow us to determine how long a car has been in the queue before it finally reaches the front. Conceptually, the queue at the core of this simulation is depicted in Figure 16.7.

FIGURE 16.7
Cars waiting at Octopus Car Wash, time-stamped with the minute of their arrival

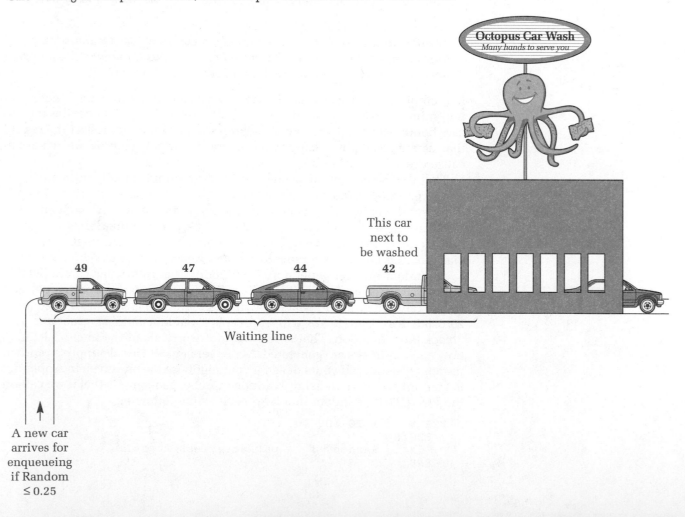

Pseudocode for the Octopus Car Wash simulation is

1. Initialize statistical counters
2. Create the queue of time-stamped cars
3. **FOR** each Minute in the day's operation
   - 3.1 Call on the random number generator to determine if a new car arrived
   - 3.2 **IF** a new car arrived **THEN**
     - 3.2.1 Time-stamp and enqueue in onto the queue of cars
   - 3.3 **IF** no car is currently being washed **AND** the queue of waiting cars is not empty **THEN**
     - 3.3.1 Dequeue a car from the queue for washing
     - 3.3.2 Use the time stamp for the car just dequeued to determine how long it waited
     - 3.3.3 Add that wait time to the accumulating total wait time
     - 3.3.4 Record that we have just begun to wash a car
   - 3.4 **IF** a car is being washed **THEN**
     - 3.4.1 Reduce by one minute the time left before we are done washing it

To refine this pseudocode into a Pascal main program, we must establish a formal Pascal interface for the queue ADT.

Pascal Interface for the Queue Abstract Data Type

```
TYPE
  QueueData = { The type of each data item in the queue };

PROCEDURE Create (var Q : Queue);

  { Given:   An arbitrary queue variable Q in unknown state        }
  { Task:    Initialize Q to the empty queue                       }
  { Return:  Q initialized to the empty queue.                     }

FUNCTION Empty (Q : Queue) : boolean;

  { Given:   A previously created queue                            }
  { Task:    Determine if Q is empty                               }
  { Return:  True if Q is empty, false otherwise.                  }

FUNCTION Full (Q : Queue) : boolean;

  { Given:   A previously created queue                            }
  { Task:    Determine if Q is full                                }
  { Return:  True if Q is full, false otherwise.                   }

PROCEDURE Enqueue (VAR Q : Queue;
                   Item : QueueData);

  { Given:   A previously created queue Q                          }
  {          An item to be added to the rear of the queue          }
  { Task:    Add the item to the queue                             }
  { Return:  Q with Item added to the rear of the queue.  If       }
  {          the queue is full, it is left unchanged.              }

PROCEDURE Dequeue (VAR Q : Queue;
                   VAR Item : QueueData);

  { Given:   A previously created queue Q                          }
  { Task:    Remove the item at the front of the queue             }
```

```
{   Return:   Q with its front value removed.                          }
{             Item  contains the value that was at the front of         }
{             queue.  If Q is empty, contents of Item are unreliable.   }
```

■ EXAMPLE 16.6

Use the preceding Pascal interface to write a main program for the Octopus
Car Wash simulation. Assume the existence of a Random function.

```
PROGRAM Octopus (input, output);

{ A program to simulate the operation of the Octopus Car Wash over      }
{ 10 hours (600 minutes) of operation.  The variables TimeForWash       }
{ and ProbOfArrival represent the time it takes to run one car through  }
{ Octopus's star car wash team and the probability that a car           }
{ arrives for a wash in any given minute.  This program assumes the     }
{ existence of a Queue data type and a random number generator invoked  }
{ by a call to the parameterless function Random.                       }

TYPE
   QueueData = integer;
   Queue = { Assume appropriate implementation };

VAR
   TimeForWash,                    { Time to wash one car }
   Minute,                         { Loop counter }
   TimeEnteredQueue,               { Used for time-stamping car in queue }
   CarsWashed,                     { Total cars washed }
   TotalQueueMin,                  { Total minutes spent waiting }
   TimeLeftOnCar : integer;        { Time left for washing current car }
   ProbOfArrival : real;
   CarQueue : Queue;
   .
   .      { Queue operations and random number generator, if needed }
   .

BEGIN
   write ('Enter time to wash one car ');
   readln (TimeForWash);
   write ('Enter probability of arrival in any minute ');
   readln (ProbOfArrival);
   Create (CarQueue);
   CarsWashed := 0;
   TotalQueueMin := 0;
   TimeLeftOnCar := 0;
   FOR Minute := 1 TO 600 DO  { Iterate through minutes of day }
     BEGIN
       IF Random < ProbOfArrival THEN  { Have new arrival in this minute }
         Enqueue (CarQueue, Minute);
       IF (TimeLeftOnCar = 0) AND NOT Empty (CarQueue) THEN
         BEGIN
           Dequeue (CarQueue, TimeEnteredQueue);
           TotalQueueMin := TotalQueueMin + (Minute - TimeEnteredQueue);
           CarsWashed := CarsWashed + 1;
           TimeLeftOnCar := TimeForWash
         END;
       IF TimeLeftOnCar <> 0 THEN
         TimeLeftOnCar := TimeLeftOnCar - 1
     END;
   writeln (CarsWashed : 4, ' cars were washed');
   writeln ('Average wait in queue ', TotalQueueMin/CarsWashed : 8 : 2)
END.
```

A sample run would appear as follows:

```
Enter time to wash one car 4
Enter probability of arrival in any minute 0.25
 150 cars were washed
Average wait in queue    15.53
```

The sample run of the program in Example 16.6 provides an indication of how the sporadic arrival of cars can cause a backlog of work at Octopus Car Wash. One of the great values of simulation programs is that they allow cost-free experimentation with various scenarios to see if a situation might improve or worsen. For instance, the program we have written for Octopus could be used to explore how adding help to the car wash team (and correspondingly reducing the amount of time it takes to wash a car) could affect the build-up of cars waiting for service. You will get a chance to explore further the use of queues for computer simulations in the Exercises and Problems.

Another noteworthy point about Example 16.6 is that it works with a queue even though we have no idea of how the queue of cars is actually implemented. Of course, this should not be surprising; this is the value of designing programs and data structures from an ADT perspective. However, given the high-level logic in our example, we should now turn our attention to ways in which the scheduling queue might be implemented.

A NOTE OF INTEREST

Computer Simulations: Blessing or Curse?

The computer's ability to condense a large span of time (such as 600 minutes in Example 16.6) into the very short time frame required for a run of a simulation program is the blessing and the curse of computer simulations. It makes the computer a very valuable experimental tool. In addition to providing a much faster means of experimentation, simulation programs allow researchers and decision-makers to set up initial conditions that would be far too risky if allowed in real life.

For example, consider the area of environmental studies. Here researchers can use simulation programs to create scenarios that would be far too time-consuming and dangerous if they were carried out in the environment. Researchers could use simulation software to see what might happen if pollution of a river were allowed to continue in an uncontrolled manner. If the results of the simulation indicate that all fish in the river would be gone within ten years, nothing has really been lost. Moreover, some valuable information has been gained; decision-makers in the environmental arena would know that some sort of pollution controls are necessary. Further experimentation with the simulation could be done to determine exactly what type and degree of controls should be imposed.

What can go wrong with decisions based on the result of computer simulation? Clearly, if the model upon which the program is based is not an accurate reflection of the situation being simulated, results could be produced that would disastrously mislead decision-makers. Additionally, we saw in Example 16.6, building the complex mathematical models used in simulation programs is a very sensitive process. Even models that seem to be relatively comprehensive can produce surprisingly inaccurate output. Hence, the real issue in using simulation results to support the decision-making process is the accuracy of the model on which the program is based. The authors of such a program must combine expertise in programming techniques with high levels of sophisticated knowledge in the relevant discipline(s). This is a situation in which computer science must truly become interdisciplinary.

The importance of simulation as an area of application within computer science is reflected in two issues of the *Communications of the ACM* that have been dedicated to this topic. The November 1985 issue (Vol. 28, No. 11) reported on simulation models in such diverse areas as molecular genetics, aviation, and seismology. The October 1990 issue (Vol. 33, No. 10) explored simulation in the context of parallel events, on-line scheduling, and semiconductor manufacturing.

Array Implementation of a Queue

From the definition of a queue, it is evident that two pointers will suffice to keep track of the data in a queue: one pointer to the front of the queue and one to the rear. This premise underlies all of the queue implementations which we will discuss in this section.

Let us consider computer jobs being scheduled in a batch processing environment, a good example of a queue in use. Suppose further that all job names are strings and that jobs are scheduled strictly in the order in which they arrive. Then an array and two pointers can be used to implement the scheduling queue. We will encapsulate the array and pointers into a single record type.

```
TYPE
   QueueData = String;
   QueueArray = ARRAY [1..MaxQueueSize] OF QueueData;
   Queue = RECORD
              List : QueueArray;
              Front, Rear : integer
           END;
VAR
   JobQueue : Queue;
```

Here MaxQueueSize would be set by a **CONST** declaration to the maximum number of entries that the field List may contain. We shall see that this is different from the actual number of entries that the queue may contain at a given time in processing.

If the Front and Rear pointers are initially set to 1 and 0 respectively, the state of the queue before any insertions or deletions appears as shown in Figure 16.8.

FIGURE 16.8
Empty queue

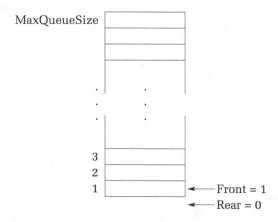

Recalling that insertions may be made only at the rear of the queue, suppose that job NEWTON now arrives to be processed. The queue then changes to the state pictured in Figure 16.9.

FIGURE 16.9
NEWTON added to the rear of
the queue

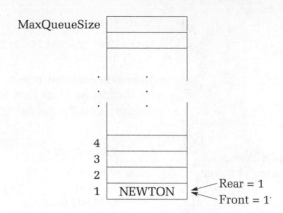

If job NEWTON is followed by PAYROLL, the queue's status must change to that of Figure 16.10, which shows that the addition of any Item to the queue requires two steps:

```
Q.Rear := Q.Rear + 1;
Q.List[Q.Rear] := Item;
```

FIGURE 16.10
PAYROLL added after NEWTON

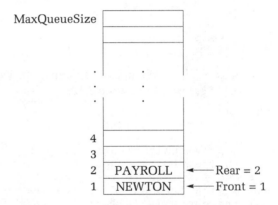

If the system is now ready to process NEWTON, the front entry must be removed from the queue to an appropriate location designated by Item in Figure 16.11.

FIGURE 16.11
NEWTON removed from the
queue

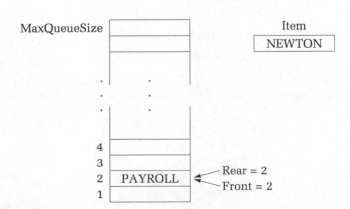

Here the instructions

```
Item := Q.List[Q.Front];
Q.Front := Q.Front + 1;
```

achieve the desired effect.

It should be clear that the conditions in Table 16.2 signal the associated boundary conditions for an array implementation of a queue.

TABLE 16.2
Boundary condition checks for array implementation of queue

Condition	Special Situation
Rear < Front	Empty queue
Front = Rear	One-entry queue
Rear = MaxQueueSize	No more entries may be added to queue

The conditions allow us to develop our brief two-line sequences for adding to and removing from a queue into full-fledged procedures. These in turn assume the existence of the Boolean-valued functions Empty and Full to check whether or not the Enqueue and Dequeue operations are possible. In the Exercises, you will be asked to write the Create, Empty, and Full operations.

■ **EXAMPLE 16.7**

Write the Enqueue and Dequeue operations for an array implementation of the queue ADT.

```
PROCEDURE Enqueue (VAR Q : Queue;
                   Item : QueueData);

{  Given:    A previously created queue Q                          }
{            An item to be added to the rear of the queue          }
{  Task:     Add the item to the queue                             }
{  Return:   Q with Item added to the rear of the queue.  If       }
{            the queue is full, it is left unchanged.              }

BEGIN
  WITH Q DO
    IF NOT Full (Q) THEN
      BEGIN
        Rear := Rear + 1;
        List[Rear] := Item
      END
END; {  of PROCEDURE Enqueue  }
```

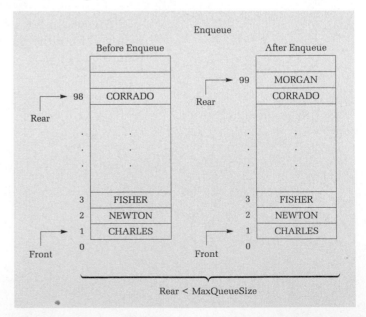

```
PROCEDURE Dequeue (VAR Q : Queue;
                   VAR Item : QueueData);

{ Given:    A previously created queue Q                          }
{ Task:     Remove the item at the front of the queue             }
{ Return:   Q with its front value removed.                       }
{           Item contains the value that was at the front of      }
{           queue.  If Q is empty, contents of Item are unreliable. }

BEGIN
  WITH Q DO
    IF NOT Empty (Q) THEN
      BEGIN
        Item := List[Front];
        Front := Front + 1
      END
END; { of PROCEDURE Dequeue }
```

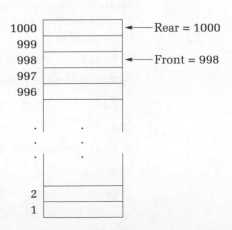

As it now stands, our implementation of a queue as a scheduling structure for jobs in a batch environment functions effectively until Rear matches MaxQueueSize. Then a call to Enqueue fails even though only a small percentage of slots in the array may actually contain data items currently in the queue structure. In fact, given the queue pictured in Figure 16.12, we should be able to use slots 1–997 again.

This is not necessarily undesirable. For example, it may be that the mode of operation in a given batch environment is to process 1,000 jobs, then print a statistical report on these 1,000 jobs, and finally clear the queue to start

FIGURE 16.12
A full queue

another group of 1,000 jobs. In this case, the queue in Figure 16.12 is the ideal structure because data about jobs are not lost even after they have left the queue.

However, if the goal of a computer installation were to provide continuous scheduling of batch jobs, without interruption after 1,000 jobs, then the queue of Figure 16.12 would not be effective. One strategy that could be employed to correct this situation is to move the active queue down the array upon reaching the condition Rear = MaxQueueSize, as illustrated in Figure 16.13.

FIGURE 16.13
Active queue moved down

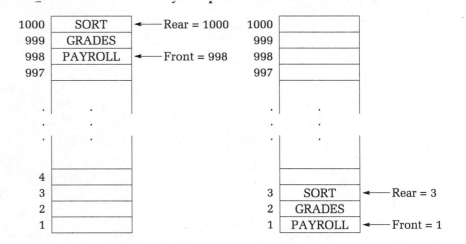

If the queue contains a large number of items, however, this strategy would not be satisfactory because it would require moving all of the individual data items. We will discuss two other strategies that allow the queue to operate in a continuous and efficient fashion: a circular implementation and a linked list implementation.

Circular Implementation of a Queue

This technique essentially allows the queue to wrap around upon reaching the end of the array. This transformation is illustrated by the addition of the Item, UPDATE, to the queue in Figure 16.14.

To handle the pointer arithmetic necessary for this implementation of a queue, we must make the Front and Rear pointers behave in a fashion analogous to an odometer in a car that has exceeded its mileage capacity. A convenient way of doing this is to use Pascal's **MOD** operator. For instance, if we replace

```
Front := Front + 1
```

in Example 16.7 with

```
Front := Front MOD MaxQueueSize + 1
```

and

```
Rear := Rear + 1
```

with

```
Rear := Rear MOD MaxQueueSize + 1
```

we will achieve the wraparound effect depicted in Figure 16.14.

FIGURE 16.14
Queue wraps around when UP-
DATE is added

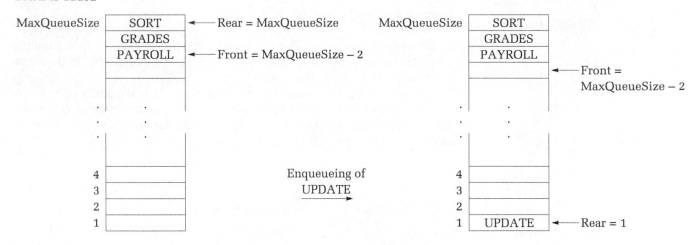

Unfortunately, it is clear from Figure 16.14 that Rear < Front will no longer suffice as a condition to signal an empty queue. To derive this condition, consider what remains after we remove an item from a queue that has only a single item in it. There are two possible situations, as illustrated in Figure 16.15.

FIGURE 16.15
Removing from one-entry queue

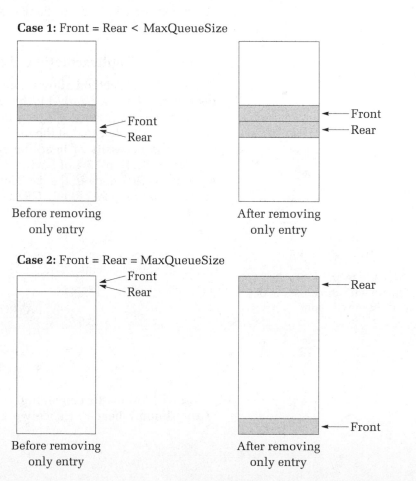

Case 1: Front = Rear < MaxQueueSize

Before removing
only entry

After removing
only entry

Case 2: Front = Rear = MaxQueueSize

Before removing
only entry

After removing
only entry

An inspection of both cases reveals that after the lone entry has been removed, the relationship

(Rear **MOD** MaxQueueSize) + 1 = Front

holds between the pointers. There is a problem, however, with immediately adopting this as a check for an empty queue. This same relationship between pointers also exists when the queue is full.

This apparent contradiction can be avoided easily if we add a counter to our encapsulation of the queue to keep track of the number of items currently in the queue. Then, as Table 16.3 indicates, tests for Empty and Full conditions need merely check this counter.

TABLE 16.3
Boundary condition checks for circular queue with encapsulated counter

Condition	Special Situation
Counter is 1	One-entry queue
Counter is 0	Empty queue
Counter is MaxQueueSize	Full queue

The actual implementation of queue operations using a circular array strategy is left for you to do in the Exercises.

Linked List Implementation of a Queue

The linked list method allows a queue to be completely dynamic with size restrictions imposed only by the pool of available nodes. Essentially, the queue is represented as a linked list with an additional rear pointer to the last node in the list so that the list need not be traversed to find this node. To reduce the necessity of handling special cases, we follow the strategy described in Section 15.4 of having a dummy header, which carries no actual data, as the first node in the list. Hence the linked list implementation of the queue containing PAYROLL, GRADES, and SORT would appear as in Figure 16.16.

FIGURE 16.16
Queue with three data nodes and dummy header

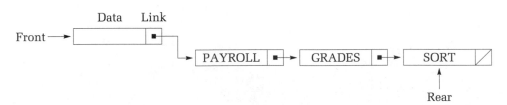

We will follow the convention that the front pointer for the queue points at the dummy header. Hence we access the first actual item in the queue through the dummy header. Table 16.4 summarizes the conditional checks that signal an empty, one-entry, or full queue.

TABLE 16.4
Conditional checks for special situations in linked list implementation (using a dummy header)

Condition	Special Situation
Rear = Front	Empty queue
Rear = Front ↑ .Link	One-entry queue
Handled by GetNode or **new** procedures of Chapter 15	Full queue

Appropriate procedures for handling additions to and removals from the queue follow. Notice that from a calling module's perspective, it would make little difference whether these low-level procedures used an array or a linked list to implement the queue. For each implementation, we have bundled all the information involved with the queue into a single record of type Queue. Hence the calling protocol for these modules is the same regardless of the implementation being used. Remember that is the essence of data abstraction: the details of how a data structure is actually implemented are hidden as deeply as possible in the overall program structure.

■ **EXAMPLE 16.8**

Code the Enqueue and Dequeue operations for a linked list implementation of a queue. Assume that a dummy header is used.

```
{  Global declarations  }

TYPE
  QueueData = { Type of data item in queue };
  QueuePointer = ^QueueNode;
  QueueNode = RECORD
                Data : QueueData;
                Link : QueuePointer
              END;
  Queue = RECORD
            Front, Rear : QueuePointer
          END;

PROCEDURE Enqueue (VAR Q : Queue;
                   Item : QueueData);

  { Given:    A previously created queue Q                        }
  {           An item to be added to the rear of the queue        }
  { Task:     Add the item to the queue                           }
  { Return:   Q with Item added to the rear of the queue.  If     }
  {           the queue is full, it is left unchanged.            }

  VAR
    P : QueuePointer;
```

```
BEGIN
  new(P);
  P^.Data := Item;
  P^.Link := NIL;
  Q.Rear^.Link := P;
  Q.Rear := P
END; {  of PROCEDURE Enqueue  }
```

Queue before Enqueue

Queue after Sort Enqueued

```
PROCEDURE Dequeue (VAR Q : Queue;
                   VAR Item : QueueData);

{  Given:    A previously created queue Q                       }
{  Task:     Remove the item at the front of the queue          }
{  Return:   Q with its front value removed.                    }
{            Item contains the value that was at the front of   }
{            queue.  If Q is empty, contents of Item are unreliable. }

VAR
  P : QueuePointer;

BEGIN
  IF NOT Empty (Q) THEN
    BEGIN
      P := Q.Front^.Link;
      Item := P^.Data;
      Q.Front^.Link := P^.Link;
```

More than one-entry Queue before Dequeue

More than one-entry Queue after Dequeue

```
      IF Q.Rear = P THEN {   Removed from one-entry queue   }
         Q.Rear := Q.Front;
      dispose(P)
   END
END; {  of PROCEDURE Dequeue   }
```

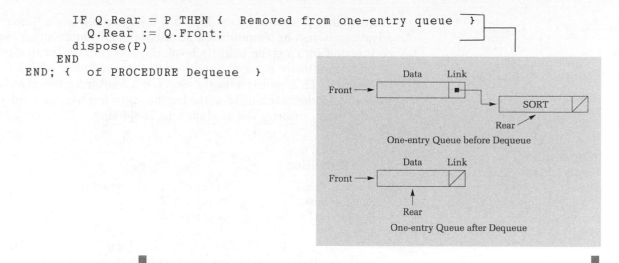

One-entry Queue before Dequeue

One-entry Queue after Dequeue

Priority Queues

So far we have used a batch scheduling application as an example of how a queue might be used in an operating system. Typically, such batch scheduling might also give higher priorities to certain types of jobs. For instance, at a university computer center, students in introductory computer science courses may receive the highest priority for their jobs to encourage a quick turnaround. Students in upper-division courses may have the next highest priority, whereas jobs related to faculty research, which require a great deal of computation, get the lowest possible priority. These jobs could be classified as types A, B, and C respectively. Any A job is serviced before any B or C job, regardless of the time it enters the service queue. Similarly, any B job is serviced before any C job. A data structure capable of representing such a queue requires just one *front pointer* but three *rear pointers,* one for each of the A, B, and C priorities.

A queue with eight jobs waiting to be serviced might appear as shown in Figure 16.17, which tells us that STATS, PRINT, and BANK are the A jobs awaiting service; COPY and CHECK, the B jobs; and UPDATE, AVERAGE, and TEST, the C jobs. If a new A job, PROB1, were to arrive for service, it would be inserted at the end of the A queue, between BANK and COPY. Because jobs can be serviced only by leaving the front of the queue, PROB1 would be processed before any of the B or C jobs.

FIGURE 16.17
Priority queue with eight jobs at three priority levels

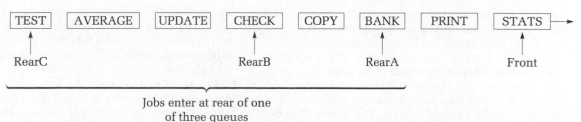

Because insertions in such a *priority queue* need not occur at the absolute rear of the queue, it is clear that an array implementation may require moving a substantial amount of data when an item is inserted at the rear of one of the higher priority queues. To avoid this, you can use a linked list to great advantage when implementing a priority queue. Whenever an item arrives to be inserted into a given priority level, the rear pointer for that priority gives us an immediately accessible pointer to the node after which the item is to be inserted. This avoids a costly sequential search for the insertion point. If a dummy leader is included at the beginning of the list, the empty conditions for any given priority are as shown in Table 16.5.

TABLE 16.5
Empty conditions for a priority queue

Condition	Priority
Front = Rear1	For priority 1, the highest priority
Rear1 = Rear2	For priority 2
Rear$(n - 1)$ = Rear$n$	For priority n

The specifics of writing a formal ADT definition of a priority queue and providing an implementation for it are included as exercises at the end of this section. In Chapter 18, we will see that priority queues may also be implemented using the special type of tree structure known as a heap (not to be confused with the heap maintained in Pascal as described in Chapter 15). Unlike the implementation we have just discussed, the heap will conveniently allow an unrestricted number of different priorities.

Operating Systems and Scheduling Resource Use in a Time-Sharing Environment

One of the primary problems facing designers of operating systems is the allocation and scheduling of resources that must be shared by a number of users. For instance, consider a simple time-sharing system which allows multiple users, each on a video terminal, and also has one shared printer. Suppose that the currently running process, called process A, makes a request to use the printer. Then, before this process completes its task on the printer, its allotted time (often called a time burst) expires, and it is replaced by process B as the currently running process. If process B requests the printer while it is running, we have a clear problem. If process B is granted the printer, its output will be interspersed with that from Process A, which did not complete its printing before its time burst expired. Obviously, we cannot let process B continue to run.

The solution developed by operating systems designers to honor both of these requests is to use multiple queues—one containing those processes that have cleared access to all resources they require to run, and one for processes that have requested a resource currently owned by another process. The former of these

queues is often called the *ready queue;* the latter is termed the *blocked queue.* Hence the solution to the scenario described in the first paragraph involves two steps.

1. Move process A from its currently running state to the ready queue when its time burst expires (because it has all the necessary resources to start running again).
2. Move process B to the blocked queue when it requests the printer already owned by process A. Here it would remain until process A is done with the printer, at which time the front entry in the blocked queue for the printer (B in this case) would be moved to the ready queue.

In practice, the addition and removal of processes to and from these queues is controlled by special flags called *semaphores.* For a thorough exposition on operating system queues and semaphores, see H. M. Deitel's *Introduction to Operating Systems,* second edition (Reading, Mass.: Addison-Wesley, 1990) and Andrew Tanenbaum's *Operating Systems: Design and Implementation* (Englewood Cliffs, N.J.: Prentice-Hall, 1987).

Exercises 16.3

1. Suppose that you are given a queue that is known to contain only positive integers. Use only the fundamental queue operations to write a procedure

   ```
   PROCEDURE Replace (VAR Queue : QueueType; Old, New : integer)
   ```

   which replaces all occurrences of the positive integer Old in the Queue with the positive integer New. Other than doing this, the queue is to remain unchanged. Avoid passing through the queue more than once.

2. Suppose that you are given a queue of real numbers. Using only the fundamental queue operations, write a function that returns the average value of an entry in the queue.

3. Augment the simulation program of Example 16.6 by
   a. Counting the number of minutes during the day when the Octopus Car Wash team is idle; that is, there are no cars in the queue waiting to be washed.
   b. Counting how many cars are left waiting in the queue at the end of the day.

   Make no assumptions about how the CarQueue might be implemented.

4. Consider a circular array implementation of a queue in which the array is declared to have an index range 1..5. Trace the status of the array and the front and rear pointers after each of the following successive operations.

   Enqueue *SMITH*
   Enqueue *JONES*
   Enqueue *GREER*
   Dequeue
   Enqueue *CARSON*
   Dequeue
   Enqueue *BAKER*
   Enqueue *CHARLES*
   Enqueue *BENSON*
   Dequeue
   Enqueue *MILLER*

5. Implement the Create, Empty, and Full operations for a (noncircular) array implementation of a queue. Be sure that your answers are consistent with the implementation of Enqueue and Dequeue in Example 16.7.

6. Provide declarations for a circular array implementation of a queue. Then use these declarations to implement each of the five basic queue operations.

7. Implement the Create, Empty, and Full operations for a linked list (with dummy header) implementation of a queue. Be sure that your answers are consistent with the implementations of Enqueue and Dequeue in Example 16.8.

8. Implement all five basic queue operations using a linked list representation that does not include a dummy header.

9. Suppose that we adopt the following conventions for the front and rear pointers associated with a queue. Front is to point at the next item to be removed from the queue. Rear is to point at the first available location, that is, the next location to be filled. Following these conventions, implement all five queue operations for a noncircular array representation of the ADT.

10. Repeat Exercise 9 for a circular array representation.

11. In a queue used to schedule batch jobs on a computer system, it is often convenient to allow users to remove a job from the queue after submitting it. (They may, for example, realize that they accidentally submitted a job with an infinite loop.) Develop a procedure header for this removal operation. Be sure

that you document it appropriately. Then implement it for a circular array representation of a queue.

12. Repeat Exercise 11 for a linked list (with dummy header) representation of a queue.

13. Provide a formal ADT definition for the priority queue. Then implement the ADT under the assumption that possible priority values are drawn from a set that could be used to index an array. See if you can make your implementation of each operation O(1) in its efficiency.

14. Discuss ways in which the Octopus Car Wash simulation of Example 16.6 does not reflect the way in which a car wash really operates. Then discuss ways in which the pseudocode logic behind this example should be modified to overcome these shortcomings.

■ ■ ■ ■

FOCUS ON
PROGRAM DESIGN

The application of the parsing algorithm described in Section 16.2 is not limited to compilers. Many of the programs typically used by scientists, engineers, and mathematicians can be greatly enhanced by allowing the user to interactively enter an algebraic expression as opposed to embedding the expression inside the program. Consider, for instance, the situation described in the following memorandum from the head of the physics department at the University of Hard Knocks.

MEMORANDUM
University of Hard Knocks

TO: Director of Computer Center
FROM: Head of Physics Department
DATE: November 22, 1996
RE: Making integration program more versatile

In physics we find frequent application to take the integral of a function $f(x)$ over the interval from a to b on the real number line. As you are aware, this essentially means that we wish to find the area under the graph of the function between endpoints a and b, as indicated in the following diagram:

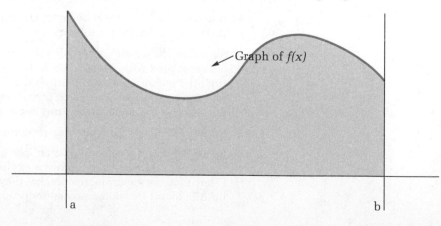

We presently have a program which obtains a good approximation of this area by adding up the areas of a large number of small rectangles, each with base along the interval from *a* to *b* and top passing through the graph of *f*(*x*). This concept is highlighted in the next diagram.

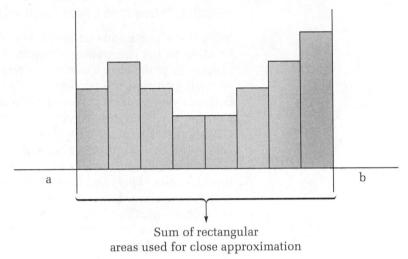

Sum of rectangular
areas used for close approximation

The user of our program can interactively enter the endpoints *a* and *b* and the number of rectangles. The result is a very good approximation when enough rectangles are used.

Our problem is not with the accuracy of the approximation but with the fact that, to change the function *f*(*x*), the user must edit the definition of the function in the source program and then recompile. Can you help us by writing a program which will allow the user to enter the function *f*(*x*) interactively? The functions we integrate in this fashion can be defined in terms of the standard arithmetic operations addition, subtraction, multiplication, division, and exponentiation. Thanks in advance for your prompt assistance.

The physics department head has presented us with a substantial task in the preceding memorandum. Consider some of the subordinate problems with which we will be faced in writing this program.

- The evaluation of integrals; that is, areas under graphs of functions. Obtaining numerical answers to mathematical problems of this variety will serve to introduce us to a subject known as *numerical analysis*.
- The interactive parsing and evaluation of a function will give us an opportunity to adapt the algorithms introduced earlier.
- For the type of functions described in the memorandum, the problem of finding the next token in the expression can become complicated. Consider, for instance, a function defined by the expression

    3.14*X^3 + X^2

where ^ is used to denote exponentiation. Here, from a stream of incoming characters, we must be prepared to select a token which may be a real number, the variable X, or an arithmetic operator. The problem of recognizing tokens in an incoming stream of characters is called *lexical analysis*.

To keep our situation relatively simple, we will assume that all tokens must be separated by a space and no other operations such as trigonometric functions may be used in defining the function f.

Modular Structure Chart for the Integral Evaluation System

With these comments in mind, we turn our attention toward designing a solution to the integration problem. Recall that the first step in this design process is to develop a modular structure chart reflecting the way in which we will partition the problem into subproblems. (See Figure 16.18). Since both conversion from infix to postfix and the evaluation of a postfix expression require fundamental stack operations, we have located our stack processing modules at the deepest level of the structure chart. Here they will be accessible by both the parsing and evaluation algorithms.

Interestingly, our system will also make use of a queue. Because the tokens in the postfix expression are now more complicated objects than single characters, we need a data structure to append tokens to as they are processed by the infix-to-postfix algorithm. A queue emerges as a very nice ADT for this purpose. Hence the structure chart also indicates the presence of fundamental queue operations at a level accessible by both the parsing and evaluation algorithms.

Data Structures for the Integral Evaluation System

We will need a queue to store the postfix expression that is built as the infix expression goes through our conversion algorithm. The data in this queue are more complex than characters, however. This is because the tokens needed from the infix string being entered by the user are not necessarily individual characters. Rather, such tokens will fall into one of the three following categories:

1. A real number. If the token is a real number, the lexical analysis phase of our algorithm must convert it from the appropriate stream of digits and decimal point as typed by the user.
2. The variable X. The infix expression defines the function in terms of this general variable. When the function is evaluated, a particular value is then substituted for X.
3. An operator. We broadly include $+$, $-$, $*$, $/$, $^$, $($, $)$, and the special delimiter $\#$ in this category.

The problem with a token that may be either a real number or a character is that we essentially need a data type that can assume one of several identities, depending upon the current token. This is exactly the purpose for which Pascal's variant record type is defined (see Section 11.4). Hence, the following declarations provide a suitable data type for all three of the categories we have described:

```
TYPE
  TokenType = (RealValue, VarX, Operator);
            { Number, variable, or operator/parenthesis  }

  TokenRec = RECORD
              CASE Token : TokenType OF
                RealValue : (Value : real);
                VarX : (XChar : char);
                Operator : (OpChar : char)
              END;
```

FIGURE 16.18
Modular structure chart for integration problem

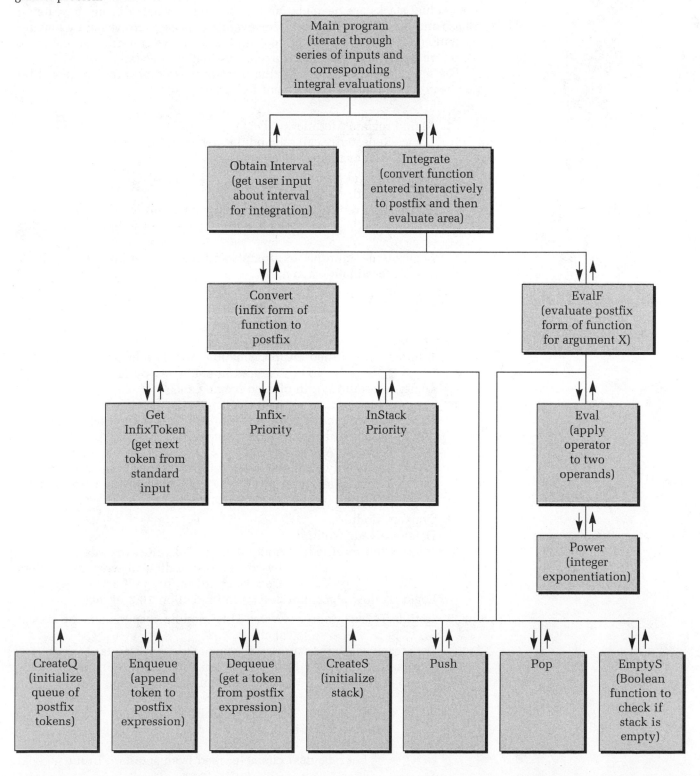

Given these declarations, an appropriate data structure for the postfix expression is a queue whose elements are of type TokenRec.

The final data structure needed by our program is a stack. Actually, two conceptual stacks are needed: one for operator symbols during the parsing phase and one for values during the evaluation phase. However, by making TokenRec the base data type of items in the stack, we can use just one stack structure for both of the conceptual stacks that are needed.

The module specifications for the integral evaluation problem posed by the head of the physics department follow.

1. Main Program Module
   Logic: Repeatedly call on modules to obtain input specifications and then evaluate integral.

2. ObtainInterval Module
   Data received: None
   Information returned: Interval endpoints a and b
   NumberOfRectangles to use in approximating area
   Logic: Issue appropriate prompts and read user input.
   Terminate when $a >= b$.

3. Integrate Module
   Data received: Endpoints a and b
   NumberOfRectangles for which area is to be accumulated
   Information returned: Approximation to area under graph of function entered interactively by user
   Logic: Compute Width of each rectangle as
   $(b - a)$/Number of Rectangles.
   Call on module Convert to convert Infix expression read from standard input to Postfix notation.
   Initialize Area to zero.
   Repeatedly evaluate f at the midpoint of the base of the current rectangle, multiply this by the width of the base, add resulting product to Area accumulation.

4. Convert Module
   Data received: Nothing
   Information returned: Postfix queue of TokenRec records, delimited by '#', corresponding to what user enters from standard input
   Logic: Follow algorithm described in Section 16.2 of text.

5. GetInfixToken Module {*Note:* This module responsible for lexical analysis.}
   Data received: Infix expression being read from standard input
   Information returned: FromInfix, a TokenRec containing the next token read from standard input
   Logic: {*Note:* We assume all tokens separated by one space.}
   Initialize Value field of FromInfix to zero.
   {In case token is a real number.}
   REPEAT
   Let c be next character read from standard input

CASE c **OF**

1. c is a space: We are done.
2. c is a 'X': Set FromInfix to c.
3. c is '+', '−', '*', '/', '^', '(', ')', '#':
     Set FromInfix to c.
4. c is decimal point: Set a Multiplier to 0.1 for future
     accumulation.
5. c is a digit:
     IF left of decimal **THEN** Set Value to
     10 * Value plus numeric form of c.
     ELSE Set Value to Value +
         Multiplier times numeric form of c.
         Divide Multiplier by 10 for next iteration.
    UNTIL c is a space

6. InfixPriority Module
   Data received: t, a TokenRec record
   Information returned: Infix priority rank of t.
   Logic: See Section 16.2 of text.

7. InStackPriority Module
   Data received: t, a TokenRec record
   Information returned: InStack priority rank of t
   Logic: See Section 16.2 of text.

8. EvalF Module
   Data received: Postfix queue representation of function f
                  x, the real number at which f is to be evaluated
   Information returned: The real number $f(x)$
   Logic: See evaluation algorithm in Section 16.2 of text.

9. Eval Module
   Data received: v1, v2: the values of two operands
                  Op: character containing operator $+$, $-$, $*$, $/$, $^$
   Information returned: Numeric result of applying Op to v1 and v2.
   Logic: Select the appropriate Pascal operation based on Op.

10. Power Module
    Data received: b, a base, and p, an integer exponent
    Information returned: b^p
    Logic: Use loop to perform appropriate number of multiplications.

In addition to these specific modules, we will need a package of procedures for stack and queue operations. To avoid name clashes between the Create, Empty, and Full operations for these ADTs, we shall use CreateS, EmptyS, and FullS for stack operations and CreateQ, EmptyQ, and FullQ for the corresponding queue operations.

The complete Pascal program for the integral evaluation system follows, with reference to the module specifications. Also included are graphic documentation and sample runs to give you a more detailed grasp of how the program functions in its interaction with a user.

```
PROGRAM TakeIntegral (input, output);

  { Program to compute area under curve of function entered          }
  { interactively.  A stack is used to convert function expression to }
  { postfix notation (which is stored in a queue) and then to         }
```

```
  {  evaluate.  Valid function expressions can contain the variable X,  }
  {  numeric constants, operators +, -, *, /, ^ (for                    }
  {  exponentiation) and appropriate parentheses.                       }

  CONST
    EndToken = '#'; {  End token corresponding to algorithm             }
                    {  described in text                                }

  VAR
    A, B : real;
    NumberOfRectangles : integer;
    Area : real;

{ *********************************************************************** }

  PROCEDURE ObtainInterval (VAR A, B : real;
                            VAR NumberOfRectangles : integer);

    {  Given:    Nothing.                                               }
    {  Task:     Issue prompts, obtain user input regarding interval    }
    {            of integration.                                        }
    {  Return:   Interval endpoints A  and B.  NumberOfRectangles,      }
    {            the number of rectangular areas to accumulate in       }
    {            approximating the area.                                }

    VAR
      K : integer;

    BEGIN
      write ('Enter left and right endpoints (left >= right to quit)--> ');
      readln (A, B);
      IF A < B THEN
        BEGIN
          write ('Enter number of rectangles for computing area--> ');
          readln (NumberOfRectangles)
        END
    END; { of PROCEDURE ObtainInterval }

{ *********************************************************************** }

  PROCEDURE Integrate (A, B : real;
                       NumberOfRectangles : integer;
                       VAR Area : real);

    {  Given:    Parameters for interval of integration:  interval      }
    {            endpoints A and B, NumberOfRectangles to accumulate     }
    {            in approximating area.                                 }
    {  Task:     Approximate area under interactively entered function  }
    {            between A and B.                                       }
    {  Return:   Approximated area.                                     }

    TYPE
      TokenType = (RealValue, VarX, Operator);
                   { Number, X, or operator/paren }
      TokenRec = RECORD
                     CASE Token : TokenType OF
                       RealValue :
                         (Value : real);
                       VarX :
                         (XChar : char);
                       Operator :
                         (OpChar : char)
                   END;
```

Token
Field

RealValue → Value Field

VarX → XChar Field

Operator → OpChar Field

Rest of record structure
depends on Token field.

```
           StackData = TokenRec;
           Stack = { A hidden implementation of the stack ADT }
           QueueData = TokenRec;
           Queue = { A hidden implementation of the queue ADT }
           PfString = Queue;    { To store postfix form of infix expression }

       VAR
         TokenStack : Stack;
         Postfix : PfString;
         Count : integer;
         Width, X : real;

{ ********************************************************************* }

         { Stack and queue operations here.  To avoid name clashes       }
         { stack operations are CreateS, EmptyS, and FullS.  Queue       }
         { operations referenced by CreateQ, EmptyQ, and FullQ.          }

{ ********************************************************************* }

       PROCEDURE Convert (VAR Postfix : PfString);

         { Given:    Infix expression being entered from standard input }
         { Task:     Apply parsing algorithm of Section 16.2            }
         {           to infix expression.                               }
         { Return:   Postfix, a queue of tokens representing the        }
         {           function in postfix notation.                      }

         VAR
           BottomStack, FromStack, FromInfix : TokenRec;

         PROCEDURE GetInfixToken (VAR FromInfix : TokenRec);

           { Given:   Nothing.                                          }
           { Task:    Get the next token from standard input.           }
           { Return:  This next token in FromInfix.                     }

         CONST Space = ' ';

         VAR
           C : char;
           Multiplier : real;
           LeftOfDecimal : boolean;

         BEGIN
           FromInfix.Value := 0;
           LeftOfDecimal := true;
           REPEAT
             IF NOT eoln THEN
               read (C)
             ELSE
               C := EndToken;
             CASE C OF
               '.':                  { Encountered decimal point }
                 BEGIN
                   LeftOfDecimal := false;
                   Multiplier := 1.0E-1
                 END;
               '+', '-', '*', '/', '^', '(', ')',
               EndToken :       { Operator }
```

> 3.14
> ↑
> We are currently here. Must prepare to accumulate digits to right of decimal.

```
      BEGIN
        FromInfix.Token := Operator;
        FromInfix.OpChar := C
      END;
     '0', '1', '2', '3', '4', '5', '6', '7', '8', '9' :
      BEGIN
        FromInfix.Token := RealValue;
        IF LeftOfDecimal THEN
          FromInfix.Value := FromInfix.Value * 10.0 + (ord(C) -
                             ord('0'))
        ELSE
          BEGIN
            FromInfix.Value := FromInfix.Value +
                              (ord(C) - ord('0')) * Multiplier;
            Multiplier := Multiplier / 10.0
          END
      END;
     'X' :                                      {  Variable X  }
      BEGIN
        FromInfix.Token := VarX;
        FromInfix.XChar := C
      END;
     Space :        {  Blank signals end of current token.    }
      BEGIN         {  So we do nothing.                      }
      END
    END {  CASE  }
  UNTIL eoln OR (C = Space) OR (C = EndToken);
  IF C = EndToken THEN
    readln
END; {  of PROCEDURE GetInfixToken  }
```

23.14
For digits to left of decimal, must multiply accumulated value by 10 and add digit.

23.14
For digits to right of decimal, add digit scaled to appropriate decimal value by Multiplier.
{ Digit }

```
{ ******************************************************************* }

    FUNCTION InfixPriority(T : TokenRec) : integer;

      {  Given:    T, a token read from the infix form of the        }
      {            function being integrated.                        }
      {  Task:     Determine infix priority value of T.              }
      {  Return:   The infix priority value.                         }

      BEGIN
        CASE T.OpChar OF
          '^' :
            InfixPriority := 3;
          '*', '/' :
            InfixPriority := 2;
          '+', '-' :
            InfixPriority := 1;
          '(' :
            InfixPriority := 4;
          ')', EndToken :
            InfixPriority := 0;
        END
      END;

{ ******************************************************************* }

    FUNCTION InStackPriority(T : TokenRec) : integer;

      {  Given:    A token T on the operator stack.                  }
      {  Task:     Determine in-stack priority of T.                 }
      {  Return:   The in-stack priority.                            }
```

6

```
              BEGIN
                CASE T.OpChar OF
                  '^' :
                    InStackPriority := 3;
                  '*', '/' :
                    InStackPriority := 2;
                  '+', '-' :
                    InStackPriority := 1;
                  '(', EndToken :
                    InStackPriority := 0
                END
              END; {  of FUNCTION InStackPriority  }

{ ********************************************************************** }

        BEGIN {  Convert  }
          CreateS (TokenStack);
          {  CreateS must push EndToken to correspond with algorithm in Section 16.2 }
          BottomStack.Token := Operator;
          BottomStack.OpChar := EndToken;
          CreateQ (PostFix);
          writeln ('Enter function with spaces between tokens, then <RETURN>');
          REPEAT
            GetInfixToken(FromInfix);
            IF (FromInfix.Token = RealValue) OR (FromInfix.Token = VarX) THEN
              {  We have an operand -- variable or number.  }
              Enqueue (Postfix, FromInfix)
            ELSE IF FromInfix.OpChar = ')' THEN
              BEGIN
                Pop(TokenStack, FromStack);
                WHILE FromStack.OpChar <> '(' DO
                  BEGIN
                    Enqueue (Postfix, FromStack);
                    Pop(TokenStack, FromStack)
                  END
              END
            ELSE IF FromInfix.OpChar = EndToken THEN
              WHILE NOT EmptyS (TokenStack) DO
                BEGIN
                  Pop(TokenStack, FromStack);
                  Enqueue (Postfix, FromStack)
                END
            ELSE
              { We have one of arithmetic operators +, -, *, /, ^  or ) }
              BEGIN
                Pop(TokenStack, FromStack);
                WHILE InStackPriority(FromStack) >=
                      InfixPriority(FromInfix) DO
                  BEGIN
                    Enqueue (Postfix, FromStack);
                    Pop(TokenStack, FromStack)
                  END;
                Push(TokenStack, FromStack);
                Push(TokenStack, FromInfix)
              END
          UNTIL (FromInfix.Token = Operator) AND
                (FromInfix.OpChar = EndToken)
        END; { of PROCEDURE Convert  }

{ ********************************************************************** }

      FUNCTION EvalF(Postfix : PfString;
                     X : real) : real;
```

```
      { Given:   Postfix, containing the postfix form of the          }
      {          function to be integrated, and X, a point            }
      {          at which the function is to be evaluated.            }
      { Task:    Evaluate the function at X.                          }
      { Return:  Result of the evaluation.                           }


      VAR
        T, T1, T2, T3 : TokenRec;
```

`{ ****************************************************************** }`

```
      FUNCTION Eval(V1, V2 : real;
                    Op : char) : real;

        { Given:   Two real operands, V1 and V2, and an              }
        {          arithmetic operator Op.                          }
        { Task:    Apply operator to the two operands.              }
        { Return:  Result of the application.                       }
```

`{ ****************************************************************** }`

```
        FUNCTION Power(B : real;
                       P : integer) : real;

          { Given:   B, a real representing a base, and P, an         }
          {          integer exponent.                               }
          { Task:    Evaluate B raised to the power P.               }
          { Return:  Result of the evaluation.                       }

          VAR
            Prod : real;
            K : integer;

          BEGIN
            Prod := 1;
            K := 1;
            WHILE K <= P DO
              BEGIN
                Prod := Prod * B;
                K := K + 1
              END;
            Power := Prod
          END; {  of FUNCTION Power  }
```

`{ ********************************************************************* }`

```
      BEGIN {  Eval  }
        CASE Op OF
          '+' :
            Eval := V1 + V2;
          '-' :
            Eval := V1 - V2;
          '*' :
            Eval := V1 * V2;
          '/' :
            Eval := V1 / V2;
          '^' :
            Eval := Power(V1, round(V2))
        END {  CASE  }
      END; {  of FUNCTION Eval  }
```

`{ ********************************************************************* }`

```
  BEGIN { EvalF }
    CreateS (TokenStack); {  Will push EndToken  }
    Dequeue (Postfix, T1);
    { Put token back into queue for next call to EvalF             }
    Enqueue (Postfix, T1);
    {  We're done when encounter operator that is                  }
    {  EndToken.  Just testing for EndToken not enough             }
    {  because coincidentally we could get match for               }
    {  EndToken when not an operator.                              }
    WHILE (T1.Token <> Operator) OR (T1.OpChar <> EndToken) DO
      BEGIN
        IF T1.Token <> Operator THEN
          IF T1.Token = RealValue THEN
            Push(TokenStack, T1)
          ELSE
            BEGIN
              T1.Token := RealValue;
              T1.Value := X;
              Push(TokenStack, T1)
            END
        ELSE
          BEGIN
            Pop(TokenStack, T2);
            Pop(TokenStack, T3);
            T.Token := RealValue;
            T.Value := Eval(T3.Value, T2.Value, T1.OpChar);
            Push(TokenStack, T)
          END;
        Dequeue (Postfix, T1);
        { Put token back into queue for next call to EvalF }
        Enqueue (postfix, T1)
      END;
    Pop(TokenStack, T);
    EvalF := T.Value
  END; {  of FUNCTION EvalF  }

{ *********************************************************************** }


  BEGIN {  Integrate  }
    Width := (B - A) / NumberOfRectangles;
    Count := 0;
    X := A;
    Area := 0;
    Convert(Postfix);
    WHILE Count < NumberOfRectangles DO
      BEGIN
        Area := Area + EvalF(Postfix, X + Width / 2.0) * Width;
        X := X + Width;
        Count := Count + 1
      END
  END; {  of PROCEDURE Integrate  }
```

Graph of function f

This height is $f(x + Width/2)$

Width

x

```
{ ******************************************************************* }
    BEGIN { Main program }
      ObtainInterval(A, B, NumberOfRectangles);
      WHILE A < B DO
        BEGIN
          Integrate(A, B, NumberOfRectangles, Area);
          writeln ('Approximation to area is ', Area: 10 : 3);
          writeln;
          ObtainInterval(A, B, NumberOfRectangles)
        END
    END.
```

Sample runs

```
Enter left and right endpoints (left >= right to quit)--> 0 3
Enter number of rectangles for computing area--> 10
Enter function with spaces between tokens, then <RETURN>
3
Approximation to area is       9.000

Enter left and right endpoints (left >= right to quit)--> 0 3
Enter number of rectangles for computing area--> 10
Enter function with spaces between tokens, then <RETURN>
X ^ 2
Approximation to area is       8.978

Enter left and right endpoints (left >= right to quit)--> 0 3
Enter number of rectangles for computing area--> 100
Enter function with spaces between tokens, then <RETURN>
X ^ 2
Approximation to area is       9.000

Enter left and right endpoints (left >= right to quit)--> 0 1
Enter number of rectangles for computing area--> 100
Enter function with spaces between tokens, then <RETURN>
( X + 2 ) ^ 3 / ( X + 1 )
Approximation to area is      10.526

Enter left and right endpoints (left >= right to quit)--> 0 0
```

RUNNING AND DEBUGGING TIPS

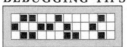

1. In applications in which the size to which a stack or queue may grow is hard to predict, use a linked list to implement the ADT. That way, you can take advantage of Pascal's dynamic memory management to avoid having to worry about a full data structure.

2. Many scientific and mathematical application programs can be enhanced by allowing users to enter function definitions at run-time. This chapter's Focus on Program Design section provides an example of how such run-time definitions of a function can be done.

3. When debugging simulations, use a random number sequence that remains the same over different runs of the program. Without such a sequence, your program will behave differently on separate runs even though you provide it with identical inputs. This is because you are getting a different pattern of random numbers. Appendix 9 indicates how you can ensure a fixed sequence of random numbers from one run of the program to the next.

■ **Summary**

Key Terms

blocked queue	parsing	ready queue
first-in, first-out (FIFO)	pop	rear pointer
front pointer	postfix	semaphores
infix	prefix	simulation
infix priority	priority queue	stack
last-in, first-out (LIFO)	push	stack priority
lexical analysis	queue	tokens
numerical analysis	random number generator	top

Key Concepts

- Conceptually, a stack is simpler than a queue since all additions and deletions are limited to one end of the structure, the top. For this reason, a stack is also known as a last-in, first-out (LIFO) list. Like a queue, a stack may be implemented using either an array or a linked list.
- The simplicity of the stack as an abstract structure belies the importance of its application. Stacks play a crucial role in the parsing done by language compilers.
- Parsing, as we have studied it in this chapter, involves the conversion of an expression from infix to postfix notation. In infix notation, an algebraic operator is located between its two operands. In postfix notation, the operator follows its two operands.
- Expressions in postfix notation do not require parentheses to override the standard hierarchy of algebraic operations.
- Stacks process procedure calls when a program executes.
- A queue is a first-in, first-out (FIFO) data structure used in processing of data such as job scheduling in a large university computer environment. There are two basic pointers, Front and Rear, associated with this structure. New data items are added to the rear of the queue, and the data item that is about to be processed is removed from the front of the queue.
- The relative advantages and disadvantages of three implementations of queues—array, circular array, and linked list—are summarized in the following table.

Implementation	Advantages	Disadvantages
Array	A record of queue entries entries remains even after they have been removed.	Static allocation of storage limits overall queue size. Array locations cannot be reused once entries are removed from queue.
Circular Array	Array locations can be reused once entries are removed from the queue.	Static allocation of storage limits overall queue size.
Linked List	With Pascal pointer variables, the queue can grow dynamically to take full advantage of all space available in Pascal's heap.	Could be less space-efficient than array implementations since each node in queue must include a pointer field as well as data fields.

- Primary applications of queues are in the areas of operating systems and computer simulation of events.

■ **Programming
Problems
and Projects**

1. Write a program that will parse infix expressions into prefix form.

2. Write a program to call for input of a decimal number and convert it to its binary equivalent using the method described in the following flowchart.

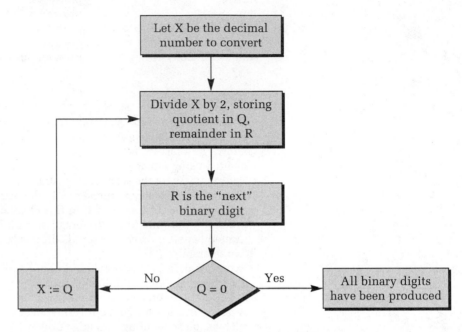

Note that this method produces the binary digits for the given number in reverse order. Use a stack to get them printed in the correct order.

3. In the Programming Problem 2 for Chapter 15, you developed a passenger list processing system for the various flights of Wing-and-a-Prayer Airlines. Wing-and-a-Prayer management would now like you to extend this system so that it processes logical combinations of flight numbers. For example, the command

LIST 1 OR 2

should list all passengers whose name appears on the flight 1 list or the flight 2 list. Your program should also accept the logical operators **AND** and **NOT** and allow parenthesized logical expressions obeying the standard logical hierarchy

**NOT
AND
OR**

4. A tax form may be thought of as a sequence of items, each of which is either a number or defined by an arbitrary mathematical formula involving other items in the sequence. To assist them in their tax-planning strategy, top management at the Fly-by-Night credit card company desire a program that would allow them to interactively enter numbers or formulas associated with given lines of a tax form. Once all such lines have been defined, users of the program may redefine the number or formula associated with a particular line, and all other lines dependent on that one should be appropriately updated.

Note that, since formulas may be entered interactively, your program will have to use a stack to evaluate them. You will in effect have written a small-scale spreadsheet program.

5. Write a program that will accept commands of the following form:
   - **INPUT** ⟨variable name⟩
   - ⟨variable name⟩ = infix expression involving variables names and arithmetic operators +, −, *, /
   - **PRINT** ⟨variable name⟩
   - **GO**

These commands are to be stored in an array of strings until the **GO** command is entered. Once the **GO** command is entered, your program should execute the previously stored commands. "Execute" here means

   - For an **INPUT** command: Send a question mark to the terminal and allow the user to enter a real number; this real number is then stored in the variable name.
   - For an assignment statement: Parse the expression into postfix form and then evaluate it, storing the results in the variable name on the left of the equality sign.
   - For a **PRINT** instruction: Write to the terminal the numerical contents of the specified variable name.

To make things relatively easy you may assume a syntax that

   - Allows variable names consisting of one uppercase alphabetical character.
   - Allows only one variable name following the commands for **INPUT** or **PRINT**.
   - Allows one blank space after the commands for **INPUT** and **PRINT** and no blank spaces anywhere else.

For an additional challenge, enable your program to handle successfully the exponentiation operator ^ within assignment statement expressions. The following example should illustrate the need for care in handling this exponentiation operator:

$3^{2^3} = 3^8$, not 9^3

6. This problem is an extension of Problem 5 for a "compiler" for a primitive programming language. Write a program that will accept commands of the following form:
   - **INPUT** ⟨variable name⟩
   - **PRINT** ⟨variable name⟩
   - ⟨variable name⟩ = infix arithmetic expression involving variable names and arithmetic operators +, −, *, /, ^
   - **GOTO** ⟨line⟩ $\begin{cases} \textbf{ALWAYS, or} \\ \textbf{IF} \text{ infix logical expression involving variable names} \\ \quad \text{and operators } +, -, *, /, \wedge, \& \text{ (for \textbf{AND}),} \\ \quad ! \text{ (for \textbf{OR})}, \sim \text{ (for \textbf{NOT}), } <, >, = \end{cases}$
   - **STOP**
   - **RUN**

These commands are to be stored in an array of strings until the **RUN** command is entered. Upon encountering the **RUN** command, your program should execute the previously stored commands. "Execute" here means:

- For an **INPUT** command: Send a question mark to the terminal and allow the user to enter a real number, which is stored in the variable name.
- For a **PRINT** command: Write to the terminal the numerical contents of the specified variable name.
- For an assignment command: Parse the expression into postfix form and then evaluate it. Store the result in the variable name on the left of the equality sign.
- For a **GOTO** command: Branch to the line number specified when the **ALWAYS** condition follows the line number or when the infix expression that follows the **IF** evaluates to true. Here "line number" refers to the relative position of the line in the sequence of lines that were entered prior to the Run command. The first line number in this sequence is "00".
- For a **STOP** command: Halt execution.

To make things relatively easy, you may assume a syntax that

- Specifies that one and only one blank space follows **INPUT**, **PRINT**, **GOTO**, and line number. No other blanks appear anywhere.
- Allows only one variable name to follow **INPUT** or **PRINT**.
- Only allows variable names consisting of one uppercase alphabetical character.
- Only allows line numbers consisting of two digits: 00 through 99.

The usual hierarchy for operators is assumed.

7. Modify **PROGRAM** TakeIntegral (Focus on Program Design section) so that it also integrates expressions involving the functions **sin, cos, tan, exp,** and **ln.** Test your modified program by having it evaluate the following integrals:
   a. **sin** (X $*$ 2) + **cos** X / 2 between 0 and 1
   b. 3 $*$ (X + 4) $^\wedge$ 2 + **tan** (X / 2) between 0 and 1
   c. 3 $*$ (X + 4) $^\wedge$ 2 + **tan** X / 2 between 0 and 1
   d. **exp ln** X $^\wedge$ 3 between 1 and 3
   e. **exp ln** (X $^\wedge$ 3) between 1 and 3

8. If you have access to a graphics library in your version of Pascal, write a program that allows a user to interactively define a function and then displays a graph of the function between two specified endpoints.

9. Develop a program to simulate the processing of batch jobs by a computer system. The scheduling of these jobs should be handled via a queue (or priority queue for more of a challenge). Examples of commands that your program should be able to process are

Command	Purpose
Add	To add an entry to queue.
Delete	To take an item out of the queue.
Status	To report on items currently in queue.

10. Back in Chapter 11 (Problem 8) you developed a program to keep track of a bank's records. Now the bank has asked you to develop a program to simulate the arrival of customers in a waiting line at the bank. Factors to consider are the average time it takes to service one customer, the average number of customers that arrive in a given time period, and the number of service windows maintained by the bank. These factors should be provided as input to your program. Statistics such as the length of time the average customer has to spend in the waiting line could be very helpful in the bank's future planning.

11. Here is a problem typically encountered in text formatting applications.

    Given a file of text, that text delimited by special bracketing symbols [and] is to be considered a footnote. Footnotes, when encountered, are not to be printed as normal text but are instead stored in a footnote queue. Then, when the special symbol # is encountered, all footnotes currently in the queue are printed and the queue should be returned to an empty state.

    What you learn in solving this problem will allow you to make good use of string storage techniques discussed in earlier chapters.

12. In order to improve their services, the Fly-by-Night credit card company (Problem 3, Chapter 15) has decided to give incentives to their customers for prompt payment. Customers who pay their bills two weeks before the due date receive top priority and a 5 percent discount. Customers who pay their bills within one week of the due date receive next priority and a 1 percent discount. Third priority is given to customers who pay their bills on or within two days after the due date. The customers who pay their bills thereafter are assigned the lowest priority. Write a program to set up a priority queue to access customer records accordingly.

13. The Bay Area Brawlers professional football team (Problem 4, Chapter 15) has been so successful in recent weeks that the team management is considering the addition of several new ticket windows at the team's stadium. However, before investing a sizable amount of money in such an improvement, they would like to simulate the operation of ticket sales with a variety of ticket window configurations. Develop a computer program that allows input of such data as number of ticket windows, average number of fans arriving each hour as game time approaches, and average length of time to process a ticket sale. Output from your program should include statistics such as the average waiting-line length each hour as game time approaches and the amount of time the average fan had to wait in line before having his or her ticket request processed. Use queues to represent each of the waiting lines.

14. Consider the design for an implementation of the radix sort algorithm and its associated bin (sublist) structure that was discussed in Chapter 15's Focus on Program Design section. Note that queues could provide an alternative implementation for the bin structure needed by radix sort. What queue implementation would provide the most space-efficient bin structure for radix sort? Why? Develop a complete radix sort program that uses queues to implement the bins needed by the

algorithm and then accesses these bins *only* through the defined ADT operations for a queue.

Is this implementation of radix sort more or less time efficient than that described in Chapter 15's Focus on Program Design section? Justify your answer in a written memorandum.

15. As Director of Computer Operations for Wing-And-A-Prayer Airlines, you receive the following memorandum. Design and write a simulation program according to the specifications in the memorandum.

MEMORANDUM
Wing-and-a-Prayer Airlines

TO: Director of Computer Operations
FROM: President, Wing-and-a-Prayer Airlines
DATE: September 30, 1996
RE: Wasted Fuel and Time

Wing-and-a-Prayer Airlines is becoming increasingly concerned about the amount of fuel being wasted as its planes wait to land at and take off from world-famous O'Hair Airport. Could you please help us write a program to simulate the operation of one day's activity at O'Hair and report on the times spent waiting to land and take off for each Wing-and-a-Prayer flight? Input data to the program should include

■ Average number of Wing-and-a-Prayer arrivals each hour
■ Average number of other airline arrivals each hour
■ Average number of Wing-and-a-Prayer departures each hour
■ Average number of other airline departures each hour
■ Number of available runways
■ Average time runway in use for an arrival
■ Average time runway in use for a departure

By appropriately adjusting these parameters, we hope to do some valuable "what-if" analyses regarding the time spent waiting for a runway by our arrivals and departures.

---

16. If an arithmetic expression is written in prefix notation, then there is no need to use parentheses to specify the order of operators. For this reason, some compilers translate infix expressions (such as 2 + 8) to prefix notation (+ 2 8) first and then evaluate the prefix string.

Write a program that will read prefix expressions and then compute and display the value of the indicated arithmetic expression. Assume that the operands are single-digit positive integers separated by blanks. The operators can be +, −, *, and /, also separated by blanks and having their usual meanings of add, subtract, multiply, and divide.

17. Implement the following robustness enhancements for **PROGRAM** TakeIntegral in this chapter's Focus on Program Design section.
   a. Make the GetInfixToken module more robust by allowing the user to separate individual tokens with an arbitrary number of zero or more spaces.

b. Make the GetInfixToken module more robust by guarding against input of an invalid arithmetic operator.

c. Make the GetInfixToken module more robust by guarding against an invalid character in a stream of characters intended to be a real number. When such an invalid character is detected, allow the user to recover from the point of error rather than forcing the user to retype the entire line.

18. This chapter's Note of Interest on "Computer Simulations: Blessing or Curse?" cites two issues of the *Communications of the ACM* that have been dedicated to the topic of simulation. Using these two issues as a starting point, research and prepare a written report on computer simulation. Your report could discuss any or all of the following:

a. Examples of disciplines and industries in which simulation has been used to great advantage.

b. Limitations and inaccuracies that arise in modeling a system by computer simulation. Techniques that can be used to measure and monitor such inaccuracies.

c. The reliance of many simulation programs on the effective generation of random numbers.

d. The potential danger in relying on the results of simulation programs without examining the validity of their underlying models.

19. This chapter's Focus on Program Design section demonstrated how a computer program can be used to solve a mathematical problem in interactive fashion. In particular, the type of problem solved by this program is the evaluation of integrals. Explore other types of mathematical problems that can be solved interactively by software systems available at your school. (The *Mathematica* program from Wolfram Research is one example of such a system available at many universities.)

Prepare a report on the results of your explorations. In keeping with the theme of this chapter's Focus on Program Design section, be sure that your report includes a discussion of the types of mathematical expressions that can be parsed and evaluated by such systems.

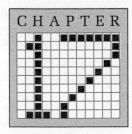

It's déjà vu all over again.
Lawrence Peter (Yogi) Berra

*Research is the process of
going up alleys to see if they
are blind.*
Marston Bates

More about Recursion

In Section 5.8, we saw that Pascal will allow a procedure or function to call itself. In computer science this form of self-reference is called *recursion.*

In our brief discussion of recursion in Chapter 5, the scope of problems we examined was often better suited to iterative control by nonrecursive methods such as **WHILE, REPEAT,** and **FOR** loops. Hence, recursion appeared mostly to be an alternative way of doing something that could be done by other iterative control strategies. There are, however, many complex problems for which recursion presents the most natural and elegant solution. We are now ready to embark on the detailed study of such problems.

In this chapter, we will first review the essentials of recursive procedures. Now that we are familiar with stack operations, we will also be able to explain more completely how recursion is implemented. The "invisible" data structure underlying *recursive procedures* is the stack used by the system to process the call-and-return pattern of procedures in a program (Section 16.1). By examining the role of this system stack more closely, you will build confidence in your ability to express algorithms recursively. In time, you will use this technique without hesitation in your problem-solving.

Then we will begin to use recursion to explore problems for which nonrecursive solutions would be exceedingly difficult to fathom. We hope that you will be amazed at the ease with which recursion handles such problems. We will demonstrate that recursion is a natural and elegant way to solve many complex problems. We will also begin to explore the price paid for this elegance: the compactness of a recursive solution to a complex problem is not necessarily an accurate statement of its time or space efficiency.

Finally, we will use recursion to develop a problem-solving methodology known as *trial-and-error,* or non-deterministic, *backtracking.* In theory this technique can solve a large variety of problems. Unfortunately, in practice, the technique is so computationally expensive that it can only be used to solve small instances of such problems in a reasonable amount of time.

■ 17.1
A Closer Look at Controlling Simple Iteration with Recursion

OBJECTIVES

- to review the essentials of controlling simple iteration by recursion.
- to be able to identify and distinguish tail-recursive algorithms.
- to understand what is meant by the stack frame associated with a procedure or function call
- to understand the role of the system stack in processing calls made to a recursive procedure, particularly a procedure that is not tail-recursive
- to be able to trace the contents of the system stack during execution of recursive procedures with only one embedded recursive call

We mentioned in Section 5.8 that any recursive algorithm must have a well-defined stopping state, or *termination condition.* Without careful logical control by means of such conditions, recursive procedures can fall prey to looping in endless circles. To illustrate this, let us suppose that we have access to an output device known as a pen plotter. Such a device is equipped with a pen held by a mechanical hand that is under control of the computer.

Typical procedures to manipulate the pen could include

Procedure	Action
Line(n)	Draw a line of length n in the current direction.
RightTurn(d)	Alter current direction by rotating d degrees in clockwise direction.

Such procedures are not unlike those found in the Logo programming language or the "turtle" graphics tool kits that accompany many popular Pascal compilers. If you have access to such a compiler, you may wish to explore developing some recursive graphic figures.

If we assume that the pen is initially set to draw a line toward the north—the top of the plotting page—then the sequence of instructions

```
Line(10);
RightTurn(90);
Line(10);
RightTurn(90);
Line(10);
RightTurn(90);
Line(10);
```

will clearly draw a square with sides of length 10.

Let us now try to predict what will happen when the following recursive procedure Draw is invoked by the initial call Draw(1).

```
PROCEDURE Draw(Side : integer);

  BEGIN
    Line(Side);
    RightTurn(90);
    Draw(Side + 3) {  Recursive call  }
  END;
```

The initial call Draw(1) will result in a line of length 1 in a northerly direction. We then rotate the pen toward the east and, via a recursive call, generate a line of length 4. This is followed by a rotation to the south and a new invocation for a line of length 7. The emerging pattern should now be clear; the resulting right-angled spiral is shown in Figure 17.1.

FIGURE 17.1
Runaway recursive spiral

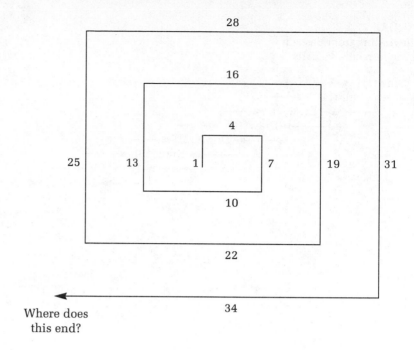

Where does
this end?

Unfortunately, our spiral-producing procedure has tumbled into a vicious circle loop of self-reference. There presently is no way to turn off the *recursive calls* made to Draw. Consider what happens, however, if we provide ourselves with a *recursive termination condition* (or recursive out) as in the following new version of Draw.

```
PROCEDURE Draw(Side : integer);

  BEGIN
    IF Side <= 34 THEN {  Recursive termination condition  }
      BEGIN
        Line(Side);
        RightTurn(90);
        Draw(Side + 3)
      END
  END;
```

Now after drawing the line of length 34 in Figure 17.1, our procedure Draw invokes itself once more, passing 37 for the parameter Side. Since the recursive termination condition is now false, no line of length 37 will be drawn. More importantly, no further recursive invocation of Draw will be made. Hence, we return immediately from the call to Draw with Side being 37. Moreover, that return triggers returns (in reverse order) from all the previous invocations of Draw, eventually ending up at the instruction following our initial call; that is, Draw(1).

The important point to stress here is that, to appropriately use recursion, we must use a recursive termination condition to avoid an infinite series of recursive calls. If we were to view each recursive call as a descent one level deeper into an algorithm's logic, we in effect must use a recursive termination condition to allow a corresponding ascent back to the level of the first call to the procedure. This concept is highlighted in Figure 17.2.

FIGURE 17.2
Unwinding from descent
through recursive calls

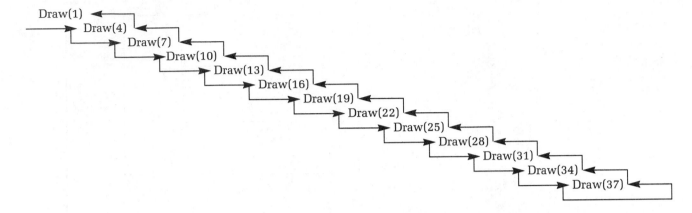

Linked Lists as Recursive Data Structures

In Section 15.1 we defined the linked list ADT. We can now reformulate that definition from a recursive perspective. The key to such a perspective is the realization that the pointer leading from each linked list node references another linked list. More formally:

> **Linked List.** A linked list is a pointer that is either *Null* (the recursive termination condition signaling an empty list) or references a node designated as the head node. The head node contains a data field and a pointer that satisfies the criteria for being a linked list.

Though an English composition teacher may find fault with our defining a linked list in terms of itself, our new definition is nonetheless completely free of ambiguity. For instance, to verify that the list in Figure 17.3 is a linked list, we note that:

1. The head node in the three-item structure contains a pointer to an embedded two-item structure, which we must verify as a linked list.
2. The head node in the two-item structure contains a pointer to an embedded one-item structure.
3. The head node in the one-node structure contains a Null pointer.
4. By the recursive termination condition, a Null pointer meets the criteria for being a linked list.
5. Hence the one-node structure in step 3 contains a pointer to a linked list and meets the criteria for being a linked list.
6. Similarly, we climb up the recursive ladder to verify that the two-node and, consequently, the three-node structures in steps 1 and 2 meet the criteria for being linked lists.

Not only does our recursive definition unambiguously specify the linked list ADT, but it also provides a natural way to implement linked list operations by recursive procedures. Consider the following example.

FIGURE 17.3
Recursive view of a linked list

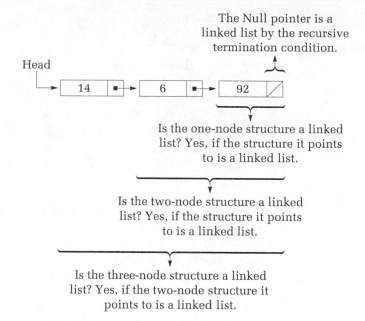

EXAMPLE 17.1

A linked list is implemented by Pascal pointer variables in the following declarations.

```
TYPE
  Pointer = ^LinkedListNode;
  LinkedListNode = RECORD
                     Data : LinkedListData;
                     Link : Pointer
                   END;
```

Develop a recursive implementation of the LinkedTraversal operation.

The implementation literally flows from our recursive definition of the linked list structure. That is, if the list we are traversing is empty there is nothing to do; otherwise we must process the data in the head node and recursively traverse the linked list referenced by the Link field in the head node. This logic is embodied in the following Pascal procedure.

```
PROCEDURE LinkedTraverse (Head : Pointer;
                PROCEDURE ProcessNode (VAR Item : LinkedListData));

{  Given:    Linked list referenced by Head pointer       }
{  Task:     Traverse the list in the linear order        }
{            determined by the links, applying the        }
{            procedure ProcessNode to each record         }
{            in the list                                  }
{  Return:   The list referenced by Head with each node   }
{            affected by ProcessNode                      }

BEGIN
  IF Head <> NIL THEN    { the only condition under which action is taken }
    BEGIN
      ProcessNode (Head^.Data);
      LinkedTraverse (Head^.Link)
    END
END;  { of PROCEDURE LinkedTraverse }
```

FIGURE 17.4
Trace of recursive
LinkedTraverse on linked list of
Figure 17.3

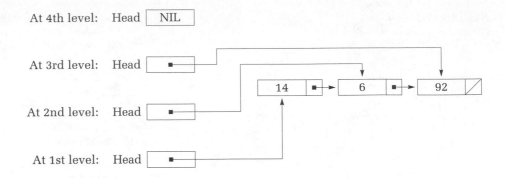

A trace of the recursive **PROCEDURE** LinkedTraverse for the list of Figure 17.3 is given in Figure 17.4. This trace shows that the procedure is initially called with a Head pointer to the node containing 14. The data are processed, and the first recursive call then passes in a Head pointer to the node containing 6. The data item 6 is processed, and a Head pointer to the node containing 92 is recursively passed to the procedure. The node containing 92 is processed, and a **NIL** head pointer is recursively passed to the procedure. Since the recursive termination condition (Head = **NIL**) is now met, we unwind from the series of recursive calls. As we return to each prior recursive level, there is nothing left to do since the recursive call is the last operation at that level.

A recursive procedure is called *tail-recursive* if only one recursive call appears in the procedure and that recursive call is the last operation performed at that procedural level. (That is, nothing else must be done after returning from a deeper recursive level.) The LinkedTraverse procedure of Example 17.1 is clearly tail-recursive. Typically, such a tail-recursive procedure can be easily recast in the form of a nonrecursive procedure using a **WHILE** or **REPEAT** control structure. We have already seen how to do this for LinkedTraverse in Chapter 15.

How Is Recursion Implemented?

As we begin to examine recursive algorithms that are not tail-recursive, we will also need to understand in detail *how* a computer language implements recursion. Here again we encounter the abstraction-implementation duality we have emphasized throughout the book. Recursion is a powerful conceptual tool. But unless you understand details of how recursion is implemented, your use of it will be limited to an intuitive approach that often employs a trial-and-error strategy to reach a solution.

In Section 16.1, we indicated that the stack is an essential data structure in a compiler's implementation of procedure calls. The role of a system stack being manipulated by the procedure calls in your program becomes even more crucial as we use recursion. To illustrate this, let us consider a problem more computationally oriented than our previous graphics and linked list examples. N factorial, denoted N!, is defined by

$$N! = N \times (N - 1) \times (N - 2) \times \ldots \times 2 \times 1$$

That is, N! is the product of the first N integers. We note that the alternate way of defining N! is by means of using (N − 1)!

$$N! = \begin{cases} 1 \text{ if } N = 1 \text{ or } N = 0 \\ N * (N - 1)! \text{ otherwise} \end{cases}$$

Language Definition

In the *Pascal User Manual and Report* (Berlin: Springer-Verlag, 1974), Kathleen Jensen and Niklaus Wirth made famous a diagrammatic way of representing Pascal syntax. By way of example, a syntax diagram which defines a Pascal statement is presented here. One interesting feature to note about this diagram is that the term *statement* is used eight times in defining statement. (Where are the recursive termination conditions in this diagram?)

Jensen and Wirth's diagrams are recursive in nature, and they point out the fact that the syntax of most computer languages can be recursively defined. This is of tremendous importance in the writing of compilers, most of which rely heavily upon stacks and recursion to parse source programs.

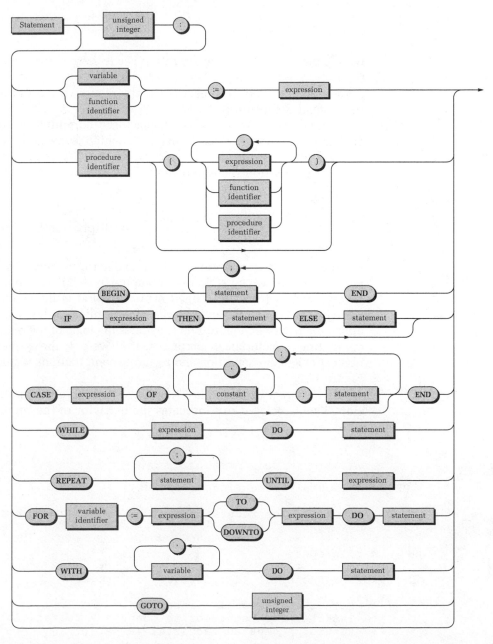

(*continued*)

Notice that this alternative definition is a *recursive definition* because it uses the notion of factorial to define factorial. Despite this circularity, we have a perfectly valid definition because of the recursive termination condition in the special definition of 1!.

To see how recursion works for factorial computation, think of the preceding definition as a series of clues which eventually will allow us to unravel the mystery of how to compute N!. That is, to compute N!, the recursive definition really tells us to

1. Remember what N is.
2. Go compute (N − 1)!.
3. Once we've computed (N − 1)!, multiply that by N to get our final answer.

Of course, when we use the definition to determine how to compute (N − 1)!, we find out that we must, in turn, compute (N − 2)!. Computing (N − 2)! will involve finding (N − 3)!. This downward spiral will eventually end with 1!, allowing us to begin the actual series of multiplications that will bring us to the appropriate answer. Figure 17.5 illustrates the logic of the recursive method for computing N factorial. In particular, if N were 4, the sequence of recursive invocations of the definition and resulting computations would be as shown in Figure 17.6.

The program in Example 17.2 calls a recursively defined Factorial function. The associated run indicates the behavior of the program for an input of 4.

■ **EXAMPLE 17.2**

```
PROGRAM RecursiveDemo (input, output);

    {  Illustrate how recursion may be used to compute factorial  }

VAR
    M : integer;

FUNCTION Factorial (N : integer) : integer;

    {  Given:    Nonnegative integer N.                         }
    {  Task:     Use recursion to compute N factorial.          }
    {  Return:   Computed factorial value.                      }
```

FIGURE 17.5
Recursive computation of N!

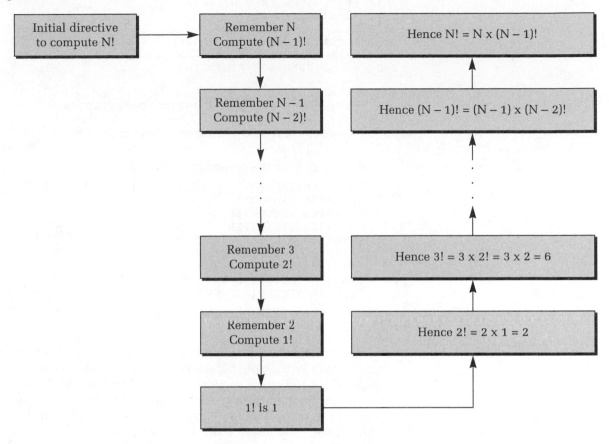

FIGURE 17.6
Recursive computation of 4!

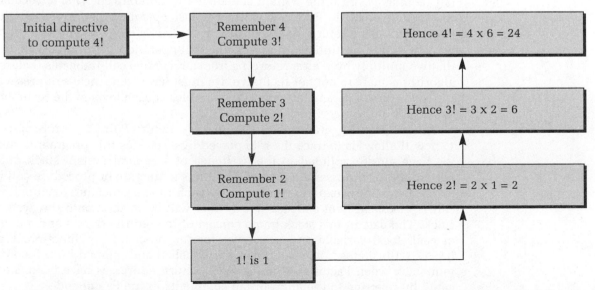

```
      BEGIN
        writeln ('ENTERING FACTORIAL WITH N = ', N);
        IF (N = 1) OR (N = 0) THEN
          Factorial := 1
        ELSE
          Factorial := N * {  Return Point 2  } Factorial (N - 1);
        writeln ('LEAVING FACTORIAL WITH N = ', N)
      END; {  of FUNCTION Factorial   }

  BEGIN {  Main program   }
    write ('ENTER NUMBER FOR FACTORIAL COMPUTATION-->');
    readln (M);
    writeln (Factorial(M)) {   Return Point 1   }
  END.
```

A sample run for the preceding code follows.

```
        ENTER NUMBER FOR FACTORIAL COMPUTATION-->4
        ENTERING FACTORIAL WITH N = 4
        ENTERING FACTORIAL WITH N = 3
        ENTERING FACTORIAL WITH N = 2
        ENTERING FACTORIAL WITH N = 1
        LEAVING FACTORIAL WITH N = 1
        LEAVING FACTORIAL WITH N = 2
        LEAVING FACTORIAL WITH N = 3
        LEAVING FACTORIAL WITH N = 4
              24
```

The **writeln** statements upon entry to and exit from **FUNCTION** Factorial in Example 17.2 are not necessary but have been included to demonstrate the precise call and return sequence triggered by the initial call of Factorial(4) in the main program. It is crucial to note that the output from **writeln** statements implies that we must in some sense have multiple copies of the variable N, one copy for each descent to a recursively deeper level. As we shall see, a stack keeps track of these multiple copies of N in the appropriate fashion.

It is also important to emphasize that **FUNCTION** Factorial would not be tail-recursive even if the **writeln** statements were removed. This is because the recursive call to Factorial is not the last operation performed by the algorithm. After a return from the call to Factorial (N − 1), we must multiply by N. It is this multiplication that is the final operation performed. The fact that we multiply by N after returning from a recursive call indicates that, for algorithms that are not tail-recursive, we must have some means of preserving the values of parameters and local variables at each level of the recursive execution of the algorithm.

The comments {   Return Point 1   } and {   Return Point 2   } in Example 17.2 will allow us to trace the role played by a stack as this program is run. We have already alluded to the existence of a general system stack onto which return addresses are pushed each time a function or procedure call is made. Let us now explain it more fully. Each time a procedure or function call is made, an item called a *stack frame* will be pushed onto the system stack. The data in this stack frame consist of the return address and a copy of each local variable and parameter for the procedure or function. Figure 17.7 illustrates how stack frames are pushed and popped from the system stack when Factorial(4) is invoked. Return addresses have been indicated by referring to the appropriate comments in the Pascal code.

FIGURE 17.7
Sequence of pushes and pops in
computing 4!

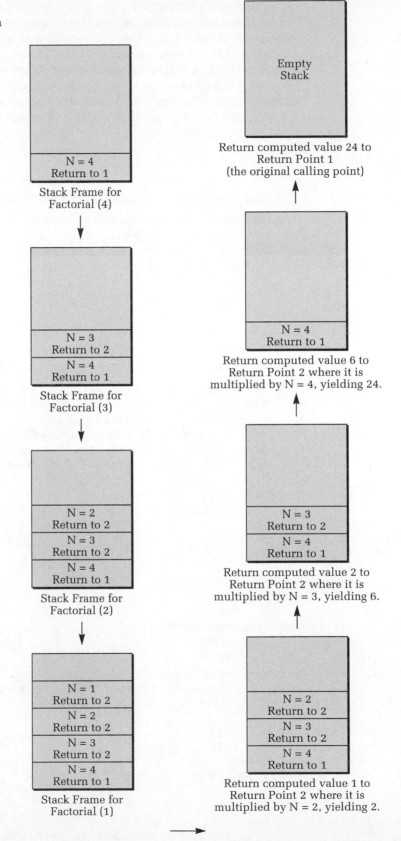

N = 4 Return to 1

Stack Frame for
Factorial (4)

N = 3 Return to 2
N = 4 Return to 1

Stack Frame for
Factorial (3)

N = 2 Return to 2
N = 3 Return to 2
N = 4 Return to 1

Stack Frame for
Factorial (2)

N = 1 Return to 2
N = 2 Return to 2
N = 3 Return to 2
N = 4 Return to 1

Stack Frame for
Factorial (1)

Empty Stack

Return computed value 24 to
Return Point 1
(the original calling point)

N = 4 Return to 1

Return computed value 6 to
Return Point 2 where it is
multiplied by N = 4, yielding 24.

N = 3 Return to 2
N = 4 Return to 1

Return computed value 2 to
Return Point 2 where it is
multiplied by N = 3, yielding 6.

N = 2 Return to 2
N = 3 Return to 2
N = 4 Return to 1

Return computed value 1 to
Return Point 2 where it is
multiplied by N = 2, yielding 2.

Although **FUNCTION** Factorial of Example 17.2 provides an illustration of an algorithm that is not tail-recursive, you could still validly argue that the computation of N! could be achieved more easily by a nonrecursive, iterative loop structure. In order to sense the real power and elegance of recursion, we must begin to explore algorithms that more subtly manipulate the stack frames hidden below the surface of recursive processing. These stack frames provide us with a "free" stack data structure; that is, a structure that we need not declare formally and that we control completely by the recursive calling pattern of our algorithm.

Exercises 17.1

1. Stand between two parallel mirrors and see how recursion works for you.

2. Consider the following function to compute N!

```
FUNCTION Factorial (N : integer) : integer;

   VAR J : integer;

   BEGIN
     Factorial := 1;
     FOR J := 2 TO N DO
       Factorial := Factorial * J
   END; { of FUNCTION Factorial }
```

Is this recursive or nonrecursive? Will it work? Explain why or why not.

3. Each of the following procedures offers a slight variation on the LinkedTraverse procedure developed in Example 17.1. For each procedure, indicate what output would be produced if the procedure were called initially with the linked list of Figure 17.3 and the ProcessNode procedure merely printed the data field of each node. If the procedure would crash with a run-time error for the data of Figure 17.3 or any other test case, explain why.

a.
```
PROCEDURE LinkedTraverse (Head : Pointer;
                          PROCEDURE ProcessNode (VAR Item : LinkedListData));

   BEGIN
     IF Head <> NIL THEN
       BEGIN
         LinkedTraverse (Head^.Link);
         ProcessNode (Head^.Data)
       END
   END; { of PROCEDURE LinkedTraverse }
```

b.
```
PROCEDURE LinkedTraverse (Head : Pointer;
                          PROCEDURE ProcessNode (VAR Item : LinkedListData));

   BEGIN
     ProcessNode (Head^.Data);
     IF Head^.Link <> NIL THEN
       LinkedTraverse (Head^.Link)
   END; { of PROCEDURE LinkedTraverse }
```

c.
```
PROCEDURE LinkedTraverse (Head : Pointer;
                          PROCEDURE ProcessNode (VAR Item : LinkedListData));
```

```
BEGIN
  IF Head^.Link <> NIL THEN
    BEGIN
      ProcessNode (Head^.Data);
      LinkedTraverse (Head^.Link)
    END
END;  {  of PROCEDURE LinkedTraverse  }
```

4. Which of the procedures in Exercise 3 are tail-recursive?

5. The following programs are intended to read a string character-by-character, put each character on the system stack, and then print out the string of characters in reverse order. Which one(s) actually achieve the intent? Which one(s) don't? Why not? What will be the output of each program for input of 'MADAM'?

a.
```
PROGRAM Palindrome (input, output);

    {  Print out a string in reverse order to check if palindrome  }

    PROCEDURE Reverse;

        {  Keep recursively stacking characters until end of string.  }
        {  Then print it out in reverse by unstacking.                }

        VAR
            c : char;  {  Here c is local to Reverse.  }

        BEGIN
          read (c);
            IF NOT eoln THEN
              Reverse;
            write(c)
        END;  {  Reverse  }

        BEGIN
          Reverse
        END.
```

b.
```
PROGRAM Palindrome (input, output);

    {  Print out a string in reverse order to check if palindrome  }

    VAR
      c : char; {  Here c is global }

    PROCEDURE Reverse;

    {  Keep recursively stacking characters until end of string.  }
    {  Then print it out in reverse by unstacking.  }

      BEGIN
        read (c);
        IF NOT eoln THEN
          Reverse;
        write (c)
      END;  {  Reverse  }

    BEGIN
      Reverse
    END.
```

6. Given the declarations for the linked list structure in Example 17.1, write a recursive procedure to search the list for a particular item and return a pointer to the item in the list if it is found. If the item is not found in the list, a **NIL** pointer should be returned.

7. Suppose that NumberArray is declared as follows:

```
TYPE NumberArray = ARRAY [1..100] OF integer;
```

Study the following function and determine what it computes. (*Hint:* Try to trace it for several small instances of the array and N values.)

```
FUNCTION Compute (A : NumberArray; N : integer) : integer;

  BEGIN
    IF N = 1 THEN
      Compute := A[N]
    ELSE IF A[N] < Compute (A, N - 1) THEN
      Compute := A[N]
    ELSE
      Compute := Compute (A, N - 1)
  END;  { of Compute }
```

8. Write a recursive function of two integer arguments M and N, both greater than or equal to zero. The function should return M^N.

9. Write a recursive function of two integer arguments M and N, $M > 1$ and $N > 0$. The function should return the integer log of N to the base M. This is defined to be the least integer L such that $M^{L+1} > N$. (*Hint:* Though your function only receives two arguments, embed within it an auxiliary function of three arguments—M, N, and L. Call on the auxiliary function initially with $L = 0$; the auxiliary function is then called recursively.)

10. Given the declaration of NumberArray in Exercise 7, write a **FUNCTION** Product that receives two arguments, one of type NumberArray and another argument N that indicates the logical size of the NumberArray. Remember that the logical size of an array is the number of indices that store well-defined data items. **FUNCTION** Product should return the product of the entries in the array from indices 1 through N.

11. Insert tracer output instructions at strategic points and use them to debug the following version of a function, which attempts to recursively compute factorials. After you've debugged the function, write a statement in which you explain the behavior of the function as originally coded and also why the function did not work in this original form.

```
FUNCTION Factorial (N : integer);

  { Given:    Integer N greater than or equal to zero.  }
  { Task:     Compute N factorial                        }
  { Return:   The computed value.                         }

  BEGIN
    IF (N=0) OR (N=1) THEN
      Factorial := 1
    ELSE
      BEGIN
        N := N - 1;
        Factorial := N * Factorial(N)
      END
  END;  { of FUNCTION Factorial  }
```

■ 17.2
Weaving More Complex Recursive Patterns

OBJECTIVES

- to recognize problems particularly suited to recursive solutions
- to be able to state the solutions to such problems as a simpler instance of the same problem
- to be able to trace the performance of a recursive algorithm using a run-time trace diagram
- to use an algorithm's run-time trace diagram to estimate the time and space efficiency of the algorithm
- to see how recursive algorithms that potentially involve more than one recursive call at each level may lead to an exponential time efficiency
- to develop an intuitive approach for developing recursive solutions to problems

The recursive algorithms we have examined so far share the property that, at each level of recursive execution of the algorithm, at most one recursive call will be made. The pattern of operations on the system stack for such algorithms is that a series of stack frames is pushed, a recursive termination condition is reached, and then all stack frames are successively popped until we return to the execution level of the main program. More complex recursive algorithms involve multiple recursive calls at each level of execution. Correspondingly, the pattern of operations on the system stack will not be a series of uninterrupted pushes followed by a series of uninterrupted pops. Instead, the system stack will initially grow a bit, then shrink, then grow again, then shrink, and so forth.

Towers of Hanoi Problem

We introduce this more complex type of recursion with a reworking of a problem we saw back in Chapter 5 (in Example 5.19). This problem, although impractical, is excellent for illustrating the technique involved. As you may recall, monks were given the painstaking task of moving a collection of N stone disks from one pillar, designated as pillar A, to another, designated as pillar C. Moreover, the relative ordering of the disks on pillar A had to be maintained as they were moved to pillar C. That is, as illustrated in Figure 17.8, the disks, all of different sizes, were to be stacked from largest to smallest, beginning from the bottom. Additionally, the monks were to observe the following rules in moving disks:

- Only one disk could be moved at a time.
- No larger disk could ever be placed on top of a smaller disk on any pillar.
- A third pillar B could be used as an intermediate to store one or more disks while they were being moved from their original source A to their destination C.

Consider the following recursive solution to this problem:

1. If N = 1, merely move the disk from A to C.
2. If N = 2, move the first disk from A to B. Then move the second disk from A to C. Then move the first disk from B to C.

FIGURE 17.8
Towers of Hanoi problem

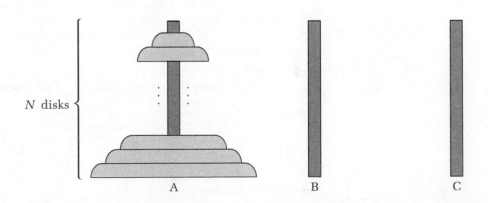

3. If N = 3, call upon the technique already established in step 2 to move the first two disks from A to B using C as intermediate. Then move the third disk from A to C. Then use the technique in step 2 to move the first two disks from B to C using A as an intermediate.

.
.
.

N. For general N, use the technique in the previous step to move N - 1 disks from A to B using C as an intermediate. Then move one disk from A to C. Then use the technique in the previous step to move N - 1 disks from B to C using A as an intermediate.

Notice that this technique for solving the Towers of Hanoi describes itself in terms of a simpler version of itself. That is, it describes how to solve the problem for N disks in terms of a solution for N - 1 disks. In general, any problem you hope to solve recursively must be approached in this fashion. This strategy is important enough to state as a principle.

> **Principle of Recursive Problem Solving.** When trying to solve a problem by recursion, always ask yourself "What could I do if I had a solution to a simpler version of the same problem?"

If you can see how to use the solution to a smaller version of the problem in solving the original problem, you have hurdled your toughest obstacle. All that remains is to determine the recursive termination conditions. This can be done by answering the question "Under what circumstances is this problem so simple that a solution is trivial?" Your answer to this question will define parameter values that trigger an immediate return from the recursive algorithm.

■ **EXAMPLE 17.3**

Implement a Pascal solution to the Towers of Hanoi problem. Our earlier discussion has indicated that the problem for N disks can be defined in terms of N - 1 if we switch the roles played by certain pillars. This switching can be achieved by altering the order in which parameters are passed when recursive calls are made. When a value of 1 is passed in for N, we have reached the recursive termination condition. The comments { Return Point 1 } and { Return Point 2 } in the following Pascal code will be used in a later trace of **PROCEDURE** Hanoi.

```
PROCEDURE HANOI (N : integer;
                 Source, Destination, Intermediate : char);

  { Given:   N, the number of disks to be transferred, and   }
  {          character representations of Source,            }
  {          Destination, and Intermediate pillars.          }
  { Task:    Apply recursive logic to specify a sequence     }
  {          of moves which will successfully transfer       }
  {          the N disks from Source to Destination.         }
  { Return:  Nothing.                                        }
```

```
BEGIN
  IF N = 1 THEN
    write ('Move disk from ', Source, 'to ', Destination)
  ELSE
    BEGIN
      Hanoi (N - 1, Source, Intermediate, Destination);
      {  In every recursive call Hanoi works with value of N less one   }


      {  Return Point 1  }
      write ('Move disk from ', Source 'to ', Destination);
      Hanoi(N - 1, Intermediate, Destination, Source)
    END
    {  Return Point 2  }
END; {  of PROCEDURE Hanoi  }
```

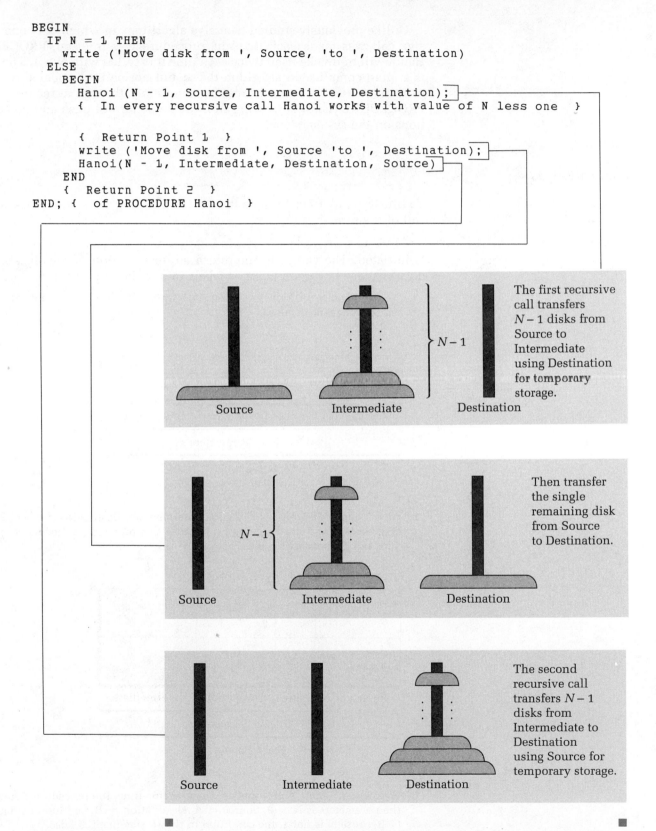

The first recursive call transfers $N-1$ disks from Source to Intermediate using Destination for temporary storage.

Then transfer the single remaining disk from Source to Destination.

The second recursive call transfers $N-1$ disks from Intermediate to Destination using Source for temporary storage.

Unlike previously studied recursive algorithms in which only one recursive call was made each time the procedure was invoked, **PROCEDURE** Hanoi will re-invoke itself twice each time it is called with N > 1. The result is a more complicated algorithm that could not be implemented easily by using mere iterative control structures. Implicitly, through its recursive calls, **PROCEDURE** Hanoi is weaving an intricate pattern of push and pop operations on the system stack.

■ EXAMPLE 17.4

To illustrate, we trace through the actions affecting the system stack when a call of the form

```
Hanoi(3, 'A', 'C', 'B')
```

is initiated. The values in the return address portion of the stack are the documentary { Return Point } labels in our Hanoi procedure.

1. We enter Hanoi with the following stack frame. N is not 1, so the condition in the **IF** statement is **false.**

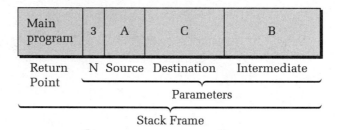

2. We encounter Hanoi(N − 1, Source, Intermediate, Destination) with A, B, C as first, second, and third arguments. Because this represents a (recursive) procedure call, some stacking must be done.

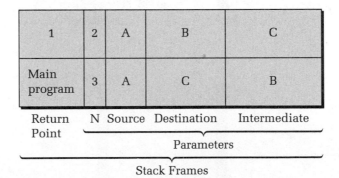

3. We reenter Hanoi. Notice that as we enter this time, the procedure's view of the parameters is N = 2, Source = A, Destination = B, and Intermediate = C. Because N is not 1, the condition in the **IF** statement is **false.**

4. We encounter Hanoi (N − 1, Source, Intermediate, Destination). Because this is a recursive call, stacking occurs.

Return Point	N	Source	Destination	Intermediate
1	1	A	C	B
1	2	A	B	C
Main program	3	A	C	B

Parameters

Stack Frames

5. We reenter Hanoi with N = 1, Source = A, Destination = C, and Intermediate = B. Because N = 1, the condition in the **IF** statement is **true.**

6. Hence

```
Move disk from A to C
```

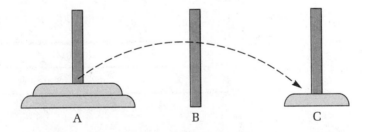

is printed and a return triggers a popping of a return address (1) and four parameters, leaving the system stack as follows:

Return Point	N	Source	Destination	Intermediate
1	2	A	B	C
Main program	3	A	C	B

Parameters

Stack Frames

7. Because the return address popped was 1

```
Move disk from A to B
```

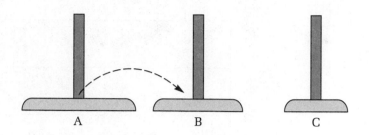

is printed and

```
Hanoi (N - 1, Intermediate, Destination, Source)
```

is encountered with N = 2, Source = A, Destination = B, and Intermediate = C.

8. The call pushes a return address and four parameters onto the system stack.

Return Point	N	Source	Destination	Intermediate
2	1	C	B	A
1	2	A	B	C
Main program	3	A	C	B

Return Point   N Source Destination Intermediate

Parameters

Stack Frames

9. We reenter Hanoi, this time with N = 1, Source = C, Destination = B, and Intermediate = A.

10. Because N = 1, the **IF** statement generates the output

```
Move disk from C to B
```

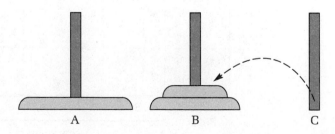

and a return.

11. The return pops a frame from the system stack and we return to the statement labeled by 2 with N = 2, Source = A, Destination = B, and Intermediate = C.

12. But statement 2 triggers a return itself, so a stack frame is popped again and we return to the statement labeled 1 with N = 3, Source = A, Destination = C, Intermediate = B.

13. Statement 1 triggers the output

    `Move disk from A to C`

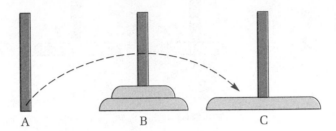

and we are immediately at another call

`Hanoi (N - 1, Intermediate, Destination, Source)`

Hence the status of the system stack is changed to

2	2	B	C	A
Main program	3	A	C	B
Return Point	N	Source	Destination	Intermediate

Parameters

Stack Frames

14. We reenter Hanoi with N = 2, Source = B, Destination = C, and Intermediate = A. Because N is not 1, another call is executed and more values are stacked.

1	1	B	A	C
2	2	B	C	A
Main program	3	A	C	B
Return Point	N	Source	Destination	Intermediate

Parameters

Stack Frames

15. We reenter Hanoi, with N = 1, Source = B, Destination = A, and Intermediate = C. Because N = 1, we print

    ```
    Move disk from B to A
    ```

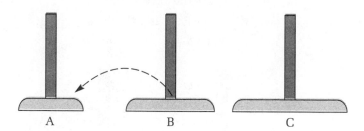

    and return.

16. The return prompts the popping of the system stack. The return address popped is the statement labeled 1. Statement 1 causes output

    ```
    Move disk from B to C
    ```

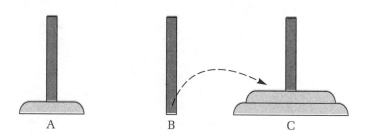

    with the stack frames left at

Return Point	N	Source	Destination	Intermediate
2	2	B	C	A
Main program	3	A	C	B

                    Parameters

              Stack Frames

17. The output from statement 1 is followed by a recursive call

    ```
    Hanoi (N - 1, Intermediate, Destination, Source)
    ```

    Hence another frame is pushed onto the stack.

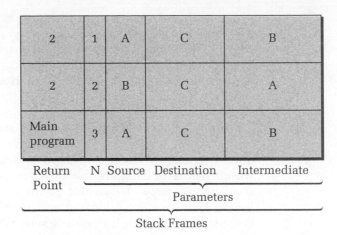

Return Point	N	Source	Destination	Intermediate
2	1	A	C	B
2	2	B	C	A
Main program	3	A	C	B

Parameters

Stack Frames

18. We reenter Hanoi (for the last time), with N = 1, Source = A, Destination = C, and Intermediate = B. Because N = 1, we output

```
Move disk from A to C
```

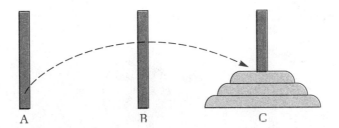

and return.

19. But now the return pops return address 2 from the stack, so return to statement 2 with the system stack given by

Return Point	N	Source	Destination	Intermediate
2	2	B	C	A
Main program	3	A	C	B

Parameters

Stack Frames

20. Statement 2 is another return, so pop the stack again. The return address popped is 2, the same return point. But this time the return will transfer control back to the original calling location—and we are done!

Long-winded as this example is, it is essential that you understand it. Recursive procedures are crucial to many of the algorithms used in computer science, and you can acquire the necessary familiarity with recursion only by convincing yourself that it really works. If you have some doubt or are not sure you understand, we recommend that you trace through the Hanoi procedure with N = 4 (be prepared to go through a lot of paper).

Efficiency Analysis of the Recursive Towers of Hanoi Algorithm An analysis of the time and space efficiency of a recursive algorithm is dependent upon two factors. The first of these is the depth, that is, number of levels, to which recursive calls are made before reaching the recursive termination condition. Clearly, the greater the depth, the greater the number of stack frames that must be allocated and the less space efficient the algorithm becomes. It is also clear that recursive calls to a greater depth will consume more computer time and hence make the algorithm less time efficient. The second factor affecting efficiency analyses (particularly time efficiency) of recursive algorithms is the amount of resource (time or space) consumed at any given recursive level.

Figure 17.9 portrays this leveled view of a recursive algorithm as a hierarchy of the recursive calls that are (potentially) made as the algorithm

FIGURE 17.9

Generalized hierarchy of calls by recursive algorithm

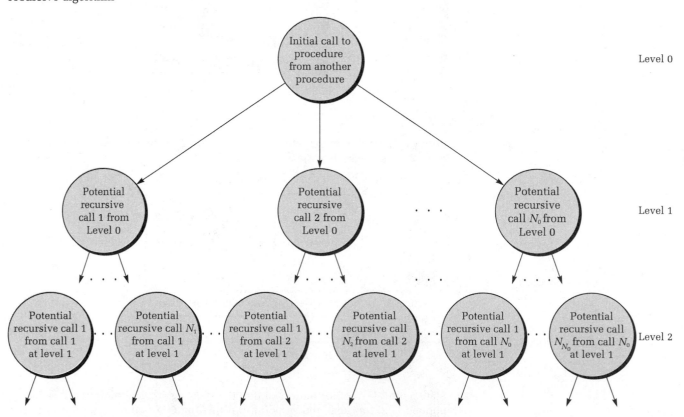

Descent continues from each potential call until recursive termination condition is reached.

Total time is sum of times spent processing at each level.

executes. Such a hierarchy can be used as a diagrammatic model of the run-time behavior of a recursive algorithm. Consequently, we will call the hierarchy associated with the execution of a particular recursive program a *run-time trace diagram* for that algorithm. Figure 17.10 presents a run-time trace diagram for the Towers of Hanoi algorithm with N = 4 disks.

FIGURE 17.10
Run-time trace of procedure Hanoi with N originally 4 (Numbers next to circles indicate order of recursive calls)

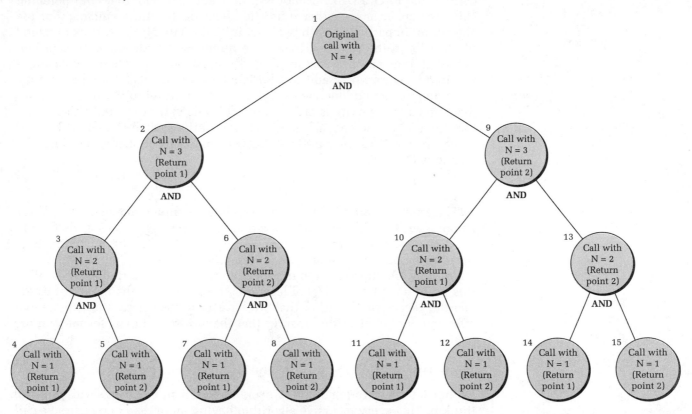

A run-time trace diagram can often be used in analyzing the time and space efficiency of an algorithm. We will provide two general principles for carrying out such analyses and then illustrate them in the context of the Towers of Hanoi algorithm.

> **Space Efficiency of a Recursive Algorithm.** Because a stack frame must be allocated at each level of recursive execution, the space efficiency of a recursive algorithm will be proportional to the deepest level at which a recursive call is made for a particular set of values; that is, the deepest level in its run-time trace diagram.

> **Time Efficiency of a Recursive Algorithm.** Because processing time is associated with each recursive call, the time efficiency of a recursive algorithm will be proportional to the sum, over all levels, of the times spent processing at each level.

Use the run-time trace diagram of **PROCEDURE** Hanoi to analyze the time and space efficiency of the algorithm.

A graphic representation of this diagram for four disks is given in Figure 17.10. Note that the two calls descending from each call are linked by **AND.** This is to emphasize that, when N is not 1, both potential recursive calls in the **PROCEDURE** Hanoi will be made. The fact that both potential calls are made has a rather dramatic effect on the time efficiency of the algorithm. In particular, calling Hanoi initially with N = 4 results in a total of 15 calls in the run-time trace. The numbers outside the circles in Figure 17.10 indicate the order in which these 15 calls are made. Increasing N to 5 in this figure would add an additional level with 16 calls to the run-time trace. In general, adding one disk adds only one level to the run-time trace diagram but doubles (plus 1) the number of calls in the diagram. This implies that the space efficiency of Hanoi relative to the system stack is O(N), but, since every call in the run-time trace diagram will be made, the time efficiency is $O(2^N)$.

■   ■

The analysis carried out in the preceding example demonstrates that the Hanoi algorithm falls into the class of exponential algorithms as defined in Section 12.3. This is the first exponential algorithm we have encountered. Recall from our discussion of algorithm efficiency in Section 12.3 that such algorithms are impractical to run for even moderate values of N. We shall at this point complete the Hanoi legend by noting that, if the monks of Hanoi use the recursive algorithm that we have described here, the exponential efficiency of the algorithm insures that the world will exist for many more centuries.

Recursive Implementation of the Binary Search Algorithm

Do not let our solution to the Towers of Hanoi problem mislead you into thinking that every recursive algorithm having more than one recursive call will be exponential in its efficiency. Consider, for example, a recursive formulation of the binary search algorithm. Recall the interface to this algorithm that we developed in Section 12.5.

```
PROCEDURE   BinarySearch (Target : KeyType;
                          N : integer;
                          SearchList : DataArray;
                          VAR InfoWanted : DataRec;
                          VAR Found : boolean);

  { Given:    List of sorted records in SearchList, Target    }
  {           storing key value being sought, and N storing    }
  {           number of records in the list.                   }
  { Task:     Apply binary search algorithm.                   }
  { Return:   DataRec associated with Target in InfoWanted.     }
  {           If not found, return false in boolean            }
  {           variable Found.                                  }
```

The principle of recursive problem-solving (stated in our discussion of the Hanoi problem) directs us to solve the binary search problem in terms of a simpler version of itself. Toward this end, we employ a perspective often used in recursive algorithms that act upon an array: we view the algorithm as occurring between a certain subrange of array indices. For the binary search, that subrange is specified by Low. .High where Low is initially 1 and High is initially N. The "simpler version" of the binary search needed for a recursive statement of the algorithm is then a version that works on a smaller subrange of array indices. This subrange ultimately may become so small that it triggers the recursive termination condition for an unsuccessful search.

An intuitive recursive statement of the binary search logic then becomes:

```
IF (recursive termination for unsuccessful search) THEN
   Found := false (and recursion terminated)
ELSE
   BEGIN
      Compute Mid index between Low and High
      IF (Target is found at Mid index) THEN
         Search is successful (and recursion terminated)
      ELSE IF (Target is less than data at Mid index) THEN
         Recursively call with same Low and Mid - 1 as High
      ELSE
         Recursively call with Mid + 1 as Low and same High
```

According to this logic, the recursive calls result in a continual narrowing of the range to be searched until either the Target is found or a recursive termination condition for an unsuccessful search is reached.

To determine what this unsuccessful recursive termination condition is, consider Figure 17.11. It portrays successive recursive calls on an array in which the Target does not exist. The shaded regions of these array snapshots indicate the index subrange in which Target = 152 could possibly be found on successive recursive calls. Note that, on the fourth recursive call, no

FIGURE 17.11
Unsuccessful search for array with 15 key values

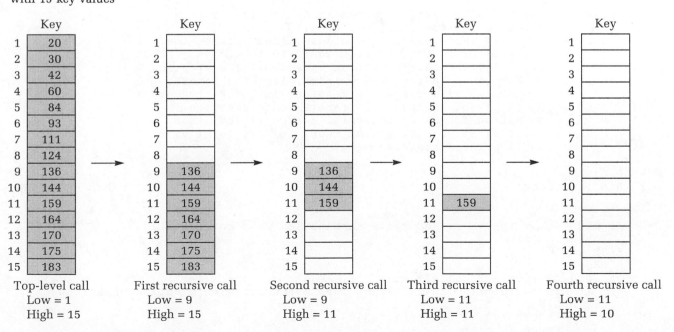

Target = 152

portion of the array is shaded; the condition High < Low exists. This condition is therefore the recursive termination check for an unsuccessful search. The following example presents the code for the recursive binary search in its entirety.

Developing a recursive version of the binary search requires that we use a local auxiliary procedure to work with the index subrange Low. .High. Using this auxiliary procedure will allow us to preserve the interface to **PROCEDURE** BinarySearch. This interface should not require its user to pass in an initial Low value of 1. Instead the user need only pass in the N: the number of records in SearchList. From there, the front-end portion of **PROCEDURE** BinarySearch need only call on its auxiliary local procedure, passing in 1 for Low and N for High.

```
PROCEDURE  BinarySearch (Target : KeyType;
                    N : integer;
                    SearchList : DataArray;
                    VAR InfoWanted : DataRec;
                    VAR Found : boolean);

  { Given:    List of sorted records in SearchList, Target   }
  {           storing key value being sought, and N storing  }
  {           number of records in the list.                 }
  { Task:     Apply binary search algorithm.                 }
  { Return:   DataRec associated with Target in InfoWanted.  }
  {           If not found, return false in boolean          }
  {           variable Found.                                }

  PROCEDURE BinarySearchAux (Low, High : integer);

    { Given:    Low and High--array indices in SearchList between  }
    {           which Target may still be found.                   }
    { Task:     Check if Target is in the middle index between Low }
    {           and High or if Low and High meet the recursive     }
    {           termination condition for an unsuccessful search.  }
    { Return:   If Target is in the middle index, then the DataRec }
    {           associated with Target is returned in InfoWanted and }
    {           Found is set to true.  If recursive termination    }
    {           condition for an unsuccessful search is met, then  }
    {           Found is false.  Otherwise recur to next level with }
    {           smaller index range.                               }

    VAR
      Mid : integer;

    BEGIN
      IF High < Low THEN     { Recursive termination when not found }
        Found := false
      ELSE
        BEGIN
          Mid := (Low + High) DIV 2;
          IF SearchList[Mid].Key = Target THEN { Recursive termination when found }
            BEGIN
              InfoWanted := SearchList[Mid];
              Found := true
            END
```

```
        ELSE IF Target < SearchList[Mid].Key THEN { Work with lower subrange }
          BinarySearchAux (Low, Mid - 1)
          ELSE                              { Work with higher subrange }
          BinarySearchAux (Mid + 1, High)
        END
  END;    { of PROCEDURE BinarySearchAux }

  BEGIN
    BinarySearchAux (1, N)
  END; {  of PROCEDURE BinarySearch  }
```

Efficiency Analysis of the Recursive Binary Search As we did for the Towers of Hanoi problem, we will use a run-time trace diagram of potential recursive calls to analyze the efficiency of the recursive implementation of the binary search algorithm. This diagram appears in Figure 17.12. For the specific case of an array with 15 data items, the run-time trace stops at level 3, as indicated in Figure 17.13. The **OR**s that appear in these two figures are

FIGURE 17.12
Run-time trace diagram of potential calls for recursive binary search algorithm

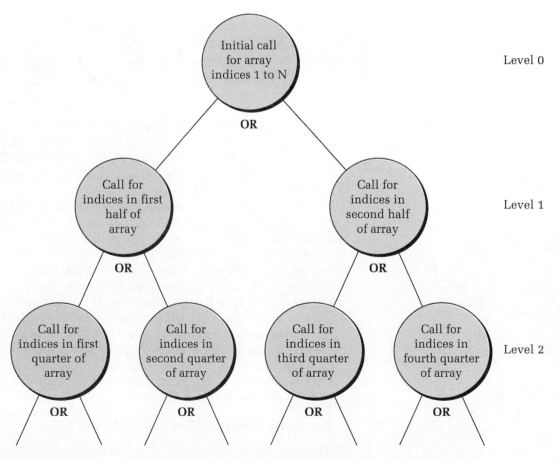

And so forth for eighths, sixteenths . . .

FIGURE 17.13
Trace of Figure 17.12 for specific case of array with 15 data items

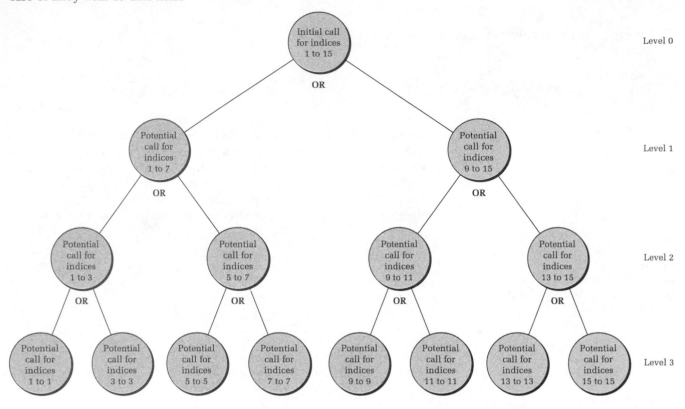

indicative of the fact that, at any given level, we will make, at most, one recursive call or the other, but not both. This is important and, as we have seen, different from the **AND** pattern of recursive calls in the Hanoi problem. It implies that the work done at any given level is simply the work done at one node along that level.

In the binary search, the work done at any node is $O(1)$ since we are merely comparing the Target item to the data at the Mid position. Hence the time efficiency of the recursive version of this algorithm will merely be proportional to the number of levels in the run-time trace for an array with N items. In Figures 17.12 and 17.13, we can see that doubling the number of items in the array will merely add one level to the run-time trace diagram. That is, the number of levels in the diagram is $\log_2 N + 1$ (truncated). With the $O(1)$ work done at each level, we can thus conclude that the time efficiency of a recursive binary search is $O(\log_2 N)$. Similarly, since a stack frame will be allocated for each recursive level, the additional space requirements of the algorithm (beyond the array itself) are $O(\log_2 N)$. Note that our earlier nonrecursive implementation of the binary search algorithm did not carry with it this additional cost in space efficiency.

Recursive Computation of "N Choose K"

The preceding discussion of the binary search algorithm has honed our ability to use the run-time trace diagram to measure the efficiency of a recursive algorithm. It did not, however, represent a solution to a problem that would be difficult to conceptualize without recursion. We close this section with an example in the latter category.

The phrase "N choose K" is often used in the combinatorics branch of mathematics to refer to the number of ways that we could choose K objects from among N different objects. For instance, "52 choose 13" represents the number of ways that you could be dealt a bridge hand (that is, 13 cards out of 52). In contrast to your solution to a similar problem in Chapter 5 (Programming Problem 45), we now seek a recursive function to compute N choose K for arbitrary N and K, K ⩽ N.

Our principle of recursive problem solving asks us to consider how we could use a solution to a simpler version of the same problem. For N choose K, a simpler version of the same problem could mean a solution for a smaller value of N or K. Let us designate our N objects as object #1, object #2, . . . , object #(N - 1), object #N. Figure 20.14 indicates that we can partition

Any selection of K − 1 objects from among these N − 1 generates a selection of K objects by adding Object #N to the K − 1 selected

Object #1	Object #2	Object #3	. . .	Object #(N − 2)	Object #(N − 1)	Object #N

Any selection of K objects from among these N − 1 objects is also a selection of K objects from among Object #1 . . . Object #N.

selections of K objects from these N as those groups of K objects that come strictly from objects 1, 2, . . . , N - 1 and those groups of K objects that include object #N in addition to K - 1 chosen among objects 1, 2, . . . , N - 1. In other words,

$$\text{Choose } (N, K) = \text{Choose } (N-1, K) + \text{Choose } (N-1, K-1)$$

Ways of selecting K objects from among the first N − 1

Ways of selecting K − 1 objects from among the first N − 1 and then including object #N

The preceding equation appears to be the recursive key we need to write our function. We need only develop recursive termination conditions to complete the puzzle. Note from the preceding equation that one of the terms being summed, Choose (N − 1, K), will recursively reduce N until it eventually equals K. But, in such a case, we are merely asking for the number of combinations of N objects selected N at a time—and there is trivially only one such combination. Hence, our first recursive termination condition is when N = K, for which we immediately return the value 1.

To develop the second recursive termination condition, we examine the second term, Choose (N − 1, K − 1), in the sum. Since both N and K will be reduced by this recursion, K will eventually reach 0. But the number of ways of choosing 0 objects from among N is again trivially 1. Consequently, the second recursive termination condition is when K = 0; this condition flags the immediate return of the value of 1.

■ **EXAMPLE 17.7**

Implement a recursive N choose K function based on the preceding discussion.

```
FUNCTION Choose (N, K : integer) : integer;

  {  Given:    N, the number of objects we are selecting from    }
  {            K, the number of objects being selected           }
  {  Task:     Compute N choose K; that is, the number of ways of }
  {            selecting K objects from N                         }
  {  Return:   The computed value of N choose K                   }

  BEGIN
    IF K = 0 THEN              { recursive termination condition  }
      Choose := 1
    ELSE IF N = K THEN         { recursive termination condition  }
      Choose := 1
    ELSE
      Choose := Choose (N - 1, K) + Choose (N - 1, K - 1)
  END;  { of FUNCTION Choose  }
```

■

■ **EXAMPLE 17.8**

FIGURE 17.15
Run-time trace diagram for
Choose (4, 2)

Trace the Choose (N, K) function by developing the run-time trace diagram for Choose (4, 2).

This diagram is provided in Figure 17.15. The numbers next to the circles indicate the order in which calls are made.

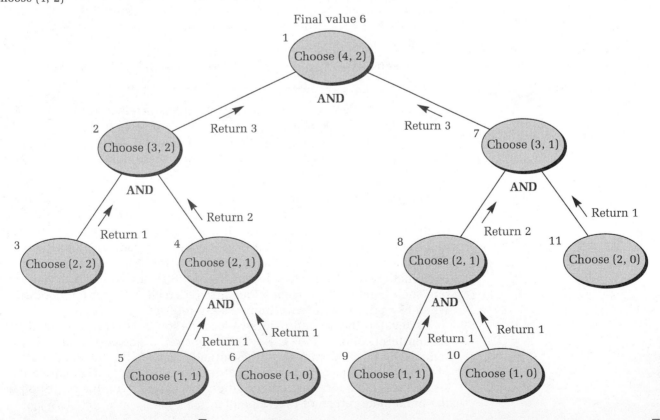

■

Exercises 17.2

1. Trace the stack frames that are pushed and popped from the system stack as the Towers of Hanoi algorithm executes for N = 4 disks.

2. Is the recursive binary search algorithm presented in this section tail-recursive? Provide a written rationale for your response.

3. Construct run-time trace diagrams in the style of Example 17.8 for a variety of values of N and K in the **FUNCTION** Choose (N, K). Judging from the run-time trace diagrams you construct, make conjectures about the time and space efficiency of this algorithm. Support these conjectures in a written statement.

4. Consider the following version of the **PROCEDURE** BinarySearchAux from Example 17.6 to which a tracer **writeln** statement has been added. What output would be produced from this tracer **writeln** if we were to call on **PROCEDURE** BinarySearch from Example 17.6 with a SearchList of 16 integers containing the key values

    12 34 67 89 113 125 169 180 191 201 225 237 256 270 299 304

    and a Target of 191?

```
PROCEDURE BinarySearchAux (Low, High : integer);

   {  Given:   Low and High--array indices in SearchList between      }
   {           which Target may still be found.                        }
   {  Task:    Check if Target is in the middle index between Low      }
   {           and High (or if Low and High meet the recursive         }
   {           termination condition)                                  }
   {  Return:  If Target is in the middle index, then DataRec          }
   {           associated with Target is in InfoWanted and Found       }
   {           is true.  If recursive termination condition is met     }
   {           then Found is false.  Otherwise recur to next level     }
   {           with smaller index range.                               }

VAR
   Mid : integer;

BEGIN
   writeln (Low, High);   { <-- Note the output added here        }
   IF High < Low THEN     { Recursive termination when not found }
     Found := false
   ELSE
     BEGIN
       Mid := (Low + High) DIV 2;
       IF SearchList[Mid].Key = Target THEN { Recursive termination when found }
         BEGIN
           InfoWanted := SearchList[Mid];
           Found := true
         END
       ELSE IF Target < SearchList[Mid].Key THEN  { Work with lower subrange }
         BinarySearchAux (Low, Mid - 1)
       ELSE                                        { Work with higher subrange }
         BinarySearchAux (Mid + 1, High)
     END
END;   { of PROCEDURE BinarySearchAux }
```

5. Repeat Exercise 4 but this time with a Target value of 6.

6. We have chosen not to include SearchList as a formal value parameter to the **PROCEDURE** BinarySearchAux in Example 17.6. Analyze what would be the cost in space and time efficiency if SearchList were to be included as a value parameter to this procedure.

7. Consider the following recursive function and associated top-level call. Comments of the form {   Return Point N   } label possible return points from recursive calls. What would a stack frame for this function contain? Show by a series of stack "snapshots" how the stack would be manipulated for the calls indicated. Finally, provide the output that would be produced by these calls.

```
PROGRAM Mystery (input, output);

  FUNCTION Weird (M, N: integer) : integer;

    BEGIN
      writeln (M, N);
      IF M = 0 THEN
        Weird := N + 1
      ELSE IF N = 0 THEN
        Weird := Weird(M - 1, 1)
                  {   Return Point 2   }
      ELSE
        Weird := Weird(M - 1,              Weird(M, N - 1))
                  {   Return Point 4   } {   Return Point 3   }
    END; { Weird }

BEGIN
  writeln (Weird(1, 3))
                {   Return Point 1   }
END.
```

8. **PROCEDURE** Hanoi developed in this section specified the sequence of disk moves that would have to be performed to complete the Towers of Hanoi problem for N disks. Now write a recursive function that computes the exact number of disk moves needed to solve the Towers of Hanoi problem for N disks. (*Hint:* Express the number of individual moves necessary to transfer N disks in terms of the number of moves necessary to transfer N − 1 disks.)

9. Write a recursive procedure to determine the minimum entry in an array of N integers.

10. Write a recursive implementation of the insertion sort algorithm.

11. Suppose we have an amount of money M that is divisible evenly by 10 cents. Write a recursive function that computes the number of ways that M can be broken down into half dollars, quarters, and dimes.

12. In essay form, discuss some of the trade-offs in terms of time and space efficiency that are made when recursion is used.

13. Both a modular structure chart and a run-time trace diagram reflect a hierarchical pattern of how procedures are called in a program. In a carefully written statement, explain the differences between these two diagrammatic techniques.

■ ■ ■ ■

■ 17.3
Recursion, Trial-and-Error Backtracking, and Generalized Nested Loops

OBJECTIVES

- to use recursion in implementing a search strategy called trial-and-error backtracking
- to realize that trial-and-error backtracking requires that loops be nested to arbitrarily deep levels
- to be able to construct a run-time trace diagram for a program that uses trial-and-error backtracking to search for solutions
- to understand what a permutation is
- to be able to use trial-and-error backtracking to develop a program that produces permutations of a size not determined until run-time
- to see how trial-and-error backtracking, as studied in the context of the permutation problem, represents a strategy that can be generalized to solve a wide variety of problems

In the previous section, we have seen examples of recursive algorithms in which the number of recursive calls at each recursive level is (potentially) more than one. In this section we shall consider what happens when the number of recursive calls made on any given level is under the control of an iterative control structure such as a **FOR, WHILE,** or **REPEAT** loop.

As an example of the class of problems we will study in this section, consider the notion of a permutation.

Permutation. A permutation of the integers 1, 2, . . . , N is an ordered arrangement of these integers in which each integer appears exactly once.

For instance, two possible permutations of the integers 1, 2, 3, 4 are

```
3   2   1   4
2   4   3   1
```

The Permutation Problem

We now pose the following problem: For input of N, devise a program that outputs all permutations of the integers 1, 2, . . . , N.

■ EXAMPLE 17.9

The following program solves this problem, but only for the special case where N = 4.

```
PROGRAM LimitedPermutations (input, output);

  {  Produce all permutations of 1, 2, 3, 4  }

  VAR K1, K2, K3, K4 : integer;

BEGIN
  FOR K1 := 1 TO 4 DO
    FOR K2 := 1 TO 4 DO
      IF K2 <> K1 THEN
        FOR K3 := 1 TO 4 DO
          IF (K3 <> K2) AND (K3 <> K1) THEN
            FOR K4 := 1 TO 4 DO
              IF (K4 <> K3) AND (K4 <> K2) AND (K4 <> K1) THEN
                writeln (K1:2, K2:2, K3:2, K4:2)
END.
```

The strategy of this program is to use a **FOR** loop to control a variable which runs through the four possibilities for each of the four permutation positions. Hence four loops emerge, nested within each other. When an inner loop generates a number that matches one at a previously generated position, the **IF** statement is used to reject that number.

∎   ∎

The program in Example 17.9 constitutes a simple and straightforward approach to the permutation problem. But it falls far short of solving the general problem as originally posed because it works only for the number 4, not for a general N to be input when the program runs. Note that the requirement that N be entered at run-time is what causes the major complication. Certainly, the strategy of using nested loops would allow us to write one program that works for $N = 2$, another that works for $N = 3$, another for $N = 4$, and so on. However, in addition to having a ridiculous number of nested **FOR** loops for reasonably large N, the decision as to which permutations to generate would instead be made at the time the appropriate program is compiled and not when it runs. Computer scientists typically call this a *binding time problem*. Here we would prefer to bind a value to N when our program runs instead of when it compiles. Clearly, the later the binding time, the more versatile the program. To do this, we need some means of simulating arbitrarily deep nested loops when the program runs.

To see how we can use recursion to achieve such a simulation, consider the diagram of permutation possibilities in Figure 17.16. This diagram bears a resemblance to what we called a run-time trace of recursive calls in the preceding section. Interpret the diagram by viewing any given path from the node labeled Start down to the base level of the diagram as a potential candidate for a permutation of $1, 2, \ldots, N$. As we progress from one level to the next along a path, we encounter the next digit in this potential permutation.

FIGURE 17.16
Candidates for permutations

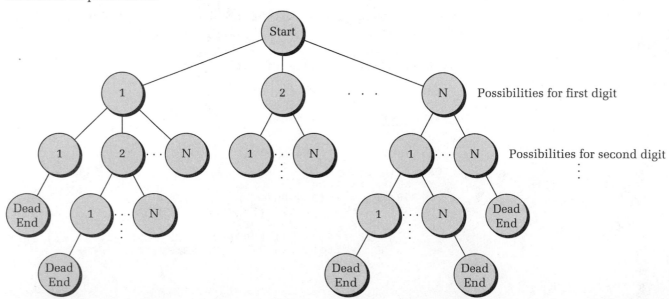

Conceptually we must use recursion to generate all the paths that appear in the figure. As soon as we generate a path with two equal numbers on it, we abandon that dead-end path and backtrack one level to continue the path along a potentially more fruitful route. If we ever complete one entire permutation along a path, we will output it, backtrack a level, and continue looking for more permutations that share the beginning of this path. At a given point in our search for a permutation, we need only store the current path. For this, a simple global array will do. Thus, the array CurrentPermutation of Figure 17.17 will store in its Jth subscript the number in the Jth position of the permutation currently being generated. The limiting factor on the size of permutations generated by our program will be the dimension of this array.

FIGURE 17.17
Current exploration of permutations beginning with 2 1 4

CurrentPermutation						MaxPermutation
1	2	3	4	5	. . .	Size
2	1	4	Undefined	Undefined	. . .	Undefined

A complete program to solve our permutation problem follows. The heart of the program is the recursive procedure Try. Try receives three parameters.

Parameter	Explanation
N	The number of numbers to be permuted in the current run.
Level	The level in the tree of Figure 20.16; that is, the position in CurrentPermutation at which Try is to attempt placement of a new value.
Possibility	The new value to be placed at this Level.

Try initially calls on a procedure AddToCurrentPath to actually place Possibility at the appropriate Level. Once this placement is made, there are three states in which the CurrentPermutation array could be.

1. The placement of the value Possibility at the designated Level could have completed a successful permutation. In this case, call on a procedure to print out the permutation and then remove Possibility from CurrentPermutation at the given Level so that we may continue seeking additional permutations.

2. The placement of the value Possibility at the designated Level did not complete a permutation but does represent a valid beginning of length Level for a potential permutation. For instance, this case would occur if *N,* Level, and Possibility were 6, 4, and 5 respectively and we called Try with CurrentPermutation as pictured in Figure 17.17. The CurrentPermutation array would be extended to contain 2 1 4 5. Here what we must do is to test the possible candidates for a value at the next position; that is, at depth (Level + 1). This is done by an iterative series of recursive calls to Try, passing a variety of values for Possibility at (Level + 1). This iterative series of recursive calls is what achieves the desired simulation of nested looping. After all of these deeper-level possibilities (that is, those below the beginning of the current permutation in Figure 17.16) have been ex-

plored, we return and can remove Possibility from CurrentPermutation at position Level since (recursively) all permutations with this beginning arrangement will have been generated.

3. The placement of the value Possibility at Level destroys the viability of the current path by adding a number that appeared earlier in the permutation. For instance, calling on Try with N = 6, Level = 4, and Possibility = 1 would cause an invalid path for the state of CurrentPermutation given in Figure 17.17. In this case we do nothing but retract from the placement of this invalid Possibility before attempting to place other possible values.

You should carefully study how these three potential cases are handled in our recursive procedure Try in the program VersatilePermutations. The modular structure chart presented in Figure 17.18 indicates how Try invokes

FIGURE 17.18
Modular structure chart for
PROGRAM VersatilePermutations

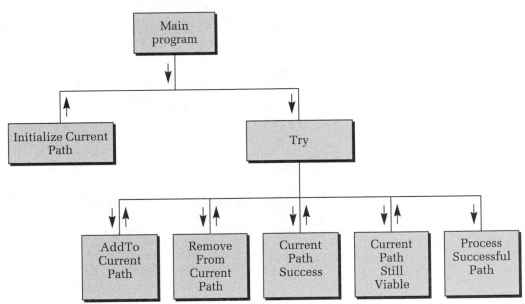

other procedures and functions. In the Focus on Program Design section, we adapt the technique illustrated here to a broader class of problems.

```
PROGRAM VersatilePermutations (input, output);

  {  Use recursion to find all permutations of 1,2, ..., N.  }

  CONST
    MaxPermutationSize = 100;
    Undefined = MaxInt;

  VAR
    N, K : integer;
    CurrentPermutation : ARRAY [1..MaxPermutationSize] OF integer;
```

```
PROCEDURE InitializeCurrentPath;

  {  Given:    CurrentPermutation array in unreliable      }
  {            state.                                       }
  {  Task:     Initialize all indices in                   }
  {            CurrentPermutation array to Undefined flag.  }
  {  Return:   Initialized array.                           }

  VAR
    K : integer;

  BEGIN
    FOR K := 1 TO MaxPermutationSize DO
      CurrentPermutation[K] := Undefined
  END; { of PROCEDURE InitializeCurrentPath  }

PROCEDURE Try (N, Level, Possibility : integer);

  {  Given:    N, the number of numbers we are trying to     }
  {            permute.  Level, the current depth of the      }
  {            solution path as portrayed in Figure 17.16.    }
  {            Possibility, the number we wish to             }
  {            place at that level.                           }
  {  Task:     After locating Possibility at specified        }
  {            Level, check if we have a permutation.  If     }
  {            so, print it.  If not, check whether or not    }
  {            a permutation is still possible for this       }
  {            placement of Possibility.  If so, attempt      }
  {            placement at deeper Level by recursive call.   }
  {  Return:   Relative to this Level, CurrentPermutation     }
  {            array is returned unaltered.  However, if      }
  {            permutation was found, contents of this        }
  {            array are printed.                             }

  VAR
    K : integer;

  PROCEDURE AddToCurrentPath (Level, Possibility : integer);

    {  Given:    Level, the current depth of the solution    }
    {            path.  Possibility, the number to place at   }
    {            that Level.                                  }
    {  Task:     Assign Possibility to this Level.            }
    {  Return:   Suitably altered CurrentPermutation array.   }

    BEGIN
      CurrentPermutation[Level] := Possibility
    END; { of PROCEDURE  AddToCurrentPath }

  PROCEDURE RemoveFromCurrentPath (Level : integer);

    {  Given:    The deepest Level to which solution path     }
    {            has grown.                                    }
    {  Task:     Remove the value at that Level.               }
    {  Return:   Suitably altered CurrentPermutation array.    }

    BEGIN
      CurrentPermutation[Level] := Undefined
    END; { of PROCEDURE RemoveFromCurrentPath }

  FUNCTION CurrentPathSuccess (N, Level : integer) : boolean;
```

```
{  Given:    CurrentPermutation array.  Level, the depth    }
{            to which solution path has grown.  N, the      }
{            number of numbers we are trying to permute.     }
{  Task:     Check if contents of CurrentPermutation array   }
{            through index Level constitute a complete        }
{            permutation of the first N numbers.             }
{  Return:   True if permutation, false otherwise.          }

VAR
  Success : boolean;
  K : integer;

BEGIN
  Success := true;
  IF N > Level THEN   {  Level must be N for successful permutation  }
    Success := false
  ELSE  {  Are all entries different from that at index Level?  }
    BEGIN
      K := 1;
      WHILE (K <= (Level - 1)) AND Success DO
        BEGIN
          Success := (CurrentPermutation[K] <> CurrentPermutation[Level]);
          K := K + 1
        END
    END;
  CurrentPathSuccess := Success
END; {  of FUNCTION CurrentPathSuccess  }

FUNCTION CurrentPathStillViable (Level : integer) : boolean;

{  Given:    CurrentPermutation array.  Level, the          }
{            depth to which solution path has grown.        }
{            N, the number of numbers we are trying to       }
{            permute.                                        }
{  Task:     Check if contents of CurrentPermutation        }
{            array through index Level constitute a          }
{            viable beginning for permutation of the         }
{            first N numbers.                                }
{  Return:   True if viable, false otherwise.               }

VAR
  Viable : boolean;
  K : integer;

BEGIN
  Viable := true;
  K := 1;
  WHILE (K <= (Level - 1)) AND Viable DO
    BEGIN
      Viable := (CurrentPermutation[K] <> CurrentPermutation[Level]);
      K := K + 1
    END;
  CurrentPathStillViable := Viable
END; {  of FUNCTION CurrentPathStillViable  }

PROCEDURE ProcessSuccessfulPath (N : integer);

{  Given:    CurrentPermutation array and N, the number     }
{            we are trying to permute.                       }
{  Task:     Write out first N indices of                    }
{            CurrentPermutation.                             }
{  Return:   Nothing.                                        }
```

```
      VAR
        K : integer;

      BEGIN
        FOR K := 1 TO N DO
          write (CurrentPermutation[K]:3);
        writeln
      END; {  of PROCEDURE ProcessSuccessfulPath  }

   BEGIN {  Try  }
     AddToCurrentPath (Level, Possibility);
     IF CurrentPathSuccess (N, Level) THEN
       ProcessSuccessfulPath (N)
     ELSE IF CurrentPathStillViable (Level) THEN
       FOR K := 1 TO N DO
         Try (N, Level + 1, K);
     RemoveFromCurrentPath (Level)
   END; {  of PROCEDURE Try  }

BEGIN {  Main program  }
  InitializeCurrentPath;
  write ('Permutation of integers from 1 to ? ');
  readln (N);
  FOR K := 1 TO N DO
    Try (N, 1, K)
END.
```

You may have noticed that certain efficiency considerations have not been taken into account in writing the previous program. For example, the initialization of the CurrentPermutation array actually is unnecessary in this particular implementation. Also, the call to RemoveFromCurrentPath could have been eliminated since the Undefined flag that this procedure assigns is quickly replaced without ever being explicitly used. Finally, additional global data could be used to keep track of information that would eliminate the necessity of using loops in the CurrentPathSuccess and CurrentPathStillViable procedures. You will be asked to rewrite the program taking these economies into account in the Exercises.

Our purpose in this section has not been to present the most compact version of a permutations program, but rather to illustrate how recursion can be used to simulate *generalized nested loops* whose nesting depth can be established at run-time. Such generalized nested loops can then be used in situations where trial-and-error backtracking is an appropriate strategy in searching for a problem's solution. In this context, we have intended the permutations program to be illustrative of a general problem-solving approach rather than a solution to a particular problem.

Consider what we must abstract from the permutations program to view it as a general template for trial-and-error backtracking instead of a mere permutation printer. Figure 17.16 presents the problem of finding permutations as a problem in finding certain types of paths through a maze. We probe deeper and deeper along a given path (that is, add new numbers to the current permutation) until we reach a predefined goal or reach a dead end. As we take a new step along the current path, we must analyze the state in which it has placed us.

1. Have we reached a goal state?
2. Have we reached a state that, though not itself a goal, is still a viable start toward that goal?
3. Have we reached a dead end?

For each of the three cases we take appropriate action such as

1. Processing a goal state; for example, printing it out, tallying a counter, or setting a flag signaling that we are done.
2. Probing further along a viable path by recursively taking another step.
3. No action in the case of a dead end.

After taking the appropriate action, we then retract from the step that led us to the current state, possibly returning to a higher recursive level where we may find ourselves in the midst of a similar three-state analysis. The essence of this trial-and-error backtracking logic is illustrated in Figure 17.19. Upon reaching a dead end for path A, you must retrace steps 9 → 8 → 7 → 6 → 5 before you can try new path B. The retracing of states that have been visited previously is conveniently done by unwinding from recursive calls.

FIGURE 17.19
Backtracking problem illustrated by maze solution

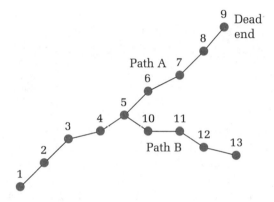

In this chapter's Focus on Program Design section and the Programming Problems, you will see how this type of logic can be used to solve a wide variety of problems.

Exercises 17.3

1. Consider the VersatilePermutations program discussed in Section 17.3. Suppose that $N = 3$ in a particular run of this program and that we printed out the contents of the CurrentPermutation array each time the Try procedure was invoked in this run. How many times would the array be printed? What would be the overall output?

2. Suppose you used the permutations procedure of this section to compute all permutations of 1, 2, 3, and 4. What would the complete run-time trace diagram of recursive procedure calls look like for such a run? Can you generalize from this diagram of procedure calls the efficiency of the permutations procedure? State your answer in big-O terms with respect to both stack size and number of stack operations. Provide justification for your answer in a written statement.

3. Rewrite **PROGRAM** VersatilePermutations in a fashion that takes into account the efficiency considerations discussed in Section 17.3. These considerations are discussed in the paragraph that follows the program.

4. What is the output from the following program?

```
PROGRAM X(output);

   PROCEDURE Y(A, B, C: integer);
      VAR K : integer;
```

```
            BEGIN
              IF B <= C THEN
                BEGIN
                  writeln(A);
                  FOR K := B TO C DO
                    Y(K, B + 1, C)
                END
            END;

          BEGIN
            Y(16,1,4)
          END.
```

5. What is the output from the following program?

```
   PROGRAM Easy(output);

     PROCEDURE Tough(B, C, D: integer);
       VAR K : integer;
       BEGIN
         IF B <= C THEN
           BEGIN
             writeln(D);
             FOR K := B TO C DO
               Tough(B + 1, C, K)
           END
       END;

     BEGIN
       Tough(1,4,12)
     END.
```

6. A car's odometer may be viewed as a physical implementation of a nested loop. Each loop cycles through the digits 0..9, with the one's digit cycling the fastest, then the ten's digit, and so forth. Write a procedure to simulate an *N*-digit odometer (*N* determined at run-time) by creating a generalized nested loop structure that will run through, in sequence, all possible settings for the odometer.

**FOCUS ON
PROGRAM DESIGN**

We have emphasized throughout this text that computer scientists must work at varying levels of abstraction. With this in mind, consider the program of the last section not merely as a permutation printer but rather as illustrative of a more abstract problem-solving technique. In fact, a careful examination of the **PROCEDURE** Try in **PROGRAM** Versatile Permutations will show that it is nearly independent of the particular problem of searching for permutations. That is, the algorithm behind Try could be used in any analogous search for a solution in which there were *N* additional possibilities at the current level. We shall now indicate the power of this abstract approach to trial-and-error backtracking by sketching a solution to another problem that could be solved with the same methodology. You will then complete the solution in the Programming Problems.

The Eight Queens Problem

Consider what has come to be known as the Eight Queens Problem. This problem has long intrigued chess fanatics. It requires determining the various ways in which eight queens could be configured on a chessboard so that none of them could capture any other queen. (The rules of chess allow a queen to move an arbitrary number of squares in a horizontal, vertical, or diagonal fashion.) Figure 17.20 illustrates one such configuration.

FIGURE 17.20
One successful eight queens configuration

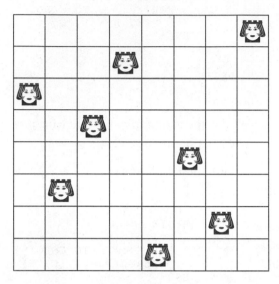

Applying backtracking logic to this problem we could attempt to find a path to a configuration by successively trying to place a queen in each column of a chessboard until we reach a dead end: a column in which the placement of queens in prior columns makes it impossible to place the queen being moved. This situation is pictured in Figure 17.21. Here, the sixth queen cannot be placed due to the placement of the first five queens.

When we reach such a dead end, we must backtrack one column (to column 5 in Figure 17.21), and attempt to find a new placement for the

FIGURE 17.21
Dead end in queen placement

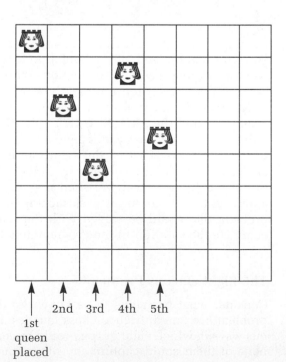

Recursion, LISP, and the Practicality of Artificial Intelligence

Artificial intelligence, the science of implementing on computers the problem-solving methods used by human beings, is one of the most rapidly expanding fields within computer science. Research in this field includes enabling computers to play games of strategy, to understand natural languages, to prove theorems in logic and mathematics, and to mimic the reasoning of human experts in fields such as medical diagnosis. Only recently has artificial intelligence become a commercially viable area of application, capable of solving some real-life problems apart from the idealized setting of a pure research environment. More and more, we are seeing artificial intelligence systems which perform such practical functions as aiding business executives in their decision-making processes and providing a "near-English" user-interface language for data-base management software.

What has sparked the sudden emergence of artificial intelligence? Why wasn't it possible to produce commercially feasible programs in this field until recently? One of the primary answers to these questions is tied to the language in which most artificial intelligence programming is done. This language is called *LISP* (for LISt Processor). Interestingly, the control structures of LISP are based almost entirely on recursion. What a Pascal programmer would view as normal iterative control structures (for example, **WHILE, REPEAT,** and **FOR** loops) appear in various versions of LISP only as infrequently used, nonstandard extensions to the language.

One of the reasons that a recursively based language such as LISP is so ideally suited to this field is that most problem-solving methods in artificial intelligence involve searching for a particular goal state; that is, searching for a path leading to a complete problem solution. This is similar to the approach we have taken in the permutation problem and the Eight Queens Problem in this chapter.

The complexity of problems studied in artificial intelligence leads to run-time trace diagrams of enormous size. Interestingly, LISP has been available as a recursive language ideally suited to such problems for a long time. It is one of the oldest high-level programming languages, having been first developed by John McCarthy in the late 1950s.

Researchers who work in artificial intelligence have realized since LISP's introduction that its ability to recursively process general data structures was, on a theoretical basis, exactly what they needed. The problem through the years has been that, because of the very high overhead associated with recursion (and some other features built into LISP), computer hardware has not been fast enough to run LISP programs in practical applications. Thus, researchers were restricted not by LISP itself but rather by the ability of computer hardware to execute LISP programs in reasonable times. One of the major reasons for the recent emergence of artificial intelligence has been the increase in speed of computing hardware and the decrease in cost of this same hardware. This has made it possible for users to have dedicated computer resources capable of meeting the demands of LISP's recursive style. As hardware continues to improve, so will applications in LISP and artificial intelligence become increasingly sophisticated.

If you are curious about LISP and the important role that it plays at some of the frontiers of research in programming languages, consult the September 1991 issue of the *Communications of the ACM* (vol. 34, no. 9). This entire issue was devoted to LISP and described its ability to adapt to many computing environments.

queen in that column. If placement in the previous column is impossible, we must backtrack yet another column to attempt the new placement. This backtracking through previous columns continues until we finally are able to reposition a queen. At that point, we can begin a new path by again attempting to position queens on a column-by-column basis until another dead end is reached or until a fully successful configuration is developed.

The key to a program that finds all possible configurations for the eight queens is a procedure that attempts to place a queen in a given square and, if successful, recursively calls itself to attempt the placement of another queen in the next column. Such a procedure in skeletal pseudocode form follows:

PROCEDURE TryQueen (K, J)

```
{     Place a queen in row K, column J. Analyze          }
{     state reached by this placement. If appropriate,   }
{     recurse to place queen in next column.             }
```

1. Actually put queen at position K, J
2. **IF** this results in successful configuration **THEN**
     Tally this configuration
   ELSE IF no queen in immediate danger **THEN**
     FOR L := 1 to 8 **DO**
       TryQueen(L, J + 1)
3. Retract from position K, J

END { of **PROCEDURE** TryQueen }

The similarities between this sketch of a solution to the Eight Queens Problem and our complete solution to the permutation problem should convince you that, from an abstract perspective, both problems are really the same. We have intentionally left the Eight Queens Problem unfinished. Still to be resolved are such issues as:

- The initial call(s) to TryQueen.
- How to represent the chessboard.
- How to check whether placing a queen at position K, J puts it in immediate danger. That is, how to determine whether there is currently another queen sharing the same row, column, or diagonal.

The resolution of these issues is left for your enjoyment in the Programming Problems at the end of the chapter. Additional problems given there further illustrate the far-reaching applicability of the trial-and-error backtracking method.

RUNNING AND DEBUGGING TIPS

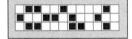

1. Recursion is an elegant and powerful tool. It combines iterative control with a built-in data structure, the system stack. To properly control that iteration, be sure that you provide an appropriate recursive termination condition for your algorithms.

2. Be sure that, when you invoke a procedure recursively, you are in some sense passing in a smaller, simpler version of the problem being solved. Otherwise, your algorithm will infinitely recur.

3. The use of tracer output can be valuable in debugging recursive algorithms. However, you must be careful not to insert so many tracer **write** statements that you become lost in the copious output they produce. Remember that recursive algorithms are often exponential in efficiency and, consequently, may be exponential in the amount of output produced by tracers also. You must be careful to insert tracer **write** statements judiciously. Where appropriate, use a Boolean constant that can be toggled to **true** or **false** to control whether or not the tracer output is produced.

■ Summary

Key Terms

binding time problem	recursive definition	stack frame
generalized nested loops	recursive procedure	tail-recursion
LISP	recursive termination	termination condition
recursive call	condition	trial-and-error
	run-time trace diagram	backtracking

Key Concepts

- Stacks process procedure calls when a program executes. Understanding the role of the stack in this application is essential to effectively using the programming technique known as recursion.

- A recursive procedure or function invokes itself with a simpler version of the same problem it was originally given. Ultimately there must be a recursive termination condition to break a series of recursive procedure calls.
- In tail-recursion, no further processing occurs at any level of recursion after a return from a recursive call is made.
- A procedure's stack frame contains memory locations for all parameters and local variables and the machine address of the point to return to after the procedure completes execution at the current level.
- A run-time trace diagram can often be used to help analyze the efficiency of a recursive algorithm. If the diagram indicates that multiple recursive calls are made at each level, there is a good chance that the algorithm is in the class of exponential algorithms.
- Recursion can be used to solve a complex class of search problems by using a trial-and-error backtracking strategy. However, often such solutions can consume a tremendous amount of resources, particularly in terms of run-time efficiency.
- Do not be misled into thinking that recursion is necessarily the most efficient programming technique because the code that expresses it is often compact and lacking in any explicit loop control statements such as **WHILE** or **REPEAT.** The very nature of a recursive call generates iteration without any need for **WHILE** or **REPEAT.** The iteration control mechanism in recursion is the recursive termination condition which triggers a series of returns before another recursive call is made. Hence, from a time-efficiency perspective, a recursive algorithm's measure of effectiveness is closely tied to the number of times it must iterate its recursive call-and-return pattern. Moreover, with recursion, we pay a price in memory efficiency that is not present in other iterative control structures. This price is system stack space.
- The value of recursion lies in the way in which it enables us to express algorithms compactly and elegantly for a certain class of problems. Since we use recursion frequently throughout the rest of this text, you will learn to acquire a feel for the type of problems particularly suitable to this powerful technique. In the next chapter, we will see that recursion is an indispensable strategy for manipulating a data structure known as a tree. In later chapters, recursion will be explored as a means of sorting and searching.

■ Programming Problems and Projects

1. Write a program to call for input of a decimal number and convert it to its binary equivalent using the method described in the following flowchart.

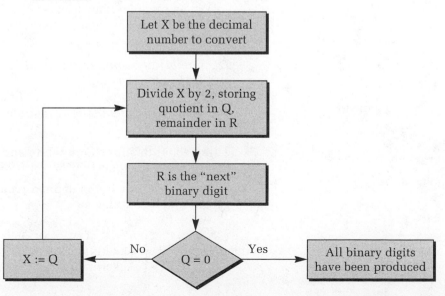

Note that this method produces the binary digits for the given number in reverse order. One strategy for printing out the digits in the correct order would be to store them in an array as they are produced and then print out the array. However, this strategy would have the drawbacks of allocating unnecessary storage for an array and then limiting the size of the binary number to the size of the array. Your program is not to employ this strategy. Rather call for input of the decimal number in your main program and then immediately transfer control to a procedure that in turn is called recursively, stacking the binary digits as they are produced. Once division by 2 yields 0, the succession of returns can be used to print out the digits one by one as they are popped from this stack.

2. The Nth Fibonacci number is defined by

1 if N is 1.
1 if N is 2.
The sum of the previous two Fibonacci numbers otherwise.

Write a recursive function to compute the Nth Fibonacci number. Then, using a run-time trace diagram, analyze the efficiency of your function.

3. Euclid devised a clever algorithm for computing the greatest common divisor of two integers. According to Euclid's algorithm,

$$GCD(M,N) = \begin{cases} GCD(N,M) \text{ if } N > M \\ M \text{ if } N = 0 \\ GCD(N,M \text{ MOD } N) \text{ if } N > 0 \end{cases}$$

Write a recursive procedure to compute greatest common divisors via Euclid's method.

4. Suppose that you have N thousand dollars and can use it to buy a combination of Orange computers (which cost $1,000 each), HAL computers (which cost $2,000 each), or MAX computers (which cost $4,000 each). How many different combinations of Orange, HAL, MAX computers could be bought with your N thousand dollars?

   Write a program that receives N as input and responds with the number of possible combinations. *Hint:* If N were 100, then the number of combinations is

The number of combinations totaling $100,000 and involving Orange and HAL computers only
PLUS
The number of combinations totaling $96,000 and involving potentially all three brands

Think about this hint for a while and extend it to a recursive function that answers this question.

5. Ackermann's function is defined recursively for two nonnegative integers m and n as follows:

$$\text{Ackermann } (m,n) = \begin{cases} n + 1 \text{ if } m = 0 \\ \text{Ackermann } (m - 1, 1) \text{ if } n = 0 \\ \text{Ackermann } (m - 1, \text{Ackermann } (m,n - 1)) \text{ otherwise} \end{cases}$$

Write a recursive version of this function. Develop a run-time trace diagram for the function when $m = 2$ and $n = 3$. Attempt to deduce the big-O efficiency of the recursive version with respect to stack size and stack operations. Justify your answer in a written statement.

6. If you have access to an appropriate graphics device, write the procedures Line and RightTurn described in Section 17.1. Then experiment by writing recursive procedures that call on these procedures (and others you may develop) to produce a variety of interesting figures.

7. Write a procedure that receives a set of N integers and then prints all subsets of this set.

8. Write a program that completes the solution of the Eight Queens Problem as sketched in the Focus on Program Design section.

9. A K-permutation of the first N positive integers, $K \leq N$, is a permutation of a K-element subset of $\{ 1, 2, \ldots, N \}$. Write a procedure to generate all possible K-permutations of the first N positive integers.

10. A continued fraction is a number of the form that follows (where each a_i is an integer):

$$a_1 + \cfrac{1}{a_2 + \cfrac{1}{a_3 + \cfrac{1}{a_4 + {\atop \ddots \atop \cfrac{1}{a_n}}}}}$$

Though a continued fraction is composed of integers a_i, it has a real value. For example, consider the following continued fraction and its indicated real value.

$$1 + \cfrac{1}{2 + \cfrac{1}{6 + \cfrac{1}{5}}} = 1 + \cfrac{1}{2 + \cfrac{1}{\frac{31}{5}}} = 1 + \cfrac{1}{2 + \frac{5}{31}} = 1 + \cfrac{1}{\frac{67}{31}} = \frac{98}{67} = 1.46$$

Provide a **TYPE** definition of your implementation of a continued fraction. Then, write a recursive function that receives a continued fraction and returns its associated real value.

11. There are five other teams in the same league as the Bay Area Brawlers (Problem 4, Chapter 15 and Problem 13, Chapter 16). Over a given five-week period, the Brawlers must play each of the other teams exactly once. Using recursion, write a program to determine the ways in which such a five-week schedule could be accomplished. For an added challenge, introduce more realistic scheduling considerations into this problem. For instance, have your program determine the ways in which a fifteen-game schedule could be constructed such that each of the six teams in the league plays each of the other teams exactly three times, but never consecutively.

12. Write a procedure that uses a random number generator to produce mazes. One way of viewing a maze is as a two-dimensional array of records.

```
RECORD
  NorthBlocked,
  EastBlocked,
  SouthBlocked,
  WestBlocked : boolean
END
```

At each square in the array, the Boolean fields are set to indicate whether or not we can proceed in the indicated direction. After your maze-generating procedure is working, develop a procedure that uses trial-and-error backtracking to solve the maze.

13. A transportation network such as the following can be represented as a two-dimensional integer array with rows and columns indexed by the cities in the network. The number stored at position (K, J) of such an array represents the distance of the link between two cities. Zero indicates that two cities are not directly linked.

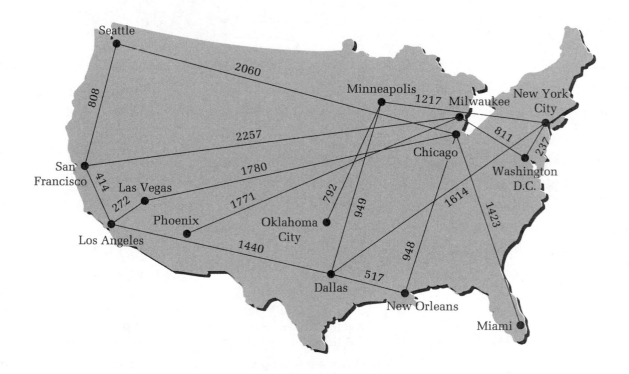

Write a program which, for input of two cities, outputs all possible paths connecting the two cities. Then modify the program so that it outputs only the shortest path linking the two cities. Use a trial-and-error backtracking strategy to do this. We will discuss a more efficient algorithm for solving this problem in the next chapter.

14. Another classic chess problem that can be solved by trial-and-error backtracking is known as the Knight's Tour. Given a chessboard with a knight initially placed at coordinates x_0, y_0, the problem is to specify a series of moves for the knight that will result in each board location being visited exactly once. From a given square on the chessboard, a knight may move to any of the eight numbered squares in the following diagram:

Write a program to find a valid Knight's Tour.

15. A famous theorem in mathematics states that four colors are enough to color any map in a fashion which allows each region on the map to be a different color from any of its adjacent neighbors. Write a program that initially allows input of a map. One way of doing this is to input each region followed by a list of its adjacent neighbors. This information can then be stored in a two-dimensional Boolean array with rows and columns indexed by region names. Store **true** at row K, column J if region K and region J are neighbors; otherwise store **false.** Once your program has appropriately stored the information associated with the input map, it should use trial-and-error backtracking to find a pattern for coloring the map with four colors. Note that the Four-Color Theorem from mathematics guarantees that such a pattern can be found.

16. Write a program to find a solution to the following stable marriage problem (or indicate that no solution exists for the input data). According to this problem, we have n men and n women, each of whom has stated distinct preferences for their possible partners. The data regarding these preferences is the input for this problem. It can be stored in two two-dimensional arrays: one in which each woman has rated each of the men as 1st choice, 2nd choice, . . . , nth choice and another in which each man has similarly rated each of the women. Given this input, a solution to the stable marriage problem is to find n couples (marriages) such that

   1. Each man is part of exactly one couple (marriage).
   2. Each woman is part of exactly one couple (marriage).
   3. There does not exist a man and a woman who are not married to each other but who would prefer each other to their current spouses.

If a pair as specified in requirement 3 does exist, then the assignment of n couples is said to be unstable and should be avoided. Note that the stable marriage problem is representative of many real-life problems in which assignments have to be made according to preferences.

17. Write a program to analyze football team scores by computing the point spread for any team A playing any team B. Your program should compute the point spreads for

Level I Analysis: Team A played B in past
Level II Analysis: Average point spreads for situations such as

> *A played C—point spread 3*
> *C played B—point spread 7*

Total point spread 10

Level III Analysis: Average point spread for situations such as

> *A played C—point spread 3*
> *C played D—point spread − 14 (C lost)*
> *D played B—point spread 7*

Total point spread − 4

Level IV Analysis: Average point spreads for situations such as

> *A played C—point spread 3*
> *C played D—point spread − 14*
> *D played E—point spread 21*
> *E played B—point spread 4*

Total point spread 14

All level II point spreads are then averaged for a final level II point spread figure. Point spreads are similarly averaged for levels III and IV. Items that potentially need to be stacked (via recursion) in this program include

- Accumulated point spread at current position.
- Number of scores reflected in the accumulated point spread at current position.
- Current position; that is, team A playing team B.
- Path to the current position; that is, teams played to get to the current position.

18. Many business phone numbers contain embedded words that correspond to the digits of the phone number and, at the same time, remind customers of the business's product name. For instance, because of the pattern of digits and letters on a phone (pictured below), the phone number for Caswell Catering and Convention Service, 227–9355, may also be interpreted as CASWELL.

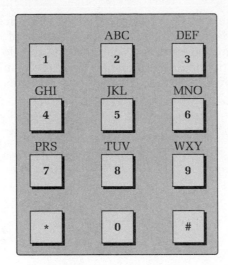

Because businesses often want to know which letter combinations are embedded in their phone number, the phone company would like you to write a procedure based upon the following:

```
TYPE
  PhoneNumber = ARRAY [1..10] OF integer; { used to store phone numbers of up to 10 digits }
  PhoneLetters = ARRAY [2..9] OF ARRAY [1..3] OF char; { used to store the three letters }
                                                       { associated with each dialing    }
                                                       { digit 2..9                       }
PROCEDURE PrintWords (NumDigits : integer;
                      Number    : PhoneNumber);

  { Given:   A phone number of up to 10 digits between 2 and 9 in Number and the actual    }
  {          number of digits in the phone number in NumDigits.                            }
  { Task:    Print out all letter combinations corresponding to this phone number.  Hence  }
  {          if Number were 56 and NumDigits were 2, your output should be the strings     }
  {          JM, JN, JO, KM, KN, KO, LM, LN, and LO. }
  { Assume:  You may assume the existence of a global array Letters of type PhoneLetters    }
  {          that has been initialized to contain 'ABC' in index 2, 'DEF' in index 3, ...,  }
  {          'WXY' in index 9, corresponding to the matchup of three letters per phone     }
  {          digit.                                                                        }
  { Hint:    Remember the generalized nested looping that can be achieved at run-time by    }
  {          recursion.  Also, though it may not be the only way to do it, consider nesting }
  {          another subordinate procedure within PrintWords, with that being the procedure }
  {          that is called recursively. Then incorporate your procedure into a main program }
  {          appropriate for testing it.                                                   }
```

19. Write a solution to the Towers of Hanoi problem in which you use a nonrecursive iterative control structure and a stack. In effect, your stack will simulate the role played by the system stack in the recursive version of the algorithm.

   In a written statement, compare the time and space efficiency of your nonrecursive solution to the recursive solution presented in this chapter. Is your solution faster than the exponential recursive solution? If so, explain why it is. Otherwise, explain why it is still exponential in its run-time.

20. If you have had a course in discrete mathematics, then you may be familiar with recurrence relations and methods for explicitly solving

them. Use your knowledge of recurrence relations to analyze the time and space efficiencies of the Towers of Hanoi and recursive binary search algorithms. Your analysis should be presented as a precise mathematical argument, citing any results that you use but do not prove.

Except during the nine months before he draws his first breath, no man manages his affairs as well as a tree does.

George Bernard Shaw
1856–1950

Binary Trees, General Trees, and Graphs

Human beings organize much of the world around them into *hierarchies*. For instance, an industrial or governmental body functions effectively only by defining a collection of supervisor-subordinate relationships among its participants. We have emphasized throughout the text that computer scientists design a software system by breaking it down into modules and defining hierarchical boss-worker relationships among those modules. In Chapter 17, we used hierarchical run-time trace diagrams to analyze the efficiency of recursive algorithms. To continue this discussion, we now introduce the idea of trees.

The familial parent-child relationship allows a natural breakdown of a family's history into a genealogical tree. In computer science, a *tree* is a data structure that represents such hierarchical relationships between data items.

To introduce some of the terminology of tree structures, consider the record of a student at a typical university. In addition to the usual statistical background information such as social security number, name, and address, a typical student record contains listings for a number of courses, exams and final grades in each course, overall grade point average, and other data relating to the student's performance at the college. Figure 18.1 is a tree structure representing such a student record. As in genealogical trees, at the highest *level* (0) of a tree is its *root* (also called the *root node*). Here STUDENT is the root node. The nodes NAME, ADDRESS, SSN, COURSE, and GPA, which are directly connected to the root node, are the *child nodes* of the *parent node* STUDENT. The child nodes of a given parent constitute a set of *siblings*. Thus NAME, ADDRESS, SSN, COURSE, and GPA are siblings. In the hierarchy represented by a tree, the child nodes of a parent are one level

891

FIGURE 18.1
Tree structure representing a
student record

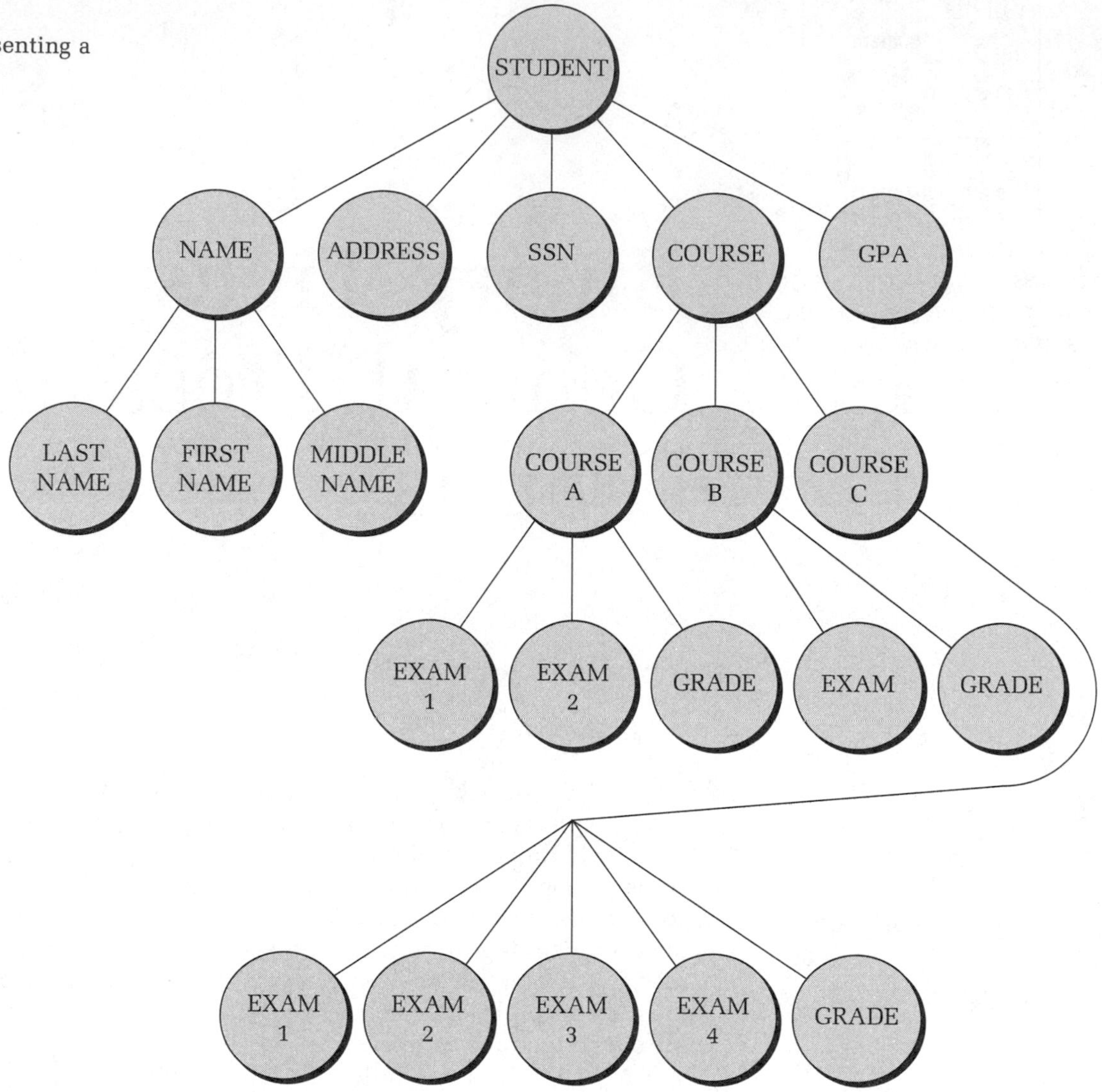

lower than the parent node. Thus NAME, ADDRESS, SSN, COURSE, and GPA are at level 1 in Figure 18.1.

A link between a parent and its child is called a *branch* in a tree structure. Each node in a tree except the root must descend from a parent node via a branch. Thus LASTNAME, FIRSTNAME, and MIDDLENAME descend from the parent node NAME. The root of the tree is the *ancestor* of all the nodes in the tree. Each node may be the parent of any number of nodes in the tree.

A node with no children is called a *leaf node*. In Figure 18.1, GPA is a leaf node. LASTNAME, FIRSTNAME, MIDDLENAME, EXAM1, and EXAM2 also are leaf nodes.

A *subtree* is a subset of a tree that is itself a tree; the tree in Figure 18.2 is a subtree of the tree in Figure 18.1. This subtree has the root node NAME. Similarly, the tree in Figure 18.3 is another subtree of the tree in Figure 18.1. Notice that the tree in Figure 18.3 is a subtree of the tree in Figure 18.1 and the tree in Figure 18.4.

FIGURE 18.2
Subtree of Figure 18.1

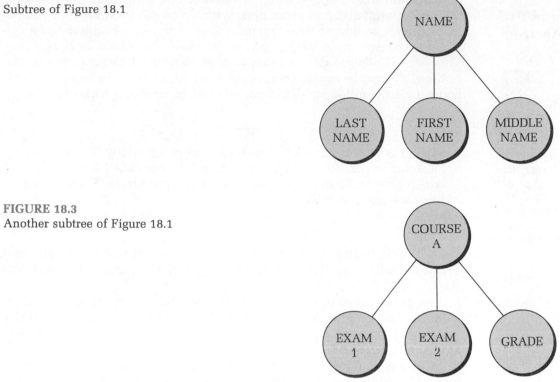

FIGURE 18.3
Another subtree of Figure 18.1

FIGURE 18.4
Another subtree of Figure 18.1

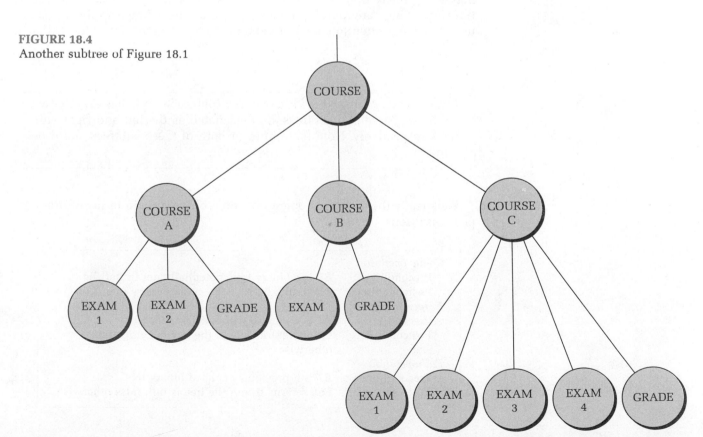

■ 18.1
General Trees and Binary Trees as Abstract Data Types

It is evident from the preceding discussion that a tree has the following interesting property: Any given node within a tree is itself the root node of a completely analogous tree structure. That is, a tree is composed of a collection of substructures, each of which also meets the criteria for being a tree. This sounds dangerously circular, and, to formally describe a tree in this fashion, we must be sure to give ourselves an escape from the recursion. This is done via the following definition of a tree as an abstract data type:

Tree. A *general tree* is a set of nodes that is either empty (the recursive termination condition), or has a designated node called the root from which (hierarchically) descend zero or more subtrees. Each subtree itself satisfies the definition of a tree.

We will defer completing the definition of a general tree to Section 18.5. There we will more formally discuss the operations associated with this ADT.

Two points about this partial definition should be emphasized. First, the recursive fashion in which a tree is defined should provide a strong hint that most tree-processing algorithms will also be recursive. Second, most operations on the tree data structure are closely linked to the hierarchical relationship among nodes for that particular tree. This hierarchical relationship may vary greatly from tree to tree. To consider some examples of such relationships which are found quite often in computer science applications, let us restrict our attention for the moment to an abstract data type called a *binary tree*.

Binary Tree. A binary tree is a tree in which each node has exactly two subtrees. These two subtrees are designated as the left and right subtrees respectively. Note that either or both of these subtrees could be empty.

We specify the following operations on a binary tree in terms of pre- and postconditions.

Create operation
  Preconditions: *BT* is a binary tree, potentially not initialized.
  Postconditions: *BT* is initialized to the empty binary tree.
Empty operation
  Preconditions: *BT* is a previously created binary tree.
  Postconditions: *Empty* returns **true** if the tree is empty, **false** otherwise.
Full operation
  Preconditions: *BT* is a previously created binary tree.
  Postconditions: *Full* returns **true** if the tree is full, **false** otherwise.

AddNode operation
 Preconditions: *BT* is a previously created binary tree based upon a
                     particular hierarchical property. *Item* is a value to
                     be inserted in *BT.*
 Postconditions: If the tree *BT* is full, *Item* is not inserted and *BT* is
                     left unaltered. Otherwise *Item* is added to *BT* in a
                     way which maintains *BT*'s hierarchical property.

PreorderTraversal operation
 Preconditions: *BT* is a previously created binary tree, and
                     ProcessNode is an algorithmic process that can be
                     applied to each node in the tree *BT.*
 Postconditions: Each node of *BT* is visited in the following order:
                     root of *BT* first, then recursively all nodes in left
                     subtree, then recursively all nodes in right subtree.
                     As each node is visited, *ProcessNode* is applied to
                     it.

InorderTraversal operation
 Preconditions: *BT* is a previously created binary tree, and
                     ProcessNode is an algorithmic process that can be
                     applied to each node in the tree *BT.*
 Postconditions: Each node of *BT* is visited in the following order:
                     first visit recursively all nodes in left subtree of *BT,*
                     then visit the root of *BT,* then recursively all nodes
                     in right subtree. As each node is visited,
                     ProcessNode is applied to it.

PostorderTraversal operation
 Preconditions: *BT* is a previously created binary tree, and
                     ProcessNode is an algorithmic process that can be
                     applied to each node in the tree *BT.*
 Postconditions: Each node of *BT* is visited in the following order:
                     first visit recursively all nodes in left subtree of *BT,*
                     then visit recursively all nodes in right subtree,
                     then visit the root of *BT.* As each node is visited,
                     ProcessNode is applied to it.

Several remarks are in order concerning this definition. First, the three
traversal procedures require some clarification. With a linked list, there is
only one obvious traversal because there was only one node that could be
reached from any given node. However, with a binary tree, at any node, there
are some choices to be made.

- Should we apply ProcessNode to the data field of the root before proceeding to the left and right subtrees?
- Should we apply ProcessNode to the nodes in the left subtree and
  right subtree before processing the data in the root?
- Should we apply ProcessNode to all the nodes in one of the subtrees,
  then to the root, and finally to all the nodes in the other subtree?

The answers to these questions determine the type of traversal. Figure 18.5
demonstrates the different orders in which nodes are visited under the three
traversals.

FIGURE 18.5
Differences between preorder,
inorder, and postorder traversals

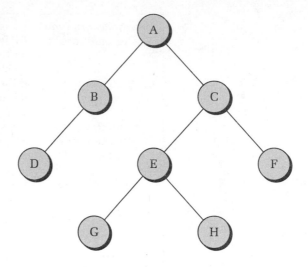

Order in which nodes are processed

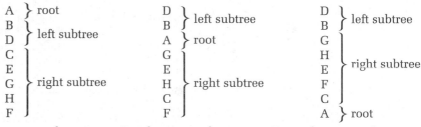

A } root		D } left subtree		D } left subtree
B } D } left subtree		B A } root		B G
C E G } right subtree H F		G E H } right subtree C F		H E } right subtree F C A } root

Preorder traversal   Inorder traversal   Postorder traversal

Second, the AddNode operation specified in our ADT definition for a binary tree provides a generic tree-building operation. That is, repeated applications of the AddNode operation on an initially empty binary tree are typically the way that a binary tree is constructed. However, it is virtually impossible to define or implement the AddNode operation in a way that is general enough for all applications that will use a binary tree. Each instance of a binary tree is highly dependent on the hierarchical relationship between nodes that defines that particular binary tree. Therefore, we have linked our specification of the AddNode operation to the hierarchical relationship underlying a particular binary tree.

The following three examples provide illustrations of hierarchical relationships that can be used in defining binary trees. We will often use trees based on these hierarchical properties as examples in the remainder of the chapter. However, these three properties should by no means be considered exhaustive—virtually every application that uses a binary tree will have its own definitional property. The point to be emphasized now is that the Add-Node operation must, in its implementation, always be tailored to the property that defines a tree.

■ **EXAMPLE 18.1**

The tree of Figure 18.6 is a binary tree. Each node of this tree has two subtrees (null or non-null) designated as the left subtree and the right subtree. The particular hierarchical relationship underlying this tree is that the data in any given node of the tree are greater than or equal to the data in its

FIGURE 18.6
Binary tree with the heap
property

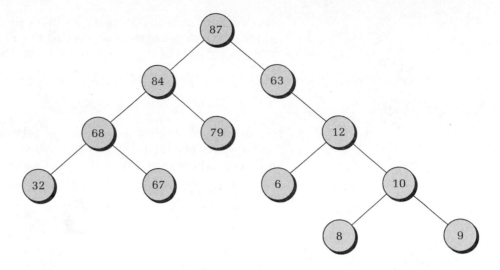

left *and* right subtrees. A tree with this property is said to be a *heap* and to
have the *heap property*. (This notion is not to be confused with the heap
maintained by Pascal for allocating space to pointer variables as described in
Chapter 15.) We will discuss heaps in more detail in the next section. Also,
they will prove particularly important in our discussion of more powerful
sorting methods in Chapter 19. The Programming Problems at the end of this
chapter also indicate how a heap may be used to implement the priority
queue abstract data structure introduced in Chapter 16. The heap property is
one example of a hierarchical relationship that can underlie a tree and hence
must be preserved when various operations are performed upon the tree.

■

■ **EXAMPLE 18.2**

A second example of a hierarchical relationship underlying a binary tree
structure is shown in Figure 18.7.

FIGURE 18.7
Binary search tree with the ordering property

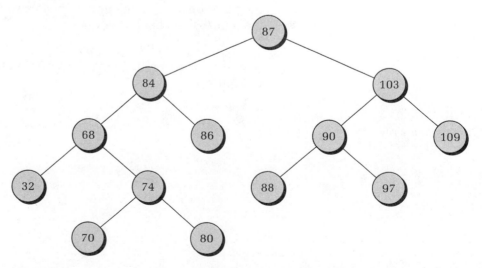

This binary tree exhibits the property known as the *ordering property;* the
data in each node of the tree is greater than all of the data in that node's left
subtree and less than or equal to all the data in the right subtree. A binary

tree with the ordering property is often called a *binary search tree*. We shall see the importance of trees possessing this property when we explore binary trees as a means of implementing a keyed list in Section 18.3.

■

■ **EXAMPLE 18.3**

As a final example of a hierarchical relationship that can determine the arrangement of data in a binary tree, consider Figure 18.8, in which we have a binary tree representation of the infix algebraic expression

$(A - B) + C * (E/F)$

FIGURE 18.8
Binary expression tree for
$(A - B) + C * (E/F)$

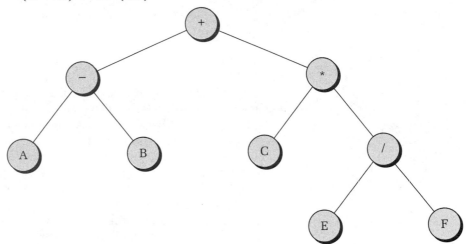

Take a moment to make particular note of Figure 18.8. Since we will be referring back to it frequently throughout this chapter, you may want to clip the page or mark it with a bookmark.

The hierarchical relationship of parent to children in this tree is that of algebraic operator to its two operands. Note that an operand may itself be an expression (that is, a subtree) which must be evaluated before the operator in the parent node can be applied. Note also that, if the order of evaluation in the expression changes as in

$(A - B) + C * E/F$

then the corresponding binary expression tree must also change as reflected in Figure 18.9.

FIGURE 18.9
Binary expression tree for
$(A - B) + C * E/F$

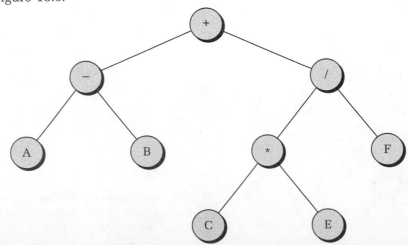

Contemporary compilers make use of tree structures in obtaining forms of an arithmetic expression for efficient evaluation. As we've seen, there are basically three forms for an arithmetic expression such as that corresponding to Figure 18.8: infix, prefix, and postfix.

Expression	Form
(A − B) + C * (E/F)	infix
+ − AB*C/EF	prefix
AB − CEF/* +	postfix

All three of these forms are immediately available to us if we know exactly how the corresponding tree should be traversed. The *inorder traversal* of the binary tree for an arithmetic expression gives us the expression in unparenthesized infix form. The *preorder traversal* of the same tree leads us to the prefix form of the expression, whereas the *postorder traversal* of the tree yields the postfix form of the expression. We shall study procedures for these three traversals in Section 18.2, when we discuss a method of implementing a binary tree.

■   ■

We close this section with a Pascal interface for the binary tree ADT. In the sections that follow, we will analyze two implementations that adhere to this interface.

Pascal Interface for the Binary Tree ADT

```
TYPE
  TreeDataNode =  { This specifies the data in a given tree node. };
  BinaryTree   =  { This is the binary tree data type.             };

PROCEDURE Create (VAR BT : BinaryTree);

  { Given:    BT a binary tree, potentially not initialized.       }
  { Task:     Initialize BT to an empty binary tree.               }
  { Return:   Initialized tree.                                    }

FUNCTION Empty (BT : BinaryTree) : boolean;

  { Given:    BT, a binary tree.                                   }
  { Task:     Check if the tree BT is empty.                       }
  { Return:   True if the tree is empty, false otherwise.          }

FUNCTION Full (BT : BinaryTree) : boolean;

  { Given:    BT, a binary tree.                                   }
  { Task:     Check if the tree BT is full.                        }
  { Return:   True if the tree is full, false otherwise.           }

PROCEDURE AddNode (VAR BT : BinaryTree;
                       Item : TreeDataNode);

  { Given:    BT, a binary tree based upon a particular            }
  {           hierarchical property.  Item, a value                }
  {           to be inserted in tree BT.                           }
  { Task:     Insert Item in tree BT maintaining the               }
  {           tree's hierarchical property.                        }
  { Return:   Appropriately altered tree.  If the tree             }
  {           BT is full, Item is not inserted and BT is           }
  {           left unaltered.                                      }
```

```
PROCEDURE PreorderTrav (BT : BinaryTree;
                        PROCEDURE ProcessNode (VAR Item : TreeDataNode));

{ Given:   Binary tree BT.                                          }
{ Task:    Perform preorder traversal--root of BT first,            }
{          then left subtree, then right subtree--                  }
{          applying ProcessNode to each Item in tree.               }
{ Return:  BT with each node affected by ProcessNode.               }

PROCEDURE InorderTrav (BT : BinaryTree;
                       PROCEDURE ProcessNode (VAR Item : TreeDataNode));

{ Given:   Binary tree BT.                                          }
{ Task:    Perform inorder traversal--left subtree                  }
{          first, then root of BT, then right subtree--             }
{          applying ProcessNode to each Item in tree.               }
{ Return:  BT with each node affected by ProcessNode.               }

PROCEDURE PostorderTrav (BT : BinaryTree;
                         PROCEDURE ProcessNode (VAR Item : TreeDataNode));

{ Given:   Binary tree BT.                                          }
{ Task:    Perform postorder traversal--left subtree                }
{          first, then right subtree, then root of BT--             }
{          applying ProcessNode to each Item in tree.               }
{ Return:  BT with each node affected by ProcessNode.               }
```

Exercises 18.1

1. Draw a binary tree for the following expression:

   A * B − (C + D) * (P/Q)

2. Represent the following StudentRec as a binary tree:

   ```
   Name = RECORD
           FirstName : ARRAY [1..10] OF char;
           LastName : ARRAY [1..10] OF char
         END;

   Year = RECORD
           FirstSem : ARRAY [1..2] OF char;
           SecondSem : ARRAY [1..2] OF char
         END;

   StudentRec = RECORD
                   StudentName : Name;
                   YearOfStudy : Year
                 END;
   ```

3. What, in an abstract sense, does a tree structure represent?

4. Indicate which of the following are binary search trees with the ordering property. Carefully explain what is wrong with those that are not.

   a.

   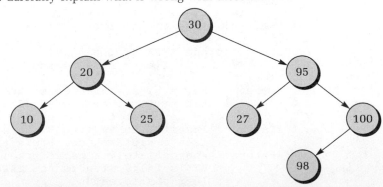

b.

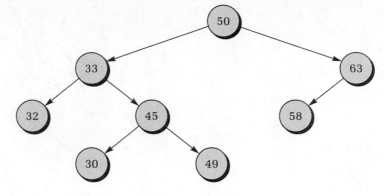

c.

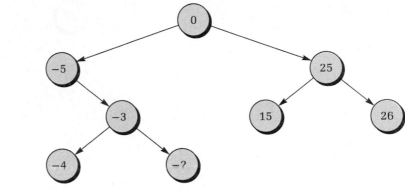

d.

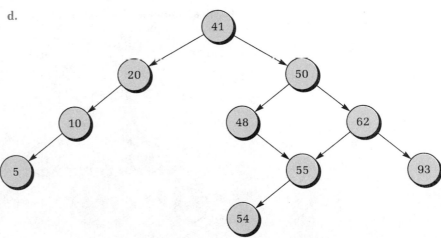

5. Indicate which of the following are binary trees with the heap property. Carefully explain what is wrong with those that are not.

a.

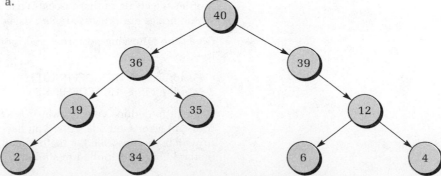

b.

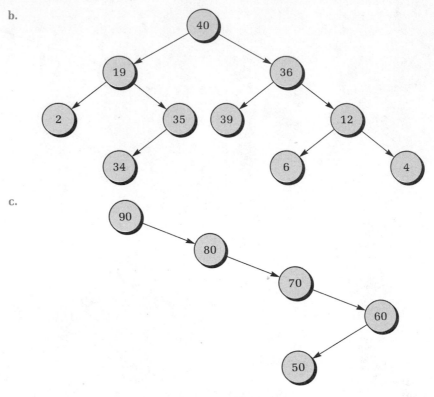

c.

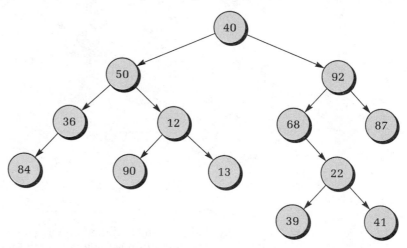

6. Given the following binary tree, indicate the order in which nodes would be processed for each of the preorder, postorder, and inorder traversals.

7. Construct some binary search trees with the ordering property. Then do some inorder traversals of these trees. What do you observe about the order in which nodes are processed? Be as specific as possible in stating your answer.

8. Given the following postorder and inorder traversals of a binary tree, draw the tree

    Postorder: ABCDEFIKJGH
    Inorder: CBAEDFHIGKJ

Attempt to deduce your answer in a systematic (and recursive) fashion, not by trial-and-error methods. After you have solved this problem, write a statement in which you describe the method you used to solve it and explain how this method could be applied to similar problems.

9. Draw binary expression trees corresponding to the algebraic expression whose:

   a. infix representation is P/(Q + R) * X − Y.

   b. postfix representation is XYZPQR* +/− *.

   c. prefix representation is + * − MNP/RS.

10. In a written statement, explain how the arrangement of data in a binary expression tree reflects the order of operations in the corresponding expression.

■ ■ ■ ■

■ 18.2
Linked Implementation of a Binary Tree

OBJECTIVES

- to become familiar with the linked implementation of the binary tree ADT
- to be able to implement the AddNode operation for a binary search tree with the ordering property
- to see how the shape of a binary search tree is dependent on the order in which data arrive for insertion into the tree
- to develop algorithms for the three traversal operations on the linked implementation of a binary tree

Consistent with the way in which we have studied other data structures, we now have a very good idea of *what* a tree is without any consideration of *how* we will implement it. This latter issue must now be explored.

There are two common methods for implementing binary trees. One method, known as *linked implementation,* uses pointers. The other, which does not require the overhead of maintaining pointers, is called a *linear implementation.* In this section and the next, we will focus on the linked implementation. We will see how this implementation is particularly well-suited for binary search trees and binary expression trees.

Because each node in a binary tree may have two child nodes, a node in a linked implementation has two pointer fields, one for each child, and one or more data fields. When a node has no children, the corresponding pointer fields are **NIL.** Figure 18.10 is a linked representation of the binary expression tree of Figure 18.8. The LeftChild and RightChild fields are pointers to (that is, memory addresses of) the left child and the right child of a node.

For the moment, let us give a detailed description of the linked representation of the binary tree of Figure 18.8, using an array of records. This is similar to the way in which we first discussed linked lists in Chapter 15. By doing this, we will actually be able to trace the values of the pointers. Once the concept is thoroughly understood, we will then return to using Pascal pointer variables for the actual implementation of binary trees. For example,

FIGURE 18.10

Linked representation of the binary expression tree of Figure 18.8

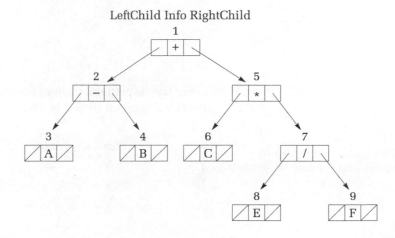

we can implement the tree of Figure 18.10 as shown in Table 18.1, using the strategy of building the left subtree for each node before considering the right subtree. The numbers on top of the cells in Figure 18.10 represent the addresses given in the LeftChild and RightChild fields.

TABLE 18.1
Implementation of Figure 21.10
using array of records

Node	Info	LeftChild	RightChild
1	+	2	5
2	−	3	4
3	A	NIL	NIL
4	B	NIL	NIL
5	*	6	7
6	C	NIL	NIL
7	/	8	9
8	E	NIL	NIL
9	F	NIL	NIL

In the linked representation, insertions and deletions involve no data movement except the rearrangement of pointers. Suppose we wish to modify the tree in Figure 18.8 to that in Figure 18.11. (This change might be needed due to some recent modification in the expression represented by Figure 18.8.) The insertion of the nodes containing − and P into the tree structure can be achieved easily by simply adding the nodes − and P in the next available spaces in the array and adjusting the corresponding pointers.

FIGURE 18.11
Desired modification of Figure 18.8

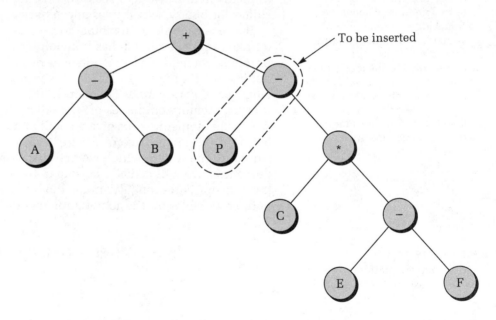

For the implementation of the tree shown in Figure 18.10, the effect of this insertion is given by Table 18.2. The adjusted pointers and data fields have

TABLE 18.2
Modification of Table 18.1 by insertions into the tree of Figure 18.8

Row	Info	LeftChild	RightChild
1	+	2	⑩
2	−	3	4
3	A	NIL	NIL
4	B	NIL	NIL
5	*	6	7
6	C	NIL	NIL
7	/	8	9
8	E	NIL	NIL
9	F	NIL	NIL
10	−	⑪	⑤
11	P	NIL	NIL

been circled. Notice that the change in row 1 of RightChild and the additional rows 10 and 11 are all that is necessary. No data were moved.

Similarly, if we wish to shorten the tree in Figure 18.8 by deleting the nodes * and C, then all we must do is rearrange the pointers to obtain the altered tree, as shown in Figure 18.12. The effect of this deletion is given in Table 18.3. As before, the adjusted pointers and data fields have been circled.

FIGURE 18.12
Another modification of Figure 18.8

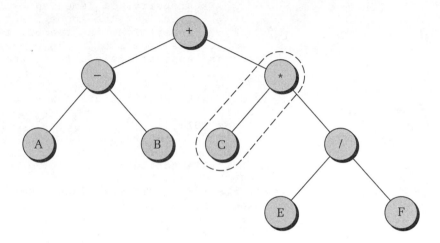

TABLE 18.3
Modification of tree of Figure 18.8

Row	Info	LeftChild	RightChild	Modified tree
1	+	2	(7)	
2	–	3	4	
3	A	NIL	NIL	
4	B	NIL	NIL	
5	*			unused space after
6	C			deletion of '*' and 'C'
7	/	8	9	
8	E	NIL	NIL	
9	F	NIL	NIL	

A more formal statement of the algorithm underlying such insertions and deletions is dependent upon the hierarchical property that forms the basis for the tree structure. We will soon examine in detail insertion and deletion algorithms for binary search trees.

Now that we have explained the linked representation of a binary tree by using arrays to contain pointer values that can be explicitly traced, we will use the following general record description with Pascal pointer variables to implement this structure in the remainder of this and the next sections.

```
TYPE
    TreeDataNode = { whatever is being stored in individual node };
    BinaryTree = ^RootNode;
    RootNode = RECORD
                   LeftChild : BinaryTree;
                   Info : TreeDataNode;
                   RightChild : BinaryTree
               END;
```

■ **EXAMPLE 18.4**

Using the linked representation of a binary tree, implement the AddNode operation for a binary search tree with the ordering property.

```
PROCEDURE AddNode (VAR BT : BinaryTree;
                       Item : TreeDataNode);

{ Given:    BT, a binary search tree with ordering         }
{           property, implemented by Pascal pointer variables. }
{           Item, a value to be inserted in tree BT.        }
{ Task:     Insert Item in tree BT, maintaining             }
{           the tree's ordering property.                   }
{ Return:   Appropriately altered tree.                     }

BEGIN
  IF BT = NIL THEN  { Add a new node  at leaf level }
    BEGIN
      new (BT);
      BT^.Info := Item;
      BT^.LeftChild := NIL;
      BT^.RightChild := NIL
    END
  ELSE IF Item < BT^.Info THEN { Move down the tree }
    AddNode (BT^.LeftChild, Item)
  ELSE
    AddNode (BT^.RightChild, Item)
END; {  of PROCEDURE AddNode  }
```

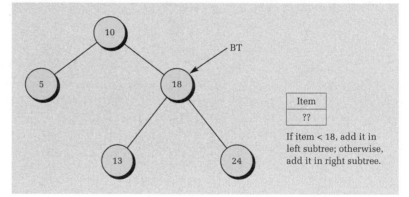

If item < 18, add it in left subtree; otherwise, add it in right subtree.

■   ■

The algorithm of Example 18.4 implies that insertion of new nodes will always occur at the leaf nodes of a tree. As with insertion into a linked list, no data are moved; only pointers are manipulated. However, unlike the steps required by a linked list, we do not have to traverse the list sequentially to determine where the new node belongs. Instead, using the *insertion rule*—if less than, go left; otherwise, go right—we need merely traverse one branch of the tree to determine the position for a new node.

For example, if the AddNode procedure of Example 18.4 is successively fed numerical items in the following order:

16 8 −5 20 30 101 0 10 18

the binary search tree that results can be traced by the sequence in Figure 18.13. Note that the shape of the binary search tree is dependent on the order in which data items are given to AddNode. This dependency of the shape of the tree on the order in which data arrive for insertion complicates any attempt to analyze the efficiency of the AddNode procedure in Example 18.4. We will provide a more detailed analysis of binary search trees with the ordering property in Section 18.3.

FIGURE 18.13
Growth of search tree when data arrive in order
16 8 − 5 20 30 101 0 10 18

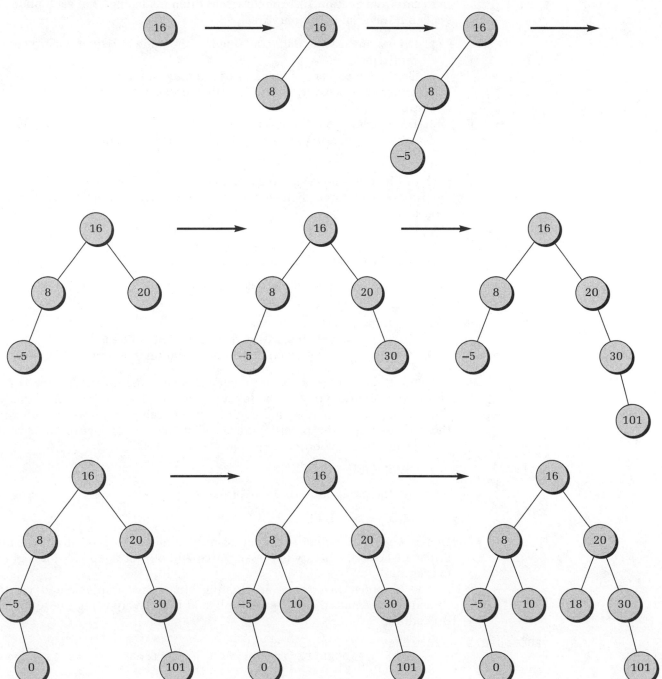

Implementing Traversal Operations on a Binary Tree

In Section 18.1 we described conceptually three different traversal operations on a binary tree: preorder, inorder, and postorder. In Example 18.3, we established correspondences between these three traversals and the prefix, infix, and postfix forms of the algebraic formula represented by a binary expression tree. However, it is important to reiterate that the three traversals apply broadly to all binary trees, regardless of the hierarchical relationship underlying their structure.

Recall from Section 18.1 the threefold dilemma facing us at each node we visit in a traversal of a binary tree.

1. Do we process the data contained in the node at which we are currently located?
2. Do we remember the location of the current node (so that we can return to process it) and visit (and process) all nodes in its left subtree?
3. Do we remember the location of the current node (so that we can return to process it) and visit (and process) all nodes in its right subtree?

Each of the three choices represents a valid choice. The route chosen out of the three-way dilemma dictates the order in which the nodes are visited and processed.

Preorder Traversal of a Binary Tree

In a preorder traversal, the three options are combined in the following order:

1. First, process the root node.
2. Then, recursively visit all nodes in the left subtree.
3. Finally, recursively visit all nodes in the right subtree.

These three ordered steps are recursive. Once the root of the tree is processed, we go to the root of the left subtree, and then to the root of the left subtree of the left subtree, and so on until we can go no farther. Following these three steps, the preorder traversal of the tree of Figure 18.8 would process nodes in the order

$$+ -AB*C/EF$$

which is the prefix form of the expression

$$(A - B) + C * (E/F)$$

Hence we conclude that if to process a node means to print it, then a preorder traversal of a binary expression tree will output the prefix form of the expression.

The preorder traversal of an existing binary tree implemented via the linked representation can be accomplished recursively using the following procedure:

```
PROCEDURE PreorderTrav (BT : BinaryTree;
                    PROCEDURE ProcessNode (VAR Item : TreeDataNode));

   {  Given:    Binary tree BT implemented by Pascal pointer variables. }
   {  Task:     Perform preorder traversal--root of BT first,           }
   {            then left subtree, then right subtree--applying         }
   {            ProcessNode to each Item in the tree.                   }
   {  Return:   BT with each node affected by ProcessNode               }
```

```
BEGIN
  IF BT <> NIL THEN
    BEGIN
      ProcessNode (BT^.Info);
      PreorderTrav (BT^.LeftChild, ProcessNode);
      PreorderTrav (BT^.RightChild, ProcessNode)
    END
END; {  of PROCEDURE PreorderTrav  }
```

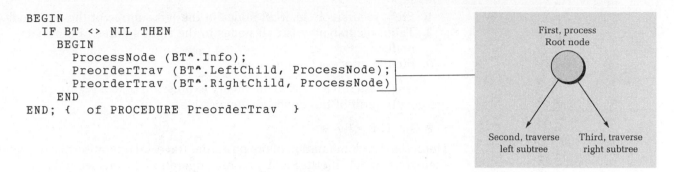

First, process
Root node

Second, traverse   Third, traverse
left subtree   right subtree

Inorder Traversal of a Binary Tree

The inorder traversal of a binary tree proceeds is outlined in the following three ordered steps:

1. First, recursively visit all nodes in the left subtree.
2. Then, process the root node.
3. Finally, recursively visit all nodes in the right subtree.

By carefully following these steps for the tree of Figure 18.8 and assuming "process" means "print," we obtain the readily recognizable infix expression

$$A - B + C * E/F$$

Unless we add parentheses, this infix expression is not equivalent to the order of operations reflected in the tree of Figure 18.8. The fact that prefix and postfix notations do not require parentheses to avoid such ambiguities makes them distinctly superior to infix notation for evaluation purposes.

An implementation of the recursive algorithm for an inorder traversal is given in the following procedure for a linked representation of a binary tree:

```
PROCEDURE InorderTrav (BT : BinaryTree;
                  PROCEDURE ProcessNode (VAR Item : TreeDataNode));

  {  Given:    Binary tree BT implemented by Pascal pointer variables. }
  {  Task:     Perform inorder traversal--left subtree first, then     }
  {            root of BT, then  right subtree--applying               }
  {            ProcessNode to each Item in the tree.                   }
  {  Return:   BT with each node affected by ProcessNode               }

BEGIN
  IF BT <> NIL THEN
    BEGIN
      InorderTrav (BT^.LeftChild, ProcessNode);
      ProcessNode (BT^.Info);
      InorderTrav (BT^.RightChild, ProcessNode)
    END
END; {  of PROCEDURE InorderTrav  }                        }
```

Second, process
Root

First, traverse   Third, traverse
left subtree   right subtree

Postorder Traversal of a Binary Tree

The third standard traversal of a binary tree, the postorder traversal, entails an arrangement of options which postpones processing the root node until last.

1. First, recursively visit all nodes in the left subtree of the root node.
2. Then, recursively visit all nodes in the right subtree of the root node.
3. Finally, process the root node.

Applying these three steps to the binary expression tree of Figure 18.8 yields the postfix form of the underlying expression:

A B − C E ∗ F / +

The actual implementation of the postorder traversal operation is completely analogous to the inorder and preorder operations. Consequently, we will leave it as an exercise.

Although we have illustrated the three traversal algorithms using binary expression trees, we emphasize that the traversals apply in general to *any* binary tree. Indeed, as we shall see in the next section, the inorder traversal when used in combination with a tree exhibiting the hierarchical ordering property of a binary search tree will neatly allow us to implement a keyed list using a binary tree.

Exercises 18.2

1. You are writing a program that uses a binary tree. To make it easy to trace the structure, you use an array of records instead of pointer variables. Consider the following binary tree:

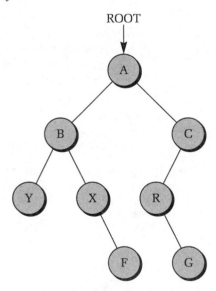

ROOT

a. Indicate the contents of Root and Avail pointers and LeftChild and RightChild fields in the array Tree that follows:

Tree

Location	Info	LeftChild	RightChild
1	C		
2	R		
3	G		
4	F		
5	X		
6	Y		
7	B		
8	A		
9			

Root

Avail

b. Show the contents of Root and Avail and LeftChild and RightChild fields after a node containing J has been inserted as the left child of X and R has been deleted with G becoming the left child of C.

2. Using a preorder traversal of the tree you derived in Exercise 1 from Section 18.1, obtain the prefix form of the expression in that exercise.

3. Sketch the binary search tree that would result when the AddNode procedure of Example 18.4 is used for data that arrive in the following orders:

   a. 100   90   80   70   60   50   40   32   20   10

   b.   60   80   30   90   70   100   40   20   50   10

   c.   60   50   70   40   80   30   90   20   100   10

   Provide a brief written statement in which you describe how the shape of the binary search tree is related to the order in which data arrive for insertion into the tree.

4. Consider the following search trees with the ordering property. For each, specify an order of arrival of data items which would result in that particular tree if the AddNode procedure of Example 18.4 is used.

   a.

   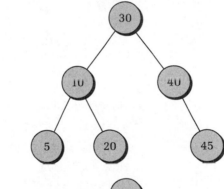

   b.

   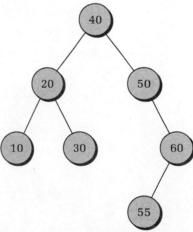

   c.

   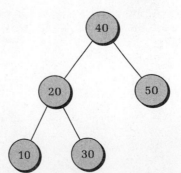

5. What is the output produced by the following procedure for the pictured tree?

```
PROCEDURE TreeWalk (BT : BinaryTree);

  BEGIN
    IF BT = NIL THEN
      writeln ('OOPS')
    ELSE
      BEGIN
        TreeWalk (BT^.RightChild);
        TreeWalk (BT^.LeftChild);
        writeln (BT^.Info)
      END
  END;
```

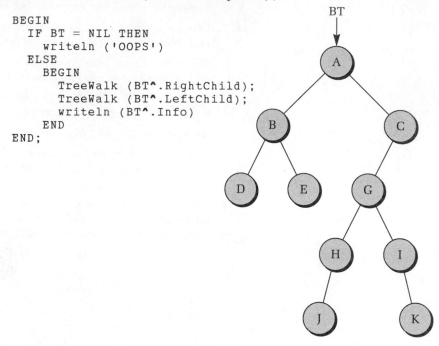

6. How does the output from Exercise 5 change if the statement

   writeln (BT^.Info)

   is moved ahead of the recursive calls to TreeWalk?

7. How does the output from Exercise 5 change if the statement

   writeln (BT^.Info)

   is located between the recursive calls to TreeWalk?

8. Repeat Exercises 5, 6, and 7 for the following tree:

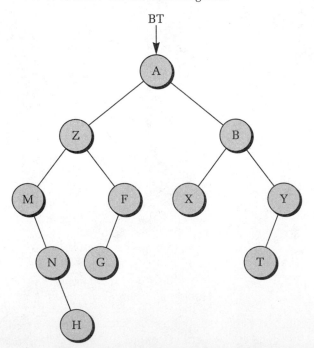

9. A *ternary tree* is a tree in which each node may have at most three children. A pointer/record structure for a linked implementation of such a tree could thus be given by the following declarations:

```
TYPE
   TreePointer = ^TreeNode;
   TreeNode = RECORD
                 LeftChild : TreePointer;
                 MiddleChild : TreePointer;
                 RightChild : TreePointer;
                 Data : char
              END;
```

What would be the output produced by the following TreeWalk procedure

```
PROCEDURE TreeWalk (Root : TreePointer);
   BEGIN
      IF Root = NIL THEN
         writeln ('NIL')
      ELSE
         BEGIN
            writeln (Root^.Data);
            TreeWalk (Root^.RightChild);
            TreeWalk (Root^.MiddleChild);
            TreeWalk (Root^.LeftChild)
         END
   END; {  of PROCEDURE TreeWalk  }
```

if it were initially called with the root pointer to the tree in the following diagram?

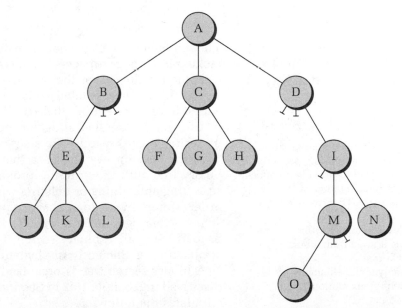

10. Write implementations of the Create, Empty, and Full operations for a binary search tree with the ordering property using the linked representation method.

11. Write an implementation of the postorder traversal operation for a linked representation of a binary tree.

12. Write a procedure that reads an algebraic expression in prefix notation and builds the binary tree corresponding to the expression (see Example 18.3). Assume that all tokens in the expression are individual characters.

13. Write a procedure that reads an algebraic expression in postfix notation and builds the binary tree corresponding to the expression (see Example 18.3). Assume that all tokens in the expression are individual characters.

14. Implement one of the traversal algorithms in a nonrecursive fashion by using a stack to keep track of pointers to nodes that must be visited when you finish processing the current subtree. Your stack will approximate the role played by the system stack in the recursive version of the algorithm.

15. Suppose that you have a binary tree representation of an algebraic expression consisting of the operators $+$, $-$, $*$, $/$ and operands that are uppercase letters. Suppose also that you have a function Value which, given an operand, will return the numeric value associated with that operand. Write a recursive function to evaluate the expression tree.

16. Write a procedure to solve the following puzzle. Assume that TreeNodeData is **char** data. Your procedure receives two strings of the same length. The first represents the order in which the nodes of a tree would be visited by a preorder traversal. The second represents the order in which nodes from the same tree would be visited by an inorder traversal. Your procedure is to construct the tree from these two traversals.

17. Write a Boolean-valued function that receives two binary trees composed of the same type of data. The function should return **true** if the two trees are identical: that is, if they have precisely the same shape and have the same values in each node. Otherwise, it should return **false**.

18. How could the inorder traversal of a binary tree be used to logically sort data? Provide your answer in the form of a precise written statement.

■ ■ ■ ■

■ 18.3
Binary Search Tree Implementation of a Keyed List

OBJECTIVES

- to realize how a binary search tree with the ordering property may be used to provide an effective implementation of the keyed list ADT introduced in Chapter 13
- to develop an algorithm for deleting a node from a binary search tree
- to analyze the efficiency of this new implementation of the keyed list ADT
- in particular, to compare the efficiency of this new keyed list implementation with the efficiencies of other implementations we have previously studied

The implementations we have considered for the keyed list have been found lacking in certain respects. The physically ordered array implementation of Chapter 12 allowed for the fast inspection of records via the binary search algorithm but necessitated excessive data movement when records were added to or deleted from the list. The linked list implementation suggested in Chapter 15 handled adds and deletes nicely but presented us with an undesirable $O(n)$ search efficiency due to the lack of random access.

In this section, we shall see that by implementing a keyed list using a binary tree with the ordering property, we can achieve efficiency in both searching and adding or deleting while at the same time keeping the list in order. Moreover, we do not have to pay too great a price in other trade-offs to achieve this best of both worlds. Indeed, binary trees with the ordering property are called binary search trees precisely because of their frequent application in efficiently implementing keyed lists.

A binary search tree is organized via the hierarchical ordering property discussed in Example 18.2 in Section 18.1. Recall that this ordering property stipulates the following:

For any given data item X in the tree, every node in the left subtree of X contains only items that are less than X with respect to a particular type of ordering. Every node in the right subtree of X contains only items that are greater than or equal to X with respect to the same ordering.

For instance, the tree of Figure 18.14 illustrates this property with respect to alphabetical ordering.

FIGURE 18.14
Ordering property with respect to alphabetical ordering

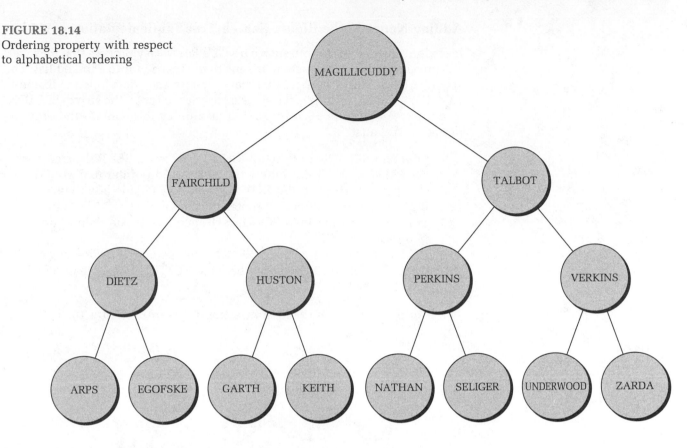

You can quickly verify that an inorder traversal of this tree (in which the processing of each node consists merely of printing its contents) leads to the following alphabetized list:

ARPS
DIETZ
EGOFSKE
FAIRCHILD
GARTH
HUSTON
KEITH
MAGILLICUDDY

NATHAN
PERKINS
SELIGER
TALBOT
UNDERWOOD
VERKINS
ZARDA

This allows us to reach the following important conclusion. That is, an inorder traversal of a binary search tree will visit nodes in ascending order. Hence such a tree may be viewed as an ordered list. The first list element is the first item visited by the inorder traversal. More generally, the nth element visited by the inorder traversal corresponds precisely to the nth element in the list. Given this view of a binary search tree as an implementation of a keyed list, let us now consider the operations of adding, deleting, and finding (retrieving) nodes in the list.

Adding Nodes to the Binary Search Tree Implementation of a List

Insertion of a new string into such a tree is a fairly easy process that may well require significantly fewer comparisons than insertion into a linked list. The specifics of the AddNode operation have already been developed in Example 18.4. Consider, for example, the steps necessary to insert the string 'SEFTON' into the tree of Figure 18.14 in such a fashion as to maintain the ordering property. We must

1. Compare SEFTON to MAGILLICUDDY. Because SEFTON is greater than MAGILLICUDDY, follow the right child pointer to TALBOT.
2. Compare SEFTON to TALBOT. Because SEFTON is less than TALBOT, follow the left child pointer to PERKINS.
3. SEFTON is greater than PERKINS. Hence follow the right child pointer to SELIGER.
4. SELIGER is a leaf node, so SEFTON may be added as one of its children. The left child is chosen because SEFTON is less than SELIGER.

The resulting tree for the sample insertion is given in Figure 18.15.

FIGURE 18.15
Tree in Figure 18.14 with the insertion SEFTON

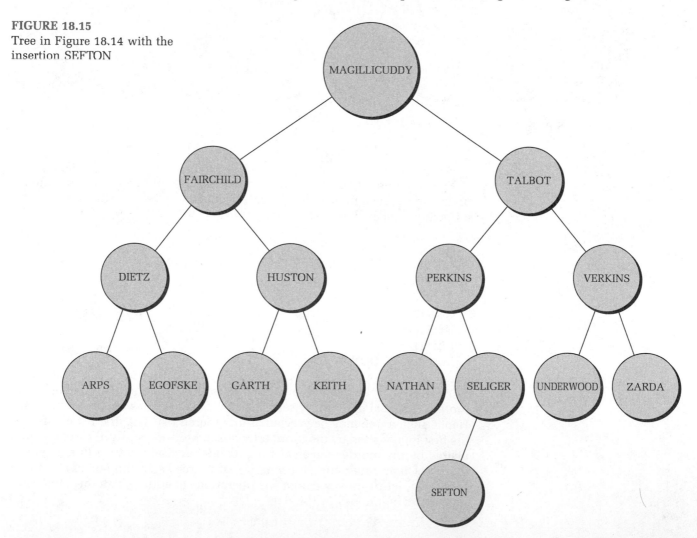

Provided that the tree maintains a full shape, the number of nodes on a given branch will be at most

$$\log_2 n + 1$$

where n is the total number of nodes in the tree. By *full* we mean that all nodes with fewer than two children must occur at level m or $m - 1$ where m is the deepest level in the tree. In other words, all nodes above level $m - 1$ must have exactly two children. Hence, adding ROBERTS to the tree of Figure 18.15 by the insertion rule would destroy its fullness.

Given this definition of full, the ($\log_2 n + 1$) figure for the maximum number of nodes on a branch emerges immediately upon inspection or, more formally, using a proof by mathematical induction. Our purpose here, however, is not to give the details of such a proof but rather to emphasize that a binary search tree presents an alternative to a linked list structure for the type of processing involved in maintaining ordered lists. Moreover, it is a particularly attractive alternative when the tree is full, because substantially fewer comparisons are needed to locate where in the structure an insertion is to be made. For instance, if n is 1,024, the linked list may require as many as 1,024 comparisons to make an insertion. Because $\log_2 1024$ is 10, the full binary search tree method will require at most 11 comparisons. This difference becomes even more dramatic as n gets larger. For an ordered list with 1,000,000 entries, a linked list may require that many comparisons, but the full binary search tree requires a mere 21 comparisons.

What happens when the tree is not full? We will comment on that situation at the end of this section, when we discuss the overall efficiency considerations for this implementation of a list. Before that, however, consider the operations of finding and deleting data in a binary search tree.

Searching for Data in a Binary Search Tree Implementation of a List

The insertion rule also dictates the search path followed through a binary search tree when we are attempting to find a given data item. Interestingly, if we trace the nodes visited on such a search path for a full tree, we will probe exactly the same items that we would in conducting a binary search on a physically ordered array containing the same data. For instance, if we are searching for SMITH in the tree of Figure 18.14, we will have to probe MAGILLICUDDY, TALBOT, and PERKINS. These are precisely the items that would be probed if the binary search algorithm were applied to the physically ordered list associated with Figure 18.14. Our analysis of such a tree has allowed us to conclude that, as long as the binary search tree remains full, search efficiency for this method of implementing a keyed list matches that of the physically ordered array implementation. That is, the search efficiency is $O(\log_2 n)$.

Deleting Data in a Binary Search Tree Implementation of a List

The deletion algorithm for a binary search tree is conceptually more complex than that for a linked list. Suppose, for instance, that we wish to remove TALBOT from the list represented by the tree of Figure 18.14. Two questions arise.

1. Can such a deletion be achieved merely by manipulating pointers?
2. If so, what does the resulting tree look like?

To answer these questions, begin by recalling that all that is necessary to represent a keyed list with a binary search tree is that, for each node in the tree

1. The left subtree must contain only items less than it.
2. The right subtree must contain only items greater than or equal to it.

With the preservation of this ordering property as the primary goal in processing a deletion, one acceptable way of restructuring the tree of Figure 18.14 after deleting TALBOT appears in Figure 18.16; essentially, SELIGER moves up to replace TALBOT in the tree. The choice of SELIGER to replace TALBOT is made because SELIGER represents the greatest data item in the left subtree of the node containing TALBOT. As long as we choose this greatest item in the left subtree to replace the item being deleted, we guarantee preservation of the crucial ordering property that enables the tree to represent the list accurately.

FIGURE 18.16
Restructuring the tree in Figure 18.14 after deleting TALBOT

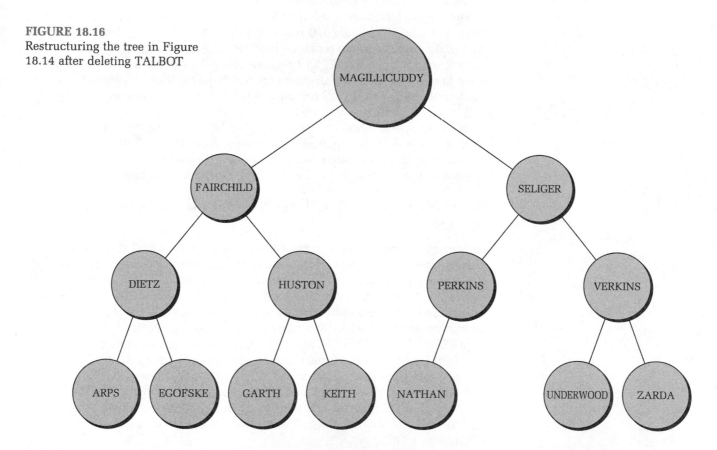

Given this general motivation for choosing a node to replace the one being deleted, let us now outline a case-by-case analysis of the deletion algorithm. Throughout this analysis, we assume that we have a pointer P to the item that we wish to delete. The pointer P may be one of the following:

1. The root pointer for the entire tree.
2. The left child pointer of the parent of the node to be deleted.
3. The right child pointer of the parent of the node to be deleted.

Figure 18.17 highlights these three possibilities; the algorithm applies whether 1, 2, or 3 holds.

FIGURE 18.17
Three possibilities for the pointer P

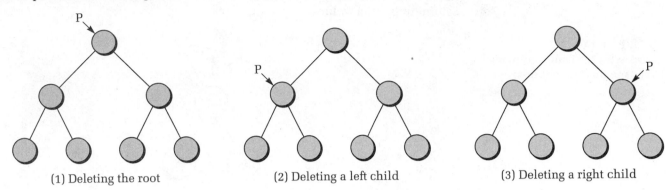

(1) Deleting the root   (2) Deleting a left child   (3) Deleting a right child

We now examine three cases of node deletion on a binary search tree.

1. The node to be deleted has no children.
2. The node to be deleted has a right child but no left child.
3. The node to be deleted has a left child.

Case 1. The node pointed to by P, that is, the node to be deleted, has no children. This is the easiest of all the cases. It can be compactly handled

```
X := P;
P := NIL;
dispose (X);
```

Case 2. The node pointed to by P, that is, the node to be deleted, has a right child but no left child. This case poses no more problems than Case 1 and is described in Figure 18.18. The node to be deleted is merely replaced by its right child. The necessary Pascal coding is

```
X := P;
P := X^.RightChild;
dispose (X);
```

FIGURE 18.18
In Case 2 the node pointed to by
P has a right but no left child

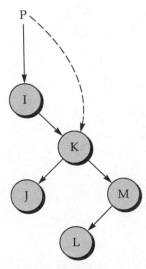

Case 3. The node pointed to by P, that is, the node to be deleted, has a left child. In Figure 18.19, node M is to be deleted, and it has left child K. In this case, because we have a non-null left subtree of the node to be deleted, our previous discussion indicates that we must find the greatest node in that left subtree. If the node pointed to by P^.LeftChild (node K in the figure) has no

right child, then the greatest node in the left subtree of P is P^.LeftChild itself. Figure 18.19 pictorially describes this situation; the dotted lines indicate new pointer values.

FIGURE 18.19
Case 3 with P^.LeftChild (node
K) having no right children

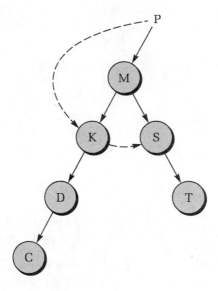

The partial coding to achieve this pointer manipulation is given by:

```
X := P;
P := X^.LeftChild;
P^.RightChild := X^.RightChild;
dispose (X);
```

If the node pointed to by P^.LeftChild does have a right child, then to find the greatest node in the left subtree of P we must follow the right branch leading from P^.LeftChild as deeply as possible into the tree. In Figure 18.20, node R is the one chosen to replace the deleted node. This figure gives

FIGURE 18.20
Case 3 with P^.LeftChild having
a right child

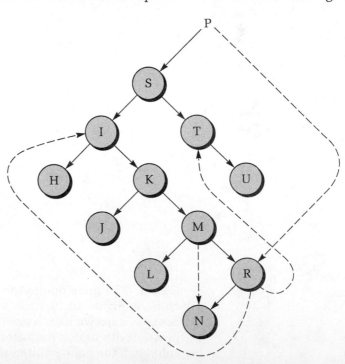

the schematic representation, with the pointer changes necessary to complete the deletion. The coding necessary for this slightly more complicated version of Case 3 is

```
X := P;
Q := X^.LeftChild^.RightChild;
QParent := X^.LeftChild;

{ Q will eventually point to node which will replace P. }
{ QParent will point to Q's parent.                      }
{ The following loop forces Q as deep as possible        }
{ along the right branch from P^.LeftChild.              }

WHILE Q^.RightChild <>NIL DO
  BEGIN
    Q := Q^.RightChild;
    QParent := QParent^.RightChild
  END;

{ Having found node Q to replace P, adjust pointers      }
{ to appropriately link it into the tree.                }

Q^.RightChild := X^.RightChild;
P := Q;
QParent^.RightChild := Q^.LeftChild;
Q^.LeftChild := X^.LeftChild;
dispose (X);
```

Efficiency Considerations for Binary Search Tree Implementation of a Keyed List

It is important to note that, in all three cases, the deletion of a node from the tree involved only pointer manipulation and no actual data movement. Hence, in a list maintained with a binary search tree, we are able to process both insertions and deletions by the same pure pointer manipulation that makes linked lists so desirable. Moreover, the binary search tree approach apparently allows us to locate data for retrieval, insertion, or deletion much faster than a linked list representation would. However, there are aspects of the binary tree method that tarnish its performance in comparison to a linked list. In particular:

- The binary search tree implementation requires more memory in two respects. First, each node has two pointers instead of the one required in a singly linked list. This proliferation of pointers is particularly wasteful because many of the pointers may be **NIL.** Second, we presently can traverse the tree in order only by using recursive techniques. Even in a language that allows recursion, a substantial amount of overhead is needed to maintain the stack used by recursive calls.
- The $O(\log_2 n)$ efficiency of the binary search tree method is only an optimal, not a guaranteed, efficiency. It is contingent upon the tree's remaining nearly full. The tree's remaining full is in turn contingent upon the order in which the data are added and deleted. In the worst possible case, data entering the tree structure in the wrong order can cause the tree to degenerate into a glorified linked list with a corresponding $O(n)$ efficiency. (The Exercises at the end of this section have you explore this relationship between the order in which data arrive for insertion and the resulting search efficiency of the binary search tree.)

Both of these drawbacks can be overcome. We can avoid the overhead associated with recursion if we use a technique (known as *threading*) that puts to good use the pointers that are otherwise wasted as **NIL.**

Moreover, by using a technique known as *height balancing,* the binary search tree may be maintained in a fashion which approaches fullness at all times, regardless of the order in which data arrive for entry. This nearly full form is enough to completely guarantee the $O(\log_2 n)$ search efficiency. Originally devised by G. M. Adelson-Velskii and Y. M. Landis, the height-balancing algorithm is sufficiently complex to be beyond the scope of this book. In-depth treatments of it and the threading technique cited above are given in *Data Structures in Pascal* by Ellis Horowitz and Sartaj Sahni (New York, N.Y.: Computer Science Press, 1990) and in *Introduction to Data Structures and Algorithm Analysis with Pascal* by Thomas L. Naps and George J. Pothering (St. Paul, Minn.: West Publishing, 1992).

Overall, the binary search tree implementation of a keyed list would seem to be the best of the three implementations we have studied for situations in which additions, deletions, and searches must all be processed efficiently. Even when steps are not taken to correct the two disadvantages we have cited, it offers the addition/deletion advantages of a linked list with a search efficiency that is bounded between $O(\log_2 n)$ and $O(n)$.

Exercises 18.3

1. Which of the following binary search trees are full?

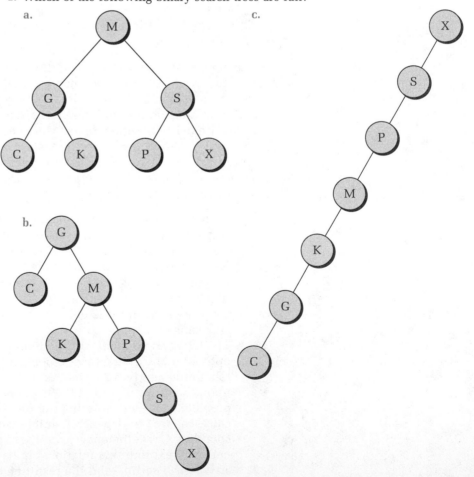

2. The key values 1 through 10 are to be inserted in a binary search tree. Specify orders of arrival for these values to create trees that correspond with each of the following shapes.

   a.

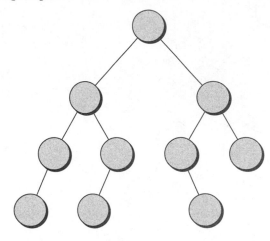

   b.   c.

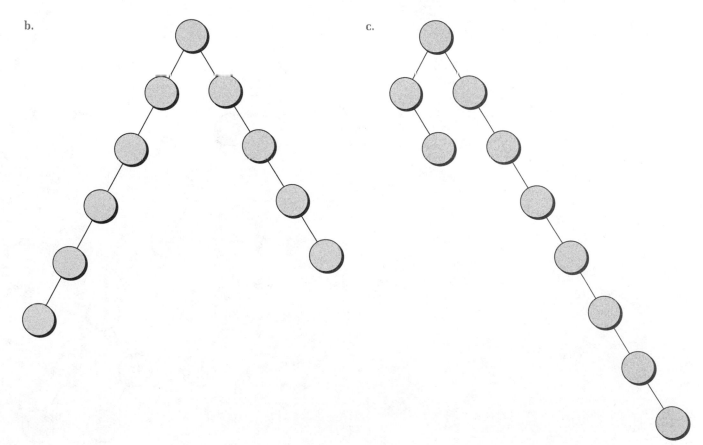

3. In an essay, discuss the relative merits of maintaining a keyed list by a binary search tree, a singly linked list, and a doubly linked list.

4. In an essay, discuss how the order in which data are entered into a binary search tree affects the fullness of the tree. Be sure to identify the best and worst possible cases. Analyze the efficiency of tree operations to add, delete, and find data for each of these cases.

5. The node containing 46 is to be deleted from each of the following binary search trees. Assuming the deletion algorithm described in this section is used, draw the tree after the deletion of 46.

a.

b.

c.

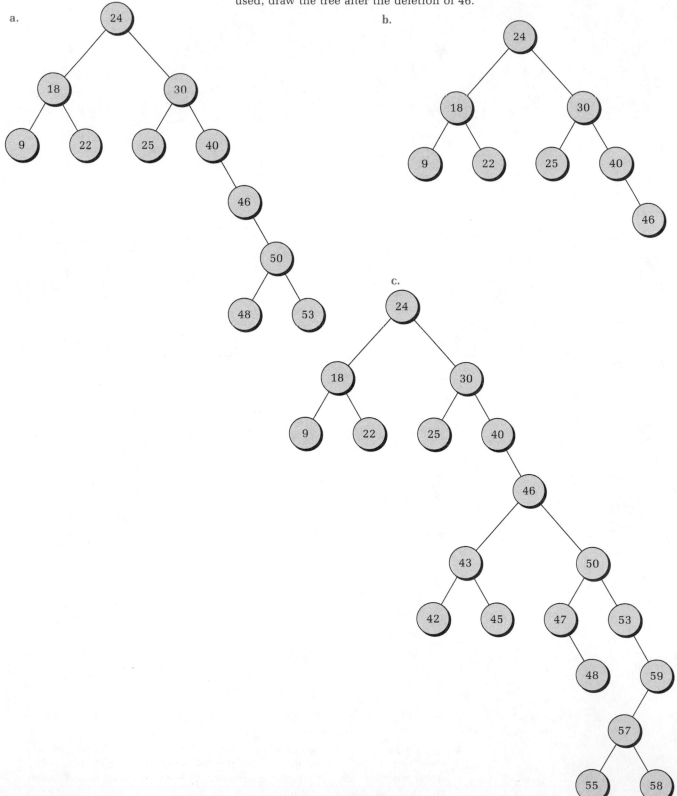

6. In Example 18.4 we provided an implementation of the AddNode operation for a binary search tree. What does the procedure in that example do when we try to insert a key value that already exists in the tree? Modify the procedure so that, when we try to insert such a key value, the tree is left unaltered.

7. The implementation of the AddNode operation for a binary search tree in Example 18.4 is recursive. Write a nonrecursive implementation of this operation.

8. Develop recursive and nonrecursive implementations of the algorithm to search for a particular data item in a binary search tree.

9. Develop a complete implementation of the algorithm to delete an item from a binary search tree. This will essentially require that you combine into one module the three cases discussed in this section. For an added challenge, try writing the procedure so that it handles deletion by using the "mirror image" of these three cases.

10. Look back to the definition of the keyed list ADT in Chapter 13. Provide a complete implementation of the keyed list operations using a binary search tree as the underlying data structure.

11. Suppose you are given a list of data in increasing order of keys. Develop a Pascal algorithm that will load this list into an optimal binary search tree.

12. A binary search tree could itself be considered an ADT that is derived from the more generic binary tree ADT defined in Section 18.1. Write a complete definition and a Pascal interface for the binary search tree as an ADT. Be sure that the set of operations you describe will allow your binary search tree ADT to be used as an implementation strategy for the keyed list ADT.

■ ■ ■ ■

■ 18.4
Linear Implementation of the Binary Tree Abstract Data Type

OBJECTIVES

- to become familiar with the linear implementation of the binary tree ADT
- to recognize the advantages and disadvantages of the linear implementation versus the linked implementation
- to see why the linear implementation is particularly well-suited to representing a binary tree with the heap property
- to analyze the efficiency of the AddNode operation for a linear implementation of a binary tree with the heap property

The linear implementation of a binary tree uses a one-dimensional array of size $(2^{(d+1)} - 1)$ where d is the depth of the tree, that is, the maximum level of any node in the tree. In the tree of Figure 18.8, the root $+$ is at the level 0, the nodes $-$ and $*$ are at level 1, and so on. The deepest level in this tree is the level of E and F, level 3. Therefore, $d = 3$ and this tree will require an array of size $2^{(3+1)} - 1 = 15$.

Once the size of the array has been determined, the following method is used to represent the tree:

1. Store the root in the first location of the array.
2. If a node is in location n of the array, store its left child at location $2n$, and its right child at location $(2n + 1)$.

With the aid of this scheme, the tree of Figure 18.8 is stored in the array BTData of size 15 shown in Figure 18.21. Locations BTData[8] through BTData[13] are not used.

An encapsulated definition of the binary tree ADT for this linear representation is given by:

```
CONST
   MaxTreeNodes = { Appropriate size for array, determined by maximum level }
                  { of any node in the tree.                                 }
   Null = { An appropriate value to signal that an array }
          { location does not  currently contain a node  }
```

FIGURE 18.21

Tree of Figure 18.8 stored in a linear representation using an array

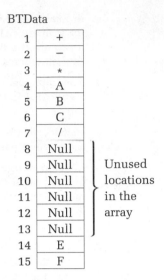

BTData

1	+
2	−
3	*
4	A
5	B
6	C
7	/
8	Null
9	Null
10	Null
11	Null
12	Null
13	Null
14	E
15	F

Unused locations in the array (8–13)

```
                    { in the tree.  Since this value is used      }
                    { as a flag, it should be chosen to be         }
                    { a value that would never actually be         }
                    { stored in the tree.                          }
        TYPE
           TreeDataNode = { Data type of each individual node };
           BTArray = ARRAY [1..MaxTreeNodes] OF TreeDataNode;
           BinaryTree = RECORD
                           BTData : BTArray;
                           NumberNodes : integer { Number of nodes currently in tree }
                        END;
```

The Create operation simply sets the NumberNodes field to zero and initializes all array locations to the Null value. The Null values are necessary to detect whether or not a given tree node has children. A tree node at location n has a left subtree if and only if location $2n$ contains a non-Null value. A similar consideration applies to the right subtree of the tree node at location n.

Efficiency Considerations for the Linear Representation

The main advantages of this method lie in its simplicity and the fact that, given a child node, its parent node can be determined immediately. If a child node is at location n in the array, then its parent node is at location n **DIV** 2.

In spite of its simplicity and ease of implementation, the linear representation method has all the costs that come with physically ordering items. Insertion or deletion of a node in a fashion that maintains the hierarchical relationships within the tree may cause considerable data movement up and down the array and hence use an excessive amount of processing time. Also, depending on the application, there may be wasted memory locations (such as locations 8 through 13 in Figure 18.21) due to partially filled trees.

Using the Linear Implementation for a Heap

One type of binary tree for which the linear implementation of a binary tree proves to be ideal is the heap, as defined in Example 18.1. The data in a heap can be embedded in an array without ever wasting any locations. To prove this claim, we will show that, given a heap with N-1 nodes embedded in an array with no gaps, we can add an Nth node and maintain the dense packing of data in the array.

To illustrate the algorithm for doing this, consider the heap with eight nodes pictured in Figure 18.22. The numbers outside the circular nodes in this figure indicate the array indices where data would be stored in the linear representation of a binary tree.

FIGURE 18.22
A heap with eight nodes

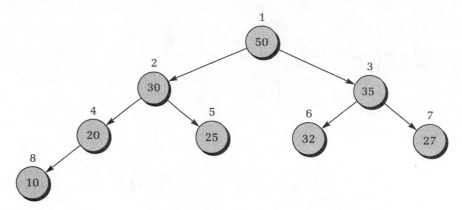

Now suppose we want to add 40 to the heap of Figure 18.22. We will begin by comparing 40 to the data in the least index which does not yet have two children: 20 at index 4 in Figure 18.22. Figure 18.23 shows a series of data interchanges that "walk 40 up" a path until the tree is transformed into a heap. The algorithm to achieve this "walking up" is given in the following example.

FIGURE 18.23
Transforming heap to accommodate insertion of 40 (Numbers outside circles indicate array index positions)

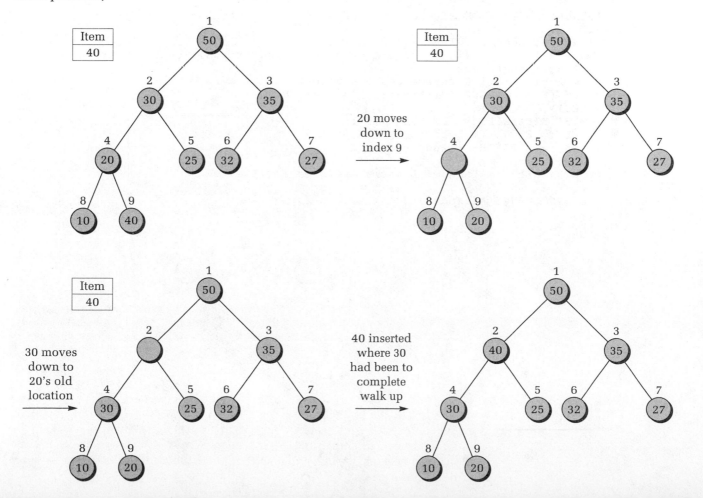

■ **EXAMPLE 18.5**

Implement the AddNode operation for a linear representation of a binary tree with the heap property.

```
TYPE
  TreeDataNode = { any data type which has < relationship between
                   its values };
  BTArray = ARRAY [1..MaxTreeNodes] of TreeDataNode;
  BinaryTree = RECORD
                 BTData : BTArray;
                 NumberNodes : integer
               END;

PROCEDURE AddNode(VAR BT : BinaryTree;
                  Item : TreeDataNode);

  { Given:    BT, a linear representation of binary tree with the   }
  {           heap property.  Item, a value to be inserted in       }
  {           tree BT.                                               }
  { Task:     Insert Item in tree BT, maintaining                   }
  {           the tree's heap property.                             }
  { Return:   Appropriately altered tree.  If there is no room      }
  {           for insertion, BT is not altered.                     }

  VAR
    K, L : integer;

BEGIN
  IF BT.NumberNodes <> MaxTreeNodes THEN  { BT is not full }
    BEGIN
      BT.NumberNodes := BT.NumberNodes + 1;
      { Now walk the new item up the tree, starting at position L }
      L := BT.NumberNodes;
      K := L DIV 2;  { K references L's parent }
      WHILE (K >= 1) AND (BT.BTData[K] < Item) DO
        BEGIN
          BT.BTData[L] := BT.BTData[K];
          L := K;       { L moves up the tree }
          K := L DIV 2  { And so does K }
        END;
      BT.BTData[L] := Item  { L marks the spot for Item }
    END
END; { of PROCEDURE AddNode }
```

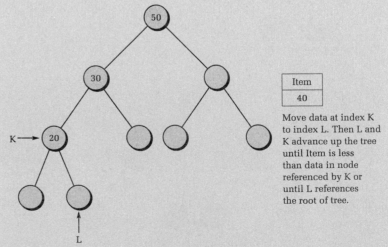

Item
40

Move data at index K to index L. Then L and K advance up the tree until Item is less than data in node referenced by K or until L references the root of tree.

A NOTE OF INTEREST

Computer Security and Tree-Structured File Systems

One of the prime concerns in developing operating systems for multiuser computers is to insure that a user cannot, in an unauthorized fashion, access system files or the files of other users. A convenient data structure to implement such a file directory system is a tree such as that pictured here.

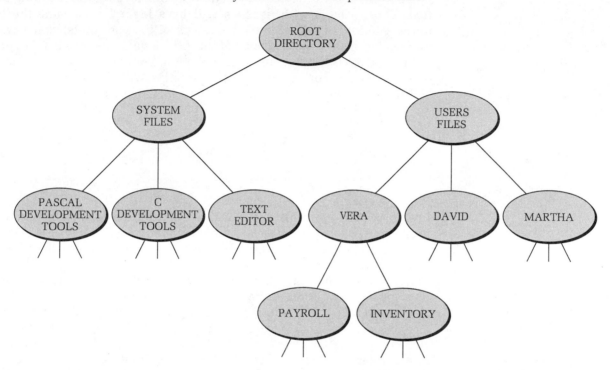

Each interior node of the tree can be viewed as a directory containing various system information about those files or subdirectories that are its descendants. Leaf nodes in the tree are the actual files. Hence, in the diagram, files can be broken down into system files and user files. System files consist of the PASCAL DEVELOPMENT TOOLS, the C DEVELOPMENT TOOLS, and the TEXT EDITOR. User directories are called VERA, DAVID, and MARTHA. One of the very convenient features of such a system is that it allows the user to extend this tree structure as deeply as desired. For instance, in the given tree directory structure, we see that user VERA has created subdirectories for files related to PAYROLL and INVENTORY. DAVID and MARTHA could have similarly partitioned subdirectories to organize their work.

In addition to offering users the convenience of being able to appropriately group their files into subdirectories, such a file system offers a very natural solution to the problem of file security. Since each individual user is, in effect, the root of a miniature subordinate file system within the overall system, a user is given, by default, free access to every node in his or her subtree. That is, the user is viewed as the owner of every node in

the subtree. To jump outside of this subtree of naturally owned files and directories requires that special permissions be given the user by other users or by the operating system itself. Hence the tree structure offers convenience as well as a means of carefully monitoring the integrity of the file system.

AT&T's UNIX operating system, developed at Bell Laboratories in the early 1970s, was one of the first to use such a tree-structured directory system. The widespread popularity of UNIX today and the adoption of this scheme by a significant number of other operating systems is evidence of the attractive way in which it combines user convenience with system security. However, this is not to say that such systems are completely free of security problems. Once the security of such a system is slightly compromised, the tree structure lends itself to a cascade of far-reaching security breaks. Brian Reid's article "Reflections on Some Recent Widespread Computer Break-ins" in the February 1987 issue of *Communications of the ACM* (Vol. 30, No. 2) provides an interesting account of how such security problems surfaced at Stanford University and spread to an entire network of computers. An entertaining narrative of another security incident is presented by Clifford Stoll in *The Cuckoo's Egg* (Doubleday, New York, 1989).

Efficiency Analysis of AddNode for Linear Representation of Heap

Clearly the time efficiency of adding an item to the heap is directly proportional to the length of the path that the item must "walk up" as its appropriate position is determined. Because the linear representation of a heap leaves no unused gaps between values stored in the array, doubling the number of items in the heap will add only one level to the resulting binary tree. Thus, a heap with n nodes will have $\log_2 n$ levels using the linear representation. In other words, the length of the path that a new item will follow, and hence the efficiency of the AddNode operation, is $O(\log_2 n)$.

In the Exercises at the end of this section, you will explore an algorithm to delete a node from a heap. That exploration will show how a heap could be used to implement the priority queue ADT defined in Chapter 16.

■ EXAMPLE 18.6

In this example, we illustrate how the postorder traversal algorithm may be implemented for a linear array implementation of a binary tree. The algorithm is slightly more difficult for this representation since the tree is the encapsulation of an array and a count of the number of nodes. Unlike the linked implementation, there is not an explicit root pointer for the tree; instead, the root of the entire tree is understood to be at index 1. The following **PROCEDURE** PostorderTrav compensates for this by acting as a mere "front-end" for a local auxillary procedure which is where the actual recursion takes place. Our front-end **PROCEDURE** PostorderTrav simply passes a root pointer value of 1 to the auxillary procedure to start the recursion. We must also assume that a flagging Null value occupies array locations that are not currently storing data in the tree. This allows the auxiliary procedure to detect when the equivalent of a **NIL** pointer is passed.

```
PROCEDURE PostorderTrav (BT : BinaryTree;
                         PROCEDURE ProcessNode (VAR Item : TreeDataNode));

  { Given:   Binary tree BT implemented by linear array representation. }
  { Task:    Perform postorder traversal--left subtree                  }
  {          first, then right subtree, then root of BT--               }
  {          applying ProcessNode to each Item in the tree.             }
  { Return:  BT with each node affected by ProcessNode                  }

PROCEDURE PostorderTravAux (NodeLocation : integer);

  { This procedure is the behind-the-scenes recursive helper            }
  { of PostorderTrav.  The interface to PostorderTravAux is not         }
  { seen by users of the ADT.  Assumption:  Array locations             }
  { not presently storing data in the tree have been flagged            }
  { with an appropriate Null value.                                     }
```

```
      BEGIN
         IF NodeLocation <= MaxTreeNodes THEN
            IF BT.BTData[NodeLocation] <> Null THEN
               BEGIN
                  PostorderTravAux (2 * NodeLocation);         { Left subtree  }
                  PostorderTravAux (2 * NodeLocation + 1);     { Right subtree }
                  ProcessNode (BT.BTData[NodeLocation])
               END
      END;  { of PROCEDURE PostorderTravAux }
```

Third, process
Root

First, traverse
left subtree

Second, traverse
right subtree

```
      BEGIN
         IF BT.NumberNodes <> 0 THEN
            PostorderTravAux (1 { The location of the root of BT } )
      END; {  of PROCEDURE PostorderTrav  }
```

Exercises 18.4

1. Suppose that items arrive for insertion into a heap in the following order:

   10 20 30 40 50 60 70 80 90 100

   Using the algorithm of Example 18.5, trace the contents of the BTData array after each item is added to the heap.

2. Write implementations of the Create, Empty, and Full operations for a binary tree with the heap property using the linear array implementation. Be sure that your Create operation is consistent with the postorder traversal algorithm of Example 18.6.

3. Write implementations of the preorder and inorder traversal operations for a linear array implementation of a binary tree.

4. The linear array implementation of a binary tree discussed in this section assumes the existence of a Null value to signal array locations that do not contain tree data. In some applications it may be impossible or highly inconvenient to determine such a Null value because you are, in effect, disallowing the Null value from ever occurring in the tree itself. Devise a strategy whereby you could still employ the linear array implementation with its mapping of $n \rightarrow 2n$ for left child and $n \rightarrow 2n + 1$ for right child but *not* have to assume the existence of a flagging Null value.

   Describe your strategy and, in a written statement, discuss why it works. Then implement the Create operation and one of the traversal operations using your strategy.

5. Implement the following operation for a linear representation of a binary tree with the heap property.

```
PROCEDURE Remove (VAR BT : Binary Tree;
                  VAR Item : TreeDataNode);
```

```
{ Given:    BT, a binary tree with the heap property      }
{ Task:     Remove the value at the root of BT, then      }
{           reshape the tree into a heap.                 }
{ Return:   The old root of BT in Item. BT with the       }
{           old root removed, reshaped to retain the      }
{           heap property.                                }
```

(*Hint:* When the root is removed, temporarily replace it by the tree node in the last active index of the array. Then develop an algorithm to walk this new root down a branch of the tree until the tree becomes a heap again.)

In a written statement, indicate how the AddNode procedure of Example 18.5 and the Remove procedure that you have written for this exercise could be used to implement a priority queue (Chapter 16) using a heap.

6. In a written statement discuss the relative advantages and disadvantages of the linear array implementation of a binary tree versus the linked implementation described in Section 18.2.

■ ■ ■ ■

■ 18.5
General Trees

OBJECTIVES

- to understand how a general tree may be implemented using a linked representation of a binary tree
- given the implementation of a general tree by a binary tree, to examine which traversal operations for the underlying binary tree make sense when it is interpreted as a general tree

We began this chapter with a discussion of the many ways in which hierarchical structures are used to organize information around us. We then quickly imposed a birth control dictate of at most two children which focused all of our attention on the seemingly restricted case of the binary tree. What about all of those applications requiring a hierarchical relationship where a parent may have an unrestricted number of children? You may have become suspicious that we are avoiding such considerations because they are too difficult.

Fortunately, we have a much more educationally sound reason. That is, we may use a binary tree to implement a general tree. The nice implication of this rather surprising statement is that we will not have to spend a significant amount of time discussing general trees because we have unknowingly studied them in our thorough analysis of binary trees. Moreover, the formal operations on a general tree may be viewed as operations derived from those associated with a binary tree.

The real key to using a restricted type of tree such as a binary tree to implement a more general type of tree is to adjust our perspective. For example, consider the general genealogical tree of Figure 18.24.

FIGURE 18.24
Genealogical tree

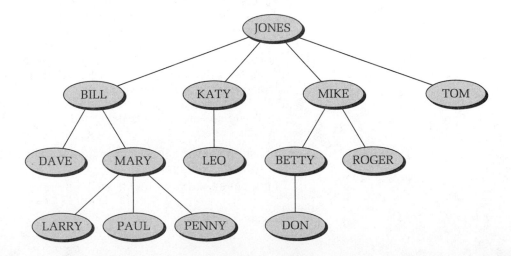

Here BILL is the first child of the JONES family, with KATY, MIKE, and TOM as BILL's siblings. Similarly, LARRY is the first child of MARY, with PAUL and PENNY as siblings. Now, in a linked representation of binary tree, we have two pointer fields associated with each node. We have called these pointer fields LeftChild and RightChild because it suited our perspective at the time. However, we shall now switch that perspective in the following way. One of the pointer fields is to be viewed as pointer to the leftmost child of a node in a general tree. The second pointer identifies the next sibling to the right of the node under consideration in the general tree. Since the children of a node taken in this context form an ordered set of nodes, we can regard the leftmost child of a node as FirstChild and the sibling to the right of this node as Sibling. We will henceforth adopt this terminology for the two link fields involved with the binary tree representation of a general tree. Figure 18.25 gives the binary representation of the general genealogical tree shown in Figure 18.24.

FIGURE 18.25
Binary tree representation of genealogical tree in Figure 18.24

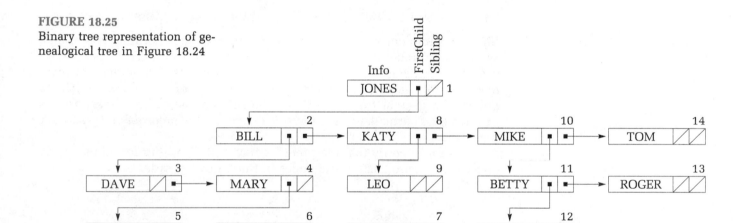

TABLE 18.4
Tree in Figure 18.24 stored in array of records for data and pointers

Location	Data	FirstChild	Sibling
1	JONES	2	0
2	BILL	3	8
3	DAVE	0	4
4	MARY	5	0
5	LARRY	0	6
6	PAUL	0	7
7	PENNY	0	0
8	KATY	9	10
9	LEO	0	0
10	MIKE	11	14
11	BETTY	12	13
12	DON	0	0
13	ROGER	0	0
14	TOM	0	0

Although we will typically use Pascal pointer variables for such a binary tree implementation of a general tree, it is worth noting that an array of records with integer pointer fields can still be used just as it was for a linked list in Chapter 15. Indeed, because this array perspective allows us to specify some actual values for pointers, we have portrayed the tree of Figure 18.24 as an array of records in Table 18.4. You should carefully check all FirstChild and Sibling values to convince yourself that the scheme used to fill this array was to store a node before any of its children, and then recursively store the leftmost child.

The analogous representation in terms of Pascal pointer variables (and the representation we shall henceforth use) requires the following type declarations:

```
GenTree = ^GenTreeNode;
GenTreeNode = RECORD
                  Info : TreeDataNode
                  FirstChild : GenTree;
                  Sibling : GenTree
              END;
```

Traversals of a General Tree Implemented via a Binary Tree

Since this implementation scheme for a general tree is nothing more than a special interpretation of a binary tree, all of the traversals defined for a binary tree clearly exist for the general tree. A more relevant question than the mere existence of a traversal, however, is the significance of the order in which the nodes of a general tree are visited when its corresponding binary tree is traversed. Of particular interest in this regard are the preorder and postorder traversals.

You should verify that the preorder traversal algorithm for a binary tree applied to Figure 18.24 visits nodes in the following order:

JONES
    BILL
        DAVE
        MARY
            LARRY
            PAUL
            PENNY
  KATY
    LEO
  MIKE
    BETTY
        DON
    ROGER
  TOM

The indentation here has been added to highlight the fact that the preorder traversal will recursively process a parent node, and then process the child nodes from left to right.

Relative to the general tree pictured in Figure 18.24, we see that the effect of the preorder traversal is to fix on a node at one level of the tree and then run through all of that node's children before progressing to the next node at the same level (the sibling). There is a hint here of a generalized nested loop situation which, as you will see, has some interesting applications in the Programming Problems.

The other traversal of interest in a binary tree representation of a general tree is the postorder traversal. In this regard, it should first be verified that the postorder traversal applied to Figure 18.24 (and its binary tree implementation in Figure 18.25) yields the following listing:

PENNY
PAUL
LARRY
MARY
DAVE
LEO
DON
ROGER
BETTY
TOM
MIKE
KATY
BILL
JONES

In general, the postorder traversal works its way up from the leaf nodes of a tree, insuring that no given node is processed until all nodes in the subtree below it have been processed.

Exercises 18.5

1. How would you implement a preorder traversal to print nodes in a fashion that has children indented under their parents?

2. Consider the following abstract graphical representation of a general tree.

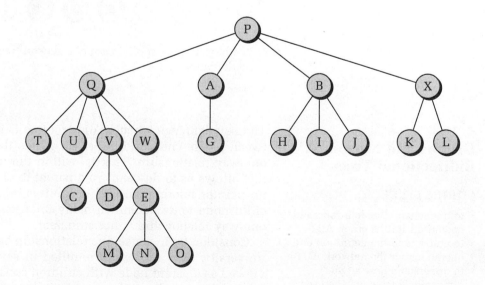

Provide a specific Pascal record description for a node in this tree as you would represent it. (Do not make any assumption about maximum possible number of children.) Then draw a specific picture of how this tree would actually be stored using the record description you have chosen.

3. Given the tree from Exercise 2, in what order would nodes be visited by a pre-order traversal? A postorder traversal?

4. For this exercise you are to assume a linked binary tree representation of a general tree. Write a procedure that meets the following specification.

```
PROCEDURE AddChild (VAR GT : GenTree;
                        ST : GenTree;
                        K : integer;
```

```
{ Given:    GT, a nonempty general tree.                        }
{           ST, another nonempty general tree.                  }
{           K>= 1.                                              }
{ Task:     Insert ST as the Kth subtree descending from        }
{           the root node of GT.                                }
{ Return:   GT with ST inserted as the Kth subtree of its       }
{           root. If the root node of GT already has            }
{           K or more subtrees, ST becomes the Kth              }
{           subtree, and the former Kth subtree becomes         }
{           the (K+1)st subtree. If the root node of GT         }
{           has fewer than K subtrees, then ST is               }
{           inserted as the last subtree of the root node.      }
```

5. Use the procedure you developed for Exercise 4 in another procedure to generate the following tree. Verify that you have generated the correct tree with a traversal procedure that outputs the tree in appropriate fashion.

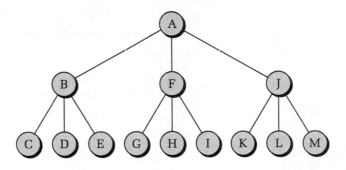

6. Is a binary tree a special case of a general tree? Provide a written rationale to justify your answer.

■ ■ ■ ■

■ 18.6
Graphs and Networks: Bidirectional Trees

The key defining characteristic of a tree is the hierarchical relationship between parent and child nodes. In a tree, this hierarchical relationship is a one-way relationship. That is, within the tree there is pointer information that allows us to descend from parent to child. However, there is generally no pointer information within the tree which allows us to ascend from a child node to its parent. In many information storage applications such a one-way relationship is not sufficient.

Consider, for instance, the relationship between students and courses at a university. Each student is enrolled in several courses and could thus be viewed as a parent node with children consisting of the courses he or she is taking. Conversely, each course enrolls many students and could thus be viewed as a parent node with children consisting of the students enrolled in that particular course. The data structure that emerges from this type of bidirectional relationship is pictured in Figure 18.26.

Objectives continued.
- to understand traversal algorithms for graphs and networks
- to understand Dijkstra's algorithm for finding the shortest path between two nodes in a network

FIGURE 18.26
Bidirectional relationship between students and courses

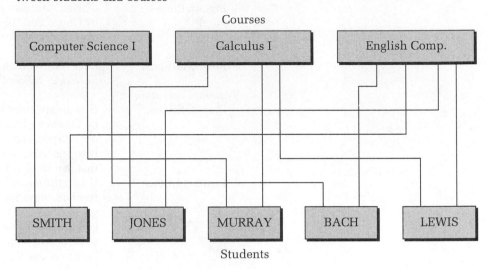

In terms of an abstract data-type, the representation of such a bidirectional relationship between nodes is called a *graph*.

> **Graph.** A graph consists of two sets. One set is a fixed set of objects called *nodes*. The other is a set of *edges,* the contents of which vary depending on the operations that have been performed upon the graph. A node is a data element of the graph, and an edge is a direct connection between two nodes. A node may also be called a *vertex* of the graph. If an edge exists between two nodes, we say that the second node is adjacent to the first node.

The operations associated with the graph ADT are specified in terms of the following pre- and postconditions:

> *Create operation*
>> Preconditions: *G* is an arbitrary graph variable.
>> Postconditions: Graph *G* initialized to a state with no edges. That is, no nodes are connected to any other nodes, including themselves.
>
> *AddEdge operation*
>> Preconditions: *G* is an arbitrary graph that has been initialized by Create and, potentially, affected by other operations. *Node1, Node2* are two nodes in graph *G*.
>> Postconditions: *G* is returned with an edge from *Node1* to *Node2*. If an edge already existed from *Node1* to *Node2*, *G* is not affected.
>
> *RemoveEdge operation*
>> Preconditions: *G* is an arbitrary graph that has been initialized by Create and, potentially, affected by other operations. *Node1, Node2* are two nodes in graph *G*.

Postconditions:	If there is an edge from *Node1* to *Node2*, it is removed. Otherwise *G* is not affected.
Edge operation	
Preconditions:	*G* is an arbitrary graph that has been initialized by Create and, potentially, affected by other operations. *Node1*, *Node2* are two nodes in graph *G*.
Postconditions:	*Edge* returns **true** if there is an edge from *Node1* to *Node2*, **false** otherwise.
Traversal operation	
Preconditions:	*G* is an arbitrary graph that has been initialized by Create and, potentially, affected by other operations. *Start* is a node at which the traversal is to start. *ProcessNode* is an algorithmic process that can be applied to each Graph node.
Postconditions:	*G* is returned with each node that can be reached from *Start* affected by *ProcessNode*. A given node can be reached from *Start* if the given node is the *Start* node or if there is a sequence of edges $E_0, E_1, \ldots, E_n$ such that E_0 begins at the *Start* node, the node at which E_{i-1} ends is the node at which E_i begins, and E_n is the given node. In effect, the sequence of edges determines a path from *Start* to the given node. The path is composed of edges between adjacent nodes. *ProcessNode* is not applied to any node more than once.

Notice that, as it relates to Figure 18.26, the formal definition of a graph does not rule out the possibility of an edge connecting two courses or connecting two students. It is merely the nature of this course-student relationship that makes the existence of such a course-to-course edge or student-to-student

FIGURE 18.27

Transportation network as graph in which edges represent flights between cities

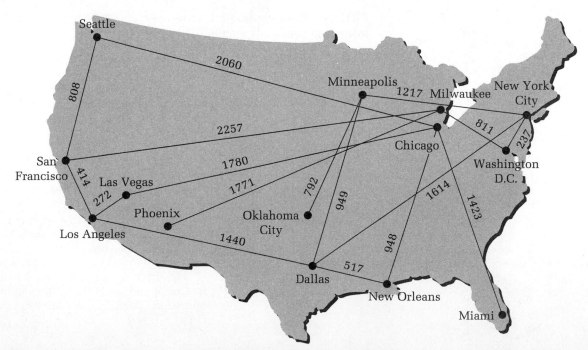

edge impractical. In other applications, such as the transportation network pictured in Figure 18.27, it may be entirely feasible for any node in the graph to have an edge connecting it to any other node.

To illustrate how a graph grows from an initial state with no edges, suppose that we start with a set of nodes labeled A, B, C, D. Figure 18.28 traces the effect of a sequence of AddEdge and RemoveEdge operations on a graph with these nodes.

FIGURE 18.28
Graph affected by sequence of AddEdge and RemoveEdge operations

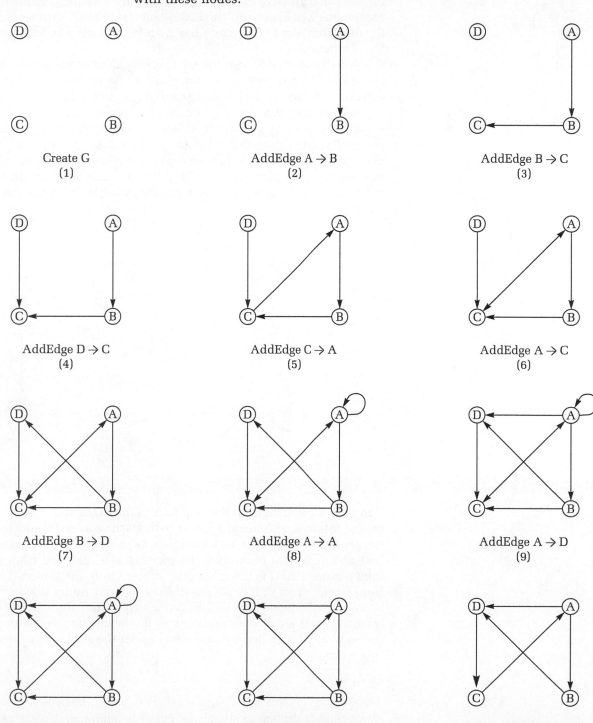

Note from this figure that the concept of an edge carries with it the notion of a direction. That is, it is possible to have an edge from Node1 to Node2 in a graph G without there being a corresponding connection in the opposite direction. Figure 18.28 (8) also illustrates that it is possible to have an edge from a node to itself.

By convention, when we draw a graph without arrows on the edges, it is implicit that all edges run in both directions. Thus, in Figure 18.27, the line connecting San Francisco and Los Angeles implicitly represents two edges— the one from San Francisco to Los Angeles and the one from Los Angeles to San Francisco.

We will sometimes use the terminology *directional graph,* or *digraph,* to emphasize that a particular graph has some edges that exist only in one direction. Figure 18.29 illustrates a digraph. In a digraph, we use arrows on edges to specify the direction of an edge between nodes.

Before providing a Pascal interface for the graph ADT, we should clarify a point of ambiguity in the definition of the traversal operation. In particular, this operation does not establish a unique order of visiting nodes that can be reached from the Start node. The following examples illustrate two potential orders in which nodes can be visited starting at A in the graph of Figure 18.29.

FIGURE 18.29
A four-node digraph

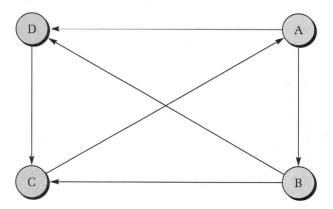

■ **EXAMPLE 18.7**

Consider a traversal from Start node A in the digraph of Figure 18.29 guided by the following strategy: a given path starting at A should be explored as deeply as possible before another path is probed. If we assume that B is the first node adjacent to A, then the traversal will proceed from A to B. If we then assume that C is the first node adjacent to B, the traversal will continue from B to C. From C, it is not possible to visit any nodes that have not already been visited. Hence, we will backtrack to B and, from there, continue the traversal to D since D is adjacent to B. Hence the overall order in which nodes would be visited by a traversal under the strategy and assumptions of this example is

A, B, C, D

The strategy exemplified here is often called a *depth-first traversal* since a given path is probed as deeply as possible before we backtrack and explore another path.

■   ■

■ **EXAMPLE 18.8**

Indicate the order in which nodes would be visited in a traversal starting at node A in the digraph of Figure 18.29 following a strategy that does not probe one path as deeply as possible but rather "fans out" to all nodes adjacent to a given node. Hence we would proceed from A to B and then to D, since both B and D are adjacent to A. Since all nodes adjacent to A have been exhausted, we would fan out from B, the first node we visited from A. This takes us to C by the edge B → C, completing the traversal in the overall order

A, B, D, C

The fan-out strategy exemplified here is often termed a *breadth-first traversal*.
■   ■

Examples 18.7 and 18.8 just begin to scratch the surface of the variety of graph traversal strategies that exist. We shall soon examine the implementation of these traversal strategies more closely. At this time the point to emphasize is that the graph traversal operation is open to a variety of implementation techniques.

Pascal Interface for the Graph ADT

Before we can develop graph algorithms in detail, we must provide a Pascal interface for this ADT. This is done in the following procedure and function headers. The interface makes the assumption that the data in graph nodes are drawn from an appropriate subrange of an ordinal data type such as **integer, char,** or an enumerated type. Our reasons for making this assumption will become apparent when we discuss ways of implementing graphs.

```
CONST
   FirstNode = {The first value in the subrange for the GraphNode type};
   LastNode  = {The last value in the subrange for the GraphNode type};

TYPE
   GraphNode = FirstNode .. LastNode;
   Graph = { An appropriate implementation of the graph ADT };

PROCEDURE Create (VAR G : Graph);
   { Given:   G -- an arbitrary graph variable.                          }
   { Task:    Initialize G.                                              }
   { Return:  Graph G initialized to a state with no edges.              }
   {          That is, no nodes are connected to any other              }
   {          nodes, including themselves.                               }

PROCEDURE AddEdge (VAR G : Graph;
                   Node1, Node2 : GraphNode);

   { Given:   G -- an arbitrary graph that has been initialized          }
   {          by Create and, potentially, affected by other            }
   {          operations.                                                }
   {          Node1, Node2 -- two nodes in graph G.                      }
   { Task:    Add an edge from Node1 to Node2 in G.                      }
   { Return:  G with an edge from Node1 to Node2.  If an edge            }
   {          already existed from Node1 to Node2, G is not             }
   {          affected.                                                  }

PROCEDURE RemoveEdge (VAR G : Graph;
                      Node1, Node2 : GraphNode);
```

```
{ Given:   G -- an arbitrary graph that has been initialized   }
{          by Create and, potentially, affected by other       }
{          operations.                                          }
{          Node1, Node2 -- two nodes in graph G.                }
{ Task:    Remove the edge from Node1 to Node2 in G.            }
{ Return:  If there is an edge from Node1 to Node2, it          }
{          is removed.  Otherwise G is not affected.            }

FUNCTION Edge (G : Graph;
               Node1, Node2 : GraphNode) : boolean;

{ Given:   G -- an arbitrary graph that has been initialized   }
{          by Create and, potentially, affected by other       }
{          operations.                                          }
{          Node1, Node2 -- two nodes in graph G.                }
{ Task:    Determine if there is an edge from Node1 to Node2.   }
{ Return:  True if there is an edge from Node1 to Node2,        }
{          false otherwise.                                     }

PROCEDURE GraphTraversal (VAR G : Graph;
                          VAR Start : GraphNode;
                          PROCEDURE ProcessNode (VAR Item : GraphNode));

{ Given:   G -- an arbitrary graph that has been initialized   }
{          by Create and, potentially, affected by other       }
{          operations.                                          }
{          Start -- a node at which the traversal is to start.  }
{          ProcessNode -- this procedure determines the        }
{          process applied to each Graph node.                  }
{ Task:    Apply ProcessNode to each node that can be reached   }
{          from Start in graph G.                               }
{ Return:  G with each node that can be reached from Start      }
{          affected by ProcessNode.  ProcessNode is not         }
{          applied to any node more than once.                  }
```

The Network ADT

Graphs such as that in Figure 18.27 are somewhat special in that the edges
have weights associated with them, here representing distances between
nodes (cities). Such a graph is an example of the *network* abstract data type.

Network. A network is a graph in which each edge has a positive
numerical *weight*. The operations associated with the network ADT are
the same as those for the graph ADT with the exceptions that the
AddEdge operation must now specify the weight of the Edge being
added and we must add an operation which, given two nodes, returns
the weight of the edge that may exist between them.

These two new operations are specified by the following pre- and postconditions.

AddEdge operation

Preconditions:
N is an arbitrary network that has been initialized by Create and, potentially, affected by other operations. *Node1, Node2* are two nodes in network *N*. *Wt* is a positive number representing the weight of an edge to be added from *Node1* to *Node2*.

Postconditions:
N has an edge of weight *Wt* from *Node1* to *Node2*. If an edge already existed from *Node1* to *Node2*, the weight of that edge is now *Wt*.

EdgeWeight operation

Preconditions:
N is an arbitrary network that has been initialized by Create and, potentially, affected by other operations. *Node1, Node2* are two nodes in network *N*.

Postconditions:
EdgeWeight returns zero if there is no edge from *Node1* to *Node2* and the numerical value of the edge if it exists.

Graphs and networks provide excellent examples of how a theoretical area of mathematics has found very relevant application in computer science. It is beyond the scope of this text to provide a comprehensive treatment of graphs and networks. Rather, our purpose in the rest of this section is to provide you with an overview of a data structure which you will no doubt encounter again as you continue your study of computer science. More in-depth treatments of graphs and networks can be found in numerous advanced texts on data structures such as *Data Structures in Pascal* by Ellis Horowitz and Sartaj Sahni (New York, N.Y.: Computer Science Press, 1990) and *Introduction to Data Structures and Algorithm Analysis with Pascal* by Thomas L. Naps and George J. Pothering (St. Paul, Minn.: West Publishing, 1992).

Implementation of Graphs and Networks

A graph may be conveniently implemented using a two-dimensional table of Boolean values. For instance, the information in Figure 18.26 is contained in the following two-dimensional table (Table 18.5). In this table, the value **true** indicates the presence of an edge between two nodes and the value **false** indicates the absence of such an edge.

TABLE 18.5
Two-dimensional table implementation of graph from Figure 18.26

Course	SMITH	JONES	MURRAY	BACH	LEWIS
Computer Science	true	false	true	true	false
Calculus I	false	true	true	false	true
English Comp.	true	true	false	true	true

In the case of a network, the two-dimensional table implementation still applies. Now, however, the data stored in the table is of a type compatible with edge weights. Such a two-dimensional table implementation of the transportation network from Figure 18.27 is given in Table 18.6. Note that the data are mirrored across the diagonal of the table because all edges are bidirectional.

TABLE 18.6
Two-dimensional table implementation of network from Figure 18.27

	NY	Wash	Miami	Milw	Chi	NOrl	Mpls	OklC	Dals	LVeg	Phex	Stl	SFran	LA
NY		237					1217		1614					
Wash	237			811										
Miami					1423									
Milw		811									1771		2257	
Chi			1423			948				1780		2060		
NOrl					948				517					
Mpls	1217							792	949					
Oklc							792							
Dals	1614					517	949							1440
LVeg					1780									272
Phex				1771										
Stl					2060									808
SFran				2257								808		414
LA									1440	272			414	

Table 18.6 illustrates a quality typically found in two-dimensional table implementations of large graphs and networks: the sparseness of nontrivial data. Hence, the methods we have discussed for implementing sparse tables actually provide alternative implementation strategies for graphs and networks. In fact, the pilot/flight data-base problem of Wing-and-a-Prayer Airlines, with which we introduced the sparse matrix ADT in Chapter 13, may now be viewed as a graph problem. This problem presented us with a bidirectional tree in which each pilot could have multiple flights as child nodes and, conversely, each flight could have multiple pilots as child nodes.

In the discussion of the two graph/network algorithms that follow, we do not tie ourselves to a particular implementation strategy for representing the underlying data structure. Rather, we discuss the algorithms in terms of the operations associated with the abstract data type involved and leave implementation considerations for the Exercises and Programming Problems at the end of the chapter.

Examples of Graph Algorithms: Depth-First and Breadth-First Traversals

In many practical applications of graphs, there is frequently a need to systematically visit all the nodes on a graph from a designated starting node. One such application occurs in a political campaign when the organizers of the campaign are interested in having their candidate visit all important political centers. The presence or absence of direct transportation routes (that is, edges) between such centers will determine the possible ways in which all the centers could be visited. At the moment, our only concern is the development of an algorithm which insures that all possible nodes are visited. Such an algorithm will provide an implementation for the graph traversal operation. Later in the chapter we investigate how to determine the shortest possible distances from one node to all others.

Depth-First Traversal. This technique was illustrated in Example 18.7. The main logic of the depth-first algorithm is analogous to the preorder traversal of a tree. It is accomplished recursively as follows:

1. Designate the starting node as the search node and mark it as visited.
2. Find a node adjacent to the search node (that is, connected by an edge from the search node) which has not yet been visited. Designate this as the new search node (but remember the previous one) and mark it as visited.
3. Repeat step 2 using the new search node. If no nodes satisfying step 2 can be found, return to the previous search node and continue from there.
4. When a return to the previous search node in step 3 is impossible, the search from the originally chosen search node is complete.

This algorithm is called a depth-first traversal because the search continues progressively deeper into the graph in a recursive manner.

To illustrate this procedure more clearly, consider Figure 18.30; its table implementation is shown in Table 18.7.

FIGURE 18.30
Graph to illustrate depth-first search

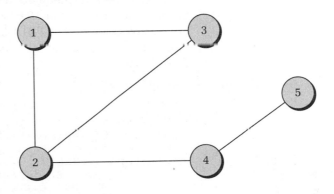

TABLE 18.7
Table implementation of Figure 18.30

	1	2	3	4	5
1	false	true	true	false	false
2	true	false	true	true	false
3	true	true	false	false	false
4	false	true	false	false	true
5	false	false	false	true	false

Suppose we have a procedure called SearchFrom which is invoked to begin a depth-first traversal from a given node on the graph. The steps followed by the algorithm are

1. We begin by marking node 1 visited and invoke SearchFrom(1).
2. Both nodes 2 and 3 are adjacent to node 1 according to the matrix implementation of the graph, but node 2 is encountered first on a left-to-right scan of the row for 1; so the search goes to node 2. We invoke SearchFrom(2), and node 2 is marked as visited.
3. Since node 3 is the first unvisited node adjacent to node 2, the search now goes to node 3, SearchFrom(3) is invoked, and node 3, is marked as visited.

4. Since there is no unvisited node adjacent to node 3, we say that this node has exhausted the search; the search goes back to its predecessor, that is, to node 2.

5. From node 2, we visit node 4.

6. From node 4, we proceed to node 5. All nodes have now been visited, and the depth-first traversal is complete.

Use Table 18.7 to verify these steps.

We note that the order in which nodes are visited in a depth-first traversal is not unique. This is because the order is dependent upon the manner in which "adjacent" nodes are chosen. That is, given two unvisited nodes adjacent to another node, which one should be chosen to invoke the Search-From procedure? In practice, this will usually be determined by the ordering of the data type used to implement the nodes in the graph.

■ **EXAMPLE 18.9**

Implement the depth-first traversal algorithm under the assumption that the GraphNode data type is a subrange of an ordinal type.

As with our implementation of the postorder traversal operation for a binary tree in Example 18.6, we use an auxiliary procedure as the real recursive workhorse. The **PROCEDURE** GraphTraversal itself is merely a front-end which appropriately sets the stage for the auxiliary **PROCEDURE** SearchFrom.

```
{  Global declarations  }

TYPE
  GraphNode = FirstNode .. LastNode;
  Graph = {  Appropriate implementation of the graph ADT  }

PROCEDURE GraphTraversal (VAR G : Graph;
                          VAR Start : GraphNode;
                          PROCEDURE ProcessNode (VAR Item : GraphNode));

  { Given:   G -- an arbitrary graph that has been initialized    }
  {          by Create and, potentially, affected by other        }
  {          operations.                                           }
  {          Start -- a node at which the traversal is to start.   }
  {          ProcessNode -- this procedure determines the         }
  {          process applied to each Graph node.                   }
  { Task:    Apply ProcessNode to each node that can be reached    }
  {          from Start in graph G.  Use a depth-first traversal to }
  {          determine these nodes.                                }
  { Return:  G with each node that can be reached from Start       }
  {          affected by ProcessNode.  ProcessNode is not          }
  {          applied to any node more than once.                   }

VAR
  K : GraphNode;
  Visited : ARRAY [GraphNode] OF boolean;

PROCEDURE SearchFrom (K : GraphNode);

  { Given:   K -- a single node in G.                              }
  { Task:    Conduct depth-first traversal from node K until all   }
  {          possibilities have been exhausted.                    }
  { Return:  Each node reachable from K affected by ProcessNode    }
```

```
VAR
  J : GraphNode;

BEGIN
  Visited[K] := true;
  ProcessNode (K);
  FOR J := FirstNode TO LastNode DO
    IF NOT Visited[J] AND Edge (G, K, J) THEN
      SearchFrom(J)  {  Recursively progress deeper into graph }
END; {  of PROCEDURE SearchFrom  }

BEGIN {  DepthFirstTraversal  }
  FOR K := FirstNode TO LastNode DO
    Visited[K] := false;  {  Initially no nodes visited  }
  {  Begin traversal from Start node.  }
  SearchFrom (Start)
END; {  of PROCEDURE DepthFirstSearch  }
```

We can now see the reason for the restriction placed upon the type Graph-Node in our Pascal interface for the graph ADT. It must be a type capable of indexing an array and an iterative loop structure. Both of these properties are assumed in the code of Example 18.9.

Breadth-First Traversal. An alternate graph traversal to the depth-first strategy is the breadth-first traversal. Instead of proceeding as deeply as possible along one path from the current node in the graph, the breadth-first traversal examines all nodes adjacent to the current node before proceeding more deeply along any given path. Hence, for the graph of Figure 18.31 implemented by Table 18.8, a breadth-first traversal starting at node 1 would visit nodes in the order 1, 2, 3, 4, 5 (as opposed to the order 1, 2, 4, 5, 3 that a depth-first traversal would dictate).

FIGURE 18.31
Graph to illustrate breadth-first traversal

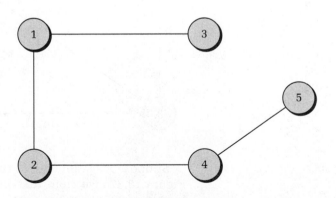

TABLE 18.8
Table implementation of Figure 18.31

	1	2	3	4	5
1	false	true	true	false	false
2	true	false	false	true	false
3	true	false	false	false	false
4	false	true	false	false	true
5	false	false	false	true	false

A breadth-first traversal of a graph involves the following steps:

1. Begin with the Start node, and mark it as visited.
2. Proceed to the next node having an edge connection to the node in step 1. Mark it as visited.
3. Come back to the node in step 1, descend along an edge toward an unvisited node, and mark the new node as visited.
4. Repeat step 3 until all nodes adjacent to the node in step 1 have been marked as visited.
5. Repeat steps 1 — 4 starting from the node visited in 2, then starting from the nodes visited in step 3 in the order visited. Keep this up as long as possible before starting a new scan.

You will be asked to explore this strategy in the Programming Problems at the end of the chapter.

Example of a Network Algorithm: Finding Shortest Paths

If the graph under consideration is a network in which edge weights represent distances, then an appropriate question is: From a given node called the Source, what is the shortest distance to all other nodes in the network?

For instance, the network of Figure 18.32 could be thought of as showing airline routes between cities. An airline would be interested in finding the most economical route between any two given cities in the network. The numbers listed on the edges would, in this case, represent distances between cities. Thus, the airline wishes to find the shortest path that can be flown from node 3 in order to reach nodes 1, 2, 4, and 5.

FIGURE 18.32

Network with edge weights representing distances

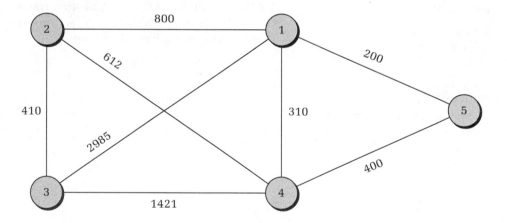

Suppose we want to find the shortest path from node 1 to node 3. From Figure 18.32, we note that this path would be 1→2→3, yielding a total weight of 800 + 410 = 1,210. An algorithm to find such a path was discovered by E. W. Dijkstra. For convenience in discussing Dijkstra's algorithm, often called the shortest path algorithm, let us assume that the nodes in the network under consideration are numbered 1, 2, . . ., NumberOfNodes. That is, the type GraphNode is the subrange of the integers given by 1 . . NumberOfNodes.

Given such a collection of nodes, Dijkstra's algorithm requires three arrays in addition to a suitable implementation of the network M. These three arrays are identified as follows:

```
VAR
    Distance, Path : ARRAY [GraphNode] OF integer;
    Included : ARRAY [GraphNode] OF boolean;
```

Identifying one node as the Source, the algorithm proceeds to find the shortest distance from Source to all other nodes in the network. At the conclusion of the algorithm, the shortest distance from Source to node J is stored in Distance[J] while Path[J] contains the immediate predecessor of node J on the path determining this shortest distance. While the algorithm is in progress, Distance[J] and Path[J] are being continually updated until Included[J] is switched from **false** to **true**. Once this switch occurs, it is known definitely that Distance[J] contains the shortest distance from Source to J. The algorithm progresses until all nodes have been so included. Hence it actually gives us the shortest distance from Source to every other node in the network.

Given the Source node in the network M, the algorithm may be divided into two phases: an initialization phase followed by an iteration phase in which nodes are included one by one in the set of nodes for which the shortest distance from Source is known definitely.

During the initialization phase, we must

1. Initialize Included[Source] to **true** and Included [J] to **false** for all other J.
2. Initialize the Distance array via the rule

$$\text{Distance[J]} = \begin{cases} 0 \text{ if J = Source} \\ \text{EdgeWeight(M,Source,J) if EdgeWeight(M,Source,J)} <> 0 \\ \text{Infinity if J is not connected to Source by a} \\ \quad \text{direct edge (that is, if} \\ \quad \text{EdgeWeight(M,Source,J)} = 0) \end{cases}$$

3. Initialize the Path array via the rule

$$\text{Path[J]} = \begin{cases} \text{Source if EdgeWeight (M,Source,J)} <> 0 \\ \text{Undefined otherwise} \end{cases}$$

Given this initialization, the iteration phase may be expressed in a generalized pseudocode form as follows:

REPEAT

1. Find the node J which has the minimal Distance among those nodes not yet Included;
2. Mark J as now Included;
3. **FOR** each R not yet Included
   3.1 **IF** there is an edge from J to R **THEN**
       3.1.1 **IF** Distance[J] + EdgeWeight (M,J,R) < Distance[R] **THEN**
             3.1.1.1 Distance[R] := Distance[J] + EdgeWeight (M,J,R)
             3.1.1.2 Path[R] := J

UNTIL all nodes are Included

The crucial part of the algorithm occurs within the innermost **IF** of the **FOR** loop. Figure 18.33 provides a pictorial representation of the logic involved here. The nodes included with the circle represent those nodes already Included prior to a given iteration of the **REPEAT** loop. The node J in Figure 18.33 represents the node found in the first step of the **REPEAT** loop; R represents another arbitrary node which has not yet been Included. The lines emanating from Source represent the paths corresponding to the current entries in the Distance array. For nodes within the circle—that is, those already Included—these paths are guaranteed to be the shortest-distance paths. If J is the node having the minimal entry in Distance among those not yet Included, we will add J to the circle of Included nodes and then check to see if J's connections to other nodes in the network which are not yet Included may result in a newly found shorter path to such nodes.

FIGURE 18.33
REPEAT loop logic in shortest-path (Dijkstra's) algorithm

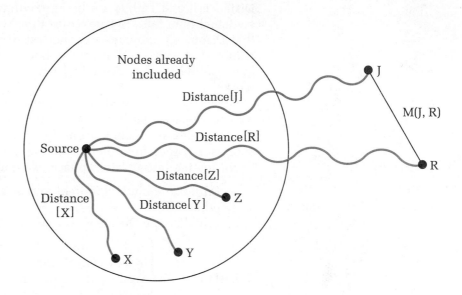

Referring to Figure 18.33 again, the sum of two sides of a triangle

Distance [J] + EdgeWeight(M,J,R)

may in fact be shorter than the third side,

Distance[R]

This geometric contradiction is possible because these are not true straight-sided triangles, but "triangles" whose sides may be very complicated paths through a network.

It is also apparent from Figure 18.33 why Dijkstra's algorithm works. As the node J in this figure is found to have the minimal Distance entry from among all those nodes not yet Included, we may now Include it among the nodes whose minimal distance from the Source node is absolutely known. Why? Consider any other path P to J containing nodes which are not yet Included at the time J is Included. Let X be the first such non-Included node on the path P. Then clearly, as the first non-Included node on the Path P, X must be adjacent to an Included node. However as Figure 18.34 indicates, the criterion that dictated the choice of J as an Included node insures that

Distance[J] ≤ The total edge weight through node X on the path P
 ≤ Total edge weight of Path P

This inequality demonstrates that, once J is Included, there exists no other path P to J through a non-Included node that can yield a shorter overall distance. Hence we have verified our claim that Including a node guarantees our having found a path of shortest possible distance to that node.

FIGURE 18.34
Guaranteeing the minimality of
Distance to J once it is Included

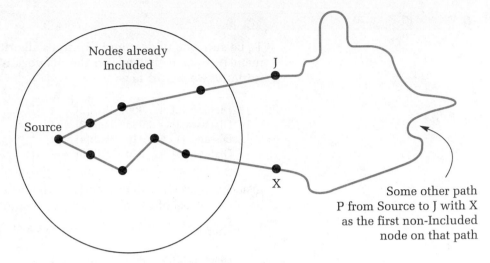

Criterion for Including J ensures
Distance [J] ≤ Distance[X] ≤ Length of path P

Computer Networks: More Than an Abstract Data Type

Beginning with ARPANET (Advanced Research Projects Agency Network) in 1969, a relatively large number of computer networks have been developed, linking computers at various sites. These networks offer users the ability to trade information between computers across electronic communications lines. Typically, this information takes the form of electronic mail and text files. Electronic mail allows users working on related projects at distant sites to keep in touch at costs that are much cheaper than long-distance phone calls and at speeds of transmission that are *much* faster than postal service.

Using electronic mail is as easy as typing your message into the computer and then specifying the electronic mail address of the recipient. Usually these electronic mail addresses are a combination of the recipient name and computer installation. For example, one of the authors has the address NAPST@LAWRENCE.EDU on the InterNet network. Anyone using a computer with access to InterNet could send electronic data to Naps by routing the message to this address.

Among the best-known networks are ARPANET and MILNET, largely for the military and defense-oriented research; CSNET for computer science research; company networks such as DEC's Easynet and Xerox's Internet;

and cooperative networks among users with common interests such as BITNET and InterNet (largely academic) and USENET (users of the UNIX operating system).

Although such networks are a godsend for users, the problems connected with their development have been monumental. One such problem concerns the routing of information from node to node along the network as data travel from originator to destination. Complicating this issue is the fact that individual networks often interconnect at so-called gateway nodes, making it possible for users on one network to relay information to someone on a completely different network. The information follows some interesting paths. For instance, to send a message from Wisconsin to New Jersey, one of the authors observed that the eventual path chosen by the routing software included computers at the University of Utah and the University of Texas. Clearly, the software does not employ Dijkstra's shortest path algorithm! (See Section 18.6.)

An excellent survey of existing computer networks appeared in *Scientific American* 265, No. 3 (September 1991). The entire issue is dedicated to articles on communications, computers, and networks. You should consult it for more information on this subject.

■ **EXAMPLE 18.10**

To be sure you understand Dijkstra's algorithm before you attempt to implement it, trace it through on the network of Figure 18.32 with Source = 1. Initially, we would have

```
Distance[2] =  800   Path[2] = 1
Distance[3] = 2985   Path[3] = 1
Distance[4] =  310   Path[4] = 1
Distance[5] =  200   Path[5] = 1
```

in accordance with steps 2 and 3 of the initialization phase. According to the iteration phase of the algorithm, we would then, in order

1. Include node 5; no change in Distance and Path needed.

```
Distance[2] =  800   Path[2] = 1
Distance[3] = 2985   Path[3] = 1
Distance[4] =  310   Path[4] = 1
Distance[5] =  200   Path[5] = 1
```

2. Include node 4; update Distance and Path to

```
Distance[2] =  800   Path[2] = 1
Distance[3] = 1731   Path[3] = 4
Distance[4] =  310   Path[4] = 1
Distance[5] =  200   Path[5] = 1
```

(Note that it is shorter to go from node 1 to node 4 to node 3 than to follow the edge directly connecting node 1 to node 3.)

3. Include node 2; update Distance and Path to

```
Distance[2] =  800   Path[2] = 1
Distance[3] = 1210   Path[3] = 2
Distance[4] =  310   Path[4] = 1
Distance[5] =  200   Path[5] = 1
```

(Now we find that traveling from node 1 to node 2 to node 3 is even better than the path determined in step 2.)

4. Finally node 3 is Included with (obviously) no changes made in Distance or Path.

■   ■

Exercises 18.6

1. Indicate the order that nodes would be visited if a depth-first traversal of the network in Figure 18.27 were initiated from SEATTLE. Use the adjacency relationships from Table 18.6.

2. Repeat Exercise 1 but initiate the traversal from MIAMI.

3. Repeat Exercise 1 for a breadth-first traversal.

4. Repeat Exercise 2 for a breadth-first traversal.

5. Trace the contents of the Distance, Path, and Included arrays as Dijkstra's shortest path algorithm is applied to the transportation network of Figure 18.27. Use PHOENIX as the Source node.

6. Repeat Exercise 5 with MILWAUKEE as the Source node.

7. Using a two-dimensional table, write procedures to implement each of the basic operations for the graph abstract data type. Then provide a big-O time efficiency analysis of each of the operations. How is this analysis affected by a particular sparse matrix technique that may be underlying the two-dimensional table? Be as specific as possible in stating your answer.

8. Using a two-dimensional table, write procedures to implement each of the basic operations for the network abstract data type.

9. In a written statement, discuss the implications of eliminating the requirement that **TYPE** GraphNode be a subrange of an ordinal type in the Pascal interface for the graph ADT. Your statement should identify problems that this would cause and outline strategies for solving such problems.

■ ■ ■ ■

FOCUS ON PROGRAM DESIGN

Throughout this text we have emphasized the importance of big-O algorithm analysis as a means of predicting beforehand the practicality of an algorithm in a given application. In this regard, big-O notation and analysis serves a vital purpose—the estimation of the time and space requirements of an algorithm in order of magnitude terms. However, when designing software systems in the very competitive and demanding real world, we often require a more detailed measurement of an algorithm's performance than that which can be achieved simply with a big-O analysis. One reason for this is the variety of complications that cannot be conveniently plugged into a big-O formula. Included among these complications are

■ The variety of hardware on which an algorithm must ultimately be executed. There will be vast differences in both the time and space limitations of such hardware. Moreover, the details of such limitations are often buried deep in system reference manuals and can be exceedingly hard to find.
■ Discrepancies that frequently arise between a user's projection of his or her computer needs and the unforeseen demands that materialize once the software system is put into use. A good systems analyst can hold those discrepancies to a minimum but not totally eliminate them.
■ The elements of chance and probability that are inherent in many algorithms.

An example of this final point is the order of arrivals for insertion into a binary search tree. We can guarantee that search efficiency in a binary search tree will be between $O(n)$ and $O(\log_2 n)$. We can specify best and worst cases. But what happens in between? When do we cross over from response times that are acceptable to those that are not? Real-life data are rarely best case or worst case. Hence the "in-between" question is often of vital importance. Yet it is also the one that a pure big-O analysis leaves relatively unanswered.

In this section, we present a program that can serve as a start toward further exploration of the questions just posed. The program reads a list of unordered integers from a file, creates a binary search tree containing those integers, and then prints the binary search tree using indentation to reflect the level at which various nodes occur in the tree. In its present form, the program will allow you to test hypotheses about the relationship of the order of arrivals for insertion into a binary search tree and the resulting shape of the tree. In the first Programming Problem, you will extend the exploratory capabilities of the program, making it a substantive experimental tool.

A modular structure chart for the program is given in Figure 18.35.

FIGURE 18.35
Modular structure chart for
PROGRAM BinarySearchTree

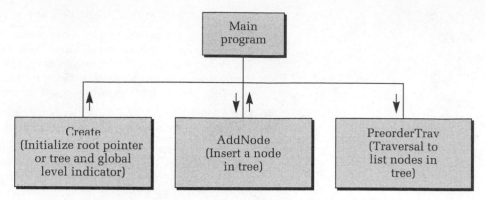

The program essentially brings together tree processing modules that we have already discussed on an individual basis; therefore, we do not provide the module specifications here. Pseudocode for the main program is

1. Create root for tree
2. **WHILE NOT eof DO**
   2.1. get a number
   2.2. add a node
3. Print the tree

One twist is needed in the preorder traversal algorithm. To achieve indentation reflecting the depth of a node in the tree, we must keep track of our current level as we recursively call and then return from **PROCEDURE** PreorderTrav. The ideal solution would be to declare a local counter in the procedure that would retain its value from one invocation of the procedure to the next. Unfortunately, this is impossible with local variables in Pascal.

We are left with two alternatives: tag the level counter along as an additional **VAR** parameter for the PreorderTrav procedure or use a global level counter. The former alternative will alter the procedural interface to the PostorderTrav operation and hence violate the ADT implementation rule (formulated in Chapter 13). Hence we choose the latter alternative—use of a global variable—as the lesser of two evils. You should be aware that the need to preserve the value of a variable between invocations of a procedure is one instance in which the use of a global variable in a procedure can be justified, provided that you carefully document its use.

The complete program and a sample run follow. You will have the chance to explore the program more thoroughly in the Problems.

```
PROGRAM BinarySearchTree (input, output);

  { This program illustrates working with a binary tree.   }
  { Input is an unordered list of integers.  Output is a   }
  { character-based representation of the binary search    }
  { tree that is constructed from the read integers.       }
  {                                                        }
  { Global variables:                                      }
  { Number--integer read from the data file                }
  { BT--pointer to indicate the tree root                  }
  { Level--global variable used to control indentation in   }
  { printing the tree                                      }

CONST
  Space = ' ';
```

```
TYPE
  TreeDataNode = integer;
  BinaryTree = ^RootNode;
  RootNode = RECORD
               LeftChild : BinaryTree;
               Info : TreeDataNode;
               RightChild : BinaryTree
             END;

VAR
  BT : BinaryTree;
  Number : TreeDataNode;
  Level : integer;

PROCEDURE Create (VAR BT : BinaryTree);

  {  Given:  BT, a binary tree, potentially not initialized.    }
  {  Task:   Initialize BT to an empty tree.                    }
  {  Return: Initialized tree.                                  }

  BEGIN
    BT := NIL;
    Level := 0  { In addition to initializing the root pointer to }
                { NIL, we initialize the Level counter used to     }
                { control indentation in printing.                 }
  END; {  of PROCEDURE Create  }

PROCEDURE AddNode (VAR BT : BinaryTree;
                   Item : TreeDataNode);

  {  Given:  BT, a binary search tree with                      }
  {          ordering property, implemented by Pascal pointer   }
  {          variables.  Item, a value to be inserted           }
  {          in tree BT.                                        }
  {  Task:   Insert Item in tree BT, maintaining                }
  {          the tree's ordering property.                      }
  {  Return: Appropriately altered tree.                        }

  BEGIN
    IF BT = NIL THEN  {  Add a new node  }
      BEGIN
        new (BT);
        BT^.Info := Item;
        BT^.LeftChild := NIL;
        BT^.RightChild := NIL
      END
    ELSE IF Item < BT^.Info THEN { Move down the list }
      AddNode (BT^.LeftChild, Item)
    ELSE
      AddNode (BT^.RightChild, Item)
  END; {  of PROCEDURE AddNode  }

PROCEDURE PreorderTrav (BT : BinaryTree;
                        PROCEDURE ProcessNode (VAR Item : TreeDataNode));

  {  Given:  Binary tree BT implemented by Pascal pointer       }
  {          variables.                                         }
  {  Task:   Perform preorder traversal--root of BT first,      }
  {          then left subtree, then right subtree--applying    }
  {          ProcessNode to each Item in the tree.              }
  {  Return: BT with each node affected by ProcessNode          }
```

```
  BEGIN
    IF BT <> NIL THEN
      BEGIN
        ProcessNode (BT^.Info);
        Level := Level + 1;   { We're recursing, so increase Level   }
        PreorderTrav (BT^.LeftChild, ProcessNode);
        PreorderTrav (BT^.RightChild, ProcessNode);
        Level := Level - 1    { Done recursing, so decrease Level     }
      END
    ELSE
      writeln (Space : Level * 4, ' NIL') { NIL to highlight end of  }
                                      { branch                       }
END; {  of PROCEDURE PreorderTrav  }

PROCEDURE PrintNode (VAR Item : TreeDataNode);

  { Given:   Item, a value in the binary search tree              }
  { Task:    Print Item, appropriately indented to reflect its    }
  {          position in the tree                                 }
  { Return:  Nothing                                              }

  BEGIN
    IF Level = 0 THEN
      writeln (Item : 4)
    ELSE
      writeln (Space : Level * 4, Item : 4)
  END;  { of PROCEDURE PrintNode }

  BEGIN  {  Main program  }
    Create (BT);
    WHILE NOT eof DO
      BEGIN
        readln (Number);
        AddNode (BT, Number)
      END;
    PreorderTrav (BT, PrintNode)
  END.  {  of main program  }
```

A sample run with the input file

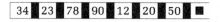

results in the following output. Graphic lines have been added to highlight how the indentation reflects the tree structure.

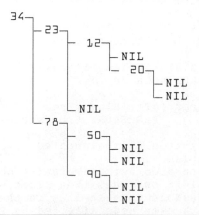

**RUNNING AND
DEBUGGING TIPS**

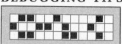

1. Trees are inherently recursive data structures, so learn to think recursively when devising algorithms that process trees.

2. When using the linear array representation of a binary tree, remember that all array locations must be initialized to a flagging Null value if the implementations of other operations are to work correctly.

3. The use of a preorder traversal to print a tree with indentation to reflect the depth of a node is a handy tracing tool to use when debugging a tree program that has gone awry. Keep such a procedure in your library, so it is readily available when the need arises. For more information, see this chapter's Focus on Program Design section.

4. When using a binary search tree to implement a keyed list, some experimentation may be necessary to determine the efficiency of this technique for the particular data of your application.

■ **Summary**

Key Terms

ancestor	edge	parent node
binary search tree	general tree	postorder traversal
binary tree	graph	preorder traversal
binary tree	heap	root
implementation of	heap property	root node
general tree	height balancing	siblings
binary	hierarchy	subtree
implementation of	inorder traversal	ternary tree
a keyed list	insertion rule	threading
branch	leaf node	tree
breadth-first traversal	level	tree traversal
child node	linear representation	vertex
depth-first traversal	linked representation	weight
digraph	network	
directional graph	ordering property	

Key Concepts

- Trees are a data structure used to reflect a hierarchical relationship among data items. Indicative of this hierarchy is the parent-child terminology used to express the relationship between items on successive levels of the tree. Trees are by nature recursive structures, with each node of a tree being itself the root of a smaller, embedded subtree.

- Binary trees are trees in which each parent may have at most two child nodes. Although this seems like a major restriction, binary trees find a wide range of applications. Three such applications are the representation of algebraic expressions, keyed lists, and priority queues.

- Two ways of implementing a binary tree are the linear representation and the linked representation. The former method uses an array and requires no pointers but is prone to wasting a large number of array locations. The latter uses pointers and consequently is able to take advantage of Pascal's dynamic memory allocation.

- There are three standard ways of traversing a binary tree: that is, three ways of visiting all nodes exactly once. These are the preorder, postorder, and inorder traversals.

- In a preorder traversal, the current root node is processed, followed recursively by the nodes in its left subtree and then its right subtree.

- In a postorder traversal, all nodes in the left subtree of the current root are recursively processed. Then all nodes in the right subtree are processed, and the root itself is processed last.
- In an inorder traversal, the nodes in the left subtree are processed first, followed by the root node, and finally the nodes in the right subtree of the root. The inorder traversal is critical in the binary tree implementation of a keyed list since the order in which it visits nodes corresponds precisely to the ordering of items as 1st, 2nd, 3rd, . . . , within the list represented by the tree.
- The binary search tree implementation of a keyed list is the third such list implementation we have studied. The other two were the array implementation (Chapter 13) and the linked list implementation (Chapter 15). The following table summarizes the relative advantages and disadvantages of the three methods.

Method	Search	Additions/ Deletions	Other Comments
Physically Ordered Array	$O(\log_2 n)$ with binary search	Excessive data movement	Data must be physically ordered
Linked List	Requires sequential search, hence $O(n)$	Only pointer manipulation required	
Binary Search Tree	Bounded between $O(\log_2 n)$ and $O(n)$ though advanced methods can guarantee the former	Only pointer manipulation required	May necessitate the overhead associated with recursive traversals

- The binary tree may be used to implement the general tree structure. The preorder and postorder traversals emerge as the most important for this particular application.
- Graphs and networks are abstract data structures that are more complex than trees because they reflect bidirectional rather than hierarchical relationships. Depth-first and breadth-first traversals and finding the shortest path are examples of algorithms that manipulate graphs and networks.

■ Programming Problems and Projects

1. Extend and experiment with the program from this chapter's Focus on Program Design section in the following ways.
   a. Use the program as it presently appears to acquire a feel for the relationship between the order of input data and the shape of the binary search tree that results.
   b. Instead of reading data from a file, randomly generate the data being inserted in the tree. Use a random number generator available in your version of Pascal or, if none is available, the random number generator that appears in Appendix 9.
   c. After a tree has been generated, add the capability to selectively delete nodes from the tree. Reprint the tree after deleting a node as verification that is has retained the critical ordering property.
   d. Use the random generation capability from part b to build some very large trees. Instead of printing out these trees after they have been generated, compute the length of the average path that must be followed to find a node in the tree.

Do the results of your experiment indicate that, for random data, binary search trees yield a search efficiency that is $O(\log_2 n)$ or $O(n)$? Justify your conclusion with a written statement that is backed up by empirical data provided from your experimental runs.

e. Extend part d by computing the maximal path length in each randomly generated tree. What percentage of randomly generated trees have a maximal path length that is $O(n)$?

f. Depending upon the availability of graphics procedures in your version of Pascal, change the present character-based tree printout into a more appealing graphical representation.

2. Use a binary tree to implement the keyed list in the registrar's system from Example 13.1.

3. Modify the airline reservation system you developed for Wing-and-a-Prayer Airlines in Problem 2, Chapter 15 so that the alphabetized lists are maintained with binary trees instead of linked lists.

4. Write a program that sorts the records of the Fly-by-Night credit card company file (Problem 3, Chapter 15) in alphabetical order by the last name and then the first name of the customer. Use a binary tree and its inorder traversal to accomplish the sort.

5. Recall the roster maintenance system that you wrote for the Bay Area Brawlers in Programming Problem 4 from Chapter 15. The system has been so successful that the league office would like to expand the system to include all the players in the league. Again the goal is to maintain the list of players in alphabetical order, allowing for frequent insertions and deletions as players are cut, picked up, and traded among teams. In addition to storing each player's height, weight, age, and university affiliation, the record for each player should be expanded to include team affiliation, years in league, and annual salary. Because the data base for the entire league is many times larger than that for just one team, maintain this list as a binary search tree to increase efficiency.

6. Write a program that reads an expression in its prefix form and builds the binary tree corresponding to that expression. Then write procedures to print the infix and postfix forms of the expression using inorder and postorder traversals of this tree. Then see if you can extend the program to evaluate the expression represented by the tree.

7. Given a file containing some arbitrary text, determine how many times each word appears in the file. Your program should print out in alphabetical order the words that appear in the file, with their frequency counts. For an added challenge, do not assume any maximum word length; this will enable you to combine trees with the string handling methods you have already learned.

8. Here is a problem you will encounter if you write statistical analysis software. Given an arbitrarily long list of unordered numbers with an arbitrary number of different values appearing in it, determine and print out the marginal distribution for this list of numbers. That is, count how many times each different value appears in the list and then print out each value along with its count (frequency). The final

output should be arranged from smallest to largest value. This problem can be solved in elegant fashion using trees.

An example of such output as produced by the COSAP (Conversationally Oriented Statistical Analysis Package) of Lawrence University follows:

```
Command?  Marginals Judge
                Pine County Criminal Cases

                    M A R G I N A L   F R E Q U E N C I E S
Variable Judge       JUDGE BEFORE WHOM CASE BROUGHT (2)
Value label          Value        Absolute         Relative
                                  Frequency        Frequency

ALLEN                  1             677             80.8%
JONES                  2              88             10.5%
KELLY                  3              26              3.1%
MURDOCK                5              47              5.6%

        838 Valid   0 Missing   838 Total Observations
```

Here the data file contained 838 occurrences of the values 1, 2, 3, and 5. Each value was a code number assigned to a particular judge.

9. Many compilers offer the services of a cross-referencing program to aid in debugging. Such a program will list in alphabetical order all the identifiers that appear in a program and the various lines of the program that reference them. Write such a cross-referencer for your favorite language using a binary tree to maintain the list of identifiers that are encountered.

10. A relatively easy game to implement with a binary tree is to have the computer try to guess an animal about which the user is thinking by asking the user a series of questions that can be answered by yes or no. A node in the binary tree to play this game could be viewed as

Yes/No pointers leading to

1. *Another question.*
2. *The name of the animal.*
3. **NIL**.

If **NIL**, have your program surrender and then ask the user for a new question that uniquely defines the animal being thought of. Then add this new question and animal to the growing binary tree data base.

11. For this problem, you are to write a program which will differentiate expressions in the variable X. The input to this program will be a series of strings, each representing an infix expression to be differentiated. Each such expression is to be viewed as a stream of tokens. Valid tokens are integers, the variable X, the binary operators (+, −, *, /, ^), and parentheses. To make scanning for tokens easy, you may assume that each token is followed by exactly one space, with the exception of the final token, which is followed by **eoln.**

First your program will have to scan the infix expression, building up an appropriate binary tree representation of it. For this you should be able to borrow significantly on the work you did in parsing expressions in Chapter 16. The major difference here is that the end result of this parse is to be a binary tree instead of a postfix string.

Once the binary expression tree is built, traverse it, building up another binary expression tree which represents the derivative of the original expression. The following differentiation rules should be used in this process:

Suppose C is a constant, and S and T are expressions in X

Diff(C) = 0
Diff(X) = 1
Diff(S + T) = Diff(S) + Diff(T)
Diff(S − T) = Diff(S) − Diff(T)
Diff(S * T) = S * Diff(T) + T * Diff(S)
Diff(S / T) = ((T * Diff(S)) − (S * Diff(T))) / (T ^ 2)
Diff(S ^ C) = (C * S ^ (C − 1)) * Diff(S) { the infamous chain rule }

Finally, once the binary expression tree for the derivative has been built, print the expression. Print it in completely parenthesized infix notation to avoid ambiguity.

Note that there are three distinct phases to this problem.

- Parsing of the original infix expression into a binary tree representation.
- Building a binary tree representation of the derivative.
- Printing out the derivative in completely parenthesized infix notation.

For an added challenge on this problem, simplify the derivative before printing it out. Simplify the expression for the derivative according to the following rules:

S + 0 = S
0 + S = S
S − 0 = S
S * 0 = 0
0 * S = 0
S * 1 = S
1 * S = S
0 / S = 0
S ^ 0 = 1
S ^ 1 = S
S − S = 0
0 / S = 0
S / S = 1
S / 0 = 'DIVISION BY ZERO'
0 / 0 = 'UNDEFINED'

12. Wing-and-a-Prayer Airlines (Problem 3) is expanding their recordkeeping data base. This data base may now be pictured hierarchically as

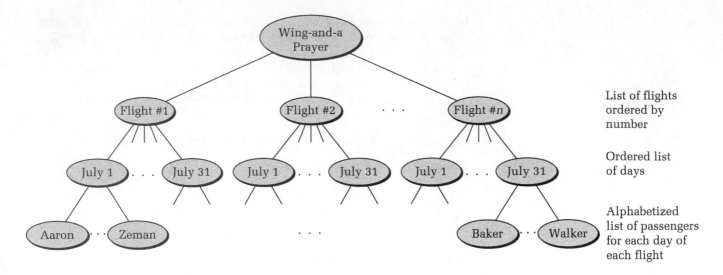

List of flights ordered by number

Ordered list of days

Alphabetized list of passengers for each day of each flight

Write a program to maintain this data base. Your program should process requests to add, delete, or list the following:

- Specified flight number.
- Specified day of the month (for a given flight number)
- Specified passenger or all passengers (for a given flight number and day of the month).

13. Many statistical analysis packages support a "cross-tabulation" command designed to explore the relationship between statistical variables. A cross-tabulation between two variables produces a two-dimensional table containing a frequency count for each possible ordered pair of values of the two variables. However, these statistical packages typically allow this type of analysis to proceed even further than merely exploring two variables. For instance, in a legal-system data base, we might be interested in cross-tabulating a defendant's age with the judge before whom the defendant stood trial. We may then wish to cross-tabulate this result with the sex of the defendant. Sex in this case is called the control variable. We would output one such cross-tabulation table for each possible value of sex.

Note that this type of output is not limited to just one control variable. There may be an arbitrary number of control variables and tables to cycle through. Moreover, the variables have an arbitrary number of observations and are all in arbitrary order. Yet for each variable the list of possible values is always printed out in smallest to largest order.

The general tree structure that emerges for handling cross-tabulation is

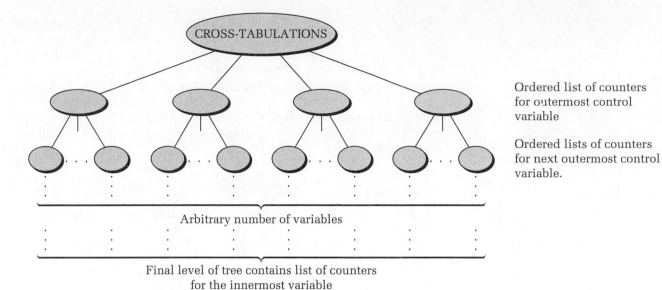

Ordered list of counters for outermost control variable

Ordered lists of counters for next outermost control variable.

Arbitrary number of variables

Final level of tree contains list of counters for the innermost variable

Write a program to handle the task of producing statistical cross-tabulations.

14. Write a program to print out the nodes of a tree level by level; that is, all level 0 nodes, followed by all level 1 nodes, followed by all level 2 nodes, and so on. *Hint:* This program will afford an excellent opportunity to practice using a queue in addition to a tree.

15. Operating systems often use general trees as the data structure on which their file directory system is based. Leaf nodes in such a system represent actual files or empty directories. Interior nodes represent nonempty directories. For instance, consider the following situation:

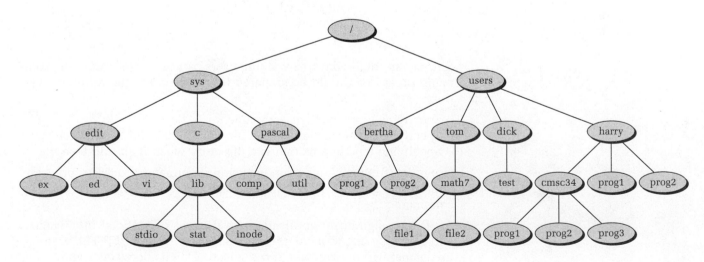

A directory entry is specified by its pathname. A pathname consists of tree node names separated by slashes. Such a pathname is absolute if it starts at the root; that is, if it starts with a slash (/). It is relative to the current directory if it does not start with a slash.

In this assignment, you are to write a command processor that will allow a user to manipulate files within such a directory structure. The commands accepted by your processor will be in the form of numbers associated with particular operations and pathnames, as shown in the following table:

Number	Operation	Pathname
1	Change directory	Absolute pathname, relative pathname, or ". ." for parent
2	Make a new directory	Absolute or relative pathname
3	Make a new file	Absolute or relative pathname
4	Remove a file	Absolute or relative pathname
5	Remove a directory, but only if it is empty	Absolute or relative pathname
6	Remove a directory and, recursively, everything below it	Absolute or relative pathname
7	Print directory entries in alphabetical order	Absolute or relative pathname
8	Recursively print directory entries in alphabetical order	Absolute or relative pathname
9	Print current directory name	
10	Quit processing commands	

Since even intelligent tree-walking users can easily get lost, your command processor should be prepared to trap errors of the following variety:

- Specifying a nonexistent pathname.
- Specifying a pathname that is a file when it should be a directory.
- Specifying a pathname that is a directory when it should be a file.

Upon detecting such an error, have your command processor print an appropriate error message and then return to accept the next user command.

16. Trees have significant applications in the area of artificial intelligence and game playing. Consider, for instance, the game of FIFTEEN. In this game, two players take turns selecting digits between 1 and 9 with the goal of selecting a combination of digits that add up to 15. Once a digit is chosen, it may not be chosen again by either player.

Rather than immediately considering a tree for the game of FIF-TEEN, let us first consider a tree for the simpler game of SEVEN with digits chosen in the range 1 to 6. A tree that partially represents the states that may be reached in this game follows:

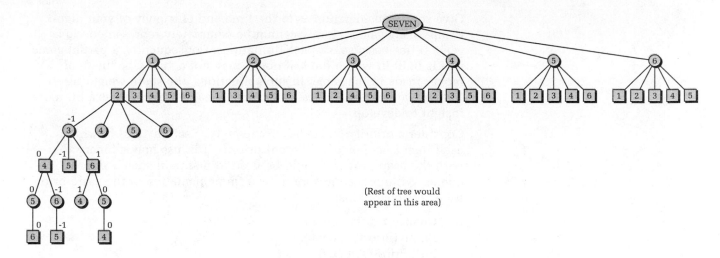

(Rest of tree would
appear in this area)

In this tree, circular nodes represent the states that may be reached by the player who moves first (the computer), and square nodes represent the states that may be reached by the player who moves second (a human opponent). The $+1$, 0, or -1 attached to each node represent weighting factors designed to help the computer choose the most advantageous move at any given stage of the game. The rules used to compute these weighting factors are

- If the node is a leaf node, its weight is determined by some static weighting function. In this case, the static weighting function used was to assign $+1$ to a leaf node representing a computer win, 0 to a leaf node representing a draw, and -1 to a leaf node representing a human win.
- If the node is a node in which the computer will move next (that is, a state occupied by the human opponent), then the weighting factor of the node is the maximum of the weighting factors of its children.
- If the node is a node in which the human opponent will move next, then the weighting factor of the node is the minimum of the weighting factors of its children.

In its turn, the computer should always choose to move to the node having the maximum possible weighting factor. The rationale behind this technique, called the minimax technique, is that the computer will move in such a way as to always maximize its chances of winning. The human opponent, if playing intelligently, will always move to a node having a minimum weighting factor. Thus in the partial game shown, the computer would choose 4 if the human had been naive enough to select the 6 node with the weighting factor of $+1$.

Write a program to build a weighted game tree for the game of FIFTEEN and then have the computer play against a human opponent. Note that this game is really the game of tic-tac-toe if one considers the following matrix.

4	9	2
3	5	7
8	1	6

All winning tic-tac-toe paths add up to 15

Give some consideration as to the time and efficiency of your algorithm. Many games simply cannot be completely represented via a general tree because of space limitations. Consequently, a partial game tree is built in which the leaf nodes may not actually be the final moves made in the game. In such situations, the static weighting function applied to the leaf nodes in the game tree requires a bit more insight to develop.

17. Consider a priority queue (see Chapter 16, Section 16.3) in which each item is assigned a different priority. Discuss how a binary tree with the heap property could be used to maintain such a priority queue. Write procedures for a heap implementation of the basic priority queue operations:

    Create(PriorityQueue)
    Empty(PriorityQueue)
    Full(PriorityQueue)
    Add(Item, PriorityQueue)
    Remove(Item, PriorityQueue)

    Categorize the run-time efficiency of the Add and Remove operations in big-O terms. Would a linear implementation or a linked implementation of the binary tree be most advantageous for this application? Explain why.
       Finally, use your priority queue implementation to solve a problem such as Programming Problem 12 in Chapter 16 or to simulate the servicing of priority-rated jobs on a time-sharing computing system.

18. Implement Dijkstra's shortest path algorithm using a suitable sparse table representation scheme to store the network data. Test your program with the transportation network pictured in Figure 18.27. Note that this same problem appeared in Chapter 17 as Problem 13. There you used a different algorithm for solving it. In a written statement, compare the efficiencies of the two algorithms.

19. A breadth-first traversal of a graph was discussed in Section 18.6. Implement this algorithm as a Pascal procedure. *Hint:* Use a queue.

20. You are given a binary tree of integers implemented by a linked representation. Such a tree is said to be *weight-balanced* if the sum of all the entries in the left subtree of the root equals the sum of all the entries in the right subtree of the root. Write a Boolean-valued function that receives a root pointer to such a tree and returns **true** if the tree is weight-balanced and **false** otherwise. Then write a complete program to test your function. Finally, adjust your procedure so that it returns **true** only when *every* subtree of the original tree is weight-balanced.

21. Explore some additional graph and network algorithms in one of the advanced texts cited earlier in this chapter (Horowitz and Sahni, *Data Structures in Pascal* (New York, N.Y.: Computer Science Press, 1990) or Naps and Pothering, *Introduction to Data Structures and Algorithm Analysis with Pascal* (St. Paul, Minn.: West Publishing, 1992)). Then prepare a written or oral report in which you explain the logic behind one of the algorithms you explore.

Never mistake motion for action.

Ernest Hemingway
1889–1961

More Powerful Sorting Methods

In Chapter 12 we analyzed three simple sorting algorithms: bubble sort, insertion sort, and selection sort. We also discussed a technique, called a pointer sort, which can be combined with any of these three algorithms to minimize data movement when large records are being sorted by a particular key field. The essence of the pointer sort is to maintain an array of pointers that dictates the logical order of the records in an array of records. When the sorting algorithm dictates a swap, only the pointers must be interchanged, not the actual records.

With all three of our sorting algorithms, however, we ran into a barrier. This barrier was a run-time efficiency of $O(n^2)$ comparisons. Since the pointer sort technique reduces data movement but not the number of comparisons, this barrier exists whether or not we incorporate the pointer sort idea into the sorting algorithm. Our goal in this chapter is to study sorting algorithms that break the $O(n^2)$ comparisons barrier. These new algorithms will make use of what we have learned since Chapter 12. In particular, both recursion and a conceptual understanding of trees are essential prerequisites to analyzing these more powerful methods.

Here we make one small simplification to the general setup for sort algorithms. Instead of sorting potentially large records with one key field, we limit ourselves to arrays consisting solely of the keys being sorted. That is, we will not worry about the other data associated with a key. This simplification will allow us to focus more directly on our primary concern in this chapter: reducing the number of comparisons made by a sorting algorithm. If you then want to generalize any of the algorithms to sorting records, the changes require only trivial syntactical considerations in Pascal.

General setup for the sort algorithms of this chapter is

```
CONST
  MaxIndex = {  Appropriate size for array to be sorted  };

TYPE
  SortType = {  Any data type with a well-defined ordering  };
  SortArray = ARRAY [1..MaxIndex] OF SortType;
```

```
PROCEDURE Sort (VAR Key : SortArray;
                    N : integer);

{  Given:    Array Key containing entries in indices        }
{            1 through N.                                    }
{  Task:     Apply appropriate sorting algorithm to these   }
{            entries.                                        }
{  Return:   Array Key with first N entries arranged in     }
{            ascending order.                                }
```

Although our algorithms for this chapter are presented in the context of sorting arrays in ascending order, they apply more generally to any list whose elements can be directly accessed (for example, random access files) and they can be easily modified to sort in descending order. Moreover, one of the methods we discuss (merge sort) actually does not require direct access into the list. Hence it could be applied to lists that are just sequentially accessible such as sequential files and linked lists.

■ 19.1
The Shell Sort Algorithm

OBJECTIVES

- to understand the logic behind the shell sort algorithm
- to see the relationship between shell sort and insertion sort
- to develop a Pascal procedure to perform shell sort
- to analyze the efficiency of the shell sort algorithm

The *shell sort,* named after its inventor D. L. Shell, incorporates the logic of the insertion sort to a certain extent. However, instead of sorting the entire array at once, it first divides the array into smaller, noncontiguous segments which are then separately sorted using the insertion sort. The advantage of doing this is twofold. First, where a comparison dictates a swap of two data items in a segment, this swap within a noncontiguous segment of the array moves an item a greater distance within the overall array than the swap of adjacent array entries in the usual insertion sort. This means that one swap is more likely to place an element closer to its final location in the array when using shell sort than when using the simple insertion sort. For instance, a large-valued entry which appears near the front of the array will more quickly move to the tail end of the array because each swap moves it a greater distance in the array. The second advantage of dividing the array into segments is tied to the first. That is, because early passes tend to move elements closer to their final destination than early passes would in a straight insertion sort, the array becomes partially sorted quite fast. The fact that the array is likely to become partially sorted relatively early then allows the embedded insertion sort logic to make more frequent use of its check for an early exit from its inner loop. (Recall that this check is what makes the insertion sort particularly efficient for arrays that are partially sorted.) An example will help clarify this shell sort rationale.

■ EXAMPLE 19.1

Suppose we have an array Key containing the following integers:

80 93 60 12 42 30 68 85 10

We first divide this into three segments of three elements each.

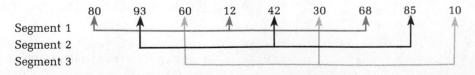

```
80    12    68→    Segment 1
93    42    85→    Segment 2
60    30    10→    Segment 3
```

and sort each of the segments.

```
12    68    80
42    85    93
10    30    60
```

The original array, partially sorted, now appears as

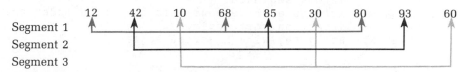

We divide this partially sorted array as

```
12    10    85    80    60    →    Segment 1
42    68    30    93          →    Segment 2
```

These segments are then sorted and the array Key takes the form

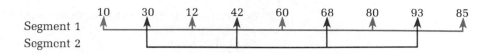

Finally, this array is sorted as one segment; 12 and 30, and 93 and 85 are swapped to give us the sorted array

10 12 30 42 60 68 80 85 93

■   ■

The key to the shell sort algorithm is that the whole array is first fragmented into K segments for some number K, where K is preferably a prime number. These K segments are given by

```
Key[1], Key[K + 1], Key[2 * K + 1], ...
Key[2], Key[K + 2], Key[2 * K + 2], ...
        .
        .
        .
Key[K], Key[2 * K], Key[3 * K], ...
```

Because each segment is sorted, the whole array is partially sorted after the first pass. For the next pass, the value of K is reduced, which increases the size of each segment, hence reducing the number of segments. Preferably, the next value of K is also chosen so that it is prime relative to its previous value, or *relatively prime*. (Two integers are said to be relatively prime to each other if they have no common factor greater than 1.) The process is repeated until K = 1, at which point the array is sorted. The insertion sort is applied to each segment, so each successive segment is partially sorted. Consequently, the later applications of the insertion sort become very efficient, dramatically increasing the overall efficiency of the shell sort.

To emphasize the fashion in which the shell sort algorithm relies on the logic of insertion sort, we present a SegmentedInsertionSort procedure which arranges each of K segments in an N-element array into ascending order. Compare this procedure with the procedure for insertion sort that was given in Chapter 12. You willl see that SegmentedInsertionSort moves an item from position J to position J + K. When K = 1, this is precisely the original insertion sort algorithm.

```
PROCEDURE SegmentedInsertionSort (VAR Key : SortArray;
                                  N, K : integer);

{  Given:    N-element array Key, viewed as being divided    }
{            into K segments.                                 }
{  Task:     Arrange each segment into ascending order using  }
{            insertion sort logic.                            }
{  Return:   Array Key with K sorted segments.                }

VAR L, J : integer;
    ItemToInsert : SortType;
    StillLooking : boolean;

BEGIN
  { On the Lth pass, insert item L into its correct position among }
  { the previous entries in its segment.                           }
  FOR L := K + 1 TO N DO
    BEGIN
      { Walk backwards through segment, looking for slot to insert Key[L] }
      ItemToInsert := Key[L];
      J := L - K;    { J counts down through current segment }
      StillLooking := true;
      WHILE (J >= 1) AND StillLooking DO
        { ItemToInsert is compared to Key[J] }
        IF ItemToInsert < Key[J] THEN
          BEGIN
            Key[J + K] := Key[J];
            J := J - K
          END
        ELSE
          StillLooking := false;
      { Upon leaving loop, J + K is the index where ItemToInsert belongs }
      Key[J + K] := ItemToInsert
    END  { FOR }
END;  { of PROCEDURE SegmentedInsertionSort }
```

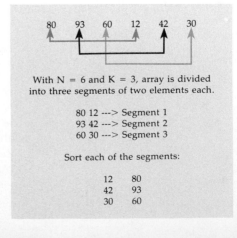

With N = 6 and K = 3, array is divided into three segments of two elements each.

```
80 12 ---> Segment 1
93 42 ---> Segment 2
60 30 ---> Segment 3
```

Sort each of the segments:

```
12    80
42    93
30    60
```

Given the SegmentedInsertionSort procedure, we now merely call on this with values of K that become successively smaller. Eventually, Segmented-InsertionSort must be called with K = 1 to guarantee that the array, viewed as one segment, is completely sorted.

The procedure ShellSort that follows illustrates these successive calls to SegmentedInsertionSort for values of K which are repeatedly halved.

```
PROCEDURE ShellSort (VAR Key : SortArray;
                     N : integer);

  { Given:   Array Key with entries in indices 1 through N.   }
  { Task:    Apply shell sort algorithm.                      }
  { Return:  Array Key with first N entries arranged in       }
  {          ascending order.                                 }

VAR
  K : integer;

PROCEDURE SegmentedInsertionSort (VAR Key : SortArray;
                                  N, K : integer);

  { This procedure would be local to ShellSort.  }

BEGIN {  PROCEDURE ShellSort  }
  K := N DIV 2;  {  K represents current number of segments.  }
  WHILE K > 0 DO
    BEGIN
      SegmentedInsertionSort (Key, N, K);
      K := K DIV 2   {  Reduce number of segments  }
    END
END;  {  of PROCEDURE ShellSort  }
```

Efficiency of the Shell Sort

The shell sort is also called the *diminishing increment sort* because the value of k (the number of segments) continually decreases. The method is more efficient if the successive values of k are kept relatively prime to each other, thereby helping to ensure that a pair of values previously compared to each other are not compared again. D. E. Knuth has mathematically estimated that, with relatively prime values of k, the shell sort will execute in an average time proportional to $O(n(\log_2 n)^2)$. (See Donald E. Knuth, *Searching and Sorting*. Vol. 3 of *The Art of Computer Programming*. (Menlo Park, Calif.: Addison-Wesley, 1973).) However, the sort will work for any values of k, as long as the last value of k is 1. For instance, note that in the version of ShellSort we have given, the successive values of k will not often be relatively prime. When the values of k are not relatively prime, then the efficiency of the shell sort is of the order $O(n^r)$, where $1 < r < 2$. The particular value of r makes the sort less efficient than $O(n(\log_2 n)^2)$ for large values of n, but better than the $O(n^2)$ methods of Chapter 12.

The shell sort is most efficient on arrays that are nearly sorted. In fact, the first chosen value of k is large to insure that the whole array is fragmented into small individual arrays, for which the insertion sort is highly effective. Each subsequent sort causes the entire array to be more nearly sorted, so that the efficiency of the insertion sort as applied to larger partially sorted arrays is increased. Trace through a few examples to convince yourself that the partially ordered status of the array for one value of k is not affected by subsequent partial sorts for a different value of k.

It is not known with what value of k the shell sort should start, but Knuth suggests a sequence of values such as 1, 3, 7, 15, . . . , for reverse values of

k; that is, the $(j + 1)$th value is two times the jth value plus 1. Knuth suggests other possible values of k, but generally the initial guess at the first value of k is all that you need. The initial guess will depend on the size of the array, and, to some extent, on the type of data being sorted.

Exercises 19.1

1. Consider the ShellSort procedure given in this section. Suppose that we were to trace the contents of the array being sorted after each call to the procedure SegmentedInsertionSort. What would we see as output if we called ShellSort with the following key array?

   60 12 90 30 64 8 6

2. Repeat Exercise 1 for a six-element array that initially contains

   1 8 2 7 3 6

3. Why is the shell sort called by that name?

4. Why is the shell sort most efficient when the original data are in almost sorted order?

5. What advantage do the relatively prime values of the increments have over other values in a shell sort? Formulate your answer in a precise written statement that explains why relatively prime values are better.

6. What property must the sequence of diminishing increments in the shell sort have to insure that the method will work?

7. Provide examples of best-case and worst-case data sets for the shell sort algorithm presented in this section. Justify your data sets by explaining why they generate best-case and worst-case performance.

8. In Chapter 12, PointerSort used an index of pointers to sort data logically without rearranging it. Identify the sort algorithm that was behind the Pascal PointerSort procedure. Adapt the pointer sort procedure to the shell sort algorithm.

9. The version of shell sort presented in this section uses the following sequence of diminishing increments

   N **DIV** 2, N **DIV** 4, . . ., 8, 4, 2, 1

   Rewrite the shell sort so that the following sequence of diminishing increments is used.

   K, . . ., 121, 40, 13, 4, 1

   Here K represents the largest member of this sequence which is < = N where N is the logical size of the array being sorted.

■ ■ ■ ■

■ 19.2
The Quick Sort Algorithm

OBJECTIVES

- to understand the logic behind the quick sort algorithm
- to understand the role played by the partitioning subalgorithm in quick sort

Objectives continued.

Even though the shell sort provides a significant advantage in run-time over its $O(n^2)$ predecessors, its average efficiency of $O(n(\log_2 n)^2)$ may still not be good enough for large arrays. The next group of methods, including the *quick sort,* have an average execution time of $O(n \log_2 n)$ which is the best that can be achieved. Compared to $O(n (\log_2 n)^2)$ or $O(n^r)$ for $1 < r < 2$, an $O(n \log_2 n)$ sort is often a good choice as the main vehicle for large sorting jobs.

The essence of the quick sort algorithm, originally devised in 1961 by C.A.R. Hoare, is to rely on a subordinate algorithm to partition the array. The process of partitioning involves moving a data item, called the *pivot,* in the correct direction just enough for it to reach its final place in the array. The

- to develop a Pascal procedure to perform quick sort
- to analyze the efficiency of the quick sort algorithm; in particular, to see the relationship between the efficiency of the quick sort algorithm and the way in which the subordinate partitioning subalgorithm splits the array.

partitioning process, therefore, reduces unnecessary interchanges and potentially moves the pivot a great distance in the array without forcing it to be swapped into intermediate locations. Once the pivot item is chosen, moves are made so that data items to the left of the pivot are less than (or equal to) it, whereas those to the right are greater (or equal). The pivot item is thus in its correct position. The quick sort algorithm then recursively applies the partitioning process to the two parts of the array on either side of the pivot until the entire array is sorted.

In the next example, we illustrate the mechanics of this partitioning logic by applying it to an array of numbers.

■ EXAMPLE 19.2

Suppose the array Key contains integers initially arranged as

15 20 5 8 95 12 80 17 9 55

Table 19.1 shows a partitioning pass applied to this array.

TABLE 19.1
Each call to QuickSort partitions an array segment

Line Number	Key[1]	Key[2]	Key[3]	Key[4]	Key[5]	Key[6]	Key[7]	Key[8]	Key[9]	Key[10]
1	15*	20	5	8	95	12	80	17	9	55 ←
2	9	20 →	5	8	95	12	80	17 ←	( )	55
3	9	( )	5 →	8	95	12	80	17	20	55
4	9	12	5	8	95 ←	( )	80	17	20	55
5	9	12	5	8	( )	95	80	17	20	55
6	9	12	5	8	15	95	80	17	20	55

The following steps are involved:

1. Remove the first data item, 15, as the pivot, mark its position, and scan the array from right to left, comparing data item values with 15. When you find the first smaller value, remove it from its current position and put in position Key[1]. (This is shown in line 2.)
2. Scan line 2 from left to right beginning with position Key[2], comparing data item values with 15. When you find the first value greater than 15, extract it and store it in the position marked by parentheses in line 2. (This is shown in line 3.)
3. Begin the right to left scan of line 3 with position Key[8] looking for a value smaller than 15. When you find it, extract it and store it in the position marked by the parentheses in line 3. (This is shown in line 4.)
4. Begin scanning line 4 from left to right at position Key[3]. Find a value greater than 15, remove it, mark its position, and store it inside the parentheses in line 4. (This is shown in line 5.)
5. Now, when you attempt to scan line 5 from right to left beginning at position Key[5], you are immediately at a parenthesized position determined by the previous left-to-right scan. This is the location to

put the pivot data item, 15. (This is shown in line 6.) At this stage, 15 is in its correct place relative to the final sorted array.

Notice that all values to the left of 15 are less than 15, and all values to the right of 15 are greater than 15. The method will still work if two values are the same. The process can now be applied recursively to the two segments of the array on the left and right of 15. Notice that these recursive calls eventually result in the entire array's being sorted. The result of any one call to **PROCEDURE** QuickSort is merely to partition a segment of the array so that the pivotal item is positioned with everything to its left being less than or equal to it and everything to its right being greater than or equal.

■   ■

The procedure Partition that follows achieves one partitioning pass in the overall QuickSort algorithm as described in Example 19.2. The indices Lo and Hi represent the pointers that move from the left and right respectively until they meet at the appropriate location for the Pivot. The pivotal value is initially chosen to be Key[Lo]. We will later discuss the possible implications of choosing a different pivotal value. Note that it is crucial for Partition to return in PivotPoint the position where the pivotal value was finally inserted. This information will allow the QuickSort procedure that calls upon Partition to determine whether or not a recursive termination condition has been reached.

```
PROCEDURE Partition (VAR Key : SortArray;
                     Lo, Hi : integer;
                     VAR PivotPoint : integer);

{ Given:   Key array, indices Lo and Hi.                   }
{ Task:    Partition Key array between indices Lo and Hi.   }
{          That is, using Key[Lo] as pivotal value, arrange }
{          entries between Lo and Hi indices so that all    }
{          values to left of Pivot are less than or equal   }
{          to it and all values to right of Pivot are       }
{          greater than or equal to it.                     }
{ Return:  Partitioned array Key, and PivotPoint            }
{          containing final location of Pivot.              }

VAR Pivot : SortType;

BEGIN
  Pivot := Key[Lo];
  { Lo and Hi start to move toward each other.  }
  WHILE Lo < Hi DO
    BEGIN
      { Begin right-to-left scan  }
      WHILE (Pivot < Key[Hi]) AND (Lo < Hi) DO
        Hi := Hi - 1;
      IF Hi <> Lo THEN
        { Move entry indexed by Hi to left side of partition.  }
        BEGIN
          Key[Lo] := Key[Hi];
          Lo := Lo + 1
        END;
```

Pivot = 12

Right-to-left scan until smaller value found here

12	8	7	6	14	20	30	5	19	13	15	Hi = 8
1	2	3	4	5	6	7	8	9	10	11	

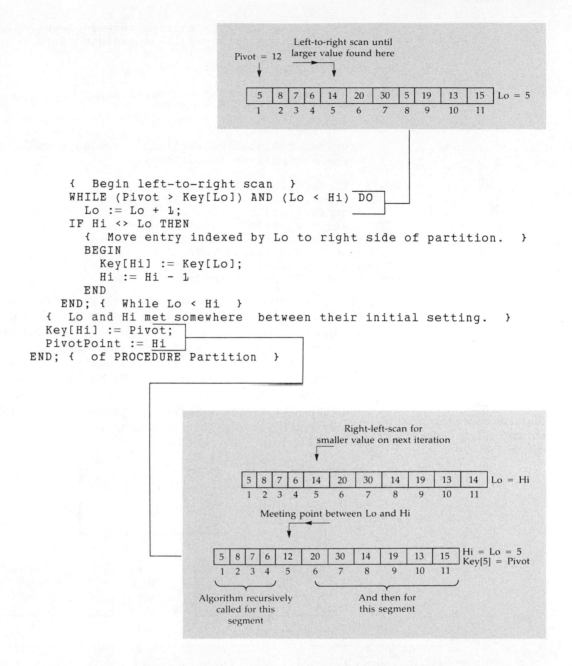

```
     {  Begin left-to-right scan  }
     WHILE (Pivot > Key[Lo]) AND (Lo < Hi) DO
        Lo := Lo + 1;
     IF Hi <> Lo THEN
        {  Move entry indexed by Lo to right side of partition.  }
        BEGIN
           Key[Hi] := Key[Lo];
           Hi := Hi - 1
        END
   END; {  While Lo < Hi  }
   {  Lo and Hi met somewhere  between their initial setting.  }
   Key[Hi] := Pivot;
   PivotPoint := Hi
END; {  of PROCEDURE Partition  }
```

Given the previous Partition procedure, QuickSort itself must call on Partition and then use the returned value of PivotPoint to decide whether or not recursive calls are necessary to perform more refined partitioning of the segments to the left and right of PivotPoint. The recursive logic for this decision is given in the following **PROCEDURE** QuickSort. Partition would be incorporated as a subordinate local procedure within QuickSort.

```
PROCEDURE QuickSort (VAR Key : SortArray;
                     Lower, Upper : integer);

{  Given:   Array Key with indices Lower and Upper.          }
{           Assume Lower <= Upper.                            }
{  Task:    Apply  quick sort logic to Key between Lower      }
{           and Upper indices.                                }
```

```
{  Return:   Array Key with entries between Lower and Upper  }
{            indices arranged in ascending order.            }

VAR  PivotPoint : integer;

PROCEDURE Partition (VAR Key : SortArray;
                     Lo, Hi : integer;
                     VAR PivotPoint : integer);

   {  Previously discussed Partition procedure would appear  }
   {  here, subordinate to QuickSort                         }

BEGIN  {  PROCEDURE QuickSort  }
   Partition (Key, Lower, Upper, PivotPoint);
   {  Recursive calls partition left and right segments  }
   IF Lower < PivotPoint THEN
      QuickSort (Key, Lower, PivotPoint - 1);
   IF Upper > PivotPoint THEN
      QuickSort (Key, PivotPoint + 1, Upper)
END; {  of PROCEDURE QuickSort  }
```

For instance, after the first call to QuickSort for a partitioning pass on the data in Table 19.1, we would then recursively call on QuickSort with Lower = 1 and Upper = 4. This would trigger deeper-level recursive calls from which we would ultimately return, knowing that the segment of the array between indices 1 and 5 is now sorted. This return would be followed by a recursive call to QuickSort with Lower = 6 and Upper = 10.

The run-time trace diagam of recursive calls to QuickSort for the data of Table 19.1 is given in Figure 19.1. You should verify this call-return pattern by walking through the preceding procedure.

FIGURE 19.1

Run-time trace diagram of (recursive) calls to QuickSort for data in Table 19.1

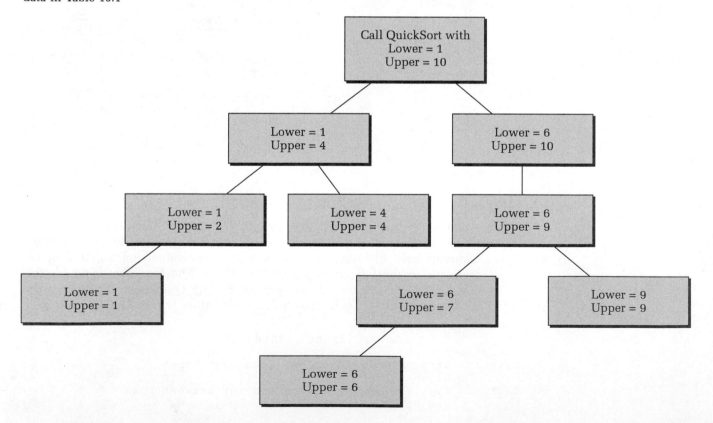

Efficiency of the Quick Sort

As mentioned earlier, the average run-time efficiency of the quick sort is $O(n\log_2 n)$, which is the best that has been achieved for a large array of size n. In the best case, it is quite easy to provide a rationale for this $O(n\log_2 n)$ figure. This best case occurs when each array segment recursively passed to QuickSort partitions at its midpoint; that is, the appropriate location for each pivotal value in the series of recursive calls is the midpoint of the segment being partitioned. In this case,

1 call to QuickSort (the first) is made with a segment of size n.
*2 calls to QuickSort are made with segments of size n **DIV** 2.*
*4 calls to QuickSort are made with segments of size n **DIV** 4.*
*8 calls to QuickSort are made with segments of size n **DIV** 8.*

$\left.\begin{array}{l} \\ \\ \\ \\ \end{array}\right\}$ *Overall* $\log_2 n$ *levels*

n calls to QuickSort are made with segments of size 1.

Since each call with a segment of size m requires $O(m)$ comparisons, it is clear that k calls with segments of size n **DIV** k will require $O(n)$ comparisons. Hence the total number of comparisons resulting from the preceding sequence of calls will be $O(n\log_2 n)$.

Privacy Issues Kill Lotus Data Base

The August 1989 issue of *Communications of the ACM* (Vol. 32, No. 8) was dedicated to the role played by ethics in the education and career of a computer scientist. What are the social responsibilities that go along with state-of-the art capabilities to sort and search through gigabytes of information? A recent incident involving Lotus Development Corporation of Cambridge, Massachusetts illustrated the importance of a social conscience in computing.

In late 1990, Lotus had planned the release of a product called MarketPlace. Designed for use on a personal computer equipped with CD-ROM storage, the so-called "Household" version of MarketPlace supposedly contained information on 120 million Americans and 80 million households. This information included data on personal income, life-style, purchasing patterns, geographic location, and marital status. This data was compiled for Lotus by Equifax, the nation's largest credit reporting agency. Lotus foresaw a great demand for MarketPlace coming from a wide variety of large and small businesses. According to Michael W. Miller in the article "MarketPlace," which appeared in the November 13, 1990 issue of the *Wall Street Journal*:

"Advances in computers are making it easier to gather and piece together minutely detailed portraits of house-

holds, and marketers are gobbling these up to help choose targets for direct-mail and telephone campaigns."

One of the early Lotus press releases for MarketPlace began with the headline "We Found You . . . And Quite Frankly, It Really Wasn't That Hard."

What Lotus had not properly anticipated was the storm of protest that would arise from consumer advocacy groups and individual consumers concerning MarketPlace's apparent insensitivity to privacy issues. Miller's *Wall Street Journal* article described these concerns:

"Privacy advocates' chief objection to MarketPlace was that it wouldn't be easy enough for consumers to delete their data, or correct any inaccuracies."

Lotus demonstrated its sensitivity to the ethical issues that had been raised by MarketPlace. In January 1991, James Manzi, Lotus's chairman, announced that Lotus was canceling the MarketPlace project. Manzi stated, "What drove our decision was the volume and tenor of the concerns that were being raised by consumers all over the U.S." Though Lotus may have exercised poor judgment in the original conception of MarketPlace, their decision to pull the plug after a sizeable investment in the enterprise illustrates a high degree of social responsibility. Such ethical dilemmas are likely to play an increasing role in the careers of many computing professionals.

If segments partition away from the midpoint, the efficiency of quick sort begins to deteriorate. In the worst-case situation, when the array is already sorted, the efficiency of the quick sort may drop down to $O(n^2)$ due to the continuous right-to-left scan all the way to the last left boundary. In the Exercises at the end of the section, you will explore how the worst-case situation is affected by your choice of the pivotal element.

You may wonder how large a stack is needed to sort an array of size n. (Remember that this stack is implicitly created even whenever you use recursion.) Knuth has mathematically estimated that the size of the stack will generally not exceed $O(\log_2 n)$. However, in the worst case, it will be $O(n)$. (See D. E. Knuth's text, *Searching and Sorting*, cited toward the end of Section 19.1.)

Exercises 19.2

1. Consider the QuickSort procedure given in this section. Suppose that we were to insert the following tracer output immediately after the initial **BEGIN** for this procedure.

```
writeln (Lower, Upper);
FOR K := Lower TO Upper DO
   write(Key[K]);
writeln;
```

   What would we see as output from these tracers if we were to call on Quick-Sort with the key array initially containing the following seven entries?

   60 12 90 30 64 8 6

2. Repeat Exercise 1 for a six-element array that initially contains

   1 8 2 7 3 6

3. When is a bubble sort better than a quick sort? Explain your answer in a written statement.

4. Under what circumstances would you not use a quick sort? Explain your answer in a written statement.

5. How does the choice of the pivotal value affect the efficiency of the quick sort algorithm? Suppose that the middle value or the last value in a segment to be partitioned were chosen as the pivotal value. How would this alter the nature of best-case and worst-case data sets? Give examples to illustrate your answer.

6. Develop run-time trace diagrams of procedure calls to QuickSort for a variety of test data sets (analogous to what was done in Figure 19.1). Use these diagrams to analyze the efficiency of QuickSort. What types of data sets yield $O(n\log_2 n)$ efficiency? What types yield $O(n^2)$ efficiency?

7. In Chapter 12, PointerSort used an index of pointers to sort data logically without rearranging it. Adapt the pointer sort procedure to the quick sort algorithm.

8. Implement QuickSort in a nonrecursive fashion.

9. Implement a variation on the quick sort algorithm presented in this section, in which the pivot is chosen to be the median of the three values:

   Key[Lo], Key[(Lo + Hi) **DIV** 2], Key[Hi]

   In a carefully written statement, explain why this variation should be more efficient than the version that chooses the pivot to be Key[Lo].

■ ■ ■ ■

■ 19.3
The Heap Sort Algorithm

OBJECTIVES

- to understand the logic behind the heap sort algorithm
- to understand the relationship between heap sort and the linear representation of a binary tree in an array
- to develop a Pascal procedure to perform the heap sort
- to analyze the efficiency of the heap sort

The *heap sort* is a sorting algorithm that is roughly equivalent to the quick sort; its average efficiency is $O(n\log_2 n)$ for an array of size n. The method, originally described by R. W. Floyd, has two phases. In the first phase, the array containing the n data items is viewed as equivalent to a full binary tree. That is, the array to be sorted is viewed as the linear representation of a full binary tree containing n items (see Chapter 18). (If you want to read Floyd's description of this method, see his article, entitled "Algorithm 245: Tree Sort 3" found in *Communications of the ACM* 7 (1964):701.)

As an example, suppose we wish to sort the following array:

11	1	5	7	6	12	17	8	4	10	2

The tree now appears as shown in Figure 19.2.

FIGURE 19.2
Full binary tree corresponding to array

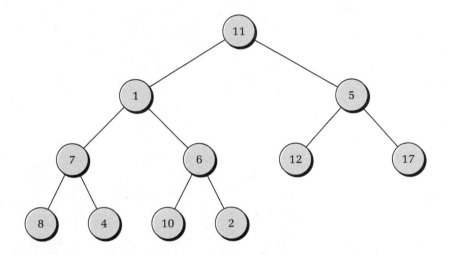

The goal of phase 1 is to sort the data elements along each path from leaf node level to the root node. If we wish to sort in ascending order, then the numbers along any path from leaf node to root should be in increasing order. Eventually, after phase 1, the tree will be a heap as described in Chapter 18. That is, the data item at each node will be greater than or equal to both of its children. To achieve this, we take the following steps:

1. Process the node that is the parent of the rightmost node on the lowest level as follows: if its value is less than the value of its largest child, swap these values; otherwise do nothing.
2. Move left on the same level. Compare the value of the parent node with the values of the children. If the parent is smaller than the largest child, swap them.
3. When the left end of this level is reached, move up a level, and, beginning with the rightmost parent node, repeat step 2. Continue swapping the original parent with the larger of its children until it is larger than its children. In effect, the original parent is being walked down the tree in a fashion that insures all numbers will be in increasing order along the path.
4. Repeat step 3 until the root node has been processed.

Figure 19.3 shows these steps applied to Figure 19.2.

FIGURE 19.3
Phase 1 of heap sort applied to
the binary tree in Figure 19.2

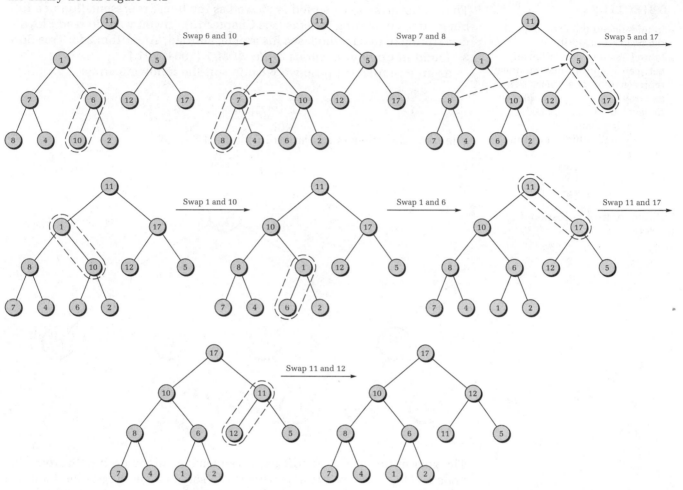

Phase 2 of the heap sort finds the node with the largest value in the tree and cuts it from the tree. This is then repeated to find the second largest value, which is also removed from the tree. The process continues until only two nodes are left in the tree; they are then exchanged if necessary. The precise steps for phase 2 are as follows:

1. Swap the root node with the bottom rightmost child, and sever this new bottom rightmost child from the tree. This is the largest value.
2. Continue swapping the new root value with the larger of its children until it is not exceeded by either child. In effect, this new root value is now being walked down a path in the tree to insure that all paths retain values arranged in ascending order from leaf node to root node. That is, the tree is being restored to a heap.
3. Repeat steps 1 and 2 until only one element is left.

Phase 2 of the heap sort begun in Figure 19.3 is shown in Figure 19.4 for the three highest values.

FIGURE 19.4
Phase 2 of heap sort for three
values

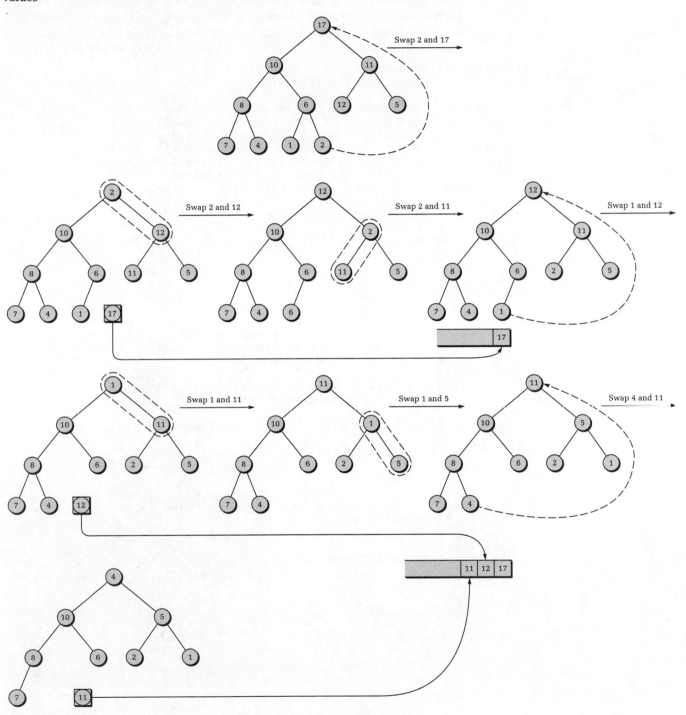

Both phase 1 and phase 2 use the same strategy of walking a parent down a path of the tree via a series of swaps with its children. The following procedure WalkDown isolates this crucial subordinate algorithm. In the linear representation of a tree assumed by WalkDown, the assignment statement K := 2 * L will make K reference the left child of the node indicated by L. That is, this statement will allow us to descend a level deeper into the tree.

```
PROCEDURE WalkDown (VAR Key : SortArray;
                    J, N : integer);

{ Given:    Array Key to be viewed as full binary tree.  N,  }
{           the number of entries in the array.  J, the      }
{           index of a parent node within the tree.          }
{ Task:     Repeatedly exchange this parent with child of     }
{           greatest value until the original parent is       }
{           greater than both of its children                 }
{ Return:   Tree array, as altered by this task.              }

VAR
  L, K : integer;
  Ref : SortType;
  FoundSpot : boolean;

BEGIN { WalkDown }
  FoundSpot := false;
  L := J;
  Ref := Key[L];
  { Key [L] will move along the appropriate path in tree.  }
  K := 2 * L; { Initially K references left child of Key[L] }
  WHILE (K <= N) AND NOT FoundSpot DO
    BEGIN
      IF K < N THEN {  Have K reference largest child  }
          IF Key[K + 1] > Key[K] THEN
            K := K + 1;
      IF Key[K] > Ref THEN {  Child must move up  }
        BEGIN
          Key[L] := Key[K];
          L := K;
          K := 2 * L
        END
      ELSE  {  Appropriate spot has been found  }
        FoundSpot := true
    END;
  Key[L] := Ref
END; {  of PROCEDURE WalkDown  }
```

Key[K]
larger
of

IF Key[K] is larger than
Ref **THEN** it moves up

With the essential WalkDown logic isolated in a separate procedure, phases 1 and 2 of HeapSort may now be developed easily. The loop for phase 1 repeatedly calls on WalkDown to form the tree into a heap. Then a loop for phase 2 repeatedly swaps the root of the tree with the last child and calls on WalkDown to allow this new root to find an appropriate position in the heap.

```
PROCEDURE  HeapSort (VAR Key : SortArray;
                         N : integer);

{  Given:    Array Key with entries in indices 1 through N.  }
{  Task:     Apply heap sort logic to array.                 }
{  Return:   Array Key with first N entries arranged in      }
{            ascending order.                                 }

VAR
  Y : integer;
  Temp : SortType;

{  Here WalkDown would be located as a procedure local to HeapSort.  }

PROCEDURE WalkDown (VAR Key : SortArray;
                        J, N : integer);

BEGIN  {  PROCEDURE HeapSort  }

  {  First phase 1 arranges the tree into a heap.  }
  Y := N DIV 2;  {  Y starts at the last node to have child.  }
  WHILE  Y > 0 DO
    BEGIN
      WalkDown (Key, Y, N);
      Y := Y - 1
    END;

  {  Phase 1 done.  Now begin phase 2.  }
  {  In phase 2, Y is used to point at the current last array slot.  }
  Y := N;
  WHILE Y > 1 DO
    BEGIN
      {  Interchange root with bottom right leaf node.  }
      Temp := Key[1];
      Key[1] := Key[Y];
      Key[Y] := Temp;
      Y := Y - 1;
      WalkDown (Key, 1, Y)
    END { of WHILE }
END; { of PROCEDURE HeapSort }
```

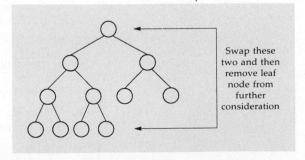

Swap these two and then remove leaf node from further consideration

Efficiency of the Heap Sort

It is relatively easy to deduce that the heap sort requires $O(n\log_2 n)$ comparisons. To see this, note that the phase 1 loop in the preceding Pascal procedure will execute $n/2$ times. Inside this loop we call WalkDown, which in turn has a loop that will execute at most $\log_2 n$ times (because it merely follows a path down a full binary tree). Hence phase 1 requires at most

$$(n/2) * \log_2 n$$

iterations at its deepest level. Phase 2 may be similarly analyzed. The phase 2 loop iterates n times. Within each iteration, WalkDown is called, again resulting in at most $\log_2 n$ operations. Thus phase 2 requires at most $n * \log_2 n$ iterations at its deepest level. Overall, we get

$$1.5\,n * \log_2 n$$

as an upper bound for the number of iterations required by the combination of phases 1 and 2.

Thus, both quick sort and heap sort yield $O(n\log_2 n)$ efficiencies. In *Searching and Sorting,* referenced in Sections 19.1 and 19.2, Knuth has shown that, on the average, quick sort will be slightly faster since its big-O constant of proportionality will be smaller than that for heap sort. However, heap sort offers the advantage of guaranteeing an $O(n\log_2 n)$ efficiency regardless of the data being sorted. As we have already noted for quick sort, worst-case data can cause its performance to deteriorate to $O(n^2)$.

Exercises 19.3

1. Consider the HeapSort procedure given in this section. Note that WalkDown is called at two points in the procedure: once in phase 1 and again in phase 2. Suppose that we were to trace the contents of the array being sorted after each call to WalkDown. What would we see as output if we called HeapSort with an array that initially contained

   60 12 90 30 64 8 6

2. Repeat Exercise 1 for a six-element array that initially contains

   1 8 2 7 3 6

3. Why is the heap sort called by that name?

4. What is a heap?

5. Is a heap sort always better than a quick sort? When is it? When isn't it? Explain your answer in a written essay.

6. What is the worst-case and average-case efficiency of the heap sort?

7. Give examples of arrays that generate the best and worst performances respectively for the heap sort algorithm. Explain why these arrays generate the best and worst performance.

8. In Chapter 12, PointerSort used an index of pointers to sort data logically without rearranging it. Adapt the pointer sort procedure to the heap sort algorithm.

■ ■ ■ ■

■ 19.4
The Merge Sort Algorithm

OBJECTIVES

- to understand the logic behind the merge sort algorithm
- to understand merge sort's reliance on a subalgorithm that merges two sorted lists
- to develop a Pascal procedure to perform the merge sort
- to analyze the efficiency of the merge sort

The essential idea behind *merge sort* is to make repeated use of a procedure that merges two lists, each already in ascending order, into a third list, also arranged in ascending order. The merge procedure itself only requires sequential access to the lists. Its logic is similar to the method you would use if you were merging two sorted piles of index cards into a third pile. That is, start with the first card from each pile. Compare them to see which one comes first, transfer that one over to the third pile, and advance to the next card in that pile. Repeat the comparison, transfer, and advance operations until one of the piles runs out of cards. At that point, merely move what is left of the remaining pile over to the third merged pile.

This logic is reflected in the generalized Merge procedure that follows. For reasons that will become apparent when we incorporate it into a full sorting procedure, this version of Merge begins with the two sorted lists stored in one array. The first list runs from subscript Lower to Mid of array Source. The second runs from subscript Mid + 1 to Upper of the same array. The merged result of the two lists is stored in a second array Destination.

```
PROCEDURE Merge (Source : SortArray;
                 VAR Destination : SortArray;
                 Lower, Mid, Upper : integer);

  { Given:   Array Source arranged in ascending order      }
  {          between indices Lower..Mid and Mid + 1..Upper  }
  {          respectively.                                   }
  { Task:    Merge the two ordered segments of Source into   }
  {          one list arranged in ascending order.           }
  { Return:  The complete ordered list in Destination.       }

VAR  S1, S2, D : integer; { Pointers into two Source lists and Destination }

BEGIN
  { Initialize pointers  }
  S1 := Lower;
  S2 := Mid + 1;
  D := Lower;

  { Repeat comparison of current item from each list.  }
  REPEAT
    IF Source[S1] < Source[S2] THEN
      BEGIN
        Destination[D] := Source[S1];
        S1 := S1 + 1
      END
    ELSE
      BEGIN
        Destination[D] := Source[S2];
        S2 := S2 + 1
      END;
    D := D + 1
  UNTIL (S1 > Mid) OR (S2 > Upper);

  { Move what is left of remaining list.  }
  IF (S1 > Mid) THEN
    REPEAT
      Destination[D] := Source[S2];
      S2 := S2 + 1;
      D := D + 1
    UNTIL S2 > Upper
  ELSE
```

```
      REPEAT
        Destination[D] := Source[S1];
        S1 := S1 + 1;
        D := D + 1
      UNTIL S1 > Mid
  END; {  of PROCEDURE Merge  }
```

Clearly Merge is an O(n) algorithm where n is the number of items in the two lists to be merged. A question remains: How can Merge be used to actually sort an entire array? To answer this we need another procedure called Order that will take the values in indices Lower through Upper of an array Source and arrange them in ascending order in subscripts Lower through Upper of another array called Destination. Notice that Order is itself almost a sorting procedure except that it produces a sorted list in a second array instead of actually transforming the array it originally receives. Our use of Order will be to obtain two sorted half-length sequences from our original array.

Then we will use the Merge procedure we have already developed to merge the two sorted half-length sequences back into the original array. Of course, this merely defers our original question of how to use Merge to sort because now we are faced with the question of how Order will be able to produce two sorted half-length sequences. Here is where recursion enters the picture. To produce a sorted half-length sequence, we use Order to produce two sorted quarter-length sequences and apply Merge to the results. Similarly, the quarter-length sequences are produced by calling on Order to produce sorted eighth-length sequences and apply Merge to the results. The recursive termination condition for this descent into shorter and shorter ordered sequences occurs when Order receives a sequence of length 1.

Given the crucial Order procedure, the MergeSort procedure itself is almost trivial. It need merely create a copy of the array to be sorted and then call on Order to sort the elements of the copy into the original. Note that, because Order continually calls on Merge and Merge cannot do its work within one array, the need to create a copy of the original array is unavoidable. Complete Pascal versions of MergeSort and Order follow:

```
PROCEDURE MergeSort (VAR Key : SortArray;
                     N : integer);

  { Given:    Array Key with entries in indices 1 through N.   }
  { Task:     Apply merge sort algorithm.                      }
  { Return:   Key arranged in ascending order.                 }

  VAR
    CopyKey : SortArray;
    K : integer;

  PROCEDURE Merge (Source : SortArray;
                   VAR Destination : SortArray;
                   Lower, Mid, Upper : integer);

    { Previously discussed Merge PROCEDURE would appear here.  }

  PROCEDURE Order (Source : SortArray;
                   VAR Destination : SortArray;
                   Lower, Upper : integer);

    { Given:    Source and Destination, two arrays that are    }
    {           initially identical between indices            }
    {           Lower..Upper.                                  }
```

```
{ Task:     Transfer Source in ascending order to       }
{           Destination, between indices Lower..Upper.   }
{ Return:   Destination arranged in order between Lower  }
{           and Upper.                                   }

    VAR Mid : integer;

    BEGIN {  PROCEDURE Order  }
      IF Lower <> Upper THEN {  Recursively call to get smaller  }
                            {  pieces which are then ordered.    }
        BEGIN
          Mid := (Lower + Upper) DIV 2;
          Order (Destination, Source, Lower, Mid);
          Order (Destination, Source, Mid + 1, Upper);
          Merge (Source, Destination, Lower, Mid, Upper)
        END
    END; {  of PROCEDURE Order  }

BEGIN  {  PROCEDURE MergeSort  }
  {  Make copy for call to Order.  }
  FOR K := 1 TO N DO
    CopyKey[K] := Key[K];
  Order (CopyKey, Key, 1, N)
END; {  of PROCEDURE MergeSort  }
```

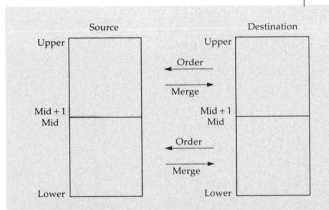

Recursively call Order to get two sorted segments in Source which are then merged into Destination. This requires that Destination originally be a copy of Source.

The run-time trace diagram of procedure calls in Figure 19.5 highlights the interaction between Order and Merge triggered by calling MergeSort with a sample array of size N = 11. The leaf nodes in this trace diagram represent the recursive termination condition reached when Lower = Upper.

Analysis of the Merge Sort

From a run-time trace of procedure calls such as that appearing in Figure 19.5, it is quite easy to deduce that merge sort requires $O(n\log_2 n)$ comparisons. The reasoning required for this deduction is as follows. All the merge operations across any given level of the trace diagram will require $O(n)$ comparisons. There are $O(\log_2 n)$ levels to the trace diagram. Hence, the

FIGURE 19.5
Run-time trace of procedure
calls to Order and Merge

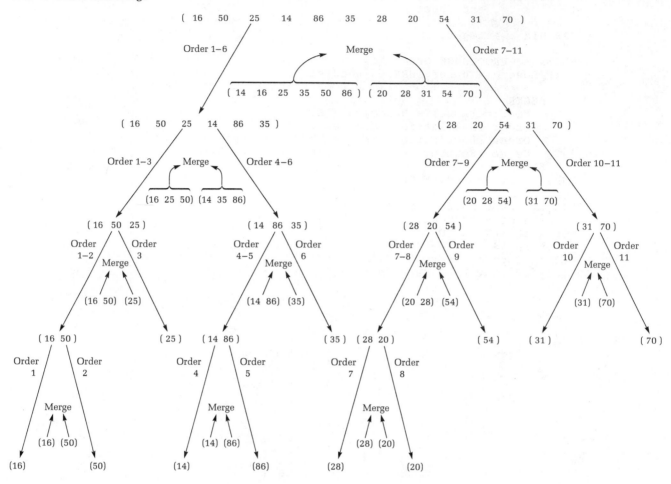

overall efficiency is the product $O(n\log_2 n)$. Notice that, like the heap sort, the merge sort can guarantee this efficiency regardless of the original data. That is, there is no worst case that can cause its efficiency to deteriorate (as there is for quick sort).

The price paid for using merge sort is in the memory space it requires. Of course, there is the stack space associated with recursion. More important, however, is the need for a duplicate copy of the array being sorted. In applications where the original array barely fits in memory, this space requirement will make merge sort totally impractical.

As steep as the memory price is, there is an added benefit to merge sort that makes it the only possible choice for certain applications: merge sort may be written in a way which necessitates only sequential access to the lists being manipulated. As we have presented it here, random access is required at only one point in the algorithm, namely, in the Merge procedure to access the second list beginning at subscript (Mid + 1) of Source. The need for this could have been eliminated by having Merge work with two separate source

A NOTE OF INTEREST

Public-Key Cryptography

The manner in which computers can sort through and in other ways manipulate information gives rise to concern over the security of electronic information. Cryptography is the science of encoding information to protect it from being viewed by unauthorized parties. Today, as an increasing amount of sensitive information is being transmitted in electronic and magnetic form, cryptography is becoming an increasingly important field. (For information on data transmission, see the Note of Interest entitled "Computer Networks: More Than an Abstract Data Type" in Chapter 18.)

A conventional encryption system works much like a mailbox with a combination lock. Anyone knowing the combination can open the box to leave a message or to read any of the messages in the box. In computerized information systems, the "combination" to the mailbox is a digital key; that is, a particular bit pattern which is applied to an electronic message to encode or decode it. In conventional systems, anyone knowing the digital key has access to the information in the electronic mailbox. Hence such systems are best suited to a small number of users and not to the networking of information among many computer installations that is possible with today's technology.

An interesting development in cryptography occurred in the early 1970s with the development of theory for public-key encryption systems. Such systems work on two different digital keys: one for writing information into the electronic mailbox and the other to read encoded information that has been left in the mailbox. As a user of such an encryption system, you could freely give out the write key to your mailbox (the public key), allowing anyone to send you an encoded letter. However, you would keep the read key (the decoding key) secret so that only you would be able to make sense out of your mail.

The best-known public-key encryption scheme is known as the RSA algorithm (after Rivest, Shamir, and Adleman, the mathematicians who developed it). This algorithm is based upon the difficulty of factoring large numbers that are the product of two prime numbers. For instance, the number $51 = 3 \times 17$ would satisfy this criterion except that it is not nearly large enough.

In the RSA system, the product of the two prime factors would be linked to your public key. However, this public key would include only the product, not the prime factors that comprise the product. Your private key would include each of the individual prime factors. Why should such numbers be large? The answer to this question lies in the present limitations of the area of mathematics known as number theory. It turns out that, given the product of two such prime factors without being told the factors themselves, number theory provides no known way of factoring the number into its prime factors in a reasonable amount of time, even using the most advanced supercomputers. From a security perspective, this means that your code could not be broken by outside agencies, even if they were using a computer to assist them.

The role of public-key cryptography in electronic data systems will no doubt become increasingly important in the future. For an excellent discussion of the method and some of the social concerns arising from it, you may want to read the article "Encryption: Technology, Privacy, and National Security," by Tom Athanasiou in *Technology Review* (August/September 1986): 57–66. A very readable description of the RSA and other encryption algorithms is presented in "Cloak and Dagger" by Rick Grehan in the June 1990 issue of *Byte* magazine (Vol. 15, No. 6: 311–324).

arrays. That is, we would merge ordered arrays Source1 and Source2 into Destination. This would be very costly with arrays since it would necessitate using three arrays to sort one array. However, it is less costly when the lists being manipulated are being implemented not by arrays but rather by dynamically allocated linked lists or sequential files. In both of these latter situations, the need to use sequential access would make the merge sort strategy the only appropriate sorting method. In the Exercises at the end of the section and the Programming Problems at the end of the chapter, you will be asked to adapt MergeSort to such sequential implementations of a list. In particular, when the list exists in a file instead of main memory, the sorting method employed is said to be an *external sort* (as opposed to the *internal sorts* we have studied in this chapter).

Exercises 19.4

1. Consider the MergeSort procedure given in this section. Note that this procedure contains a subordinate procedure called Order. Suppose that we were to insert the following tracer output immediately after the initial **BEGIN** for this procedure.

```
writeln (Lower,Upper);
FOR K := Lower to Upper DO {  K  declared as scratch variable.  }
    write (Source[K]);
writeln;
```

What would we see as output from these tracers if we were to call on Merge-Sort with an array that initially contained

60 12 90 30 64 8 6

2. Repeat Exercise 1 for a six-element array that initially contains

1 8 2 7 3 6

3. Explain in what sense **PROCEDURE** MergeSort of this section would be more efficient if the Source parameter for the subordinate **PROCEDURE** Order were a **VAR** parameter instead of a value parameter.

4. Implement MergeSort in a nonrecursive fashion.

5. In Chapter 12, PointerSort used an index of pointers to sort data logically without rearranging it. Adapt the pointer sort procedure to the merge sort algorithm.

6. Identify and give an example of best-case and worst-case data sets for the merge sort algorithm. Explain why your data sets generate best- and worst-case performance.

7. A sorting method is said to be stable if two data items of matching value are guaranteed not to be rearranged with respect to each other as the algorithm progresses. For example, in the four-element array

$60\ 42_1\ 80\ 42_2$

a stable sorting method would guarantee a final ordering of

$42_1\ 42_2\ 60\ 80$

Classify each of the sorting algorithms studied in this chapter and in Chapter 12 as to their stability. (To see why stability may be important, consider Programming Problems 5 and 9 at the end of this chapter.)

8. You are to sort an array in a program in which the following considerations are to be taken into account. First, there is a large amount of data to be sorted. The amount of data to be sorted is so large that frequent $O(n^2)$ run-times will prove unsatisfactory. The amount of data will also make it impossible for your program to use a large amount of overhead data (for example, stack space) to make the sort efficient in its run-time. This is because the space required by the overhead data would potentially take up space needed by the array to be sorted. Second, you are told that the array to be sorted is often nearly in order to start with. For each of the seven sorting methods indicated, specify whether or not that method would be appropriate for this application and, in a brief statement, explain why your answer is correct.

   a. Bubble sort
   b. Insertion sort
   c. Selection sort
   d. Shell sort
   e. Quick sort

f. Heap sort

g. Merge sort

■ ■ ■ ■

**FOCUS ON
PROGRAM DESIGN**

We have stressed repeatedly that analysis of algorithms combines formal mathematical techniques with experimental methodology. Certainly, nowhere is this better illustrated than in the analysis of sorting algorithms. For instance, among the four algorithms studied in this chapter, only two—heap sort and merge sort—can be placed with certainty in the $O(n\log_2 n)$ category by purely mathematical analysis. The other two—shell sort and quick sort—are apparently much more dependent on the original arrangement of the data being sorted.

In this section, we present components of a program whose structure facilitates experimentation with a sorting algorithm. In particular, our program will be useful in the exploration of the shell sort algorithm. However, the underlying structure of the program makes it easy to incorporate other sorting algorithms. All that must be altered is the procedure that implements the particular sorting algorithm being studied. This procedure must not only do the sorting, but also profile the algorithm in the sense described in Chapter 12. All the other modules in the program are geared toward construction of an environment in which you can experiment with the sorting algorithm. These modules remain the same regardless of which sorting algorithm is chosen.

Input to the program is the list of integers to be sorted. This input may be provided in one of three forms:

1. A randomly generated permutation of the integers from

    1, 2, 3, . . . Size–1, Size

    where Size is the logical size of the list being sorted. Recall that a permutation is an arrangement of the integers in which no repetitions occur.
2. A list of integers entered interactively, allowing input of particular data sets for which you want to profile the sorting algorithm.
3. A list of integers read one per line from a text file.

This final form of input, coupled with the program's ability to save a particular data set in the text file form which can later be read, allows you to fine-tune the sorting algorithm for data sets that proved particularly interesting from an efficiency perspective. That is, if you encounter a randomly generated or interactively input data set for which the efficiency of the sort algorithm seems to deteriorate, you can save that data set in a text file. Then you can adjust the sort algorithm to allow for the characteristics of that data set and rerun the program, loading the saved data set to see if your adjustments made a substantial improvement. This mode of experimental use of the program is illustrated in the following sample runs:

First run:

```
1 - Load a random array
2 - Interactively load an array
3 - Load array from previous round
```

```
              Enter 1, 2, or 3 -->1

              Enter the number of values -->10
              Do you want to see the array? (Y/N) -->y

       ARRAY[ 1] =  1
       ARRAY[ 2] =  3
       ARRAY[ 3] =  2
       ARRAY[ 4] =  4
       ARRAY[ 5] =  5
       ARRAY[ 6] =  8
       ARRAY[ 7] =  6
       ARRAY[ 8] =  9
       ARRAY[ 9] =  7
       ARRAY[10] = 10

  Sort required 51 loop interation(s).
  Sort required 4 swap(s) of data.
  Sort required 78 comparison(s).

  Do you want to see the array after sorting? (Y=N) -->y

           ARRAY[ 1] =  1
           ARRAY[ 2] =  2
           ARRAY[ 3] =  3
           ARRAY[ 4] =  4
           ARRAY[ 5] =  5
           ARRAY[ 6] =  6
           ARRAY[ 7] =  7
           ARRAY[ 8] =  8
           ARRAY[ 9] =  9
           ARRAY[10] = 10

  Save this list for another run? (Y/N) -->y
  Name for save file -->test.dat
  Another Shell Sort? (Y/N) -->n
```

Then fine-tune the program to improve efficiency, and run again.

Second run:

```
           1 - Load a random array
           2 - Interactively load an array
           3 - Load array from previous round

           Enter 1, 2, or 3 -->3

           Enter the name of the file -->test.dat
           Do you want to see the array? (Y/N) -->y

       ARRAY[ 1] =  1
       ARRAY[ 2] =  3
       ARRAY[ 3] =  2
       ARRAY[ 4] =  4
       ARRAY[ 5] =  5
       ARRAY[ 6] =  8
       ARRAY[ 7] =  6
       ARRAY[ 8] =  9
       ARRAY[ 9] =  7
       ARRAY[10] = 10

  Sort required 42 loop interation(s).
  Sort required 4 swap(s) of data.
  Sort required 61 comparisons(s).
```

```
Do you want to see the array after sorting? (Y/N) -->n

Save this list for another run? (Y/N) -->n
Another Shell Sort? (Y/N) -->n
```

Notice how the profiling output gives evidence of the improved efficiency of the second run.

The modular structure chart for our program is given in Figure 19.6. Modular specifications and a partial program listing follow. In the Programming Problems, you will be asked to complete the program and then use it in various forms of exploration with the shell sort. You will also be asked to incorporate the design of the program into a vehicle for exploring other sorting algorithms.

FIGURE 19.6
Modular structure chart for
PROGRAM ShellExperimentation

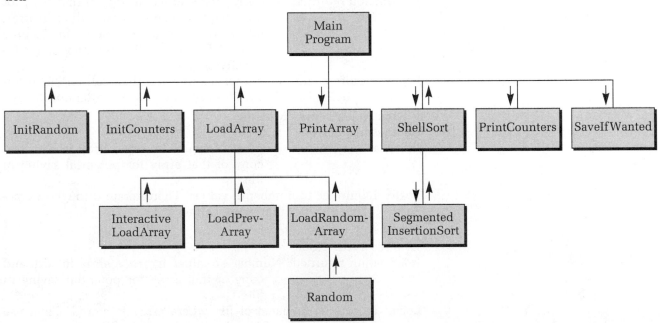

A first-level pseudocode development for the main program is

1. Initialize the random number generator (if necessary—see Appendix 9)
2. **REPEAT**
    2.1   Initialize the global profiling counters.
    2.2   Load the array by user-chosen method. Also return a duplicate copy of the array for potential saving in a file.
    2.3   Print the array if user wants to see it.
    2.4   Apply shell sort to the array.
    2.5   Output the global profiling counters.
    2.6   Print the sorted array if the user wants to see it.
    2.7   Save the copy of the original array if the user wants to.
    2.8   Inquire if the user wants to shell sort another array.
    UNTIL   user indicates no more sorts.

Modular specifications corresponding to the modular structure chart of Figure 19.6 are as follows:

1. <u>InitRandom Module</u>
   Data received: None
   Information returned: None
   Logic: Initialize the random number generator as described in Appendix 9. May be unnecessary if your version of Pascal provides a random number generator.

2. <u>InitCounters Module</u>
   Data received: Profiling counters as global variables—for number of comparisons, number of swaps, and number of loop iterations.
   Information returned: Profiling counters set to zero.
   Logic: Obvious.

3. <u>LoadArray Module</u>
   Data received: None
   Information returned: The array to be sorted, a copy of that array for potential saving, number of values in array, integer indicating user choice for loading array: 1 for random permutation, 2 for interactive, 3 for file.
   Logic: Inquire about method for loading and then call on one of InteractiveLoadArray, LoadPrevArray, or LoadRandomArray.

4. <u>InteractiveLoadArray Module</u>
   Data received: None
   Information returned: Number of values in array, array to sort, and copy of that array for potential saving in file.
   Logic: Inquire as to number of values. Then iterate through interactive input of that many values.

5. <u>LoadPrevArray Module</u>
   Data received: None
   Information returned: Number of values in array, array to sort, and copy of that array for potential saving in file.
   Logic: Inquire as to name of file where array is stored. Then use **WHILE NOT eof** loop to read data from file into array.

6. <u>RandomLoadArray Module</u>
   Data received: None
   Information returned: Number of values in array, array to sort, and copy of that array for potential saving in file.
   Logic: Inquire as to size of array. Generate a random permutation of the values 1, 2, . . ., Size. There are several algorithms to do this. We leave it for you to discover one in the Programming Problems.

7. <u>Random Module</u>
   Data received: None
   Information returned: Randomly generated value.
   Logic: Use algorithm in Appendix 9 or random number generator provided with your version of Pascal.

8. PrintArray Module
    Data received: Array and its logical Size.
    Information returned: None
    Logic: Iterate through output of each array value.

9. ShellSort and SegmentedInsertionSort Modules
    Data received: Array of values and its logical Size.
    Information returned: Array sorted in ascending order.
    Logic: See Section 19.1.

10. PrintCounters Module
    Data received: Global profiling counters.
    Information returned: None.
    Logic: Print profiling counters to report on efficiency of algorithm for data set just sorted.

11. SaveIfWanted Module
    Data received: Copy of original array, logical Size of that array, integer indicating how user loaded array.
    Information returned: None.
    Logic: Inquire if user wants to save this list for further exploration. **IF** user wants to save and list not originally loaded from file **THEN** write array to file in form compatible with LoadPrevArray module.

A partial program listing follows:

```
PROGRAM ShellExperimentation(input, output, f);

  { This program allows the user to experiment with the ShellSort    }
  { algorithm on a variety of different arrays of data.  The sort    }
  { algorithm has been augmented to keep track of the number of      }
  { swaps, comparisons, and loop iterations necessary to sort the    }
  { current array. These can be used as a measure of comparison      }
  { among various initial data arrays or among different sorting     }
  { methods.  This method of measuring the amount of work required   }
  { to sort the array is used because standard Pascal has no built-in }
  { method of timing program execution.                              }
  {                                                                  }
  { The data file created by the program when an array is saved is   }
  { simply a text file with one element of the array per line of the }
  { file.  Similarly, the program expects any file from which it is to }
  { read an array to have this format.                               }

  CONST { ShellExperimentation }
    MaxArraySize = 500;        { Maximum size of data array       }
    NameSize = 30;             { Maximum size of file name string }

  TYPE { ShellExperimentation }
    SortType = integer;
    SortArray = ARRAY [1..MaxArraySize] OF SortType;
    NameString = PACKED ARRAY [1..NameSize] OF char;

  VAR { ShellExperimentation }
    Key, CopyOfKey: SortArray;  { Arrays to hold the data           }
    ArraySize: integer;         { Current size of array             }
    Query: char;                { User's response                   }
    f: text;                    { File variable                     }
    Seed: integer;              { Seed for random number generator  }
    ChoiceOfLoad: integer;      { User's choice for loading array   }
```

```
{ Global counters used to measure the amount of work required    }
{ to sort the data array.                                        }
NumIterations: integer;    { Number of loop iterations           }
NumSwaps: integer;         { Number of swaps of data             }
NumComparisons: integer;   { Number of comparisons made          }


{ ************************************************************************ }
{                 Random number modules appear here.                      }
{                 See Appendix 9 or use function provided with            }
{                        your version of Pascal.                          }
  .
  .
  .

{ ************************************************************************ }
{                 Procedures to handle the data arrays                    }

PROCEDURE SaveIfWanted(ArraySize: integer;
                       VAR ArrayToSave: SortArray;
                       ChoiceOfLoad: integer);

  { Given:   Array to save, Size of array, type of load performed.   }
  { Task:    Write the array out to a file if the user indicates     }
  {          that he wants to save it for future runs.  The file     }
  {          handling may require modification on some systems.      }
  { Return:  Nothing.                                                }


  .
  .
  .


PROCEDURE LoadArray(VAR Size: integer;
                    VAR Original, Copy: SortArray;
                    VAR ChoiceOfLoad: integer);

  { Given:   Nothing.                                                }
  { Task:    Determine which method the user wants to use to         }
  {          load the array of data and call the appropriate         }
  {          procedure.                                              }
  { Return:  Both arrays, the size of the arrays, and the            }
  {          user's selection of type of load to be performed.       }

  VAR { LoadArray }
    Valid: boolean;

  PROCEDURE InteractiveLoadArray(VAR Size: integer;
                                 VAR Orig, Copy: SortArray);

    { Given:   Nothing.                                              }
    { Task:    Prompt the user to input the data for the array,      }
    {          read it in, and make a copy of it.                    }
    { Return:  Both arrays along with their size.                    }


      .
      .
      .


  PROCEDURE LoadPrevArray(VAR Size: integer;
                          VAR Orig, Copy: SortArray);

    { Given:   Nothing.                                              }
    { Task:    Open the file containing the previous array the       }
```

```
    {                 user desires to use, read the data into the        }
    {                 array, and make a copy of the array.  The file     }
    {                 handling may require modification on some           }
    {                 systems.                                            }
    { Return:  Both arrays along with their size.                         }


                     .
                     .
                     .


  PROCEDURE LoadRandomArray(VAR Size: integer;
                            VAR Orig, Copy: SortArray);

    { Given:   Nothing.                                                   }
    { Task:    Fill the array with a randomly generated permutation of    }
    {          the integers between 1..Size, and then make a copy of      }
    {          the array.                                                 }
    { Return:  Both arrays along with their size.                         }


                     .
                     .
                     .


  BEGIN { LoadArray }
    REPEAT
      writeln;
      writeln;
      writeln;
      writeln('          1 - Load a random array');
      writeln('          2 - Interactively load an array');
      writeln('          3 - Load array from previous round');
      writeln;
      write('          Enter 1, 2, or 3 --> ');
      readln(ChoiceOfLoad);
      Valid := ((ChoiceOfLoad > 0) AND (ChoiceOfLoad < 4));
      IF Valid THEN
        CASE ChoiceOfLoad OF
          1:
            LoadRandomArray(Size, Original, Copy);
          2:
            InteractiveLoadArray(Size, Original, Copy);
          3:
            LoadPrevArray(Size, Original, Copy);
        END { CASE }
      ELSE
        writeln('\', ChoiceOfLoad: 1,
                '\ is not a valid response - try again')
    UNTIL Valid
  END; { of PROCEDURE LoadArray }

PROCEDURE PrintArray(VAR A: SortArray;
                     Low, High: integer);

  { Given:   Array of data, low and high ends of the range of            }
  {          indices of the array to be printed.                         }
  { Task:    Print the contents of the specified range of                }
  {          the array to the terminal.                                  }
  { Return:  Nothing.                                                     }


             .
             .
             .
```

```
{*********************************************************************** }
{                   Procedures for the global counters                  }

PROCEDURE InitCounters;

  { Given:    Nothing.                                                   }
  { Task:     Initialize the global counters.                            }
  { Return:   Nothing.                                                   }

  BEGIN { InitCounters }
    NumIterations := 0;
    NumSwaps := 0;
    NumComparisons := 0
  END; { InitCounters }

PROCEDURE PrintCounters;

  { Given:    Nothing.                                                   }
  { Task:     Print the statistics regarding the sort.                   }
  { Return:   Nothing.                                                   }

  BEGIN { PrintCounters }
    writeln;
    writeln('Sort required ', NumIterations: 1, ' loop iteration(s).');
    writeln('Sort required ', NumSwaps: 1, ' swap(s) of data.');
    writeln('Sort required ', NumComparisons: 1, ' comparison(s).');
    writeln
  END; { PrintCounters }

{*********************************************************************** }
{                    Procedures for ShellSort                           }

PROCEDURE ShellSort(Size: integer;
                    VAR Key: SortArray);

  { Given:    Array Key with entries in indices 1 through Size.          }
  { Task:     Apply shell sort algorithm.                                }
  { Return:   Array Key with first "Size" entries arranged in            }
  {           ascending order.                                           }

  VAR { ShellSort }
    K: integer;

  PROCEDURE SegmentedInsertionSort(VAR Key: SortArray;
                                   N, K: integer);

    { Given:    N-element array Key, viewed as being divided             }
    {           into K segments.                                         }
    { Task:     Arrange each segment into ascending order using          }
    {           insertion sort logic.                                    }
    { Return:   Array Key with K sorted segments.                        }

    VAR L, J : integer;
        ItemToInsert : SortType;
        StillLooking : boolean;

    BEGIN
      { On the Lth pass, insert item L into its correct position among   }
      { the previous entries in its segment.                             }
      FOR L : = K + 1 TO N DO
        BEGIN
          NumIterations := NumIterations + 1;          { Update Efficiency Stats }
```

```
         { Walk backwards through segment, looking for slot to insert Key[L]  }
         ItemToInsert := Key[L];
         J := L - K;    { J counts down through current segment  }
         StillLooking := true;
         NumComparisons := NumComparisons + 1;           { Update Efficiency Stats}
         WHILE (J >= 1) AND StillLooking DO
           BEGIN
             NumIterations := NumIterations + 1;         { Update Efficiency Stats}
             { ItemToInsert is compared to Key[J] }
             NumComparisons := NumComparisons + 1;       { Update Efficiency Stats}
             IF ItemToInsert < Key[J] THEN
               BEGIN
                 Key[J + K] := Key[J];
                 NumSwaps := NumSwaps + 1;               { Update Efficiency Stats}
                 J := J - K
               END
             ELSE
               StillLooking := false;
             NumComparisons := NumComparisons + 1        { Update Efficiency Stats}
           END;  { WHILE }
         { Upon leaving loop, J + K is the index where ItemToInsert belongs  }
         Key[J + K] := ItemToInsert
       END { FOR }
   END; { of PROCEDURE SegmentedInsertionSort }

  BEGIN { ShellSort }
    K := Size DIV 2;           { K represents current number of segments. }
    NumComparisons := NumComparisons + 1;              { Update Efficiency Stats}
    WHILE K > 0 DO
      BEGIN
        NumIterations := NumIterations + 1;            { Update Efficiency Stats}
        SegmentedInsertionSort(Key, Size, K);
        K := K DIV 2; { Reduce number of segments }
        NumComparisons := NumComparisons + 1           { Update Efficiency Stats}
      END
  END; { of PROCEDURE ShellSort }

{************************************************************************ }
{                    The main program                                    }

BEGIN { Main }
  InitRandom;
  REPEAT
    InitCounters;
    LoadArray(ArraySize, Key, CopyOfKey, ChoiceOfLoad);
    write('Do you want to see the array? (Y/N) --> ');
    readln(Query);
    IF (Query = 'Y') OR (Query = 'y') THEN
      PrintArray(Key, 1, ArraySize);
    ShellSort(ArraySize, Key);
    PrintCounters;
    write('Do you want to see the array after sorting? (Y/N) --> ');
    readln(Query);
    IF (Query = 'Y') OR (Query = 'y') THEN
      PrintArray(Key, 1, ArraySize);
    SaveIfWanted(ArraySize, CopyOfKey, ChoiceOfLoad);
    write('Another Shell Sort? (Y/N) --> ');
    readln(Query)
  UNTIL (Query = 'N') OR (Query = 'n')
END. { Main }
```

RUNNING AND
DEBUGGING TIPS

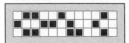

1. To describe and understand the more complex sort algorithms, it is helpful to present them via subordinate algorithms and stepwise refinement. To this end, we have found it convenient to initially focus on subalgorithms (SegmentedInsertion-Sort for ShellSort, Partition for QuickSort, WalkDown for HeapSort, and Merge for MergeSort). Our method is illustrative of the stepwise refinement approach to problem solving: break a complex problem down into smaller problems, solve these smaller problems, and then tie their solutions together to solve the original large problem.

2. Describing and understanding algorithms is a separate issue from their actual implementation in a specific programming language and on a real machine. One implication of this separation of algorithm description and algorithm implementation is the run-time cost associated with a procedure call. We must consider the hidden costs of making a procedure call and how deeply embedded the procedure call is in the iterative structure of the calling module.

3. Depending upon the machine you are using, calling a procedure instead of directly inserting the code necessary may mean that your program spends more run-time handling the hidden cost of procedure calls than it does in actually interchanging data items. If large data sets are being sorted and if run-time efficiency is of primary importance, then we should implement our algorithm without actually calling on a procedure.

4. Keep in mind the distinction between algorithm description and algorithm implementation when making decisions about whether or not to proceduralize a given sequence of instructions. What may be appropriately isolated as a trivial subalgorithm at the time when a designer is concerned with describing an algorithm may carry with it a steep price if implemented as a trivial procedure that is called upon many times when the resulting program is put into use.

5. In making the decision whether to use procedures or in-line code when implementing an algorithm, carefully weigh run-time considerations with respect to the clarity and readability of code. A useful rule of thumb is that only in exceptional circumstances should the code associated with a module exceed one printed page in length. This guideline allows in-line insertion of code for simple algorithmic units and assures that the overall software system does not become unwieldy.

■ Summary

Key Terms

diminishing increment sort	merge sort	quick sort
external sort	partition	relatively prime
heap sort	pivot	shell sort
internal sort		

Key Concepts

- This chapter has added four sorting algorithms to those already presented in Chapter 12. This gives us a large variety of tools from which to choose when we need to perform a sorting job.
- The following comparison table summarizes the pros and cons of each sorting method we've covered.

Sorting Method	Chapter	Number of Comparisons in Terms of the Number of Data Items Being Sorted (n)	Space Requirement	Additional Comments
Binary tree	21	Between $O(n^2)$ and $O(n\log_2 n)$ depending on original data and whether tree height-balanced	Pointers for tree and possible stack space for recursive traversals	
Bubble	15	$O(n^2)$	No additional overhead	Loop check allows early exit as soon as array is ordered.
Heap	22	$O(n\log_2 n)$	No additional overhead	
Insertion	15	$O(n^2)$	No additional overhead	Loop check allows early exit as soon as item is correctly placed.
Merge	22	$O(n\log_2 n)$	Requires duplicate array and stack space for recursion	Since only requires sequential access, can be used for linked lists and sequential files.
Pointer	15	Depends on method with which it is combined	Required list of pointers to maintain logical order	Can be combined with any method to substantially reduce size of data items being interchanged.
Quick	22	$O(n\log_2 n)$ on the average but $O(n^2)$ for worst cases	Stack space for recursion	
Radix	15, 18	$O(n)$	Space for bins	Though $O(n)$, large constant of proportionality. Not generalizable to all types of data, for example, **real**.
Selection	15	$O(n^2)$	No additional overhead	
Shell	22	Between $O(n(\log_2 n)^2)$ and $O(n^{1.5})$ depending on increments used	No additional overhead	

■ Programming Problems and Projects

1. Complete the partial program presented in this chapter's Focus on Program Design section. Then use the completed program to explore empirically the shell sort algorithm. In particular, experiment with different sequences of diminishing increments.

   Write a report on your exploration. In your report you should compare various sequences of diminishing increments and rate them as to their performance on a variety of data sets.

2. Modify the shell sort so that it employs bubble sort logic on segments instead of insertion sort. Incorporate this change into the program presented in this chapter's Focus on Program Design section. Compare the observed efficiency of this new version of shell sort with the original on a variety of data sets. Which performs better? Explain your answer in a carefully written statement.

3. Modify the program presented in this chapter's Focus on Program Design section so that it becomes an experimental tool for quick sort, heap sort, or merge sort. Then use the modified program to conduct an experiment similar to that which you did for shell sort in Problem 1. For instance, for quick sort, you could experiment with the selection of a pivot element or try invoking insertion sort when the size of the array segment to be partitioned becomes sufficiently small. Whatever experimentation you choose to do, write a report on your exploration. In your report, draw conclusions about the efficiencies of various strategies. Support your conclusions with empirical data obtained from your exploratory runs.

4. Given a sequential file containing an unordered list of passengers and their flight numbers for Wing-and-a-Prayer Airlines (Problem 2, Chapter 15; Problems 3 and 12, Chapter 18), produce a listing arranged in flight-number order. Passengers on the same flight should be ordered by last name. The easy version of this program assumes that all information will fit in memory, allowing the use of an internal sort. For an added challenge, write the program using an external sort algorithm. (*Hint:* Adapt MergeSort along the lines discussed in the text.)

5. The Bay Area Brawlers professional football team (Problem 4, Chapter 15; Problem 5, Chapter 18) has stored the records of all the players who have played on the team during the history of the team. One player's record consists of

   Name
   Total points scored
   Number of touchdowns
   Number of field goals
   Number of safeties
   Number of extra points

   Write a program that lists players in order from the highest scorer in the team's history down to the lowest. Those players who have scored the same number of points should then be arranged in alphabetical order.

6. Take N randomly generated integers. Now apply a bubble sort, a shell sort, a quick sort, a heap sort, and a merge sort. Observe, compare, and plot their execution time for N = 100; N = 1,000; N = 10,000; N = 100,000, ...

7. Put some hypothetical data in an external file and apply a modified merge sort to them.

8. Write a Pascal program to complete the following steps.

   - Artificially create a file with a large number of randomly chosen names.
   - Read into an array all those names which begin with *A* through some letter, say *G*, chosen so that all the names will fit in the array.
   - Sort this array with one of the sorting algorithms from this chapter and store this sorted array into another file.
   - Now read into the array all those names from the file which begin with *H* through another appropriate letter.
   - Sort the array and append it to the end of the new file.

   Repeat this process until all names from the original file have been processed. The new file will be the sorted version of the original. Observe the execution time of your program. Analyze its efficiency in big-O terms.

9. Consider a list of records, each containing four fields.

   Name
   Month of birth
   Day of birth
   Year of birth

   Write a program to sort this list in oldest-to-youngest order. People with the same birth date should be arranged alphabetically. One strategy you could employ would be to concatenate strategically the four fields into one, and then sort just that one field. Another strategy would be to sort the list four times, each time by a different field. (Think carefully about which field to sort first.) Which of the strategies would require that you choose a stable sorting algorithm? (See Exercise 7 in Section 19.4.)

10. Modify MergeSort so that it will sort a linked list instead of an array.

I do not search, I find.
Pablo Picasso

More Powerful Search Methods

In earlier chapters, we've analyzed three methods of searching for items within a list: sequential search, binary search, and binary search tree. The sequential search, though easy to implement and applicable to short lists, is limited in many practical situations by its $O(n)$ search efficiency. The binary search offers a much faster $O(\log_2 n)$ search efficiency but also has limitations. Foremost among these limitations are the need to maintain the list in physically contiguous order and the need to maintain a count of the number of records in the list. Both of these limitations are particularly restrictive for volatile lists; that is, lists in which insertions and deletions are frequently made. In Chapter 18, a binary search tree emerged as offering the best of both worlds. Insertions and deletions can be done on a binary search tree by merely manipulating pointers instead of moving data, and an $O(\log_2 n)$ search efficiency can be achieved if the tree remains close to full. Unfortunately, to guarantee that the tree remains nearly full and hence insure the $O(\log_2 n)$ efficiency, a sophisticated technique known as height balancing (see Chapter 18) is required. The complications involved in implementing this technique frequently dictate that it not be used. Essentially, you must weigh the significant cost in development time to implement a height-balanced tree against the risk that the order in which data arrive for insertion may cause search efficiency to deteriorate from $O(\log_2 n)$ to $O(n)$. If data items arrive in a relatively random order, then taking that risk may well be the prudent choice.

The efficiency of all three of these techniques is dependent on the number of items in the list being searched. In this chapter, we shall study another alternative, called *hashing*. Its efficiency is measurable in terms of the amount of storage you are willing to waste. In this sense, hashing can achieve phenomenally fast search times regardless of how much data you have, provided that you can afford to keep a relatively large amount of unused list space available.

We shall also explore some of the special considerations that enter into searching for data stored in a disk file instead of main memory. These considerations lead to a variety of search schemes, all of which employ some variation of a data structure known as an *index*.

■ 20.1
Density-Dependent Search Techniques

OBJECTIVES

- to understand what is meant by a key-to-address transformation, that is, a hashing function
- to develop techniques for constructing hashing functions
- to understand why, for most applications, hashing functions cannot transform all possible keys to a unique address
- to understand what the term *collision* means relative to hashing
- to develop methods for processing collisions: linear probing, quadratic probing, rehashing, linked (chained) probing, and bucket hashing
- to understand what the term *clustering* means relative to hashing

In an ideal data processing world, all identifying keys such as product codes, Social Security numbers, and so on, would start at 1 and follow in sequence thereafter. Then, in any given list, we would merely store the key and its associated data at the position that matched the key. The search efficiency for any key in such a list would be one access to the list, and all data processors could live happily ever after! Unfortunately, in the real world, users (not being concerned with the happiness of data processing personnel) desire keys that consist of more meaningful characters, such as names, addresses, region codes, and so on. For instance, it may be that in a given inventory-control application, product codes are numbered in sequence beginning with 10,000 instead of 1. A moment's reflection should indicate that this is still a highly desirable situation since, given a key, we need merely locate the key at position

KeyValue − 9999

in the list, and we still have a search efficiency of 1. What we have done here is to define what is known as a *key-to-address transformation,* or *hashing function.* The idea behind a hashing function is that it acts upon a given key in such a way as to return the relative position in the list where we expect to find the key.

Most hashing functions are not as straightforward as the preceding one and present some additional complications which we can quickly illustrate. Suppose we use the following hashing function:

Hash(KeyValue) = (KeyValue **MOD** 4) + 1

Then the set of keys 3, 5, 8, and 10 will be scattered as illustrated here.

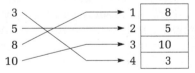

However, if we happen to have 3, 4, 8, and 10 as keys instead of 3, 5, 8, and 10, a problem arises: 4 and 8 hash to the same position. They are said to be *synonyms,* and the result is termed a *collision.* This situation, here a collision at position 1, is shown in the following illustration.

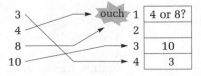

Clearly, one of the goals of the hashing functions we develop should be to reduce the number of collisions as much as possible.

The Construction of Hashing Functions

The business of developing hashing functions can be quite intriguing. The essential idea is to build a mathematical black box that will take a key value as input and issue as output the position in the list where that key value should be located. The position emitted should have a minimal probability of colliding with the position that would be produced for a different key. In addition, the black box we create must insure that a given key will always produce the same position as output. You should begin to note a similarity between some of the properties possessed by a good hashing function and a good random number generator such as that used in our simulation case study in Chapter 16. Indeed, list access via a hashing function is sometimes called *randomized storage,* and the first type of hashing function we discuss makes direct use of a random number generator.

Method 1: Use of a Random Number Generator. Many high-level languages provide a random number generator to produce random sequences of real values between 0 and 1. If one is not provided, you may easily write one using a method such as that described in Appendix 9. (For readable discussions of other methods of random number generation, see Chapter 7 of *Numerical Recipes* by William H. Press, Brian P. Flannery, Saul A. Teukolsky, and William T. Vetterling (Cambridge, England: Cambridge University Press, 1986).) Typically, all of these methods rely on having a global seed to start the process of generating random numbers. Computations done on this seed produce the random number. At the same time, the computations alter the value of the seed so that the next time the random number generator is called, a different random number will almost surely be produced.

In typical applications of random number generation, you need merely initialize the seed to some arbitrary value to start the random sequence. Once the seed is supplied, the random sequence is completely determined. If you have access to a system procedure that returns the current time, day, month, and year, this can be called to initialize the seed in a fashion that insures there is only a very small likelihood of generating the same random sequence twice.

How does all of this relate to hashing? For a hashing application, we must slightly alter the definition of our random number generator so that the seed is supplied as a value parameter. Then we supply the values of search keys as the seeds. The nature of the random number algorithm insures that

- Each time the same key is passed to the function, the same random value will be returned.
- It is unlikely that two different keys will yield the same random value.

The random number between 0 and 1 which is correspondingly produced can then be appropriately multiplied, truncated, and shifted to produce a hash value within the range of valid positions.

Method 2: Folding. In situations where the key to be positioned is not a pure integer, some preliminary work may be required to translate it into a usable form. Take, for instance, the case of a Social Security number such as

387–58–1505

Viewed as one integer, this would cause overflow on many machines. By a method known as *shift folding,* this Social Security number would be viewed as three separate numbers to be added

```
   387
    58
+ 1505
```

producing the result 1,950. This result could either be regarded as the hash position itself or, more likely, as a pure integer which now could be further acted upon by Method 1 or 4 to produce a final hash position in the desired range.

Another often-used folding technique is called *boundary folding.* The idea behind boundary folding is that, at the boundaries between the numbers making up the key under consideration, every other number is reversed before being added to the accumulated total. Applying this method to our Social Security number example, we would have

```
   387
    58 (this number reversed)
+ 1505
```

yielding a result of 1,977. Clearly, the two methods do not differ by much, and a choice between them must often be made on the basis of some experimentation to determine which will produce more scattered results for a given application.

Regardless of whether shift or boundary folding is used, one of the great advantages of the folding method is its ability to transform noninteger keys into an integer suitable for further hashing action. For keys such as names which contain alphabetic characters, the type of folding just illustrated may be done by translating characters into their ASCII (or other appropriate) codes.

Method 3: Digit or Character Extraction. In certain situations, a given key value may contain specific characters that are likely to bias any hash value arising from the key. The idea in *digit or character extraction* is to remove such digits or characters before using the result as a final hash value or passing it on to be further transformed by another method. For instance, a company may choose to identify the various products it manufactures by using a nine-character code which always contains either an A or B in the first position and either a 1 or 0 in the fourth position. The rest of the characters in the code tend to occur in less predictable fashion. Character extraction would remove the biased first and fourth characters, leaving a seven-character result to pass on to further processing.

Method 4: Division-Remainder Technique. All hashing presupposes a given range of positions that can be valid outputs of the hash function. In the remainder of this section, we assume the existence of a global constant RecordSpace which represents the upper limit of our hashing function. That is, the function should produce values between 1 and RecordSpace. It should than be evident that

Hash(KeyValue) = (KeyValue **MOD** RecordSpace) + 1

is a valid hashing function for integer KeyValue.

To begin examining criteria for choosing an appropriate RecordSpace, let us load the keys 41, 58, 12, 92, 50, and 91 into a list with RecordSpace 15. Figure 20.1 shows the results. In this array, zeros are used to denote empty positions.

FIGURE 20.1

Array with RecordSpace 15 loaded using a division remainder hashing function

Position	Key
1	0
2	91
3	92
4	0
5	0
6	80
7	0
8	0
9	0
10	0
11	0
12	41
13	12
14	58
15	0

However, if we keep RecordSpace the same and try to load the keys 10, 20, 30, 40, 50, 60, and 70, we have many collisions, as shown in Figure 20.2.

FIGURE 20.2

Array from Figure 20.1, loaded differently, with several collisions

Position	Key	
1	30	← 60 (collision)
2	0	
3	0	
4	0	
5	0	
6	20	← 50 (collision)
7	0	
8	0	
9	0	
10	0	
11	10	← 40 ← 70 (collision)
12	0	
13	0	
14	0	
15	0	

Hence a different set of keys can cause disastrous results even though the list seemingly has plenty of room available. On the other hand, if we choose RecordSpace to be 11, we have a list with considerably less room but no collisions. Figure 20.3 indicates the hashing positions when the same set of keys is acted upon by 11 instead of by 15.

Position	Key
1	0
2	0
3	0
4	0
5	70
6	60
7	50
8	40
9	30
10	20
11	10

Although these examples of the *division-remainder technique* are far from conclusive, they suggest that choosing a prime number for RecordSpace may produce a more desirable hashing function. The Exercises at the end of this section have you explore this question more deeply. Apart from considerations of whether or not RecordSpace should be prime, it is clear that the nature of a particular application may dictate against the choice of certain RecordSpace values. For instance, in a situation where the rightmost digits of key values happen to follow certain recurring patterns, it would be unwise to choose a power of 10 for RecordSpace. (Why?)

Despite such considerations, usually a hashing function cannot rule out the possibility of collisions; it can only make them less likely. You should quickly be able to imagine a key value that will produce a collision for the hashing function used in determining the list of Figure 20.3. Notice that, as the list becomes more full, the probability that collisions will occur increases. Hence, when using hashing as a search strategy, one must be willing to waste some positions in the list; otherwise search efficiency will drastically deteriorate. How much space to waste is an interesting question that we will soon discuss. Further, since hashing functions generally cannot eliminate collisions, we must be prepared to handle them when they occur.

Collision Processing

The essential problem in collision processing is to develop an algorithm that will position a key in a list when the position dictated by the hashing function itself is already occupied. Ideally, this algorithm should minimize the possibility of future collisions; that is, the problem key should be located at a position that is not likely to be the hashed position of a future key.

However, the nature of hashing makes this latter criterion difficult to meet with any degree of certainty, since a good hashing function does not allow prediction of where future keys are likely to be placed. We will discuss five methods of collision processing: linear, quadratic, rehashing, linked, and buckets. In all of the methods, it will be necessary to detect when a given list position is not occupied. To signify this, we use a global constant Empty to distinguish unoccupied positions. As you read, give some thought to the question of how deletions could be processed from a list accessed via one of these hashing methods. In particular, will the Empty flag suffice to denote positions that have never been occupied *and* positions previously occupied but now vacant? This question is explored in the Exercises and Programming Problems.

Linear Collision Processing

The linear method of resolving collisions is the simplest to implement (and, unfortunately, the least efficient). *Linear collision processing* requires that, when a collision occurs, we proceed down the list in sequential order until a vacant position is found. The key causing the collision is then placed at this first vacant position. If we come to the physical end of our list in the attempt to place the problem key, we merely wrap around to the top of the list and continue looking for a vacant position. For instance, suppose we use a hashing function of

$$\text{Hash}(\text{KeyValue}) = (\text{KeyValue} \textbf{ MOD } \text{RecordSpace}) + 1$$

with RecordSpace equal to 7, and attempt to insert the keys 18, 31, 67, 36, 19, and 34. The sequence of lists in Figure 20.4 shows the results of these insertions. When a collision occurs at the third insert, it is processed by the linear method; 67 is thus loaded into position 6.

FIGURE 20.4
Insertion with linear collision processing

1	0		1	0		1	0		1	0		1	0		1	34
2	0		2	0		2	0		2	36		2	36		2	36
3	0		3	0		3	0		3	0		3	0		3	0
4	0		4	31		4	31		4	31		4	31		4	31
5	18		5	18		5	18		5	18		5	18		5	18
6	0		6	0		6	67		6	67		6	67		6	67
7	0		7	0		7	0		7	0		7	19		7	19

First insert Hash(18) = 5	Second insert Hash(31) = 4	Third insert Hash(67) = 5	Fourth insert Hash(36) = 2	Fifth insert Hash(19) = 6	Sixth insert Hash(34) = 7

■ EXAMPLE 20.1

Suppose that an array has been loaded with data using the linear collision processing strategy illustrated in Figure 20.4. Write a Pascal algorithm to seek a Target key in this array.

```
{  Global declarations  }

CONST
  RecordSpace = {  Appropriate size  };
  Empty       = {  Appropriate flagging value  };

TYPE
  KeyType = {  Appropriate data type for key field in record  };
```

```
DataRec = RECORD
            Key : KeyType;
            OtherData : {  Appropriate type  }
          END;
DataArray = ARRAY [1..RecordSpace] OF DataRec;

PROCEDURE  LinearHash (Target : KeyType;
                       SearchList : DataArray;
                       VAR InfoWanted : DataRec;
                       VAR Found : boolean);

{  Given:    List of records loaded by linear hashing method  }
{            in SearchList.  Target, the value of a key        }
{            field to be found in SearchList.                  }
{  Task:     Use linear hashing algorithm to search           }
{            SearchList for Target.                            }
{  Return:   If record with key field matching Target is      }
{            found, return Found as true and return           }
{            associated information for that record in         }
{            InfoWanted.  Otherwise return Found as false.     }

VAR
  K, J : integer;
  Traversed : boolean;

BEGIN
  Found := false;       {  Assume failure  }
  Traversed := false; {  Toggled to true if entire list is traversed  }
  K := Hash (Target); {  Call on hashing function  }
  J := K;               {  J is used to probe list  }
  WHILE (SearchList[J].Key <> Empty) AND NOT (Traversed OR Found) DO
    IF Target = SearchList[J].Key THEN
      BEGIN
        InfoWanted := SearchList[J];
        Found := true
      END
    ELSE
      BEGIN
        J := (J MOD RecordSpace) + 1; {  MOD insures wraparound  }
        Traversed := (J = K)
      END
END; {  OF PROCEDURE LinearHash  }
```

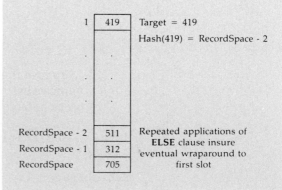

1	419	Target = 419
		Hash(419) = RecordSpace - 2
.	.	
.	.	
.	.	
RecordSpace - 2	511	Repeated applications of
RecordSpace - 1	312	**ELSE** clause insure
RecordSpace	705	eventual wraparound to
		first slot

Several remarks are in order concerning the procedure in Example 20.1. First, note that the procedure as it stands would not handle list processing in which it was necessary to process deletions. In such a situation, an additional flagging value would be needed to indicate a list position that had once been occupied and is now vacant because of a deletion. Without this distinction, we would not know whether or not to exit the search loop upon encountering an empty slot. You will explore the problem of deletions from a list maintained by hashing in greater detail in the Exercises and Programming Problems. Second, note that the linear method is not without its flaws. In particular, it is prone to a problem known as *clustering*. Clustering occurs when a collision processing strategy relocates keys that have a collision at the same initial hashing position to the same region (known as a cluster) within the storage space. This usually leads to further collisions with other relocated values until everything is resolved. With linear collision processing, the clustering problem is compounded because, as one cluster expands, it can run into another cluster, immediately creating a larger cluster. This one large cluster ultimately causes collision resolutions to be drawn out longer than they would otherwise be. Hence, linear hashing is more likely to result in the clustering phenomenon pictured in Figure 20.5 than the other methods we discuss.

FIGURE 20.5

Clustering due to biased hashing function and linear processing

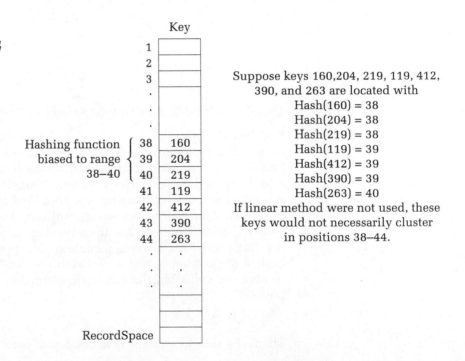

Suppose keys 160, 204, 219, 119, 412, 390, and 263 are located with

Hash(160) = 38
Hash(204) = 38
Hash(219) = 38
Hash(119) = 39
Hash(412) = 39
Hash(390) = 39
Hash(263) = 40

If linear method were not used, these keys would not necessarily cluster in positions 38–44.

Efficiency Considerations for Linear Hashing. A final point to note about the linear hashing method is its search efficiency. Knuth has shown that the average number of list accesses for a successful search using the linear method is

$$(1/2) * (1 + 1/(1 - D))$$

where

$$D = (\text{Number of currently active records})/\text{RecordSpace}$$

(See Donald E. Knuth, *Searching and Sorting*. Vol. 3 of *The Art of Computer Programming*. (Menlo Park, Calif.: Addison-Wesley, 1973).) An interesting fact about this search efficiency is that it is not solely dependent upon the number of records in the list but rather upon the density ratio of the number of records currently in the list divided by the total record space available. In other words, no matter how many records there are, a highly efficient result can be obtained if one is willing to waste enough vacant records. This is what is meant by a *density-dependent search technique*. In the case of searching for a key that cannot be found, Knuth's results indicate that the average search efficiency will be

$$(1/2) * (1 + 1/(1 - D)^2)$$

Table 20.1 illustrates the effectiveness of linear collision resolution by showing the computed efficiencies for a few strategic values of D.

TABLE 20.1
Average search efficiency for linear collision processing

D	Efficiency for Successful Search (number of accesses)	Efficiency for Unsuccessful Search (number of accesses)
0.10	1.06	1.18
0.50	1.50	2.50
0.75	2.50	8.50
0.90	5.50	50.50

Quadratic and Rehashing Methods of Collision Processing

Both the *quadratic* and *rehashing collision processing methods* attempt to correct the problem of clustering. They force the problem-causing key to immediately move a considerable distance from the initial collision. By the rehashing method, an entire sequence of hashing functions may be applied to a given key. If a collision results from the first hashing function, a second is applied, then a third, and so on, until the key can be successfully placed.

The quadratic method has the advantage of not requiring numerous hashing functions for its implementation. Suppose that a key value initially hashes to position K and a collision results. Then, on its first attempt to resolve the collision, the quadratic algorithm attempts to place the key at position

$$K + 1^2$$

Then, if a second attempt is necessary to resolve the collision, position

$$K + 2^2$$

is probed. In general, the Rth attempt to resolve the collision probes position

$$K + R^2$$

(with wraparound taken into account). Figure 20.6 highlights this scattering pattern. At this point you should verify that, if the hashing function

$$\text{Hash(KeyValue)} = (\text{KeyValue } \textbf{MOD } \text{RecordSpace}) + 1$$

is used with RecordSpace equal to 7, the keys 17, 73, 32, and 80 will be located in positions 4, 5, 6, and 1 respectively.

FIGURE 20.6
Quadratic collision processing

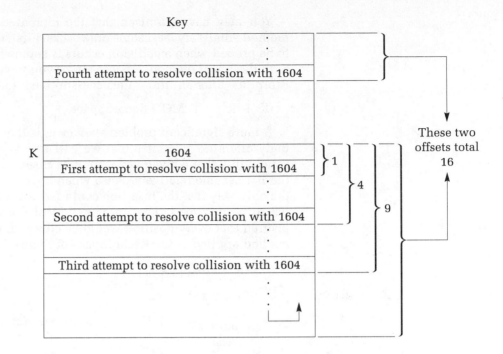

Efficiency Considerations for the Quadratic and Rehashing Methods. Knuth's results (see *Searching and Sorting,* cited earlier in this section) demonstrate the effectiveness of the rehashing and quadratic methods versus the linear method. For the quadratic method, average search efficiencies improve to

$$1 - \log_e(1 - D) - (D/2)$$

for the successful case and

$$1/(1 - D) - D - \log_e(1 - D)$$

for an unsuccessful search, where D is density ratio defined earlier in this section and e is the base for the natural logarithm function.

Rehashing with a completely random sequence of rehashing locations for each key improves slightly the efficiencies of the quadratic method to

$$-(1/D) * \log_e(1 - D)$$

for the successful case and

$$1/(1 - D)$$

for an unsuccessful search. Compare the numbers presented in Table 20.2 for quadratic collision processing and (ideal) random rehashing to those in Table 20.1 for linear collision processing.

TABLE 20.2
Average search efficiency for quadratic and rehashing collision processing

D	Efficiency for Successful Search (number of accesses)		Efficiency for Unsuccessful Search (number of accesses)	
	Quadratic	Rehashing	Quadratic	Rehashing
0.10	1.05	1.05	1.11	1.11
0.50	1.44	1.39	2.19	2.00
0.75	2.01	1.84	4.64	4.00
0.90	2.85	2.56	11.40	10.00

You may have surmised that the increased efficiency of the quadratic method entails aty least some drawbacks. First, the computation of a position to be probed when a collision occurs is somewhat more obscure than it was with the linear method. We leave it for you to verify that the position for the Rth probe after an initial unsuccessful hash to position K is given by

$$(K + R^2 - 1) \textbf{ MOD } RecordSpace + 1$$

A more significant problem, however, is that the quadratic method seemingly offers no guarantee that we will try every position in the list before concluding that a given key cannot be inserted. With the linear method, as the list became relatively dense when keys and insertions were attempted, the only way that the insertion could fail would be for every position in the list to be occupied. The linear nature of the search, although inefficient, insured that every position would be checked. However, with the quadratic method applied to the RecordSpace of Figure 20.7, you can confirm that an

FIGURE 20.7
Quadratic probing after initial hash to 4

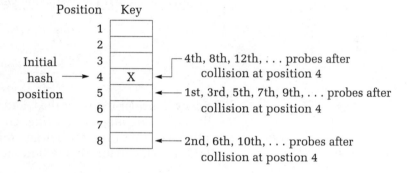

initial hash to position 4 will lead to future probing of positions 4, 5, and 8 only; it will never check positions 1, 2, 3, 6, or 7.

A satisfactory answer to the question of what portion of a list will be probed by the quadratic algorithm was fortunately provided by Radke for values of RecordSpace that are prime numbers which satisfy certain conditions. Radke's results and their application to the quadratic algorithm are explored in the Exercises at the end of the section. (If you wish to read Radke's results, see C. E. Radke, "The Use of Quadratic Residue Research." *Communications of the ACM* 13, No. 2, (February 1970): 103–105.)

Linked Method of Collision Processing

The logic of *linked collision processing* completely eliminates the possibility that one collision begets another. It requires a storage area divided into two regions: a *prime hash area* and an *overflow area*. Each record requires a Link field in addition to the Key and OtherData fields. The global constant RecordSpace is applicable to the prime hash area only. This storage concept is illustrated in Figure 20.8.

Initially, the hashing translates function keys into the prime hashing area. If a collision occurs, the key is inserted into a linked list with its initial node in the prime area and all following nodes in the overflow area (no dummy header is used). Figure 20.9 shows how this method would load the keys 22, 31, 67, 36, 29, and 60 for a RecordSpace equal to 7 and hashing function

$$Hash(KeyValue) = (KeyValue \textbf{ MOD } RecordSpace) + 1$$

FIGURE 20.8
Storage allocation for linked collision processing

FIGURE 20.9
Loading keys with KeyValue
MOD 7 + 1 and linked collision
processing

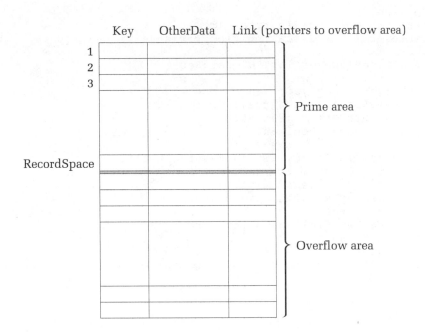

	Key	Link
1	0	NULL
2	22	8
3	0	NULL
4	31	NULL
5	67	10
6	0	NULL
7	0	NULL
8	36	9
9	29	NULL
10	60	NULL
11	0	NULL
12	0	NULL
13	0	NULL
14	0	NULL
15	0	NULL
16	0	NULL
17	0	NULL

■ **EXAMPLE 20.2**

Suppose that an array has been loaded with data using the linked collision processing strategy illustrated in Figures 20.8 and 20.9. Write a Pascal procedure to find a Target key in this array.

We have made the Link fields integer pointers to other array locations instead of Pascal dynamic memory pointers to facilitate using the algorithm with a random access file. As written, the procedure assumes that all key locations in the prime area have had their corresponding Key and Link fields initialized to appropriate constant flags for Empty and Null respectively. The assumption is also made that no keys will be deleted.

```
{  Global declarations  }

CONST
  RecordSpace = {  Appropriate size for prime area  };
  PrimePlusOverflow = {  Actual array size  };
```

```
                Empty = {  Appropriate flag for key field of empty record  };
                Null = {  Appropriate flag for end-of-list pointer  };

           TYPE
             KeyType = {  Appropriate type for key field in record  };
             DataRec = RECORD
                          Key : KeyType;
                          OtherData : {  Appropriate type  };
                          Link : integer {  or Pascal pointer variable if desired  }
                       END;
             DataArray = ARRAY [1..PrimePlusOverflow] OF DataRec;

           PROCEDURE  LinkedHash (Target : KeyType;
                                  SearchList : DataArray;
                                  VAR InfoWanted : DataRec;
                                  VAR Found : boolean);

             {  Given:    List of records loaded by linked hashing method  }
             {            in SearchList.  Target, the value of a key        }
             {            field to be found in SearchList.                  }
             {  Task:     Use linked hashing algorithm to search           }
             {            SearchList for Target.                            }
             {  Return:   If record with key field matching Target is       }
             {            found, return Found as true and return            }
             {            associated information for that record in         }
             {            InfoWanted.  Otherwise return Found as false.      }

             VAR
               K : integer;

             BEGIN
               Found := false;      {  Assume failure  }
               K := Hash (Target); {  Call on hashing function, use K to probe list}
               REPEAT
                 IF Target = SearchList[K].Key THEN
                   BEGIN
                     InfoWanted := SearchList[K];
                     Found := true
                   END
                 ELSE
                   K := SearchList[K].Link
               UNTIL Found OR (K = Null)
             END; {  of PROCEDURE LinkedHash  }
```

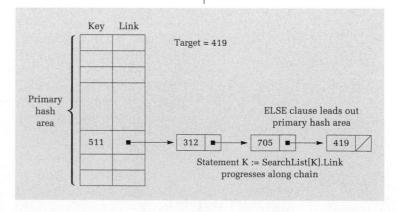

Key   Link

Target = 419

Primary
hash
area

ELSE clause leads out
primary hash area

511   312   705   419

Statement K := SearchList[K].Link
progresses along chain

Efficiency Considerations for Linked Hashing. Knuth's efficiency results for the linked hashing method depend on a density factor (D) which is computed using the RecordSpace in the prime hashing area only. Hence, unlike the other hashing methods we have discussed, the linked method allows a density factor greater than 1. For example, if the RecordSpace for the primary hash area were 200 and the overflow area contained space for 300 additional records, then 400 active records would yield a density factor of 2. Given this variation, average search efficiencies for the successful and unsuccessful cases are $1 + D/2$ and D respectively. Table 20.3 shows computations of this

TABLE 20.3
Average search efficiencies for the linked method

D	Efficiency for Successful Search (number of accesses)	Efficiency for Unsuccessful Search (number of accesses)
2	2	2
5	3.5	5
10	6	10
20	11	20

search efficiency for selected values of D, and should be compared to the corresponding results for the linear and quadratic methods, which were presented in Table 20.1 and Table 20.2, respectively.

A NOTE OF INTEREST

Machine Translation

When the search algorithms discussed in this chapter were first discovered, they sparked a flurry of activity in an area known as machine translation. Programs in this area attempt to translate text from one natural language to another, for example, English to German. Early attempts at machine translation tended to view the process as essentially the searching of a large dictionary. Hence, to translate the English sentence

The sun is yellow.

the program would simply find each of the words in a disk-based version of an English-to-German dictionary and arrive at the German sentence

Die Sonne ist gelb.

However, machine translation activity was soon slowed by the complexities of syntax (grammar) and semantics (meanings) in natural language. The translation of some sentences by these early systems produced some rather humorous results. According to computer folklore cited in the article "Computers Gain as Language Translators Even Though Perfect Not They Always" by William M. Bulkeley (*Wall Street Journal,* February 6, 1985, p. 25), the following translations occurred in an early English-to-Russian system.

English Phrase	Russian Translation
The spirit is willing but the flesh is weak.	The vodka is good but the meat is rotten.
Out of sight, out of mind	Invisible maniac.

Results such as these caused a government panel to declare, in 1966, that computerized translation would never be practical. Today, as linguists have more successfully formalized rules of syntax and semantics, machine translation is making somewhat of a comeback. In restricted domains, such as the translation of language specific to technology and business, products are being developed as time-saving aids to human translators.

Two recent issues of the *Communications of the ACM*—Vol. 33, No. 5 (May, 1990) and Vol. 33, No. 8(August, 1990)—contain a variety of articles describing progress that has been made in processing natural languages. These articles provide an excellent starting point for you to explore this topic more thoroughly.

Bucket Hashing

In the bucket hashing strategy of collision processing, the hashing function transforms a given key to a physically contiguous region of locations within the list to be searched. This contiguous region is called a *bucket*. Thus, instead of hashing to the Kth location, a key would hash to the Kth bucket of locations. The number of locations contained in this bucket would depend upon the bucket size. (We assume that all buckets in a given list are the same size.) Figure 20.10 illustrates this concept for a list with seven buckets and a bucket size of 3.

FIGURE 20.10

Storage allocation for bucket hashing

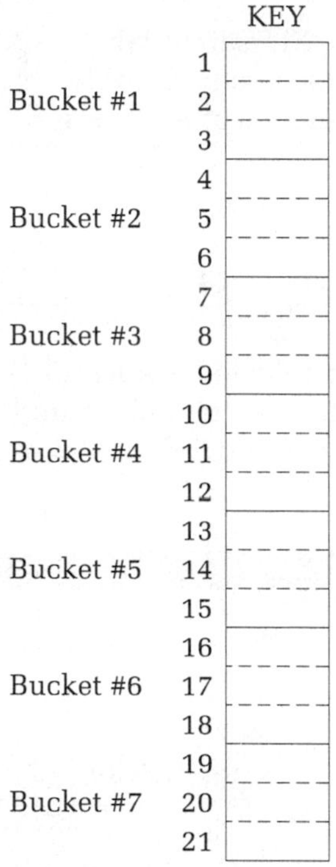

Having hashed to a bucket, the Target must then be compared in sequential order to all of the keys in that bucket. On the surface, it would seem that this strategy could do no better than duplicate the efficiency of the linked hash method discussed earlier. Indeed, because a sequential search is conducted in both cases after the initial hash is made, the average number of list accesses for a successful or unsuccessful search cannot be improved by using buckets. Moreover, provisions for linking to some sort of overflow area must still be made in case a series of collisions consumes all of the space in a given bucket.

What then could be a possible advantage of using buckets? If the list to be searched resides entirely in main memory, there is no advantage. However, if the list resides in a disk file, the bucket method will allow us to take advantage of some of the physical characteristics of the storage medium itself. To see this, we must realize that a one-surface disk is divided into concentric *tracks* and pie-shaped *sectors* as indicated in Figure 20.11.

There are two ways in which the bucket hashing strategy may take advantage of the organization of the data on the disk. First, when records in a contiguous random access file are stored on a disk, they are generally located in relative record number order along one track, then along an adjacent track,

FIGURE 20.11
One-surface disk

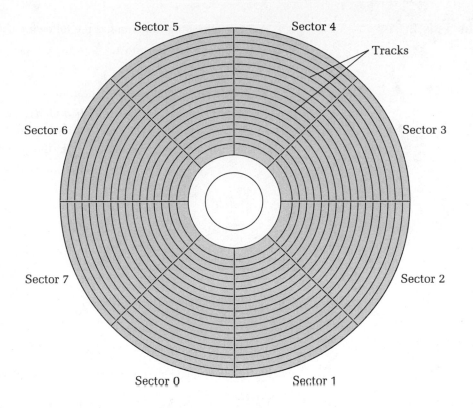

and so on. The movement of the read-write head between tracks is generally the cause of the most significant delays in obtaining data from a disk. The farther the movement, the greater the delay. Hence, if our knowledge of the machine in question allows us to make a bucket coincide with a track on the disk, then hashing to the beginning of a bucket and proceeding from there using a sequential search within the bucket (that is, the track) will greatly reduce head movement. A linked hashing strategy, on the other hand, could cause considerable movement of the read-write head between tracks on the disk, thereby slowing program execution. This consideration is an excellent example of how one must examine more than just the number of list accesses when measuring the efficiency of a program involving disk files.

A second advantage in using the bucket hashing algorithm when disk files are being searched is related to the way in which records are transferred between the disk and main memory. Frequently, programming languages create the illusion that each record accessed requires a separate disk access. However, records are frequently blocked, that is, positioned in contiguous regions on a track of the disk, so that a fixed number of them are brought into main memory when a record in that block is requested. This means that, if the record requested happens to be part of the block presently in main memory, a program statement that requests a record may not even require a disk access but only a different viewing window applied to the block already in main memory. Since main memory manipulations are orders of magnitude faster than the rate of data transfer to and from a disk, this means that positioning our buckets to coincide with a disk block will necessitate only one disk access each time an entire bucket is sequentially searched. Here again, the more scattered nature of a purely linked hashing algorithm would not allow this disk-oriented efficiency consideration to be taken into account.

Exercises 20.1

1. Assume a hashing function has the following characteristics:

Keys 459 and 333 hash to 1.
Key 632 hashes to 2.
Key 1090 hashes to 3.
Keys 1982, 379, 238, and 3411 hash to 10.

Assume that insertions into a hashed file are performed in the order 1982, 3411, 333, 632, 1090, 459, 379, and 238.

a. Indicate the position of the keys if the linear method is used to resolve collisions.

Record No.	Key
1	
2	
3	
4	
5	
6	
7	
8	
9	
10	
11	

b. Indicate the position of the keys if the quadratic method is used to resolve collisions.

Record No.	Key
1	
2	
3	
4	
5	
6	
7	
8	
9	
10	
11	

c. Indicate the position of the keys and the contents of the link fields if the chaining (that is, linked) method is used to resolve collisions. Use zeros to represent **NIL** links and assume that the first record used in the overflow area is 12, then 13, then 14, and so on.

Record No.	Key	Link
1		
2		
3		
4		
5		
6		
7		
8		
9		
10		
11		

Prime Area

Record No.	Key	Link
12		
13		
14		
15		
16		
17		
18		
19		
20		
21		
22		

Overflow Area

2. Repeat Exercise 1 with the order of insertion of keys reversed.

3. We have covered binary search, linked lists, binary trees, and hashing as methods of implementing a keyed list ADT. Choose the method you would use to implement the data list involved for each of the following three real-world applications. In each case you should choose the most appropriate implementation technique. "Most appropriate" here means efficiently handling all of the required operations while not being too powerful; that is, not doing something that should be easy in an overly complicated way. Then provide a written rationale as to why yours would be the appropriate method.

   a. The list to be maintained is the card catalog of a library. Frequent additions to and deletions from this catalog are made by the library. Additionally, users are frequently searching for the data associated with a given book's key. However, the library rarely prints out an ordered list of all its holdings. Hence ordering the list is not to be considered a high priority.

   b. You are writing a program that maintains the lists of passengers on flights for an airline company. Passengers are frequently added to these lists. Moreover, quite often passengers cancel flight plans and must be removed from a list. You are also told that the airline frequently wants alphabetized listings of the passengers on a given flight and often needs to search out a particular passenger by name when inquiries are received from individuals.

   c. You are writing a program to access a large customer data base and build up counts for the numbers of customers from each of the 50 states (plus the District of Columbia). To do this you will use a list of records consisting of the two-character state abbreviation and an integer representing the count of customers from that state. For each customer you read in from the data base, you must find the customer's home state in your list and increase the corresponding count field. At the end, print out the counts in order alphabetized by the two-character state abbreviation.

4. Write procedures to insert a key into a list to be searched by
   a. Linear hashing.
   b. Quadratic hashing.
   c. Linked hashing.
   d. Bucket hashing.

5. Write procedures to search for a key via
   a. Quadratic hashing.
   b. Bucket hashing.

6. Devise strategies to delete keys from a list being maintained by each of the four hashing strategies in Exercise 4. Write Pascal versions for each of these algorithms. Given your deletion strategy, describe in detail the modifications (if any) that must be made in the various search and insertion procedures of Exercises 4 and 5.

7. In Section 20.1 we mentioned a result by Radke that answered the question of how many array slots would be probed by the quadratic hashing algorithm for certain values of RecordSpace. In particular, Radke showed that if RecordSpace is a prime number of the form $4m + 3$ for some integer m, then half of the array slots would be probed by the sequence of probes

$$K, K + 1^2, K + 2^2, K + 3^2, \ldots$$

where K is the original hash position. Radke also showed that the other half would be probed by the sequence

$$K - 1^2, K - 2^2, K - 3^2, \ldots$$

Rewrite your insertion and search procedures for the quadratic method in Exercises 4 and 5 to take into account Radke's result.

8. a. Given the arrival of integer keys in the order 67, 19, 4, 58, 38, 55, 86 and RecordSpace = 9 with

   Hash(KeyValue) = (KeyValue **MOD** RecordSpace) + 1

   trace the insertion steps of linearly processing collisions.

   Index   KeyValue

Index	KeyValue
1	0
2	0
3	0
4	0
5	0
6	0
7	0
8	0
9	0

   (0 indicates empty position)

   b. Given the arrival of integer keys in the order 32, 62, 34, 77, 6, 46, 107 and RecordSpace = 15 with

   Hash(KeyValue) = (KeyValue **MOD** RecordSpace) + 1

   trace the insertion steps of quadratically processing collisions.

   Index   KeyValue

Index	KeyValue
1	0
2	0
3	0
4	0
5	0
6	0
7	0
8	0
9	0
10	0
11	0
12	0
13	0
14	0
15	0

   (0 indicates empty position)

   c. Given the arrival of integer keys in the order 5, 3, 16, 27, 14, 25, 4 and RecordSpace = 11 with initial hashing function

   $Hash_1$(KeyValue) = (KeyValue **MOD** RecordSpace) + 1

   trace the insertion steps of the rehashing collision processing method where the secondary hashing function is

   $Hash_2$(KeyValue) = (5*KeyValue **MOD** RecordSpace) + 1

   Assume that, if the secondary hashing function is not successful in locating a position for the key, then linear collision processing is used from the address indicated by the secondary hashing function.

Index	KeyValue
1	0
2	0
3	0
4	0
5	0
6	0
7	0
8	0
9	0
10	0
11	0

(0 indicates empty position)

Comment on the effectiveness of rehashing with this particular secondary hashing function. Can you think of a better one? Explain why yours is better.

9. In a written statement explain how hashing could be used to search for keys that were not unique. For instance, you might have several people identified by the same name.

■ ■ ■ ■

■ 20.2
Two Abstract Data Types Revisited

OBJECTIVES

- to discuss how hashing could be used to implement the keyed list ADT
- to evaluate the efficiency of hashing as an implementation strategy for the keyed list ADT
- to discuss how hashing could be used to implement the sparse table ADT

We can analyze hashing from a pragmatic perspective by considering how it might be used to implement two ADTs introduced in Chapter 13. the keyed list and the sparse table. You will then be asked to carry out these implementations in the Exercises and Programming Problems at the end of the chapter.

The Keyed List ADT Implemented by Hashing

In this context, hashing emerges as yet another list maintenance strategy to be evaluated and compared to those strategies we have already discussed: array (or random access file) with binary search, linked list, and binary tree. Hence we must examine its performance with respect to the same Add, Retrieve, Delete, and TraverseInOrder operations that were introduced in Chapter 13 and then used to evaluate these other list implementation techniques. Assuming the existence of an appropriate hashing function to act on the key and a willingness to waste enough storage to allow for fast searching, hashing will clearly perform very well in all of these areas with the exception of ordering data. Here is where we have to pay a price for the scattered storage of records that are located via a hashing function.

Nonetheless, there are strategies that can be used to allow hashing and ordering of data to coexist. One such strategy would simply be to use a pointer sort algorithm (see Chapter 12) to logically sort the data when an ordered list is needed. This strategy has the drawback of not maintaining the list in order but actually performing a potentially costly sort algorithm each time an ordering is requested. Clearly, this strategy would not be wise if such an ordering were requested frequently and unpredictably.

In situations where requests for ordering would come frequently enough to make maintaining the list in order (as opposed to sorting) a necessity, we could follow a strategy that would combine the search speed of hashing with the ordered list advantages offered by a linked list implementation. This combination would have us use hashing to search for an individual record but would add link fields to each record so that a linked list for each desired ordering could be woven through the collection of hashed records. Implementing this combination of hashing and linked list would entail the following considerations with respect to the keyed list operations:

- Add. In effect, the hashing/collision processing algorithm would provide us with an available node to store data. Each linked list involved would then have to be traversed to link the node into each ordering in the appropriate logical location.
- Retrieve. There is no problem here because the hash algorithm should find the desired record quickly.
- Delete. This is similar to the retrieve operation. Use hashing to find the record to be deleted, then adjust the link field appropriately. A doubly linked list could prove to be particularly valuable here. (Why?)
- TraverseInOrder. There is no problem here because the linked lists constantly maintain the appropriate orderings.

The Sparse Table ADT Implemented by Hashing

We have already suggested two implementation strategies for sparse tables.

1. In Section 13.3 we described a strategy that would simply create a list of the rows and columns corresponding to nontrivial values in the table. Thus, determining the value of the data at a conceptual row/column location is simply a matter of searching this list.
2. In Chapter 15, we described a strategy that would form a linked list of the nontrivial columns in each row. Here, determining the value of the data at a conceptual row/column location is reduced to the problem of sequentially searching a relatively small linked list.

At the time we explored these two strategies, the first one appeared to be less attractive. Because the data in the list of row/column coordinates corresponding to nontrivial values are likely to be volatile, physically ordering the data for a binary search would not be practical. Yet, without a binary search, requests to inspect the value at any given location are met with the $O(n)$ response time of a sequential search. Hashing allows us to search for a row/column coordinate in the list of the first strategy in a very efficient fashion, probably faster than the sequential search along the linked list representing a given row required by the second strategy. Moreover, since the order of the data in the list is not important for this application, the scattered nature of hashed storage does not present any obstacle at all.

The considerations we have discussed with respect to these two ADTs make it evident that hashing is a very attractive list implementation technique. It will be extremely efficient in regard to the add, retrieve, and delete list operations if we are willing to pay the price of wasting enough storage to get a reasonably low density ratio. The only other drawback to hashing, in addition to this wasted storage, is the price that must be paid if various orderings of the data are frequently needed.

Exercises 20.2

1. Suppose that we combine hashing with a linked list in the fashion described in Section 20.2 so that all keyed list operations can be efficiently performed. Which of the variations on a linked list structure would be most effective in this context? Explain why in a carefully worded statement. (*Hint:* Think about the retrieve and delete operations.)

2. Give an example of an application where the hashing implementation of a two-dimensional table described in this section would be less efficient (overall) than the linked list implementation described in Chapter 15. Explain why in a carefully worded statement.

3. Provide implementations of all keyed list operations using the hashing strategy described in this section. Provide alternative implementations of the TraverseInOrder operations: one should invoke a pointer sort and another should combine hashing with a linked list.

4. Provide implementations of all sparse table operations defined in Chapter 13 using the hashing strategy described in this section.

■ ■ ■ ■

■ 20.3
Indexed Search Techniques (Optional)

OBJECTIVES

■ to understand the differences between searching in main memory and in random access disk storage
■ to understand how an index may be used to advantage when searching for data in a random access file
■ to study how the indexed sequential search methodology is implemented
■ to discuss the efficiency of the indexed sequential search strategy
■ to understand how the B-tree data structure may be used to implement an index for a random access file
■ to discuss the efficiency of B-trees
■ to understand how the trie data structure may be used to implement the index for a random access file keyed by strings of variable length
■ to discuss the efficiency of tries

All of the search strategies we have studied up to this point could be applied to lists implemented in main memory or on a random access disk. However, with the exception of bucket hashing, none of the methods we have studied actually take into account physical characteristics of disk storage in an attempt to enhance their efficiency. In practice, because retrieval of data from a disk file is orders of magnitude slower than retrieval from main memory, we often cannot afford to ignore these special characteristics of disk files if we want reasonable response time for our searching efforts. The indexing schemes that we are about to discuss in this section are primarily directed toward file-oriented applications and thus will take into account the operational properties of this storage medium. We encourage you to reread the discussion of bucket hashing at the end of Section 20.1 for a summary analysis of file storage considerations.

The idea behind the use of an index is analogous to the way in which we routinely use an address book to find a person whom we are seeking. That is, if we are looking for a person, we do not knock on the doors of numerous houses until we find the one where that person lives. Instead, we apply a search strategy to an address book. There we use the name of the person as a key to find a pointer—that is, an address—which swiftly leads us to where the person can be found. Only one actual "house access" must be made, although our search strategy may require numerous accesses into the address book index.

In a computer system, records (or more precisely blocks) could play the role of houses in the search scenario just described. Data records on disk are (when compared to main memory) terribly slow and awkward creatures to access. One of the reasons for this is that there is often so much data that must be moved from disk to main memory every time a record is accessed. Because of this, the conceptual picture for the general setup of an indexed search must be revised. The list of keys is no longer parallel to the actual data with which they are logically associated but rather is parallel to a list of pointers which will lead us to the actual data. The revised picture is presented in Figure 20.12.

The general strategy of an indexed search is to use the key to efficiently search the index, find the relative record position of the associated data, and from there make only one access into the actual data. Because the parallel lists of keys and relative record positions require much less storage than the data itself, frequently the entire index can be loaded and permanently held in main memory, necessitating only one disk access for each record being

FIGURE 20.12
General setup for an indexed search

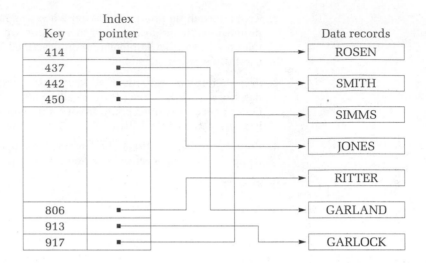

sought. For larger indices, it still remains true that large blocks of keys and associated pointers may be manipulated in main memory, thereby greatly enhancing search efficiency.

Indexed Sequential Search Technique

The *indexed sequential search* technique is also commonly recognized by the acronym *ISAM,* which stands for *Indexed Sequential Access Method.* Essentially it involves carefully weighing the disk-dependent factors of blocking and track size to build a partial index. The partial index, unlike some other index structures we will study, does not reduce to one the number of probes which must be made into the actual data.

To continue the analogy between searching for data and searching for a person, the indexed sequential strategy is somewhat like an address book that would lead us to the street on which a person lives but leave it to us to check each of the houses on that street. The ISAM method correspondingly leads us to an appropriate region (often a track or a cylinder containing multiple tracks within a disk pack) and then leaves it to us to search sequentially within that region.

As an example, let us suppose that we can conveniently fit the partial index, or directory, pictured in Figure 20.13 into main memory and that the organization of our disk file allows six records per track. This directory is formed by choosing the highest key value in each six-record track along with a pointer indicating where that track begins. Here our pointers are simply relative record numbers; in practice they could well be a more disk-dependent locator. The strategy to conduct an indexed sequential search is to

1. Search the main memory directory for a key which is greater than or equal to the Target.
2. Then follow the corresponding pointer out to the disk and there search sequentially until we find a match (success) or the key that the directory maintains as the high key within that particular region (failure).

For the data given in Figure 20.13, this technique would mean that the 36-record file would require no more than six main memory index accesses plus six disk accesses, all of which are located in the same track.

FIGURE 20.13
One-level indexed sequential file

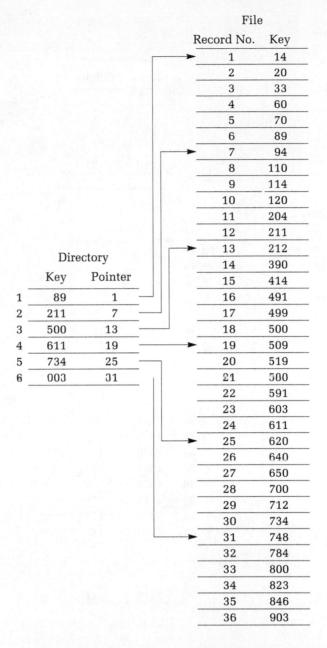

For larger files, it may be advantageous to have more than one level of these directory structures. Consider, for instance, the two-level directory structure for a file with 216 records given in Figure 20.14. Here we might suppose that storage restrictions allow the entire primary directory to be kept in main memory, the secondary directory to be brought in from a disk file in blocks of six key-pointer pairs each, and the actual data records to be stored six per track. The primary directory divides the file into regions of 36 records each. The key in the primary directory represents the highest-valued key in a given 36-record region, but the pointer leads us into the subdirectory instead of the actual file. So, we search the primary directory for a key greater than or equal to the target we are seeking. Once this is done, we follow the primary directory pointer into the secondary directory. Beginning at the

FIGURE 20.14
Two-level directory structure

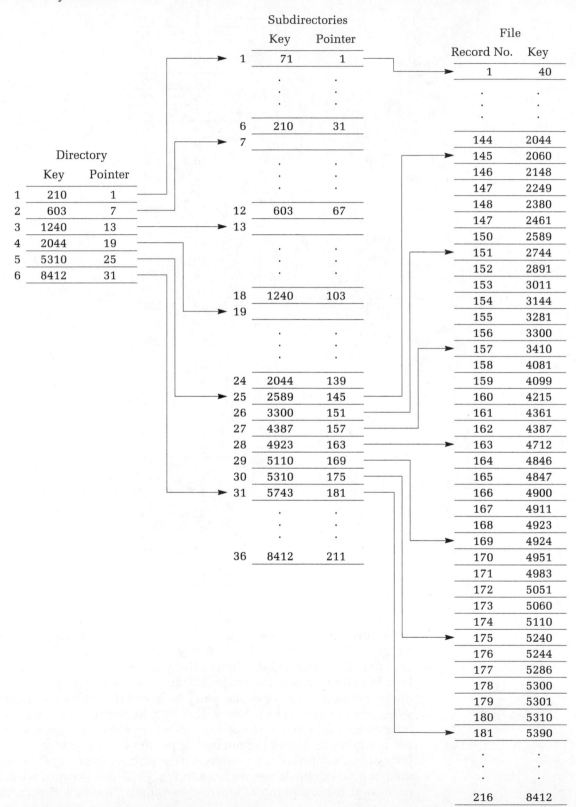

position indicated by the primary directory's pointer, we again search for a key greater than or equal to the target. Notice that fetching one block of six key-pointer pairs from the subdirectory has necessitated one disk access in our hypothetical situation. In return for this single disk access, we are able to subdivide the 36-record region determined by the primary directory into six 6-record regions, each of which will lie entirely on one track by the time we get out to the actual disk file. Following the subdirectory's pointer to the file, we end up with a relatively short sequential search on the storage medium itself. In this example, the maximum number of disk accesses required to find any record would be seven, and six of those would be isolated on one track of the disk.

Efficiency Considerations for the Indexed Sequential Search. It should be clear from the preceding discussion that the search efficiency of the indexed sequential technique depends on a variety of factors. Included among them are

- To what degree the directory structures are able to subdivide the actual file.
- To what degree the directory structures are able to reside in main memory.
- The relationship of data records to physical characteristics of the disk such as blocking factors, track size, cylinder size, and so on.

It should also be clear that the indexed sequential method may not be ideal for a highly volatile file. This is because, as implicitly indicated in Figures 20.13 and 20.14, the actual data records must be physically stored in increasing (or decreasing) key order. The requirement for physical ordering is obviously not conducive to frequent insertions and deletions. In practice, the solution to this problem is that each file subregion which is ultimately the subject of a sequential search is equipped with a pointer to an overflow area. Insertions are located in this overflow area and linked to the main sequential search area. As the overflow area builds up, the search efficiency tends to deteriorate. In some applications, this deterioration can be so severe that data processing personnel have been known to refer to the ISAM technique as the Intrinsically Slow Access Method.

The way to avoid deterioration is to periodically reorganize the file into a new file with no overflow. However, such reorganization cannot be done dynamically. It requires going through the file in key sequential order and copying it into a new one. Along the way, the indices must be rebuilt, of course. These types of maintenance problems involved with the ISAM structure have led to the development of several more dynamic indexing schemes.

Binary Search Tree Indexing

The concept of a binary search tree has already been covered in Chapter 18. The only twist added when the binary tree plays the role of an index is that each node of the tree contains a key and a pointer to the record associated with that key in some larger data aggregate. The advantages of using a binary search tree as an index structure include:

- A search efficiency potentially proportional to $\log_2 n$.
- The ability to traverse the list indexed by the tree in key order.
- Dynamic insertion and deletion capabilities.

Data Integrity, Concurrent Updates, and Deadlock

The problems of finding and allowing a user to access a particular record in a file are complicated somewhat in a system that allows several users to access that file simultaneously. To see why this is so, it is important to recall that when you actually manipulate a record or part of an index from a file, you really have a copy of that portion of the file in your main memory area. Now suppose that two users are not only accessing the same file simultaneously but also the same record in that file simultaneously. A scenario such as the following could emerge:

Memory Area for User 1   Memory Area for User 1

XYZ Record   Disk file   XYZ Record

User 1 requests record associated with key XYZ.
User 2 requests record associated with key XYZ.
User 1 updates address field of that record.
User 2 updates inventory field of that record.
User 1 makes change in the file by writing that record to disk.
User 2 makes changes in the file by writing that record to disk.

What will be wrong with the new record that exists in the disk file? Clearly, the address change made by User 1 will have been destroyed when User 2's copy of the record is written back to the disk. We have what is known as a *data integrity* problem caused by the *concurrent updating* of the same record by two users. The situation can become much worse than merely losing an address change. Imagine the havoc created if one of the users deleted the record while the other was processing it or if the portion of the file being simultaneously updated by two users was not a data record but instead part of the file index.

The concurrent update problem must be avoided in any multiuser system if data integrity is to be insured. The solution used in many systems is that of a *record lock facility*. With such a facility, the user who has a file record in main memory for updating is considered the owner of that record to the exclusion of any other users accessing that record. That lock on the record exists until the user writes the (perhaps altered) record back to the disk file. Hence, in our scenario, User 2 would not have been able immediately to obtain the record for key XYZ. Instead, that user would sit idle in a wait state until the record became available.

Although the record-locking approach guarantees data integrity, it is not without its own set of problems. For instance, consider the following scenario:

User 1 requests and gets record for key XYZ.
User 2 requests and gets record for key ABC.
To process record XYZ, User 1 needs data associated with record ABC.
  Because record is owned by User 2, User 1 must wait in idle state.
To process record ABC, User 2 needs data associated with record XYZ.
  Because record is owned by User 1, User 2 must wait in idle state.

Though data integrity has been maintained, we now have two users in an infinite wait state known as a *deadlock* or, more glamorously, *fatal embrace*. The avoidance and/or detection of deadlock situations in a multiuser environment is a nontrivial problem. If you are interested in exploring it more deeply, see Harvey M. Deitel's *An Introduction to Operating Systems*. 2nd ed. (Reading, Mass.: Addison-Wesley, 1990).

These qualities make the binary search tree the ideal index structure for situations in which the entire tree can fit in main memory. However, if the data collection is so large that the tree index must itself be stored on disk, the efficiency of the structure is less than optimal. This is because each node of the index may lie in a disk block separate from the other nodes and hence require a separate disk access. Using an example of 50,000 keys, a search of a *binary tree index* could require 16 disk accesses. To solve this problem, we would like to cluster those nodes along a given search path into one, or at least relatively few, disk blocks. The *B-tree* index structure is a variation on the tree index which accomplishes this goal.

B-Tree Indexing

We begin this discussion of B-trees by reminding you that one index entry requires nothing more than a key and a pointer. Moreover, we have assumed that both the key and the pointer are integers, and we continue to operate under this assumption during our discussion of B-trees. We emphasize this point here because, in a B-tree, a given tree node will in fact contain many such key-pointer pairs. This is because a given B-tree node will in fact coincide with one disk block. The idea behind a B-tree is that we will somehow group key-pointer pairs which are related in the search algorithm into a few strategic B-tree nodes, that is, disk blocks. At this point, we make a formal definition; later, we'll clarify this definition via some examples.

B-Tree of Order *n*. A B-tree of order *n* is a structure with the following properties:

1. Every node in the B-tree has sufficient room to store $n - 1$ key-pointer pairs.
2. Additionally, every node has room for n pointers to other nodes in the B-tree (as distinguished from the pointers within key-pointer pairs, which point to the position of a key in the file).
3. Every node except the root must have at least $(n - 1)$ **DIV** 2 key-pointer pairs stored in it.
4. All terminal nodes are on the same level.
5. If a nonterminal node has m key-pointer pairs stored in it, then it must contain $m + 1$ nonnull pointers to other B-tree nodes.
6. For each B-tree node, we require that the key value in key-pointer pair KP_{i-1} be less than the key value in key-pointer pair KP_i, that all key pointer pairs in the node pointed to by P_{i-1} contain keys that are less than the key in KP_i, and that all key-pointer pairs in the node pointed to by P_i contain key values that are greater than the key in KP_i.

According to property 5 of the definition, we can think of a B-tree node as a list

$$P_0, KP_1, P_1, KP_2, P_2, KP_3, \ldots, P_{m-1}, KP_m, P_m$$

where P_i represents the *i*th pointer to another B-tree node and KP_i represents the *i*th key-pointer pair. Note that a B-tree node will always contain one more pointer to another B-tree node than it does key-pointer pairs. With this picture in mind, the sixth and final property of our definition makes sense. Figure 20.15 illustrates how this rather involved definition applies to a B-tree node with three key-pointer pairs.

As a further illustration of this definition, a complete B-tree of order 6 serving as an index structure for the 36-record file of Figure 20.13 appears in

FIGURE 20.15
Example of a B-tree node with
three key-pointer pairs

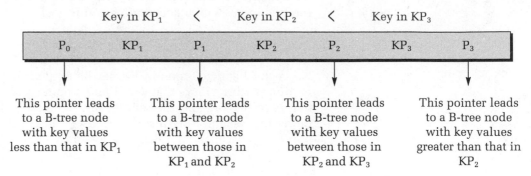

Figure 20.16. (In this figure, the slash between numbers denotes a key-pointer pair; ⊢ denotes a null pointer.) Carefully verify that all six defining properties are satisfied.

The choice of order 6 for Figure 20.16 was made only for the purposes of making the figure fit on a page of text. In practice, the order chosen would be the maximum number of B-tree pointers and key-pointer pairs that we could fit into one disk block. That is, the choice should be made to force a disk block to coincide with a B-tree node. It is also worth noting that B-trees of order 3 have special application as a data structure apart from indexing considerations. This application will be covered in the Programming Problems at the end of the chapter.

Efficiency Considerations for B-Tree Indexing. Let us now consider what is involved in searching a B-tree for a given key. Within the current node (starting at the root), we must search sequentially through the key values in the node until we come to a match, a key value that is greater than the one being sought, or the end of the key values in that particular node. If a match is not made within a particular B-tree node, we have a pointer to follow to an appropriate follow-up node. Again, you should verify this algorithm for several of the keys appearing at various levels of Figure 20.16. The sequential search on keys within a given node may at first seem unappealing. However, the important fact to remember here is that each B-tree node is a disk block which is loaded entirely into main memory. Hence, it may be possible to search sequentially on hundreds of keys within a node in the time it would take to load one new node from disk. Our main concern is to minimize disk accesses, and here we have achieved a worst-case search for our 36-entry file in three disk accesses.

What in general is the search efficiency for a B-tree index? It should be clear from the nature of the structure that the maximum number of disk accesses for any particular key will simply be the number of levels in the tree. So the efficiency question really amounts to knowing the maximum number of levels that the six defining criteria would allow for a B-tree containing n key-pointer pairs. That is, this number would be the worst-case search efficiency. To determine this number, we use the minimum number of nodes that must be present on any given level. Let L be the smallest integer greater than or equal to K/2 where K is the order of the B-tree in question.

FIGURE 20.16
B-tree index of order 6 for file in
Figure 20.13

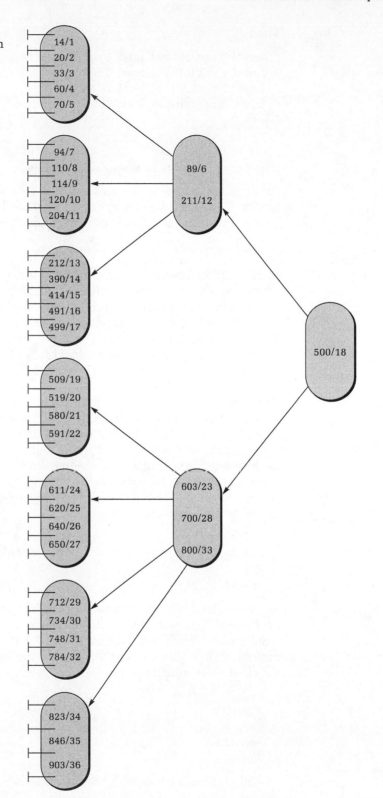

Then

Level 0 contains at least 1 node.
Level 1 contains at least 2 nodes.
Level 2 contains at least 2L nodes.
Level 3 contains at least $2L^2$ nodes.

.   .
.   .
.   .

Level m contains at least $2L^{m-1}$ nodes.

An argument based on Knuth's research (see *Searching and Sorting,* cited in Section 20.1) uses this progression to show that the maximum number of levels (and thus the worst-case search efficiency) for n key-pointer pairs is

$$\log_K((n + 1)/2)$$

Thus, a B-tree search has an $O(\log_K n)$ efficiency where n is the number of records and K is the order of the B-tree. Note that this can be considerably better than an $O(\log_2 n)$ search efficiency. As an example, the index for a file of 50,000 records which would require on the order of 16 disk accesses using a binary tree structure could be searched with 3 disk accesses using a B-tree of order 250. Note that, given typical block sizes for files, the choice of order 250 for this example is not at all unrealistic.

Unlike ISAM, the B-tree index can dynamically handle insertions and deletions without a resulting deterioration in search efficiency. We next discuss how B-tree insertions are handled; making deletions is left for an exercise. The essential idea behind a B-tree insertion is that we must first determine which bottom-level node should contain the key-pointer pair to be inserted. For instance, suppose that we want to insert the key 742 into the B-tree of Figure 20.16. By allowing this key to walk down the B-tree from the root to the bottom level, we could quickly determine that this key belongs in the node presently containing

712/29
734/30
748/31
784/32

Since, by the definition of a B-tree of order 6, this node is not presently full, no further disk accesses would be necessary to perform the insertion. We would merely need to determine the next available record space in the actual data file (37 in this case) and then add the key-pointer pair 742/37 to this terminal node, resulting in

712/29
734/30
742/37
748/31
784/32

A slightly more difficult situation arises when we find that the key-pointer pair we wish to add should be inserted into a bottom-level node that is already full. For instance, this would occur if we attempted to add the key 112 to the B-tree of Figure 20.16. We would load the actual data for this key into file position 38 (given the addition already made in the preceding paragraph) and then determine that the key-pointer pair 112/38 belongs in the bottom-level node

94/7
110/8
114/9
120/10
204/11

The stipulation that any B-tree node except the root have at least $(n - 1)$ **DIV** $2 = 2$ key-pointer pairs allows us to split this node, creating one new node with two key-pointer pairs and one with three key-pointer pairs. We also have to move one of the key-pointer pairs up to the parent of the present node. The resulting B-tree is given in Figure 20.17.

Although it does not happen in this particular example, note that it would be entirely possible that the moving of a key-pointer pair up to a parent node that is already full would necessitate a split of this parent node, using the same procedure. Indeed it is possible that key-pointer pairs could be passed all the way up to the root and cause a split of the root. This is in fact how a new level of the tree would be introduced. A split of the root would force the creation of a new root which would only have one key-pointer pair and two pointers to other B-tree nodes. However, at the root level this is still a sufficient number of pointers to retain the B-tree structure. Because the insertion algorithm for a B-tree requires checking whether a given node is full and potentially moving back up to a parent node, it is convenient to allow space within a node to store both of the following:

- A count of the number of key-pointer pairs in the node.
- A back pointer to the node's parent.

Trie Indexing

In all of the indexing applications we have discussed so far, the keys involved have been integers. In practice, however, we must be prepared to deal with keys of different types. Perhaps the worst case is that of keys that are variable length character strings. *Trie indexing* has developed as a means of retrieving keys in this worst case. (The term itself is derived from the four middle letters of "retrieve," though it is usually pronounced "try.")

Let us suppose that the strings in the following list represent a set of keys. Each string may be thought of as a last name followed by initials and a delimiting $.

ADAMS BT$
COOPER CC$
COOPER PJ$
COWANS DC$
MAGUIRE WH$
MCGUIRE AL$
MEMINGER DD$
SEFTON SD$
SPAN KD$
SPAN LA$
SPANNER DW$
ZARDA JM$
ZARDA PW$

FIGURE 20.17
B-tree of Figure 20.16 after insertion of 112/38 and 742/37

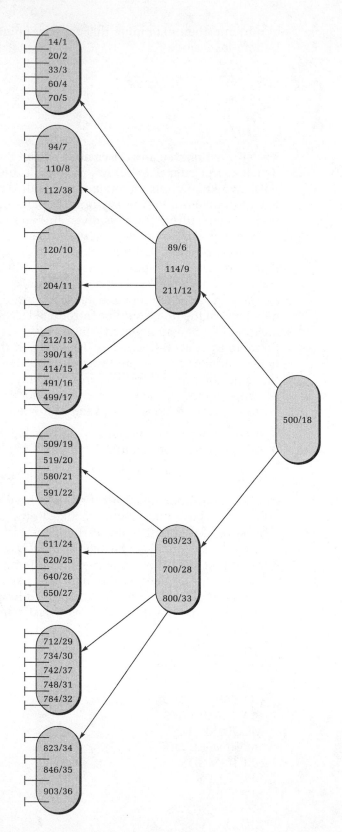

An individual node in a trie structure for these keys follows:

$ ♭ A B C D E F G H I J K L M N O P Q R S T U V W X Y Z

Trie Node

It is essentially a fixed length array of 28 pointers: one for each letter of the alphabet, one for a blank, and one for the delimiter. Each pointer within one of these nodes can lead to one of two entities—either another node within the trie or the actual data record for a given key. Hence it may be convenient to embed a Boolean flag in each pointer indicating the type of entity to which it is pointing. The trie structure for the preceding list of keys is given in Figure 20.18. In this figure, pointers to nodes labeled as data records lead us outside of the trie structure itself.

FIGURE 20.18
Trie index structure

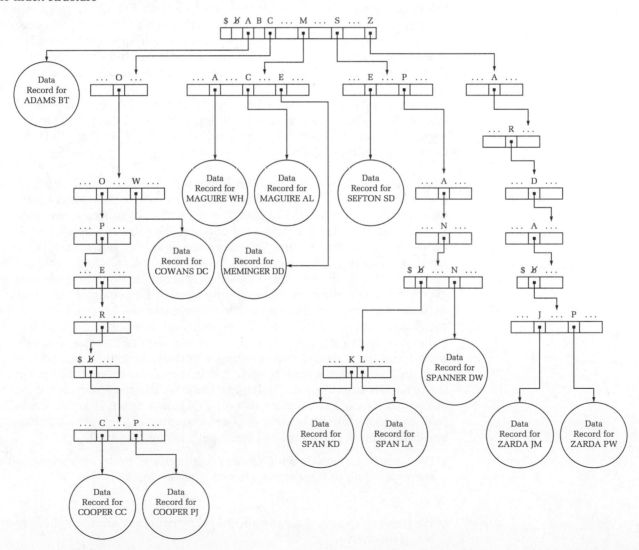

The logic behind a trie structure may best be seen by tracing through an example. This search algorithm involves examining the target key on a character-by-character basis. Let us begin by considering the easy case of finding the data record for ADAMS BT$. In this case, we look at A, the first character in the key, and follow the A pointer in the root node to its destination. From what we have previously said, we know that its destination will be either another node within the trie structure or an actual data record. If it were a node within the trie, it would be a node on the search path for all keys that begin with A. In this case, there is only one key in our list that begins with A, so the A pointer in the root node leads us directly to the actual data record for ADAMS BT$.

On the other hand, the search path to find the key COOPER CC$ in the trie is somewhat longer. We follow the C pointer from the root node down a level to a node shared by all keys starting with C. From there, the O pointer is followed to a trie node shared by all keys that start with CO. The process continues down level by level, following the O pointer to a trie node shared by all keys starting with COO, then the P pointer to a node for all keys starting with COOP, the E pointer to a node for all keys starting with COOPE, the R pointer to a node for all keys starting with COOPER, and the blank pointer to a node shared by all keys starting with COOPER followed by a blank. Notice that, as each character is read in, we must continue following these pointers from trie node to trie node (instead of from trie node to actual data record) until we finally reach a point where the next character to be read will uniquely define the key. At this point, the key in question need no longer share its pointer with other keys that match it on an initial substring. Hence the pointer may now lead to an actual data record. This is what happens in our example when we read in the next C to form the uniquely defined substring COOPER C.

Efficiency Considerations for Trie Indexing. The search efficiency for the trie index is quite easily determined. The worst case occurs when a key is not uniquely defined until its last character is read in. In this case, we may have as many disk accesses as there are characters in the key before we finally locate the actual data record. You may have observed, however, that there is another efficiency consideration to take into account when using the trie method. This is the amount of wasted storage in the trie nodes. In our example using a short list of keys, only a small percentage of the available pointers are ever used. In practice, however, a trie would only be used for an extremely large file, such as the list represented by a phone book with names as keys. In such a situation, a much larger number of character combinations occurs and the resulting trie structure is correspondingly much less sparse.

A final point to consider relative to trie indexes is their ability to dynamically handle insertions and deletions. Here, we discuss insertions; deletions are left as an exercise. Insertions may be broken down into two cases. For both we must begin by reading the key to be inserted, character by character, and following the appropriate search path in the trie until

- We come to a trie node which has a vacant pointer in the character position corresponding to the current character of the insertion key.

or

- We come to an actual data record for a key different from the one which is being inserted.

The first case is illustrated by trying to insert the key COLLINS RT$ into the trie of Figure 20.18. We would follow the search path pointers until we came to the trie node shared by all keys starting with CO. At this point, the L pointer is null. The insertion is completed by merely aiming the presently null L pointer to a data record for the key COLLINS RT$. The second case is illustrated by trying to insert the key COOPER PA$ into the trie of Figure 20.18. Here, following the search path of the trie would eventually lead us to the data record for the key COOPER PJ$. The dynamic solution is to get a new trie node, aim the P pointer presently leading to the data record for COOPER PJ$ to this new trie node, and use the A and J pointers in the new trie node to lead us to data records for COOPER PA$ and COOPER PJ$ respectively. Both the COLLINS RT$ and COOPER PA$ insertions are shown with the resulting trie in Figure 20.19.

FIGURE 20.19
Trie of Figure 20.18 after inserting COLLINS RT$ and COOPER PA$

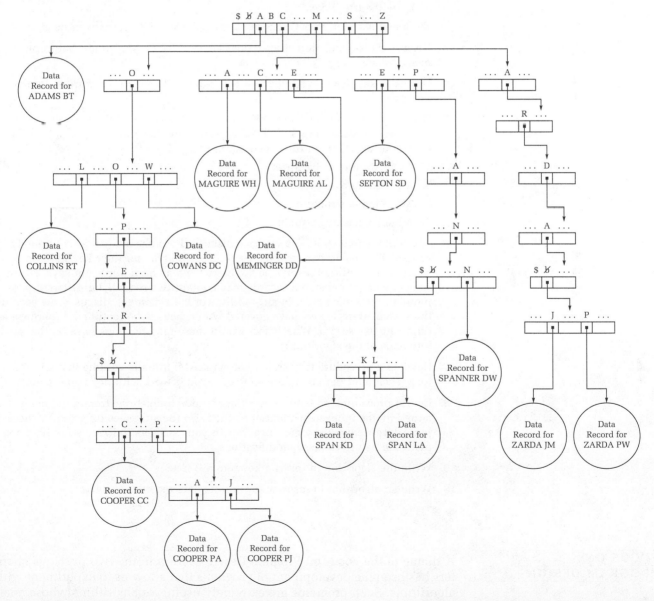

Exercises 20.3

1. a. Suppose that the records associated with keys 810, 430, 602, 946, 289, 106, and 732 are stored in positions 1, 2, 3, 4, 5, 6, and 7 respectively of a file. Draw a B-tree index of order 8 for this file.

   b. Suppose the key 538 then arrives for insertion in position 8. Redraw your B-tree of order 8 after this insertion.

2. Suppose that the following strings arrive for insertion into a trie index.

   CARTER
   HERNANDEZ
   HERMAN
   HERMANSKI
   HERSCHEL
   HALL
   CARSON
   CARSWELL
   CARSEN

   a. Draw the trie index.

   b. Draw the index after CARSWELL and HERMANSKI have been deleted.

3. Discuss the key deletion strategy for B-trees. Write a procedure that implements your strategy.

4. Discuss a key deletion strategy for trie indexes. Write a procedure to implement your strategy.

5. Carefully read your system reference material concerning the specifics of how disk file records are blocked. Then explain how this knowledge would influence your decisions in the construction of

   a. An ISAM index structure.

   b. A B-tree index structure.

   c. A trie index structure.

   d. A bucket hashing structure.

6. All of the search strategies we have discussed assume a key that is uniquely valued. That is, no two records have the same value for their key field. In practice this will not always be the case. We may have duplicate keys. For instance, a list of personnel records may contain two records for different people with the same name. In a carefully worded statement, discuss how each of the search strategies we have covered would have to be modified to perform a duplicate key search. What effect would these modifications have on the performance of the algorithm?

7. Develop a procedure to search a list via ISAM. Initially assume just one directory. Then alter the procedure so that it would work with one subdirectory.

8. Devise procedures to handle insertions into and deletions from a list maintained by the indexed sequential method. Do the strategies reflected by these procedures require any modifications in your answers to Exercise 7? If so, explain the nature of these modifications.

9. Write the algorithm to insert a key into a B-tree.

10. Write an algorithm to insert a key and its data record into a trie.

■ ■ ■ ■

FOCUS ON PROGRAM DESIGN

A theme of the Focus on Program Design section in the two previous chapters has been the development of programs that allow us to experiment with algorithms. Such programs are extremely useful for algorithms whose analysis defy purely mathematical techniques. Certainly the strategy of hashing, presented in Section 20.1, falls into this category of algorithms. The efficiency of hashing is dependent on a variety of factors: the randomness with which your hashing function scatters keys into the record space, the amount of space you are willing to sacrifice to empty storage locations, and the effectiveness of your collision-processing strategy in reducing clustering.

Because of hashing's dependency on these factors, an experimental tool for testing various hashing strategies can be very valuable in predicting how effective hashing will be for a particular application. In this section, we discuss the design of such an experimental program for situations in which we wish to study the effectiveness of hashing on keys that are strings.

As with the previous chapter's Focus on Program Design program, we want to choose between three forms of input for our experimentation:

1. A sequence of randomly generated string keys
2. A sequence of string keys that we enter interactively, so that we can enter specific data sets particularly relevant to our experimentation.
3. A sequence of string keys read one per line from a file

From last chapter's program, we will also borrow the facility to save a particularly interesting data set in a text file form that can later be read by the program. This will allow you to fine-tune the algorithm by altering the hashing function or selecting a different collision-processing method and then testing the new program with the same set of data. An example of such experimental runs with the program follows:

First Run: Hash Table with Record Space for 40, 30 Slots Filled with Random Strings.

```
How large is record space for hash table? 40
Choose method for loading hash table:

        1 - Load table with random strings
        2 - Interactively load the table
        3 - Load the table from a file

Enter 1, 2 or 3 --> 1

Enter number of values in table --> 30
Print the table? (Y/N) --> y
NONEMPTY SLOTS OF THE TABLE:

        ARRAY[ 2] = \TUFqY]Y-t1LcTIxGRnPHUjikDzoxy    { Note random strings }
        ARRAY[ 1] = UVo{texGxxYSbwNMqI\-O7¨≠(??D4E
        1≠≠1?[ 4] = Qrfh[O46×53S0=DCOTQO×AO4{paxhN
        ARRAY[ ι] = OTSK{onLIBZ^U'VfDwdKrmOhqbSjBx
        ARRAY[ 6] = MID\argowZc-Z[vMF[hZzBxkJiohiD
        ARRAY[ 7] = Pr]Rncs{CXOREpjkyYRtmmFRaXHbWv
        ARRAY[10] = 'kgP1^[lJrmTsSfbw\JBXrVOVDTose
        ARRAY[14] = O'S'[SL^sVJn'Pdw'aJ^votElbqLFZ
        ARRAY[15] = J[lsvd{LwcRvQyiF{SPPKLDyrIIpGl
        ARRAY[16] = LkYsfFhnyvdKPnPe'Niiup{xXHMxGj
        ARRAY[18] = pKiWMJzLLNfho-jYGcPxJzVsDRDiqE
        ARRAY[19] = YC's^ZPOXZEnHe{BnbI'Xp'uEvOgr\
        ARRAY[20] = bT{bZGcKmhwGfdFxH]IOPrIbHQJ]oS
        ARRAY[21] = NILYPSQnhr-H'u{CuDnErrunYr[kif
        ARRAY[22] = \]kmBdbnLhSQBN{ncqjtwe\II\WFPe
        ARRAY[23] = fByLV{fqOhOLSfotfZYZReHYTn{Wp\
        ARRAY[24] = ^NSsPsYp\{kSKOUw[ISOWOjnzHbIVU
```

```
ARRAY[25] = eLWstIC'ZLPsUwHXgvhk\jzWpsHwlx
ARRAY[26] = IxV'GzjKFeq[IXptTukEjhdbuQ-wSQ
ARRAY[27] = HPyGpLkGZINJEh-pnVghemjPgZlJxx
ARRAY[28] = XPDHfZTwyCzk\fGCMokZNEv]dCllXN
ARRAY[29] = GvpO^bWgPubRY]\jEsI[OddGCRzM^]
ARRAY[30] = EZzxgV'ih'nLJ-nCLsdnqISzHvyMJl
ARRAY[31] = qwbs{HblUTCIwEzfox-nB^iHfRbPmu
ARRAY[32] = KWQcS[WdJSyZl]FeJbpl\HMVjiTCzs
ARRAY[35] = RUhjdEgb{x]d''NWPXx\OGjZaMcpOP
ARRAY[36] = ysb[z-gCgghfDskqOiqKRiFOPZ'bM^
ARRAY[37] = PngO'I\efYtwfJykbvnc-PWE'mqkiz
ARRAY[38] = KB]Uiq]kLxmylwUdXUTLMmlSOkh-cq
ARRAY[39] = iJtgsTbicsFueT]{uRqZdRKZGwdc\m
```

```
Average length for successful search    2.13
Average length for unsuccessful search    4.87


Save the input values for this table? (Y/N)--> y
Name for save file --> test.dat
Another table? (Y/N) --> n
```

Second Run: Now Adjust Hashing Function and/or Collision Processing, and Run Again.

```
How large is record space for hash table? 40
Choose method for loading hash table:

        1 - Load table with random strings
        2 - Interactively load the table
        3 - Load the table from a file

Enter 1, 2 or 3 --> 3

Enter the name of the file --> test.dat
Print the table? (Y/N) --> n
Average length for successful search 1.92
Average length for unsuccessful search 4.76

Save the input values for this table? (Y/N) --> n
Another table? (Y/N) --> n
```

Note the slight improvement in efficiency for the second run.

A modular structure chart for **PROGRAM** HashingExperimentation appears in Figure 20.20. Notice from the modular structure chart that a package of queue modules is used in the program. As a sequence of string keys is loaded into the hash table by the program, the keys are also placed on the queue. Then, after the hash table has been loaded, these keys are removed from the queue. As each key is removed from the queue, we search the hash table for it, accumulating a profiling counter as the search for the key is performed. The key is then returned to the tail of the queue. If the user chooses to save the sequence of string keys to a text file, we merely proceed through the queue, writing each key to the file as it is removed from the queue.

To accumulate the statistics for the average unsuccessful search, the program generates a fixed number of additional random keys—assuming that the probability of any such key matching one already in the table is virtually zero. The program is exercised by sending each of these randomly generated keys through the search algorithm. A profiling accumulator for unsuccessful searches is maintained as these keys are processed.

FIGURE 20.20
Modular structure chart for
PROGRAM HashingExperimen-
tation

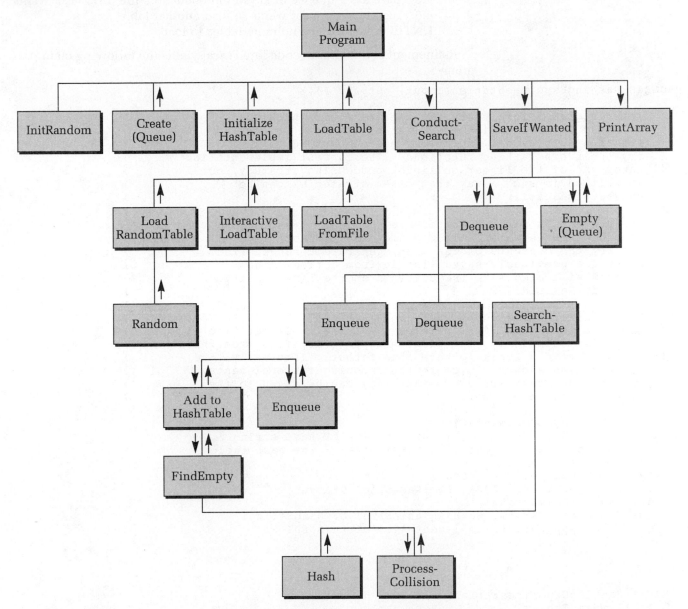

A first-level pseudocode development for the main program is given by:

1. Intialize the random number generator (See Appendix 9)
2. Create the queue used to store a copy of keys in order of generation
3. Initialize the value used to flag an empty slot
4. **REPEAT**
    4.1   Initialize hash table to all empty slots
    4.2   Load the table of a specified logical record space with number of
          keys specified by user, also returning a queue containing the
          sequence of keys generated

4.3   If the user wants, print the hash table

4.4   Conduct searches: accumulate and print profiling counters for successful and unsuccessful searches

4.5   Save the sequence of keys from queue to a file if the user wants

4.6   Inquire if the user wants to load another table

UNTIL user indicates no more tables to load

Refinement of this pseudocode into Pascal yields the following main program:

```
PROGRAM HashingExperimentation(input, output, F);

   { This program allows users to experiment with hashing on      }
   { an array implementation of a list of strings.  A hashing     }
   { function is provided, but users are encouraged to            }
   { try their own hashing functions.  The current implementation }
   { makes use of the linear collision processing strategy, but   }
   { is written in such a way that other strategies can be        }
   { substituted easily.                                          }
   {                                                              }
   { The program is designed to create the list of strings        }
   { in one of three ways:  allow a user to interactively         }
   { specify the contents of the list, generate a random list,    }
   { or read a previously-saved list in from a file.  The         }
   { program will also save the contents of the list for later    }
   { reuse if desired.                                            }
   {                                                              }
   { The data file created by the program when a table is saved is }
   { simply a text file with one element of the table per line of  }
   { the file.  Similarly, the program expects any file from which }
   { it is to read a table to have this format.  Internally, the   }
   { program uses a queue to store the incoming table elements     }
   { in the order they arrive so that they can be saved to the     }
   { file in that same order.                                     }

   CONST { HashingExperimentation }
      NameSize = 30;              { Maximum size of name string      }
      MaxHashTableSize = 2000;  { Maximum size of the hash table   }

   TYPE { HashingExperimentation }
      NameString = PACKED ARRAY [1..NameSize] OF char;
      InfoType = NameString;
      HashTable = ARRAY [1..MaxHashTableSize] OF NameString;
      Queue = { Appropriate implementation of this ADT }
      .
      .
      .


   VAR { HashingExperimentation }
      Table: HashTable;          { Hash table                       }
      Query: char;               { User's response                  }
      F: text;                   { File variable                    }
      ChoiceOfLoad: integer;     { User's choice for loading table  }
      EmptySlot: NameString;     { String for empty hash table entry }
      AveSearchLength: real;     { Statistics for search efficiency }
      HashTableSize : integer;   { Logical size of hash table       }
      Copy : Queue;              { Copy of keys which are generated }
      .
      .

   { You will fill procedures as part of programming problem        }
      .
      .
```

```
{*************************************************************}
{                   The Main Program                        }
BEGIN { Main program }
  InitRandom;
  CreateQueue(Copy);
  InitString(EmptySlot);
  REPEAT
    InitializeHashTable(Table, EmptySlot);
    LoadTable(Table, ChoiceOfLoad, Copy);
    write('Print the table? (Y/N) --> ');
    readln(Query);
    IF (Query = 'Y') OR (Query = 'y') THEN
      PrintArray(Table, 1, HashTableSize);
    ConductSearch(Table);
    SaveIfWanted(Copy, ChoiceOfLoad);
    write('Another table? (Y/N) --> ');
    readln(Query)
  UNTIL (Query = 'N') OR (Query = 'n')
END. { of main program }
```

Specifications for individual modules in the program follow. You will implement these specifications in the Programming Problems, thereby providing yourself with a means of exploring the effectiveness of a variety of hashing functions and collision processing methods.

1. InitRandom Module
   Data received: None
   Information returned: None
   Logic: Initialize the random number generator as described in Appendix 9. This may be unnecessary if your version of Pascal provides a random number generator.

2. Create, Enqueue, Dequeue, Empty Modules
   Standard modules for performing operations on a queue.

3. InitializeHashTable Module
   Data received: Hash table in arbitrary state.
   Information returned: Hash table with all slots initialized to emtpy indicator.
   Logic: For each index in table, assign empty slot flag.

4. LoadTable Module
   Data received: Table, an empty hash table, and Copy, an empty queue.
   Information returned: An integer indicating the user's chice for loading the hash table: 1 for randomly generated strings, 2 for interactively loaded strings, 3 for strings read from file. Table is returned loaded with strings generated by chosen method. Copy contains sequence of strings generated by chosen method.
   Logic: Determine logical size of record space in table and choice for loading. Dispatch to LoadRandomTable, InteractiveLoadTable, or LoadTableFromFile respectively.

5. LoadRandomTable Module
   Data received: None
   Information returned: Hash table loaded with randomly generated strings and a queue Copy which contains each of the strings in the order of their generation.

Logic: 1. Inquire as to number of strings to generate.
 2. For each string,
  2.1 Fill it with randomly generated characters.
  2.2 Call on AddToHashTable to load string into Table.
  2.3 Call on Enqueue operation to add string to Copy queue.

6. Random Module
 Data received: None
 Information returned: Randomly generated value.
 Logic: Use algorithm of Appendix 9 or random number generator provided with your version of Pascal.

7. InteractiveLoadTable Module
 Data received: None
 Information returned: Hash table loaded with strings entered interactively by user and a queue Copy which contains each of the strings in the order they were entered.
 Logic: 1. Inquire as to number of strings that will be entered.
  2. For each string,
   2.1 Allow user to enter it interactively.
   2.2 Call on AddToHashTable to load string into Table.
   2.3 Call on Enqueue operation to add string to Copy queue.

8. LoadTableFromFile Module
 Data received: None.
 Information returned: Hash table loaded with strings read from file and a queue Copy which contains each of the strings in the order they were read.
 Logic: 1. Inquire as to name of file to load.
  2. **WHILE NOT eof**
   2.1 Read string from file.
   2.2 Call on AddToHashTable to load string into Table.
   2.3 Call on Enqueue operation to add string to Copy queue.

9. AddtoHashTable Module
 Data received: Hash table.
  NewItem to be inserted in hash table.
 Information returned: Table with NewItem added.
 Logic: 1. Call on FindEmpty module to obtain index position for NewItem.
  2. **IF** FindEmpty reports that Table is full or NewItem already in Table **THEN**
   2.1 Print error message.
  ELSE
   2.2 Store NewItem at index position.

10. FindEmpty Module
 Data received: Hash table.
  Target value for which empty Index position in Table is needed.
 Information returned: Boolean Found set to **true** if such an index position could be found. Boolean Exists set to **true** if Target already in Table.
  Index: the position for Target when Found returned as **true**.

Logic: 1. Call on Hash function for initial placement of target.
2. **WHILE** (Target does not already exist in Table)
   AND (Empty slot not found)
   AND (All possible slots have not been checked)
   2.1 Call on ProcessCollision module to obtain next index position.

11. Hash Module
    Data received: A string key.
    Information returned: Hashed index position for key.
    Logic: Many possibilities exist; these are left for your experimentation in the Problems.

12. ProcessCollision Module
    Data received: Previous index position visited.
    Information returned: Next index position to check.
    Logic: Determined by collision processing technique; left for your experimentation in the Problems.

13. ConductSearch Module
    Data received: Hash table.
    Copy queue containing string keys in order generated by LoadTable module.
    Information returned: None.
    Logic: Perform empirical testing on hashing method for this particular data.
    1. For each queue in Copy queue.
       1.1 Dequeue that key.
       1.2 Call on SearchHashTable to find that key, accumulating a profiling count of number of probes into table that are required to find the key.
       1.3 Enqueue that key back into Copy queue.
    2. Report on average length for successful searches conducted in step 1.
    3. For a fixed number of unsuccessful searches
       3.1 Randomly generate a key not in Table.
       3.2 Call on SearchHashTable to attempt to find that key, accumulating a profiling count of the number of probes into table that are required to determine that the key cannot be located.
    4. Report profiling information for unsucessful searches.

14. SearchHashTable Module
    Data received: Hash table.
    Target to be found in Table.
    Information returned: Index position of Target in Table if Found set to **true**.
    Found set to **false** if Target not in Table.
    Logic: 1. Call on Hash function for initial position of Target.
    2. Increment profiling counter of number of table probes.
    3. **WHILE** (EmptySlot not encountered)
       AND (Target not found)
       AND (All possible positions not checked)
       3.1 Call on ProcessCollision to determine next index to check.
       3.2 Increment profiling counter of number of table probes.

15. <u>SaveIfWanted Module</u>
Data received: Copy queue containing keys in order originally generated.
Information returned: None.
Logic: Inquire if user wants to save this data set for further exploration.
IF user wants to save and data set was not originally loaded from file **THEN**
write Copy queue to file in form compatible with Load TableFrom File module.

16. <u>PrintArray Module</u>
Data received: Hash table.
Low and High: indices of table between which nonempty table positions are to be printed.
Information returned: None.
Logic: Iterate through Table from Low to High, printing nonempty slots.

RUNNING AND DEBUGGING TIPS

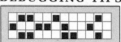

1. When using hashing as a search strategy, provide yourself with a means of experimenting with your hashing function and collision-processing strategy. This will allow you to tailor your program to the particular kind of keys that are stored in the hash table.

2. Searching for data in a random access file involves different criteria than searching for data in main memory. Programs that search for data in random access files should minimize file accesses at the expense of main memory accesses. Indexed searches provide ways of doing this.

3. If a search program has to handle duplicate keys, that is, different records associated with the same key value, the search algorithm will have to be adjusted appropriately. Be sure you know and decide in advance whether this added complexity is necessary.

■ Summary

Key Terms

boundary folding	hashing	quadratic collision
buckets	hashing function	processing
clustering	index	randomized storage
collision	key-to-address	rehashing
density-dependent	transformation	rehashing collision
search techniques	linear collision	processing
digit/character	processing	sectors
extraction	linked collision	shift folding
division-remainder	processing	synonyms
technique	overflow area	tracks
folding	prime hash area	

Key Terms (Optional)

binary tree index	fatal embrace	indexed sequential
B-tree	Indexed Sequential	search
concurrent updating	Access Method	record lock facility
data integrity	(ISAM)	trie indexing
deadlock		

Key Concepts

■ The following table gives a concise synopsis of the search strategies that have been discussed in this and earlier chapters. Additional comments emphasize particular strengths or weaknesses of the strategy in terms of the keyed list operations we have considered throughout the text.

Method	Efficiency (n = Number of Records)	Other Components Regarding Keyed List Operations
Binary	$O(\log_2 n)$	Data must be maintained in physical order, hence making insertions and deletions inefficient.
Binary tree index	$O(\log_2 n)$ index probes, 1 file probe	Guaranteeing this efficiency requires height balancing.
B-tree index order K	Worst case requires $1 + \log_K((n + 1)/2)$ disk accesses for index	Choose K so that index node coincides with disk block.
Indexed sequential	O(size of index) index probes, $O(n/$(size of index)) file probes	Index and file require physical ordering to maintain efficiency.
Linear hashing	Average successful: $(1/2) * (1 + 1/(1 - D))$ Average unsuccessful: $(1/2) * (1 + 1/(1 - D)^2)$ where density $D = n/\text{RecordSpace}$	Data not maintained in any order.
Linked hashing	Average successful: $1 + D/2$ Average unsuccessful: D (where RecordSpace used in computation of D is that in primary hash area)	Data not maintained in any order.
Quadratic hashing	Average successful: $1 - \log_e(1 - D) - (D/2)$ Average unsuccessful: $1/(1 - D) - D - \log_e(1 - D)$	Data not maintained in any order.
Rehashing	Average successful: $-(1/D) * \log_e(1 - D)$ Average unsuccessful: $1/(1 - D)$	Data not maintained in any order.
Sequential	$O(n)$	
Trie index	O(number of characters in Target)	Specifically suited for character strings.

- In addition to hashing, other search strategies specifically oriented toward file structures include indexed sequential search, B-trees, and tries.
- As an implementation strategy for keyed lists, hashing fares very well in all of the operations except ordering. It thus represents a very viable addition to the list implementation strategies discussed in earlier chapters: array or random files with binary search, linked lists, and binary trees.

■ Programming Problems and Projects

1. Complete the program designed in this chapter's Focus on Program Design section. Then use the program as a means of conducting experiments on hashing. In your experiments, you should try a variety of hashing functions and collision-processing strategies. You might also try to adjust the generation of random strings so that, although

still random, the strings conform to rules for particular kinds of data. That is, if the data consist of names of the form

COOPER, J. C.

the random generation of characters could be modified based on the probabilities of certain letters being used and on the average length of last names.

Write up a report in which you analyze each of the hashing functions and collision-processing strategies you use. Back up your analysis with empirical profiling data obtained from the ConductSearches module of your program.

2. Implement the registrar's system described in Example 13.1 using hashing as a list maintenance technique. Be sure that you devise an appropriate strategy to output the ordered listings that the registrar must have.

3. Implement the Wing-and-a-Prayer flight/pilot data base (Section 13.3) using the implementation technique described in Section 20.2. For an added challenge, assume that the rows of the flight/pilot table are indexed by pilot name instead of pilot number. How could this complication be handled in a way which minimizes the memory needed to store the implementation of a sparse table?

4. A B-tree of order 3 is often called a 2-3 tree since each node has 2 or 3 children. Because of its low order, a 2-3 tree is not particularly applicable as a file index. However, if we store up to two actual data records in each node instead of up to two key-pointer pairs, then a 2-3 tree becomes an alternative to an ordered binary tree for implementing a list. Develop search, insertion, and deletion algorithms for such a 2-3 tree structure. Compare its performance characteristics with those of an ordered binary tree.

5. Implement the registrar's system of Problem 2 using a 2-3 tree representation of a list. (See Programming Problem 4.)

6. Wing-and-a-Prayer Airlines has the records of all its customers stored in the following form:

   - Last name.
   - First name.
   - Address.
   - Arbitrarily long list of flights on which reservations have been booked.

   Using a trie index, write a search-and-retrieval program that will allow input of a customer's last name (and, if necessary, the first name and address to resolve conflicts created by matching last names) and then output all flights on which that customer has booked reservations.

7. SuperScout Inc. is a nationwide scouting service for college football talent to which the Bay Area Brawlers professional team subscribes. As the pool of college talent increases in size, SuperScout has found that its old recordkeeping system has deteriorated considerably in its ability to quickly locate the scouting record associated with a given player in its file. Rewrite their scouting record system using a trie to

look up the record location of the data associated with a given player's name.

8. Using a large collection of randomly generated keys, write a series of programs that will test various hashing functions you develop. In particular, your programs should report statistics on the number of collisions generated by each hashing function. This information could be valuable in guiding future decisions about which hashing functions and techniques are most effective for your particular system.

9. Consider a student data record which consists of

   - Student identification number.
   - Student name.
   - State of residence.
   - Sex.

   Choose an index structure to process a file of such records. Then write a program to maintain such a file as a keyed list.

10. Suppose that data records for a phone book file consist of a key field containing both name and address, and a field containing the phone number for that key. Devise an appropriate index for such a file. Then write a program which calls for input of
    a. A complete key.
    b. If a complete key is not available, as much of the initial portion of a key as the inquirer is able to provide.

    In the case of situation **a**, your program should output the phone number corresponding to the unique key. In the case of situation **b**, have your program output all keys (and their phone numbers) that match the provided initial portion.

11. Consider the following problem faced in the development of a compiler. The source program contains many character-string symbols such as variable names, procedure names, and so on. Each of these character-string symbols has associated with it various attributes such as memory location, data type, and so on. However, it would be too time-consuming and awkward for a compiler to actually manipulate character strings. Instead, each string should be identified with an integer which is viewed as an equivalent to the string for the purpose of compiler manipulation. In addition to serving as a compact equivalent form of a string symbol within the source program, this integer can also serve as a direct pointer into a table of attributes for that symbol. Devise such a transformation that associates a string with an integer, and which in turn serves as a pointer into a table of attributes. Test the structure(s) you develop by using them in a program that scans a source program written in a language such as Pascal. You will in effect have written the symbol table modules for a compiler.

12. Write a spelling checker program. Such a program must scan a file of text, looking up each word it finds in a dictionary of correctly spelled words. When a word cannot be found in the dictionary, the spelling checker should convey this fact to its user, giving the user the opportunity to take one of the following steps:
    a. Skip the word.
    b. Change the spelling of the word in the text file.

c. Add the word to the dictionary so it will not be reported as incorrectly spelled in the future.

Since the dictionary for such a program will be searched frequently and is likely to become quite large, an efficient search algorithm is an absolute necessity. One possibility in this regard is to use a trie index with pointers into a large string workspace instead of the pointers to data records described in Section 20.3. Test your program with a text file and dictionary large enough to handle all of the possibilities your algorithm and data structure may encounter.

13. If you solved one of the problems from Chapter 13 that involved maintaining a keyed list, redo that problem using hashing combined with linked lists as an implementation technique. When finished, write a report in which you empirically compare the performance of your two implementations.

14. If you solved one of the problems from Chapter 13 that involved maintaining a sparse matrix, redo that problem using hashing of row and column indices as an implementation technique. When finished, write a report in which you empirically compare the performance of your two implementations.

▦ Appendixes

Appendix 1 Reserved Words

The following words have predefined meanings in standard Pascal and cannot be changed. Each of these, except **GOTO** and **LABEL,** have been developed in the text. These statements are discussed in Appendix 7.

AND	**END**	**MOD**	**REPEAT**
ARRAY	**FILE**	**NIL**	**SET**
BEGIN	**FOR**	**NOT**	**THEN**
CASE	**FORWARD**	**OF**	**TO**
CONST	**FUNCTION**	**OR**	**TYPE**
DIV	**GOTO**	**PACKED**	**UNTIL**
DO	**IF**	**PROCEDURE**	**VAR**
DOWNTO	**IN**	**PROGRAM**	**WHILE**
ELSE	**LABEL**	**RECORD**	**WITH**

Appendix 2
Standard Identifiers

The standard identifiers for constants, types, files, functions, and procedures are set forth in this appendix. All have predefined meanings that could (but probably should not) be changed in a program. Summary descriptions are given for the functions and procedures.

Constants	*Types*	*Files*
false	**boolean**	**input**
maxint	**char**	**output**
true	**integer**	
	real	
	text	

Functions

Function	Parameter Type	Result Type	Value Returned
abs(x)	**integer**	**integer**	Absolute value of x
	real	**real**	
arctan(x)	**integer**	**real**	Arctangent of x
	real		(radians)
chr(a)	**integer**	**char**	Character with ordinal a
cos(x)	**integer**	**real**	Cosine of x (radians)
	real		
eof(F)	**file**	**boolean**	End-of-file test for F
eoln(F)	**file**	**boolean**	End-of-line test for F
exp(x)	**integer**	**real**	e^x
	real	**real**	
ln(x)	**integer** (positive)	**real**	Natural logarithm of x
	real (positive)		
odd(a)	**integer**	**boolean**	Tests for a an odd integer
ord(x)	nonreal scalar	**integer**	Ordinal number of x
pred(x)	nonreal scalar	same as x	Predecessor of x

Functions (continued)

Function	Parameter Type	Result Type	Value Returned
round(x)	real	integer	Rounds off x
sin(x)	integer real	real	Sine of x
sqr(x)	integer real	integer real	Square of x
sqrt(x)	integer real	real	Square root of x
succ(x)	nonreal scalar	same as x	Successor of x
trunc(x)	real	integer	Truncated value of x

Procedures

Procedure Call	Purpose of Procedure
dispose (Ptr)	Returns variable referenced by Ptr to available space list
get (F)	Advances the file pointer for the file F and assigns the new value to F^
new (Ptr)	Creates a variable of the type referenced by Ptr and stores a pointer to the new variable in Ptr
pack (U, J, P)	Copies unpacked array elements from U into the packed array P; copying starts with P[1] := U[J]
page (F)	Starts printing the next line of text F at the top of a new page
put (F)	Appends the current value of F to the file F
read (F, variable list)	Reads values from file F into indicated variables; if F is not specified, **input** is assumed
readln (F, variable list)	Executes the same as **read** and then advances the file pointer to the first position following the next end-of-line marker
reset (F)	Resets the pointer in file F to the beginning for the purpose of reading from F
rewrite (F)	Resets the pointer in file F to the beginning for the purpose of writing to F
unpack (P, U, J)	Copies packed array elements from P into the unpacked array U; copying starts with U[J] := P[1]
write (F, parameter list)	Writes values specified by parameter list to the text file F; if F is not specified, **output** is assumed
writeln (F, parameter list)	Executes the same as **write** and then places an end-of-line marker in F

Appendix 3
Syntax Diagrams

Syntax diagrams in this appendix are listed in the following order:

```
Program
      Identifier
      File List
Declarations and Definitions
      Label Declaration
      Constant Definition
      Type Definition
            Type
                        Enumerated Type
                        Subrange Type
                        Pointer Type
                        Array Type
                        Record Type
                              Field List
                                    Fixed Part
                                    Variant Part
                                          Variant Description
                        File Type
                        Set Type
            Variable Declaration
            Procedure and Function Declarations
                  Formal Parameter List
Body
      Compound Statement
            Statement
                  Assignment Statement
                        Expression
                              Term
                                    Factor
                                          Variable
                                          Set Value
                  Boolean Expression
            read or readln Statement
```

```
write or writeln Statement
Procedure Statement
IF Statement
CASE Statement
    Case Label
WHILE Statement
REPEAT Statement
FOR Statement
WITH Statement
GOTO Statement
Empty Statement
```

Program

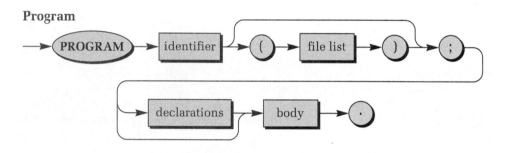

Identifier

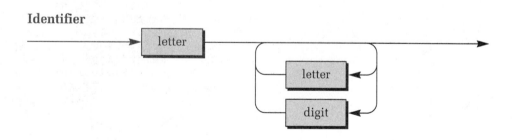

File List

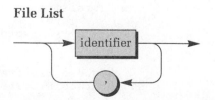

Declarations and Definitions

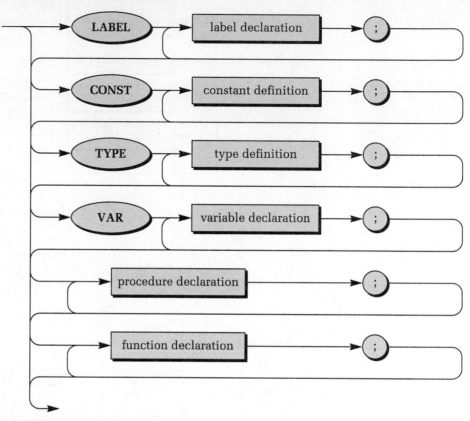

Label Declaration

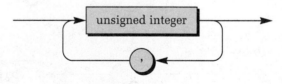

Constant Definition

Type Definition

Type

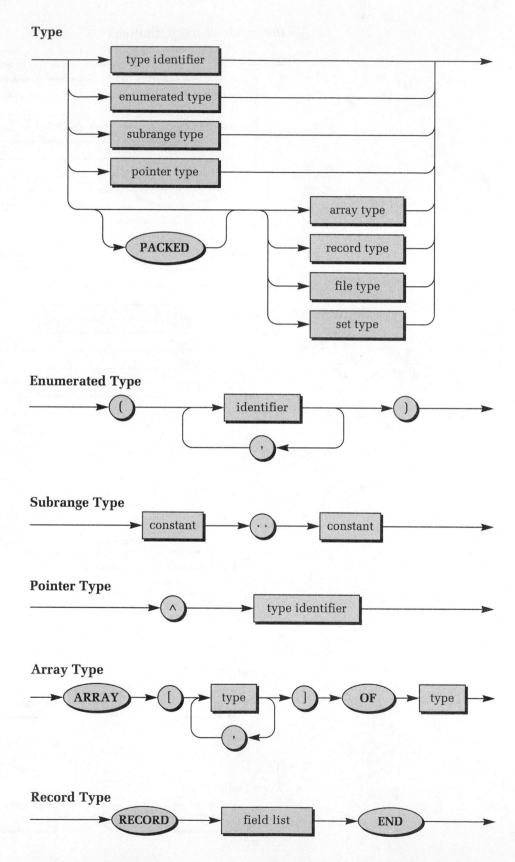

Enumerated Type

Subrange Type

Pointer Type

Array Type

Record Type

Appendix 13.NANCE (15% PMS 173)

Field List

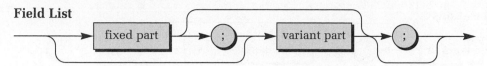

Fixed Part

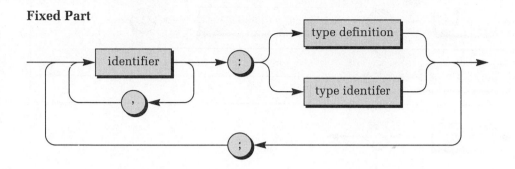

Variant Part

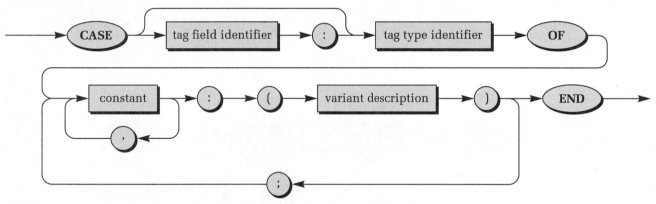

Variant Description

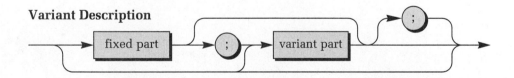

File Type

Set Type

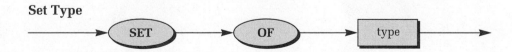

Variable Declaration

Procedure and Function Declarations

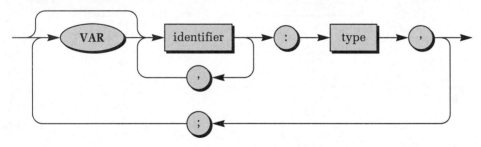

Formal Parameter List

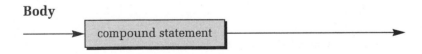

Body

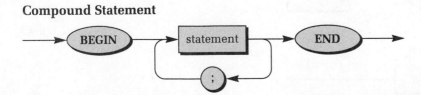

Compound Statement

Statement

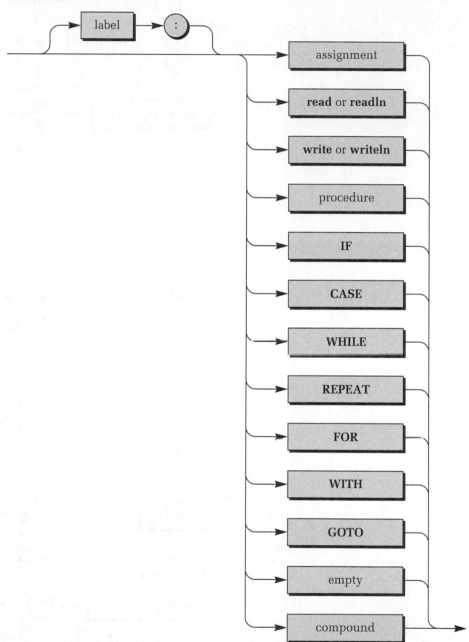

Assignment Statement

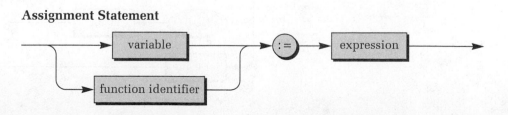

Expression

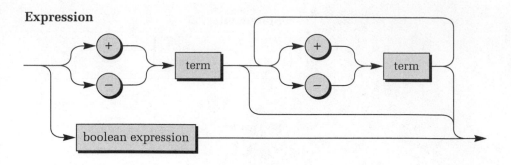

Term

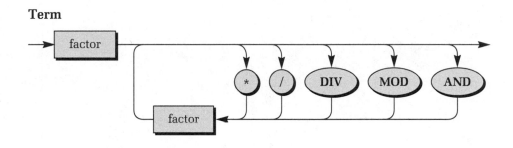

Factor

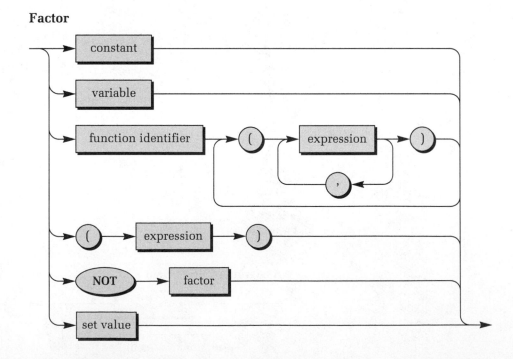

Variable

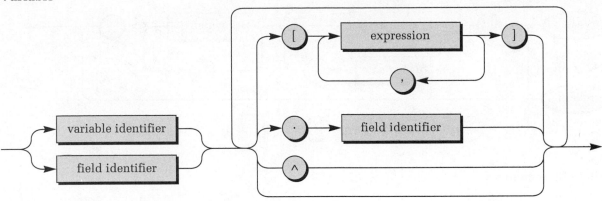

jendix 3ummarunct

Set Value

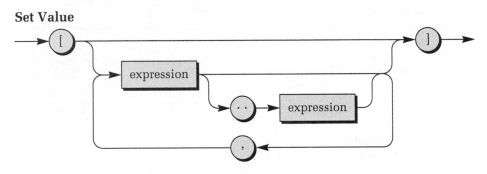

Boolean Expression

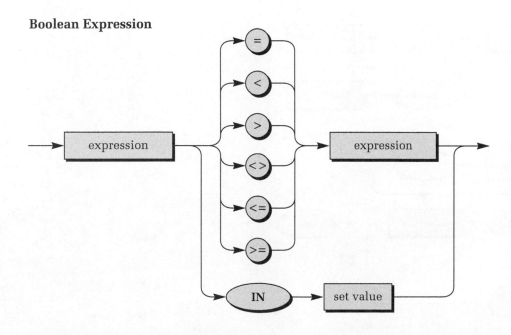

read or readln Statement

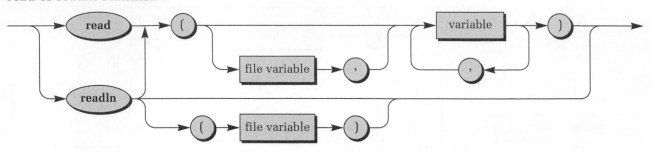

write or writeln Statement

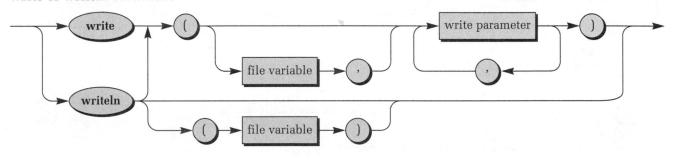

Procedure Statement

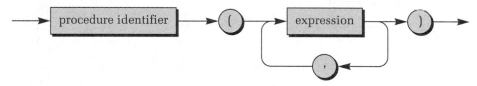

IF Statement

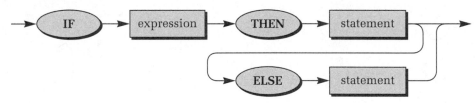

CASE Statement

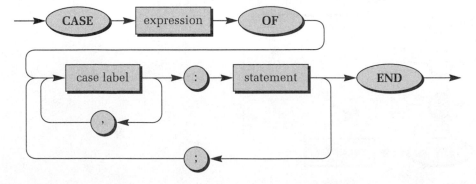

Case Label

WHILE Statement

REPEAT Statement

FOR Statement

WITH Statement

GOTO Statement

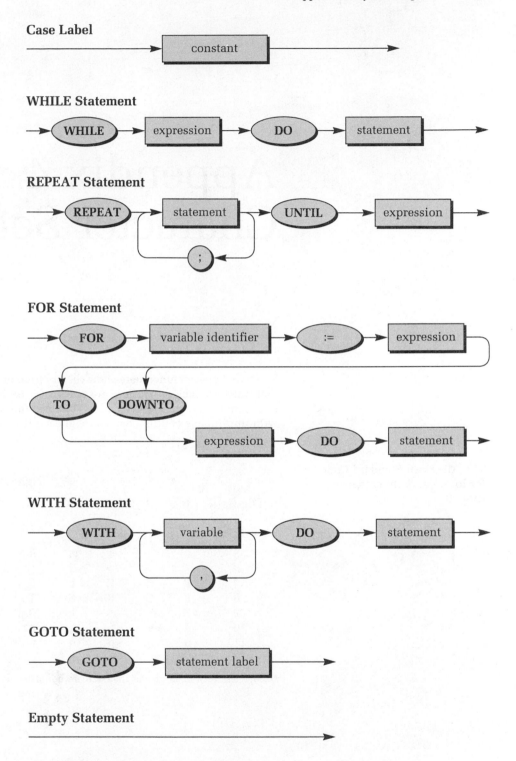

Empty Statement

⊞ Appendix 4 Character Sets

The two tables included here show the ordering of two common character sets. Note that only printable characters are shown for each set. Ordinals without character representations either do not have standard representation, or they are associated with unprintable control characters. In each list, the blank is denoted by "♭".

The American Standard Code for Information Interchange (ASCII)

Left Digit(s)	Right Digit									
	0	1	2	3	4	5	6	7	8	9
3			♭	!	"	#	$	%	&	'
4	(	)	*	+	,	—	.	/	0	1
5	2	3	4	5	6	7	8	9	:	;
6	<	=	>	?	@	A	B	C	D	E
7	F	G	H	I	J	K	L	M	N	O
8	P	Q	R	S	T	U	V	W	X	Y
9	Z	[	\	]	^	—	`		a	b	c
10	d	e	f	g	h	i	j	k	l	m
11	n	o	p	q	r	s	t	u	v	w
12	x	y	z	{			}	~			

*Codes less than 32 or greater than 126 are nonprintable.

The Extended Binary Coded
Decimal Interchange Code
(EBCDIC)

Left Digit(s)	Right Digit									
	0	1	2	3	4	5	6	7	8	9
6					ƀ					
7					¢	.	<	(	+	|
8	&									
9	!	$	*	)	;	¬	-	/		
10							^	,	%	—
11	>	?								
12			:	#	@	'	=	"		a
13	b	c	d	e	f	g	h	i		
14						j	k	l	m	n
15	o	p	q	r						
16			s	t	u	v	w	x	y	z
17								\	{	}
18	[	]								
19				A	B	C	D	E	F	G
20	H	I								J
21	K	L	M	N	O	P	Q	R		
22							S	T	U	V
23	W	X	Y	Z						
24	0	1	2	3	4	5	6	7	8	9

*Codes not listed in this table are nonprintable.

Appendix 5 Compiler Error Messages

The following are typical error messages used by a compiler to identify compilation errors. Such errors will be identified by number with appropriate messages produced at the bottom of a compilation listing. Different compilers produce different error messages.

```
 1   ERROR IN SIMPLE TYPE.
 2   IDENTIFIER EXPECTED.
 3   'PROGRAM' EXPECTED.
 4   ')' EXPECTED.
 5   ' ' EXPECTED.
 6   UNEXPECTED SYMBOL.
 7   ERROR IN PARAMETER LIST.
 8   'OF' EXPECTED.
 9   '(' EXPECTED.
10   ERROR IN TYPE.
11   '[' EXPECTED.
12   ']' EXPECTED.
13   'END' EXPECTED.
14   ';' EXPECTED.
15   INTEGER CONSTANT EXPECTED.
16   '=' EXPECTED.
17   'BEGIN' EXPECTED.
18   ERROR IN DECLARATION PART.
19   ERROR IN FIELD-LIST.
20   ',' EXPECTED.
21   '..' EXPECTED.

40   VALUE PART ALLOWED ONLY IN MAIN PROGRAM.
41   TOO FEW VALUES SPECIFIED.
42   TOO MANY VALUES SPECIFIED.
43   VARIABLE INITIALIZED TWICE.
44   TYPE IS NEITHER ARRAY NOR RECORD.
45   REPETITION FACTOR MUST BE GREATER THAN ZERO.
```

```
50    ERROR IN CONSTANT.
51    ':=' EXPECTED.
52    'THEN' EXPECTED.
53    'UNTIL' EXPECTED.
54    'DO' EXPECTED.
55    'TO' OR 'DOWNTO' EXPECTED.
57    'FILE' EXPECTED.
58    ERROR IN FACTOR.
59    ERROR IN VARIABLE.
60    FILE TYPE IDENTIFIER EXPECTED.

101   IDENTIFIER DECLARED TWICE.
102   LOWBOUND EXCEEDS HIGHBOUND.
103   IDENTIFIER IS NOT OF APPROPRIATE CLASS.
104   IDENTIFIER NOT DECLARED.
105   SIGN NOT ALLOWED.
106   NUMBER EXPECTED.
107   INCOMPATIBLE SUBRANGE TYPES.
108   FILE NOT ALLOWED HERE.
109   TYPE MUST NOT BE REAL.
110   TAGFIELD TYPE MUST BE SCALAR OR SUBRANGE.
111   INCOMPATIBLE WITH TAGFIELD TYPE.
112   INDEX TYPE MUST NOT BE REAL.
113   INDEX TYPE MUST BE SCALAR OR SUBRANGE.
114   BASE TYPE MUST NOT BE REAL.
115   BASE TYPE MUST BE SCALAR OR SUBRANGE.
116   ERROR IN TYPE OF STANDARD PROCEDURE PARAMETER.
117   UNSATISFIED FORWARD REFERENCE.
119   FORWARD DECLARED; REPETITION OF PARAMETER LIST NOT ALLOWED.
120   FUNCTION RESULT TYPE MUST BE SCALAR, SUBRANGE, OR POINTER.
121   FILE VALUE PARAMETER NOT ALLOWED.
122   FORWARD DECLARED FUNCTION; REPETITION OF RESULT TYPE NOT
      ALLOWED.
123   MISSING RESULT TYPE IN FUNCTION DECLARATION.
124   FIXED-POINT FORMATTING ALLOWED FOR REALS ONLY.
125   ERROR IN TYPE OF STANDARD FUNCTION PARAMETER.
126   NUMBER OF PARAMETERS DOES NOT AGREE WITH DECLARATION.
127   INVALID PARAMETER SUBSTITUTION.
128   PARAMETER PROCEDURE/FUNCTION IS NOT COMPATIBLE WITH
      DECLARATION.
129   TYPE CONFLICT OF OPERANDS.
130   EXPRESSION IS NOT OF SET TYPE.
131   TESTS ON EQUALITY ALLOWED ONLY.
132   '<' AND '>' NOT ALLOWED FOR SET OPERANDS.
133   FILE COMPARISON NOT ALLOWED.
134   INVALID TYPE OF OPERAND(S).
135   TYPE OF OPERAND MUST BE BOOLEAN.
136   SET ELEMENT MUST BE SCALAR OR SUBRANGE.
137   SET ELEMENT TYPES NOT COMPATIBLE.
138   TYPE OF VARIABLE IS NOT ARRAY.
139   INDEX TYPE IS NOT COMPATIBLE WITH DECLARATION.
140   TYPE OF VARIABLE IS NOT RECORD.
141   TYPE OF VARIABLE MUST BE FILE OR POINTER.
142   INVALID PARAMETER SUBSTITUTION.
143   INVALID TYPE OF LOOP CONTROL VARIABLE.
144   INVALID TYPE OF EXPRESSION.
145   TYPE CONFLICT.
146   ASSIGNMENT OF FILES NOT ALLOWED.
147   LABEL TYPE INCOMPATIBLE WITH SELECTING EXPRESSION.
148   SUBRANGE BOUNDS MUST BE SCALAR.
149   INDEX TYPE MUST NOT BE INTEGER.
150   ASSIGNMENT TO THIS FUNCTION IS NOT ALLOWED.
151   ASSIGNMENT TO FORMAL FUNCTION IS NOT ALLOWED.
```

```
152   NO SUCH FIELD IN THIS RECORD.
155   CONTROL VARIABLE MUST NOT BE DECLARED ON AN INTERMEDIATE
      LEVEL.
156   MULTIDEFINED CASE LABEL.
157   RANGE OF CASE LABELS IS TOO LARGE.
158   MISSING CORRESPONDING VARIANT DECLARATION.
159   REAL OR STRING TAGFIELDS NOT ALLOWED.
160   PREVIOUS DECLARATION WAS NOT FORWARD.
161   MULTIPLE FORWARD DECLARATION.
164   SUBSTITUTION OF STANDARD PROCEDURE/FUNCTION NOT ALLOWED.
165   MULTIDEFINED LABEL.
166   MULTIDECLARED LABEL.
167   UNDECLARED LABEL.
168   UNDEFINED LABEL IN THE PREVIOUS BLOCK.
169   ERROR IN BASE SET.
170   VALUE PARAMETER EXPECTED.
172   UNDECLARED EXTERNAL FILE.
173   FORTRAN PROCEDURE OR FUNCTION EXPECTED.
174   PASCAL PROCEDURE OR FUNCTION EXPECTED.
175   MISSING FILE 'INPUT' IN PROGRAM HEADING.
176   MISSING FILE 'OUTPUT' IN PROGRAM HEADING.
177   ASSIGNMENT TO FUNCTION ALLOWED ONLY IN FUNCTION BODY.
178   MULTIDEFINED RECORD VARIANT.
179   X-OPTION OF ACTUAL PROCEDURE/FUNCTION DOES NOT MATCH
      FORMAL DECLARATION.
180   CONTROL VARIABLE MUST NOT BE FORMAL.
181   ARRAY SUBSCRIPT CALCULATION TOO COMPLICATED.
182   MAGNITUDE OF CASE LABEL IS TOO LARGE.
183   SUBRANGE OF TYPE REAL IS NOT ALLOWED.

198   ALTERNATE INPUT NOT FOUND.
199   ONLY ONE ALTERNATE INPUT MAY BE ACTIVE.

201   ERROR IN REAL CONSTANT DIGIT EXPECTED.
202   STRING CONSTANT MUST BE CONTAINED ON A SINGLE LINE.
203   INTEGER CONSTANT EXCEEDS RANGE.
204   8 OR 9 IN OCTAL NUMBER.
205   STRINGS OF LENGTH ZERO ARE NOT ALLOWED.
206   INTEGER PART OF REAL CONSTANT EXCEEDS RANGE.
207   REAL CONSTANT EXCEEDS RANGE.

250   TOO MANY NESTED SCOPES OF IDENTIFIERS.
251   TOO MANY NESTED PROCEDURES AND/OR FUNCTIONS.
255   TOO MANY ERRORS ON THIS SOURCE LINE.
256   TOO MANY EXTERNAL REFERENCES.
259   EXPRESSION TOO COMPLICATED.
260   TOO MANY EXIT LABELS.
261   TOO MANY LARGE VARIABLES.
262   NODE TO BE ALLOCATED IS TOO LARGE.
263   TOO MANY PROCEDURE/FUNCTION PARAMETERS.
264   TOO MANY PROCEDURES AND FUNCTIONS.

300   DIVISION BY ZERO.
302   INDEX EXPRESSION OUT OF BOUNDS.
303   VALUE TO BE ASSIGNED IS OUT OF BOUNDS.
304   ELEMENT EXPRESSION OUT OF RANGE.

350   ONLY THE LAST DIMENSION MAY BE PACKED.
351   ARRAY TYPE IDENTIFIER EXPECTED.
352   ARRAY VARIABLE EXPECTED.
353   POSITIVE INTEGER CONSTANT EXPECTED.

397   PACK AND UNPACK ARE NOT IMPLEMENTED FOR DYNAMIC ARRAYS.
398   IMPLEMENTATION RESTRICTION.
```

Appendix 6
GOTO Statement

In your work with computers, you may have heard of a **GOTO** statement. It is another statement in Pascal that allows a programmer to transfer control within a program. The **GOTO** statement has the effect of an immediate unconditional transfer to an indicated designation. You should not use **GOTO** statements in a Pascal program, but for the sake of completeness, you should be aware of their existence and how they work.

Early programming languages needed a branching statement; therefore, both FORTRAN and BASIC were designed using a **GOTO** statement for branching. Subsequent languages, particularly Pascal, included more sophisticated branching and looping statements. These statements led to an emphasis on structured programming, which is easier to design and read. If you are a beginning programmer and have not used the **GOTO** statement in another language, you should continue to develop your skills without including this statement. If you have already written programs in a language that uses **GOTO** statements, you should still attempt to write all Pascal programs without **GOTO** statements.

One instance in which **GOTO** statements might be appropriate is in making a quick exit from some part of the program. For example, if you are getting data from somewhere within a program and you have a check for valid data, your design could include a program segment such as

```
read data
IF (<bad data>) THEN
  BEGIN
    <write error message>;
    GOTO <end of program>
  END
ELSE
  <process data>
```

With the previous admonitions against using **GOTO** statements in mind, we will now briefly examine the form, syntax, and flow of control for these statements.

GOTO statements require the use of numerically labeled statements. Thus, your program could contain

```
LABEL
   <label 1>,
   <label 2>;
      .
      .
      .
GOTO 100;
      .
      .
      .
100: <program statement>;
      .
      .
      .
```

All labels must be declared in a label declaration section that precedes the constant definition section in a program. Each label can only be used for a single program statement. The form for the label declaration section is

```
LABEL
   ⟨label 1⟩,
   ⟨label 2⟩,
      .
      .
      .
   ⟨label n⟩;
```

Correct form for a **GOTO** statement is

```
GOTO ⟨numerical label⟩;
```

where numerical label is an integer from 1 to 9999 inclusive. Declared labels are then used with appropriate statements in a program. Proper syntax for labeling a statement is

```
⟨label⟩ : ⟨program statement⟩;
```

Consider the fragment

```
BEGIN
   read (Num);
   IF Num < 0 THEN
      GOTO 100
   ELSE
      Sum := Sum + Num;
         .
         .
         .
   100: writeln ('Data include a negative number,':40)
END.
```

In this instance, when a negative number is encountered as a data item, an appropriate message is printed and the program is terminated.

GOTO statements permit you to immediately transfer out of any control structure. As stated, we recommend you avoid the use of this statement whenever possible. However, if you must use it, use it only for an immediate exit from some point in the program; never use it to construct a loop in Pascal.

Appendix 7
Turbo Pascal Notes

This text is written using standard Pascal. The decision to use standard Pascal rather than some other version was made for three reasons.

1. Standard Pascal is still frequently used at many colleges and universities.
2. Although many different versions of Pascal are available, no single one is dominant.
3. Standard Pascal is the easiest version from which to adapt if some other version is being used.

Recently, however, Turbo Pascal has begun to grow rapidly in popularity. Turbo's popularity is a function of the increasing use of personal computers, good compiler programs, and Turbo's relatively low cost.

The second edition of this text has responded to the increasing use of Turbo Pascal by expanding this appendix on Turbo Pascal. Here, reference is made to parts of the text where specific differences occur between standard and Turbo Pascal. These differences are explained in some detail.

Using Turbo Pascal

Using a properly formatted disk containing Turbo Pascal, boot the system. When the prompt appears, enter 'TURBO' and press ⟨RETURN⟩. Next enter 'Y' or 'N' for error messages. At this stage, several options are available. Enter 'W' and you will be asked to enter a work file name. Enter 'Prac1' and press ⟨RETURN⟩. Then enter 'E' and you will be in the edit mode ready to write a program.

To see how the compiler works, input the following sample program. Enter this program exactly as written—complete with the error!

```
PROGRAM Practice;
  VAR
    A, B, Sum : integer;
  BEGIN
    A := 20
    B := 30;
```

```
        Sum := A + B;
        writeln ('Sum is', Sum:5)
    END.
```

Exit the edit mode by pressing Ctrl-K-D. Enter 'C' to compile the program. The error message

```
    "Error 85: ';' expected. Press <Esc>"
```

appears. Press ⟨Esc⟩ and you will be returned to the program in the edit mode with the cursor under the 'B' of B := 30;. Move the cursor to where the missing semicolon belongs (after 20), enter the semicolon, and press Ctrl-K-D to exit. Compile again by entering 'C'. You now have an error-free program and can run it by entering 'R'.

You can save the program by entering 'S'. It will be saved as PRAC1.PAS. You can then exit by pressing 'Q'. Prac1 is now a permanent file. If you need to use it again, enter 'TURBO' and type in 'Prac1' when a work file name is requested.

Versions 5.0 and 6.0 have significantly different environments. After leaving the edit mode, menus are available for running and compiling. You run and/or compile a program by selecting the appropriate menu choice. A little practice with these menus should make you comfortable with their use.

The remainder of this appendix consists of specific page references in bold type, followed by appropriate comments. Turbo logos (shown to the left) are used throughout the text to indicate a reference to this appendix.

Turbo Notes

Page 28: Turbo does not require a file list with the program heading.

```
    PROGRAM <name>;
```

is sufficient.

Page 35: maxint is 32767. Most versions of Turbo also include the integer data types **byte, word, shortint,** and **longint.** For those versions, the constant **longmaxint** is 2147483647.

Page 35: Most versions of Turbo also include the real data types **single, double, extended,** and **comp: single** is a floating-point type with a range of $1.5 * 10^{-45}$ to $3.4 * 10^{38}$ (positive and negative); **double** is a floating-point type with a range of $5.0 * 10^{-324}$ to $1.7 * 10^{308}$ (positive and negative); **extended** is a floating-point type with a range from $3.4 * 10^{-4932}$ to $1.1 * 10^{4932}$ (positive and negative); and **comp** is an integral type with a range from $-9.2 * 10^{18}$ to $9.2 * 10^{18}$.

Page 36: string data types may be defined. For an explanation and illustration of declaring and using strings, see the comment for page 331.

Page 37: See Turbo note for page 36.

Page 37: Default output is to the monitor. Output can be directed to the printer by using lst (short for list) within a **writeln** statement. Thus,

```
    writeln ('Hello');
```

goes to the screen and

```
    writeln (lst, 'Hello');
```

outputs to the printer.

In later versions of Turbo, the use of lst to send output to the printer is only available by linking a library procedure to your program. lst is defined in the unit Printer and is linked by:

```
    Uses Printer;
```

following the program header. Using lst, however, is not practical while debugging.

For ease in directing output between the CRT and printer, Marilyn Jussel, Kearney State College, suggests a standard procedure that allows one to select output destination without changing code. While debugging, the output goes to the screen; otherwise the output goes to the printer.

The version that requires the library unit CRT is

```
Uses CRT

PROCEDURE Output_To_Where;

  VAR
    OutFile : text;
    Choice : char;

  BEGIN

    writeln ('Do you want printer output?');
    write ('Please enter choice (Y or N)');
    readln (Choice);
    IF (upcase(Choice) = 'Y') THEN
      assign (OutFile, 'prn')
    ELSE
      AssignCRT (OutFile);  {  Procedure defined in Unit CRT  }
    rewrite (OutFile)

END;  {  of PROCEDURE Output_To_Where  }
```

The second version does not require a library unit. The only change to the code is the line following **ELSE.**

```
assign (OutFile, 'con');
```

The distinction should be made that on the screen the command

```
writeln;
```

gives a blank line, but on the printer the programmer must include the output file name:

```
writeln (OutFile)
```

Page 38: The last line of output for Example 1.1 is

```
Pittsburgh, PA15238
```

Page 40: writeln (123.456:4:3) produces 123.456.

Page 46: The **MOD** operator returns the remainder obtained by dividing its two operands; that is

```
i MOD j = i - (i DIV j) * j
```

The sign of the result of **MOD** is the same as the sign of i. An error occurs if j is zero. To better illustrate the difference, consider the expression -17 **MOD** 3. In standard Pascal, the result is 1; in Turbo Pascal, the result is -2.

Page 50:

```
writeln (maxint + 1);
```

produces

```
-32768
```

Page 60: The standard file **input** is not required as part of the heading. When omitted, the default input file is the keyboard.

Page 65: Interactive programs should use **readln** rather than **read.** In order for **read** to be used in an interactive program, a compiler directive ({$B-}) should be used. This, however, restricts editing. For best results, use separate **readln**s for character data.

Page 66: See Turbo note for page 331.

Page 136: Output in Turbo is **true**.

Page 172: **ELSE** is optional inside a **CASE** statement.

Page 173: Turbo Pascal does not include an **OTHERWISE** option for a **CASE** statement. However, an equivalent **ELSE** option is available. Syntax for the **ELSE** option is

```
CASE ⟨selector⟩ OF
   ⟨label 1⟩ : ⟨statement 1⟩;
          .
          .
          .
   ⟨label 2⟩ : ⟨statement n⟩
ELSE
   BEGIN
      ⟨statement 1⟩;
          .
          .
          .
      ⟨statement m⟩
   END {    of ELSE option    }
END {    of CASE statement    }
```

Page 200: All variables are initialized to zero as a default setting. When a loop has been exited, the loop index retains the last assigned value.

Page 263: Text files are written using the Turbo editor. You can create a data disk by using the Turbo editor in the same way as you would write a program. However, instead of program lines, you enter appropriate lines of data. When finished, you exit the editor and save the file on the disk by entering 'S'.

When this is saved on the disk, it would be listed in the directory as DATA1.PAS [unless some other designator is specified]. You can then use the data file by declaring a file of type **text** in the variable declaration section. The file name does not have to be listed in the program heading. Thus, you could have

```
PROGRAM UseData;
VAR
   DataFile : text;
```

Within the program you must then assign the file name on the directory to the declared file. This can be accomplished by

```
assign (DataFile, 'DATA.PAS');
reset (DataFile);
```

Notice that DataFile is **reset** to guarantee the pointer is at the beginning of the file. At this stage, you can use **read** or **readln** to get input from the text file DataFile. You can accomplish this by including the file name in the **read** or **readln** command. Thus, you might have

```
WHILE NOT eof(DataFile) DO
   BEGIN
      readln (DataFile, Num);
      writeln (Num)
   END;
```

When you finish reading from a text file, you should close it with a **close** command. In the previous example, this would be

```
close (DataFile);
```

eoln and **eof** can be used with text files. The text file must be included as an argument. Thus, you might have statements such as

```
        WHILE NOT eof(Data);
```
or
```
        WHILE NOT eoln(Data);
```

When reading from a text file, you must include the file name as an argument. Typical statements are

> **read** (Data, ⟨variables here⟩);
> or
> **readln** (Data, ⟨variables here⟩);

Page 265: See Turbo for Page 263.

Page 284: Subrange limits may be ignored. Assignment of a value outside the specified range will not cause a compilation error. However, since you cannot predict what value will be stored, you should not use subranges as a form of program protection. This can lead to program crashes caused by inappropriate values.

Page 341: A **string** data type is available in Turbo Pascal. Correct syntax is

```
    VAR
       Name : string;
```
or
```
    VAR
       Name : string[n];
```

for early versions of Turbo where *n* specifies the string length (from 1 through 255). With this declaration, you could have a statement such as

```
    readln (Data, Score, Name);
```

as part of a program. There are several string functions and procedures available in Turbo. They include **delete, insert, str, concat(+), copy, length, pos, val,** and **numstr.** Students working in a Turbo environment are encouraged to become familiar with each of these.

Page 342: All variables are automatically packed in Turbo. Thus, packed arrays need not be declared and procedures **pack** and **unpack** have no effect. (For a discussion of **pack** and **unpack,** see Appendix 8.)

Page 343: For the first reference, see Turbo note for page 341. In Turbo, the length of a string variable is dynamic. The actual length is determined by the current string value assigned to that variable. Therefore, even though Name may be declared as string[20], if Name is assigned 'Sue', its length will be 3.

Page 343: See Turbo note for page 341.

Page 384: Since **string** is a data type available in Turbo Pascal, packed arrays of characters are not needed. An array of **strings** can be thought of as a one-dimensional array.

Page 429: Loops are not needed for reading names when using a **string** data type. The code on this page could be replaced by

```
    WITH Student DO
      BEGIN
        read (Data, Name);
        FOR J := 1 TO 3 DO
          read (Data, Score[J]);
        readln (Data);
        Average := (Score[1] + Score[2] + Score[3] / 3)
      END;
```

Page 473: File names are not required as part of a program heading. If information is stored in a binary file named DATA, it is listed in the directory as DATA.PAS.

Assuming such a file of integers exists, the following program illustrates how the data can be accessed.

```
PROGRAM UseData;
VAR
  DataFile : FILE OF integer;
  Num : integer;
BEGIN
  assign (DataFile, 'DATA.PAS');
  reset (DataFile);
  WHILE NOT eof(DataFile) DO
    BEGIN
      read (DataFile, Num);
      writeln (Num)
    END;
  close (DataFile)
END.
```

The effect of this program is to print the integers in DATA.PAS to the screen.

Turbo Pascal permits random access of binary files. Using the procedure **seek**, a particular file component can be located by

```
seek (<file name>, <position - 1>);
```

The component can then be obtained by

```
read (<file name>, <component>);
```

Random access files can be opened for reading (**read**) and writing (**write**) at the same time. Thus, if you are updating a file, after processing a component, you reposition the pointer by

```
seek (<file name>, <position - 1>);
```

and then **write** the updated component to the file by

```
write (<file name>, <component>):
```

When you are finished, you should close the file by

```
close (<file name>);
```

Page 477: Files in Turbo may be created in two ways. Files of type **text** are created by using the Turbo editor with an appropriately named data file. Both numeric and nonnumeric data may be entered in a text file. Both **read** and **readln** may be used when retrieving data from a text file.

Binary files must be created from a program by writing to a defined file. A sample program that creates a binary file of integers from a text file follows.

```
PROGRAM FilePrac;

VAR
  Num : integer;                { Integers moved between files }
  NewFile : FILE OF integer; {  Binary file of integers       }
  OldFile : text;               {  Existing text file          }

BEGIN

  assign (OldFile, 'INTDATA.PAS');
  assign (NewFile, 'NEWDATA.PAS');
  reset (OldFile);
  rewrite (NewFile);
  writeln ('OldFile', 'Values to NewFile':29);
  writeln ('-------', '-----------------':29);
  WHILE NOT eof(OldFile) DO
    BEGIN
      readln (OldFile, Num);      {  read from the text file   }
      write (Num);                {  display the number        }
```

```
              Num := Num * 10;
              writeln (Num:20);              { display the new number    }
              write (NewFile, Num)           { write to the binary file  }
           END;
      close (OldFile);
      close (NewFile);
      reset (NewFile);
      writeln; writeln;

      {  Now display contents of the binary file.                       }

      writeln ('Values from NewFile');
      writeln ('-------------------');
      WHILE NOT eof(NewFile) DO
        BEGIN
          read (NewFile, Num);
          writeln (Num)
        END;
      close (NewFile)

 END.  { of main program  }
```

Output from this program is

```
      OldFile              Values to NewFile
      -------              -----------------
      2                    20
      4                    40
      6                    60
      8                    80
      10                   100


      Values from NewFile
      -------------------
      20
      40
      60
      80
      100
```

Page 477: get and **put** are not used in Turbo Pascal. All files are accessed using **read, readln, write,** or **writeln.** This simplifies working with files since you no longer must work with file windows and buffer variables.

Page 482: There are no internal files in Turbo Pascal.

Page 489: The following program is included as a sample of creating a file of records in Turbo. Specifically, it creates a file of records for Programming Problem 9 from Chapter 10.

```
    PROGRAM CreateDataFile;

    TYPE
      Flight = RECORD
                  FlightNumber : integer;
                  ETA : 0..2400;
                  ETD : 0..2400;
                  Orig, Dest : string[15]
               END;  { of RECORD }

    VAR
      FlightFile : FILE OF Flight;
      FlightRec : Flight;
      MoreData : boolean;
      Continue : char;
```

```
BEGIN

    assign (FlightFile, 'NewFile.pas');
    rewrite (FlightFile);
    MoreData := true;
    WHILE MoreData DO      { Get one flight record }
      BEGIN
        WITH FlightRec DO
          BEGIN
            ClrScr;
            writeln ('Enter a data line');
            writeln ('Origin        *Destination  * ETA   ETD   Flight Num');
            readln (Orig, Dest, ETA, ETD, FlightNumber)
          END;
        write (FlightFile, FlightRec);   {  write one record to the file }
        write ('Continue? y or n   ');
        readln (Continue);
        MoreData := (Continue = 'y') OR (Continue = 'Y')
      END; {  of getting data  }
    close (FlightFile);
    reset (FlightFile);     { Print contents of the binary file }

    {  Display contents of the binary file  }

    WHILE NOT eof(FlightFile) DO
      BEGIN
        read (FlightFile, FlightRec);
        WITH FlightRec DO
          writeln (Orig:12, Dest:12, ETA:5, ETD:5, FlightNumber:5)
      END

END. {  of PROGRAM  }
```

A sample run of this program produces the binary file

```
Detroit        Chicago        752  756  521
Chicago        Tampa         1157  857  911
```

Page 514: The maximum number of elements in a set is 256, and the ordinal values of the base type must be within the range 0 through 255.

Page 586: Turbo Pascal provides five predefined integer types. Each type denotes a specific subset of the whole numbers, as shown here:

Type	Range	Size
byte	0..255	8 bit
integer	$-32768..32767$	16 bit
longint	$-2147483648..2147483647$	32 bit
shortint	$-128..127$	8 bit
word	0..65535	16 bit

Page 589: Turbo's Random function may be used to return either a real or integer random number.

```
Syntax:
  Random [ ( Range: word) ]
```

If the optional word argument is used, then the result is a word random number within the range $0 <= x <$ Range. For a description of the word data type in Turbo, see the previous Turbo note. If the optional word argument is omitted, then a real random number in the range $0 <= x < 1$ is returned.

To initialize the random number generator, call Randomize, or assign a value to the global Turbo variable RandSeed.

Page 600: Turbo provides its own String data type with a library of operations. The caution here is that this makes String a reserved word in Turbo. Hence, if you work in Turbo, you will need to identify the String ADT in Chapter 13 by a different name.

Page 613: UNITs are the basis of modular programming with ADTs in Turbo Pascal. You use UNITs to create libraries and to divide large programs into logically related modules. The syntax for defining a UNIT file is as follows:

```
UNIT identifier;            { Heading }

INTERFACE                   { Public symbols that define the interface for your ADT }
  USES . . . ;              { This clause specifies other UNITs used by this one }
  CONST . . . ;             { Constants }
  TYPE . . . ;              { Types }
  VAR . . . ;               { Variables }
  PROCEDURE . . . ;         { Procedure headers for provided operations }
  FUNCTION . . . ;          { Function headers for provided operations }

IMPLEMENTATION              { Private symbols that define your implementation of the
                              ADT. Users of your ADT cannot access symbols in the
                              IMPLEMENTATION section.   }

  USES . . . ;
  CONST . . . ;             { Constants }
  TYPE . . . ;              { Types }
  VAR . . . ;               { Variables }
  PROCEDURE                 { Procedure definitions to implement headers specified
  . . . ;                     in INTERFACE section }
  FUNCTION . . . ;          { Function definitions to implement headers specified in
                              INTERFACE section }

BEGIN                       { Initialization necessary for implementation of ADT }
  Statement;                { Statements }
  . . .
  Statement
END.
```

Page 630: Unfortunately, Turbo does not obey the syntax of standard Pascal when it comes to passing procedures as parameters to other procedures. Instead of directly including information about the number and type of a procedure's parameters in the formal parameter list of the procedure that is receiving another procedure as a parameter, Turbo requires that you define a type that includes this information. For instance, the following type declarations define a FUNCTION TYPE PrecedesRelation.

```
TYPE
  ElementType = integer;
  Sortarray = ARRAY [1..IndexLimit] of ElementType;
  { The following type is for the function parameter }
  PrecedesRelation = FUNCTION (A, B : ElementType) : boolean;
                  { Given:   Two values to compare                  }
                  { Return:  True if A precedes B in order          }
                  {          relationship on ElementType            }
```

Then, in the function that is to receive a function or procedure as a parameter, this type identifier must be used. The following example illustrates this usage.

```
PROCEDURE Sort ( VAR A : SortArray;
                 N : integer;
                 Precedes : PrecedesRelation);
```

```
{  Given:     Array of values to be returned in order     }
{             according to Precedes relation and N, the   }
{             number of values in array.                  }
{  Task:      Sort the array using a sort algorithm       }
{  Return:    The array arranged in order by the Precedes }
{             relation passed in as parameter             }
```

Finally, note that Turbo requires that you enable the *far call model* when you are using parameters that are functions or procedures. See your Turbo reference manual as to how to set this switch in your version of the Turbo compiler.

Page 685: read and **write** must be used to access file records in Turbo. **get** and **put** are not supported in Turbo.

Page 686: Remember when using a **seek** statement in Turbo, such as

```
seek (Students, K)
```

that records in a file are numbered starting with zero. Hence, to access the fourteenth record in a file, K in the above example would be set to the value 13.

Page 693: In Turbo, an object is a data structure that contains data fields (like a record) and methods (unlike a record). These methods constitute ADT operations that are owned by the object.

The nature of this Appendix prevents any kind of detailed exposition on object-oriented programming. Briefly, the syntax would be as follows:

```
OBJECT
  <field declaration>;
  <field declaration>;
  .
  .
  .
  <method declaration>;
  <method declaration>
END;
```

For further information, you are encouraged to consult your Turbo reference manual. Note that only Turbo versions 5.5 or higher offer such object-oriented extensions.

Page 799: Refer to the previous Turbo note for page 589.

Appendix 8 Random Access File in Various Versions of Pascal

The original standard for Pascal developed by Kathleen Jensen and Niklaus Wirth (*Pascal User Manual and Report* (Berlin: Springer-Verlag, 1974)) made no provision for random (direct) access files. From the perspective of leaning structured programming concepts, this is not a serious omission. From the perspective of applying data structure concepts in the real world, however, it is a major omission. This is because most programs with a database orientation involve storing large amounts of data in files and then accessing the data by a search strategy that guarantees a quick response time. Without direct access, a tedious sequential search is the only method possible. Hence, what has emerged is that most implementors of Pascal compilers have developed their own procedures for directly accessing records that reside in a disk file. A general picture that applies in all of these various implementations appears at right.

A record from a random access file may be acted upon (for instance, updated) only when it has been retrieved as the currently available record in the main memory buffer associated with that file. (Actually, application programmers may think of the currently available record and the file's buffer as coinciding, though this is an oversimplification that can affect the efficiency of the search technique being considered. See Chapter 23 for a discussion of this point.) Hence the problem of programming in Pascal with random access files becomes one of being able to

1. Retrieve the Kth record from the file as the currently available record in main memory (where K is an arbitrary positive integer less than or equal to the number of records in the file).

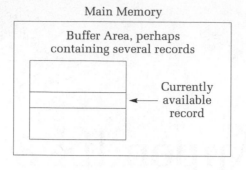

2. Update the currently available record in main memory.
3. Write the currently available record in memory to the Kth position in the file.

Step 2 may typically be accomplished by using standard Pascal's up-arrow notation for a file variable. (See Chapter 12 for a discussion of this notation.) For example,

```
F↑.IDNumber := 4918;
```

will assign the value 4918 to the IDNumber field of the record currently available in main memory. Note that this assignment is only made in memory; nothing is altered in the file until this record is written out to the appropriate file position.

Thus, only steps 1 and 3 require special nonstandard Pascal procedures. Once such procedures exist, search algorithms that apply to arrays may also be appropriately applied to random access files. Hence, a random access file may be conceptually thought of as a large array that resides on disk.

In the following examples, we assume that *F* is a Pascal file variable associated with records of an appropriate type (other than text). For each implementation of Pascal specified, we describe how to open, retrieve, and update records for random access file processing. If you do not see your system specified, the examples should nonetheless provide points of comparison to help you understand the local documentation describing similar facilities for your environment.

DEC's VAX-Pascal

- To open a file for random access:

```
open (F, access_method := direct, organization := relative);
```

- To fetch Kth record as currently available record:

```
find(F, K);
```

- To write currently available record to Kth position

```
locate(F, K)
put(F);
```

or

```
update(F); { if file already positioned at Kth record }
```

Macintosh and Lightspeed Pascal for the Apple Macintosh Family

- To open a file for random access:
  ```
  open(F, filename);
  ```
- To fetch Kth record as currently available record:
  ```
  seek(F, K);
  ```
- To write currently available record to Kth file position:
  ```
  seek(F, K);
     .
     .
     .
  put(F);
  ```

Oregon Software's (OMSI) Pascal-1 and Pascal-2

- To open a file for random access:
  ```
  reset(F, filename specified with '=seek' switch);
  ```
- To retrieve Kth record as currently available record:
  ```
  seek (F, K)
  ```
- To write currently available record to Kth file position:
  ```
  seek (F, K)
    .
    . [ Appropriate updating ]
    .
  put(F);
  ```

Turbo Pascal

- To open a file for random access:
  ```
  assign(F, filename);
  resest(F);
  ```
  (Keep in mind that in Turbo Pascal, records are numbered beginning at 0.)
- To fetch Kth record into TempRec as the currently available record:
  ```
  seek(F, K);
  read(F, TempRec);
  ```
  (In Turbo, the record is accessed in a declared record location, such as TempRec, instead of by accessing the buffer directly via F↑.)
- To write the currently available record in TempRec to Kth file position:
  ```
  seek(F, K);
  write (F, TempRec);
  ```

(For further information on Turbo Pascal, see Appendix 7.)

Glossary

abstract data type (ADT) A form of abstraction that arises from the use of defined types. An ADT consists of a class of objects, a defined set of properties of those objects, and a set of operations for processing the objects.

abstraction The description of data structures at a conceptual level, apart from their implementation using a particular technique and language.

abstract syntax tree *See* **parse tree**.

acceptance testing That testing phase in which the full system is released to the end users for their evaluation.

accumulator A variable used for the purpose of summing successive values of some other variable.

actual parameter A variable or expression contained in a procedure or function call and passed to that procedure or function. *See also* **formal parameter**.

Ada A newer, package-oriented programming language developed by the U.S. Defense Department.

address Once called address of a memory location, this is an integer value that the computer can use to reference a location. *See also* **value** and **pointer**.

ADT *See* **abstract data type**.

ADT implementation rule An implementation of an ADT must provide an interface that is entirely consistent with the operations specified in the ADT's definition.

ADT use rule An algorithm that uses an ADT should access variables of that abstract data type only through the operations provided in the ADT definition.

algorithm A finite sequence of effective statements that, when applied to the problem, will solve it.

analysis phase The first phase of the software system life cycle in which the systems analyst determines the user's needs and develops formal specifications describing the proposed system and its requirements.

ancestor A tree node which is hierarchically related to another tree node at a lower level in the tree.

application software Programs designed for a specific use.

argument A value or expression passed in a function or procedure call.

arithmetic/logic unit (ALU) The part of the central processing unit (CPU) that performs arithmetic operations and evaluates expressions.

array A structured variable designed to handle data of the same type.

array index The relative position of the components of an array.

array of records An array whose component type is a record.

artificial intelligence (AI) The field of computer science in which the goal is to program the computer to mimic intelligent human behavior.

ASCII collating sequence The American Standard Code for Information Interchange ordering for a character set.

assembler A computer program that automatically converts assembly language instructions to machine language.

assembly language A computer language that allows words and symbols to be used in an unsophisticated manner to accomplish simple tasks.

assertion Special comments used with selection and repetition that state what you expect to happen and when certain conditions will hold.

assignment statement A method of putting values into memory locations.

assignment, string The copying of one string variable to another.

automatic program synthesis Situation in which one computer program can be given the specifications for another computer program, generate the code to satisfy those specifications, and then prove the correctness of that code.

Backus-Naur grammar A standard form for defining the formal syntax of a language.

batch input Input for a program being run in batch mode. Also referred to as stream input.

batch processing A technique of executing the program by reading data from a file that has been created. User interaction with the computer is not required during execution. Also referred to as stream input.

BEGIN . . . END block The segment of code between **BEGIN** and **END** that, when a compound statement is executed within a program, is treated as a single statement.

best case The arrangement of data items prior to beginning a sort procedure that allows the sort procedure to finish in the least amount of time for that particular set of items. *See also* **worst case.**

big-O analysis A technique in which the time and space requirements of an algorithm are estimated in order of magnitude terms.

big-O notation Saying that an algorithm is O($f(n)$) indicates that the function $f(n)$ may be useful in characterizing how efficiently the algorithm performs for large n. For such n, we are assured that the operations required by the algorithm will be bounded by a constant times $f(n)$.

bin sort *See* **radix sort.**

binary buddy system System used to coalesce blocks of memory in which all blocks have size 2^k for some integer k.

binary code A term often used as a synonym for machine language.

binary digit A digit, either 0 or 1, in the binary number system. Program instructions are stored in memory using a sequence of binary digits. Binary digits are called bits.

binary search The process of examining a middle value of a sorted array to see which half contains the value in question and halving until the value is located.

binary search tree A binary tree with the ordering property.

binary tree A tree such that each node can point to at most two children.

binary tree index A binary tree with the ordering property used as an index for the positions of keys in a random access file.

binary tree search A search algorithm driven by the hierarchical relationships of data items in a tree with the ordering property.

binding time The time at which a program variable is bound to a particular value. This can occur either at compile time or run time.

bit *See* **binary digit.**

black box testing The method of testing a module in which the tester is aware of only what the module is supposed to do, not the method of implementation or internal logic. *See also* **white box testing.**

block A contiguous area on a magnetic disk capable of storing a fixed amount of data.

block A program in Pascal can be thought of as a heading and a block. The block contains an optional declaration part and a compound statement. The block structure for a subprogram is a subblock. *See also* **subblock.**

blocked queue In an operating system, the queue of processes that have requested a resource currently owned by another process.

Boolean expression An expression whose value is either true or false. *See also* **compound Boolean expression** and **simple Boolean expression.**

bottom-up testing Independent testing of modules.

boundary conditions Values that separate two logical possibilities. These are important cases to check when testing a module.

boundary folding A variation on shift folding; in boundary folding, the digits in every other numeric section are reversed before the addition is performed.

boundary tag buddy system System for coalescing blocks of memory in which each block contains bookkeeping information at both its upper and lower boundaries.

branch In a tree, a link between a parent and its child node.

breadth-first traversal A visiting of all nodes in a graph; it proceeds from each node by first visiting all nodes adjacent to that node.

B-tree An efficient, flexible index structure often used in data-base management systems on random access files.

bubble sort Rearranges elements of an array until they are in either ascending or descending order. Consecutive elements are compared to move (bubble) the elements to the top or bottom accordingly during each pass. *See also* **heap sort, insertion sort, merge sort, quick sort, radix sort, selection sort,** and **shell sort.**

bucket In bucket hashing, an contiguous region of storage locations.

bucket hashing Method of handling collisions in which the hashing function sends the key to a bucket of locations rather than a single location. The key is then placed by performing a sequential search within the bucket.

buddy system Name applied to a variety of techniques which coalesce blocks of memory being returned from users.

buffer variable The actual vehicle through which values are passed to or from a file component.

built-in function *See* **standard function.**

bus A group of wires imprinted on a circuit board to facilitate communication between components of a computer.

byte A sequence of bits used to encode a character in memory. *See also* **word.**

call Any reference to a subprogram by an executable statement. Also referred to as invoke.

central processing unit (CPU) A major hardware component that consists of the arithmetic/logic unit (ALU) and the control unit.

character set The list of characters available for data and program statements. *See also* **collating sequence.**

child node A node that descends from another node in a tree.

children Nodes pointed to by an element in a tree.

circular linked list A linked list in which the last node of the list points to the first node in the list.

class object In object-oriented programming, the bundling of both the data fields and the operations for an ADT into the ADT's declaration.

cluster In a linked list implementation of a character string, the placement of more than one character per data node forms a cluster of data.

clustering Occurs when a hashing function is biased toward the placement of keys in a given region of the storage space.

coalescing The process by which two adjacent available blocks of memory are combined into one larger block.

code (writing) The process of writing executable statements that are part of a program to solve a problem.

coding phase The third phase of the software system life cycle. The code necessary to implement the system design specifications is produced in this phase.

cohesive subprogram A subprogram designed to accomplish a single task.

collating sequence The particular order sequence for a character set used by a machine. *See also* **ASCII** and **EBCDIC.**

collision Condition in which more than one key hashes to the same position with a given hashing function.

column major Implementation of a two-dimensional array as a one-dimensional array so that the columns are arranged in sequential order with all entries of the same column being adjacent.

comment A nonexecutable statement used to make a program more readable.

compaction The process of collecting all fragments of available memory and moving them to one end of memory to create one large block.

compatible (type) Variables that have the same base type. A value parameter and its argument must be of compatible type. *See also* **identical (type).**

compilation error An error detected when the program is being compiled. A complete list of compilation error messages is set forth in Appendix 5. *See also* **design error, run-time error,** and **syntax error.**

compiler A computer program that automatically converts instructions in a high-level language to machine language.

compiler symbol table A table kept by a compiler; it contains the identifiers used in the source program currently being compiled.

component of a file One element of the file data type.

component of a linked list *See* **node.**

component of an array One element of the array data type.

compound Boolean expression Refers to the complete expression when logical connectives and negation are used to generate Boolean values. *See also* **Boolean expression** and **simple Boolean expression.**

compound statement Uses the reserved words **BEGIN** and **END** to make several simple statements into a single compound statement.

computer graphics The use of computers to produce pictures.

concatenation, string The joining together of two character strings.

concurrent updating When two users each update the same record of a file at the same time.

conditional statement *See* **selection statement.**

constant The contents of a memory location whose contents cannot be changed.

constant definition section The section where program constants are defined for subsequent use.

control structure A structure that controls the flow of execution of program statements.

control unit The part of the central processing unit (CPU) that controls the operation of the rest of the computer.

counter A variable used to count the number of times some process is completed.

coupling The amount of interaction between a pair of modules.

cubic algorithm A polynomial algorithm in which the highest nonzero term is n^3.

data The particular characters that are used to represent information in a form suitable for storage, processing, and communication.

data about data Data that a program stores (for example, a pointer) in order to keep track of the data it is designed to be storing.

data abstraction The separation between the conceptual definition of a data structure and its eventual implementation.

data flow diagram A graphic tool used by a systems analyst to represent data flow and transformations in a conceptual process. Also referred to as a bubble diagram.

data integrity The problem of ensuring that no data are lost or corrupted due to concurrent updating.

data movement The physical transfer of data stored in computer memory from one location to another.

data type A formal description of the set of values that a variable can have.

data validation The process of examining data prior to use of the data in a program.

deadlock An infinite wait state in which two processes each own system resources the other needs and will not release these until they have obtained the remaining resources they need. Also referred to as fatal embrace.

debugging The process of eliminating errors or "bugs" from a program.

declaration section The section used to declare (name) all symbolic constants, data types, variables, and subprograms that are necessary to the program.

decrement To decrease the value of a variable.

deletion, string In text editing applications, removing a substring from the middle of string.

density The density is the number of storage locations used divided by the number of total storage locations available.

density-dependent search technique Search technique whose efficiency is determined solely by the density of the data.

depth-first traversal A visiting of all nodes in a graph; this traversal proceeds from each node by probing as deeply as possible along one path leading from that node.

design error An error such that a program runs, but unexpected results are produced. Also referred to as a logic error. *See also* **compilation error, run-time error,** and **syntax error.**

design phase Second phase of the software system life cycle. In this phase, a relatively detailed design plan is created from the formal specifications of the system as produced in the analysis phase.

difference The difference of set A and set B is A − B where A − B contains the elements that are in A but not in B. *See also* **intersection, subset,** and **union.**

digit/character extraction In creating a hashing function, the process of removing from a key those digits or characters that may bias the results of the hashing function.

digraph A graph in which some edges exist only in one direction.

diminishing increment sort A sort in which the number of segments on which the sort works on any one pass decreases with each successive pass. *See also* **shell sort.**

directional graph *See* **digraph.**

disk file A file that resides on a secondary storage medium (usually a magnetic disk) rather than in main memory.

division-remainder technique A technique used in creating hashing functions to ensure that the result will be a valid output. It uses the **MOD** function to scale the value into the proper range. *See also* **integer arithmetic operations.**

documentation The insertion of explanatory remarks into the program code to make maintenance of the program easier.

dominant term The highest power of n in a polynomial. For large n, the behavior of the entire polynomial will approach the behavior of the polynomial that contains only that term.

doubly-linked list A linked list in which each node has two pointers instead of one. One pointer points to the node preceding that node in the list and the other points to the node following that node in the list.

driver *See* **driver module.**

driver module A module used in testing another module. The driver module calls on the module being tested, sends it the values it needs, and then reports the values returned from that module.

dummy header A node preceding the first actual data node in a list and often containing information about the list.

dynamic memory manangement The allocation and reclamation of computer memory locations as necessary during program execution.

dynamic structure A data structure that may expand or contract during execution of a program.

dynamic variable Frequently designed as Ptr^ or Ptr ↑ , a dynamic variable is a variable accessed by a pointer variable.

EBCDIC collating sequence The Extended Binary Coded Decimal Interchange Code ordering for a character set.

echo checking A debugging technique in which values of variables and input data are displayed during program execution.

edge A direct connection between two nodes in graph.

effective statement A clear, unambiguous instruction that can be carried out.

efficiency ratio For a sparse table implementation method, the efficiency ratio is the number of storage locations used by that method divided by the number of storage locations used by standard row-major form.

element of an array *See* **component of an array.**

element of a set A value that has been assigned to a set.

embedded length implementation An implementation of the string ADT in which the length of the string is stored and maintained as part the record encapsulating the string.

empty set A set containing no elements. Also called a null set.

empty statement A semicolon used to indicate that no action is to be taken. Also referred to as a null statement.

encapsulation Grouping into a single record description all those data items necessary to implement an ADT.

encapsulation principle Whenever the implementation of an ADT involves several data items, these data items should be grouped into a record by which the ADT is identified to high-level logic.

end-of-file marker (eof) A special marker inserted by the machine to indicate the end of the data file. In this text it is represented by a black square (■).

end-of-line marker (eoln) A special marker inserted by the machine to indicate the end of a line in the data. In this text it is represented by a black column (▮).

entrance controlled loop *See* **pretest loop.**

enumerated data type A data type that is defined in the **TYPE** definition section by the programmer. Also referred to as user-defined data type.

equivalence classes A partitioning of all the logical possibilities that can be checked when testing a module. All test cases within a single equivalence class are identical from the standpoint of the logic of the module.

error *See* **compilation error, design error, run-time error,** and **syntax error.**

executable section Contains the statements that cause the computer to do something. Starts with the reserved word **BEGIN** and concludes with the reserved word **END.**

executable statement The basic unit of grammar in Pascal consisting of valid identifiers, standard identifiers, reserved words, numbers, and/or characters, together with appropriate punctuation.

execute To perform a program step-by-step.

exit controlled loop *See* **posttest loop.**

expert system Program able to reason as an expert in a limited domain world.

exponential algorithm An algorithm whose efficiency is dominated by a term of the form a^n.

exponential form *See* **floating point.**

extended IF statement Nested selection where additional **IF . . . THEN . . . ELSE** statements are used in the **ELSE** option. *See also* **nested IF statement.**

external file A file used to store data in secondary storage between runs of a program. *See also* **internal file.**

external sort A sort in which the list being sorted resides in a file rather than in memory.

factorial The product of the first N positive integers (denoted N!).

fatal embrace *See* **deadlock.**

Fibonacci buddy system System of coalescing blocks of memory in which all blocks of memory have a size corresponding to one of the numbers in the Fibonacci sequence.

field A component of a record.

field width The phrase used to describe the number of columns used for various output. *See also* **formatting.**

FIFO *See* **queue.**

file A data structure that consists of a sequence of components all of the same type.

file buffer An area in main memory associated with a file; the file buffer is capable of storing exactly one record from that file.

file window A term used in this book, though not designated by Pascal, to indicate an imaginary window through which values of a file component can be transferred.

finite state automata Algorithms driven by a table indexed by the possible states that can exist and the possible categories of input characters are called finite state algorithms. Machines that operate under such algorithms are called finite state automata.

finite state machine A method that conveniently employs enumerated types to perform a robustness check on strings of characters entered by a user.

first-in, first-out (FIFO) *See* **queue.**

fixed length method A method of storing strings in which a fixed amount of space is allocated for each string regardless of its actual length.

fixed repetition loop A loop used if the number of times a segment of code needs to be repeated is known in advance. **FOR . . . TO . . . DO** is a fixed repetition loop. Also referred to as an iterated loop.

fixed parts Fields in a record that exist for all records of a particular type. *See also* **variant part.**

fixed point A method of writing decimal numbers where the decimal is placed where it belongs in the number. *See also* **floating point.**

floating point A method for writing numbers in scientific notation to accommodate numbers that may have very large or very small values. Exactly one nonzero digit must appear on the left of the decimal. *See also* **fixed point.**

folding A method of constructing a hashing function in cases where the key is not an integer value whereby the nonnumeric characters are removed and the remaining digits are combined to produce an integer value.

FOR loop A fixed repetition loop causing a fragment of code to be executed a predetermined number of times. **FOR . . . TO . . . DO** and **FOR . . . DOWNTO . . . DO** are FOR loops.

formal parameter A variable, declared and used in a procedure or function declaration, that is replaced by an actual parameter when the procedure or function is called.

formal verification The use of the basic principles and axioms of logic to produce a proof of the correctness of an algorithm.

formatting Designating the desired field width when printing integers, reals, Boolean values, and character strings. *See also* **field width.**

forward reference A method of listing a subprogram heading without writing the subprogram. This allows a subprogram to be referenced by other subprograms before it appears as a complete subprogram in the list of subprograms.

fragmentation problem Problem faced by an operating system where after frequent allocation of memory to and reclamation of memory from users, the overall pattern of available memory is one of relatively small, disconnected fragments of available space.

front pointer The pointer to the front of a queue.

function *See* **standard function** and **user-defined function.**

functionally cohesive A functionally cohesive module achieves one particular predefined task without having unexpected side effects on the performance of other modules in the system.

general list A collection of data items, all of the same type, which are related to each other by their relative position in the list.

general tree A set of nodes that is either empty or has a designated node (called the root) from which descend zero or more subtrees.

generalized nested loops Nested loops whose nesting depth is determined at run-time using recursive logic.

global identifier An identifier that can be used by the main program and all subprograms in a program.

global variable *See* **global identifier.**

graph A set of data elements called nodes and the paths between those data elements called edges.

halting problem Problem concerned with determining whether or not a given program will terminate or loop indefinitely when provided with a given set of input data.

hardware The actual computing machine and its support devices.

hashing A density-dependent search technique in which the key for a given data item is transformed using a hashing function to produce the address in which that item is stored in memory.

hashing function A key-to-address transformation.

head pointer A pointer to the head or front of the list.

heap The portion of computer memory not required to store the program instructions, predeclared data storage locations, or various operating system requirements. The heap contains the memory used for dynamic memory requests.

heap A binary tree with the heap property.

heap property A binary tree has the heap property when the data at any given node are greater than or equal to the data in its left and right subtrees.

heap sort Sort in which the array is treated like the array implementation of a binary tree and the items are repeatedly manipulated to create a heap from which the root is removed and added to the sorted portion of the array. *See also* **bubble sort, insertion, merge sort, quick sort, radix sort, selection sort,** and **shell sort.**

height balancing A technique for ensuring that an ordered binary tree remains as full as possible in form.

heterogeneous A set of elements is heterogeneous if the elements are not all of the same type.

heuristics Rules of thumb which cut down on the number of possible choices to examine. They often lead to quick solutions but do not guarantee a solution the way an algorithm does.

hierarchy A relationship between nodes in which one is viewed as above or prior to another.

high-level language Any programming language that uses words and symbols to make it relatively easy to read and write a program. *See also* **assembly language** and **machine language.**

higher-dimensional array An array of more than two dimensions.

homogeneous A set of elements is homogeneous if the elements are all of the same type.

identical (type) Variables that are declared with the same type identifier. A variable parameter and its argument must be of identical type.

identifiers Words that must be created according to a well-defined set of rules but can have any meaning subject to these rules. *See also* **standard identifiers.**

implementation The process representing the abstract model of the system and its abstract data types in terms of declarations and instructions in a particular computer language.

index *See* **array index** or **loop index.**

indexed sequential access method (ISAM) The most common method of indexed sequential search.

indexed sequential search Use of a partial index based on disk-dependent factors to find the proper portion of the disk on which to sequentially search for the key.

index sort Sorting an array by ordering the indices of the components rather than exchanging the components.

index type The data type used for specifying the range for the index of an array. The index type can be any ordinal data type that specifies an initial and final value.

inductive assertion A method of formally proving the correctness of an algorithm by using an inductive proof.

infinite loop A loop in which the controlling condition is not changed in such a manner to allow the loop to terminate.

infix Algebraic notation in which the arithmetic operator appears between the two operands upon which it will be applied.

infix priority Function to hierarchically rank algebraic operators in order of precedence.

information hiding Characteristic of a package which allows it to be used by a calling program without that program requiring knowledge of how the package achieves the implementation.

inorder predecessor The node preceding a given node in an inorder tree traversal.

inorder successor The node following a given node in an inorder tree traversal.

inorder threads Pointers to the inorder predecessor and inorder successor of a node.

inorder traversal A binary tree traversal in which at any node, that node's left subtree is visited first, then that node is processed, and finally that node's right subtree is visited.

input Data obtained by a program during its execution. *See also* **batch input** and **interactive input.**

input assertion A precondition for a loop.

input device A device that provides information to the computer. Typical devices are keyboards, disk drives, card readers, and tape drives. *See also* **I/O device** and **output device.**

insertion rule For binary trees, rule whereby a new item is placed in the left subtree of an item greater than it or in the right subtree of an item less than it.

insertion sort Sorts an array of elements in either ascending or descending order. Starts with an empty array and inserts elements one at a time in their proper order. *See also* **bubble sort, heap sort, merge sort, quick sort, radix sort, selection sort,** and **shell sort.**

insertion, string In text editing applications, placing one string in the middle of another string.

instance In object-oriented programming, a specifically declared variable that belongs to a particular class of objects.

integer arithmetic operations Operations allowed on data of type **integer.** This includes the operations of addition, subtraction, multiplication, **MOD,** and **DIV** to produce integer answers.

interactive input A method of getting data into the program from the keyboard. User interaction is required during execution.

interface A formal statement of how communication occurs between subprograms, the main driver, and other subprograms.

interface for an ADT A collection of Pascal procedure and function headers for the operations which act on ADT objects.

internal file A file, also called a temporary or scratch file, that is used for processing only and not saved in secondary storage. *See also* **external file.**

internal sort A sort in which the list being sorted resides in memory.

intersection The intersection of set A and set B is A * B where A * B contains the elements that are in both A and B. *See also* **difference, subset,** and **union.**

invariant expression An assertion that is true before the loop and after each iteration of the loop.

invoke *See* **call.**

I/O device Any device that allows information to be transmitted to or from a computer. *See also* **input device** and **output device.**

iterated loop *See* **fixed repetition loop.**

iteration *See* **loops.**

key Field in a general list that is used to order or access elements of the list.

keyed list A collection of records, each of which is the same type. The records in the list are organized around a designated key field. This key field must take on a unique value for each record and have a well-defined ordering. The records are to be viewed as arranged in logical order by this key field.

keyed ordering Ordering imposed on the entries in a list by the value of a key field.

key-to-address transformation Transformation in which the key of the data item is transformed to provide the address at which the data are actually stored.

keywords Either reserved words or predefined identifiers.

last-in, first-out (LIFO) *See* **stack.**

leaf In a tree, a node that has no children.

length (of an array) The number of components of an array.

level All nodes in a tree with the same length path from the root node.

lexical analysis The task of recognizing valid language tokens in an incoming stream of characters.

LIFO *See* **stack.**

linear algorithm A polynomial algorithm in which the highest nonzero term is n.

linear collision processing Method of handling a collision in which the storage space is searched sequentially from the location of the collision for an available location where the new key can be placed.

linear ordering Any ordering of data in which there is an identifiable first element, second element, and so forth.

linear representation (of binary tree) An implementation of a binary tree in an array. For a given node stored at index position K, that node's left child is at position 2 * K, and the right child is at position 2 * K + 1.

linear search *See* **sequential search.**

link A pointer from one node to another.

linked collision processing Method of handling a collision in which the second key is stored in a linked list located in an overflow area.

linked list A collection of elements called nodes, each of which contains a data portion and a pointer to the node which follows that one in the linear ordering of the list.

linked representation An implementation of a binary tree in which pointer fields are used to reference the right and left child of a node in the tree (as opposed to the linear representation of a binary tree).

LISP (LISt Processor) A highly-recursive computer programming language used heavily in artificial intelligence (AI).

list traversal The process of sequentially visiting each node in a list.

local identifier An identifier that is restricted to use within a subblock of a program.

local variable *See* **local identifier.**

logarithmic algorithm An algorithm whose efficiency is dominated by a term of the form $\log_a n$.

logic error *See* **design error.**

logical operator Either logical connective (**AND, OR**) or negation (**NOT**).

logical order An ordering of data items according to some defined criterion such as alphabetic, increasing numeric, and so forth. That logical order of the data may or may not be the physical order of the data as stored in the computer.

logically sorted Data have been logically sorted when pointers to the data have been sorted, even though the data itself have not been touched. Hence, items that the sort places consecutively need not be physically adjacent.

$\log_2 n$ search algorithm A search algorithm whose efficiency is dominated by a term of the form $\log_2 n$.

loop goal expression *See* **invariant expression.**

loop index Variable used for control values in a **FOR** loop.

loop invariant An assertion that expresses a relationship between variables that remain constant throughout all iterations of the loop.

loops Program statements that cause a process to be repeated. *See also* **FOR loop, REPEAT . . . UNTIL loop,** and **WHILE . . . DO loop.**

loop variant An assertion whose truth changes between the first and final execution of the loop.

loop verification The process of guaranteeing that a loop performs its intended task.

low-level language *See* **assembly language.**

machine language This language is used directly by the computer in all its calculations and processing.

main block The part of a program consisting of both the declaration and executable sections.

main driver The main program when subprograms are used to accomplish specific tasks.

main memory Memory contained in the computer. *See also* **memory** and **secondary memory device.**

main unit A computer's main unit contains the central processing unit (CPU) and the main (primary) memory; it is hooked to an input device and an output device.

mainframe Large computers typically used by major companies and universities. *See also* **microcomputer** and **minicomputer.**

maintenance phase The fifth phase of the software system life cycle. In this phase, changes must be made in the original program either to fix errors discovered by the users of the program or to meet new user needs.

mapping function A function that transforms row-column array coordinates to the linear address of that array entry.

master file An existing external file.

maxint The largest integer constant available to a particular system.

memory The ordered sequence of storage cells that can be accessed by address. Instructions and variables of an executing program are temporarily held here. *See also* **main memory** and **secondary memory device.**

memory location A storage cell that can be accessed by address. *See also* **memory.**

merge The process of combining lists. Typically refers to files or arrays.

merge sort Sort in which the array is repeatedly split in half and then these pieces are merged together. *See also* **bubble sort, heap sort, insertion sort, quick sort, radix sort, selection sort,** and **shell sort.**

message In object-oriented programming, a signal to perform an operation on an object.

message-passing In object-oriented programming, one object's telling another object to perform an operation that is part of its encapsulation.

method of inductive assertions Method of formally verifying the correctness of an algorithm by identifying the input assertions, output assertions, and loop invariants of the algorithm and constructing a verification proof by mathematical induction.

microcomputer A personal computer with relatively limited memory, generally used by one person at a time. *See also* **mainframe** and **minicomputer.**

minicomputer A small version of a mainframe computer. It can be used by several people at once. *See also* **mainframe** and **microcomputer.**

mixed-mode Expressions containing data of both **integer** and **real** types; the value will be given as a real and not as an integer.

Modula-2 A newer, package-oriented programming language developed by Nicklaus Wirth (of Pascal fame).

modular development The process of developing an algorithm using modules. *See also* **module.**

modular specifications A description of the data received by, information returned from, and logic of a module within a system's design.

modular structure chart A graphic tool used by software designers to display the hierarchical relationships among the modules of the software system.

modular testing A method of testing in which each module is tested immediately after it has been completed rather than when the entire system has been completed.

modularity The property possessed by a program which is written using modules.

module An independent unit that is part of a larger development. Usually a procedure or function. *See also* **modular development.**

module specifications A description of data received, information returned, and logic used in the module.

multilinked list A linked list in which each node has two or more link fields.

natural language A language by which humans normally communicate (such as English), as opposed to a formal programming language (such as Pascal).

negation The use of the logical operator **NOT** to negate the Boolean value of an expression.

nested IF statement A selection statement used within another selection statement.

nested loop A loop as one of the statements in the body of another loop.

nested record A record as a field in another record.

nested selection Any combination of selection statements within selection statements. *See also* **selection statement.**

nested subprograms Functions or procedures within functions or procedures.

network A graph in which the edges have weight values associated with them.

node One data item in a linked list, tree, graph, or network.

null set *See* **empty set.**

null statement *See* **empty statement.**

numerical analysis A field concerned with obtaining numerical answers to mathematical problems which involve much computation.

object code *See* **object program.**

object-oriented programming A programming paradigm in which a data object is viewed as the owner of operations, as opposed to procedural programming in which an operation is passed data objects as actual parameters. Object-oriented programming emphasizes the ADT approach and allows the users of an ADT to extend the operations of an ADT library in a convenient and efficient fashion.

object program The machine code version of the source program.

opened for reading Positions a pointer at the beginning of a file for the purpose of reading from the file.

opened for writing Positions a pointer at the beginning of a file for the purpose of writing to the file.

opening a file Positions a pointer at the beginning of a file. *See also* **opened for reading** and **opened for writing.**

operating system A large program that allows the user to communicate with the hardware.

operations Actions to be performed on an abstract data type.

order of magnitude Power of ten. Two numbers have the same order of magnitude if their representations in scientific notation have identical exponents to designate the power of ten.

ordering A means of arranging the elements in a list.

ordering property In a binary tree, the data in each node of the tree are greater than or equal to all of the data in that node's left subtree and less than or equal to all of the data in its right subtree.

ordinal data type A data type ordered in some association with the integers; each integer is the ordinal of its associated character.

output Information that is produced by a program.

output assertion A postcondition for a loop.

output device A device that allows you to see the results of a program. Typically it is a monitor or printer. *See* **input device** and **I/O device.**

overflow In arithmetic operations, a value may be too large for the computer's memory location. A meaningless value may be assigned or an error message may result. *See also* **underflow.**

overflow area In linked collision processing, the area in which keys that cause collisions are placed.

packed array An array that has had data placed in consecutive bytes.

packed array implementation An implementation of the string ADT in which no data other than the characters composing the string are stored in the encapsulation of the string.

parallel arrays Arrays of the same length but with different component data types.

parallel processing The use of more than one processor to execute parts of a program concurrently. The effect is that these parts are completed in parallel rather than in sequence.

parameter *See* **argument.**

parameter list A list of parameters. An actual parameter list is contained in the procedure or function call. A formal parameter list is contained in the procedure or function heading.

parent In a tree, the node that is pointing to its children.

parse tree Tree representation of the syntactic structure of a source program produced by a compiler. Also referred to as abstract syntax tree.

parser A program that checks the syntax of an expression and represents that expression in a unique form.

parser generator A program that can take the input grammar for a language and produce the parser for that language.

parsing The procedure of checking the syntax of an expression and representing it in one unique form.

partition In quick sort, the process of moving the pivot to the location where it belongs in the sorted array and arranging the remaining data items to the left of the pivot if they are less than or equal to the pivot and to the right if they are greater than the pivot.

passed by reference When variable parameters are used in subprograms.

path A sequence of edges which connect two nodes in a graph or network.

peripheral memory *See* **secondary memory device** and **memory.**

permutation An ordered arrangement of the first n positive integers in which each integer appears exactly once.

physically ordered array implementation An implementation of the keyed list ADT in which the logical order of the items in the list matches their physical position in an array.

physically sorted Data are physically sorted when the sort routine has actually manipulated the data so that items that the sort places consecutively are also physically adjacent.

pivot Item used to direct the partitioning in quick sort.

pointer A memory location containing the location of another data item.

pointer sort A sort in which pointers to the data are manipulated rather than the data itself.

pointer variable A special data type used in Pascal to reference the location of other data. *See also* **address** and **dynamic variable.**

polymorphism That feature of object-oriented programming which allows one operation to have different meaning for different kinds of objects.

polynomial algorithm An algorithm whose efficiency can be expressed in terms of a polynomial.

pop A procedure that removes an item from the top of the stack.

postcondition An assertion written after a segment of code.

postfix Unambiguous algebraic notation in which the arithmetic operator appears after the two operands upon which it is to be applied.

postorder traversal A binary tree traversal in which at any node, that node's left subtree is visited first, then that node's right subtree is visited, and finally that node is processed.

posttest loop A loop where the control condition is tested after the loop is executed. **REPEAT . . . UNTIL** is a posttest loop. Also referred to as an exit controlled loop.

precondition An assertion written before a particular statement.

prefix Unambiguous algebraic notation in which the arithmetic operator appears before the two operands upon which it is to be applied.

preorder traversal A binary tree traversal in which at any node, that node is first processed, then that node's left subtree is visited, and finally that node's right subtree is visited.

pretest condition A condition that controls whether the body of the loop is executed before going through the loop.

pretest loop A loop where the control condition is tested before the loop is executed. **WHILE . . . DO** is a pretest loop. Also referred to as an entrance controlled loop.

primary memory *See* **main memory** and **memory.**

prime hash area In linked collision processing, the main storage area in which keys are placed if no collision occurs.

priority queue A queue in which the entries on the queue are ranked into groups according to priority. Such a queue requires a rear pointer for each different possible priority value.

procedural abstraction The process of considering only what a procedure is to do rather than details of the procedure.

procedure A subprogram designed to perform a specific task as part of a larger program. Procedures are not limited to returning a single value to the main program.

profile an algorithm A means of empirically measuring the execution of an algorithm by inserting counters to keep track of the number of times certain instructions are executed during a run of the program.

program A set of instructions that tells the machine (the hardware) what to do.

program heading The first statement of any Pascal program; it must contain the reserved word **PROGRAM.**

program proof An analysis of a program that attempts to verify the correctness of program results.

program protection A method of using selection statements to guard against unexpected results.

program walk-through The process of carefully following, using pencil and paper, steps the computer uses to solve the problem given in a program. Also referred to as a trace.

programmer-supplied identifier *See* **identifier.**

programming by personification In object-oriented programming, invoking an operation by sending a message to the object to perform an operation that is part of its encapsulation. The object is viewed as an actor who is told to perform a particular scene in a play.

programming language Formal language that computer scientists use to give instructions to the computer.

prompt A marker on the terminal screen that requests input data.

proportional Term applied to two algebraic functions whose quotient is a constant.

protection *See* **program protection.**

pseudocode A stylized half-English, half-code language written in English but suggesting Pascal code.

push A procedure that adds an item to the top of the stack.

quadratic algorithm A polynomial algorithm in which the highest nonzero term is n^2.

quadratic collision processing Method of handling a collision in which the storage space is searched in the k^2 place, for successive integer values of k starting at the location of the collision, until an available spot is found.

queue A dynamic data structure where elements are entered at one end and removed from the other end. Referred to as a FIFO (first-in, first-out) structure.

quick sort A relatively fast sorting technique that uses recursion. *See also* **bubble sort, heap sort, insertion sort, merge sort, radix sort, selection sort,** and **shell sort.**

radix sort Sorts integer data by repeatedly placing the items into bins and then collecting the bins, starting with the least significant digit for the first pass and finishing with the most significant digit. Also referred to as bin sort. *See also* **bubble sort, heap sort, insertion sort, merge sort, quick sort, selection sort,** and **shell sort.**

random access Ability to access any elements in a list without first accessing all preceding elements.

random access file A file whose components can be accessed using random access.

random number generator A function that returns a real number between 0 and 1 each time it is called. The numbers it returns are statistically random in that after repeated calls to the function, the sequence of numbers returned is evenly distributed over the interval yet each one is completely unpredictable.

randomized storage A name given to list access via a hashing function.

reading from a file Retrieving data from a file.

ready queue In an operating system, the queue of processes with cleared access to all the resources the processes require to run.

real arithmetic operations Operations allowed on data of type **real.** This includes addition, subtraction, multiplication, and division.

rear pointer The pointer to the rear of a queue.

record A data structure that is a collection of fields that may be treated as a whole or that will allow you to work with individual fields.

record lock facility Method used on many systems to maintain data integrity by allowing only one user at a time to have access to a record. Any other user wishing that same record must wait until the first user has released it.

recursion The process of a subprogram calling itself. A clearly defined stopping state must exist. Any recursive subprogram can be rewritten using iteration and a stack.

recursive call A statement in a procedure which invokes that same procedure.

recursive definition *See* **recursive definition.** (A definition that uses the term being defined to define itself.)

recursive out A condition that terminates a series of recursive calls and hence prevents an infinite series of such calls. Also referred to as recursive termination condition.

recursive procedure A procedure which contains a call to itself.

recursive step A well-defined step that leads to the stopping state in the recursive process.

recursive subprogram *See* **recursion.**

recursive termination condition A condition that signals the end of a series of recursive calls. Also referred to as recursive out.

rehashing Method of handling a collision in which a sequence of new hashing functions is applied to the key that caused the collision until an available location for that key is found.

rehashing collision processing Resolving a collision by invoking a sequence of hashing functions on a key.

relational operator An operator used for comparison of data items of the same type.

relative ordering Ordering imposed on the entries in a list by their relative positions in that list.

relatively prime Two numbers are relatively prime if and only if their only common factor is 1.

REPEAT . . . UNTIL loop A posttest loop examining a Boolean expression after causing a fragment to be executed. *See also* **FOR loops, loops,** and **WHILE . . . DO loop.**

repetition *See* **loops.**

reserved words Words with predefined meanings that cannot be changed. They are highlighted in text by capital boldface print; a list of Pascal reserved words is set forth in Appendix 1.

return type The data type for a function name.

robust The state in which a program is completely protected against all possible crashes from bad data and unexpected values.

root The first or top node in a tree.

row major Implementation of a two-dimensional array as a one-dimensional array so that the rows are arranged in sequential order with all entries of the same row adjacent.

run-time error Error detected when, after compilation is completed, an error message results instead of the correct output. *See also* **compilation error, design error,** and **syntax error.**

run-time trace diagram The leveled hierarchy of procedure calls associated with the execution of a particular recursive program. Such diagrams can help in analyzing the efficiency of recursive algorithms.

scope of identifier The largest block in which the identifier is available.

scratch file *See* **internal file.**

search algorithm An algorithm designed to find a particular data item in a large collection of such items.

secondary memory device An auxiliary device for memory, usually a disk or magnetic tape. *See also* **main memory** and **memory.**

sector A particular portion of a magnetic disk used at the machine language level in addressing information stored on the disk.

seed A global number used as the basis for generating random numbers in random number generating function.

selection sort A sorting algorithm that sorts the components of an array in either ascending or descending order. This process puts the smallest or largest element in the top position and repeats the process on the remaining array components. *See also* **bubble sort, heap sort, insertion sort, merge sort, quick sort, radix sort,** and **shell sort.**

selection statement A control statement that selects some particular logical path based on the value of an expression. Also referred to as a conditional statement.

self-documenting code Code that is written using descriptive identifiers.

semantics The semantics of an algorithmic statement is the action dictated by that statement.

semaphore In an operating system, special flags that regulate the addition and removal of processes to and from the blocked and ready queues.

sentinel value A special value that indicates the end of a set of data or of a process.

sequential access Requirement that elements of a list must be accessed according to the list's ordering so that before a particular element can be accessed, all preceding elements must be accessed first.

sequential access file A file whose components must be accessed using sequential access.

sequential algorithm *See* **straight-line algorithm.**

sequential search The process of searching a list by examining the first component and then examining successive components in the order in which they occur. Also referred to as a linear search.

set A structured data type that consists of a collection of distinct elements from an indicated base type (which must be ordinal).

shaker sort A variation on the bubble sort in which each pass through the data positions the (current) largest element in the (current) last array index *and* the (current) smallest element in the (current) first array index.

shell sort Sort that works by dividing the array into smaller, noncontiguous segments. These segments are separately sorted using the insertion sort algorithm. The number of these segments is repeatedly reduced on each successive pass until the entire array has been sorted. *See also* **bubble sort, heap sort, insertion sort, merge sort, quick sort, radix sort,** and **selection sort.**

shift folding A variation on folding in which each numeric part of the key is treated as a separate number, and these numbers are added to form an integer value. *See also* **boundary folding.**

siblings The child nodes of a given node.

side effect An unintentional change in a variable which is the result of some action taken in a program.

sieve of Eratosthenes A technique devised by the Greek mathematician Eratosthenes for finding all prime numbers greater than 2 and less than or equal to a given number.

simple Boolean expression An expression where two numbers or variable values are compared using a single relational operator. *See also* **Boolean expression** and **compound Boolean expression.**

simulation A computer model of a real-life situation.

simulation of system stack Technique used to eliminate recursion by making a program explicitly perform the duties of the system stack.

software Programs that make the machine (the hardware) do something, such as word processing, data-base management, or games.

software engineering The process of developing and maintaining large software systems.

software system A large program, typically composed of numerous modules that interact to solve one complex problem.

software system life cycle The process of development, maintenance, and demise of a software system. Phases include analysis, design, coding, testing/verification, maintenance, and obsolescence.

sort-merge The process of repeatedly subdividing a long list, sorting shorter lists, and then merging to obtain a single sorted list.

source program A program written by a programmer. *See also* **system program.**

sparse table A table in which a high percentage of data storage locations will be of one uniform value.

stack A data structure where access can be made from only one end. Referred to as a LIFO (last-in, first-out) structure.

stack frame The information placed on the system stack by the operating system when a procedure call is made.

stack priority Function to hierarchically rank algebraic operators in order of precedence.

standard function A built-in function available in most versions of Pascal.

standard identifiers Predefined words whose meanings can be changed if needed. Standard identifiers are highlighted in text by lowercase boldface print; a list of Pascal standard identifiers is set forth in Appendix 2.

standard simple types The predefined data types **integer, real, char,** and **boolean.**

state space The space of all possible states which can be generated in the solution to a given problem.

state-transition diagram A diagram used to model the logic of a finite state machine.

static variable A variable whose size (for example, array length) is fixed at compilation time. A certain memory area is reserved for each variable, and these locations are retained for the declared variables as long as the program or subprogram in which the variable is defined is active.

stepwise refinement The process of breaking a complex problem down into smaller problems, solving those smaller problems, and then tying those solutions together to solve the original large problem.

stopping state *See* **termination condition.**

straight-line algorithm Also called sequential algorithm, this algorithm consists of a sequence of simple tasks.

stream input *See* **batch input.**

string A list of characters that are related in linear fashion and that can be manipulated using string operations.

string ADT A sequence of characters viewed as a data object, along with the operations that may be performed on them.

string constant One or more characters used as a constant in a program.

string data type A data type that permits a sequence of characters. This is not available in standard Pascal, but can be simulated using a packed array of characters.

string operations Operations that manipulate character strings. *See* **assignment, string; concatenation, string; deletion, string; insertion, string.**

structure chart A graphic method of indicating the relationship between modules when designing the solution to a problem.

structured English A means of specifying the logic of a module using an English-like pseudocode description.

structured programming Programming that parallels a solution to a problem achieved by top-down design. *See also* **stepwise refinement** and **top-down design.**

stub module A module used to aid in testing another module. The stub module reports the values it was sent and sends back the values needed by the module being tested so it can continue execution.

stub programming A no-frills, simple version of a final program.

subblock A block structure for a subprogram. *See also* **block.**

subprogram A program within a program. Procedures and functions are subprograms.

subrange The defined subset of values of an existing ordinal data type.

subscript *See* **array index** and **loop index.**

subset Set A is a subset of set B if all the elements in A are also in B. *See also* **difference, intersection,** and **union.**

substring A portion of a string that is itself a string.

subtree A subset of a tree that is itself a tree.

symbol table A list of identifiers maintained by a compiler as it parses a source program.

synonyms Two keys that hash to the same position and therefore cause a collision.

syntax The formal rules governing construction of valid statements.

syntax diagramming A method to formally describe the legal syntax of language structures; syntax diagrams are set forth in Appendix 3.

syntax error An error in spelling, punctuation, or placement of certain key symbols in a program. *See also* **compilation error, design error,** and **run-time error.**

system program A special program used by the computer to activate the compiler, run the machine code version, and cause output to be generated. *See also* **source program.**

system software The programs that allow users to write and execute other programs, including operating systems such as DOS.

system testing Exercising the interfaces between modules instead of the logic of a particular module.

systems analyst The person responsible for analyzing the needs of the users and then formally specifying the system and its requirements to meet those needs.

tag field A field used in defining variant records. Values of the tag field determine the variant record structure.

tail recursion A type of recursion in which an initial return operation triggers a series of returns uninterrupted by further recursive calls.

temporary file *See* **internal file.**

termination condition *See* **recursive termination condition.**

test cases Collection of sets of test data that will exercise all the logical possibilities the module will encounter. Each test case has a corresponding expected result called the test oracle.

testing phase The fourth phase of the software system life cycle. In this phase, the program code is thoroughly tested in an effort to discover errors both in the design of the program and in the code itself.

test oracle The expected result for a particular test case when a module is being tested.

test program A short program written to provide an answer to a specific question.

text file A file of characters that is divided into lines.

thread A pointer contained in a tree node which leads to the predecessor or successor of the node relative to a specified traversal.

threaded tree A tree in which threading is used.

threading A technique of avoiding recursion in tree traversal algorithms whereby the pointers unused in tree formation are turned into pointers to the inorder predecessor and inorder successor of that node.

time/space trade-off The maxim that an attempt to make a program more efficient in terms of time will only come as a result of a corresponding decrease in efficiency in terms of space, and vice versa.

token A language symbol comprised of one or more characters in an incoming stream of characters. The basic unit in lexical analysis.

top The end of a stack at which entries are added and removed.

top-down design A design methodology for solving a problem whereby you first state the problem and then proceed to subdivide the main task into major subtasks. Each subtask is then subdivided into smaller subtasks. This process is repeated until each remaining subtask is easily solved. *See also* **stepwise refinement** and **structured programming.**

trace *See* **program walk-through.**

tracer output The values of the data received by and returned from a module through the use of **write** statements at the beginning and end of that module.

track A particular portion of a magnetic disk used at the machine language level in addressing information stored on the disk.

transaction file A file containing changes to be made in a master file.

transitions In a finite state machine, the possible actions taken upon encountering a particular character.

tree *See* **general tree.**

tree of recursive calls *See* **run-time trace diagram.**

tree traversal A means of processing every node in the tree.

trial-and-error backtracking Recursion in which more recursive calls may be made after the first return operation occurs.

trie index A type of indexing used when the keys are variable-length character strings. Although taken from the word *retrieve,* trie is pronounced "try."

Turing machine A hypothetical computing machine which consists of input and output units, and infinite memory in the form of a sequentially organized tape to store characters from a finite alphabet, a finite collection of states in which the machine could exist in at any given time, and a control unit capable of checking and potentially modifying the contents of any memory cell.

two-dimensional array An array in which each element is accessed by a reference to a pair of indices.

two-dimensional table A collection of data of the same type arranged as a rectangular grid whose rows and columns are each indexed by a separate contiguous range of an ordinal data type. Each entry in the grid can be specified by giving its row and column coordinates.

two-way merge The process of merging two sorted lists.

type *See* **data type.**

undecidable proposition A statement within an axiomatic system such that neither that statement nor its negation can be proven by reasoning within the system itself.

underflow If a value is too small to be represented by a computer, the value is automatically replaced by zero. *See also* **overflow.**

union The union of set A and set B is A + B where A + B contains any element that is in A or that is in B. *See also* **difference, intersection,** and **subset.**

universal set Any set that contains all possible values of the base type.

unordered array implementation An implementation of a keyed list in which data are stored in an array but not physically ordered to match the logical ordering of the list.

unpacked array An array in which data are not in consecutive bytes.

user-defined data type *See* **enumerated data type.**

user-defined function A subprogram (function) written by the programmer to perform a specific task. Functions return one value when called.

user-friendly A phrase used to describe an interactive program with clear, easy-to-follow messages for the user.

value Often called value of a memory location. Refers to the value of the contents of a memory location. *See also* **address.**

value parameter A formal parameter that is local to a subprogram. Values of these parameters are not returned to the calling program.

variable A memory location, referenced by an identifier, whose value can be changed during a program.

variable condition loop A repetition statement in which the loop control condition changes within the body of the loop.

variable declaration section The section of the declaration section where program variables are declared for subsequent use.

variable dictionary A listing of the meaning of variables used in a program.

variable parameter A formal parameter that is not local to a subprogram. Values of these parameters are returned to the calling program.

variant part The part of a record structure in which the number and type of fields can vary. *See also* **fixed part.**

vertex A data object (or node) in a graph.

volatile list A list that undergoes frequent insertions and deletions.

weight The numeric value associated with an edge in a network.

WHILE . . . DO loop A pretest loop examining a Boolean expression before causing a fragment to be executed.

white box testing The method of testing a module in which the tester is aware of the method of implementation and internal logic of that module. *See also* **black box testing.**

word A unit of memory consisting of one or more bytes. Words can be addressed.

workspace-index method A method of storing strings in which one large workspace is provided for storing all the strings and an index keeps track of the starting locations and lengths of each of the individual strings.

worst case The arrangement of data items prior to the beginning of the sort procedure which causes that procedure to take the longest amount of time for that particular set of items. *See also* **best case.**

writing to a file The process of entering data to a file.

Answers to Selected Exercises

This section contains answers to selected exercises from the exercise sets at the end of each section. In general, answers to odd-numbered problems are given.

CHAPTER 1

Section 1.3

1. **a.** and **c.** are effective statements.

   b. is not effective because you cannot determine when to perform the action.

   d. is not effective because there is no smallest positive fraction.

   e. is not effective because you cannot determine in advance which stocks will increase in value.

3. **a.** 1. Select a topic
   2. Research the topic
   3. Outline the paper
   4. Refine the outline
   5. Write the rough draft
   6. Read and revise the rough draft
   7. Write the final paper

   c. 1. Get a list of colleges
   2. Examine criteria (programs, distance, money, and so on)
   3. Screen to a manageable number

   4. Obtain further information
   5. Make a decision

5. **a.** First-level development
   1. Get information for first employee
   2. Perform computations for first employee
   3. Print results for first employee
   4. ⎫
   5. ⎬ repeat for second employee
   6. ⎭

   Second-level development
   1. Get information for first employee
      1.1 get hourly wage
      1.2 get number of hours worked
   2. Perform computations for first employee
      2.1 compute gross pay
      2.2 compute deductions
      2.3 compute net pay
   3. Print results for first employee
      3.1 print input data
      3.2 print gross pay
      3.3 print deductions
      3.4 print net pay
   4. ⎫
   5. ⎬ repeat for second employee
   6. ⎭

   Third-level development
   1. Get information for first employee
      1.1 get hourly wage
      1.2 get number of hours worked
   2. Perform computations for first employee
      2.1 compute gross pay
      2.2 compute deductions
         2.2.1 federal withholding
         2.2.2 state withholding
         2.2.3 social security
         2.2.4 union dues
         2.2.5 compute total deductions
      2.3 compute net pay
         2.3.1 subtract total deductions from gross
   3. Print results for first employee
      3.1 print input data
         3.1.1 print hours worked
         3.1.2 print hourly wage
      3.2 print gross pay
      3.3 print deductions
         3.3.1 print federal withholding
         3.3.2 print state withholding
         3.3.3 print social security
         3.3.4 print union dues
         3.3.5 print total deductions
      3.4 print net pay

4.
5. } repeat for second employee
6. }

7. There are several ways to solve this problem, one of which follows:
1. Get the numbers as input
2. Put them in order - Small, Large
3. Check for a divisor
   3.1 **IF** Small is a divisor of Large **THEN**
      3.1.1 GCD is Small
      ELSE
      3.1.2 Decrease Small until a common divisor is found
4. Print the results
   3.1.2 can be further refined as
   3.1.2 Decrease Small until a common divisor is found
      3.1.2.2 **REPEAT**
         IF GCDCandidate is a common divisor **THEN**
         GCD is GCDCandidate
         ELSE
         Decrease GCDCandidate by 1
      UNTIL a common divisor is found

Section 1.4

3. a., b., and e. are valid; however, a semicolon must be used between the heading in a. and the next line of code.

c. does not begin with the reserved word **PROGRAM**.

d. is missing an identifier for the program name.

f. and g. use improper identifiers for the program name.

5. A typical constant definition statement is

```
CONST
   Name = 'Julie Adams';
   Age = 18;
   BirthDate = 'November 10, 1973';
   Birthplace = 'Carson City, MI';
```

Section 1.5

1. a., d., e., and g. are valid.

b. has a decimal.

c. has a comma.

f. is probably larger than **maxint**

3. a. 1.73E2

b. 7.43927E11

c. −2.3E−8

d. 1.4768E1

e. −5.2E0

5. a. and d. are **intigers.** b., c., and g. are **reals.** e. and f. are string constants.

7. a.
```
writeln ('Score':14);
writeln ('-----':14);
writeln (86:13);
writeln (82:13);
writeln (79:13);
```

CHAPTER 2

Section 2.1

1. a. 11

b. −41

c. 3

d. 24

e. 126

f. 63

g. 48

h. 140

i. 1

j. 7

3. a. and b. are valid, type **integer.**

c., e., f., g., h., and i. are valid, type **real.**

d. and j. are invalid.

5. Output will vary according to local implementation.

Section 2.2

1. a., b., e., f., and h. are valid assignment statements.

c. is invalid. A real cannot be assigned to an integer variable.

d. is invalid. An operand cannot be on the left of an assignment statement.

g. is invalid. IQ/3 is a real.

3. a.

3	−5
A	B

b.

26	31
A	B

c.

−3	−5
A	B

d.

9	9
A	B

5.
```
Sex        M
Age        23
Height     73 inches
Weight     186.5 lbs
```

7. column 11
```
******************************
*                            *
*    Name       Age    Sex   *
*    ----       ---    ---    *

*    Jones       21     M     *
*                            *
******************************
```

9.   column 10
                   ↓
```
             This  reviews string formatting.
When a letterAis used,
             Oops! I forgot to format.
             When a letter A is used,
             it is a string of length one.
```

Section 2.3

5. (Answers are system dependent.)

a.
```
  83       95      ' '     100.0
Num1     Num2      Ch      Num3
```

b.
```
  83       95      '.'      0.0
Num1     Num2      Ch      Num3
```

c.
```
  83      -72      ' '      93.5
Num1     Num2      Ch      Num3
```

d.
```
  83      -72      ' '      93.5
Num1     Num2      Ch      Num3
```

e. Error. Not enough values.

f.
```
  70       73      '-'      80.5
Num1     Num2      Ch      Num3
```

g.
```
  91       92      ' '      93.0
Num1     Num2      Ch      Num3
```

h.
```
 -76      -81      '-'      16.5
Num1     Num2      Ch      Num3
```

Section 2.4

3.
```
   CPS 150                TEST #2
   ----------------------------------
   Total points           100
   My score                93
   Class average          82.3
```

Section 2.5

1. a. 15.2

   b. 14

   c. 0

   d. 36

   e. −4.5

   f. −11.98

3. a. `sqrt(A*A+B*B)`

   b. `(-B + sqrt(B*B-4*A*C)) / (2 * A)`
      and
      `(-B - sqrt(B*B-4*A*C)) / (2 * A)`

5. `(round(10*X)) / 10.0`

7. a. `-4.30 4.30 -4 -4`

   b. `4` (depends on character set— 65 in ASCII)

   c. Depends on character set

9. a. `Uppercase := chr(ord(Lowercase) - ord('a') + ord('A'));`

   b. `IntValue := ord(Digit) - ord('0');`

CHAPTER 3

Section 3.2

3. a. A and B are variable parameters. X is a value parameter.

   b. A and X are variable parameters. B and Ch are value parameters.

   c. X, Y, and Z are variable parameters. A, B, and Ch are value parameters.

5. a. `Prob5 (Num1, Num2, Letter);`

   b. `PrintHeader;`

   c. `FindMax (Num1, Num2, Max);`

   d. `Switch (Num1, Num2);`

7. b.
```
PROCEDURE MaxAndAver (X, Y, Z : real;
                          VAR Max, Aver : real);
    BEGIN
      Max := X;
      IF Y > Max THEN
        Max := Y;
      IF Z > Max THEN
        Max := Z;
      Aver := (X + Y + Z) / 3.0
    END;
```

Section 3.3

7. Identifiers for this program are represented schematically by the figure at right.

9. 10
    20
    10
    30
    30

11. a. Average cannot be used as a procedure name since it has already been declared as an identifier with scope that includes that procedure.

   b. No errors. The variables declared in the procedure heading are local to it.

   c. No errors.

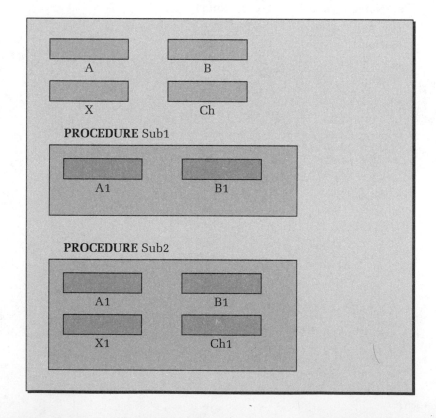

13. The main program is trying to access an identifier that is not available. The line

    ```
    writeln (X1:20:2);
    ```

    in the main program is inappropriate because the scope of X1 is **PROCEDURE** Sub1.

Section 3.4

3. c. and d. are valid.

    a. is invalid. The data type for what will be returned to the calling program must be listed.

    ```
    FUNCTION RoundTenth (X : real) : real;
    ```

    b. is invalid. Data types must be listed for X and Y.

    e. is invalid. The comma following **char** should be a semicolon.

CHAPTER 4

Section 4.1

1. true true false
            false

3. Only c. and f. are valid.

5. a., b., d., and g. are **true**.

    c., e., and f. (which compare as reals) are **false**.

7. a., b., and c. are **true**.

    d. and e. are **false**.

Section 4.2

1. a. 10   5
   b. no output
   c. 5   Since B has no value, the result will vary.
   d. 10   5
   e. 15   4
      15   4
   f. 10   5

3. a. should be

    ```
    IF A = 10 THEN ...
    ```

   b. 3 < X < 10

    cannot be evaluated. This should be

    ```
    (3 < X) AND (X < 10)
    ```

   c. This expression needs a **BEGIN ... END** to be consistent with indenting. It should be

    ```
    IF A > 0 THEN
      BEGIN
        Count := Count + 1;
        Sum := Sum + A
      END;
    ```

   d. IF Ch = 'A' OR 'B' THEN

    should be

    ```
    IF (Ch = 'A') OR (Ch = 'B') THEN
    ```

5. Yes.

9.
    ```
    BEGIN
      readln (Num1, Num2, Num3);
      Total := Total + Num1 + Num2 + Num3;
      writeln (Num1:5, Num2:5, Num3:5);
      writeln;
      writeln (Total)
    END;
    ```

11.
    ```
    read (Ch1, Ch2, Ch3);
    IF (Ch1 <= Ch2) AND (Ch2 <= Ch3) THEN
      writeln (Ch1, Ch2, Ch3);
    ```

    This can also be written as

    ```
    read (Ch1, Ch2, Ch3);
    IF Ch1 <= Ch2 THEN
      IF Ch2 <= Ch3 THEN
        writeln (Ch1, Ch2, Ch3);
    ```

Section 4.3

1. a. −14   14
   b. 50   25
      1   75
   c. 10   5
      5   0

3. a. Since the intent appears to be a statement that counts characters other than periods, a **BEGIN ... END** block should be included in the **IF ... THEN** option.

    ```
    IF Ch <> '.' THEN
      BEGIN
        CharCount := CharCount + 1;
        writeln (Ch)
      END
    ELSE
      PeriodCount := PeriodCount + 1;
    ```

   b. The semicolon between **END** and **ELSE** should be omitted.

   c. Technically this fragment will run. However, since it appears that OldAge := OldAge + Age is to be included in the **ELSE** option, the programmer probably meant

```
      ELSE
        BEGIN
          OldCount := OldCount + 1;
          OldAge := OldAge + Age
        END;
```

Section 4.4

	X	Y
1. a.	38.15	763.0
b.	- 21.0	21.0
c.	600.0	1200.0
d.	3000.0	9000.0

```
3. a. IF Ch = 'M' THEN
        IF Sum > 1000 THEN
          X := X + 1
        ELSE
          X := X + 2
      ELSE IF Ch = 'F' THEN
        IF Sum > 1000 THEN
          X := X + 3
        ELSE
          X := X + 4;

   b. read (Num);
        IF Num > 0 THEN
          IF Num <= 10000 THEN
            BEGIN
              Count := Count + 1;
              Sum := Sum + Num
            END
          ELSE
            writeln ('Value out of range':27)
        ELSE
          writeln ('Value out of range':27);

   c. IF A > 0 THEN
        IF B > 0 THEN
          writeln ('Both positive':22)
        ELSE
          writeln ('Some negative':22)
      ELSE
        writeln ('Some negative':22);

   d. IF C <= 0 THEN
        IF A > 0 THEN
          IF B > 0 THEN
            writeln ('Option one':19)
          ELSE
            writeln ('Option two':19)
        ELSE
          writeln ('Option two':19)
      ELSE
        writeln ('Option one':19);

5. IF Average < 90 THEN
     IF Average < 80 THEN
       IF Average < 70 THEN
         IF Average < 55 THEN
           Grade := 'E'
         ELSE Grade := 'D'
       ELSE Grade := 'C'
     ELSE Grade := 'B'
   ELSE Grade := 'A';
```

This could be written using sequential **IF ... THEN** statements. For example,

```
IF (Average <= 100) AND (Average >= 90) THEN
   Grade := 'A';
IF (Average < 90) AND (Average >= 80) THEN
   Grade := 'B';
      .
      .
      .
```

The disadvantage of this method is that each Boolean expression of each statement will always be evaluated. This is relatively inefficient.

7. | 8 | | 13 | | 104 |

    A   B   C

Section 4.5

3.
```
IF ((Age DIV 10) > 10) OR ((Age DIV 10) < 1) THEN
   writeln ('Value of age is', Age)
ELSE
   .
   . (CASE statement here)
   .
```

5. a. 5   3   125

   b. You have purchased   Super Unleaded gasoline

   c. 3   -3

   d. 5   10   -5

7. Assume there is a variable ClassType. The design of the fragment to compute fees is

```
read (ClassType);
CASE ClassType OF
   'U' :
   'G' :
   'F' :   (list options here)
   'S' :
END;  {  of CASE ClassType  }
```

CHAPTER 5

Section 5.2

1. a.
```
*
 *
  *
   *
    *
     *
```

b.
```
1 :      9
2 :      8
3 :      7
4 :      6
5 :      5
6 :      4
7 :      3
8 :      2
9 :      1
10 :     0
```

c.
```
** 2
** 3
** 4
** 5
** 6
** 7
** 8
** 9
** 10
** 11
** 12
** 13
** 14
** 15
** 16
** 17
** 18
** 19
** 20
```

d.
```
1
2
3
4
5
6
7
8
9
10
11
12
13
14
15
16
17
18
19
20
21
```

3. a.
```
FOR J := 1 TO 4 DO
   writeln ('*':2);
```

b.
```
FOR J := 1 TO 8 DO
   writeln ('***':J+3);
```

c.
```
writeln ('*':6);
FOR J := 1 TO 3 DO
   writeln ('*':6-J, '*':2*J);
writeln (' **** ****');
FOR J := 1 TO 2 DO
   writeln ('* *':7);
writeln ('***':7);
```

d. This is a "look ahead" problem that can be solved by a loop within a loop. This idea is developed in Section 5.6.
```
FOR J := 5 DOWNTO 1 DO
   BEGIN
      write (' ':(6-J)); {  Indent a line  }
      FOR K := 1 TO (2*J-1) DO {  Print a line  }
         write ('*');
      writeln
   END;
```

5. a.
```
FOR J := 1 TO 5 DO
   write (J:3);
FOR J := 5 DOWNTO 1 DO
   write (6-J:3);
```

b.
```
FOR J := 1 TO 5 DO
   writeln ('*':J);
FOR J := 5 DOWNTO 1 DO
   writeln ('*':(6-J));
```

7.
```
FOR J := 2 TO 10 DO
   writeln (12-J:12-J);
```

9. The key loop in this program will be something like
```
FOR J := -10 TO 10 DO
   BEGIN
      Num := 5*J;
      writeln (Num:10, Num * Num:10, Num * Num * Num:10)
   END; {  of printing the chart  }
```

Section 5.3

3. a.
```
1
2
3
4
5
6
7
8
9
10
```

b.
```
1          0
2          1
3          2
4          1
5          2
```

c. 54   50

d. The partial sum is   1
   The partial sum is   3
   The partial sum is   6
   The partial sum is   10
   The partial sum is   15
   The count is   5

e.   96.00   2.00

5. a. WHILE Num > 0 DO
      BEGIN
         writeln (Num:10:2);
         Num := Num - 0.5
      END;

   c. read (Num1, Num2);
      Sum := Num1 + Num2;
      writeln (Sum);
      WHILE (Num1 > 0) OR (Num2 > 0) DO
         BEGIN
            read (Num1, Num2);
            Sum := Num1 + Num2;
            IF (Num1 > 0) OR (Num2> 0) THEN
               writeln (Sum)
         END;

Section 5.4

1. A pretest loop tests the Boolean expression before executing the loop. A posttest loop tests the Boolean expression after the loop has been executed.

3. a. 1   9
      2   8
      3   7
      4   6
      5   5
      6   4

   b.   2
         4
         8
        16
        32
        64
       128

   c.   1
         2
         3
         4
         5
         6
         7
         8
         9
        10

   d. 1   0
      2   1
      3   2
      4   1
      5   2

5. a. IF Num > 0 THEN
      REPEAT
         writeln (Num:10:2);
         Num := Num - 0.5
      UNTIL Num <= 0;

   c. read (Num1, Num2);
      REPEAT
         Sum := Num1 + Num2;
         writeln (Sum);
         read (Num1, Num2)
      UNTIL (Num1 <= 0) AND (Num2 <= 0);

Section 5.5

1. a. FOR K := 1 TO 5 DO
      BEGIN
         write (' ':K);
         FOR J := K TO 5 DO
            write ('*');
         writeln
      END;

   c. FOR K := 1 TO 7 DO
      IF K < 5 THEN
         BEGIN
            FOR J := 1 TO 3 DO
               write ('*');
            writeln
         END
      ELSE
         BEGIN
            FOR J := 1 TO 5 DO
               write ('*');
            writeln
         END;

3. 4   5   6   7
    4   5   6   7
    4   5   6   7
    4   5   6   7

    5   6   7
    5   6   7
    5   6   7

    6   7
    6   7

Section 5.6

1. a. This is an infinite loop.

   b. The loop control variable, K, is unassigned once the **FOR ... TO** loop is exited. Thus, the attempt to use K in the expression K **MOD** 3 = 0 may result in an error.

CHAPTER 6

Section 6.1

3. The variables should be formatted so the integers will be separated by blanks.

You should check your answers to Exercises 5–7 on your computer due to possible differences in reading text files.

11.
```
PROGRAM DeleteBlanks (input, output, NoBlank ,Data);
  VAR
    NoBlank,Data : text;
    Ch : char;
  BEGIN
    reset (Data);
    rewrite (NoBlank);  {  Open for writing  }
    WHILE NOT eof(Data) DO
      BEGIN
        WHILE NOT eoln(Data) DO
          BEGIN
            read (Data,Ch);
            IF Ch <> ' ' THEN
              write (NoBlank, Ch)
          END;  { of WHILE NOT eoln  }
        readln(Data);
        writeln (NoBlank)
      END  { of WHILE NOT eof  }
END.  { of main program  }
```

Section 6.2

3. a. Jane is listed in both types Names and People.

b. Red is listed twice in type Colors.

c. Parentheses are needed around the values. Thus, it should be

```
TYPE
   Letters = (A, C, E);
```

5. a., d., and e. are valid.

b. is invalid; Tues + Wed is not defined.

c. is valid (but a poor choice).

f. is invalid; you cannot **write** user-defined values.

g. is invalid; you cannot **read** user-defined ordinals.

h. is invalid; the operation Tues + 1 is not defined.

Section 6.3

1. a. The definition is invalid; 10 .. 1 is not a subrange of an existing ordinal data type.

b. Bases and Double are valid. Score is invalid because Second .. Home is not a subrange.

c. All definitions and declarations are valid. However,

```
Hue := Blue
```

is an invalid use because Blue is not in the subrange defined for Stripes.

d. The definitions are invalid because the type Days must be defined before the subrange Weekdays.

e. All definitions and declarations are valid, but

```
Score2 := Score1 + 5
```

will produce a run-time error because the intended value (65) is not in the defined subrange.

3. a. Dependents usually refers to the number of single-family dependents for tax purposes. Twenty is a reasonable maximum.

b. Assuming hours worked in one week, 0 to 60 is a reasonable range.

c. The subrange was chosen for a maximum score of ten. This would vary for other maximum scores.

d. The subrange could be used if the total points were a maximum of 700. This might be used in some grading programs.

5. a. and b. are compatible. The base type is ChessPieces.

c. and f. are incompatible.

d. and e. are compatible. The base type is **integer.**

Section 6.4

1. a. Oak

b. Cotton

c. 2

d. Invalid

e. 3

f. Invalid

g. 0

3. a. 'D'

b. 10

c. '0'

d. Invalid; addition of characters is not defined.

e. Invalid; **pred**('K') is a character; thus, the operation, '+', is not defined.

f. 'Z'

5. a.
```
Weekend
Weekday
Weekday
Weekday
Weekday
Weekday
```

b. For a **WHILE** loop, you could use the Boolean expression **WHILE** Day < Sat **DO**.

```
Day := Sun;
WHILE Day < Sat DO
  BEGIN
    .
    .        (body of loop here)
    .
  END;
```

A **FOR** loop could be controlled by the Boolean expression

```
FOR Day := Sun TO Fri DO
  BEGIN
    .
    .        (body of loop here)
    .
  END;
```

c. This can be accomplished by using ordinal values. For example, if OrdValue has been declared, the loop could be

```
OrdValue := 0;
  REPEAT
    CASE OrdValue OF
      0          : (action here)
      1,2,3,4,5 :
    END;  {  of CASE OrdValue  }
    OrdValue := OrdValue + 1
  UNTIL OrdValue = 6;
```

d. The last value (Sat) is not being considered. This could be altered by using a **FOR** loop and including Sat or using a variable control loop and adding a **writeln** statement such as

```
writeln ('Weekend':20);
```

outside the loop.

7. Assume variables MonthNum and Month have been appropriately declared. A function could be

```
FUNCTION Month (MonthNum : integer) : MonthName;
  BEGIN
    CASE MonthNum OF
```

```
      1 : Month := Jan;
      2 : Month := Feb;
              .
              .
              .
     12 : Month := Dec
   END   {  of CASE MonthNum  }
END;  {  of FUNCTION Month  }
```

CHAPTER 7

Section 7.1

1. a. TYPE
```
      ScoreList = ARRAY [1..35] OF integer;
   VAR
      Score : ScoreList;
```

   b. TYPE
```
      PriceList = ARRAY [1..20] OF real;
   VAR
      CarCost : PriceList;
```

   c. CONST
```
      NumQuestions = 50;
   TYPE
      AnswerList = ARRAY [1..NumQuestions] OF char;
   VAR
      Answer : AnswerList;
```

   Note: It is possible to use an array of element type **boolean** here.

   d. TYPE
```
      GradeList = ARRAY [1..6] OF char;
   VAR
      Grade : GradeList;
```

3. a. There is no error if Hours has been defined as a constant.

   b. No error.

   c. No index range has been given for the array.

   d. The index range should be [1 .. 10] rather than [1 **TO** 10].

   e. The index range is not appropriate; something like **ARRAY** [⟨index range⟩] **OF boolean** should be used.

   f. [1 . . . 5] should be [1 . . 5]

5. a. TYPE
```
      LetterList = ARRAY [1..100] OF 'A'..'Z';
   VAR
      Letter : LetterList;
```

   b. TYPE
```
      Name = ARRAY [1..30] OF char;
   VAR
      CompanyName : Name;
```

   c. TYPE
```
      ScoreList = ARRAY [30..59] OF real;
   VAR
      Score : ScoreList;
```

7. a.   Money

183.25	Money[1]
10.04	Money[2]
17.32	Money[3]

b.   Money

10.04	Money[1]
19.26	Money[2]
17.32	Money[3]

c.   Money

19.26	Money[1]
10.04	Money[2]
2.68	Money[3]

Section 7.2

1. a.   List

0	List[1]
0	List[2]
1	List[3]
1	List[4]
1	List[5]

b.   List   Score

5	List[1]	1	Score[1]
6	List[2]	2	Score[2]
7	List[3]	2	Score[3]
8	List[4]	2	Score[4]
9	List[5]	3	Score[5]

c.   Answer

false	Answer[1]
true	Answer[2]
false	Answer[3]
true	Answer[4]
false	Answer[5]
true	Answer[6]
false	Answer[7]
true	Answer[8]
false	Answer[9]
true	Answer[10]

d. The contents of this array depend on the character set being used.

3. The section counts the number of scores greater than 90.

5.
```
TYPE
   ListOfLetters = ARRAY [1..20] OF char;
VAR
   Letter : ListOfLetters;
```
A **FOR** loop could be used as follows:
```
FOR J := 1 TO 20 DO
   read (Letter[J]);
```

7.
```
FOR J := 1 TO 100 DO
   A[J] := 0.0;
```

9. a. JOHN SMITH

b. SMITH, JOHN

c. HTIMS NHOJ

11.
```
writeln ('Test Number', 'Score':10);
writeln ('-----------', '-----':10);
writeln;
FOR J := 1 TO 50 DO
   writeln ('<':4, J:2, '>', TestScore[J]:11);
```

Section 7.3

1. a. after one pass   after two passes

−20
10
0
10
8
30
−2

−20
−2
0
10
8
30
10

b. Three exchanges are made.

3. A high to low sort is achieved by changing

```
IF A[K] < A[Index] THEN
```

to

```
IF A[K] > A[Index] THEN
```

Section 7.4

1. a. is valid; it can be called by

```
NewList (List1, Aray);
```

b. is invalid; a semicolon is needed after Row.

c. is invalid; array declaration cannot be included in the heading.

d. is valid; can be called by

```
NewList (List1, List2);
```

e. is invalid; Column cannot be used as a variable name.

f. is invalid; array declaration cannot be included in the heading.

g. is invalid; Name is not a data type.

h. is valid; can be called by

```
Surnames (Name1, Name2);
```

i. is invalid; Name is not a data type.

j. is valid; can be called by

```
Table (List1, List2);
```

3. a.
```
PROCEDURE OldList (X : Row;
                   Y : Column);
```

b.
```
PROCEDURE ChangeList (X : Row;
                      N : String20;
                      D : Week);
```

c. This call is inappropriate because the data type for A and B has not been defined in the **TYPE** section.

d. This call is inappropriate because the argument, String20, is a data type rather than a variable.

5. a.

List1	List2
1	0
4	0
9	0
16	0
25	0
36	0
49	0
64	0
81	0
100	0

Section 7.5

1. a., c., d., and f are valid; **true.**

   b. and e. are invalid.

3. a. ```To err is human. Computers do not forgive.```

   b. ```
   To err is human. Computers do not forgive.
   There are 15 blanks.
   ```

   c. ```    To err is human.                   **********```
   ↑        (20 blanks)                    (10 asterisks)
   (position 18)

   d. ```
   To err is human. Computers do not forgive.
           .evigrof ton od sretupmoC .namuh si rre oT
   ```
   (8 blanks)

5. ```
   MCount := 0;
   FOR J := 1 TO 100 DO
     IF Message[J] = 'M' THEN
       MCount := MCount + 1;
   ```

Section 7.6

1. ```
   FOR J := 1 TO Length DO
     IF Num = A[J] THEN
       writeln (Num, ' is in position', J:5);
   ```

3. The value of Index in the loop can be used as a counter.

5. a. ```Num = 18```

	First	Last	Mid	A[Mid]	Found
Before loop	1	5	Undefined	Undefined	**false**
After first pass	1	2	3	37	**false**
After second pass	1	2	1	18	**true**

c. ```Num = 76```

	First	Last	Mid	A[Mid]	Found
Before loop	1	5	Undefined	Undefined	**false**
After first pass	4	5	3	37	**false**
After second pass	4	3	4	92	

Since First > Last, the loop will be exited and an appropriate message should be printed.

7. Algorithmic developments for this problem follow.

   a. 1. Copy file components into an array
      2. Get number to look for
      3. Search sequentially for a match

   c. 1. Copy file components into an array
      2. Get new number
      3. Use a binary search until Last < First

      4. Assign First to Position
      5. Move array components ahead one from Position to the end of the list

         ```
         FOR J := Length DOWNTO Position DO
           A[J + 1] := A[J];
         ```

      6. Assign new number to

         ```A[Position];```

      9. There will be a maximum of five passes.
         ```

CHAPTER 8

Section 8.1

1. **a.** DrugPrice = ARRAY [1 ..4, 1..5] OF real;
   DrugPrice = ARRAY [1..4] OF ARRAY [1..5] OF real;

   b. Grade = ARRAY [1..20, 1..6] OF char;
   Grade = ARRAY [1..20] OF ARRAY [1..6] OF char;

   c. QuizScore = ARRAY [1..30, 1..12] OF integer;
   QuizScore = ARRAY [1..30] OF ARRAY [1..12 OF integer;

3. **a.**   ShippingCost   GradeBook

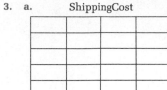

   40 locations available

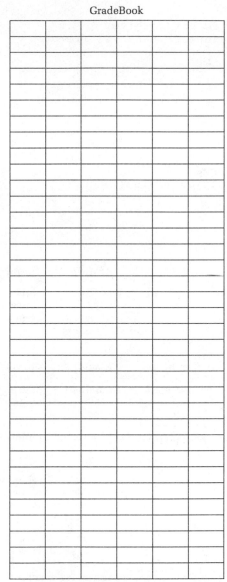

   210 locations available

b.   A

15 locations available

c.   Schedule

25 locations available

d.   AnswerSheet

250 locations available

5. a.
```
FOR J := 1 TO 3 DO
   FOR K := 1 TO 6 DO
   A[J,K] := 2 * J + K;
```

b.
```
FOR J := 1 TO 3 DO
   FOR K := 1 TO 6 DO
      A[J,K] := 0;
```

c.
```
FOR J := 1 TO 3 DO
   FOR K := 1 TO 6 DO
      A[J,K] := 2 * J;
```

7.
```
TYPE
   String20 = PACKED ARRAY [1..20] OF char;
   NameList = ARRAY [1..50] OF String20;
VAR
   Name: NameList;

FOR J := 1 TO 50 DO            {  Loop to get data  }
   BEGIN
      FOR K := 1 TO 20 DO       {  Read one line  }
         read (Name[J,K]);
      readln
   END;
```

9. a.
```
FOR J := 1 TO 4 DO
    BEGIN
       MinRow[J] := Table[J,1];
       FOR K := 2 TO 5 DO
          IF Table[J,K] < MinRow[J] THEN
             MinRow[J] := Table [J,K]
    END;
```

c.
```
Total := 0;
FOR J := 1 TO 4 DO
   FOR K := 1 TO 5 DO
      Total := Total + Table[J,K];
```

11. a.
```
TYPE
    Table = ARRAY [1..3, 1..8] OF integer;
```

b.
```
PROCEDURE Replace (VAR A : Table);
    VAR
       J, K : integer;
    BEGIN
       FOR J := 1 TO 3 DO
          FOR K := 1 TO 8 DO
             IF A[J,K] < 0 THEN
                A[J,K] := 0
    END;  {  of PROCEDURE Replace  }
```

c. **PROCEDURE** Replace of **b.** could be called by

```
Replace (Table3X5);
```

13. a. Reading values into *A* and *B* depends on how data are arranged in the data file.

b.
```
FOR H := 1 TO M DO
   FOR J := 1 TO P DO
      BEGIN
         Sum := 0;
         FOR K := 1 TO N DO
            Sum := Sum + A[H,K] * B[K,J];
         C[H,J] := Sum
      END;
```

Section 8.2

1. a. This prints an alphabetical listing of the states whose first letter is O.

   b. This prints every fifth state in reverse alphabetical order.

   c. This lists the first two letters of each state.

   d. This counts all occurrences of the letter A in the names of the states.

3. Assume the number of data lines is in NumLines.

   a.
```
FOR J := 1 TO NumLines DO
   BEGIN
      read (Name[J,1]);
      K := 1;
      WHILE Name[J,K] <> '*' DO
        BEGIN
           K := K + 1;
           read (Name[J,K])
        END;
      Length := K;
      FOR K := Length TO 20 DO
        Name[J,K] := ' ';
      readln
   END;
```

   c.
```
FOR J := 1 TO NumLines DO
   BEGIN
      FOR J := 1 TO 20 DO
        read (Name[J,K]);
      readln
   END;
```

Section 8.3

1. a. These declarations are not appropriate because Names is an array of 10 elements while Amounts is an array of 15 elements.

   b. These are appropriate because both Table and Names represent an array of size 12 × 10.

3. b. Assume an array type is defined as
```
TYPE
   GradeCount = ARRAY ['A'..'E'] OF integer;
```
   If Count is a variable of type GradeCount, the frequency of each grade can be determined by
```
FOR Ch := 'A' TO 'E' DO  { Initialize  }
   Count[Ch] := 0;
FOR J := 1 TO ListLength DO
   CASE Grade[J] OF
      'A' : Count['A'] := Count['A'] + 1;
      'B' : Count['B'] := Count['B'] + 1;
      'C' : Count['C'] := Count['C'] + 1;
      'D' : Count['D'] := Count['D'] + 1;
      'E' : Count['E'] := Count['E'] + 1
   END;  {  of CASE Grade[J]  }
```

Section 8.4

1. a. 2 * 3 * 10 = 60

   b. 6 * 3 * 4 = 72

   c. 3 * 2 * 11 = 66

   d. 4 * 10 * 15 = 600

3.
```
TYPE
   Floor = 1..4;
   Wing = 1..5;
   Room = 1..20;
   FloorPlan = ARRAY [Floor, Wing, Room] OF char;
VAR
   RoomType : FloorPlan;
```

5. There are 10 schools, 12 sports and 2 genders. Thus, there are 10 * 12 * 2 (240) memory locations reserved.

7. a.
```
{  Initialize to zero  }
FOR School := 'A' TO 'J' DO
   NumGrants[School] := 0;
FOR School := 'A' TO 'J' DO  { Consider each school  }
   FOR Sport := Baseball TO Wrestling DO  { Consider each sport  }
      FOR Gender := Male TO Female DO  { Consider each gender  }
         NumGrants[School] := NumGrants[School] +
                           Grants[School, Sport, Gender];
```

CHAPTER 9

Section 9.1

5. a. Employee

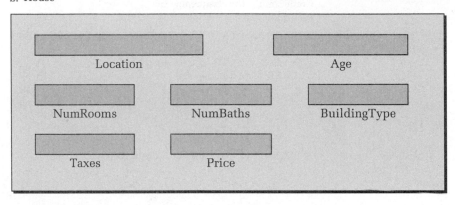

   b. House

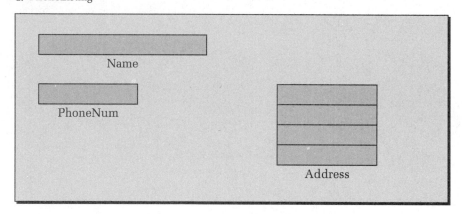

   c. PhoneListing

7. a.   `Info : RECORD`

       should be

            `Info = RECORD`

       and

            `Name = PACKED`

       should be

            `Name : PACKED`

   b. Member is used as both a variable and a data type.

   c.   `IQ = 50..200`

       should be

            `IQ : 50..200`

Section 9.2

1. a., c., and d. are valid.

    b. is invalid; Cust2 and Cust3 are not of identical type.

    e. is valid but demonstrates a poor practice. For better readability, you should always determine precisely which fields are being used.

3. a. The three different methods you
       could use are

    (1) ```
        Employee2 := Employee1;
        ```

    (2) ```
        WITH Employee2 DO
           BEGIN
              Name := Employee1.Name;
              SSN := Employee1.SSN;
              Age := Employee1.Age;
              HourlyWage := Employee1.HourlyWage;
              Volunteer := Employee1.Volunteer
           END;  {  of WITH...DO  }
        ```

    (3) ```
        WITH Employee1 DO
           BEGIN
              Employee2.Name := Name;
              Employee2.SSN := SSN;
              Employee2.Age := Age;
              Employee2.HourlyWage := HourlyWage;
              Employee2.Volunteer := Volunteer
           END; { of WITH...DO }
        ```

    b. Did you consider

    ```
    WITH Employee2 DO
       BEGIN
         Temp := HoursWorked;
         Employee2 := Employee1;
         HoursWorked := Temp
       END;
    ```

5.  ```
    FUNCTION Grade (Pts : integer) : char;
       VAR
          Percent : real;
       BEGIN
          Percent := Pts / 5;  {  Compute percent  }
          IF Percent < 60 THEN
             Grade := 'E'
          ELSE IF Percent < 70 THEN
             Grade := 'D'
          ELSE IF Percent < 80 THEN
             Grade := 'C'
          ELSE IF Percent < 90 THEN
             Grade := 'B'
          ELSE
             Grade := 'A'
       END;
    ```

    This can be called by

    ```
    With Student DO
       LetterGrade := Grade(TotalPts);
    ```

Section 9.3

1. a. See figure at right.

    b. i, iii, iv, viii, ix, and x are valid
       references

    ii, v, vi, and vii are invalid refer-
    ences

3. TYPE
```
    String20 = PACKED ARRAY [1..20] OF char;
    Status = ('S', 'M', 'W', 'D');
    NumKids = 0..15;
    FamilyRec = RECORD
                    MaritalStatus : Status;
                    Children : NumKids
                END;  {  of FamilyRec  }
    AddressRec = RECORD
                    Street : String20;
                    City : String20;
                    State : PACKED ARRAY [1..2] OF char;
                    ZipCode : integer
                END;  {  of AddressRec  }
    CustomerInfo  = RECORD
                    Name : String20;
                    Address : AddressRec;
                    SSN : PACKED ARRAY [1..11] OF char;
                    AnnualIncome : real;
                    FamilyInfo : FamilyRec
                END;  {  of CustomerInfo  }
VAR
    Customer : CustomerInfo;
```

5. CONST
```
    SquadSize = 15;
TYPE
    String20 = PACKED ARRAY[1..20] OF char;
    AgeRange = 15..25;
    HeightRange = 70..100;
    WeightRange = 100..300;
    PlayerInfo = RECORD
                    Name : String20;
                    Age : AgeRange;
                    Height : HeightRange;
                    Weight : WeightRange;
                    ScoringAv : real;
                    ReboundAv : real
                END;  {  of PlayerInfo  }
    PlayerList = ARRAY [1..SquadSize] OF PlayerInfo;
VAR
    Player : PlayerList;
```

7. a. Student

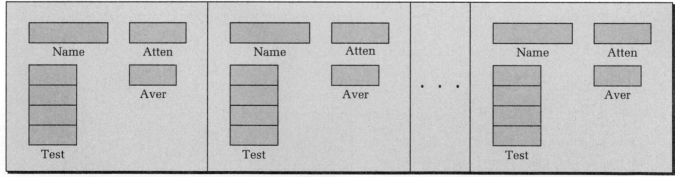

b. This function computes the test average for one student. It could be called by

```
WITH Student[K] DO
  Aver := GuessWhat(Test);
```

c. Format and headings will vary according to personal preference. However, your procedure should include

```
WITH St DO  {  Printout for St  }
  BEGIN
     .
     .
     .
     write ('Your attendance was ');
     CASE Atten OF
        Excellent : writeln ('excellent.');
        Average   : writeln ('average.');
        Poor      : writeln ('poor.')
     END;  {  of CASE  }
     .
     .
     .
   END;  {  of WITH...DO  }
```

Section 9.4

3. a. The type TagType for the tag field Tag has not been defined.

   b. There is no value listed for the C of the tag field.

   c. There is a syntax error. A semicolon is needed between **boolean** and **CASE**. A type has not been given for the tag field. It should be

   ```
   CASE Tag : TagType OF
   ```

   d. Only one variant part can be defined in a record

5. a. Figure

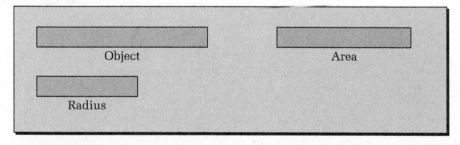

   b. Figure

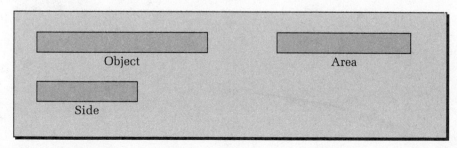

c. Figure

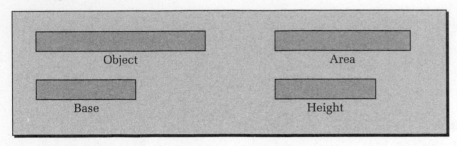

7.  ```
    PubType = (Book, Article);
    DataRange = 1600..2000;
    PublicationInfo = RECORD
                        Author : String30;
                        Title : String30;
                        Date : DataRange;
                        CASE Pub : PubType OF
                          Book    : (Publisher : String30;
                                        City : String30);
                          Article : (JournalName : String30;
                                        VolumeNumber : integer)
                      END;
    ```

CHAPTER 10

Section 10.1

3. a. is valid; the component type is an integer in the subrange 0 .. 120

    b. is invalid; no file type has been defined.

    c. is invalid; component type for a file cannot be another file.

    d. is invalid; the expression **FILE**[1 .. 100] has no meaning.

    e. is valid; the component type is **integer.**

5.  ```
    TYPE
        String20 = PACKED ARRAY [1..20] OF char;
        AddressType = ARRAY [1..3] OF String20;
        GenderType = (M, F);
        PatientInfo = RECORD
                        Name : String20;
                        Address : AddressType;
                        Height : 0..200;
                        Weight : 0..300;
                        Age : 0..120;
                        Gender : GenderType;
                        InsuranceCo : String20
                      END;  { of PatientInfo }
        PatientFile = FILE OF PatientInfo;
    VAR
        Patient : PatientFile;
    ```

Section 10.2

3.  ```
    TYPE
        FileType = FILE OF 0..100;
    VAR
        SevenMult : FileType;
    ```

    A fragment of code for this problem is

    ```
    rewrite (SevenMult);  { Open the file }
    Num := 1;
    Sevens := 7;
    WHILE Sevens < 100 DO
      BEGIN
        SevenMult^ := Sevens;
        put (SevenMult);
        Num := Num + 1;
        Sevens := 7 * Num
      END;  { of WHILE...DO }
    ```
    ```

5. Using **get** we have

```
reset (FivesFile);
A := FivesFile^;
get (FivesFile);
B := FivesFile^;
get (FivesFile);
C := FivesFile^;
get (FivesFile);
D := FivesFile^;
```

Using **read** we have

```
reset (FivesFile);
read (FivesFile, A);
read (FivesFile, B);
read (FivesFile, C);
read (FivesFile, D);
```

7. The **reset** procedure opens a file so that values may be read from the file. Contents of the file are not altered by this command. When **reset**(⟨file name⟩) is executed, the value of the first component is copied into the buffer variable.

   The **rewrite** procedure opens a file so that values may be written to the file. When **rewrite**(⟨file name⟩) is executed, any previous contents are lost.

9. **a.** The **reset** procedure opens the file for reading from the file, and **put** is used to write to the file. It appears that

```
reset(File1);
```

should have been

```
rewrite(File1);
```

   b. No errors.

c. The buffer variable is not properly written.

```
File1 := 10 * J;
```

should be

```
File1^ := 10 * J;
```

d. This loop will execute, but nothing happens. In order to put the values into File1, the loop should be

```
FOR J := 1 TO 5 DO
  BEGIN
    File1^ := J * 10;
    put (File1)
  END;
```

e. The files are mixed up. It appears that the intent is to copy the contents of File1 into File2.

f. No errors. This is a correct version of a problem similar to that posed in **e.**

11. The output is

```
-17
-4
```

The files contain the following values.

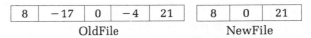

8	−17	0	−4	21		8	0	21

        OldFile   NewFile

Section 10.3

1. **b.** TYPE

```
    String20 = PACKED ARRAY [1..20] OF char;
    BookInfo = RECORD
                  Author : String20;
                  Title : String20;
                  StockNumber : integer;
                  Price : real;
                  Quantity : 0..500
               END;  {  of RECORD BookInfo  }
    BookFile = FILE OF BookInfo;
VAR
    Book : BookFile;
```

3. a. TYPE

```
     String20 = PACKED ARRAY [1..20] OF char;
     QuizList = ARRAY [1..10] OF 0..10;
     TestList = ARRAY [1..4] OF 0..100;
     StudentRec = RECORD
                      Name : String20;
                      Number : integer;
                      Quiz : QuizList;
                      Test : TestList
                  END;  {  of RECORD StudentRec  }
     StudentFile = FILE OF StudentRec;
   VAR
     Student : StudentFile;
```

b.
```
   PROCEDURE GetData (VAR St : StudentFile);
     VAR
       J : integer;
     BEGIN
       rewrite (St);      {  Open St for writing  }
       WHILE NOT eof(input) DO
         BEGIN
           WITH St^ DO   {  Get data for one student  }
             BEGIN
               FOR J := 1 TO 20 DO
                 read (Name[J]);  {  Get a name  }
               read (Number);      {  Get student ID  }
               FOR J := 1 TO 10 DO
                 read (Quiz[J]);  {  Get quiz scores  }
               FOR J := 1 TO 4 DO
                 read (Test[J])  {  Get test scores  }
             END;  {  of WITH...DO  }
           readln;
           put (St)  {  Move data to file  }
         END  {  of WHILE NOT eof  }
     END;  {  of PROCEDURE GetData  }
```

c. The basic design for this task is
to
(1) Transfer records to an array
(2) Sort the array
(3) Transfer records from the array back to the file

Assuming suitable definitions and declarations have been made, a procedure for this is

```
   PROCEDURE SortFile (VAR St : StudentFile);
     VAR
       Temp : StudentRec;
       J, K, Length, Index : integer;
       TempList : ARRAY [1..MaxSize] OF StudentRec;
     BEGIN
       reset (St);
       J := 0;
       WHILE NOT eof(St) DO  {  Copy to array  }
         BEGIN
           J := J + 1;
           TempList[J] := St^;
           get (St)
         END;
       Length := J;

       {  Now sort the array  }
```

```
   FOR J := 1 TO Length-1 DO
      BEGIN
        Index := J;
        FOR K := J + 1 TO Length DO
          IF TempList[K].Name < TempList[Index].Name THEN
            Index := K;
        IF Index <> J THEN
          BEGIN
            Temp := TempList[Index];
            TempList[Index] := TempList[J];
            TempList[J] := Temp
          END  {  of exchange  }
      END;  {  of one pass  }

   {  Now copy back to the file  }

      rewrite (St);
      FOR J := 1 TO Length DO
        BEGIN
          St^ := TempList[J];
          put (St)
        END
   END;  {  of PROCEDURE SortFile  }
```

CHAPTER 11

Section 11.1

1. a. **real** is not an ordinal data type.

    b. **integer** will exceed maximum size for a set.

    c. : should be =.

    d. Brackets should not be used.

    e. No errors.

3. a. `A := ['J', 'I', 'M'];`

    b. `A := ['P', 'A', 'S', 'C', 'L'];`

    c. The elements are 'T', 'O', and 'Y'. The eight subsets are [], ['T'], ['O'], ['Y'], ['T', 'O'], ['T', 'Y'], ['O','Y'], ['T', 'O', 'Y']

5. a. Brackets are needed, as

    `A := ['J'..'O']`

    b. No errors.

    c. Single quotation marks are needed, as

    `B := ['A'..'Z'];`

    d. 'E' and 'I' are listed more than once.

    e. [ ] is not a set variable.

    f. Since 'S' is in the subrange 'A' .. 'T', it is listed more than once.

7. a.
```
TYPE
   Hues = (Red, Orange, Yellow, Green, Blue, Indigo, Violet);
   RainbowSet = SET OF Hues;
VAR
   Rainbow : RainbowSet;
```

c. TYPE
```
    SomeFruits = (Apple, Orange, Banana, Grape, Pear, Peach,
                     Strawberry);
    FruitSet = SET OF SomeFruits;
  VAR
    Fruit : FruitSet;
```

Section 11.2

1. No. When A = B, both A >= B
   and A <= B are **true**.

3. a. A + B = [−3..4, 7..10]
      A * B = [0,1,2,8,10]
      A − B = [−3,−2,−1]
      B − A = [3,4,7,9]

   c. A + B = B
      A * B = A
      A − B = A
      B − A = B

5. All of these are **true**.

7. Code for this is

```
VowelsUppercase := ['A', 'E', 'I', 'O', 'U'];
VowelCount := 0;
WHILE NOT eof(Data) DO
  BEGIN
    read(Data, Ch);
    IF Ch IN VowelsUppercase THEN
       VowelCount := VowelCount + 1
  END;
```

Section 11.3

3. Modify **PROGRAM** DeleteBlanks
   presented in Section 8.1, Example
   8.4, by changing

```
IF Ch = ' ' THEN
  Ch := '*';
```

   to

```
IF Ch IN Vowels THEN
  write '*'
ELSE
  write (Ch);
```

7.
```
FUNCTION AllOddDigits (Num : integer) : boolean;
   TYPE
     Digits = SET of 0..9;
   VAR
     EvenDigits : Digits;
     NumDigits, J, Digit : integer;
   BEGIN
     EvenDigits := [0,2,4,6,8,10];
     IF Num DIV 1000 = 0 THEN   {  Num < 1000  }
       IF Num DIV 100 = 0 THEN  {  Num < 100   }
         IF Num DIV 10 = 0 THEN  {  Num < 10   }
           NumDigits := 1
         ELSE NumDigits := 2
       ELSE NumDigits := 3
     ELSE NumDigits := 4;
     AllOddDigits := true;
     FOR J := 1 TO NumDigits DO
       BEGIN
         Digit := abs(Num MOD 10);
         IF Digit IN EvenDigits THEN
           AllOddDigits := false;
         Num := Num DIV 10
       END  {  of FOR loop  }
   END;  {  of FUNCTION AllOddDigits  }
```

CHAPTER 12

Section 12.2

1. Insertion sort provides for a possible early exit from its inner loop. This early exit can potentially reduce the number of comparisons necessary, especially for data that are "almost" in order.

3. Selection sort does not provide for an early exit from either the outer or the inner loop; however, it does guarantee that only n data exchanges will be made—fewer than either insertion or selection sort can guarantee (both require n^2 data exchanges on average).

5.

K=1	K=2	K=3	K=4	K=5	K=6
43 → 12	12	12	12	12	12
40 → 40	18	18	18	18	18
18 → 18	40	24	24	24	24
24 → 24	24	40	39	39	39
39 → 39	39	39	40	40	40
60 → 60	60	60	60	60	43
12 → 43	43	43	43	43	60

7. This sort algorithm resembles a bubble sort, but is different in that small array entries "bubble up" instead of having large array entries "bubble down" on each successive pass. That is, in the bubble sort we can guarantee that after the kth pass, the *largest k* array entries are in their rightful place; whereas, in this sort algorithm, we can guarantee that after the kth pass, the *smallest k* entries are in their rightful place.

Original	k=1	k=2	k=3	k=4	k=5	k=6
43	12	12	12	12	12	12
40	43	18	18	18	18	18
18	40	43	24	24	24	24
24	18	40	43	39	39	39
39	24	24	40	43	40	40
60	39	39	39	40	43	43
12	60	60	60	60	60	60

9. This sort algorithm resembles insertion sort in that it, too, positions the kth element in its rightful place among $k-1$ entries already in order. The difference between the two sorts lies in the section of the array each has sorted with each successive iteration. In insertion sort, the *first $k+1$* entries are in order after the kth pass; in this sort, the *last k* entries are in order after the kth pass.

Original	k=1	k=2	k=3	k=4	k=5	k=6
43	43	43	43	43	43	12
40	40	40	40	40	12	18
18	18	18	18	12	18	24
24	24	24	12	18	24	39
39	39	12	24	24	39	40
60	12	39	39	39	40	43
12	60	60	60	60	60	60

11. The integers

20
30
40
50
10

or any such arithmetically or alphabetically ordered data cause the
bubble sort to make comparisons,
but no data are interchanged until
the 10 is "bubbled up" to the top.
For the insertion sort, the inner
loop is shut off after a single comparison, until the final 10 is
reached. Then the 10 is inserted at
the top.

13.

```
PROCEDURE ModifiedInsertionSort (N:integer; VAR List:SortArray);
    { Same Given, Task, and Return as given in text for InsertionSort  }
    { New logic:  Move element only after all comparisons per loop are }
    {                finished                                          }

VAR  I,K,J: integer;
     Done: boolean;
     Remember: integer;

BEGIN
   FOR K := 2 TO N DO
     BEGIN
       J := K;
       Remember := J;              { remember the position being tested }
       Done := false;
       WHILE (J >=2) AND NOT Done DO
           IF List[Remember].Key < List[J-1].Key THEN
              J := J-1
           ELSE
              Done := true;
       IF J <> Remember THEN               { shuffle data from bottom up }
          BEGIN
            FOR K := Remember DOWNTO J+1 DO
              List[K] := List[K-1];
            List[J] := List[Remember]         { place in correct location }
          END
     END
END;
```

Section 12.3

1. a. Inner loop: $m - 6$ repetitions.
Outer loop: n repetitions. For
each outer loop repetition, the inner loop is traversed $m - 6$ times.
Therefore, $(m - 6) \times n$ overall
repetitions are performed. This is
$O(n^2)$.

b. The inner loop will be executed
$\log_2 n$ times and the outer loop
will be executed n times. Thus
the loops are $O(n \log_2 n)$.

c. The inner **REPEAT** is executed
$n/2$ times for each execution of
the outer loop. The outer **REPEAT**
is executed n times. Thus there
are $n \times (n/2)$ repetitions. Thus
the loops are $O(n^2)$.

3. The efficiency of the algorithm in question is constant—32 operations—for all input. Remembering that in big-O analysis, we are concerned primarily with the order of magnitude of the algorithm's efficiency, we write this algorithm's efficiency as O(1) * 32. And recalling that constants bear no importance except in comparing algorithms with the same big-O, we drop the constant 32 to arrive at the big-O that most accurately characterizes the algorithm—O(1).

5. a. The $n^3\log_2 n$ term dominates and this is $O(n^3\log_2 n)$.

   b. The 4^n exponential term will (eventually) dominate any polynomial terms. Thus this is $O(4^n)$.

   c. The 2^n exponential term will (eventually) dominate any polynomial terms. Thus this is $O(2^n)$.

7. For this small set of integers, the trace of the insertion sort is

20	20	20	20	10
30	30*	30	30	20
40	40	40*	40	30
50	50	50	50*	40
10	10	10	10	50

The inner loop of the insertion sort is "shut off" after one comparison for each value of K, until the "bottom" 10 is reached. At that point, four swaps are required to move it into the "top" position. For this almost ordered data, the insertion sort is $O(n)$.

9. Since n^2 dominates $n^2 + \log_2 n$, $O(n^2 + \log_2 n)$ is the same as $O(n^2)$. Hence, we have the following answers for a–d.

   a. You are both correct for any algorithm whose performance is dominated by a term such as n^k for $k \geq 2$ or a^n for any base a > 1.

   b. You are both wrong for any linear or logarithmic algorithm.

   c. No.

   d. No.

Section 12.4

1.

	K=1 J=1	K=1 J=2	K=1 J=3	K=1 J=4	K=1 J=5	K=1 J=6
1	2	2	2	2	2	2
2	1	3	3	3	3	3
3	3	1	4	4	4	4
4	4	4	1	5	5	5
5	5	5	5	1	6	6
6	6	6	6	6	1	7
7	7	7	7	7	7	1

K=2 J=1	K=2 J=2	K=2 J=3	K=2 J=4	K=2 J=5
3	3	3	3	3
2	2	2	2	2
4	4	5	5	5
5	5	4	6	6
6	6	6	4	7
7	7	7	7	4
1	1	1	1	1

K=3 J=1	K=3 J=2	K=3 J=3	K=3 J=4
3	3	3	3
2	5	5	5
5	2	2	2
6	6	6	7
7	7	7	6
4	4	4	4
1	1	1	1

K=4 J=1	K=4 J=2	K=4 J=3
3	3	3
5	5	5
2	2	7
7	7	2
6	6	6
4	4	4
1	1	1

K=5 J=1	K=5 J=2
3	3
5	7
7	5
2	2
6	6
4	4
1	1

K=6 J=1
7
3
5
2
6
4
1

3. Ten passes would be made through the outer **WHILE** loop of
the radix sort algorithm because the length of the longest data
item is ten characters. It is assumed that strings are padded
with space beyond their last alphabetical character.

Pass 0:

List: CHOCOLATE VANILLA CARAMEL PEACH STRAWBERRY CHERRY

Pass 1:

Bins: Space: CHOCOLATE VANILLA CARAMEL PEACH CHERRY
      Y: STRAWBERRY
List: CHOCOLATE VANILLA CARAMEL PEACH CHERRY STRAWBERRY

Pass 2:

Bins: Space: VANILLA CARAMEL PEACH CHERRY
      E: CHOCOLATE
      R: STRAWBERRY
List: VANILLA CARAMEL PEACH CHERRY CHOCOLATE STRAWBERRY

Pass 3:

Bins: Space: VANILLA CARAMEL PEACH CHERRY
      R: STRAWBERRY
      T: CHOCOLATE
List: VANILLA CARAMEL PEACH CHERRY STRAWBERRY CHOCOLATE

Pass 4:

Bins: Space: PEACH CHERRY
      A: VANILLA CHOCOLATE
      E: STRAWBERRY
      L: CARAMEL
List: PEACH CHERRY VANILLA CHOCOLATE STRAWBERRY CARAMEL

Pass 5:

Bins: Space: PEACH
      B: STRAWBERRY
      E: CARAMEL
      L: VANILLA CHOCOLATE
      Y: CHERRY
List: PEACH STRAWBERRY CARAMEL VANILLA CHOCOLATE CHERRY

Pass 6:

Bins: H: PEACH
       L: VANILLA
       M: CARAMEL
       O: CHOCOLATE
       R: CHERRY
       W: STRAWBERRY
List: PEACH VANILLA CARAMEL CHOCOLATE CHERRY STRAWBERRY

Pass 7:

Bins: A: CARAMEL STRAWBERRY
       C: PEACH CHOCOLATE
       I: VANILLA
       R: CHERRY
List: CARAMEL STRAWBERRY PEACH CHOCOLATE VANILLA CHERRY

Pass 8:

Bins: A: PEACH
       E: CHERRY
       N: VANILLA
       O: CHOCOLATE
       R: CARAMEL STRAWBERRY
List: PEACH CHERRY VANILLA CHOCOLATE CARAMEL STRAWBERRY

Pass 9:
        Bins: A: VANILLA CARAMEL
                     E: PEACH
                     H: CHERRY CHOCOLATE
                     T: STRAWBERRY
       List: VANILLA CARAMEL PEACH CHERRY CHOCOLATE STRAWBERRY

Pass 10:
        Bins: C: CARAMEL CHERRY CHOCOLATE
                     P: PEACH
                     S: STRAWBERRY
                     V: VANILLA
       List: CARAMEL CHERRY CHOCOLATE PEACH STRAWBERRY VANILLA

5. An application in which the array of data items consumed all available memory would not have the space necessary to store the array of pointers.

7. Although the introduction of pointers into the bubble sort routine will not improve its $O(n^2)$ nature, there will most likely be an increase in run-time efficiency. This is because physical swapping of data is drastically reduced. If the data to be swapped were records with numerous fields of records themselves, many machine operations would be involved. But with pointers, only integers need be swapped, involving many fewer machine operations.

9. The pointer strategy would have the least effect on selection sort, because it guarantees a fewer number of data exchanges (only one per outer loop iteration) than either of the other sorts. Since the pointer sort affects the efficiency of data exchanges, and since fewer swaps are made with selection sort, less overall time is saved with selection sort than with the other two sorting algorithms; these sorting algorithms swap more often, and would therefore benefit more significantly from improved swapping efficiency.

11.
```
PROCEDURE PointerSelectionSort (N : integer;
                                VAR Pointers : IntegerArray;
                                List : SortArray);

{ Given:   Array List containing entries in locations 1 through N. }
{          Array Pointers that are integers pointing to the data   }
{          in array List.                                          }
{ Task:    Selection sort logic using pointers instead of actual   }
{          data movement.                                          }
{ Return:  Array Pointers that point to the correctly arranged     }
{          data or array List.                                     }
VAR    K, J, MinPosition: integer;
       Temp: integer;

BEGIN
  FOR K := 1 TO N DO
    Pointer[K] := K;
  FOR K := 1 TO N-1 DO
    BEGIN
      MinPosition := Pointer[K];
      FOR J := K+1 TO N DO
        IF List[ Pointer[J] ].Key < List[MinPosition].Key  THEN
          MinPosition := Pointer[J];
      Temp := Pointer[K];
      Pointer[K] := Pointer[MinPosition];
      Pointer[MinPosition] := Temp
    END
END;
```

13.
```
FUNCTION Digit (Number,K: integer): SingleDigit;

  { Given:   Integers Number and K                        }
  { Task:    Determine the Kth digit of Number             }
  { Return:  The Kth digit of Number                       }

  VAR P,Q: integer;

          FUNCTION PowerOfTen (I: integer): integer;

             { Given:   Integer I                      }
             { Task:    Computer 10 to the I power      }
             { Return:  10 to the I power               }

             VAR Count,Total: integer;

             BEGIN
               IF I = 0 THEN PowerOfTen := 1
               ELSE
                 BEGIN
                   Total := 1;
                   FOR Count := 1 TO I DO
                     Total := Total * 10;
                   PowerOfTen := Total
                 END
             END;

  BEGIN
    P := PowerOfTen (K);    {Determine 10 to the K power  }
    Q := PowerOfTen (K-1);  {Determine 10 to the K-1 power}
    Digit := (Number - P*(Number DIV P)) DIV Q
  END;
```

Section 12.5

1. Initial array with Low, High, and Middle = (High + Low) **DIV** 2. Target is 43. Found is **false** to begin.

Low				Mid					High
1	2	3	4	5	6	7	8	9	10
18	40	46	50	52	58	63	70	77	90

Since 43 < 52, High points to "4".

Low	Mid		High						
1	2	3	4	5	6	7	8	9	10
18	40	46	50	52	58	63	70	77	90

Since 43 > 40, Low points to "3".

		Mid Low High							
1	2	3	4	5	6	7	8	9	10
18	40	46	50	52	58	63	70	77	90

Since 43 < 46, High points to "2" and the search ends with Found = **false.**

3. A symbol table is a list of the identifiers that have been declared in a program and which the compiler continually searches as the program is compiled. Since the sequential search is $O(n)$, the continual searching of the symbol table uses up too much time to be practical.

5. 21 or fewer times.

7. This version of the binary search will work correctly provided the variable N never comes in as 0 (indicating an empty list). In this situation, Middle will be computed to be 0, which will generate an array index out-of-range error.

11. Although still $O(n)$ in its efficiency, the code for this version of the algorithm can reduce the number of comparisons by a factor of 2. This is because we need not test for the sentinel *and* the target data each time through the loop.

13. When an array is passed by value, a physical copy of that array must be generated and passed to the procedure each time it is called. When an array is passed by reference, on the other hand, only the address of the array—an integer—need be passed to the procedure. Clearly, passing an integer (which can be quickly looked up) is far more time and space efficient than passing an entire copy of an array (which must be generated on the spot).

CHAPTER 13

Section 13.1

1. Characteristics of the software engineering approach to system development are

   ■ Analysis of the situation (interviews, observations, research, and so on).
   ■ Design of a solution (beginning with a completely abstract non-physical design).
   ■ Construction of a model (to anticipate various construction problems).
   ■ Construction of actual solution.
   ■ Maintenance.

3.

MEMORANDUM

TO: Recalcitrant Team Member
FROM: Dedicated Software Engineer
RE: Tactful note defending software engineering principles

As a dedicated team member whose paycheck depends on "getting it done" on time, I am as committed as you to meeting the deadlines set forth for this project. At the same time, I do not care to fall prey to the unreliable, inelegant methods of our predecessors in this company, whose lack of planning often resulted in software products with serious flaws—flaws that ended up costing this company dearly. Let me offer two sound reasons why delving into the details of Pascal code without a conceptual model, as you have suggested, would spell disaster.

First, without a conceptual model, our team would not be able to work as a team. With potentially differing ideas of the system design, individual members would inevitably waste time writing pieces of the system that did not fit together. Moreover, since team members would not have laid out the system beforehand, they would not be cognizant of what basic tasks are done frequently throughout the system. Hence, many lines of redundant code would be written, thus wasting time as well as space.

Second, what if the final system we've coded turned out not to work? Flaws that we could have detected with a conceptual model would not have been discovered until the system was up and running. And by that time, all of our hours of coding would have been wasted.

In short, if it is your interest to implement a reliable, working system—and to do so on time—creating a conceptual design simply cannot be avoided. Although it may seem like a waste of time initially, it will more than pay for itself in the end by ensuring that our final system has the best design possible, and is reliable enough to deserve the trust our company will need to place in it.

Our team will meet at 9:00 A.M. tomorrow morning to begin carving out a conceptual design. We hope to see you there.

Section 13.2

3. If users of the String ADT choose not to include calls to the Create operation because they know that certain String ADT implementations do not actually require String variable initialization, they can no longer be sure that their high-level logic will be plug-compatible with all possible String ADT implementations. Having violated the principle of information hiding, they lose one of the most valuable features of ADTs: the ability to experiment with various implementations of an ADT without recoding the high-level logic.

Section 13.3

1. For the simple two-row, four-column table

```
1  2  3  4
5  6  7  8
```

the row-major implementation would be 1 2 3 4 5 6 7 8; the column-major implementation would be 1 5 2 6 3 7 4 8.

3. Any situation in which a high percentage of the cell entries are either zeros for arithmetic values or one particular Boolean value calls for a sparse table implementation.

An example would be a table listing medical patients across the top and serious illnesses down the side. If a patient had the serious illness, then a 1 is registered; otherwise a 0 indicates the patient has not had the serious illness.

5. Allowing subscripts for an arbitrary range of ordinal values, not necessarily always integers starting at one, does not cause problems in translating two-dimensional table coordinates into linear positions. It simply requires another function to translate the arbitrary range to the range the mapping function would use.

For example,

```
TYPE Rows = 3..8;
     Columns = 23..49;
     Numbers = ARRAY [Rows,Columns] OF integer;
```

would require translating the range 3..8 for Rows to 1..6, which is what the mapping function would need, and translating the range 23..49 for Columns to 1..27. Other ordinal types would need a similar translation so that the mapping function could locate the correct linear position.

7.
```
PROCEDURE Create(VAR T : TwoDTable);

   { Given:  T, a two-dimensional table in an arbitrary state.  }
   { Task:   Initialize T to be an empty sparse table.          }
   { Return: T, an initialized, empty sparse table.             }

   BEGIN
     T[1].PilotNum := HighPilotPlus1
   END;
```

11. If a table were R rows by C columns, then a row-major implementation would require R × C locations in a linear list of the table's contents.

By implementing the sparse table with a one dimensional array of records, we could in the worst case of a table absolutely full, need R × C locations to hold records, each of which contains two integer fields. Thus for a full, or nearly full table, the row-major implementation seems to be more space efficient.

But as the percentage of **false** values increases, fewer pairs are in the array of records. The break-even point seems to be roughly 50 percent. (This is a rough estimate because of system requirements to keep track of array indicies, and so on.)

13. These implementations are imperfect for at least three reasons. First, they necessarily impose a specific ordinal type—the integers—as the table index type. The two-dimensional table definition stipulates that these indices can be *any* ordinal type, and clearly a perfect two-dimensional table ADT would provide users with a way to specify the index type in the Create operation.

Second, whereas the two-dimensional table definition states that the rows and columns are each indexed by a separate contiguous range, the implementations discussed in this chapter impose a specific range on users. The definition would seem to imply that a perfect two-dimensional table implementation would allow an arbitrary index range to be specified at the time of creation, perhaps as parameters to the Create operation.

And third, whereas the formal two-dimensional table definition imposes no restriction on the data stored in the table (other than all data must be of the same type) the implementations in this chapter have restricted the data type determined by the ADT author at compile time. Again, a "perfect" implementation should allow the ADT user to determine an appropriate data type to be stored in the table; perhaps this data type could be passed as a parameter to the Create operation.

15. The radix sort requires a sparse table because approximately 90 percent of the bin capacity can be wasted. Suppose there are 100 four-digit integers to sort with the radix sort. There must be 10 bins, each bin capable of holding all 100 four-digit integers. Suppose, that, all 100 four-digit integers happened to have a "3" in the ten's place. Then the 3-bin would be filled and the other nine bins totally empty—a waste of 90 percent of the storage capability. Since so much space is unused, a sparse table would be appropriate.

Section 13.4

1. The number and type of formal parameters associated with Print-Node must exactly match the declaration of ProcessNode in TraverseInOrder's formal parameter list. In this case, the parameter Item is declared as a **VAR** parameter instead of a Value parameter. Since PrintNode's parameter list does not exactly match the declaration in TraverseInOrder's parameter list, PrintNode cannot be legally passed to TraverseInOrder. Unless PrintNodes's Item parameter is changed to a **VAR** parameter, the code as it stands will generate a syntax error.

3.
```
PROCEDURE ChangeNegToZero(VAR ITEM : ListNode);

   { Given:  A ListNode Item                              }
   { Task:   Test OtherData field for being negative      }
   { Return: If OtherData < 0, then Item with OtherData := 0; }
   {         item unchanged otherwise.                    }

   BEGIN
     IF Item.OtherData < 0 THEN
       Item.OtherData := 0
   END;
```

Assuming the existence of a keyed list L, one could call TraverseInOrder as follows:

```
TraverseInOrder(L,ChangeNegToZero);
```

5. Instead of shifting all array elements from K to L.NumberRec down one slot, this modification has the disastrous effect of clobbering all data below the Kth slot (that is, in indices > K). When the (J+1)st slot is assigned the contents of the Jth slot, the corrupted value of the Jth slot (itself a copy of the datum in the Kth slot) merely "slides down" one more slot, permanently clobbering the datum previously in that slot. This chain reaction continues all the way down the array; when it's over, indices K+1 through L.NumberRec contain a copy of the datum in index K.

11.

> MEMORANDUM
>
> TO: My Supervisor
> FROM: Me
> RE: Keyed list implementation for zip code application
>
> I strongly recommend that we employ a physically ordered array to implement the zip code keyed list application. You have told me that users of this application will often want to see the information associated with a particular zip code; therefore, fast retrieval time is extremely important. Using a physically ordered array, we can achieve the excellent $O(\log_2 N)$ retrieval efficiency of the binary search.
>
> You might argue that we will pay dearly for such efficiency in the form of poor add and delete efficiency. Although the Add and Delete operations in the physically ordered array strategy require $O(N)$ comparisons and $O(N)$ data exchanges—clearly unacceptable for an array that will contain all of our nation's zip codes—I would argue that this slow efficiency really shouldn't be a factor in this application. How often does one hear about a new U.S. zip code? And how often does our postal service delete one? To my knowledge, the United States zip codes haven't changed in years.
>
> The point is, once a record for each zip code has been added to the list, the list will remain virtually static. So while it may take a while initially to build up the list, the slow add efficiency will be only a temporary nuisance; we will begin reaping the benefits of $O(\log_2 N)$ retrievals in no time!

13. The Success Boolean parameter for the Add operation could be returned as **false** for at least two reasons. First, Success would be **false** if the list were already full. Second, Success would be **false** if the key field of the record being added were the same as the key field of a record already in the list.

CHAPTER 14

Section 14.1

3. Here is one possible way to depict the flow of information:

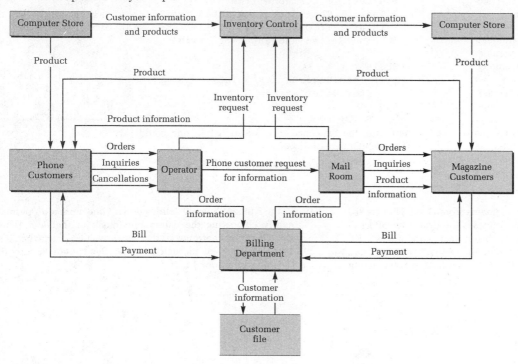

Section 14.2

1. A module that is functionally cohesive performs exactly one predefined task and does it without unexpected outcomes.

3. Since one of the modules performs two tasks, the system is not functionally cohesive. A better design would be

5. Using global variables is a poor strategy from a data coupling perspective because one procedure might corrupt the data needed by other procedures.

7. Data flow diagrams and modular structure charts are similar in that both are used as devices to partition the system logically into a set of subcomponents, each with a well-defined, specific task. The fundamental difference between these two modeling tools lies in the way in which each depicts the interaction among system subcomponents. Data flow diagrams present the system's subcomponents as a (more or less) linear sequence of modules through which system data flow and by which they are processed; modular structure charts present the system as a hierarchy depicting relationships among high-level (boss) and low-level (worker) modules. Thus, modular structure charts more accurately represent how the system will be designed in a computer language; they constitute the next logical refinement of the system in its evolution from abstraction to implementation.

Section 14.3

1. In the analysis phase, the system analyst, through interviews, inspections, observations, and so on reports what the user's needs are.

   In the design phase, the designer studies the analyst's report and designs a solution for the user.

   In the coding phase, the programmer codes the design provided by the design phase.

   In the testing phase, the system is checked for performance under varying conditions, especially boundary conditions in the data being used.

   In the maintenance phase, the system is modified and updated to meet changing user needs and/or to correct errors in the system.

3. A robust module is one that does not "bomb" when it receives invalid data. If every module in a system were completely robust, the system would most likely be too slow to be of practical use: too much time would be consumed by each module in checking to make certain that the data it received were valid.

7. Test data for **PROCEDURE** ReadReal could be as follows. (Note that a space is indicated by "_".)

Val	Rationale	Expected Results
_00.000	a form of 0	valid
0.0	a form of 0	valid
−0.0	a form of 0	valid
+0	a form of 0	valid
5.356	"conventional" number	valid
0.002	"conventional" number	valid
_.05	nothing left of decimal	valid
0_5_.703	spaces between digits	invalid
56	no decimal	valid
75.	unguarded decimal	valid
.	decimal only	invalid
−7	− without decimal	valid
−.5	unguarded decimal	valid
+7	+ without decimal	valid
Hi.there	test a string	invalid
−.	test no digit case	invalid
+.	test no digit case	invalid
−_5.7	test space trailing sign	valid

Note that the current algorithm would accept "−.", ".", and "+." all of which would be invalid numbers.

11.

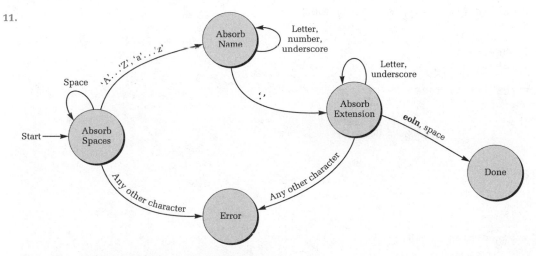

Note that this finite state machine accepts digits only in the string before the '.'; in the extension, only letters and the underscore are acceptable (including the '_' immediately following the '.'). The associated procedure follows:

```
{ Assume the following Type: }
TYPE
  FileString = PACKED ARRAY [1..MaxStringLength] OF char;

PROCEDURE ReadFileName(VAR FileName : FileString);

  { Given:  FileName a FileString.  Assume  that Chr(O) marks end of  }
  {         string, and that MaxStringLength is 1 greater than the    }
  {         length of string the user will attempt to input.          }
  { Task:   Prompt user for a valid file name until one is entered,   }
  {         employing finite state logic to verify that the input is  }
  {         valid.                                                     }
  { Return: FileName, a string containing a valid file name.          }

  TYPE
    States = (AbsorbSpaces, AbsorbName, AbsorbExtension, Error, Done);

  VAR
    S : States;
    K : integer;
    ch : char;

  BEGIN
    REPEAT
      writeln('Please enter a valid file name below:');
      K := O;
      S := AbsorbSpaces;
      REPEAT
        read(ch);
        CASE S OF
          AbsorbSpaces:
            IF eoln THEN
              S := Error
            ELSE IF (ch IN ['A'..'Z','a'..'z']) THEN
              BEGIN
                K := K + 1;
                FileName[K] := ch;
                S := AbsorbName
              END
            ELSE IF (Ch <>' ') THEN
              S := Error;
          AbsorbName:
            .
            .
            .

          AbsorbExtension:
            .
            .
            .

          Error:
            BEGIN { Do nothing } END;
          Done:
            BEGIN { Do nothing } END
        END { CASE }
      UNTIL (S = Done) OR (S = Error);
      IF (S = Done) THEN
        FileName[K+1] := Chr(O)
      ELSE
        BEGIN
          readln;
          writeln('Invalid file name -- please reenter.')
        END
    UNTIL (S = Done)
  END;
```

Section 14.4

1. Advantages of an array implementation of a list over a random access file include cleaner code (fewer statements) and fast execution time. A disadvantage of an array is its lack of permanence.

5. Altering just one component of a sequential file requires copying all of the records in the file into a new file. This is, quite simply, impractical for large files. A random access file, in contrast, allows us to work with a single record; its contents can be modified and rewritten to the file without affecting the remainder of the file. Typical syntax is

```
seek(FileName, Position);
get(FileName);
FileName^ := UpdatedRecord;
seek(FileName,Position);
put(FileName);
```

Section 14.5

3. It could. Proofs of correctness do not take into account the limitations of a particular machine. Factors such as rounding errors in arithmetic computation, faulty user input, and exceeding the overflow and underflow cutoffs for numeric storage can all cause a "proven" algorithm to fail.

Section 14.6

1. The answer to this question would depend on the object-oriented extensions available at your institution.

CHAPTER 15

Section 15.1

1. The array involved in the PointerSort of Chapter 15 is not a linked list because its cells do not store links (to other array cells) that indicate the order in which the cells are to be traversed (the pointer array is always traversed sequentially). Instead, the pointers stored in the pointer array serve as indices to cells in a separate array (which contains the real data of interest).

3. With respect to search efficiency, both the linked list and unordered array implementations provide $O(n)$ access to list nodes; both require a sequential search. However, whereas both implementations require $O(n)$ comparisons to find a node, the linked list strategy requires only $O(1)$ data exchanges actually to delete the node. Compare this to the $O(n)$ exchanges needed by the array implementation.

   With respect to add efficiency, the linked list implementation strategy is at a disadvantage, requiring $O(n)$ operations to find a node's rightful place in the list, and $O(1)$ operations actually to insert it. The unordered array, on the other hand, provides $O(1)$ add efficiency, since nodes are always added to the end of the array.

   With respect to sort efficiency, the linked list is maintained in sequential order, so no sort is required to traverse it sequentially. In contrast, the unordered array requires an $O(n^2)$ pointer sort before it can be traversed sequentially. Here, the linked list strategy is at an advantage.

5. Merely write a procedure that receives a **real** parameter and prints this parameter only when it is positive. Then pass this procedure as the actual parameter associated with ProcessNode in LinkedTraverse.

Section 15.2

1. a.

79	→	55	→	89	→	13	→	19	→	178

b.

	Data	Link
1	47	3
2	89	5
3	66	7
4	833	2
5	912	10
6	55	2
7	112	4
8	912	0
9	79	6
10	912	8

3.

Head			Data	Link
5		1	LOCKE	3
		2	MILLER	3
		3	SMITH	Null
		4	FOSTER	1
		5	ALLEN	4

(Cell 2 should be returned to the available pool of nodes.)

5.

Head			Data	Link
1		1	JAMES	Null

Head			Data	Link
2		1	JAMES	Null
		2	CHILTON	1

Head			Data	Link
2		1	JAMES	3
		2	CHILTON	1
		3	SEFTON	Null

Head			Data	Link
2		1	JAMES	4
		2	CHILTON	1
		3	SEFTON	Null
		4	LEE	3

Head			Data	Link
1		1	JAMES	4
		2	CHILTON	1
		3	SEFTON	Null
		4	LEE	3

Head			Data	Link
1		1	JAMES	4
		2	WAGNER	Null
		3	SEFTON	2
		4	LEE	3

Head			Data	Link
4		1	JAMES	4
		2	WAGNER	Null
		3	SEFTON	2
		4	LEE	3

Head			Data	Link
1		1	AARON	4
		2	WAGNER	Null
		3	SEFTON	2
		4	LEE	3

7. PROCEDURE LinkedTraverse(VAR Head : Pointer;
                            PROCEDURE ProcessNode(VAR Item :
                                             LinkedListData));

```
{ Given:   Linked list reference by Head pointer.           }
{ Task:    Traverse the list in the linear order determined by  }
{          the links, applying PROCEDURE ProcessNode to each    }
{          record in the list.                                  }
{ Return:  The list referenced by Head with each node affected  }
{          by ProcessNode.                                      }

VAR
  P : Pointer;

BEGIN
  P := Head;
  WHILE (P <> NIL) DO
    BEGIN
      ProcessNode(Nodes[P].Data);
      P := Space.Nodes[P].Link
    END
END;
```

9. PROCEDURE FindNodeToDelete(VAR Head, P, Prev : Pointer;
                              DeleteData : LinkedListData;
                              VAR Found : boolean);

```
{ Given:   A linked list referenced by Head, and DeleteData, the data  }
{          contained in the node to delete.                            }
{ Task:    Search linked list for node containing DeleteData.          }
{ Return:  Found = true, P pointing to node containing DeleteData       }
{          and Prev pointing to the node preceding P; or Found = false }
{          if node with DeleteData could not be found.                 }

BEGIN
  P := Head;
  Prev := Null;
  Found := false;
  WHILE (NOT Found) AND (P <> Null) DO
    IF (Space.Nodes[P].Data = DeleteData) THEN
      Found := true
    ELSE
      BEGIN
        Prev := P;
        P := Space.Nodes[P].Link
      END
END;
```

13. For each of the n values we inserted into the sorted list, we would have to perform a sequential search (requiring O(n) comparisons) to find its rightful place. Keep in mind that with each insertion into the sorted list, n would grow by 1, so that only the last node inserted would have a worst-case efficiency of O(n); all previous nodes would have been inserted into smaller lists. Since for the linked list sort, we will have to carry out n O(n) sequential searches, the efficiency of this algorithm is O(n^2). As is always the case for linked lists, each of the insertions has O(1) efficiency, giving us O(n) total data interchanges. Compare this to the efficiencies of the other sorts we have studied: insertion sort—O(n^2) comparisons and data interchanges; bubble sort—O(n^2) comparisons and data interchanges; selection sort—O(n^2) comparisons and O(n) data interchanges; and radix sort—O(cn) comparisons and

O(cn) data exchanges, where c = the maximum length of the data being sorted.

Section 15.3

1. a., c., f., and i. are correct.

   b. Incorrect—cannot assign a Ptr to an integer.

   d. Incorrect—one disposes a Ptr, not what it points to.

   e. Incorrect—cannot dispose an integer.

   g. Incorrect—cannot **writeln** a Ptr variable.

   h. Incorrect—cannot **writeln** a complete record, only its fields.

3. `A^.Next^.Next := A^.Next^.Next^.Next`

effects the deletion of the third node.

5.
```
BEGIN
   B := A^.Next^.Next^.Next;
   A^.Next^.Next^.Next := NIL;
   B^.Next := A;
   A := B
END;
```

11.
```
PROCEDURE DestroyList(VAR Head : ListNodePtr);

   { Given:   Linked list referenced by Head.                     }
   { Task:    Return all dynamically allocated memory associated with }
   {          the list via dispose.                                }
   { Return:  Head, a pointer in an unreliable state.              }

   VAR
      temp : ListNodePtr;

   BEGIN
      WHILE (Head <> NIL) DO
         BEGIN
            temp := Head;
            Head := Head^.Link;
            dispose(temp)
         END
   END;
```

One couldn't dispose of the list by passing the **dispose** procedure LinkedTraverse because **dispose**'s parameter list does not exactly match that of formal parameter ProcessNode (**dispose** accepts a pointer whereas ProcessNode accepts a record).

LinkedTraverse is set up to process the current node before moving to the next node in the list. If the process were actually the **dispose** procedure, a reference to the current node would be destroyed before we advanced to the next node. With no reference to the current node, we could not access its link field, and thus we could not get to the next node in the list.

13. The array implementation of linked lists (Example 18.9) differs from the pointer variable implementation in that the method by which it allocates and deallocates pointers isn't as well encapsulated as it is in the pointer variable implementation. We can ascertain, from the declaration of the Space-Structure record, exactly how the dynamic memory is maintained. One way we could redefine the linked list ADT to make the different implementations more consistent would be to require the linked list type to encapsulate the dynamic memory scheme it employs. In this way, users of the ADT would not have to concern themselves with the details of dynamic memory management.

15. Traversing a Pascal pointer linked list node by node while writing the data portion and the link portion to a disk file will not work. Although the data and the memory address (the link) can be written to a disk file, when the disk file is read, there is no guarantee that the data will be placed into exactly the same memory locations as when the data were originally in memory.

An alternative solution would be simply to store the structure in the file in a way that would allow a program to read it in and recapture its original form. For linked structures, this might mean storing the data nodes in the file sequentially, perhaps with special flags at the head and the tail of the list.

Section 15.4

1.

	Data	Link
0	*DUMMY	1
1	JAMES	end of list
2		3
3		4
4		5
5		6
6		7
7		8
8		end of list

Head: 0
Avail: 2

	Data	Link
0	*DUMMY	1
1	JAMES	4
2		5
3	SEFTON	end of list
4	LEE	3
5		6
6		7
7		8
8		end of list

Head: 0
Avail: 2

	Data	Link
0	*DUMMY	2
1	JAMES	end of list
2	CHILTON	1
3		4
4		5
5		6
6		7
7		8
8		end of list

Head: 0
Avail: 3

	Data	Link
0	*DUMMY	1
1	JAMES	4
2	WAGNER	end of list
3	SEFTON	2
4	LEE	3
5		6
6		7
7		8
8		end of list

Head: 0
Avail: 5

	Data	Link
0	*DUMMY	2
1	JAMES	3
2	CHILTON	1
3	SEFTON	end of list
4		5
5		6
6		7
7		8
8		end of list

Head: 0
Avail: 4

	Data	Link
0	*DUMMY	4
1		5
2	WAGNER	end of list
3	SEFTON	2
4	LEE	3
5		6
6		7
7		8
8		end of list

Head: 0
Avail: 1

	Data	Link
0	*DUMMY	2
1	JAMES	4
2	CHILTON	1
3	SEFTON	end of list
4	LEE	3
5		6
6		7
7		8
8		end of list

Head: 0
Avail: 5

	Data	Link
0	*DUMMY	1
1	AARON	4
2	WAGNER	end of list
3	SEFTON	2
4	LEE	3
5		6
6		7
7		8
8		end of list

Head: 0
Avail: 5

3.

	Data	FLink	BLink		Head
0	*DUMMY	1	end		0
1	JAMES	end	0		
2		3	end		Avail
3		4	2		2
4		5	3		
5		6	4		
6		7	5		
7		8	6		
8		end	7		

	Data	FLink	BLink		Head
0	*DUMMY	1	end		0
1	JAMES	4	2		
2		5	end		Avail
3	SEFTON	end	4		2
4	LEE	3	1		
5		6	2		
6		7	5		
7		8	6		
8		end	7		

	Data	FLink	BLink		Head
0	*DUMMY	2	end		0
1	JAMES	end	2		
2	CHILTON	1	0		Avail
3		4	end		3
4		5	3		
5		6	4		
6		7	5		
7		8	6		
8		end	7		

	Data	FLink	BLink		Head
0	*DUMMY	1	end		0
1	JAMES	4	2		
2	WAGNER	end	3		Avail
3	SEFTON	2	4		5
4	LEE	3	1		
5		6	end		
6		7	5		
7		8	6		
8		end	7		

	Data	FLink	BLink		Head
0	*DUMMY	2	end		0
1	JAMES	3	2		
2	CHILTON	1	0		Avail
3	SEFTON	end	1		4
4		5	end		
5		6	4		
6		7	5		
7		8	6		
8		end	7		

	Data	FLink	BLink		Head
0	*DUMMY	4	end		0
1		5	end		
2	WAGNER	end	3		Avail
3	SEFTON	2	4		1
4	LEE	3	0		
5		6	1		
6		7	5		
7		8	6		
8		end	7		

	Data	FLink	BLink		Head
0	*DUMMY	2	end		0
1	JAMES	4	2		
2	CHILTON	1	0		Avail
3	SEFTON	end	4		5
4	LEE	3	1		
5		6	end		
6		7	5		
7		8	6		
8		end	7		

	Data	FLink	BLink		Head
0	*DUMMY	1	end		0
1	AARON	4	0		
2	WAGNER	end	3		Avail
3	SEFTON	2	4		5
4	LEE	3	1		
5		6	end		
6		7	5		
7		8	6		
8		end	7		

5.
```
PROCEDURE InsertNodeDouble(Point1, Point2 : Pointer);

  { See Example 18.18 for Given-Task-Return documentation }

  BEGIN
    Point1^.BLink := Point2^.BLink;
    Point1^.FLink := Point2;
    Point2^.BLink^.FLink := Point1;
    Point2^.BLink := Point1
  END;


PROCEDURE DeleteNodeDouble(Point1 : Pointer);

  { See Example 18.19 for Given-Task-Return documentation }

  BEGIN
    Point1^.BLink^.FLink := Point1^.FLink;
    Point1^.FLink^.BLink := Point1^.BLink;
    dispose(Point1)
  END;
```

Section 15.5

1. The assignment strategy discussed in this section is unsafe because only one actual copy of the string exists in memory. Therefore, any change in that copy affects all string variables pointing to it—even those not directly involved in the change. The situation outlined in this problem is an excellent example. Because the Assign operation only adjusts pointers—it causes S1 and S2 to reference the same physical copy—ReadAString(S1) affects both S1 and S2. Even though only S1 was passed to ReadAString, S2 also points to what is read into S1^; WriteAString(S2), therefore, will output the result of ReadAString(S1). If "Coffee" is read in for the first ReadAString and "Tea" is read in for the second, the output is "Tea."

5. b. We merely compare the efficiency of both methods' insert operation. Recall that in order to insert string T into string S, we need three pointers: (a) a pointer to the node in S after which to insert T; (b) a pointer to the first node in T; and (c) a pointer to the last node in T. The insert operations for both methods are equally efficient at obtaining (a) and (b), both requiring "Place" comparisons to get (a) and 0 com-

parisons to get (b). However, whereas the singly linked list method requires Length(T) comparisons to obtain (c), the doubly linked list method requires 0 comparisons. Because the doubly linked list method avoids having to walk to the end of T, it is more time efficient.

Section 15.6

5. In Example 16.14, replace the **FOR** loops in the cases for 'F' and 'P' with calls to TraverseColumn and TraverseRow respectively. Each of these calls to the traverse operations would require that you pass a procedure as a parameter. That procedure should be designed to write the pilot (for TraverseColumn) whenever it finds a **true** entry in the column of the table that is being traversed. Similarly, the procedure passed to TraverseRow should write the flight whenever it finds a **true** entry in the row that is traversed.

9. The implementation becomes space efficient only when

$$N < \frac{NRow * NCol - NRow - NCol}{5}$$

CHAPTER 16

Section 16.1

1.

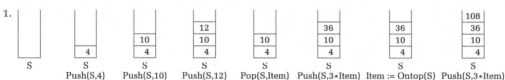

S   Push(S,4)   Push(S,10)   Push(S,12)   Pop(S,Item)   Push(S,3*Item)   Item := Ontop(S)   Push(S,3*Item)

3. { Global declarations }

```
CONST
    StackSize = { Appropriate size };

TYPE
   StackType = RECORD
                   List : Array [1..StackSize] of
                            { Appropriate type };
                   Top  : integer
               END;
```

a.
```
   PROCEDURE Create(Var S : StackType);

   { Given :   An array implementation of a stack. }
   { Task  :   Initialize the stack.               }
   { Return:   An initialized stack.               }

   BEGIN
      S.Top := 0;
   END;
```

c.
```
   FUNCTION Empty(S : StackType) : boolean;

   { Given   :  An array implementation of a stack. }
   { Task    :  Test whether the stack is empty.    }
   { Return  :  true if empty; false if not empty.  }

   BEGIN
      Empty := ( S.Top = 0 );
   END;
```

5. The stack would grow and shrink as follows:

Section 16.2

1. Infix: $A + B*C - D/P - R$
Postfix: $ABCD - PR - /* +$
Prefix: $+ A * B / - CD - PD$

3.

Ch	OpStack	Postfix	Commentary
#			Push #
P			Read Ch
		P	Append Ch to Postfix
+			Read Ch
	+		Push Ch
	#		
(			Read Ch
	(		Push Ch
	+		
	#		
Q			Read Ch
		PQ	Append Ch to Postfix
−			Read Ch
	−		Push Ch
	(		
	+		
	#		
F			Read Ch
		PQF	Append Ch
)		Read Ch	
	+	PQF −	Pop and Append
	#		
/			Read Ch
	/		Push Ch
	#		
Y			Read Ch
		PQF − Y	Append Ch
#			Read Ch
		PQF − Y/ + #	Pop and Append rest of stack

7. Assume the following declarations:

```
SNptr = SNode;
SNode = RECORD
          ch : char;
          next : SNptr
        END;

PostfixString = ^StringRec;
StringRec = RECORD
              Head,
              Tail : SNptr;
            END;
```

```
PROCEDURE Append(VAR Postfix : PostfixString;
                      ch : char);

{ Given:   Postfix String, and character ch.   }
{ Task:    Append ch to end of Postfix.         }
{ Return: Postfix string with ch appended.      }
{ Note:    This procedure assumes that Postfix  }
{          has been created.                     }

VAR P : SNptr;
BEGIN
  New(P);
  P^.ch := ch;
  P^.next := NIL;
  IF (Postfix.Head = NIL) THEN { Empty String }
    BEGIN
      Postfix.Head := P;
      Postfix.Tail := P
    END
  ELSE
    BEGIN
      Postfix.Tail^.Next := P;
      Postfix.Tail := P
    END
END;
```

9. If operand 'A' has a stack priority that is greater than or equal to the infix priority of operand 'B,' then 'A' has equal or greater operator precedence; therefore, it is appended to the postfix string before B, and will be applied before B. Such precedence, however, can be overridden by parentheses, which force the operators between them to be unconditionally appended to the postfix string, regardless of their stack priority.

In summary, the order in which operators are appended to the postfix string is dictated by stack priority relative to infix priority; equal or greater stack priority indicates either higher operator precedence (if the two operators being compared are different) or left-associativity, if the two operators being compared are the same.

Hence, if we want to make the '^' operator right associative, we merely make its infix priority greater than its stack priority. Our infix and stack priority functions would then appear as follows:

Priority:	*	/	+	–	(	)	^	#
Infix	2	2	1	1	5	0	4	0
Stack	2	2	1	1	0	undefined	3	0

The adjusted infix and stack priorities reflect both the fact that exponentiation has the highest operator precedence, and the fact that all operators except exponentiation are left-associative.

Section 16.3

3. a. Introduce an integer variable MinutesIdle, which is initialized to 0 before entering the **FOR** loop. We then add the following **ELSE** clause to the **IF** (TimeLeftOnCar = 0) AND Empty(CarQueue) clause:

```
ELSE IF (TimeLeftOnCar = 0) AND (Empty(CarQueue) THEN
  { This minute is idle }
  MinutesIdle := MinutesIdle + 1
```

b. To make this count, we merely dequeue the CarQueue until it is empty after we have exited the **FOR** loop. In Pascal, this amounts to introducing an integer variable "CarsRemaining," which we initialize to zero before dequeuing begins:

```
CarsRemaining := 0;
```

Now we are prepared to execute a **WHILE** loop:

```
WHILE NOT Empty(CarQueue) DO
  BEGIN
    Dequeue(CarQueue,Minute);
    CarsRemaining := CarsRemaining + 1
  END;
```

7. PROCEDURE Create(VAR Q : Queue);

```
    { Given:  An arbitrary queue variable Q in an unknown state.  }
    { Task:   Initialize Q to the empty queue.                    }
    { Return: Q initialized to the empty queue.                   }

    BEGIN
      New(Q.Front);
      Q.Front^.Link := NIL;
      Q.Rear := Q.Front
    END;

  FUNCTION Empty (Q : Queue) : boolean;

    { Given:  A previously created queue.                         }
    { Task:   Determine if Q is empty.                            }
    { Return: true if Q is empty; false otherwise.                }

    BEGIN
      Empty := (Q.Front = Q.Rear)
    END;

  FUNCTION Full(Q : Queue) : boolean;

    { Given:  A previously create queue.                          }
    { Task:   Determine if Q is full.                             }
    { Return: true if Q is full; false otherwise.                 }
    { Note:   Assume that the GetNode or New procedure handles    }
    {         this appropriately.                                 }
```

CHAPTER 17

Section 17.1

3. **a.** 92
      6
      14

   b. 14
      6
      92

   Note, however, that because this procedure neglects to test Head for being **NIL** before referencing Head^., a run-time "attempt to access **NIL** pointer" error will occur when the empty list is passed in for Head.

   c. 14
      6

   Note that because this procedure neglects to test Head itself for being **NIL** before it references Head^.Link, a run-time "attempt to access **NIL** pointer" error will occur when the empty list is passed in for Head.

5. Program (a) will achieve the original intent presented. Its output is

   MADAM

   Program (b) will fail because it globally declares the characters being read so the recursive calls do not result in copies of the characters being pushed onto the system stack. Consequently, only the last character read is remembered and written when the recursion unwinds. Its output is

   MMMMM

7. This function computes the smallest value in NumberArray within the subrange 1 . . N, where N is the value originally passed in.

11. We could insert tracer output instructions into factorial as follows:

```
FUNCTION Factorial(N : integer);

  { Given-Task-Return as in the problem statement. }

  BEGIN
    writeln('Entering Factorial with N = ',N:2);
    IF (N = 0) OR (N = 1) THEN
      BEGIN
        writeln('Computed Factorial: 1');
        Factorial := 1
      END
    ELSE
      BEGIN
        N := N - 1;
        writeln('Computing Factorial of: ',N:2, ' * ','Factorial(',N:2,')');
        Factorial := N * Factorial(N)
      END
  END;
```

These tracers should clearly reveal that the factorial function is incorrectly subtracting one from N prior to the recursive call

```
Factorial := N * Factorial(N).
```

The problem, of course, is that factorial, by definition, equals

```
N * Factorial(N - 1),
```

not

```
(N - 1) * Factorial(N - 1),
```

as in the current algorithm. Hence, the problem can be easily corrected by replacing the two statements under the **ELSE** clause with the statement

```
Factorial := N * Factorial(N - 1)
```

Section 17.2

5. The output is as follows:

```
1   16
9   16
9   11
9   16
```

7. The stack frames for this function should contain three pieces of information: The current value of M, the current value of N, and the point in the program to which to return.

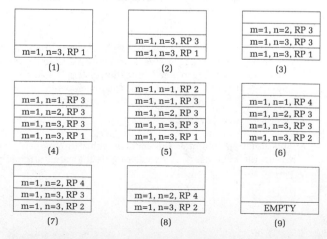

(1)   (2)   (3)

(4)   (5)   (6)

(7)   (8)   (9)

The output is as follows:

```
1   3
1   2
1   1
1   0
0   1
0   2
0   3
0   4
5
```

11. *Hint:* Consider the number of ways that M can be broken down into quarters and dimes plus the number of ways that (M − 50¢) can be broken down into half dollars, quarters, and dimes. The total of these two provide the answer in terms of quantities that are (recursively) easier to compute.

Section 17.3

5. The output is as follows:

```
12   1   2   3   4   3   3   4
     4   3   4   2   2   3   4   3
     3   4   4   3   4   3   2   3
     4   3   3   4   4   3   4   4
     2   3   4   3   3   4   4   3
     4
```

CHAPTER 18

Section 18.1

1.

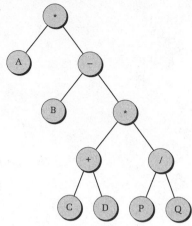

3. A tree is a hierarchically ordered data structure consisting of nodes and links to nodes. A tree is accessed by a node called the root.

5. a. and **c.** are binary trees with the heap property.

   b. is not, because the node containing 35 is a subtree of the node containing 19. Similar situation for the node containing 39.

Section 18.2

1. a.

Location	Data	LeftChild	RightChild
1	C	2	–
2	R	–	3
3	G	–	–
4	F	–	–
5	X	–	4
6	Y	–	–
7	B	6	5
8	A	7	1
9		–	–

Root
8

Avail
9

b.

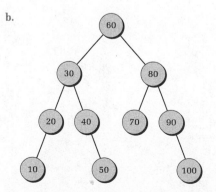

The shape of the search tree is dependent on the order in which data arrive because the first element determines the shape. The tree will give good search results if the root has a value that is the median relative to the criteria used to

9. a.

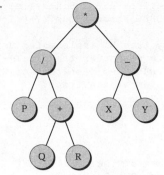

c.

search the tree. If the elements added after the root alternate between the value of the root, a tree with good search results is constructed.

5. G
K
I
J
H
C
E
D
B
A

7. C
K
I
G
H
J
A
E
B
D

11. PROCEDURE PostorderTrav (BT : BinaryTree;
              PROCEDURE ProcessNode (VAR Item : TreeNodeData));

```
    { Given:  Binary tree BT implemented using Pascal Pointer variables  }
    { Task:   Perform postorder traversal--left subtree first, then the  }
    {         right subtree, then root of BT*applying ProcessNode to     }
    {         each Item in the tree.                                     }
    { Return: Nothing.                                                   }

    BEGIN
    IF BT <> NIL THEN
      BEGIN
        PostorderTrav (BT^.LeftChild);
        PostorderTrav (BT^.RightChild);
        ProcessNode (BT^.Root)
      END
    END; { of PROCEDURE PostorderTrav }
```

15. FUNCTION Eval (BT : BinaryTree) : real;

```
    { Given:  A nonempty algebraic expression tree.                      }
    { Task:   Evaluate the tree using a function Value to obtain         }
    {         numeric values for the operands in the tree.               }
    { Return: The value of the evaluated algebraic expression tree.      }

    { Assume a function Value is defined. }

    BEGIN
      IF BT^.Data is an operand THEN
        Eval := Value(BT^.Data)
      ELSE
        CASE BT^.Data OF
          '+' :
            Eval := Eval(BT^.LeftChild) + Eval(BT^.RightChild);
          '*' :
            Eval := Eval(BT^.LeftChild) * Eval(BT^.RightChild);
          '-' :
            Eval := Eval(BT^.LeftChild) - Eval(BT^.RightChild);
          '/' :
            Eval := Eval(BT^.LeftChild) / Eval(BT^.RightChild)
        END { of CASE statement }
    END; { of FUNCTION Eval }
```

Section 18.3

1. a. is full. b. and c. are not full.

5. b.

Section 18.4

1.

Item	1	2	3	4	5	6	7	8	9	10
10	10									

Item	1	2	3	4	5	6	7	8	9	10
20	20	10								

Item	1	2	3	4	5	6	7	8	9	10
30	30	10	20							

Item	1	2	3	4	5	6	7	8	9	10
40	40	30	20	10						

Item	1	2	3	4	5	6	7	8	9	10
50	50	40	20	10	30					

Item	1	2	3	4	5	6	7	8	9	10
60	60	40	50	10	30	20				

Item	1	2	3	4	5	6	7	8	9	10
70	70	40	60	10	30	20	50			

Item	1	2	3	4	5	6	7	8	9	10
80	80	70	60	40	30	20	50	10		

Item	1	2	3	4	5	6	7	8	9	10
90	90	80	60	70	30	20	50	10	40	

Item	1	2	3	4	5	6	7	8	9	10
100	100	90	60	70	80	20	50	10	40	30

3.
```
PROCEDURE PreorderTrav (BT : BinaryTree;
                 PROCEDURE ProcessNode (VAR Item: TreeDataNode));

  { Given:  Binary tree BT implemented by linear array            }
  {         representation.                                        }
  { Task:   Perform preorder traversal--root of BT, left subtree,  }
  {         then right subtree--applying ProcessNode to each Item in }
  {         the tree.                                              }
  { Return: Nothing.                                               }

  PROCEDURE PreorderTravAux (Nodelocation : integer);

  { This procedure is the behind-the-scenes recursive helper of    }
  { PreorderTrav.  The interface to PreorderTravAux is not seen     }
  { by users of the ADT.  Assumption:  Array locations which are    }
  { not presently storing data in the tree have been flagged with   }
  { an appropriate Null value.                                      }

    BEGIN
      IF NodeLocation <= MonTreeNodes THEN
        IF BT.BTData[NodeLocation] <> Null THEN
          BEGIN
            ProcessNode(BT.BTData[NodeLocation]);
            PreorderTravAux(2*NodeLocation); {  left subtree  }
            PreorderTravAux(2*NodeLocation+1); {  right subtree  }
          END
    END; { of PROCEDURE PreorderTravAux }

BEGIN
  IF BT.NumberNodes <> 0 THEN
    PreorderTravAux(1 {  location of the root of BT  })
END;  { of PROCEDURE PreorderTrav }
```

Section 18.5

1. The indentation can be obtained by increasing the indentation before traversing the left (child) subtree and decreasing the indentation again before traversing the right (sibling) subtree.

3. Preorder traversal
```
P  Q  T  U  V  C  D  E
M  N  O  W  A  G  B  H
I  J  X  K  L
```

Section 18.6

1. The order of the nodes would be Seattle, Chicago, Miami, New Orleans, Dallas, New York, Washington, Milwaukee, Phoenix, San Francisco, Los Angeles, Las Vegas, Minneapolis, Oklahoma City.

3. One way the cities could be visited is as follows: Seattle, Chicago, San Francisco, Miami, New Orleans, Las Vegas, Milwaukee, Los Angeles, Dallas, Washington, Phoenix, Minneapolis, New York City, Oklahoma City.

9. Eliminating the requirement that **TYPE** GraphNode be a subrange of an ordinal type would mean that there would not be a convenient way to index the nodes in the graph, making the normal operations more difficult to perform. One strategy to overcome that problem would be to build an indexing scheme that would make indexing the nodes very convenient.

CHAPTER 19

Section 19.1

```
1. 60  12  90  20  64   8   6
    8  12   6  20  64  90  60
    6  12   8  20  60  90  64
    6   8  12  20  60  64  90
```

3. The shell sort is named after its inventor D. L. Shell.

5. Relatively prime values of the increments are better because they insure distinct increments that will not divide evenly into each other so that data that have been compared to each other are less likely to be compared again.

7. The best case for the shell sort algorithm presented in this section would be a data set with the data already in order: each segment would be in order and no data would be swapped. The worst case would be a data set arranged in descending order because every data element would be out of order and there would be a maximum number of data swaps.

9. The body of the ShellSort procedure would be as follows:

```
VAR
  K : integer;

BEGIN
  K := 1;
  WHILE K < N DO
    K := (3*K) + 1;
  K := K DIV 3;
  WHILE K > 0 DO
    BEGIN
      SegmentedInsertionSort(Key, N, K);  { same procedure as before }
      K := K DIV 3  { Reduce  number of segments }
    END;
END;  { of PROCEDURE ShellSort }
```

Section 19.2

1. The output would be as follows:

```
 1   7
60  12  90  30  64   8   6

 1   4
 6  12   8  30

 2   4
12   8  30

 2   2
 8

 4   4
30

 6   7
64  90

 7   7
90
```

3. The bubble sort is better than the quick sort when the data are already in order. The bubble sort can safely conclude that the data are in order after the first pass through the data; the quick sort must perform the entire sort even if the data are already in order.

5. The choice of the pivotal point will not change the overall efficiency of the quick sort; however, it does dramatically change the best and worst data sets.

9. All of the quick sort procedure would remain the same as in the book. One line in the partition procedure would change from

```
Pivot := Key[Lo];
```

to

```
{ Assume the FUNCTION median gives the median of three values. }
Pivot := Median(Key[Lo], Key[(Lo+Hi) DIV 2], Key[Hi]);
```

This variation should be more efficient because the pivot value is more likely to split the array being sorted more evenly. Quick sort is most efficient when the array is split at the midpoint.

Section 19.3

1.
```
60  12  90  30  64   8   6
60  12  90  30  64   8   6
60  64  90  30  12   8   6
 6  64  60  30  12   8  90
 8  30  60   6  12  64  90
12  30   8   6  60  64  90
 6  12   8  30  60  64  90
 8   6  12  30  60  64  90
 6   8  12  30  60  64  90
```

3. The sort derives its name from the heap structure that it uses in sorting the data.

5. The heap sort is not always as efficient as the quick sort. On average, the quick sort is slightly better than the heap sort because its big-O constant of proportionality will be smaller. However, the heap sort handles data already sorted much faster than the quick sort.

Section 19.4

1. The output for MergeSort would be

```
 1   7
60  12  90  30  64   8   6

 1   4
60  12  90  30

 1   2
60  12

 1   1
60

 2   2
60  12

 2   2
60  12
```

and so on . . .

3. **PROCEDURE** MergeSort would be more efficient if the Source parameter for the subordinate **PROCEDURE** Order were a **VAR** parameter because then the address of the array would be sent to the procedure. With Source as a value parameter, the procedure makes a local copy of the entire array upon each call. Since the procedure is recursive, many such copies may exist on the system stack at a given time. In fact, if the Source array is very large, this can lead to an overflow of the system stack and hence an execution error.

7. Heap sort, quick sort, and shell sort are unstable. Merge sort is unstable as written but can be modified so that it is stable. Bubble sort, insertion sort, and selection sort are stable.

CHAPTER 20

Section 20.1

1. a. The keys would have the following positions:

Record No.	Key
1	333
2	632
3	1090
4	459
5	379
6	238
7	
8	
9	
10	1982
11	3411

c. With the chaining method, the keys and links would be

Record No.	Key	Link	Record No.	Key	Link
1	333	13	12	3411	14
2	632	0	13	459	0
3	1090	0	14	379	15
4			15	238	0
5			16		
6			17		
7			18		
8			19		
9			20		
10	1982	12	21		
11			22		

3. a. The best method to implement the card catalog in this situation would be hashing. Hashing allows for very quick searches and is fairly good at handling additions and deletions. Since the library rarely prints out an ordered list of books, the time it takes to sort the list doesn't really matter.

c. The best method to implement the data base would be the binary search. The states are kept in order by two-letter code. All the program need do is access the record quickly, increment a field, and be able to print the list out in order. All these are handled very well by a binary search.

5. a.
```
PROCEDURE QuadraticHash (Target : KeyType;
                         SearchList : DataArray;
                         VAR InfoWanted : DataRec;
                         VAR Found : boolean);

  { This solution will search until it finds Target, finds empty location,
    or visits original hash location for a second time }

  VAR
    K, J, R : integer;
    Traversed : boolean;

  BEGIN
    Found := false; { Assume failure }
    Traversed := false; { Toggled to true if entire list is traversed }
    K := Hash(Target); { Call on hashing function }
    J := K;
    R := 0;
    WHILE (SearchList[J].Key <> Empty) AND NOT (Traversed OR Found) DO
      IF Target = SearchList[J].Key THEN
        BEGIN
          InfoWanted := SearchList[J];
          Found := true
        END
      ELSE
        BEGIN
          R := R + 1;
          J := ((J + R*R - 1) MOD RecordSpace) + 1; { MOD insures wraparound }
          Traversed := (J = K)
        END
  END; { OF PROCEDURE QuadraticHash }
```

Section 20.2

1. As suggested in the text, the doubly linked list is the best choice for implementing linked lists with hashing. When the order of the list is disturbed during a change of a key field or during a deletion of an item in the list, the linked list must be rebuilt. If a doubly linked list is not used, the list would have to be traversed to find the predecessor node in the linked list. The doubly linked list makes rebuilding lists more efficient.

Section 20.3

1. a.

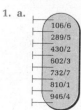

5. a. For the ISAM index, this knowledge will enable us to set the index so that the subsequent search on the disk will be more efficient.

c. The trie is constructed the same no matter what the disk structure may be.

⊞ Index

Credits

TABLE OF ABSTRACT DATA TYPES AND THEIR IMPLEMENTATIONS

ADT OPERATIONS IMPLEMENTED IN PASCAL

Operation		Page Reference
FUNCTION Choose	{ Recursive implementation of N-choose-K computation }	868
FUNCTION Evaluate	{ Evaluate postfix string }	796
FUNCTION Length	{ Length operation - packed array implementation of string }	605
FUNCTION Length	{ Length operation - embedded length implementation of string }	611
FUNCTION Next	{ Move to next node for array implementation of linked list }	725
FUNCTION Next	{ Move to next node - Pascal pointer impl. of linked list }	744
FUNCTION Retrieve	{ Retrieve operation - list implementation of 2-D table ADT }	625
FUNCTION Retrieve	{ Retrieve operation for linked list impl. of 2-D table }	763
PROCEDURE Add	{ Add operation - ordered array implementation of keyed list }	635
PROCEDURE AddNode	{ Add an item to a binary search tree }	906
PROCEDURE AddNode	{ Add an item to a linear implementation of a heap }	928
PROCEDURE Assign	{ Assign operation for linked list impl. of 2-D table }	762
PROCEDURE BinarySearch	{ Recursive implementation of binary search algorithm }	864
PROCEDURE BinarySearch	{ Binary search on ordered array }	573
PROCEDURE BubbleSort	{ Implements bubble sort algorithm }	542
PROCEDURE Convert	{ Convert infix string to postfix }	793
PROCEDURE Create	{ Create operation - packed array implementation of string }	604
PROCEDURE Create	{ Create operation - embedded length implementation of string }	610
PROCEDURE Create	{ Create operation for an array implementation of linked list }	724
PROCEDURE Create	{ Create operation - Pascal pointer impl. of linked list }	743
PROCEDURE Delete	{ Delete operation - packed array implementation of string }	609
PROCEDURE Delete	{ Delete operation - embedded length implementation of string }	612
PROCEDURE DeleteNodeDouble	{ Delete operation for doubly linked list }	754
PROCEDURE DeleteNode	{ Delete operation for array implementation of linked list }	730
PROCEDURE DeleteNode	{ Delete operation - Pascal pointer impl. of linked list }	744
PROCEDURE Dequeue	{ Remove an item from array implementation of a queue }	807
PROCEDURE Dequeue	{ Remove an item from a linked list implementation of queue }	812
PROCEDURE Euqueue	{ Add an item to array implementation of a queue }	806
PROCEDURE Euqueue	{ Add an item to linked list of implementation of a queue }	811
PROCEDURE FindInsertionSlot	{ Find insertion location - array impl. of linked list }	727
PROCEDURE FindNodeToDelete	{ Locate node to delete - Pascal pointer impl. of linked list }	745
PROCEDURE GetNode	{ Operation that obtains a pointer to an available node }	723
PROCEDURE GraphTraversal	{ Depth-first implementation of graph traversal }	946
PROCEDURE Hanoi	{ Recursive implementation of Towers of Hanoi algorithm }	852
PROCEDURE HeapSort	{ Implementation of heap sort algorithm }	983
PROCEDURE InitializeSpace	{ Initialization operation for array-based pointers }	722
PROCEDURE InOrderTrav	{ Inorder traversal of binary tree implemented by pointers }	909
PROCEDURE Insert	{ Insert operation for linked list impl. of string ADT }	758
PROCEDURE InsertionSort	{ Implements insertion sort algorithm }	547
PROCEDURE InsertNode	{ Insert operation for array implementation of linked list }	725
PROCEDURE InsertNode	{ Insert operation - Pascal pointer impl. of linked list }	744
PROCEDURE InsertNodeDouble	{ Insert operation for doubly linked list }	753
PROCEDURE LinearHash	{ Retrieve item from hash table - linear collision processing }	1012
PROCEDURE LinkedHash	{ Retrieve item from hash table - linked collision processing }	1018
PROCEDURE LinkedTraverse	{ Recursive implementation of linked list traversal }	841
PROCEDURE Merge	{ Algorithm that is subordinate to merge sort }	985
PROCEDURE MergeSort	{ Merge sort algorithm }	986
PROCEDURE Partition	{ Algorithm that is subordinate to quick sort }	974
PROCEDURE PointerBubbleSort	{ Implements bubble sort with pointers }	564
PROCEDURE Pop	{ Pop operation for array implementation of stack }	784
PROCEDURE PreOrderTrav	{ Preorder traversal of binary tree implemented by pointers }	908